What's New in 2009

Standard Deduction. The standard deduction amounts for 2009 are $11,400 for married individuals filing jointly (and surviving spouses), $8,350 for heads of households, and $5,700 for unmarried individuals and married individuals filing separately. An additional standard deduction may also be claimed in 2009 for real estate taxes, motor vehicle sales and excise taxes, and net disaster losses.

Itemized Deductions and Exemption Amounts. For 2009, the phaseout of itemized deductions will begin when a taxpayer's AGI reaches $166,800 ($83,400 for married individuals filing separately). The amount for each personal and dependency exemption claimed is $3,650 ($2,433 for taxpayers with an AGI in excess of the maximum phaseout amount).

Standard Mileage Rates. The standard mileage rate for business miles driven from January 1, 2009, through December 31, 2009, is 55¢ per mile, while the rate for deductible moving and medical expenses is 24¢ per mile. The rate for business miles driven for charity remains at 14¢ per mile, unless the charity work is related to Midwest disaster relief efforts then it is 70 percent of the standard business mileage rate.

Homebuyer Credit. The first-time homebuyer credit is extended to purchases before May 1, 2010, or July 1, 2010, for binding written contracts entered into before May 1, 2010, to close a purchase before July 1, 2010. The deadlines are extended one year for taxpayers on qualified official extended duty. The maximum credit is $8,000 ($4,000 if married filing separately) for purchases by a first-time homebuyer after 2008. For purchases after November 6, 2009, individuals who owned and used the same principal residence for five consecutive years during the eight years prior to the purchase may claim a maximum credit of $6,500 ($3,250 if married filing separately). The repayment requirement is generally waived for all taxpayers for purchases after 2008 and for purchases made during 2008 for taxpayers on qualified official extended duty.

Section at a Glance

Tax Preparer's Checklist

- ☐ Ensure that all Form W-2s and 1099s are available. Be sure to compare prior year accounts with those in the current year.
- ☐ Ensure that the Social Security number is correct on all Form W-2s and 1099s.
- ☐ Be sure to request paperwork for the purchase of any stock sold appearing on Form 1099-B.

Relevant IRS Publications

- ☐ IRS Publication 3, *Armed Forces' Tax Guide*
- ☐ IRS Publication 17, *Your Federal Income Tax*
- ☐ IRS Publication 501, *Exemptions, Standard Deduction, and Filing Information*
- ☐ IRS Publication 504, *Divorced or Separated Individuals*
- ☐ IRS Publication 519, *U.S. Tax Guide for Aliens*
- ☐ IRS Publication 521, *Moving Expenses*
- ☐ IRS Publication 525, *Taxable and Nontaxable Income*

2009 Tax Brackets by Filing Status

Tax Rate*	Single	MFJ or SS	MFS	HOH
10%	$ 0 – 8,350	$ 0 – 16,700	$ 0 – 8,350	$ 0 – 11,950
15%	8,351 – 33,950	16,701 – 67,900	8,351 – 33,950	11,951 – 45,500
25%	33,951 – 82,250	67,901 – 137,050	33,951 – 68,525	45,501 – 117,450
28%	82,251 – 171,550	137,051 – 208,850	68,526 – 104,425	117,451 – 190,200
33%	171,551 – 372,950	208,851 – 372,950	104,426 – 186,475	190,201 – 372,950
35%	Over $372,950	Over $372,950	Over $186,475	Over $372,950

* See Tab 17 for complete tax rate schedules and tax tables.

Taxpayer Information

Form 1040 is the principal form for use by individual taxpayers. Even if a taxpayer is eligible to file Form 1040A or Form 1040EZ, Form 1040 may still be used. See MTG ¶124 for requirements to be eligible to file Form 1040A or Form 1040EZ.

Who Must File Form 1040

Individuals who are U.S. citizens or resident aliens, and whose gross income exceeds the amount shown in the following table for their filing status and age, must file an income tax return for 2009. However, even if gross income is less than the amount shown, an individual must still file a return if he or she:

- had net earnings from self-employment of at least $400;
- received any advance earned income credit (EIC) payments from an employer; or
- had wages of $108.28 or more from a church or qualified religious organization that is exempt from employer Social Security and Medicare taxes.

In addition, any taxpayer who owes any of the following special taxes must file a return:

- Social Security and Medicare taxes on tips not reported to an employer;
- uncollected Social Security, Medicare or railroad retirement tax on tips reported to an employer;
- the alternative minimum tax;
- household employment taxes;
- additional tax on a qualified retirement plan, including an IRA;
- additional tax on a health savings account (HSA), Archer MSA, Coverdell education savings account (ESA) or qualified tuition program; or
- recapture of certain tax credits and other benefits as reported on line 44 (see page 1-36) and line 60 (see page 1-39), such as the education credit, investment credit, first-time homebuyer credit, and the credit for employer-provided child care facilities.

If a taxpayer must file a return only due to the additional tax owed on a qualified retirement plan or IRA, then Form 5329 may be filed by itself. Similarly, if the taxpayer is filing a return only because household employment taxes are due, then Schedule H may be filed by itself. If an individual had income from a U.S. possession, then see IRS Publication 570.

Who Must File a Return in 2009

Filing Status	Age	Gross Income of at Least
Single	Under 65	$ 9,350
	65 or older	10,750
Married Filing Jointly[1]	Under 65 (both spouses)	18,700
	65 or older (one spouse)	19,800
	65 or older (both spouses)	20,900
Qualifying Widow(er) with dependent child	Under 65	15,050
	65 or older	16,150
Married Filing Separately	Any age	3,650
Head of Household	Under 65	12,000
	65 or older	13,400
Single, if may be claimed as a dependent on another return	Under 65	Greater of $950 or earned income (up to $5,400) + $300[2]
	65 or older or blind	Greater of $950 or earned income (up to $5,400) + $1,700[3]
	65 or older and blind	Greater of $950 or earned income (up to $5,400) + $3,100[4]
Married, if may be claimed as a dependent on another return[5]	Under 65	Greater of $950 or earned income (up to $5,400) + $300[2]
	65 or older or blind	Greater of $950 or earned income (up to $5,400) + $1,400[6]
	65 or older and blind	Greater of $950 or earned income (up to $5,400) + $2,500[7]

[1] If spouses lived apart at the end of 2009, Married Filing Separately floor applies.
[2] Taxpayer must also file if unearned income is over $950.
[3] Taxpayer must also file if unearned income is over $2,350.
[4] Taxpayer must also file if unearned income is over $3,750.
[5] Taxpayer must also file if income is greater than $5 and spouse itemizes deductions on a separate return.
[6] Taxpayer must also file if unearned income is over $2,050.
[7] Taxpayer must also file if unearned income is over $3,150.

Special Filing Requirements

Children. If a child is required to file a return, then the investment income of the child may be taxed at the parents' highest marginal rate. This is referred to as the "kiddie tax" and is discussed at Tab 13 and MTG ¶114. However, the child's parents may elect to report the child's income on their return if the child had only interest and dividend income of more than $950 and less than $9,500, had no federal income tax withheld, and made no estimated tax payments. The parents make the election on Form 8814 which must be filed with their return. If the election is made, the child does not need to file a separate return.

> **Planning Tip.** The election to report a child's income on a parent's return has consequences for the parent's AGI dependent deductions (for example, medical expenses). Thus, it is best to figure the tax consequences of the whether to make the election or not.

Resident and Nonresident Aliens. A resident alien is subject to the same filing requirements that apply to U.S. citizens. A nonresident alien, on the other hand, is taxed only on U.S.-source income and must use Form 1040NR to file a tax return if the individual has more than $3,650 in gross income for 2009 or was engaged in a trade or business in the United States during the year. Students, teachers, or trainees under F, J, M, or Q visas are required to file Form 1040NR only if they have taxable income.

For this purpose, an individual (other than a U.S. citizen) is considered a resident alien if he or she:

- is a lawful permanent resident of the United States during the tax year (has a "green card"); or
- was present in the United States for 31 days in the current tax year and a total of 183 days during the current and two proceeding calendar years (all of the days of physical presence in the United States during the current year count as one full day, while each day in the proceeding year counts as one-third of a day, and each day in the second proceeding year counts as one-sixth of a day).

Any alien individual that fails to meet either of these requirements will be considered a nonresident alien. However, even if the substantial presence test is met, an individual can still be treated as a nonresident alien if they can establish (using Form 8840) that during the tax year they: were present in the United States for less than 183 days, had a tax home in a foreign country, and had a closer connection to a foreign country in which they had the tax home. See MTG ¶2409.

A nonresident alien may also elect to be treated as a resident alien for the entire tax year if the individual is married to a U.S. citizen or resident alien on the last day of the tax year. Both spouses must join in the election and the couple must file a joint tax return. The election is effective for the current tax year and all subsequent tax years.

A nonresident alien may also elect resident status for the current calendar year if they were a nonresident alien for the entire preceding year. The election can only be made if the individual was present for at least 31 consecutive days during the year and 75 percent of the days in the year beginning with the first day of the 31-day period through the end of the year. See MTG ¶2410.

> **Caution.** Practitioners should always consult the applicable tax treaty, if any, prior to preparing an income tax return of a nonresident alien.

Expatriates. U.S. citizens who have relinquished their citizenship and long-term residents whose residency has been terminated may be subject to special rules following their expatriation from the United States. For example, if expatriation occurs after June 16, 2008, the individual will be subject to a mark-to-market tax regime under which they are considered to have sold all of their property on the date before expatriation. See MTG ¶2412. If expatriation occurs before June 17, 2008, the individual will continue to be subject to U.S. income and alternative minimum taxes for 10 years following the date of expatriation and must file Form 1040NR. See MTG ¶2413.

IRS Label and SSN

The taxpayer's Social Security number (SSN) must be written on Form 1040 in the space provided. If filing a joint return, the SSNs of both individuals must be provided in the same order as the taxpayers' names. The order should be used on all forms and documents submitted to the IRS.

> **Planning Tip.** The same order should also be used in all subsequent tax years to avoid any problems.

ITINs. The IRS will issue an individual taxpayer identification number (ITIN) to any resident or nonresident alien who does not have and is not eligible to get an SSN. Form W-7 is used to apply for an ITIN. This number is used on a tax return wherever an SSN is requested.

Taxpayer's Address. Taxpayers whose address changes from the address shown on their last return may use Form 8822 to notify the IRS. The IRS also uses the U.S. Post Office's database to update taxpayer addresses.

Presidential Election Campaign Contribution

Each taxpayer, who is required to file an income tax return, may elect to designate $3 to the presidential election campaign fund. In the case of joint filers, each spouse may make their own designation. The amount of refund or tax owed is unaffected by this choice.

Filing Status, Lines 1-5

There are five categories of filing status that apply to individual taxpayers to determine tax rates, standard deduction, and eligibility for certain deductions. Filing status for the 2009 tax year is determined as of December 31, 2009. If more than one filing status applies to a taxpayer, choose the one that results in the lowest tax.

Filing Tip. Tax return preparers must be sure that the taxpayer provides all information relevant to determining filing status. See sample interview in Tab 16.

Single

A taxpayer may file as single if he or she was never married during the tax year, was divorced or legally separated as of December 31, 2009, or was widowed before January 1, 2009, and did not remarry during the year. However, a single taxpayer may file as a head of household (see page 1-5) or qualifying widow(er) (see page 1-7) if certain requirements are met.

Married Filing Jointly

Couples who are married and not legally separated as of December 31, 2009, may elect to file a joint return for the year, even if the couple lived apart at the end of the year. See MTG ¶152. For federal tax purposes, marriage is the legal union of a man and woman as husband and wife. Same-sex couples cannot file a joint return, even if their union is recognized under state law. However, a common-law marriage recognized under state law does entitle a couple to file a joint return.

Generally, a joint return may not be filed if either spouse is a nonresident alien during the year. However, if a nonresident alien or dual-status alien is married to a U.S. citizen or resident at the end of the year, the nonresident may elect to be treated as a resident alien in order for the couple to file a joint return (see page 1-3).

Caution. Annulment is treated differently than divorce. Because an annulment means the couple was never legally married, any tax returns that were filed as married filing separately or married filing jointly must be amended if the tax year is still open.

If a couple files a joint return, then both spouses are generally responsible for the tax and any interest and penalties due on the return. For this reason, both spouses must generally sign the return (see page 1-44). Once a joint return is filed, the couple cannot choose to file separate returns for that year if the due date for the return has passed. However, the executor of a deceased spouse may disaffirm a joint return and file a late separate return.

Surviving Spouse. If a married taxpayer dies during the year, the surviving spouse may elect to file a joint return with the deceased spouse provided the surviving spouse did not remarry during the year. For the next two years, the taxpayer may then be able to file as a qualifying widower provided there is a qualifying child dependent who resides with them in their principal residence (see page 1-7). In the case of a spouse of a member of the Armed Forces serving in a combat zone and listed as missing, a joint return may be filed for up to two years following the termination of combat activities (the return is valid even if it is later determined that the missing spouse died before the year covered in the return). See MTG ¶175.

Married Filing Separately

Married individuals who do not elect to file a joint return usually have to file as married filing separately. Married filing separately status generally results in higher tax liability than filing a joint return. However, in some cases, filing separate returns may result in a lower tax liability (such as when one spouse has deductions that are subject to an AGI limitation). See the table on page 1-6 and MTG ¶156 for information related to the decision to file jointly or separately.

If a married individual lives apart from his or her spouse at the end of the tax year, then the individual may elect head of household filing status if certain conditions are met (see page 1-5). However, a married couple must file separately when one spouse is a nonresident alien, unless the election to be treated as a resident alien is made (see page 1-3).

Caution. When one spouse uses the married filing separately status, the other spouse must also. Tax preparers should request that their client make every effort to ascertain the filing status of the other spouse and whether they are going to itemize their deductions. This is because if one spouse itemizes deduction, then the other must also itemize unless they qualify for head-of-household filing status. A good practice is to always explain thoroughly the consequences of the married filing separately status to your client. Be sure to note on the file that you had this discussion or, even better, have the client sign a statement to the effect that you have explained the consequences.

How To File. If a couple files as married filing separately, each spouse must report only his or her own income, exemptions, deductions and credits on their return. In most states, income is allocated to the spouse who earned it. Interest is allocated to the spouse who owned the property or account that earned the interest. Expenses paid from separate funds are treated as paid by the spouse who owned the funds. Expenses paid from joint funds are treated as though each spouse paid half unless otherwise proven.

If the couple resides in a community property state, then income is geconsidered community income, and half is allocable to each spouse regardless of who earned it. See MTG ¶710 and ¶711, and IRS Publication 555. Community property states include Arizona, California, Idaho, Louisiana, Nevada, New Mexico, Texas, Washington, and Wisconsin. A registered domestic partner in California must report only his or her own wages, salaryand other compensation received on his or her own return.

Head of Household

An unmarried person who provides a home for a qualifying person(s) may file as head of household entitling the individual to a lower tax rate and higher standard deduction than allowed for single individuals or married individuals filing separately. See MTG ¶173. A taxpayer may file as head of household only if:

- he/she is a U.S. citizen or resident alien for the entire tax year;
- he/she is unmarried or "considered unmarried;"
- he/she paid more than half the cost of keeping up a home in which he or she lives for the year; and
- the taxpayer's household is the principal place of abode for a "qualifying person" for more than half of the year.

Filing Tip. Assuming all other requirements are met, a taxpayer may qualify as head of household if he or she maintains a household for a father or mother for whom a dependency exemption may be claimed, even if the parent does not live in the taxpayer's home. Instead, the taxpayer may maintain a household for the parent by providing more than half the cost of maintenance of any home that is the parent's principal place of abode.

Considered Unmarried. To qualify for head of household status, an individual must actually be unmarried or "considered unmarried" on the last day of the tax year. An individual is considered unmarried if:

- he/she file a separate return;
- he/she paid more than half the cost of keeping up his or her home for the tax year;
- his/her spouse did not live in the home during the last six months of the tax year;
- his/her home was the principal place of abode of their child, stepchild, adopted child, or foster child for more than half of the tax year; *and*
- he/she can claim the child as a dependent (unless the child's other parent can claim the child under the rules for divorced or separate parents, see page 1-11).

If an individual's spouse was a nonresident alien at any time during the year, then the taxpayer will be considered unmarried and eligible for head of household filing status unless the election is made to treat the nonresident alien spouse as a resident alien (see page 1-3). However, the nonresident alien spouse is not a qualifying person for head of household purposes. In addition, the taxpayer will still be considered married for purposes of the earned income credit.

Caution. A taxpayer must actually be unmarried (as opposed to being "considered unmarried") to claim any person other than their child as a qualifying person for head of household status. Thus, a married taxpayer who claims someone other than their child as the qualifying person (parent, niece, nephew, etc.) does not qualify for head of household status, even if all of the other head of household requirements are met.

Keeping Up a Home. To qualify for head of household status, an individual must have paid more than half of the cost of keeping up his or her home during the tax year. For this purpose, the cost of keeping up a home includes rent, property tax, mortgage interest, utilities, repairs, food consumed on the premises, and other household expenses. It does not include the costs for education, medical treatment, life insurance, transportation, or clothing.

Qualifying Person. For purposes of head of household filing status, a qualifying person with whom the taxpayer must live with includes:

- any qualifying child of the taxpayer (see page 1-8) if:
  - the child is single (whether or not the taxpayer can claim an exemption for them) or
  - the child is married and the taxpayer can claim an exemption for them;
- the taxpayer's parent for whom he or she can claim an exemption for; or
- any qualifying relative of the taxpayer other than a parent (see page 1-9) who lived with the taxpayer for more than half of the tax year, is related to the taxpayer, and for whom an exemption can be claimed.

A person cannot be a qualifying person for more than one taxpayer for the tax year for purposes of the head of household filing status. Also, if an exemption can be claimed for a person only because of a multiple support agreement, that person cannot be a qualifying person.

Example. Jonathan is an unmarried individual. His sister Margaret lived in a home for the developmentally disabled for all of 2009. Margaret had no income during the year and Jonathan provided all of her support. Jonathan can claim Margaret as a dependent on his tax return since she is a *qualifying relative* under the definitions for a dependent (see page 1-7). Margaret, however, is not a *qualifying person* for Jonathan for purposes of the head of household filing status since she did not live with him for more than half the year. Jonathan must file as a single individual.

Choosing Married Filing Separately Filing Status

Advantages

- No joint liability. Married taxpayers who file separate returns are not liable for the accuracy of their spouse's returns or for the payment of their spouse's tax.
- If one spouse owes child support or federal debts for which a tax refund may be offset, the other spouse's refund is not at risk.
- Some couples pay less tax. If one spouse has large itemized deduction subject to AGI limits (medical expenses or employee expenses), these deductions may result in a lower tax when the spouses file separately.

Disadvantages

- Tax rate is generally higher than on a joint return.
- The standard deduction is half the amount allowed on a joint return.
- If one spouse itemizes deductions, the other cannot claim the standard deduction.
- The first-time homebuyer credit is limited to $4,000 (instead of $8,000 if a joint return is filed).
- Exemption amount for figuring the AMT is half of that allowed on a joint return.
- Capital loss deduction limit is $1,500 (instead of the $3,000 limit for a joint return).
- Amount excluded from income under an employer's dependent care assistance program is limited to $2,500 (instead of the $5,000 limit for a joint return).

Deductions and credits reduced at lower income levels:

- Deduction for personal exemptions
- Itemized deductions
- Child tax credit
- Retirement savings contributions credit

Ineligible for:

- Credit for child and dependent care expenses, in most cases
- Earned income credit
- Exclusion or credit for adoption expenses, in most cases
- Hope scholarship credit, lifetime learning credit, deduction for student loan interest, and tuition and fees deduction
- Cannot exclude any interest income from qualified U.S. savings bonds that was used for higher education expenses

If spouses lived together at any time during the tax year:

- Ineligible for credit for the elderly or the disabled
- Must include in income up to 85% of Social Security benefits or equivalent railroad retirement benefits
- Cannot roll over amounts from a traditional IRA into a Roth IRA

Qualifying Widow(er)

An individual may file as a qualifying widow(er) in 2009 if all of the following apply:

- the taxpayer's spouse died in 2007 or 2008 and the taxpayer did not remarry as of December 31, 2009;
- the taxpayer was entitled to file a joint return with the deceased spouse for the year in which the spouse died (it does not matter whether a joint return was actually filed); and
- the taxpayer paid over half of the cost of maintaining his or her home during 2009, and the home was the principal residence of the taxpayer's child or stepchild for whom the taxpayer may claim an exemption (foster children do not qualify).

Exemptions, Lines 6a-6d

For tax year 2009, the amount allowed for each personal and dependent exemption is generally $3,650. The amount of the exemption is reduced for high-income taxpayers (see page 1-35). The exemption is not reduced in the event of the death of the taxpayer, spouse, or dependent during the tax year. See MTG ¶149.

An additional exemption amount of $500 may also be claimed for providing housing free of charge to each individual displaced by the severe storms and flooding in the Midwest during the summer of 2008 (up to $2,000 over 2008 and 2009) (see page 1-35). The taxpayer must include the displaced individual's taxpayer identification number on the return for the year the additional exemption is claimed.

Personal Exemptions

A taxpayer can claim a personal exemption if he or she cannot be claimed as a dependent by anyone else. On a joint return, a personal exemption can be claimed for each spouse. If married individuals file separate returns, each spouse claims their own personal exemption. However, one spouse may claim the personal exemption of the other spouse on a separate return if the other spouse has no gross income, is not filing a return, and is not a dependent of another taxpayer. If one spouse dies during the year, then the surviving spouse may still claim the personal exemption of the deceased spouse on either a joint or separate return as described, but only if the surviving spouse does not remarry during the year.

> **Caution.** A taxpayer (or their spouse) who *may* be claimed as a dependent on another person's return may not claim his or her own personal exemption (or spouse's personal exemption) even if the exemption is not actually claimed on the other person's return. This is particularly important to remember in the case of college students living at home. See Tab 13.

Dependency Exemption

A taxpayer is allowed to claim an exemption for each person he or she can claim as a dependent. For 2009, a person can be claimed as a dependent only if he or she is a "qualifying child" or a "qualifying relative" of the taxpayer. However, even if a person is a qualifying child or qualifying relative, a taxpayer cannot claim a dependency exemption for them if:

- the taxpayer (or spouse, if filing a joint return) can be claimed as a dependent by another person;
- the qualified child or qualified relative is not a U.S. citizen, U.S. national, U.S. resident alien, or a resident of Canada or Mexico, for part of the year (however, an exception exists for a child legally adopted by a U.S. citizen or U.S. national if the child is a member of the taxpayer's household for the entire year);
- the qualified child or qualified relative is married and files a joint return for the tax year (unless the joint return was only filed as a claim for refund or there is no tax liability for either spouse on separate returns).

A Social Security number (SSN) must be reported by the taxpayer for each person he or she claims as a dependent. If the dependent does not have a SSN or cannot get one as in the case of a resident or non-resident alien, as well as adoptee, then the taxpayer must provide the dependent's taxpayer identification number (ITIN) or adoption taxpayer identification number (ATIN) in the case of a domestic adoption still pending.

If a child was born and died during the tax year and no SSN was obtained, then enter "DIED" in column (2) of line 6c next to the child's name and attach a copy of the child's birth certificate, death certificate, or hospital records. A child born alive during the year may be claimed as an exemption for the entire year, even if he or she dies during the year. However, a still-born child may not be claimed.

> **Caution.** The dependency exemption amount is denied to claimants who fail to provide the dependent's correct SSN or ITIN on the return. The exemption may also be denied if the SSN or ITIN fails to match the name on file with the Social Security Administration.

Qualifying Child. There are five requirements for an individual to be considered a qualifying child of a taxpayer for the 2009 tax year.

> **Filing Tip.** An individual who is not a "qualifying child" of the taxpayer because of failure to meet any one of these requirements may still be claimed as a dependent by the taxpayer if the child meets the requirements for being a "qualifying relative" of the taxpayer (see page 1-9).

1. *Relationship.* In order to be a qualifying child, the child must be the taxpayer's:

- child, stepchild, adopted child, foster child, or a descendant of any such child; or
- brother, sister, step-brother, step-sister, half-brother, half-sister, or a descendant of any such person (for example, niece or nephew).

An adopted child includes any child legally placed with the taxpayer by an authorized agency. A foster child is any child placed with the taxpayer by an authorized placement agency or by a judgment or decree issued by a court.

2. *Residency.* A qualifying child must have resided with the taxpayer for more than one-half of the year in the same principal place of abode. Temporary absences for illness, school, vacation, or military service may count as time lived with the taxpayer. Special rules apply in the case of children of divorced or separated parents (see page 1-11). In addition, a child who is born or dies during the tax year will be considered as living with the taxpayer for the entire year if the taxpayer's home was the child's home for the entire time he or she was alive.

If a child is presumed by law enforcement authorities to have been kidnapped by someone who is not a member of the family of the child or the taxpayer, and the child shared the same principal place of abode as the taxpayer for more than half of the portion of the year preceding the kidnapping, then the child satisfies the residency test for all tax years ending during the period in which the child is missing. A missing child ceases to satisfy the residency test in the taxpayer's first tax year beginning after the calendar year in which the child is determined to be dead or, if earlier, in which the child would have attained the age of 18.

3. *Age Requirement.* A qualifying child is an individual who is:

- under the age of 19 at the end of the calendar year;
- under the age of 24 at the end of the calendar year and a full-time student for at least five calendar months during the year; or
- permanently and totally disabled at any time during the calendar year, regardless of age.

Beginning in 2009, the individual must also be younger than the taxpayer in order to be claimed as a qualifying child. For example, a taxpayer's older brother or sister cannot be the taxpayer's qualifying child.

4. *Support.* The qualifying child must **not** provide over one-half their own support during the year. For this purpose, a scholarship received by a child who is a full-time student is not considered. This test is different from the support test to be a qualifying relative or to be eligible for head of household filing status (see page 1-10).

> **Example.** Jasmine is 19 years old and a full-time student. She lives with her father but only receives one-third of her support from him. The remaining two-thirds of her support comes from a trust set up by her grandmother. As a result, Jasmine is not a qualifying child of her father. The trust income is attributable to Jasmine and she therefore provides more than half of her own support.

5. *Joint Return.* Beginning in 2009, an individual cannot be a qualifying child of another taxpayer if they file a joint tax return with his or her spouse for the year unless the joint return is filed *solely* as a claim for refund (for example, a refund of taxes withheld from wages).

> **Caution.** A taxpayer is already prohibited from claiming a dependency exemption for an individual who files a joint tax return for the year; thus, the separate return requirement does not affect who is a qualifying child for the purposes of claiming a dependency exemption. However, because the definition of a qualifying child is used for claiming other tax benefits, the separate return requirement applies to claiming those benefits (see page 1-9).

Qualifying Child of More Than One Person. A child may meet the requirements to be a qualifying child of more than one taxpayer. However, only one taxpayer can claim the child as a qualifying child for purposes of the following tax benefits (unless the special rule for children of divorced or separated parents applies, see page 1-11):

- dependency exemption;
- child tax credit;
- head of household filing status;
- dependent care credit;
- exclusion of dependent care benefits; and
- earned income tax credit.

If two individuals have the same qualifying child, they cannot agree to divide these tax benefits between themselves. Instead, they can only decide who will treat the child as a qualifying child for purposes of all of the tax benefits. However, if the individuals cannot agree and more than one tax return is filed claiming the same child as a qualifying child, then the IRS will disallow all but one of the claims based on the following ordering rules:

- if only one of the taxpayers is the child's parent, then the child is the qualifying child of the parent;
- if child's parents do not file a joint return, then the child is the qualifying child of the parent with whom the child lived with the longest during the year;
- if the child resided with both parents equally during the year and the parents do not file a joint return, then the child is the qualifying child of the parent with the highest AGI;
- if none of the taxpayers claiming the child are the child's parent, then the child is the qualifying child of the person with the highest AGI; or
- if the parents may claim the child as a qualifying child, but do not actually do so, then the child may be the qualifying child of any other taxpayer but only if his or her AGI is higher than the AGI of either parent.

Special rules apply in determining how a noncustodial parent may claim a child as a qualified child (see page 1-11).

Qualifying Relative(s). There are four requirements for a person to be considered a qualifying relative of a taxpayer for purposes of the dependency exemption

1. *Not a Qualifying Child.* A person is not a qualifying relative of a taxpayer if that person meets the requirements for being a qualifying child of any other taxpayer. However, if the other taxpayer is not required to file a return for the year or files a return *solely* as a claim for refund, then the child is not a qualifying child of the other taxpayer.

Example. Mary and her infant son from another relationship move in with her boyfriend Jeff in 2009. Mary has $8,500 of earned income in 2009 from which income taxes were withheld. Even though she is not required to file a return for the year, she files one anyway to obtain a refund of the withheld taxes and to claim the earned income tax credit. If Mary and Jeff remain unmarried to each other during the year, the child is the qualifying child of Mary. The child cannot be the qualifying relative of Jeff even if all other requirements are met because Mary did not file her return solely as a claim for refund.

2. *Relationship or Member of Household Test.* To be a qualifying relative, a person must have either lived in the taxpayer's home all year as a member of the household or be related to the taxpayer (or spouse, if filing a joint return) by one of these relationships:

- child, stepchild, adopted child, foster child, or a descendant of any such child;
- brother, sister, half brother, half sister, stepbrother, or stepsister;
- parent, grandparent, or other direct ancestor (other than foster parent), as well as any stepparent;
- brother or sister of the taxpayer's parent (aunt or uncle), as well as any son or daughter of the taxpayer's brother or sister (niece or nephew); or
- father-in-law, mother-in-law, son-in-law, daughter-in-law, brother-in-law, or sister-in-law.

A person is considered to live in the taxpayer's home as a member of the household even if he or she (or the taxpayer) is temporarily absent due to vacation, school, business, illness, or military service. A person who died during the tax year, but lived in the taxpayer's home as a member of household until death also qualifies. Likewise, a dependent born during the year who becomes a member of the household immediately after birth is considered a member a household member for the entire year.

3. *Gross Income Test.* To be a qualifying relative, a dependent's gross income for 2009 must be less than $3,650. Gross income includes all income in the form of money, property, and services that is not exempt from tax, such as receipts from rental property, a partner's share of gross partnership income, and unemployment compensation. Gross income does not include income received by a disabled individual for services performed at a sheltered workshop, if the availability of medical services is the primary reason for participation. See MTG ¶143.

4. *Support Test.* In order for a person to be a qualifying relative, the taxpayer must have provided over half of the person's total support during the calendar year. Thus, it is the taxpayer's responsibility to prove not only the support he or she provided to the person, but also the total support the person received during the year from. See MTG ¶147.

"Total support" includes amounts spent to provide food, shelter, clothing, education, medical and dental care, transportation, and similar necessities. Expenses that are not directly related to any one member of a household must be divided among members of the household.

Items ***not*** included in total support include:

- the person's own funds which are not actually spent for support;
- federal, state, and local income taxes paid by persons from their own income;
- Social Security and Medicare taxes paid by persons from their own income;
- life insurance premiums;
- funeral expenses;
- scholarships received by a taxpayer's child if the child is a full-time student;
- Survivors' and Dependents' Educational Assistance and Aid to Families with Dependent Children (AFDC) payments used for support of the child who receives them; and
- governmental or charitable assistance received due to the storms and flooding in the Midwestern disaster area in 2008.

Example. Grace lives with her son David and his two children during the year. She had $4,400 in Social Security income during the year, which she used to pay $1,200 in life insurance premiums and $2,200 in medical expenses. The fair rental value of the lodging provided to Grace is $2,400 for the year. David paid all of his mother's other expenses, including an additional $1,200 in medical expenses and $1,000 for other items such as clothing, transportation, and entertainment. He also spent $5,200 in total food expenses for the household. Grace's total support for the year was $7,900. The support David provides to his mother is than half of her total support ($2,400 lodging + $1,200 medical expenses + $1,300 share of food + $1,000 miscellaneous items).

In most cases, a child of divorced or separated parents will be the qualifying child of one of the parents. However, if the child does not meet the requirements to be a qualifying child of either parent, the child may be a qualifying relative of one of the parents. In this case, the parent who has custody of the child for the greater part of the year as determined under the most recent divorce decree or separate maintenance agreement is generally treated as providing more than half of the child's support for the year, regardless of whether they did or not.

Example. Dana and Casey, a divorced couple, jointly provided for all of their child's total support for 2009. Dana provided 25 percent of the support and Casey provided 75 percent. For the first eight months of the year, Dana had custody of the child under the couple's 2003 divorce decree. On August 31, 2009, a new custody decree granted custody to Casey. Because Dana had custody for the greater part of the year, she is considered to have provided more than half of the child's support during the year.

For special rules on how a noncustodial parent may claim a child as a qualified child or qualified relative, see the discussion on page 1-11.

Multiple Support Agreements. Sometimes no one taxpayer provides more than half of the support of a dependent in order to be a qualifying relative. Instead, two or more persons, each of whom would be able to take the exemption except for the support test, together may provide more than half of the person's support.

When this happens, the taxpayers who provide more than 10 percent of the dependent's support can agree that any one of them may claim the exemption. Each of the other taxpayers must sign a statement agreeing not to claim the exemption for that year. The person who claims the exemption must keep these statements with his or her tax records. A multiple support declaration identifying each of the others who agreed not to claim the exemption must also be attached to the return of the taxpayer claiming the exemption. Form 2120 is used for this purpose.

Example. Three children provided the entire support for their mother for the tax year. Alice provided 55 percent, Bob provided 35 percent and Cliff provided 10 percent. Provided the other requirements for the qualifying relative test are met, either Alice or Bob may claim a dependency exemption for their mother, so long as the other one signs a statement agreeing not to take the exemption. Because Cliff did not provide more than 10 percent of the support, he cannot claim the exemption and Alice or Bob do not have to get a signed statement from him to claim the exemption.

Planning Tip. Several things should be taken into consideration in determining which taxpayer will claim a dependent under a multiple support agreement.

First, due to the phaseout of the dependency exemption, some high income taxpayers may not receive the full benefit of the deduction. In such cases, the taxpayer may choose to release the exemption. On the other hand, low-income taxpayers do not receive as large a tax advantage because their tax rate is lower. For example, it is generally more advantageous for a taxpayer in the 15 percent tax bracket to relinquish the exemption to a taxpayer in the 28 percent tax bracket.

Second, medical expenses paid by a taxpayer for someone who is claimed as a dependent by another taxpayer under a multiple support agreement are not deductible. Only the taxpayer claiming the exemption is entitled to deduct medical expenses paid on behalf of the dependent.

Children of Divorced or Separated Parents. Generally, a child of divorce or separated parents is the qualifying child or qualifying relative of the parent who has primary custody of the child during the year. However, a child may be treated as the qualifying child or qualifying relative of the noncustodial parent if:

- the parents are divorced, legally separated, separated under a written separation agreement, or lived apart at all times during the last six months of the calendar year;
- one or both parents provide more than half of the child's total support for the calendar year (determined without regard to any multiple support agreement);
- one or both parents have custody of the child for more than half of the calendar year; and
- the custodial parent makes a written declaration that he or she will not claim the exemption and noncustodial parent attaches the declaration to his or her tax return for each year the exemption is claimed.

For this purpose, the custodial parent is the parent with whom the child resides for the greater number of nights during the calendar year. Temporary absences count toward the parent the child would have resided with for the night (for example, sleepover at a friend's home or nights on vacation). If the child resides with each parent for an equal number of nights during the year, then the parent with the highest AGI is the custodial parent.

Caution. A State court order or divorce decree will not apply to allocate the dependency exemption between divorced or separated parents. The rules discussed above are the sole means for determining which parent may claim the exemption.

Form 8332 or similar statement must be used by the custodial parent to make a written declaration to release the dependency exemption to the noncustodial parent. The release must be signed by the custodial parent and specify the year or years for which it is effective. If it specifies that it applies to all future years, then it is effective the first tax year after the year it is executed. The release must not be conditioned on the noncustodial parent meeting some obligation such as the payment of child support or alimony. The custodial parent may revoke the release for future tax years by providing a written notice of the revocation to the noncustodial parent. A copy of the revocation must be attached to the custodial parent's return for any year he or she claims the exemption as a result of the revocation.

Planning Note. The noncustodial parent must attach the signed Form 8332 or similar statement to his or her return to claim the dependency exemption for the child. If the exemption is released for more than one year, then the original release must be attached to the return for the first year, and a copy must be attached for each later year. Beginning with 2009 tax returns, the noncustodial parent can no longer attach pages from the divorce decree or separation agreement to claim a dependency exemption.

If all of the above requirements are met, the noncustodial parent may only claim a child as a qualifying child for purposes of the dependency exemption and the child tax credit. The noncustodial parent may not claim the child as a qualifying child for purpose of head of household filing status, dependent care credit, the exclusion of dependent care benefits, earned income credit, and the health coverage tax credit.

However, the child may be claimed as a dependent by both parents for purposes of deducting and excluding certain medical and fringe benefits from gross income regardless of whether or not the custodial parent releases the dependency exemption. This includes:

- itemized medical deductions of the taxpayer's child;
- employer medical reimbursements for medical care of an employee's child;

- employer-provided health insurance on behalf of the employee's children;
- fringe benefits for no-additional-cost services or qualified employee discounts due to use by an employee's child; and
- distributions from HSAs and Archer MSAs used to pay qualified medical expenses of the account beneficiary's child.

Planning Note. Without this rule, a noncustodial parent could not deduct or exclude the medical and fringe benefits from gross income without a release of the dependency exemption from the custodial parent. This relief applies for any tax year beginning after 2004. Thus, parents may claim a refund for any prior tax year so long as the statute of limitations has not expired.

Overview of the Rules for Claiming an Exemption for a Dependent

• If the taxpayer, or the taxpayer's spouse if filing a joint return, can be claimed as a dependent by another taxpayer, then the taxpayer cannot claim any dependent.

• The taxpayer cannot claim a married person who files a joint return as a dependent unless that joint return is only a claim for refund and there would be no tax liability for either spouse on separate returns.

• The taxpayer cannot claim a person as a dependent unless that person is a U.S. citizen, U.S. resident, U.S. national, or a resident of Canada or Mexico, for some part of the year.[1]

• The taxpayer cannot claim a person as a dependent unless that person is a qualifying child or qualifying relative.

Tests to Be a Qualifying Child	Tests to Be a Qualifying Relative
1. The child must be the taxpayer's son, daughter, stepchild, eligible foster child, brother, sister, half brother, half sister, stepbrother, stepsister, or descendant of any of them.	1. The person cannot be the qualifying child of any other taxpayer unless the other taxpayer is not required to file a return for the year or files solely as a claim for refund.
2. The child must be younger than the taxpayer and (a) under age 19 at the end of the calendar year, (b) under age 24 at the end of the calendar year and a full-time student, or (c) any age if permanently and totally disabled.	2. The person must either (a) live with the taxpayer the entire year as a member of the taxpayer's household,[2] or (b) be related to the taxpayer (or spouse, if filing a joint return) as their child or descendent of the child, sibling, parent, grandparent, stepparent, aunt, uncle, niece, nephew, or in-law.
3. The child must have lived with the taxpayer for more than half of the year.[2]	3. The person's gross income for the year must be less than $3,650.[3]
4. The child must not have provided more than half of his or her own support for the year.	4. The taxpayer must provide more than half of the person's total support for the tax year.[4]
5. If the child meets the rules to be a qualifying child of more than one taxpayer, only one of them may claim the child as a qualifying child for the dependency exemption and other tax benefits.	

[1] There is an exception for certain adopted children.
[2] There are exceptions for temporary absences, children who were born or died during the year, children of divorced or separated parents, and kidnapped children.
[3] There is an exception if the person is disabled and has income from a sheltered workshop.
[4] There is an exception for multiple support agreements.

Income, Lines 7-22

Generally, all income from whatever source except those items specifically exempted are taxable. Note that some types of income may not be reported to the taxpayer. Not all payers are required to provide an information return (e.g., Form W-2 or 1099) to the recipient. This does not excuse the taxpayer from reporting these unreported amounts as income. See the chart beginning on page 1-23 of common gross income inclusions and exclusions, and where to report includible income.

Line 7, Wages, Salaries, Tips, Etc.

Report on line 7, the taxpayer's (and spouse if filing a joint return) wages, salaries, fees, and other compensation for personal services for the year, including taxable fringe benefits, employee bonuses or awards, employer reimbursements, etc (see MTG ¶713). For most people, the amount to enter is reported in box 1 of Form W-2. However, other amounts to report on line 7 include:

- wages earned as a household employee for which the employer was not required to issue a Form W-2 because the amount was less than $1,700 in 2009 (enter "HSH" and the amount not reported on Form W-2 on the dotted line next to line 7);

- taxable dependent care benefits (box 10 of Form W-2 and Form 2441);
- taxable adoption assistance provided by an employer (box 12 of Form W-2, code T, and Form 8839);
- strike and lockout benefits provided by a union;
- elective salary deferrals (box 12 of Form W-2 codes D, E, F, G, H, or S) to the extent they exceed the excludable amount for the year (see Tab 9); or
- disability pensions received before retirement age (Form 1099-R).

Filing Tip. If the "statutory employee" box on Form W-2 is checked, do not enter the amount from box 1 on Form 1040, line 7. Instead, enter the amount on Schedule C, line 1. For a discussion of statutory employees see Tab 3 and MTG ¶941B.

Missing or Incorrect Form W-2. Employers are required to report wages and other earnings paid to an employee in 2009 on Form W-2 by February 1, 2010. A taxpayer who does not receive the form by that date, or receives an incorrect form, should always first contact the employer. If the taxpayer has not received a Form W-2 or corrected Form W-2 by February 15, 2010, then the taxpayer should contact the IRS.

If the taxpayer does not receive a Form W-2 or corrected Form W-2 from the employer by April 15, 2010, then Form 4852 should be used as a substitute for Form W-2 to estimate wages and earnings for the year, as well as taxes withheld from wages. The substitute can usually be created from the taxpayer's last paycheck received from the employer for 2009. The taxpayer should also check his or her Social Security Statement received after the end of the tax year.

Filing Tip. If the taxpayer receives a Form W-2 from the employer after their tax return is filed, and the information differs from that reported on Form 4852, then the taxpayer must file an amended return to match the information reported on Form W-2.

If the taxpayer is convinced that amounts reported to him or her by an employer as self-employment income on Form 1099 are actually wages, then Form 8919 should be used to calculate the taxpayer's unreported Social Security and Medicare taxes from the income. This occurs if the employer misclassifies the taxpayer as an independent contractor, rather than an employee. The income the taxpayer receive should be reported as wages on line 7 and the taxes are included on line 57 (see page 1-37).

Filing Tip. If the taxpayer is convinced that income he or she receives is from wages and not self-employment, Form SS-8 should be submitted to request a determination from the IRS of the taxpayer's status for purposes of federal employment taxes and income tax withholding. Submission of Form SS-8, however, does not relieve the taxpayer from timely filing and paying any income and employment taxes due.

Tips. All tips received by the taxpayer are income subject to tax including tips paid by cash, check, debit or credit card, or received in noncash items such as tickets or passes. If the taxpayer received $20 or more of tips in a month, then the tips must be reported to the taxpayer's employer on Form 4070 by the 10th day of the following month. If the taxpayer worked for more than one employer in any month, then the $20 rule applies separately to the tips received while working for each employer and not the total received. The taxpayer may use Form 4070A (found in IRS Publication 1244) to maintain a daily record of tips received.

Tips reported to an employer are included in box 1 of Form W-2 and reported on line 7 of Form 1040. The taxpayer must also include on line 7, all tips not reported to the employer on Form 4070. In addition, the taxpayer's employer may allocate tips to employees under a tip-splitting or tip-pooling arrangement. Allocated tips are reported separately in box 8 of Form W-2 and must be included as wages on line 7, unless the taxpayer can prove a lesser amount was received. See IRS Publication 531 for more information.

Example. John Allen began working at the Diamond Restaurant (his only employer for the year) on June 30 and received $10,000 in wages during the year. John kept a daily tip record showing that his tips for June were $18 and his tips for the rest of the year totaled $7,000. He was not required to report his June tips to his employer, but he reported all of the rest of his tips to his employer as required. John's Form W-2 from Diamond Restaurant shows $17,000 ($10,000 in wages plus $7,000 in reported tips) in box 1. He adds the $18 in unreported tips to that amount and reports $17,018 on line 7 of his tax return.

If the taxpayer received $20 or more in tips in a month from any one job and did not report all of those tips to his or her employer, then Social Security and Medicare taxes on the unreported tips must be paid. The taxpayer must also pay Social Security and Medicare taxes on all allocated tips reported on line 8 of Form W-2. Form 4137 is used to figure these taxes. They are then reported on line 57 of Form 1040 (See page 1-37). In addition, if an employer can not collect all the Social Security and Medicare taxes the taxpayer owes on tips reported for the tax year, then the uncollected taxes will be shown in box 12 of Form W-2 (Codes A and B). Those taxes must also be reported on line 57 of Form 1040 (see page 1-37).

Scholarships and Fellowship Grants. A taxpayer who is a candidate for a degree can exclude from income amounts received as a scholarship or fellowship grant which is used for tuition to attend school or fees, books, supplies and equipment required for his or her studies. Any amount used for other expenses, such as room and board, is taxable and must be included on line 7 (enter "SCH" and the taxable amount next to line 7). See Tab 13 and MTG ¶879.

Military Personnel. Generally, any payment a taxpayer receives as a member of the U.S. Armed Forces is treated as wages and reported in box 1 of Form W-2 and on line 7 of Form 1040. However, certain items are excluded from income including retirement pay (which is taxed as a pension), certain allowances (living, moving, traveling, family, death), and combat zone pay (see MTG ¶895). In addition, the taxpayer may elect to treat excludable combat pay as earned income for purposes of determining the earned income credit, the refundable portion of the child tax credit (see Tab 10) and deductible contributions to an IRA (see page 1-31).

Planning Tip. Beginning in 2009, differential wage payments made by an employer to an active member of the U.S. uniformed services will be reported as wages in box 1 of Form W-2 for income tax withholding purposes. However, the wages will not be subject to FICA or FUTA taxes.

Workers' Compensation. Amounts received as workers' compensation for an occupational sickness or injury are fully exempt from tax if they are paid under a workers' compensation act or similar statute. The exemption also applies to survivors. The exemption, however, does not apply to retirement plan benefits received based on age, length of service, or prior contributions to the plan, even if retirement was due to an occupational sickness or injury. In addition, if part of the workers' compensation reduces Social Security or equivalent railroad retirement benefits, that part is considered Social Security benefits and may be taxable. For more information, see MTG ¶851 and IRS Publication 915.

Filing Tip. Sick pay received by a taxpayer is taxable, depending on how his or her employer's plan. The employer, union, or employee benefits guide should be consulted.

Lines 8a and 8b, Interest

Interest income is generally reported to the taxpayer on Form 1099-INT (or Form 1099-OID), or on Schedule K-1 of Form 1065 or Form 1120S. The taxpayer's total taxable interest is reported on line 8a. However, the taxpayer must also complete Schedule B of Form 1040 if he or she:

- received more than $1,500 of taxable interest or ordinary dividends during the year;
- is claiming the exclusion from gross income of interest from Series EE or I U.S. savings bonds;
- has accrued interest on a bond between interest payment dates;
- received interest from a seller-financed mortgage and the buyer who used the property as a personal residence;
- received interest or ordinary dividends as a nominee;
- is reporting original issue discount interest less than the amount shown on Form 1099-OID;
- is reducing the interest income on a bond by the amount of the amortizable premiums; or
- has a foreign bank account or received a distribution from a foreign trust, was the grantor of a foreign trust, or transferred property to a foreign trust (see Tab 2 for more information).

Tax-exempt interest is reported on line 8b, such as interest from a municipal bond or exempt-interest dividends from a mutual fund.

Caution. Do not include interest earned on a individual retirement account (IRA), health savings account (HSA), Archer or Medicare Advantage MSA, or Coverdell education savings account on line 8a or line 8b.

Original Issue Discount (OID). Original issue discount (OID) is reported to the taxpayer in box 1 of Form 1099-OID. For a more detailed discussion of treatment of OID interest, see Tab 2 and MTG ¶1952-¶1956.

Lines 9a and 9b, Dividends

Dividends are distributions of money, stock, or other property paid by a corporation on stock or received through a partnership, an estate, a trust, or an association that is taxed as a corporation. Dividend income is generally reported to the taxpayer on Form 1099-DIV, or on Schedule K-1 of Form 1065 or Form 1120S. There are two types of dividends.

Ordinary Dividends. Ordinary dividends are reported in box 1a of Form 1099-DIV and are fully includible in gross income. A taxpayer reports his or her total ordinary dividends on line 9a of Form 1040. However, the taxpayer must also complete Schedule B if the total amount of ordinary dividends received during the year is over $1,500 or the ordinary dividends were received as a nominee. See Tab 2 and MTG ¶733.

Caution. Some distributions that a taxpayer receives are called dividends but are actually interest income that must be report on line 8a (for example, dividends on deposits in credit unions, mutual savings banks). Similarly, other distributions that may be called dividends should be reported as other income on line 21 (patronage dividends of cooperative, Alaska Permanent Fund dividends, see page 1-20).

Filing Tip. Some distributions with respect to corporate stock is a return of the taxpayer's cost and reduces the taxpayer's basis of the stock. Once such basis is recovered, the distribution may be considered capital gains and the taxpayer will be required to file Schedule D of Form 1040. See Tab 4 and MTG ¶1736.

Qualified Dividends. Certain qualified dividends are eligible to be taxed at the lower capital gains rates, rather than tax rates that apply to ordinary income. A taxpayer's qualified dividends are shown in box 1b of Form 1099-DIV and reported on line 9b of Form 1040. Qualified dividends are either subject to a 15 percent tax rate or not taxed at all depending on the ordinary income rate that would otherwise apply. The worksheet reproduced on page 1-57 is used to calculate the tax on qualified dividends and capital gains. See also Tab 4.

To qualify for the reduced tax rate, the dividends must have been paid by a U.S. corporation or a qualified foreign corporation. In addition, the taxpayer must have held the stock for at least 61 days during the 121-day period that begins 60 days before the ex-dividend date (the first date following the declaration of a dividend on which the seller, not the buyer, of a stock will receive the next dividend payment). When counting the number of days the stock was held, include the day the stock was disposed, but not the day it was acquired.

Example. Joshua bought 10,000 shares of ABC Mutual Fund common stock on July 1, 2009. ABC Mutual Fund paid a cash dividend of 10 cents a share. The ex-dividend date was July 9, 2009. The ABC Mutual Fund advises Joshua that the portion of the dividend eligible to be treated as qualified dividends equals two cents per share. His Form 1099-DIV from ABC Mutual Fund shows total ordinary dividends of $1,000 and qualified dividends of $200. However, Joshua sold the 10,000 shares on August 4, 2009. He therefore has no qualified dividends from ABC Mutual Fund because he held the ABC Mutual Fund stock for less than 61 days.

Caution. In the case of preferred stock with dividends attributable to periods totaling more than 366 days, the required holding period is at least 91 days during the 181-day period that begins 90 days before the ex-dividend date 366 days.

For this purpose, the following dividends will not be considered qualified dividends even if they are shown in box 1b of Form 1099-DIV:

- capital gain distributions (see line 13 on page 1-16 and Tab 4);
- dividends paid on deposits with mutual savings banks, cooperative banks, credit unions, U.S. building and loan associations, federal savings and loan associations, and similar financial institutions (see line 8b on page 1-14);
- dividends from a corporation that is a tax-exempt organization or farmer's cooperative during the corporation's tax year in which the dividends were paid or during the corporation's previous tax year;
- dividends paid by a corporation on employer securities that are held on the date of record by an employee stock ownership plan (ESOP) maintained by that corporation;
- dividends on any share of stock to the extent that the taxpayer is obligated (whether under a short sale or otherwise) to make related payments for positions in substantially similar or related property; and
- payments in lieu of dividends, if the taxpayer knows or has reason to know that the payments are not qualified dividends.

Dividends Received in January. If a mutual fund or real estate investment trust (REIT) declares a dividend (including any interest-exempt dividend or capital gain distribution) in October, November, or December payable to shareholders of record on a date in one of those months but actually pays the dividend during January of the next calendar year, the taxpayer is considered to have received the payments in the year in which they were announced.

Line 10, Taxable Refunds, Credits, or Offsets of State and Local Income Taxes

If the taxpayer received a refund, credit or offset of state or local *income* taxes in 2009, then a portion may be included in gross income if the taxpayer deducted the taxes in 2008. Generally, the taxpayer should receive Form 1099-G indicating the amount of any refund in box 2.

The worksheet reproduced on page 1-49 is used to calculate the taxable portion of a taxpayer's refund and the result is entered on line 10 of Form 1040. However, the taxpayer must treat the refund the same as the recovery of any other itemized deduction (see page 1-21) and report it as "Other Income" on line 21 if any of the following applies:

- the refund is for a tax year other than 2008;
- the refund is for state or local general sales tax, real property taxes, or motor vehicle taxes;
- the amount on line 42 (the total of personal and dependent exemptions) of the taxpayer's 2008 Form 1040, is more than the amount on line 41 (adjusted gross income less either the standard or itemized deduction) of the 2008 Form 1040;
- the refund of 2008 state and local income taxes was more than the amount deducted in 2008 by the taxpayer (less the amount of 2008 state and general sales taxes that the taxpayer could have deducted);
- the taxpayer's last payment of 2008 estimated state or local income taxes was made in 2009;
- the taxpayer owed alternative minimum tax in 2008;
- the taxpayer could not deduct the full amount of credits he or she was entitled to in 2008;
- the taxpayer could be claimed as a dependent by someone else in 2008; or
- the taxpayer could not deduct all of his or her itemized deduction in 2008 because their AGI exceeded $159,950 ($79,975 if married filing separately) and the amount of line 8 on the 2008 Itemized Deduction Worksheet exceeded the amount on line 4 of the worksheet if that amount were reduced by 80 percent of the refund received by the taxpayer in 2009.

Line 11, Alimony Received

Alimony (also called spousal support, separate maintenance, or maintenance and support) is taxable income of the spouse who receives the payment (and deductible for the spouse who makes the payment; see line 31a). Child support is not alimony and is not taxable to the recipient. The recipient of alimony is required to provide his or her SSN to the payer. For a discussion of the requirements for alimony to be reported on line 11, see Tab 13 and MTG ¶771-¶777.

Line 12, Business Income or Loss

Income from a trade or business is calculated on Schedule C or C-EZ and reported on line 12. See Tab 3 for more information.

> **Caution.** If an activity is engaged in for profit, it is treated as a business and Schedule C is required. Other proceeds, such as hobby income, are reported on line 21. The IRS may apply strict tests to determine whether an activity is a business or a hobby.

Line 13, Capital Gain or Loss

Schedule D is required to be completed for any capital gain or loss realized during the year, including any capital gain distributions or capital loss carryover from 2008, unless both of the following apply:

- the taxpayer received only capital gain distributions shown in box 2a of Form(s) 1099-DIV or substitute statements, and
- none of the Forms 1099-DIV or substitute statements received by the taxpayer have an amount in box 2b (unrecaptured Section 1250 gain), box 2c (Section 1202 gain), or box 2d (collectibles gain).

If both of the requirements apply, the taxpayer is not required to file Schedule D, but instead enters his or her total capital gain distributions received other than as a nominee (from box 2a of Form(s) 1099-DIV) on line 13 and by checking the box. The taxpayer may then use the Qualified Dividends and Capital Gain Tax Worksheet reproduced at page 1-57 to figure his or her tax. See also Tab 4 for instructions for filling out Schedule D.

Line 14, Other Gains or Losses

Include on line 14 other gains and losses recognized from the sale or exchange of property used in a trade or business and calculated on Form 4797. See Tab 4 for more information.

Lines 15a and 15b, IRA Distributions

Generally, distributions from a taxpayer's IRA are included in income including distributions from a traditional IRA, Roth IRA, simplified employee pension (SEP) IRA, and savings incentive match plan for employees (SIMPLE IRA). The amount of the distribution is reported to the taxpayer on Form 1099-R. The total amount of the distribution should be entered on line 15(b) and line 15(a) should be left blank, unless the distribution meets one of the following exceptions. See Tab 9 and MTG ¶2178.

Filing Tip. If more than one than one exception applies, a statement should be attached to the taxpayer's return showing the amount of each exception, instead of making a separate entry next to line 15b. In addition, if the taxpayer (or spouse if filing jointly) received more than one distribution, then figure the taxable amount of each distribution and enter the total on line 15b.

Caution. If the distribution is made before the taxpayer is age 59½, then a 10-percent additional tax will generally apply (25-percent for SIMPLE IRAs). In addition, if the amount received from a traditional, SEP, or SIMPLE IRA by a taxpayer's who is at least age 70½ is less than their required minimum distribution, then an additional 50 percent tax would also generally apply. However, the required minimum distributions rules have been waived for 2009. The additional taxes are reported on Line 59 (see page 1-38 and Tab 9 for more information).

Rollovers. A qualified IRA distribution is not taxable if it is rolled over: from one IRA to another IRA of the same type (for example, from one traditional IRA to another traditional IRA); from a SEP or SIMPLE IRA to a traditional IRA or from an IRA to a qualified plan other than an IRA. If the total distribution was rolled over, then enter the total amount distribution on line 15a, write -0- on line 15b, and write "Rollover" next to line 15b. However, if only a portion of a distribution was rolled over, then enter the amount rolled over on line 15a and the amount not rolled over on 15b (unless the exception for nondeductible contribution or for returned or recharacterized contributions applies to the part not rolled over).

Generally, a qualified rollover must be made within 60 days from when the distribution is received by the taxpayer. In addition, the taxpayer cannot roll over any later distribution from the same IRA within one year. For this purpose, a direct transfer from the IRA to another IRA is not considered a distribution and therefore is not a rollover and not subject to the one year limit. On the other hand, required minimum distributions are not eligible to be rolled over (see Tab 9).

Filing Tip. Be sure to include any IRA distribution rolled over to any qualified plan other than an IRA on line 15a. Even though the rollover amount is not subject to income tax or additions to tax, it needs to be reported because the IRS matches Forms 1099-R to insure that all retirement income is properly taxed. In such circumstances, the taxpayer should attach a statement to his or her return explaining what they did.

Nondeductible Contributions. Distributions received by the taxpayer from a traditional or SEP IRA that relate to nondeductible contributions are not taxable. Thus, if the taxpayer made nondeductible contributions to the IRA, then the total amount of any distribution should be reported on line 15a and Form 8606 should be used to calculate the taxable portion to report on line 15b. If a distribution is received from a Roth IRA, Form 8606 does not have to be used and -0- should be entered on line 15b if box 7 of Form 1099-R indicates that the distributions is a qualified Roth IRA distribution (code Q) or the distribution is otherwise not taxable (code T).

Planning Tip. There is no required form for a taxpayer to keep track of nondeductible contributions to an IRA. However, in the case of a Roth IRA, a record should be kept by the taxpayer to determine if a distribution from the IRA meets the five-year holding period and to determine how much, if any, of the distribution is taxable (see page 9-12 for more information).

Return or Recharacterization of Contributions. Report on line 15a the amount of 2008 or 2009 IRA contributions returned to the taxpayer (including any earnings or less any loss) prior to the due date (including extensions) for filing the return for the particular year. The taxpayer should also include on line 15a any distribution related to the conversion of a traditional, SEP, or SIMPLE IRA to a Roth IRA, or the recharacterization of a contribution to a Roth or traditional IRA. Form 8606 should be used to be taxable portions of such distributions.

Charitable Distributions. For 2009, taxpayer's age 70½ or older can have up to $100,000 directly distributed from their IRA(s) (other than a SEP or SIMPLE IRA) to a charitable organization without recognizing income. However, the total amount of qualified charitable distributions from all IRAs cannot be more than $100,000 for the year. On a joint return the total qualified charitable distributions for the year may be up to $100,000 for each spouse.

The total amount distributed is reported on line 15a. If the distribution meets all of the requirements, enter -0- on line 15b and "QCD" next to line 15b. If only part of the distribution is a qualified charitable deduction, then enter the part that is not qualified on line 15b (unless one of the other exceptions above applies). If the taxpayer made nondeductible contributions to the IRS, then a distribution is first considered paid out of otherwise taxable income.

HSA Transfers. A taxpayer is allowed to make a one-time rollover of a distribution from an IRA (other than a SEP or SIMPLE IRA) to his or her health savings account (HSA). The amount of the distribution must be included in the total amount of IRA distributions reported on line 15a. It may be excluded from the taxable amount reported on line 15b, but only up to the HSA contribution limit for the year or the amount that would otherwise be taxable (unless another exception excludes it from income). Write "HFD" next to line 15b when excluding any portion of a HSA rollover. If the taxpayer made nondeductible contributions to the IRA, then any rollover of a distribution to an HSA is first considered paid out of otherwise taxable income.

Caution. An IRA distribution is eligible to be rolled over to HSA only if it made directly from the IRA trustee to the HSA trustee. The taxpayer can only make one such transfer during his or her lifetime. The amount rolled over reduces the amount that the taxpayer can contribute to the HSA for the year. If the taxpayer fails to maintain eligibility for the HSA for the 12 months following the rollover, then the amount rolled over will be included in gross income and subject to an additional 10-percent tax. See Form 8889.

Disaster Distributions. Qualified recovery assistance distributions from an IRA may be included in income ratably over three years and will not be subject to the 10-percent additional tax on early distributions (25-percent for SIMPLE plans). Any amount repaid within three years may be treated as a qualified rollover and is not subject to the one-rollover-per-year-limitation. The total amount of qualified disaster distributions that may be received from all qualified retirement plans and IRAs is limited to $100,000. Disasters covered by these rule include Hurricanes Katrina, Rita, or Wilma in 2005, Kansas tornadoes on May 4, 7007; and Midwest storms and floods in 2008. See Form 8915 or Form 8930 for more information.

Lines 16a and 16b, Pensions and Annuities

Form 1099-R indicates the amount of pension and annuity payments received by the taxpayer including distributions from a qualified retirement plan such as a 401(k), 403(b), or governmental 457(b) plan. Pension and annuity payments are fully taxable (including military retirement pay) and entered on line 16b if the taxpayer did not pay any part of the cost or taxpayer received the entire cost back before 2009. Line 16a should be left blank in such cases.

Filing Tip. A corrective distribution (including earnings) of excess salary deferrals or contributions to a retirement plan, as well as a disability pension received before minimum retirement age, are considered wages and reported on line 7 of Form 1040. Similarly, railroad retirement benefits reported to the taxpayer on Form RRB-1099 may be taxed as Social Security benefits or as a pension or annuity benefit. See MTG ¶716 and ¶839, as well as IRS Publication 915.

Partly Taxable Payments. If the taxpayer did pay part of the cost of the pension or annuity, then part of the payment received represents a return of the cost. If the Form 1099-R does not show the taxable amount, then the taxpayer must use either the Simplified Method or the General Rule to figure the taxable and nontaxable portions of the annuity payment. See Tab 9 and MTG ¶817 for a discussion of these methods, as well as a worksheet that must be completed if the Simplified Method is used. The total distribution is entered on line 16a and the taxable part on line 16b.

A taxpayer who is a retired public safety officer (police, firefighter, emergency responder), can elect to exclude up to $3,000 of income distributions made from a qualified retirement plan to pay accident and health insurance premiums (as well as for long-term care insurance) for themselves, their spouse or dependents. The amount reported in box 2a of Form 1099-R may not reflect the exclusion. Thus, the taxpayer must report their total distributions on line 16a and the taxable amount on line 16b with "PSO" next to line 16b.

Filing Tip. If the taxpayer is retired on disability and reporting disability income on line 7, then include only the taxable amount on line 7 and enter "PSO" and the excluded amount on the dotted line next to line 7.

Rollovers. A distribution from a qualified retirement plan that is rolled over to another qualified plan (including an IRA or SEP, but not a Roth IRA) is generally not taxable. If the taxpayer receives the distribution from the plan directly, then it must be rolled over within 60 days in order to be tax-free. Certain distributions, however, may not be rolled over including required minimum distributions, hardship distributions, and a distribution under a series of substantially equal period payments paid at least once a year over the participant's life expectancy or over a period of 10 years or more.

In the case of a rollover to a plan (other than a Roth IRA or designated Roth account), report on line 16a the total amount of the distribution as indicated in box 1 of Form 1099-R. From that subtract the amount rolled over and any after-tax contributions made by the taxpayer (box 5 of Form 1099-R). Enter the remaining amount, even if zero (-0-) on line 16b and write "Rollover" next to line 16b.

In the case of a rollover to a Roth IRA other than from a designated Roth account, follow the same procedures as above. However, in the case of rollover to a Roth IRA or designated Roth account from a designated Roth account, report on line 16a the total amount of the distribution before income tax or other deductions are withheld. From that amount subtract the amount of the qualified rollover distribution. Enter the remaining amount, even if zero (-0-) on line 16b and write "Rollover" next to line 16b.

Planning Tip. A taxpayer planning on rolling over a distribution from an employer's plan should elect a direct rollover to another plan or IRA (trustee to trustee transfer). A rollover distribution that is directly paid to the taxpayer is generally subject to a 20 percent withholding rate and may also be subject to the additional tax on early distributions.

Lump-Sum Distributions. If the taxpayer received a lump-sum distribution from a retirement plan, then the box 2b "Total Distribution" should be checked on Form 1099-R. Enter the total distribution on line 16a and the taxable part on line 16b. Generally, taxable lump-sum distributions are treated as ordinary income and taxed at ordinary income tax rates. However, certain older taxpayers may be eligible to tax a portion of their distributions at capital gains tax rates and may employ a 10-years tax option on the portion of the distribution not taxed at capital gains rates. This optional method is available only to taxpayers born before January 2, 1937. Use Form 4972 to figure the tax using the optional method. The tax figured on Form 4972 is added to any other amounts on line 44 (see page 1-36).

Loans from Qualified Retirement Plans. Loans of less than $50,000 or 50 percent of the taxpayer's vested account balance are not taxable if certain requirements are met. The portion of loans in excess of this limit is treated as a taxable distribution. See Tab 9 for more information.

Planning Tip. If the taxpayer's main home was located in the Midwest disaster area, then loans from a qualified retirement plan will not be taxable if less than $100,000 or 100 percent of the taxpayer's vested account balance (or $10,000, whichever is greater).

Disaster Distributions. Qualified disaster distributions received from a qualified retirement plan are subject to similar rules that apply to such distributions from IRAs (see page 1-18).

Line 17, Rental Real Estate, Royalties, Partnerships, S Corporations, Trusts, Etc.

Calculate rental and royalty income, as well as gains and losses from partnerships, S corporations, estates, and trusts on Schedule E. See Tab 5.

Line 18, Farm Income or Loss

Calculate income from farming activities on Schedule F and report on line 18. See Tab 3 and MTG ¶767.

Line 19, Unemployment Compensation

A taxpayer should receive a Form 1099-G if he or she received any unemployment compensation during the tax year. Unemployment compensation is taxable except to the extent that any overpayment received was repaid during the year. In other words, do not include any unemployment compensation repaid in 2009 on line 19. Instead, enter "Repaid" and the nontaxable amount next to line 19. In addition, for tax years beginning in 2009, the taxpayer may excluded up to $2,400 of unemployment compensation received during the year.

If the taxpayer repaid unemployment compensation in 2009 which was included in gross income in an earlier year, then the amount repaid may be deducted as an itemized deduction on Schedule A (see Tab 2). However, if the repayment was more than $3,000, the taxpayer may choose to either claim the repayment as an itemized deduction or claim a tax credit for the difference in tax that would have resulted had the income not been claimed in the earlier year. Claim the credit on line 70 and enter "I.R.C. 1341" in the column to the right.

Employer and Private Benefits. Employer payments of supplemental unemployment benefits and guaranteed wages paid under a union agreement are treated as taxable wages and reported on line 7. Unemployment benefits paid to union members from regular union dues are reported as income on line 21. However, benefits received from a special union fund for unemployment is reported as income on line 21 only to the extent they exceed any deductible contributions made by the taxpayer.

Lines 20a and 20b, Social Security Benefits

Social Security and Railroad Retirement benefits paid to the taxpayer during the year are reported in box 3 of Form SSA-1099 and Form RRB-1099, respectively. The total amount must be reported on line 20a. The worksheet reproduced on page 1-50 is generally used to calculate the portion of the benefits which are taxable and reported on line 20b. In the case of IRA deductions, repayment of benefits and lump-sum distributions, special rules apply to determine the taxable amount reported on line 20b. See Tab 9 and MTG ¶716 for more information.

> **Filing Tip.** If the taxpayer is married, filing separately and lived apart from his or her spouse for all of 2009, they must enter "D" next to "benefits" reported on line 20a. If the taxpayer lived with his or her spouse during the tax year, then up to 85 percent of Social Security benefits received must be included in income.

> **Planning Tip.** If the taxpayer excludes any of the following from gross income, then Worksheet 1 in IRS Publication 915 must be used to calculate the taxable portion of Social Security or Railroad Retirement benefits received:
> - employer-provided adoption benefits;
> - interest from series EE or I U.S. Savings Bonds;
> - foreign earned income; or
> - income from sources within Puerto Rico or American Samoa.

IRA Deduction. If the taxpayer received Social Security benefits, contributed to a traditional IRA and is covered by an employer-sponsored retirement plan (or the taxpayer's spouse, see page 1-31), then the taxable portion of Social Security benefits is computed using a three step process. First, figure the taxable portion of the Social Security benefits as if no IRA deduction is taken. Second, calculate the IRA deduction on line 32 of Form 1040 using the taxable Social Security amount determined in step 1. Finally, recompute the taxable portion of the Social Security benefits using the IRA deduction calculated in step 2. See IRS Publication 590.

Repayments. If the taxpayer repaid any Social Security benefits during the year (box 4) and the total amount of repayments exceeds the total benefits received in the year (box 3), then none of the benefits are taxable (enter -0- on line 20b). The excess can be used to offset any net benefits of the taxpayer's spouse (box 5) if a joint return is filed. If any more excess remains, the taxpayer can claim a deduction similar to the deduction for the repayment of unemployment compensation (see page 1-19).

Lump-Sum Payments. If the taxpayer received a lump-sum payment of Social Security benefits in 2009 that includes benefits for an earlier tax year, then the taxpayer may elect to calculate the taxable portion of the payment for the earlier year separately (using the income for the earlier year) if it would lower the amount of taxable benefits. See IRS Pub. 915 on how to use the lump-sum election method.

Line 21, Other Income

All taxable income not included on lines 7 through 20 (and related schedules) is reported on line 21. List the type and amount of income included (attach a statement if necessary). The following are examples of the more common types of income reported on line 21.

> **Filing Tip.** Items of income which are not taxable and which do not need to be reported on line 21 include: (1) economic recovery payments of $250 made to recipients of Social Security benefits, supplemental security income, railroad retirement benefits, or certain veterans disability compensation or pension; and (2) vouchers or payments made for such vouchers of $3,500 or $4,500 received under the CARS "cash for clunkers" program to buy or lease a new fuel-efficient automobile.

Cancelled Debts. Generally, any debt of the taxpayer which is canceled or forgiven will be considered income, unless it is gift. A debt includes any indebtedness for which the taxpayer is personally liable or which attaches to property he or she holds. Income from the cancellation of debt is reported in box 2 of Form 1099-C and should be included on line 21 of Form 1040 if it is a nonbusiness debt. If it is a business debt, report the income on Schedule C or F, as appropriate.

If interest is forgiven with the debt (box 3), then the net amount of the debt (box 2 less box 3) is reported on line 21 but only if the interest would otherwise be deductible by the taxpayer. If the interest would not otherwise be deductible by the taxpayer, then the total amount of cancelled debt cannot be offset by the interest cancelled or forgiven.

Filing Tip. For this purpose, a discount provided for the early payment on a mortgage is considered cancelled debt and must be included on line 21. On the other hand, if a corporation cancels a shareholder's debt, the amount canceled is a constructive dividend and reported as dividend income on line 9a.

The discharge of a mortgage when the taxpayer disposes of their property (including by foreclosure or repossession) will generally result in cancellation of debt income to the extent the mortgage discharge exceeds the fair market value of the property. However, effective for 2009 through 2012, a taxpayer may exclude from gross income up to $2 million ($1 million for a married taxpayer filing a separate return) of any income realized from the cancellation or discharge of a qualified principal residence indebtedness. The taxpayer must reduce their basis in the home by the amount excluded.

A qualified principal residence indebtedness is a mortgage personally incurred by the taxpayer to acquire, construct, or substantially improve his or her principal residence, and which is not more than the cost of the home (plus improvements). It also includes the cost to refinance a qualified mortgage.

Caution. The exclusion is only available if the taxpayer is personally liable for the mortgage (recourse debt). If the taxpayer is not personally liable for the mortgage (nonrecourse debt), the amount of the mortgage that is discharged when the taxpayer disposes of their property (including by foreclosure or repossession) is included in the amount realized on the sale of the property.

Caution. The discharge of a qualified mortgage is not eligible for the exclusion if it is as a result of service performed by the taxpayer for the lender or other factors unrelated to the financial condition of the taxpayer or decline in value in the property. It is also not available if the taxpayer is in Chapter 11 bankruptcy or insolvent.

There are several other exceptions to the inclusion of canceled debt in income. These include:

- debt discharged (before 2010) in response to damage suffered from Midwest storms and flooding in 2008;
- student loans if the discharge is contingent on the taxpayer working for a specified period of time for certain employers such as the government, educational institutions;
- debt cancelled in a Chapter 11 bankruptcy or if the taxpayer is insolvent; or
- qualified farm debt or qualified real property business debt. See MTG ¶791 and IRS Publications 225 and 334.

Recoveries. The taxpayer must include on line 21 refunds, recoveries, and rebates of amounts deducted or claimed as a credit in an earlier tax year. Interest earned on the recovery must be reported as interest income in the year received on line 8a. If the recovery and expense occur in the same tax year, the recovery reduces the deduction or credit and is not reported as income. If the recovery is for amounts paid in more than one prior year, then the recovered amount must be allocated between years.

The most common recoveries are refunds, reimbursements and rebates of itemized deductions. (Special rules apply to the recovery of state and local income taxes, see page 1-16.) Generally, the full amount of the recovery must be included in income in the year received if the taxpayer itemizes deductions in the current year. However, the taxpayer may be able to exclude a portion of a recovery from income in the following circumstances:

- only itemized deductions that exceed the standard deduction for the earlier year are subject to recovery; thus, the amount included in income is the smaller of the recovery or the amount by which the taxpayer's itemized deductions for the earlier year exceeded the standard deduction;
- if the taxpayer had negative taxable income in the earlier year, the amount of the recovery included in income is reduced by the negative amount;
- the amount recovered cannot exceed the taxpayer's deduction in the earlier year; thus, the amount included in income is the smaller of the recovery or the amount deducted on Schedule A in the earlier year;
- if the taxpayer's itemized deductions in the earlier tax year were subject to the AGI limits, then the amount recovered that must be included in income is the difference between the amount of itemized deductions actually allowed in the earlier year and the deductions (standard or itemized) that would have been claimed had the taxpayer paid the proper amount in the earlier year; and
- if the taxpayer had any unused tax credits or was subject to the alternative minimum tax in the earlier tax year, then his or her tax liability for the earlier year must be recomputed by adding the recovered amount to taxable income; if the

recomputed tax liability is increased, then the recovery is included in income in the current tax year up to the amount of the deduction that reduced the tax in the earlier year.

Example. Martin incurred $3,000 in medical expenses in 2008. However, due to the 7.5 percent AGI threshold, he was only eligible to claim $500 as an itemized deduction. If Martin receives $2,000 in 2009 as a reimbursement for his prior year medical expenses, then he must include $500 in income on line 21 on his 2009 return (assuming he itemizes deductions).

Example. Brian, a single individual, had an AGI of $349,950 in 2008. His only allowable itemized deduction was $10,000 for state income taxes. However, using the 2008 Itemized Deduction Worksheet for Schedule A, Brian determined he could only claim $8,100 of the itemized deductions.

In 2009, Brian receives a refund of $3,000 of his state income taxes for 2008. If he had used the net amount of $7,000 of his state income taxes to figure his itemized deductions for 2008, then the amount he would have been allowed to claim would have been $5,100 and he should instead have claimed the standard deduction amount of $5,450. Therefore, by deducting $8,100 for his state income taxes in 2008, Brian derived a tax benefit of $2,650 ($8,100 - $5,450) and he should include this amount of the refund on line 21 of his 2008 return.

Filing Tip. If a taxpayer is not required to include all of his or her recoveries in income, and he or she has both a recovery of state and local income taxes and other itemized deduction, then the total amount recovered for the year must be allocated for reporting purposes. Recoveries of state and local income taxes are reported on line 10 of Form 1040. Recoveries of other itemized deductions are reported as other income on line 21 of Form 1040.

Barter Income. A taxpayer should report on line 21 the fair market value of any property or services received in a barter transaction to the extent not reportable on another schedule (for example, Schedule C or E). Taxpayers who receive goods or services through a barter exchange should receive a Form 1099-B by February 16, 2010, that shows the value of goods and services received through the exchange during the year. This includes barter exchanges conducted through the internet (for example, eBay sellers with PayPal barter exchanges). The IRS will also receive a copy of Form 1099-B.

Disaster Payments. Do not include in income on line 21 any amount received that is a qualified disaster relief payment or disaster grant. A payment is excluded if it is paid to reimburse or pay reasonable and necessary personal, family, living or funeral expenses that result from a qualified disaster. See MTG ¶897.

Foreign Earned Income. A qualifying individual may elect to exclude a limited amount of foreign earned income and employer-provided housing expenses from gross income. The amount of the exclusions are calculated on Form 2555 and reported in parentheses on line 21 and subtracted from the taxpayer's income to arrive at the total income on line 22 (enter "Form 2555" in the space provided). See MTG ¶2402.

Other Examples. Additional items of other income to report on line 21 include:

- income from an activity not engaged in for profit (hobby income);
- prizes, awards, and gambling winnings including lump-sum payment received from sale of future lottery payments;
- taxable distributions from an HSA or Archer MSA, as well as amounts deemed to be income from an HSA because the taxpayer did not remain eligible to contribute during a testing period;
- taxable distributions from a qualified tuition program or Coverdell ESA (see Tab 13);
- rental income from the lease of personal property if the taxpayer was not in the business of renting such property (see also line 36 on page 1-34);
- net operating loss (NOL) carryforward (enter as negative amount and attach statement about NOL);
- loss on a corrective distribution of an excess deferral distributed to taxpayer (include loss as a negative amount and identify it as "Loss on Excess Deferral Distribution");
- recapture of a charitable contribution deduction of a fractional interest in tangible personal property (see also line 60 on page 1-39) or charitable organization disposes of the property within three years (see Tab 2);
- dividends on insurance policies to extent they exceed net premiums paid;
- alternative trade adjustment assistance payments (box 5 of Form 1099-G);
- Alaska Permanent Fund dividends; and
- jury duty pay (if jury duty pay is surrendered to an employer in exchange for regular compensation, then it is included in income on line 21, but deducted on line 36).

Common Gross Income Inclusions and Exclusions

Type of Income	Taxable	Nontaxable	How Reported to Taxpayer	Where Taxpayer Reports Income
Advance payments	• Advance earned income tax credit payments • All payments received during tax year if taxpayer uses cash method of accounting	• Some advance payments for taxpayers who use the accrual method of accounting	Earned income credit: Form W-2, box 9 Other payments: Form W-2, box 1	Earned income credit: Form 1040, line 60 Other payments: Form 1040, line 7
Alimony	• Full amount received that is not child support, noncash property settlement, and payment of spouse's part of community income. Alimony is deductible by the payor.	• Amounts received for child support, noncash property settlements, and payment of spouse's part of community income	No IRS form is used to report alimony	Recipient: Form 1040, line 11 Payor: Form 1040, line 31a
Barter	• Fair market value of property or services received	• Portion that is a gift	Form 1099-B, box 3	Schedule C, E, or F, depending on the services provided
Bond interest	• Generally, full amount accrued or received during the tax year depending on the taxpayer's method of accounting	• Interest from municipal bonds • Interest from Series EE or I U.S. Education Savings Bonds	Form 1099-INT	Schedule B, generally Form 8815: Education Saving Bond Interest Exclusion
Bonuses and awards	• Full amount received except for certain noncash employee achievement awards	• Achievement awards of tangible personal property of up to $1,600 annually or $400 for qualified plan awards. • Token goodwill bonuses	Employee award: Form W-2, box 1 Nonemployee award: Form 1099, box 3 or 7	Employee award: Form 1040, line 7 Nonemployee award: Schedule C or F
Canceled debt	• Entire amount of debt forgiven, including interest that would not be deductible by the taxpayer • Discount for prepayment of mortgage loans	• Amount for which the taxpayer was not personally liable (nonrecourse), that was a gift, or that was forgiven due to bankruptcy or insolvency • Qualified principal residence indebtedness or qualified mortgage (see page 1-20) • Student loans forgiven for performance of certain work • Amount that was qualified farm indebtedness or qualified real property business indebtedness • Canceled debt that would have been deductible	Form 1099-C, box 2, generally; box 3, interest	Form 1040, line 21, for nonbusiness debt Schedule C or F of Form 1040 for business- or farm-related debt

Common Gross Income Inclusions and Exclusions (Continued)

Type of Income	Taxable	Nontaxable	How Reported to Taxpayer	Where Taxpayer Reports Income
Disability benefits and pensions	• Amounts of disability pension received under health plan which were paid for by the taxpayer's employer	• Amounts of disability pension received under health plan paid for the taxpayer • Military and government disability pensions such as VA disability benefits or benefits received as a result of active service in the Armed Forces • Compensation for permanent loss of a part or function of the body or its use, calculated without regard to period of absence from work or lost wages • Benefit payments from a public welfare trust, including payments received under a worker's compensation or similar law • Compensatory (but not punitive damages) for physical injury or sickness, as well as compensation for permanent loss or loss of use of part or function of body, or permanent disfigurement • Benefits receive under a "no-fault" car insurance policy for loss of income or earning capacity	Taxable amounts: Form W-2, box 1 or Form 1099-R Nontaxable amounts: Form W-2, box 12, code J or Form 1099-MISC, box 3	Disability pension received before retirement, Form 1040, line 7 Disability pension received after retirement, Form 1040, line 16a and 16b
Employee and nonemployee compensation	• Amount of cash payments, including wages, salaries, fees, commissions, and tips received for personal services performed – Offerings and fees received by member of the clergy unless earned as agent of religious order – Reimbursement, allowance, or advance paid under employer's nonaccountable plan • FMV of any property or services received in return for services performed, including any restricted property (see ¶MTG 1681) • Incentive stock options (taxed when stock is sold, see ¶MTG 1930) • Nonstatutory stock options (taxed when granted if is has ascertainable FMV, see ¶MTG 1923)	• Reimbursement, allowance, or advance paid under employer's accountable plan • Military retirement pay (taxed as a pension) or veterans benefits • Member of the clergy's housing or parsonage allowance (nontaxable for income-tax purposes only)	Employee compensation, generally: W-2, box 1 Nonemployee compensation, generally: 1099-MISC, box 7 Member of the clergy's housing allowance: W-2, box 14	Form 1040, line 7 Schedule C or F for business- or farm-related services

Common Gross Income Inclusions and Exclusions (Continued)				
Type of Income	**Taxable**	**Nontaxable**	**How Reported to Taxpayer**	**Where Taxpayer Reports Income**
Employer-paid benefits	• Adoption benefits in excess of $12,150 (subject to phaseout) • Death benefits, not part of pension or retirement plan • Dependent care benefits in excess of $5,000 ($2,500 for married individuals filing separately) • Disability benefits • Educational assistant payments in excess of $5,250 • Financial counseling fees • Fringe benefits (unless fair market value is paid by taxpayer) • Group-term life insurance cost in excess of $50,000 in coverage • Sickness and injury benefits (including disability) received through an accident or health plan due to employer's contributions	• Accident and health plan coverage provided by employer, including contributions to HSAs, MSAs, health FSAs, HRAs, and long-term care coverage • *De minimis* (minimal) benefits (for example, food discounts, holiday gifts, company picnics) • Employee discounts (for example, reduced sales prices on products or services sold by the employer) • Meals and lodging furnished on employer's premises and for its convenience • Military base realignment and closure benefit payments • Moving expense reimbursement (see page 1-29) • No-additional-cost services (services offered to customers in ordinary course of work provided by employer) • Retirement plan contributions (qualified plan) and retirement planning services • Transportation fringe benefits – for any month beginning before February 18, 2009, $120 per month for commuter vehicles, transit passes, and $230 per month for parking – for any month beginning after February 17, 2009, $230 per month for commuter vehicles, transit passes, and parking – beginning in 2009, $20 per month for bicycle commuting • Working condition fringe benefits (for example, use of company car for business purposes)	Taxable amounts, generally: Form W-2, box 1 Adoption: Form W-2, box 12, code T Death: Form 1099-R, box 1, 2a and 7, code 4 Dependent care: Form W-2, box 10 Education: Form W-2, box 14 Fringe benefits, Form W-2, box 1 and 14 Group-term life insurance, Form W-2, box 12, code C Insurance premiums, generally: Form W-2, box 14 Insurance premiums, retirement: Form 1099-R, box 1 and 2a MSA: Form W-2, box 12, code R	Taxable amounts, generally: Form W-2, line 7 Adoption: Form 8839, line 22 Dependent care: Form 2441, line 12 MSA and long-term care insurance: Form 8853
Foster care payments	• Full amount of payments received for the care of more than five individuals age 19 or older • Full amount of difficultly-of-care payments received for the care of more than five individuals age 19 or older, or more than 10 individuals under age 19	Full amount, if received from a state or government agency or qualified foster care placement agency for care in taxpayer's home	Taxable amounts: Form 1099-MISC	Schedule C

Common Gross Income Inclusions and Exclusions (Continued)

Type of Income	Taxable	Nontaxable	How Reported to Taxpayer	Where Taxpayer Reports Income
Foreign-source income	• All foreign earned income (wages, salaries, etc.), as well as unearned income (interest, dividends, rents, capital gains, etc.) unless exempted by U.S. law or tax treaty	• Up to $91,400 of foreign earned income, as well as certain amount of foreign housing expenses	Form W-2 or Form 1099, if used by the foreign payer, otherwise no IRS form is generally used	Form 1040, line 21, and Form 2555 or Form 2555-EZ
Gambling winnings, prizes and award	• Full amount of gambling winnings, including winnings from lotteries and raffles • Prizes and awards received in goods or services other than as an employee (fair market value) • Scholarship prizes if taxpayer is not required to use for education	• Prize for accomplishment in religious, charitable, scientific, education, literary or civic field if taxpayer is not required to perform substantial future services and the prize is directly transferred to a tax-exempt organization	Gambling: Form W-2G, box 1 Prizes and awards: Form 1099-MISC, box 3	Form 1040, line 21
Gifts and inheritance	• Income in respect of decedent that would have been taxable if received by the decedent prior to death	• Property received as a gift, bequest, or inheritance, unless a pension or IRA is inherited, interest in an expected inheritance from a living person is sold, or bequest is for services performed while the decedent was alive	None	Taxable amounts, Form 1040, line 21
Life insurance	• Life insurance proceeds from a policy transferred for valuable consideration prior to the death of the insured • Proceeds from an endowment contract paid in lump-sum at maturity if exceeds the cost of the policy • Cash proceeds from surrender of life insurance policy if exceeds the cost of the policy • Benefits received under a credit card disability or unemployment insurance plan if exceeds premiums paid during the tax year	• Life insurance proceeds paid as a result of the death of the insured unless the policy was transferred for valuable consideration prior to the death of the insured • Accelerated death benefits if the insured is terminally or chronically ill	Life insurance, annuity, and endowment contracts: Form 1099-R Long-term care and accelerated death benefits: Form 1099-LTC	Generally: Form 1040, line 21 Accelerated death benefits: Form 8853
Scholarships, fellowships, and educational grants	• Full amount received if not a degree candidate • Amount used for room, board, travel, or other expenses not required for enrollment • Amount received as payment for services (for example, teaching, research) • Amount received as a prize if not required to use for educational purposes	• Amount received if a degree candidate and used for tuition, fees, books, and other course related expenses • Reduced tuition received by an undergraduate because the student or parent is an employee of the institution, if the tuition program does not favor highly paid employees, and reduced tuition received by graduate students that is not payment for services	Received as payment for services: Form W-2, box 1 Other taxable payments: Not required to be reported	Generally, Form 1040, line 7 (write "SCH" and taxable amount on the dotted line next to line 7) Prizes, Form 1040, line 21 (whether or not used for educational purposes)
Tips and gratuities	• Full amount, including allocated tips (see page 1-13)	• Allocated tips when taxpayer can prove less was actually received	Form W-2, box 1 or box 8	Form 1040, line 7

Common Gross Income Inclusions and Exclusions (Continued)				
Type of Income	Taxable	Nontaxable	How Reported to Taxpayer	Where Taxpayer Reports Income
Unemployment compensation	• For 2009, amounts in excess of $2,400 paid under a governmental program including state unemployment benefits, railroad unemployment benefits, disability payments under a government program paid as a substitute for unemployment compensation, trade readjustment allowances, and disaster unemployment payments (see page 1-19) • Unemployment benefits paid from union fund, unless contributions to the fund were not deductible • Benefits paid from a private fund (nonunion) to the extent they exceed voluntary contributions made by the taxpayer • Benefits received from an employer-financed fund (to which employees did not contribute)	• Workers' compensation paid to an injured worker or survivors • Railroad sick pay for an injury that is job-related	Form 1099-G, box 1	Form 1040, line 19
Welfare and public assistance	• Welfare payments received as compensation for services or that are obtained by fraud • Full amount of work training program benefits if the amount received exceeds welfare benefits that would otherwise have been paid • Alternative trade adjustment assistance (ATAA) payments	• Public assistance or welfare payments that are based on need • Medicare benefits, Parts A and B • Disaster relief payments received as a result of a federally declared disaster or terrorist/military act • Disaster relief grants	Taxable, generally: Form W-2, box 1 ATAA payments: Form 1099-G	Generally: Form 1040, line 7 ATAA payments: Form 1040, line 21
Workers' compensation	• Salary payments received for performing light duties as a result of an occupational sickness or injury	• Amounts received for an occupational sickness or injury if paid under a workers' compensation or similar law	Salary for light duty work: Form W-2, box 1	Form 1040, line 7

Adjusted Gross Income, Lines 23-37

Amounts deductible against gross income in arriving at adjusted gross income (AGI) are called "above-the-line" deductions. Since these deductions reduce AGI, they may also affect other items with AGI-related thresholds, such as the deduction for medical expenses, casualty losses, and miscellaneous itemized deductions. See Tab 2.

Line 23, Teachers' Classroom Expenses

Eligible educators may deduct up to $250 of qualified expenses paid or incurred during the year as an adjustment to gross income, rather than as a miscellaneous itemized deduction. In the case of married taxpayers filing a joint return, if both spouses are eligible educators, the maximum deduction is $500 but neither spouse can deduct more than $250 of his or her qualified expenses. Qualified expenses incurred in excess of the limits may be deducted as unreimbursed employee expenses on line 21 of Schedule A.

A taxpayer is eligible to claim the deduction if for at least 900 hours during a school year, the individual was a kindergarten through grade 12 teacher, instructor, counselor, principal or aide in a school that provides elementary or secondary education as determined under state law. Qualified expenses include ordinary and necessary expenses paid for books, supplies, equipment (including computer equipment, software and services), and other materials used in the classroom. Expenses for homeschooling and nonathletic supplies for courses in health or physical education do not qualify. In addition, qualified expenses must be reduced by:

- any reimbursements received for the expenses that were not reported on Form W-2;
- excludable series EE and I U.S. savings bonds interest from Form 8815;
- nontaxable earnings from a qualified state tuition program; and
- nontaxable earnings from Coverdell ESAs.

Line 24, Certain Business Expenses of Reservists, Performing Artists, and Fee-Based Government Officials

The performance of services as an employee is considered to be a trade or business and expenses related to that business are generally deductible as miscellaneous itemized deductions (after completing Form 2106). Special rules, however, permit certain taxpayers to deduct expenses as an adjustment to gross income. Such individuals must still complete Form 2106.

Armed Forces Reservists. Reserve members of Armed Forces of the United States, including the National Guard, who periodically travel (typically one weekend per month and two weeks in the summer) for duty may incur significant travel expenses. To the extent the individual is not reimbursed by the military, he or she may deduct the travel expenses associated with such duty if they travel more than 100 miles from the taxpayer's home. Deductible expenses include meals, lodging and incidentals up to the federal per diem rate for the applicable local and the standard mileage rate for car expenses (plus any parking fees, ferry fees or tolls). See MTG ¶941E.

Qualified Performing Artists. The deductible business expenses of a qualified performing artist are deductible as an adjustment against gross income if the taxpayer:

- receives wages from at least two employers of at least $200 from each during the tax year in exchange for services in the performing arts;
- has total business expense deductions attributable to the performance of those services exceeding 10 percent of the income received from those services; and
- has an AGI of $16,000 or less (determined before deducting the expenses) from all sources.

If the performing artist is married, the couple must file a joint return in order to deduct the performer's business expense against gross income. If both spouses are performing artists, their expenses and income from performing services are computed separately, but the $16,000 AGI limitation applies to the couple's combined income. See MTG ¶941A.

Fee-Based Public Officials. Expenses paid or incurred with respect to services performed by an official as an employee of a state or local government are deductible, provided that the official is compensated in whole or in part on a fee basis. These expenses are also deductible for alternative minimum tax purposes. See MTG ¶941D.

Line 25, Health Savings Account Deduction

Health Savings Accounts (HSAs) are a type of medical savings account set up to pay for qualified medical expenses of individuals and their families covered by a high-deductible health plan (HDHP). A taxpayer may be able to claim a deduction for his or her contributions (and contributions made by any other person other than the taxpayer's employer) to an HSA.

The maximum deductible contribution that can be made to a taxpayer's HSA for calendar year 2009 is $3,000 for an individual with self-only coverage and $5,950 for an individual with family coverage. If the taxpayer is age 55 or older at the end of the year, then the limit is increased by $1,000. In the case of married taxpayer's, if either spouse has family coverage, then both are considered as having family coverage and the limit is split equally between them (unless they agree to a different division). If both spouses are age 55 or older, then each spouse's limit is increased by the additional contribution (thus, a total contribution limit of $7,950 for 2009). If a taxpayer has more than one HSA, then contributions to all HSAs cannot be more than the limits described.

The contribution limits will be reduced by any employer contributions to the taxpayer's HSA, any contributions made to the taxpayer's Archer MSA (including employer contributions), and any qualified HSA funding distributions from a traditional or Roth IRA (see page 1-18). In addition, the limit will be reduced if the taxpayer was not considered eligible to contribute to the HSA for the entire year. Rollover contributions from Archer MSAs and other HSAs will not reduce the contribution limits. However, beginning with the first month the taxpayer is enrolled in Medicare, the contribution limit is zero. Form 8889 is used to compute the taxpayer's contribution limit for the tax year and the amount of the deduction that is reported on line 25.

For this purpose, contributions through a salary reduction plan (cafeteria plan) are treated as employer contributions. On the other hand, contributions by a partnership to a partner's HSA, or by an S corporation to a two-percent shareholder-employee's HSA, for services rendered are treated as guaranteed payments and may be deducted by the partner or shareholder. In addition, general contributions by a partnership are not employer contributions but instead treated as a distribution of money and not included in the partner's gross income.

Planning Tip. Excess contributions to an HSA are not deductible and will be subject to a six percent excise tax reported on line 58 (see page 1-38). Excess employer contributions not included in the taxpayer's income on Form W-2 should be reported as "Other Income" on line 21. The taxpayer may avoid the excise tax if he or she withdraws the excess contributions by the due date of the return (including extensions) for the year contributions are made and any income earned on the contributions is included on line 21.

Line 26, Moving Expenses

A taxpayer may deduct certain expenses of moving to a new home because of a changed job location or to start a new job if a distance and time test are met. Form 3903 is used to calculate the deduction. If a taxpayer is reimbursed by his or her employer for moving expenses, then use the chart on page 1-30 to determine how to report the expenses. See MTG ¶1073.

Filing Tip. Members of the Armed Forces do not have to meet the distance and time tests if the move is due to a permanent change of duty station.

Deductible moving expenses include the reasonable cost of moving household goods and personal effects of the taxpayer and members of his or her household. This includes the cost of storing and insuring goods for up to 30 consecutive days during the move. It also may include the cost of traveling (including lodging but not meals) from the old home to the new home. Travel expenses are limited to one trip per person but not all of the members of the household must travel together or at the same time. If the taxpayer uses his or her own car to travel, then the standard mileage rate of 24 cents-per-mile (plus parking and tolls) may be used to calculate the travel expenses incurred in 2009.

Caution. In order to deduct moving expenses, they must generally be incurred within one year from the date the taxpayer first reported to work at the new location.

Distance Test. Moving expenses are deductible only if the taxpayer's new principal workplace is at least 50 miles farther from his or her old home then their old workplace was. For example, if the old workplace was three miles from the taxpayer's former home, then the new workplace must be at least 53 miles from the former home.

Time Test. If the taxpayer is an employee, then he or she must work full-time in the general area of the new workplace for at least 39 weeks during the 12 months after the move in order for moving expenses to be deductible. A self-employed person must work full-time in the general area of the new workplace for at least 78 weeks during the 24 months right after the move. The time test does not have to met if:

- the taxpayer's job was transferred for the employer's benefit;
- the taxpayer's job ends because of death or disability;
- the taxpayer is laid-off or discharged for a reason other than willful misconduct; or
- the taxpayer is a retiree or survivor living outside the United States.

Filing Tip. Moving expenses can be deducted in the year of the move if the taxpayer expects to meet the time test. If the taxpayer later discovers that he or she did not meet the time test, then an amended return must be filed for the year the deduction was claimed or the taxpayer may report as income the amount of moving expense deduction claimed in the year of the move.

Reporting Your Moving Expenses and Reimbursements		
IF your Form W-2 shows...	**AND you have . . .**	**Tests to Be a Qualifying Relative THEN . . .**
your reimbursement reported only in box 12 with code P	moving expenses greater than the amount in box 12	file Form 3903 showing all allowable expenses and reimbursements
your reimbursement reported only in box 12 with code P	moving expenses equal to the amount in box 12	do not file Form 3903
your reimbursement divided between box 12 and box 1	moving expenses greater than the amount in box 12	file Form 3903 showing all allowable expenses but only the reimbursements reported in box 12
your entire reimbursement reported as wages in box 1	moving expenses	file Form 3903 showing all allowable expenses, but no reimbursements
no reimbursement	moving expenses	file Form 3903 showing all allowable expenses

Line 27, One-Half of Self-Employment Tax

A self-employed taxpayer who files Schedule SE may deduct one-half of the self-employment taxes paid for the tax year (Schedule SE, line 6). See Tab 3 for more information.

Line 28, Self-Employed SEP, SIMPLE, and Qualified Plans

A self-employed taxpayer (including partner in a partnership) who makes contributions to their own SEP, SIMPLE, or other qualified retirement plan may claim a deduction for such contributions. The deduction is calculated using the worksheets in IRS Publication 560 or IRS Publication 517 if the taxpayer is a minister. See Tab 9 for more information.

Line 29, Self-Employed Health Insurance Deduction

A self-employed taxpayer may deduct amounts paid for health insurance (including qualified long-term care insurance) for themselves, their spouse, and their dependents if they are:

- self-employed with a net profit reported on Schedule C or F;
- a partner with net earnings from self-employment (box 14, Code A, Schedule K-1 of Form 1065); or
- a shareholder owning more than 2 percent of an S corporation and who receives wages from the corporation.

The insurance plan must be established under the taxpayer's business. This means the policy can be in the name of the individual or the business. However, in the case of a partner or more-than-2-percent shareholder, the partnership or S corporation must either pay the premiums or reimburse the taxpayer for payment of the premiums. The amount paid or reimbursed by a partnership will be reported to the taxpayer as guaranteed payments on Schedule K-1 of Form 1065. The amounts paid or reimbursed by an S corporation will be reported to the taxpayer as wages in box 1 of Form W-2.

The deduction for health insurance is not permitted for any month in which the self-employed person was eligible to participate in any subsidized health plan provided by an employer of the taxpayer or the taxpayer's spouse. Amounts paid for health insurance coverage from retirement plan distributions for retired public safety officers also cannot be used to figure the deduction (see page 1-18).

Generally, a worksheet in the Form 1040 instructions is used to calculate the amount of the deduction. However, if the taxpayer is a trade adjustment assistance (TAA) or Pension Benefit Guaranty Corporation (PBGC) recipient, then Form 8885 must be completed before using the worksheet. In addition, Worksheet 6-A in IRS Pub. 535 must be used if the taxpayer had more than one source of income subject to self-employment tax, paid for qualified long-term care insurance, or is filing Form 2555 to claim the exclusion foreign earned income or housing costs. If the taxpayer has more than one health plan and each plan is established under a different business, then a separate Worksheet 6-A must be used to figure each plan's net earnings limit.

Line 30, Penalty on Early Withdrawal of Savings

Enter any penalty for early withdrawal of savings or certificates from Form 1099-INT or Form 1099-OID on line 30.

Lines 31a and 31b, Alimony Paid

Alimony (also called spousal support, separate maintenance or maintenance and support) is deductible for the spouse who makes the payment on line 31 and taxable income of the spouse who receives the payment reported on line 11 (see page 1-16). Enter the amount of alimony paid on line 31a and the recipient's SSN on line 31b. For a discussion of the requirements for alimony, see Tab 13 and MTG ¶771-¶777.

Filing Tip. Taxpayers who claim a deduction for alimony paid should be sure to place all documentation related to making this payment with their tax records. The IRS frequently will request documentation from a taxpayer to substantiate the amount paid to insure that the correct amount was declared by the former spouse.

Line 32, IRA Deduction

A taxpayer may claim a deduction for contributions to a traditional IRA (but not a Roth IRA). For 2009, the maximum contribution that can be made to an IRA is limited to the lesser of $5,000 ($6,000 for taxpayers who will be at least age 50 by the end of the year) or the taxpayer's taxable compensation for the year. If the taxpayer has more than one IRA, the limit applies to the total contributions made to all of his or her IRAs for the year.

Compensation for this purpose includes wages, salaries, tips, professional fees, bonuses, or other compensation reported in box 1 of Form W-2 (including scholarships and fellowships, but reduced by income received from a nonqualified deferred compensation plan or 457 plan as shown in box 11 of Form W-2, box 12 of Form W-2 with Code Z, or box 15b of Form 1099-MISC). It also includes net earnings from self employment (reduced by contributions made to retirement plans and the deduction for one-half of self-employment taxes reported on line 29), as well as any alimony or separate maintenance payments reported on line 11. Members of the U.S. Armed Forces may elect to include combat pay (normally excluded from gross income and reported in box 12 of Form W-2, Code Q) as part of their compensation for purposes of determining their maximum IRA contributions.

In the case of married taxpayers filing a joint return, each spouse may have a separate IRA. For 2009, the maximum contribution limit for the spouse with the least amount of compensation is the lesser of $5,000 (or $6,000 if age 50 or older) or the total compensation of both spouses. For this purpose, total compensation is reduced by:

- the IRA deduction for the year of the spouse with the greater compensation;
- any nondeductible contributions made for the year on behalf of the spouse with the greater compensation; and
- any contributions to a Roth IRA on behalf of the spouse with the greater compensation.

Example. Kris is 25 years old and is a full-time student with no taxable income. During 2009, she marries Chad who is 30 years old and has taxable income of $35,000. If the couple files a joint return for the tax year, they may both contribute $5,000 to a traditional IRA. This is because Kris can add Chad's compensation to her own (reduced by the amount of his IRA contribution) to figure her maximum contribution to a traditional IRA. In this case, her contribution limit is $5,000 because it is less than her compensation ($30,000).

Deduction Limit. A taxpayer's contributions to a traditional IRA may be deductible up to the maximum contribution limit. However, the deduction may be reduced or eliminated if the taxpayer (or his or her spouse) is covered by an employer-provided retirement plan such as a 401(k) plan, depending on the taxpayer's filling status and modified AGI. The worksheet reproduced on pages 1-51 and 1-52 is generally used to calculate the amount of the deduction. However, if the taxpayer receives Social Security benefits, then use the worksheets in Appendix B of IRS Publication 590 to calculate the deduction.

2009 Phaseout- Ranges for IRA Deduction

Filing Status	Modified AGI
Single or head of household	$55,000 to $65,000
Married filing jointly (taxpayer covered by employer plan)	$89,000 to $109,000
Married filing jointly (taxpayer not covered by employer plan but spouse is)	$166,000 to $176,000
Married filing separately*	Less than $10,000

*If the taxpayer did not live with his or her spouse at any time during the year, their filing status is considered Single for this purpose. Under such circumstances, the taxpayer should enter "D" next to the dotted line next to line 32.

Caution. An individual only has to be eligible to participate in an employer-provided retirement plan for the limitation on deducting IRA contributions to apply. It does not matter if the individual actually does participate in the plan. For purposes of a defined contribution plan (for example, 401(k)), if any amount is contributed or allocated to the account by the taxpayer or the employer, then the taxpayer is considered covered by the plan. The taxpayer's employer should inform the taxpayer if he or she is eligible to participate in an employer-provided plan by checking box 13 of the individual's Form W-2. However, if box 13 is checked and the taxpayer believes that he or she is not covered, they should check with their employer and obtain a revised Form W-2 if needed.

Nondeductible Contributions. Although a taxpayer's deduction for contributions to a traditional IRA may be reduced or eliminated, contributions can still be made up to the maximum limit. Nondeductible contributions to a traditional IRA must be reported on Form 8606. A taxpayer has until the due date for filing their tax return (not including extensions) to make a contribution to an IRA for the year (for example, April 15, 2010, for the 2009 tax year). Thus, the taxpayer does not have to designate a contribution to a traditional IRA as nondeductible until he or she files their return. See MTG ¶2170-¶2172.

Caution. Contributions to either a traditional or Roth IRA in excess of the maximum limit (whether deductible or nondeductible) are subject to a six percent excise tax reported on line 58 (see page 1-38). To avoid the tax, the taxpayer may withdraw any excess contribution by the due date of the return (including extensions) for the year contributions are made. Any income earned on the excess contributions, however, must also be withdrawn and reported as 'Other Income' on line 21.

Caution. Taxpayers who are age 70 1/2 or older at the end of the tax year may not deduct contributions to traditional IRAs or treat them as nondeductible contributions.

Line 33, Student Loan Interest Deduction

Individuals are allowed to deduct interest paid during the tax year on any qualified student loan. The maximum deduction is $2,500. However, the deduction is phased out in 2009 for taxpayers with modified (AGI) of $60,000 to $75,000 ($120,000 to $150,000 for married individuals filing a joint return). Generally, the taxpayer should receive a Form 1098-E from any person (including a bank or government agency) indicating the amount of interest paid on a qualified student loan. The worksheet reproduced on page 1-49 is used to calculate the deduction. See MTG ¶1082.

The deduction can only be claimed if the taxpayer is legally obligated to pay the interest on a qualified student loan. The interest must also be actually paid by the taxpayer or by someone else on the taxpayer's behalf. The deduction, however, cannot be claimed if someone else claims the taxpayer as a dependent in the tax year or if the interest can be deducted elsewhere (for example, as home mortgage interest). Married taxpayers must file a joint return in order to claim the deduction.

Example. Josh received a Form 1098-E from his bank indicating that he paid $1,100 of interest on his qualified student loan in 2009. Only he is legally obligated to make the payments on the loan. If Josh's parents claim him as a dependent on their 2009 return, then neither Josh nor his parents may deduct the student loan interest Josh paid in 2009. However, if Josh's parents do not claim him as a dependent on their return, then Josh may deduct the interest on his return.

Example. Darla obtained a qualified student loan to attend college. After Darla's graduation from college, she worked as an intern for a nonprofit organization. As part of the internship program, the nonprofit organization made an interest payment on behalf of Darla. This payment was reported in box 1 of her Form W-2. Assuming all other qualifications are met, Darla can deduct this payment of her student loan interest on her return.

Qualified Student Loan. A qualified student loan is a loan for qualified higher education expenses including tuition, fees, room and board, and related expenses such as books and supplies. The expenses must be for a degree, certificate or similar program at a college, university or vocational school eligible to participate in federal student aid programs. The student must be the taxpayer, the taxpayer's spouse, any person who was the taxpayer's dependent at the time the loan was taken out, or any person who could have been claimed as a depedent at the time the loan was taken out except that the person filed a joint return, had gross income of at least $3,650 for the year, or if taxpayer is married filing a joint return and either spouse could be claimed as a dependent on someone else's return. The student must carry at least half the normal full-time workload for the degree or certificate they are pursuing.

Line 34, Tuition and Fees Deduction

A deduction may be claimed for qualified tuition expenses paid in 2009 for the taxpayer, the taxpayer's spouse, or the taxpayer's dependent for whom an exemption is claimed. The maximum deduction is $4,000 for taxpayers with an adjusted gross income (AGI) at or below $65,000 ($130,000 for joint filers). The maximum deduction is $2,000 for taxpayers whose AGI exceeds $65,000 but less than or equal to $80,000 ($130,000 and $160,000, respectively, for joint filers). Taxpayers whose AGI exceed these limits, married taxpayers filing separately, nonresident aliens, and taxpayers who may be claimed as a dependent on another person's return are not allowed to claim the deduction. Form 8917 is used to calculate the deduction.

Qualified tuition expenses are amounts paid in 2009 (or in the first three months of 2010) for tuition and fees required for the student's enrollment at a college, university or vocational school during the year. They do not include expenses for room and board, insurance, medical expenses (including student health fees), transportation or other similar personal expenses. Qualified expenses also do not include books, supplies, equipment, or expenses for courses involving sports, games or hobbies, unless such courses are part of the student's degree program. The taxpayer should receive a Form 1098-T from the school indicating the amount of qualified expenses paid.

Qualified education expenses cannot be deducted on line 34 to the extent:

- the expenses are deducted elsewhere, for example as a business expense;
- the American Opportunity (modified Hope) or lifetime learning Credit is claimed for the same student for the year (see Tab 13);
- the expenses are used to figure the tax-free portion of a distribution from a Coverdell ESA or qualified tuition program (529 plan);
- the expenses are paid with tax-free educational assistance such as scholarships and fellowships that were not included on line 7, employer-provided or other nontaxable educational assistance (for example, Pell grants or veterans' educational assistance), or other tax-free payments such as gifts or inheritance; or
- the expenses are paid with tax-free interest on U.S. savings bonds.

Line 35, Domestic Production Activities Deduction

For 2009, individuals engaged in a trade or business may deduct six percent of the lesser their adjusted gross income (determined without regard to the deduction) or qualified production activities income (QPAI). However, the deduction may not exceed 50 percent of the W-2 wages paid by the taxpayer attributable to domestic production gross receipts.

Filing Tip. Form 8903 is used to figure the deduction. Married individuals filing a joint return use only one Form 8903 using the applicable items of both spouses. If the individual is a member of a pass-through entity, information needed to figure the deduction should be provided on his or her Schedule K-1.

Qualified Activities. A taxpayer's QPAI is their domestic production gross receipts (DPGR), less the cost of goods sold allocable to DPGR and other expenses, losses or deductions allocable to DPGR. Generally, an individual's gross receipts derived from the following activities are DPGR:

- construction of real property performed by the taxpayer in the United States in a construction trade or business;
- engineering or architectural services performed by the taxpayer in the United States in a engineering or architectural services trade or business for the construction of real property in the United States; and
- any lease, rental, license, sale, exchange or other disposition of:
  - tangible personal property, computer software, and sound recordings that the taxpayer manufactured, produced, grew, or extracted in whole or in significant part in the United States;
  - qualified film produced by the taxpayer; or
  - electricity, natural gas, or potable water the taxpayer produced in the United States.

Activities from which the gross receipts will **not** be DPGR include:

- the sale of food and beverages at a retail establishment;
- property leased, rented or licensed between certain persons treated as a single employer;
- the lease, rental, license, sale, exchange or other disposition of land; and
- the transmission or distribution of electricity, natural gas, or potable water.

Allocation methods. To compute the deduction, a taxpayer must allocate all of its gross receipts between DPGR and non-DPGR. Any reasonable method may be used so long as it accurately identifies which gross receipts are DPGR. However, if less than five percent of the taxpayer's gross receipts are DPGR, all of the gross receipt may be treated as either DPGR or non-DPGR.

The taxpayer must use the same method to allocate cost of goods sold (COGS) to DPGR as used to allocate gross receipts, unless another method is more accurate. To allocate other deductions, expenses or losses (other than COGS and employee business expenses), one of three methods can be used.

Small business simplified overall method. Under this method, COGS and other deductions, expenses and losses are allocated ratably between DPGR and non-DPGR based on relative gross receipts. A taxpayer can use this method if he or she:

- has average annual gross receipts of $5 million or less;
- is engaged in a farming trade or business and is not required to use the accrual-method of accounting; or
- has average annual gross receipts of $10 million or less and is eligible to use the cash method of accounting under Rev. Proc. 2008-52 and Rev. Proc. 2002-28.

Simplified deduction method. Under this method, trade or business deductions, expenses and losses (other than COGS and employee business expenses) are allocated ratably between DPGR and non-DPGR based on relative gross receipts. A taxpayer can use this method if total trade or business assets are $10 million or less at the end of the tax year or average annual gross receipts are $100 million or less.

Section 861 method. Under this method, trade or business expenses and losses (other than COGS and employee business expenses) are allocated using the tracing rules under Code Sec. 861.

Lines 36, 37, and 38, Adjusted Gross Income Calculations

Include in the sum on line 36 any of the following write-in adjustments, including on the dotted line next to line 36 the amount and identity of the deduction.

- expenses related to income from rental of personal property reported on line 21 and engaged in for profit (identify as "PPR");
- jury duty pay surrendered to an employer in exchange for regular compensation (identify as "Jury Pay");
- deductible contributions to Archer MSAs as determined on Form 8853 (identify as "MSA");
- repayment of supplemental unemployment benefits under the Trade Act of 1974 (identify as "Sub-Pay TRA");
- contributions to certain pension plans under IRC §§403(b) or 501(c)(18)(D) (identify as "403(b)" and "501(c)(18)(D)," respectively);
- attorney fees and court costs paid for prosecuting unlawful discrimination claims, but only to extent of gross income from such actions (identify as "UDC");
- attorney fees and courts costs paid in connection with IRS whistle-blower award that substantially contributed to detection of tax law violations, but only to the extent of the amount of the award included in gross income (identify as "WBF");
- reforestation amortization and expenses (see Tab 8 for more information) (identify as "RFST"); and
- foreign housing deduction for qualified self-employed taxpayers as calculated on Form 2555 (identify as "Form 2555").

See MTG ¶1005 for a comprehensive list of above-the-line deductions.

Adjusted Gross Income. Lines 37 and 38 are the taxpayer's AGI. This is the primary value used in tax calculations, including calculation of the alternative minimum tax.

Tax and Credits, Lines 38-55

After AGI is determined, additional deductions may be taken to determine the taxpayer's taxable income. From this amount the taxpayer's tentative tax liability is calculated before any tax credits are subtracted dollar for dollar to determine the taxpayer's actual tax liability.

Lines 39 and 40, Itemized or Standard Deductions

Generally, a taxpayer will lower their federal income tax liability by taking the larger of their itemized deductions on Schedule A (see Tab 2) or a standard deduction listed in the table below. Additions to the standard deduction are allowed if the taxpayer (or spouse if filing a joint return) is age 65 or older (born before January 2, 1945), or is totally or partially blind on the last day of the year. Check the appropriate box(es) on line 39a and enter the total number checked.

2009 Standard Deductions

Filing Status	Standard Deduction	Age 65 or Older or Blind (Each)
Single	$5,700	$1,400
MFJ or QW/SS	$11,400	$1,100
MFS	$5,700	$1,100
HOH	$8,350	$1,400

The standard deduction may also be increased if the taxpayer paid state or local real estate taxes, paid state or local motor vehicle sales or excise taxes, or had a net disaster loss from a federally declared disaster. To claim any of these increased standard deduction amounts, check box 40b and use Schedule L reproduced on page 1-54 to determine the amount to enter on line 40a. However, if the taxpayer may be claimed as a dependent on someone else's return, the standard deduction amount will be limited and the worksheet reproduced on page 1-53 must be used to compute the amount to enter on line 40a.

Filing Tip. If the taxpayer is married filing a separate return and his or her spouse itemizes deductions for the year, then the taxpayer's standard deduction amount is zero (-0-), even if the taxpayer was age 65 or older, blind, paid real estate or motor vehicle taxes, or had a net disaster loss. The individual should itemize deductions under such circumstances. In either case, the box on line 39b must be checked.

Filing Tip. The standard deduction amount for a taxpayer who is a dual-status alien (both nonresident and resident alien during portions of the year) will also be zero (-0-), even if the taxpayer was age 65 or older, blind, paid real estate or motor vehicle taxes, or had a net disaster loss. Under such circumstance, the box on line 39b must be checked and "Dual-Status Return" should be written across the top of the taxpayer's return. However, a nonresident alien married to a U.S. citizen or resident alien at the end of the year may elect to be treated as a resident alien (see page 1-3).

Real Estate Taxes. The standard deduction claimed by a homeowner may be increased for any state and local real property taxes paid in 2009 which are unrelated to any business use of the home (including as a rental expense). The deduction is the lesser of the amount that could be claimed as an itemized deduction or $500 ($1,000 for joint filers). To claim the deduction, check the box on line 40b and complete Schedule L reproduced on page 1-54.

Motor Vehicle Taxes. The standard deduction claimed by a taxpayer may be increased for any state or local sales, or excise taxes paid in 2009 for the purchase of a qualified motor vehicle after February 16, 2009. The additional deduction is limited to the portion of the taxes imposed on the first $49,500 of the purchase price of the vehicle. A qualified vehicle includes any new (not used) passenger vehicle, light truck, or motorcycle with a gross vehicle weight of 8,500 pounds or less, or a motor home of any weight. To claim the deduction, check the box on line 40b and complete Schedule L reproduced on page 1-54.

Disaster Losses. The standard deduction claimed by a taxpayer may be increased by the amount of his or her net disaster loss for the year. This is the excess of the taxpayer's personal casualty losses attributable to a federally declared disaster occurring in a disaster area, over any personal casualty gains and reported on line 18a of Form 4684. To claim the deduction, check the box on line 40b and complete Schedule L reproduced on page 1-54.

Line 42, Calculation of Exemptions

In 2009, a taxpayer may be able to claim a deduction of up to $3,650 for each exemption claimed in line 6d. The deduction, however, will be reduced or eliminated if the taxpayer's AGI exceeds the appropriate threshold amount (based on filing status). The worksheet reproduced on page 1-53, is used to figure the amount to enter on line 42 in these circumstances. See MTG ¶133 for more information. The exemption amounts begin to phase out in 2009 when AGI reaches:

- $250,200 for married individuals filing joint returns and surviving spouses;
- $208,500 for heads of households;
- $166,800 for unmarried individuals; and
- $125,100 for married individuals filing separate returns.

Planning Tip. For 2009, the deduction is reduced by only 1/3 of the amount that would otherwise be required under the phase out rules. As a result, taxpayers with AGI in excess of the maximum phase out amounts may claim a deduction of $2,433 for each exemption claimed on line 6d. This adjustment to the exemption deduction is also computed on the worksheet on page 1-53.

Midwest Displaced Individuals. Taxpayers who housed Midwestern displaced individuals (other than spouse or dependents) from the 2008 flood disaster free of charge for 60 consecutive days in their principal residence are entitled to claim an additional $500 exemption per evacuee, up to $2,000 per taxpayer over 2008 and 2009. The additional exemption amount is not subject to the income-based phaseouts and is allowed as a deduction in computing the alternative minimum tax. Form 8914 reproduced on page 1-55 is used to figure the amount to enter on Line 42.

A Midwestern displaced individual is an individual who had his or her main home in one of the counties listed in Table 1 or Table 2 on page 1-56 on the applicable disaster date shown in the table for that county, and was displaced from that home. In addition, if the individual's main home was in a county listed in Table 2, the home must have been damaged by the storms, tornadoes, or flooding that gave rise to the disaster declaration for that county, or the individual must have been evacuated from the home because of the storms, tornadoes, or flooding.

Line 43, Taxable Income

Subtract line 42 from line 41 to determine the taxpayer's taxable income. If line 42 is more than line 41, enter zero (-0-).

Line 44, Tax Rates

A taxpayer's tentative tax liability is reported on line 44. Generally, if taxable income (line 43) is less than $100,000, then the tax table reproduced in Tab 17 is used to determine the taxpayer's tentative liability. If taxable income is $100,000 or more, then the tax rate schedule reproduced in Tab 17 is used. Certain taxpayers, however, are required to calculate their tentative tax liability using alternative methods.

- Form 8615 must generally be used for certain children who had more than $1,900 of investment income (unless neither of the child's parents was alive at the end of 2009 or the child files a joint return for the year). See Tab 13.
- Schedule D Worksheet must be used if the taxpayer is required to file Schedule D and has gains which are subject to the 28 percent capital gains rate or any unrecaptured section 1250 gain. See Tab 4.
- Qualified Dividends and Capital Gain Tax Worksheet, reproduced on page 1-57, must be used if the taxpayer does not have to use the Schedule D Worksheet, but reports qualified dividends on line 9b or capital gains on line 13. The Worksheet must also be used if the taxpayer is filing Schedule D and has net-long term capital gains or losses, or long-term capital loss carryovers. See Tab 4.
- Schedule J may be used by taxpayers who had income from farming or fishing. See Tab 3 and MTG ¶767.
- Foreign Earned Income Tax Worksheet reproduced on page 1-58 must be used by taxpayers who claimed the foreign earned income exclusion, housing exclusion, or housing deduction on Form 2555.

Include in the total on line 44 (checking the appropriate box) any of the following:

- tax from Form 8814, relating to a parent's election to report a child's investment income (see Tab 13);
- tax from Form 4972, relating to the tax on lump-sum distributions (see page 1-20); and
- recapture of an education credit if the credit was claimed in an earlier year and a refund or tax-free educational assistance was received in 2009 for that year (enter the amount and write "ECR" in the space on the dotted line next to line 44). See Form 8863 for more information

Line 45, Alternative Minimum Tax

All taxpayers subject to the regular federal income tax are also subject to the alternative minimum tax (AMT). Alternative minimum taxable income (AMTI) is calculated according to a different system than that for income subject to the regular tax. See Tab 10 for more information, as well as a worksheet to be used to determine whether the taxpayer must complete Form 6251 to calculate their AMT liability.

Line 46, Calculation of Tax Liability

Add line 44, regular income tax, and 45, alternative minimum tax, to determine the taxpayer's total tax liability.

Line 47, Foreign Tax Credit

Taxpayers who paid or accrued foreign income taxes on foreign-source income subject to U.S. tax may choose to claim a credit for such taxes or to include them as an itemized deductions on Schedule A. Form 1116 is generally used to calculate the credit. See Tab 10 for more information.

Line 48, Child and Dependent Care Credit

Taxpayers who paid someone to care for their child under age 13 or other qualifying dependent so they (or spouse, if filing a joint return) could work or look for work may claim a credit for such expenses. Form 2441 is used to calculate the credit. See Tab 10 for more information.

Caution. A taxpayer cannot receive a double benefit by claiming a credit on dependent care benefits that are excluded from income on line 7 of Form 1040. Thus, a taxpayer must first calculate the exclusion in Part III of Form 2441 first. Then the credit may be calculated in Part II of Form 2441 on any child and dependent care expenses not excluded from income.

Line 49, Education Credits

The American Opportunity (modified Hope) and lifetime learning credits are available to taxpayers who incurred qualifying educational expenses during the tax year. Form 8863 is used to calculate the credits. A taxpayer may take only one of these credits for each student each year. For 2009, 40 percent of the American Opportunity (modified Hope) credit is refundable and reported on line 66 (see page 1-41). See Tab 10 for more information.

Line 50, Retirement Savings Credit

Certain low and middle-income taxpayers may be able to claim a nonrefundable credit for contributions made to a retirement plan. Form 8880 is used to calculate the credit. See Tab 10 for more information.

Line 51, Child Tax Credit

Taxpayers who have one or more qualifying child (see page 1-8) under the age of 17 may be entitled to a credit of $1,000 per child, subject to a phaseout limitation. A taxpayer should have checked the box in column 4 of line 6c for each dependent for whom the child tax credit is claimed. Generally, the credit is nonrefundable. However, a taxpayer may qualify for an additional child tax credit which may be refundable on line 65 (see page 1-41). See Tab 10 for more information.

Lines 52 and 53, Other Tax Credits

A taxpayer reports the following various credits on lines 52 and 53 by checking the appropriate box(es) and completing the form(s) indicated. If the taxpayer checks box c on line 53, then enter the form number in the space provided. See Tab 10 for more information about these credits.

- **Form 8396**, *Mortgage Interest Credit.* The credit can only be claimed if the taxpayer was issued a Mortgage Credit Certificate (MCC) by a state or local government.
- **Form 8839**, *Qualified Adoption Expenses.* The form is used to figure the amount of the credit and any employer-provided adoption benefits that may be excluded from income on line 7. While the exclusion and credit may be claimed for the same adoption, the taxpayer cannot claim both for the same expenses.
- **Form 5695,** *Residential Energy Efficient Property Credit.* The form is used to figure the amount of the taxpayer's nonbusiness energy property credit, and the residential energy efficient property credit.
- **Form 3800**, *General Business Credit.* The credit consists of a number of credits that usually only apply to individuals who are partners, S corporation shareholders, self-employed, or have rental property. If the taxpayer claims only one business credit, Form 3800 need not be filed unless the taxpayer has one or more of the business credits to claim in a single year or a carryback or carryforward from previous years.
- **Schedule R, Form 1040**, *Credit for the Elderly or the Disabled.* Write "Sch R" in space next to box c. See Tab 10 for more information.
- **Form 8834**, *Qualified Electric and Plug-in Electric Vehicle Credit.* The qualified plug-in electric vehicle credit is available for vehicles acquired and placed in service after February 17, 2009. A credit may also be claimed for a passive activity electric vehicle carried forward from a prior year.
- **Form 8936**, *Qualified Plug-in Electric Drive Motor Vehicle Credit.* The qualified plug-in electric drive motor vehicle credit is available for placed in service in 2009.
- **Form 8910**, *Alternative Motor Vehicle Credit.* The credit can only be claimed if the taxpayer placed an alternative motor vehicle in service in 2009. See also Form 8911, *Alternative Fuel Vehicle Refueling Property Credit.*
- **Others.** Form 8801, *Credit for Prior Year Minimum Tax–Individuals, Estates, and Trusts;* Form 8859, *District of Columbia First-Time Homebuyer Credit (see also line 67);* Form 8912, *Credit for Clean Renewable Energy and Gulf Tax Credit Bonds.*

Lines 54 and 55, Total Credits

Lines 47 through 53 are added together to determine the taxpayer's total amount of tax credits claimed on line 54. This total is then subtracted from the taxpayer's tentative tax liability (line 46) and the result is entered on line 55. However, if the total amount of tax credits claimed on line 54 is more than the taxpayer's tentative liability, then enter zero (-0-) on line 55.

Other Taxes, Lines 56-60

Line 56, Self-Employment Tax

Self-employed taxpayers who have more than $400 of net earnings must pay a self-employment tax. The tax is computed on Schedule SE. See Tab 3 for more information. A taxpayer may claim a deduction from gross income for one-half of the self-employment tax paid on line 27 (see page 1-30).

Line 57, Unreported Social Security and Medicare Tax

A taxpayer must figure and report his or her share of uncollected Social Security and Medicare taxes due on tip income or wages received during the year. Check the appropriate box and enter the total amount of taxes from Form 4137 and Form 8919 for this purpose.

Form 4137 is used if the taxpayer received cash or charge tips of $20 or more in any month and did not report the full amount to their employer. The taxpayer must also pay uncollected Social Security and Medicare taxes on allocated tips shown on his or her Form W-2(s) and that are included on line 7.

Form 8919 is used if the taxpayer was an employee but was incorrectly treated as an independent contractor by his or her employer resulting in no Social Security or Medicare taxes being withheld from compensation received from the employer.

Caution. If the taxpayer did not report tips to their employer as required, then he or she may be charged a penalty equal to 50 percent of the taxes calculated on Form 4137. To avoid the penalty, attach a statement to the return explaining why the taxpayer had reasonable cause for not reporting the tips to their employer.

Line 58, Additional Tax on IRAs and Other Qualified Retirement Plans, Etc.

Report on line 58 any additional taxes on qualified retirement plans (including IRAs), HSAs, Archer MSAs, Coverdell ESAs, and qualified tuition plans (529 plans) as calculated on Form 5329. In the case of a joint return, a separate Form 5329 must be completed for each spouse. The additional taxes include:

- the 10-percent additional tax on early distributions from a qualified retirement plan or IRA (including an early distribution from a Roth IRA that is not a qualifying distribution);
- the six-percent tax on excess contributions to a traditional IRA, Roth IRA, HSA, Archer MSA, or Coverdell ESA; and
- the 10-percent additional tax on distributions from a Coverdell ESA or qualified tuition plan (529 plan) which are not used for qualified education expenses.

If the taxpayer is only subject to the 10-percent additional tax on early distributions (code 1 in box 7 of Form 1099-R), then Form 5329 does not need to be filed. Instead, on line 58 enter 10 percent of the taxable amount of the distribution (as reported on line 15b, 16b or Form 4972) and enter "No" to the left of line 58. However, if code 1 is incorrectly shown in box 7 of Form 1099-R or an exception to the early distribution penalty applies (code 2 in box 7 of Form 1099-R), then Form 5329 must be filed (see Tab 9).

Planning Tip. For 2009, a taxpayer will generally not be subject to the 50-percent tax for failing to take a required minimum distribution (RMD) from an IRA or employer-provided qualified retirement plan that is normally reported on Form 5329. The temporary waiver applies to plan participants and beneficiaries including individuals who turned 70 1/2 in 2009 and would not receive their RMD until April 1, 2010. If a taxpayer receives a distribution in 2009 that would otherwise be a RMD, it can be rolled over to a qualified retirement plan or IRA within 60 days of the distribution.

Line 59, Additional Taxes

Report on line 59 any advanced earned income credit (EIC) received (see Tab 10) and any household employment taxes from Schedule H. Check the appropriate box.

Advanced EIC. An eligible taxpayer can receive an advance of the EIC in their wages by completing Form W-5 and providing it to their employer. The advance EIC the taxpayer receives is shown in box 9 of Form W-2. The taxpayer must report the advanced EIC received even if it later determined that he or she was not eligible for the EIC.

Household Employment Taxes. If the taxpayer pays cash wages of $1,700 or more in 2009 to any one household employee, then Social Security and Medicare (FICA) taxes must be paid. Similarly, if the taxpayer pays cash wages of $1,000 or more in any one calendar quarter in 2008 or 2009 to all household employees, then federal unemployment taxes (FUTA) must be paid. Schedule H is used to calculate the taxes and the amount reported on line 59. However, Schedule H does not have to be used and no amount is required to be reported on line 59 if the taxpayer chooses to pay the taxes for household employees with business or farm employment taxes on Form 941, Form 943, or Form 944.

Planning Tip. A taxpayer is not required to withhold federal *income* taxes from wages paid to a household employee unless the employee requests the taxpayer to do so (using Form W-4) and the taxpayer agrees. If the withholding tables show no income tax should be withheld, then a notice (Copy B of Form W-2) should be given to the employee about the earned income credit (EIC).

Filing Tip. If the taxpayer is otherwise not required to file a tax return for 2009, Schedule H must be filed by itself by April 15, 2010, along with a payment of the employment taxes by check or money order. If Schedule H is filed by itself, then the paid preparer must sign the Schedule and provide the information requested in the Paid Preparer's Use Only section.

Wages paid to certain household employees will not be subject to employment taxes. This includes wages paid to the taxpayer's spouse, the taxpayer's child who is under the age of 21, or the taxpayer's parent. However, FICA taxes must be paid if the parent is caring for the taxpayer's minor child who has a physical of mental condition and the taxpayer is divorced, a widow(er) or living with a spouse who is physically or mentally disabled. FICA taxes also do not have to paid for any employee under the age of 18 at any time during the year, unless providing household services is their principal occupation.

Planning Tip. The taxpayer must make advance EIC payments to a household employee who provides the taxpayer with a completed Form W-5. The payment should be included in the employee's net pay, but it is not subject withholding of income or employment taxes.

For these purposes, a household employee is any person hired by the taxpayer to do household work in and around their home. Examples include housekeepers, nannies, health aides, maids, yard workers, and similar domestic workers. However, the taxpayer must be able to control what work the individual does and how they do it in order to be considered an employee. For example, workers from an agency or a self-employed individual who can control how their work is done are not considered household employees.

A separate Form W-2 must be filed with the Social Security Administration (SSA) for each household employee the taxpayer paid wages of $1,700 or more subject to FICA or wages from which federal income tax is withheld. A copy must also be given to the employee. If the taxpayer files one or more Form W-2, then Form W-3 must also be filed with the SSA. The taxpayer must obtain an employment identification number (EIN) to file Form W-2 or Schedule H. The taxpayer must also have verified that the employee can legally work in the United States by completing with the employee Form I-9 obtained from the U.S. Citizenship and Immigration Services.

Line 60, Total Tax

A taxpayer computes his or her total tax liability by adding lines 55 through 59 together and entering the result on line 60. Include in the total, all of the following that apply. On the dotted line next to line 60, enter the amount of the tax and identify as indicated.

- Additional tax on distributions from
  - health savings accounts, "HSA" (Form 8889)
  - Archer medical savings accounts, "MSA" (Form 8853)
  - Medicare Advantage MSAs, "Med MSA" (Form 8853)
  - nonqualified deferred compensation plan, "NQDC" (Form W-2, box 12, Code Z or Form 1099-MISC, box 15b)
- Additional tax for failure to maintain HDHP for a HSA, "HDHP" (Form 8889, Part III))
- Recapture of federal mortgage subsidy, "FMSR" (Form 8828)
- Section 72(m)(5) excess benefits tax, "72(m)(5)"
- Uncollected Social Security and Medicare tax on tips or group-term life insurance, "UT" (Form W-2, box 12, codes A and B or M and N)
- Golden parachute payments, "EPP" (Form W-2, box 12, code K or Form 1099-MISC, box 13)
- Tax on accumulation distribution of trusts, "ADT" (Form 4970)
- Interest on tax due on installment income from the sale of certain residential lots and timeshares "453(l)(3)"
- Interest on deferred tax on gain from certain installment sales over $150,000, "453A(c)"
- Recapture of the following credits
  - first-time homebuyer credit, "FTHCR" (Form 5450) (see Tab 10 for more information)
  - investment credit, "ICR" (Form 4255)
  - low-income housing credit, "LIHCR" (Form 8611)
  - qualified electric vehicle credit, "QEVCR" (Form 8834)
  - Indian employment credit, "IECR" (Form 8845)
  - new markets credit, "NMCR" (Form 8874)
  - credit for employer-provided child care facilities, "ECCFR" (Form 8882)
  - alternative motor vehicle credit, "AMVCR" (Form 8910)
  - alternative motor vehicle refueling property credit, "APRCR" (Form 8911)
  - excise tax on insider stock compensation from an expatriated corporation, "ISC", and
  - additional tax on recapture of charitable contribution deduction relating to fractional interest in tangible personal property, "FITPP".

Caution. Eligible employees who have lost their jobs may qualify for a 65 percent subsidy for COBRA continuation premiums for up to nine months. Generally, the premium subsidy is not included in gross income. However, the subsidy must be recaptured as an addition to tax on line 60 and identified as "COBRA" when the individual's modified AGI exceeds $125,000 ($250,000 for joint returns). If the individual's modified AGI exceeds $250,000 ($290,000 for joint returns), then the full-amount of the subsidy is recaptured. See MTG ¶896B for more information.

Payments, Lines 61-71

Line 61, Federal Income Tax Withheld

Report on line 61 the sum of the federal income tax withheld shown in:

- box 2 of Forms W-2 and W-2G;
- box 4 of most types of Form 1099 (1099-DIV, 1099-G, 1099-R, etc.); and
- box 6 of Form SSA-1099.

If the taxpayer is married filing a separate return, enter only the tax withheld from his or her own income. Do not include any amount withheld from the income of the taxpayer's spouse unless the couple lives in a community property state. In such cases, each spouse can claim half of the total income tax withheld from their combined wages since each can report half of the wages.

Line 62, Estimated Tax Payments

Enter on line 62, estimated federal income tax payments made using Form 1040-ES and any overpayment from the taxpayer's 2008 return that was applied to his or her 2009 estimated tax. Also include any estimated taxes credited to the taxpayer from an estate or trust (box 13 of Schedule K-1 of Form 1041).

Planning Note. If any estimated taxes are credited to the taxpayer from an estate or trust, then they must be reported on Schedule E (see Tab 5). However, the taxes do not need to be included on line 37 of Schedule E. Instead, enter "ES payment claimed" and the amount next to line 37.

Married Filing Separate Returns. Joint estimated payments made by married taxpayers who are filing separate returns or who are divorced may be divided between the spouses in any way they agree. If the spouses cannot agree, then the couple must divide the joint payments in proportion to each spouse's individual tax as shown on their separate 2009 returns.

Example. Richard and Paula filed a joint return for 2008 that showed a $3,000 overpayment, which they applied to their 2009 estimated tax. The couple, however, are filing separate returns for 2009. Richard's tax liability for 2009 is $4,000 and Paula's tax liability for 2009 is $1,000. If the couple does not agree on how to divide the $3,000 overpayment made in 2008, then Richard's share will be $2,400 (80 percent of $3,000) and Paula's share will be $600 (20 percent of $3,000).

If the taxpayer claims a joint estimated payment on a separate return, then the other spouse's Social Security number (SSN) must be reported in the space provided on page 1 of the return. However, if a divorced taxpayer has remarried during the year, enter the present spouse's SSN on page 1 of their separate return. Enter the former spouse's SSN, followed by "DIV" to the left of line 62.

If a married couple paid separate estimated tax payments for 2009 but are filing a joint return, then the separate amounts may be added together on the return. However, if a married couple made separate estimated tax payments for 2009 and file separate returns for 2009, then each spouse may only claim credit for the estimated payments he or she made.

Example. Carla and Nick filed a joint return for 2008 that showed a $1,100 overpayment which they applied to their 2009 estimated tax. The couple, however, are filing separate returns for 2009. Carla's W-2 shows $1,000 withheld for 2009 and she has a tax liability of $2,700. Nick's W-2 shows $300 withheld for 2009 but he has no tax liability. Carla can enter $2,100 on line 62, claiming $1,000 for the amount withheld from her wages and the entire $1,100 of the 2008 overpayment since Nick has no tax liability for 2009. Carla, however, cannot claim the $300 withheld from Nick's wages even though she would have a tax liability of $600 remaining. Instead, Nick must claim the $300 on his separate return.

Name Change. If a taxpayer's name changed, and estimated payments were made using the former name, attach a statement to the return explaining all the payments made by the taxpayer (and spouse, if applicable), and the names and SSNs under which they were made.

Line 63, Making Work Pay and Government Retiree Credits

For the 2009 tax year, taxpayers with earned income (including self-employed) are eligible for a refundable credit of up to $400 for individuals and $800 for joint filers called the Making Work Pay credit. Similarly, taxpayers who are not eligible for Social Security but receive a pension or annuity payment in 2009 for service performed for the federal government, or state or local government, are entitled to refundable credit of up to $250 ($500 if spouses on a joint return are government retirees). To claim the credits, the taxpayer must complete Schedule M and provide his or her Social Security number (or the number of the taxpayer's spouse if filing a joint return) on the return. See Tab 10 for more information.

> **Filing Tip.** The majority of taxpayers already received the Making Work Pay credit during 2009 through reduced income tax withholding. However, an individual must still complete Schedule M and attach it to his or her return.

Line 64, Earned Income Credit

A refundable credit is available to certain low-income individuals who have earned income. See Tab 10 for more information including a worksheet and tables to determine the amount of credit that may be claimed on line 64a.

Members of the U.S. armed forces may elect to treat nontaxable combat pay as earned income for purposes of the credit. A taxpayer's nontaxable combat pay should be shown in box 12 of Form W-2, Code Q. The amount of pay that the taxpayer elects to be included as earned income is reported on line 64b. In the case of joint return where both spouses receive nontaxable combat pay, both spouses may make the election and the total is reported on line 64b.

> **Filing Tip.** Since electing to include nontaxable combat pay could potentially decrease the amount of earned income credit, the credit amount should be calculated both with and without the nontaxable combat pay included.

Line 65, Additional Child Tax Credit

Taxpayers who have at least one qualifying child for the child tax credit on line 51 (see page 1-37) may also qualify for the additional child tax credit. The additional child tax credit may give the taxpayer a refund even if no tax is owed. If the taxpayer claimed the child tax credit, or was not entitled to take the child tax credit only because no tax was owed, use Form 8812 to determine the amount of the additional child tax credit. See Tab 10 and MTG ¶1302 for more information.

Line 66, Refundable Education Credit

Report on line 66 the refundable portion of the American Opportunity (modified Hope) education credit shown on line 16 of Form 8863. For 2009, 40 percent of the American Opportunity (modified Hope) credit is refundable. See Tab 10 for more information.

Line 67, First-Time Homebuyer Credit

A taxpayer who may qualify for a refundable income tax credit for the purchase of a principal residence made in 2009. The maximum amount of the credit is the lesser of 10 percent of the purchase price or $8,000 ($4,000 for married taxpayers filing separately). Form 5404 is used to calculate the credit. See Tab 10 for more information.

Line 68, Payments Made With Extension Request

If the taxpayer filed Form 4868 or Form 2350 to get an automatic extension to file his or her 2009 return, enter on line 68 any amount paid with the forms or by electronic funds withdrawal or credit card. If an amount was paid by credit card, the convenience fee is not included.

Line 69, Excess Social Security and Tier 1 RRTA Tax Withheld

If the taxpayer had more than one employer during 2009 and total wages of more than $106,800, too much Social Security or tier 1 Railroad Retirement taxes may have been withheld. For 2009, no more than $6,621.60 should have been withheld. Any excess may be claimed as a credit on line 69. Withheld Social Security and tier 1 RRTA taxes are reported in box 4 and box 14 of Form W-2, respectively. The taxpayer must include in the total on line 69 any uncollected Social Security or tier 1 RRTA taxes on tips or group-term life insurance from line 43 (see page 1-36). For taxpayers filing a joint return, each spouse must figure the excess separately. A taxpayer cannot add Social Security or tier 1 RRTA tax withheld from their spouse's income to the amount withheld from their own income.

> **Caution.** If any one employer withheld too much Social Security or tier 1 RRTA taxes, then the taxpayer cannot claim the credit. Instead, the employer should adjust the amount withheld. If the employer does not, the taxpayer must file a claim for refund using Form 843. If the taxpayer has any excess tier 2 RRTA taxes, Form 843 must also be used. For 2009, the maximum amount of tier 2 RRTA taxes that should have been withheld and reported in box 14 of Form W-2 is $4,165.20.

Line 70, Other Payments

Check the appropriate box(es) and enter the amount from the following forms to receive credit for the payment of certain taxes:

- Form 2439, *Notice to Shareholders of Undistributed Long-Term Capital Gains* (box 2).
- Form 4136, *Credit for Federal Tax Paid on Fuels* (line 17).
- Form 8801, *Credit for Prior Year Minimum Tax* (line 29) (see Tab 10).
- Form 8885, *Health Coverage Tax Credit* (line 7).

Line 71, Total Payments

Add lines 61, 62, 63, 64a, and 65 through 70. This is the amount of 2009 federal income tax prepaid by the taxpayer (including refundable credits).

Refund or Amount Due, Lines 72-76

Line 72, Overpayment

If line 71 is more than line 60, then the taxpayer is entitled to a refund. However, if the overpayment is less than $1, the IRS will send a refund only on written request.

Planning Tip. If the amount of overpayment is large, the taxpayer may want to file a new Form W-4 or recalculate the estimated tax amounts that will be paid with Form 1040-ES. See Tab 11 for more details.

Refund Offsets. All or part of a taxpayer's overpayment may be used to pay past-due debts including federal tax, state income tax, child or spousal support, or federal non-tax debts such as student loans and unemployment benefits received by fraud. If offsets are made, the taxpayer will receive a notice showing the amount of the offset and the agency receiving it.

A spouse who files a joint return may file an injured-spouse claim using Form 8379 to obtain a refund of his or her part of the overpayment if an offset is taken to pay the other spouse's debts. If the form is attached to the taxpayer's return, then write "Injured Spouse" on page 1 of the return. Form 8379 may also be filed by itself. In such cases, it must show the Social Security numbers of both spouses in the same order as they appear on the taxpayer's return. Injured spouse relief is different from innocent spouse relief request made on Form 8857.

Line 73, Amount of Refund

On line 73a, enter the portion of any overpayment that the taxpayer would like refunded (if any). The taxpayer may also have the overpayment applied to his or her 2010 estimated taxes (see line 74).

Direct Deposit. Normally, the IRS will issue a paper check to the taxpayer for any refund. However, a taxpayer may have the entire refund directly deposited into an account maintained in his or her name at a U.S. financial institution (such as a mutual fund, brokerage firm, or credit union). A taxpayer can choose to have a refund directly deposited into a checking or savings account, brokerage account, any type of IRA (except a SIMPLE IRA), health savings account (HSA), Archer MSA, or Coverdell ESA.

Caution. Generally, a taxpayer cannot directly deposit a refund into someone else's account (even the account of the preparer for any fees preparing the return). The only exception is in the case of a joint return where the taxpayers can designate deposits to a joint account or to an account of only one spouse. In such cases, married taxpayers appoint their spouse as an agent to receive a refund of taxes.

Caution. A taxpayer should check with his or her financial institution to make sure a direct deposit will be accepted. For example, some financial institutions will not allow a joint refund to be deposited into an individual account. If the direct deposit is rejected by the financial institution, the IRS will issue a paper check instead.

Split Refund. A taxpayer may choose to have a refund directly deposited in up to three different accounts in his or her name. To deposit the refund in a single account, include the routing and account number on line 73b and 73d, respectively (leaving any unused boxes blank). If the deposit is to an IRA, HSA, MSA, Coverdell, or brokerage account, the taxpayer must confirm with their financial institution as to whether the "Checking" or "Savings" box should be checked on line 73c.

Caution. The taxpayer should also verify the correct routing and accounting numbers with their financial institution. The IRS is not responsible for a lost refund if incorrect account information is provided with the return.

If a taxpayer chooses to have a refund directly deposited into more than one account, then the check the box at the end of line 73a and complete Form 8888. On the form, the taxpayer should indicate the amount of the refund allocated to each account, as well as the routing number, account type, and account number of each account. If the total amount allocated on Form 8888 does not equal the amount the taxpayer wants refunded as indicated on line 73a, then no direct deposit will occur and the IRS will send a paper check to the taxpayer. Also, if the taxpayer's refund is adjusted (such as math error or refund offset), this will be reflected in the last account listed.

Caution. A taxpayer cannot have a refund deposited into more than one account if he or she has filed for an injured spouse allocation using Form 8379.

Deposits in IRAs. For a refund to be deposited in an IRA, the account must be established before the request for the direct deposit. The deposit will count towards the taxpayer's annual deductible limit for contributions to his or her traditional IRAs. Thus, the taxpayer must notify the trustee of the account of the year to which the deposit applies. The taxpayer must also verify that the direct deposit is actually made to the IRA by the due date or his or her return (without regard to extensions).

Example. Leon Rice files his 2009 individual return on April 9, 2010, indicating a $5,500 overpayment. Leon files Form 8888 with his return, indicating that he would like $5,000 of the overpayment directly deposited in his traditional IRA and the remaining $500 directly deposited into his savings account. Leon directs the trustee of his IRA that the deposit is a contribution to his IRA for the 2009 tax year.

The IRS deposits Leon's refund into his IRA and savings account on April 20, 2010. Because the deposit is made after the due date for Leon to file his return, the deposit cannot be considered a contribution to his IRA for 2009, but instead is a contribution for 2010. If Leon claimed the $5,000 deposit into his traditional IRA as a deductible contribution made in 2009, then he must file an amended 2008 return to reduce his IRA deduction and any retirement savings credit he claimed.

Planning Tip. To ensure that a deposit of a refund into an IRA may be claimed as deductible contribution on the taxpayers return in the same year the return is filed, a taxpayer should be sure to file their return as soon as possible. Normally, taxpayers who file their returns electronically and opt for direct deposit can receive their refund in two weeks or less. However, the closer to the filing deadline a taxpayer waits to submit their return to the IRS, the longer it may take to deposit a refund into an IRA.

Line 74, Applied to 2010 Estimated Tax

Instead of having an overpayment of taxes refunded, a taxpayer may request that part or all of the overpayment be applied to the taxpayer's 2010 estimated tax by entering the appropriate amount on line 74. A married taxpayer may request that any overpayment be applied to a spouse's 2010 estimated tax instead of his or her own by attaching a statement to that effect and including the other spouse's Social Security number in the attachment.

Caution. The election to apply part or all of any overpayment to 2010 estimated tax cannot be changed later.

Line 75, Amount Owed

If the amount of a taxpayer's total tax (line 60) is more than the total payments (line 71), then the taxpayer owes taxes and the amount is reported on line 75. Include any estimated tax penalty from line 76 in the amount reported on line 75.

Payment Methods. If the amount of taxes owed is less than $1, the taxpayer does not have to pay. However, if the taxpayer must pay taxes, they must be paid in full by April 15, 2010, to avoid interest and penalties. Payments may be made by check, money order, credit card, or electronic fund transfer through the Electronic Federal Tax Payment System (EFTPS) or Electronic Funds Withdrawal (EFW).

Make checks or money orders payable to the "United States Treasury." Include the taxpayer's name, address, daytime phone, Social Security number (SSN) and write "2009 Form 1040" on the front of the check or money order. If filing a joint return, enter the SSN shown first on the return. Enter the full amount tax owed from line 75 as $XXX.XX. Do not use dashes or lines. Form 1040-V is an optional payment voucher that may also be used which allows the IRS to process the payment more accurately.

Credit Card Payments. A taxpayer can pay any tax liability by American Express, Discover, MasterCard, or Visa. To pay by credit card, call or visit the website of one of the following service providers: Link2Gov Corporation (888-PAY-1040 or www.PAY1040.com); and Official Payments Corporation (800-2PAY-TAX or www.officialpayments.com). A convenience fee will be charged by the service provider based on the amount of tax being paid.

Filing Tip. If a taxpayer cannot pay the full amount shown on line 75 by the due date, he or she may ask to make monthly installment payments by filing Form 9465. Generally, the IRS will respond to an installment payment request within 30 days. Even if the IRS agrees to let the taxpayer make installment payments, interest and penalties will still accrue on any unpaid amounts.

Line 76, Estimated Tax Penalty

The IRS will assess a penalty against the taxpayer if he or she failed to pay enough tax during the tax year either through withholding of by making estimated tax payments. The penalty will apply if *either* of the following applies:

- Line 75 is at least $1,000 and more than 10 percent of the tax shown on the return.
- The taxpayer did not pay enough estimated tax by any of the due dates even if the taxpayer is due a refund.

Planning Tip. Form 2210 (Form 2210-F for farmers and fisherman) is used by a taxpayer to determine if he or she owes a penalty for underpayment of taxes and to figure the amount of the penalty. Because the penalty is complicated, line 76 may be left blank and the IRS will compute any penalty amount required to be paid.

Safe Harbor. No penalty will be owed if the taxpayer's 2008 tax return was for 12 full months, any estimated tax payments were made on time, and *either* of the following applies:

- the taxpayer had no tax liability for 2008 and was a U.S. citizen or resident for all of 2008; or
- the total tax withheld on lines 61, 62, and 69 on the taxpayer's 2009 return is at least as much as the tax liability shown on the 2008 return, or is at least 110 percent of the tax liability shown on the 2008 return if the 2008 AGI was over $150,000 (over $75,000 if married filing separately) and the taxpayer is not a farmer or fisherman.

See Tab 11 and MTG ¶2682 for more information.

Third Party Designee

A taxpayer may designate any person to discuss his or her 2009 tax return with the IRS by checking "Yes" in the "Third Party Designee" section. Also, enter the designee's name, phone number, and any five-digits the designee chooses as his or her personal identification number. However, if the taxpayer wants to allow the paid preparer who signed the return (see page 1-45) to discuss it with the IRS, enter only "Preparer" in the space for the designee's name.

By checking the "Yes" box, the taxpayer (and spouse, if filing a joint return) is authorizing the following:

- the IRS may call the designee to answer any questions that may arise during the processing of the taxpayer's return;
- the designee may provide any information that is missing on the return to the IRS;
- the designee may request information about the processing of the return or the status of the refund or payment;
- the IRS may send copies of notices or transcripts related to the return, upon request; and
- the designee may respond to certain IRS notices about math errors, offsets, and return preparation.

The designee is not authorized to receive any refund check or to represent the taxpayer before the IRS. In addition, the authorization is only good for one year after the due date of the return without extension (April 15, 2010, for most taxpayers). The authorization may be revoked at any time by the sending a written statement signed by both the taxpayer and the third-party designee to the IRS. See IRS Publication 947.

Signature Requirements

All returns must be signed and dated by the taxpayer. The taxpayer must also enter his or her occupation. A daytime telephone number may be provided to help speed the processing of the return.

If a joint return is filed, then both spouses must generally sign and date the return, even if only one spouse had income. In addition, both spouses must enter their respective occupations. However, a domestic spouse may sign a joint return on behalf of the spouse serving in the U.S. Armed Forces oversees if the other spouse is:

- in a combat zone or qualified hazardous duty area;
- missing in a combat zone (domestic spouse can sign return for up to two years after end of combat zone activities);
- incapacitated; or
- died during the tax year, so long as the surviving spouse did not remarry before the end of the year.

Filing Tip. Generally, the domestic spouse must attach a dated statement to the return for the reason he or she is signing the return for the other spouse. However, for military personnel who have died during the tax year, the surviving spouse must simply write "Filing as surviving spouse" in the signature area of the return.

Form 2848. An agent may be appointed to sign the return on the taxpayer's behalf if the taxpayer is unable to sign because of a disease or injury, the taxpayer is absent from the United States for at least 60 days before the due date of the return, or the taxpayer is given the authority to have an agent sign on his or her behalf by the IRS. A return signed by an agent must have a power of attorney on Form 2848 attached to the return and it must state that the agent is granted authority to sign the return. There are several exceptions to this requirement.

Child. If the taxpayer is a child and cannot sign the return, either parent may sign the child's name and add "By (parent's signature), parent for minor child."

Deceased Taxpayer. If the taxpayer is deceased, then the return must be signed by the taxpayer's personal representative (executor or administrator). If it is a joint return, the surviving spouse must also sign. If no personal representative has been appointed, the surviving spouse should sign the return and write in the signature area "Filing as surviving spouse." If there is no personal representative or surviving spouse, the person in charge of the decedent's property must file and sign the return as "personal representative."

Filing Tip. In the case of deceased taxpayer's return, the word "DECEASED," the decedent's name, and the date of death should be written across the top of the return.

Paid Preparers. An individual who prepares the return for a taxpayer(s) for a fee must also sign the return and provide his or her identifying information (e.g., name, address, Social Security number or preparer tax identification number (PTIN)). If the return is signed by a representative for the taxpayer, then a power of attorney (Form 2848) must also be attached to the return.

Electronic Returns. A taxpayer may sign an electronically filed income tax return by directly entering onto the return a self-selected personal identification number (PIN). If filing a joint return, both spouses must enter a self-selected PIN. A taxpayer establishes a five-digit PIN by verifying his or her identity and AGI from their originally filed federal income tax return from the prior year.

Alternatively, the practitioner may enter the taxpayer's PIN on the return or the electronic return originator (ERO) may select the taxpayer's PIN to be entered on the return. In either case, the taxpayer authorizes the practitioner or ERO to enter the PIN by completing the appropriate sections of Form 8879. The form does not have to be filed with the IRS, but must be retained by the practitioner or ERO for up to three years.

Filing Tip. Form 8453 is used to send certain required paper forms or supporting documentation with an electronically filed return, including Form 2848, and Schedule D-1. Form 8453 and supporting documents must be transmitted to the IRS within three business days after the taxpayer's electronically filed return has been accepted.

If the taxpayer signs the return using an electronic signature method, then the preparer must also sign the return with a PIN. The PIN may be manually inputed or automatically entered by software. The identifying information of the preparer (e.g., name, address, SSN or PTIN) must be entered in the e-file return.

Caution. Tax preparation software may automatically enter the preparer's identifying information onto a return. However, some software may enter the preparer's business entity name and not the practitioner's name for the "name" area of the return. Sole proprietors often change this to their individual names.

Filing Details

For most individuals, Form 1040 must be filed for the 2009 tax year by April 15, 2010. For fiscal-year filers, the return must be filed on or before the 15th day of the fourth full month following the close of the tax year. Individuals are entitled to an automatic *six-month* extension of time to file their income tax return. The extension can be obtained by filing Form 4868 on or before the due date of the tax return. No reason must be given for the need for the extension, but a good-faith estimate of the tax liability must be provided.

> **Caution.** The automatic extension of time to file does not extend the amount of time to pay the tax. Thus, interest is charged from the original due date. Penalties may also apply.

Outside of the Country. U.S. citizens and residents outside the country will have an additional two months to file their return and pay taxes. For tax year 2009, this means the return is not due until June 15, 2010. To qualify, the individual must be living outside the United States and Puerto Rico, and their main place of business or post of duty is outside the United States and Puerto Rico on the due date of the return. Individuals in military or naval service on duty outside the United States also qualify for this extension. If a joint return is filed, only one spouse has to qualify. If married taxpayers file separate returns, the extension only applies to the spouse who qualifies.

> **Caution.** No form is required for a taxpayer "outside of the country" to obtain the automatic two-month extension to file or pay taxes for the tax year. Instead, the taxpayer must attach a statement to his or her return showing that he or she meets the requirements for the extension. If any tax remains unpaid, interest is charged from the original due date of the return.

A taxpayer who is "out of the country" is generally given only an additional four-month extension (for a total of six months) if he or she files Form 4868. However, the individual may get an extension of time beyond the normal six-month period if he or she expects to qualify for the foreign earned income or foreign housing exclusion and file Form 2555 by meeting either the bona fide resident or physical presence test after the due date for their return. In these circumstance, the taxpayer who is "out of the country" may request for additional time by filing Form 2350.

> **Caution.** If false or misleading information is provided on Form 2350, then any extension of time granted by the IRS is voided and the taxpayer will be responsible for late filing penalties.

Serving in Combat Zone. The deadline for filing a tax return, paying any tax owed, and filing a claim for refund is automatically extended for taxpayers serving in a combat zone. This applies to members of the U.S. Armed Forces, as well as merchant marines serving aboard vessels under the operational control of the Department of Defense, Red Cross personnel, accredited correspondents, and civilians under the direction of the Armed Forces in support of the Armed Forces.

If a member of the Armed Forces is serving in a designated combat zone or is deployed in a contingency operation, or is hospitalized outside the United States due to injury received while serving in a combat zone or in a contingency operation, the due date of the member's return is postponed for the period of the combat service or hospitalization plus 180 days. The deadline will also be extended by the number of days the taxpayer had left to take action with the IRS before entering the combat zone. No interest or penalties will be assessed during this period. The extension is also available to the spouse of such service members wishing to file a joint return. See MTG ¶895 for a listing of combat zones.

Where to File Form 1040

If the taxpayer did not move during the year and received an envelope addressed to the "Internal Revenue Service Center" with their tax booklet, then use the envelope to mail in the taxpayer's return. If the taxpayer did not receive an envelope or moved during the year, then mail the Form 1040 or Form 4868 for the 2009 tax year to the "Internal Revenue Service Center" at the address listed in the following chart. Different addresses are required depending on whether the taxpayer files their own returns, a paid preparer files the return on behalf of a taxpayer, or a payment is included with the return. See MTG ¶3.

Where Taxpayers File Form 1040 and Form 4868 for 2009

State of Taxpayer's Residence	Form 1040 and 4868 (Taxpayer Prepared) No Payment Enclosed	Form 1040 (Taxpayer Prepared) Payment Enclosed	Form 4868 (Taxpayer Prepared) Payment Enclosed
Florida, Georgia, North Carolina, South Carolina	Atlanta, GA 39901-0002	Atlanta, GA 39901-0102	P.O. Box 105050 Atlanta, GA 30348-5050
Alabama, Kentucky, Louisiana, Mississippi, Tennessee, Texas	Austin, TX 73301-0002	Austin, TX 73301-0102	P.O. Box 1302 Charlotte, NC 28201-1302
Alaska, Arizona, California, Colorado, Hawaii, Nevada, New Mexico, Oregon, Utah, Washington	Fresno, CA 93888-0002	Fresno, CA 93888-0102	P.O. Box 7122 San Francisco, CA 94120-7122
Idaho, Illinois, Indiana, Iowa, Kansas, Michigan, Minnesota, Montana, Nebraska, North Dakota, Oklahoma, South Dakota, Wisconsin, Wyoming	Fresno, CA 93888-0002	Fresno, CA 93888-0102	P.O. Box 802503 Cincinnati, OH 45280-2503
Arkansas, Connecticut, Delaware, District of Columbia, Maryland, Missouri, Ohio, Rhode Island, Virginia, West Virginia	Kansas City, MO 64999-0002	Kansas City, MO 64999-0102	P.O. Box 970028 St. Louis, MO 63197-0028
Maine, Massachusetts, New Hampshire, New Jersey, New York, Pennsylvania, Vermont	Kansas City, MO 64999-0002	Kansas City, MO 64999-0102	P.O. Box 37009 Hartford, CT 06176-0009
A foreign country, American Samoa, or Puerto Rico (or is excluding income under Code Sec. 933); use an APO or FPO address, or file Form 2555, 2555-EZ, or 4563, or are a dual-status alien or nonpermanent resident of Guam of the U.S. Virgin Islands	Austin, TX 73301-0215	Austin, TX 73301-0215	P.O. Box 1302 Charlotte, NC 28201-1302

1 Permanent residents of Guam should use: Department of Revenue and Taxation, Government of Guam, P.O. Box 23607, GMF, GU 96921.
2 Permanent residents of U.S. Virgin Islands should use: V.I. Bureau of Internal Revenue, 9601 Estate Thomas, Charlotte Amalie, St. Thomas, VI 00802.

Where Tax Professionals File Form 1040 and Form 4868 for 2009

State of Taxpayer's Residence	Form 1040 and 4868 (Filed by Preparer) No Payment Enclosed	Form 1040 (Filed by Preparer), Payment Enclosed	Form 4868 (Filed by Preparer) Payment Enclosed
Florida, Georgia, North Carolina, South Carolina	Atlanta, GA 39901-0002	P.O. Box 105017 Atlanta, GA 30348-5017	P.O. Box 105050 Atlanta, GA 30348-5050
Alabama, Kentucky, Louisiana, Mississippi, Tennessee, Texas	Austin, TX 73301-0002	P.O. Box 1214 Charlotte, NC 28201-1214	P.O. Box 1302 Charlotte, NC 28201-1302
Alaska, Arizona, California, Colorado, Hawaii, Nevada, New Mexico, Oregon, Utah, Washington	Fresno, CA 93888-0002	P.O. Box 7704 San Francisco, CA 94120-7704	P.O. Box 7122 San Francisco, CA 94120-7122
Idaho, Illinois, Indiana, Iowa, Kansas, Michigan, Minnesota, Montana, Nebraska, North Dakota, Oklahoma, South Dakota, Wisconsin, Wyoming	Fresno, CA 93888-0002	P.O. Box 802501 Cincinnati, OH 45280-2501	P.O. Box 802503 Cincinnati, OH 45280-2503
Arkansas, Connecticut, Delaware, District of Columbia, Maryland, Missouri, Ohio, Rhode Island, Virginia, West Virginia	Kansas City, MO 64999-0002	P.O. Box 970011 St. Louis, MO 63197-0011	P.O. Box 970028 St. Louis, MO 63197-0028
Maine, Massachusetts, New Hampshire, New Jersey, New York, Pennsylvania, Vermont	Kansas City, MO 64999-0002	P.O. Box 37008 Hartford, CT 06176-0008	P.O. Box 37009 Hartford, CT 06176-0009
A foreign country, American Samoa, or Puerto Rico (or is excluding income under Code Sec. 933); use an APO or FPO address, or file Form 2555, 2555-EZ, or 4563, or are a dual-status alien or nonpermanent resident of Guam of the U.S. Virgin Islands	Austin, TX 73301-0215	P.O. Box 1303 Charlotte, NC 28201-1303	P.O. Box 1302 Charlotte, NC 28201-1302

1 Permanent residents of Guam should use: Department of Revenue and Taxation, Government of Guam, P.O. Box 23607, GMF, GU 96921.
2 Permanent residents of U.S. Virgin Islands should use: V.I. Bureau of Internal Revenue, 9601 Estate Thomas, Charlotte Amalie, St. Thomas, VI 00802.

State and Local Income Tax Refund Worksheet—Line 10

Keep for Your Records

Before you begin: √ Be sure you have read the **Exception** above to see if you can use this worksheet instead of Pub. 525 to figure if any of your refund is taxable.

1. Enter the income tax refund from **Form(s) 1099-G** (or similar statement). But **do not** enter more than the amount of your state and local income taxes shown on your 2008 Schedule A, line 5 . . . . **1.** ______
2. Enter your total allowable itemized deductions from your 2008 Schedule A, line 29 . . . . **2.** ______

Note. If the filing status on your 2008 Form 1040 was married filing separately and your spouse itemized deductions in 2008, skip lines 3 through 9, enter the amount from line 2 on line 10, and go to line 11.

3. Enter the amount shown below for the filing status claimed on your **2008** Form 1040.
   - Single or married filing separately—$5,450
   - Married filing jointly or qualifying widow(er)—$10,900
   - Head of household—$8,000 } **3.** ______
4. Did you fill in line 39a on your 2008 Form 1040?
   ☐ **No.** Enter -0-.
   ☐ **Yes.** Multiply the number in the box on line 39a of your 2008 Form 1040 by $1,050 ($1,350 if your 2008 filing status was single or head of household). } **4.** ______
5. Enter any state or local real estate taxes shown on your 2008 Schedule A, line 6. **Do not** include foreign real estate taxes . . . . **5.** ______
6. Enter $500 ($1,000 if married filing jointly) . . . . **6.** ______
7. Enter the smaller of line 5 or line 6 . . . . **7.** ______
8. Enter any net disaster loss from your 2008 Form 4684, line 18a . . . . **8.** ______
9. Add lines 3, 4, 7, and 8 . . . . **9.** ______
10. Is the amount on line 9 less than the amount on line 2?
    ☐ **No.** STOP None of your refund is taxable.
    ☐ **Yes.** Subtract line 9 from line 2 . . . . **10.** ______
11. **Taxable part of your refund.** Enter the **smaller** of line 1 or line 10 here and on Form 1040, line 10 . . **11.** ______

Student Loan Interest Deduction Worksheet—Line 33

Keep for Your Records

Before you begin:
√ Figure any write-in adjustments to be entered on the dotted line next to line 36 (see the instructions for line 36 on page 35).
√ Be sure you have read the **Exception** above to see if you can use this worksheet instead of Pub. 970 to figure your deduction.

1. Enter the total interest you paid in 2009 on qualified student loans (see above). **Do not** enter more than $2,500 **1.** ______
2. Enter the amount from Form 1040, line 22 . . . . **2.** ______
3. Enter the total of the amounts from Form 1040, lines 23 through 32, plus any write-in adjustments you entered on the dotted line next to line 36 . . . . **3.** ______
4. Subtract line 3 from line 2 . . . . **4.** ______
5. Enter the amount shown below for your filing status.
   - Single, head of household, or qualifying widow(er)—$60,000
   - Married filing jointly—$120,000 } . . . . **5.** ______
6. Is the amount on line 4 more than the amount on line 5?
   ☐ **No.** Skip lines 6 and 7, enter -0- on line 8, and go to line 9.
   ☐ **Yes.** Subtract line 5 from line 4 . . . . **6.** ______
7. Divide line 6 by $15,000 ($30,000 if married filing jointly). Enter the result as a decimal (rounded to at least three places). If the result is 1.000 or more, enter 1.000 . . . . **7.** ___ . ___
8. Multiply line 1 by line 7 . . . . **8.** ______
9. **Student loan interest deduction.** Subtract line 8 from line 1. Enter the result here and on Form 1040, line 33. **Do not** include this amount in figuring any other deduction on your return (such as on Schedule A, C, E, etc.) . . . . **9.** ______

Social Security Benefits Worksheet—Lines 20a and 20b

Keep for Your Records

Before you begin:

- √ Complete Form 1040, lines 21 and 23 through 32, if they apply to you.
- √ Figure any write-in adjustments to be entered on the dotted line next to line 36 (see the instructions for line 36 on page 35).
- √ If you are married filing separately and you lived apart from your spouse for all of 2009, enter "D" to the right of the word "benefits" on line 20a. If you do not, you may get a math error notice from the IRS.
- √ Be sure you have read the **Exception** on page 27 to see if you can use this worksheet instead of a publication to find out if any of your benefits are taxable.

1. Enter the total amount from **box 5** of **all** your **Forms SSA-1099** and **Forms RRB-1099.** Also, enter this amount on Form 1040, line 20a . . . . . . **1.** ______
2. Enter one-half of line 1 . . . . . . **2.** ______
3. Enter the total of the amounts from Form 1040, lines 7, 8a, 9a, 10 through 14, 15b, 16b, 17 through 19, and 21 . . . . . . **3.** ______
4. Enter the amount, if any, from Form 1040, line 8b . . . . . . **4.** ______
5. Add lines 2, 3, and 4 . . . . . . **5.** ______
6. Enter the total of the amounts from Form 1040, lines 23 through 32, plus any write-in adjustments you entered on the dotted line next to line 36 . . . . . . **6.** ______
7. Is the amount on line 6 less than the amount on line 5?
   - ☐ **No.** STOP None of your social security benefits are taxable. Enter -0- on Form 1040, line 20b.
   - ☐ **Yes.** Subtract line 6 from line 5 . . . . . . **7.** ______
8. If you are:
   - Married filing jointly, enter $32,000
   - Single, head of household, qualifying widow(er), or married filing separately and you **lived apart** from your spouse for all of 2009, enter $25,000
   - Married filing separately and you lived with your spouse at any time in 2009, skip lines 8 through 15; multiply line 7 by 85% (.85) and enter the result on line 16. Then go to line 17

   . . . . . . **8.** ______
9. Is the amount on line 8 less than the amount on line 7?
   - ☐ **No.** STOP None of your social security benefits are taxable. Enter -0- on Form 1040, line 20b. If you are married filing separately and you **lived apart** from your spouse for all of 2009, be sure you entered "D" to the right of the word "benefits" on line 20a.
   - ☐ **Yes.** Subtract line 8 from line 7 . . . . . . **9.** ______
10. Enter: $12,000 if married filing jointly; $9,000 if single, head of household, qualifying widow(er), or married filing separately and you **lived apart** from your spouse for all of 2009 . . **10.** ______
11. Subtract line 10 from line 9. If zero or less, enter -0- . . . . . . **11.** ______
12. Enter the **smaller** of line 9 or line 10 . . . . . . **12.** ______
13. Enter one-half of line 12 . . . . . . **13.** ______
14. Enter the **smaller** of line 2 or line 13 . . . . . . **14.** ______
15. Multiply line 11 by 85% (.85). If line 11 is zero, enter -0- . . . . . . **15.** ______
16. Add lines 14 and 15 . . . . . . **16.** ______
17. Multiply line 1 by 85% (.85) . . . . . . **17.** ______
18. **Taxable social security benefits.** Enter the **smaller** of line 16 or line 17. Also enter this amount on Form 1040, line 20b . . . . . . **18.** ______

TIP *If any of your benefits are taxable for 2009* ***and*** *they include a lump-sum benefit payment that was for an earlier year, you may be able to reduce the taxable amount. See Pub. 915 for details.*

IRA Deduction Worksheet—Line 32

Keep for Your Records

CAUTION

If you were age 70½ or older at the end of 2009, you cannot deduct any contributions made to your traditional IRA or treat them as nondeductible contributions. ***Do not*** *complete this worksheet for anyone age 70½ or older at the end of 2009. If you are married filing jointly and only one spouse was under age 70½ at the end of 2009, complete this worksheet only for that spouse.*

Before you begin:

- √ Be sure you have read the list on page 31. You may not be eligible to use this worksheet.
- √ Figure any write-in adjustments to be entered on the dotted line next to line 36 (see the instructions for line 36 on page 35).
- √ If you are married filing separately and you lived apart from your spouse for all of 2009, enter "D" on the dotted line next to Form 1040, line 32. If you do not, you may get a math error notice from the IRS.

		Your IRA	Spouse's IRA
1a.	Were you covered by a retirement plan (see page 31)?	**1a.** ☐ Yes ☐ No	
b.	If married filing jointly, was your spouse covered by a retirement plan?		**1b.** ☐ Yes ☐ No

Next. If you checked "No" on line 1a (and "No" on line 1b if married filing jointly), skip lines 2 through 6, enter the applicable amount below on line 7a (and line 7b if applicable), and go to line 8.

- $5,000, if under age 50 at the end of 2009.
- $6,000, if age 50 or older but under age 70½ at the end of 2009.

Otherwise, go to line 2.

2. Enter the amount shown below that applies to you.

- Single, head of household, or married filing separately and you **lived apart** from your spouse for all of 2009, enter $65,000
- Qualifying widow(er), enter $109,000
- Married filing jointly, enter $109,000 in both columns. But if you checked "No" on either line 1a or 1b, enter $176,000 for the person who was not covered by a plan
- Married filing separately and you lived with your spouse at any time in 2009, enter $10,000

2a. ________ **2b.** ________

3. Enter the amount from Form 1040, line 22 . . . . **3.** ________

4. Enter the total of the amounts from Form 1040, lines 23 through 31a, plus any write-in adjustments you entered on the dotted line next to line 36 . . . . **4.** ________

5. Subtract line 4 from line 3. If married filing jointly, enter the result in both columns **5a.** ________ **5b.** ________

6. Is the amount on line 5 less than the amount on line 2?

☐ **No.** STOP None of your IRA contributions are deductible. For details on nondeductible IRA contributions, see Form 8606.

☐ **Yes.** Subtract line 5 from line 2 in each column. Follow the instruction below that applies to you.

- If single, head of household, or married filing separately, and the result is $10,000 or more, enter the applicable amount below on line 7 for that column and go to line 8.
  - **i.** $5,000, if under age 50 at the end of 2009.
  - **ii.** $6,000, if age 50 or older but under age 70½ at the end of 2009.

  Otherwise, go to line 7.
- If married filing jointly or qualifying widow(er), and the result is $20,000 or more ($10,000 or more in the column for the IRA of a person who was not covered by a retirement plan), enter the applicable amount below on line 7 for that column and go to line 8.
  - **i.** $5,000, if under age 50 at the end of 2009.
  - **ii.** $6,000 if age 50 or older but under age 70½ at the end of 2009.

  Otherwise, go to line 7.

6a. ________ **6b.** ________

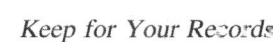

IRA Deduction Worksheet—*Continued*

		Your IRA		Spouse's IRA
7. Multiply lines 6a and 6b by the percentage below that applies to you. If the result is not a multiple of $10, increase it to the next multiple of $10 (for example, increase $490.30 to $500). If the result is $200 or more, enter the result. But if it is less than $200, enter $200. • Single, head of household, or married filing separately, multiply by 50% (.50)(or by 60% (.60) in the column for the IRA of a person who is age 50 or older at the end of 2009) • Married filing jointly or qualifying widow(er), multiply by 25% (.25) (or by 30% (.30) in the column for the IRA of a person who is age 50 or older at the end of 2009). But if you checked "No" on either line 1a or 1b, then in the column for the IRA of the person who was not covered by a retirement plan, multiply by 50% (.50) (or by 60% (.60) if age 50 or older at the end of 2009)	**7a.**		**7b.**	
8. Enter the total of your (and your spouse's if filing jointly): • Wages, salaries, tips, etc. Generally, this is the amount reported in box 1 of Form W-2. See page 31 for exceptions • Alimony and separate maintenance payments reported on Form 1040, line 11 • Nontaxable combat pay. This amount should be reported in box 12 of Form W-2 with code Q	**8.**			
9. Enter the earned income you (and your spouse if filing jointly) received as a self-employed individual or a partner. Generally, this is your (and your spouse's if filing jointly) net earnings from self-employment if your personal services were a material income-producing factor, minus any deductions on Form 1040, lines 27 and 28. If zero or less, enter -0-. For more details, see Pub. 590	**9.**			
10. Add lines 8 and 9	**10.**			

CAUTION *If married filing jointly and line 10 is less than $10,000 ($11,000 if one spouse is age 50 or older at the end of 2009; $12,000 if both spouses are age 50 or older at the end of 2009), **stop here** and see Pub. 590 to figure your IRA deduction.*

11. Enter traditional IRA contributions made, or that will be made by April 15, 2010, for 2009 to your IRA on line 11a and to your spouse's IRA on line 11b	**11a.**		**11b.**	
12. On line 12a, enter the **smallest** of line 7a, 10, or 11a. On line 12b, enter the **smallest** of line 7b, 10, or 11b. This is the most you can deduct. Add the amounts on lines 12a and 12b and enter the total on Form 1040, line 32. Or, if you want, you can deduct a smaller amount and treat the rest as a nondeductible contribution (see Form 8606)	**12a.**		**12b.**	

Standard Deduction Worksheet—Line 40a

Keep for Your Records

CAUTION Do not complete this worksheet if you checked the box on line 39b; your standard deduction is zero. Also, do not complete this worksheet if you must use Schedule L to figure your standard deduction (see *Exception* on page 35).

1. Enter the amount shown below for your filing status.
- Single or married filing separately—$5,700
- Married filing jointly or Qualifying widow(er)—$11,400
- Head of household—$8,350

. . . . **1.** ______

2. Can you (or your spouse if filing jointly) be claimed as a dependent on someone else's return?

☐ **No.** Enter the amount from line 1 on line 4, skip line 3, and go to line 5.

☐ **Yes.** Go to line 3.

3. Is your **earned income*** more than $650?

☐ **Yes.** Add $300 to your earned income. Enter the total

☐ **No.** Enter $950

. . . . **3.** ______

4. Enter the **smaller** of line 1 or line 3. . . . . **4.** ______

5. If born before January 2, 1945, or blind, multiply the number on Form 1040, line 39a, by $1,100 ($1,400 if single or head of household). Otherwise, enter -0- . . . . **5.** ______

6. Add lines 4 and 5. Enter the total here and on Form 1040, line 40a . . . . **6.** ______

***Earned income** includes wages, salaries, tips, professional fees, and other compensation received for personal services you performed. It also includes any amount received as a scholarship that you must include in your income. Generally, your earned income is the total of the amount(s) you reported on Form 1040, lines 7, 12, and 18, minus the amount, if any, on line 27.*

Deduction for Exemptions Worksheet—Line 42

Keep for Your Records

1. Is the amount on Form 1040, line 38, more than the amount shown on line 4 below for your filing status?

☐ **No.** STOP Multiply $3,650 by the total number of exemptions claimed on Form 1040, line 6d, and enter the result on Form 1040, line 42.

☐ **Yes.** *Continue*

2. Multiply $3,650 by the total number of exemptions claimed on Form 1040, line 6d . . . . **2.** ______

3. Enter the amount from Form 1040, line 38 . . . . **3.** ______

4. Enter the amount shown below for your filing status.
- Single—$166,800
- Married filing jointly or qualifying widow(er)—$250,200
- Married filing separately—$125,100
- Head of household—$208,500

. . . . . . **4.** ______

5. Subtract line 4 from line 3 . . . . **5.** ______

6. Is line 5 more than $122,500 ($61,250 if married filing separately)?

☐ **Yes.** Multiply $2,433 by the total number of exemptions claimed on Form 1040, line 6d. Enter the result here and on Form 1040, line 42. **Do not** complete the rest of this worksheet.

☐ **No.** Divide line 5 by $2,500 ($1,250 if married filing separately). If the result is not a whole number, increase it to the next higher whole number (for example, increase 0.0004 to 1) . . . . **6.** ______

7. Multiply line 6 by 2% (.02) and enter the result as a decimal . . . . **7.** ___.___

8. Multiply line 2 by line 7. . . . . **8.** ______

9. Divide line 8 by 3.0 . . . . **9.** ______

10. **Deduction for exemptions**. Subtract line 9 from line 2 Enter the result here and on Form 1040, line 42 . . . . **10.** ______

SCHEDULE L
(Form 1040A or 1040)

Department of the Treasury
Internal Revenue Service (99)

Standard Deduction for Certain Filers

▶ Attach to Form 1040A or 1040. ▶ See instructions on back.

OMB No. 1545-0074

2009

Attachment Sequence No. **57**

Name(s) shown on return | **Your social security number**

CAUTION *File this form **only** if you are increasing your standard deduction by certain state or local real estate taxes, new motor vehicle taxes, or a net disaster loss. It may be better for you to itemize your deductions instead. See the Instructions for Schedule A (Form 1040).*

1 Enter the amount shown below for your filing status.
- Single or married filing separately—$5,700
- Married filing jointly or Qualifying widow(er)—$11,400
- Head of household—$8,350

. . . **1** ______

2 Can you (or your spouse if filing jointly) be claimed as a dependent on someone else's return?
☐ **No.** Enter the amount from line 1 on line 4, skip line 3, and go to line 5.
☐ **Yes.** Go to line 3.

3 Is your earned income more than $650 (see instructions)?
☐ **Yes.** Add $300 to your earned income. Enter the total
☐ **No.** Enter $950
. . . **3** ______

4 Enter the **smaller** of line 1 or line 3 . . . **4** ______

5 Multiply the number on Form 1040, line 39a, or Form 1040A, line 23a, by $1,100 ($1,400 if single or head of household). If blank, enter -0- . . . **5** ______

6 Form 1040 filers only, enter any net disaster loss from Form 4684, line 18 . . . **6** ______

7 Enter the state and local real estate taxes you paid. **Do not** include foreign real estate taxes (see instructions) . . . **7** ______

8 Enter $500 ($1,000 if married filing jointly) . . . **8** ______

9 Enter the smaller of line 7 or line 8 . . . **9** ______

10 Did you (or your spouse if filing jointly) pay any state or local sales or excise taxes in 2009 for the purchase of a new motor vehicle **after** February 16, 2009 (see instructions)?
☐ **No.** Skip lines 10 through 19, enter -0- on line 20, and go to line 21.
☐ **Yes.** If Form 1040, line 38, or Form 1040A, line 22, is less than $135,000 ($260,000 if married filing jointly), enter the amount of these taxes paid. Otherwise, skip lines 10 through 19, enter -0- on line 20, and go to line 21 **10** ______

11 Enter the purchase price (**before taxes**) of the new motor vehicle(s) (see instructions) . . . **11** ______

12 Is the amount on line 11 more than $49,500?
☐ **No.** Enter the amount from line 10.
☐ **Yes.** Figure the **portion** of the tax from line 10 that is attributable to the first $49,500 of the purchase price of each new motor vehicle and enter it here (see instructions) . . **12** ______

13 Enter the amount from Form 1040, line 38, or Form 1040A, line 22 **13** ______

14 Form 1040 filers only, enter the total of any—
- Amounts from Form 2555, lines 45 and 50; Form 2555-EZ, line 18; and Form 4563, line 15, and
- Exclusion of income from Puerto Rico . . . **14** ______

15 Add lines 13 and 14 . . . **15** ______

16 Enter $125,000 ($250,000 if married filing jointly) . . . **16** ______

17 Is the amount on line 15 more than the amount on line 16?
☐ **No.** Skip lines 17 through 19, enter the amount from line 12 on line 20, and go to line 21.
☐ **Yes.** Subtract line 16 from line 15 . . . **17** ______

18 Divide the amount on line 17 by $10,000. Enter the result as a decimal (rounded to at least three places). If the result is 1.000 or more, enter 1.000 . . . **18** ___ . ___

19 Multiply line 12 by line 18 . . . **19** ______

20 Subtract line 19 from line 12 . . . **20** ______

21 Add lines 4, 5, 6, 9, and 20. Enter the total here and on Form 1040, line 40a, or Form 1040A, line 24a. Also check the box on Form 1040, line 40b, or Form 1040A, line 24b . . . **21** ______

For Paperwork Reduction Act Notice, see Form 1040A or 1040 instructions. Cat. No. 49875F **Schedule L (Form 1040A or 1040) 2009**

Form **8914**

Department of the Treasury
Internal Revenue Service

Exemption Amount for Taxpayers Housing Midwestern Displaced Individuals

▶ Attach to Form 1040, Form 1040A, or Form 1040NR.

OMB No. 1545-0074

2009

Attachment Sequence No. 55

Name(s) shown on your return | Your social security number

Part I **Information on Midwestern Displaced Individuals for Whom You Provided Housing in Your Main Home for at Least 60 Consecutive Days**

Do not enter information for more than four individuals, for anyone included on line 6d of Form 1040 or 1040A (line 7d of Form 1040NR), or for anyone included on a Form 8914 you filed for 2008.

1	(a) First and last name	(b) Social security number (see instructions)	(c) Former address in disaster area (number and street, city or town, state, and ZIP code)	(d) Number of consecutive days housed in your main home

Part II **Exemption Amount**

2 **Maximum exemption amount.** Enter $2,000 ($1,000 if married filing separately) **2**

3 Did you file Form 8914 for 2008?
☐ **Yes.** Enter the amount from your 2008 Form 8914, line 2.
☐ **No.** Enter -0- **3**

4 Subtract line 3 from line 2 . . . . **4**

5 Multiply $500 by the total number of individuals listed in Part I above **5**

6 Enter the smaller of line 4 or line 5 . . . . **6**

7 Multiply $3,650 by the total number of exemptions claimed on line 6d of Form 1040 or Form 1040A (line 7d of Form 1040NR) **7**

8 Add lines 6 and 7 . . . . **8**

9 Is the amount on Form 1040, line 38 (Form 1040A, line 22; or Form 1040NR, line 36), more than the amount shown on line 10 below for your filing status?

☐ **No.** (STOP) Enter the amount from line 8 above on Form 1040, line 42 (Form 1040A, line 26; or Form 1040NR, line 39).

☐ **Yes.** Enter the amount from Form 1040, line 38 (Form 1040A, line 22; or Form 1040NR, line 36) **9**

10 Enter the amount shown below for your filing status.
- Single—$166,800
- Married filing jointly or Qualifying widow(er)—$250,200
- Married filing separately—$125,100
- Head of household—$208,500

Form 1040NR filers, see instructions **10**

11 Subtract line 10 from line 9 . . . . **11**

12 Is line 11 more than $122,500 ($61,250 if married filing separately)?
☐ **No.** Skip line 13; go to line 14.
☐ **Yes.** Multiply $2,433 by the total number of exemptions claimed on line 6d of Form 1040 or Form 1040A (line 7d of Form 1040NR) . . **12**

13 Add lines 6 and 12. Enter the result here and on Form 1040, line 42; Form 1040A, line 26; or Form 1040NR, line 39. Do not complete the rest of this form . . . **13**

14 Divide line 11 by $2,500 ($1,250 if married filing separately). If the result is not a whole number, increase it to the next higher whole number (for example, increase .0004 to 1) **14**

15 Multiply line 14 by 2% (.02) and enter the result as a decimal rounded to at least three places . . . . **15** .

16 Multiply line 7 by line 15 . . . . **16**

17 Divide line 16 by 3.0 . . . . **17**

18 **Exemption amount.** Subtract line 17 from line 8. Enter the result here and on Form 1040, line 42; Form 1040A, line 26; or Form 1040NR, line 39 . . . . **18**

For Paperwork Reduction Act Notice, see page 3. Cat. No. 37724X Form **8914** (2009)

Table 1

The counties listed in Table 1 below are Midwestern disaster areas. You may be eligible for the additional $500 exemption for housing a Midwestern displaced individual if that individual had his or her main home in one of the counties listed in this table on the applicable disaster date shown for that county and was displaced from that home.

Applicable Disaster Date*	State	Affected Counties — Midwestern Disaster Areas
05/02/2008	Arkansas	Arkansas, Benton, Cleburne, Conway, Crittenden, Grant, Lonoke, Mississippi, Phillips, Pulaski, Saline, and Van Buren
06/01/2008	Illinois	Adams, Calhoun, Clark, Coles, Crawford, Cumberland, Douglas, Edgar, Hancock, Henderson, Jasper, Jersey, Lake, Lawrence, Mercer, Rock Island, Whiteside, and Winnebago
06/06/2008	Indiana	Adams, Bartholomew, Brown, Clay, Daviess, Dearborn, Decatur, Gibson, Grant, Greene, Hamilton, Hancock, Hendricks, Henry, Huntington, Jackson, Jefferson, Jennings, Johnson, Knox, Lawrence, Madison, Marion, Monroe, Morgan, Owen, Parke, Pike, Posey, Putnam, Randolph, Ripley, Rush, Shelby, Sullivan, Tippecanoe, Vermillion, Vigo, Washington, and Wayne
05/25/2008	Iowa	Adair, Adams, Allamakee, Appanoose, Audubon, Benton, Black Hawk, Boone, Bremer, Buchanan, Butler, Cass, Cedar, Cerro Gordo, Chickasaw, Clarke, Clayton, Clinton, Crawford, Dallas, Davis, Decatur, Delaware, Des Moines, Dubuque, Fayette, Floyd, Franklin, Fremont, Greene, Grundy, Guthrie, Hamilton, Hancock, Hardin, Harrison, Henry, Howard, Humboldt, Iowa, Jackson, Jasper, Johnson, Jones, Keokuk, Kossuth, Lee, Linn, Louisa, Lucas, Madison, Mahaska, Marion, Marshall, Mills, Mitchell, Monona, Monroe, Montgomery, Muscatine, Page, Polk, Pottawattamie, Poweshiek, Ringgold, Scott, Story, Tama, Union, Van Buren, Wapello, Warren, Washington, Webster, Winnebago, Winneshiek, Worth, and Wright
05/10/2008	Missouri	Barry, Jasper, and Newton
06/01/2008	Missouri	Adair, Andrew, Callaway, Cass, Chariton, Clark, Gentry, Greene, Harrison, Holt, Johnson, Lewis, Lincoln, Linn, Livingston, Macon, Marion, Monroe, Nodaway, Pike, Putnam, Ralls, St. Charles, Stone, Taney, Vernon, and Webster
05/22/2008	Nebraska	Buffalo, Butler, Colfax, Custer, Dawson, Douglas, Gage, Hamilton, Holt, Jefferson, Kearney, Lancaster, Platte, Richardson, Sarpy, and Saunders
06/05/2008	Wisconsin	Adams, Calumet, Columbia, Crawford, Dane, Dodge, Fond du Lac, Grant, Green, Green Lake, Iowa, Jefferson, Juneau, Kenosha, La Crosse, Manitowoc, Marquette, Milwaukee, Monroe, Ozaukee, Racine, Richland, Rock, Sauk, Sheboygan, Vernon, Walworth, Washington, Waukesha, and Winnebago

* In some cases, the date will be later due to the continuation of the severe storms, tornadoes, or flooding that began on the above date. For more details, go to *www.fema.gov*.

Table 2

The counties listed in Table 2 below are Midwestern disaster areas. You may be eligible for the additional $500 exemption for housing a Midwestern displaced individual if that individual had his or her main home in one of the counties listed in this table on the applicable disaster date shown for that county and was displaced from that home and either:

- That home was damaged by the storms, tornadoes, or flooding that gave rise to the disaster declaration for that county, or
- The individual was evacuated from that home because of the storms, tornadoes, or flooding.

Applicable Disaster Date*	State	Affected Counties — Midwestern Disaster Areas
06/01/2008	Illinois	Greene, Madison, Monroe, Pike, Randolph, St. Clair, and Scott
06/06/2008	Indiana	Benton, Boone, Fountain, Franklin, Jay, Montgomery, Ohio, Switzerland, Union, and Wabash
05/25/2008	Iowa	Carroll, Cherokee, Lyon, Palo Alto, Pocahontas, Taylor, and Wayne
05/22/2008	Kansas	Barber, Barton, Bourbon, Brown, Butler, Chautauqua, Cherokee, Clark, Clay, Comanche, Cowley, Crawford, Decatur, Dickinson, Edwards, Elk, Ellis, Ellsworth, Franklin, Gove, Graham, Harper, Haskell, Hodgeman, Jackson, Jewell, Kingman, Kiowa, Lane, Linn, Logan, Mitchell, Montgomery, Ness, Norton, Osborne, Pawnee, Phillips, Pratt, Reno, Republic, Riley, Rooks, Rush, Saline, Seward, Sheridan, Smith, Stafford, Sumner, Thomas, Trego, Wallace, and Wilson
06/06/2008	Michigan	Allegan, Barry, Eaton, Ingham, Lake, Manistee, Mason, Missaukee, Osceola, Ottawa, Saginaw, and Wexford
06/07/2008	Minnesota	Cook, Fillmore, Freeborn, Houston, Mower, and Nobles
06/01/2008	Missouri	Atchison, Audrain, Bates, Buchanan, Cape Girardeau, Carroll, Christian, Daviess, Grundy, Howard, Jefferson, Knox, Mercer, Miller, Mississippi, Morgan, New Madrid, Pemiscot, Perry, Pettis, Platte, Polk, Randolph, Ray, Saline, Schuyler, Scotland, Shelby, St. Genevieve, St. Louis, the Independent City of St. Louis, Scott, Sullivan, and Worth
04/23/2008	Nebraska	Gage, Johnson, Morrill, Nemaha, and Pawnee
05/22/2008	Nebraska	Adams, Blaine, Boone, Boyd, Brown, Burt, Cass, Chase, Cherry, Cuming, Dundy, Fillmore, Frontier, Furnas, Garfield, Gosper, Greeley, Hall, Hayes, Howard, Johnson, Keya Paha, Lincoln, Logan, Loup, Merrick, McPherson, Morrill, Nance, Nemaha, Otoe, Phelps, Polk, Red Willow, Rock, Saline, Seward, Sherman, Stanton, Thayer, Thomas, Thurston, Valley, Webster, Wheeler, and York
06/27/2008	Nebraska	Dodge, Douglas, Sarpy, and Saunders
06/05/2008	Wisconsin	Lafayette

* In some cases, the date will be later due to the continuation of the severe storms, tornadoes, or flooding that began on the above date. For more details, go to *www.fema.gov*.

Qualified Dividends and Capital Gain Tax Worksheet—Line 44

Keep for Your Records

Before you begin:

√ See the instructions for line 44 that begin on page 37 to see if you can use this worksheet to figure your tax.

√ If you do not have to file Schedule D and you received capital gain distributions, be sure you checked the box on line 13 of Form 1040.

1. Enter the amount from Form 1040, line 43. However, if you are filing Form 2555 or 2555-EZ (relating to foreign earned income), enter the amount from line 3 of the worksheet on page 38 . . . . . **1.** ______

2. Enter the amount from Form 1040, line 9b* . . . . . **2.** ______

3. Are you filing Schedule D?*

☐ **Yes.** Enter the **smaller** of line 15 or 16 of Schedule D. If either line 15 or line 16 is a loss, enter -0-

☐ **No.** Enter the amount from Form 1040, line 13 . . . . . **3.** ______

4. Add lines 2 and 3 . . . . . **4.** ______

5. If you are claiming investment interest expense on Form 4952, enter the amount from line 4g of that form. Otherwise, enter -0- . . . . . **5.** ______

6. Subtract line 5 from line 4. If zero or less, enter -0- . . . . . **6.** ______

7. Subtract line 6 from line 1. If zero or less, enter -0- . . . . . **7.** ______

8. Enter the **smaller** of:

- The amount on line 1, or
- $33,950 if single or married filing separately, $67,900 if married filing jointly or qualifying widow(er), $45,500 if head of household. . . . . . **8.** ______

9. Is the amount on line 7 equal to or more than the amount on line 8?

☐ **Yes.** Skip lines 9 and 10; go to line 11 and check the "No" box.

☐ **No.** Enter the amount from line 7 . . . . . **9.** ______

10. Subtract line 9 from line 8 . . . . . **10.** ______

11. Are the amounts on lines 6 and 10 the same?

☐ **Yes.** Skip lines 11 through 14; go to line 15.

☐ **No.** Enter the **smaller** of line 1 or line 6 . . . . . **11.** ______

12. Enter the amount from line 10 (if line 10 is blank, enter -0-) . . . . . **12.** ______

13. Subtract line 12 from line 11 . . . . . **13.** ______

14. Multiply line 13 by 15% (.15) . . . . . **14.** ______

15. Figure the tax on the amount on line 7. Use the Tax Table or Tax Computation Worksheet, whichever applies . . . . . **15.** ______

16. Add lines 14 and 15 . . . . . **16.** ______

17. Figure the tax on the amount on line 1. Use the Tax Table or Tax Computation Worksheet, whichever applies . . . . . **17.** ______

18. **Tax on all taxable income.** Enter the **smaller** of line 16 or line 17. Also include this amount on Form 1040, line 44. If you are filing Form 2555 or 2555-EZ, do not enter this amount on Form 1040, line 44. Instead, enter it on line 4 of the worksheet on page 38 . . . . . **18.** ______

**If you are filing Form 2555 or 2555-EZ, see the footnote in the worksheet on page 38 before completing this line.*

Foreign Earned Income Tax Worksheet—Line 44

Keep for Your Records

If Form 1040, line 43, is zero, do not complete this worksheet.

1. Enter the amount from Form 1040, line 43	**1.**	
2. Enter the amount from your (and your spouse's, if filing jointly) Form 2555, lines 45 and 50, or Form 2555-EZ, line 18	**2.**	
3. Add lines 1 and 2	**3.**	
4. Tax on the amount on line 3. Use the Tax Table, Tax Computation Worksheet, Qualified Dividends and Capital Gain Tax Worksheet*, Schedule D Tax Worksheet*, or Form 8615, whichever applies. See the instructions for line 44 that begin on page 37 to see which tax computation method applies. (Do not use a second Foreign Earned Income Tax Worksheet to figure the tax on this line)	**4.**	
5. Tax on the amount on line 2. Use the Tax Table or Tax Computation Worksheet, whichever applies	**5.**	
6. Subtract line 5 from line 4. Enter the result. If zero or less, enter -0-. Also include this amount on Form 1040, line 44	**6.**	

**Enter the amount from line 3 above on line 1 of the Qualified Dividends and Capital Gain Tax Worksheet or Schedule D Tax Worksheet if you use either of those worksheets to figure the tax on line 4 above. Complete the rest of that worksheet through line 6 (line 10 if you use the Schedule D Tax Worksheet). Next, you must determine if you have a capital gain excess. To find out if you have a capital gain excess, subtract Form 1040, line 43, from line 6 of your Qualified Dividends and Capital Gain Tax Worksheet (line 10 of your Schedule D Tax Worksheet). If the result is more than zero, that amount is your capital gain excess.*

If you do not have a capital gain excess, complete the rest of either of those worksheets according to the worksheet's instructions. Then complete lines 5 and 6 above.

If you have a capital gain excess, complete a second Qualified Dividends and Capital Gain Tax Worksheet or Schedule D Tax Worksheet (whichever applies) as instructed above but in its entirety and with the following additional modifications. Then complete lines 5 and 6 above. These modifications are to be made only for purposes of filling out the Foreign Earned Income Tax Worksheet above.

1. Reduce (but not below zero) the amount you would otherwise enter on line 3 of your Qualified Dividends and Capital Gain Tax Worksheet or line 9 of your Schedule D Tax Worksheet by your capital gain excess.

2. Reduce (but not below zero) the amount you would otherwise enter on line 2 of your Qualified Dividends and Capital Gain Tax Worksheet or line 6 of your Schedule D Tax Worksheet by any of your capital gain excess not used in (1) above.

3. Reduce (but not below zero) the amount on your Schedule D (Form 1040), line 18, by your capital gain excess.

4. Include your capital gain excess as a loss on line 16 of your Unrecaptured Section 1250 Gain Worksheet on page D-9 of the Instructions for Schedule D (Form 1040).

What's New in 2009

State and Local Sales Tax Deduction. The election to deduct state and local sales taxes in lieu of state and local income taxes, originally set to expire after 2007, has been extended through 2009.

Mortgage Insurance Deduction. The deduction for premiums paid on qualified mortgage insurance, originally set to expire after 2007, has been extended through 2010.

Casualty/Theft Losses. The 10-percent limitation on personal casualty losses attributable to federally declared disasters is waived for 2009. Victims of criminally fraudulent "Ponzi" schemes have been provided guidance on deducting qualified losses as theft losses. Qualified investors who meet certain conditions may elect an optional safe harbor that provides a uniform approach for determining the year in which the loss is deemed to have occurred and a simplified means of computing the amount of the loss.

Section at a Glance

Tax Preparer's Checklist

The following items are required:

- ☐ Records of medical expenses
- ☐ State tax returns or receipts showing sales tax paid
- ☐ Statement of mortgage interest and points (Form 1098)
- ☐ Required records for charitable contributions
- ☐ Detailed gambling logs
- ☐ Records of property tax payments
- ☐ Spouse's Schedule A if filing status is MFS

Relevant IRS Publications

- ☐ IRS Publication 463, *Travel, Entertainment, Gift, and Car Expenses*
- ☐ IRS Publication 502, *Medical and Dental Expenses*
- ☐ IRS Publication 514, *Foreign Tax Credit for Individuals*
- ☐ IRS Publication 523, *Selling Your Home*
- ☐ IRS Publication 526, *Charitable Contributions*
- ☐ IRS Publication 529, *Miscellaneous Deductions*
- ☐ IRS Publication 547, *Casualties, Disasters, and Thefts*
- ☐ IRS Publication 550, *Investment Income and Expenses*
- ☐ IRS Publication 561, *Determining the Value of Donated Property*
- ☐ IRS Publication 936, *Home Mortgage Interest Deduction*

Itemized Deductions—2009 Schedule A

Category	Other Forms Needed	Limits and Reductions	High-Income Phaseout
Medical and dental expenses	None	Reduced by 7.5%-of-AGI floor	Not subject to high-income phaseout
Taxes paid	None	No reduction or floor	Subject to high-income phaseout
Interest paid	Form 4952 (investment interest)	Investment interest limited to net investment income with carryover	Subject to high-income phaseout, except investment interest paid
Gifts to charity	Form 8283 (noncash gifts greater than $500)	Maximum of 50%, 30%, or 20% of AGI, depending on receiver of gift	Subject to high-income phaseout
Casualty and theft losses	Form 4684	Reduced by $100 per occurrence, then reduced by 10% of AGI	Not subject to high-income phaseout
Job expenses and most other misc. deductions	Form 2106 (certain job expenses)	Reduced by 2%-of-AGI floor	Subject to high-income phaseout, except gambling losses to extent of winnings
Other misc. deductions	None	No reduction or floor	Not subject to high-income phaseout

Schedule A: Itemized Deductions

If the total of a taxpayer's itemized deductions is greater than the standard deduction for the applicable filing status, Schedule A should be used. If a taxpayer is married and filing as MFS and his or her spouse itemizes deductions, no standard deduction is allowed and Schedule A should be used to deduct any allowable deductions. The standard deduction for 2009 is $5,700 for Single and MFS filers, $11,400 for MFJ or QW filers, and $8,350 for HOH filers. Additional deductions for individuals who are over the age of 65 or blind are also available to those who take the standard deduction. See Tab 1.

In 2007, the last year for which the IRS has published detailed information, 34.9% of all individual returns itemized deductions, claiming an average of $25,136 in deductions, after limitation.

National Guard and Reserve. Before 2003, National Guard and Reserve members had to use Schedule A to claim deductions for their nonreimbursable expenses for transportation, meals, and lodging when they had to travel away from home (and stay overnight) to attend meetings or drills. They now have an above-the-line deduction for these expenses, meaning that even fewer members of the military will now benefit from itemizing deductions. These expenses are tabulated on Form 2106 or 2106-EZ and reported on line 24 of Form 1040. See Tab 1 and MTG ¶941E for details.

Medical and Dental Expenses, Lines 1-4

Medical and Dental Expense Deduction Facts

As medical costs have increased, so has use of the medical and dental expense deduction on Schedule A. The average itemized deduction for medical and dental expenses was $7,140 in 2007 (the last year for which information is available). More than 10.5 million returns claimed the deduction, an increase of more than 400,000 from 2006.

Line 1, Medical and Dental Expenses

Whose Medical Expenses Are Deductible? The medical expenses of the taxpayer, the taxpayer's spouse, and dependents can all be included in this deduction. For the purpose of medical deductions on Schedule A, persons whom the taxpayer could have claimed as a dependent except for the fact that they had gross income above the threshold or that they filed a joint return with their spouses can be considered "dependents."

A child of divorced parents is treated as the dependent of both parents, regardless of which parent claims the child as a dependent.

See MTG ¶1015.

Example. John Griffin contributes $9,000 per year toward his brother Joe's support, and he pays Joe's dental bills of $400. Because Joe has gross income of $7,000, John may not claim Joe as a dependent. However, John does contribute more than half of Joe's support ($9,400 out of $16,400, assuming Joe spends all of his income on his own support and receives no other support), so he can deduct the $400 as a medical expense on Schedule A.

Example. Sylvia Khalid furnished over half the support of her daughter Angela in 2009. Angela was married in October 2009 and filed a 2009 return jointly with her husband, who was required to file a 2009 return. Therefore, Sylvia cannot claim an exemption for Angela. She can claim all medical expenses that she paid for Angela during the year on line 1 of Schedule A because all other dependency tests were met.

What Qualifies as a Deductible Medical Expense? As a general rule, deductible medical expenses are the costs of diagnosis, cure, mitigation, treatment, or prevention of disease, and the costs for treatments affecting any part or function of the body. The following are some of the rules that apply to medical expenses (including dental expenses):

- They must be primarily for the purpose of alleviating or preventing a physical or mental defect or illness.
- In many cases, the necessity of care or medicines must be determined by a licensed doctor.
- They exclude expenses that are merely beneficial to general health, such as vitamins or a vacation.
- They can include the premiums paid for insurance that covers the expenses of medical care, and the amounts for transportation to obtain medical care. They can also include medical expenses paid for qualified long-term care services and limited amounts paid for a qualified long-term care insurance contract.
- They include all physician-prescribed drugs and therapies for the purpose of treating medical conditions.

The IRS has clarified that, for purposes of the medical-expense deduction: (1) the deduction is not limited to amounts paid for the least expensive form of medical care applicable; and (2) a physician's recommendation, while often important to determine whether certain expenses are for medical or personal reasons, is unnecessary when the expenditures are for items wholly medical in nature and that serve no other function.

> **Gray Area.** Prescription drugs obtained from alternative sources (e.g., Canada) are deductible if prescribed by a physician for the treatment of a medical condition and, if imported from another country, the FDA has approved that they can be legally imported. Offlabel and alternative-source prescriptions are not treated differently for tax purposes provided they are FDA-approved drugs.

The following table provides an alphabetical list of the medical and dental expenses listed in IRS Publication 502, *Medical and Dental Expenses*, along with their treatment as specified by Code Sec. 213. MTG ¶59 and ¶1016 also list medical expenses.

Deductibility of Medical and Dental Expenses on 2009 Schedule A

Expense	Deductible (Subject to 7.5%-of-AGI floor)?
Abortion	Costs of legal abortion deductible
Acupuncture costs	Deductible
Alcoholism treatment	Inpatient costs deductible, including meals and lodging; travel costs to AA meetings deductible
Ambulance costs	Deductible
Artificial limb costs	Deductible
Artificial teeth costs	Deductible
Babysitting, child care, and nursing services for a normal, healthy baby	Not deductible; such services for a sick child may be deductible
Bandages	Deductible
Breast reconstruction surgery	Deductible following a mastectomy
Birth control pills	Deductible
Braille books and magazines	Cost of such editions over and above the cost of regular publications of the same material deductible
Capital expenses	If reasonable and mainly for medical purposes; see discussion on page 2-6
Car	Modifications to accommodate disability, and medical transportation; see discussion on page 2-5
Chiropractor fees	Deductible
Christian Science practitioner fees	Deductible
Contact lenses	Costs for contact lenses for which there is a medical reason (i.e., for vision correction but not for solely cosmetic purposes)
Controlled substances	No substances taken in violation of federal law (e.g., marijuana, even in states where its medical use is legal) qualify for deduction
Cosmetic surgery	All costs of cosmetic surgery to correct the effects of an accident or disease; routine, elective cosmetic surgery is not deductible
Crutches	Costs of buying or renting are included [need not be prescribed (Rev. Rul. 2003-58)]
Dancing lessons	Not deductible, even if prescribed, if only for the improvement of general health, but deductible if prescribed as part of physical therapy to treat specific condition
Dental treatment	Nearly all expenses except teeth whitening
Diagnostic devices	Deductible, including self-monitoring devices
Diaper service	Not deductible, unless needed for the effects of a disease
Disabled dependent care expenses	Can be deducted as a medical expense or can be applied to a credit for dependent care (cannot be used for both)
Drug addiction treatment	Inpatient costs, including meals and lodging
Drugs	Prescribed drugs and insulin, but not over-the-counter or those for improvement of general health
Electrolysis or hair removal	Not deductible
Eye exams	Deductible if needed for medical reasons
Eyeglasses	Deductible if needed for medical reasons

Deductibility of Medical and Dental Expenses on 2009 Schedule A (Continued)	
Expense	**Deductible (Subject to 7.5%-of-AGI floor)?**
Eye surgery	Deductible if used to treat defective vision, including corrective laser surgery
Fertility enhancement	All costs deductible, including those associated with in vitro fertilization or reversal of prior sterilization procedures
Founder's fee (advance payments to a retirement home)	Amount allocable to medical care deductible
Funeral expenses	Not deductible on a living person's return, but may be deductible on a decedent's return (see Tab 14)
Future medical care	Not deductible, but see exception under *Long-Term Care*, page 2-7
Guide dog or other, similar animal	All costs for purchase and care deductible
Hair transplant	Not deductible, except to correct effects of disease or accident
Health club dues	Not deductible, unless related to a specific medical condition
Health institute	Deductible only if prescribed by a physician; physician must also provide a statement of support
Health maintenance organization (HMO) fees	Deductible as insurance premiums
Health savings accounts (HSAs) contributions	Contributions not deductible as itemized medical expense (deductible directly on Form 1040)
Hearing aids	All costs, including batteries, deductible
Home care	See *Nursing Services*, page 2-8
Home improvements	See *Capital Expenses*, page 2-6
Household help	Not generally deductible, although there may be exceptions; see *Long-Term Care*, page 2-7 or *Nursing Services*, page 2-8
Illegal operations and treatments	Not deductible
Hospital services	Deductible, including meals and lodging
Insurance premiums	Generally deductible; see discussion on page 2-6
Laboratory fees	Deductible
Lead-based paint removal	Deductible only if necessary to keep such paint away from a child who has been diagnosed with lead poisoning; may be treated as capital expense (page 2-6) if covered (e.g., with wallboard or paneling) rather than removed
Learning disability	Costs of tutoring a child with a physician-diagnosed learning disability
Legal fees	Deductible only if necessary to authorize treatment of mental illness; other legal fees not generally deductible
Lifetime care advance payments	Amount allocable to medical care
Lodging	Lodging outside a hospital, up to $50 per night per person if the trip is made to enable treatment by a physician; if the person being treated needs to be accompanied (e.g., child accompanied by a parent), up to a total of $100 per night
Long-term care	See discussion on page 2-7
Maternity clothes	Not deductible
Meals and lodging	See discussion on page 2-6
Medical conferences	Costs of travel and admission to medical conferences concerning chronic condition of taxpayer, spouse, or dependent deductible; meals and lodging connected with the conference not deductible
Medical information plan	Deductible
Medical savings accounts (MSAs)	Contributions not deductible, nor are expenses paid with tax-free distributions
Medicines	Prescribed medicines deductible
Mentally retarded, special home for	Deductible, if recommended by a psychiatrist
Nonprescription drugs and medicines	Only insulin is deductible; other nonprescription drugs are not deductible, even if recommended by a physician
Nursing home	All costs deductible if the primary purpose of admission is medical; otherwise, only the medical costs are deductible
Nursing services	See discussion on page 2-8

Deductibility of Medical and Dental Expenses on 2009 Schedule A (Continued)	
Expense	**Deductible (Subject to 7.5%-of-AGI floor)?**
Nutritional supplements	Deductible only if recommended by a medical practitioner for a condition diagnosed by a physician; not deductible if taken only to enhance general health
Organ donors	All expenses deductible for taxpayer who is a donor or potential donor, or for patient who pays donor's expenses, including transportation
Osteopath	Deductible
Oxygen and related equipment	Deductible
Personal use items	Disposable personal use items, such as toothbrushes, not generally deductible
Physical therapy	All costs of physical therapy received as medical treatment are deductible
Prostheses	Deductible
Psychiatric care	Deductible, including costs of support of a mentally ill dependent in a special medical facility
Psychoanalysis	Deductible, unless part of training to be a psychoanalyst
Special education	Costs of tutoring a child with a physician-diagnosed learning disability are deductible; costs associated with sending such a child to a special school (meals, lodging, tuition) are also deductible [doctor's recommendation may not be necessary (*Lawrence F. Fay*, CCH Dec. 37,721, Feb. 25, 1981)]
Sterilization	Deductible
Stop-smoking programs	Fees for programs are deductible, but nonprescription drugs to aid smokers in quitting are not deductible
Surgery	Costs for all but unnecessary cosmetic surgery are deductible
Swimming lessons	Not deductible, even if prescribed, if only for the improvement of general health [may be deductible for therapeutic reasons (*R. Emanuel*, T.C. Summary Opinion, 2002-127)]
Teeth whitening	Not deductible, even if done by a dentist
Telephone	Special equipment for hearing-impaired is deductible
Television	Cost of equipment to display audio for hearing-impaired individual is deductible; if a specially equipped set is purchased, the deductible portion is the excess over the cost for a similar television without the special equipment
Transplants	All expenses deductible for taxpayer who is a donor or potential donor, or for patient who pays donor's expenses, including transportation
Transportation	If for essential medical care; see discussion below
Trips	If for essential medical care; see discussion below
Vasectomy	Deductible (reversal also deductible)
Veterinary fees	Not deductible, except for the care of guide dogs and other animals trained to help people with disabilities
Weight-loss program	Deductible if used to treat a physician-diagnosed disease; cost of special dietary food in such programs is generally not deductible without supporting statement from a physician
Wheelchair	Deductible, if used for a medical condition and not just for transportation
Wig	Deductible if hair loss is the result of disease
X-rays	Deductible

Medical Transportation and Trips. Transportation expenses are deductible for trips that are primarily for and essential to medical care. The following expenses are included:

- Bus, taxi, train, plane, or ambulance service
- Travel of parent who must go with a child needing medical care
- Travel of a nurse or other person who can give injections, medications, or other treatments required by a patient who is traveling to get medical care and is unable to travel alone
- Regular visits to see a mentally ill dependent, if these visits are recommended as a part of treatment
- Travel expenses to a medical conference concerning a chronic condition of taxpayer, spouse, or dependent

For this purpose, the standard mileage rate is 24¢ per mile during 2009.

Meals and Lodging. Costs of meals and lodging at a hospital or similar institution are deductible if a principal reason for being there is to receive medical care. Lodging elsewhere than at a hospital may be deductible if all of the following apply:

- The lodging is primarily for and essential to the seeking of medical care.
- The medical care is provided by a doctor in a licensed hospital or in a medical care facility related to, or the equivalent of, a licensed hospital.
- The lodging is not lavish or extravagant under the circumstances.
- There is no significant element of personal pleasure, recreation, or vacation in the travel away from home.

The amount for lodging cannot be more than $50 each night for each person.

The taxpayer can include lodging for a person traveling with the person receiving medical care. For example, a parent traveling with a sick child can deduct a total of $100 per night for lodging. Meals that are not part of inpatient care are not deductible.

Capital Expenses for Medical Care. Costs for special equipment installed in a home, or for improvements to a home, are deductible if their main purpose is medical care for the taxpayer, spouse, or a dependent. Only reasonable costs are considered medical care related; expenses incurred for personal reasons, such as for architectural or aesthetic purposes, are not deductible. Also, costs for permanent improvements must be reduced by resulting increases in property value.

Example. Willie Smith has heart problems, and the Smiths' doctor recommends that they install an elevator in their home so that Willie does not have to climb stairs. In addition, the Smiths have some landscaping done to improve the grade from the driveway to the front door. The elevator costs $10,000 to construct, and the grading costs $1,000. An appraisal shows that the elevator increases the value of their home by $5,000 but the grading has no effect. The medical expense calculation for this scenario is as follows:

Total cost of the improvements	$11,000
Value of home with improvement	150,000
Value of home before the improvement	145,000
Increase in value of home	5,000
Medical expense (cost of improvement less increase in value)	6,000

Expenses to improve a home to accommodate disabled conditions usually do not increase the value of the home and are thus fully deductible. These improvements include the following:

- Constructing entrance or exit ramps
- Widening doorways at entrances or exits
- Widening or otherwise modifying hallways and interior doorways
- Installing railings, support bars, or other modifications in bathrooms
- Lowering or modifying kitchen cabinets and equipment
- Moving or modifying electrical outlets and fixtures
- Installing porch lifts and other forms of lifts (elevators generally do add value to the house)
- Modifying fire alarms, smoke detectors, and other warning systems
- Modifying stairways
- Adding handrails or grab bars anywhere
- Modifying hardware on doors
- Modifying areas in front of entrance and exit doorways
- Grading the ground to provide access to the residence

Medical Insurance Premiums. Medical expenses can include insurance premiums paid for policies that cover medical care. Policies may provide payment for any of the following:

- Hospitalization, surgical fees, X-rays, etc.
- Prescription drugs
- Replacement of lost or damaged contact lenses
- Membership in an association that gives cooperative, or "free-choice," medical service
- Group hospitalization and clinical care
- Qualified long-term care insurance contracts (subject to additional limitations); see *Qualified Long-Term Care Insurance Contracts*, page 2-7

If the policy provides payments that are not medically related, the premiums for the medical care part of the policy can be included if the charge for the medical part is reasonable. The cost of the medical part must be separately stated in the insurance contract or provided in a separate statement. For example, no part of the premiums for an automobile insurance policy that lumps all medical and nonmedical costs together will be deductible.

Caution. If advance payments of the health coverage tax credit were made on the taxpayer's behalf by an insurance company, these payments are not included in medical expense deductions.

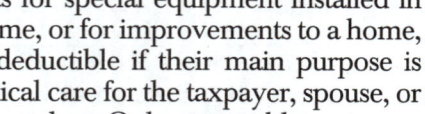

The following premiums can be included as medical expenses:

- Medicare Part B
- Medicare A tax (if taxpayer was not previously covered and then enrolled voluntarily)
- Medicare Part D

The following premiums cannot be included:

- Employer-sponsored health insurance plan (pretax plan) payments (unless included on the taxpayer's W-2 in box 1)
- Flexible spending arrangement where contributions are made by the taxpayer's employer to provide coverage for qualified long-term care services under a flexible spending or similar arrangement
- Health reimbursement arrangement (HRA) funded solely by employer
- Medicare A tax (unless taxpayer was not previously covered and then enrolled voluntarily)
- Life insurance policies
- Policies providing payment for loss of earnings
- Policies for loss of life, limb, sight, etc.
- Policies that pay the taxpayer a guaranteed amount each week for a stated number of weeks if the taxpayer is hospitalized for sickness or injury
- The part of the taxpayer's car insurance premiums that provides medical insurance coverage for all persons injured in or by the taxpayer's car, because the part of the premium for the taxpayer, the taxpayer's spouse, and the taxpayer's dependents is not stated separately from the part of the premium for medical care for others

Planning Tip. The fees paid to a dependent's educational institution generally include a fee for insurance and medical care. The applicable part is deductible as a part of medical expenses.

Unused Sick Leave Used to Pay Premiums. If the taxpayer elects to use unused sick leave pay to pay for the cost of continuing participation in a health plan, this cost can be included as a medical expense, but it would also count as income. If this participation is required by the employer, however, it cannot be included as a medical expense, but the pay will not count as income.

Prepaid Insurance Premiums. Premiums paid before age 65 for medical insurance for medical care after the taxpayer reaches age 65 are medical care expenses in the year paid if both of the following are true:

- The premiums are payable in equal yearly or more frequent installments.
- Premiums are payable for at least 10 years, or until the taxpayer reaches age 65 (but not for less than five years).

Qualified Long-Term Care Insurance Contracts. A qualified long-term care insurance contract is an insurance contract that provides coverage only for qualified long-term care services. The contract must:

1. Be guaranteed renewable;
2. Not provide for a cash surrender value;
3. Provide that refunds, other than refunds on the death of the insured or complete surrender or cancellation of the contract, be used only to reduce future premiums or increase future benefits; and
4. Generally not pay or reimburse expenses incurred for services or items that would be reimbursed under Medicare, unless Medicare is a secondary payor, and not pay per diem or other periodic payments without regard to expenses.

See MTG ¶1019.

Limit on Long-Term Care Premiums the Taxpayer May Deduct in 2009

Age at End of 2009	Maximum Deduction
40 or under	$ 320
41-50	600
51-60	1,190
61-70	3,180
71 or older	3,980

Qualified Long-Term Care Services. Qualified long-term care services are necessary diagnostic, preventive, therapeutic, curing, treating, mitigating, or rehabilitative services, and maintenance and personal care services (defined below) that are required by a *chronically ill individual* and are provided according to a plan of care prescribed by a *licensed health care practitioner*. For these services, all unreimbursed expenses are deductible on Schedule A, as are insurance premiums up to the limits in the above table.

According to IRS Publication 502, an individual is defined as *chronically ill* if, within the previous 12 months, a licensed health care practitioner has certified that the individual meets either of the following descriptions:

- For at least 90 days, he or she is unable to perform at least two activities of daily living without substantial assistance from another individual, due to a loss of functional capacity. Activities of daily living are eating, toileting, transferring, bathing, dressing, and continence.
- He or she requires substantial supervision to be protected from threats to health and safety due to severe cognitive impairment.

Maintenance or personal care services consist of care that has as its primary purpose the providing of a chronically ill individual with needed assistance for his or her disabilities (including protection from threats to health and safety due to severe cognitive impairment).

Nursing Services. Nursing services provided in the home or in another facility are deductible. These services need not be performed by a nurse as long as they are services generally performed by a nurse–such as giving medicine or changing bandages–or if they are services connected with a disability, such as bathing a patient. Also includible as a medical expense are any payments of Social Security tax, FUTA, Medicare tax, and state employment taxes for nursing services.

If an attendant also provides household services such as cleaning or cooking, the wages and taxes paid for time spent on these tasks are not deductible, and the percentage of time spent on these tasks will have to be calculated.

Reimbursements as a Subtraction from Medical Expenses. Medical expenses can be deducted only if there was no insurance or other reimbursement payment made during the tax year. This includes payments from Medicare, but it does not include amounts received for loss of earnings or damages for injuries. Even if a policy overpays for certain expenses, the overpayment must be counted against other services that are not reimbursed.

Health Reimbursement Arrangement (HRA). A health reimbursement arrangement is an employer-funded plan that reimburses employees for medical care expenses and allows unused amounts to be carried forward. An HRA is funded solely by the employer, and the reimbursements for medical expenses, up to a maximum dollar amount for a coverage period, are not included in income and should not be included in deductions.

> **Example.** Betty Wiggins has insurance policies that cover her hospital and doctors' bills but not her nursing bills. After an operation that disables her for a while, she receives payment of $6,500 for her hospital and doctors' bills, which is $150 more than their charges. Her policy does not include the home nursing services she requires after the operation. For these, she pays $800 to a nursing agency, which includes $100 for cleaning services. She can claim a deduction of $550: $800 minus the $100 nonqualified nursing services minus the $150 insurance payment.

Other Reimbursements That Do Not Reduce Medical Expenses. Generally, medical expenses are not reduced by payments received for the following:

- Permanent loss or loss of use of a member or function of the body (loss of limb, sight, hearing, etc.) or disfigurement to the extent the payment is based on the nature of the injury without regard to the amount of time lost from work, or
- Loss of earnings

However, the taxpayer must reduce medical expenses by any part of these payments that is designated for medical costs.

Insurance Reimbursements More than Medical Expenses. If a reimbursement from insurance is greater than the total medical expenses, the excess may or may not be taxable, depending on who paid for the policy. If the policy was paid for by the taxpayer, the excess is tax-free and need not be reported. If, however, the taxpayer's employer paid for the policy, the excess is taxable and is reported on line 21 of Form 1040. If both the taxpayer and the employer paid for the policy (the usual arrangement), the excess is taxable in the proportion that the employer paid.

Insurance Reimbursements in a Different Taxable Year. It often happens that medical expenses are paid in one year but not reimbursed until the next. In this case, the expenses are deductible in the year paid. The reimbursement, when it comes, however, must then be treated as "other income" and reported on line 21 of Form 1040. The reimbursement is, of course, taxfree if no deduction was taken for the expense.

Decedent Considerations. Medical expenses paid before death by the decedent are included in figuring any deduction for medical and dental expenses on the decedent's final income tax return. This includes expenses for the decedent's spouse and dependents. The survivor or personal representative of a decedent can choose to treat certain expenses paid by the decedent's estate for the decedent's medical care as paid by the decedent at the time the medical services were provided. The expenses must be paid within the one-year period beginning with the day after the date of death. The survivor or personal representative who is making this choice must attach a statement to the decedent's Form 1040 (or the decedent's amended return, Form 1040X) saying that the expenses have not been and will not be claimed on the estate tax return. See MTG ¶1018.

What if the decedent's return had been filed and the medical expenses were not included? Form 1040X can be filed for the year or years the expenses are treated as paid, unless the period for filing an amended return for that year has passed. Generally, an amended return must be filed within three years of the date the original return was filed, or within two years from the time the tax was paid, whichever date is later.

Caution. Qualified medical expenses paid before death by the decedent are not deductible if paid with a tax-free distribution from any HSA or Archer MSA.

Example. Willis Ferguson died on June 1, 2009. He had incurred $8,000 in medical expenses: $5,000 in 2008 and $3,000 in 2009. He had filed his 2008 return on April 15, 2009, and did not claim the $5,000 in medical expenses. His executor paid the entire $8,000 in August 2009. The executor can then file an amended return for 2008, claiming the $5,000 as a deduction in order to get a refund from the increase in deductions. This amended return must be accompanied by a waiver of the estate tax deduction. The remaining $3,000 may be deducted on Willis's final return.

What if the taxpayer paid medical expenses of a deceased spouse or dependent? If the taxpayer paid medical expenses for the taxpayer's deceased spouse or dependent, the expenses should be treated as medical expenses on Form 1040 in the year paid, whether they are paid before or after the decedent's death.

Lines 2-4, Calculation

The amount of the allowed deduction on line 4 will be the amount of line 1 that exceeds 7.5% of line 2, which is the taxpayer's adjusted gross income (AGI). (See Tab 1 for a discussion of AGI.)

Note that, for AMT purposes (see Tab 10), medical expenses are deductible only to the extent that they exceed 10% (rather than 7.5%) of AGI.

Partly because of the 7.5%-of-AGI subtraction, it may be beneficial for married couples who have medical expenses to file separately.

Caution. Filing separate returns can have many other adverse tax consequences. When making the decision whether clients should file separate returns, take all parts of the return into consideration. In the example below, Mrs. Miranda cannot elect to use the standard deduction and this may result in an increase in overall tax liability. See Tab 1 for considerations regarding MFS filing status.

Example. Leoni Wheeler's AGI is $50,000 and her deductible medical expenses are $5,000 (all of which she paid in 2009). The allowed deduction would be calculated as follows:

Line	Amount
1	$5,000
2	50,000
3	3,750
4	1,250

Amount of medical expenses not deductible due to 7.5%-of-AGI reduction:

$50,000 × 7.5% = $3,750

Deductible amount:

$5,000 – $3,750 = $1,250

Planning Tip. If a client is filing as MFS and is using Schedule A, it's a good idea to ask for the spouse's Schedule A to ensure that both are itemizing, as required.

Taxes Paid, Lines 5-9

Taxes Paid Deduction Facts

The deduction for taxes paid was the most frequently claimed itemized deduction for 2007. Taxpayers who itemized deductions in 2007 deducted an average of

Example. Jorge Miranda paid $1,100 for his own medical expenses, $800 for his wife Esperanza's medical expenses, and $1,450 for his dependent mother's medical expenses in 2009. Jorge's 2009 AGI is $22,000, and his wife's AGI is $23,000. If he and his wife file jointly, they cannot deduct any of the expenses [$3,350 of medical expenses – $3,375 (7.5% of $45,000 AGI) is less than zero].

If they file separate returns, however, their total medical deductions will be $900. While Esperanza cannot deduct her medical expenses [$800 of medical expenses - $1,725 (7.5% of $23,000 AGI) is less than zero], Jorge's deduction is $900 [$2,550 of medical expenses -$1,650 (7.5% of $22,000 AGI) = $900].

If the couple had records substantiating payment of Esperanza's medical expenses solely from Jorge's funds, the deduction could be as much as $1,700. Careful and detailed records are required.

$3,324 in taxes paid if they had AGIs under $50,000, and $11,291 if their AGIs were over $50,000.

Taxes not directly connected with a business or with property held for production of income are generally deducted on lines 5-9 of Schedule A. See MTG ¶1021.

Nondeductible Taxes

The following taxes are not deductible:

- Federal income and excise taxes
- Social Security, Medicare, federal unemployment (FUTA), and railroad retirement (RRTA) taxes
- Customs duties
- Federal estate and gift taxes
- Gasoline tax
- Car inspection fees
- Assessments for sidewalks or other improvements to the taxpayer's property
- Taxes paid for others
- License fees (marriage, driver's, dog, etc.)

Who Can Deduct Taxes?

Taxes are deductible only by the person who paid them. Taxes paid on a child's property are not deductible by the parent, because they are not the parent's obligation, or by the child, because the child did not pay them, unless the parent paid on the child's behalf (the child treats the amount as a gift).

If, as part of a rental arrangement, a tenant pays taxes for his or her landlord on a business property, the taxes will be deductible by the tenant, not as a tax expense but as additional rent (provided that the rent is deductible).

When Are Taxes Deducted?

Cash-basis taxpayers deduct taxes in the year they are paid. Accrual-basis taxpayers deduct taxes in the year they are accrued. Amended returns must be filed to deduct taxes in the correct year if they were not claimed on the original return.

Line 5, State and Local Income Taxes or General Sales Taxes

The deduction for state and local income taxes is reported on line 5a. The Emergency Economic Stabilization Act of 2008 extended, through December 31, 2009, the election by individuals to deduct state and local general sales taxes in lieu of state and local income taxes. If elected, the deduction for general sales taxes is reported on line 5b. Unless extended by new legislation, the deduction for state and local general sales taxes will expire after 2009.

State and local income taxes include the following: 1) amounts withheld from the taxpayer's salary (Form W-2) or other earnings (Form 1099) in 2009; 2) taxes paid in 2009 for a prior year (not including penalties or interest); 3) state and local estimated tax payments made during 2009, including any part of a prior year's refund that the taxpayer chooses to have credited to the current year's state or local income taxes; and 4) mandatory contributions made to the Alaska, New Jersey, or Pennsylvania unemployment fund; California, New Jersey, or New York Nonoccupational Disability Benefit Fund; Rhode Island Temporary Disability Benefit Fund; or Washington State Supplemental Workmen's Compensation Fund.

Planning Tip. The choice to deduct either state and local sales taxes paid or state and local income taxes paid is available to all taxpayers. A number of factors must be taken into consideration, including the sales and income tax rates and also less obvious circumstances such as the savings level of the taxpayer, the number of major purchases made during the year (such as homes, cars and boats), and whether sufficient documentation is available for sales tax paid over and above the amounts in the IRS sales tax tables to be found in the 2009 Instructions for Schedule A. In the event that the deductible amount of income taxes and sales taxes are fairly equal and that currently deducting income taxes would result in a taxable refund for the following year, the taxpayer may be better off deducting the sales taxes in the current year.

Planning Tip. The taxpayer can often make adjustments in paying the fourth-quarter estimated taxes to maximize deductions in one year and minimize them in another. Estimating whether itemizing deductions for 2009 will be advantageous in December allows planning for maximum benefit.

If a state tax refund was received in 2009 and a state tax deduction was claimed in 2008, the refund amount does not reduce the Schedule A tax deduction. Instead, the refund is included in gross income on Form 1040, line 10. If a standard deduction was claimed in 2008, the refund is not taxable.

Caution. Some practitioners use the actual state income tax due rather than the total state tax withheld for Schedule A, thereby avoiding making the refund taxable in the subsequent year. Although doing so can be more favorable to the taxpayer, it could lead to a document matching inquiry by the IRS.

If the taxpayer elects to deduct state and local sales tax rather than income tax, the total amount substantiated by receipts may be claimed. IRS tables of allowed amounts are also available in the Instructions to Schedule A and are reproduced on pages 2-48 through 2-50. Taxpayers may use those amounts plus state and local sales taxes paid on the purchase of a motor vehicle, boat, or other items to be determined by the IRS. A worksheet for computing the deduction for sales tax also appears in the Instructions and is reproduced on page 2-47. Instead of completing the worksheet, taxpayers can use the IRS Sales Tax Calculator at www.irs.gov.

Caution. A taxpayer who elects to deduct state and local sales taxes in lieu of deducting state and local income taxes may not "double dip" and also claim the deduction for qualified motor vehicle taxes (see, below, under "Line 7, New Motor Vehicle Taxes").

Line 6, Real Estate Taxes

Taxes (state, local, or foreign) paid on real estate owned by the taxpayer (or spouse, if MFJ) that was not used for business are reported on line 6, but only if the taxes are based on the assessed value of the property. Also, the assessment must be made uniformly on property throughout the community, and the proceeds must be used for general community or governmental purposes. The following amounts are not included:

- Itemized charges for services to specific property or persons. For example, a $20 monthly charge per house for trash collection, a $5 charge for every 1,000 gallons of water consumed, or a flat charge for mowing a lawn that had grown higher than permitted under a local ordinance, would be excluded.
- Charges for improvements that tend to increase the value of the taxpayer's property (for example, an assessment to build a new sidewalk). The cost of a property improvement is added to the basis of the property. However, a charge is deductible if the funds are used only to maintain an existing public facility in service (for example, a charge to repair an existing sidewalk, and any interest included in that charge, if it meets the general requirements for deductible taxes).
- Amounts for refunds and rebates of current-tax-year real estate taxes.

If mortgage payments include real estate taxes, only the amount the mortgage company actually paid to the taxing authority during the tax year may be deducted.

Caution. States or municipalities may impose regular, uniform, or specific-purpose "benefit" taxes. Both intent of the tax and uniformity of application must be scrutinized to determine deductibility.

Real Estate Taxes Paid at Settlement or Closing. If real estate is sold, the deduction for real estate taxes is apportioned according to the number of days during the tax year that the buyer and seller each owned the home. For federal income tax purposes, the seller is treated as paying the property taxes up to, but not including, the date of sale. The buyer's tax-paying portion begins on the date of sale. The seller's and buyer's share of these taxes are each fully deductible, if each itemizes deductions. See MTG ¶¶1032-1038.

Planning Tip. Examine real estate closing documents carefully to ensure that proration between buyer and seller follows the expected pattern.

For federal income tax purposes, the buyer and the seller each are considered to have paid their own share of the taxes, even if one or the other paid the entire amount. If the buyer pays delinquent back taxes that have been imposed on the seller, the buyer may not deduct these payments, but they should be added to the basis of the property.

Example. Mr. and Mrs. Larsen bought their home on September 1, 2009. The property tax year (the period to which the tax relates) in their area is the calendar year. The tax for the year was $1,000 and was due and paid by the seller on August 15. The deduction calculation would be as follows:

Total real estate taxes	$1,000
Number of days in the home (from September 1 to December 31)	122
Portion of the year (days in the home divided by days in the year: 122/365)	0.334
Total deduction	$ 334

Construction Period Taxes. Taxes (and interest) on real property paid during the construction period generally must be capitalized. See MTG ¶991 and ¶993.

Line 7, New Motor Vehicle Taxes

Taxpayers can claim an itemized deduction for state or local sales or excise taxes paid on purchases of new (not used) automobiles, light trucks and motorcycles with a gross vehicle weight of no more than 8,500 pounds, and motor homes, but only for purchases made on or after February 17, 2009, and before January 1, 2010. As enacted under the American Recovery and Reinvestment Tax Act of 2009 (P.L. 111-5), the deduction is not available to taxpayers who elect to deduct state and local sales taxes in lieu of state and local income taxes. For taxpayers who do not itemize, the motor vehicle sales tax deduction can be claimed as an increase in the standard deduction (see Tab 1).

Only taxes on the first $49,500 of the vehicle's purchase price can be deducted. The deduction begins to phase-out for a taxpayer with modified adjusted gross income (MAGI) over $125,000 ($250,000 for a married couple filing jointly), and it is reduced to zero when MAGI reaches $135,000 ($260,000 for joint filers). MAGI for this purpose is the taxpayer's AGI plus any excluded income of a United States citizen or resident living abroad, and any excluded income from sources within Guam, American Samoa, the Northern Mariana Islands or Puerto Rico.

For taxpayers who itemize, the deduction for qualified motor vehicle taxes is computed on a worksheet located on the back of Schedule A.

Line 8, Other Taxes

Any other deductible taxes not listed on line 5, 6, or 7 should be listed on line 8 by type and amount. Taxes paid to a foreign country or U.S. possession are included on this line.

Planning Tip. The taxpayer may want to take a credit for the foreign tax instead of a deduction. See the discussion of Form 1040, line 47 in Tab 1.

If the foreign tax credit is taken for any eligible foreign taxes, the taxpayer generally may not take any part of the year's foreign taxes as a deduction. However, even if the foreign tax credit is claimed, a deduction may be taken if:

- Foreign taxes are not allowed as a credit because of boycott provisions
- Taxes are paid to certain foreign countries for which a credit has been denied (listed in IRS Publication 514)
- Taxes are paid on dividends that are not creditable because the taxpayer does not meet the stock holding period requirement (generally more than 15 days during a 30-day period), as described in IRS Publication 514
- Certain taxes are paid or accrued to a foreign country in connection with the purchase or sale of oil or gas extracted in that country, as described in IRS Publication 514

Planning Tip. Although a taxpayer claiming the credit for foreign taxes on an accrual basis will ordinarily use the average exchange rate for the relevant tax year, the taxpayer may elect to use the exchange rate on the date the taxes were paid, rather than an annual average.

See IRS Publication 514 and Tab 10 for details.

Filing Tip. Individuals subject to AMT should usually take the foreign tax credit, which can be used to reduce the AMT, rather than the foreign tax deduction, which will only reduce regular income taxes.

Also included on line 8 are state and local personal property taxes. To be deductible, personal property taxes must be based on value alone and must be charged on a yearly basis.

Example. Taxpayers in Larimer County, Colorado, pay a vehicle registration tax that includes an ownership tax based on the vehicle's value and a license fee based on the weight of the vehicle. If Jason of Fort Collins paid a fee of $225 when registering his new $10,000 car, the deductible amount would be the portion attributable to the value of the car, $178 ($10,000 × 0.85 × 0.021). The $46.50 he paid based on the weight of the vehicle is not deductible.

Line 9, Add Lines 5 through 8

The total of deductible taxes is entered on line 9.

Example. Leon Jones has had $1,220 in state income taxes withheld from his income in 2009, and he paid an additional $250 with his state tax return. He bought a new residence on May 15, 2009, and sold his previous residence (in the same state) on June 12, 2009. The annual real estate taxes on his first residence were $1,725 and on his second residence, $2,150. In addition, his new municipality levies an annual garbage collection charge of $250 with its property tax bill. In his new city of residence, he has also paid a vehicle registration tax, based entirely on book value, of $19. The calculation of his real estate tax is shown below. His total tax deductions would amount to $3,615.30 ($1,470 in state income taxes + $2,126.30 in real estate taxes + $19 in personal property taxes).

Days in first residence (January 1–June 11)	162
Tax deductible for first residence (162/365 × $1,725)	$765.62
Days in second residence (May 15–December 31)	231
Tax deductible for second residence (231/365 × $2,150)	$1,360.68
Total real estate tax (garbage collection fee not includible)	$2,126.30

Where to Deduct Interest on 2009 Return

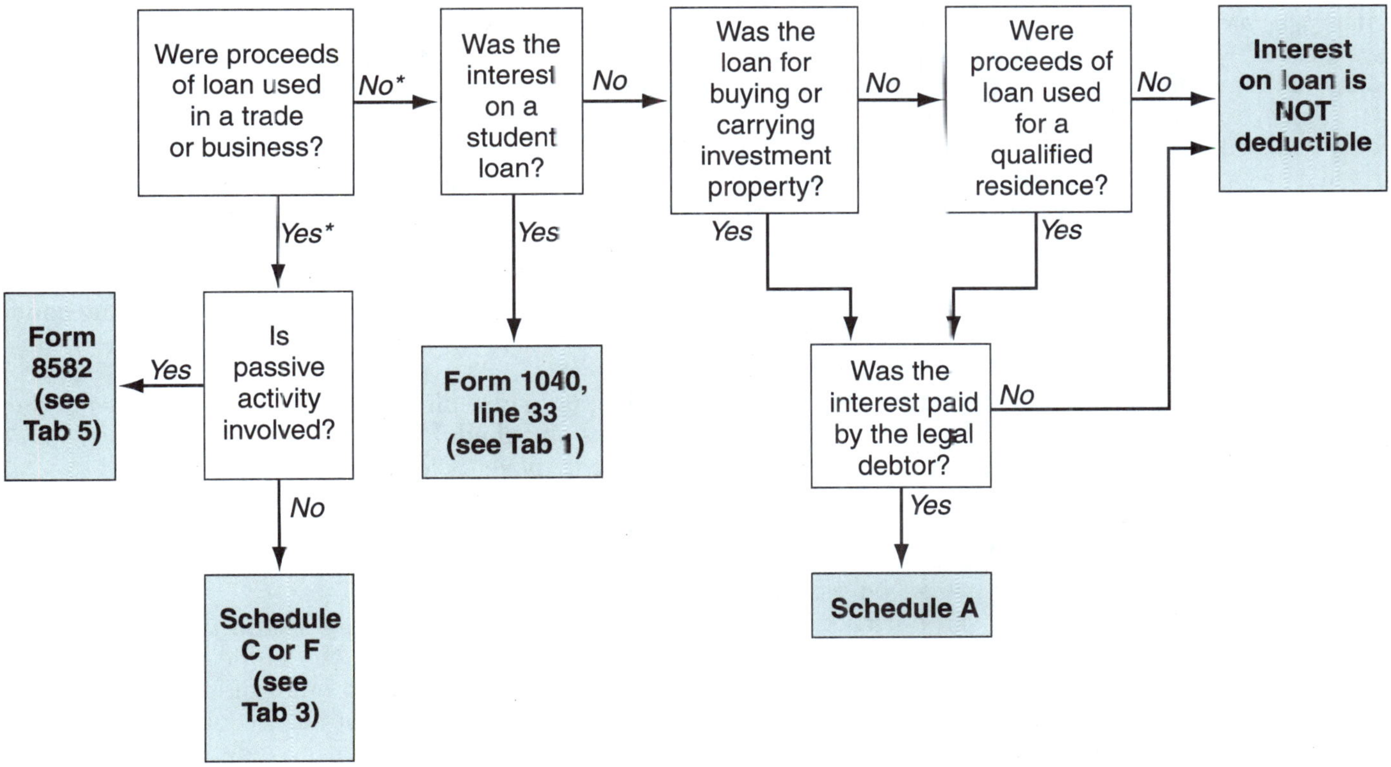

* If proceeds were used for both business and personal use, the interest must be allocated; see Reg. §1.163-8T and IRS Publication 535.

Interest Paid, Lines 10-15

Interest Paid Deduction Facts

For 2007, interest paid was the largest itemized deduction taken by individual taxpayers. Total interest paid was $502 billion for 2007. Taxpayers who itemized deductions in 2007 deducted an average of $9,328 in interest paid if they had AGIs under $50,000, and $13,280 if their AGIs were over $50,000.

What Can Be Deducted on Schedule A?

Whether interest is deductible depends on the type and purpose of the debt on which the interest is paid.

- *Personal interest,* which is interest paid on nonbusiness car loans, credit cards, and the like, is not deductible.
- *Student loan interest,* although generally considered as personal interest, may be deductible from gross income on Form 1040 (see Tab 1).
- *Business interest* is interest incurred on debts that are used in a trade and business; it is deductible on Schedule C or F (see Tab 3), or, if the business involves rentals or other passive activities, on Schedule E or Form 4835 (see Tab 5).
- *Investment interest* is interest paid on money borrowed to buy or carry property held for investment that generates income such as interest, dividends, annuities, and royalties. Investment interest is figured on Form 4952 and is generally reportable on Schedule A; it is deductible up to the amount of net investment income (see discussion on page 2-20).
- *Mortgage interest* is deductible on Schedule A, regardless of whether the proceeds were used to pay personal expenses, if the mortgage is on a qualified residence. In fact, outstanding personal loans can be converted into loans with deductible interest (for regular tax purposes only) if they are consolidated into qualified home equity loans or lines of credit. Premiums paid on mortgage insurance may be treated as deductible mortgage interest.

Treatment of Tax Penalties and Tax Refunds

Interest paid as tax penalties, no matter what the jurisdiction, has been consistently ruled by the courts as personal interest and thus not deductible. Interest on tax refunds is counted as investment income to be netted against investment expenses.

Filing Tip. Interest earned on federal refunds is reported with other interest income on line 1 of Schedule B. IRA maintenance fees not debited directly from the IRA and other mutual fund and investment expenses are reported on line 23 of Schedule A, and investment interest paid on line 14 of Schedule A, up to the amount of taxable interest income (after first making a loop through Form 4952).

An individual may deduct all interest paid (for cash-basis taxpayers) or accrued (for accrual-basis taxpayers) on a debt that he or she is legally obligated to pay. Interest paid on another's debt, however, is treated as a gift, so it is not deductible. Also, mortgage payments made by a former spouse will probably be treated as taxable alimony, and the interest will not be deductible by either party (*Linda J. Baxter*, TC Memo 1999-190). See Tab 13.

Filing Tip. An individual who wishes to help someone by paying off a debt should not pay the money directly to the creditor. Instead, they should give the money to the debtor, who can then deduct the interest portion of the payment to the creditor.

See IRS Publication 550, *Investment Income and Expenses*, and IRS Publication 936, *Home Mortgage Interest Deduction*, for more information.

Line 10, Home Mortgage Interest and Points Reported to You on Form 1098

Mortgage interest and points reported on Form 1098 are entered on line 10. If this form shows any refund of overpaid interest, the deduction does not have to be reduced. See Tab 1 for instructions on reporting it on Form 1040, line 21.

Home mortgage interest is any interest the taxpayer pays on a loan secured by his or her main home or second home. The loan may be a mortgage to buy the home, a second mortgage, a home equity line of credit, or a home equity loan. Home mortgage interest can be deducted only if all four of the following conditions are met:

- The taxpayer files Form 1040 and itemizes deductions on Schedule A.
- The taxpayer is legally liable for the loan.
- Both the taxpayer and the lender intend that the loan be repaid. In addition, there must be a true debtor-creditor relationship between the taxpayer and the lender.
- The mortgage must be a *secured debt* on a *qualified* home. To be qualified, the home must be the taxpayer's main or second home, and it must be a structure (mobile or not) that has sleeping, cooking, and toilet facilities. Note that the debt is not considered secured by the taxpayer's home if it is a security interest that attaches to the property without the taxpayer's consent (such as a mechanic's lien or judgment lien).

There are three types of qualified debt: home acquisition debt, home equity debt, and grandfathered debt.

Home Acquisition Debt. Home acquisition debt is a mortgage taken out after October 13, 1987, to buy, build, or substantially improve a qualified home (main or second home). It must be secured by that home. If the amount of the mortgage is more than the cost of the home plus the cost of any substantial improvements, only the debt that equals the cost of the home plus improvements qualifies as home acquisition debt. The additional debt may qualify as *home equity debt.*

- *Home acquisition debt limit*–The total amount the taxpayer can treat as home acquisition debt at any time on the main home and second home cannot be more than $1 million ($500,000 for MFS). This limit is reduced (but not below zero) by the amount of *grandfathered debt.* Debt over this limit may qualify as *home equity debt.*
- *Refinanced home acquisition debt*–Any secured debt the taxpayer uses to refinance home acquisition debt is treated as home acquisition debt. The new debt, however, will qualify as home acquisition debt only up to the balance of the old mortgage principal just before the refinancing. Any additional debt is not home acquisition debt, but may qualify as *home equity debt.* The IRS has confirmed that qualified home mortgage interest, which is deductible for AMT purposes, includes interest paid on a repeatedly refinanced home mortgage to the extent the amount of the mortgage indebtedness is not increased (Rev. Rul. 2005-11).

Home Equity Debt. If the taxpayer took out a loan for reasons other than to buy, build, or substantially improve the main or second home, it may qualify as home equity debt. In addition, debt that the taxpayer incurred to buy, build, or substantially improve the home, to the extent that it is more than the home acquisition debt limit, may qualify as home equity debt. Home equity debt is a mortgage the taxpayer took out after October 13, 1987, that is secured by a qualified home but does not qualify as home acquisition debt.

- *Home equity debt limit*–The limit on the amount of debt that can be treated as home equity debt is the smaller of $100,000 ($50,000 if married filing separately) or the total of each home's fair market value (FMV) reduced (but not below zero) by the amount of its home acquisition debt and grandfathered debt. (FMV and the outstanding home acquisition and grandfathered debt for each home are determined on the date that the last debt was secured by the home.)

Grandfathered Debt. If the taxpayer took out a qualified mortgage before October 14, 1987, or refinanced a qualified mortgage, it will qualify as grandfathered debt if it was secured by the qualified home on October 13, 1987, and at all times after that date. All of the interest paid on grandfathered debt is fully deductible home mortgage interest, but the amount of grandfathered debt reduces the limits for home acquisition debt and home equity debt.

- *Refinanced grandfathered debt*–If grandfathered debt was refinanced after October 13, 1987, for an amount that was not more than the mortgage principal left on the debt, then it is still grandfathered debt. To the extent the new debt is more than the mortgage principal, it is treated as home acquisition or home equity debt, and the mortgage is a mixed-use mortgage. Grandfathered debt that was refinanced after October 13, 1987, is treated as grandfathered debt only for the term left on the debt that was refinanced. Then it has to be treated as home acquisition debt or home equity debt, depending on how the proceeds are used. (There is an exception for balloon notes; see IRS Publication 936.)
- *Line-of-credit mortgage*–If the taxpayer had a line-of-credit mortgage on October 13, 1987, and borrowed additional amounts against it after that date, the additional amounts are either home acquisition debt or home equity debt depending on how the proceeds were used. The balance on the mortgage before the taxpayer borrowed the additional amounts is grandfathered debt.

Home Considerations. An individual may consider interest on loans secured by two homes as deductible home mortgage interest:

- *Main home*–This is the home where the taxpayer ordinarily lives (only one at a time).
- *Second home*–A second home is a home that the taxpayer chooses to treat as a second home.

The following circumstances may affect mortgage interest deductibility:

- *Office in the home*–Only the part of the home used for residential living is considered a qualified home. Taxpayers who use part of it as a home office must divide both the cost and fair market value of the home between the part that is a qualified home and the part that is not. This allocation may affect the amount of home acquisition debt.
- *Renting out part of home*–If the taxpayer rents out part of a qualified home, the entire value of the home will still be qualified as long as there is not a separate unit for the tenant to live in. See IRS Publication 936 for details.
- *Home under construction*–The taxpayer can treat a home under construction as a qualified home for a period of up to 24 months, but only if it becomes a qualified home when it is ready for occupancy. The 24-month period can start any time on or after the day construction begins.

Example. William and Jennifer Qian bought a home in 2002. Its current FMV is $125,000, and the balance on the mortgage on July 1, 2009, is $105,000. In order to consolidate some personal debts, they look into taking out a home mortgage loan. The best deal they find is from BBB Bank, which offers a loan of 120% of the FMV over the outstanding mortgage debt. (There are no other liens attached to the property.)

Currently, the Qians have $105,000 in home acquisition debt. Their loan from BBB is 120% × $125,000 – $105,000 = $45,000. Because their home acquisition debt is $105,000, their home equity debt is limited to $20,000, which is the amount by which their home's FMV exceeds the home acquisition debt. The interest they pay on their new home mortgage loan will have to be allocated between the qualified home equity part ($20,000), which will be fully deductible on Schedule A, and the rest ($25,000), which will be considered as personal interest and will not be deductible.

Is Home Mortgage Interest Fully Deductible on Schedule A?

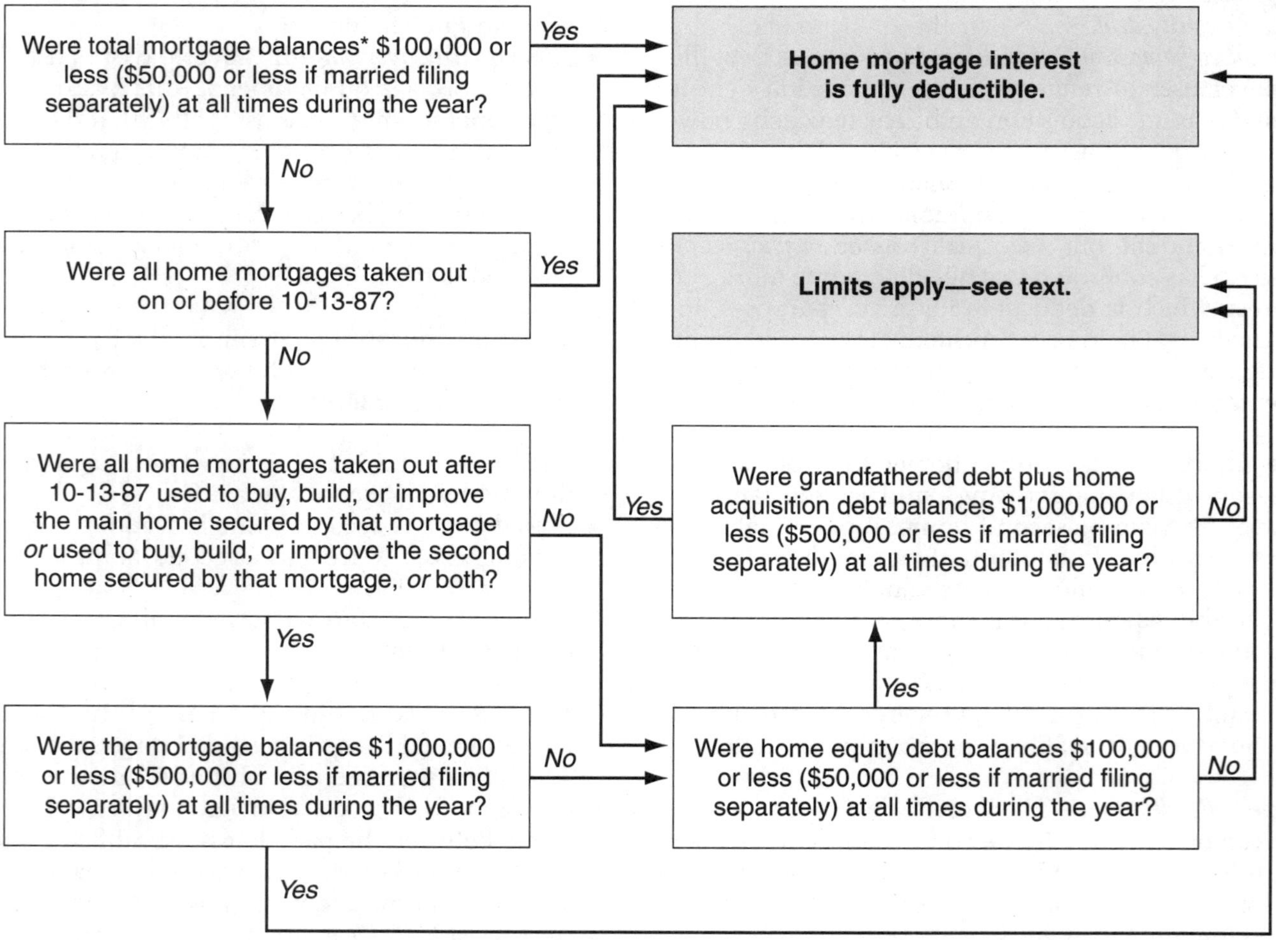

*Balances of ALL mortgages secured by main home and second home

- *Home destroyed*–The taxpayer may be able to continue treating a home as a qualified home even after it is destroyed in a fire, storm, tornado, earthquake, or other casualty. See IRS Publication 936 for details.
- *Tenant-stockholders in a cooperative project*–Tenant-stockholders in an apartment house can deduct their portion of interest payments on the indebtedness of the cooperative. (They can also deduct their share of the real estate taxes on the building.)

The following considerations apply to second homes:

- *Second home not rented out at any time during the year*–The taxpayer can treat it as a qualified home, even if the home is not used during the year.
- *Second home rented out part of the year*–The taxpayer must use this home more than 14 days or more than 10% of the number of days during the year that the home is rented at a fair rental, whichever is greater. If this condition is not met, the unit is considered rental property rather than a second home.
- *More than one second home*–If the taxpayer has more than two homes, only one can be treated as the qualified second home during any year.
- *Time-sharing arrangements*–A time-shared home can be treated as a qualified home if it meets the requirements for a second home that is rented out.

Filing Tip. A second home is any "structure" deemed by the taxpayer to be a second home. An RV, time share, or condominium may qualify, but the chosen second home may not be in violation of local ordinance as a qualified residence.

Example. Heather Brooks owns and occupies an apartment in a cooperative project. Her yearly carrying charges total $1,700: $1,000 for her share of the interest on the building's mortgage and $700 for her share of the real estate taxes. The $1,000 would be deductible on line 10 of Schedule A, and the $700 would be deductible on line 6 of Schedule A.

Limits on Home Mortgage Interest Deduction. Limits apply to the home mortgage interest expense if the taxpayer has a home mortgage that does not fit into any of the previously discussed categories (see flowchart). The home mortgage interest deduction is limited to the interest on the part of the home mortgage debt that is not more than the qualified loan limit. This is the part of the taxpayer home mortgage debt that is grandfathered debt or that is not more than the limits for home acquisition debt and home equity debt.

In most cases, all of the home mortgage interest will be deductible. Whether it is all deductible depends on the date the taxpayer took out the mortgage, the amount of the mortgage, and the taxpayer's use of its proceeds. If all of the taxpayer's mortgages fit into one or more of the three categories already discussed at all times during the year, the taxpayer can deduct all of the interest on those mortgages.

The dollar limits for the home acquisition debt and the home equity debt categories apply to the combined mortgages on the taxpayer's main home and second home.

Caution. Interest deducted for the home equity debt payments is subject to alternative minimum tax.

Line 11, Home Mortgage Interest Not Reported on Form 1098

Deductible mortgage interest for which there is no Form 1098 is reported on line 11. If the home was purchased from the recipient of that interest, the recipient's name, identifying number, and address go on the dotted lines next to line 11. If the recipient is an individual, the identifying number is his or her Social Security number (SSN); otherwise, it is the employer identification number.

Filing Tip. The taxpayer may have to pay a $50 penalty if he or she fails to show the required information about the recipient or fails to inform the recipient of his or her SSN. If another person (other than the taxpayer's spouse if filing jointly) was liable for, and paid interest on, the mortgage, and the other person received the Form 1098, a statement must be attached to the return showing the name and address of that person and the notation "See attached" added to the right of line 11.

Line 12, Points Not Reported on Form 1098

"Points," used to describe certain charges paid, or treated as paid, by a borrower (homebuyer) to obtain a mortgage for the purchase, construction, or substantial improvement of a main or second home, are deductible as interest in the year paid, if the following conditions are met:

Example. The Qians paid a total of $12,000 of debt on their original home mortgage and their consolidation loan in 2009, and they use Table 1 from IRS Publication 936 (reproduced below) to figure the amount of interest that is deductible, $8,640. Because the consolidation loan was entirely for personal reasons, none of the $3,360 nonallowable mortgage interest is deductible anywhere. In addition, the Qians paid $800 of points on the consolidation loan, but they cannot claim that amount as a deduction because it was not paid to purchase or improve their home. The total average balance of both mortgages on their home is $284,700. The Qians also paid $13,900 in investment interest in 2009. On their Schedule A, the Qians enter the $8,640 in mortgage interest on line 10 and the $13,900 in investment interest on line 14. The total of these amounts, $22,540, is entered on line 15.

Part I	**Qualified Loan Limit**		
1.	Enter the average balance of all your grandfathered debt. See line 1 instructions . .	1.	-------------
2.	Enter the average balance of all your home acquisition debt. See line 2 instructions	2.	105,000
3.	Enter $1,000,000 ($500,000 if married filing separately)	3.	1,000,000
4.	Enter the **larger** of the amount on line 1 or the amount on line 3	4.	1,000,000
5.	Add the amounts on lines 1 and 2. Enter the total here	5.	105,000
6.	Enter the **smaller** of the amount on line 4 or the amount on line 5	6.	105,000
7.	Enter $100,000 ($50,000 if married filing separately). See the line 7 instructions for a limit that may apply	7.	100,000
8.	Add the amounts on lines 6 and 7. Enter the total. This is your qualified loan limit . .	8.	205,000
Part II	**Deductible Home Mortgage Interest**		
9.	Enter the total of the average balances of all mortgages on all qualified homes. See line 9 instructions	9.	284,700
	• If line 8 is less than line 9, go on to line 10. • If line 8 is equal to or more than line 9, stop here. All of your interest on all the mortgages included on line 9 is deductible as home mortgage interest on Schedule A (Form 1040).		
10.	Enter the total amount of interest that you paid. See line 10 instructions	10.	12,000
11.	Divide the amount on line 8 by the amount on line 9. Enter the result as a decimal amount (rounded to three places)	11.	× .720
12.	Multiply the amount on line 10 by the decimal amount on line 11. Enter the result. This is your **deductible home mortgage interest.** Enter this amount on Schedule A (Form 1040)	12.	8,640
13.	Subtract the amount on line 12 from the amount on line 10. Enter the result. This is **not** home mortgage interest. See line 13 instructions	13.	3,360

1. The amount is clearly shown on the settlement statement (such as the HUD-1 Settlement Statement) as points charged for the mortgage. The points may be shown as paid from either the taxpayer's funds or the seller's.
2. Amounts are computed as a percentage of the stated principal loan amount.
3. Paying points is an established business practice in the area where the loan was made, and the points conform to the amounts generally charged in that area.
4. The loan is used to buy, build, or make substantial improvements to the taxpayer's main home, and it is secured by that home.
5. The amounts are paid directly by the taxpayer (or by the seller for the borrower's mortgage; see discussion in text).

Planning Tip. If the five tests for full deductibility of points in the year paid are met, the taxpayer still has the option to deduct the points over the loan's lifetime. This option should be used in years in which deductions are otherwise insufficient to itemize in the year that the points were paid.

Points may also be called loan origination fees, maximum loan charges, loan discount, or discount points. Points paid to obtain a loan for the purchase of a principal residence are generally reported on Form 1098. A borrower is treated as having paid any points that a home seller pays for the borrower's mortgage.

Caution. All points paid on loans secured by the taxpayer's second home must be deducted only over the life of the loan.

Not Considered Points. Certain amounts charged by the lender for specific services connected to a loan are not considered interest:

- Appraisal fees
- Notary fees
- Preparation costs for the mortgage note or deed of trust
- Mortgage insurance premiums
- VA funding fees, unless paid directly by the buyer

These fees cannot be deducted as points either in the year paid or over the life of the mortgage.

Gray Area. Points paid to refinance a mortgage, regardless of the arrangement to pay them, are not deductible in full in the year paid unless they are in connection with the purchase or improvement of a home, even if the refinancing is secured by the taxpayer's home. They are deductible over the term of the loan. One appeals court, however, has allowed a current deduction for the refinancing of a short-term mortgage because it viewed the refinancing as an integral part of the process of financing a home purchase. *J.R. Huntsman*, 90-2 USTC ¶50.340, 905 F2d 1182 (8th Cir. 1990). A taxpayer or return preparer taking this position may want to disclose this position in order to avoid imposition of the accuracy-related penalty if challenged by the IRS.

Points Paid by the Seller. The term "points" also includes loan placement fees that the seller pays to the lender to arrange financing for the buyer.

- *Treatment by seller*–The seller cannot deduct these fees as interest, but can use them as a selling expense that reduces the gain realized (see Tab 4)
- *Treatment by buyer*–The buyer reduces the basis of the home by the amount of the points paid by the seller and treats them as if he or she had paid them.

Example. Wilson Williams has interest income derived from investments. His investment income totals $15,000. His investment expenses were directly connected with the production of this income, and these expenses total to $1,050 after the 2%-of-AGI floor is taken into account. He has also paid $12,500 of investment interest in 2009, and carried forward $1,500 of disallowed interest from 2008. He figures the deduction for line 14 as follows:

Form **4952** — Department of the Treasury, Internal Revenue Service (99)

Investment Interest Expense Deduction

▶ Attach to your tax return.

OMB No. 1545-0191 — **2009** — Attachment Sequence No. **51**

Name(s) shown on return: **Wilson Williams** — Identifying number: **000-00-0000**

Part I	**Total Investment Interest Expense**				
1	Investment interest expense paid or accrued in 2009 (see instructions)			1	12,500
2	Disallowed investment interest expense from 2008 Form 4952, line 7			2	1,500
3	**Total investment interest expense.** Add lines 1 and 2			3	14,000
Part II	**Net Investment Income**				
4a	Gross income from property held for investment (excluding any net gain from the disposition of property held for investment)	4a	15,000		
b	Qualified dividends included on line 4a	4b			
c	Subtract line 4b from line 4a			4c	15,000
d	Net gain from the disposition of property held for investment	4d			
e	Enter the **smaller** of line 4d or your net capital gain from the disposition of property held for investment (see instructions)	4e			
f	Subtract line 4e from line 4d			4f	
g	Enter the amount from lines 4b and 4e that you elect to include in investment income (see instructions)			4g	
h	Investment income. Add lines 4c, 4f, and 4g			4h	15,000
5	Investment expenses (see instructions)			5	1,050
6	**Net investment income.** Subtract line 5 from line 4h. If zero or less, enter -0-			6	13,950
Part III	**Investment Interest Expense Deduction**				
7	Disallowed investment interest expense to be carried forward to 2010. Subtract line 6 from line 3. If zero or less, enter -0-			7	50
8	**Investment interest expense deduction.** Enter the **smaller** of line 3 or 6. See instructions			8	13,950

Line 13, Qualified Mortgage Insurance Premiums

Premiums paid for qualified mortgage insurance can be treated as mortgage interest and deducted, subject to certain restrictions. "Qualified mortgage insurance" refers to mortgage insurance provided by the Veterans Administration (VA), the Federal Housing Administration (FHA), the Rural Housing Administration (RHA), and private mortgage insurance (as defined under section 2 of the Homeowners Protection Act of 1998 (12 U.S.C. Sec. 4901)).

To be deductible, the premiums must be paid or accrued for qualified mortgage insurance obtained in connection with acquisition indebtedness on a qualified residence. The premiums must be paid or accrued after 2006 with respect to mortgage insurance contracts issued after 2006. Although the deduction was originally scheduled to terminate for premiums paid or accrued after December 31, 2007, or properly allocable to any period after December 31, 2007, it has been extended for premiums paid or accrued after December 31, 2010, or properly allocable to any period after December 31, 2010.

The deduction for mortgage insurance premiums is also subject to a phaseout. For every $1,000 or fraction thereof by which the taxpayer's adjusted gross income (AGI) exceeds $100,000, the amount of mortgage insurance premiums that can be treated as qualified residence interest is reduced by 10 percent. In the case of a married taxpayer filing separately, the preceding amounts are lowered to $500 and $50,000. The effect of this phaseout is that interest treatment is not allowed for most taxpayers with AGI in excess of $109,000 ($54,500 for a married taxpayer filing separately).

A Qualified Mortgage Insurance Premium Deduction Worksheet appears in the Instructions to Schedule A and is reproduced on page 2-46.

Example. Gina Garcia has deductible mortgage insurance premiums in the amount of $2,000, but has AGI of $102,100. She is subject to the phaseout and must reduce the otherwise deductible amount by 30 percent. The amount of her mortgage insurance premium deduction is $1,400.

In the case of prepaid mortgage insurance, except contracts issued by the VA or RHA, amounts paid that are allocable to periods beyond the year in which they are paid are charged to a capital account and treated as paid in the allocable year. The allocation rule provides that an individual may allocate the prepaid premium ratably over the shorter of the stated term of the mortgage, or 84 months, which is the average life of a mortgage insurance contract. This rule applies to prepaid qualified mortgage insurance premiums paid or accrued on or after January 1, 2008, and on or before December 31, 2010, for mortgage insurance provided by the Federal Housing Administration or private mortgage insurers issued on or after January 1, 2007. If the mortgage is satisfied before the end of its term, no deduction will be allowed for the unamortized balance of the capital account.

Line 14, Investment Interest

If the taxpayer borrows money to buy property held for investment purposes, the interest on that loan is investment interest. The taxpayer can deduct investment interest subject to the limit of net investment income. The taxpayer cannot deduct interest incurred to produce tax-exempt income (see MTG ¶1055 and ¶1056).

Investment interest is deductible in the year paid for cash-basis taxpayers and in the year accrued for accrual-basis taxpayers. Interest paid in advance beyond year's end must be apportioned over the tax years to which the payment relates (see MTG ¶1055 and ¶1056).

Allocation of Interest Expense. If the same loan covers business or personal purposes in addition to investment purposes, the debt must be allocated among those purposes. Regardless of what kind of property is used to secure the debt, the interest expense on the part of the debt used for investment purposes is the only interest that can be deducted on line 14 of Schedule A.

Limit on Deduction. The deduction for investment interest expense cannot exceed net investment income. The amount that cannot be deducted may be carried forward to the next tax year. The interest carried over is treated as investment interest paid or accrued in that next year. The taxpayer can carry over disallowed investment interest to the next tax year even if it is more than the taxpayer's taxable income in the year the interest was paid or accrued.

Form 4952. The investment interest expense deduction is figured on Form 4952, which is attached to Schedule A, and reported on line 14. See the Example on page 2-19.

Definitions

- *Investment property*–Qualified investment property is property that produces interest, dividends, annuities, or royalties not derived in the ordinary course of a trade or business (but not an interest in a passive activity). Investment property also includes any interest in a trade or business activity in which the taxpayer did not materially participate (other than a passive activity).
- *Net investment income*–This is determined by subtracting investment expenses (other than interest expense) from all investment income.

- *Investment income*–This generally includes gross income derived from property held for investment. It does not include qualified dividends or net capital gain unless an election is made to include them–in which case capital gains and dividend rates do not apply.
- *Investment expenses*–Included in investment expenses are all income-producing expenses (other than interest expense) related to investment property after the 2%-of-AGI floor is applied (see discussion of miscellaneous itemized deductions on page 2-30).

Line 15, Total Interest Deduction

The sum of lines 10 through 14 is reported on line 15. This is the total amount of deductible interest.

Gifts to Charity, Lines 16-19

Charitable Contributions Deduction Facts

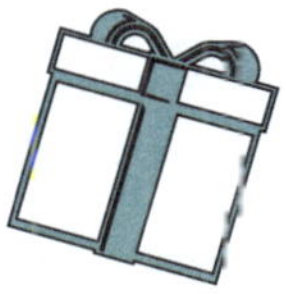

Charitable contributions were the third-largest itemized deduction. The charitable contribution deduction increased from 2006 to 2007, to $174.5 billion. Taxpayers who itemized deductions in 2005 deducted an average of $1,991 in charitable contributions if they had AGIs under $50,000, and $5,022 if their AGIs were over $50,000.

Deductible Contributions

Generally, taxpayers can deduct contributions of money or property made to a qualified organization. A gift or contribution may also be deductible if given "for the use of" a qualified organization if held in a legally enforceable trust for the qualified organization or in a similar legal arrangement. The contributions must be made to a qualified organization and not set aside for use by a specific person. The fair market value of property given to a qualified organization is also deductible.

Qualified Organizations. Contributions can qualify for a charitable deduction only if made to one of the following:

- A corporation, trust, community chest, fund, or foundation that is organized and operated exclusively for a charitable, religious, educational, scientific, or literary purpose or for the prevention of cruelty to children or animals (up to a limit of 50% of AGI)
- The United States, a state, a territory, a city, or a political subdivision of any of these, if the contribution is made for a public purpose (up to a limit of 50% of AGI)
- Certain veterans' organizations or auxiliaries (up to a limit of 30% of AGI)
- Certain nonprofit cemetery companies (up to a limit of 30% of AGI)
- A domestic fraternity operating under the lodge system if the contribution is used solely for public purposes (up to a limit of 30% of AGI)

See MTG ¶1059 and ¶1061 for further details.

In addition, any qualifying organization must meet these requirements:

- No part of the net earnings may go for the benefit of a private shareholder or individual.
- No substantial part of the activities of the organization may consist of carrying on lobbying activities or otherwise attempting to influence legislation.

Caution. A qualified charitable entity cannot act as a conduit to an individual regardless of the desires of the giver or the worthiness of the recipient. The IRS may disallow contributions it deems directed to an individual even if the gift was made through an organization.

Organizations should make their charitable status known when soliciting funds. IRS Publication 78, which can now be searched online at www.irs.gov, has information on whether an organization is a qualified charity. If an organization is not listed on the IRS list, an inquiry may be sent to the Commissioner of Internal Revenue, Washington, DC 20224, Attention T:R:EO. The following organizations are usually qualified charities:

- Churches, temples, synagogues, mosques, and other religious organizations
- Public recreation and park funds
- Red Cross, Goodwill, Salvation Army, United Way, Boy/Girl Scouts, Boys/Girls Clubs of America, and other well-known charitable organizations
- Established veterans' groups such as the American Legion, the VFW, and Disabled American Veterans, although many newer veterans' groups should be checked for qualification in Publication 78

Caution. The IRS lists charities that have had their tax-exempt status revoked recently. The list is published on a monthly basis in the Internal Revenue Bulletin. When an organization has had its exempt status revoked, contributions by individuals unaware of the revocation will still be deductible (1) until the date an announcement is published or (2) until the termination date stated in the announcement.

See IRS Publication 526, *Charitable Contributions*, and IRS Publication 561, *Determining the Value of Donated Property*, for more information.

Nondeductible Contributions

Contributions to the following are not deductible:

- Civic leagues (although membership dues to some civic organizations may be deductible as a business expense on Schedule C)
- Social clubs
- Any international or foreign organization

Caution. Contributions to an individual—no matter how needy that individual may be—are never deductible. This rule applies even to donations to qualified organizations if the gift is designated for the benefit of a specific individual.

Tuition for a Religious School. Tuition is never deductible on Schedule A. The IRS considers that all tuition payments go solely to the value of education. In the only significant challenge to this stance, a taxpayer tried to deduct 55% of his children's tuition to a religious school because that amount was for religious studies. However, the IRS prevailed in circuit court (*Sklar*, 279 F.3d 697 (9th Cir. 2002).

Contributions made directly to a religious school aside from tuition, such as at a fundraiser, are deductible.

Services Rendered. The value of services rendered to any organization is not deductible, but unreimbursed expenses related to those services are deductible:

- Cost of uniforms required to be worn by Red Cross workers
- Transportation expenses incurred (the standard automobile charitable mileage rate is 14 cents per mile)
- Expenses (travel, meals, lodging, etc.) incurred while attending a qualified organization's convention as a delegate or officer of the organization (no expenses are deductible for attending in an unofficial capacity)

Contributions from Which the Donor Benefits. A taxpayer who receives a benefit as a result of making a contribution to a qualified organization can deduct only the amount of the contribution that exceeds the value of the benefit received. If the taxpayer pays more than fair market value to a qualified organization for merchandise, goods, or services, the amount paid over the value of the item can be deducted. For the excess amount to qualify, the taxpayer must pay it with the intent to make a charitable contribution.

Example. John and Mary Kinsey pay $100 for two tickets to a dinner at their church. The church (as it should do) provides all contributors with a good-faith statement that says the FMV of the two dinners is $40. The Kinseys may take a $60 deduction on their joint return (or, if filing separately, whoever paid for the tickets may take the deduction).

Token Items. If the value received in return for a contribution is a small item, such as a calendar or a mug, the benefit can be ignored in calculating the deduction. The 2009 value limit on the value of token benefits was $9.50; the IRS fixes a new amount every year. Any contribution is fully deductible in 2009 if the benefit received by the donor is no more than the lesser of $9.50 or 2% of the amount of the contribution.

Gray Area. Raffle tickets, a common fundraiser, benefit donors even if they do not win. Amounts paid for chances to participate in raffles do not qualify as charitable contributions. Although in theory the amount by which the price of a raffle ticket exceeds the value of the chance to win the prize may be deductible if the taxpayer establishes the value of the chance of winning the prize, the taxpayer's unsubstantiated opinion of the chances of winning is not sufficient to satisfy the burden of proof.

Privilege to Purchase Athletic Tickets. If a donor gives money to a college and receives as a benefit the right to purchase game tickets, only 80% of the donation may be claimed (subject to limits on AGI discussed below). The cost of the tickets is, of course, not deductible.

Limits on Charitable Deductions

The amount of deductible charitable contributions is limited to 50% of AGI, and may be limited to 30% or 20% of AGI, depending on the type of property given and the type of organization receiving it.

50% Limit. The deduction for charitable contributions cannot be more than 50% of AGI for the year.

Filing Tip. An "exception" occurs for certain awards that are excludable from income (and therefore not deducted on Schedule A). Awards for scientific, artistic, literary, or civic achievement transferred unused to a government unit or tax-exempt charitable organization are nontaxable without regard to AGI. See MTG ¶785.

For organizations listed as 50% limit organizations, total contributions up to 50% of AGI are permissible, except that a 30% limit applies to gifts of capital gain property for which the deduction is figured by using fair market value without reduction for appreciation. Examples of 50% limit organizations are churches and religious organizations, hospitals, medical research organizations, educational organizations (including public or private schools), and organizations that receive a substantial amount of public support, such as libraries, museums, and symphony orchestras. Also qualifying as 50% limit organizations are private foundations that distribute all contributions during the taxable year in which they were received or within a 2.5-month period after the end of the year, and private foundations such as the United Way that pool contributions and allow contributors to name charities, as long as their income is distributed by within 2.5 months of the end of the year.

30% Limit. A 30%-of-AGI limit applies to gifts to all qualified organizations other than 50% limit organizations. This includes gifts to veterans' organizations, fraternal societies, nonprofit cemeteries, and certain private nonoperating foundations.

20% Limit. A 20%-of-AGI limit applies to gifts to 30%-of-AGI organizations of capital gain property for which the deduction is figured by using fair market value without reduction for appreciation.

Figuring the Deduction When Limits Apply. If contributions are subject to more than one of the limits to a percentage of AGI, they can be deducted in the following order:

1. Contributions subject only to the 50% limit, up to 50% of the taxpayer AGI
2. Contributions subject to the 30% limit, up to the lesser of (a) 30% of AGI, or (b) 50% of AGI minus contributions to 50% limit organizations, including contributions of capital gain property subject to the special 30% limit
3. Contributions of capital gain property subject to the special 30% limit, up to the lesser of (a) 30% of AGI, or (b) 50% of AGI minus other contributions to 50% limit organizations
4. Contributions subject to the 20% limit

Amounts of qualified contributions not allowable in 2009 may be carried over; see discussion on page 2-26.

Example. Nancy Holdrege has AGI of $10,000. During 2009, she donates $700 to her church, $800 to her alma mater (both 50% organizations), and $3,300 to the Holdrege Family Foundation, a "private," 30% organization. Her deduction is calculated as follows: First, the $1,500 total contribution to 50% organizations is figured ($700 + $800). Because it is below the 50%-of- AGI maximum, she can also deduct the 30% maximum of $3,000 for her contribution to the family's foundation, for a total of $4,500. The unused portion of the latter contribution can be carried over.

Contributions of Property

If the taxpayer contributes property to a qualified organization, the amount of the taxpayer's charitable contribution for deduction purposes is generally the fair market value of the property at the time of the contribution. However, if the property has increased in value, the taxpayer may have to make some adjustments to the amount of deduction.

Caution. Charitable deductions for donated vehicles that have a value in excess of $500 are limited. Written acknowledgment by the donee is also required. Form 1098-C, *Contributions of Motor Vehicles, Boat, and Airplanes,* may be used for this purpose. The donor is required to attach the written acknowledgment to his or her return. In general, the deduction cannot be more than the price the organization receives when it sells the vehicle. If the organization does not sell the vehicle, it must provide certification of its intended use. See MTG ¶1059.

In general, two questions have to be answered about gifts of property. What is the amount of the contribution based on—cost or value? What is the percentage limitation on the gift?

Capital Gain Property. Gifts of these types of property held long-term are deductible at their FMV on the date of donation. Examples include personal property, stocks and other capital assets held long-term, and a portion of a business-use property that would generate long-term gains if sold. In a sense, the appreciation is not taxed, but it is taken into account when figuring the amount of contribution. If given to a 50% limit organization, these gifts can-

Example. Ben Halpern has an AGI of $50,000 in 2009. During 2009, he contributes $18,000 cash and $2,000 of artwork to his synagogue (a 50%-of-AGI limit organization) and $10,000 cash to a 30% limit organization. He has no other charitable contributions during the year and no carryover from prior year. He may deduct a total of $25,000 for 2009, allocated first to his $20,000 contribution to the 50% limit organization and then to $5,000 of the 30% limit contribution. He fills out Form 8283 for his $2,000 noncash contribution. On his Schedule A, Ben enters $23,000 on line 16 (gifts by cash or check), $2,000 on line 17 (gifts other than by cash or check), zero on line 18 (carryover from prior year), and $25,000 on line 19 (total of lines 16, 17, and 18).

For 2010, Ben projects an AGI of $60,000. He plans to contribute $10,000 to the synagogue and $16,000 to the 30% limit organization. He will be able to deduct both contributions in full because their total is under the $18,000 (30% of $60,000) limit. Of his $5,000 carryover, he can deduct only $2,000 (i.e., $18,000 – $16,000) because it is a 30% limit carryover, and 30% of $60,000 is $18,000. The remaining $3,000 will be carried over to 2011 as 30% limit contributions.

not exceed 30% of AGI (20% if given to a 30% limit organization).

If stock is donated to a private foundation, no more than 10% of the outstanding stock may be given.

Election for Raising Limit. Instead of applying the 30% (or 20%) limit, a 50% limit may be used if the amount of contribution is reduced by *all* of the appreciation. If this election is made, all gifts–including carryovers–must be reduced by appreciation. The election is made with an attachment to Form 1040 simply stating that the election is being made. This election is not usually advisable unless there is minimal appreciation on all property donated.

Ordinary Income Property. If property would not result in long-term capital gain if sold, it is considered ordinary income property. It is deductible at cost, and it is limited to 50% or 30% of AGI depending on the organization receiving it. Examples include capital assets held short term, inventory, taxpayer-produced creative works, and portions of business-use property that generate ordinary income if sold.

Tangible Personal Property. The amount of deduction depends on how the recipient uses the donation. For the FMV to be deductible, the organization must use the gift for its exempt purpose. Otherwise, the deduction is limited to the original cost to the taxpayer. If the FMV is used, the 30% (or 20%) limit of AGI is used; otherwise, the 50% limit of AGI may be used.

Example. George Reeder gives an old book to his church. He paid $100 for the book years ago, but it has appreciated in value to $5,000. The church sells it at a rummage sale. George can deduct only the $100 cost, up to the 50%-of-AGI limit. If, however, he had donated it to a library, he could have taken a $5,000 deduction, subject to the 30%-of-AGI limit.

Line 16, Gifts by Cash or Check

Cash contributions include any amounts paid by cash, check, credit card, or payroll deduction. They also include out-of-pocket expenses incurred while donating services. (Noncash contributions are contributions of tangible property.)

Caution. Owners of IRAs who are 70-1/2 or older can give as much as $100,000 from their IRA or Roth IRA to charitable organizations in 2009 without recognizing any income on the distribution. This means that the distribution will not be included in gross income. A charitable contribution deduction is *not* permitted, and, therefore, the distributed amount should *not* be reported on line 16. For further information on this provision, see Tab 9.

Contributions of Less than $250. Substantiation requirements are as follows:

- A canceled check or a "legible and readable" account statement
- A receipt (or a letter or other written communication) from the organization showing its name, date of the contribution, and amount of the contribution
- Other reliable (i.e., made near the time of contribution and regularly kept) written records with the relevant information just described

Donors may not deduct contributions made in cash or by check or other monetary gifts unless they can produce a bank record or a receipt, letter or other written communication from the charitable organization.

Contributions of $250 or More. A deduction for a contribution of $250 or more in any one day must have an acknowledgment from the qualified organization or certain payroll deduction records.

The acknowledgment must be written, and it must be received by the earlier of the date the return is filed for the year of the contribution or the due date, including extensions, for filing the return.

For payroll deductions, a pay stub, Form W-2, or other document is required, accompanied by a pledge card or other document from the organization stating that the organization does not provide goods or services in return for any contribution made to it by payroll deduction.

Unreimbursed Expenses. For unreimbursed out-of-pocket expenses related to services performed for a charitable organization, the taxpayer must have adequate records to prove the amount of the expenses. The organization also has to provide, by the due date of the return, a written acknowledgment of those services.

Line 17, Other than by Cash or Check

For noncash contributions, the taxpayer must have records that show all the following:

- The name of the charitable organization
- The date and location of the charitable contribution
- A reasonably detailed description of the property
- FMV of the property and the appraisal method
- Any required reductions to the FMV (see discussion on page 2-23)

Gifts of Partial Interest. In general, deductions cannot be claimed for property in which the giver retains an interest. There are, however, several exceptions, including the following:

- *Charitable remainder trusts*–The donor may deduct the present value of the remainder interest in a trust in which an income interest is retained for life or a term of not more than 20 years. It can be set up as a charitable remainder annuity trust or a charitable remainder unitrust and must meet strict requirements; see IRC §664(d) and Tab 14.
- *Pooled income funds*–The donor may deduct the present value of the remainder interest in a pooled income fund in which an income interest is retained for life.
- *Charitable interest in a personal residence or farm*–The donor may deduct the present value of the remainder interest in a home or farm in which the right to use the property is retained for life.

If less than the taxpayer's entire interest in the property is donated, there are additional requirements for record keeping: the amount claimed as a deduction for the tax year as a result of the contribution, the amount claimed as a deduction in any earlier years, the name of any person in possession of the property other than the organization to which it was contributed, and the name and address of each organization to which it was contributed.

Clothing and Household Items. Any donations of clothing and household items that are made to a charitable organization are not deductible unless the donated items are in "good" or better condition. This means that the IRS may deny a deduction for any item that has minimal monetary value. It also means that a donor of such items should be prepared to prove both the condition and the value of the donated items. (Taxpayers who make several donations of clothing and household goods would be well-advised to take a digital photograph and keep the memory card with their tax records as insurance in the event of an audit.) There is one exception to this rule: if a single donated item is not in at least good condition, but it is, nevertheless, worth more than $500, it is deductible, so long as a qualified appraisal is obtained at the time of the donation.

For purposes of this provision, "household items" include furniture, furnishing, electronics, appliances, linens, and other similar items. The term does not include food, paintings, antiques, other objects of art, jewelry, gems, or collections.

Contributions of Less than $250. Although all of the general recordkeeping requirements apply, it is not necessary to have a receipt if getting one would be difficult, such as at a drop-off site for donations or for a church-plate offering. Otherwise, a receipt showing the same things as the requirements for larger donations is needed.

Contributions of $250 to $500. For contributions of $250 and above, the taxpayer must get and keep an acknowledgment from the qualified organization showing the name and address of the organization, the date and location of the contribution, and a description of the property for each separate contribution of $250 or more. In addition, the acknowledgment must state whether the taxpayer received any goods or services in return for the donation.

Contributions of $501 to $5,000. In addition to the records necessary for the previous category, recordkeeping requirements include the following:

- How the taxpayer originally obtained the property
- The approximate date the property was obtained or completed
- The cost or other basis, and any adjustments to the basis, of any property held less than 12 months and
- The cost or other basis, and any adjustments to the basis, of property held 12 months or more (except publicly traded securities)

If the last requirement cannot be met, a statement of explanation must be attached to the return.

Caution. If the total deduction of noncash contributions is over $500, Form 8283 must be attached.

Contributions of More than $5,000. To calculate whether the deduction is over $5,000, combine the claimed deductions for all similar items donated to any charitable organization during the year. All the requirements for lesser donations apply, and the taxpayer must obtain a qualified written appraisal of the donated property from a qualified appraiser (except for publicly traded stock; non-publicly traded stock needs an appraisal only if over $10,000).

Filing Tip. The taxpayer must know when appraisal is required and have the proper documentation. If there is no proof of cost or FMV, the value should be documented in some other way, such as with photographs. See IRS Publication 561, *Determining the Value of Donated Property.*

Line 18, Carryover from Prior Year

Contributions that cannot be deducted in the current year because they exceed the limitation on itemized deductions based on AGI (see line 29, later) can be carried forward for up to five years. Contributions for the current year are always deducted before the contributions that are carried over. If there are carryovers from two or more prior years, the earliest year's must be used first.

Contributions carried over are subject to the same percentage limits in the year to which they are carried. For example, contributions subject to the 20% limit in the year in which they are made are 20% limit contributions in the year to which they are carried. See MTG ¶1060.

Line 19, Calculation

Add lines 16 through 18. This is the total deductible gifts to charity. The total on line 19 must be limited by any applicable 50%, 30%, or 20% AGI limitation.

Casualty and Theft Losses, Line 20

Casualty and Theft Deduction Facts

Casualty and theft loss deduction amounts can vary greatly from year to year. In 1993, Midwest flooding caused $23.1 billion in damage, and deductions in constant dollars grew by 23.2% from 1992. In 2001, multiple hurricanes and a national drought contributed to a 63.5% annual growth rate, in constant dollars, from 2000. The series of hurricanes and tropical storms affecting Florida, Louisiana and other states in 2004 and 2005 led to another record increase in casualty loss claims.

Casualties

A casualty is the damage, destruction, or loss of property resulting from an identifiable event that is sudden, unexpected, or unusual.

Deductible Losses. Examples of deductible casualty losses are losses due to automobile collisions, fires, floods, storms, shipwrecks, explosions, and hurricanes.

See IRS Publication 547, *Casualties, Disasters, and Thefts*, and MTG ¶1124 for more information.

Loss on Deposits. Loss on deposits occurs when a bank, credit union, or other financial institution becomes insolvent or bankrupt. If this happens, the taxpayer can choose whether to treat the loss as a casualty loss, an ordinary loss, or a nonbusiness bad debt. [Ordinary loss is limited to $20,000 ($10,000 MFS), and it cannot be claimed if any part of the deposit is federally insured.] See MTG ¶1128 for more information.

Gray Area. Although usually limited to physical damage, casualty damages have been extended by courts to include permanent loss of FMV to a home [*Finkbohner v. United States*, 788 F.2d 723 (11th Cir. 1986)]. This is a difficult case to prove, but even if it is not proven, there may be no penalty for claiming it [*Gerald Chamales v. Commissioner*, T.C. Memo 2000-33 (Feb. 3, 2000)].

Nondeductible Losses. Deteriorations that occur gradually through a steadily operating cause of damage from a normal process do not qualify as casualty losses. For example, the weakening of a building brought on by ordinary wind or weather conditions is not a casualty loss, nor is damage from moths or termites. Deductions of losses from "sudden" infestations of termites and beetles have, however, occasionally been upheld in court [*Rosenberg v. Commissioner*, 198 F.2d 46 (8th Cir. 1952) (termites); *Black v. Commissioner*, 36 T.C.M. 1347 (1977) (beetles)].

Similarly, loss from drought is sometimes deductible and sometimes not. It is generally deductible if the drought is not of long duration (i.e., it meets the "suddenness" condition) and it involves reduction to FMV in the form of damaging permanent landscaping features such as trees or shrubs or damaging the building itself (*Winters v. U.S.*, D.C. Okla. 1958; *Stevens*, T.C. Memo 1984-365).

The taxpayer's culpability in the incident is sometimes a factor. Losses resulting from a filer's drunk driving are not deductible, nor are those from a filer's deliberately setting a fire.

Theft

Theft losses are deductible if the taking of the property is classified as a theft under state law. Losses from fraud, for example, are deductible; when a contractor disappears after taking a down payment for a repair he never performs, the victim is allowed a deduction.

The following are not allowable theft deductions:

- The loss of another's property in the filer's care, even if the filer had to pay the owner for the loss. The owner may deduct the loss, if the filer does not pay him or her for the loss.
- Anything confiscated by a foreign government. Such losses will qualify as business or investment losses if the property is used for business or investment, but not as theft losses of personal property.
- Anything legally confiscated by another. In some states, spouses who take personal property when permanently leaving a shared home are not committing a crime.

Mislaid or Lost Property. The mere disappearance of money or property is not a theft. However, an accidental loss or disappearance of property can qualify as a casualty if it results from an identifiable event, such as dropping a diamond ring down the drain.

"Ponzi" Schemes. Qualified investors who sustained losses from certain criminally fraudulent investment arrangements known as "Ponzi" schemes may claim them as a theft loss. The loss is deductible as a loss on a transaction entered into for profit; therefore, deductibility is not limited to losses that exceed $100 ($500 in 2009) or that exceed 10% of the investor's AGI (see page 2-28). Further, the loss is not subject to the overall limitation on itemized deductions (see page 2-36) or to the two-percent-of-AGI limit for miscellaneous itemized deductions (see page 2-35).

Guidance to assist victims of Ponzi-type investment schemes has been provided by the IRS. Although the guidance makes no mention of the Bernard Madoff scandal by name, Rev. Rul. 2009-9 clarifies the favorable tax treatment to which investors in that and similarly-situated schemes are entitled. Rev. Proc. 2009-20 provides optional safe harbor treatment that allows investors to deduct up to 95% of qualified losses from a fraudulent investment scheme, calculated by detailed definitions and formulas, if certain requirements are met. The procedure, which also provides guidance for investors choosing not to use the safe harbor, applies to investment fraud losses discovered in tax years after 2007.

A taxpayer who wishes to make the safe harbor election must mark "Revenue Procedure 2009-20" at the top of Form 4684, Casualties and Thefts, for the tax year of the investor in which the indictment, information, or complaint is filed against the lead figure. The taxpayer must also complete and sign the statement provided in Appendix A of Rev. Proc. 2009-20 and attach the statement to the taxpayer's return. See MTG ¶1125 for further details.

When to Report

Casualty and theft losses are usually deductible only in the year they occur. This is true even if the property is not replaced or repaired until the following year. However, if a theft loss is discovered later than the year in which it occurs, the year of discovery is the only year in which it is deductible.

If the extent of loss cannot be ascertained before the tax return's due date, Form 4868 can be filed for an automatic six-month extension of time to file.

Insurance and Other Reimbursement

The loss deduction must be reduced by the amount of reimbursement received. If the taxpayer expects with reasonable certainty to receive insurance or other compensation payments after the due date of the return, the loss must be reduced by the estimated amount. If the amount ultimately received is less than the expected amount, the difference is deductible as a casualty loss in the following year.

Note: If property is covered by an insurance policy, the loss cannot be deducted unless an insurance claim has been made. For example, if a driver does not want to report an accident to his or her insurance company in order to keep rates low, the loss cannot be deducted on line 20.

If the reimbursement is greater than the loss, the excess is reportable as income in the current year, unless the reimbursement is under $100,000 and is reinvested in similar property within two years, in which case it will not be reportable until the new property is sold.

New York Liberty Zone Property. The reinvestment time limit for property in the New York Liberty Zone is five years rather than two.

Caution. If a loss is claimed in one year and an unexpected insurance or other recovery is received in the following year, the amount of recovery will have to be reported as income in the year it is obtained. The return for the loss year cannot be amended in this case, even if the tax year of the return is still open for amendment. However, for an exception to this rule, see, below, under "Gulf Opportunity (GO) Zone Property."

Gulf Opportunity (GO) Zone Property. As a result of Hurricanes Katrina, Rita and Wilma in 2005, many taxpayers took a casualty loss deduction on their federal tax returns (in most cases, their 2005 federal tax return, or, if elected, their 2004 return) to account for hurricane damage to their personal residences. The Housing Assistance Tax Act of 2008 (P.L. 110-289) provides that a taxpayer who claimed a casualty loss deduction on his or her principal residence resulting from any of these hurricanes, and who subsequently received a grant (under Public Laws 109-148, 109-234 or 110-116) as reimbursement for the loss, may elect to file an amended income tax return for the tax year in which the deduction was taken (and for any tax year to which the deduction was carried) and reduce the amount of the deduction (but not below zero) by the amount of the reimbursement. The amended income tax return must be filed by the later of (1) the due date for filing the tax return for the tax year in which the taxpayer received the grant, or (2) July 30, 2009.

Records to Keep

To claim a deduction on line 20, the claimant must have records to show the following:

Casualty Loss Proof

- Type of casualty (car accident, fire, storm, etc.) and when it occurred.
- That the loss was a direct result of the casualty.
- That the taxpayer was the owner of the property, or if the taxpayer leased the property from someone else, that the taxpayer was contractually liable to the owner for the damage.
- Whether a claim for reimbursement exists for which there is a reasonable expectation of recovery.

Theft Loss Proof

- When it was discovered that the property was missing.
- That the property was stolen.
- That the taxpayer was the owner of the property.
- Whether a claim for reimbursement exists for which there is a reasonable expectation of recovery.

Planning Tip. The costs of creating and keeping these records are reportable on line 23 of Schedule A.

Figuring the Loss

The following steps are required to figure the amount of the loss:

- Determine the adjusted basis in the property before the casualty or theft (see Tab 4 for a discussion of adjusted basis).
- Determine the decrease in FMV of the property as a result of the casualty or theft (for personal losses and nontotal business losses).
- Take the smaller of 1 and 2.
- Subtract any insurance or other reimbursement received or that the taxpayer is eligible to receive.
- Determine whether the loss is a personal or business loss and apply the appropriate reduction ($100 per incident followed by 10% of AGI for personal losses).

Example. Gale and Harry Adams purchased their main residence for $112,000 in 1998, which in this case is also the adjusted basis. They had a kitchen fire in 2009 that reduced their home's value from $188,000 before the fire to $175,000 immediately thereafter. They collected $10,000 from their insurance company and expect no more insurance payments. Their AGI for the year was $47,500.

1 The adjusted basis is $112,000.
2. The decrease in value is $188,000 – $175,000 = $13,000.
3. $13,000 is the smaller value.
4. $13,000 – $10,000 insurance = $3,000.
5. The loss is clearly a personal loss, so it has a $100 floor and a reduction by 10% of AGI (discussed below). The deduction is thus $3,000 – $100 – (0.10 × $47,500 = $4,750) < 0. Thus, they cannot claim a casualty deduction.

Personal Casualty Losses. Personal casualty losses are deductible only to the extent that the loss exceeds 10% of AGI; also, each separate casualty must be reduced by $100 (however, see below, under "Federally Declared Disaster Areas"). If the taxpayer sustains more than one loss as the result of one casualty, or when the events of the casualty are closely related in origin, the resulting losses are subject to only one $100 reduction.

Example. Jo Manning's vacation home sustained wind damage of $1,800 and flood damage of $1,200 from a single storm. Her AGI for 2009 was $28,000, and she had no insurance on the home. She reduces her $3,000 loss by only $100 because the damage was caused by closely related events, so the deduction she can take is $2,900 – (0.10 × $28,000 = $2,800) = $100.

For purposes of applying the limitations, a husband and wife with status MFJ are treated as one individual: only one $100 floor applies to each casualty. Couples with filing status MFS must apply all limitations separately. The $100 floor also applies to all individuals involved in a casualty loss, even if they are victims of the same event.

Filing Tip. When reporting losses with multiple parts, the incident is the numbering sequence for electronic filing purposes, not the number of items related to the incident.

Business Casualty Loss. If business or income-producing property, such as rental property is stolen or completely destroyed, the decrease in FMV is not considered. The loss is figured as follows:

It is often advantageous to claim a business loss if possible, because there is no $100 floor and the 10%-of-AGI limit does not apply. Business casualty losses are netted against Section 1231 gain and reported above the line (see Tab 4).

Employee Education Expenses

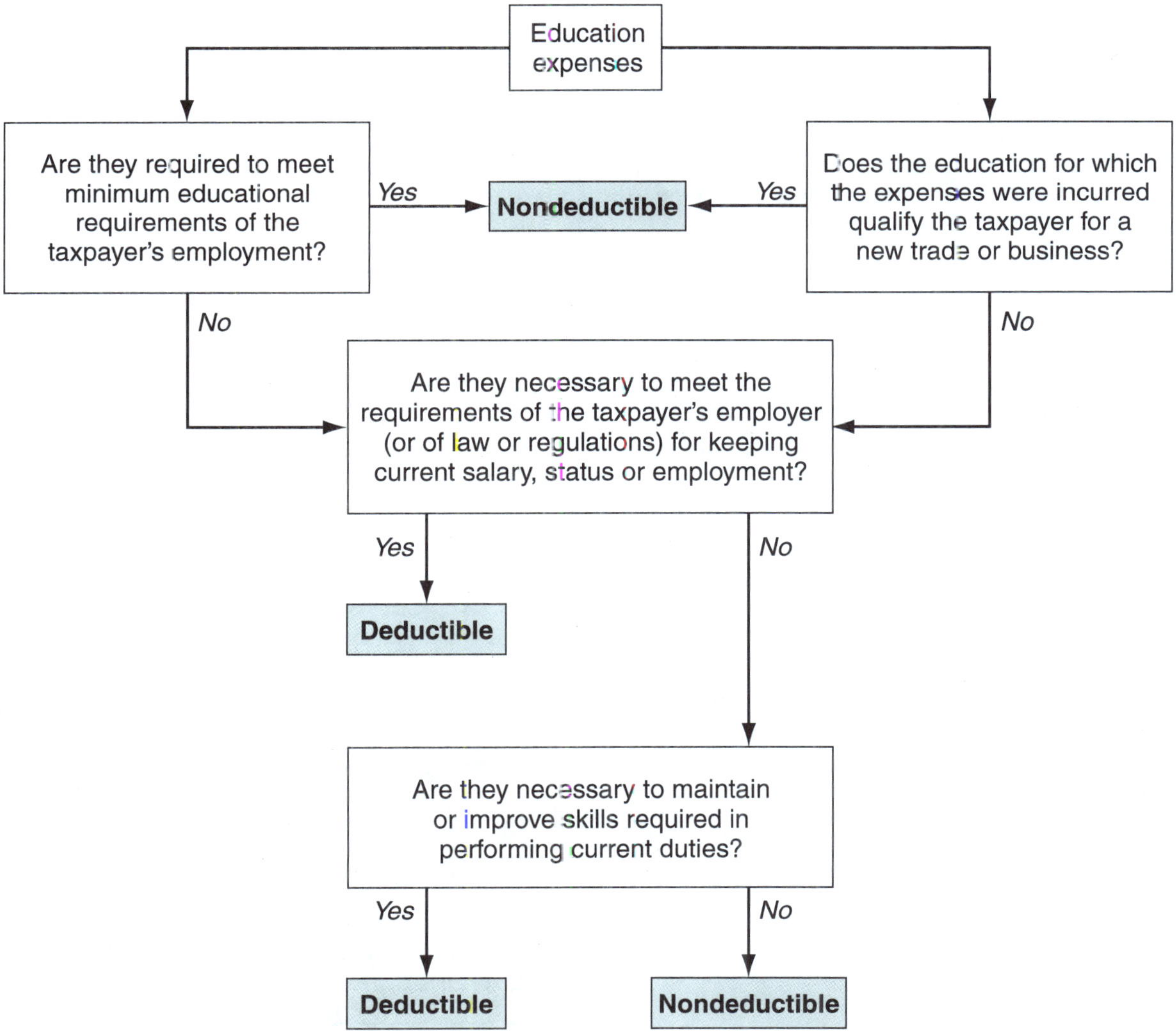

If property is held for both business and personal use, the $100 floor and the 10%-of-AGI limit apply proportionally to the loss for the personal-use part.

Example. Roland and Rebecca Provenzano own a car used 50% in Mr. Provenzano's business and 50% for personal use. It sustains $1,000 damage in a collision in early 2009. The adjusted basis of the auto is $2,000, and the Provenzanos collected $900 from the insurance company, for a net loss of $100. The $50 business loss is deductible, but the personal loss of $50 is reduced by the $100 floor and is therefore not deductible. Nothing is reported on line 20 of Schedule A, although the Provenzanos will fill out and file Form 4684 to deduct their business loss.

Form 4684. Form 4684 must be filled out and attached to the return if any casualty or theft loss is claimed. For any claim on line 20 of Schedule A, only Part A need be filled out.

Federally Declared Disaster Areas

For property in a federally declared disaster area (previously referred to as a presidentially declared disaster area), a special rule permits quick tax relief. Disaster losses during the current tax year can be deducted on the tax return filed for the previous year. The taxpayer may choose which of the two years to take the deduction.

If the previous year is elected for taking the casualty loss, the deadline for filing the amended return is the due date, without extensions, for filing the return for the year in which the loss was incurred. For a calendar-year taxpayer who lives in an area that is declared a disaster area in 2009, the deadline for filing an amended 2008 return would be April 15, 2010.

Other advantages for taxpayers with involuntary conversions are available in federal disaster zones (see Tab 4).

Caution. The taxpayer's AGI for the year of the return elected will determine the 10% reduction amount.

If such disasters occur during tax-filing season, the IRS may postpone deadlines for up to 120 days.

Planning Tip. Taxpayers claiming the disaster loss on the previous year's return should put the disaster designation in red ink at the top of the amended return so that the IRS can expedite the refund.

Personal Casualty Losses. Under the Emergency Economic Stabilization Act of 2008 (P.L. 110-343), personal casualty losses attributable to a federally declared disaster occurring in 2008 and 2009 are deductible without regard to whether the losses exceed 10 percent of a taxpayer's AGI. The 10-percent-of-AGI limitation continues to apply to casualty or theft losses that are not attributable to a federally declared disaster.

The deduction for any casualty attributable to a federally declared disaster occurring in 2008 remained limited to the amount of the loss that exceeds $100. The deduction for any casualty attributable to a federally declared disaster occurring in 2009, however, is limited to the amount of the loss that exceeds $500. The limitation amount for tax years beginning after 2009, however, will return to $100.

Job Expenses and Most Other Miscellaneous Deductions, Lines 21-27

Miscellaneous Deduction Facts

Employee business expenses typically represent the largest part of miscellaneous deductions subject to the 2%-of-AGI floor.

Line 21, Unreimbursed Employee Expenses

The taxpayer can deduct only unreimbursed employee expenses that meet the following three criteria:

1. They are paid or incurred during the tax year.
2. They are for carrying on the taxpayer's trade or business of being an employee.
3. They are ordinary and necessary: An expense is ordinary if it is common and accepted in the taxpayer's type of trade or business. An expense is necessary if it is appropriate and helpful to the taxpayer's trade or business.

Caution. Many employee claims for business expense deductions have been denied when the employees could not prove that the employers *expected* them to make the expenditures. Taxpayers should request written authorization from the employer at the time the expense is incurred.

See IRS Publication 463, *Travel, Entertainment, Gift, and Car Expenses*, for more information.

Form 2106. Form 2106 (see Tab 6) must be completed and attached if either of the following applies:

- Travel, transportation, meal, or entertainment expenses are claimed.
- The employer has reimbursed any of the job expenses reportable on line 21.

If Form 2106 need not be attached, the expenses should be listed directly on the dotted lines by line 21; a separate page can be attached if there are too many to fit.

Work-Related Education. Education expenses are deductible, even if the education may lead to a degree, if the education meets at least one of the following two tests:

- It maintains or improves skills required in the taxpayer's present work.
- It is required by the taxpayer's employer or the law in order for the taxpayer to keep his or her salary, status, or job, and the requirement serves a business purpose of the taxpayer's employer.

If the education meets either of these tests, expenses for tuition, books, supplies, laboratory fees, and similar items, and even certain transportation costs, are deductible.

Nondeductible Job-Related Education. The taxpayer cannot deduct expenses for education, even if one or both of the preceding tests are met, if either of the following is true:

- The education is needed to meet the *minimum educational requirements* to qualify the employee in his or her trade or business.
- The education will lead to qualifying the taxpayer for a new trade or business. (If the education qualifies the taxpayer for a new trade or business, expenses are not deductible even if there is no intention to enter that trade or business.)

The "new trade or business" disqualification does not disqualify expenses of the education if new duties involve the same general type of work.

Example. A teacher who is required by his or her district to take summer school courses can deduct expenses. A teacher who takes courses to become qualified in an additional subject area or grade level has deductible expenses.

A teacher who takes courses to obtain a basic teaching certificate does not have qualified education expenses.

A computer technician who takes computer programming courses probably cannot deduct expenses, unless it could be shown that the programming was connected to his or her present position.

A dentist's expenses in studying to become an orthodontist have been ruled as deductible (Rev. Rul. 74-78).

A lawyer who takes a course to become qualified in another state has deductible educational expenses, but an accountant taking a CPA prep course does not (Rev. Rul. 69-292).

Planning Tip. The cost of travel for educational benefit is not by itself a deductible expense. However, it may be a deductible business expense if it is linked to the trade or business of the traveler (e.g., a professor of Russian history traveling to do research in Russia).

Employee Home Expenses

- The cost of household employees such as maids or babysitters is not deductible on Schedule A (it may qualify for a credit; see Tab 10).
- The cost of long-distance phone calls made for business usually is deductible, as is the cost of business-related features such as call forwarding.

Planning Tip. Basic telephone service is always considered a personal expense. A cell phone used for business will be deductible only to the extent long distance and specific overage charges are attributable to the business if no other personal phone line is maintained by the taxpayer.

Example. George works day shift as a typesetter. His computer is shared with a night-shift worker, but his employer wants him to occasionally put in overtime. However, the employer has no extra computer for George to work on, so George buys one to meet the employer's needs. William also works as a typesetter, but for a company that provides him with a computer and access to the building 24 hours per day. The employer permits William to work at home in the evenings to care for his children, but does not require him to. George may deduct depreciation on his computer, but William may not, because his computer is not being used for the employer's convenience.

- The cost of installing a second phone exclusively for business is deductible.
- Depreciation on a computer or cell phone (or other IRC §179 property), if required by an employer, is deductible. In this case Form 4562, Part V, must also be submitted, and the straight-line method over the ADS recovery period must be used. This deduction is available even if the device is used less than 50% of the time for business. If it is used more than 50% for business or is part of a home office, the accelerated depreciation deduction may be claimed. See Tab 7.
- Expenses for keeping an office at home for the employer's convenience are deductible.

Job Search Expenses. Certain expenses of looking for a new job in the taxpayer's present occupation are deductible, even if the search is not successful. The taxpayer has to be currently employed or recently unemployed. The following are deductible:

- Employment agency fees
- Resume expenses–amounts spent for typing, printing, and mailing copies of a resume to prospective employers
- Advertising expenses
- Career counseling costs
- Meal and entertainment expenses, 50%
- Travel and transportation expenses directly related to employment search. The amount of time spent on personal activity compared with the amount of time spent in looking for work is important in determining whether a trip is primarily personal or is primarily to look for a new job. Even if the travel expenses to and from an area are not deductible, the expenses of looking for a new job while in the area are deductible.

Caution. In general, expenses of seeking a job outside one's current trade or business are not deductible.

Miscellaneous Expenses 2009

Expense	Is It Deductible?
Annuities, unrecovered cost of, on decedent's return	Fully deductible
Appraisal fees (charitable contributions and casualty losses)	Deductible, subject to 2%-of-AGI floor
Business bad debt	Deductible, subject to 2%-of-AGI floor
Cell phone	Depreciation is deductible, subject to 2% floor if cell phone is required by employer (line 21), or if used to produce other income (line 23)
Club dues	Not deductible (with certain exceptions)
Collecting interest or dividends, fees for	Deductible, subject to 2%-of-AGI floor
Commuting expenses, to regular place of employment	Not deductible
Commuting expenses, to temporary place of employment	Deductible subject to 2%-of-AGI floor (with Form 2106)
Computer	Depreciation is deductible, subject to 2%-of-AGI floor if computer is required by employer (line 21), or if used to produce other income (line 23)
Convenience fee charged by the card processor for paying income tax (including estimated tax payments) by credit or debit card	Deductible, subject to 2%-of-AGI floor
Credit card fees to pay taxes	Not deductible
Damages paid to former employer for breach of employment contract	Deductible, subject to 2%-of-AGI floor

Miscellaneous Expenses 2009 (Continued)

Expense	Is It Deductible?
Dividend reinvestment plans, service charges for	Deductible, subject to 2%-of-AGI floor
Employee business expenses: travel, 50% of meals and entertainment, professional books and journals, home office deductions, supplies, depreciation on property used for business	Deductible, subject to 2%-of-AGI floor
Estate taxes	Fully deductible, if already collected on the same taxable income reported on return
Funeral expenses	Not deductible
Gambling losses	Deductible, up to amount of winnings
Handicapped job-related expenses	Fully deductible
Hobby expenses	Deductible, subject to 2%-of-AGI floor and up to amount of hobby income
Homeowners' associations assessments	Not deductible except as business expense
House repairs or improvements (personal residence)	Not deductible
Investments, expenses (e.g., office help) for maintaining	Deductible, subject to 2%-of-AGI floor
IRA investments, loss on	Deductible, subject to 2%-of-AGI floor
Job-hunting expenses	Deductible, subject to 2%-of-AGI floor
Job-related education expenses	Deductible, subject to 2%-of-AGI floor
Legal fees: divorce, representation before IRS and courts, estate planning not related to tax matters, representation in lawsuits, except to protect business reputation	Not deductible
Legal fees: for collecting or producing taxable income, keeping a job, obtaining tax advice, filing business-related voluntary bankruptcy	Deductible, subject to 2%-of-AGI floor
Licenses (marriage, drivers, dog, etc.)	Not deductible
Life insurance	Not deductible
Loss on deposits	Deductible, subject to 2%-of-AGI floor
Malpractice insurance premiums	Deductible, subject to 2%-of-AGI floor
Medical exams, if required by employer	Deductible, subject to 2%-of-AGI floor
Miscellaneous investment expenses	Deductible, subject to 2%-of-AGI floor
Parking tickets and other fines for illegal acts, even if incurred for business purposes	Not deductible
Passport expense, if job-related	Deductible, subject to 2%-of-AGI floor
Pass-through entities, indirect miscellaneous deductions	Deductible, subject to 2%-of-AGI floor
Personal living expenses	Not deductible
Personal residence, loss on sale of	Not deductible
Political contributions	Not deductible
Professional dues	Deductible, subject to 2%-of-AGI floor
Repayment of income	Deductible, netted against reportable income, subject to 2%-of-AGI floor if under $3,000, or fully deductible over $3,000 (see page 2-34)
Research expenses (college professor)	Deductible, subject to 2%-of-AGI floor
Safe deposit box fees	Deductible, subject to 2%-of-AGI floor
Safe in home, installation costs	Deductible, subject to 2%-of-AGI floor
Sales tax, unless added to cost of business expenses	Not deductible (see page 2–10)
Tax preparation and other personal tax assistance	Deductible, subject to 2%-of-AGI floor
Teacher's classroom expenses	Deductible, subject to 2%-of-AGI floor and up to $250 may be taken as above-the-line deduction (see Tab 1)
Telephone expenses of first line to personal residence	Not deductible, even if used for business
Tools, disposable within one year	Deductible, subject to 2%-of-AGI floor

Miscellaneous Expenses 2009 (Continued)

Expense	Is It Deductible?
Tools, useful life more than one year	Depreciation deductible, subject to 2%-of-AGI floor
Trust administration fees	Deductible, subject to 2%-of-AGI floor
Undeveloped land management, expenses	Deductible, subject to 2%-of-AGI floor
Union dues	Deductible, subject to 2%-of-AGI floor
Work clothes and uniforms, if not suitable for wear outside work	Deductible, subject to 2%-of-AGI floor

Work Clothes and Uniforms

- Wearing work clothes or uniforms must be a condition of employment.
- The clothes must not be suitable for everyday wear.
- The cost of protective clothing, such as safety shoes or boots, safety glasses, hard hats, and work gloves, is deductible.
- *Examples:* delivery workers, firefighters, health care workers, law enforcement officers, letter carriers, professional athletes, and transportation workers (air, rail, bus, etc.). Musicians and entertainers can deduct the cost of theatrical clothing and accessories that are not suitable for everyday wear. However, according to the IRS, work clothing consisting of white cap, white shirt or jacket, white bib overalls, and standard work shoes, which a painter might be required by his union to wear on the job, is not distinctive in character or in the nature of a uniform.

Commuting

- Not deductible for travel between the home and the regular workplace.
- Deductible if traveling to a temporary workplace outside the metropolitan area that contains both the taxpayer's home and the permanent workplace. Work locations are considered temporary if the work is expected to last less than one year.
- Deductible if the taxpayer works at two places in a day, whether or not for the same employer; you can generally deduct the expenses of getting from one workplace to the other.

Caution. A taxpayer who reports to a central dispatching location and then goes to a worksite is considered to be commuting. This travel is not deducible.

Line 22, Tax Preparation Fees

These fees are usually deductible in the year paid. Thus, on the 2009 return, fees paid in 2009 for preparing the taxpayer's 2008 return may be deducted. These fees can include the cost of tax preparation software programs and tax publications, legal and accounting fees, and any fee paid for electronic filing. Expenses for preparing Schedules C, E, and F should be deducted on the respective schedules; all other expenses are deducted on line 22.

Line 23, Other Expenses

The three basic categories for "other expenses" listed by the IRS in Publication 529 are expenses incurred for the following:

- To produce or collect income that must be included in gross income
- To manage, conserve, or maintain property held for producing such income
- To determine, contest, pay, or claim a refund of any tax

Items listed as deductible subject to the 2% floor in the table on page 2-32 are listed on line 23 if they are not employee related.

Return of Income. A taxpayer may sometimes have to return income that he or she was not entitled to (such as Social Security payments or unemployment compensation). If the mistake is found in the same year and the taxpayer repays it in the same year, the amount repaid is simply not entered on any form.

Under Code Sec. 1341, if the money is repaid in a later year, and it is $3,000 or less, the taxpayer has to deduct the repayment amount on line 23. There is no way to recover the tax benefit if the taxpayer does not itemize deductions.

If the amount repaid in a later year is greater than $3,000, and the taxpayer can establish a claim of right (i.e., he or she appeared to have a right to the money), the taxpayer has a choice: claim the money on line 28 (no 2%-of-AGI floor) or claim a tax credit for the difference caused by the added income in the previous year's taxes.

Example. Roger Hahn was mistakenly awarded $3,500 of unemployment compensation in 2008. This added $750 to his and his wife's joint tax total for 2008. He repaid all the money in 2009. He and his wife itemize deductions, and they do not exceed the AGI limitation. They first figure their tax using the $3,500 as a deduction, but they do not have enough other deductions to make itemizing advantageous over taking the standard deduction. Therefore, they will take a tax credit for $750, the amount that they overpaid in 2008.

Code Sec. 1341 does not apply to the following:

- Deductions for bad debts
- Deductions for sales to customers, such as returns and allowances
- Deductions for legal expenses of contesting the repayment

Hobby Loss. Losses from hobbies that produce income are deducted here, but only to the extent that income was reported above the line. Making the distinction between a hobby and a business (where all expenses are deductible on different forms) can be a difficult call. See Tabs 3 and 16 for information on factors that go into determining whether an activity is a business or a hobby.

Lines 24-27, Calculation

Example. John and Mary Wysocki have an AGI of $47,500 for 2009. Mary was required to use a cell phone and a laptop computer in her work, and she can claim $135 of depreciation on them for the year. In addition, they had an uninsured casualty loss of $8,000 on their personal residence, which required a $200 appraisal to calculate. John, a high school teacher, paid $240 in union dues and $975 in education expenses (including travel) for a course that he was required to take by his district. He had $125 in additional travel and meal expenses for attending required seminars. Also, 2010 is the first year that they have paid for tax preparation assistance.

They can claim a $3,150 casualty loss on line 20, calculated as $8,000 – $100 – (0.10 × $47,500 = $4,750). They will also submit a Form 4684. They can claim a deduction of $1,475 on line 21 (they will also submit Forms 4562 and 2106) and a deduction of $200 on line 23. They get no deduction on line 22 because they did not pay any fees in 2009. Because 2% of their income is $950 (line 26), they enter $725 on line 27.

Other Miscellaneous Deductions, Line 28

Deductions Not Subject to the 2% Limit

- Amortizable premium on taxable bonds (usually claimed as an offset to investment income, but can be deducted here instead if an election to do so was made after 1998)
- Casualty and theft losses on income-producing property (note that this deduction is not subject to the $100 subtraction or the 10% personal casualty floor)
- Federal estate tax on income in respect of a decedent
- Gambling losses up to the amount of gambling winnings
- Impairment-related work expenses of persons with disabilities
- Repayments of more than $3,000 under a claim of right
- Unrecovered investment in an annuity

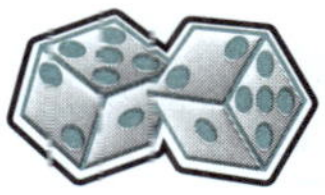

Gambling Losses. No gambling losses may be deducted unless gambling winnings are reported above the line. Gambling winnings must be reported as income even if no Form W-2G is issued.

Form W-2G must be issued by the payor when there is

- $600 or more of winnings and the payout is 30 times or more greater than the stake
- $1,200 or more in winnings from bingo or slot machines
- $1,500 net winnings from keno
- Any other net winnings over $5,000

Gambling winnings and losses include lotteries, raffles, bets on athletic contests, bingo, bets on horse or dog racing, and all casino wagering, among other activities. Office pools and similar personal wagering activities are not included.

The taxpayer should keep an adequate log of winnings and losses. The log should include the date, location, amount, type of gambling, and results. Because winnings must be reported in full, not netted against losses, as income, winnings and losses should be kept separate on the log.

The IRS suggest the following notations in the diary for the following gambling activities:

- **Keno:** Copies of the keno tickets purchased that were validated by the gambling establishment, copies of casino credit records, and copies of your casino check-cashing records
- **Slot machines:** A record of the machine number and all winnings by date and time the machine was played
- **Table games (twenty-one, blackjack, craps, poker, baccarat, roulette, wheel of fortune, etc.):** The number of the table; casino credit card data in-

dicating whether the credit was issued in the pit or at the cashier's cage

- **Bingo:** A record of the number of games played, cost of tickets purchased, and amounts collected on winning tickets, plus receipts from the casino, parlor, etc.
- **Racing (horse, harness, dog, etc.):** A record of the races, amounts of wagers, amounts collected on winning tickets and amounts lost on losing tickets, plus unredeemed tickets and payment records from the racetrack
- **Lotteries:** A record of ticket purchases, dates, winnings and losses, plus unredeemed tickets, payment slips, and winnings statements

Planning Tip. Getting information on losses and winnings is a vital part of the initial interview of new clients, and a vital part of planning for subsequent years.

Note: Travel, meal, and entertainment expenses are not deductible for a nonprofessional gambler.

Caution. For a joint gambling lottery venture, all participants should sign up in advance with allocations preset. Doing so after the fact can be a real problem.

Impairment-Related Work Expenses. Work expense as the result of a physical or mental disability that limits the taxpayer from being employed or substantially limits one or more of the taxpayer's major life activities–such as performing manual tasks, walking, speaking, breathing, learning, or working–is fully deductible on line 28. The definition of work expense for this deduction is the same as for other employee-related expenses: "ordinary" and "necessary."

Unrecovered Investment in Annuity. A retiree who contributed to the cost of an annuity can exclude from income a part of each payment received as a tax-free return of the retiree's investment. If the retiree dies before the entire investment is recovered tax-free, any unrecovered investment can be deducted on the retiree's final income tax return.

Filing Tip. Statutory employees (e.g., certain insurance agents and outside salespersons) can claim their business expenses on Schedule C and, therefore, are not subject to the 2% floor. See Tab 3 for more details on whether the client qualifies.

Filing Tip. If an expense is an annual payment, double up by paying on January 1 and December 31 one year and not at all the next, then repeat. This may get the deduction over the applicable limitation for itemizing.

Total Itemized Deductions, Lines 29-30

The overall AGI limitation on itemizing for 2009 is $166,800 for all taxpayers, except that for MFS it is $83,400. The total of certain itemized deductions is reduced by 3% of the amount of AGI above these thresholds. The total of affected deductions cannot, however, be reduced by more than 80%.

The reduction does not apply to medical expenses, casualty, theft, or gambling losses, or investment interest.

Example. Pragnya Chakravarti received the interest payments shown on the following Schedule B. She also received nominee interest of $400.

			Amount
1	List name of payer. If any interest is from a seller-financed mortgage and the buyer used the property as a personal residence, see instructions on back and list this interest first. Also, show that buyer's social security number and address ▶		
	State Bank 1		400
	State Bank 2		1,500
	U.S. Government		730
	Local Bank A		950
	Subtotal		3,580
	Nominee Distribution	1	400
2	Add the amounts on line 1	2	3,180

It does apply to real estate and income (or sales) taxes, interest paid on home mortgages, charitable contributions (but not for qualified contributions for relief efforts in the Midwestern disaster area), and miscellaneous deductions. Other limitations already discussed are, of course, applied before this reduction due to AGI.

Phase-out of itemized deduction limits. The high income limitation on itemized deductions is being phased out from 2006 through 2009. For tax years beginning in 2009, the limit will be reduced by two-thirds. Thus, for 2009, after the regular limitation is determined, the taxpayer must take this amount and multiply it by one-third. This resulting fractional amount of the limitation is the amount by which the taxpayer's otherwise allowable itemized deductions must be reduced.

The reduction for exceeding the AGI limit is computed as follows for 2009:

1. The excess of the AGI over $166,800 (or $83,400) is computed.
2. The sum of the medical expenses, casualty or theft losses, gambling losses, and investment interest deductions is computed and subtracted from the total deductions.
3. The 3% reduction is computed by multiplying 0.03 by the amount from step 1.
4. The 80% limit is found by multiplying the amount in step 2 by 0.8.
5. The two-thirds "phase-out" reduction is computed by multiplying the lesser of steps 3 and 4 by 1/3.
6. The result from step 5 is subtracted from the total amount of itemized deductions.

See MTG ¶ 1014.

Example. David and Harriet Green file a joint return. They have AGI of $200,000 in 2009. Their total deductions of $22,250 include $4,200 in medical costs and $800 in investment interest. The rest is entirely attributable to charitable contributions and state income tax, so the amount subject to reduction is $22,250 – $5,000 = $17,250. Their total is reduced by 3% × ($200,000 – $166,800) = $996. Since this total is less than 80% of $17,250, it is multiplied by 1/3 = $332. As a result, their itemized deductions (subject to reduction) are reduced to $17,250 – $332 = $16,918. Therefore, their total itemized deductions are $16,918 + $5,000 = $21,918.

Line 30 directs the taxpayer to check a box if the taxpayer elects to itemize deductions even though they are less than the taxpayer's standard deduction. This might be the case if, for example, the taxpayer would pay less total tax because the excess of the taxpayer's state standard deduction over the taxpayer's state itemized deductions was greater than the excess of the Federal itemized deductions over the Federal standard deduction.

Schedule B: Interest and Ordinary Dividends

Part I: Interest, Lines 1-4

Part I must be filled out if (a) taxable interest income is greater than $1,500; (b) the exclusion of interest from series EE bonds issued after 1989 is being used; (c) any interest is being received as a nominee; (d) any interest was received from a seller-financed mortgage on a property the buyer used as a home; (e) a Form 1099-INT was received for interest on a bond bought between interest payment dates, for interest on frozen deposits, or for U.S. savings bond interest that was reported before 2003; (f) the taxpayer had any foreign account; (g) the taxpayer elects to reduce interest from bonds acquired after 1987 by any amortizable bond premium; or (h) there is a discrepancy between OID reported by the taxpayer and that shown on Form(s) 1099-OID.

See IRS Publication 550, *Investment Income and Expenses*, for detailed information.

Nominee Interest

A taxpayer may receive a Form 1099 as a nominee, meaning that the taxpayer does not own the proceeds. The following procedure must be used for reporting nominee interest:

- Report the amount of interest as usual on line 1 of Schedule B.
- Under the last amount listed on line 1, total up all the amounts entered.
- On the line under this subtotal, write "Nominee Distribution" and enter the total interest received as a nominee.
- Subtract the nominee interest and enter the result on line 2.
- Issue a 1099-INT to the actual owner of the interest (unless the owner is the taxpayer's spouse).
- File a 1099-INT and Form 1096, *Annual Summary and Transmittal of U.S. Information Returns*, with the IRS.

An example illustrating the reporting of nominee interest appears below.

Planning Tip. If your client is assigning someone as a nominee, he or she should do so in writing, which should lessen the chance of confusion in coming years

Original Issue Discount (OID)

If a bond is issued at a price lower than its stated redemption value, the difference is called OID. This is simply a form of interest. The issuer of the bond reports a portion of OID each year to the bondholder on Form 1099-OID.

- **Debt instruments issued after 1954 and before May 28, 1969 (before July 2, 1982, if a government instrument)**–OID is not reported until the year the obligation is sold, exchanged, or redeemed. If a gain results and the instrument is a capital asset, the amount of the gain equal to the OID is ordinary interest income and the rest is capital gain. If there is a loss on the sale, the entire loss is a capital loss and no reporting of OID is required. If a bond is purchased in the secondary market, the interest shown on the Form 1099-OID is not accurate unless the bond was purchased at exactly its original price, and the total OID has to be adjusted. Rules for adjusting the OID depend on when the debt instrument was issued and what kind it is.
- **Debt instruments issued after May 27, 1969 (after July 1, 1982, if a government instrument), and before 1985**–If held as capital assets, include any discount on these debt instruments as a part of the discount in gross income each year that the taxpayer owns the instruments. The taxpayer's basis in the instrument is increased by the amount of OID included in gross income.
- **Debt instruments issued after 1984**–Report the total OID that applies each year regardless of whether the taxpayer holds the debt instrument as a capital asset. The taxpayer's basis in the instrument is increased by the amount of OID included in gross income.

Details for calculating OID where necessary can be found in IRS Publication 1212, *List of Original Issue Discount Instruments*.

The OID reporting rules do not apply to the following debt instruments:

- Tax-exempt obligations (but must be accrued for increasing holder's basis to determine gain/loss if sold before maturity)
- U.S. savings bonds
- Short-term debt instruments (less than one year to maturity)
- Obligations issued by an individual before March 2, 1984
- Most loans between individuals

Stripped Bonds and Coupons. A *stripped bond* is a bond from which all of the interest coupons have been detached. *Stripped coupons* are the detached interest coupons. Without special rules, a bondholder could sell a stripped bond for less than he paid for the bond with the coupons and recognize a capital loss. Current law, however, prevents this scenario by mandating that the bondholder allocate between the bond without the coupons and the coupons. The bond and the coupons are then treated as having been issued with an OID. The allocation must be based on the FMV of the bond and of the coupons on the date that either the bond or a coupon is sold without the other. In addition, the bondholder must report any accrued interest at the time of the sale of the bond, and the basis of the bond is adjusted accordingly. See MTG ¶1952.

Figuring the OID. A full discussion of the OID rules is contained in IRC §§1271–1288. The rules provide a formula for allocating the OID attributable to a bond (or other debt instrument) over the expected term of the bond. The objective of this formula is to amortize OID in a manner approximating the way in which interest would accrue on a bond that was issued for its face amount and paid a market interest rate.

The formula for allocating OID to particular taxable periods is contained in IRC §1272(a)(3) and explained in the many pages of Proposed Regulations under that section. This statutory formula provides a method for spreading the total OID attributable to a bond over the bond's term.

Line 1, List Name of Payer

Form 1099-INT. Interest income is generally reported on Form 1099-INT or Form 1099-OID, or a similar statement, by banks, savings and loans, and other payors of interest. This form, which shows the interest received during the year, should be kept for the taxpayer's records, but does not have to be attached to the tax return.

> **Planning Tip.** The name of the company or institution that issued the Form 1099 should always be used. Otherwise, the IRS's computer matching program will show unreported income.
>
> Note that electronic filing enhances IRS access to matching 1099 information, leading to much faster CP-2000 follow-up letters.

Seller-Financed Mortgage. If the taxpayer has financed the sale of his or her personal residence during 2009, all interest paid by the buyer must be listed on line 1, along with the buyer's name, address, and Social Security number. In order to avoid a penalty, the seller must provide all the information just mentioned, and must also give the buyer the same information.

This information should precede all other entries on line 1.

Bank Accounts and Certificates of Deposit. Interest is usually taxable in the year it is earned. Thus, interest earned on a passbook savings account on December 31, 2009, is taxable in 2009, even though the depositor did not present the passbook for the crediting of interest until 2010.

Interest on CDs is taxable in the year earned if the taxpayer has the right to use the income. Some short-term CDs do not give the depositor the right to use the interest until after the full maturity.

Example. Josh Brown purchases a six-month CD on August 15, 2009. He does not have the right to access the interest until the CD matures. Even though he earns interest from August 15 through December 31, 2009, that interest will not be taxed until 2010.

Note: Amounts received from money market funds are taxable as dividends, not as interest income. Report them on line 5 of Schedule B.

REMICs and CMOs. Holders of REMICs (real estate mortgage investment conduits) or CMOs (collateralized mortgage obligations) have special reporting rules. Holders of these instruments should not count on written information on amounts to include until March 15, 2010, and then should follow instructions accompanying the written information.

Refunds on Adjustable-Rate Mortgages. If a taxpayer with an adjustable-rate mortgage on his or her principal residence receives a refund as a result of recalculation of the interest rate, the refund is considered interest income in the year paid.

Caution. Failure to report interest income in the year received can result in backup withholding on future interest and dividends. The backup withholding rate for 2009 is 28%.

U.S. Treasury Bills, Notes, and Bonds

Treasury bills, notes, and bonds are direct debt obligations of the U.S. government, and interest on these is subject to federal income tax. However, interest income from Treasury bills, notes, and bonds is exempt from all state and local income taxes.

U.S. savings bonds currently offered to individuals include the following:

- Series HH bonds–The U.S. Treasury stopped issuing Series HH bonds after August 31, 2004. Bonds already held will continue to earn interest until maturity. These bonds were issued at face value. Interest is paid twice a year by direct deposit to a holder's bank account. A cash-method taxpayer must report interest on these bonds as income in the year received. Series HH bonds were first offered in 1980 and mature in 20 years.

Example. Devon purchases a $1,000 Giganto Corp. bond from Oliver on June 1, 2009. This bond bears interest of 6%, payable semiannually, on January 1 and July 1. Devon pays Oliver $1,025 for the bond, because $25 of the $30 payment due on July 1 has already accrued.

Oliver will report $55 of interest income on the bond for 2009 ($30 January 1 payment and $25 accrued interest). Capital gain and loss rules do not apply to his sale of the bond. Devon will report interest income of only $5 from the bond. On Schedule B, he follows the method outlined for nominees (see page 2–37), but he writes "Accrued Interest" instead of "Nominee Distribution."

Lines 1 and 2 of Devon's Schedule B will show the entire $55 of interest and the reduction by $50 of accrued interest:

			Amount
1	List name of payer. If any interest is from a seller-financed mortgage and the buyer used the property as a personal residence, see instructions on back and list this interest first. Also, show that buyer's social security number and address ▶		
	State Bank 1		**5,000**
	Giganto Corp		**55**
	Subtotal		**5,055**
	Accrued Interest	1	**50**
2	Add the amounts on line 1	2	**5,005**

- Series EE bonds–Interest on these bonds is payable when the bond is redeemed. The difference between the purchase price and the redemption value is taxable interest. Series EE bonds were first offered in July 1980 and have a maturity period of 30 years.
- Series I bonds–Series I bonds were first offered in 1998. These are inflation-indexed bonds issued at their face amount with a maturity period of 30 years. The face value plus all accrued interest is payable at maturity.

Treasury Inflation-Indexed Debt Securities (TIPs). This relatively new type of Treasury obligation gives investors current interest and adjusts for inflation as well. If there is no significant purchase discount (less than $25 for a 10-year bond), these securities produce income each year (usually twice a year) that will be regarded as regular interest. Any adjustment based on inflation is then taken into account under the rules for OID (Reg. §1.1275-7). If the premium is greater than the *de minimis* amount, all income will be considered OID.

Filing Tip. TIP bonds can produce significant income, and should usually be purchased for IRAs or other retirement plans in which the income tax can be deferred.

Series E and EE Bonds. These U.S. savings bonds are issued at less than face value (i.e., at a discount) (series E bonds are no longer issued). The increase in value each year represents interest but for cash-basis taxpayers is not reportable until maturity (30 years) unless the bond is cashed before that year. No further interest will be paid after maturity.

There is an election to report the income in each year instead of reporting the entire amount at maturity. This election to report annually may be made in the year the bond is purchased or in any year thereafter. If the election is made in a later year, the entire amount of interest accrued to that time must be reported in that year. Also, once this election is made, it applies to all bonds currently owned or acquired in the future, unless permission is given to change back to the lump-sum reporting method.

Filing Tip. The election to report income annually is generally attractive for low-income elderly taxpayers and children not subject to the "kiddie tax," because the small yearly interest may escape taxation altogether.

Changing the method of reporting is done by filing Form 3115, *Application for Change in Accounting Method*, with the tax return for the year of change, noting at the top that it is "Filed under Rev. Proc. 2008-52" and listing all bonds to which the change applies. Note that accrual-basis taxpayers cannot change the way they account for this bond income, because they automatically report income when it accrues.

Planning Tip. For children who may be subject to the "kiddie tax," the use of series EE or I savings bonds is a way to defer interest income.

State or Local Government Obligations

Interest received on an obligation issued by a state or local government is generally not taxable for federal tax purposes. The issuer of tax-exempt state or local bond interest is required to furnish to the buyer Form 1099-INT (or a substitute statement) reporting the aggregate amount of tax-exempt interest. If the taxpayer invested in the obligation through a trust, fund, or other organization, that organization should issue this information.

Interest on state and local government bonds is taxable if the bonds are "private activity" bonds, unless a specific exemption is included in the IRC. The following state and local government bonds are nontaxable:

- Bonds for exempt facilities, such as airports and other commuting facilities, water-furnishing facilities, sewage facilities, residential rental projects, local furnishing of energy resources, and qualified hazardous-waste disposal facilities
- Mortgage revenue bonds
- Qualified small-issue bonds (less than $10 million and available for manufacturing facilities)
- Student loan bonds
- Qualified development bonds
- Qualified 501(c)(3) bonds

Caution. Interest on "private activity" bonds issued after August 7, 1986, is a preference item that may be subject to AMT.

Interest on a bond used to finance government operations generally is not taxable if the bond is issued by a state, the District of Columbia, a U.S. possession, or any of their political subdivisions. Political subdivisions include:

- Port authorities
- Toll road commissions
- Utility services authorities
- Community redevelopment agencies

Example. Bette Saver received $2,700 of Series EE bond interest on bonds bought in January 1997 and redeemed in December 2009. She used the entire $2,700 on the expenses incurred for college costs of her son, Brett, in excess of those that she used to calculate the Hope credit. She did not, however, use all of the principal of these bonds ($12,300) toward these expenses. Her modified AGI for 2009 is $71,850. To calculate the exclusion of Series EE bond interest, she multiplies the fraction ($71,850 – $69,950 = $1,900)/$15,000 = 0.127 by the interest on the total bond proceeds used to pay Brett's qualified education expenses ($2,700 × 0.233 = $630) and gets $80. The excludable interest is thus $630 – $80 = $550. This is figured on Form 8815, which must be attached to Schedule B:

Form **8815**

Department of the Treasury
Internal Revenue Service (99)

Exclusion of Interest From Series EE and I U.S. Savings Bonds Issued After 1989
(For Filers With Qualified Higher Education Expenses)
▶ Attach to Form 1040 or Form 1040A.

OMB No. 1545-0074
2009
Attachment Sequence No. **167**

Name(s) shown on return	Your social security number
Bette Saver	000-00-0000

1 (a) Name of person (you, your spouse, or your dependent) who was enrolled at or attended an eligible educational institution	(b) Name and address of eligible educational institution
Brett Saver	University of Illinois Urbana, IL

If you need more space, attach a statement.

2	Enter the total qualified higher education expenses you paid in 2009 for the person(s) listed in column (a) of line 1. See the instructions to find out which expenses qualify			2	8,000
3	Enter the total of any nontaxable educational benefits (such as nontaxable scholarship or fellowship grants) received for 2009 for the person(s) listed in column (a) of line 1 (see instructions)			3	4,500
4	Subtract line 3 from line 2. If zero or less, **stop.** You **cannot** take the exclusion			4	3,500
5	Enter the total proceeds (principal and interest) from all series EE and I U.S. savings bonds **issued after 1989** that you **cashed during 2009**			5	15,000
6	Enter the interest included on line 5 (see instructions)			6	2,700
7	If line 4 is equal to or more than line 5, enter "1.000." If line 4 is less than line 5, divide line 4 by line 5. Enter the result as a decimal (rounded to at least three places)			7	× .233
8	Multiply line 6 by line 7			8	630
9	Enter your modified adjusted gross income (see instructions) **Note:** *If line 9 is $84,950 or more if single or head of household, or $134,900 or more if married filing jointly or qualifying widow(er),* ***stop.*** *You* ***cannot*** *take the exclusion.*	9	71,850		
10	Enter: $69,950 if single or head of household; $104,900 if married filing jointly or qualifying widow(er)	10	69,950		
11	Subtract line 10 from line 9. If zero or less, skip line 12, enter -0- on line 13, and go to line 14	11	1,900		
12	Divide line 11 by: $15,000 if single or head of household; $30,000 if married filing jointly or qualifying widow(er). Enter the result as a decimal (rounded to at least three places)			12	× .127
13	Multiply line 8 by line 12			13	80
14	**Excludable savings bond interest.** Subtract line 13 from line 8. Enter the result here and on Schedule B (Form 1040A or Form 1040), line 3 ▶			14	550

- Qualified volunteer fire departments (for certain obligations issued after 1980)

Nongovernment Bonds

Interest on all nongovernment types of bonds is taxable.

Selling a Bond. If a bond is sold during 2009, part of its sale price is attributable to interest accrued up to the date of sale. The seller must report the interest accrued up to that time, and the buyer subtracts the accrued interest to that point from the full interest amount listed on Schedule B. (The buyer's basis in the bond is also reduced by the amount of interest accrued up to the point of sale.)

Below-Market Loans and Imputed Interest

Interest on below-market loans is considered interest income, and an additional amount of interest may be added to taxable interest income. A below-market loan is one on which interest is charged at a rate lower than market value (or the applicable federal rate, or AFR), sometimes at no interest whatsoever. If such loans were allowed without tax consequences, it could result in an untaxed shift of income from the lender to the borrower. It could also result in the recharacterization of income from interest income to capital gain income, which may be more favorably taxed. Under current law, however, the lender is treated as having (1) made a loan to the borrower at the statutory rate and (2) made a payment to the borrower. This payment is treated as a gift, dividend, contribution to capital, compensation, or other payment, depending on the type of transaction. The size of the deemed payment depends on the imputed interest, which is based on how much the government has to spend to borrow money in a given month.

K-1 filers must be careful in handling loans. In the absence of documents showing intent or agreed process, the IRS can reclassify the "loan" as wages and assess accordingly or impute interest and then assess tax, penalty, and interest for under-reporting.

Exceptions. If the loan is considered a "gift loan," there is no imputed interest if the amount of the loan is not over $10,000. Nor is there any imputed interest if a gift loan up to $100,000 is made to a child to help pay for a principal residence, if the child's investment income does not exceed $1,000. If the child's investment income is greater than $1,000, the imputed interest cannot be greater than the child's total investment income.

> **Example.** Jonas Livemore loaned his daughter $50,000 interest-free to help purchase her home. If her investment income is $750 in 2009, Jonas has no tax liability on the imputed interest. If her investment income is $1,500, Jonas's imputed interest will be no more than $1,500.

The IRS, in Revenue Rulings, publishes AFR tables every month for short-, mid-, and long-term loans. In the case of demand loans that were outstanding for all of 2009 with the principal balance constant, the IRS interest rate is 0.82%.

Demand Loans versus Term Loans. A demand loan is any loan that is payable in full on demand of the lender, including those with indefinite maturity dates. Term loans are any other loans.

> **Filing Tip.** The $10,000 "gift loan" limit is unrelated to the $13,000 annual gift-tax limit for 2009 (see Tab 14). However, the $10,000 limit does apply to all outstanding loans from the lender to a single borrower, including those charging interest.

Line 3, Excludable Interest on Series EE and I U.S. Savings Bonds Issued after 1989

Interest on series EE or I U.S. savings bonds cashed in 2009 and issued after 1989 may be excludable from interest income if used to pay qualified higher education costs. The following tests have to be met:

- The bondholder cashed qualified U.S. savings bonds in 2009 that were issued after 1989.
- The bondholder paid qualified higher education expenses in 2008 for self, spouse, or dependents, or to a qualified state tuition program or education IRA.
- The bondholder's filing status is any status except married filing separately. The bondholder's modified AGI is less than $84,950 if single or HOH, or $134,900 if MFJ or QW; exclusion is phased out beyond $69,950 for single or HOH and $104,900 for MFJ and QW. ("Modified" in this case means without regard to the foreign income exclusion and income from U.S. possessions.)
- The bondholder was at least 24 years old when the bonds were purchased.

The excludable portion of interest on Series EE or I U.S. savings bonds is computed on Form 8815. See the example on page 2-41.

> **Caution.** The amount of higher education costs taken into account for figuring the exclusion of interest on college savings bonds has to be reduced by the expenses taken into account in figuring the Hope credit or the lifetime learning credit (see Tab 10).

Phaseout. The phaseout is calculated by multiplying a fraction by the amount of interest on series EE bonds bought after 1989 and used for qualified education purposes, then subtracting the result from the amount otherwise excludable. The numerator of the fraction is the excess of modified AGI over the phaseout trigger, and the denominator is $15,000 for single or HOH and $30,000 for MFJ or QW.

Line 4, Subtract Line 3 from Line 2

If this amount is over $1,500, then Part III must be completed. The result entered on line 4 is also entered on line 8a of Form 1040.

Part II: Ordinary Dividends, Lines 5-6

See IRS Publication 550, Investment Income and Expenses, for detailed information.

Ordinary Dividends. Ordinary (taxable) dividends are the most common type of distribution from a corporation. They are paid out of the earnings and profits of a corporation and are ordinary income. This means that they are not capital gains. Any dividend received on common or preferred stock is an ordinary dividend unless the paying corporation tells the taxpayer otherwise. Ordinary dividends will be shown in box 1a of Form 1099-DIV.

Qualified Dividends. Qualified dividends are the ordinary dividends received in tax years beginning after 2002 that are subject to the same 0% or 15% maximum tax rate that applies to net capital gains. They will be shown in box 1b of Form 1099-DIV. Qualified dividends are subject to the 15% rate if the regular tax rate that would apply is 25% or higher. If the regular tax rate that would apply is lower than 25%, qualified dividends are subject to the 0% rate.

> **Caution.** Even though dividends are taxable at the long-term capital gain rate, they may not be used to offset capital losses.

> **Filing Tip.** The holding period for eligibility of dividends for 0% or 15% treatment is more than 60 days; be sure the client knows how to count the holding period (i.e., don't count the day of acquisition). Also, the holding period is reduced if holdings are offset by a corresponding short position.

Nonqualified Dividends. Not all dividends are qualified for the capital gain rates. Common stock must be owned for at least 61 days during the 121-day period beginning 60 days before the ex-dividend date (see Tab 4). (Some preferred stock has a longer holding period; see IRS Publication 550.) Dividends paid by a foreign corporation qualify only if its stock trades on a U.S. exchange. The following are also not qualified dividends, even if shown as such in box 1b of Form 1099-DIV:

- Dividends from money market funds (for balanced funds, the portion allocated to stock holdings does qualify)
- Dividends from benevolent life insurance associations, credit unions, certain trusts, and tax-exempt farmers' cooperatives
- Dividends paid on deposits in mutual savings banks, cooperative banks, domestic building savings and loan associations, and similar savings institutions
- Dividends paid on employer securities held in retirement plans
- Dividends received from REITs if certain requirements are met
- Dividends generated by regulated investment companies
- The extent to which a taxpayer is under a payment obligation, as in a covered call

Distributions from Savings Accounts. Distributions from savings accounts are not considered dividends. They should be reported as interest income and reported in Part I, if Part I has to be filled out.

"Dividends" on Insurance Policies. So-called dividends paid by insurance companies to holders of annuity, endowment, or unmatured life insurance policies are not true dividends. Because they serve simply to reduce the cost of the policy, they are not reportable as income, whether they are applied toward payment of the premiums or received in cash.

If total dividends *do* exceed the premiums paid, however, the excess is taxable as interest, not dividends. All dividends received after the policy has matured are also taxable as interest.

Dividends in Additional Stock. A corporation may issue dividends in the form of additional stock in the company rather than in cash. Such dividends are tax free unless they raise the receiver's proportion of ownership in the company. If an option is offered to take either cash or stock, however, the dividends are taxable.

A dividend in the form of a right to acquire stock (*stock rights*) is taxed in much the same way as a stock dividend. They are not taxable unless there is a cash option, or percentage-of-ownership increases, or the distribution can be converted to preferred stock.

Liquidating Dividends. These dividends are paid when a corporation dissolves and disposes of all its assets. They are a return of the investor's capital and are not taxable unless they exceed the investment, in which case they are taxable as a capital gain on Form 1040. Upon complete liquidation, if total distributions are less than invested, it may be treated as a capital loss on Schedule D.

Mutual Fund Dividends. Distributions from a mutual fund could be of three kinds: ordinary dividends, nontaxable distributions (return of capital), and capital gain distributions. A mutual fund will notify its stockholders within 60 days of the close of its tax year what portion of the dividends distributed should be reported as long-term capital gains. It will also report what portion of the undistributed capital gains should be reported as long-term capital gains.

Ordinary dividends are reported as dividend income. Capital gains are reported as long-term capital gain (see Tab 4).

If the mutual fund has paid a tax on an undistributed capital gain, shareholders are entitled to a credit or refund of the tax, since it is deemed as paid by them. In such a case, the company should send Form 2439,

Notice to Shareholder of Undistributed Long-Term Capital Gains, to indicate the tax paid.

Planning Tip. If dividends are not distributed to the investor, be sure to add the undistributed dividends to the basis of the fund shares.

Foreign Tax Paid. If a mutual fund invests overseas, it may be able to allocate foreign tax to its shareholders, as reported in box 6 of Form 1099-DIV. An investor who receives a foreign tax allocation has a choice: claim the foreign tax as an itemized deduction, or claim a foreign tax credit. The itemized deduction provides a small benefit (and none at all for some taxpayers) but is easy to take. The tax credit usually provides a larger benefit; see Tab 10 for calculation of the foreign tax credit.

Filing Tip. Calculation of a foreign tax credit of over $300 ($600 for MFJ) requires knowledge of the names of countries the mutual fund was investing in. Such information is not usually available on the Form 1099-DIV but should be available in the fund's annual report.

Part III: Foreign Accounts and Trusts

Because the IRS is concerned about abusive tax shelters in other countries, it wants to know about every taxpayer's foreign investments. Because tax shelters tend to be used primarily by people with significant investment income, the IRS puts this mini-information return at the bottom of Schedule B.

Caution. Clients with foreign accounts and trusts merit close detail checking, since the IRS has placed these accounts near the top of its audit priorities.

Line 7, Signature Authority over Foreign Account

Line 7 asks taxpayers, "At any time during 2009, did you have an interest in or a signature or other authority over a financial account in a foreign country, such as a bank account, securities account, or other financial account? ... If 'Yes,' enter the name of the foreign country."

A taxpayer must check the "Yes" box on line 7a if either of the following applies:

1. The taxpayer owns more than 50% of the stock in any corporation that owns one or more foreign bank accounts.
2. At any time during the year the taxpayer had an interest in or signature or other authority over a financial account in a foreign country (such as a bank account, securities account, or other financial account). This does not apply to foreign securities held in a U.S. securities account.

A taxpayer with a foreign account has to check "Yes" here, unless one of the IRS's exceptions is met:

- The combined value of all accounts was $10,000 or less during the entire year.
- The accounts were with a U.S. military banking facility operated by a U.S. financial institution.
- The taxpayer was an officer or employee of a commercial bank supervised by the Comptroller of the Currency, the Board of Governors of the Federal Reserve System, or the Federal Deposit Insurance Corporation; the account was in an employer's name; and the taxpayer did not have a personal financial interest in the account.
- The taxpayer was an officer or employee of a domestic corporation with securities listed on national securities exchanges or with assets of more than $1 million and 500 or more shareholders of record; the account was in the employer's name; the taxpayer did not have a personal financial interest in the account; *and* the corporation's chief financial officer has given the taxpayer written notice that the corporation has filed a current report that includes the account.

Form TD F 90-22.1 contains information needed to determine who is considered to have an interest in or signature or other authority over a financial account in a foreign country.

Anyone who checked the "Yes" box on line 7a must file Form TD F 90-22.1 with the Department of the Treasury, at the address shown on that form, by June 30, 2010. Do not attach it to Form 1040.

Line 8, Foreign Trusts

Line 8 asks taxpayers, "During 2009, did you receive a distribution from, or were you the grantor of, or transferor to, a foreign trust? If 'Yes,' you may have to file Form 3520."

A taxpayer who received a distribution (including a loan) from a foreign trust must provide additional information, on either Form 3520, *Annual Return to Re-*

port Transactions with Foreign Trusts and Receipt of Certain Foreign Gifts, or Form 926, *Return of a U.S. Transferor of Property to a Foreign Corporation.*

Caution. Anyone required to file Form TD F 90-22.1 who fails to do so may have to pay a penalty of up to $10,000 (more in some cases). If a taxpayer may meet any of the requirements listed for checking "Yes" on line 7a, review Form TD F 90-22.1 carefully.

Taxpayers who checked the "Yes" box on line 7a must also enter the name of the foreign country or countries in the space provided on line 7b. A separate statement may be attached if more space is required.

Qualified Mortgage Insurance Premiums Deduction Worksheet—Line 13

Keep for Your Records

Before you begin: √ See the instructions for line 13 on page A-7 to see if you must use this worksheet to figure your deduction.

1. Enter the total premiums you paid in 2009 for qualified mortgage insurance for a contract issued after December 31, 2006 . . . . . . **1.** ______
2. Enter the amount from Form 1040, line 38 . . . . . . **2.** ______
3. Enter $100,000 ($50,000 if married filing separately) . . . . . . **3.** ______
4. Is the amount on line 2 more than the amount on line 3?
   - ☐ **No.** Your deduction is not limited. Enter the amount from line 1 above on Schedule A, line 13. **Do not** complete the rest of this worksheet.
   - ☐ **Yes.** Subtract line 3 from line 2. If the result is not a multiple of $1,000 ($500 if married filing separately), increase it to the next multiple of $1,000 ($500 if married filing separately). For example, increase $425 to $1,000, increase $2,025 to $3,000; or if married filing separately, increase $425 to $500, increase $2,025 to $2,500, etc. . . . . . . **4.** ______
5. Divide line 4 by $10,000 ($5,000 if married filing separately). Enter the result as a decimal. If the result is 1.0 or more, enter 1.0 . . . . . . **5.** ___ . ___
6. Multiply line 1 by line 5 . . . . . . **6.** ______
7. **Qualified mortgage insurance premiums deduction.** Subtract line 6 from line 1. Enter the result here and on Schedule A, line 13 . . . . . . **7.** ______

State and Local General Sales Tax Deduction Worksheet—Line 5b
(See the *Instructions for Line 5b Worksheet* that begin on page A-3.) *Keep for Your Records*

Before you begin: See the instructions for line 1 on page A-3 if you:
- √ Lived in more than one state during 2009, or
- √ Had any **nontaxable** income in 2009.

1. Enter your **state** general sales taxes from the applicable table on page A-12 or A-13 (see page A-3) . . **1.** $______

Next. If, for all of 2009, you lived only in Connecticut, the District of Columbia, Indiana, Kentucky, Maine, Maryland, Massachusetts, Michigan, New Jersey, Rhode Island, or West Virginia, skip lines 2 through 5, enter -0- on line 6, and go to line 7. Otherwise, go to line 2.

2. Did you live in Alaska, Arizona, Arkansas, California (Los Angeles County only), Colorado, Georgia, Illinois, Louisiana, Missouri, New York State, North Carolina, South Carolina, Tennessee, Utah, or Virginia in 2009?

☐ **No.** Enter -0-

☐ **Yes.** Enter your **local** general sales taxes from the applicable table on page A-14 (see page A-3) . . . . **2.** $______

3. Did your locality impose a **local** general sales tax in 2009? Residents of California and Nevada see page A-5.

☐ **No.** Skip lines 3 through 5, enter -0- on line 6, and go to line 7.

☐ **Yes.** Enter your **local** general sales tax rate, but omit the percentage sign. For example, if your local general sales tax rate was 2.5%, enter 2.5. If your local general sales tax rate changed or you lived in more than one locality in the same state during 2009, see page A-5. (If you do not know your local general sales tax rate, contact your local government.) . . . . **3.** __.__

4. Did you enter -0- on line 2 above?

☐ **No.** Skip lines 4 and 5 and go to line 6.

☐ **Yes.** Enter your **state** general sales tax rate (shown in the table heading for your state), but omit the percentage sign. For example, if your state general sales tax rate is 6%, enter 6.0 . . . . **4.** __.__

5. Divide line 3 by line 4. Enter the result as a decimal (rounded to at least three places) **5.** __.__

6. Did you enter -0- on line 2 above?

☐ **No.** Multiply line 2 by line 3

☐ **Yes.** Multiply line 1 by line 5. If you lived in more than one locality in the same state during 2009, see the instructions on page A-5 . . . . **6.** $______

7. Enter your state and local general sales taxes paid on specified items, if any (see page A-5) . . . . **7.** $______

8. **Deduction for general sales taxes.** Add lines 1, 6, and 7. Enter the result here and the total from all your state and local general sales tax deduction worksheets, if you completed more than one, on Schedule A, line 5. Be sure to check **box b** on that line . . . . **8.** $______

2009 Optional State and Certain Local Sales Tax Tables

Income / Exemptions

Alabama 4.0000%

At least	But less than	1	2	3	4	5	Over 5
$0	$20,000	203	239	264	282	298	319
20,000	30,000	310	362	397	424	446	477
30,000	40,000	365	425	465	496	521	557
40,000	50,000	413	479	524	558	586	626
50,000	60,000	458	530	578	615	645	688
60,000	70,000	500	576	627	667	700	746
70,000	80,000	540	621	675	717	752	800
80,000	90,000	578	663	720	764	801	852
90,000	100,000	615	704	763	809	848	901
100,000	120,000	666	759	822	870	910	967
120,000	140,000	737	836	903	955	998	1059
140,000	160,000	801	906	977	1032	1077	1141
160,000	180,000	868	978	1053	1110	1158	1225
180,000	200,000	930	1045	1122	1183	1232	1302
200,000 or more		1271	1407	1499	1571	1630	1713

Arizona 5.6000%

At least	But less than	1	2	3	4	5	Over 5
$0	$20,000	219	237	249	258	265	274
20,000	30,000	364	393	412	425	436	451
30,000	40,000	443	478	499	516	529	546
40,000	50,000	514	553	577	596	610	630
50,000	60,000	579	623	650	670	686	708
60,000	70,000	641	688	718	739	757	781
70,000	80,000	702	752	783	807	825	851
80,000	90,000	759	812	846	871	890	917
90,000	100,000	815	871	906	932	953	982
100,000	120,000	891	951	988	1016	1039	1069
120,000	140,000	999	1064	1105	1135	1159	1192
140,000	160,000	1098	1167	1210	1242	1268	1303
160,000	180,000	1200	1273	1319	1353	1380	1418
180,000	200,000	1295	1372	1420	1456	1485	1524
200,000 or more		1816	1910	1970	2014	2050	2099

Arkansas 6.0000%

At least	But less than	1	2	3	4	5	Over 5
$0	$20,000	287	319	340	356	368	386
20,000	30,000	475	526	559	584	604	631
30,000	40,000	574	635	674	704	727	760
40,000	50,000	662	731	775	809	835	872
50,000	60,000	742	818	867	904	934	975
60,000	70,000	816	899	952	992	1025	1069
70,000	80,000	887	976	1034	1077	1111	1159
80,000	90,000	954	1049	1110	1156	1193	1243
90,000	100,000	1017	1118	1183	1231	1270	1324
100,000	120,000	1103	1211	1280	1332	1374	1431
120,000	140,000	1222	1339	1415	1472	1518	1580
140,000	160,000	1327	1454	1535	1596	1645	1712
160,000	180,000	1434	1569	1656	1721	1774	1846
180,000	200,000	1532	1675	1767	1835	1891	1967
200,000 or more		2039	2221	2337	2424	2495	2591

California[1, 2] 8.0034%

At least	But less than	1	2	3	4	5	Over 5
$0	$20,000	285	309	323	334	343	355
20,000	30,000	482	519	542	559	573	591
30,000	40,000	589	633	660	681	697	719
40,000	50,000	686	736	767	790	808	833
50,000	60,000	776	831	865	891	911	939
60,000	70,000	862	921	958	986	1008	1038
70,000	80,000	945	1009	1049	1078	1102	1134
80,000	90,000	1025	1092	1135	1166	1191	1226
90,000	100,000	1102	1174	1218	1251	1278	1314
100,000	120,000	1208	1284	1332	1367	1395	1434
120,000	140,000	1358	1441	1493	1531	1562	1604
140,000	160,000	1496	1584	1639	1680	1713	1758
160,000	180,000	1638	1731	1790	1834	1869	1916
180,000	200,000	1771	1869	1931	1977	2014	2064
200,000 or more		2504	2624	2701	2757	2803	2865

Colorado 2.9000%

At least	But less than	1	2	3	4	5	Over 5
$0	$20,000	105	114	119	123	127	131
20,000	30,000	171	184	193	200	205	212
30,000	40,000	206	223	233	240	246	254
40,000	50,000	239	257	268	276	283	292
50,000	60,000	269	288	301	310	317	327
60,000	70,000	297	318	331	341	349	360
70,000	80,000	324	347	361	372	380	392
80,000	90,000	351	375	390	401	410	422
90,000	100,000	376	401	417	429	438	451
100,000	120,000	411	438	454	467	477	491
120,000	140,000	461	490	508	521	532	547
140,000	160,000	506	537	556	570	582	597
160,000	180,000	554	586	606	621	633	650
180,000	200,000	598	631	653	668	681	698
200,000 or more		842	882	908	927	943	963

Connecticut 6.0000%

At least	But less than	1	2	3	4	5	Over 5
$0	$20,000	216	229	238	244	249	256
20,000	30,000	369	392	406	416	424	435
30,000	40,000	452	479	496	508	518	531
40,000	50,000	526	557	576	590	601	616
50,000	60,000	593	628	649	665	677	694
60,000	70,000	656	694	717	735	748	766
70,000	80,000	717	758	783	802	816	836
80,000	90,000	774	818	845	865	880	901
90,000	100,000	829	875	904	925	942	964
100,000	120,000	902	952	983	1006	1024	1048
120,000	140,000	1005	1060	1094	1119	1139	1166
140,000	160,000	1096	1156	1193	1220	1241	1270
160,000	180,000	1189	1254	1293	1322	1345	1376
180,000	200,000	1274	1343	1385	1416	1440	1473
200,000 or more		1718	1807	1862	1902	1933	1976

District of Columbia[1] 5.8130%

At least	But less than	1	2	3	4	5	Over 5
$0	$20,000	177	188	194	199	203	208
20,000	30,000	303	320	330	337	343	352
30,000	40,000	373	393	405	414	421	430
40,000	50,000	436	458	472	482	490	501
50,000	60,000	495	519	534	546	554	566
60,000	70,000	550	577	593	605	615	628
70,000	80,000	604	633	651	664	674	688
80,000	90,000	656	686	705	719	730	745
90,000	100,000	706	738	758	773	784	800
100,000	120,000	774	808	830	845	858	874
120,000	140,000	871	908	931	948	962	980
140,000	160,000	959	999	1023	1042	1056	1075
160,000	180,000	1049	1092	1118	1137	1153	1174
180,000	200,000	1133	1178	1206	1227	1243	1265
200,000 or more		1590	1647	1681	1707	1727	1754

Florida 6.0000%

At least	But less than	1	2	3	4	5	Over 5
$0	$20,000	228	249	263	272	280	291
20,000	30,000	385	419	440	456	469	486
30,000	40,000	471	512	537	556	571	591
40,000	50,000	549	594	623	644	662	685
50,000	60,000	621	671	703	727	746	771
60,000	70,000	689	744	778	804	824	852
70,000	80,000	755	814	851	878	901	931
80,000	90,000	819	881	920	950	973	1005
90,000	100,000	880	946	987	1018	1043	1077
100,000	120,000	964	1034	1078	1112	1138	1175
120,000	140,000	1083	1159	1207	1244	1273	1312
140,000	160,000	1191	1273	1325	1363	1394	1437
160,000	180,000	1303	1390	1445	1486	1519	1565
180,000	200,000	1408	1499	1557	1601	1636	1683
200,000 or more		1982	2096	2168	2222	2265	2325

Georgia 4.0000%

At least	But less than	1	2	3	4	5	Over 5
$0	$20,000	147	160	169	175	179	186
20,000	30,000	240	260	272	281	289	299
30,000	40,000	290	313	328	339	347	359
40,000	50,000	335	361	377	389	399	412
50,000	60,000	377	405	423	436	447	461
60,000	70,000	416	447	466	480	492	507
70,000	80,000	454	487	507	523	535	552
80,000	90,000	491	525	547	563	576	594
90,000	100,000	527	563	586	602	616	635
100,000	120,000	575	614	638	656	670	690
120,000	140,000	645	686	712	731	747	768
140,000	160,000	708	752	779	800	816	839
160,000	180,000	774	820	849	870	888	912
180,000	200,000	835	883	914	936	955	979
200,000 or more		1174	1232	1269	1296	1318	1349

Hawaii 4.0000%

At least	But less than	1	2	3	4	5	Over 5
$0	$20,000	245	280	302	319	333	353
20,000	30,000	388	440	474	500	521	551
30,000	40,000	462	523	562	593	618	652
40,000	50,000	526	594	639	673	700	739
50,000	60,000	583	658	707	745	775	817
60,000	70,000	637	718	771	811	844	889
70,000	80,000	687	774	830	873	908	957
80,000	90,000	735	826	886	932	969	1020
90,000	100,000	780	876	939	987	1026	1080
100,000	120,000	840	943	1010	1061	1102	1160
120,000	140,000	923	1035	1107	1162	1208	1270
140,000	160,000	997	1116	1193	1252	1300	1367
160,000	180,000	1071	1197	1280	1342	1393	1464
180,000	200,000	1139	1272	1358	1424	1478	1552
200,000 or more		1487	1652	1759	1841	1907	1999

Idaho 6.0000%

At least	But less than	1	2	3	4	5	Over 5
$0	$20,000	300	353	388	415	437	469
20,000	30,000	466	544	596	636	670	716
30,000	40,000	553	643	703	750	788	842
40,000	50,000	630	730	797	849	892	951
50,000	60,000	700	809	882	939	985	1050
60,000	70,000	766	883	961	1022	1072	1142
70,000	80,000	830	954	1037	1101	1155	1229
80,000	90,000	890	1021	1109	1176	1232	1311
90,000	100,000	949	1086	1178	1248	1307	1389
100,000	120,000	1028	1173	1270	1345	1407	1494
120,000	140,000	1140	1296	1400	1481	1548	1641
140,000	160,000	1242	1406	1517	1603	1673	1772
160,000	180,000	1346	1520	1637	1727	1802	1906
180,000	200,000	1444	1626	1748	1842	1920	2030
200,000 or more		1977	2196	2343	2457	2552	2684

Illinois 6.2500%

At least	But less than	1	2	3	4	5	Over 5
$0	$20,000	233	259	276	289	299	314
20,000	30,000	376	416	442	461	477	498
30,000	40,000	453	500	530	552	570	595
40,000	50,000	522	574	607	633	653	681
50,000	60,000	586	643	680	707	729	760
60,000	70,000	647	708	747	777	801	833
70,000	80,000	706	771	813	844	869	904
80,000	90,000	763	831	875	908	935	972
90,000	100,000	817	889	935	970	998	1037
100,000	120,000	892	968	1017	1054	1084	1125
120,000	140,000	999	1080	1133	1173	1205	1249
140,000	160,000	1096	1183	1238	1280	1314	1361
160,000	180,000	1197	1288	1347	1391	1427	1477
180,000	200,000	1292	1387	1449	1495	1533	1584
200,000 or more		1816	1930	2003	2059	2105	2167

Indiana 7.0000%

At least	But less than	1	2	3	4	5	Over 5
$0	$20,000	280	307	325	338	348	363
20,000	30,000	454	496	523	544	560	582
30,000	40,000	547	597	628	652	671	697
40,000	50,000	628	685	720	747	768	798
50,000	60,000	703	765	805	834	857	890
60,000	70,000	773	840	883	914	940	975
70,000	80,000	840	912	958	992	1019	1056
80,000	90,000	904	980	1028	1064	1093	1133
90,000	100,000	965	1045	1096	1134	1164	1206
100,000	120,000	1046	1132	1187	1227	1260	1304
120,000	140,000	1161	1254	1313	1357	1393	1441
140,000	160,000	1264	1364	1427	1474	1512	1563
160,000	180,000	1368	1475	1542	1592	1632	1687
180,000	200,000	1465	1577	1647	1700	1743	1801
200,000 or more		1972	2112	2201	2268	2321	2394

Iowa 6.0000%

At least	But less than	1	2	3	4	5	Over 5
$0	$20,000	255	279	294	305	313	326
20,000	30,000	433	471	495	513	527	547
30,000	40,000	528	574	603	624	641	665
40,000	50,000	612	665	697	722	742	768
50,000	60,000	690	748	784	812	834	863
60,000	70,000	762	825	865	895	919	951
70,000	80,000	831	899	943	975	1001	1036
80,000	90,000	896	969	1015	1050	1077	1115
90,000	100,000	959	1036	1085	1122	1151	1191
100,000	120,000	1042	1126	1179	1218	1249	1292
120,000	140,000	1159	1251	1309	1352	1386	1433
140,000	160,000	1264	1363	1425	1471	1508	1559
160,000	180,000	1370	1475	1542	1592	1632	1686
180,000	200,000	1467	1579	1650	1702	1745	1802
200,000 or more		1971	2116	2207	2275	2329	2403

Kansas 5.3000%

At least	But less than	1	2	3	4	5	Over 5
$0	$20,000	285	332	364	389	410	438
20,000	30,000	453	525	574	612	643	686
30,000	40,000	540	625	682	726	762	812
40,000	50,000	616	712	775	824	865	921
50,000	60,000	685	790	860	913	958	1020
60,000	70,000	749	862	937	995	1043	1110
70,000	80,000	810	930	1011	1073	1124	1195
80,000	90,000	867	994	1079	1145	1199	1275
90,000	100,000	921	1056	1145	1214	1271	1351
100,000	120,000	994	1137	1232	1306	1366	1451
120,000	140,000	1095	1249	1353	1432	1498	1590
140,000	160,000	1184	1349	1459	1544	1614	1712
160,000	180,000	1274	1449	1566	1656	1731	1834
180,000	200,000	1357	1541	1664	1758	1837	1946
200,000 or more		1781	2010	2163	2280	2377	2513

Kentucky 6.0000%

At least	But less than	1	2	3	4	5	Over 5
$0	$20,000	220	242	257	268	276	288
20,000	30,000	363	399	421	438	451	470
30,000	40,000	442	483	510	529	545	567
40,000	50,000	512	559	588	611	629	653
50,000	60,000	577	629	661	686	706	733
60,000	70,000	639	695	730	756	778	807
70,000	80,000	699	759	796	825	848	879
80,000	90,000	757	820	860	890	914	947
90,000	100,000	813	879	921	953	978	1013
100,000	120,000	889	959	1004	1038	1065	1102
120,000	140,000	997	1074	1122	1159	1188	1229
140,000	160,000	1097	1178	1229	1268	1300	1343
160,000	180,000	1199	1285	1340	1381	1415	1460
180,000	200,000	1295	1385	1443	1486	1521	1569
200,000 or more		1824	1935	2005	2059	2102	2161

Louisiana 4.0000%

At least	But less than	1	2	3	4	5	Over 5
$0	$20,000	159	172	180	186	191	198
20,000	30,000	271	292	306	316	324	334
30,000	40,000	333	358	374	386	395	408
40,000	50,000	388	416	435	448	459	473
50,000	60,000	439	471	491	506	517	534
60,000	70,000	487	521	543	559	572	590
70,000	80,000	533	570	594	611	625	644
80,000	90,000	577	617	642	661	676	696
90,000	100,000	620	662	689	708	724	745
100,000	120,000	677	723	751	772	789	812
120,000	140,000	759	808	839	862	881	906
140,000	160,000	832	885	919	944	963	990
160,000	180,000	907	964	1000	1027	1048	1077
180,000	200,000	977	1037	1075	1103	1126	1156
200,000 or more		1351	1427	1475	1511	1539	1578

Maine 5.0000%

At least	But less than	1	2	3	4	5	Over 5
$0	$20,000	149	159	166	170	174	179
20,000	30,000	252	268	278	285	291	299
30,000	40,000	309	328	340	348	355	365
40,000	50,000	361	382	396	405	413	423
50,000	60,000	410	433	448	458	467	478
60,000	70,000	456	481	497	508	518	530
70,000	80,000	502	528	545	557	567	580
80,000	90,000	545	574	591	604	615	629
90,000	100,000	588	618	636	650	661	675
100,000	120,000	646	678	697	712	723	739
120,000	140,000	730	763	785	800	813	830
140,000	160,000	806	842	864	881	894	912
160,000	180,000	886	924	947	965	979	998
180,000	200,000	961	1000	1025	1043	1058	1078
200,000 or more		1378	1425	1454	1476	1494	1518

Maryland 6.0000%

At least	But less than	1	2	3	4	5	Over 5
$0	$20,000	215	236	250	261	269	280
20,000	30,000	349	382	402	418	431	448
30,000	40,000	421	460	484	502	517	537
40,000	50,000	487	529	557	577	594	616
50,000	60,000	548	594	624	646	664	689
60,000	70,000	606	656	688	711	731	757
70,000	80,000	662	715	749	775	795	823
80,000	90,000	717	773	808	835	857	886
90,000	100,000	770	828	866	894	916	947
100,000	120,000	843	904	943	973	997	1030
120,000	140,000	947	1013	1055	1087	1112	1147
140,000	160,000	1043	1112	1157	1190	1217	1254
160,000	180,000	1143	1216	1262	1297	1326	1365
180,000	200,000	1238	1313	1361	1398	1428	1468
200,000 or more		1769	1856	1912	1955	1990	2038

Massachusetts[1] 5.5240%

At least	But less than	1	2	3	4	5	Over 5
$0	$20,000	166	178	186	191	196	202
20,000	30,000	269	288	299	308	315	324
30,000	40,000	326	347	361	370	378	389
40,000	50,000	378	401	416	426	435	447
50,000	60,000	426	451	467	479	488	501
60,000	70,000	472	498	515	528	538	551
70,000	80,000	517	545	562	576	586	601
80,000	90,000	560	589	607	621	632	647
90,000	100,000	602	632	651	666	677	693
100,000	120,000	659	691	711	726	738	755
120,000	140,000	742	775	796	812	825	843
140,000	160,000	817	852	874	891	904	923
160,000	180,000	896	932	955	973	987	1006
180,000	200,000	971	1008	1031	1049	1063	1083
200,000 or more		1384	1425	1451	1471	1487	1509

Michigan 6.0000%

At least	But less than	1	2	3	4	5	Over 5
$0	$20,000	215	236	249	258	266	277
20,000	30,000	351	382	402	417	429	446
30,000	40,000	424	461	485	502	516	535
40,000	50,000	490	532	558	578	593	615
50,000	60,000	552	597	626	647	665	688
60,000	70,000	610	659	690	713	732	757
70,000	80,000	667	719	752	776	796	823
80,000	90,000	721	776	811	837	858	886
90,000	100,000	774	831	868	895	918	948
100,000	120,000	846	907	946	975	998	1030
120,000	140,000	948	1014	1056	1087	1113	1147
140,000	160,000	1042	1112	1156	1190	1217	1253
160,000	180,000	1139	1213	1260	1295	1324	1362
180,000	200,000	1230	1308	1357	1394	1424	1464
200,000 or more		1734	1827	1887	1932	1968	2017

Minnesota[1] 6.6890%

At least	But less than	1	2	3	4	5	Over 5
$0	$20,000	224	239	248	255	261	268
20,000	30,000	387	411	427	438	447	459
30,000	40,000	476	505	524	537	548	562
40,000	50,000	555	589	610	625	638	654
50,000	60,000	628	666	689	707	720	739
60,000	70,000	696	738	764	783	798	818
70,000	80,000	762	807	835	856	872	894
80,000	90,000	825	873	903	925	942	966
90,000	100,000	885	936	968	991	1010	1035
100,000	120,000	966	1021	1056	1081	1101	1128
120,000	140,000	1080	1141	1179	1206	1228	1258
140,000	160,000	1182	1248	1289	1319	1342	1374
160,000	180,000	1286	1357	1401	1433	1458	1493
180,000	200,000	1382	1457	1504	1538	1565	1602
200,000 or more		1887	1985	2046	2090	2126	2173

Mississippi 7.0000%

At least	But less than	1	2	3	4	5	Over 5
$0	$20,000	393	451	489	519	543	576
20,000	30,000	628	717	776	821	858	909
30,000	40,000	750	855	924	976	1020	1079
40,000	50,000	857	975	1052	1111	1160	1227
50,000	60,000	954	1083	1168	1233	1286	1360
60,000	70,000	1043	1183	1274	1345	1402	1482
70,000	80,000	1128	1278	1376	1451	1512	1598
80,000	90,000	1208	1366	1470	1550	1615	1705
90,000	100,000	1284	1451	1561	1644	1713	1808
100,000	120,000	1385	1563	1680	1770	1843	1944
120,000	140,000	1526	1719	1846	1943	2022	2132
140,000	160,000	1651	1857	1993	2096	2181	2298
160,000	180,000	1777	1996	2140	2250	2340	2465
180,000	200,000	1892	2123	2274	2390	2485	2616
200,000 or more		2483	2772	2961	3105	3223	3387

Missouri 4.2250%

At least	But less than	1	2	3	4	5	Over 5
$0	$20,000	161	181	194	204	212	223
20,000	30,000	265	296	316	331	343	360
30,000	40,000	320	357	380	398	413	432
40,000	50,000	370	411	438	458	474	496
50,000	60,000	417	462	491	513	531	555
60,000	70,000	461	509	541	564	584	610
70,000	80,000	503	555	589	614	635	663
80,000	90,000	544	599	634	661	683	713
90,000	100,000	584	641	679	707	730	762
100,000	120,000	638	699	739	769	793	827
120,000	140,000	714	781	824	856	883	919
140,000	160,000	784	855	901	935	964	1002
160,000	180,000	856	931	980	1017	1047	1088
180,000	200,000	924	1003	1054	1092	1124	1167
200,000 or more		1296	1393	1455	1503	1542	1595

Nebraska 5.5000%

At least	But less than	1	2	3	4	5	Over 5
$0	$20,000	233	252	263	272	279	289
20,000	30,000	395	426	446	460	471	487
30,000	40,000	483	520	543	560	574	593
40,000	50,000	560	603	629	649	665	686
50,000	60,000	632	679	708	730	748	772
60,000	70,000	698	750	782	806	825	851
70,000	80,000	761	817	852	878	899	927
80,000	90,000	821	881	918	946	968	998
90,000	100,000	879	942	982	1011	1035	1067
100,000	120,000	956	1024	1067	1099	1124	1158
120,000	140,000	1064	1139	1186	1220	1248	1286
140,000	160,000	1160	1241	1291	1329	1359	1399
160,000	180,000	1257	1344	1398	1438	1471	1514
180,000	200,000	1347	1439	1496	1539	1573	1619
200,000 or more		1812	1931	2005	2060	2104	2163

(Continued on next page)

2009 Optional State and Certain Local Sales Tax Tables *(Continued)*

Income		Nevada[1,3] 6.6764%						New Jersey[4] 7.0000%						New Mexico 5.0000%						New York 4.0000%						North Carolina[1] 4.8973%					
At least	But less than	1	2	3	4	5	Over 5	1	2	3	4	5	Over 5	1	2	3	4	5	Over 5	1	2	3	4	5	Over 5	1	2	3	4	5	Over 5
$0	$20,000	239	262	276	287	296	307	244	260	271	278	284	292	218	236	248	256	263	273	145	154	159	163	166	171	206	225	237	246	253	263
20,000	30,000	389	423	445	462	475	493	418	444	460	472	481	494	372	402	421	435	446	461	247	261	270	276	281	288	340	371	390	404	415	430
30,000	40,000	470	510	536	555	571	592	514	544	563	577	588	603	455	491	513	530	543	561	303	320	330	338	344	352	412	448	471	487	501	519
40,000	50,000	543	588	617	633	656	679	600	634	656	671	684	701	528	569	595	614	629	650	353	372	384	393	399	409	476	516	542	561	576	597
50,000	60,000	611	660	692	715	734	760	679	717	741	759	773	791	595	641	670	691	708	731	399	421	434	443	451	461	534	579	607	628	645	668
60,000	70,000	675	728	762	787	808	836	754	796	821	840	856	876	658	708	739	763	781	807	443	466	480	491	499	510	589	637	668	691	709	734
70,000	80,000	737	794	830	857	879	909	827	872	899	919	936	958	718	772	806	831	851	879	486	510	526	537	546	558	641	693	726	751	770	797
80,000	90,000	797	857	895	924	947	978	897	944	973	994	1012	1035	774	832	869	896	917	947	526	552	568	580	590	603	690	746	781	807	828	856
90,000	100,000	855	918	958	983	1013	1045	964	1013	1044	1067	1085	1110	828	890	929	958	981	1012	565	593	610	622	632	646	738	796	833	861	883	913
100,000	120,000	934	1001	1044	1076	1101	1136	1055	1107	1140	1165	1184	1211	907	968	1009	1040	1065	1099	618	647	666	679	690	704	801	864	904	933	957	989
120,000	140,000	1048	1120	1166	1200	1227	1265	1183	1241	1276	1303	1324	1353	1003	1076	1122	1156	1183	1220	693	725	745	759	771	787	890	959	1002	1035	1061	1096
140,000	160,000	1151	1227	1276	1312	1342	1382	1300	1361	1399	1427	1450	1481	1093	1172	1222	1258	1288	1327	760	794	816	831	844	861	970	1044	1090	1125	1153	1190
160,000	180,000	1258	1339	1390	1429	1460	1502	1419	1484	1525	1555	1579	1611	1185	1270	1323	1362	1394	1436	829	866	888	905	918	936	1051	1130	1179	1216	1246	1286
180,000	200,000	1359	1443	1497	1537	1570	1614	1530	1598	1641	1673	1698	1732	1270	1360	1416	1458	1491	1536	894	932	956	973	987	1006	1125	1209	1261	1300	1332	1374
200,000 or more		1915	2017	2082	2131	2170	2224	2125	2210	2263	2302	2333	2376	1708	1824	1897	1951	1994	2052	1238	1286	1315	1337	1355	1378	1517	1623	1690	1739	1779	1333

Income		North Dakota 5.0000%						Ohio 5.5000%						Oklahoma 4.5000%						Pennsylvania 6.0000%						Rhode Island 7.0000%					
At least	But less than	1	2	3	4	5	Over 5	1	2	3	4	5	Over 5	1	2	3	4	5	Over 5	1	2	3	4	5	Over 5	1	2	3	4	5	Over 5
$0	$20,000	168	191	206	217	226	239	225	242	253	261	268	277	223	259	282	300	315	336	203	218	227	234	239	246	239	258	269	278	285	294
20,000	30,000	276	311	334	351	365	385	376	404	422	434	445	459	356	411	447	474	497	529	340	362	376	386	395	406	387	415	433	446	457	471
30,000	40,000	335	376	403	423	440	463	459	491	512	527	539	556	427	491	533	565	592	628	414	440	457	469	479	492	466	499	520	536	548	564
40,000	50,000	389	434	464	487	506	531	532	569	592	610	623	642	490	561	608	644	674	715	481	510	529	542	553	568	535	573	596	614	628	646
50,000	60,000	439	489	521	546	567	595	600	641	667	686	701	721	548	626	677	717	749	795	543	575	595	610	622	639	599	641	666	685	701	721
60,000	70,000	486	540	575	602	624	654	664	708	736	757	773	795	602	686	741	784	819	868	601	636	658	674	687	704	659	704	731	752	768	791
70,000	80,000	533	590	628	656	680	712	725	773	803	825	843	867	655	744	803	849	886	938	657	695	718	735	749	768	716	764	794	816	834	857
80,000	90,000	577	638	677	708	732	767	784	834	866	890	909	934	705	799	862	910	950	1005	711	751	775	794	808	828	770	821	853	876	895	920
90,000	100,000	621	684	726	758	784	820	840	894	927	952	972	999	754	853	918	969	1010	1068	763	805	831	850	865	886	823	876	909	934	954	980
100,000	120,000	681	748	792	826	853	892	916	974	1010	1036	1058	1086	820	924	994	1048	1092	1154	834	878	905	926	942	964	893	950	985	1011	1032	1061
120,000	140,000	767	839	887	923	953	994	1024	1087	1126	1155	1178	1209	913	1026	1102	1160	1207	1274	934	981	1011	1033	1051	1075	991	1053	1091	1120	1143	1173
140,000	160,000	846	923	973	1011	1043	1086	1121	1188	1230	1261	1286	1319	999	1119	1199	1260	1311	1382	1024	1075	1106	1130	1149	1174	1079	1145	1186	1217	1241	1274
160,000	180,000	929	1010	1062	1103	1136	1182	1221	1292	1337	1370	1396	1432	1087	1214	1298	1363	1417	1492	1117	1171	1204	1229	1249	1276	1168	1239	1283	1315	1341	1376
180,000	200,000	1008	1091	1146	1189	1224	1272	1313	1389	1435	1470	1498	1536	1170	1303	1391	1459	1515	1594	1203	1259	1295	1321	1342	1370	1251	1325	1372	1406	1433	1470
200,000 or more		1448	1547	1613	1664	1705	1763	1808	1902	1961	2004	2039	2087	1627	1786	1893	1976	2044	2140	1668	1736	1779	1811	1837	1871	1686	1780	1838	1881	1915	1961

Income		South Carolina 6.0000%						South Dakota 4.0000%						Tennessee 7.0000%						Texas 6.2500%						Utah 4.7000%					
At least	But less than	1	2	3	4	5	Over 5	1	2	3	4	5	Over 5	1	2	3	4	5	Over 5	1	2	3	4	5	Over 5	1	2	3	4	5	Over 5
$0	$20,000	244	263	274	283	290	299	227	261	283	300	314	333	341	393	427	454	475	505	259	284	300	312	322	335	226	256	276	291	303	319
20,000	30,000	408	438	457	470	481	496	363	415	449	475	496	526	541	619	671	711	743	789	438	479	505	525	541	562	369	416	446	469	488	514
30,000	40,000	497	532	554	570	583	601	433	494	534	565	590	624	646	737	798	844	882	934	534	584	615	638	657	683	446	500	536	563	585	616
40,000	50,000	575	615	640	658	673	693	495	563	608	642	671	710	739	841	909	960	1002	1061	620	676	712	738	760	789	513	575	615	645	670	705
50,000	60,000	647	691	719	739	756	778	551	626	675	713	744	786	825	936	1010	1066	1112	1177	698	761	800	830	854	886	575	643	687	721	748	786
60,000	70,000	713	762	792	814	832	856	602	683	737	777	811	857	905	1024	1103	1164	1214	1283	771	839	882	915	941	976	633	707	754	791	820	861
70,000	80,000	778	830	863	887	906	932	651	738	795	839	874	924	981	1109	1193	1258	1311	1384	841	915	961	996	1024	1063	689	768	819	858	889	933
80,000	90,000	839	895	929	955	975	1003	697	789	850	896	934	986	1054	1188	1277	1346	1402	1480	907	985	1035	1073	1103	1144	742	825	880	921	954	1001
90,000	100,000	897	956	993	1020	1042	1071	741	838	902	950	990	1046	1124	1265	1358	1430	1489	1571	970	1054	1107	1146	1178	1221	793	881	938	982	1017	1066
100,000	120,000	976	1039	1079	1108	1131	1162	800	903	971	1023	1065	1124	1218	1368	1467	1543	1606	1692	1055	1145	1202	1244	1278	1325	862	955	1016	1063	1100	1153
120,000	140,000	1086	1155	1199	1231	1256	1290	881	993	1067	1123	1169	1233	1350	1512	1619	1701	1768	1862	1173	1272	1334	1381	1418	1469	958	1060	1126	1176	1217	1274
140,000	160,000	1185	1259	1306	1340	1367	1404	953	1072	1151	1211	1260	1329	1469	1641	1755	1842	1914	2013	1279	1385	1452	1502	1543	1598	1045	1153	1224	1278	1322	1382
160,000	180,000	1285	1365	1415	1451	1481	1520	1025	1153	1236	1300	1352	1425	1590	1772	1893	1985	2061	2167	1386	1500	1572	1626	1669	1728	1133	1249	1324	1381	1428	1492
180,000	200,000	1378	1462	1515	1554	1585	1626	1092	1226	1313	1381	1436	1512	1703	1894	2020	2117	2197	2307	1485	1605	1681	1738	1784	1847	1215	1337	1416	1476	1525	1593
200,000 or more		1863	1972	2039	2089	2128	2182	1432	1600	1709	1793	1862	1957	2302	2536	2691	2810	2908	3043	1997	2151	2250	2323	2382	2462	1651	1802	1901	1976	2037	2122

Income		Vermont 6.0000%						Virginia 4.0000%						Washington 6.5000%						West Virginia 6.0000%						Wisconsin 5.0000%					
At least	But less than	1	2	3	4	5	Over 5	1	2	3	4	5	Over 5	1	2	3	4	5	Over 5	1	2	3	4	5	Over 5	1	2	3	4	5	Over 5
$0	$20,000	140	147	151	154	156	159	161	182	196	207	215	227	259	282	297	308	317	329	283	318	342	359	373	393	209	227	238	246	253	262
20,000	30,000	241	251	257	262	266	271	256	288	309	325	338	355	440	478	502	520	534	554	465	520	556	583	606	636	356	385	403	416	427	441
30,000	40,000	296	308	316	322	326	332	307	344	369	387	402	422	539	585	613	634	651	674	562	627	670	702	728	764	435	469	491	507	520	537
40,000	50,000	346	360	369	375	380	386	353	394	421	442	458	481	628	679	712	736	755	782	648	722	770	806	835	876	505	544	569	587	602	622
50,000	60,000	392	408	417	424	430	437	395	440	469	492	510	535	710	767	803	830	851	880	727	809	861	901	934	978	569	613	641	661	677	699
60,000	70,000	436	453	463	471	477	485	434	483	515	539	558	585	788	849	888	917	941	973	801	890	947	990	1025	1073	629	677	707	729	747	771
70,000	80,000	478	497	508	516	523	531	473	525	558	584	605	633	862	929	971	1002	1027	1062	873	967	1028	1075	1112	1164	686	738	771	795	814	840
80,000	90,000	518	538	550	559	566	575	510	564	600	627	649	679	933	1004	1049	1082	1109	1146	941	1041	1106	1155	1195	1250	741	796	831	856	877	905
90,000	100,000	557	578	591	600	608	618	545	602	640	668	691	723	1002	1077	1125	1160	1188	1227	1006	1111	1180	1232	1274	1332	793	851	888	916	937	967
100,000	120,000	610	632	646	656	664	675	594	654	694	724	748	782	1095	1175	1226	1264	1294	1336	1094	1206	1279	1335	1380	1442	862	925	965	995	1018	1050
120,000	140,000	684	709	724	735	744	756	663	728	770	803	829	865	1226	1314	1369	1411	1444	1489	1217	1340	1419	1479	1528	1596	959	1029	1073	1105	1131	1156
140,000	160,000	751	778	795	807	816	829	726	795	840	874	902	940	1344	1439	1498	1543	1578	1627	1328	1459	1544	1608	1661	1733	1046	1121	1168	1203	1231	1259
160,000	180,000	820	849	867	880	890	903	791	864	911	947	977	1018	1466	1566	1630	1678	1716	1768	1442	1581	1672	1740	1796	1872	1134	1215	1265	1303	1332	1373
180,000	200,000	884	915	934	947	958	972	852	928	978	1016	1047	1089	1578	1685	1752	1802	1842	1897	1547	1694	1789	1861	1920	2000	1215	1300	1354	1394	1425	1458
200,000 or more		1225	1265	1289	1307	1321	1339	1188	1280	1340	1386	1423	1475	2180	2315	2400	2464	2515	2584	2106	2289	2408	2498	2571	2672	1635	1746	1815	1866	1907	1962

Income		Wyoming 4.0000%					
At least	But less than	1	2	3	4	5	Over 5
$0	$20,000	154	167	175	181	186	193
20,000	30,000	264	285	298	308	316	327
30,000	40,000	324	349	365	377	386	399
40,000	50,000	378	407	425	438	449	463
50,000	60,000	428	460	480	495	506	523
60,000	70,000	475	510	532	548	561	578
70,000	80,000	521	558	581	599	613	632
80,000	90,000	564	604	629	647	662	682
90,000	100,000	606	648	675	694	710	731
100,000	120,000	663	708	736	757	774	797
120,000	140,000	743	792	823	846	865	890
140,000	160,000	816	869	902	926	946	973
160,000	180,000	890	946	982	1008	1030	1058
180,000	200,000	959	1019	1056	1084	1107	1137
200,000 or more		1328	1404	1452	1487	1516	1554

Note. Alaska does not have a state sales tax. Alaska residents should follow the instructions on the next page to determine their local sales tax amount.

1 The rates for California, the District of Columbia, Massachusetts, Minnesota, Nevada, and North Carolina increased during 2009, so the rates given are averaged over the year.

2 The California table includes the 1% uniform local sales tax rate in addition to the 7.0034% state sales tax rate.

3 The Nevada table includes the 2.25% uniform local sales tax rate in addition to the 4.4264% state sales tax rate.

4 Residents of Salem County should deduct only half of the amount in the state table.

Which Optional Local Sales Tax Table Should I Use?

IF you live in the state of...	AND you live in...	THEN use Local Table...
Alaska	Any locality	C
Arizona	Mesa, Phoenix, or Tucson	A
	Chandler, Gilbert, Glendale, Peoria, Scottsdale, Tempe, Yuma, or any other locality	B
Arkansas	Any locality	C
California	Los Angeles County	A
Colorado	Arvada, Aurora, City of Boulder, Fort Collins, Greeley, Longmont, Thornton, or Westminster	B
	Adams County, Arapahoe County, Boulder County, Centennial, Colorado Springs, Denver City/Denver County, El Paso County, Jefferson County, Lakewood, Larimer County, City of Pueblo, Pueblo County, or any other locality	A
Georgia	Any locality	B
Illinois	Any locality	A
Louisiana	Any locality	C
Missouri	Any locality	C
New York	New York City, or one of the following counties: Albany, Allegany, Cattaraugus, Cayuga, Chemung, Clinton, Cortland, Erie, Essex, Franklin, Fulton, Genesee, Herkimer, Jefferson, Lewis, Livingston, Monroe, Montgomery, Nassau, Niagara, Oneida, Onondaga, Ontario, Orange, Orleans, Oswego, Otsego, Putnam, Rensselaer, Rockland, St. Lawrence, Saratoga, Schenectady, Schoharie, Seneca, Steuben, Suffolk, Sullivan, Tompkins, Ulster, Warren, Washington, Westchester, Wyoming, or Yates	A
	Any other locality	D
North Carolina	Any locality	A
South Carolina	Cherokee, Chesterfield, Darlington, Dillon, Horry, Jasper, Lee, Lexington, or Myrtle Beach	B
	Any other locality	C
Tennessee	Any locality	C
Utah	Any locality	B
Virginia	Any locality	B

2009 Optional Local Sales Tax Tables for Certain Local Jurisdictions

(Based on a local sales tax rate of 1 percent)

Income At least	But less than	Local Table A Exemptions						Local Table B Exemptions						Local Table C Exemptions						Local Table D Exemptions					
		1	2	3	4	5	Over 5	1	2	3	4	5	Over 5	1	2	3	4	5	Over 5	1	2	3	4	5	Over 5
$0	$20,000	37	41	44	46	47	49	45	51	55	59	61	65	56	64	69	73	76	81	36	39	40	41	42	43
20,000	30,000	61	67	71	74	76	79	72	82	88	93	96	102	89	101	109	115	120	126	62	65	68	69	70	72
30,000	40,000	74	81	85	89	91	95	86	98	105	110	115	121	106	120	129	136	142	150	76	80	83	85	86	88
40,000	50,000	85	93	98	102	105	109	99	112	120	126	131	138	121	137	147	155	162	170	88	93	96	98	100	102
50,000	60,000	96	105	110	114	117	122	111	124	133	140	146	153	135	152	164	172	179	189	100	105	109	111	113	115
60,000	70,000	106	115	121	126	129	134	122	136	146	153	159	168	148	167	179	188	196	206	111	117	120	123	125	128
70,000	80,000	116	126	132	137	141	146	132	148	158	166	172	181	160	180	193	203	211	222	122	128	132	134	137	140
80,000	90,000	125	136	142	147	151	157	142	159	170	178	185	194	172	193	207	217	226	237	132	138	142	145	148	151
90,000	100,000	134	145	152	157	162	167	152	170	181	190	197	207	183	205	219	230	239	252	141	148	153	156	158	162
100,000	120,000	147	158	166	171	176	182	165	184	196	205	213	223	198	221	237	248	258	271	155	162	167	170	173	176
120,000	140,000	164	177	185	191	196	202	184	204	217	227	235	246	219	244	261	273	284	298	173	181	186	190	193	197
140,000	160,000	180	194	202	209	214	221	201	222	236	247	255	267	237	264	282	296	307	322	190	199	204	208	211	215
160,000	180,000	197	211	220	227	232	240	218	241	256	267	276	289	256	285	304	318	330	346	207	217	222	226	230	234
180,000	200,000	213	227	237	244	249	257	235	258	274	285	295	308	274	304	323	339	351	368	224	233	239	243	247	252
200,000 or more		298	316	327	336	343	352	323	351	370	385	397	413	365	402	427	445	461	482	310	322	329	334	339	345

Schedules C, F and SE

What's New in 2009

Increased Section 179 Limit Extended. The maximum Section 179 deduction that can be elected for property purchased and placed in service in 2009 remains at $250,000. The threshold for reducing the deduction also remains at $800,000.

Temporary Bonus Depreciation. Qualifying taxpayers may claim a 50-percent bonus depreciation of the adjusted basis of qualifying property. The original use of the property must begin with the taxpayer and the property must be placed in service after December 31, 2007, and before January 1, 2010. For property with a recovery period of 10 years or longer, transportation property, and certain aircraft, the date is extended through December 31, 2010.

Vehicle Expense Deduction Changes. The standard mileage rate for the cost of operating a vehicle after December 31, 2008, and before January 1, 2010, is 55 cents per mile. The rate is 24 cents per mile for medical and moving expense deductions. The standard mileage rate for charitable purposes remains at 14 cents per mile. For 2009, the bonus depreciation cap remains at $8,000 which results in a maximum first-year depreciation of $10,960 for autos and $11,060 for trucks and vans.

Self-Employment Income Subject to Social Security. For 2009, Social Security tax must be paid on the first $106,800 of self-employment income.

Section at a Glance

Relevant IRS Publications

- ☐ IRS Publication 15, Circular E, *Employer's Tax Guide*
- ☐ IRS Publication 51, *Circular A, Agricultural Employer's Tax Guide*
- ☐ IRS Publication 225, *Farmer's Tax Guide*
- ☐ IRS Publication 334, *Tax Guide for Small Business*
- ☐ IRS Publication 535, *Business Expenses*
- ☐ IRS Publication 583, *Starting a Business and Keeping Records*

Tax Preparer's Checklist

- ☐ Existing businesses should have a taxpayer identification number; submit Form SS-4 if they do not.
- ☐ New businesses should obtain EINs as an identity protection issue for the business owners even if they do not have employees or retirement plans that would otherwise require them.
- ☐ Have copies of filed payroll documents to crosscheck: Forms 940, 941, W-3, SUI, and other state and local tax filings.
- ☐ Have copies or a record of state and local filing documents such as sales taxes.
- ☐ Request 1099-MISC and 1098 documents received and look for 1099-MISC filings.
- ☐ Keep and collect business mileage records.
- ☐ Keep records of ending inventory, if applicable.

3 Schedules C, F and SE

Key 2009 Figures Relating to Self-Employment Income	
Net earnings threshold for filing Schedule SE	$ 400 ($433 x 92.35%)*
Income subject to Social Security or 6.2% railroad retirement tier 1 tax	$106,800
Self-employment tax rate Social Security portion Medicare portion	15.3% 12.4% 2.9%
Form 1040, line 27, deduction for one-half of self-employment tax paid	50%

*Church employee net income threshold is $100 ($108.28 x 92.35%).

Other 2009 Schedules and Forms that May Have to Be Filed with or because of Schedule C, C-EZ, or F	
Schedule SE	To pay self-employment tax on income from any trade or business
Form 1065	In Lieu of a Schedule C if a business is a partnership
Form 4562	To claim depreciation and amortization deductions, to make an election under Section 179 to expense the cost of certain tangible property, and to provide information on the business and/or investment use of cars and other listed property (see Tab 7)
Form 4684	To report a casualty or theft gain or loss involving property used in trade or business or income-producing property (see Tab 2)
Form 4797	To report sales, exchanges and involuntary conversions (not from a casualty or theft) of trade or business property and to document recapture of Code Sec. 179 deductions (see Tab 4)
Form 8300	To report the receipt of more than $10,000 cash in one or more related transactions
Form 8824	To report like-kind exchanges (see Tab 4)
Form 8829	To claim expenses for business use of taxpayer's home
Form 8903	To take a deduction for income from domestic production activities
Employment Returns	Form 941, *Employer's Quarterly Federal Tax Return* Form 940, *Employer's Annual Federal Unemployment (FUTA) Tax Return* Form 943, *Employer's Annual Federal Tax Return for Agricultural Employees* Form 944, *Employer's Annual Federal Tax Return* Form W-2, *Wage and Tax Statement* Form W-3, *Transmittal of Wage and Tax Statements*
Information Returns	Form 1099-MISC, *Miscellaneous Income* Form 1096, *Annual Summary and Transmittal of U.S. Information Returns*

When to File Schedule C, Schedule C-EZ, Schedule F, and Schedule SE

Schedule C, *Profit and or Loss from Business* (Sole Proprietorship), Schedule C-EZ, *Net Profit from Business* (Sole Proprietorship), and Schedule F, *Profit or Loss from Farming,* are filed with Form 1040, *U.S. Individual Income Tax Return,* to report the income and expenses generated by an individual's participation as a sole proprietor in an active trade or business, along with pertinent information about the business. Income from separate businesses, even though owned by the same individual, must be reported on separate copies of Schedule C. Combining businesses on one Schedule C could lead to a tax penalty (IRC §6662 and Rev. Rul. 81-90).

An individual with a net self-employment income of $400 or more must file an income tax return and use Schedule SE to report that income, even if filing would not otherwise be required.

Business Owned Jointly by Spouses

Spouses who jointly own and operate an unincorporated business and share in the profits and losses are considered to be operating a partnership, even if no formal partnership agreement exists. A Form 1065, *U.S. Return of Partnership Income,* should be filed in such situations, with the profit/loss and other items flowing through on Form 1065 Schedule K-1, *Partner's Share of Income, Credits, Deductions, etc.*

A qualified joint venture where the only members are a husband and wife filing a joint return can elect *not* to be treated as a partnership for federal tax purposes. Each spouse would take into account his or her income, gain, loss and other items as a sole proprietor and report their share of income on a separate Form 1040, *Schedule C.* A qualified joint venuture is a joint venture involving the conduct of a trade or business if:

- the only members of the joint venture are the husband and wife;
- both spouses materially participate in the trade or business; and
- both spouses elect to have the qualified joint venture provision apply.

If the material participation requirement is not satisfied, a married couple living in community property states can elect *not* to be treated as a partnership for federal tax purposes if their business is a qualified entity. To be a qualified entity:

- the business must be 100% owned by the couple as community property under the laws of a state, a foreign country, or a possession of the United States;
- no person, other than one or both spouses, may have an ownership interest in the property for federal tax purposes; and
- the business must not be treated as a corporation (Rev. Proc. 2002-69).

When one Schedule C is filed for a jointly owned business under these rules, self-employment income must be allocated on two Schedules SE.

Filing Tip. Community property states are Arizona, California, Idaho, Louisiana, Nevada, New Mexico, Texas, Washington, and Wisconsin.

Shared and Allocated Expenses

If an individual operates a business in the same profession in which he or she is employed by someone else, records of expenses must be carefully allocated. Specific identification of expenses allocable to each activity is preferred, in order to properly file Schedule C (or C-EZ) and Form 2106, *Employee Business Expenses.* If specific identification is not possible, such expenses may be allocated on the basis of the relative gross income from each activity.

Sole Member of a Limited Liability Company (LLC)

The owner of a single-member domestic limited liability company (LLC) must file a Schedule C, C-EZ, or F, unless an election has been made to treat the LLC as a corporation. (Form 8832, *Entity Classification Election,* is used to make that election.) If the election has been made, the business income and expenses are reported on Form 1120, *U.S. Corporation Income Tax Return,* or Form 1120-S, *U.S. Income Tax Return for an S Corporation,* as appropriate.

Caution. States handle LLCs in different ways. Some even require a separate return for a single member LLC and charge annual fees.

Statutory Employees

The Form W-2, *Wage and Tax Statement,* of a statutory employee will have a checkmark in box 13. Wages and expenses of a statutory employee are reported on Schedule C or C-EZ.

Congress has declared certain employees to be statutory employees. Their position of being able to deduct expenses on Schedule C obviously gives them an advantage over other employees, who must itemize their deductions, subject to certain limitations, on Schedule A (see Tab 2).

Employers must withhold Social Security and Medicare taxes on the income of statutory employees and must give them a Form W-2 that reports this income and shows the payroll taxes that were withheld. Statutory employees must pay estimated income taxes on their net income since their employers are not required to withhold income taxes from their pay.

The following employees are considered statutory employees:

- Full-time traveling or local salespersons who solicit orders from wholesalers, retailers, contractors or operators of hotels, restaurants, or other similar establishments on behalf of a principal, if the goods sold are merchandise for resale or supplies for use in the customer's business;
- Drivers who distribute beverages other than milk, or who distribute meat, vegetable, fruit, or bakery products, or who pick up and deliver laundry or dry cleaning as an agent for the business or on commission;
- Full-time life insurance sales agents whose principal business is selling life insurance or annuity contracts primarily for one life insurance company; and
- Home workers performing work on material or goods furnished by the employer and to the employer's specifications.
- For more information see MTG ¶941B.

When to File Schedule C-EZ?

Schedule C-EZ is a simpler, less detailed version of Schedule C. Schedule C-EZ may be used in place of Schedule C on a 2009 return, provided that all of the following are true:

- The business had expenses of no more than $5,000.
- The business uses the cash method of accounting.
- The business did not have an inventory at any time during the year.
- The business did not have a net loss for the year.
- The taxpayer had only one business as either a sole proprietor or statutory employee during the year.
- The business had no employees during the year.
- The business is not required to file Form 4562, *Depreciation and Amortization (Including Information on Listed Property).*
- The taxpayer does not deduct expenses for the business use of his or her home.
- There are no prior years' unallowed passive activity losses from this business.

When to File Schedule C?

Taxpayers who do not qualify to file Schedule C-EZ should file Schedule C to report income from a nonfarm business.

When to File Schedule F?

Schedule F is used to report income generated and the related expense from the active conduct of a business involved in producing agricultural or horticultural commodities. Items to be reported include the following:

- Sales of livestock and other items bought for resale.
- Sales of livestock, produce, grains and so on that the taxpayer raised or produced.
- Distributions from cooperatives related to the farm business (from Form 1099-PATR).
- Government farm program payments, including commodity credit loans and certificates, disaster assistance, crop insurance proceeds and other income replacement insurance; also payments for damages to standing crops or crop replacement payments by responsible parties.
- Payments for custom hire or machine work (machine operator furnishes equipment).
- Federal and state fuel tax refunds and credits.

Gains from the sale of livestock held for draft, breeding, sport or dairy are reported on Form 4797, *Sales of Business Property*, as are the sales of farmland and depreciable farm equipment.

Rental of farmland and facilities that is based on a share of crops or livestock produced by a tenant is normally reported on Form 4835, *Farm Rental Income and Expenses,* and is not subject to SE tax, providing the owner does not materially participate in the operation or management of the farm.

Cash rent that represents a flat charge for the use of farmland and is not based on production is reported on Schedule E, *Supplemental Income and Loss,* and is not subject to SE tax.

Rental of farm equipment, soil testing, computer consulting, and other "farm-related" activities that are conducted as a separate trade or business are normally Schedule C activities.

Income from the rental of personal property, if not conducted for profit, is reported on Form 1040, line 21. Related expense is reported on Schedule A of Form 1040.

When to File Schedule SE

Schedule SE, *Self-Employment Tax,* is used to report net earning of $400 or more from self-employment. An individual is self-employed if they are in business for themselves or are a farmer. Receipt of Form 1099-MISC, *Miscellaneous Income,* does not necessarily mean that a Schedule SE must be filed. Often the sender of the 1099-MISC has mischaracterized the nature of the payment.

An individual is self-employed if:

- The taxpayer carried on a trade or business as a sole proprietor or an independent contractor;
- The taxpayer is a member of a partnership that carries on a trade or business; or
- The taxpayer is otherwise in business for themselves.

A trade or business is generally an activity carried on for a livelihood or in good faith to make a profit. The facts and circumstances of each case determine whether or not an activity is a trade or business. The regularity of activities and transactions and the production of income are important elements. A taxpayer does not need to actually make a profit to be in a trade or business as long as the taxpayer has a profit motive. However, the taxpayer does need to make ongoing efforts to further the interests of their business.

A taxpayer does not have to carry on regular full-time business activities to be self-employed. Having a part-time business in addition to a regular job or business may also be self-employment.

A taxpayer is a sole proprietor if they own an unincorporated business by themselves, in most cases. If the taxpayer is the sole member of a domestic limited liability company (LLC), they are a sole proprietor unless they elect to treat the LLC as a corporation. For more information see IRS Form 8832.

If the taxpayer is a member of a partnership that carries on a trade or business, the partnership should report the taxpayer's earnings subject to self-employment tax in box 14, of Form 1065, Schedule K-1 (using code A) or in box 9 of Form 1065-B, Schedule K-1 (using code J1), *Partner's Share of Income (Loss) From an Electing Large Partnership.* If the taxpayer is a general partner, the taxpayer may need to reduce these unreported earnings by the amounts the taxpayer has claimed as Code Sec. 179 deductions, unreimbursed partnership expenses, or depletion on oil and gas properties. If the amount reported is subject to the loss limitation rules (see Tab 5), the taxpayer should only include the deductible amount when figuring their total earnings subject to self-employment tax.

People such as doctors, dentists, veterinarians, lawyers, accountants, contractors, subcontractors, public stenographers, or auctioneers who are in an independent trade, business, or profession in which they offer services to the general public are generally independent contractors. However, whether these people are independent contractors or employees depends on the facts in each case. The general rule is that an individual is an independent contractor if the service recipient has the right to control or direct only the result of the work and not how it will be done. The earnings of a person who is working as an independent contractor are subject to self-employment tax.

A taxpayer is not an independent contractor if they perform services that can be controlled by an employer (i.e., what will be done and how it will be done). This applies even if the taxpayer is given freedom of action. What matters is that the employer has the legal right to control the details of how the services are performed. For more information regarding independent contractors, see IRS Publication 15-A, *Employer's Supplemental Tax Guide.*

Net earnings from self-employment consist of:

- Gross income derived from any trade or business, less allowable deductions attributable to the trade or business; and
- The taxpayer's distributive share of ordinary income or loss of a partnership engaged in a trade or business.

The term "trade or business" does not include services performed as an employee other than services relating to certain: (1) newspaper or magazine sales, (2) sharing of crops, (3) foreign organizations and (4) sharing of fishing catches.

Schedule SE must also be filed if an individual had church employee income of $108.28 or more. Self-employment tax must also be paid on certain partnership income and guaranteed payments. See IRS Publication 334, *Tax Guide for Small Business (For Individuals Who Use Schedule C or Schedule C-EZ)* and MTG ¶2670 for more information.

Rents from real estate and personal property leased with the real estate, and the attributable deductions are excluded from net earnings from self-employment unless received by the individual in his course of business as a real estate dealer. Termination payments received by former insurance salespeople are excluded under certain circumstances. For more information see MTG ¶2670.

There is also a Farm Optional Method for calculating net earnings from self-employment. See page 3-32.

The following are not subject to self-employment tax:

- Income from a hobby.
- Income received by a minister, member of the clergy, or member of a religious organization provided they have obtained an exemption.
- Wages earned as an employee.
- Retirement pay.
- Wages earned by a railroad employee.
- A distributive share of income or loss from a trade or business allocated to a limited partner.
- A distributive share of S corporation income or loss allocated to a shareholder and included on Schedule K-1.
- Periodic retirement payments.
- Some fishing crew members.
- State and local government employees.
- Public officials.
- Corporate employees.
- Nonprofessional fiduciaries such as an administrator or an executor of an estate.
- Indian fishing rights.
- Nonresident aliens, unless they are subject to an international agreement or are residents of a U.S. possession.

US citizens or resident aliens residing abroad who are subject to the social security laws of the foreign country under a totalization agreement.

Chart of Business Entity Comparisons

Entity	Sole Proprietorship	General Partnership	Limited Partnership	C Corporation	S Corporation	Limited Liability Company
Tax Form	Form 1040–Schedule C, C-EZ, or F	Form 1065	Form 1065	Form 1120	Form 1120S	Forms 1065/1040 (Schedule C)/1120 or 1120S (election)
Taxation	Direct to proprietor	Flow-through	Flow-through	Direct to corporation	Flow-through	Various, based on election
Ownership	One owner	Unlimited number of general partners	Unlimited–must have one general partner	Unlimited number of stockholders	Up to 100 stockholders	Single-member or unlimited number of members

Chart of Business Entity Comparisons (Continued)

Entity	Sole Proprietorship	General Partnership	Limited Partnership	C Corporation	S Corporation	Limited Liability Company
Liability	Unlimited personal liability	Unlimited liability for general partners	Unlimited liability for general partners–limited to investment for limited partners	Shareholders have no personal liability for corporate obligations	Shareholders have no personal liability for corporate obligations	Members generally have no personal liability for business obligations
Management	Owner has complete control	Partners normally have equal voice unless otherwise agreed to	General partners manage business–possible restrictions from limited partners in agreement	Board of directors overall–officers day to day are responsible to board	Board of directors overall–officers day to day are responsible to board	Operating agreement with designated manager(s)
Legal Requirements	Easy to set up, easy to liquidate; minimal legal requirements	Few legal requirements; should have partnership agreement (not required in all states)	Distinction between general partners and limited partners	Must have board of directors, officers, and annual meetings–articles of incorporation and by-laws	Must have board of directors, officers, and annual meetings–articles of incorporation and by-laws	Organizational documentation–normally articles of organization; also operating agreement

Recordkeeping and Substantiation Requirements

A separate bank account should be kept for each business, in addition to a personal account for family living.

Planning Tip. Although it is not required by law, an audit normally goes more smoothly if business and personal accounts are kept separate.

There is no requirement that business books be double-entry. A double-entry system, however, will make reconciliation of ending asset and liability balances easier.

No matter how the records are kept–(13-column analysis pads, the traditional handwritten general ledger with supporting journals, basic computer spreadsheets, or sophisticated computer accounting programs), it is imperative that the supporting documentation be kept in an organized manner. In addition to the checkbook, canceled checks, deposit slips, and bank statements, the records that need to be maintained include sales slips, invoices, receipts, delivery receipts, inventory records, cost calculations and financial statements.

Canceled Checks. It is now rare that a bank returns the original canceled check to the customer. Copies of the cleared checks are normally included with the bank statement, along with a listing of the cleared checks by number. The taxpayer should request that a copy of the check backs, in addition to the fronts, be included. Some banks are making the electronic images, front and back, available to the account holder online. Since a canceled check alone may not be sufficient documentation, the taxpayer should match the canceled check copies to the invoices and not the check number on the invoice.

To the extent possible, all disbursements should be made by check, rather than cash. Personal expenses should never be paid from the business account.

Accounting Methods

The taxpayer's accounting method is a set of rules as to when and how income and expenses are reported. Generally the same accounting method used for keeping the business's records must be used for completing Schedule C. The accounting method used in the year for which the first income tax return that includes the Schedule C for the business is filed is the accounting method the business is required to use in subsequent years. From then on, most changes in accounting method will require IRS approval. Kinds of accounting methods include the following:

- Cash method–used by most sole proprietors with no inventory. Items are included in income as they are actually or constructively received. Property or services received (i.e., bartering) must be valued and included in income at fair market value. Expenses

are deducted in the tax year in which they are actually paid. There are some restrictions on advance payments that may not be deducted until applicable and some items (such as depreciable equipment) that must be capitalized.
- Accrual method–income is reported in the year earned (not necessarily received), and expenses are deducted in the year incurred.
- Special methods for certain items of income and expense.
- Combination method using elements of two or more of the above. It is quite common for taxpayers who must maintain an inventory in order to properly reflect income and expense to use the cash method for other expenses. The bottom line is that the method of accounting selected must be used consistently and must clearly show the income and expenses of the business.

Business and Personal Items

A taxpayer may account for business and personal items using different accounting methods. For example, a Schedule C business may be on the accrual method, while the taxpayer reports his or her personal items on a cash basis.

Planning Tip. The timing of both receipt of income and payment of expenses can shift profits/losses to a more desirable year for a cash-basis taxpayer. It can also greatly influence other deductions or related expenditures, including Section 179 and bonus depreciation or retirement plan funding.

Determining how the client reports income can be simplified: cash if the client works from his or her checkbook balance, or accrual if the client reports/posts income and expenses by transactions/sales.

Two or More Businesses

If a taxpayer has two or more separate and distinct businesses, with separate books and records, he or she may use a different accounting method for each. The accounting method used must clearly reflect the income of each business. If the books are kept together and allocated at the end of the year in order to file the return, the books are not separate and distinct.

How Long Must Records Be Kept?

The statute of limitations for a tax return and supporting documentation is three years. The time frame increases to six years if gross income is understated by more than 25%. There is no limit if fraud is involved or false or fraudulent information is entered on the tax return. The statute of limitations does not begin to run until the return is filed, so if a return has not been filed, the statute remains open.

Some other events or items extend the statute of limitations:

- Net operating loss (NOL) or capital loss carryback extends the limitations period to three years after the filing of the return for the loss year.
- Support and documentation of items that affect future returns extend the time as well. The support for depreciable assets must be kept for the statutory period after the last return on which depreciation for the asset is claimed. If like-kind exchanges are involved, the documentation for an asset originally purchased many years ago may need to be retained through subsequent trades.

Special Documentation for Some Business Deductions

Meals, entertainment, travel and gifts are subject to some special documentation requirements Such expenditures must be ordinary and necessary expenses of carrying on the business to be deductible

For *entertainment and meal expenses*, the following information should be maintained:

- Date and location.
- Business purpose or business benefit.
- Nature of business discussion or activity.
- If entertainment was directly before or after business discussion, keep the names of individuals who participated, as well as the date, place and nature of the business discussion.
- Record the professions/occupations/business relationship to the taxpayer of individuals present. Documentation must also show that the taxpayer or an employee participated if the entertainment was a business meal.

For *travel expenses*:

- Dates of departure and return and days spent for business versus personal days.
- Cost by category of expense, i.e., travel, lodging, meals and incidental expenses.
- Destination or travel area.
- Business purpose or business benefit of trip.
- See Tab 8 for additional rules.

For *gifts*:

- Date of gift.
- Description and cost of gift.
- Business purpose or business benefit of gift.
- Business relationship of taxpayer to recipient.

Schedule C Line-by-Line Instructions

General Business Information

Name of Proprietor and SSN

Be sure to include the name and Social Security number of the proprietor.

Lines A and B, Principal Business or Profession and Code

Enter on line A the activity that provided the principal source of income to be reported on line 1. The six-digit Principal Business or Professional Activity Codes are based on the North American Industry Classification System (NAICS) and are reproduced beginning on page 3-18 for convenience. Enter the code for the business on line B.

Lines C, D, and E, Business Name, EIN, and Address

If a business name is used, it goes on line C. If there is no separate business name or "doing business as"-type designation ("/dba"), line C is left blank.

The employer ID number (EIN) is entered on line D. This is required only if the business has a qualified retirement plan or is required to file an employment, excise, estate, trust, or alcohol, tobacco, and firearms tax return. If there is no EIN for the business and none is required, leave the line blank. Do not enter the taxpayer's Social Security number again.
There are several ways to apply for an EIN:

- Apply online at the IRS Web site: Go to www.irs.gov/businesses/index.html and click on "Employer ID Numbers" under "Businesses Topics."
- Apply via fax: Complete Form SS-4 online, print it, and fax it to the taxpayer's state fax number.
- Apply via telephone at 800-829-4933. Have the completed SS-4 form in front of you ready to read the information to the IRS representative. The person making the call must be authorized to sign the form or be an authorized designee. The representative may or may not request that the signed Form SS-4 be mailed or faxed.
- Apply by mail. The processing time frame for an EIN application received by mail is four weeks. Ensure that the Form SS-4 contains all of the required information. A copy of Form SS-4 with signature authorization should be maintained in a practitioner's records.

Note: Form SS-4 and the instructions may be downloaded from the IRS Web site at www.irs.gov for specific line-by-line instructions.

On line E, enter the address of the business, including suite or room number, as well as city, state, and zip.

Line F, Accounting Method

On line F, check Cash, Accrual, or Other. The mechanics of various accounting methods are discussed on page 3-6. Of primary concern to the IRS is that the method used clearly reflects income. Unless the taxpayer meets the requirements as a qualifying taxpayer or a qualifying small business, the accrual method must be used for sales and purchases of inventory items. Exceptions apply to taxpayers with average annual gross receipts of $1 million or less and to service-type businesses with average annual gross receipts of $10 million or less.

It is possible to change accounting methods. Some changes require IRS approval. To change accounting methods, file Form 3115, *Application for Change in Accounting Method.* If a change is made, there may be adjustments to items of income and expense in order to prevent duplication or omission of any items. The adjustment is made under Code Sec. 481(a).

Line G, Material Participation

In general, material participation includes any work done in connection with an activity by an individual who owned an interest in the activity at the time the work was done. Marking this box "No" identifies the business as a passive activity. If the business is classified as a passive activity, allowable losses may be limited. See Tab 5 for information on passive activity losses and Form 8582, *Passive Activity Loss Limitations,* used to calculate the allowable loss.

According to the instructions for Schedule C, for purposes of the passive activity rules, the taxpayer materially participated in the operation of the trade or business activity during the year if he or she met any of the following seven tests:

1. The taxpayer participated in the activity for more than 500 hours during the tax year.
2. The taxpayer's participation in the activity for the tax year was substantially all of the total individual participation (including individuals who did not own any interest in the activity) for the tax year.
3. The taxpayer participated in the activity for more than 100 hours during the tax year, and participated at least as much as any other person for the tax year.
4. The activity is a significant participation activity for the tax year and the taxpayer participated in all significant participation activities for more than 500 hours during the year. An activity is a "significant participation activity" if it involves the conduct of a trade or business, the taxpayer participated in the activity for more than 100 hours during the tax year, and the taxpayer did not materially participate under any of the material participation tests other than this one.

5. The taxpayer materially participated in the activity for any five of the 10 tax years prior to the taxyear in question.
6. The activity is a personal service activity in which the taxpayer materially participated for any three prior tax years. A personal service activity is an activity that involves performing personal services in the fields of health, law, engineering, architecture, accounting, actuarial science, performing arts, consulting or any other trade or business in which capital is not a material income-producing factor.
7. Based on all the facts and circumstances, the taxpayer participated in the activity on a regular, continuous, and substantial basis during the tax year. Participation in managing the activity does not count in determining if this test is met if anyone other than the taxpayer (a) received compensation for performing management services in connection with the activity, or (b) spent more hours during the tax year than the taxpayer spent performing management services in connection with the activity (regardless of whether the person was compensated for the services).

A taxpayer will not be treated as significantly participating in an activty if the taxpayer participated in the activty for 100 hours or less during any tax year.

Working interest in oil or gas property. There is an exception for a working interest in oil or gas property. The box should be checked "Yes" whether the working interest is owned directly or indirectly through an entity that does not limit liability. No matter the level of participation, the activity of owning a working interest is not a passive activity.

Investors. Work done as an investor in an activity is not treated as participation unless the individual was directly involved in the day-to-day management or operations of the activity. Work done as an investor includes:

- studying and reviewing financial statements or reports on the operation of the activity;
- preparing or compiling summaries or analyses of the finances or operations of the activity for the individual's own use; and
- monitoring the finances or operations in a nonmanagerial capacity.

Line H, New Business

If 2009 is the first year for the business for this taxpayer, check the box on line H. If a Schedule C or C-EZ was filed for the same business in 2008, leave the box blank.

> **Planning Tip.** If a taxpayer operates multiple businesses, he or she may choose to include tax items from related businesses on the same Schedule C or to report tax items from each business on separate Schedule Cs. When a taxpayer's records cannot be separated by individual business, shared expenses are generally allocated on a pro rata basis by revenue.

Part I: Income

What Constitutes Business Income?

The term "trade or business" is used over and over again in the Internal Revenue Code. In most instances, there is no explanation or definition of the term. The explanations that do exist are not consistent across the Code.

Most tax professionals look at trade or business income as income that is generated by regular and continuous activity, not performed as an employee, and that is done with a profit motive. Trade or business activity may be engaged in on a full or part time basis. Many individuals have one or more Schedule C or F businesses in addition to full-time employment. Normally, investment activity is not considered trade or business activity.

Line 1, Gross Receipts or Sales

The term "gross receipts" includes all amounts received for the sale of goods or services (produced or purchased) in the normal course of business. Whether or not accounts receivable are a factor depends on the accounting method used for the business.

Income reported on Form 1099-MISC is normally reported as a part of gross receipts. All Forms 1099-MISC with entries in box 7 (nonemployee compensation) should be totaled and verified to ensure that they are included in gross receipts. If the total of the forms is more than income reported, attach an explanation and reconciliation of the totals. If a 1099-MISC is incorrect or was issued in error, the issuer should be contacted and a request for a correction made.

Bartering is a perfectly legal activity, but both parties must report their respective income for tax purposes. Include in gross receipts the fair market value (FMV) of property or services received in a bartering transaction. In order to avoid problems, both parties should agree to the FMV of items or services in advance of the actual trade.

Form 1099-B, *Proceeds from Broker and Barter Exchange Transactions*, or Form 1099-MISC, *Miscellaneous Income*, should be filed in bartering situations.

An individual may be a statutory employee, with income reported on a W-2, but reportable by him or her on a

Schedule C or C-EZ. (See discussion on page 3-3.) Line 13 of Form W-2 contains a box that should be checked, if the individual is a statutory employee. The income and related expenses are reported on Schedule C or C-EZ and the "Statutory Employee" box is checked on Line 1 of Part I.

Social Security and Medicare tax is withheld and matched by the employer, so no self-employment tax is due on such earnings.

> **Filing Tip.** If an individual has both income from self-employment and statutory employee income, he or she must file two Schedule Cs. The activities may not be combined on one Schedule C, and Schedule C-EZ is not allowed.

Line 2, Returns and Allowances

Report on line 2 returns, sales discounts, allowances, rebates and other items that reduce sales.

Line 3, Calculation

Subtract line 2 from line 1 and enter the result on line 3.

Line 4, Cost of Goods Sold

Line 4 is carried from line 42, Part III.

Line 5, Gross Profit

Subtract line 4 from line 3 and enter the result on line 5. This is the gross profit for the business.

Line 6, Other Income

Report as "Other income" income related to the trade or business, but not generated as a direct result of the principal trade or business activity. "Other income" items include the following:

- Federal fuel tax credit claimed on 2008 Form 1040
- State gasoline or fuel tax refunds received in 2009
- Finance reserve income
- Bad debts recovered
- Patronage dividends reported on Form 1099-PATR related to prior business purchases or business transactions with a cooperative sale of scrap or by-products
- Discount earned on timely sales tax filing
- Interest generated by accounts receivable finance charges
- Recapture of excess depreciation when business use of listed property falls below 50% before the end of the asset's recovery period (The recapture amount is calculated on Form 4797, Part III. See Tab 4.)
- *Note:* Not all receipts of money or property are included in income.

Sales tax is generally not reported as income. The tax is collected on sales and remitted to a state or local government authority. The amount is a flow-through. Most states require that the business owner remit to the state any excess sales tax collected. Some states do allow a discount for timely filing and remittance of sales tax. This discount should be reported on line 6, Other Income. Some states require that sales tax collected be reported as income, and the amount paid to the state is deducted.

The following items are **not income** and should not be reported as such:

- *Loans.* Money borrowed for operations or capital items, whether on a line of credit or a traditional note, is not income.
- *Asset appreciation.* Unrealized appreciation is not income until the asset is disposed of. At that point the disposition is reported on Form 4797, not Schedule C. See Tab 4.
- *Leasehold improvements.* Improvements paid for by a tenant on business or investment property may increase the value of the property, but are not considered income at that time. There is an exception if the facts and circumstances show that the improvements were actually a barter for rent payments.
- *Construction allowances.* Often a landlord will provide a tenant with a "construction allowance." The allowance is excluded from income provided both these conditions are met:
  - The arrangement is under a short-term lease (15 years or less) of retail space.
  - The allowance is to be used for constructing or improving nonresidential real property for use in the business at that retail space.
- *Like-kind exchange.* When business property is traded for like-kind replacement property (such as a business vehicle for a business vehicle), a gain is not taxable and a loss is not deductible. Form 8824, *Like-Kind Exchanges (and Section 1043 Conflict-of-Interest Sales)*, does need to be included as part of the tax return for the year of trade. (See the discussion in Tabs 4 and 8.)
- *Consignments.* The title to merchandise consigned to someone else remains with the consignor until property is sold by the consignee. The property is considered inventory for the consignor until that time. Likewise, merchandise received on consignment is not a part of the consignee's inventory. The profit or commission is income to the consignee when the property is sold or payment received (subject to accounting method).

> **Caution.** Gross receipts (reported sales or revenues) should equal other reported receipts that the entity submits to any other third party: sales tax, workers' compensation payments and payments from the U.S. Department of Commerce, for example. Exceptions or deviations may be explained to the IRS in attached documentation.

Part II: Expenses

What Constitutes a Deductible Business Expense?

Ordinary and Necessary Business Expense. "Ordinary" and "necessary" have specific meanings with regard to business expenses.

- An **ordinary** expense is one that is common and accepted in that particular business or activity.
- A **necessary** expense is one that is helpful and appropriate for the trade or business. The expense does not have to be indispensable to be considered necessary.

Start-up Costs. For expenses incurred on or after September 8, 2008, a taxpayer is deemed to have made an election to deduct and amortize start-up and/or organizational expenses for the taxable year in which the active trade or business to which the expenditures relate begins. Up to $5,000 of such expenses may be deducted, with the remainder amortized over the 180-month period beginning with the month in which the trade or business begins. A taxpayer may choose to forego the deemed election by clearly electing to capitalize its start-up and/or organizational expenditures on a timely filed federal income tax return, including extensions, for the taxable year in which the active trade or business to which the expenditures relate begins.

Expenses Paid after Business Is Closed and Ceases to Generate Revenue. For a cash-basis taxpayer, expenses incurred in prior years, but paid in the current year, are considered deductible. The taxpayer may continue to file a Schedule C in order to claim these expenses.

Line 8, Advertising

Expenditures for advertising costs are deducted on line 8 and must be reasonably related to the products and services offered by the business.

Lobbying. Note that advertising to influence legislation, contributions to candidates or office holders, and other such expenditures are not deductible for federal income tax.

Line 9, Car and Truck Expenses

Expenses related to the use of a car or truck may be deducted on Schedule C using one of two methods:

- *Standard mileage method.* The standard mileage method allows the taxpayer to deduct 55 cents per mile for 2009 business miles on up to four vehicles. This mileage amount covers all costs of owning and operating the vehicle except for interest on a vehicle loan, property taxes for the business percentage of the vehicle, parking, and tolls.
- *Actual cost method.* The actual cost method multiplies the percentage of business use by the actual cost of owning and operating the vehicle–depreciation, fuel, oil, repairs, insurance, license, maintenance and so on. Depreciation is reported on line 13 of schedule C, along with other business depreciation. If the vehicle is rented or leased, that expense goes on line 20a.

Information relative to the vehicle is reported in Part V of Form 4562, *Depreciation and Amortization (Including Information on Listed Property)*, providing that form is required for the return. If Form 4562 is not required for the return, complete the information in Part IV of Schedule C, *Information on Your Vehicle.*

This written information includes the date the vehicle was placed in service, the number of business, commuting, and other miles driven during the year, and questions regarding personal use and supporting evidence as to the business miles claimed.

Line 10, Commissions and Fees

Enter commissions and fees paid by the taxpayer on line 10.

Line 11, Contract Labor

On line 11, deduct the cost of services provided or labor performed by any individual who is not an employee. Contract labor normally does not include parts or materials.

A Form 1099-MISC must be filed if $600 or more is paid to one individual during 2009. A copy of Form 1099-MISC must be provided to the worker by February 1, 2010, and submitted to the IRS, along with a Form 1096 transmittal, by March 1, 2010.

Filing Tip. Be sure to report 1099-MISC income revenues as a separate line entry so that it may be identified easily.

1099-MISC nonemployee payouts should be segregated by activity, reported to the recipient, and shown as either a cost of goods (where appropriate) or as a business expense.

Form 1099-MISC is not required and should not be issued for any of the following:

- Payments to corporations.
- Payments for products, supplies, materials, or inputs.
- Payments to individuals for nonbusiness services, such as a plumber doing work on one's personal residence.
- Payments to employees.

Caution. Because 1099-MISC nonreporting of compensation over $600 can result in a serious nonfiling penalty, obtain provider identification numbers. Use Form W-9 to obtain required SSNs as nonemployee workers are hired.

Line 12, Depletion

A depletion deduction is taken to offset the decrease in value of a taxpayer's economic interest in certain natural properties. These include mineral property, oil, gas, or geothermal wells and standing timber.

The depletion of standing timber is claimed on Form T (Timber), *Forest Activities Schedules.*

Line 13, Depreciation and Section 179 Expense Deduction

Depreciation and Section 179 expense deductions are taken on line 13 and detailed on Form 4562. Form 4562 must be completed and attached to the 2009 return only if one of the following applies:

- Bonus depreciation is claimed in 2009.
- A Section 179 expense deduction is claimed.
- Depreciation is claimed on property placed in service during 2009.
- Depreciation is claimed on listed property for 2009, regardless of when the property was placed in service.

Depreciation spreads the recovery of the cost of property with an identifiable useful life over a period of years. Depreciation is not taken on inventory, stock in trade, land, or personal assets. See Tab 7.

Planning Tip. Optional reporting of depreciation or election to expense of newly acquired assets should usually be a profit-based decision; discourage clients from making such depreciation decisions *only* on the basis of current tax consequences.

Temporary Bonus Depreciation. The maximum Section 179 deduction that can be elected for property placed in service in 2009 is $250,000. The threshold for reducing the deduction is $800,000.

The first-year limit on depreciation for passenger automobiles is raised by $8,000 if bonus depreciation is claimed for a qualifying vehicle for a maximum first-year depreciation of not more than $10,960 ($11,060 for vans or trucks).

Line 14, Employee Benefit Programs

Contributions to employee benefit programs (other than pension and profit-sharing plans) are taken on line 14. These include accident and health plans, medical insurance, medical reimbursement plans, group term-life insurance, and dependent care assistance for employees.

Do not claim such expenses for the sole proprietor. In recent years, a popular move has been to hire the sole proprietor's spouse and provide family plan health insurance coverage to him or her as an employee benefit under a cafeteria plan. For the deduction to be allowable, the following conditions must be met:

- The spouse must be a true employee and must provide services as an employee to the business.
- The spouse must meet participation rules under an established medical reimbursement plan.
- The insurance coverage must be issued in the employee-spouse's name, not in the name of the employer-spouse.
- The employee-spouse may not be a joint owner, co-owner, or partner in the business.

Line 15, Insurance

Premiums paid for business insurance are reported on line 15. Insurance policies that qualify include the following:

- Casualty insurance–fire, theft, flood, and so on
- Credit insurance
- Business interruption insurance
- Overhead insurance
- Liability insurance
- Malpractice insurance
- Employee bonding
- Merchandise and inventory insurance
- Workers' compensation insurance

The following types of insurance policies do *not* qualify:

- Amounts credited to a reserve for self-insurance
- Premiums for a policy that pays for lost earnings due to the sickness or disability of the business owner
- Debt-driven life insurance on the business owner
- Health insurance for the business owner
- Long-term-care insurance for the business owner

Filing Tip. Employing the taxpayer's spouse and providing health insurance benefits may increase deductions.

Line 16, Interest

Mortgage interest on business real property is deducted on line 16a. Generally, report on line 16a interest for which a bank or financial institution issued a Form 1098 to the taxpayer. The portion of home mortgage interest that applies to the business use of the taxpayer's personal residence is taken on Form 8829, *Expenses for Business Use of Your Home.* The personal portion of the home mortgage interest goes on Schedule A, *Itemized Deductions.*

Other business interest is reported on line 16b. This includes the interest on business operating loans, lines of credit, and the business-use portion of vehicle loans.

Generally, borrowing for business expenses is deductible and can be documented by using the tracing rules. Under the tracing rules, the use of the loan proceeds determines the nature of the interest and where and if it is deductible. IRS Publication 535, *Business Expenses,* gives details on tracing interest costs.

Interest charged on income tax owed is not deductible. It makes no difference that the tax problem that generated the interest charges was related to Schedule C.

Line 17, Legal and Professional Services

The cost of accounting and tax preparation related to Schedule C, Schedule E, *Supplemental Income and Loss,* and Schedule F, *Profit or Loss From Farming,* are properly deductible on each schedule. Ideally, the professional will provide information as to the portion of the fees allocable to each schedule. If not, allocation on the basis of income (including nonbusiness income) may be used. The personal portion of the tax preparation fee is reported on Schedule A.

Legal fees incurred in the normal operation of the business are deducted on the appropriate business schedule. Legal fees to acquire business assets must be added to the basis of depreciated assets over the life of the assets.

Line 18, Office Expenses

Office expenses, telephone, maintenance, office supplies, small tools, paper products, and so on are taken on line 18. This does not include business use of the home, which is reported on Form 8829 and flows to line 30 on Schedule C.

Line 19, Pension and Profit-Sharing Plans

Contributions made to pension, profit-sharing, and other retirement plans for the benefit of employees are claimed on line 19. Note that, even though a part of the same plan or program, contributions made for the benefit of the sole proprietor are claimed on the first page of Form 1040 as an adjustment to gross income.

Line 20, Rent or Lease

Line 20a is used for the rental of vehicles, machinery, and equipment.

Caution. Rent-to-own contracts and purchase contracts are sometimes disguised as lease or rental arrangements. It is often necessary to look beneath the name of the contract or arrangement to its substance. If at the end of the lease or rental period, the asset belongs to the lessor for a small payment or no payment at all, the taxpayer has purchased the property. It is appropriately treated as acquired property and set up for depreciation. It may be necessary to add an inclusion amount to income. See Tab 8 for tables of inclusion amounts.

Line 20b is for amounts paid to rent or lease other property–office space, a retail shop, an entire building–used in the Schedule C business.

Line 21, Repairs and Maintenance

The cost of repairs and maintenance–ordinary upkeep, rather than improving or extending the life of the property involved–is a current deduction on line 21. Repairs related to an office in the home go on Form 8829 and ultimately on line 30 of Schedule C.

Line 22, Supplies

The cost of supplies purchased during the year for use in the ordinary course of business is deductible on line 22. The taxpayer may have a small amount of incidental supplies on hand, with no inventories or records of use and still deduct the cost of supplies purchased during the year, provided that this treatment clearly reflects income.

Line 23, Taxes and Licenses

The following taxes and licenses are deductible on line 23:

- Real estate tax and personal property tax on business assets
- Licenses and regulatory fees, if paid every year
- Matching Social Security taxes (employer's share)
- Matching unemployment taxes (employer's share)
- Federal highway use tax

The following items are *not* deductible on line 23:

- Federal income tax
- Self-employment tax
- Estate or gift taxes
- Taxes on personal use property
- Sales tax on purchase of business assets (add to basis and depreciate)
- Taxes assessed to pay for improvements–paving and so on (reported on Form 4562)
- Employees' share of Social Security and Medicare tax, as well as federal income tax withheld

from employees' wages (reported as part of gross wages on line 26)

Caution. Many taxpayers list net wages here and also incorrectly report Social Security taxes under taxes. Withholdings are often omitted. Taxpayers and practitioners must carefully review. Be sure to reconcile payroll tax returns to numbers shown on Schedule C.

Line 24, Travel, Meals, and Entertainment

Lodging and transportation costs for overnight travel on business are reported on line 24a. The cost of travel for the taxpayer's spouse, dependent, or any other individual is not an allowable deduction unless the travel is for a bona fide business purpose, the person is an employee of the taxpayer, and the travel cost would have been deductible if the individual had paid for it himself or herself.

Expenses for foreign travel are not deductible unless directly related to the taxpayer's trade or business.

On line 24b, enter the cost of business meals and entertainment. In lieu of actual cost, the taxpayer may use the standard meal allowance.

Planning Tip. Be aware that records documenting the time, place, and purposes of the business meal or meals while traveling must still be kept, even if standard allowances are used.

A per diem that includes both meals and incidental expenses (M&IE) may be used. There is also a per diem that includes lodging–but that allowance may not be used by self-employed individuals. Actual facility receipts must support the lodging deduction.

The per diem rates can be found in Tab 6 and at www.gsa.gov/perdiem. IRS Publication 463 shows how to calculate the standard meal allowance. In order to be deductible, the business meals must be directly related to or associated with the active conduct of the trade or business, not lavish or extravagant, and they must be incurred while either the owner or an employee is present.

The following items are deductible without regard to whether they are directly related to or associated with the active conduct of the business (IRC §274(e)):

- Food and drink furnished on the employer's business premises primarily for employees (e.g., costs of a holiday office party).
- Recreational or social activities, including facilities primarily for employees (e.g., a summer golf outing, a company health club or an annual picnic).
- Entertainment and meal expenses for an employee if the employee reports their value as taxable compensation (e.g., a company-provided vacation for the top salesperson).
- Entertainment and meal expenses at business meetings of employees, stockholders, and directors (e.g., refreshments at a directors' meeting).
- Costs of items made available to the general public (e.g., soft drinks at a grand opening, free ham to the first 50 customers).
- Costs of entertainment and meals sold to customers (e.g., costs of food sold at an event).
- Reimbursed expenses if the employer does not include the reimbursements as compensation.
- Expenses directly related to and necessary for attendance at a business meeting of any tax-exempt group, such as a chamber of commerce, real estate board, or board of trade.
- Expenses incurred for goods, services, and facilities provided to nonemployees.

Because only 50% of the cost of business meals and entertainment is deductible, 50% of line 24b is shown on line 24c. Line 24b less line 24c gives the deductible portion of meals and entertainment on line 24d.

Exceptions to the 50% Limitation. There are a number of situations involving meal and entertainment expenses when the 50% disallowance rule does not apply.

Reimbursement of expenses. The limitation does not apply to the extent the expense is reimbursed under an accountable plan. Instead, the limitation is imposed on the party making the reimbursement.

Excludable fringe benefits. The 50% limitation does not apply to fringe benefits that can be excluded, such as:

- De minimis fringe benefits (e.g., holiday turkeys, hams, and fruitcakes) given to employees
- Subsidized employee cafeterias
- Meals provided on the employer's premises for the convenience of the employer (e.g., for restaurant employees)

Self-employed. Taxpayers who are self-employed are not subject to the 50% limit if all of the following apply:

- The expenses are incurred as an independent contractor.
- The taxpayer's customer or client reimburses him or her for meal and entertainment expenses incurred in connection with services performed.
- The taxpayer provides adequate records of the expenses to the customer or client.

Advertising expenses. The limitation does not apply if the taxpayer provides meals and entertainment as a means of advertising (i.e., promoting goodwill in the community).

Sales of meals or entertainment. The limitation does not apply if the taxpayer actually sells the meals or entertainment to the general public.

Charitable sporting events. The costs of tickets to a sporting event are generally not subject to the reduction rule if the event is for charity.

Department of Transportation workers. For workers subject to the Department of Transportation hours of service limitations, the deduction for 2009 is 80% of the total meal cost. This includes air transportation workers subject to Federal Aviation Administration regulations, as well as truck drivers, railroad workers, and others.

Line 25, Utilities

Direct utility costs for the business are deducted on line 25. Utilities costs for the business portion of the taxpayer's personal residence are reported on Form 8829.

If the taxpayer's home phone is used for business, the base rate of the first phone line into the residence is not deductible. The cost of a second line into the home is deductible to the extent of business use, including the base charges.

Line 26, Wages

Report on line 26 the gross wages paid to employees, reduced by employment credits and wages deducted under the calculation of the cost of goods sold. This is the net of the reportable wages, plus the employee's share of Social Security and Medicare withheld, the federal income tax withheld, and the state income tax withheld.

Reconcile the amount on line 26 to the Forms W-2 and W-3 filed for the business. For a cash-basis taxpayer, the gross wages are deductible when the net wages are paid to the employee. The employer's match for Social Security and Medicare is deductible when the government deposit is made.

Filing Tip. Match reported wages—Forms 941 and W-2—with taxpayer's summarized wages. Do not include non-W-2 compensation with W-2 wages.

Line 27, Other Expenses

Deductible expenses not elsewhere identified on Schedule C are listed in Part V, with the total carried forward to line 27. This includes such items as bad debts, bank service charges, dues and subscriptions, trash removal, and others. It also includes the amortization of start-up costs.

Charitable contributions are not normally deductible on Schedule C; rather, they are claimed by the taxpayer on Schedule A. There are possible exceptions, however, that convert an otherwise charitable contribution to a business expense. A common situation is a contribution to a charity, for which in return the business is listed or featured in a program brochure or advertised or promoted in some other way.

Lines 28 and 29, Calculations

Total expenses before including business use of home, the sum of lines 8 through 27 except lines 24b and 24c, are reported on line 28. This amount is then subtracted from line 7 to determine tentative profit or loss, which is reported on line 29.

Line 30, Expenses for Business Use of Home

Form 8829 is used to calculate the allowable expenses for the business use of the taxpayer's personal residence to be deducted on line 30 of Schedule C. The form also documents the carryover to the following year of amounts not deductible in the current year.

In order to qualify for the deduction, the taxpayer must meet two tests.

The business part of the home must be used in all of the following ways:

- *Exclusively.* The use of the specified portion of the home must be exclusive. That area must be used only for the trade or business. The area can be a room, or a portion of a room. It should be separately identifiable, but does not have to have a permanent partition.
- *Regularly.* The space must be used consistently and regularly for the business. Occasional or incidental use does not meet the test.
- *For the trade or business.* If the space is used for a profit-seeking activity that is not a trade or business, the deduction is not allowable.

The business part of the home must be one of the following:

- The principal place of business. The space qualifies as the principal place of business if it is used exclusively and regularly for administrative or management activities of the trade or business and there is no other fixed location where substantial administrative or management activities of the trade or business are conducted.

- A place used to meet or deal with patients, clients, or customers in the normal course of the trade or business.
- A separate structure, not attached to the home, and used for the trade or business.

Planning Tip. Maintaining a guest book for all business visitors in which clients or customers sign in and out will support the deduction.

The business percentage of the home is calculated on Form 8829. The area of the home used for business is divided by the total area. The resulting percentage is the percentage applied to indirect expenses.

Expenses that can be included in calculating the business cost of the home include casualty losses, mortgage interest, real estate taxes, insurance, repairs and maintenance, utilities, and other operating expenses, including a security system.

Form 8829 has two columns so that expenses can be listed as direct or indirect in each category. Direct expenses are those that benefit only the business portion of the home. Examples would be painting only the business area or putting in special security for that room only.

Indirect expenses are those that involve both the business and personal portions of the home. The full amount is entered in column b, with the business percentage from line 7 then applied to that amount.

A taxpayer who provides day care in the home may deduct a part of the home and take an appropriate percentage for day care expense, even if the area is not used exclusively for business. The room may be used by family members in the evening and for day care during the day or vice versa. The percentage calculation for day care also takes into consideration the hours that day care is provided, rather than the square footage.

Line 31, Net Profit or (Loss)

Net profit or loss is entered on Form 1040, line 12, to become a part of the AGI calculation. The profit or loss is also entered on Schedule SE in order to calculate self-employment tax.

Hobby Loss. The gain or loss generated by the business is effectively netted against other income on the first page of Form 1040. However, IRC §183 says that a loss that is generated by an activity not engaged in for profit may not be deducted against other income. There is a "safe harbor" for determining whether an activity is engaged in for profit: if a business generates a profit in three out of five consecutive years, the IRS will not question the profit motive. (It is two out of seven years for horse breeding, showing, and training.)

Planning Tip. What a lot of people think is the sole test is just a safe harbor; clients may therefore be overly timid about declaring hobby losses.

Failing to meet the safe harbor provision does not mean an automatic disallowance–only that the IRS may look into the situation and could disallow the loss. The IRS applies a facts and circumstances test to make a determination. Although the following list is not exhaustive, taken as a whole it does help gauge the existence of a profit motive. The IRS will look at the following items:

1. Does the time and effort put into the activity indicate an intention to make a profit?
2. Does the taxpayer depend upon income from the activity?
3. If there are losses, are they due to circumstances beyond the taxpayer's control or did they occur in the start-up phase of the business?
4. Has the taxpayer changed methods of operation to improve profitability?
5. Does the taxpayer or his/her advisors have the knowledge needed to carry on the activity as a successful business?
6. Has the taxpayer made a profit in similar activities in the past?
7. Does the activity make a profit in some years?
8. Can the taxpayer expect to make a profit in the future from the appreciation of assets used in the activity? (IRS Fact Sheet, FS-2008-23).

Planning Tip. Any client claiming consistent losses on a business should have, at the very least, a business plan that he or she can show to the IRS if necessary.

Line 32, Is Investment at Risk?

If the business generates a loss and there are amounts for which the taxpayer is not at risk, that point is answered by checking the appropriate box for line 32. If there are amounts for which the taxpayer is not at risk, Form 6198, *At-Risk Limitations,* is used to calculate the allowable loss. Under the at-risk rules, the amount of loss that can be claimed is limited to what could actually be lost in the business.

Some possible non-at-risk items are the following:

- Nonrecourse loans used in the business, to acquire the business or to finance aspects of the business, but not secured by the taxpayer's own property (but there is an exception for some nonrecourse financing borrowed in connection with holding real property).
- The existence of a stop-loss agreement, guarantee, or other arrangement (other than insurance) that protects cash, property, or borrowed amounts used in the business.
- Amounts borrowed for business use from an individual who has an interest in the business, other than as a creditor.

Any loss that is disallowed under the at-risk rules on the 2008 return will be available to use as a deduction in the business for 2009. See Tab 5 for a discussion of the at-risk rules.

Part III: Cost of Goods Sold

If the production, purchase, or sale of merchandise is an income-producing factor for the business, inventories must be taken into account at the beginning and end of the tax year.

A taxpayer whose average annual gross receipts for the three previous years are $1 million or less, and whose business is not a tax shelter, may account for inventories in the same manner as materials and supplies that are not incidental. So may a qualifying small business taxpayer whose average annual gross receipts for the three prior tax years are more than a $1 million but not more than $10 million, whose business is not a tax shelter, and whose principal business activity in not an ineligible activity per Rev. Proc. 2002-28.

Line 33, Inventory Method

The inventories may be valued at cost, the lower of cost or market, or any other method approved by the IRS.

Caution. Note that taxpayers using the cash method of accounting are required to use cost.

Line 34, Changes in Inventory Method

An explanation must be attached if there was a change in determining quantities, costs, or valuations between the opening and closing inventory.

Line 35, Inventory at Beginning of Year

Enter the inventory at the beginning of the year and attach an explanation if the 2009 opening inventory differs from the 2008 closing inventory.

Line 36, Purchases Less Cost of Items Withdrawn for Personal Use

Enter the amount paid for purchasing items of inventory, less the cost of items used personally by the taxpayer.

Filing Tip. Some inventory items, such as cosmetics, readily lend themselves to personal use by the taxpayer or as gifts. Take special note if this might be the case and verify inventory records.

Line 37, Cost of Labor

Be certain that amounts entered as labor here are not duplicated on line 26, Wages. Do not include any amount paid to the sole proprietor. If $600 or more was paid to one noncorporate entity, the 1099-MISC must be attached to the return.

Line 38 Materials and Supplies

Enter on line 38 the cost of materials and supplies used to produce or support inventory items.

Line 39 Other Costs

Enter other costs attributable directly to inventory or to the cost of goods sold on line 39. Warehousing costs or fees are included here.

Line 40, Calculation

The sum of lines 35 through 39 (costs related to inventory) is reported on line 40.

Line 41, Inventory at End of Year

The value of the inventory at year's end, preferably the result of a physical inventory, should be entered on line 41.

Caution. Make sure you know whether the client is giving you retail or wholesale inventory numbers. Discourage anything but cost basis.

Table of Common Activity Codes

These codes for the Principal Business or Professional Activity classify sole proprietorships by the type of activity they are engaged in to facilitate the administration of the Internal Revenue Code. These six-digit codes are based on the North American Industry Classification System (NAICS).

Select the category that best describes your primary business activity (for example, Real Estate). Then select the activity that best identifies the principal source of your sales or receipts (for example, 531210, the code for offices of real estate agents and brokers) and **enter the six-digit code assigned to the activity on line B of Schedule C or C-EZ.**

Note. If your principal source of income is from farming activities, you should file **Schedule F**, *Profit or Loss From Farming.*

Accommodation, Food Services, & Drinking Places

Accommodation

721310 Rooming & boarding houses

721210 RV (recreational vehicle) parks & recreational camps

721100 Travel accommodation (including hotels, motels, & bed & breakfast inns)

Food Services and Drinking Places

722410 Drinking places (alcoholic beverages)

722110 Full-Service restaurants

722210 Limited-service eating places

722300 Special food services (including food service contractors & caterers)

Administrative & Support and Waste Management & Remediation Services

Administrative & Support Services

561430 Business service centers (including private mail centers & copy shops)

561740 Carpet & upholstery cleaning services

561440 Collection agencies

561450 Credit bureaus

561410 Document preparation services

561300 Employment services

561710 Exterminating & pest control services

561210 Facilities support (management) services

561600 Investigation & security services

561720 Janitorial services

561730 Landscaping services

561110 Office administrative services

561420 Telephone call centers (including telephone answering services & telemarketing bureaus)

561500 Travel arrangement & reservation services

561490 Other business support services (including repossession services, court reporting, & stenotype services)

561790 Other services to buildings & dwellings

561900 Other support services (including packaging & labeling services, & convention & trade show organizers)

Waste Management & Remediation Services

562000 Waste management & remediation services

Agriculture, Forestry, Hunting, & Fishing

112900 Animal production (including breeding of cats and dogs)

114110 Fishing

113000 Forestry & logging (including forest nurseries & timber tracts)

114210 Hunting & trapping

Support Activities for Agriculture & Forestry

115210 Support activities for animal production (including farriers)

115110 Support activities for crop production (including cotton ginning, soil preparation, planting, & cultivating)

115310 Support activities for forestry

Arts, Entertainment, & Recreation Amusement, Gambling, & Recreation Industries

713100 Amusement parks & arcades

713200 Gambling industries

713900 Other amusement & recreation services (including golf courses, skiing facilities, marinas, fitness centers, bowling centers, skating rinks, miniature golf courses)

Museums, Historical Sites, & Similar Institutions

712100 Museums, historical sites, & similar institutions

Performing Arts, Spectator Sports, & Related Industries

711410 Agents & managers for artists, athletes, entertainers, & other public figures

711510 Independent artists, writers, & performers

711100 Performing arts companies

711300	Promoters of performing arts, sports, & similar events
711210	Spectator sports (including professional sports clubs & racetrack operations)

Construction of Buildings

236200	Nonresidential building construction
236100	Residential building construction

Heavy and Civil Engineering Construction

237310	Highway, street, & bridge construction
237210	Land subdivision
237100	Utility system construction
237990	Other heavy & civil engineering construction

Specialty Trade Contractors

238310	Drywall & insulation contractors
238210	Electrical contractors
238350	Finish carpentry contractors
238330	Flooring contractors
238130	Framing carpentry contractors
238150	Glass & glazing contractors
238140	Masonry contractors
238320	Painting & wall covering contractors
238220	Plumbing, heating & air-conditioning contractors
238110	Poured concrete foundation & structure contractors
238160	Roofing contractors
238170	Siding contractors
238910	Site preparation contractors
238120	Structural steel & precast concrete construction contractors
238340	Tile & terrazzo contractors
238290	Other building equipment contractors
238390	Other building finishing contractors
238190	Other foundation, structure, & building exterior contractors
238990	All other specialty trade contractors

Educational Services

611000	Educational services (including schools, colleges, & universities)

Finance & Insurance

Credit Intermediation & Related Activities

522100	Depository credit intermediation (including commercial banking, savings institutions, & credit unions)
522200	Nondepository credit intermediation (including sales financing & consumer lending)
522300	Activities related to credit intermediation (including loan brokers)

Insurance Agents, Brokers, & Related Activities

524210	Insurance agencies & brokerages
524290	Other insurance related activities

Securities, Commodity Contracts, & Other Financial Investments & Related Activities

523140	Commodity contracts brokers
523130	Commodity contracts dealers
523110	Investment bankers & securities dealers
523210	Securities & commodity exchanges
523120	Securities brokers
523900	Other financial investment activities (including investment advice)

Health Care & Social Assistance

Ambulatory Health Care Services

621610	Home health care services
621510	Medical & diagnostic laboratories
621310	Offices of chiropractors
621210	Offices of dentists
621330	Offices of mental health practitioners (except physicians)
621320	Offices of optometrists
621340	Offices of physical, occupational & speech therapists, & audiologists
621111	Offices of physicians (except mental health specialists)
621112	Offices of physicians, mental health specialists
621391	Offices of podiatrists
621399	Offices of all other miscellaneous health practitioners
621400	Outpatient care centers
621900	Other ambulatory health care services (including ambulance services, blood, & organ banks)

Hospitals

622000	Hospitals

Nursing & Residential Care Facilities

623000	Nursing & residential care facilities

Social Assistance

624410	Child day care services
624200	Community food & housing, & emergency & other relief services
624100	Individual & family services
624310	Vocational rehabilitation services

Information

511000	Publishing industries (except Internet)

Broadcasting (except Internet) & Telecommunications

515000	Broadcasting (except Internet)
517000	Telecommunications

Internet Publishing & Broadcasting

516110	Internet publishing & broadcasting

Internet Service Providers, Web Search Portals, & Data Processing Services

518210	Data processing, hosting, & related services
518111	Internet service providers
518112	Web search portals
519100	Other information services (including news syndicates and libraries)

Motion Picture & Sound Recording

512100	Motion picture & video industries (except video rental)
512200	Sound recording industries

Manufacturing

315000	Apparel mfg.
312000	Beverage & tobacco product mfg.
334000	Computer & electronic product mfg.
335000	Electrical equipment, appliance, & component mfg.
332000	Fabricated metal product mfg.
337000	Furniture & related product mfg.
333000	Machinery mfg.
339110	Medical equipment & supplies mfg.
322000	Paper mfg.
324100	Petroleum & coal products mfg.
326000	Plastics & rubber products mfg.
331000	Primary metal mfg.
323100	Printing & related support activities
313000	Textile mills
314000	Textile product mills
336000	Transportation equipment mfg.
321000	Wood product mfg.
339900	Other miscellaneous mfg.

Chemical Manufacturing

325100	Basic chemical mfg.
325500	Paint, coating, & adhesive mfg.

325300	Pesticide, fertilizer, & other agricultural chemical mfg.
325410	Pharmaceutical & medicine mfg.
325200	Resin, synthetic rubber, & artificial & synthetic fibers & filaments mfg.
325600	Soap, cleaning compound, & toilet preparation mfg.
325900	Other chemical product & preparation mfg.

Food Manufacturing

311110	Animal food mfg.
311800	Bakeries & tortilla mfg.
311500	Dairy product mfg.
311400	Fruit & vegetable preserving & speciality food mfg.
311200	Grain & oilseed milling
311610	Animal slaughtering & processing
311710	Seafood product preparation & packaging
311300	Sugar & confectionery product mfg.
311900	Other food mfg. (including coffee, tea, flavorings, & seasonings)

Leather & Allied Product Manufacturing

316210	Footwear mfg. (including leather, rubber, & plastics)
316110	Leather & hide tanning & finishing
316990	Other leather & allied product mfg.

Nonmetallic Mineral Product Manufacturing

327300	Cement & concrete product mfg.
327100	Clay product & refractory mfg.
327210	Glass & glass product mfg.
327400	Lime & gypsum product mfg.
327900	Other nonmetallic mineral product mfg.

Mining

212110	Coal mining
212200	Metal ore mining
212300	Nonmetallic mineral mining & quarrying
211110	Oil & gas extraction
213110	Support activities for mining

Other Services

Personal & Laundry Services

812111	Barber shops
812112	Beauty salons
812220	Cemeteries & crematories
812310	Coin-operated laundries & drycleaners
812320	Drycleaning & laundry services (except coin-operated) (including laundry & drycleaning dropoff & pickup sites)
812210	Funeral homes & funeral services
812330	Linen & uniform supply
812113	Nail salons
812930	Parking lots & garages
812910	Pet care (except veterinary) services
812920	Photofinishing
812190	Other personal care services (including diet & weight reducing centers)
812990	All other personal services

Repair & Maintenance

811120	Automotive body, paint, interior, & glass repair
811110	Automotive mechanical & electrical repair & maintenance
811190	Other automotive repair & maintenance (including oil change & lubrication shops & car washes)
811310	Commercial & industrial machinery & equipment (except automotive & electronic) repair & maintenance
811210	Electronic & precision equipment repair & maintenance
811430	Footwear & leather goods repair
811410	Home & garden equipment & appliance repair & maintenance
811420	Reupholstery & furniture repair
811490	Other personal & household goods repair & maintenance

Professional, Scientific, & Technical Services

541100	Legal services
541211	Offices of certified public accountants
541214	Payroll services
541213	Tax preparation services
541219	Other accounting services

Architectural, Engineering, & Related Services

541310	Architectural services
541350	Building inspection services
541340	Drafting services
541330	Engineering services
541360	Geophysical surveying & mapping services
541320	Landscape architecture services
541370	Surveying & mapping (except geophysical) services
541380	Testing laboratories

Computer Systems Design & Related Services

541510	Computer systems design & related services

Specialized Design Services

541400	Specialized design services (including interior, industrial, graphic, & fashion design)

Other Professional, Scientific, & Technical Services

541800	Advertising & related services
541600	Management, scientific, & technical consulting services
541910	Market research & public opinion polling
541920	Photographic services
541700	Scientific research & development services
541930	Translation & interpretation services
541940	Veterinary services
541990	All other professional, scientific, & technical services

Real Estate & Rental & Leasing

Real Estate

531100	Lessors of real estate (including miniwarehouses & self-storage units)
531210	Offices of real estate agents & brokers
531320	Offices of real estate appraisers
531310	Real estate property managers
531390	Other activities related to real estate

Rental & Leasing Services

532100	Automotive equipment rental & leasing
532400	Commercial & industrial machinery & equipment rental & leasing
532210	Consumer electronics & appliances rental
532220	Formal wear & costume rental
532310	General rental centers
532230	Video tape & disc rental
532290	Other consumer goods rental

Religious, Grantmaking, Civic, Professional, & Similar Organizations

813000	Religious, grantmaking, civic, professional, & similar organizations

Retail Trade

Building Material & Garden Equipment & Supplies Dealers

444130	Hardware stores
444110	Home centers

444200 Lawn & garden equipment & supplies stores
444120 Paint & wallpaper stores
444190 Other building materials dealers

Clothing & Accessories Stores

448130 Children's & infants' clothing stores
448150 Clothing accessories stores
448140 Family clothing stores
448310 Jewelry stores
448320 Luggage & leather goods stores
448110 Men's clothing stores
448210 Shoe stores
448120 Women's clothing stores
448190 Other clothing stores

Electronic & Appliance Stores

443130 Camera & photographic supplies stores
443120 Computer & software stores
443111 Household appliance stores
443112 Radio, television, & other electronics stores

Food & Beverage Stores

445310 Beer, wine, & liquor stores
445220 Fish & seafood markets
445230 Fruit & vegetable markets
445100 Grocery stores (including supermarkets & convenience stores without gas)
445210 Meat markets
445290 Other specialty food stores

Furniture & Home Furnishing Stores

442110 Furniture stores
442200 Home furnishings stores

Gasoline Stations

447100 Gasoline stations (including convenience stores with gas)

General Merchandise Stores

452000 General merchandise stores

Health & Personal Care Stores

446120 Cosmetics, beauty supplies, & perfume stores
446130 Optical goods stores
446110 Pharmacies & drug stores
446190 Other health & personal care stores

Motor Vehicle & Parts Dealers

441300 Automotive parts, accessories, & tire stores
441222 Boat dealers
441221 Motorcycle dealers
441110 New car dealers
441210 Recreational vehicle dealers (including motor home & travel trailer dealers)
441120 Used car dealers
441229 All other motor vehicle dealers

Sporting Goods, Hobby, Book, & Music Stores

451211 Book stores
451120 Hobby, toy, & game stores
451140 Musical instrument & supplies stores
451212 News dealers & newsstands
451220 Prerecorded tape, compact disc, & record stores
451130 Sewing, needlework, & piece goods stores
451110 Sporting goods stores

Miscellaneous Store Retailers

453920 Art dealers
453110 Florists
453220 Gift, novelty, & souvenir stores
453930 Manufactured (mobile) home dealers
453210 Office supplies & stationery stores
453910 Pet & pet supplies stores
453310 Used merchandise stores
453990 All other miscellaneous store retailers (including tobacco, candle, & trophy shops)

Nonstore Retailers

454112 Electronic auctions
454111 Electronic shopping
454310 Fuel dealers
454113 Mail-order houses
454210 Vending machine operators
454390 Other direct selling establishments (including door-to-door retailing, frozen food plan providers, party plan merchandisers, & coffee-break service providers)

Transportation & Warehousing

481000 Air transportation
485510 Charter bus industry
484110 General freight trucking, local
484120 General freight trucking, long distance
485210 Interurban & rural bus transportation
486000 Pipeline transportation
482110 Rail transportation
487000 Scenic & sightseeing transportation
485410 School & employee bus transportation
484200 Specialized freight trucking (including household moving vans)
485300 Taxi & limousine service
485110 Urban transit systems
483000 Water transportation
485990 Other transit & ground passenger transportation
488000 Support activities for transportation (including motor vehicle towing)

Couriers & Messengers

492000 Couriers & messengers

Warehousing & Storage Facilities

493100 Warehousing & storage (except leases of miniwarehouses & self-storage units)

Utilities

221000 Utilities

Wholesale Trade

Merchant Wholesalers, Durable Goods

423600 Electrical & electronic goods
423200 Furniture & home furnishing
423700 Hardware, & plumbing & heating equipment & supplies
423940 Jewelry, watch, precious stone, & precious metals
423300 Lumber & other construction materials
423800 Machinery, equipment, & supplies
423500 Metal & mineral (except petroleum)
423100 Motor vehicle & motor vehicle parts & supplies
423400 Professional & commercial equipment & supplies
423930 Recyclable materials
423910 Sporting & recreational goods & supplies
423920 Toy & hobby goods & supplies
423990 Other miscellaneous durable goods

Merchant Wholesalers, Nondurable Goods

424300 Apparel, piece goods, & notions
424800 Beer, wine, & distilled alcoholic beverage
424920 Books, periodicals, & newspapers
424600 Chemical & allied products
424210 Drugs & druggists' sundries
424500 Farm product raw materials
424910 Farm supplies

424930 Flower, nursery stock, & florists' supplies	424100 Paper & paper products	424990 Other miscellaneous nondurable goods	425120 Wholesale trade agents & brokers
424400 Grocery & related products	424700 Petroleum & petroleum products	**Wholesale Electronic Markets and Agents & Brokers**	999999 Unclassified establishments (unable to classify)
424950 Paint, varnish, & supplies	424940 Tobacco & tobacco products	425110 Business to business electronic markets	

Schedule F Line-by-Line Instructions

Schedule F is filed to report income and related expenses from the sale of livestock and other items bought for resale; the sale of livestock, produce, and other items raised; distributions from cooperatives; government farm program payments; and other income generated by the active conduct of production agriculture.

Schedule F may also be used to report the farm income for a trust or partnership.

> **Gray Area.** When is a farmer not a farmer? A farmer is one who is engaged primarily in the business of farming. A taxpayer was not considered a farmer, due to his wife's separate income, because less than two-thirds of the aggregate gross income on the couple's joint return was from farming. Where only one spouse has substantial nonfarm income, the two-thirds farm income rule can be avoided by filing separate returns.

Farming and Self-Employment Tax

The net profit on Schedule F is subject to self-employment tax. Farmers who have a loss can use the "farm optional method SE tax." This method allows individuals to continue paying SE tax for their Social Security coverage when their net profit for the year is small or they have a loss.

To qualify to use the "farm optional method SE tax", gross income from farming must be $6,540 or less, or net farm profits must be less than $4,721. The amount that may be considered net earnings from farm self-employment income, and be taxed for SE purposes, is the smaller of $4,360 and two-thirds of gross farm income (not less than zero).

Farm Income Averaging

Farm income averaging was designed to allow farmers to "average" their income from a high-income year back over the last three years. Schedule J of Form 1040 is used to calculate 2009 tax by averaging, over the base years (the three previous years), all or part of a taxpayer's income from the trade or business of farming.

Farm income averaging may be used by an individual engaged in a farming business, a partner in a farm partnership, or a shareholder in an S corporation that is engaged in farming. Corporations, partnerships, S corporations, estates, and trusts cannot use farm income averaging.

Farm income, gains, losses, and deductions reported on the following forms are generally eligible for averaging:

- Form 1040, line 7–to the extent of wages and other compensation received as a shareholder in an S corporation engaged in a farming business
- Schedule D
- Schedule E, Part II
- Schedule F
- Form 4797
- Form 4835

Note two recent developments:

- Negative income in a base year now counts as negative income, rather than just zero.
- In calculating AMT, the regular tax before income averaging is compared to the tentative minimum tax.

Information About Farm Business

Name of Proprietor and SSN

The name of the proprietor goes on the first line of Schedule F, followed by the Social Security number at the end of that line (see line D). When Schedule F is used as a part of a Form 1041, 1065, or 1065B, use Employer ID Number, rather than a Social Security number.

Lines A and B, Principal Product and Code

Enter the principal crop or activity for 2009 on line A. On line B, enter one of the 14 principal agricultural codes. Select the code from the table below that best describes the largest source of income from Part IV of Schedule F.

Agricultural Principal Product Codes	
Crop Production	
111100	Oilseed and grain farming
111210	Vegetable and melon farming
111300	Fruit and tree nut farming
111400	Greenhouse, nursery, and floriculture production
111900	Other crop farming
Animal Production	
112111	Beef cattle ranching and farming
112112	Cattle feedlots
112120	Dairy cattle and milk production
112210	Hog and pig farming
112300	Poultry and egg production
112400	Sheep and goat farming
112510	Animal aquaculture
112900	Other animal production
Forestry and Logging	
113000	Forestry and logging (including forest nurseries and timber tracts)

Line C, Accounting Method

Schedule F gives the taxpayer a choice of cash or accrual basis.

With the cash method, income is reported in the year it is actually or constructively received. Expenses are reported in the year they are paid, unless the expenditure creates an asset that has a useful life beyond the current year. In that case, the items may be only partially deductible in the current year. One example is the purchase of a tractor. It must be set up for depreciation. Another example is payment for liability insurance that includes the current year and the following two years. Only the portion applying to the current year is deductible on that year's return. A cash-basis taxpayer marks the "Cash" box and completes Parts I and II of Schedule F.

Caution. Is that farm implement a depreciable asset or a leased piece of equipment? Read the contract and also follow the payment and trade-in documentation.

Under the accrual method of accounting, income is reported in the year earned, while expenses are deducted in the year incurred. Accrual-basis taxpayers are on a cash basis for deducting business expenses owed to a related cash-basis taxpayer. A taxpayer who keeps an inventory must generally use an accrual method of accounting to determine gross income. There is an exception for farmers who average annual gross receipts of $1 million or less.

Under the accrual method of accounting, expenses are generally deducted or capitalized when the *all-events* test has been met and economic performance has occurred. The all-events test is met when all events have occurred that fix the fact of liability and the liability can be determined with reasonable accuracy.

An accrual basis farmer marks the "Accrual" box and completes Parts II, III, and line 11 of Schedule F.

Line D, EIN

Enter an employer identification number only if the business has a qualified retirement plan or is required to file an employment, excise, estate, trust, partnership, or alcohol, tobacco, and firearms tax return. If you do not have an EIN, leave Line D blank.

Line E, Material Participation

See the discussion of material participation under Schedule C, page 3-8.

Part I: Farm Income—Cash Method

For items 1 through 10 of this section, include both cash actually or constructively received and the FMV of goods or other property received for these items. When an amount is credited to the taxpayer's account, or is set aside for his or her benefit, it is considered constructively received.

There is an exception for farm production flexibility contract payments received under the Federal Agriculture Improvement and Reform Act of 1996. They must be reported as income only in the year of actual receipt.

Do not include sales of livestock held for draft, breeding, sport, or dairy purposes on Schedule F. The sale or disposition of these animals is reported on Form 4797.

There is a special provision for livestock sold due to drought, flood, or other weather-related conditions. A Schedule F filer may elect to report the income from the sale in the year after the sale if all of these conditions are met:

- The taxpayer's main business is farming.
- Schedule F is filed on a cash basis.
- The excess animals would not have been sold under the taxpayer's normal business practices, but were instead sold solely because of the weather-related condition.
- The weather-related condition caused the area to be designated as eligible for federal assistance.

Line 1, Sales of Livestock and Other Items Purchased for Resale

Enter on line 1 livestock, grain, and other items purchased for resale. These animals should not have been on the depreciation schedule. A common example is feeder cattle, purchased at a given number of pounds, fed for a period of time, and sold at an increased number of pounds.

Line 2, Cost or Other Basis of Livestock and Other Items Reported on Line 1

Enter on line 2 the cost or basis of items sold and reported on line 1. Note that, for cash-basis taxpayers, lines 1 and 2 are for reporting the sale and cost of the same animals, or other items. Items purchased in 2009 but not sold until 2010 are reported on line 2 in 2010. Similarly, both the sale and the cost of animals or other items purchased in 2008 but not sold until 2009 are reported on the 2009 Schedule F.

Line 3, Calculation

Subtract line 2 from line 1 and enter the result on line 3.

Line 4, Sales of Livestock, Produce, Grains, and Other Products You Raised

Sales proceeds from livestock, produce, grains, and so on raised by the taxpayer are reported on line 4.

Lines 5a and 5b, Cooperative Distributions [Form(s) 1099-PATR, *Taxable Distributions Received From Cooperatives*]

Patronage dividends reported by cooperatives are reported to the taxpayer on a 1099-PATR.

Filing Tip. Such distributions are often made in a combination of cash (check) and stock in the co-op. Both must be reported. Taxpayers often forget to report the stock portion, since it is quite likely not recorded in the record book.

Two spaces are provided on line 5 for patronage refunds (dividends). The entire amount reported to the taxpayer (received by the taxpayer) is reported on line 5a, the taxable portion is reported on line 5b. Only the amount that was generated by farming activity or purchases is reported on line 5b. Income generated from buying personal or family items or personal assets is included on line 5a, but not on line 5b.

Lines 6a and 6b, Agricultural Program Payments

Government farm program payments are reported to recipients on Form 1099-G, *Certain Government Payments,* or CCC-1099-G. The payments reported may be from price support payments, market gain on CCC loans, diversion payments, cost-share payments, conservation reserve payments, payments in the form of materials or services, and other farm program payments.

There are two spaces for line 6: 6a is for reporting the total amount received and 6b is for reporting the taxable amount.

Example. Marvin Phillips elected to report CCC loan proceeds as income in 2008, the year he received it. There is no gain from redemption of the commodity in 2009 because the CCC loan proceeds have previously been reported as income. Marvin is treated as having repurchased the commodity for the amount of the loan repayment. The transaction is thus shown on line 6a.

If Marvin had not reported the CCC loan proceeds under the election in 2008, then he would have to report the market gain on line 6b.

Lines 7a, 7b, and 7c, Commodity Credit Corporation (CCC) Loans

Schedule F has three spaces for reporting CCC loans. Line 7a is for CCC loans taken out in 2009 which the taxpayer is electing to report as income. CCC loans forfeited are reported in full on 7b, whether or not an election was made and the original loan was reported as income. The taxable amount of the loans forfeited is reported on 7c; if the taxpayer did not elect to report the loan proceeds as income when the loan was taken out, then the loan is reported as income here.

Normally, there will not be an entry on line 7c if the loan proceeds were reported as income under the election. However, even if the election was made, if the amount forfeited is different from the basis in the commodity, there may be an entry on line 7c.

Lines 8a, 8b, 8c, and 8d, Crop Insurance Proceeds and Certain Disaster Payments

There are four spaces for reporting crop insurance proceeds. The total of all crop insurance payments (and certain disaster payments) received during the tax year is entered on line 8a. The taxable amount is reported on 8b.

Caution. Dating of contracts, CCC loans, and leases must be tied to actual service times and not as shell dates for contingency arrangements for income recognition or placed in service scheduling.

Line 8b may be "0" if, on line 8c, the taxpayer elects to defer insurance proceeds received in the current year to the following year.

Line 8d is for reporting the amount deferred from the prior year and is fully taxable.

Note that the Form 1099 received from the insurance company may well show more than the total of the checks received. This may happen because many companies net the amount of the insurance claim against the deferred premium. When crop insurance proceeds are reported, check to reconcile the amount received with the Form 1099. The remittance advice received with the check should detail the deduction for the premium. Enter the full 1099 amount as above and show the amount deducted as an expense on line 22 of Part II as crop insurance premiums.

Line 9, Custom Hire (Machine Work) Income

Report on line 9 payments from those for whom the taxpayer performed farm-related services and, in some cases, used the farm machinery for which depreciation is claimed on Schedule F. There may be some 1099-MISCs issued by other farmers to the taxpayer.

Line 10, Other Income

Items that are reported on line 10 include federal fuel tax credits and state gasoline or fuel tax refunds. Also reported here is any recapture of excess depreciation or Section 179 expense if the business use of any listed property decreases to 50% or less during 2009 (from Part IV, Form 4797). Gain or loss on the sale of commodity futures contracts is reported on line 10 as well, provided the transactions were truly hedges and not speculation. If the amount to be reported is a loss, put it in brackets and subtract that item when totaling down the column. Also include rebates from vendors, reimbursement from landlords, and other farm-related income not reported elsewhere on Schedule F.

Cancellation of Farm Debt. Cancellation of farm debt may also be reported on line 10. However, it is normally more complex than that. If a debt is canceled, other than as a gift or bequest, it must generally be included in gross income. If it is a nonbusiness debt, it is reported on line 21 of Form 1040. There are some exceptions:

- If the seller of property reduces the amount owed, this is considered a purchase price (basis) adjustment.
- If the payment of the debt would have resulted in a deductible expense, the forgiveness of the debt is not reported as income.

There are some exclusions for which the cancellation of debt is not included in income:

- The cancellations is a part of a bankruptcy under title 11 of the U.S. Code.
- The cancellation takes place when the individual is insolvent.
- The canceled debt is a qualified farm debt. The *Qualified farm debt* exclusion applies when at least 50% of the taxpayer's total gross receipts for the three tax years preceding the year of debt cancellation were from the farming business for which the debt was incurred.
- The canceled debt is a qualified real property business debt.

These exclusions are claimed on Form 982 and in some cases require a reduction in tax attributes.

Caution. Uses of working capital loans for payment of personal, nonbusiness debt can change the nature of the loan from business to personal.

Line 11, Gross Income

Cash-method taxpayers add lines 3, 4, 5b, 6b, 7a, 7c, 8b, 8d, 9, and 10 and enter the result on line 11. Accrual-method taxpayers enter the amount from line 51 on line 11. This is the gross income from the farm business.

Part II: Farm Expenses—Cash and Accrual Method

Do not deduct the following in this section: personal or living expenses (such as taxes, insurance or home repairs costs) that do not produce income, expenses of raising anything that was used by the taxpayer or his or her family, the value of animals raised that died, inventory losses or personal losses. If the taxpayer was repaid for any part of an expense the taxpayer must subtract the amount that was repaid from the deduction.

Filing Tip. Segregate recordkeeping for personal and farming activities to avoid subsequent confusion of source and use.

Line 12, Car and Truck Expenses

See Tab 8 for a full discussion of autos and listed property.

- Taxpayers may use the standard mileage rate for vehicles operated in 2009 (55 cents per mile for business travel, 24 cents per mile for medical or moving mileage; 14 cents per mile for charitable mileage) or track actual operating expenses.
- The standard mileage rate covers depreciation, fuel, oil, repairs, insurance, license, tires, and so on. Only

tolls, parking, and the appropriate part of interest and personal property taxes paid are additional expenses.

Actual costs include all costs. A log of business use must be kept in order to determine the appropriate allocation between business and personal use.

There is a special rule (Temporary Reg. §1.274-6T(b)) under which a farmer may consider a pickup truck, used the majority of each day for farm business, as a business vehicle.

Line 13, Chemicals

The cost of chemicals is shown on line 13. Report the total amount paid on line 13. Report any reimbursements from a landlord on line 10, Part I.

Line 14, Conservation Expenses

Deductible soil and water conservation expenses include the cost of leveling, grading and terracing; contour furrowing; the construction, control and protection of diversion channels, drainage ditches, earthen dams, watercourses, outlets and ponds; the eradication of brush; and the planting of windbreaks. All these are expenses paid to prevent erosion of land used for farming. In order to be deductible, they must be consistent with a conservation plan approved by the Natural Resources Conservation Service of the U.S. Department of Agriculture.

The deduction may not exceed 25% of gross income from farming in each year (excluding gains from selling assets, such as machinery or land). Any amount that cannot be taken in the current year is carried forward and deducted in a later year.

Endangered species recovery expenditures. The Heartland, Habitat, Harvest, and Horticulture Act of 2008 (Farm Act) added the endangered species recovery expenditures to the category of expenditures that qualify for the deduction allowed by Code Sec. 175 for soil and water conservation expenditures and land erosion prevention expenditures. However, endangered species recovery expenditures are expenses paid or incurred after December 31, 2008, and, therefore, not available for the 2008 tax year.

Planning Tip. Section 179 planning should look beyond deferring tax liability in the current year; it should also watch the impact on future years. Instant gratification is not always the best theory here.

Line 15, Custom Hire (Machine Work)

On line 15, enter the amount paid to a nonemployee to do a custom job for the taxpayer or to bring in his equipment and operate it. This includes both the cost of the machinery or implement and the cost of the operator.

Caution. A taxpayer should not report the amount paid for rental or lease of equipment that he or she operates himself or herself on line 15. That is machine rental to be reported on line 26a.

Line 16, Depreciation and Section 179 Expense Deduction

See Tab 7 for a complete discussion of depreciation.

Planning Tip. Land-clearing costs, costs of draining or filling wetlands, costs involved in preparing the land for center pivot irrigation systems, and other related costs are added to the basis of the land.

The expanded Section 179 expensing election has worked very well for farmers in helping to even out the ups and downs of farming.

Unicap refers to uniform capitalization rules under IRC §263A for both farmers and other businesses. There are some special unicap rules for farmers. For more discussion see MTG ¶999.

For individuals with a farming business, the unicap rules apply only for plants that have a preproductive period of more than two years. They also do not apply to the cost of replanting plants bearing a crop for human consumption that are damaged or lost due to freezing, disease, drought, pests or casualty.

For unicap, a farming business is defined as a trade or business involving the cultivation of land or the raising or harvesting of any agricultural or horticultural commodity.

Caution. Section 263A costs for raising an animal needs specialized attention.

- The preproductive period for plants begins when the plant is first acquired or the seed is first planted and ends when a marketable crop is produced.

The rules for depreciating farm property may be found in IRS Publication 225, *Farmer's Tax Guide.*

Line 17, Employee Benefit Programs Other Than Pension and Profit-Sharing Plans

Here report accident and health insurance, group-term life insurance and other employee benefits not reportable elsewhere. Pension and profit-sharing plans are reported on line 25.

Do not include any contribution made on behalf of the sole proprietor or self-employed individual.

Line 18, Feed Purchased

Report the cost of feed purchased during the current year.

Prepaid feed (as well as fertilizer, lime, chemicals and other crop and livestock input items) to be used in the following year may be deducted. There are some rules that must be followed:

- This must be an actual purchase, not a deposit. Indicators of a deposit, rather than a payment, are the following:
  - The absence of specific quantity terms.
  - The right to a refund of any unapplied payment credit at the end of the contract.
  - The seller's treatment of the payment as a deposit.
  - The right to substitute other goods or products for those specified in the contract.

- The product must be delivered to the business, or if it remains with the vendor, it should be separately accounted for by the vendor. There is an exception here for feed that does allow for some substitute ingredients to vary the particular feed to the livestock's current diet requirements: neither this, nor a price adjustment to reflect market value at the date of delivery is, by itself, proof of a deposit when dealing with prepaid feed.
- There must be a business purpose for the prepayment. (Saving taxes is not a business purpose.) The purpose could be concern about a possible supply shortage or a concern about a price increase. It may even be some other preferential treatment. But there should be a business benefit for the purchase.
- The purchase should not materially distort income.

For a cash-basis business, the deduction for prepaid farm supplies, feed, seed, etc. in the year they are paid for 2009 is generally limited to 50% of the other deductible farm expenses for 2009 (that is, all Schedule F deductions except prepaid farm supplies). Any excess is deducted in the year of use. The 50% limit does not apply if:

- The prepaid farm supplies expense is more than 50% of other deductible farm expenses because of a change in business operations caused by unusual circumstances.

- The total prepaid farm supplies expense for the preceding three years is less than 50% of the total other deductible farm expenses for those three years.

Farm Property Recovery Periods

Assets	Recovery Period in Years	
	GDS	ADS
Agricultural structures (single purpose)	10	15
Airplanes (including helicopters)[1]	5	6
Automobiles	5	5
Calculators and copiers	5	6
Cattle (dairy or breeding)	5	7
Communication equipment[2]	7	10
Computer and peripheral equipment	5	5
Cotton ginning assets	7	12
Drainage facilities	15	20
Farm buildings[3]	20	25
Farm machinery and equipment	7	10
Fences (agricultural)	7	10
Goats and sheep (breeding)	5	5
Grain bin	7	10
Hogs (breeding)	3	3
Horses (age when placed in service)		
Breeding and working (12 years or less)	7	10
Breeding and working (more than 12 years)	3	10
Racing horses (more than 2 years)	3	12
Horticultural structures (single purpose)	10	15
Logging machinery and equipment[4]	5	6
Nonresidential real property	39[5]	40
Office equipment (not calculators, copiers, or typewriters)	7	10

Farm Property Recovery Periods (Continued)

Assets	Recovery Period in Years	
	GDS	ADS
Office furniture or fixtures	7	10
Residential rental property	27.5	40
Trees or vines bearing fruit or nuts	10	20
Truck (heavy duty, unloaded weight 13,000 lbs. or more)	5	6
Truck (actual weight less than 13,000 lbs)	5	5
Typewriter	5	6
Water wells	15	20

1 Not including airplanes used in commercial or contract carrying of passengers.
2 Not including communication equipment listed in other classes.
3 Not including single purpose agricultural or horticultural structures.
4 Used by logging and sawmill operators for cutting of timber.
5 For property placed in service after May 12, 1993; for property placed in service before May 13, 1993, the recovery period is 31.5 years.

These exceptions apply only to farm-related taxpayers. A farm-related taxpayer is one who either makes his or her main home on a farm or has farming as his or her principal business. Any individual will qualify if a family member meets either qualification.

Line 19, Fertilizers and Lime

Enter on this line the cost of fertilizer and lime applied or purchased during the current year.

Line 20, Freight and Trucking

On line 20 enter the amount paid for freight and trucking. Do not include the cost of transportation incurred in purchasing livestock held for resale–those costs should be added to the cost of the livestock and taken as a deduction when the animal is sold. Similarly, additional freight costs incurred in getting a depreciable farm asset to the farm should not be taken as freight and trucking, but rather added to the basis of the machinery or equipment and taken along with and in the same manner as the depreciation of the item.

Line 21, Gasoline, Fuel, and Oil

The cost of gasoline, fuel, and oil is entered here.

Filing Tip. Be certain that documentation exists for any personal use of these items. This is something the IRS will question on audit. Separate tanks for farm and personal fuels can banish this problem. Another solution is to routinely buy personal fuel in town and keep the receipts.

Line 22, Insurance (Other Than Health)

Take farm liability insurance here–and be sure to separate out the portion that applies to the home if it is covered under the same policy. Also report crop insurance costs–and be sure to check whether the crop insurance premium was deducted from the benefits check. If that is the case, it may not appear in the taxpayer's records. Note that amounts credited to a reserve for self-insurance or premiums paid for a policy that pays for any lost earnings due to sickness or disability are not deductible.

Line 23, Interest

Two lines are provided for interest. Mortgage interest is reported on 23a. This is interest paid to a financial institution and for which the taxpayer received a Form 1098, *Mortgage Interest Statement.* Be sure to separate out the home mortgage portion if both farm and home are part of the mortgage. Interest for which no Form 1098 was received and other farm interest–on operation loans, equipment acquisitions and so on–is reported on 23b.

Line 24, Labor Hired (Less Employment Credits)

The gross amount of labor hired is reported on line 24. The employer matching portion for Social Security and Medicare is reported with taxes on line 31. Cross-check the amounts with Form 943, *Employer's Annual Federal Tax Return for Agricultural Employees,* and all W-2s issued, and also with other records.

If payments for work performed are paid to a spouse or children, they should be paid as wages, not as contract labor. They should be reported with a W-2, not a 1099-MISC. If the payments are reported with the 1099-MISC, the recipient will have to pay self-employment tax. This is especially significant for children under 18, since children under age 18 may work for a parent in a sole proprietorship and not be subject to Social Security or Medicare withholding or payment.

It is possible to pay "wages in commodities." This means that the employee receives his or her pay as a certain quantity of commodities: 5,000 bushels of soybeans, and so on. When using wages in commodities, it is important that the employee have "dominion and control" over the commodities. He or she should make decisions as to where, when, and for what price the commodities are sold. The employee is also generally responsible for the cost of storage and trucking.

Line 25, Pension and Profit-Sharing Plans

Report on line 25 the amount of contributions to employee pension, profit-sharing, or annuity plans. The sole proprietor's contribution for himself or herself is not reported here, but rather is taken as an above-the-line adjustment on Form 1040.

Some of these plans require reporting on a Form 5500, *Annual Return/Report of Employee Benefit Plan,* or a Form 5500-EZ, *Annual Return of One Participant (Owners and Their Spouses) Retirement Plan.*

Line 26, Rent or Lease

The rental or lease of vehicles, machinery and equipment is reported on line 26a. Be sure to check that items listed as being rented or leased are documented by an instrument that bears out the nature of the arrangement. Often a document that says "Lease" at the top is in reality a sale.

If the item is truly a purchase, rather than a lease, it should be set up for depreciation over the appropriate life.

Line 26b is for "Other" rentals. This is normally where cash rent for land and pasture is recorded.

Line 27, Repairs and Maintenance

The cost of repairs of farm assets and maintenance is reported here.

Filing Tip. This is an area that the IRS likes to look at on audit. The reason is that they often find large amounts in this account that should actually have been depreciated over a period of time. Repairs and small fixes to the home sometimes end up in this account. Be sure they are taken out.

Line 28, Seeds and Plants Purchased

Purchases of seeds and plants are reported on line 28.

Line 29, Storage and Warehousing

Storage and warehousing of commodities are reported on line 29.

Line 30, Supplies Purchased

Line 30 is for general farm supplies and may be anything from soap to ledger paper to a longer telephone cord. Often this is referred to as "supplies and small tools," and hammers, pliers, and so on are included as well.

Line 31, Taxes

Report on line 31 real estate taxes, personal property tax, and other assessments on farm business assets. Be sure to eliminate real estate taxes on the home and anything else that is personal or family property rather than a part of the farm business.

Report also the employer portion of Social Security and Medicare taxes, as well as federal unemployment tax and federal highway use tax.

Caution. Personal taxes cannot be taken here. Do not deduct federal income tax, estate and gift taxes, taxes assessed for improvements, such as for sewers, paving, and so on not related to the farm.

Line 32, Utilities

Deduct the business portion of payments for electricity, water, telephone, and gas. It is a great help if the taxpayer can have the farm and home electricity (and possibly gas) billed separately and recorded on separate meters.

Telephone. The base cost of having the first telephone line in a residence is not deductible. The cost of a second line, provided it is used entirely for farm business, is fully deductible.

Line 33, Veterinary, Breeding, and Medicine

The cost of veterinary service, medicine, breeding, and so on is taken on line 33.

Line 34, Other Expenses

Farm expenses and costs that do not fit anywhere else on Schedule F are taken on line 34 and should be separately itemized to the extent possible. These items include, but are not limited to, the following:

- Amortization
- At-risk deduction disallowed from prior year
- Bad debts
- Business use of home (use the worksheet in IRS Publication 587 to calculate the deduction–do not use Form 8829)
- Legal and professional fees
- Travel, meals, and entertainment–noting that meals and entertainment costs must be reduced by 50%
- Preproductive period expenses

Line 35, Total Expenses

The sum of lines 12 through 34f is the total expenses for the farm business and is entered on line 35.

Line 36, Net Farm Profit or (Loss)

Subtract line 35 from line 11, and enter the result on line 36. This is the net farm profit or loss. Net farm profit is entered on Form 1040, line 18, and also on Schedule SE, line 1. If the amount on line 36 is a loss, the question on line 37 must be answered to determine where to report the loss.

Schedule F loss limitation. The Heartland, Habitat, Harvest, and Horticulture Act of 2008 limits the amount of net farm losses that can be claimed for any tax year in which a taxpayer, other than a C corporation, has received "applicable subsidies" to the "excess farm loss." However, this loss limitation is only available for tax years after December 31, 2009.

Line 37, At-Risk Investment

If Schedule F shows a loss and the taxpayer was not at risk for the activity, Form 6198 must be completed. If all of the amounts are at risk in this business, enter the loss on line 36, check box 37a, and enter the loss on Form 1040, line 18, and on Schedule SE, line 1. If box 37b is checked, Form 6198 must be completed to determine how much of the loss will be allowable on this return.

Part III: Farm Income—Accrual Method

Taxpayers using the accrual method of accounting report income when it is earned, not when it is received. The taxpayer must include animals and crops in inventory if the accrual method is used.

Line 38, Sales of Livestock, Produce, Grains, and Other Products

Enter on line 38 the amount earned from selling livestock, produce, grains and other products raised by the farm business.

Lines 39a and 39b, Cooperative Distributions

Same as 5a and 5b.

Lines 40a and 40b, Agricultural Program Payments

Same as 6a and 6b.

Lines 41a through 41c, Commodity Credit Corporation (CCC) Loans

Same as 7a, 7b, and 7c.

Line 42, Crop Insurance Proceeds

Report crop insurance proceeds received during 2009 for 2008 and those receivable at the end of 2009 for 2009.

Line 43, Custom Hire Income

Report custom hire income received during 2008, less that on receivables from prior years and that earned in 2008 and recorded as a receivable at year's end.

Line 44, Other Income

Same as line 10, except any items listed that have been earned, but not received at year's end, should be recorded as receivables.

Line 45, Calculation

The sum of lines 38, 39b, 40b, 41a, 41c, 42, 43, and 44 is entered on line 45.

Line 46, Inventory of Livestock, Produce, Grains, and Other Products at Beginning of the Year

The amount on line 46 should match the final inventory on the taxpayer's 2008 return. If it does not, attach a statement explaining the discrepancy.

Line 47, Cost of Livestock, Produce, Grains, and Other Products Purchased during the Year

Enter the cost of livestock, produce, grains, and other products purchased during the year on line 47. Include those for which a liability has been incurred, but has not yet been paid.

Line 49, Inventory of Livestock, Produce, Grains, and Other Products at End of Year

A physical inventory should be taken if possible. Enter the total inventory of livestock, produce, grains, and other products at year's end.

There are four common methods for valuing farm inventory:

- Cost
- Lower of cost or market price
- Farm-price method
- Unit-livestock method

In the farm-price method, each item is valued at its market price less the direct cost of disposition. Market price is the current price at the nearest market and cost includes commissions, freight, and other costs of disposition. In the unit-livestock method, the livestock are grouped according to type and age and a standard unit price is applied to each animal in a group.

Line 50, Calculation

The cost of livestock, produce, grains, and other products sold is calculated by subtracting line 49 from line 48. The result is entered on line 50. Exception: If the taxpayer uses the unit-livestock-price method or the farm-price method of valuing inventory and the amount on line 49 is larger than the amount on line 48, enter the result on line 50 as a positive amount.

Line 51, Gross Income

Subtract line 50 from line 45 and enter the result on line 51, unless the exception just mentioned applies. In that case, add lines 45 and 50 and enter the result on line 51.

The gross farm income for accrual-method taxpayers on line 51 is also entered on line 11.

Schedule SE Line-by-Line Instructions

Schedule SE is comprised of two sections. For each taxpayer required to file the schedule, either Section A (Short Schedule SE) or Section B (Long Schedule SE) must be completed. Individuals generally may report self-employment income from multiple businesses on a single form. Joint filers must report their self-employment income separately, though they may use the same form if one must use the long form and the other may use the short form. The Schedule includes a flow chart to determine which form to use.

Schedule SE Short Form

Line 1

Enter the net farm profit or loss from Schedule F, line 36 and Schedule K-1, box 14, code A.

Line 2

Enter net profit or loss from Schedule C line 31, Schedule C-EZ line 3, Schedule K-1 (Form 1065) box 14, code A, and Schedule K-1 (Form 1065-B) box 9, code J1. Ministers need to include on this line the rental value of a home or allowance for a home, including utilities, furnished to them as well as the value of meals and lodging provided to them, their spouse and their dependents. Retired ministers should not include their retirement benefits or the value of a housing allowance that has been provided to them during retirement.

Line 3, Calculation

Add lines 1 and 2.

Line 4, Calculation

Multiply line 3 by 92.35%. If the amount is less than $400, self-employment tax is not owed.

Line 5, Self-employment Tax

If line 4 is $106,800 or less, multiply line 4 by 15.3%. Enter this result here and on Form 1040, line 57.

If line 4 is more than $106,800, multiply line 4 by 2.9%. Then add $13,243.20 to the result. Enter the total here and on Form 1040, line 56.

Line 6, Self-Employment Tax Deduction

Multiply line 5 by 50%. Enter the result here and on Form 1040, line 27.

Schedule SE Long Form

Part I: Self-Employment Tax

If the individual's income is only church employee income, skip lines 1-4b. Enter 0 on line 4c and go to line 5a. Income from services performed as a minister or member of a religious order is not church employee income.

Box A

If the individual is a minister, member of a religious order or Christian Science practitioner and filed Form 4361, *Application for Exemption From Self-Employment for Use by Ministers, Members of Religious Orders and Christian Scientist Practitioners*, but had $400 or more of other net earnings from self-employment, check the box.

Line 1

Enter the net farm profit or loss from Schedule F, line 36 and Schedule K-1 (Form 1065), box 14, code A. If the individual uses the farm optional method this line can be skipped.

Line 2

Enter net profit or loss from Schedule C line 31, Schedule C-EZ line 3, Schedule K-1 (Form 1065) box 14, code A, and Schedule K-1 (Form 1065-B) box 9, code J1. Ministers need to include on this line the rental value of a home or allowance for a home, including utilities, furnished to them as well as the value of meals and lodging provided to them, their spouse and their dependents. Retired ministers should not include their retirement benefits or the value of a housing allowance that has been provided to them during retirement.

If the individual uses the nonfarm optional method this line can be skipped.

Line 3, Calculation

Add lines 1 and 2.

Line 4a, Calculation

If line 3 is more than 0, multiply line 3 by 92.35%. Otherwise enter the amount from line 3.

Line 4b

If the individual elected one or both of the optional methods, enter the totals from line 15 and 17 here,

Line 4c, Calculation

Add lines 4a and 4b. If the amount is less than $400 no self-employment tax is owed. The exception to this is if an individual also had church employee income. If so, enter 0 on this line and continue.

Line 5a

Enter church employee income. Church employee income is wages received as an employee (other than a minister or a member of a religious order) of a church or qualified church-controlled organization that has a certificate in effect electing an exemption from employer Social Security and Medicare taxes.

Line 5b, Calculation

Multiply line 5a by 92.35%. If the amount is less than $100, enter 0.

Line 6, Net Earnings from Self-Employment

Add lines 4c and 5b,

Line 7

The maximum amount of combined wages subject to social security tax or tier 1 of the railroad retirement tax is $106,800.

Line 8a

Enter the total of boxes 3 and 7 on Form W-2 (social security wages and tips) and railroad retirement (tier 1) compensation. If $106,800 or more skip line 8b-10 and go to line 11.

Line 8b

Enter unreported tips subject to social security tax (from Form 4137, line 10).

Line 8c

Enter wages subject to social security tax (from Form 8919, Line 10).

Line 8d, Calculation

Add line 8a, 8b and 8c.

Line 9, Calculation

Subtract line 8d from line 7. If zero or less, enter 0 here and on line 10 and go to line 11.

Line 10, Calculation

Multiply the smaller of line 6 or line 9 by 12.4%.

Line 11, Calculation

Multiply line 6 by 2.9%.

Line 12, Self-employment Tax

Add lines 10 and 11. Enter here and on Form 1040 line 56.

Line 13, Self-employment Tax Deduction

Multiply line 12 by 50%. Enter the result here and on Form 1040, line 27.

Part II: Optional Methods to Figure Net Earnings

Farm Optional Method

This method can only be used if (a) the individual's gross farm income was not more than $6,540 or (b) the net farm profits were less than $4,721.

Line 14

The maximum income for the optional methods is $4,360.

Line 15

Enter the smaller of two-thirds of gross farm income (cannot be less than zero) or $4,360. Include this amount on line 4b.

Nonfarm Optional Method

This method can be used only if the individual's net farm profits were less than $4,721 and less than 72.189% of the individual's gross nonfarm income and the individual had net earnings from self-employment of at least $400 in 2 of the prior 3 years. This method can be used no more than 5 times.

Line 16, Calculation

Subtract line 15 from line 14.

Line 17

Enter the smaller of two-thirds of gross nonfarm income (not less than zero) or the amount on line 16. Also include this amount on line 4b above.

KEY FACTS: Home Office Deduction

Expenses that qualify for the home office deduction (to the extent of the area reserved for the business relative to the total size of the home) include:

- Operating expenses
- Depreciation
- Mortgage interest
- Real estate taxes
- Rent (with the exception of rent paid by the employer for the area in question)
- Casualty and theft losses
- Utilities charges
- Cleaning and other services
- Homeowner's insurance
- Security system costs
- Repair costs (labor and supplies)

To qualify for the deduction, the area must meet the following conditions:

- The area is used *regularly* and *exclusively* for *trade or business purposes* as opposed to other profit-making activity.
  - **Exception:** The home is used as a day care facility for children, adults 65 or over, or individuals who are mentally or physically incapacitated.
  - **Exception:** The area is used for inventory or storage of produce (must be regular but not exclusive).
- The area is used for the *convenience of the employer.*
- The area represents the *primary place of business, or* the area is the *place of contact* with clients or customers in the normal course of the trade or business, *or* the area is a *separate structure* used in connection with the trade or business.

Direct vs. Indirect Expenses

Direct expenses are those that affect only the part of the home used for the trade or business, such as the cost of painting or furnishing an office. Direct costs are deductible in full. **Indirect** expenses involve the costs of maintaining the entire home of which the office is a part. Only the business use percentage of an indirect expense is deductible.

Formulas

$$\text{Business use \%} = \frac{\text{Area used for business}}{\text{Total area of home}}$$

$$\text{Day care deduction} = \text{Total costs to maintain the home}$$

$$\frac{\text{Area available and used regularly for day care each day}}{\text{Total area of home}}$$

$$\frac{\text{Total hours used for day care per year}}{\text{Total hours in year (8,760)}}$$

KEY FACTS: Hobby vs. Business

Are you starting a business that may not turn a profit for several years?

OR

Does your home business consistently lose money?

The IRS may classify your business as a hobby

Do you use business losses to offset income? If yes, read on.

Is your business a:

- Farm run on spare time?
- Craft business run from home?
- Distributor of household items?

Yes → **The IRS is LIKELY to question whether it's a hobby**

No → **You may have to prove to the IRS that it's a business**

"Safe" Ways to Prove It's a Business

- You conduct the activity in a businesslike manner (for example, with thorough accounting and recordkeeping
- You or your advisors possess the requisite expertise to operate the business profitably
- The time and effort you spend pursuing the activity suggest the intent to make a profit
- You rely on income from the activity for your livelihood
- You realized profits from conducting similar activities in the past
- The activity results in significant profits in some years
- Appreciation of assets used in the activity can be expected to bring a profit in the future
- The activity lacks elements of recreation and personal pleasure

What happens if your business is classified as a hobby?

Hobby

- **Losses are deductible ONLY to extent of gain**
- **Deductibility is subject to 2% of AGI floor**

Business

- **Losses are generally deductible**
- **Losses beyond income may be carried over**
- **You have to pay Social Security tax**

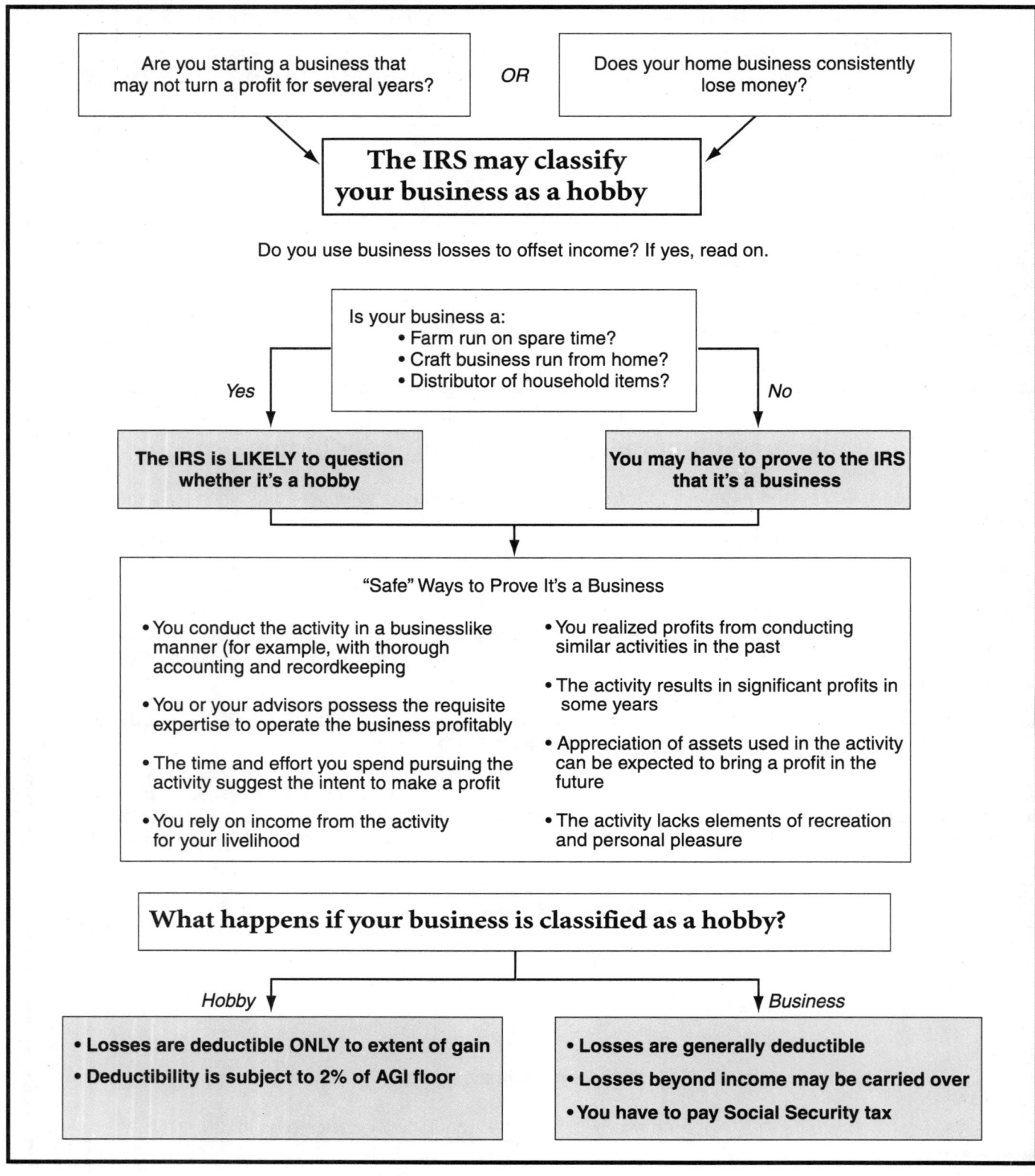

What's New in 2009

Zero Capital Gains Rate Continues. The zero-percent maximum tax rate on capital gains and qualified dividends for taxpayers in the 10- and 15-percent tax brackets continues for 2009. The zero-percent rate also continues to apply for the alternative minimum tax (AMT).

IRC §179 Expensing Election Increase Extended for 2009. The $250,000 maximum amount of newly acquired business asset costs that may be expensed under IRC §179 has been extended by the American Recovery and Reinvestment Act of 2009 (P.L. 111-5) for tax years beginning in 2009. The increased phaseout threshold amount of $800,000 was also extended.

Bonus Depreciation Extended to Assets Placed in Service in 2009. The American Recovery and Reinvestment Act of 2009 (P.L. 111-5) extended the 50% bonus or additional depreciation allowance regime for assets placed in service in 2009. This special depreciation must be claimed unless the taxpayer elects out on the original return.

Gain on Sale of Principal Residence Allocated to Nonqualified Use Is Not Excludable. Gain from the sale of a principal residence that is allocable to periods of nonqualified use after January 1, 2009, is not excludable from gross income.

Relevant IRS Publications

- ☐ IRS Publication 463, *Travel, Entertainment, Gift, and Car Expenses*
- ☐ IRS Publication 523, *Selling Your Home*
- ☐ IRS Publication 537, *Installment Sales,* and Instructions to Form 6252, *Installment Sale Income*
- ☐ IRS Publication 544, *Sales and Other Dispositions of Assets*
- ☐ IRS Publication 550, *Investment Income and Expenses (Including Capital Gains and Losses)*
- ☐ IRS Publication 551, *Basis of Assets*
- ☐ IRS Publication 564, *Mutual Fund Distributions*
- ☐ IRS Publication 946, *How to Depreciate Property*
- ☐ Instructions to Form 4684, *Casualties and Thefts*
- ☐ Instructions to Form 6781, *Gains and Losses from Section 1256 Contracts and Straddles*
- ☐ Instructions to Form 4797, *Sales of Business Property (Also Involuntary Conversions and Recapture Amounts Under Section 179 and 280F(b)(2))*
- ☐ Instructions to Form 8824, *Like-Kind Exchanges (and section 1043 conflict-of-interest sales)*

Section at a Glance

Tax Preparer's Checklist

- ☐ Documents with the original purchase date and sale date for the purchase and sale of capital assets are vital.
- ☐ Double-check basis calculation; seek all available records that may affect basis including those for improvements or reinvestments since original acquisition.
- ☐ Verify if any stock splits or reverse stock splits occurred during the holding period of the taxpayer.
- ☐ Assemble all Schedule K-1s received with respect to distributions from Forms 1041, 1065, and 1120S.
- ☐ 2008 Form 1040, Schedule D, and the Capital Loss Carryover Worksheet, for any capital losses to be carried forward to 2009.

General Summary of Basis Rules by Type of Acquisition

Type of Acquisition	Basis for Gain or Loss
Accounts receivable	
Accrual-basis taxpayer	Face value
Cash-basis taxpayer	Zero
Bequest	
Property acquired from decedent's estate	FMV on date of death or alternate valuation date
Property acquired in lieu of specific bequest	Value assigned in settlement
Cash purchase	Cost
Community property survivor	see "Bequest" and Tab 14
Gift property	Donor's basis plus gift tax paid on appreciated property, **but** basis for loss is *limited* to the lesser of the donor's basis or FMV at time of gift
Inherited property	see "Bequest" and Tab 14
Inventory goods	Last inventory value
Joint tenancy between spouses	Survivor's cost basis in one-half of property increased by one-half FMV at date of death or on alternative valuation date (full estate tax value for property purchased by decedent before 1977)
Joint tenancy in general	
After death of one tenant after 1953	FMV on date of death or alternative valuation date of portion included in estate
Life estate	Zero, if disposed of after October 9, 1969
Livestock	
Inventoried	Last inventory value
Purchased	Cost
Raised by accrual-basis farmers	Cost of raising
Raised by cash-basis farmers	Zero, if costs expensed
Mortgage assumed (or property taken subject to mortgage)	Full price, including mortgage
Nontaxable exchange	Basis of property given up plus any recognized gain less any boot received
Marital property settlements	Transferor's basis
Repossessed property after installment sale	
Personal property	FMV
Real property reacquired to satisfy purchaser's indebtedness secured by property	Adjusted basis of indebtedness plus gain resulting from reacquisition and reacquisition costs
Stock	
Acquired in wash sale	Cost of acquired stock plus loss not recognized
Nontaxable stock dividend	Basis allocated among new total shares of stock on date declared
Received for services	Amount reported in income plus cash paid
Stock rights	
Taxable	FMV when issued
Nontaxable	Allocable share of basis of stock, unless right's value is less than 15% of stock value, in which case basis is zero

Introduction to Capital Gains and Losses

Capital and Noncapital Assets

Capital assets consist of any property owned for personal purposes or for the purpose of generating income. A taxpayer's home, for example, is a capital asset, as is virtually everything in it. Stocks and bonds and all other investment instruments are also capital assets, as are collectibles.

The only property not regarded as a capital asset (i.e., a noncapital asset) is listed in IRC §1221, and is generally property that is used in a trade or business:

- Assets held as inventory in a trade or business.
- Property held primarily for sale to customers in the ordinary course of the taxpayer's trade or business.
- A note or account receivable acquired in the ordinary course of trade or business for services rendered or from the sale of stock in trade or property held for sale in the ordinary course of business.
- Depreciable property used in a trade or business, even if fully depreciated.
- Real property used in taxpayer's trade or business.
- A U.S. government publication (including the Congressional Record) held by a taxpayer who received it (or by another taxpayer in whose hands the publication would have a basis determined in whole or in part by reference to the taxpayer's basis) other than by purchase at the price at which the publication is offered to the public.
- Certain commodities derivative financial instruments held by a dealer.
- Hedging transactions entered into during the normal course of a trade or business.
- Supplies of a type regularly used or consumed by the taxpayer in the ordinary course of business.
- A copyright; a literary, musical, or artistic composition; a letter or memorandum; or similar property (but not a patent or invention) held by the taxpayer who created it.

Planning Note. Taxpayers may elect to treat the proceeds from the sale or exchange of a musical composition, or its copyright, that has been created by the taxpayer's personal efforts (or that has a basis determined by reference to the basis in the hands of the taxpayer whose personal efforts created the musical composition or copyright) as received in exchange for a capital asset (IRC §1221(b)(3)).

Gain or loss from the disposition of these noncapital assets is generally treated as ordinary income and not reported on Schedule D or Form 4797. (See Tab 3 and MTG ¶1741.)

General Rules Regarding Gain/Loss

Sale or exchange of a capital asset will produce a capital gain or loss. The following general rules apply:

- The amount of gain or loss depends on the taxpayer's basis in the asset at the time of acquisition and at the time of disposition (see the discussion of basis beginning on page 4-21).
- The tax rate depends on the holding period, type of capital asset, and taxpayer's tax bracket.
- After offsetting short-term losses against short-term gains and long-term losses against long-term gains, and then any remaining losses against remaining gains, any remaining losses up to $3,000 are deductible against ordinary income.
- Unused net capital losses can be carried forward indefinitely and may be used to offset capital gains and/or up to $3,000 of ordinary income in each future year.
- Capital gains and losses are recognized on the *trade date*, ***not*** the settlement date.

Schedule D or Form 4797?

Use Schedule D of Form 1040, *Capital Gains and Losses*, to report the following:

- The sale or exchange of capital assets *not* reported elsewhere on the return.
- Gains from involuntary conversions (other than from casualty or theft) of capital assets *not* held for business or profit.
- Capital gain distributions *not* reported directly on Form 1040, line 13.
- Nonbusiness bad debts (see Tab 1 for exceptions).

Filing Tip. Before completing Schedule D, the taxpayer may have to complete other forms; see the *Forms 2439, 4684, 6252, 6781, and 8824* section following.

Use Form 4797, *Sales of Business Property (Also Involuntary Conversions and Recapture Amounts under Sections 179 and 280F(b)(2))*, to report gain or loss from a sale or exchange of:

- Property used in a trade or business.
- Depreciable and amortizable property.
- Oil, gas, geothermal, or other mineral properties.
- IRC §126 cost-sharing property including property used in the following federal progams:
  - the Rural Clean Water Program,
  - the Rural Abandoned Mine Program,
  - the Water Bank Program,
  - the Emergency Conservation Program,
  - the Agricultural Conservation Program,
  - the Great Plains Conservation Program,
  - the Resource Conservation and Development Program,
  - the Forestry Incentives Program, and
  - certain small watershed programs administered by the Agriculture Department.

In addition to the federal programs listed above, IRC §126 property includes property used in state programs under which payments are made to individuals primarily for the purpose of conserving soil, protecting or restoring the environment, improving forests, or providing a habitat for wildlife.

Form 4797 is also used for reporting the following:

- Dispositions of noncapital assets (other than inventory or property held primarily for sale to customers in the taxpayer's trade or business).
- Dispositions of capital assets not reported on Schedule D.
- Involuntary conversions (from other than casualty or theft) of property used in a trade or business and capital assets held in connection with a trade or business or a transaction entered into for profit.
- Gain or loss allocated to partners and S corporation shareholders from dispositions of section 179 property by partnerships and S corporations.
- The computation of recapture amounts under IRC §179 and §280F(b)(2), when the business use drops to 50% or less.

Caution. Traders in securities, including day traders (for definition, see "Traders in Securities," in the instructions for Schedule D) must report gains or losses on Schedule D unless they choose to change to the mark-to-market method of accounting (see page 4–30 and MTG ¶1903). If that election is made, the transactions must be reported on Form 4797.

Forms 2439, 4684, 6252, 6781, and 8824

Form 2439, *Notice to Shareholder of Undistributed Long-Term Capital Gains,* is sent by regulated investment companies and real estate investment trusts to inform shareholders of their portion of undistributed capital gains and tax paid. See MTG ¶2305.

Form 4684, *Casualties and Thefts,* is used to report gains or losses from casualties and thefts. Casualty and theft gains and losses for personal property are reported on Schedule A, and those for business property are reported on Schedule C or F. Schedule E and Form 4835, *Farm Rental Income and Expenses,* may also be required. Gains may be deferred if insurance proceeds are used to purchase replacement property. See MTG ¶1137 and ¶1713.

Form 6252, *Installment Sale Income,* is used to report casual sales of real or personal property (other than inventory) if payments will be received in a tax year after the year of sale. For more details on installment sales, see the discussion on page 4-23 and MTG ¶1801.

Form 6781, *Gains and Losses from IRC §1256 Contracts and Straddles,* is used to report gains and losses on any regulated futures contract, foreign currency contract, nonequity option, dealer equity option, or dealer securities futures contract (IRC §1256 contracts). An IRC §1256 contract held at the end of the tax year will generally be treated as sold at its FMV on the last business day of the tax year, and any gain or loss that results must be recognized. That gain or loss is taken into account in figuring gain or loss when the contract is later disposed of. A *straddle* is any set of offsetting positions on personal property. For example, a straddle may consist of a purchased option to buy and a purchased option to sell on the same number of shares of a security, with the same exercise price and period. Use Part II of Form 6781 to figure gains and losses on straddles before entering these amounts on Schedule D.

Form 8824, *Like-Kind Exchanges,* is used to report exchanges of qualifying business or investment property (not personal property) for property of a like-kind/like-class. Properties are of like kind if they are of the same nature or character, even if they differ in grade or quality. The IRS interpretation of "same nature or character" is typically quite liberal. Real properties are generally of like kind, regardless of whether they are improved or unimproved. However, real property in the United States and real property outside the United States are not like-kind properties. (See full discussion of like-kind exchanges on page 4-18 and MTG ¶1721.)

Filing Tip. A trade-in of a business automobile for the purchase of a new business car or truck is a tax-free like-kind/like-class exchange, but it must nevertheless be reported on Form 8824.

Caution. When trading in a used business vehicle for a newer business vehicle care must be taken to insure that both vehicles fall into the same depreciation class to satisfy the like-kind/like-class requirement. Thus, trading in a used small panel truck of less than 13,000 lbs. (Class Life 4) for a medium-sized panel truck of more than 13,000 lbs. (Class Life 6) fails the like-class requirement and does not qualify as a tax-free exchange.

Sale of Principal Residence

Reporting Rules/Excluding Gain

Generally, the home one lives in most of the time is one's principal residence; it can be a house, houseboat, mobile home, cooperative apartment, or condominium. In order to exclude gain on the sale of a home, a taxpayer generally must have owned and lived in the property as his or her main home for at least two years during the five-year period ending on the date of sale. The maximum gain that can be excluded is $250,000 for individuals and $500,000 for married couples filing jointly. For more details, see page 4-30 and MTG ¶ 1705.

Exceptions

A taxpayer who has owned and lived in the property as his main home for less than two years can still claim an exclusion if he sold or exchanged the home because of changes in employment, health, or unforeseen circumstances. The maximum amount that can be excluded will, however, be reduced. See also the **Planning Tip** under "*Reduced Exclusion Rules*" at page 4-33.

Surviving spouses may claim the $500,000 exclusion on the sale of the main home provided that the sale occurs within two years of the date of deceased spouse's death.

Military personnel, members of the foreign service, certain employees of the intelligence community, and certain members of the Peace Corps may suspend the five-year test for up to 10 years while they are on qualified extended duty.

A principal residence originally acquired through the use of a like-kind exchange must be owned for at least five years from the date of acquisition for the gain from the sale to qualify for the exclusion.

Planning Tip. Gain from the sale of a principal residence allocable to the nonqualified use of the property after January 1, 2009, will not be excludable from gross income.

Nondeductible Losses

Losses from transactions between related parties are nondeductible. Do *not* deduct a loss from the direct or indirect sale or exchange of property between any of the following:

- Members of a family.
- A corporation and an individual owning more than 50% of the corporation's stock (unless the loss is from a distribution after the corporation has undergone complete liquidation).
- A grantor and a fiduciary of a trust.
- A fiduciary and a beneficiary of the same trust.
- A fiduciary and a beneficiary of another trust created by the same grantor.
- An executor of an estate and a beneficiary of that estate, unless the sale or exchange was to satisfy a bequest of money.
- An individual and a tax-exempt organization controlled by the individual or the individual's family.

Schedule D

Short-Term Capital Gains and Losses, Lines 1-7

Short-Term versus Long-Term Capital Gains

The holding period for the property determines whether capital gains are short or long term. If the holding period is one year or less, the gain is short-term. If the holding period is more than one year, the gain is long term. Begin counting the holding period on the day after the taxpayer acquired the property and include the day on which it was disposed of. If the taxpayer disposed of property acquired by inheritance, the disposition is reported as a long-term gain or loss, regardless of the holding period for the property.

Caution. Nonbusiness bad debts are reported as short-term capital losses. Worthless securities are treated as though they were capital assets sold on the last day of the tax year.

Example. On March 15, 2009, Vasily Cherokov sold shares of stock A for $700 gain and shares of stock B for $400 gain. He had purchased the shares of stock A on March 15, 2008, and the shares of stock B on February 1, 2008. His gain on stock A is short-term gain because he held the stock one day less than one year, but his gain on the stock B shares is long-term gain because he held the stock at least one day more than one year after purchase.

Line 1(a), Description of Property

Enter here a brief description of the property's nature, For example, for a block of stock indicate the number of shares and the company name.

Line 1(b), Date Acquired

Enter in this column the date the asset was acquired. Use the trade date for stocks and bonds traded on an exchange or over-the-counter market. For stock or other property sold short (see **Short Sales**, following), enter the date the stock or property was delivered to the broker or lender to close the short sale.

If the property was acquired by inheritance, the date acquired is reported as "INHERITED" on line 8(b).

For the sale of a block of stocks that were acquired over a period of time, "VARIOUS" may be entered for the date of acquisition, but the short- and long-term gain for each acquisition must still be reported in the appropriate part of Schedule D.

Short Sales. A *short sale* is a sale of stock in which the seller borrows the stock that is delivered to the buyer. At a later date, the seller "closes" the short sale by covering the loan either with stock purchased for that purpose or with stock the seller held at the time of the short sale but did not wish to transfer at the earlier date. An investor who enters into a short sale realizes profits when the price of the stock declines. *The taxable event in a short sale is the closing of the transaction.* Any gain or loss realized upon closing a short sale is treated as a capital gain or loss, provided that the stock used to close the short sale is a capital asset in the investor's hands.

See MTG ¶1944 for more details.

Example. On January 2, 2009, Sara O'Loughlin enters into an agreement to sell 100 shares of QQ Corporation for $10 a share to Buyer 1. Sara does not own any QQ shares, so she borrows the 100 shares from her broker and delivers these shares to Buyer 1. On May 1, 2009, Sara purchases 100 shares of QQ at a price of $15 a share. On the same day, she delivers these shares to her broker in order to replace the shares she had borrowed (i.e., she closes out her short sale). Her recognized loss of $500 is short term because her holding period of the QQ shares is determined by the amount of time she held the shares (less than one day in this case).

Line 1(c), Date Sold

Enter in this column the date the asset was sold. Use the trade date for stocks and bonds traded on an exchange or over-the-counter market. For stock or other property sold short, enter the date the taxpayer sold the stock or property borrowed to open the short-sale transaction.

In real estate sales, a sale occurs when the deed passes or when possession and the burdens and benefits of ownership are, from a practical standpoint, transferred to the buyer, whichever occurs first. The same rules apply to an executory contract, such as one involving a purchase option. The transaction is usually not considered to be closed until unconditional liability of the buyer for the purchase price is created by acquisition of title and right of possession (MTG ¶1742).

Line 1(d), Sales Price

Brokers and barter exchanges use Form 1099-B to report proceeds from transactions to the taxpayer and the IRS. Form 1099-S is used to report the sale or exchange of real estate. Brokers are also allowed to issue substitute statements listing information that is identical to what appears on Form 1099-B.

Enter under line 1(d) either the gross sales price or the net sales price from the sale. If the taxpayer sold stocks or bonds and received a Form 1099-B from his or her broker that shows the gross sales price, enter that amount in column (d). But if Form 1099-B (or substitute statement) indicates that gross proceeds minus commissions and option premiums were reported to the IRS, enter that net amount in column (d). If the net amount is entered in column (d), do not include the commissions and option premiums from the sale in column (e).

Line 1(e), Cost or Other Basis

The cost or other basis is the cost of the property plus purchase commissions and improvements, minus depreciation, amortization, and depletion. If the taxpayer inherited the property, got it as a gift, or received it in a tax-free exchange, involuntary conversion, or wash sale of stock, he or she may not be able to use the actual cost as the basis. If the actual cost is not used, attach an explanation of the basis used; see IRS Publication 550, *Investment Income and Expenses (Including Capital Gains and Losses)*, for specific instructions.

Increase the cost or other basis by any expense of sale, such as broker's fees, commissions, state and local transfer taxes, and option premiums, before making an entry in column (e), unless the net sales price was reported in column (d).

Inherited Property. The basis of property acquired from a decedent is generally the fair market value at the date of death. If elected by the executor, the basis is determined six months after the date of death, or, if the property is sold prior to that time, the date of sale.

See Tab 14 for more information.

Stock. If the taxpayer sold stock, adjust the basis by subtracting all nontaxable distributions received before the sale, while adjusting the basis for stock splits, if any.

Mutual Funds. There are two ways to determine a taxpayer's basis in shares of a mutual fund: cost basis or average basis.

- **Cost Basis Method.** A taxpayer may elect to use this method for determining their basis in mutual-fund shares only if they have *not* used the average basis method in a pervious sale, exchange or redemption of other shares of the same mutual fund. They have a choice of two methods:
  - **Specific Share Identification**, or
  - **First-in, First-out**.
- **Specific Share Identification.** This method is just as the name indicates, the taxpayer must adequately

specify the shares to be sold. This allows them to use their adjusted cost basis for each lot of shares. They must specify to their broker the particular shares sold and receive a written confirmation from the broker within a reasonable time after having instructed them to sell the particular shares. This method is generally the most advantageous but does require the most effort to elect and *must be done before the sale.*

  - **First-in, First-out (FIFO).** This method is used if the shares were acquired at different times and different prices and the shares were not specifically identified at the time of sale. The basis of the sold shares will be equal to the basis of the oldest shares owned at the time of the sale.

- **Figuring an Average Basis.** The average basis is simply the total adjusted basis of all shares owned in a fund divided by the total number of shares owned. To figure the average basis, one of the following methods must be used:

  Single-category method, or
  Double-category method.

  - **Single-category method.** The single-category method computes the average on all shares held, regardless of length of time held, for each disposition. This method does not change the requirement to calculate the holding period for each share sold. For the purposes of determining the holding period, the shares sold are considered to be the shares acquired first.
  - **Double-category method.** The double-category method divides the shares held into long-term and short-term baskets. Thus, any shares held one year or less are in the short-term basket and any shares held for more than one year are in the long-term basket. The taxpayer must specify to the broker which shares to sell and the broker must send a confirmation of the sale of those shares. Failure to specify before the transaction, means that all shares sold come out of the long-term basket first. The holding period is determined at the time of disposition and, thus, shares can move from the short-term basket to the long-term basket upon being held for more than one year prior to disposition.

Once the taxpayer elects to use an average basis, it must be used for all accounts in the same fund and the same method must continue to be used. However, the cost basis (or a different method of figuring the average basis) may be used for shares in other funds, even those within the same family of funds.

Filing Tip. When the taxpayer chooses to use the average basis method for reporting the sale of shares in a mutual fund be sure to include "AVGB" in column (a) of Schedule D.

Example. Reginald and Sara Logan sold 250 shares of Mutual Fund Z on April 1, 2009. They received $35 per share, for a total of $8,750. They had purchased 200 shares in 2005 at $25 per share, another 200 shares in 2006 at $21 per share, and another 10 shares at $30 per share in September 2008.

Using the FIFO cost basis method, their basis in the 250 shares sold in 2009 would be the cost of the first 200 (200×$25 = $5,000) plus the cost of 50 shares bought in 2006 (50×$21 = $1,050), which would be $6,050.

Using the single-category method, their average basis would be the total of the basis of all shares ($5,000 + $4,200 + $300) divided by the total number of shares: $9,500/410 = $23.17. Their basis in the 250 shares sold on April 1, 2009, would be $5,792.50.

Using the double-category method, their average basis would not take into account the 10 shares purchased in September 2008. Thus, the average of the long-term shares would be $9,200/400 = $23, and the average basis of the 250 shares would be $5,750.

In this case, Reginald and Sara should choose the FIFO cost basis if they wish to minimize 2009 gain. If they do, they will have to use the FIFO cost basis on subsequent sales of Mutual Fund Z shares. If they had chosen a specific identification method prior to the sale and wanted to minimize their gain, they would identify the 250 most expensive shares to sell, for a total basis of $6,140.

OID. Increase the cost or other basis of an original issue discount (OID) debt instrument by the amount of OID included in gross income for that instrument.

Line 1(f), Gain or (Loss) for the Entire Year

Line 1(f) is for recording the taxpayer's short-term and long-term gain or loss for the year as a whole. It is the result of subtracting column (e) from column (d).

Filing Tip. Be sure to reconcile all Form 1099-Bs to insure that all transactions have been reported on the Form 1040. Combining information on single lines of Schedule D will lead to IRS follow up and added attention; use Schedule D-1 instead. Transaction by transaction listings allows the IRS to match all reported Form 1099-Bs and avoids the problem of future inquiries regarding net information.

Example. Mr. and Mrs. Jones sold securities in 2008. The sales resulted in a long-term capital loss of $7,000. This was their only capital transaction. Their taxable income was $26,000. On their joint 2008 return, they can deduct $3,000 as an offset to ordinary income. The unused portion of the loss, $4,000 ($7,000 – $3,000), can be carried over as a long-term loss to 2009. In 2009, their net long-term gains amount to $2,000, and their net short-term gains to $1,500. They will first offset the $2,000 long-term gains and then the $1,500 short-term gains. This will leave them $500 to use as an offset to ordinary income.

Planning Tip. When reconciling all Forms 1099-Bs, be sure to obtain the necessary basis information for each transaction. The IRS is increasingly following up on transactions reported on Schedule D to insure proper reporting of gains and losses.

Line 2, Schedule D-1

Enter combined totals from all Schedules D-1, *Continuation Sheet for Schedule D.* Its columns (a) through (f) are the same as Schedule D's.

Line 3, Total Short-Term Sales Price Amounts

From column (d), Sales Price, add lines 1 and 2. Enter the amount on line 3.

Line 4, Short-Term Gain from Form 6252 and Short-Term Gain or (Loss) from Forms 4684, 6781, and 8824

See page 4-4 for a discussion of these forms.

Line 5, Net Short-Term Gain or (Loss) from Partnerships, S Corporations, Estates, and Trusts from Schedule(s) K-1

Enter amount from Schedule K-1, Forms 1041, 1065, and 1120S. Instructions are included with Schedule K-1. See Tab 5 for a discussion of Schedule K-1.

Line 6, Short-Term Capital Loss Carryover

The allowable capital loss deduction, figured on Schedule D, is the lesser of;

(1) $3,000 ($1,500 if married filing separately) or
(2) the total net loss as shown on line 16 of Schedule D.

The total net loss can be used to reduce ordinary income dollar for dollar, up to the $3,000 ($1,500 if married filing separately) limit.

Individuals and other noncorporate taxpayers may carry over a net capital loss to future tax years until the loss is used. A capital loss that is carried over to a later tax year retains its original character as either long term or short term in the year to which it is carried. The amount of the of capital loss to be carried over to the next tax year is equal to the excess of the total net loss over the lesser of;

(1) the allowable capital loss deduction for the current tax year, or
(2) the taxable income increased by the allowable capital loss deduction for the current tax year plus the personal exemption deductions. If the deductions are more than the gross income for the tax year, use the negative taxable income in computing this item.

The carryover can be figured on the Capital Loss Carryover Worksheet in Publication 550, *Investment Income and Expenses (Including Capital Gains and Losses)*, or in the Schedule D Instructions. A sample worksheet is reproduced on page 4-38.

The result is that a short-term capital loss carryover first offsets short-term gain in the carryover year. If a net short-term capital loss remains, this loss then offsets net long-term capital gain, and then up to $3,000 of ordinary income. A long-term capital loss carryover first reduces long-term capital gain in the carryover year, then net short-term capital gain, and finally up to $3,000 of ordinary income.

Filing Tip. When calculating the amount of a capital loss carryover to the next tax year, the allowable capital loss deduction for the current year must be taken into account regardless of whether you claimed it in, or filed a return for, the current tax year.

Line 7, Net Short-Term Capital Gain (or Loss)

Add lines 1(f), 2(f), 4, 5, and 6. Enter total on line 7.

Example. Joel and Susan Cramer filed a joint return with an AGI of $30,000 and deductions of $11,000 in 2009. Their Schedule D shows a net short-term capital loss of $1,000 and a net long-term capital loss of $5,000. The $1,000 net short-term loss will be used to offset $1,000 of ordinary income; then the $2,000 of the net long-term capital loss will be used to offset $2,000 of ordinary income. The remaining $3,000 of the net long-term capital loss will be carried over to 2010.

Long-Term Capital Gains and Losses, Lines 8-15

Line 8, Description of Transactions

Line 8 consists of essentially the same parts as line 1, except they apply to long-term gains or losses. See discussion beginning on page 4-5.

Long-term gains or losses are those from the disposition of assets held more than one year. The holding period begins on the day after acquisition and ends on the day of disposition.

> **Caution.** In a leap year, the question may come up as to whether the necessary holding period is more than 365 days or more than one year. The Code states that the holding period is more than one year, and does not consider whether the year contains 365 or 366 days.

> **Filing Tip.** Inherited property is reported as a long-term gain or loss, regardless of the decedent's or heir's holding period for the property.

Line 9, Schedule D-1

From Schedule D-1, line 9, enter any long-term totals.

Line 10, Total Long-Term Sales Price Amounts

Add line 8, column (d), and line 9, column (d), and enter the total on line 10.

Line 11, Gain from Form 4797, Part I, and Other Long-Term Gains

See the later discussion of Form 4797, *Sales of Business Property.* Also include long-term gains from Form 2439, *Notice to Shareholder of Undistributed Long-Term Capital Gains,* and all other forms from which short-term gains are reported on line 4.

Line 12, Net Long-Term Gain from Schedule(s) K-1

Long-term gain from partnerships, S corporations, estates, and trusts reported to the taxpayer on a Schedule K-1 is reported on line 12.

Line 13, Capital Gain Distributions

Distributions paid by a mutual fund (or other regulated investment company) or REIT (real estate investment trust) from its net realized long-term capital gains are recorded on line 13. They are reported on Form 1099-DIV in boxes 2a–2d. The total in box 2a is the amount that is entered on line 13.

Distributions of net realized short-term capital gains are not treated as capital gains at all. They are included on Form 1099-DIV as ordinary dividends and are reported on Schedule B.

Capital gains received as a nominee are reported on Schedule D but in only the amount that belongs to the taxpayer. A statement must be attached showing the full amount received and the amount received as a nominee. See Tab 2 for filing requirements by a nominee.

Line 14, Long-Term Capital Loss Carryover

When a loss is carried over, it remains long or short term. A long-term capital loss carried over to the next year will reduce that year's long-term capital gain prior to reducing that year's short-term gains.

Change in Filing Status. Married taxpayers who file a joint return for 2009 after filing separate returns in 2008 are entitled to carry over any net capital losses from their 2008 returns.

For a husband and wife who have consistently made joint returns from year to year, the carryover of their combined net capital losses is computed as if they were one taxpayer. If a joint return is filed in one year with a resulting capital loss to be carried to a subsequent tax year for which separate returns are filed, however, the carryover is allocated to the husband and wife on the basis of their respective net capital losses for the preceding year.

> **Example.** Jon and Margery Wilhelm filed joint returns from 2005 to 2008, but they chose married filing separately in 2009. Their 2008 return has a long-term capital loss of $6,000: $5,000 for Jon's investment activities and $1,000 for Margery's. The couple cannot split the $6,000 carryover equally; Margery can use only $1,000 of the total carryover in 2009, and Jon, assuming he can use the maximum $1,500 to offset gain or income, will carry over $3,500 of loss to 2010.

Line 15, Net Long-Term Capital Gain (or Loss)

In column f, combine lines 8 through 14. Enter total on line 15 and proceed to Part III.

Part III, Summary, Lines 16-22

Lines 16 and 17

Combine line 7, net short-term capital gain/loss, and line 15, net long-term capital gain/loss, and enter the result on line 16. Answer whether both lines 15 and 16 are gains and mark line 17 accordingly.

Line 18, Amount of 28% Rate Gain

Collectibles. A *collectibles gain or loss* is a long-term gain or loss from the sale or exchange of a collectible that is a capital asset.

For capital gains purposes, the definition of "collectibles" is very comprehensive; examples include works of art, rugs, antiques, metals (such as gold, silver, and platinum bullion), gems, stamps, coins, alcoholic beverages, and certain other tangible property.

Caution. Note that, although certain gold, silver, and platinum coins and bullion are not classified as collectibles for IRA investment purposes, these items are considered collectibles for purposes of the 28% capital gains rate.

The maximum rate of 28% remains in effect for collectibles gains despite the reduction in the general capital gain rates to 15 or zero percent.

Gains (but not losses) from any sale of a partnership, S corporation, or trust that is attributable to unrealized appreciation of collectibles will also be taxed at up to 28%.

IRC §1202 Exclusion (QSB Stock). A taxpayer who realizes a gain on qualified small business (QSB) stock may exclude a portion of the gain on Schedule D. The amount of gain that may be excluded is 50% of the gain on Schedule D for stock acquired on or before February 17, 2009, or 75% for stock acquired after February 17, 2009, and before January 1, 2011. 60% of the gain on stock may be excluded if the underlying business is located in an empowerment zone. For details on how to report the IRC §1202 exclusion on line 8, see the 2009 Schedule D instructions; for details on what stock is eligible for this exclusion, see MTG ¶2396.

Planning Tip. For qualified small buisness stock acquired after February 17, 2009, and before January 1, 2011, the percentage of exclusion of gain increases to 75%. This increase exclusion percentage does not apply to the sale or exchange of certain empowerment zone stock.

The exclusion may be partially recaptured on the 28% Rate Gain Worksheet.

28% Rate Gain Worksheet. This worksheet, in the instruction for Schedule D (a sample worksheet is reproduced at page 4-39), matches the net of collectibles gain (including collectible gain from Form 1099-DIV, box 2d; Form 2439, box 1f; and Schedule K-1), IRC §1202 exclusions, and net long-term losses from line 15 of Schedule D. This net is then netted against short-term losses, if any; if the result is positive, the amount has to be entered on line 18.

Line 19, Unrecaptured IRC §1250 Gain

The IRC §1250 Gain Worksheet (a sample worksheet is reproduced on page 4-39) must be completed if *any* of the following conditions applied for 2009:

- Taxpayer sold or otherwise disposed of IRC §1250 property (generally, real property that the client depreciated) held more than one year (reported on Form 4797, Parts I and III).
- Taxpayer received installment payments for IRC §1250 property held more than one year for which taxpayer reported gain on the installment method (reported on Form 6252, *Installment Sale Income*).
- Taxpayer received Schedule K-1 from an estate or trust, partnership, or S corporation that shows "unrecaptured Section 1250 gain."
- Taxpayer received Form 1099-DIV or Form 2439 from a REIT or regulated investment company (including a mutual fund) that reports "unrecaptured Section 1250 gain."
- Taxpayer reported long-term capital gain from the sale or exchange of an interest in a partnership that owned IRC §1250 property.

As with the 28% Rate Gain Worksheet, the Unrecaptured IRC §1250 Gain Worksheet nets these unrecaptured gains against long-term and short-term capital gains from lines 15 and 7. If the net is positive, that number will figure into tax liability for the year.

For more information on IRC §1250 property, see the discussion on page 4-16 and MTG ¶1736.

Planning Tip. Some broker-dealer reports are thorough and others are poorly organized and incomplete. These reports require a lot of analysis and data entry. By having the client request a detailed report in advance of year-end reporting, you will help prevent reporting errors and minimize preparation time.

Form 4797

Purpose of Form

Form 4797 is used to report the following:

- Gain or loss to partners and S corporation shareholders from property dispositions by partnerships and S corporations, including any related recapture of IRC §179 expense deductions.

Where To Make First Entry for Certain Items Reported on This Form		
(a) Type of property	**(b) Held 1 year or less**	**(c) Held more than 1 year**
1 Depreciable trade or business property		
a Sold or exchanged at a gain	Part II	Part III (1245, 1250)
b Sold or exchanged at a loss	Part II	Part I
2 Depreciable residential rental property:		
a Sold or exchanged at a gain	Part II	Part III (1250)
b Sold or exchanged at a loss	Part II	Part I
3 Farmland held less than 10 years upon which soil, water, or land clearing expenses were deducted:		
a Sold at a gain	Part II	Part III (1252)
b Sold at a loss	Part II	Part I
4 All other farmland	Part II	Part I
5 Disposition of cost-sharing payment property described in section 126	Part II	Part III (1255)
6 Cattle and horses used in a trade or business for draft, breeding, dairy, or sporting purposes:	**Held less than 24 months**	**Held 24 months or more**
a Sold at a gain	Part II	Part III (1245)
b Sold at a loss	Part II	Part I
c Raised cattle and horses sold at a gain	Part II	Part I
7 Livestock other than cattle and horses used in a trade or business for draft, breeding, dairy, or sporting purposes:	**Held less than 12 months**	**Held 12 months or more**
a Sold at a gain	Part II	Part III (1245)
b Sold at a loss	Part II	Part I
c Raised livestock sold at a gain	Part II	Part I

- The computation of recapture amounts under IRC §179 and §280F(b)(2), when the business use drops to 50% or less.
- The sale or exchange of:
  (a) property used in a trade or business;
  (b) depreciable and amortizable property;
  (c) oil, gas, geothermal, or other mineral properties; and
  (d) IRC §126 property.
- The involuntary conversion (from other than casualty or theft) of property used in a trade or business and capital assets held in connection with a trade or business or a transaction entered into for profit.
- The disposition of noncapital assets (other than inventory or property held primarily for sale to customers in the ordinary course of a trade or business).
- The disposition of capital assets not reported on Schedule D.

It is divided into four main parts (Form 4797 is reproduced at pages 4–41 and 4–42). The table on page 4-11 from the Form 4797 instructions gives some examples of where to begin reporting most transactions.

General Information and Line 1

Line 1, Gross Proceeds from Form(s) 1099-B or 1099-S

The taxpayer enters gross proceeds from all sales or exchanges that were reported on Form 1099-B or Form 1099-S or substitute statement on line 1. These amounts are then included on line 2, line 10, or line 20, whichever is applicable.

Part I, Lines 2-9

Part I is used to determine gains or losses from the sales or exchanges of IRC §1231 property (see definitions following) that are not required to be reported in Part III.

Line 2, Description of Transaction

Holding Period. As with capital assets, the holding period begins the day after purchase and ends on the day of disposition. To qualify for Part I, most business property must be held for one day longer than a full calendar year.

IRC §1231 Property. IRC §1231 property includes the following:

- Property used in a trade or business, subject to depreciation and held more than one year.
- Real property used in a trade or business and held for more than one year (but excluding property includible in inventory or held primarily for sale to customers).
- Trade or business property (defined in the previous two items) held for more than one year and involuntarily converted.
- Capital assets held for more than one year.
- A crop sold with the land when the land has been held for more than one year.

- Livestock.
- Timber, domestic iron ore, or coal under certain conditions.

See MTG ¶ 1741–¶ 1772 for details and explanations.

Line 2(a), Description of Property

List any property sales or exchanges that the taxpayer made in the trade or business. Examples would be cutting or disposal of timber, disposal of coal, sale or exchange of livestock such as cattle or horses (unless held more than a year), and sales or exchanges of unharvested crops.

IRC §1231 transactions do not include sales or exchanges of inventory or property held primarily for sale to customers; copyrights; literary, musical, or artistic compositions; letters or memoranda; or similar property. Also not included are U.S. government publications, including the Congressional Record, received from the government other than by purchase at the normal sales price or from someone who had received it in a similar way.

> **Filing Tip.** Taxpayers may elect to treat the proceeds from the sale or exchange of a musical composition or its copyright as received from the sale or exchange of a capital asset. The election is available to the composer and to anyone whose basis in the composition or copyright is determined by reference to the composer's basis.

Involuntary Conversions. Also entered in Part I are involuntary conversions of trade or business property or capital assets held more than one year in connection with a trade or business or a transaction entered into for profit. These conversions may result from;

(a) part or total destruction,
(b) theft or seizure, or
(c) requisition or condemnation (whether threatened or carried out).

If any recognized losses were from involuntary conversions from fire, storm, shipwreck, or other casualty or from theft and the losses exceed the recognized gains from the conversions, any gains or losses should not be included in figuring IRC §1231 losses.

Line 2(b), Date Acquired

Note that the actual date acquired should be listed on line 2(b), even though the following day is used to determine length of holding period.

If the property was inherited, the word "INHERITED" should be written in column (b) instead of the actual date acquired.

Line 2(c), Date Sold

The date of sale is entered on line 2(c).

Line 2(d), Sales Price

Profit from the sale of livestock or other items bought by a farmer is computed by deducting the cost from the sales price. For the sale of animals that were originally bought as draft or work animals, or for breeding or dairy purposes and not for resale, the profit is the difference between the sale price and the depreciated basis of the animal sold.

See also Schedule D, line 1(d) on page 4-6.

Line 2(e), Depreciation Allowed or Allowable since Acquisition

If depreciable or amortizable property was disposed of at a gain, all or part of the gain (even if otherwise nontaxable) may have to be recaptured and treated as ordinary income.

> **Caution.** The allowable depreciation will be subtracted from the unadjusted basis to determine gain or loss, even if the depreciation has never been taken.

Line 2(f), Cost or Other Basis

The cost or other basis is the cost of the property plus purchase commissions, improvements, and sale expenses. An explanation of any basis used that is not the cost has to be attached. This may be necessary if the property was inherited, received as a gift, or received in a tax-free exchange, involuntary conversion, or wash sale of stock.

For more information, see the discussion of basis beginning on page 4-21.

Line 2(g), Gain or (Loss)

To calculate a client's gain or loss for the entire year, subtract line (f) from the sum of lines (d) and (e). Enter total on line (g).

Line 3, Gain, If Any, from Form 4684, Line 39

Form 4684, *Casualties and Thefts*, is used to report gains and losses from casualties and thefts. See discussion in Tab 2.

Line 4, Section 1231 Gain from Installment Sales

See installment sales discussion on page 4-23.

Line 5, Section 1231 Gain from Like-Kind Exchanges from Form 8824

See discussion of like-kind exchanges beginning on page 4-18.

Line 6, Gain from Line 32 from Other than Casualty or Theft

This line represents the total long-term gain reported in Part III, other than from casualty or theft.

Line 7, Net Gain/Loss

If line 7 is zero or a loss, it is carried to Part II (line 11), where it is netted against short-term gain/loss. If line 7 is a gain and there are no prior year IRC §1231 losses, the gain is reported on Schedule D, and there are no long-term losses to offset short-term gains reported in Part II.

Line 8, Nonrecaptured Net Section 1231 Losses from Prior Years

IRC §1231 gain on line 7 is treated as ordinary income to the extent of nonrecaptured IRC §1231 losses, which are simply net IRC §1231 losses sustained during the *five preceding tax years* that have not yet been applied against any net IRC §1231 gain.

Example. Raphael LaTurcio had net IRC §1231 losses of $4,000 and $5,000 in 2004 and 2006, respectively, and net IRC §1231 gains of $3,000 in 2008. After filing his 2008 return, he has $6,000 of unrecaptured loss ($9,000 – $3,000). In 2009, he had a net IRC §1231 gain of $2,000 which is entered on line 7, and the nonrecaptured net IRC §1231 loss of $6,000 is entered on line 8. The entire $2,000 net IRC §1231 gain on line 7 is treated as ordinary income and is entered on line 12 of Form 4797. For recordkeeping purposes, $1,000 was recaptured from 2004 and $1,000 from 2006. Thus, the $4,000 loss from 2004 is entirely recaptured ($3,000 in 2008 and $1,000 in 2009), and $4,000 of IRC §1231 losses from 2006 are left to be recaptured ($5,000 minus the $1,000 recaptured in 2009) in 2010.

Line 9, Net Gain (or Loss)

Subtract line 8 from line 7. If the result is zero or less, enter -0-. Whenever this line is greater than zero, all net IRC §1231 losses from prior years have been recaptured.

Part II, Lines 10-18

Gain or loss reported in Part II is ordinary income, reported on line 14 of Form 1040.

Line 10, Ordinary Gains and Losses Not Included in Parts I and III

Report other ordinary gains and losses, including gains/losses from property held one year or less, here.

Securities or Commodities Held by a Trader Who Made a Mark-to-Market Election. Report on line 10 all gains and losses from sales and dispositions of securities or commodities held in connection with a trading business, including gains and losses from marking to market securities and commodities held at the end of the tax year. Attach a statement that shows the details of each transaction, using the same format as line 10 (that is, columns (a) through (g)). Separately show and identify securities or commodities held and marked to market at the end of the year. On line 10, enter *"Trader–see attached"* in column (a) and the totals from the statement in columns (d), (f), and (g).

Small Business Investment Company Stock. Report on line 10 ordinary losses from the sale or exchange (including worthlessness) of stock in a small business investment company operating under the Small Business Investment Act of 1958 (IRC §1242).

Also attach a statement that includes the name and address of the small business investment company and, if applicable, the reason the stock is worthless and the approximate date it became worthless.

IRC §1244 (Small Business) Stock. Individuals report losses, up to $50,000 ($100,000 for joint filers) from the sale or exchange (including worthlessness) of IRC §1244 (small business) stock as ordinary losses on line 10.

To qualify as IRC §1244 stock, certain requirements apply:

- The corporation's equity cannot exceed $1 million at the time of stock issuance.
- The stock must have been acquired directly by the taxpayer at original issue for money or property other than stock or securities.
- In the five years preceding the loss, the corporation must have derived over half of its gross receipts from business operations (not simply from investments).

Special rules may limit the amount of IRC §1244 ordinary loss if:

(a) IRC §1244 stock was received in exchange for property with a basis in excess of its FMV; or
(b) the holder's stock basis increased because of contributions to capital or otherwise.

See Publication 550, *Investment Income and Expenses (Including Capital Gains and Losses)*, for more details.

Report on Schedule D losses in excess of the maximum amount that may be treated as an ordinary loss (and all gains) from the sale or exchange of IRC §1244 stock.

> **Filing Tip.** It is advisable to include a statement with the return on which you are claiming a loss (including worthlessness) on the sale or exchange of stock in a small business investment company. The statement should include the name and address of the company. If declaring the stock worthless, an explanation of why the stock is worthless along with the approximate date it became worthless.

Lines 11-17, Net Gain (or Loss) from All Transactions

Line 11 has the net capital loss from Part I, and line 12 is the gain or unrecaptured IRC §1231 losses from Part I. See the discussion of Part III below regarding gain reported on line 13. Lines 14-16 are for *ordinary gain or loss* from casualty and theft, installment sales, and like-kind exchanges.

Line 18a, Subtraction of Casualty/Theft Losses

Enter here the smaller of the loss on Form 4797, line 11, or the loss on Form 4684, line 39, column (b)(ii). To figure which loss is smaller, treat both losses as positive numbers. If the casualty loss is from income-producing property, the loss will be reported on line 28 of Schedule A and will not be subject to the 2% adjusted-gross-income (AGI) floor. If the loss was sustained as an employee, the loss is reported on line 23 of Schedule A but is subject to the 2% AGI floor. Be sure to identify the amount as from "Form 4797, line 18a." The taxpayer must redetermine the gain or loss, including any gain reported on line 3 of Form 4797, to account for the loss taken on line 18a. The results will be reported as ordinary income or loss on line 14 of Form 1040.

> **Caution.** If deductions are not itemized in 2009, these losses will not be recovered.

Part III, Lines 19-32

Part III is used to determine the recapture of depreciation and certain other items that must be reported as ordinary income upon the disposition of property.

Line 19, Description of Property

List each property separately, including dispositions of property for which the IRC §179 expense deduction was separately reported on Schedule K-1 by a partnership or S corporation. If there are more than four properties to report, use additional Forms 4797.

> **Filing Tip.** Do not combine properties; each property must have its own line.

Line 20, Gross Sales Price

The gross sales price includes money, the FMV of other property received, and any existing mortgage or other debt the buyer assumes. For casualty or theft gains, include insurance or other reimbursement received or expected for each item. As with all casualty reporting, insurance coverage must be considered in expected payments even if no claim has been submitted or will be submitted.

For IRC §1255 property disposed of in a sale, exchange, or involuntary conversion, enter the amount

Categories of Property on Form 4797, Parts III and IV

IRC Section	Description	Examples
1245	Any property that has been subject to an allowance for depreciation or amortization	Personal property, either tangible or intangible; manufacturing equipment; oil-drilling equipment; storage facilities; single-purpose agricultural structures such as livestock barns or silos
1250	Real estate property subject to depreciation that is not IRC §1245 property	Rental property, leaseholds
1252	Farm land on which soil or water conservation or land-clearing write-offs have been allowed	Improvements to farm land
1254	Interest in oil, gas, geothermal, or other mineral properties	Drilling or mining rights
1255	Certain improvements to property authorized under IRC §126 for conservation	Reforestation, wetlands preservation
179 and 280F	IRC §1245 property for which treatment as a current expense may be elected	Autos and other motor vehicles, computers, computer software

Example. Emil Garza sold the building and land in which he housed and repaired equipment used in his roofing business in 2009. He had purchased the building and land in 2002 for $70,000. He had also paid $1,000 in sales commissions and $500 in legal fees, so his original basis in the building and land was $71,500, of which $10,000 was allocated to the land. He immediately remodeled the building for $15,000. In 2006, Emil had a loss of $2,000 beyond his insurance compensation to repair flood damage, an amount that he claimed as a deduction on his 2006 return. He then spent an additional $1,000 on improving the building in 2007. Between the time he bought the building and the time he sold it, he had been allowed $12,500 of depreciation on the building. He incurred $400 worth of expenses to sell the building in 2009.

When he sells the property, his basis shown on line 21 will be $75,900 ($61,500 (original cost of building plus fees less land allocation) + $16,000 (improvement costs) – $2,000 (casualty loss) + $400 (expense of sale). The depreciation amount, $12,500, will be entered on line 22 and subtracted to produce the adjusted basis, $63,400, on line 23.

As a reminder, the land is Section 1231 property and any gain or loss will be calculated in Part I of Form 4797.

realized. For IRC §1255 property disposed of in any other way, enter the FMV.

Line 21, Cost or Other Basis Plus Expense of Sale

Any increase in the cost or other basis of the property from expenditures with respect to the property must be reduced by the amount of any enhanced oil recovery credit or disabled access credit claimed with respect to such property. However, no adjustment is made to the cost or other basis for any of the items taken into account on Line 22.

Line 22, Depreciation (or Depletion) Allowed or Allowable

Depreciation allowed must be reported here (and recaptured) even if it was not taken.

Planning Tip. Taxpayers who have failed to claim depreciation or claimed an impermissible amount can correct this error even in the year of disposition by filing Form 3115, *Application for Change of Accounting Method*, and requesting an automatic change. Details can be found in the form instructions and Rev. Proc. 2008-52, as modified by Rev. Proc. 2009-39. To determine the correct amount to enter on Line 22, first you add any amounts from the following list of items:

- Deductions allowed or allowable for depreciation (including any special depreciation allowance), amortization, depletion, or preproduction expenses.
- The IRC §179 expense deduction.
- The commercial revitalization deduction.
- The downward basis adjustment under IRC § 50(c) (or the corresponding provision of prior law).
- The deduction for qualified clean-fuel vehicle property or refueling property placed in service before January 1, 2006.
- Deductions claimed under IRC §§190, 193, or 1253(d)(2) or (3) (as in effect before the passage of the Omnibus Budget Reconciliation Act of 1993 (August 10, 1993)).
- The basis reduction for the qualified electric vehicle credit for property placed in service before January 1, 2007.
- The basis reduction for the qualified plug-in electric vehicle credit.
- The basis reduction for the employer-provided childcare facility credit.
- The deduction for qualified energy-efficient commercial building property.
- The basis reduction for the alternative motor vehicle credit.
- The basis reduction for the alternative fuel vehicle refueling property credit.

From this total, subtract any amounts from the following list of items:

- Any investment credit recapture amount, if the basis of the property was reduced in the tax year the property was placed in service under IRC §50(c)(1) (or the corresponding provision of prior law).
- Any IRC §§179 or 280F(b)(2) recapture amount included in gross income in a prior tax year because the business use of the property decreased to 50 percent or less.
- Any qualified clean-fuel vehicle property or refueling property deduction you were required to recapture.
- Any basis increase for qualified electric vehicle credit recapture.
- Any basis increase for recapture of the employer-provided childcare facility credit.
- Any basis increase for recapture of the alternative motor vehicle credit.
- Any basis increase for recapture of the alternative fuel vehicle refueling property credit.
- Any qualified disaster expense recapture under IRC §198A.

To insure the correct amounts are recaptured as depreciation allowed or allowable, IRS Publication 544, *Sales and Other Dispositions of Assets,* should be reviewed.

A taxpayer may be a partner or an S corporation shareholder, and the partnership or S corporation may have given him or her a Schedule K-1 that separately reports information on the sale, exchange, or other disposition of property for which the IRC §179 expense deduction was claimed. This information will be separately reported on line 20 of Schedule K-1 (Form 1065) or on line 17 of Schedule K-1 (Form 1120S).

If this is the case, the taxpayer should complete the worksheet in the instructions to Form 4797.

Filing Tip. It is possible that this calculation will turn a gain into a loss. If it does, that loss will be reported in Part I, not Part III.

Lines 23 and 24, Adjusted Basis and Total Gain

For IRC §1255 property, enter the adjusted basis of the IRC §126 property disposed of.

Lines 25a and 25b, Section 1245 Property Depreciation

IRC §1245 property is property that is depreciable or amortizable and is one of the following:

- Personal property.
- Elevators and escalators placed in service before 1987.
- Real property (other than property described under tangible real property below) subject to amortization or deductions under IRC §§169, 179, 179A, 179B, 179C, 179D, 185 (repealed), 188 (repealed), 190, 193, or 194.
- Tangible real property (except buildings and their structural components) if used in any of the following ways:
  - As an integral part of manufacturing, production, or extraction or of furnishing transportation, communications, or certain public utility services.
  - As a research facility in these activities.
  - For the bulk storage of fungible commodities (including commodities in a liquid or gaseous state) used in these activities.
- A single-purpose agricultural or horticultural structure, as defined in IRC §168(i)(13).
- A storage facility (not including a building or its structural components) used in connection with the distribution of petroleum or any primary petroleum product.
- Any railroad grading or tunnel bore, as defined in IRC §168(e)(4).

See IRC §1245(b) for exceptions and limits involving the following:

- Gifts.
- Transfers at death.
- Certain tax-free transactions.
- Certain like-kind exchanges, involuntary conversions, etc.
- Property distributed by a partnership to a partner.
- Transfers to tax-exempt organizations where the property will be used in an unrelated business.
- Timber property.

For example, if a taxpayer transfers IRC §1245 property to another by gift and the recipient later sells the property for a gain, the recipient must take into account any depreciation deducted by the donor in computing IRC §1245 income.

A special rule must be applied when disposing of IRC §197 intangibles (IRC §1245(b)(8)).

Example. Joanna Chung purchased IRC §1245 property in 2006 for $10,000. She takes depreciation deductions of $2,000 before giving the property to her son, Bruce. The adjusted basis to the son is $8,000, the same as the mother's. Bruce later takes an additional $1,000 of depreciation, reducing his basis to $7,000. In 2009, he sells the property for $10,500, realizing a recognized gain of $3,500.

Lines 26a-d, Section 1250 Property

IRC §1250 property is depreciable real property (other than IRC §1245 property). IRC §1250 recapture applies if the taxpayer used an accelerated depreciation method or claimed the 30% or 50% special depreciation allowance, or the commercial revitalization deduction. IRC §1250 recapture does not apply to dispositions of the following property placed in service after 1986 (or after July 31, 1986, if elected):

- 27.5-year (or 40-year, if elected) residential rental property (except for 27.5-year qualified New York Liberty Zone property acquired after September 10, 2001).
- 22-, 31.5-, or 39-year (or 40-year, if elected) nonresidential real property (except for 39-year qualified New York Liberty Zone property acquired after September 10, 2001, and property for which the taxpayer elected to claim a commercial revitalization deduction).

Real property depreciable under ACRS (pre-1987 rules) is subject to recapture under IRC §1245, except for the following, which are treated as IRC §1250 property:

- 15-, 18-, or 19-year real property and low-income housing that is residential rental property.
- 15-, 18-, or 19-year real property and low-income housing that is used mostly outside the United States.

- 15-, 18-, or 19-year real property and low-income housing for which a straight-line election was made.
- Low-income rental housing described in IRC §1250(a)(1)(B).

See IRC §1250(d) for exceptions and limits involving the following:

- Gifts.
- Transfers at death.
- Certain tax-free transactions.
- Certain like-kind exchanges, involuntary conversions, etc.
- Property distributed by a partnership to a partner.
- Disposition of qualified low-income housing.
- Transfers of property to tax-exempt organizations if the property will be used in an unrelated business.
- Dispositions of property as a result of foreclosure proceedings.

Additional Depreciation after 1975. For line 26a, *additional depreciation* is the excess of actual depreciation (including any special depreciation allowance or commercial revitalization deduction) over depreciation figured using the straight-line method. For this purpose, the basis under IRC §50(c)(1) (or the corresponding provision of prior law) should not be reduced to figure straight-line depreciation. Also, if a commercial revitalization deduction was claimed, figure straight-line depreciation using the property's applicable recovery period under IRC §168.

Applicable Percentage. The percentage entered on line 26b will be 100%, except for low-income housing described in IRC §1250(a)(1)(B), where the applicable percentage can be found.

Additional Depreciation after 1969 and before 1976. If straight-line depreciation is more than the actual depreciation for the period after 1975, line 26d is reduced by the excess, but not below zero.

Line 27, Section 1252 Property

The taxpayer may have ordinary income on the disposition of certain farmland held more than a year but less than 10 years. Line 27 may be skipped if such farmland was disposed of during the tenth or later year after acquisition.

Enter 100% of line 27a on line 27b except as follows:

- 80% if the farmland was disposed of within the sixth year after it was acquired.
- 60% if disposed of within the seventh year.
- 40% if disposed of within the eighth year.
- 20% if disposed of within the ninth year.

Partners enter applicable amounts in accordance with instructions from the partnership.

Line 28, Section 1254 Property

If the taxpayer had a gain on the disposition of oil, gas, or geothermal property placed in service before 1987, all or part of the gain is treated as ordinary income. Include on line 22 of Form 4797 any depletion allowed (or allowable) in determining the adjusted basis of the property.

If the taxpayer had a gain on the disposition of oil, gas, geothermal, or other mineral properties (IRC §1254 property) placed in service after 1986, he or she must recapture all expenses that were deducted as intangible drilling costs, depletion, mine exploration costs, and development costs.

If the property was placed in service before 1987, enter on line 28a the total expenses after 1975 that were deducted by the taxpayer or any previous owner as intangible drilling and development costs under IRC § 263(c) (except previously expensed mining costs that were included in income upon reaching the producing state) and would have been reflected in the adjusted basis of the property if they had not been deducted.

If the property was placed in service after 1986, enter on line 28a the total expenses that were deducted under IRC §§263, 616, or 617 by the taxpayer or any other person, and that would have been included in the basis of the property if there had been no deduction, plus the deduction under IRC §611 that reduced the adjusted basis of the property.

Lines 29a and 29b, Section 1255 Property

Applicable Percentage. Enter 100% of the payments on line 29a if the property is disposed of less than 10 years after receipt of payments excluded from income. Enter 100% minus 10% of the amount for each year, or part of a year, that the property was held over 10 years after receipt of the excluded payments; enter zero if 20 years or more.

Recapture for Part III Properties. If any part of the gain shown on line 24 is treated as ordinary income under IRC §§1231 through 1254 (for example, IRC §1252), enter the smaller of line 24 reduced by the part of the gain treated as ordinary income under the other provision, or line 29a.

Lines 30-32, Total Gains for All Properties

The recapture amounts are totaled on line 31 and subtracted from total gains on the transactions listed on line 24. The amount is then added to long-term capital gains in Part I.

Part IV, Lines 33-35

General Rules

If the taxpayer took an IRC §179 expense deduction for property placed in service after 1986 (other than listed property defined by IRC §280F(d)(4)), and the business use of the property decreased to 50 percent or less in 2008, complete column (a) of lines 33 through 35 to figure the recapture amount.

Filing Tip. IRC §179 expense deduction recapture rules also apply to any qualified Gulf Opportunity Zone (GO Zone) property on which the 50 percent bonus depreciation was claimed and which has ceased to be qualified GO Zone property (Code Sec. 1400N(d)(5); MTG ¶1208 and ¶1237).

If the client has listed property placed in service in a prior year and the business use decreased to 50 percent or less in 2009, figure the amount to be recaptured under IRC §280F(b)(2). Complete column (b), lines 33 through 35. See IRS Publication 463, *Travel, Entertainment, Gift, and Car Expenses*, for more details on recapture of excess depreciation.

Filing Tip. If the client has more than one property subject to the recapture rules, figure the recapture amounts separately for each property. Show these calculations on a separate statement and attach it to the tax return.

Line 33, Section 179 Expense

In column (a), enter the IRC §179 expense deduction claimed when the property was placed in service. In column (b), enter the depreciation allowable on the property in prior tax years (plus any IRC §179 expense deduction claimed when the property was placed in service).

Line 34, Recomputed Depreciation

In column (a), enter the depreciation that would have been allowable on the IRC §179 property from the year the property was placed in service through (and including) the current year. See Tab 7, MTG ¶1208, and IRS Publication 946, *How to Depreciate Property.*

In column (b), enter the depreciation that would have been allowable if the property had not been used more than 50% in a qualified business. Figure the depreciation from the year it was placed in service up to (but not including) the current year.

Line 35, Recapture Amount

Subtract line 34 from line 33 and enter the recapture amount as "other income" on the same form or schedule on which client took the deduction (Schedule C (Form 1040), for example).

Caution. The recapture amount may be subject to self-employment tax if the taxpayer filed Form 1040, Schedule C or F. If your client has filed either Schedule C or F and the property was used in both the client's trade or business and for the production of income, the portion of the recapture amount attributable to the trade or business is subject to self-employment tax. The recapture amount on Line 35 needs to be properly allocated to the appropriate schedule. Finally, be sure to increase the basis in the property by the recapture amount.

Sales and Exchanges

Definitions

Gain/Loss Realized. The difference between the amount received for property and the amount of basis in the property.

Gain/Loss Recognized. The portion of a gain or loss that is reported for tax purposes.

Recapture. The reversal of all or part of the effect of a tax benefit.

Like-Kind Exchanges

For personal property, it makes no tax difference whether the property changed hands by a sale or an exchange. When business property changes hands, it may make a great deal of difference in the taxes paid.

If a taxpayer sells business or investment property, both gain and loss are recognized. If a taxpayer exchanges business or investment property for other "like-kind/like-class" business or investment property, the gain or loss that is realized on the exchange is not recognized. See **"What Constitutes a Like-Kind Exchange?"** which follows for a discussion of on what sorts of properties may be exchanged to qualify as like kind.

Remember, to qualify as a tax-free exchange, both the property given and the property taken in exchange must be held for business or investment purposes–*not* for personal use.

The provisions for nonrecognition of gain or loss do not apply to property held for sale in the ordinary course of a taxpayer's trade or business or to inventory items. Thus, if an automobile dealer exchanges one of his or her cars held for sale to a customer for another automobile, the full amount of gain or loss realized will be recognized by the dealer for tax purposes. The same is true if a *dealer* in real estate exchanges one real estate property (if held for sale to customers) for another piece of real estate.

If it were not for this restriction, storekeepers, dealers, and other sellers of merchandise could simply trade or barter their goods, instead of selling them outright, in order to avoid paying taxes on their profits.

What Constitutes a Like-Kind Exchange? As mentioned previously, the provision for nonrecognition of gain or loss on the exchange of business or investment property applies only if the property given and the property taken in exchange are of like-kind or like-class. Thus, an exchange of real property for real property, and the exchange of specific class of personal property (i.e., non-real estate) for personal property in the same class are exchanges of like property. This means that the exchange of an apartment house for a factory building, or of improved land for an unimproved piece of land, would qualify because both are real properties used in trade, business, or investment. For the types of personal property that are treated as like-class property, taxpayers should refer to the North American Industry Classification System (NAICS). For additional information regarding the exchange of like-kind or like-class property, see IRS Publication 544, *Sales and Other Dispositions of Assets*.

Foreign realty cannot be treated as like-kind property. Similarly, personal property used predominantly in the United States can be exchanged *only* for other like-kind property in a similar location. So, for example, a computer used within the United States exchanged for a computer used in Canada does not qualify for like-kind treatment.

Similarly, the exchange of a business car for a sports utility vehicle (SUV) is a like-kind exchange because both items are of the same class of property used in a trade or business or for investment. However, the exchange for a pick-up truck for a panel truck may not be a like-kind exchange because they are of different NAICS classifications, even though they are both trucks used in a trade or business.

Time Limit on Like-Kind Exchanges. For transfers to qualify as like-kind exchanges, a 180-day time limit is imposed for completing the exchange following the relinquishment of the property to be exchanged. Also, the property to be received in the exchange must be identified within 45 days after the original property transfer. *Identification* means delivering to the other party involved in the exchange a written description of the property.

Caution. There are no extensions available for the 45- and 180-day identification and closing requirements for like-kind exchanges. The IRS strictly enforces the like-kind requirements.

Trade or Exchange Involving Both Property and Money

The simple exchange of one property for another is just the least complex case of the like-kind exchange. It frequently happens that a taxpayer will pay or receive *money* in addition to the property traded or received in trade. Also, at times, several items of property are involved in one combined transaction. The money and other unlike property received are generally referred to as *boot*.

Here are a few short rules that give a general view of such transactions. Rules 1 to 3 cover situations in which the taxpayer realizes a *gain*; Rule 4 deals with the treatment of a *loss*.

Rule 1. No gain is recognized on a like-kind exchange if the taxpayer *pays* money (so-called boot) in addition to the property given in the trade.

Planning Tip. To qualify, the transaction must be conducted by a third party, usually a qualified intermediary such as a bank. Neither the buyer nor the seller receives any money directly from the other.

Example. A printer trades in his old printing press, which has a basis of $3,400, for a new press that costs $5,600. He is given a trade-in allowance of $3,600 and pays $2,000 "boot" in cash to make up the difference. The amount realized is $5,600 (the value of the new press). Since the total basis of the assets given up is only $5,400 ($3,400, the basis of the old press, plus $2,000 cash), the printer realizes a gain of $200. However, because the press is held for productive use in a trade or business, the gain is not recognized.

Note that if the printer had sold his original press for $3,600 and then added $2,000 to purchase the new machine for $5,600, the $200 gain would have been recognized, because it would have been realized on a sale, not an exchange.

Rule 2. If a taxpayer *receives* property, plus money, in exchange for property and realizes a gain, the gain is recognized, but only to the extent of the money received. In other words, the taxpayer must either report the gain realized or the amount of money received, whichever is less.

Example. A butcher exchanges his refrigerator, which has a basis of $600, and receives in return $150 in cash plus a meat-cutting machine with an FMV of $700. He realizes a gain of $250 on this transaction [$850 amount realized ($700 + $150), less the basis of property traded in ($600) = $250]. Since the refrigerator and the meat-cutting machine are items of the same class and both are held for productive use in the taxpayer's trade or business, the exchange is tax free. However, because the butcher also received cash, the gain is recognized to the extent of the money received. Thus, the amount of the recognized gain is $150, which was the amount received in cash.

The reason for Rule 2 will be better understood if we consider a transaction in which the taxpayer receives both like-kind property and money–a combination sale and exchange. To the extent of the cash received, there is a sale; to the extent property is received, there is an exchange. Because gain on a sale is always recognized, it follows that to the extent of the cash received, the gain is recognized.

Rule 3. If a taxpayer, in exchange for property, receives both like-kind property and property that is not like kind, the FMV of the non-like-kind property is treated as cash. This means that a gain, if any, is recognized only to the extent of the FMV of the other property received.

Example. An investor exchanges farm property having a basis of $35,000 for a vacant building lot worth $36,000, an automobile worth $2,000, and a diamond ring worth $500. The amount realized is $36,000 plus $2,000 plus $500, a total of $38,500. Consequently, the investor realizes a gain of $3,500. The farm and the lot are like-kind property, but the automobile and ring are other kinds of property. Thus, the gain will be recognized only to the extent of $2,500, the sum of the FMVs of the automobile and ring.

Rule 4. A loss is never recognized on the exchange of like-kind property held for productive use in a trade or business, even though other property or money is received or paid in addition to the exchange.

Example. A farmer exchanges a combine with a basis of $15,000 for a tractor worth $10,000, a parcel of land worth $2,000, and $1,000 cash. The amount realized is $13,000, and the realized loss is, therefore, $2,000, no part of which is recognized.

Where the exchange involves related parties (spouse, siblings, descendants, ancestors, or controlled entities) and property is disposed of within two years of that exchange, gain on the original exchange is triggered. Exceptions apply to dispositions because of death or involuntary conversion.

Planning Tip. The nonrecognition of gain on a like-kind transaction is a two-edged sword. On the one hand, it defers the immediate recognition (and tax) of the taxpayer's gain, which is usually beneficial to the taxpayer. On the other hand, it reduces the taxpayer's basis and increases the taxpayer's gain in the event of a future taxable disposition.

The only way to tell whether nonrecognition in a given situation is desirable is to project the taxpayer's future income and tax picture. If it appears that nonrecognition would do more harm than good, it may be possible to sidestep the nonrecognition provisions by arranging the transaction in the form of a sale rather than as an exchange.

Exchanges of Securities

Although corporate stocks (shares) are usually held for investment, an exchange of stock for stock is not a tax-free, like-kind exchange, unless the stock is exchanged for the same class of stock in the same corporation.

This means that the exchange of stock in one corporation for stock in another corporation or the exchange of common stock for preferred stock in the same corporation, or of stocks for bonds or vice versa, is not a like-kind exchange. Any gain or loss is therefore fully recognized.

Exchanges of Insurance Policies

No gain or loss is recognized if a taxpayer exchanges a life insurance policy for another life insurance policy, an endowment, or an annuity contract. This is so even if there is an outstanding loan on the policy, as long as the new policy has similar loan provisions. The same rule applies when one annuity contract is exchanged for another annuity contract, so long as the insured (the annuitant) remains the same. Where one endowment policy is exchanged for another endowment policy, no gain or loss is recognized if the beginning date under the new contract is no later than the beginning date under the old contract. Nonrecognition also applies to the exchange of an endowment policy for an annuity contract.

Caution. The exchange of an annuity contract for a life insurance policy or an endowment policy does not fall under this tax-free exchange rule.

If the insurance company is financially troubled (in rehabilitation, insolvency, conservatorship, or other state proceeding), a policyholder can surrender the policy and make a tax-free reinvestment of the proceeds in a new policy if the transfer is completed within 60 days

How Nonrecognition of Gain or Loss Affects Basis

The basis of the property that a taxpayer receives in a fully or partially tax-free exchange must be reduced by the amount of any gain that was realized but not recognized.

The reason for this reduction in the basis of the new asset makes economic sense in that the new property is merely a continuation or substitution of the old. In other words, for tax purposes, the exchange never took place (which is the theory for nonrecognition of gain or loss on a like-kind exchange).

Example. Joan Haslan had a nonrecognized gain of $1,400 on the exchange of her truck, which had a basis of $12,600, for another truck worth $14,000. The basis of the new truck would be $12,600 ($14,000 less the $1,400 nonrecognized gain).

Thus, if she shortly thereafter sold the new truck for $14,000, she would have a recognized gain of $1,400.

Computing Gain or Loss

Basis

The basis for computing gain or loss or depreciation on property acquired in most common transactions is outlined here, with references to the MTG paragraphs where additional details appear. This basis, after adjustments described on page 4-6 and MTG ¶1611–¶1617, is subtracted from the amount realized to determine the amount of gain or loss from a sale or exchange. Except where other rules are prescribed, the basis for gain or loss is determined under the law in effect when the property is sold.

Fair Market Value

Fair market value (FMV) is the standard for valuing property acquired by a corporation for its stock and for valuing a decedent's property at date of death. It is also used in determining whether and to what extent property received in an exchange is the equivalent of cash. The IRS has recognized a judicial definition of FMV as being the price that property will bring when offered for sale by a willing seller to a willing buyer, neither being obliged to buy or sell. Only in rare and extraordinary cases (see Treas. Reg. §1.1001-1) does property have no determinable FMV.

Planning Tip. If the FMV of an asset received in an exchange (such as a contract to receive royalties) cannot be determined with certainty, gain is not realized on the exchange until after the total payments received under the contract exceed the cost (or other basis) of the property surrendered in exchange. The Tax Court has applied the *Cohan* rule (estimated or approximate value) to estimate the value of patents, patent applications, and stock rights when the taxpayer could not prove their exact value. *G.M. Cohn*, CA-2, 2 USTC ¶489 (1930).

Nonrecourse Indebtedness

In determining the amount of gain or loss (or deemed gain or loss) realized on the sale or exchange of any property, the FMV of such property is deemed to be not less than the amount of any nonrecourse indebtedness to which the property is subject (IRC §7701(g)).

See, **Amount Realized on a Nonrecourse Debt,** page 4-26 and MTG ¶791.

Property Acquired by Gift

If property was acquired by gift, the basis to the donee for gain is the same as it would be in the hands of the donor or the last preceding owner by whom it was not acquired by gift. The basis for loss is the basis determined in the same way or the FMV of the property at the time of the gift, whichever is lower.

Filing Tip. The potential exists that a taxpayer will recognize neither gain nor loss on the sale of property received by gift because the selling price is less than the basis for gain and more than the basis for loss.

If a gift tax was payable on a gift made after September 1, 1958, and before 1977, the basis of the property is increased by the amount of the gift tax, but not above the FMV of the property at the time of the gift. As to gifts made before September 2, 1958, and held by the donee on that date, the basis is also increased by the amount of the gift tax, but not by more than any excess of the

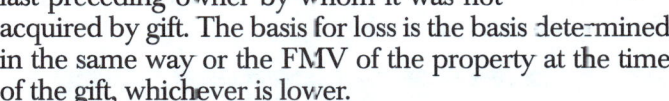

FMV at the time of the gift over the basis of the property in the hands of the donor at the time of the gift.

In the case of a gift made after 1976 on which the gift tax is paid, the basis of the property is increased by the amount of gift tax attributable to the net appreciation in value of the gift. The net appreciation for this purpose is the amount by which the fair market value of the gift exceeds the donor's adjusted basis immediately before the gift.

For the basis of a life estate acquired by gift, see MTG ¶1633.

Additions to Basis of Property

In computing gain or loss on the sale of business or investment property or gain on the sale of personal property, the cost or other basis must be *adjusted* for any expenditure, receipt, loss, or other item properly chargeable to the capital account. For example, an addition for improvements made to the property since its acquisition must be made. The cost of capital improvements such as an addition or new roof on a home, installation of central air conditioning, or rewiring of a home is added to its basis. Other capital charges such as brokers' commissions and lawyers' fees incurred in buying real estate are added to its basis. Generally, expenditures incurred in defending or perfecting title to property are also a part of the cost of the property. The basis of property is also increased by zoning costs and the capitalized value of a redeemable ground rent.

Cost basis also includes sales tax, freight, installation and testing costs, excise taxes, and revenue stamps.

Settlement Fees and Other Costs. The basis of real property includes settlement fees and closing costs including the following:

- Abstract fees.
- Charges for installing utility services.
- Legal fees (including title search and preparation of the sales contract and deed).
- Recording fees.
- Surveys.
- Transfer taxes.
- Owner's title insurance.

Amounts owed by the seller but paid by the buyer, such as back taxes or interest, recording or mortgage fees, charges for improvements or repairs, and sales commissions also add to the basis.

In addition, the following rules apply:

- A buyer may claim a current deduction for reimbursing the seller for real estate taxes paid by the seller for the buyer.
- Amounts placed in escrow for future payments of items such as insurance and taxes do *not* increase basis.
- A buyer increases basis by the amount of an existing mortgage that the buyer assumes and becomes liable for (*B.B. Crane*, S.Ct., 47-1 USTC ¶9217). Fees and costs related to getting a loan to purchase the property are *not* included in the basis of the property.

Assessments. An assessment for improvements or other items that increase the value of a property are added to the basis of the property and not deducted as a tax. Such improvements may include streets, sidewalks, water mains, sewers, and public parking facilities. The amount of such an assessment may be a depreciable asset. For example, the cost of a mall enclosure paid for by a business taxpayer through an assessment is depreciable. Assessments for maintenance or repair or meeting interest charges on the improvements are currently deductible as a real property tax.

Examples of Increases and Decreases to Basis

Increases to Basis	Decreases to Basis
o Capital improvements: Putting an addition on home Replacing an entire roof Paving driveway Installing central air conditioning Rewiring home o Assessments for local improvements: Water connections Sidewalks Roads o Casualty losses: Restoring damaged property o Legal fees: Cost of defending and perfecting a title Zoning costs	o Exclusion from income of subsidies for energy conservation measures o Casualty or theft loss deductions and insurance reimbursements o Credit for qualified electric vehicles o Section 179 deduction o Deduction for clean-fuel vehicles and clean-fuel vehicle refueling property o Depreciation o Nontaxable corporate distributions

Legal fees for obtaining a decrease in an assessment levied against property to pay for local improvements are also added to the basis of the property (Rev. Rul. 70-62).

Taxes. Any tax paid in connection with the acquisition of a property is included in the basis of the property. A tax paid in connection with the disposition of a property reduces the amount realized on the disposition.

Valuation of Securities and Real Estate

- The FMV of securities *traded on the open market*, or on a recognized exchange, is ordinarily the average of the high and low quoted prices on the valuation date. If only a minimal number of shares are traded on the valuation date, or if other abnormal market conditions exist, an alternative valuation method may be necessary.
- When corporate stock is *not sold on the open market*, its FMV depends on many factors, including the nature and history of the business, economic outlook and condition of the industry, book value of stock and financial condition of the business, earning capacity of the company, dividend-paying capacity, goodwill, prior sales, size of the block to be valued, and market price of similar but listed stock. Isolated sales of small portions of the stock or forced sales are not considered evidence of fair market value.
- *Restrictive sales agreements* must be considered in the valuation of stock. If the stock is subject to a repurchase option, its value may *not* exceed the amount for which it may be repurchased. If there are restrictions making sale of stock impossible, and its value is highly speculative, it does not have a FMV.
- Accepted evidence of the FMV of real estate includes sales of similar property in the same locality, testimony of real estate experts, and offers to purchase. Appraisal affidavits of a retrospective nature, standing alone, are generally not accorded great weight.

Property Transferred Between Spouses or Incident to Divorce

No gain or loss is recognized on a transfer of property from an individual to, or in trust for the benefit of, a spouse or a former spouse if the transfer to the former spouse is incident to the divorce of the parties. (See Tab 13 and MTG ¶1734.) In such a case, the basis of the transferred property in the hands of the transferee is the transferor's adjusted basis in the property. This nontaxable carryover basis provision does not, however, apply to a spouse (or former spouse) who is a nonresident alien.

Nonrecognition of gain is *not* permitted with respect to the transfer of property in trust to the extent that the sum of the amount of any liabilities assumed, plus the amount of any liabilities to which the property is subject, exceeds the total of the adjusted basis of the property transferred. The transferee's basis is adjusted to take into account any gain recognized.

Installment Sales

Figuring Adjusted Basis for Installment Sale Purposes. Use the following worksheet to figure adjusted basis in the property for installment sale purposes. The worksheet also determines the gross profit percentage necessary to figure installment sale income (gain) for the current year.

Worksheet for Figuring Adjusted Basis and Gross Profit Percentage on Installment Sales	
1. Enter the selling price for the property.	
2. Enter adjusted basis for the property.	
3. Enter selling expenses.	
4. Enter any depreciation recapture.	
5. Add lines 2, 3, and 4. This is the **adjusted basis for installment sale purposes**.	
6. Subtract line 5 from line 1. If $0 or less, enter -0-. This is **gross profit**.	
If the amount entered on line 6 is $0, **Stop** here. The installment method cannot be used.	
7. Enter the contract price for the property.	
8. Divide line 6 by line 7. This is the **gross profit percentage**.	

Caution. Care must be taken when structuring an installment sale agreement to insure a sufficient payment in the first year to avoid a cash-flow problem in paying taxes caused by the recapture of preferences for alternative minimum tax purposes.

Form 6252, Installment Sale Income. The installment method can be used to defer some tax on capital gains, as long as the seller received at least one payment for a piece of property after the year of the sale. It cannot be used if the sale results in a loss. The bad news is that payments for many (or even most) of the assets of a client's business are not eligible for installment sale treatment. In most cases, only gain on assets that have appreciated in value beyond their original purchase price will be eligible for installment sale treatment.

A separate Form 6252 should be filed for each asset sold using this method. This form must be filed in the year the sale occurs, and in every later year in which a payment is received.

Part I, Gross Profit and Contract Price, should be completed for the year of sale only.

Part II, Installment Sale Income, should be completed for the year of sale and for any year in which payment is received or certain debts must be treated as a payment on installation obligations.

Part III, Related Party Installment Sale Income, should not be completed if final payment is received in the current tax year.

Planning Tip. An installment sale may be much more advantageous than an outright sale whenever recapture rates apply. Spreading out gain can significantly minimize tax impact.

Electing Out of Installment Sale Treatment. Do not file Form 6252 if the taxpayer elects not to report the sale on the installment method. To elect out, report the full amount of gain on a timely filed return, including extensions, on Form 4797 or Schedule D. If the original form was filed on time without the election being made, the election may be made on an amended return filed no later than six month after due date of the tax return, excluding extensions. Write "Filed pursuant to section 301.9100-2" at the top of the amended return.

Because this is an election, look at the sale agreement to see if the potential exists for a favorable allocation of the selling price.

Planning Tip. Other consideration that need to be taken into account when determining whether to use an installment sale are: dealing with elderly clients who may inadvertently leave the installment agreement in their estate; clients having capital losses that are being carried forward; and the potential of an increase in capital gains rates in the future when the balance of the installment sale agreement is paid.

Involuntary Conversions

An involuntary conversion occurs when property is destroyed, stolen, condemned, or disposed of under the threat of condemnation and the taxpayer receives other property or money in payment (e.g., insurance proceeds or a condemnation award).

There are two specific sets of circumstances under which gain from compulsory, or involuntary, conversion of property is not recognized for tax purposes.

1. When property is converted involuntarily or by compulsion into other property that is similar or related in service or use, no gain is currently recognized. The basis of the old property is simply transferred to the new property. This nonrecognition rule is mandatory.
2. When property is involuntarily converted into money (e.g., insurance proceeds after fire destroys a building) or into unlike property, the owner may elect to postpone gain by buying qualified property within a specified replacement period. (See MTG ¶1715 for information concerning replacement property and replacement periods.) When the involuntary conversion results in a gain, the taxpayer may make an election to recognize gain only to the extent that the amount realized from the converted property exceeds the cost of the replacement property. The election to defer all or part of the gain realized in the involuntary conversion is made by excluding the gain from gross income on the tax return for the year in which it is realized. A taxpayer who has realized gain from an involuntary conversion must provide details of it on the tax return for the tax year in which the gain is realized (see **"Required Statement,"** following).

Planning Tip. Victims of Hurricane Katrina were given an extended period of time to replace both businesses and personal residences destroyed in the hurricane. The replacement period for both individuals and businesses is five years from August 25, 2005, if the property was originally located with the disaster area and the replacement property is also substantially located within the disaster area.

The same replacement period relief has been extended to the victims of the tornados and storms that struck Kansas in the spring of 2007 and to the parts of the Midwest struck by violent weather in the spring of 2008 (the Midwestern disaster area).

Loss. Loss from an involuntary conversion is deductible only if the converted property is used in a business or for the production of income. However, casualty or theft losses on personal property may be deductible.

Residence. When an individual's principal residence has been involuntarily converted, the individual may exclude any realized gain, up to the $250,000/$500,000 maximum (see page 4-30) as if the home had been sold. If the total realized gain is more than the maximum exclusion, the individual may defer recognizing the excess if replacement property is purchased.

The sale of land within a reasonable period of time following the destruction of a principal residence qualifies as part of the involuntary conversion of the residence (Rev. Rul. 96-32, 1996- CB 177).

Planning Tip. The IRS has provided for automatic extensions of the four-year replacement period for livestock treated as involuntarily converted. For farmers and ranchers in designated severe drought areas, the replacement period is extended to the first tax year ending after the first drought-free year for the applicable region. See Notice 2006-82 (2006-2 CB 529) for details.

Livestock. The destruction of livestock by disease, or the sale or exchange of livestock because of disease, is also treated as an involuntary conversion. Sales or exchanges of livestock (except poultry) solely on account of drought, flood, or other weather-related conditions that exceed the number normally sold may also be entitled to involuntary conversion treatment. If, because of soil or other environmental contamination, it is not feasible for a farmer to reinvest the proceeds from involuntarily converted livestock in property similar or related in service or use, the proceeds may be invested in other property, including real property, used for farming. The replacement property will then be treated as property similar or related in service or use to the converted livestock.

Filing Tip. The IRS has released Notice 2009-81 (2009-40 IRB 455), declaring that the 12-month period ending on August 31, 2009, is not a drought-free year for the listed regions. The replacement period will be extended for any county listed in the applicable regions. A list of counties in affected states is attached to this notice.

Reporting Requirements. Form 4797, *Sale of Business Property*, is used to report the gain or loss from an involuntary conversion (other than from casualty or theft) of:

(a) business property,
(b) capital assets used in a business, or
(c) capital assets used in connection with a transaction entered into for profit.

Form 4684, *Casualties and Thefts*, is used to report involuntary conversions from casualties and thefts.

Schedule D is used to report gains from involuntary conversions (other than from casualty or theft) of capital assets not held for business or profit.

Required Statement. A taxpayer is required to attach a statement to the tax return for the year in which gain is realized (e.g., the year in which insurance proceeds are received). The statement should include such information as the date and details of the involuntary conversion and the insurance or other reimbursement received. If replacement property is acquired before the tax return is filed, the statement must include information concerning a description of the replacement property, the date of acquisition, and the cost of the replacement property. If replacement is to be made after the year in which the gain is realized, the statement should also state that the taxpayer intends to replace the property within the required replacement period.

Foreclosures

If a borrower does not make payments owed on a loan secured by property, the lender may foreclose on the loan and/or repossess the property. The foreclosure and/or repossession is treated as a sale or exchange from which the borrower may realize gain or loss, even if the property is voluntarily returned to the lender. The borrower may also realize ordinary income from cancellation of debt if the loan balance is more than the FMV of the property.

Worksheet for Foreclosures and Repossessions *Keep for Your Records*

Part 1. Complete Part 1 only if you were personally liable for the debt (even if none of the debt was canceled). Otherwise, go to Part 2.	
1. Enter the amount of outstanding debt immediately before the transfer of property reduced by any amount for which you remain personally liable immediately after the transfer of property	______
2. Enter the fair market value of the transferred property	______
3. Ordinary income from the cancellation of debt upon foreclosure or repossession.* Subtract line 2 from line 1. If less than zero, enter zero. Next, go to Part 2	______
Part 2. Gain or loss from foreclosure or repossession.	
4. Enter the **smaller** of line 1 or line 2. If you did not complete Part 1 (because you were not personally liable for the debt), enter the amount of outstanding debt immediately before the transfer of property	______
5. Enter any proceeds you received from the foreclosure sale	______
6. Add line 4 and line 5	______
7. Enter the adjusted basis of the transferred property	______
8. Gain or loss from foreclosure or repossession. Subtract line 7 from line 6	______

* The income may not be taxable.

Filing Tip. For an overview on the treatment of an individual's tax issues related to foreclosure or cancellation of debt, review IRS Publication 4681, Canceled Debts, Foreclosures, Repossessions, and Abandonments (for Individuals).

Buyer's (Borrower's) Gain or Loss. Figure and report gain or loss from a foreclosure or repossession in the same way as gain or loss from a sale or exchange. The gain or loss is the difference between borrower's adjusted basis in the transferred property and the amount realized.

Use the worksheet located on page 4-25 to figure gain or loss from a foreclosure or repossession.

Amount Realized on a Nonrecourse Debt. If the borrower is not personally liable for repaying the debt (nonrecourse debt) secured by the transferred property, the amount realized includes the full debt canceled by the transfer. The full canceled debt is included even if the FMV of the property is less than the canceled debt.

Example. Chet Ambler bought a new car for personal use for $15,000. He paid $2,000 down and borrowed the remaining $13,000 from the dealer's credit company. Chet is not personally liable for the loan (nonrecourse), but he pledged the new car as security. The credit company repossessed the car in 2009 because he stopped making loan payments. The balance due after taking into account the payments Chet made was $10,000. The FMV of the car when repossessed was $9,000. The amount Chet realized on the repossession is $10,000 (the amount of debt canceled by the repossession), even though the car's FMV is less than $10,000.

Amount Realized on a Recourse Debt. If the borrower is personally liable for the debt (recourse debt), the amount realized on the foreclosure or repossession does not include the canceled debt that is income from cancellation of debt. However, if the FMV of the transferred property is less than the canceled debt, the amount realized includes the canceled debt up to the FMV of the property. The taxpayer is treated as receiving ordinary income from the canceled debt for the part of the debt that is more than the FMV. See **"Cancellation of Debt,"** following.

Seller's (Lender's) Gain or Loss on Repossession. If the seller financed a buyer's purchase of property and later acquires an interest in it through foreclosure and/or repossession, the seller may have a gain or loss on the acquisition. For more information, see "Repossession" in IRS Publication 537, *Installment Sales.*

Cancellation of Debt. If property that is repossessed or foreclosed on secures a debt for which the borrower is personally liable (recourse debt), the borrower must generally report as ordinary income the amount by which the canceled debt exceeds the FMV of the property. This income is separate from any gain or loss realized from the foreclosure or repossession. Income from cancellation of a debt related to a business or rental activity is business or rental income. Report the income from cancellation of a nonbusiness debt as "other income" on line 21, Form 1040.

However, income from cancellation of debt is not taxed if any of the following conditions apply:

- The cancellation is intended as a gift.
- The debt is qualified farm debt (see IRS Publication 225, *Farmer's Tax Guide*).
- The debt is qualified real property business debt (see IRS Publication 334, *Tax Guide for Small Business*).
- The buyer is insolvent or bankrupt (see IRS Publication 908, *Bankruptcy Tax Guide*).
- The debt is qualified principal residence indebtedness (see IRS Publication 4681, *Canceled Debts, Forclosures, Repossessions, and Abandonments*).

- The debt is qualified Midwestern disaster area indebtedness (see IRS Publication 4681, *Canceled Debts, Forclosures, Repossessions, and Abandonments*).

Forms 1099-A and 1099-C

A lender who acquires an interest in a borrower's property in a foreclosure or repossession should send a Form 1099-A showing the information needed to figure gain or loss. However, if the lender also cancels part of the debt, they must also file Form 1099-C. The lender may include the information about the foreclosure or repossession on that form instead of on Form 1099-A. The lender must file Form 1099-C and send a copy to the borrower if the amount of debt canceled is $600 or more and the lender is a financial institution, credit union, federal government agency, or any organization that has a significant trade or business of lending money.

Filing Tip. Be sure to account for all 1099's that your clients receive, even if they have completed a bankruptcy proceeding. This is accomplished by filing a Form 982, *Reduction of Tax Attributes Due to Discharge of Indebtedness (and Section 1082 Basis Adjustment).*

Securities Transactions

Wash Sales

Losses cannot be deducted from sales or trades of stock or securities in a wash sale.

A wash sale occurs when a taxpayer sells or trades stock or securities at a loss and within 30 days before or after the sale does one of the following:

- Buys substantially identical stock or securities.
- Acquires substantially identical stock or securities in a fully taxable trade.
- Acquires a contract or option to buy substantially identical stock or securities.

If stock is sold and a spouse or closely held corporation buys substantially identical stock under the same conditions, the seller again has a wash sale.

Caution. Watch for notes on Forms 1009-B or 1099-DIV from mutual funds; reinvestment of dividends can trigger wash sale treatment.

If a loss was disallowed because of the wash sale rules, the disallowed loss will be added to the cost of the new stock or securities. The result is the basis in the new stock or securities. This adjustment postpones the loss deduction until the disposition of the new stock or securities. The holding period for the new stock or securities begins on the same day as the holding period of the stock or securities sold, not the date of purchase of the new stock.

Example. Dolores Hays buys 100 shares of ABC stock for $1,000. She sells these shares for $750 on May 19, 2009, and buys 100 shares of the same stock for $800 on June 13, 2009. Because Dolores bought substantially identical stock, the loss of $250 on the sale cannot be deducted. However, she adds the disallowed loss of $250 to the cost of the new stock, $800, to obtain a basis of $1,050 in the new stock.

Example. Rory Hanh, an employee of Corporation Z, has an incentive pay plan. Under this plan, Rory was given 10 shares of the corporation's stock as a bonus. He included the FMV of the stock, $600, in his gross income for 2008 as additional pay. Those shares are sold on April 8, 2009, for $500. He gets another 10-share bonus award at the end of April, at which time the stock has bounced back to $60 per share. He must again include the $600 in his gross income for 2009, but he cannot deduct his loss on the April 8 sale. His basis in the new stock is $700.

Related-Party Transactions

Special rules apply to the sale or trade of property between related parties. The gain from the sale or trade of property to a related party may be ordinary income, rather than capital gain, if the property can be depreciated by the party receiving it, and losses are not deductible.

A related party is a family member, a partnership in which the individual owns more than 50% of the capital interest or profits interest, a corporation in which the individual owns more than 50% in value or outstanding stock, or a tax-exempt or charitable organization controlled by the individual.

The rules do not apply to dispositions owing to the death of either related party; involuntary conversions; or trades and subsequent dispositions whose main purpose is not the avoidance of federal income tax.

Example. Donald Werth sells his sister some stock for $7,600. The stock's cost basis was $10,000 before the sale. Donald cannot deduct the $2,400 loss. Later, his sister sells the stock to an unrelated person for $10,500, realizing a gain of $2,900. Her reportable gain is $500: the $2,900 gain less the $2,400 loss not allowed to the brother.

Options

An option is a right to buy or sell property at a stipulated price on or before a specified date. A taxpayer has a capital gain or loss from the sale or exchange of an option or a loss on failure to exercise it only if the property covered by the option would be a capital asset in the taxpayer's hands. When a taxpayer fails to exercise an option, the option is deemed sold or exchanged on the day it expired.

In the case of an option on stock, securities, commodities, or commodity futures, any gain of a non-dealer grantor on the lapse of options is short-term capital gain. Also, any gain or loss of a non-dealer grantor from a closing transaction is short-term capital gain or loss. The capital gain and loss provisions do not apply if the taxpayer is in a business of which granting options is a normal part.

Gain or loss is recognized on the exercise of an option on IRC §1256 contracts, which include regulated futures contracts, foreign currency contracts, non-equity options, and dealer equity options.

Planning Tip. Extensive capital loss carryforwards should be considered in a taxpayer's investment strategy. Gain on options is essentially tax free if loss carryforwards are available.

Puts and Calls

A put is an option to sell a specified number of shares of stock to the writer of the option at a specific price within a certain time. A call is an option to purchase a certain number of shares of stock from the writer at a stated price within a certain time. The buyer of an option is called the "holder." The seller of an option is called the "writer."

Example. A call purchased on April 23, 2008, would have to be exercised on April 24, 2009, or later for the gain on the call to be characterized as long term. How long the stock is subsequently held is immaterial. Any exercise or sale of the option prior to that date would be deemed a short-term gain or loss.

The cost of purchasing a put or call is a nondeductible capital expenditure (Rev. Rul. 71-521, 1971-2 CB 313).

Example—Expiration. Ten call options were issued to Ronnie Hunt on April 8, 2009, for $4,000 from Scott Turner. These equity options expired in December 2009 without being exercised. Ronnie recognizes a short-term capital loss of $4,000. Scott recognizes a short-term capital gain of $4,000.

Example—Closing Transaction. Assume the same facts as in the previous example, except that on May 10, 2009, the options were sold for $6,000 to a third party. Ronnie, the original buyer of the options, recognizes a short-term capital gain of $2,000. If Scott had bought them back, he would recognize a short-term capital loss of $2,000.

Employee Stock Options

Corporations may grant their employees the option to purchase stock in the corporation. Stock options may be given to employees and may also be *sold* to employees.

Stock Option Defined. There are two classifications of employee stock options:

(1) statutory or qualified options (that is, the tax treatment of the options is governed by IRC §§421–424), and
(2) nonstatutory or nonqualified options (the tax treatment of the options is governed by IRC §83).

Basically, a stock option is an agreement through which the employee who holds the option has the right, but not the obligation, to purchase corporate shares at a fixed price on a fixed date or within a range of dates (Treas. Reg. §1.421-7(a)(1)).

Nonqualified Stock Options

A nonqualified stock option is one that does not meet the requirements of, and is not governed by, the rules of IRC §§421–424. For nonqualified stock options, the recipient usually owes no taxes when the options are granted, but pays tax on the gain realized when the options are exercised. Employers can deduct this amount as a compensation expense. Subsequent appreciation in the stock is taxed at capital gains rates when the recipient sells the shares. These options can be granted at a discount to the current stock price, and they are transferable to children and charity if the employer allows it.

Taxation upon Grant. A nonqualified stock option is taxed when it is granted if the option has a "readily ascertainable fair market value" at that time. An option that is not actively traded on an established market has a readily ascertainable fair market value only if all of the following requirements are met:

- The option must be transferable.
- The option must be exercisable immediately and in full when it is granted.
- There can be no condition or restriction on the option that would have a significant effect on its FMV.

Because these requirements are seldom satisfied, few nonqualified options that are not traded on an established market are taxed when granted.

Nonqualified Options without Readily Ascertainable FMV. If the nonqualified option does not have a readily ascertainable FMV, it is the exercise of the option, and not the grant, that triggers the taxable event (Treas. Reg. §1.83-7(a)). When the employee exercises the option, the employee recognizes ordinary income in the amount of the fair market value of the stock purchased minus any amount paid for the stock or the option. Later, when the employee sells the stock, any gain or loss recognized is treated as capital gain or loss. The employee's holding period of the stock begins the day after the option was exercised. See MTG ¶1681 for information concerning the tax consequences to the employee when stock or other property is received in payment for the employee's services.

Nonqualified Options with Readily Ascertainable Fair Market Value. If a nonqualified option has a readily ascertainable fair market value, the employee must recognize ordinary income in the amount of the fair market value in the year the option is granted (Treas. Reg. §1.83-1(a)). If the employee paid for the option, he recognizes the value of the option minus its cost. The employee is not taxed again when he exercises the option and buys corporate stock. However, the employee is taxed when he sells the stock. The employee's basis in the stock is the fair market value of the option on which he paid taxes, plus the amount he paid for the stock. Capital gain or loss is recognized when the stock is sold.

Determining the Holding Period. In determining whether a capital gain or loss on stock is long term or short term, the taxpayer's holding period begins on the date after the option is exercised. See MTG ¶1777 for rules used to determine holding period of various types of capital assets.

Qualified Options. For qualified options, or incentive stock options (ISOs), no income tax is due when the options are granted or when they are exercised. Instead, the tax is deferred until the stock is sold, at which time the entire gain is taxed. As long as the employee sells at least two years after the options were granted and at least one year after they were exercised, all gain will be taxed at the long-term capital gains rate. If these holding period requirements are not satisfied, the sale is considered a "disqualifying disposition," the gain at exercise will be taxed as ordinary income, and any subsequent appreciation is taxed as capital gains.

Qualified options may not be granted at a discount to the current stock price, and they are not transferable, except through a will.

Caution. Although there may be no immediate regular tax consequences upon the exercise of an incentive stock option (ISO), there are significant alternative minimum tax (AMT) consequences. Stock acquired through the exercise of an ISO carries a dual basis. The exercise of an ISO is considered a preference item of income under the AMT rules. The AMT income is increased by the difference between the incentive price and the FMV of the date of exercise. Unaware taxpayers will find they owe a larger than expected tax liability because of the increase in tax generated by the "phantom" income. In addition, the basis of the ISO stock must be tracked for the purpose of calculating gain or loss upon sale or exchange for both the regular tax and for the alternative minimum tax.

Market Discount Rules

In order to determine whether a taxpayer's gains or losses are ordinary or capital in nature, it must be determined whether the taxpayer entered into the transaction as an investor, dealer, or trader.

Investors. An investor is a taxpayer whose activities are limited to occasional transactions for his or her own account. The level of activity is less than that associated with a trade or business. Gains and losses of an investor are subject to the capital gain and loss rules.

Dealers. Capital gain and loss treatment does *not* apply to securities owned by a dealer, except for securities that are held primarily for personal investment. Securities that are held by a dealer for investment purposes must be clearly identified in the dealer's records before the close of the day on which they were acquired and must *never* be held primarily for sale to the dealer's customers. A dealer regularly purchases securities from, and sells securities to, customers in the ordinary course of a trade or business. Because dealers are in the business of buying and selling, their gains and losses are classified as ordinary gain or loss.

Capital gain and loss treatment does not apply to real estate sales by a dealer in realty, except for property held as an investment.

Traders. A securities trader (including a "day trader") buys and sells securities for his or her own account. A trader's expectation of making a profit depends upon such circumstances as a rise in value or an advantageous purchase that will allow him or her to sell at a price in excess of cost. Because the securities that traders buy and sell are not held primarily for sale to customers, the gains and losses are generally treated as capital in nature and are reported on Schedule D. Traders may make a mark-to-market election that allows them to treat gains and losses as ordinary (see MTG ¶1901). Traders claim their business expenses on Schedule C, *Profit or Loss From Business*, because they are in the business of trading. For the rules concerning the commissions paid by traders when buying and selling securities, see MTG ¶1983.

Mark-to-Market (MTM) Rules

Dealers must follow MTM rules, and investors and traders may elect to use the rules. Investors and traders make an MTM election by attaching a statement to an original and timely (not including an extension) filed tax return for the tax year directly preceding the election. If an election is made, the gains and losses are treated as ordinary income and are deemed to be sold on the last business day of the year at FMV.

Traders in Securities

Special rules apply if the taxpayer is a trader in securities, that is in the business of buying and selling securities for his own account. To be engaged in business as a trader in securities, all of the following conditions must be met:

- The taxpayer must seek to profit from daily market movements in the prices of securities and not from dividends, interest, or capital appreciation.
- The taxpayer's activity must be substantial.
- The taxpayer must carry on the activity with continuity and regularity.

The following facts and circumstances should be considered in determining if the taxpayer's activity is a securities trading business:

- Typical holding periods for securities bought and sold.
- Frequency and dollar amount of trades during the year.
- The extent to which the activity is pursued to produce income for a livelihood.
- The amount of time devoted to the activity.

Real Estate

Planning Tip: Even though the rules for exclusion of gain on the sale of a principal residence mean that the majority of taxpayers will feel they do not need to keep detailed records on improvements to their homes and other additions to basis, all homeowners should be encouraged to keep such records. This is especially true in areas experiencing rapid appreciation in housing prices or when plans call for a long-term occupancy. Also, the exclusion could be modified or eliminated in the future and the current exclusion amounts are not inflation adjusted, leading to devaluation over time.

Sale of Residence

The reporting rules presented in the following table apply.

- Schedule D–If any taxable gain on the sale of a primary residence cannot be excluded (more than $250,000, or $500,000 for joint filers), then the entire gain realized is reported on Schedule D. The allowed exclusion, if any, is reported as a IRC §121 exclusion directly below the line where the gain is reported.
- Form 4797–If the home was used in part as a home and in part as a business or rental during the year of sale, the sale of the business or rental portion is reported on Form 4797.
- Form 6252–If the home was sold using the installment sale method, the part of the gain that cannot be excluded is reported on Form 6252.

Caution. Beginning on January 1, 2009, gain from the sale of a principal residence that is allocable to periods of nonqualified use (periods before the residence was ever the principal home of the taxpayer or the taxpayer's spouse when neither the taxpayer, the taxpayer's spouse nor the taxpayer's former spouse used the property as a principal residence) is no longer excludable (IRC §121(b)). This rule prevents the exclusion from applying to gain accumulated while a home was being used as a vacation home before being used as a primary residence. There are exceptions to the general rule and IRC §121 should be reviewed.

Ownership and Use Test. To claim the exclusion, the seller must meet the ownership and use tests. This means that during the five-year period ending on the date of the sale, the seller must have done both of these:

- Owned the home for at least two years (the ownership test).
- Lived in the home as a main home for at least two years (the use test).

Gray Area. A taxpayer with more than one home should have records that support the treatment of one home as his or her main residence for any given period of time. It may be advantageous for planning purposes to select the home that will be sold first as the main home. A main home is not necessarily the location where one spends the most time, but if the taxpayer spent the most time at another location, then proof of principal residency must be available supporting the exclusion.

The exclusion may be claimed only once every two years. However, there are exceptions that allow a taxpayer to prorate the exclusion under special circumstances. See **"Reduced Exclusions Rules,"** following.

Caution. The regulations for IRC §121 allow "short temporary absences, such as for vacation or other seasonal absence" to be counted toward the two year use test. However, long absences, whether accompanied by renting the home out or not, will not be counted toward the two-year rule. For example, a professor on a one-year sabbatical spent continuously in a foreign country would not be deemed to have occupied the house during the year.

Caution. If a residence has been acquired in a like-kind exchange, the ownership test increases to five years, rather than the usual two-year test.

Reporting Residence Sales: Scenarios and Forms to Use

Situation	How to Report
Client had any taxable gain on the sale of his or her main home that cannot be excluded	Report the entire gain realized on Schedule D [in column (f) of line 1 or line 8, depending on how long client owned the home]
Client qualifies for an exclusion	Do not report sale if entire gain is excluded
Client used the home partly or entirely for business or rental income	Report the sale of the business or rental part (or the sale of the entire property if used entirely for business or rental) on Form 4797
The sale was an installment sale, providing for part or all of the selling price to be paid in a later year	Report the sale on Form 6252; enter the exclusion on line 15 of Form 6252

Treatment of Real Estate Sales

Type of Real Estate	Gain on Sale Reported On . . .	Exceptions	Loss on Sale Reported On . . .
Principal residence	Reportable as capital gain on Schedule D	Gains up to $250,000 ($500,000 MFJ) are excluded from income when ownership and use tests met	None recognized
Principal residence rented less than 15 days per year or partly used as home office (assume within the same dwelling unit)	Reportable as capital gain on Schedule D	Gains up to $250,000 ($500,000 for MFJ) are excluded from income when ownership and use tests met; gain attributable to depreciation after May 6, 1997, not excludable	None recognized
Principal residence, partially rented more than 15 days per year (separate part of dwelling unit)	Reportable as capital gain on Schedule D and Form 4797	Gains up to $250,000 ($500,000 for MFJ) are all excluded from income when ownership and use tests meet all portion allowable to principal residence	None recognized
Second home, rented less than 15 days annually	Reportable as capital gain on Schedule D	No exclusion	None recognized
Second home, rented more than 15 days annually	Part ordinary gain (Schedule E) and part capital gain (Schedule D)	No exclusion	All losses deductible, including unallowed passive losses from prior years (i.e., ordinary loss)
IRC §1221 asset (investment not used personally or in trade or business)	Reportable as capital gain on Schedule D	None	Schedule D; capital loss limited to $3,000 per year
IRC §1231 asset–not rented but used in a trade or business (commercial real estate)	Form 4797, Part III	None	Form 4797, Part I

Grantor Trust. If a residence is owned by a trust, for the period in which the taxpayer is treated as the owner of the trust or the portion of the trust that includes the residence, the taxpayer will be treated as owning the residence for purposes of satisfying the two-year ownership requirement. A sale or exchange by the trust will be treated as if made by the taxpayer.

Caution. Irrevocable Trust. Generally an irrevocable trust is not entitled to IRC §121, Exclusion of Gain from Sale of Principal Residence, benefits. The IRS denied full exclusion to a taxpayer who held a personal residence in an irrevocable trust in one instance. A wedded couple originally set up a revocable trust that included their primary residence. After one spouse died, the residence was transferred to an irrevocable trust that allowed the surviving spouse to withdraw up to the greater of $5,000 or 5% of the trust principal each year. The trust wished to sell the residence and asked for a ruling on whether the gain from the sale was excludable. The IRS said that the power to withdraw from the trust vested a portion of the irrevocable trust's body in the husband (IRS Letter Ruling 200104005). Each year in which he failed to exercise this power resulted in his owning an increased portion of the trust corpus and being, therefore, eligible to exclude a larger portion of the gain; however, he was not able to take the entire $250,000 exclusion.

Widowed Taxpayer. A surviving spouse can exclude up to $500,000 in gain if the marital principal residence is sold within two years after the death of the spouse (IRC §121(b)(4)). A taxpayer's period of ownership and use of a residence includes the period during which the taxpayer's deceased spouse owned and used the residence as a principal residence.

Example. Jorge Estrada owned and lived in a house as his principal residence since 1996. Jorge and Miranda were married in 2008 and used Jorge's house as their principal residence. Jorge died on August 15, 2009, and Miranda inherited the residence. She sold the house for a $200,000 gain two weeks later, on September 1, 2009. Even though Miranda owned and used the house for less than two years, she is considered to have satisfied the ownership and use requirements because her period of ownership and use includes the time period that Jorge owned and used the property prior to his death.

Newlyweds. The rule limiting the exclusion to one sale every two years nevertheless allows a husband and wife filing a joint return to each exclude up to $250,000 of gain from the sale of each spouse's principal residence so long as each spouse would be permitted to exclude up to $250,000 of gain if they filed separate returns.

Transfers Incident to Divorce. If a residence is transferred following a divorce, the time during which the taxpayer's spouse or former spouse owned the residence is added to the taxpayer's period of ownership. Also, a taxpayer who owns a residence is deemed to use it as a principal residence while the taxpayer's spouse or former spouse is given separate use of the residence under the terms of a divorce or separation decree. Thus, if the former spouse maintains an ownership interest and the other spouse is allowed to use the residence as a principal residence under a decree of divorce and separation for a number of years, each spouse will be allowed to exclude the gain from the later sale of the former marital principal residence.

Example. Jack and Laetitia Ryan divorced in 2004. Under terms of the divorce agreement, their house and adjacent property were divided equally between them, each retaining 50% ownership. Laetitia was allowed the full use of the house. They sold the house in 2009 at a gain of $90,000. Even though Jack had not met the use test of the IRC §121 rules, both he and Laetitia are allowed to exclude their respective shares of the gain.

Unmarried Joint Owners. Taxpayers who jointly own a principal residence, but are not married, may each exclude up to $250,000 of gain attributable to their respective interests in the property.

Military, Foreign Service, Intelligence Community, and Peace Corps Personnel. A special exception to the two-out-of-five- year rule exists for certain members of the military and the Peace Corps. Foreign Service personnel, and certain employees of the intelligence community. A qualified taxpayer in one of these groups may elect to suspend the five-year test period by up to 10 years. To qualify, the taxpayer or the taxpayer's spouse must be serving on qualified official extended duty. The term extended duty refers to any active duty lasting for a period in excess of 90 days or for an indefinite period, at a location which is at least 50 miles from the residence or requiring residence in Government quarters. The election to extend the five-year test period is made by the taxpayer in the year of the sale by not including the gain in gross income.

Filing Tip. The members of the intelligence community that may take advantage of the 10-year suspension are those employed by the:

- Office of the Director of National Intelligence,
- Central Intelligence Agency,
- National Security Agency,
- Defense Intelligence Agency,
- National Geospacial-Intelligence Agency,
- National Reconnaissance Office,
- Bureau of Intelligence and Research of the Department of State,
- Any other office within the Department of Defense for the collection of specialized national intelligence through reconnaissance programs,
- Any of the intelligence elements of the Army, Navy, Air Force, Marines, Federal Bureau of Investigation, Department of Treasury, Department of Energy, and Coast Guard, or
- Any element of the Department of Homeland Security concerned with the analysis of foreign intelligence.

Filing Tip. The members of the Peace Corps that may take advantage of the 10-year suspension period are individuals who are serving outside the United States;

- as an employee of the Peace Corps on qualified official extended duty, or
- as an enrolled volunteer leader under section 5 or 6 of the Peace Corps Act (22 U.S.C. 2504, 2505).

For members of the intelligence community, the suspension of the five-year rule applies for sales after December 20, 2006 and, for member of the Peace Corps, the suspension applies to sales or exchanges after December 31, 2007.

Reduced Exclusion Rules

An individual who fails to meet the ownership and use test but who qualifies for an exception may be entitled to a reduced exclusion. The reduced exclusion is computed by multiplying the maximum allowable exclusion ($250,000 or $500,000 if filing jointly) by a fraction.

The numerator of the fraction is the shortest of (a) the period of time that the individual owned the property as a principal residence during the five-year period ending on the date of sale or exchange; (b) the period of time that the individual used the property as a principal residence during the five-year period ending on the date of sale; or (c) the period between the date of the most recent prior sale to which the exclusion applied and the date of the current sale or exchange. The numerator may be expressed in days or months.

The denominator of the fraction is either 730 days or 24 months (depending on the measure of time used in the numerator) (Treas. Reg. §1.121-3(a)).

The following events are "safe harbors" for entitlement to the use of the reduced exclusion. Other unforeseen events may also qualify.

- Involuntary conversion.
- Natural or man-made disaster, acts of war or terrorism, etc.
- Death of a member of the household.
- Change of employment.
- Change in income that leaves the owner unable to meet household expenses.
- Divorce or legal separation.
- Multiple births from same pregnancy.

Planning Tip. The IRS has issued several taxpayer-friendly letter rulings describing circumstances in which a reduced exclusion of gain from the sale of a residence would be allowed. Although letter rulings have no precedential value they provide significant insight into the IRS's position on what are acceptable "unforeseen circumstances." Some of the taxpayers in the rulings included:

- a retired couple selling a recently purchased residence in an age-restricted community to move back to their home state to assist a recently unemployed, divorced daughter with a young child (IRS Letter Ruling 200601023);
- a couple who sold a residence, which they had been renting out in what was intended to be a temporary arrangement, because the birth of another child rendered their plan to return to it impractical (IRS Letter Ruling 200601022);
- a couple with one son who sold their residence after experiencing numerous death threats and a physical attack on their son (IRS Letter Ruling 200601009);
- a police officer who sold a residence after a high profile arrest of a powerful narcotics dealer because of the fear for the safety of his family (IRS Letter Ruling 200615011); and
- a couple who shortly after moving into the home were approved to adopt another child but, under state law, were required to have a larger house to provide sufficient privacy for the adopted child (IRS Letter Ruling 200613009).

Example. Mr. Cheadle is an unmarried taxpayer who owned and used a house for 385 days before he moved out of the house in December 2007 because he was unable to care for himself after sustaining injuries in an auto accident. He sold the house in January 2009. Mr. Cheadle had not excluded gain from the sale of a residence within the previous two years. He may exclude up to $131,849 of any gain that he realizes from the sale ($250,000 × 385/730 = $131,849). Even though he owned the house for more than 385 days, he must use the smaller of the days of use or the days of ownership.

Example—Personal- and Business-Use Portion in Same Dwelling Unit. Amanda bought her house in 2004. She used a room in her home for her business, but it did not qualify as a home office because she also used it for other purposes. She sold her house in 2009 for a gain of $50,000. Because she did not qualify for depreciation deductions, and because she does not need to allocate gain between the business portion and the residential portion of the house within the same dwelling unit, the entire $50,000 may be excluded.

If she had qualified to take depreciation on her home office, she would not be able to exclude the amount of depreciation taken. For example, had she been allowed $4,000 of depreciation on her office space, she would not have to allocate gain, but she would have to subtract the depreciation taken from the amount of her exclusion and could exclude only $46,000 ($50,000 – $4,000).

Example. James and Amy Wickham buy a house near an airport with considerable jet traffic. After one year, they come to the conclusion that they can no longer live with the noise of the airplanes, so they sell their house. They are not eligible for even a partial exclusion on the gain from the sale. The airplane noise could not be considered an unforeseen circumstance since it existed at the time they purchased the home.

Business Use of Home

A part of the home is considered a place of business if it is *used exclusively on a regular basis* in at least one the following ways:

- As the principal place of any business carried on by the taxpayer.
- As a place of business that is used by patients, clients, or customers in meeting or dealing with the taxpayer in the normal course of business.

In addition, use of a separate structure that is appurtenant to, but not attached to, the home may also qualify as being a business use of the home (IRC §280A(c)).

Generally, a specific portion of the taxpayer's home must be used solely for the purpose of carrying on a trade or business in order to satisfy the exclusive-use test. This requirement is not met if the portion is used for both business and personal purposes. However, an exception is provided for a wholesale or retail seller whose dwelling unit is the sole fixed location of the trade or business. In this situation, a space within the dwelling unit that is used as a storage unit for inventory or product samples is considered a business use provided that the space is used on a regular basis and is a separately identifiable space suitable for storage.

Business Use of Dwelling Unit. If part of the home used for business *is within the same dwelling unit* as the residence part of the home, the taxpayer is deemed as having used the entire home as a principal residence for purposes of the home exclusion rules. Thus, no allocation of basis and amount realized from the sale is required.

If the part of the home used for business *is not within the same dwelling unit* as the residential part, the taxpayer must treat the sale of the home as a sale of two distinct properties and allocate gain accordingly.

Caution. Post–May 6, 1997, depreciation is treated as an unrecaptured IRC §1250 gain, regardless of where the business portion of the home is located. Depreciation taken before that date can, however, be excluded if all other tests are met.

Although the taxpayer may take deductions of various kinds on such a business use of the home (see Tab 3 for deducting expenses on a home office), the exclusion on the sale of a residence will *not* apply to the business portion of the home, unless the office is within the same dwelling unit.

In most cases, the apportionment is made according to respective square footage occupied by each business

Example. Barry bought a property in 2003 that included a house, a barn, and four acres of land. Barry used the house and four acres as his principal residence and the barn for his snow removal business. In 2007, Barry moved out of the house and rented it to tenants. He sold the property in 2009, realizing a gain of $21,000. Between 2003 and 2009, Barry has claimed depreciation deductions of $4,500 attributable to the snow removal business, and between 2007 and 2009 has claimed depreciation deductions of $3,000 attributable to the house. Barry has no other Section 1231 or capital gains or losses for 2009.

Because the portion of the property used in the snow removal business is separate from the dwelling unit, Barry has to allocate basis and gain on the sale between the portion of the property that he used as his principal residence and the portion of the property that he used for nonresidential purposes. Barry determines that $4,000 of the gain is allocable to the nonresidential portion of the property and that $17,000 of the gain is allocable to the portion of the property that he used as his principal residence.

Barry must recognize the entire $4,000 of gain allocable to the nonresidential portion of the property. In addition, Barry must subtract from his exclusion the amount of depreciation taken on the residential portion of the property for periods after May 6, 1997, which is $3,000. Therefore, Barry may exclude only $14,000 ($17,000 gain allocable to principal residence - $3,000 depreciation claimed after May 6, 1997) of the gain from the sale of the property. His overall recognized gain from the transaction is $7,000, of which $4,000 is ordinary income.

and the home. Other methods of apportionment may, however, be used if they give a more realistic indicator of the relative worth of each space and have been used in computing depreciation or other expenses.

If the business is within the same dwelling unit, the entire gain is excludable unless depreciation has been taken after May 6, 1997.

If business use of the home ceases for two years prior to the sale, the entire property can be considered a residence eligible for the exclusion, because the two-year use test is met for the whole dwelling. However, any depreciation that has been claimed on a business use must be used to reduce basis of the entire residence, thus increasing gain.

See MTG ¶961–¶967.

Reporting the Sale of a Residence

Gain on Personal-Use Portion. The entire gain should be reported on line 1 (short term) or line 8 (long term) of Schedule D, unless it is entirely excludable. The excludable portion of the gain is then entered on the next line as a loss; write "Section 121 exclusion" in column (a) of that line.

Gain on Business-Use Portion. If there was a gain on the sale, fill out lines 20–24 of Form 4797 based on the business-use portion only. If there has been post-May 6, 1997, depreciation allowed, this will be reported on line 26.

Gain on Personal-Use and Business-Use Portion in Same Dwelling Unit. Report only on Schedule D, as above; this does not need to be reported on Form 4797 even if there was depreciation allowed.

Loss on Business-Use Portion. A loss on the business-use portion of a residence is reported on line 2 (long term) or line 10 (short term).

Filing Tip. Barry, in the previous example, will report $17,000 on line 8 of Schedule D, followed by ($14,000) in column (g) and "Section 121 exclusion" in column (a) on the next line. The resulting $3,000 is a long-term capital gain. He will report the $4,000 gain on the business-use portion on Form 4797, lines 20–24. His depreciation would be reported as $4,000 on line 26 of Form 4797 (the lesser of depreciation taken, $4,500, and gain realized). It would be transferred to line 13, from which it will be reported as ordinary income on Form 1040. Line 32 will be zero, assuming that this is the only transaction listed on the Form 4797. Thus, Barry will have $4,000 of ordinary income and $3,000 of long-term capital gains to recognize on his return.

Basis of the Residence

Additions to Basis. Expenditures to increase the value of a residence are generally added to basis. The answer to the question of what constitutes a part of the cost or basis of real estate depends on the law of the particular state in which the property is located; the law may or may not classify the improvement as a *fixture*. Also, many settlement costs are treated as additions to basis.

Subtractions from Basis. The following must be subtracted from the basis of a residence:

- Depreciation allowed or allowable on the portion of the home used for business;
- Casualty deductions;
- Residential energy credits claimed between 1978 and 1985;

- District of Columbia first-time homebuyer credit (but not the national first-time homebuyer credit under IRC §36); and
- Credits claimed under either or both the nonbusiness energy and residential energy credits for energy property placed into service after 2005.

Note that no settlement costs serve to decrease the buyer's basis.

Settlement Cost Table—Sale of Personal Residence

Cost	Impact on Seller	Impact on Buyer
Attorneys' fees–finding property	Reduce amount realized	Increase basis
Attorneys' fees–obtaining mortgage	Reduce amount realized	No impact
Commissions	Reduce amount realized	Increase basis
Expenses owed by seller and paid by buyer	Adjust deductions on Schedule A	Increase basis
Points (loan origination)	Reduce amount realized	Deductible on Schedule A (even if paid by seller)
Loan processing fee	Reduce amount realized	No impact
Miscellaneous expenses concerning title or deed	Reduce amount realized	Increase basis
Miscellaneous closing costs	Reduce amount realized	No impact
Real estate taxes (see Tab 2)	Deductible on Schedule A	Deductible on Schedule A
Title policy fees or insurance	Reduce amount realized	Increase basis

Sale of Investment Properties

Real estate held as an investment is a capital asset. Thus, gain or loss on its sale or exchange must be reported as a capital gain or loss. Investment property may be held for the production of income without loss of its capital asset status. In such a case, depreciable real property is treated as being used in the taxpayer's trade or business and is considered IRC §1231 property. If gains exceed the losses from sales of such property, all the gains and losses are treated as capital gains and losses. If the losses exceed the gains, all the losses and gains are treated as ordinary losses and gains.

Whether property is held for investment or for sale depends upon a number of factors, such as;

1. continuity of sales over a period of time,
2. frequency of sales as opposed to isolated transactions,
3. general activities of the seller or those acting under his instructions,
4. the extent or substantiality of the transactions, and
5. the purpose for which the property was acquired.

Depreciation. Most real property used in a taxpayer's trade or business and placed in service after December 31, 1980, and before March 16, 1984, was depreciable over 15 years (18 years if placed in service after March 15, 1984, and before May 9, 1985, and 19 years if placed in service after May 8, 1985, and before 1987) under the accelerated cost recovery system (ACRS) method or, at the taxpayer's election, under a statutory straight-line method over the regular recovery period or an optional, longer recovery period of 35 or 45 years and without regard to useful life or salvage value. Under MACRS, the cost of such property placed in service after 1986 and before May 13, 1993, is recovered over 31.5 years under the straight-line method. Property placed into service on or after May 12, 1993, has a 39-year recovery period. Land is never depreciable. See Tab 7 for more details on depreciation.

Recapture. Generally, excess depreciation is recaptured as ordinary income under the following rules:

- **Rule 1:** Post-1975 excess depreciation is 100% recaptured. No further computation is necessary if the recapture equals or exceeds the gain on the sale of such property. All of the gain will be ordinary income.
- **Rule 2:** Excess depreciation after 1969 and before 1976 may be partially recaptured or fully recaptured if the post-1975 recapture under Rule 1 is less than the gain. The amount of this recapture will be a percentage of the 1970–1975 excess depreciation or the unrecaptured gain (gain less recapture under Rule 1), whichever is less. The percentage is 100% for housing held more than 12 months and less than 101 months. The percentage decreases by 1% for each month that the property has been held over 100 full months, and there is no recapture under this rule after 16 years and eight months.
- **Rule 3:** Excess depreciation after 1963 and before 1970 may be partially or fully recaptured if the amounts recaptured under Rules 1 and 2 are less than the gain. The amount of this pre-1970 recapture will be a percentage of the 1964–1969 excess depreciation or the unrecaptured gain (gain less amounts recaptured under Rules 1 and 2), whichever is less. The percentage is 100% for realty held for more than 12 months and less than 21 months. The percentage decreases by 1% for each full month that the property has been held over 20 months. Thus, there is no Rule 3 recapture if the property is held for more than 10 years. Certain categories of low-income housing are excluded from Rule 1 recapture.

Sale of Rental Properties

IRC §1250 Property. Depreciable real property, other than that included within the definition of IRC §1245 property, is subject to depreciation recapture under IRC §1250. Gain on the sale or other disposition of IRC §1250 property is treated as ordinary income, rather than capital gain, to the extent of the excess of post-1969 depreciation allowances over the depreciation that would have been available under the straight-line method. See MTG ¶1780. However, if IRC §1250 property is held for one year or less, all depreciation (and not just the excess over straight-line depreciation) is recaptured. See MTG ¶1736 and ¶1780 for capital gains treatment of unrecaptured IRC §1250 gain.

Special recapture rules phase out the recapture by reducing it by 1% for each full month the IRC §1250 property is held over a specified period in the case of:

(1) residential rental property,
(2) certain types of subsidized housing, and
(3) IRC §1250 property for which rapid depreciation of rehabilitation expenditures was claimed (IRC §1250(a)(1)(B) and (2)(B)).

The recapture rules apply notwithstanding any other provision of the Code. In the case of a sale to a related party (see page 4-27), gain that is not recaptured may still be treated as ordinary income.

Calculating Basis in Stock

Stock Basis

Part of the process of figuring gain or loss on stock sales is determining the stock basis–a value that starts out as the original cost of the stocks (what the buyer paid for them, plus any commissions), then gets adjusted up or downas the shares pay dividends, split, or rare subject to certain other events.

Here are the basic steps.

1. Gather all those brokerage statements from the time the stocks were purchased until the time they were sold.
2. Figure out how much was paid for the shares, including any purchase costs such as commissions. (The result is known as the *starting basis.*)
3. If the company issued dividends in the form of shares of stock, or a return on capital, reduce the starting basis by those amounts. If the stock split, divide the basis accordingly. The result is an adjusted basis for computing the capital gain or loss.
4. Figure out the net proceeds from selling the shares–the money received for the shares, minus any commission paid.
5. Subtract the stock basis from the net proceeds to determine the capital gain or loss.

But what if, as often happens, the records have been lost, misplaced, or thrown out? Or what if the shares were inherited, or a gift?

Inherited Stock

If the shares of stock were inherited, the starting basis is the FMV of the stock on the date the original owner died. An interesting wrinkle: If the stocks grew in value while the original owner was alive, there are no taxes on the increase in value of the stocks while the original owner had them.

Gifts of Stock

If the shares of stock were a gift, then generally the starting basis is the same as the basis for the person who gave the stock. However, if the FMV of the stock on the date of the gift is lower than the basis of the person who gave the stock, then the FMV is the recipient's basis.

The FMV is usually determined by taking the midpoint of the opening and closing quotes on the stock for that day.

The Adjusted Basis

If the stock has been held for a while, it may have gone through several stock splits, issued dividends, perhaps distributed a return of capital, or maybe a subsidiary has been spun off in a corporate reorganization. If any of these events has occurred while the client owned and held the stock, he or she must make adjustments to the starting basis in those shares.

- *Stock splits:* These make the basis per share less than it was, at the same time increasing the number of shares owned. For example, if Bette paid $80 per share for Hot Item stock and the company subsequently split 2 for 1 on two occasions, her basis per share is now $20 ($80 x 1/2 x 1/2).
- *Stock dividends:* The shares (not cash payments) earned as dividends reduce the basis in the stock; it is only dividends in the form of stocks that adjust the basis. For example, Willie owns 100 shares of High Echelon stock that he bought for $20 per share, total cost $2,000. High Echelon issues a dividend in the form of stock, and Willie gets 10 more shares as his "dividend." So Willie now has 110 shares of stock, but he still only paid $2,000. His basis per share now is $2,000 divided by 110, or $18.18 per share, so his basis per share actually went down. Even though those extra 10 shares were "free," Willie must allocate his original basis to cover those "free" shares as well.
- *Return of capital:* A return-of-capital distribution reduces basis dollar for dollar.
- *Spin-offs:* If a large company spins off a subsidiary to form a new company, with its own stock, the com-

pany will send out an announcement telling how to allocate the basis.

Making Adjustments

If no records exist, it is still possible to calculate basis. One possible method is to check your local public library for a copy of CCH's *Capital Changes Reporter,* which tracks these corporate transactions. There are also websites available that can be used to track a specific companies stock history. Using the data, you are able to make the necessary adjustments to the basis of the stock.

Capital Loss Carryover Worksheet—Lines 6 and 14

Keep for Your Records

Use this worksheet to figure your capital loss carryovers from 2008 to 2009 if your 2008 Schedule D, line 21, is a loss and **(a)** that loss is a smaller loss than the loss on your 2008 Schedule D, line 16, **or (b)** the amount on your 2008 Form 1040, line 41 (or your 2008 Form 1040NR, line 38, if applicable), reduced by any amount on your 2008 Form 8914, line 2, is less than zero. Otherwise, you do not have any carryovers.

1. Enter the amount from your 2008 Form 1040, line 41, or your 2008 Form 1040NR, line 38. If a loss, enclose the amount in parentheses . . . . . **1.** ______

2. Did you file Form 8914 (to claim an exemption amount for housing a Midwestern displaced individual) for 2008?
☐ **No.** Enter -0-
☐ **Yes.** Enter the amount from your 2008 Form 8914, line 2 } . . . . . **2.** ______

3. Subtract line 2 from line 1. If the result is less than zero, enclose it in parentheses . . . . . **3.** ______

4. Enter the loss from your 2008 Schedule D, line 21, as a positive amount . . . . . **4.** ______

5. Combine lines 3 and 4. If zero or less, enter -0- . . . . . **5.** ______

6. Enter the **smaller** of line 4 or line 5 . . . . . **6.** ______

If line 7 of your 2008 Schedule D is a loss, go to line 7; otherwise, enter -0- on line 7 and go to line 11.

7. Enter the loss from your 2008 Schedule D, line 7, as a positive amount . . . . . **7.** ______

8. Enter any gain from your 2008 Schedule D, line 15. If a loss, enter -0- . . . **8.** ______

9. Add lines 6 and 8 . . . . . **9.** ______

10. **Short-term capital loss carryover for 2009.** Subtract line 9 from line 7. If zero or less, enter -0-. If more than zero, also enter this amount on Schedule D, line 6 . . . . . **10.** ______

If line 15 of your 2008 Schedule D is a loss, go to line 11; otherwise, skip lines 11 through 15.

11. Enter the loss from your 2008 Schedule D, line 15, as a positive amount . . . . . **11.** ______

12. Enter any gain from your 2008 Schedule D, line 7. If a loss, enter -0- . . . . **12.** ______

13. Subtract line 7 from line 6. If zero or less, enter -0- . . . . . **13.** ______

14. Add lines 12 and 13 . . . . . **14.** ______

15. **Long-term capital loss carryover for 2009.** Subtract line 14 from line 11. If zero or less, enter -0-. If more than zero, also enter this amount on Schedule D, line 14 . . . . . **15.** ______

28% Rate Gain Worksheet—Line 18

Keep for Your Records

1. Enter the total of all collectibles gain or (loss) from items you reported on line 8, column (f), of Schedules D and D-1	**1.**	
2. Enter as a positive number the amount of any section 1202 exclusion you reported on line 8, column (f), of Schedules D and D-1, for which you excluded 50% of the gain, plus ⅔ of any section 1202 exclusion you reported on line 8, column (f), of Schedules D and D-1, for which you excluded 60% of the gain	**2.**	
3. Enter the total of all collectibles gain or (loss) from Form 4684, line 4 (but only if Form 4684, line 15, is more than zero); Form 6252; Form 6781, Part II; and Form 8824	**3.**	
4. Enter the total of any collectibles gain reported to you on: • Form 1099-DIV, box 2d; • Form 2439, box 1d; and • Schedule K-1 from a partnership, S corporation, estate, or trust.	**4.**	
5. Enter your long-term capital loss carryovers from Schedule D, line 14, and Schedule K-1 (Form 1041), box 11, code C	**5.**	( )
6. If Schedule D, line 7, is a (loss), enter that (loss) here. Otherwise, enter -0-	**6.**	( )
7. Combine lines 1 through 6. If zero or less, enter -0-. If more than zero, also enter this amount on Schedule D, line 18	**7.**	

Unrecaptured Section 1250 Gain Worksheet—Line 19

Keep for Your Records

If you are not reporting a gain on Form 4797, line 7, skip lines 1 through 9 and go to line 10.

1. If you have a section 1250 property in Part III of Form 4797 for which you made an entry in Part I of Form 4797 (but not on Form 6252), enter the **smaller** of line 22 or line 24 of Form 4797 for that property. If you did not have any such property, go to line 4. If you had more than one such property, see instructions			**1.**	
2. Enter the amount from Form 4797, line 26g, for the property for which you made an entry on line 1			**2.**	
3. Subtract line 2 from line 1			**3.**	
4. Enter the total unrecaptured section 1250 gain included on line 26 or line 37 of Form(s) 6252 from installment sales of trade or business property held more than 1 year (see instructions)			**4.**	
5. Enter the total of any amounts reported to you on a Schedule K-1 from a partnership or an S corporation as "unrecaptured section 1250 gain"			**5.**	
6. Add lines 3 through 5			**6.**	
7. Enter the **smaller** of line 6 or the gain from Form 4797, line 7	**7.**			
8. Enter the amount, if any, from Form 4797, line 8	**8.**			
9. Subtract line 8 from line 7. If zero or less, enter -0-			**9.**	
10. Enter the amount of any gain from the sale or exchange of an interest in a partnership attributable to unrecaptured section 1250 gain (see instructions)			**10.**	
11. Enter the total of any amounts reported to you on a Schedule K-1, Form 1099-DIV, or Form 2439 as "unrecaptured section 1250 gain" from an estate, trust, real estate investment trust, or mutual fund (or other regulated investment company)			**11.**	
12. Enter the total of any unrecaptured section 1250 gain from sales (including installment sales) or other dispositions of section 1250 property held more than 1 year for which you did not make an entry in Part I of Form 4797 for the year of sale (see instructions)			**12.**	
13. Add lines 9 through 12			**13.**	
14. If you had any section 1202 gain or collectibles gain or (loss), enter the total of lines 1 through 4 of the **28% Rate Gain Worksheet** on page D-8. Otherwise, enter -0-	**14.**			
15. Enter the (loss), if any, from Schedule D, line 7. If Schedule D, line 7, is zero or a gain, enter -0-	**15.**	( )		
16. Enter your long-term capital loss carryovers from Schedule D, line 14, and Schedule K-1 (Form 1041), box 11, code C*	**16.**	( )		
17. Combine lines 14 through 16. If the result is a (loss), enter it as a positive amount. If the result is zero or a gain, enter -0-			**17.**	
18. **Unrecaptured section 1250 gain.** Subtract line 17 from line 13. If zero or less, enter -0-. If more than zero, enter the result here and on Schedule D, line 19			**18.**	

*If you are filing Form 2555 or 2555-EZ (relating to foreign earned income), see the footnote in the Foreign Earned Income Tax Worksheet on page 38 of the Form 1040 instructions before completing this line.

Schedule D Tax Worksheet

Keep for Your Records

Complete this worksheet only if line 18 or line 19 of Schedule D is more than zero. Otherwise, complete the Qualified Dividends and Capital Gain Tax Worksheet on page 39 of the Instructions for Form 1040 (or in the Instructions for Form 1040NR) to figure your tax.

Exception: Do not use the Qualified Dividends and Capital Gain Tax Worksheet **or** this worksheet to figure your tax if:

- Line 15 or line 16 of Schedule D is zero or less **and** you have no qualified dividends on Form 1040, line 9b (or Form 1040NR, line 10b); **or**
- Form 1040, line 43 (or Form 1040NR, line 40) is zero or less.

Instead, see the instructions for Form 1040, line 44 (or Form 1040NR, line 41).

1. Enter your taxable income from Form 1040, line 43 (or Form 1040NR, line 40). (However, if you are filing Form 2555 or 2555-EZ (relating to foreign earned income), enter instead the amount from line 3 of the Foreign Earned Income Tax Worksheet on page 38 of the Form 1040 instructions) . . . **1.** ______
2. Enter your qualified dividends from Form 1040, line 9b (or Form 1040NR, line 10b) . . . **2.** ______
3. Enter the amount from Form 4952 (used to figure investment interest expense deduction), line 4g . . . **3.** ______
4. Enter the amount from Form 4952, line 4e* **4.** ______
5. Subtract line 4 from line 3. If zero or less, enter -0- . . . **5.** ______
6. Subtract line 5 from line 2. If zero or less, enter -0-** . . . **6.** ______
7. Enter the **smaller** of line 15 or line 16 of Schedule D . . . **7.** ______
8. Enter the **smaller** of line 3 or line 4 . . . **8.** ______
9. Subtract line 8 from line 7. If zero or less, enter -0-** . . . **9.** ______
10. Add lines 6 and 9 . . . **10.** ______
11. Add lines 18 and 19 of Schedule D** . . . **11.** ______
12. Enter the **smaller** of line 9 or line 11 . . . **12.** ______
13. Subtract line 12 from line 10 . . . **13.** ______
14. Subtract line 13 from line 1. If zero or less, enter -0- . . . **14.** ______
15. Enter the **smaller** of:
    - The amount on line 1 **or**
    - $33,950 if single or married filing separately; $67,900 if married filing jointly or qualifying widow(er); or $45,500 if head of household

    . . . **15.** ______
16. Enter the **smaller** of line 14 or line 15 . . . **16.** ______
17. Subtract line 10 from line 1. If zero or less, enter -0- . . . **17.** ______
18. Enter the **larger** of line 16 or line 17 . . . ▶ **18.** ______
    If lines 15 and 16 are the same, skip line 19 and go to line 20. Otherwise, go to line 19.
19. Subtract line 16 from line 15 . . . ▶ **19.** ______
    If lines 1 and 15 are the same, skip lines 20 through 32 and go to line 33. Otherwise, go to line 20.
20. Enter the **smaller** of line 1 or line 13 . . . **20.** ______
21. Enter the amount from line 19 (if line 19 is blank, enter -0-) . . . **21.** ______
22. Subtract line 21 from line 20. If zero or less, enter -0- . . . ▶ **22.** ______
23. Multiply line 22 by 15% (.15) . . . **23.** ______
    If Schedule D, line 19, is zero or blank, skip lines 24 through 29 and go to line 30. Otherwise, go to line 24.
24. Enter the **smaller** of line 9 above or Schedule D, line 19 . . . **24.** ______
25. Add lines 10 and 18 . . . **25.** ______
26. Enter the amount from line 1 above . . . **26.** ______
27. Subtract line 26 from line 25. If zero or less, enter -0- . . . **27.** ______
28. Subtract line 27 from line 24. If zero or less, enter -0- . . . ▶ **28.** ______
29. Multiply line 28 by 25% (.25) . . . **29.** ______
    If Schedule D, line 18, is zero or blank, skip lines 30 through 32 and go to line 33. Otherwise, go to line 30.
30. Add lines 18, 19, 22, and 28 . . . **30.** ______
31. Subtract line 30 from line 1 . . . **31.** ______
32. Multiply line 31 by 28% (.28) . . . **32.** ______
33. Figure the tax on the amount on **line 18**. Use the Tax Table or Tax Computation Worksheet, whichever applies . . . **33.** ______
34. Add lines 23, 29, 32, and 33 . . . **34.** ______
35. Figure the tax on the amount on **line 1**. Use the Tax Table or Tax Computation Worksheet, whichever applies . . . **35.** ______
36. **Tax on all taxable income (including capital gains and qualified dividends).** Enter the **smaller** of line 34 or line 35. Also include this amount on Form 1040, line 44 (or Form 1040NR, line 41). (If you are filing Form 2555 or 2555-EZ, do not enter this amount on Form 1040, line 44. Instead, enter it on line 4 of the Foreign Earned Income Tax Worksheet in the Form 1040 instructions) . . . **36.** ______

*If applicable, enter instead the smaller amount you entered on the dotted line next to line 4e of Form 4952.

**If you are filing Form 2555 or 2555-EZ, see the footnote in the Foreign Earned Income Tax Worksheet on page 38 of the Form 1040 instructions before completing this line.

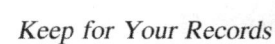

Form **4797**

Department of the Treasury
Internal Revenue Service (99)

Sales of Business Property

(Also Involuntary Conversions and Recapture Amounts Under Sections 179 and 280F(b)(2))

► Attach to your tax return. ► See separate instructions.

OMB No. 1545-0184

2009

Attachment Sequence No. 27

Name(s) shown on return | **Identifying number**

1	Enter the gross proceeds from sales or exchanges reported to you for 2009 on Form(s) 1099-B or 1099-S (or substitute statement) that you are including on line 2, 10, or 20 (see instructions)	1	

Part I **Sales or Exchanges of Property Used in a Trade or Business and Involuntary Conversions From Other Than Casualty or Theft—Most Property Held More Than 1 Year** (see instructions)

2	**(a)** Description of property	**(b)** Date acquired (mo., day, yr.)	**(c)** Date sold (mo., day, yr.)	**(d)** Gross sales price	**(e)** Depreciation allowed or allowable since acquisition	**(f)** Cost or other basis, plus improvements and expense of sale	**(g) Gain or (loss)** Subtract (f) from the sum of (d) and (e)

3	Gain, if any, from Form 4684, line 43	3	
4	Section 1231 gain from installment sales from Form 6252, line 26 or 37	4	
5	Section 1231 gain or (loss) from like-kind exchanges from Form 8824	5	
6	Gain, if any, from line 32, from other than casualty or theft	6	
7	Combine lines 2 through 6. Enter the gain or (loss) here and on the appropriate line as follows:	7	
	Partnerships (except electing large partnerships) and S corporations. Report the gain or (loss) following the instructions for Form 1065, Schedule K, line 10, or Form 1120S, Schedule K, line 9. Skip lines 8, 9, 11, and 12 below.		
	Individuals, partners, S corporation shareholders, and all others. If line 7 is zero or a loss, enter the amount from line 7 on line 11 below and skip lines 8 and 9. If line 7 is a gain and you did not have any prior year section 1231 losses, or they were recaptured in an earlier year, enter the gain from line 7 as a long-term capital gain on the Schedule D filed with your return and skip lines 8, 9, 11, and 12 below.		
8	Nonrecaptured net section 1231 losses from prior years (see instructions)	8	
9	Subtract line 8 from line 7. If zero or less, enter -0-. If line 9 is zero, enter the gain from line 7 on line 12 below. If line 9 is more than zero, enter the amount from line 8 on line 12 below and enter the gain from line 9 as a long-term capital gain on the Schedule D filed with your return (see instructions)	9	

Part II **Ordinary Gains and Losses** (see instructions)

10 Ordinary gains and losses not included on lines 11 through 16 (include property held 1 year or less):

11	Loss, if any, from line 7	11	( )
12	Gain, if any, from line 7 or amount from line 8, if applicable	12	
13	Gain, if any, from line 31	13	
14	Net gain or (loss) from Form 4684, lines 35 and 42a	14	
15	Ordinary gain from installment sales from Form 6252, line 25 or 36	15	
16	Ordinary gain or (loss) from like-kind exchanges from Form 8824	16	
17	Combine lines 10 through 16	17	
18	For all except individual returns, enter the amount from line 17 on the appropriate line of your return and skip lines a and b below. For individual returns, complete lines a and b below:		
a	If the loss on line 11 includes a loss from Form 4684, line 39, column (b)(ii), enter that part of the loss here. Enter the part of the loss from income-producing property on Schedule A (Form 1040), line 28, and the part of the loss from property used as an employee on Schedule A (Form 1040), line 23. Identify as from "Form 4797, line 18a." See instructions	18a	
b	Redetermine the gain or (loss) on line 17 excluding the loss, if any, on line 18a. Enter here and on Form 1040, line 14	18b	

For Paperwork Reduction Act Notice, see separate instructions. Cat. No. 13086I Form **4797** (2009)

Part III Gain From Disposition of Property Under Sections 1245, 1250, 1252, 1254, and 1255 (see instructions)

19 (a) Description of section 1245, 1250, 1252, 1254, or 1255 property:	(b) Date acquired (mo., day, yr.)	(c) Date sold (mo., day, yr.)
A		
B		
C		
D		

These columns relate to the properties on lines 19A through 19D. ▶		Property A	Property B	Property C	Property D
20 Gross sales price (**Note:** *See line 1 before completing.*)	20				
21 Cost or other basis plus expense of sale	21				
22 Depreciation (or depletion) allowed or allowable	22				
23 Adjusted basis. Subtract line 22 from line 21	23				
24 Total gain. Subtract line 23 from line 20	24				
25 **If section 1245 property:**					
a Depreciation allowed or allowable from line 22	25a				
b Enter the **smaller** of line 24 or 25a	25b				
26 **If section 1250 property:** If straight line depreciation was used, enter -0- on line 26g, except for a corporation subject to section 291.					
a Additional depreciation after 1975 (see instructions)	26a				
b Applicable percentage multiplied by the **smaller** of line 24 or line 26a (see instructions)	26b				
c Subtract line 26a from line 24. If residential rental property **or** line 24 is not more than line 26a, skip lines 26d and 26e	26c				
d Additional depreciation after 1969 and before 1976	26d				
e Enter the **smaller** of line 26c or 26d	26e				
f Section 291 amount (corporations only)	26f				
g Add lines 26b, 26e, and 26f	26g				
27 **If section 1252 property:** Skip this section if you did not dispose of farmland or if this form is being completed for a partnership (other than an electing large partnership).					
a Soil, water, and land clearing expenses	27a				
b Line 27a multiplied by applicable percentage (see instructions)	27b				
c Enter the **smaller** of line 24 or 27b	27c				
28 **If section 1254 property:**					
a Intangible drilling and development costs, expenditures for development of mines and other natural deposits, mining exploration costs, and depletion (see instructions)	28a				
b Enter the **smaller** of line 24 or 28a	28b				
29 **If section 1255 property:**					
a Applicable percentage of payments excluded from income under section 126 (see instructions)	29a				
b Enter the **smaller** of line 24 or 29a (see instructions)	29b				

Summary of Part III Gains. Complete property columns A through D through line 29b before going to line 30.

30 Total gains for all properties. Add property columns A through D, line 24	30	
31 Add property columns A through D, lines 25b, 26g, 27c, 28b, and 29b. Enter here and on line 13	31	
32 Subtract line 31 from line 30. Enter the portion from casualty or theft on Form 4684, line 37. Enter the portion from other than casualty or theft on Form 4797, line 6	32	

Part IV Recapture Amounts Under Sections 179 and 280F(b)(2) When Business Use Drops to 50% or Less (see instructions)

		(a) Section 179	(b) Section 280F(b)(2)
33 Section 179 expense deduction or depreciation allowable in prior years	33		
34 Recomputed depreciation (see instructions)	34		
35 Recapture amount. Subtract line 34 from line 33. See the instructions for where to report	35		

Form **4797** (2009)

What's New in 2009

Transactions of Interest. A taxpayer is required to report "transactions of interest" entered into after November 1, 2006. A transaction of interest is a transaction that is the same as or substantially similar to one of the types of transactions that the IRS has identified by notice, regulation, or other form of published guidance as a transaction of interest. It is a transaction that the IRS believes has a potential for tax avoidance or evasion, but for which there is not enough information to determine if the transaction should be identified as a tax avoidance transaction. In Notice 2009-55, the IRS has provided a list of transactions identified as transactions of interest. The IRS may issue new guidance that identifies a transaction as a transaction of interest; see the IRS web page at www.irs.gov/businesses/corporations and click on "Abusive Tax Shelters and Transactions."

Section at a Glance

Relevant IRS Publications

- ☐ IRS Publication 527, *Residential Rental Property*
- ☐ IRS Publication 535, *Business Expenses*
- ☐ IRS Publication 544, *Sales and Other Dispositions of Assets*
- ☐ IRS Publication 550, *Investment Income and Expenses (Including Capital Gains and Losses)*
- ☐ IRS Publication 555, *Community Property*
- ☐ IRS Publication 925, *Passive Activity and At-Risk Rules*

Tax Preparer's Checklist

- ☐ Assemble all Forms 1099-MISC and 1098 payee documents and inquire whenever other evidence indicates that a document may be missing.
- ☐ Identify business versus investment activity sources.
- ☐ Assemble Schedule K-1 documents.

Supplemental Forms That May Be Required with Schedule E

Form	When Required
Form 6198, *At-Risk Limitations*	The taxpayer reports a loss from a trade or business activity or from an activity engaged in for the production of income when some amounts invested in the activity are not at risk.
Form 8082, *Notice of Inconsistent Treatment or Administrative Adjustment Request (AAR)*	The taxpayer has received apparently incorrect partnership, S corporation, estate, or trust information.
Form 8582, *Passive Activity Loss Limitations*	The taxpayer reports a loss from activities in which the taxpayer did not materially participate.
Form 8621, *Return by a Shareholder of a Passive Foreign Investment Company or a Qualified Electing Fund*	The taxpayer is a direct or indirect shareholder of a PFIC and recognizes gain on a direct or indirect disposition of PFIC stock, receives certain direct or indirect distributions from a PFIC, or is making an election reportable in Part I of the form.
Form 8886, *Reportable Transaction Disclosure Statement*	The taxpayer's federal income tax liability is affected by participation in any transaction that falls into one or more of the reportable categories (see page 5–5).

At-Risk Rules

Deductions or losses from any activity are limited to the investor's amount at risk. Any losses in excess of that amount are suspended until there is an increase in the amount at risk. The suspension is another form of carryforward. The suspended losses cannot be carried back. See MTG ¶2045 for further information.

Caution. The at-risk rules cover any trade or business or investment activity other than certain real estate activities or equipment leasing activities. They are not limited to investments that produce portfolio income or loss or to those that produce passive income or loss.

Amount at Risk Defined

The amount at risk includes money contributed to the activity, debts for which the taxpayer is personally liable, and certain qualified nonrecourse financing. If the taxpayer has no personal liability but has pledged property that is not used in the activity as security for repayment of the debt, the amount at risk is the fair market value of the pledged property, less any superior liens. If the taxpayer pledges property that is used in the activity, the amount at risk does not include the value of the pledged property. A related rule provides that any loan from a co-venturer in the activity usually does not increase the borrower's amount at risk, even if the borrower is personally obligated to repay the loan.

Example. Susan acquires stock in SHV Corporation, an S corporation. She invests $10,000 of her own money and borrows $90,000 from SHV to purchase a total of $100,000 worth of stock. Her basis is $100,000 but her amount at risk is only $10,000 because the loan is from a co-venturer.

A taxpayer's amount at risk is increased for additional contributions of cash or property. It is also increased by the individual's share of any income that the venture produces.

In addition, a taxpayer can increase his or her amount at risk by changing a loan from nonrecourse to recourse. This refinancing would not affect the taxpayer's adjusted basis in his or her partnership interest, and it is unlikely that it would affect the basis of a shareholder in his or her S corporation stock or debt.

Finally, a rule that is a complete departure from the basis rules increases a taxpayer's amount at risk for any gain recognized on the disposition of the taxpayer's interest in the activity.

Worksheet: Amount at Risk	
1. Amount at risk at beginning of year, or at acquisition date if acquired during year	1. $
2. Additions to amount at risk (CAUTION: Make sure that any debt amount at risk has been restored to the extent of prior reductions.)	2. $
a. Add all taxable items	2a. $
b. Add all tax-exempt income	2b. $
c. Add any nonrecourse financing that has been reduced by cash payment or by refinancing with recourse debt	2c. $
d. Add any gain from the sale of part or all of an interest in the activity	2d. $
3. Subtotal (1 + 2 + 2a + 2b + 2c + 2d)	3. $
4. Reductions of amount at risk	4. $
a. Nondeductible expenses, not capitalized	4a. $
b. Subtotal (3 - 4 - 4a)	4b. $
c. Deductible expenses and losses	4c. $
d. Amounts carried forward from last year	4d. $
e. Subtotal (4b - 4c - 4d) (CAUTION: Do not reduce amount at risk below zero. Carry forward any excess expense to next year.)	4e. $
f. Refinancing of amount at risk by nonrecourse debt	4f. $
5. Ending amount at risk (4e - 4f)	5. $
6. Amount carried forward to next year.	6. $

Example. During the previous year, Ken invested $125,000 cash in KPB Partnership and received a 25% partnership interest, using $25,000 of his own funds plus $100,000 loaned to him by one of the other partners. In the current year, the partnership used cash plus $500,000 borrowed from First One Bank to purchase an office building for $1,000,000. The debt on the building was secured by a mortgage and was payable over 20 years with an interest rate of 6 percent. None of the partners were personally liable on the debt. Also during the current year, the partnership suffered a loss of $700,000.

Worksheet: Amount at Risk

1. Amount at risk at beginning of year, or at acquisition date if acquired during year	1.	$ 25,000
2. Additions to amount at risk (CAUTION: Make sure that any debt amount at risk has been restored to the extent of prior reductions.)	2.	125,000
a. Add all taxable items	2a.	0
b. Add all tax-exempt income	2b.	0
c. Add any nonrecourse financing that has been reduced by cash payment or by refinancing with recourse debt	2c.	0
d. Add any gain from the sale of part or all of an interest in the activity	2d.	0
3. Subtotal (1 + 2 + 2a + 2b + 2c + 2d)	3.	150,000
4. Reductions of amount at risk	4.	0
a. Nondeductible expenses, not capitalized	4a.	0
b. Subtotal (3 - 4 - 4a)	4b.	150,000
c. Deductible expenses and losses	4c.	175,000
d. Amounts carried forward from last year	4d.	0
e. Subtotal (4b - 4c - 4d) (CAUTION: Do not reduce amount at risk below zero. Carry forward any excess expense to next year.)	4e.	0
f. Refinancing of amount at risk by nonrecourse debt	4f.	0
5. Ending amount at risk (4e - 4f)	5.	0
6. Amount carried forward to next year.	6.	25,000

Ken's at-risk amount includes his $25,000 cash contribution plus his 25% of the partnership's $500,000 qualified nonrecourse debt. It does not include the $100,000 amount borrowed from the other partner. Since the building loan was borrowed from an unrelated commercial lender and not the seller, the loan is considered qualified nonrecourse financing. Ken's share of the partnership's loss is $175,000. However, his deduction is limited to his $150,000 at-risk amount and the remaining $25,000 is carried over until his at-risk basis is increased.

Passive Activity Loss (PAL) Rules

According to IRC §469, expenses related to passive activities can be deducted to the extent of passive activity income. Suspended losses and credits (not available because of limitations) can be carried forward to offset passive income from future years. Suspended losses from a passive activity are allowed in full once the taxpayer disposes of his or her interest in the activity.

Example. Susan Johnson incurred a $25,000 passive loss and reported no passive income in the previous tax year. However, the loss was not deductible in that year. Assume Susan reports $25,000 of passive income for the current tax year. Of the suspended loss, $25,000 will be allowed in the current year.

Passive Activity Defined

A passive activity is one that involves the conduct of a trade or business in which the taxpayer does not materially participate. In addition, a rental activity (whether or not the taxpayer materially participates) is generally considered a passive activity. Special rules apply to real estate rentals. See MTG ¶2059 for more details.

Example. John Smith is a self-employed real estate appraiser. In the current tax year his appraisal business sustained a loss of $6,000. He had interest income of $10,000 and a $5,000 loss from an equipment rental business in which he did not materially participate. The loss from his appraisal business is allowable in full in the current tax year. However, the $5,000 loss from his rental activity is a passive loss and cannot offset John's interest income. John must report $4,000 of income for the current year, and carry the $5,000 passive loss forward.

Nonpassive Activity Defined

A trade or business activity in which the taxpayer materially participates is a nonpassive activity.

In addition, a working interest in any oil or gas property that the taxpayer holds directly or as a general partner is considered nonpassive.

Example. Attorney Sam Jones owns and operates K&B Corporation, a law firm for which Sam works full-time. Sam and his wife lease a building that they own jointly to K&B Corporation. The corporation was the sole tenant. The rents received in the current tax year totaled $24,000. The amount received would not be considered passive income since Sam materially participates in the business of the corporation.

Material Participation

If a taxpayer materially participates in the operations of an activity on a regular, continuous and substantial basis, the income is not considered passive and losses generated are currently deductible against other forms of income. Treasury Regulations Sec. 1.469-5T outlines objective standards that look to the actual number of hours spent in the activity. An individual who meets the requirements of any one of seven tests is deemed to materially participate in an activity:

1. The individual participates for more than 500 hours during the tax year.
2. The individual's participation in the tax year constitutes substantially all of the participation in the activity.
3. The individual participates for more than 100 hours and no other individual spends more time on the activity.
4. Total participation in all significant participation activities exceeds 500 hours. A significant participation activity is defined as one in which the taxpayer participates for more than 100 hours.
5. The individual materially participated in the activity for five of the past ten years.
6. The individual materially participated in a personal service activity for three years prior to the current year.
7. The individual participated in an activity for more than 100 hours and based on all facts and circumstances, the individual participates on a regular, continuous, and substantial basis.

Example. Phil Smart is a teacher who earns extra income by contracting with some of his neighbors to plow private roads and driveways. He maintains and drives the truck. Assume that in the current tax year there is little snow and he only operates the truck for 10 hours. He is considered a material participant in the snow plowing business under the second test listed above.

Special Rules for Real Estate Rentals

$25,000 Limit. Rental operations are generally classified as passive. If a taxpayer who owns an interest in a rental real estate property does not satisfy the material participation standards described above but does actively participate in the management of that property, the activity will still be classified as passive. In this case, however, the taxpayer will be allowed a deduction for up to $25,000 in losses from the activity, in excess of income from other real estate activities. This relief is provided to individuals and certain estates, but not to trusts or corporations.

"Active" Participation. The difference between active participation and material participation is that the active participation test can be satisfied without regular, continuous and substantial involvement in operations, as long as the taxpayer participates in making management decisions or arranging for others to provide tenant services (such as repairs) in a significant and bona fide manner. The approvals of tenants, terms, major repairs, and capital expenditures are all evidence of active participation.

To qualify as actively participating, the taxpayer must also have at least a 10% ownership in the rental activity.

Example. Sidney owns and rents out an apartment that he formerly used as his primary residence. He hires a rental agent and uses a contractor to handle routine repairs. Sidney is likely to meet the active participation test.

AGI Phaseout. The $25,000 allowance starts being phased out when a taxpayer's adjusted gross income reaches $100,000. Once the adjusted gross income exceeds that amount, the allowance is reduced by 50% of the excess. Once adjusted gross income reaches $150,000, losses from rental real estate with active participation are treated in the same manner as other losses from passive activities. For this measurement, adjusted gross income is computed before any contribution to an IRA is deducted, before any Social Security benefits are included, and before any net passive loss is allowed. See MTG ¶2063 for further information.

Example. Lisa Miller reports income of $10,000 from a passive activity on her current year tax return. She also reports a $47,000 loss from an apartment building that she owns and actively manages. She will use $10,000 of the loss from the rental property to offset income from the other passive activity. Of the remaining $37,000 loss, $25,000 may be claimed as a current year deduction and $12,000 will be carried forward.

Rental Activities as Nonpassive

Persons engaged in active real estate trades or businesses are allowed to treat real estate rental activities as nonrental trades or businesses. Thus, a qualifying owner can treat these activities as nonpassive if he or she meets the requirement of a material participation test.

A real estate professional is someone who performs more than half of the personal services he or she performs in all trades or businesses during the tax year in real property trades or businesses in which he or she materially participated. He or she must also spend more than 750 hours during the year in real estate business activities, which include management, operation, development, redevelopment, construction, conversion, rental, leasing and brokering.

Even if the taxpayer meets the real estate professional standard, he or she must still meet one of the material participation tests for the particular activity in question.

Example. John retired from the medical profession in 2007. Since then, he has acquired several properties that he has renovated and rented. He spent a total of 500 hours overseeing and working on renovations during 2008. During 2009, John bought several more properties and spent a total of 1,400 hours on renovations. John rented out all the properties purchased and renovated in 2008; however, he had vacant units in the properties purchased in 2009. In that year, John sustained a loss of $15,000 due to the vacant units. John did not qualify as a real estate professional in 2008, but in 2009 he meets the requirements as a real estate professional and therefore he can deduct the $15,000 loss.

Where to Report Passive Activity Losses

Not all passive activity losses are reported on Schedule E. Some other forms on which these losses may be reported are Schedule C for PALs related to a business, Schedule D for capital gains and losses, Schedule F for PALs related to farming, Form 4797 for sales of business property, and Form 6252 for installment sales. See IRS Publication 925, *Passive Activity and At-Risk Rules* for more information.

Gray Area. Multiple rental unit activity may require proper licensing (as a realtor or property manager). An investor must be able to substantiate tax treatment of rental income. Records should include how the property is managed, by whom, and time spent.

Taxpayers with rental losses, or losses incurred in a trade or business, must be careful to review the various participation rules. The definition of a real estate professional is not precise. At least one person who was a partial owner in several closely held businesses has found that merely inspecting and managing company-owned real estate does not constitute being a real estate professional. Thus the taxpayer was unable to deduct losses on certain real estate activities, even though he had met the material participation test, since the real estate rents were per se passive.

Form 8886—Reportable Transaction Disclosure Statement

There are always creative new ways to avoid taxes. The financial press has been full of stories about abusive tax shelters, which have gone far beyond the legitimate structuring of businesses and investment matters. Promoters, which have included major accounting and law firms, have been penalized severely. Some have even gone out of existence. Part of the government's response has been to require specific reporting by persons who promote such transactions and by persons who have invested in these ventures. The transaction categories that require this special reporting are

1. "Listed" transactions, specifically designated by the IRS in published documents (Notice 2004-67 and subsequent modifications thereto) and any transactions "substantially similar" to those listed.
2. "Confidential transactions" for which the investor has signed an agreement with the advisors, agreeing to a limit of disclosure of the tax treatment of the transaction. In addition, the taxpayer must have paid the advisor a fee of at least $50,000, except in the case of corporations, in which case the fee must be at least $250,000.
3. "Transactions with contractual protection" for which the promoter has guaranteed a refund of the fee if the IRS disallows the anticipated tax treatment.
4. "Loss transactions" that result in a loss of at least $2 million in one year or $4 million in multiple years to an individual (except for foreign currency transactions that result in a loss of at least $50,000 in a single year). Different limits apply to other types of taxpayers.

5. "Transactions of interest," which are those identified by the IRS in published guidance. In Notice 2009-55, the IRS has provided a list of transactions identified as transactions of interest. For updates, see the IRS web page at www.irs.gov/businesses/corporations and click on "Abusive Tax Shelters and Transactions."

Filing Tip. "Transactions with a brief holding period" (i.e., the taxpayer holds an asset for 45 days or less) were eliminated as a category of transaction required to be disclosed on Form 8886, effective for transactions entered into on or after August 3, 2007. "Transactions with a significant book-tax difference" (i.e., more than $10 million) were required to be disclosed on returns filed with due dates (including extensions) of January 5, 2006, or before. However, effective for returns due after that date, they are no longer considered reportable transactions and are not required to be disclosed. However, a significant book-tax difference transaction must still be reported if it either (1) should have been disclosed on a return due prior to January 6, 2006; or (2) is also described in any of the five categories above.

The taxpayer who participates in one of the five reportable ventures must file Form 8886 and disclose the category, the person(s) to whom the taxpayer paid a fee for tax advice, and the nature and projected amount of tax benefits. Form 8886 does not feed directly into any other schedule. The losses and credits claimed from these ventures are reported on the usual schedules. Accordingly, if any of these transactions relate to rental or royalty activities, or are conducted through partnerships or S corporations, the losses would be reported on Schedule E.

Planning Tip. Having a taxpayer describe in writing the results they anticipated from particular financial or investment activities will greatly aid the preparer in addressing those unique tax issues. The preparer will also be able to incorporate the source of the intent and show during filer review whether the tax benefits were a principal factor in the transaction.

Schedule E

Part I: Income or Loss from Rental Real Estate or Royalties

Line 1, Type and Location of Rental Real Estate

On line 1, the taxpayer identifies each real estate property from which rental income was received, or for which expense was incurred at any time during the tax year. If the taxpayer has more than three properties that produced rental income or royalties, he or she may use additional schedules but enters the total on only one form.

Rentals of personal property, except for rentals incidental to real estate, are not entered on Schedule E. The IRS instructs the lessor of personal property to report the related income and expenses on Schedule C or Schedule C-EZ if the rentals constitute a trade or business, and to enter the amounts directly on Form 1040 as other income on line 21 if it is not. Rentals incidental to real property would include furniture and appliances in a rental home or office space, if the use of the property is included in the real estate rental arrangement.

If an individual taxpayer is a co-owner of one or more of the rental real estate properties listed on this line, he or she needs to disclose the percentage ownership on line 1.

Line 2, Personal Use Definition and Limits

On this line, the taxpayer must give the information necessary to determine whether or not the income and expense from the real property are subject to the vacation home rules, which limit most of the deductions so that they cannot exceed the gross rental income from the property. In other words, any net income is reportable, but a net loss under the vacation home rules does not even enter into the calculations on Form 8582.

If the taxpayer uses the home for more than 14 days, it may pass the test only if the taxpayer's use is fewer than 10% of the days for which it is rented to others at a fair market rate. If it passes the non-personal-use test, it is treated as a rental activity and all deductions in connection with the rental property are allowed, subject to the at-risk and passive activity loss restrictions, discussed below.

If the owner's use exceeds the greater of 14 days or 10% of the days the property was rented, the expenses may offset the gross income from the property. However, allowable deductions cannot exceed gross income from the property. The statute prescribes that the gross income shall be offset in the following order:

1. Interest, taxes, and casualty losses that are deductible without regard to the vacation home limits. Advertising, rental commissions, and such other expenses that can be associated only with rental income. If these expenses create a net loss, the loss may be deductible, subject to the passive activity loss limits.

2. Repairs and maintenance, utilities, and insurance, but only to the extent of the income remaining after the first category of expenses has been subtracted.
3. Depreciation, but only to the extent of the income remaining after the first two categories of expenses have been subtracted.

If the taxpayer cannot get beyond step 1, there is possible additional relief. If the interest is on a second (but not a third) home, the taxpayer may claim a deduction for the interest that is left over from Schedule E as an itemized deduction on Schedule A. Real property taxes are also deductible on Schedule A, without limit as to the number of properties.

Gray Area. When the personal usage of a rental unit exceeds the greater of either 14 days or 10 percent of the rental days, according to the IRS, expenses attributable to the use of the rental unit are limited so that the total deductions may not exceed the gross rental income and only a percentage of expenses equalling the total days rented divided by the total days used is deductible. However, the Tax Courtn and the Ninth and Tenth Circuit Courts of Appeals, have rejected this formula and stated that mortgage interest and real estate taxes are not subject to the same percentage limitations as are other expenses because they are assessed on an annual basis without regard to the number of days that the property is used. The formula employed by the courts computes the percentage limitation for interest and taxes by dividing the total days rented by the total days in the year. Generally, the courts' formula allows higher expense deductions.

Line 3, Rents Received

Line 3 shows the amount of gross rental income from each property in the current year. Most individual taxpayers use the cash method of accounting. By this method, only amounts actually received during the reporting year are shown as income. Thus, if a tenant is late and makes a December payment in the following January, the income is not reported by the landlord until the tax year in which it is actually received. However, if a tenant pays early, the landlord must report that in the year received.

Example. Ms. Jones owns a duplex and rents both halves in 2009. One tenant does not pay the December rent until January 5, 2010. The other tenant pays her January rent on December 17, 2009. Ms. Jones reports only the amounts she received in 2009 on line 3 of Schedule E.

Payments are usually in cash, although some lessors receive payment in the form of other property or services. The fair market value of these noncash payments is reportable as income. One item that is usually not included as rental income is any improvement made by the lessee. The landlord takes no cost basis in this item and is unable to claim any deduction or depreciation related to the cost.

A landlord who receives a security deposit that may be returned to the tenant at the end of the rental period usually must report the deposit as income when received and as a deduction when it is returned. However, if the landlord receives a deposit, segregates it in the accounting records, and actually pays the tenant interest on the deposit when all or a part of it is refunded, the landlord need not report the deposit as income until it is determined that all or a part of the deposit will not be returned. Any other deposit, for which no return is anticipated, must be reported in the year received, even if it is to cover more than one year of the lease term.

Line 4, Royalties Received

Royalty income from oil, gas, mineral, copyright, or patent properties is reported on line 4. However, if a payment for patent rights is termed a royalty, but is actually consideration for a sale of the patent rights, the seller may be able to claim capital gain treatment. Enter the gross amount of royalty income; any taxes withheld are reported on line 16.

Royalties received in the ordinary course of the business of being an author, composer, or other creator of intellectual property are reported as self-employment income on Schedule C or C-EZ.

Line 5, Advertising

A cash-method taxpayer deducts advertising expenses when they are actually paid and not when they are billed by the agency or media outlet. These could be newspaper, radio, magazine, or other media promotions. They could also include fees paid to an advertising agency or fees paid to a property manager that are designated as advertising expense.

Line 6, Auto and Travel

Automobile expenses are deductible to the extent that the taxpayer uses his or her personal automobile for travel related to the rental activity. If the rental property is located away from the taxpayer's home, the taxpayer must be careful to separate business from rental purposes for a trip. This is an especially hot issue when there is a vacation home and the taxpayer deducts travel to that home. See Tab 3 and Tab 8.

Example. Mr. Gray lives in Indiana and owns a condominium in Florida. After severe storms and tornadoes in early 2008, he drove to Florida to inspect damage and make arrangements for repairs to the condominium. If the majority of the days on this trip were devoted to the business matters of the condominium, he may deduct the expenses.

A taxpayer who uses his or her personal automobile for rental activities may use the standard mileage rate for trade or business expense (55 cents per mile for 2009), assuming he or she meets all of the conditions for that election in the tax year. Alternatively, he or she may keep track of mileage and the actual expenses of owning and operating the automobile and apportion the expenses to valid rental usage.

Documentation of automobile expense for any type of deduction is often challenged by the IRS. A mileage log, which has been filled out contemporaneously, may be essential to preserving this deduction.

Line 7, Cleaning and Maintenance

Cleaning and maintenance expenses are deductible in the year paid. These can sometimes be subject to challenge. The taxpayer is advised to keep careful records to distinguish maintenance from improvements to the property.

Line 8, Commissions

Commissions may be paid to real estate agents, owners' groups, or other property managers, based on the amounts of rent collected. If the agent is entitled to collect a portion of a tenant's rent, then the income is received and the commission is paid when the agent receives the rental income from the tenant.

Line 9, Insurance

Most property owners carry hazard insurance on property. The insurance premiums are deductible when paid. If they are paid by the lender out of an escrow account, the taxpayer claims the deduction in the year in which the lender pays the amount out of escrow. If a premium covers more than one year on a policy, the taxpayer should prorate it among the years covered. As a practical matter, the IRS approves the deduction of a one-year premium in the year paid.

Example. In February, a taxpayer pays a one-year premium for hazard insurance. Assuming that the taxpayer follows the practice consistently, he or she may deduct the cost in the current year.

In addition to hazard insurance, a property owner may also carry personal liability insurance, private mortgage insurance, business interruption insurance and other specialty policies. These are generally deductible under the same rules as hazard insurance. However, credit life insurance, which will pay off the mortgage in the event of the insured's death or disability, is not deductible.

Line 10, Legal and Other Professional Fees

Legal expenses paid in the ordinary course of operating the rental property, such as those incurred for dealing with tenants, vendors, contractors, neighbors or other periodic concerns, are deductible when paid. The taxpayer must be careful to segregate fees paid in connection with rental property from those incurred in connection with other business operations or those related to personal or family matters. Legal fees paid in connection with the purchase of the property must be added to the property's cost and may be deductible through depreciation, discussed below, on line 20. Legal fees connected with the sale of the property are treated as reductions of the sale price and are reflected in determining the gain or loss on the sale or other disposition of the property.

Legal, accounting, and other professional fees related to tax preparation or tax advice are also deductible. If these fees are commingled with the owner's other tax and legal fees, there should be some sustainable method of segregating the portion of the fees attributable to the rental property.

Planning Tip. Tax preparation and other professional fees may have alternative minimum tax consequences when posted on Schedule A. Allocation of these expenses to income schedules (Schedules C, E, and F) can minimize AMT impact.

Line 11, Management Fees

Management fees have no special rules that are not applicable to deductions generally. If a property manager charges periodic fees for monitoring or supervision of the property, or for conducting business with tenants, these are deductible when paid. Amounts paid to family members may qualify, as long as the recipient reports it in his or her taxable income. Self-charged time, or the value of the owner's personal services, is not deductible under management fees or any other category of expenses.

Line 12, Mortgage Interest Paid to Banks, etc.

Mortgage interest paid to banks and commercial lenders is deductible when paid. Any points paid at the time of loan origination are not immediately deductible but must be amortized over the entire term of the loan. If the property owner refinances the mortgage, the points paid at that time must be amortized over the life of the new loan. Any amortization remaining from prior financing should be deducted.

The lender should send Form 1098 to the borrower if the borrower paid $600 or more in mortgage interest during the year. If the amount on Form 1098 does not agree with the borrower's records, the borrower should prepare a note explaining the difference and attach it to his or her tax return. Mortgage interest paid to private lenders or when Form 1098 is not issued in the taxpayer's name should be reported on line 13.

Line 13, Other Interest

Interest paid to private lenders and other interest paid in connection with the rental activity is reported on line 13. Examples include interest paid on loans to improve, repair, or furnish the property, to replace appliances, and other expenditures. This line should also include interest paid to the seller of the property, and any other source of credit that is not required to file Form 1098.

Line 14, Repairs

This line shows the amount paid for repairs to the property, furnishings, or appliances. A taxpayer should be careful to distinguish repairs from improvements. Any expenditure that improves a property's income potential beyond what it was when the taxpayer acquired it is suspect as a repair deduction. However, repairs that merely restore the property to its normal operating condition are completely deductible. These can result from tenant damage, storms, vandalism, or any other occurrence. If the expenditure in question is an improvement, the taxpayer may be able to recover its cost gradually by claiming depreciation deductions. See line 20 for further discussion.

> **Gray Area.** Work done to prevent damage and protect an investment may qualify as repair expense rather than capital investment if the work prolongs the life of the property in its normal operating condition.

Line 15, Supplies

Supplies for cleaning, maintenance, tenant comfort, and other needs may be deducted when they are purchased. On occasion, the IRS may challenge the immediate deductibility of a large purchase of items in bulk quantities that may last more than one year. This is another area where the taxpayer needs to distinguish routine supplies, such as furnace filters, from capital improvements, such as a new furnace. The former would be deductible when purchased, whereas the latter would need to be capitalized and depreciated according to its MACRS recovery period (see Tab 7).

Line 16, Taxes

Taxes assessed on the property by a local government, county, school district, or other taxing authority are deductible when paid. If paid by the lender from an escrow account, the taxes are deductible when the lender pays the tax. The primary trouble spots for this deduction are assessments for improvement of the property, which are not deductible. They must be added to the cost of the land. On occasion, a taxpayer attempts to deduct a portion of state or local income tax, to the extent it is attributable to net rental income. Personal income taxes are deductible only on Schedule A.

Sales taxes paid on supplies or services are deductible as part of those expenditures. Sales taxes paid on appliances, furnishings, or other long-lived assets must be added to the property's cost and recovered either through depreciation deductions or upon selling the property.

Line 17, Utilities

Utilities paid by the landlord for tenant use are deductible when the rental agreement provides that the landlord will pay the utilities. Any utility charges imposed on the landlord during a period of vacancy would also be deductible.

Line 18, Other Expenses

As innocuous as the title for this line may appear, it may be the only location where some extremely important items can be reported. Other expenses not listed above may be deductible if they are ordinary and necessary to the conduct of the rental activity. These might include the following:

- Wages and salaries paid in connection with the rental real estate activity.
- Some prizes or other incentives given to tenants, although there are strict substantiation requirements for anything construed as entertainment.
- The cost of an event such as a holiday picnic (may be subject to the 50% disallowance for meals and entertainment).

Line 19, Total Expenses

On this line, the taxpayer merely sums the expenses reported above. Note that this is computed before depreciation expense.

Line 20, Depreciation Expense or Depletion

Depreciation expense is computed for property used in the trade or business of renting. There is some depreciation on royalty-producing property, although it is not as common as depletion. Depletion is allowed only for oil, gas, or mineral royalty property. As similar as the terms depreciation and depletion may sound, they are really quite different.

Depreciation on real estate rental property is often divided into two major components: building and land. The building component is depreciated using the real property depreciation allowance rules. These generally allow deductions over 27.5 years, using the straight-line method for any residential property placed in service after 1986. Nonresidential property, which includes short term lodging facilities such as hotels and motels, is subject to a longer depreciation period. For most buildings placed in service after May 12, 1993, this period is 39 years. There are different rules for properties placed in service before these dates.

Personal property used in connection with the rental property may be depreciated over much shorter MACRS lives. Thus, it is wise to segregate the cost of furnishings, appliances and mechanical equipment from the cost of the building itself.

There is no depreciation deduction for the cost of the land. The only tax benefit resulting from land cost is its effect on the gain or loss from the sale of the property.

A taxpayer with depletable oil, gas, timber, or mineral interests should consult IRS Publication 535 for the rules governing these computations. They can become quite complicated, and they may vary by the nature of the property, the involvement of the royalty interest holder, and other conditions.

Line 21, Total Expenses

Add lines 19 and 20.

Line 22, Income or Loss from Rental Real Estate and Royalties

Fill out line 22 using only the current year's income and deduction items. Subtract line 21 from either line 3 (rents) or line 4 (royalties). If the result on line 22 is positive income for any property, no more work may be necessary. However, failure to examine all of the records may result in a loss of hidden possible deductions. Be sure to check prior years' Forms 6198 and 8582 for any previous losses.

In general, the income and loss items from line 22 should also be posted to Form 8582 and its worksheets to determine the amount to report on line 23. However, if there are no properties for which losses are reported in the current year and no properties where there have been disallowed losses, the taxpayer may not need to fill out Form 8582.

If any rental or royalty activity shows a loss, the taxpayer must check the at-risk limitations. If a loss is limited by this rule, the loss on line 22 should be the amount from Form 6198, line 21.

Line 23, Deductible Rental Real Estate Loss

Caution. Losses from royalty interests should not be reported on line 23. Royalty losses should be reported on line 22 and line 25.

This line includes a net loss that has run through Form 8582 and is deductible on Schedule E for the current year. Up to $25,000 of passive activity loss may be deducted as a result of the taxpayer's passive activity income or according to the active participation rule. This line is also the proper place for deducting losses for which the taxpayer qualifies by meeting the "real estate professional" status, which allows the taxpayer to treat these rental operations as a trade or business, rather than *per se* passive activities.

Line 23 should also include any prior-year loss that was disallowed under the passive activity loss rules, if the activity is completely disposed of in the current year. Also, report disallowed passive activity losses from prior years when there is passive income in the current year that can offset those losses.

Gray Area. The instructions to Form 6198 provide that prior-year losses that were not deductible due to at-risk limitations should be reported on the appropriate form or schedule of the taxpayer's current year tax return. In most cases, prior-year unallowed losses from rental real estate activities will be reported on line 3c of Form 8582. However, they may be reported elsewhere on Form 8582 for some activities, and if the taxpayer is not required to file Form 8582 for the current tax year, generally these losses are entered directly on line 23 with an explanation on the dotted line next to line 23. The IRS recommends "PYA" for prior-year unallowed losses entered in Part II, so this is the recommended notation.

Lines 24, 25, and 26, Income and Loss Calculations

These totals involve self-evident calculations. If the taxpayer has no income or losses reportable in Part II, III, IV, or line 40, the amount from line 26 goes to Form 1040, line 17. If the taxpayer has income or deductions from partnerships, S corporations, trusts, estates, or residual interests in real estate mortgage investment conduits (REMICs; see page 5-14), the total from line 26 becomes part of the amount entered on Schedule E, line 41.

Part II: Income or Loss from Partnerships and S Corporations

Partnerships

Each partnership must provide Form 1065, Schedule K-1 to every partner. Most K-1s report income or loss that should be entered on Schedule E. However, there are other forms on which a taxpayer may need to report income or loss from his or her interest in a partnership. Schedule K-1 has fairly detailed instructions on where to report the amount from each line item. For example, interest income must be reported by the individual taxpayer on Form 1040, line 8a or Schedule B. If a partnership realizes interest income, it must report it as such to the partners on Schedule K-1. However, this interest is not reported on the individual partner's Schedule E, but on Form 1040, line 8a or Schedule B.

> **Filing Tip.** Processing of Schedule K-1 (Form 1065) may delay preparation of the individual's Form 1040. If a partnership has not provided Schedule K-1, the individual should contact the person responsible. Individuals may estimate the information, file Form 1040, and file a later amended return if information on the K-1 is different from the estimate. Filing an extension until all information is received is the other option.

Not all income or loss may progress directly from Schedule K-1 to Schedule E. For example, any net rental income from a partnership, or net trade or business income from a partnership in which the taxpayer does not materially participate, must be routed through Form 8582 in order to compute the allowable losses from passive activities owned by the taxpayer.

> **Example.** A taxpayer has net ordinary income of $15,000 from ABC Partnership. He also has $14,000 of ordinary losses from XYZ Partnership. Both of these items need to be entered on Schedule E. However, if the taxpayer does not materially participate in these activities or if they are rental activities, he must also report them on Form 8582.

A Schedule K-1 may show ordinary income or ordinary loss. If there is a loss, the taxpayer must ensure that the loss does not exceed his or her basis in the partnership interest. If the loss exceeds basis, the partner may deduct only the portion of the loss that does not exceed basis. Next, the partner must make sure that the loss does not exceed his or her amount at risk in the partnership. Only the portion that does not exceed the amount at risk moves to the next step, which is the passive activity loss limit, and only if the partner does not materially participate in the partnership's trade or business or if the loss is incurred in connection with a rental activity. Only the portion of the loss that is allocable from Form 8582 and its worksheets actually flows to Schedule E.

It is always a good idea to check prior years' tax returns for any losses or deductions that might have been disallowed due to one of these provisions. If the partner has acquired basis, increased his or her amount at risk, or currently meets one of the passive activity loss allowance criteria, he or she may be able to claim a deduction on the current year's return for prior year items.

A partnership must also report the partner's share of self-employment income. This amount is not always identical to the ordinary income shown in box 1 of Schedule K-1. Enter the amount from box 14 (with code A) of Schedule K-1 of Form 1065 or from box 9 (with code J1) of Schedule K-1 of Form 1065-B on Schedule SE after reducing this amount by any allowable expenses. These expenses may also qualify as an adjustment to self-employment income flowing from Schedule K-1. The self-employment income amount goes directly to Schedule SE and does not enter into any other calculations, including those on Form 8582.

In general, income from a partnership is not community income, but is the separate income of the partner. See IRS Publication 555. However, if the partnership is community property, the income or loss from the partnership is community income.

A U.S. citizen who is a member of a foreign partnership may be required to file Form 8865 to provide information similar to Form 1065, which U.S. partnerships must file. There are several categories of filers of this form. The level of required information varies with the level of ownership in the foreign partnership.

A partner may bear certain expenses outside of the partnership on its behalf, such as for the use of a personal automobile, or interest paid on loans to acquire the investment in the partnership. The partner should report these on line 28 of Schedule E with an appropriate explanation. Line 28 should also include any loss or deduction that had been disallowed in any prior year due to basis, at-risk, or passive activity loss limits.

S Corporations

The rules for reporting income and other items from S corporations are almost identical to the partnership reporting rules, with the following important differences.

There is no self-employment income reportable from the S corporation, so there is no feed to Schedule SE. If the S corporation shareholder is also an employee and incurs employee business expenses related to the S corporation, these are treated in the same manner as any other employee expenses. If the S corporation reimburses the shareholder-employee, the reimbursements do not appear on the return. If not reimbursed, the shareholder-employee must complete Form 2106 and enter the appropriate items on Schedule A as miscellaneous itemized deductions. This is quite different from the partner, who reports these items on Line 28 of Schedule E. However, if the shareholder borrows money to purchase stock in the S corporation, the interest paid on these loans is reported on Schedule E, in the same manner as a partner who has borrowed money to finance his or her interest in the partnership.

A final major difference between partnership income and S corporation income arises when there are distributions of accumulated earnings and profits from years before the corporation became an S corporation. These may be dividend income to the shareholder when received and should be reported on Form 1040, line 9a or 9b, or on Schedule B in the same manner as dividends from regular C corporations. They should not be duplicated on Schedule E. The S corporation should send Form 1099 to notify the shareholder of these distributions.

Caution. Persons who are sole shareholders in S corporations have often made the mistake of trying to avoid social security taxes by taking little or no wages or salaries from the corporation, but by taking the profits out in the form of distributions. The IRS has had an active program of monitoring these corporations, and assessing FICA and FUTA taxes on the corporations. Often the penalties alone for failure to pay these taxes are more than the income that the shareholders have attempted to divert. Many of these assessments have been challenged in the courts, but to date the IRS has won every single case. Thus, every shareholder in an S corporation who performs services for the corporation, and withdraws money from the corporation should make sure to establish and maintain a reasonable level of compensation for the services he or she performs.

Losses from S corporations are subject to similar limitations as partnership losses. Therefore the shareholder should check prior years' tax returns for losses that may have been disallowed in an earlier year. If they are deductible in the current year they should be entered on line 28, Schedule E.

Line 27, Prior-Year Losses

Line 27 is a box that should be checked if the taxpayer is reporting any prior year losses on the current return. These prior year losses must have been disallowed due to the basis, at-risk, or passive activity loss limits in earlier years. These items will not appear on Schedule K-1 or any other correspondence from a partnership or S corporation in the current year, so the taxpayer must be able to consult prior years' records to determine if it is necessary to check this box. It is not necessary to check this box if the taxpayer has prior years' losses but is unable to claim any of them in the current year.

Line 28, Income and Loss Details

Line 28 is divided into two sets of columns, passive and nonpassive. Nonpassive income or loss, as well as IRC §179 asset expensing, will be from partnerships and S corporations in which the taxpayer materially participates. However, even these entities might have some rental income that does not meet the active business exception. If that is the case, the income or loss might be divided between passive and nonpassive. This information should be readily available from the Schedule K-1 of the partnership or S corporation, possibly on attachments to the official form.

Example. A taxpayer owns an interest in a limited liability company (LLC), which is treated as a partnership for federal income tax purposes. This year's Schedule K-1 shows that her share of the LLC's ordinary income from its business was $40,000 and her share of IRC §179 asset expensing was $15,000. The LLC also owned a rental property, which was separate from its business. The taxpayer was allocated $3,000 of net income from the rental activity this year. She will make three separate entries on line 28 for the LLC's activities reported on the K-1. These will include nonpassive income of $40,000, a nonpassive IRC §179 deduction of $15,000, and passive income of $3,000.

There may be two reasons why a prior year's disallowed nonpassive loss is reported in the current year. A taxpayer who lacked basis in his or her partnership interest or S corporation stock and debt in one or more prior years may have either invested additional amounts or reported income from the same entity in the current year. In either of these cases, some or all of the prior year's suspended loss may be deductible in the current year. If so, it is reported on line 28 with the notation PYA (for prior year amount).

Example. A taxpayer owns stock in an S corporation. Last year the taxpayer's share of ordinary losses from the S corporation was $40,000, but his basis was only $25,000. His suspended loss from this corporation was $15,000. This year, he reports $60,000 of ordinary income from the S corporation. The taxpayer materially participated in the S corporation's business in both years. On line 28 this year he reports $60,000 of nonpassive income. On a separate line, with the notation "PYA," he should report a loss of $15,000.

A passive loss could have been disallowed in the prior year for lack of basis, lack of amount at risk, or from the passive activity loss (PAL) limits. The first two limits should not appear on the prior year's worksheet for Form 8582, but the PAL limit should come from that worksheet.

Lines 29-32, Calculations

Passive and nonpassive income from Schedule K-1 are totaled separately in columns (g) and (j) of line 29a, and the total of these is reported on line 30. Allowed passive loss is totaled on line 29b in column (f), and nonpassive losses from Schedule K-1 are totaled on line 29b in column (h). Totals of IRC §179 expense deductions in column (i) are also reported on line 29b. The total of the three sums on line 29b is reported on line 31, shown in parentheses to indicate it represents a loss.

Line 32 is the total partnership and S corporation income or loss, the result of combining lines 30 and 31. This amount is included in line 41.

Part III: Income or Loss from Estates and Trusts

Part III is quite similar to Part II. However, the information for this part is from the taxpayer's Schedule K-1 from estates and trusts. The flow-through amount from an estate or trust is calculated quite differently from partnership or S corporation amounts. The fiduciary bears the responsibility for those calculations. The taxpayer who receives income from these fiduciary entities will find that the estate and trust reporting requirements are almost identical to those for partnerships.

One principal difference is that a taxpayer will not normally report a loss from an estate or trust, unless the fiduciary entity is terminated in the reporting year. Another reporting difference is that there is no place for a IRC §179 asset expensing deduction, since this provision is prohibited for estates and trusts.

Trusts Not Reported on Schedule E. There are two types of trusts that do not require the taxpayer to report income or expenses on Schedule E. A grantor trust is one in which the taxpayer has sufficient control and the trust is disregarded entirely for tax purposes. A revocable living trust is a popular example of this type of trust. The taxpayer should report all items of income of the trust directly on his own return. Thus, the income from a grantor trust will be reported on Schedule E only if the income source is from a partnership, S corporation, another trust or estate, rental, or royalty activities.

The other type of trust not reporting to Schedule E is the electing small business trust (ESBT). An ESBT's sole purpose is to hold stock in one or more S corporations. This trust does not pass income or loss to its beneficiaries. Distributions from these trusts are not taxable to the beneficiary and are not reported on the individual beneficiary's tax return.

The taxation of trust activities can be quite complicated. A trust may pass through some of its income to a beneficiary on Schedule K-1 and may report that part of the income is from a grantor trust. This is reported directly by the beneficiary on the source schedule, such as Schedule B. Some trusts are actually split into three parts for one beneficiary, with some trust income reported on Schedule E, Part III, some reportable as grantor trust income, and some as distributions from an ESBT.

Line 33, Income and Loss Details

Line 33 serves the same purpose as line 28 does for income and deductions from partnerships and S corporations. Again, there is no column for IRC §179 expensing, since this deduction is not allowed for fiduciaries. The passive or nonpassive status of the income or loss is usually determined by the fiduciary's participation, rather than by the taxpayer's participation.

Lines 34a-37, Calculations

Line 35 is total income and line 36 is total loss from estates and trusts. The combination on line 37 is also included on line 41.

Form 8082

Form 8082 is filed by a taxpayer when he or she receives apparently incorrect partnership, S corporation, estate, or trust information, or does not receive a Schedule K-1. In this situation, the taxpayer will not be reporting the same amounts that are reported by the entity. He or she should use this form to explain the difference.

Form 3520 and Form 3520-A

These forms are filed by taxpayers who have certain dealings with foreign trusts, partnerships, or corporations. Preparation of these forms requires substantial knowledge of the tax and nontax laws of the affected jurisdiction.

Part IV: Income or Loss from Real Estate Mortgage Investment Conduits (REMICs)

Distributions from a REMIC are not reported on Schedule E. If the distribution does not exceed the taxpayer's basis in the REMIC, the holder reduces his or her basis in the REMIC investment. If a distribution from the REMIC exceeds the taxpayer's basis, the excess is reported as a gain from the sale of the interest in a REMIC. For the casual investor, this would be reported as a capital gain on Schedule D.

REMICs Defined

A REMIC is an entity formed for holding a pool of mortgages secured by real estate. For income tax purposes, its treatment is generally the same as that of a partnership, although it may be subject to certain taxes on its holdings.

REMIC income or loss is not passive activity income or loss. Therefore, it does not enter onto Form 8582, although some of it may be reported on Schedule E. The income from a "regular" interest is interest income. The taxpayer receives a Form 1099 from the REMIC and reports that amount on Form 1040, line 8a or Schedule B.

For the residual interest, the holder is treated like a partner in a partnership. Rather than sending a K-1 annually, the REMIC sends Form 1066, Schedule Q, each quarter. The holder's treatment of this income or loss is not passive activity income or loss, but has other complications.

If the taxpayer does not agree with the amounts reported by the REMIC, he or she should file Form 8082, discussed previously under Part III, to notify the IRS of the contrary position on the return. Note that this greatly increases the probability of examination, so Form 8082 should be filed with great care. However, it is probably better to file this form than to merely ignore the figures on Form 1066, Schedule Q, or to knowingly report erroneous items on a tax return.

Line 38, Income and Loss Details

Form 1066, Schedule Q, line 2c is the smallest amount reportable as taxable income or as alternative minimum taxable income (AMTI). This is really a black box calculation made by the REMIC. The holder reports this total for the year on Schedule E, line 38, column (c). The taxpayer must compare this total with his or her taxable income on line 43, Form 1040, as computed without this item. If this amount does not exceed the otherwise taxable income on line 43 of Form 1040, it does not enter into the income tax calculation, *per se.* However, the taxpayer must also compare this figure with the alternative minimum taxable income, calculated without regard to this amount, which is found on Form 6251, line 29. If line 29 exceeds column (c), no further action is necessary. However, if line 29 of Form 6251 is less than column (c), AMTI must be increased up to this amount.

Form 1066, Schedule Q lists the holder's share of net residual income on line 1b and the share of investment expenses on line 3b. These are entered on Schedule E, line 38, columns (d) and (e), respectively.

The individual holder must add these two together, even though it is intuitively illogical to include an item that is designated as an expense on Schedule Q as income on Schedule E. However, the amount on line 1b is net of the investment expenses, so the individual holder must gross it up for the amount of these expenses, and then report the expenses as a Schedule A itemized deduction, subject to the 2% adjusted gross income (AGI) limit.

Line 39, REMIC Total

Only columns (d) and (e) of line 38 are combined on line 39.

Part V: Summary

Line 40, Net Farm Rental Income or Loss

A taxpayer who receives rental income from farming may have up to three places to report his or her income.

A taxpayer who materially participates in the farming business and receives crop rents must report the income and deductions on Schedule F.

Cash rents that are not dependent upon production are reported on Schedule E, Part I, in the same manner as other real estate rental income.

Cash rents based on production, where the owner (or sublessor) does not materially participate, are reported on Form 4835 and then on Schedule E, line 40. This net income or loss from each identifiable farming activity must also be reported on Form 8582, unless the taxpayer is not required to submit this form. If this rental activity shows a loss for the year, it is subject to the cutback imposed by the passive activity loss rules before the amount allowable is transferred to line 40.

Line 41, Total Income or Loss

This line shows the total of all ordinary income or deductible loss from all of the activities reported on Schedule E. Although there are two additional lines on Schedule E, this is the final amount that flows to

Form 1040. The taxpayer must enter this total on Form 1040, page 1, line 17.

Line 42, Reconciliation of Farming and Fishing Income

On line 42, the taxpayer shows the amount of gross income from farming and fishing. This amount is taken from Form 4835, line 7 and includes any gross income from farming and fishing reported to the taxpayer by partnerships, S corporations, estates, and trusts.

The major significance of this amount is its effect on estimated tax payments. To calculate estimated tax payments required, the amount from line 42 of Schedule E must be combined with gross income from Schedule F and with the gains from the sales of certain livestock on Form 4797. However, cash rents reported in Part I of Schedule E are not included in farming or fishing income. If less than two-thirds of the taxpayer's gross income from all sources is from farming and fishing, this figure has no other significance. However, if the gross income from farming and fishing is at least two-thirds of the taxpayer's gross income, there are special estimated tax rules.

If the taxpayer pays all tax due by January 15 of the following year, there is no penalty for failing to pay quarterly estimates. If the taxpayer misses this date, but files Form 1040 by March 1 of the succeeding year, and pays the tax due in full with the return, there is no penalty for failure to pay estimated tax.

If the taxpayer does not pay all tax due by January 15 and does not file and pay by March 1, the penalty period is from January 15 of the subsequent year to April 15, or three months. In addition, the required estimate is only two-thirds of the current tax, as opposed to 90% for most taxpayers. See Tabs 3 and 11 for more information about these special rules that apply to farmers and fishermen.

Example. Alistair Brown has $10,000 in tax liability for 2009, including all income tax, self-employment tax, and alternative minimum tax, after subtracting credits. His 2008 tax was higher than $10,000, so he does not qualify for an underpayment exception based on the prior year's tax. He files his return and pays his tax on April 15, 2010.

If he does not meet the farming gross income test, his estimated tax payments must be at least 90% of the tax due, or $9,000. The penalty dates for 2009 are April 15 for 25% of the $9,000, or $2,250; June 16 for $2,250; September 15 for $2,250; and January 15, 2010, for $2,250. If he does qualify for the farming exception his required estimated tax payment is only $6,667 and the penalty period for the entire amount runs from January 15 to April 15, 2010.

Line 43, Reconciliation for Real Estate Professionals

This line does not directly feed into any other schedule or form. It is the net income from real estate rental activities in which the taxpayer materially participated, if he or she is a real estate professional. The significance of this is that real estate rentals are treated as trades or businesses, rather than *per se* rental activities, if the taxpayer qualifies for this status.

Planning Tip. Electronic filing limits the number of Schedule Es to five forms. If more forms are required a paper return must be filed.

Comprehensive Example of Schedule E

Pam Stanley is a real estate dealer. In addition to $175,000 in real estate commissions reported on Form 1099, she has the following items for the current tax year:

Activity	Income and Loss
A number of rental duplexes that she actively manages. She spent 800 hours in the current year. No other person participates in management of this activity.	Current income $14,000, deductions $18,000. In the previous tax year, $2,500 was disallowed due to at-risk limits. She invested an additional $10,000 in this activity in the current tax year. No passive activity loss deductions suspended from prior year.
Limited real estate partnership interest, in which she does not participate.	Schedule K-1 shows $3,000 rental loss and $2,000 interest income. $1,800 deductions suspended from prior year.
Equipment leasing partnership. Pam holds a limited interest.	Schedule K-1 shows $4,000 net rental loss. Suspended passive activity loss of $6,000 from prior years.
Joint ownership in apartment complex. She participated about 50 hours this year, and others participated more.	$2,500 net rental loss, and $7,000 gain from sale of her entire interest to an unrelated party this year. $1,500 suspended passive activity loss from prior year.

Each of these items will be treated as follows:

Activity	Information Comes From	Where Reported
Rental duplexes	Books and records, last year's Form 6198	All to Schedule E Part I. None of these items go to Form 8582, since she is a material participant, using the real estate professional rules.
Limited real estate partnership	Form 1065, Schedule K-1, last year's Form 8582	Interest income does not go to Schedule E or Form 8582, but directly to Form 1040, Line 8a and Schedule B. Net rental loss from current year and prior year will go to Form 8582, and any allowable amount will be reported on Schedule E, Part II.
Equipment leasing partnership	Form 1065, Schedule K-1, last year's Form 8582	Net rental loss from current year and prior year will go to Form 8582, and any allowable amount will be reported on Schedule E, Part II.
Apartment complex	Books and records, last year's Form 8582, closing statement on sale	Gain from sale goes to Form 8582, and then to Form 4797. Current and last year's loss will go to Form 8582, but only to offset gain. Net loss will be allowed in full on Schedule E, Part I, because the joint ownership arrangement does not constitute a partnership.

Pam needs to fill out the following schedules.

Schedule E Part I	
Rental duplex, line 3	$ 14,000
Lines 5 through 21	18,000
Line 22, and 23, including $2,500, noted on line 23 with notation "PYA." This does not feed into Form 8582, since she materially participates, and is a real estate professional.	(6,500)

Form 8582, Worksheets

There are no entries to worksheets 1 and 2, since Pam does not have any passive real estate rentals in which she actively participates. Moreover, her AGI is too high to claim any active participation loss. She has no commercial revitalization deduction expenses which would qualify for that special deduction. Worksheet 3 is where she will begin her inputs for this form.

Real Estate Partnership		Apartment	
Worksheet 3, column b	$ 3,000	Worksheet 3, column a	$7,000
Worksheet 3, column c	1,800	Worksheet 3, column b	2,500
Worksheet 3, column e	4,800	Worksheet 3, column c	1,500
		Worksheet 3, column d	3,000
Equipment Leasing Partnership		**Totals for This Worksheet**	
Worksheet 3, column b	$ 4,000	Column a	$7,000
Worksheet 3, column c	6,000	Column b	9,500
Worksheet 3, column e	10,000	Column c	9,300

These totals then go to the front page of Form 8582.

Line 3a	$ 7,000
Line 3b	(9,500)
Line 3c	(9,300)

Line 3d shows a loss of ($11,800.00). Since there are no entries on lines 1d or 2d, the same ($11,800.00) goes to line 4.

Line 15	$7,000
Line 16	7,000

Now she must return to the worksheets, and will use worksheet 5. This worksheet requires that she apportion the losses between all passive activities, and determine the disallowed portion. It is not an obvious transition from page 1. The loss in column a comes from the losses in column e of worksheet 3. The total of these losses is then prorated by percentage in column b. The total in column c is the total passive activity loss for the year from line 4 of page 1 ($11,800) less the sum of the special allowance for rental real estate activities with active participation from line 10 of page 1 ($0) and the special allowance for commercial revitalization deductions from rental real estate activities ($0).

Activity	Form or Schedule Where Reported	(a) Loss	(b) Ratio	(c) Unallowed Loss
Limited real estate partnership	E	$ 4,800	.3243	$ 3,827
Equipment leasing partnership	E	10,000	.6757	7,973
Total		14,800	1.00	11,800

For this year, Pam's final step in completing Form 8582 is to fill out worksheet 6, as follows:

Activity	Form or Schedule Where Reported	(a) Loss	(b) Unallowed Loss	(c) Allowed Loss
Limited real estate partnership	E	$ 4,800	$ 3,827	$ 973
Equipment leasing partnership	E	10,000	7,973	2,027
Total		14,800	11,800	3,000

Now Pam returns to Schedule E, where she needs to complete the following:

Part I, line 25		$ 10,500
Part I, line 26		(10,500)
Part II, line 27		Check no
Part II, line 28	a	(name of partnership)
	b	Enter p
	c	Check if foreign
	d	EIN
	e	Do not check
	f	973
		2,027
Part II, line 29	f	3,000
Part II, line 31		3,000
Part II, line 32		(3,000)
Part V, line 41		(13,500)
Schedule E, line 43		(10,500)

Form 2106

What's New in 2009

Business Mileage Rate. In 2009, the standard rate for business miles driven is 55 cents per mile.

High-Low Rates. In 2009, for travel from January 1 through September 30, the per diem rates under the "high-low" substantiation method are $256 for "high-cost" localities and $158 for all other localities. For travel on and after October 1, the rates are $258 for "high-cost" localities and $163 for all other localities.

"Bumping" Rights. An airline mechanic who was laid off from his Minneapolis job but who "bumped" more junior mechanics from their jobs in other cities was not "away from home" and could not deduct travel and lodging expenses incurred while he worked those jobs (*D.A. Wilbert*).

Tax Preparer's Checklist

The following items are required:

- ☐ Review employer pay stubs for deductions and reimbursements.
- ☐ Verify employer's policy for travel and entertainment reimbursements.
- ☐ Interview filer for ordinary and necessary work-related expenses.
- ☐ Compile mileage records, with vehicle type and odometer readings.
- ☐ Review meal and entertainment expense documentation.

Section at a Glance

Relevant IRS Publications

- ☐ IRS Publication 463, *Travel, Entertainment, Gift, and Car Expenses*
- ☐ IRS Publication 529, *Miscellaneous Deductions*
- ☐ IRS Publication 535, *Business Expenses*
- ☐ IRS Publication 1542, *Per Diem Rates*

2009 Federal Per Diem Rates for Some Common U.S. Destinations

City		Maximum Lodging		Meals and Incidentals Rate		Max Per Diem Rate	
		Before Oct. 1*	After Sept. 30	Before Oct. 1*	After Sept. 30	Before Oct. 1*	After Sept. 30
Chicago, IL	*Jan. 1 – Apr. 30*	157	158	64	71	221	229
	May 1 – Jun. 30	209	211	64	71	273	282
	Jul. 1 – Aug. 31	177	176	64	71	241	247
	Sep. 1 – Nov. 30	218	205	64	71	282	276
	Dec. 1 – Dec. 31	157	158	64	71	221	229
Houston, TX		110	118	59	71	169	189
Las Vegas, NV	*Jan. 1 – May 31*	126	118	64	71	190	189
	Jun. 1 – Dec. 31	105	109	64	71	169	180
Los Angeles, CA		128	135	64	71	192	206
Manhattan, NY	*Jan. 1 – Mar.31*	285	209	64	71	349	280
	Apr. 1 – Jun. 30	285	318	64	71	349	389
	Jul. 1 – Aug. 31	259	279	64	71	323	350
	Sep. 1 – Dec. 31	360	340	64	71	424	411
Orlando, FL	*Jan. 1 – Mar. 31*	133	117	49	56	182	173
	Apr. 1 – Dec. 31	109	108	49	56	158	164

* Note that this rate may be used for all of 2009; see text. Complete per diem listings begin on page 6-17.

Employee Business Expenses

Substantiation and Reporting of Expenses

The treatment and reporting of an employee's business expenses differs depending on whether and how the expenses are reimbursed.

Most employees account for their expenses to their employers and then receive reimbursements. If the reimbursement arrangement constitutes an "accountable plan" as defined by the IRS, the reimbursement normally is equivalent to the expenses, and nothing appears on the employee's tax return. If the expenses are not reimbursed or the reimbursement is less than the expenses incurred, or the reimbursement arrangement does not qualify as an "accountable plan," the unreimbursed expenses are reported on Form 2106 and are treated as miscellaneous itemized deductions on Schedule A. (See page 6-13, "Accountable and Nonaccountable Plans".)

If the reimbursements received from the employer are reported in box 1 of Form W-2 as gross wages, a determination should be made as to whether this is the proper treatment. Normally, reimbursements for expenses that are properly accounted for should not be treated as wages. See MTG ¶942 and ¶952A.

Substantiation Requirements for 2009 Expenses

Category of Expense	Details Required in Records			
	Amount	**Time**	**Place or Description**	**Business Purpose and Business Relationship**
Travel	Cost of each separate expense for travel, lodging, and meals. Incidental expenses may be totaled in reasonable categories such as taxis, daily meals for traveler, etc.	Dates taxpayer left and returned for each trip and number of days spent on business.	Destination or area of taxpayer's travel (name of city, town, or other designation).	**Purpose:** Business purpose for the expense or the business benefit gained or expected to be gained. **Relationship:** N/A
Entertainment	Cost of each separate expense. Incidental expenses such as taxis, telephones, etc., may be totaled on a daily basis.	Date of entertainment. (Also see *Business Purpose.*)	Name and address or location of place of entertainment. Type of entertainment if not otherwise apparent. (Also see *Business Purpose.*)	**Purpose:** Business purpose for the expense or the business benefit gained or expected to be gained. For entertainment, the nature of the business discussion or activity. If the entertainment was directly before or after a business discussion: the date, place, nature, and duration of the business discussion, and the identities of the persons who took part in both the business discussion and the entertainment activity. **Relationship:** Occupations or other information (such as names, titles, or other designations) about the recipients that shows their business relationship to taxpayer. For entertainment, must also prove that taxpayer or taxpayer's employee was present if the entertainment was a business meal.
Gifts	Cost of the gift. (Deduction limited to $25 per recipient per year.)	Date of the gift.	Description of the gift.	(See Entertainment, above.)
Transportation	Cost of each separate expense. For car expenses: cost of the car and any improvements, date taxpayer started using it for business, mileage for each business use, and total miles for the year.	Date of the expense. For car expenses, the date of the use of the car.	Taxpayer's business destination.	**Purpose:** Business purpose for the expense. **Relationship:** N/A

Statutory Employees. An important rule applies to "statutory employees," such as outside salesmen (e.g., traveling salesmen), life insurance salesmen, certain agent or commission drivers and certain homeworkers. These taxpayers can report their unreimbursed deductible expenses on Schedule C. Thus a statutory employee avoids both having to itemize deductions and the 2% of AGI limitation imposed on miscellaneous itemized deductions. Employers normally check box 13 on Form W-2 to indicate that the taxpayer is a statutory employee. If the employee is a statutory employee and the employer has failed to check this box, the employee should contact the employer to obtain a corrected Form W-2 with box 13 checked. See Tab 3.

> **Caution.** Don't assume that the taxpayer is a "statutory employee" simply because he or she fits into a category mentioned above. Advise the employee to verify the classification with his or her employer.

Employee Business Expenses That Are Not Reimbursed

Unreimbursed employee expenses are treated as miscellaneous itemized deductions and are deductible to the extent that total miscellaneous itemized deductions exceed 2% of AGI. Miscellaneous itemized deductions are subject to the 3% cutback on total itemized deductions, and are added back to the income base in determining the alternative minimum tax. See Tabs 2 and 10.

Employee Business Expenses Reimbursed under an Accountable Plan

Employee expenses reimbursed under an accountable plan are not deductible by the employee, but the reimbursement is excludable from gross income. In effect, the reimbursement and expense offset each other, and there is no effect on the taxpayer's return.

An expense is considered "reimbursed" and eligible for this treatment only if the employer has an accountable plan.

Documentation

Under the *Cohan* rule, a reasonable estimate of an expense is normally considered sufficient documentation. However, the *Cohan* rule does not apply to travel and entertainment expenses. A taxpayer cannot deduct expenses for travel (including meals, unless the standard meal allowance is used), entertainment, gifts, or use of a car or other listed property (such as a computer) unless the taxpayer maintains records to prove five elements of the expense:

- Time;
- Place;
- Business purpose;
- Business relationship (for entertainment and gifts); and
- Amount.

The taxpayer must also keep receipts for all lodging expenses regardless of the amount (unless per diem allowances for lodging, meals and incidental expenses are used under an accountable plan); and for any other expense of $75 or more. The IRS provides a table in Publication 463 (reproduced on page 6-2) explaining the documentation required.

Note that documentation is required to substantiate the time, place, and purpose of travel (but not actual amounts paid), even if a per diem rate is used. See MTG ¶953 and ¶954.

> **Planning Tip.** By itself, a receipt is insufficient to meet the substantiation standards. A diary or some other type of record should be used to document the five elements, particularly the business purpose and business relationship, which are never included on the receipt. Records should be prepared at or near the time of the expense in order to meet the contemporaneous recordkeeping requirement. Court decisions have allowed calendars and other types of substantiation. A pocket calendar, PDA, or any other recordkeeping mechanism should work.

Per Diems and Car Allowances

The taxpayer can use a per diem or car allowance to satisfy the adequate accounting requirements for employee business expense amounts only if all of the following conditions apply:

- The employer reasonably limits payments of the taxpayer's expenses to those that are ordinary and necessary in the conduct of the business.
- The allowance is similar in form to and not more than the federal rate.
- The taxpayer proves the time, place and business purposes of his or her employee expenses to the employer within a reasonable time.
- The taxpayer is not related to his or her employer.

The taxpayer is related to the employer if any of the following apply:

- The employer is the taxpayer's spouse, brother, sister, half-brother, half-sister, ancestor or lineal descendant.
- The employer is a corporation in which the taxpayer owns, directly or indirectly, more than 10% in value of the outstanding stock.
- A grantor, fiduciary or beneficiary relationship exists between the taxpayer, a trust, and the employer.

Who Must File 2009 Form 2106?

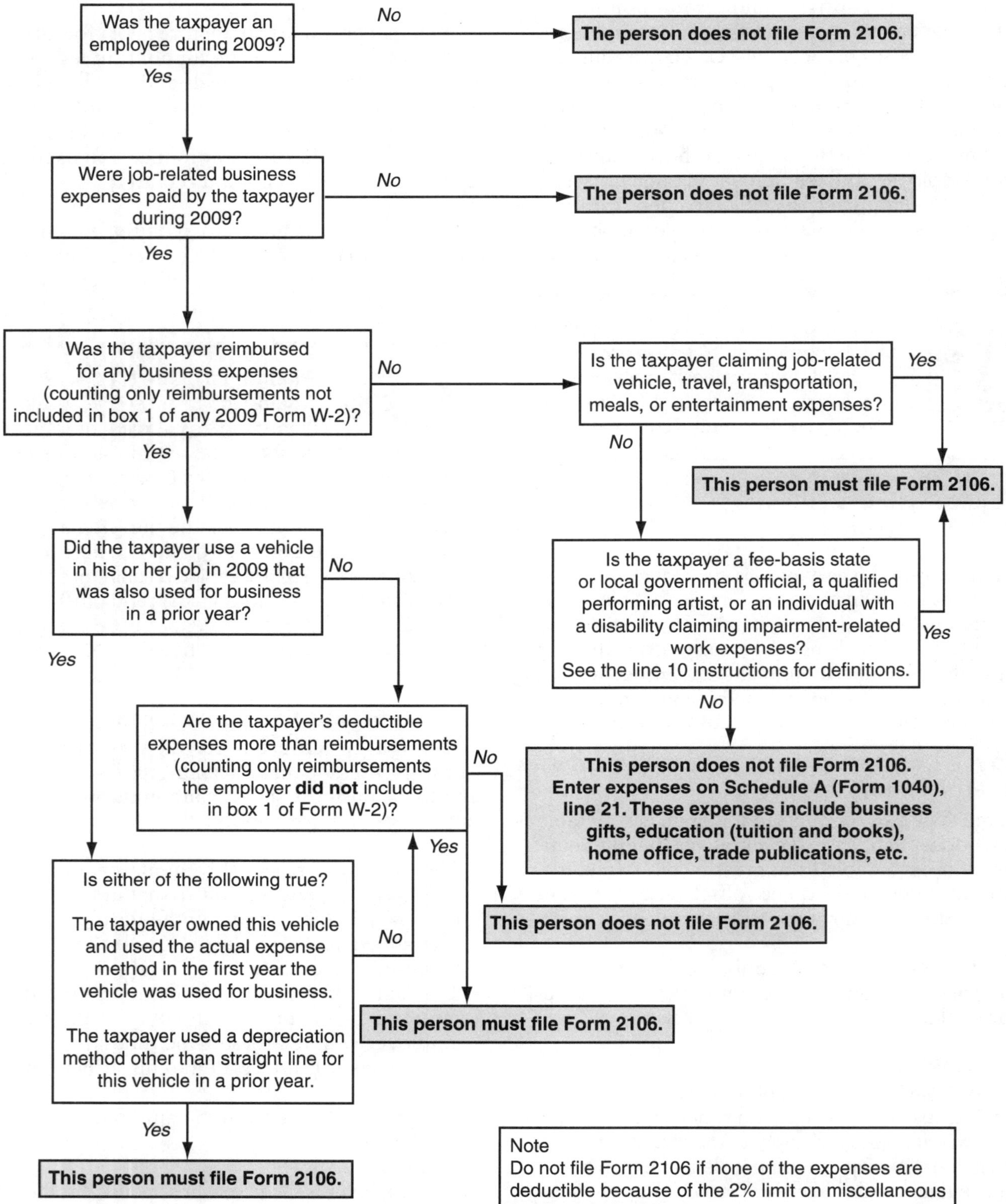

Note
Do not file Form 2106 if none of the expenses are deductible because of the 2% limit on miscellaneous itemized deductions.

Per Diems for Travel. For business travel within the continental United States (CONUS), the IRS provides taxpayers a choice of two per diem methods: high-low and regular federal per diem rate. Under the high-low method, expenses for travel to certain localities (see Tables 1 and 2, beginning at page 6-17) are deductible at a higher rate: $256 ($198 for lodging, $58 for meals and incidental expenses (M&IE)), effective through September 30, 2009; $258 ($193 for lodging, $65 for M&IE), effective October 1, 2009. Expenses for travel to localities that are within CONUS but not specifically listed in the per diem tables or within the boundary definition of a listed locality are deductible at a lower rate: $158 ($113 for lodging, $45 for M&IE), effective through September 30, 2009; $163 ($111 for lodging, $52 for M&IE), effective October 1, 2009.

The regular federal per diem rate method provides specific rates for many localities (see Tables 3 and 4, beginning at page 6-19). For localities that are within CONUS but not specifically listed in the per diem tables or within the boundary definition of a listed locality, a standard rate applies. Before October 1, 2009, the standard rate is $109 ($70 for lodging, $39 for M&IE); after September 30, 2009, the standard rate is $116 ($70 for lodging, $46 for M&IE). See MTG ¶954 and ¶954A.

Planning Tip. Taxpayers can find per diem rates for locations within CONUS in IRS Publication 1542, and at the U.S. General Services Administration website (www.gsa.gov). For locations outside the continental U.S. (OCONUS), such as Alaska, Hawaii, Guam, etc., and for foreign locations, rates are published at the Department of Defense Per Diem, Travel and Transportation Allowance Committee website (http://www.defensetravel.dod.mil/perdiem/perdiemrates.html).

Use by Employees and the Self-Employed. Employees and self-employed individuals who are not reimbursed may compute their allowable deductions for *meals and incidental expenses* while away from home by using the applicable federal M&IE rate. The time, place, and business purpose of the travel must still be substantiated. However, for *lodging expenses,* they must apply the actual amount, not the per diem rate, and must substantiate with the required documentation. See MTG ¶954B.

Prorated M&IE Rate. The M&IE rate is for a full 24-hour day of travel (i.e., 12:01 a.m. to 12 midnight). If the travel is only for a partial day, compute the M&IE rate (or the M&IE portion of the high-low or regular federal per diem rates) by either (1) allowing 75% of the M&IE rate for each partial day during which the employee or self-employed individual is traveling away from home on business, or (2) prorating the M&IE rate by using any method that is consistently applied and in accordance with reasonable business practice. See MTG ¶954A.

Standard Mileage Rate. See "Section B: Standard Mileage Rate" on page 6-15 for details.

Do You Need Form 2106?

Taxpayers normally report employee business expenses on Form 2106, Employee Business Expenses. The preparer should consult the flowchart on page 6-4 (similar to that in the Instructions to Form 2106) for determining whether or not the form should be filed.

Form 2106 is divided into Part I and Part II:

- Part I (page 1) is used to report deductible employee business expenses and reimbursements related to those expenses.
- Part II (page 2) is used to report information that must be provided if deductions are claimed for employee vehicle expenses. Total vehicle expenses calculated here are entered on line 1 of Part I.

Filing Tip. Form 2106-EZ, Unreimbursed Employee Business Expenses, is a one-page form which may be used if the taxpayer uses the standard mileage rate (if claiming vehicle expenses) and was not reimbursed for *any* expenses.

Part I: Employee Business Expenses and Reimbursements

Step 1: Enter Your Expenses

Unreimbursed employee business expenses are miscellaneous itemized deductions. This treatment is reflected in Part I of Form 2106. All expenses are reported in step 1 (lines 1-6). All reimbursements are reported in step 2 (line 7). The expenses identified in step 1 are reduced by any reimbursement reported in step 2, and the net amount appears in step 3 (line 8). The net effect is that neither the reimbursements nor the reimbursed expenses have any effect on the taxpayer's taxable income.

Part I includes two columns: column A, "Other Than Meals and Entertainment," and column B, "Meals and Entertainment." Column A requires information about all employee business expenses except those for meals and entertainment. Meals and entertainment are reported separately in column B, to accommodate the limitation imposed on their deduction. The deduction for unreimbursed meals and entertainment expenses is generally limited to 50% of their actual cost. Note that the 50% limitation is applied before the 2% of AGI floor for miscellaneous itemized deductions.

Line 1, Vehicle Expenses

This information is carried over from line 22 or line 29. The costs of operating a vehicle in a trade or business are generally deductible (see Tab 8 for more information). Such expenses are computed in Part II and the total is entered here.

Rural Mail Carriers. Employees of the U.S. Postal Service (USPS) who collect and deliver the mail on rural routes are subject to a special rule. If the employee received qualified reimbursements (i.e., certain equipment maintenance allowance amounts) for vehicle expenses incurred in performing services for USPS, he or she may deduct actual expenses that exceed the qualified reimbursements. In such case, total vehicle expenses from line 29 of Part II are carried over to line 1, and the qualified reimbursement amount is entered on line 7.

If vehicle expenses are less than or equal to the qualified reimbursement amount, the rural mail carrier does not have to file Form 2106 unless he or she has deductible employee business expenses other than vehicle expenses. In such case, the qualified reimbursement amount is not entered on line 7.

Caution. Rural mail carriers who receive qualified reimbursements cannot use the standard mileage rate.

Line 2, Parking Fees, Tolls, and Transportation

The costs of transportation incurred in a trade or business are deductible to the extent they are not the costs of commuting to and from work. Transportation expenses that do not involve overnight travel are reported on line 2. (Travel expenses that involve overnight stays are reported on line 3.) See MTG ¶945. Examples of expenses to report on line 2 include:

- Parking fees incurred while visiting customers or clients, but not those for parking at the taxpayer's regular place of business, which are considered nondeductible commuting costs.
- Tolls.
- Fares for transportation by train, bus, subway, taxi, or other form of paid conveyance.

Commuting. Costs of commuting between the taxpayer's home and his or her place of employment are nondeductible personal expenses, regardless of how far the taxpayer lives from work.

If the taxpayer carries tools, equipment, or similar items while commuting to and from work, a deduction may be allowed for additional expenses incurred (such as renting a trailer towed by the taxpayer's car to carry the equipment), notwithstanding the ban on deducting commuting expenses.

The IRS measures the taxpayer's "additional expenses" by applying the "same mode" test. Under this test, a deduction is allowed for the excess cost of commuting by one mode with the tools over the cost of commuting by the same mode without the tools. Thus, a carpenter who drives a truck would not be allowed a transportation deduction simply by loading it with tools, since carrying the tools created no additional expense. The fact that the carpenter might or would have used a less expensive mode of transportation were it not for the tools is immaterial.

Commuting from Home Office. If the taxpayer maintains an office in his or her home and qualifies for the home office deduction, the IRS permits a deduction specifically for the costs of transportation from the home to another work location in the same trade or business.

Commuting to a Temporary Work Location. If a taxpayer commutes to a temporary work location, the commuting expenses are deductible transportation costs if either of the following conditions is met:

- The taxpayer has no regular place of work, and the temporary work location is *outside* the metropolitan area where the taxpayer lives and normally works.
- The taxpayer has one or more regular work locations away from his or her residence and the temporary work location is *in the same trade or business*, regardless of the distance. If this condition applies, then the expenses of commuting between the taxpayer's residence and a temporary work location *within* the metropolitan area where the taxpayer lives and normally works are deductible.

A taxpayer's work location is *temporary* if he or she is realistically expected to be (and is in fact) employed at that location for one year or less.

Example. Marguerite is a claims adjuster for an insurance company that has its office in downtown Dallas. Marguerite works about 20% of the time in her employer's office, and the remaining 80% is spent at various sites throughout the state. Marguerite may deduct the costs of commuting between her residence and the site of an insurance claim because the site is a temporary work location and Marguerite otherwise has a regular place of business (i.e., her employer's office).

Example. Ed is an electrician. He works for EZS Inc. as an electrical contractor. Most of his assignments are located within about 25 miles of his employer's office. This year he spent most of his time installing electrical systems at two apartment complexes. Although Ed is assigned to temporary work locations, he is not allowed to deduct any of his commuting expenses because he does not otherwise have a regular place of business.

Union Members' Trips from a Union Hall. If a taxpayer obtains work assignments at a union hall and then proceeds to the assigned place of work, the costs of getting from the union hall to the place of work are nondeductible commuting expenses.

Caution. Merely displaying advertising on an automobile does not convert use of the car from personal to business use. Similarly, the cost of using a taxpayer's car in a nonprofit car pool are not deductible. Any payments received from passengers are not included in income but are considered reimbursements of expenses.

Line 3, Travel Expenses

Deductible expenses for overnight travel include lodging, airline, car rental, and similar costs. *Do not* include meals and entertainment on line 3. See MTG ¶952.

Travel Away from Home. A deduction is permitted for travel expenses while "away from home" in the pursuit of a trade or business. The taxpayer is considered to be "away from home" if (1) the taxpayer's duties require him or her to be away from his or her "tax home" for substantially longer than an ordinary day's work, and (2) the taxpayer needs sufficient time to sleep or rest to meet the demands of work while away from home. The taxpayer does not need to be away from his or her tax home for a whole day or even from dusk to dawn, as long as the taxpayer is relieved from work duties long enough to get necessary sleep or rest. Taking naps in the car does not satisfy the rest requirement. See MTG ¶949.

The IRS and the Tax Court have defined the term *tax home* to mean the business location of the taxpayer or the general vicinity of the taxpayer's employment, regardless of the location of the taxpayer's personal residence. If the taxpayer has more than one regular place of business, his or her tax home is the main place of business.

Example. Sasha is a traveling salesman living in St. Louis. His employer's office is also in St. Louis. The majority of his customers live in St. Louis. Sasha drove to Kansas City to call on several customers. He spent the night there and drove back home to St. Louis the next day. St. Louis is Sasha's tax home, the general vicinity of his employment. Sasha meets the away-from-home test since he was away overnight from his tax home, St. Louis. Thus Sasha may deduct his travel expenses to and from Kansas City as well his meals and lodging.

If the taxpayer has no principal place of business, his or her tax home is normally his or her residence. But if the taxpayer has no permanent place of residence, the taxpayer is considered an itinerant whose tax home is wherever his or her work is done.

Caution. An airline mechanic who was laid off from his Minneapolis job but who "bumped" more junior mechanics from their jobs in other cities for short periods could not deduct travel and lodging expenses incurred while he worked those jobs, because he was not "away from home." Unless the taxpayer has a business rather than a personal reason to live in two places, he cannot deduct his travel expenses if he decides not to move (*D.A. Wilbert*, CA-7).

Local Lodging Expenses. The IRS will allow deduction of lodging expenses *not* incurred while an employee is "traveling away from home" if (1) the lodging is temporary, and necessary for the employee to participate in or be available for the employer's bona fide business meeting or function; and (2) the expenses are or would otherwise be deductible by the employee as a business expense.

Business Straddling Weekend. A taxpayer may have away-from-home business that straddles a weekend.

For example, the taxpayer may have to attend business meetings on Friday and Monday. If the taxpayer remains at the location for business reasons (i.e., to attend the Monday meeting), the weekend days (Saturday and Sunday) should be treated as business days, the travel expenses for which are deductible.

Weekend Travel Home. If a taxpayer is out of town on a temporary business assignment for an extended period of time, he or she may decide to fly home for a weekend. The costs of the weekend trip home (transportation, plus meals and lodging en route) are deductible up to the amount the traveler would have spent on meals and lodging at the out-of-town location. Note, however, that this rule applies only if the traveler checks out of the out-of-town hotel before leaving for the weekend trip home and then re-registers. If the traveler retains the hotel room, the cost of the hotel room is deductible, and the deduction for the trip home (e.g., the airfare) is limited to what the traveler would have spent on meals during the weekend at the out-of-town location. The costs of meals and lodging purchased while at home for the weekend are not deductible.

Temporary Assignments. Taxpayers may deduct travel expenses incurred away from the principal place of business if an assignment away from home is temporary and not indefinite. Assignments in a single location lasting more than one year are not temporary but are considered indefinite. If a taxpayer anticipates an assignment to last more than a year or it actually exceeds one year, none of the taxpayer's travel expenses is deductible. See MTG ¶951.

Combined Business and Personal Travel. If a taxpayer travels within the United States (including all 50 states and the District of Columbia) combining business and personal activities, the taxpayer may deduct *all* of the costs of travel to and from the destination if the trip is *primarily* for business. The costs of side trips for personal purposes are not deductible. If the travel is primarily for personal purposes, none of the travel costs is deductible even though some business is conducted. However, any expenses incurred while at the destination that are directly related to business may be deducted. Observe that the taxpayer deducts either *all* of the *to-and-from* travel expenses or none of them–there is no allocation.

Travel Expenses for Another Individual. The taxpayer generally cannot deduct the travel expenses of a spouse, dependent, or other individual who accompanies the taxpayer on a business trip. However, a deduction is allowed for the travel expenses of someone who goes with the taxpayer if that person: (1) is the taxpayer's employee or a business associate (e.g., a current or prospective customer, client, supplier, agent, partner, or professional advisor); (2) has a bona fide business purpose for the travel; and (3) would otherwise be allowed to deduct the travel expenses. A bona fide business purpose exists if the taxpayer can prove a real business purpose for the individual's presence; incidental services are not enough to make the expenses deductible. See MTG ¶952.

Example. David drives to Philadelphia on business and takes his wife, Linda, with him. Linda is not David's employee, but occasionally types notes and performs other similar services for David, and joins him for lunches and dinners. Linda's services do not establish that her presence on the trip is necessary to the conduct of David's business, so her expenses are not deductible. David pays $105 per day for a double room; a single room costs $90 per day. He can deduct the total cost of driving his car to and from Philadelphia, but only $90 per day for his hotel room. If he uses public transportation, David can deduct only his fare.

Saturday Night Stayovers. Although an employee's out-of-town business work concludes on Friday, he or she may be asked to extend the business trip to take advantage of a low-priced airfare requiring a "Saturday night stayover." The savings in airfare may outweigh the costs of the additional meals and lodging. Meals and lodging expenses for a Saturday night stayover are deductible to the same extent as they would be for "normal" business travel away from home.

Travel Outside the United States. Transportation expenses incurred for travel to and from a foreign destination and other travel expenses must be allocated between business and personal activities. However, the foreign travel will be considered "entirely for business" and travel expenses will be fully deductible without allocation, even if the taxpayer did not spend all of his or her time on business activities, if *at least one* of the following conditions is satisfied:

- *Travel outside the United States does not exceed one week* (seven consecutive days). In counting the days outside of the United States, the day of departure from the United States is excluded but the day of return to the United States is included.
- *More than 75% of the days on the trip were devoted to business.* In determining whether a day is business or personal, a day is treated as a business day if during any part of the day the taxpayer's presence is required at a particular place for a business purpose, even if the taxpayer spends more time during normal working hours engaged in nonbusiness activity than in business activity. Weekends, holidays, or other "standby" days that fall between the taxpayer's business days are also

considered business days. However, such days are not business days if they fall at the end of the taxpayer's business activities and the taxpayer elects to stay merely for personal purposes. The day of departure and the day of return are both treated as business days.

- *A personal vacation was not a major consideration in making the trip.*
- *The taxpayer had no substantial control over arranging the business trip.* The taxpayer does not have "substantial control" over the trip if he or she is an employee who was reimbursed or paid a travel expense allowance, is not related to the employer, and is not a managing executive.

If none of those conditions is satisfied, the to-and-from travel expenses must be allocated. A deduction for the to-and-from travel expenses is not allowed if the trip is primarily personal. However, expenses that are directly related to the taxpayer's business upon arriving at the destination are deductible. See MTG ¶955.

> **Example.** Claudia is the chief financial officer of an international company located in Los Angeles. She called a meeting of the controllers of the European units, to be held in Madrid. Claudia leaves Los Angeles on Monday morning, and arrives in Madrid on Tuesday morning. On Tuesday afternoon, she takes a sightseeing tour of the city. On Wednesday, Claudia meets all day with the controllers. On Thursday, she leaves Madrid and arrives back in Los Angeles. Because Claudia was outside of the U.S. for less than a week, her trip is considered entirely for business. She may deduct all of her travel expenses subject to the normal rules for travel expenses.

Luxury Water Travel. Deductions for transportation by water are limited to twice the highest per diem amount allowable at the time of travel to federal employees while away from home but serving in the 48 contiguous states. See MTG ¶957.

Foreign Conventions. No deduction is allowed for travel expenses to attend a convention, seminar, or similar meeting outside of North America unless the taxpayer establishes *both* of the following:

- The meeting is directly related to the active conduct of his or her trade or business.
- It is as reasonable to hold the meeting outside North America as within North America.

North America includes the United States, its possessions, Canada, Mexico, jurisdictions that have entered into Compacts of Free Association with the U.S., and certain beneficiary countries (see IRS Publication 463 for a complete list). See MTG ¶960.

Cruise Ships. No deduction is allowed for the cost of attending a meeting conducted on a cruise ship unless all four of the following conditions are met:

- The ship is a vessel registered in the United States and sails *only* between ports in the United States or its possessions;
- The meeting is directly related to the taxpayer's business;
- The taxpayer signs and attaches to the return a statement regarding total days of the trip, total hours each day devoted to scheduled business activities, and a program of the activities; and
- The taxpayer attaches to the return a written statement signed by an officer of the organization or group sponsoring the meeting which includes a schedule of business activities of each day of the meeting, and the number of hours which the taxpayer attended the scheduled business activities.

For qualifying cruises, the maximum deduction is $2,000 per calendar year for each taxpayer.

> **Example.** Teresa traveled by cruise ship to Nassau for a business meeting in September 2009. The cruise took five days at a total cost of $5,000. Since the highest federal per diem rate allowed in September 2009 is $424, under the luxury water travel limitation, Teresa's deduction can be no more than ($424 × 2) × 5 = $4,240. However, because she did not attend a conference or similar meeting *on* the cruise ship, her trip is not subject to the $2,000 annual deduction limit for meetings held on cruise ships.

Line 4, Business Expenses Not Included on Lines 1 through 3

All deductible employee business expenses not listed on any other line of the form are entered on line 4. These include such expenses as business gifts, education (tuition and books), home office costs, trade publications, union dues, professional license fees, etc. Do not include the costs of meals and entertainment on line 4. Also, do not include any tuition and fees that the taxpayer deducted on line 34 of Form 1040, or educator expenses deducted on line 23 of Form 1040. See Tab 2 for details on other common employee business expenses.

Qualifying Education Expenses. An employee may deduct education expenses if the expenses satisfy *either* of the following conditions *and* are not considered personal or capital in nature, as discussed below:

- The education maintains or improves skills required of the taxpayer in his or her present work.
- The education meets express requirements imposed by either the individual's employer or applicable law, and the taxpayer must meet such requirements to retain his or her job, position, or rate of compensation.

Education expenses that meet either of these conditions are *not* deductible if they are considered personal or capital expenditures under either of the following two tests:

- The education is necessary to meet the minimum educational requirements of the taxpayer's trade or business.
- The education qualifies the taxpayer for a new trade or business.

Travel as a form of education. No deduction is allowed for travel alone, notwithstanding the fact that it may be educational. Deductions are allowed for travel only when the education activity otherwise qualifies and the travel expense is necessary to pursue such activity. For example, a deduction for travel expenses would be allowed where a professor of French literature travels to France to take courses that are offered only at the Sorbonne.

Types of deductible education expenses. Typical deductible education expenses are for continuing professional education programs, professional development courses, college courses related to the taxpayer's trade or business, vocational courses, or similar courses or seminars. Deductible expenses include costs of tuition, books, supplies, typing, transportation, and travel (including meals, lodging, and similar expenses).

Transportation expenses for going between the taxpayer's place of work and the educational location are deductible. If the taxpayer goes home before going to the educational location, however, the expense of going from home to the location is deductible, but only to the extent that it does not exceed the costs of going directly to the location from work.

According to IRS Publication 970, *Tax Benefits for Education,* if the taxpayer is regularly employed and goes directly from home to school on a temporary basis, the cost of round-trip transportation between home and school is deductible, regardless of the school's location, the distance traveled, or whether the taxpayer attends school on nonwork days. A taxpayer attends school on a "temporary basis" if his or her attendance is realistically expected to last–and does last–one year or less. If, at a later date, the taxpayer later reasonably expects attendance to last longer, attendance is temporary only up to that later date. Attendance is not temporary if facts and circumstances indicate otherwise.

Caution. The Tax Court has both disallowed the deduction for transportation costs between home and school (*E.J. Zimmerman; D.M. Jouett*), and allowed the deduction to the extent of the excess of commuting costs between home and work (*G.F. Boerner; O. Gilliam*).

Line 5, Meal and Entertainment Expenses

Although meal and entertainment expenses may contain personal elements, such costs may be deducted if they are business related. Generally, expenses for meals are deductible if the taxpayer is traveling away from home on business and must stop for substantial sleep or rest to properly perform his or her duties, and the meals are not lavish or extravagant under the circumstances. See MTG ¶949 and ¶952.

Entertainment includes any activity generally considered to provide entertainment, amusement or recreation. Expenses for entertainment and "entertainment-related" meals (see "Entertainment-Related Business Meals" discussion on page 6-11) are deductible only if they:

- Represent an ordinary and necessary expense incurred in carrying on the taxpayer's trade or business; *and*
- Are *either* "directly related to" *or* "associated with" the taxpayer's business.

The taxpayer must meet strict substantiation requirements. For exceptions to the entertainment rules, see Tab 3 and MTG ¶915.

Directly Related Expenses. Expenses for entertainment and entertainment-related meals are considered *directly related* to the business if the taxpayer can show all of the following:

- More than a general expectation of deriving some income or other specific benefit (other than goodwill) existed as a result of making the expenditure; no resulting benefit must be shown, however.
- Business was actually discussed or engaged in during the entertainment or meal.
- The main purpose of the combined business and entertainment or meal was the active conduct of business.

"Associated With" Expenses. Expenses for entertainment and entertainment-related meals are considered *associated with* the taxpayer's business if the taxpayer can show that:

- He or she had a clear business purpose in making the expenditure, such as to obtain new business or to encourage the continuation of an existing business relationship; and
- The entertainment or meal occurs immediately before or after a substantial and bona fide business discussion.

In determining whether the expenses are "immediately before or after," it is sufficient if the entertainment or meal takes place on the same day as the business activity. In some cases, the entertainment or meal may take place on the day before or after the business activity.

> **Example.** The Cadillac division of General Motors provides a golf clinic for its franchise owners on the day before a business meeting. The clinic is deductible under the "associated with" test.

Entertainment-Related Business Meals. Entertainment includes the cost of a meal the taxpayer *provides to a customer or client,* whether the meal is part of other entertainment or by itself. Like other entertainment expenses, entertainment-related meal expenses are deductible only if they satisfy the "directly related" or "associated with" test. In addition, the meal must not be lavish or extravagant under the circumstances, and the taxpayer or his or her employee normally must be present at the meal. For example, if the taxpayer merely reserves a table for dinner at a restaurant for a customer but does not attend the dinner, no deduction is allowed. See MTG ¶914.

The IRS allows the taxpayer a deduction for his or her own business meal except in abusive situations where it is apparent that substantial personal expenditures are being deducted. The taxpayer cannot claim the cost of his or her business meal both as an entertainment expense and a travel expense.

Entertainment Facilities. Costs related to the ownership, rental or use of any entertainment facility (e.g., yacht, skybox, hunting lodge) are not deductible. However, out-of-pocket expenses incurred while at the entertainment facility for such items as food or beverage are deductible, assuming they meet the "directly related" or "associated with" test. See MTG ¶913.

Club Dues. No deduction is allowed for the cost of membership in any club organized for business, pleasure, recreation, or any other social purpose. The rule applies not only to country clubs but to all types of clubs, including luncheon, social, athletic, airline, and hotel clubs. However, dues paid to civic organizations, such as the Kiwanis or Rotary Club, or to professional organizations, such as a bar association, are deductible as long as the organization's principal purpose is not entertainment. Any specific expense incurred at a club, such as a business meal, is deductible to the extent that it meets the other applicable requirements for business expenses. See MTG ¶913A.

Standard Meal Allowance. To calculate the amount of meal expenses, before reimbursement and application of the 50% limit, taxpayers may either use the actual cost of their meals or a "standard meal allowance" provided by the IRS. The standard meal allowance allows taxpayers to use a set amount for their daily meals and incidental expenses (M&IE) incurred in connection with business travel away from home. The amount differs by travel location. The standard meal allowance cannot be used if the taxpayer is related to his or her employer, unless the taxpayer receives an allowance from the employer *only* for M&IE. There are two methods for determining M&IE under the standard meal allowance: high-low and the regular federal per diem rate (see "Per Diems and Car Allowances" on page 6-3 for more details).

Meals & Incidentals Breakdown until 9/30/09

M&IE Rate	$39	$44	$49	$54	$59	$64
Breakfast	7	8	9	10	11	12
Lunch	11	12	13	15	16	18
Dinner	18	21	24	26	29	31
Incidentals	3	3	3	3	3	3

Meals & Incidentals Breakdown effective 10/1/09

M&IE Rate	$46	$51	$56	$61	$66	$71
Breakfast	7	8	9	10	11	12
Lunch	11	12	13	15	16	18
Dinner	23	26	29	31	34	36
Incidentals	5	5	5	5	5	5

"Incidental expenses" means:

- fees and tips to porters, baggage carriers, bellhops, hotel maids, stewards or stewardesses and others on ships, and hotel servants in foreign countries;
- the costs of transportation between places of lodgings or business and places where meals are taken; and
- mailing costs associated with filing travel vouchers and paying employer-sponsored charge card billings.

A taxpayer has the option of deducting only incidental expenses if no meal expenses are incurred. The amount of this deduction is $3 a day for travel during 2009, $5 a day for travel during 2010. See MTG ¶954B.

Per diem rates change on October 1 of each year, but a taxpayer may elect to use the "before Sept. 30" rates for the entire year. See the "transition rule" for the high-low substantiation method on page 6-17, and for the standard federal per diem method on page 6-37.

Transportation industry workers. A special standard meal allowance applies to taxpayers whose work (1) directly involves moving people or goods by airplane, barge, bus, ship, train, or truck; and (2) regularly requires travel away from home which, during any single trip, usually involves travel to localities with differing federal M&IE rates. Before October 1, 2009, the special rate is $52 per day ($58 per day for travel outside the continental United States (OCONUS)); after September 30, 2009, the special rate is $59 per day ($65 per day for OCONUS travel).

Entertainment Expenses for Spouses. The taxpayer generally cannot deduct the cost of entertainment for his or her spouse or for the spouse of a customer. However, these costs are deductible if the taxpayer can show that he or she had a clear business purpose for providing the entertainment, rather than a personal or social purpose.

Example. Kevin entertains a customer. The cost is an ordinary and necessary business expense and is allowed under the entertainment rules. The customer's spouse joins them because it is impractical to entertain the customer without the spouse. Kevin can deduct the cost of entertaining the customer's spouse. If Kevin's spouse joins the party because the customer's spouse is present, the cost of entertaining Kevin's spouse is also deductible.

50% Limitation. The amount that can be deducted for meals and entertainment is limited to 50% of the allowable expense. For employees whose entertainment expenses are *not reimbursed* or are reimbursed under a nonaccountable plan, the 50% limitation is applied before the 2% of AGI floor for itemized deductions. See Tab 2.

Expenses subject to the 50% limitation include the costs of taxes, tips, and parking related to a meal or an entertainment activity. Costs of transportation to and from the activity are not subject to the limitation.

The 50% reduction is calculated on column B of line 9. Therefore, the full amount of qualifying meal and entertainment expenses should be entered on line 5.

Example. Dale, an employee, pays $2,500 for entertaining clients, including meals. He was not reimbursed. The amount of the 50% limitation is calculated as follows:

Total unreimbursed meals and entertainment expenses	$2,500
Less: 50% reduction (50% × $2,500)	(1,250)
Amount reported on line 9 (col. B) of Form 2106	1,250

Certain transportation workers are allowed to deduct more than 50% of the cost of their meals consumed while away from home. Individuals subject to Department of Transportation hours of service rules may deduct 80% of their meal expenses. The hours of service rules apply to such workers as airplane pilots, crew, dispatchers, mechanics, and control tower operators under Federal Aviation Administration regulations; interstate truck operators and bus drivers under Department of Transportation regulations; certain railroad employees such as engineers, conductors, train crews, dispatchers, and control operations personnel under Federal Railroad Administration regulations; and certain merchant mariners under Coast Guard regulations. The special rule exists because workers in these industries are frequently forced to eat meals away from home in circumstances where their choices are limited, prices are comparatively high, and the opportunity for lavish meals is remote.

For exceptions to the 50% limitation on meal and entertainment expenses, see Tab 3 and MTG ¶917.

Line 6: Total Expenses

In column A, the sum of lines 1 through 4 is entered on line 6. In column B, the amount from line 5 is entered on line 6.

Step 2: Enter Reimbursements Received from Your Employer for Expenses Listed in Step 1

Line 7, Employer Reimbursements

Note: If the taxpayer was not reimbursed for any expenses in step 1, skip line 7 and enter the amount from line 6 on line 8.

Enter reimbursements received from an employer that were not reported in box 1 of Form W-2. If the amounts were included in gross wages on the W-2, they are not reported here.

Include any reimbursements reported under code L in box 12 of Form W-2. The code L amounts are reimbursements made to the employee under an accountable plan arrangement. Reimbursements paid under an accountable plan are not reported as income.

Accountable and Nonaccountable Plans. The tax treatment of an employee's business expenses depends upon whether his or her employer's reimbursement or expense allowance arrangement is an accountable or nonaccountable plan. An arrangement is an *accountable plan* if it satisfies the following:

- The employee must properly substantiate the expenses to the employer;
- In the case of advances or allowances (i.e., per diems), the employee must return to the employer any amount in excess of substantiated expenses; and
- The expenses must have a business connection.

Amounts paid under an accountable plan are excluded from gross income, are not reported on the employee's Form W-2, and are exempt from employment taxes (i.e., Social Security and unemployment). If expenses equal reimbursements, the taxpayer does not need to complete Form 2106 and has no business expense deduction.

If the arrangement does not meet one or more of the accountable plan requirements, it is considered a *nonaccountable plan*, in which case the following treatment applies:

- Reimbursements and advances made to the employee must be reported in the employee's gross income, are included on Form W-2, and are subject to employment taxes.
- The employee taxpayer must complete Form 2106 or Form 2106-EZ and itemize deductions in order to deduct his or her business expenses. The taxpayer must substantiate the full amount of his or her expenses, including any that are treated as reimbursed under an accountable plan.
- The expense is treated as a miscellaneous itemized deduction subject to the 2% of AGI floor, and meals and entertainment expenses are subject to the 50% limitation.

Planning Tip. Taxpayers should encourage their employers to establish accountable plans if such arrangements are not offered, or they could face greater tax burdens. If the employer's plan is not accountable or if there is no plan, all or part of the business expense deduction could be lost if the taxpayer cannot meet the 2% of AGI floor, or if the taxpayer's AGI is above the threshold amount that subjects miscellaneous itemized deductions to the 3% cutback. See Tab 2.

The taxpayer is deemed to have properly substantiated an expense if either:

- The employer gave the taxpayer a fixed travel allowance, such as a per diem, that falls within the government guidelines, and the taxpayer reports the time, place, and business purpose of the expenditure. In this case, the employee need not return any allowance received that exceeded expenses.
- The employer reimburses vehicle expenses at the standard mileage rate, and the taxpayer substantiates the date of each trip, mileage, and business purpose of the vehicle use.

Step 3: Figure Expenses to Deduct on Schedule A (Form 1040)

Line 8, Subtract Line 7 from Line 6

If the result is zero or less, enter -0-. However, if line 7 is greater than line 6 in column A, report the excess as income on Form 1040, line 7.

Note: If both columns of line 8 are zero, do not deduct employee business expenses. Stop here and attach Form 2106 to the return.

In step 3, the taxpayer compares the total reimbursements to total expenses. If reimbursements exceed expenses, the taxpayer reports the excess as income on line 7 of Form 1040. If the expenses exceed the reimbursements, the taxpayer proceeds with the computation of the final deduction to be claimed on line 21 of Schedule A. The amount in column A representing all business expenses other than meals and entertainment is the amount of the deduction subject to the 2% of AGI limitation on miscellaneous itemized deductions that is applied on Schedule A. No other calculation is required. The amount in column B is the deduction for meals and entertainment before reduction for the 50% disallowance.

Line 9

In Column A, Enter the Amount from Line 8. This is the amount of the deduction for employee business expenses, other than meals and entertainment, that is subject to the 2% of AGI limitation on Schedule A.

In Column B, Multiply Line 8 by 50% (0.50). In line 9, column B, the 50% limitation on meals and entertainment expenses is computed. The 50% limitation applies only to the unreimbursed expenses, and is applied before the 2% of AGI limitation is applied on Schedule A.

The deductible percentage of the cost of meals consumed while away from home on business is increased to 80% for transportation workers subject to Department of Transportation hours-of-service rules.

For more details, see “50% Limitation” on page 6-12.

Line 10, Add the Amounts on Line 9 of Both Columns

Total employee business expenses are the combination of the meals and entertainment expenses (after taking into account the appropriate percentage limitation) on line 9, column B, and all other employee business expenses in line 9, column A. This total is entered on line 10, and is transferred to line 21 of Schedule A (Form 1040), where it is aggregated with all other miscellaneous itemized deductions. This aggregate amount is potentially deductible as an itemized deduction to the extent it exceeds 2% of AGI. See Tab 2.

Special Rules for Certain Occupations

Armed Forces Reservists. Members of an armed forces reserve component who travel *more than 100 miles away from home* in connection with the performance of services as reservists can include those line 10 expenses for travel over 100 miles from home as an above-the-line deduction on line 24 of Form 1040. The expenses are not miscellaneous itemized deductions subject to the 2% of AGI limitation. The above-the-line deduction is limited to the regular federal per diem rate (for lodging, meals, and incidental expenses; see page 6-5) and the standard mileage rate (for car expenses; see page 6-15) plus any parking fees, ferry fees, and tolls. Any excess over those amounts is treated as a miscellaneous itemized deduction. See MTG ¶941E.

Members of a reserve component include individuals in the Army, Navy, Marine Corps, Air Force, or Coast Guard Reserve; the Army National Guard; the Air National Guard; or the Reserve Corps of the Public Health Service.

Fee-Basis State or Local Government Officials. A fee-basis state or local government official is an official who is an employee of a state or political subdivision of a state and is compensated in whole or in part on a fee basis. These individuals are entitled to include their line 10 employee business expenses incurred in that job on line 24 of Form 1040. The expenses are not miscellaneous itemized deductions subject to the 2% of AGI limitation. See MTG ¶941D.

Qualified Performing Artists. Employee business expenses of qualified performing artists should be reported on line 10 and also in the total on line 24 of Form 1040. A qualified performing artist meets all of the following tests:

(1) Performs services in the performing arts for at least two employers during the tax year;
(2) Has earnings of at least $200 from each employer;
(3) Has total performing-arts business deductions that exceed 10% of gross income from such services; and
(4) Has AGI before business deductions of $16,000 or less.

If the individual is married, he or she must file a joint return, and tests (1), (2) and (3) must be determined separately for each spouse; test (4) is determined using the spouses' combined AGIs.

If the individual fails to meet these tests, any unreimbursed employee business expenses are considered miscellaneous itemized deductions. See MTG ¶941A.

Disabled Individuals. Handicapped individuals are entitled to deduct the ordinary and necessary business expenses incurred for attendant care services at their place of employment, or for other expenses in connection with the place of employment that are necessary for the individual to be able to work. Handicapped persons include individuals who have a physical or mental disability (including those who are blind or deaf) that limits employment, or a physical or mental impairment (including sight or hearing impairment) that substantially limits one or more major life activities. See MTG ¶1013.

If an employee is not reimbursed for these impairment-related work expenses, they are treated as itemized deductions but are not subject to the 2% of AGI limitation. The portion of the total employee business expenses from line 10 of Form 2106 that constitutes impairment-related work expenses is reported on line 28 of Schedule A (Form 1040), rather than line 21 for miscellaneous itemized deductions.

Part II: Vehicle Expenses

Section A: General Information, Lines 11-21

An employee's vehicle expenses are reported in Part II of Form 2106. There are two methods for computing vehicle expenses: the actual expense method and the standard mileage rate. See Tab 8 for more details on vehicle expenses.

Part II has four sections:

- Section A requests general information about mileage driven, including business use, personal use, and commuting. Section A also asks whether evidence exists to support the deduction for vehicle expenses and whether it is written.
- Section B is used to compute the deduction using the standard mileage rate.
- Section C is used to compute the deduction using actual expenses.
- Section D is used to compute the amount of depreciation to be reported in Section C.

Only the sections necessary for the reporting method selected should be completed.

Line 11, Enter the Date the Vehicle Was Placed in Service

The date the vehicle was placed in service is generally the date the taxpayer first started using the vehicle for business. See Tab 8.

Line 12, Total Miles Driven in 2009

Record the total number of miles driven for each vehicle used during 2009 (both business and personal). If the taxpayer converted a vehicle during the year from personal to business use (or from business to personal use), record the total miles for only the months the taxpayer drove the vehicle for business.

Line 13, Business Miles

Record the total business miles driven during the year. Do not include commuting mileage, which is not considered business mileage. (See the discussion of line 15, below, for what constitutes "commuting.")

Line 14, Percent of Business Use

Determine the business use percentage by dividing line 13 business miles by line 12 total miles.

Caution. If the taxpayer has converted the vehicle from personal use to business use during the tax year but does not have mileage records for the period before the change, an additional calculation may be required to determine the business use percentage for the depreciation deduction. See IRS Pub. 463.

Line 15, Average Daily Round-Trip Commuting Distance

Report the taxpayer's daily round-trip commuting distance. If the taxpayer commutes to more than one work location, the average daily commuting distance should be reported.

According to the IRS, commuting is travel between the taxpayer's home and a work location. However, travel in the following situations is not "commuting":

- The taxpayer has at least one regular work location away from home (e.g., an insurance agent has an office), and the travel is to a temporary work location in the same trade or business regardless of the distance (e.g., a client's location). A temporary work location is one where employment is expected to last one year or less.
- The travel is to a temporary work location outside the metropolitan area where the taxpayer lives and normally works.
- The taxpayer maintains a qualified home office that is the principal place of business (see Tab 3), and the travel is to another work location in the same trade or business, regardless of whether that location is regular or temporary and regardless of distance.

Line 16, Commuting Miles

Report the total actual miles that the taxpayer used the vehicle for commuting during the year. If the actual commuting miles are unknown, multiply the average daily commuting miles by the number of days during the year that the vehicle was used for commuting. However, if the taxpayer converted the vehicle during the year from personal to business use (or vice versa), only the commuting miles for the period the vehicle was driven for business are reported.

Line 17, Other Miles

Add the business miles on line 13 and commuting miles on line 16, subtract this sum from the total miles on line 12, and enter the result on line 17.

Lines 18-21, Vehicle Business Expense Support

Due to the strict recordkeeping requirements of IRC § 274(d), the IRS must ask the following questions concerning substantiation:

	Yes	No
Line 18: Was your vehicle available for personal use during off-duty hours?	❐	❐
Line 19: Do you (or your spouse) have another vehicle available for personal use?	❐	❐
Line 20: Do you have evidence to support your deduction?	❐	❐
Line 21: If "Yes," is the evidence written?	❐	❐

Section B: Standard Mileage Rate

Line 22: Multiply Line 13 by 55¢

A taxpayer may use the standard mileage rate for a vehicle that is either owned or leased by the taxpayer. The taxpayer may deduct an amount equal to the standard rate times the number of business miles driven during the year. The deduction is in lieu of all actual vehicle expenses allocable to business use (i.e., maintenance, repairs, depreciation, insurance, license fees, etc.). Parking fees, tolls, personal property taxes, and interest relating to the vehicle's purchase may be deducted separately. Interest on a vehicle loan is deductible only if the taxpayer is self-employed and used the vehicle in the business.

To use the standard mileage rate, the taxpayer generally must do so in the first year the vehicle is placed in service. The standard mileage rate may not be available for all vehicles. See Tab 8.

Section C: Actual Expenses, Lines 23-29

In lieu of using the standard mileage rate to determine the vehicle expense deduction, taxpayers may report actual expenses, which normally include the costs for gas, oil, tires, repairs, insurance, depreciation, etc. See MTG ¶946.

Business-related parking fees and tolls that were not incurred in overnight travel or commuting to and from work are listed separately on line 2 of Form 2106.

Business-related personal property taxes on motor vehicles may be deductible on Schedule A (Form 1040). See Tab 2.

An employee cannot deduct any interest paid on a car loan, even if the car is used 100% for business. A self-employed taxpayer may be able to deduct the business-use part of car loan interest, but that deduction would appear on Schedule C (Form 1040), not Form 2106. See Tab 3.

Actual expenses are reported on the following lines:

- *Line 23:* Gasoline, oil, repairs, vehicle insurance, etc.
- *Line 24a:* Vehicle rentals. Enter the cost of renting or leasing the vehicle if the taxpayer rented the vehicle.
- *Line 24b:* Inclusion amount. The rent deduction for certain leased vehicles might be reduced by an inclusion amount if the lease term is 30 days or more. To prevent taxpayers from avoiding the limitation on the depreciation deduction for luxury automobiles, a certain amount must be included in income as an offset to the lease expense deduction. To determine the inclusion amount, see IRS Publication 463 and MTG ¶1215. See Tab 8 for inclusion amount tables.
- *Line 24c:* Subtract line 24b from line 24a.
- *Line 25:* Value of employer-provided vehicle. If the employer provided the taxpayer with a vehicle for business use and included 100% of its annual lease value in box 1 of the taxpayer's W-2, enter that amount on line 25. If less than 100% was included in box 1, then skip line 25.
- *Line 26:* Add lines 23, 24c, and 25.
- *Line 27:* Multiply line 26 by the business use percentage on line 14.
- *Line 28:* Depreciation. Enter amount from line 38 below if applicable.
- *Line 29:* Add lines 27 and 28. Enter total here and on line 1.

Filing Tip. If the taxpayer has the option of using either the standard mileage rate or the actual expenses method, he or she should calculate expenses both ways, and then fill in the form using the method that provides the larger vehicle expense amount.

Section D: Depreciation of Vehicles, Lines 30-38

Note: Use Section D only if the taxpayer owned the vehicle and is using actual expenses rather than the standard mileage rate to calculate the vehicle expense deduction.

Line 30, Enter the Cost or Other Basis

Enter the vehicle's actual cost (including sales tax) or other basis, unadjusted for prior years' depreciation. If the taxpayer converted the vehicle from personal to business use, the basis for depreciation is the smaller of the vehicle's adjusted basis or its fair market value on the conversion date. See Tab 8 for more details.

Line 31, Enter Section 179 Deduction and Special Depreciation Allowance

An employee using the actual expense method to compute vehicle expenses is entitled to claim a deduction for depreciation, subject to a variety of limitations. The depreciation deduction, including the Section 179 limited expensing amount and the 50% special allowance for 2009, is computed on lines 32-38. Calculation of vehicle depreciation, the Section 179 expense and the special allowance is covered in detail in Tab 8.

Lines 32-38, Calculations

Line 32: Multiply line 30 by line 14 (the business use percentage) to determine the basis for depreciation, then subtract the full amount of any Section 179 deduction and special allowance.

Line 33: Enter depreciation method and percentage. See Tab 8 for the applicable vehicle depreciation methods and percentages.

Line 34: Multiply line 32 by the depreciation percentage on line 33. If the taxpayer sold or exchanged a vehicle during the year, see IRS Publication 463 for special rules.

Line 35: Add lines 31 and 34.

Line 36: Enter applicable depreciation limit. See Tab 8 and MTG ¶1214 for depreciation limits.

Line 37: Multiply line 36 by the percentage on line 14.

Line 38: Enter the smaller of line 35 or line 37. If lines 36 and 37 were skipped, enter amount from line 35. Enter the line 38 amount on line 28.

Planning Tip. The taxpayer should retain the following information for each vehicle for at least four years after it is removed from service:

- Vehicle's bill-of-sale from purchase, or lease contract;
- Receipts from all maintenance or repairs;
- Total mileage driven each year, broken down into personal, commuting, and business miles; and
- Dates of each use for business, with an explanation of the purpose of the expense.

The taxpayer should keep a daily log or diary to achieve adequate substantiation of vehicle expenses.

Table 1. Localities Eligible for $256 ($58 M&IE) Per Diem Amount Under the High-Low Substantiation Method (Effective October 1, 2008 – September 30, 2009)[1,2]

Note: The standard ("low") rate of $158 ($113 for lodging and $45 for M&IE) applies to all locations within the continental United States (CONUS) not specifically listed below or encompassed by the boundary definition of a listed point.

State	Key City	County and/or Other Defined Location	Effective Date of $256 Rate
Arizona	Phoenix, Scottsdale	Maricopa	1/1 - 4/30
	Sedona	City limits of Sedona	3/1 - 4/30
California	Napa	Napa	All year
	San Diego	San Diego	1/1 - 8/31
	San Francisco	San Francisco	All year
	Santa Barbara	Santa Barbara	All year
	Santa Monica	City limits of Santa Monica	All year
	South Lake Tahoe	El Dorado	1/1 - 3/31; 12/1 - 12/31
Colorado	Aspen	Pitkin	1/1 - 4/30; 12/1 - 12/31
	Crested Butte, Gunnison	Gunnison	1/1 - 3/31; 12/1 - 12/31
	Silverthorne, Breckenridge	Summit	1/1 - 4/30; 12/1 - 12/31
	Steamboat Springs	Routt	1/1 - 3/31; 12/1 - 12/31
	Telluride	San Miguel	1/1 - 3/31; 10/1 - 12/31
	Vail	Eagle	1/1 - 7/31; 12/1 - 12/31
District of Columbia	Washington, DC (also the cities of Alexandria, Fairfax, and Falls Church, and the counties of Arlington and Fairfax, in Virginia; and the counties of Montgomery and Prince George's in Maryland)		All year
Florida	Fort Lauderdale	Broward	1/1 - 4/30; 10/1 - 12/31
	Fort Walton Beach, DeFuniak Springs	Okaloosa, Walton	6/1 - 7/31
	Key West	Monroe	All year
	Miami	Miami-Dade	1/1 - 2/28; 10/1 - 12/31
	Naples	Collier	2/1 - 3/31
	Palm Beach	Palm Beach (also the cities of Boca Raton, Delray Beach, Jupiter, Palm Beach Gardens, Palm Beach Shores, Singer Island, and West Palm Beach)	1/1 - 4/30; 12/1 - 12/31
Illinois	Chicago	Cook, Lake	All year
Maryland	Counties of Montgomery and Prince George's		All year
	Baltimore	Baltimore City	All year
	Cambridge, St. Michaels	Dorchester, Talbot	5/1 - 8/31
	Ocean City	Worcester	6/1 - 9/30
Massachusetts	Boston, Cambridge	Suffolk; City of Cambridge	All year
	Martha's Vineyard	Dukes	6/1 - 8/31
	Nantucket	Nantucket	6/1 - 9/30
New York	Floral Park, Garden City, Glen Cove, Great Neck, Roslyn	Nassau	All year
	Manhattan (includes the boroughs of Manhattan, Brooklyn, the Bronx, Queens, and Staten Island)	Bronx, Kings, New York, Queens, Richmond	All year
	Saratoga Springs, Schenectady	Saratoga, Schenectady	7/1 - 8/31
	Tarrytown, White Plains, New Rochelle, Yonkers	Westchester	All year
Pennsylvania	Philadelphia	Philadelphia	All year
Rhode Island	Jamestown, Middletown, Newport	Newport	6/1 - 9/30
Utah	Park City	Summit	1/1 - 3/31
Virginia	Cities of Alexandria, Falls Church, and Fairfax; counties of Arlington and Fairfax		All year
Washington	Seattle	King	All year
Wyoming	Jackson, Pinedale	Teton, Sublette	7/1 - 8/31

Transition rule. A payor who uses the high-low substantiation method in Table 1 for an employee during the first 9 months of calendar year 2009 must continue to use the high-low substantiation method for the remainder of calendar year 2009 for that employee. For travel on or after October 1, 2009, and before January 1, 2010, the payor may continue to use the rates and high-cost localities published in Table 1 or the updated rates and high-cost localities published in the revenue procedure that supersedes Revenue Procedure 2008-59, as long as those rates and localities are used consistently during this period for all employees reimbursed under this method.

Revenue Procedure 2008-59 in Internal Revenue Bulletin No. 2008-41.

Table 2. Localities Eligible for $258 ($65 M&IE) Per Diem Amount Under the High-Low Substantiation Method (Effective October 1, 2009)[1,2]

Note: The standard ("low") rate of $163 ($111 for lodging and $52 for M&IE) applies to all locations within the continental United States (CONUS) not specifically listed below or encompassed by the boundary definition of a listed point.

State	Key City	County and/or Other Defined Location	Effective Date of $258 Rate
Arizona	Phoenix/Scottsdale	Maricopa	1/1 - 5/31
	Sedona	City limits of Sedona	3/1 - 4/30
California	Monterey	Monterey	All year
	Napa	Napa	4/1 - 11/30
	San Diego	San Diego	All year
	San Francisco	San Francisco	All year
	Santa Barbara	Santa Barbara	All year
	Santa Monica	City limits of Santa Monica	All year
	South Lake Tahoe	El Dorado	1/1 - 3/31; 12/1 - 12/31
Colorado	Aspen	Pitkin	1/1 - 4/30; 12/1 - 12/31
	Denver/Aurora	Denver, Adams, Arapahoe, and Jefferson	All year
	Steamboat Springs	Routt	1/1 - 3/31; 12/1 - 12/31
	Telluride	San Miguel	1/1 - 3/31; 6/1 - 9/30; 12/1 - 12/31
	Vail	Eagle	1/1 - 3/31; 12/1 - 12/31
District of Columbia	Washington D.C. (also the cities of Alexandria, Falls Church, and Fairfax, and the counties of Arlington and Fairfax, in Virginia; and the counties of Montgomery and Prince George's in Maryland) (See also Maryland and Virginia)		All year
Florida	Fort Lauderdale	Broward	1/1 - 4/30; 10/1 - 12/31
	Fort Walton Beach/De Funiak Springs	Okaloosa and Walton	6/1 - 7/31
	Key West	Monroe	All year
	Miami	Miami-Dade	1/1 - 3/31
	Naples	Collier	1/1 - 4/30
Illinois	Chicago	Cook and Lake	All year
Maine	Bar Harbor	Hancock	7/1 - 8/31
Maryland	Baltimore City	Baltimore City	3/1 - 11/30
	Cambridge/St. Michaels	Dorchester and Talbot	6/1 - 8/31
	Ocean City	Worcester	6/1 - 8/31
	Washington, DC Metro Area	Montgomery and Prince George's	All year
Massachusetts	Boston/Cambridge	Suffolk, City of Cambridge	All year
	Martha's Vineyard	Dukes	6/1 - 8/31
	Nantucket	Nantucket	6/1 - 9/30
New Hampshire	Conway	Carroll	7/1 - 8/31
New York	Floral Park/Garden City/Great Neck	Nassau	All year
	Glens Falls	Warren	7/1 - 8/31
	Lake Placid	Essex	7/1 - 8/31
	Manhattan (includes the boroughs of Manhattan, Brooklyn, the Bronx, Queens and Staten Island)	Bronx, Kings, New York, Queens, Richmond	All year
	Saratoga Springs/Schenectady	Saratoga and Schenectady	7/1 - 8/31
	Tarrytown/White Plains/New Rochelle	Westchester	All year
Pennsylvania	Hershey	City of Hershey	6/1 - 8/31
	Philadelphia	Philadelphia	All year
Rhode Island	Jamestown/Middletown/Newport	Newport	5/1 - 10/31
Utah	Park City	Summit	1/1 - 3/31
Virginia	Washington, DC Metro Area	Cities of Alexandria, Fairfax, and Falls Church; counties of Arlington and Fairfax	All year
Washington	Seattle	King	All year
Wyoming	Jackson/Pinedale	Teton and Sublette	7/1 - 8/31

[1] **Transition rule.** A payor who uses the high-low substantiation method in Table 2 for an employee during the first 9 months of calendar year 2010 must continue to use the high-low substantiation method for the remainder of calendar year 2010 for that employee. For travel on or after October 1, 2010, and before January 1, 2011, the payor may continue to use the rates and high-cost localities published in Table 2 or the updated rates and high-cost localities published in the revenue procedure that supersedes Revenue Procedure 2009-47, as long as those rates and localities are used consistently during this period for all employees reimbursed under this method.

[2] Revenue Procedure 2009-47, in Internal Revenue Bulletin 2009-42.

Table 3. Maximum Federal Per Diem Rates (Effective 10/1/2008 - 9/30/2009)

State	Primary Destination	County	Begin	End	Lodging	M&IE	Total
	Standard CONUS Rate applies to all destinations or counties not specifically listed				$70	$39	$109
Alabama	Birmingham	Jefferson and Shelby			$94	$44	$138
Alabama	Gulf Shores	Baldwin	10/01/08	05/31/09	$110	$39	$149
Alabama	Gulf Shores	Baldwin	06/01/09	07/31/09	$139	$39	$178
Alabama	Gulf Shores	Baldwin	08/01/09	09/30/09	$110	$39	$149
Alabama	Huntsville	Madison and Limestone			$84	$44	$128
Alabama	Mobile	Mobile			$94	$49	$143
Alabama	Montgomery	Montgomery			$80	$39	$119
Arizona	Grand Canyon / Flagstaff	Coconino (except the city limits of Sedona), Yavapai	10/01/08	10/31/08	$93	$44	$137
Arizona	Grand Canyon / Flagstaff	Coconino (except the city limits of Sedona), Yavapai	11/01/08	02/28/09	$75	$44	$119
Arizona	Grand Canyon / Flagstaff	Coconino (except the city limits of Sedona), Yavapai	03/01/09	09/30/09	$93	$44	$137
Arizona	Kayenta	Navajo	10/01/08	04/30/09	$75	$54	$129
Arizona	Kayenta	Navajo	05/01/09	09/30/09	$86	$54	$140
Arizona	Phoenix / Scottsdale	Maricopa	10/01/08	12/31/08	$122	$59	$181
Arizona	Phoenix / Scottsdale	Maricopa	01/01/09	04/30/09	$160	$59	$219
Arizona	Phoenix / Scottsdale	Maricopa	05/01/09	08/31/09	$96	$59	$155
Arizona	Phoenix / Scottsdale	Maricopa	09/01/09	09/30/09	$122	$59	$181
Arizona	Sedona	City Limits of Sedona	10/01/08	02/28/09	$135	$64	$199
Arizona	Sedona	City Limits of Sedona	03/01/09	04/30/09	$157	$64	$221
Arizona	Sedona	City Limits of Sedona	05/01/09	09/30/09	$135	$64	$199
Arizona	Sierra Vista	Cochise			$78	$39	$117
Arizona	Tucson	Pima	10/01/08	01/31/09	$106	$49	$155
Arizona	Tucson	Pima	02/01/09	05/31/09	$124	$49	$173
Arizona	Tucson	Pima	06/01/09	08/31/09	$83	$49	$132
Arizona	Tucson	Pima	09/01/09	09/30/09	$106	$49	$155
Arizona	Yuma	Yuma			$86	$39	$125
Arkansas	Hot Springs	Garland			$98	$49	$147
Arkansas	Little Rock	Pulaski			$88	$54	$142
California	Antioch / Brentwood / Concord / Lafayette / Martinez / Pleasant Hill / Richmond / San Ramon / Walnut Creek	Contra Costa			$113	$49	$162
California	Bakersfield / Delano (Naval Weapons Center and Ordnance Test Station, China Lake)	Kern			$78	$44	$122
California	Barstow / Ontario / Victorville	San Bernardino			$97	$59	$156
California	Benicia / Dixon / Fairfield / Vacaville / Vallejo	Solano			$93	$44	$137
California	Brawley / Calexico / El Centro / Imperial	Imperial			$76	$39	$115
California	Death Valley	Inyo			$81	$49	$130
California	Eureka / Arcata / McKinleyville	Humboldt			$89	$54	$143

Table 3. Maximum Federal Per Diem Rates (Effective 10/1/2008 - 9/30/2009) (Continued)

State	Primary Destination	County	Begin	End	Lodging	M&IE	Total
California	Fresno	Fresno			$95	$54	$149
California	Los Angeles	Los Angeles, Orange, Ventura, and Edwards AFB			$128	$64	$192
California	Mammoth Lakes	Mono	10/01/08	11/30/08	$113	$54	$167
California	Mammoth Lakes	Mono	12/01/08	01/31/09	$142	$54	$196
California	Mammoth Lakes	Mono	02/01/09	09/30/09	$113	$54	$167
California	Mill Valley / San Rafael / Novato / Corte Madera / Sausalito / Tiburon / Larkspur	Marin			$122	$54	$176
California	Modesto	Stanislaus			$89	$49	$138
California	Monterey	Monterey			$133	$64	$197
California	Napa	Napa			$146	$64	$210
California	Oakhurst	Madera	10/01/08	04/30/09	$75	$39	$114
California	Oakhurst	Madera	05/01/09	08/31/09	$90	$39	$129
California	Oakhurst	Madera	09/01/09	09/30/09	$75	$39	$114
California	Oakland	Alameda			$106	$59	$165
California	Palm Springs	Riverside	10/01/08	12/31/08	$114	$59	$173
California	Palm Springs	Riverside	01/01/09	04/30/09	$139	$59	$198
California	Palm Springs	Riverside	05/01/09	08/31/09	$97	$59	$156
California	Palm Springs	Riverside	09/01/09	09/30/09	$114	$59	$173
California	Point Arena / Gualala	Mendocino			$81	$54	$135
California	Redding	Shasta			$86	$44	$130
California	Sacramento	Sacramento			$114	$59	$173
California	San Diego	San Diego	10/01/08	12/31/08	$137	$64	$201
California	San Diego	San Diego	01/01/09	08/31/09	$147	$64	$211
California	San Diego	San Diego	09/01/09	09/30/09	$137	$64	$201
California	San Francisco	San Francisco	10/01/08	10/31/08	$185	$64	$249
California	San Francisco	San Francisco	11/01/08	08/31/09	$164	$64	$228
California	San Francisco	San Francisco	09/01/09	09/30/09	$185	$64	$249
California	San Luis Obispo	San Luis Obispo	10/01/08	06/30/09	$109	$54	$163
California	San Luis Obispo	San Luis Obispo	07/01/09	08/31/09	$131	$54	$185
California	San Luis Obispo	San Luis Obispo	09/01/09	09/30/09	$109	$54	$163
California	San Mateo / Foster City / Belmont	San Mateo			$123	$54	$177
California	Santa Barbara	Santa Barbara	10/01/08	06/30/09	$149	$59	$208
California	Santa Barbara	Santa Barbara	07/01/09	08/31/09	$194	$59	$253
California	Santa Barbara	Santa Barbara	09/01/09	09/30/09	$149	$59	$208
California	Santa Cruz	Santa Cruz			$102	$54	$156
California	Santa Monica	City limits of Santa Monica			$212	$64	$276
California	Santa Rosa	Sonoma			$118	$64	$182
California	South Lake Tahoe	El Dorado	10/01/08	11/30/08	$132	$54	$186
California	South Lake Tahoe	El Dorado	12/01/08	03/31/09	$153	$54	$207
California	South Lake Tahoe	El Dorado	04/01/09	06/30/09	$118	$54	$172
California	South Lake Tahoe	El Dorado	07/01/09	09/30/09	$132	$54	$186
California	Stockton	San Joaquin			$83	$44	$127

Table 3. Maximum Federal Per Diem Rates (Effective 10/1/2008 - 9/30/2009) (Continued)

State	Primary Destination	County	Begin	End	Lodging	M&IE	Total
California	Sunnyvale / Palo Alto / San Jose	Santa Clara			$132	$59	$191
California	Tahoe City	Placer			$105	$59	$164
California	Truckee	Nevada	10/01/08	11/30/08	$94	$59	$153
California	Truckee	Nevada	12/01/08	03/31/09	$109	$59	$168
California	Truckee	Nevada	04/01/09	09/30/09	$94	$59	$153
California	Visalia / Lemoore	Tulare and Kings			$83	$49	$132
California	West Sacramento	Yolo			$100	$44	$144
California	Yosemite National Park	Mariposa	10/01/08	12/31/08	$126	$64	$190
California	Yosemite National Park	Mariposa	01/01/09	07/31/09	$133	$64	$197
California	Yosemite National Park	Mariposa	08/01/09	09/30/09	$126	$64	$190
Colorado	Aspen	Pitkin	10/01/08	11/30/08	$85	$64	$149
Colorado	Aspen	Pitkin	12/01/08	04/30/09	$223	$64	$287
Colorado	Aspen	Pitkin	05/01/09	09/30/09	$111	$64	$175
Colorado	Boulder / Broomfield	Boulder and Broomfield			$105	$54	$159
Colorado	Colorado Springs	El Paso			$88	$44	$132
Colorado	Cortez	Montezuma	10/01/08	05/31/09	$83	$39	$122
Colorado	Cortez	Montezuma	06/01/09	08/31/09	$102	$39	$141
Colorado	Cortez	Montezuma	09/01/09	09/30/09	$83	$39	$122
Colorado	Crested Butte / Gunnison	Gunnison	10/01/08	11/30/08	$77	$49	$126
Colorado	Crested Butte / Gunnison	Gunnison	12/01/08	03/31/09	$188	$49	$237
Colorado	Crested Butte / Gunnison	Gunnison	04/01/09	05/31/09	$72	$49	$121
Colorado	Crested Butte / Gunnison	Gunnison	06/01/09	08/31/09	$96	$49	$145
Colorado	Crested Butte / Gunnison	Gunnison	09/01/09	09/30/09	$77	$49	$126
Colorado	Denver / Aurora	Denver, Adams, Arapahoe, and Jefferson			$149	$49	$198
Colorado	Douglas County	Douglas			$104	$54	$158
Colorado	Durango	La Plata	10/01/08	05/31/09	$94	$49	$143
Colorado	Durango	La Plata	06/01/09	09/30/09	$125	$49	$174
Colorado	Fort Collins / Loveland	Larimer			$93	$44	$137
Colorado	Glenwood Springs / Grand Junction	Garfield / Mesa			$91	$49	$140
Colorado	Montrose	Montrose	10/01/08	05/31/09	$76	$39	$115
Colorado	Montrose	Montrose	06/01/09	09/30/09	$93	$39	$132
Colorado	Silverthorne / Breckenridge	Summit	10/01/08	11/30/08	$96	$54	$150
Colorado	Silverthorne / Breckenridge	Summit	12/01/08	04/30/09	$157	$54	$211
Colorado	Silverthorne / Breckenridge	Summit	05/01/09	09/30/09	$96	$54	$150
Colorado	Steamboat Springs	Routt	10/01/08	11/30/08	$103	$54	$157
Colorado	Steamboat Springs	Routt	12/01/08	03/31/09	$212	$54	$266
Colorado	Steamboat Springs	Routt	04/01/09	09/30/09	$103	$54	$157
Colorado	Telluride	San Miguel	10/01/08	12/31/08	$155	$59	$214
Colorado	Telluride	San Miguel	01/01/09	03/31/09	$211	$59	$270
Colorado	Telluride	San Miguel	04/01/09	05/31/09	$99	$59	$158
Colorado	Telluride	San Miguel	06/01/09	09/30/09	$128	$59	$187
Colorado	Vail	Eagle	10/01/08	11/30/08	$127	$64	$191
Colorado	Vail	Eagle	12/01/08	01/31/09	$268	$64	$332

Table 3. Maximum Federal Per Diem Rates (Effective 10/1/2008 - 9/30/2009) (Continued)

State	Primary Destination	County	Begin	End	Lodging	M&IE	Total
Colorado	Vail	Eagle	02/01/09	03/31/09	$233	$64	$297
Colorado	Vail	Eagle	04/01/09	07/31/09	$225	$64	$289
Colorado	Vail	Eagle	08/01/09	09/30/09	$127	$64	$191
Connecticut	Bridgeport / Danbury	Fairfield			$122	$64	$186
Connecticut	Cromwell / Old Saybrook	Middlesex			$88	$44	$132
Connecticut	Hartford	Hartford			$112	$49	$161
Connecticut	Lakeville / Salisbury	Litchfield			$95	$64	$159
Connecticut	New Haven	New Haven			$96	$64	$160
Connecticut	New London / Groton	New London			$105	$64	$169
Connecticut	Putnam / Danielson / Storrs / Mansfield	Windham / Tolland			$75	$59	$134
Delaware	Dover	Kent	10/01/08	05/31/09	$83	$44	$127
Delaware	Dover	Kent	06/01/09	09/30/09	$99	$44	$143
Delaware	Lewes	Sussex	10/01/08	06/30/09	$81	$39	$120
Delaware	Lewes	Sussex	07/01/09	08/31/09	$117	$39	$156
Delaware	Lewes	Sussex	09/01/09	09/30/09	$81	$39	$120
Delaware	Wilmington	New Castle			$119	$39	$158
District of Columbia	District of Columbia	Washington DC (also the cities of Alexandria, Falls Church and Fairfax, and the counties of Arlington and Fairfax, in Virginia; and the counties of Montgomery and Prince George's in Maryland) (See also Maryland and Virginia)	10/01/08	10/31/08	$233	$64	$297
District of Columbia	District of Columbia	Washington DC (also the cities of Alexandria, Falls Church and Fairfax, and the counties of Arlington and Fairfax, in Virginia; and the counties of Montgomery and Prince George's in Maryland) (See also Maryland and Virginia)	11/01/08	06/30/09	$209	$64	$273
District of Columbia	District of Columbia	Washington DC (also the cities of Alexandria, Falls Church and Fairfax, and the counties of Arlington and Fairfax, in Virginia; and the counties of Montgomery and Prince George's in Maryland) (See also Maryland and Virginia)	07/01/09	08/31/09	$165	$64	$229
District of Columbia	District of Columbia	Washington DC (also the cities of Alexandria, Falls Church and Fairfax, and the counties of Arlington and Fairfax, in Virginia; and the counties of Montgomery and Prince George's in Maryland) (See also Maryland and Virginia)	09/01/09	09/30/09	$233	$64	$297

Table 3. Maximum Federal Per Diem Rates (Effective 10/1/2008 - 9/30/2009) (Continued)

State	Primary Destination	County	Begin	End	Lodging	M&IE	Total
Florida	Altamonte Springs	Seminole	10/01/08	12/31/08	$88	$39	$127
Florida	Altamonte Springs	Seminole	01/01/09	03/31/09	$101	$39	$140
Florida	Altamonte Springs	Seminole	04/01/09	09/30/09	$88	$39	$127
Florida	Boca Raton, Delray Beach, Jupiter, Palm Beach Gardens, Palm Beach, Palm Beach Shores, Singer Island and West Palm Beach	Palm Beach	10/01/08	11/30/08	$99	$64	$163
Florida	Boca Raton, Delray Beach, Jupiter, Palm Beach Gardens, Palm Beach, Palm Beach Shores, Singer Island and West Palm Beach	Palm Beach	12/01/08	04/30/09	$145	$64	$209
Florida	Boca Raton, Delray Beach, Jupiter, Palm Beach Gardens, Palm Beach, Palm Beach Shores, Singer Island and West Palm Beach	Palm Beach	05/01/09	09/30/09	$99	$64	$163
Florida	Bradenton	Manatee	10/01/08	12/31/08	$85	$39	$124
Florida	Bradenton	Manatee	01/01/09	04/30/09	$115	$39	$154
Florida	Bradenton	Manatee	05/01/09	09/30/09	$85	$39	$124
Florida	Cocoa Beach	Brevard			$106	$44	$150
Florida	Daytona Beach	Volusia	10/01/08	01/31/09	$93	$39	$132
Florida	Daytona Beach	Volusia	02/01/09	07/31/09	$117	$39	$156
Florida	Daytona Beach	Volusia	08/01/09	09/30/09	$93	$39	$132
Florida	Fort Lauderdale	Broward	10/01/08	04/30/09	$176	$54	$230
Florida	Fort Lauderdale	Broward	05/01/09	09/30/09	$118	$54	$172
Florida	Fort Myers	Lee	10/01/08	12/31/08	$88	$49	$137
Florida	Fort Myers	Lee	01/01/09	04/30/09	$128	$49	$177
Florida	Fort Myers	Lee	05/01/09	09/30/09	$88	$49	$137
Florida	Fort Pierce	Saint Lucie	10/01/08	10/31/08	$96	$49	$145
Florida	Fort Pierce	Saint Lucie	11/01/08	04/30/09	$118	$49	$167
Florida	Fort Pierce	Saint Lucie	05/01/09	09/30/09	$96	$49	$145
Florida	Fort Walton Beach / De Funiak Springs	Okaloosa and Walton	10/01/08	10/31/08	$118	$44	$162
Florida	Fort Walton Beach / De Funiak Springs	Okaloosa and Walton	11/01/08	02/28/09	$83	$44	$127
Florida	Fort Walton Beach / De Funiak Springs	Okaloosa and Walton	03/01/09	05/31/09	$135	$44	$179
Florida	Fort Walton Beach / De Funiak Springs	Okaloosa and Walton	06/01/09	07/31/09	$176	$44	$220
Florida	Fort Walton Beach / De Funiak Springs	Okaloosa and Walton	08/01/09	09/30/09	$118	$44	$162
Florida	Gainesville	Alachua			$93	$44	$137
Florida	Gulf Breeze	Santa Rosa	10/01/08	02/28/09	$105	$39	$144
Florida	Gulf Breeze	Santa Rosa	03/01/09	05/31/09	$124	$39	$163
Florida	Gulf Breeze	Santa Rosa	06/01/09	07/31/09	$150	$39	$189
Florida	Gulf Breeze	Santa Rosa	08/01/09	09/30/09	$105	$39	$144

Table 3. Maximum Federal Per Diem Rates (Effective 10/1/2008 - 9/30/2009) (Continued)

State	Primary Destination	County	Begin	End	Lodging	M&IE	Total
Florida	Jacksonville / Jacksonville Beach / Mayport Naval Station / Fernandina Beach / Atlantic Beach	Duval, City of Jacksonville and Nassau			$89	$49	$138
Florida	Key West	Monroe	10/01/08	11/30/08	$167	$64	$231
Florida	Key West	Monroe	12/01/08	01/31/09	$202	$64	$266
Florida	Key West	Monroe	02/01/09	03/31/09	$243	$64	$307
Florida	Key West	Monroe	04/01/09	09/30/09	$167	$64	$231
Florida	Kissimmee	Osceola	10/01/08	12/31/08	$79	$39	$118
Florida	Kissimmee	Osceola	01/01/09	07/31/09	$85	$39	$124
Florida	Kissimmee	Osceola	08/01/09	09/30/09	$79	$39	$118
Florida	Lakeland	Polk			$87	$39	$126
Florida	Leesburg	Lake			$77	$44	$121
Florida	Miami	Miami-Dade	10/01/08	02/28/09	$149	$59	$208
Florida	Miami	Miami-Dade	03/01/09	09/30/09	$121	$59	$180
Florida	Naples	Collier	10/01/08	01/31/09	$134	$64	$198
Florida	Naples	Collier	02/01/09	03/31/09	$221	$64	$285
Florida	Naples	Collier	04/01/09	09/30/09	$120	$64	$184
Florida	Ocala	Marion			$91	$44	$135
Florida	Orlando	Orange	10/01/08	12/31/08	$109	$49	$158
Florida	Orlando	Orange	01/01/09	03/31/09	$133	$49	$182
Florida	Orlando	Orange	04/01/09	09/30/09	$109	$49	$158
Florida	Panama City	Bay	10/01/08	02/28/09	$85	$49	$134
Florida	Panama City	Bay	03/01/09	05/31/09	$125	$49	$174
Florida	Panama City	Bay	06/01/09	07/31/09	$146	$49	$195
Florida	Panama City	Bay	08/01/09	09/30/09	$85	$49	$134
Florida	Pensacola / Pensacola Beach	Escambia			$107	$49	$156
Florida	Punta Gorda	Charlotte	10/01/08	01/31/09	$88	$44	$132
Florida	Punta Gorda	Charlotte	02/01/09	03/31/09	$115	$44	$159
Florida	Punta Gorda	Charlotte	04/01/09	09/30/09	$88	$44	$132
Florida	Sarasota	Sarasota	10/01/08	01/31/09	$101	$49	$150
Florida	Sarasota	Sarasota	02/01/09	03/31/09	$143	$49	$192
Florida	Sarasota	Sarasota	04/01/09	09/30/09	$101	$49	$150
Florida	Sebring	Highlands	10/01/08	12/31/08	$76	$39	$115
Florida	Sebring	Highlands	01/01/09	03/31/09	$137	$39	$176
Florida	Sebring	Highlands	04/01/09	09/30/09	$76	$39	$115
Florida	St. Augustine	St. Johns			$105	$54	$159
Florida	Stuart	Martin	10/01/08	12/31/08	$93	$49	$142
Florida	Stuart	Martin	01/01/09	04/30/09	$129	$49	$178
Florida	Stuart	Martin	05/01/09	09/30/09	$93	$49	$142
Florida	Tallahassee	Leon			$89	$44	$133
Florida	Tampa / St. Petersburg	Pinellas and Hillsborough	10/01/08	12/31/08	$104	$54	$158
Florida	Tampa / St. Petersburg	Pinellas and Hillsborough	01/01/09	03/31/09	$127	$54	$181
Florida	Tampa / St. Petersburg	Pinellas and Hillsborough	04/01/09	09/30/09	$104	$54	$158
Florida	Vero Beach	Indian River	10/01/08	01/31/09	$95	$49	$144

Table 3. Maximum Federal Per Diem Rates (Effective 10/1/2008 - 9/30/2009) (Continued)

State	Primary Destination	County	Begin	End	Lodging	M&IE	Total
Florida	Vero Beach	Indian River	02/01/09	03/31/09	$127	$49	$176
Florida	Vero Beach	Indian River	04/01/09	09/30/09	$95	$49	$144
Georgia	Athens	Clarke			$90	$39	$129
Georgia	Atlanta	Fulton, Dekalb and Cobb			$141	$49	$190
Georgia	Augusta	Richmond			$79	$39	$118
Georgia	Columbus	Muscogee			$92	$39	$131
Georgia	Conyers	Rockdale			$77	$39	$116
Georgia	Duluth / Norcross / Lawrenceville	Gwinnett			$80	$44	$124
Georgia	Jekyll Island / Brunswick	Glynn	10/01/08	02/28/09	$120	$49	$169
Georgia	Jekyll Island / Brunswick	Glynn	03/01/09	09/30/09	$146	$49	$195
Georgia	Peachtree City / Jonesboro / Morrow / Newnan	Fayette / Coweta / Clayton			$77	$44	$121
Georgia	Savannah	Chatham			$108	$49	$157
Idaho	Bonner's Ferry/Sandpoint	Boundary/Bonner	10/01/08	03/31/09	$70	$39	$109
Idaho	Bonner's Ferry/Sandpoint	Boundary/Bonner	04/01/09	06/30/09	$76	$59	$135
Idaho	Bonner's Ferry/Sandpoint	Boundary/Bonner	07/01/09	08/31/09	$104	$59	$163
Idaho	Bonner's Ferry/Sandpoint	Boundary/Bonner	09/01/09	09/30/09	$76	$59	$135
Idaho	Boise	Ada			$86	$49	$135
Idaho	Coeur d'Alene	Kootenai	10/01/08	06/30/09	$75	$59	$134
Idaho	Coeur d'Alene	Kootenai	07/01/09	08/31/09	$109	$59	$168
Idaho	Coeur d'Alene	Kootenai	09/01/09	09/30/09	$75	$59	$134
Idaho	Driggs/Idaho Falls	Teton/Bonneville/Fremont	10/01/08	03/31/09	$70	$39	$109
Idaho	Driggs/Idaho Falls	Teton/Bonneville/Fremont	04/01/09	09/30/09	$76	$44	$120
Idaho	Sun Valley / Ketchum	Blaine			$84	$59	$143
Idaho	Twin Falls	Twin Falls			$86	$39	$125
Illinois	Bolingbrook / Romeoville / Lemont / Lockport / Homer Glen / Mokena / New Lenox	Will			$91	$44	$135
Illinois	Chicago	Cook and Lake	10/01/08	11/30/08	$218	$64	$282
Illinois	Chicago	Cook and Lake	12/01/08	04/30/09	$157	$64	$221
Illinois	Chicago	Cook and Lake	05/01/09	06/30/09	$209	$64	$273
Illinois	Chicago	Cook and Lake	07/01/09	08/31/09	$177	$64	$241
Illinois	Chicago	Cook and Lake	09/01/09	09/30/09	$218	$64	$282
Illinois	Elgin / Aurora	City of Elgin, Kane			$87	$44	$131
Illinois	Oak Brook Terrace	Dupage			$106	$49	$155
Illinois	O'Fallon / Fairview Heights / Collinsville	Bond, Calhoun, Clinton, Jersey, Macoupin, Madison, Monroe and St. Clair			$111	$59	$170
Illinois	Springfield	Sangamon			$83	$49	$132
Indiana	Bloomington	Monroe			$96	$44	$140
Indiana	Brownsburg / Plainfield	Hendricks			$78	$44	$122
Indiana	Ft. Wayne	Allen			$90	$39	$129
Indiana	Hammond / Munster / Merrillville	Lake			$93	$44	$137

Table 3. Maximum Federal Per Diem Rates (Effective 10/1/2008 - 9/30/2009) (Continued)

State	Primary Destination	County	Begin	End	Lodging	M&IE	Total
Indiana	Indianapolis / Carmel	Marion, Hamilton, Fort Benjamin Harrison military base			$94	$44	$138
Indiana	Lafayette	Tippecanoe			$87	$39	$126
Indiana	Michigan City	La Porte			$82	$39	$121
Indiana	South Bend	St. Joseph			$95	$44	$139
Indiana	Valparaiso / Burlington Beach	Porter			$82	$49	$131
Iowa	Cedar Rapids	Linn			$80	$39	$119
Iowa	Des Moines	Polk			$86	$44	$130
Kansas	Kansas City / Overland Park	Wyandotte and Johnson			$107	$44	$151
Kansas	Wichita	Sedgwick			$86	$49	$135
Kentucky	Boone County	Boone			$98	$44	$142
Kentucky	Kenton County	Kenton			$117	$44	$161
Kentucky	Lexington	Fayette			$91	$49	$140
Kentucky	Louisville	Jefferson	10/01/08	05/31/09	$103	$49	$152
Kentucky	Louisville	Jefferson	06/01/09	09/30/09	$94	$49	$143
Louisiana	Baton Rouge	East Baton Rouge Parish			$101	$44	$145
Louisiana	Covington / Slidell	St. Tammany Parish			$96	$49	$145
Louisiana	Lafayette	Lafayette Consolidated Government			$86	$49	$135
Louisiana	Lake Charles	Calcasieu Parish			$80	$39	$119
Louisiana	New Orleans	Orleans, St. Bernard, Jefferson and Plaquemine Parishes	10/01/08	06/30/09	$140	$59	$199
Louisiana	New Orleans	Orleans, St. Bernard, Jefferson and Plaquemine Parishes	07/01/09	09/30/09	$101	$59	$160
Maine	Bar Harbor	Hancock	10/01/08	06/30/09	$87	$49	$136
Maine	Bar Harbor	Hancock	07/01/09	09/30/09	$143	$49	$192
Maine	Kennebunk / Kittery / Sanford	York	10/01/08	10/31/08	$93	$54	$147
Maine	Kennebunk / Kittery / Sanford	York	11/01/08	03/31/09	$70	$54	$124
Maine	Kennebunk / Kittery / Sanford	York	04/01/09	06/30/09	$83	$54	$137
Maine	Kennebunk / Kittery / Sanford	York	07/01/09	08/31/09	$126	$54	$180
Maine	Kennebunk / Kittery / Sanford	York	09/01/09	09/30/09	$93	$54	$147
Maine	Portland	Cumberland / Sagadahoc	10/01/08	06/30/09	$89	$44	$133
Maine	Portland	Cumberland / Sagadahoc	07/01/09	09/30/09	$113	$44	$157
Maine	Rockport	Knox	10/01/08	06/30/09	$70	$49	$119
Maine	Rockport	Knox	07/01/09	08/31/09	$78	$49	$127
Maine	Rockport	Knox	09/01/09	09/30/09	$70	$49	$119
Maryland	Aberdeen / Bel Air / Belcamp / Edgewood	Harford			$83	$44	$127
Maryland	Annapolis	Anne Arundel			$126	$64	$190
Maryland	Baltimore City	Baltimore City	10/01/08	10/31/08	$172	$59	$231
Maryland	Baltimore City	Baltimore City	11/01/08	08/31/09	$157	$59	$216
Maryland	Baltimore City	Baltimore City	09/01/09	09/30/09	$172	$59	$231
Maryland	Baltimore County	Baltimore			$106	$54	$160

Table 3. Maximum Federal Per Diem Rates (Effective 10/1/2008 - 9/30/2009) (Continued)

State	Primary Destination	County	Begin	End	Lodging	M&IE	Total
Maryland	Cambridge / St. Michaels	Dorchester and Talbot	10/01/08	10/31/08	$140	$54	$194
Maryland	Cambridge / St. Michaels	Dorchester and Talbot	11/01/08	04/30/09	$105	$54	$159
Maryland	Cambridge / St. Michaels	Dorchester and Talbot	05/01/09	08/31/09	$163	$54	$217
Maryland	Cambridge / St. Michaels	Dorchester and Talbot	09/01/09	09/30/09	$140	$54	$194
Maryland	Columbia	Howard			$125	$49	$174
Maryland	Frederick	Frederick	10/01/08	03/31/09	$89	$39	$128
Maryland	Frederick	Frederick	04/01/09	09/30/09	$90	$39	$129
Maryland	Hagerstown	Washington			$76	$39	$115
Maryland	La Plata / Indian Head	Charles			$90	$39	$129
Maryland	Lexington Park / Leonardtown / Lusby	St. Mary's and Calvert			$97	$39	$136
Maryland	Ocean City	Worcester	10/01/08	05/31/09	$82	$64	$146
Maryland	Ocean City	Worcester	06/01/09	09/30/09	$181	$64	$245
Maryland	Washington, DC Metro Area	Montgomery and Prince George's	10/01/08	10/31/08	$233	$64	$297
Maryland	Washington, DC Metro Area	Montgomery and Prince George's	11/01/08	06/30/09	$209	$64	$273
Maryland	Washington, DC Metro Area	Montgomery and Prince George's	07/01/09	08/31/09	$165	$64	$229
Maryland	Washington, DC Metro Area	Montgomery and Prince George's	09/01/09	09/30/09	$233	$64	$297
Massachusetts	Andover	Essex			$90	$59	$149
Massachusetts	Boston / Cambridge	Suffolk, city of Cambridge	10/01/08	10/31/08	$256	$64	$320
Massachusetts	Boston / Cambridge	Suffolk, city of Cambridge	11/01/08	08/31/09	$203	$64	$267
Massachusetts	Boston / Cambridge	Suffolk, city of Cambridge	09/01/09	09/30/09	$256	$64	$320
Massachusetts	Burlington / Woburn	Middlesex			$119	$59	$178
Massachusetts	Falmouth	City limits of Falmouth	10/01/08	06/30/09	$100	$49	$149
Massachusetts	Falmouth	City limits of Falmouth	07/01/09	08/31/09	$142	$49	$191
Massachusetts	Falmouth	City limits of Falmouth	09/01/09	09/30/09	$100	$49	$149
Massachusetts	Hyannis	Barnstable	10/01/08	06/30/09	$85	$59	$144
Massachusetts	Hyannis	Barnstable	07/01/09	08/31/09	$118	$59	$177
Massachusetts	Hyannis	Barnstable	09/01/09	09/30/09	$85	$59	$144
Massachusetts	Martha's Vineyard	Dukes	10/01/08	10/31/08	$123	$64	$187
Massachusetts	Martha's Vineyard	Dukes	11/01/08	05/31/09	$106	$64	$170
Massachusetts	Martha's Vineyard	Dukes	06/01/09	08/31/09	$186	$64	$250
Massachusetts	Martha's Vineyard	Dukes	09/01/09	09/30/09	$123	$64	$187
Massachusetts	Nantucket	Nantucket	10/01/08	05/31/09	$119	$64	$183
Massachusetts	Nantucket	Nantucket	06/01/09	09/30/09	$206	$64	$270
Massachusetts	Northampton	Hampshire			$91	$39	$130
Massachusetts	Pittsfield	Berkshire			$109	$59	$168
Massachusetts	Plymouth / Taunton / New Bedford	Plymouth / Bristol			$95	$54	$149
Massachusetts	Quincy	Norfolk			$123	$44	$167
Massachusetts	Springfield	Hampden			$96	$44	$140
Massachusetts	Worcester	Worcester			$96	$49	$145
Michigan	Ann Arbor	Washtenaw			$91	$44	$135

Table 3. Maximum Federal Per Diem Rates (Effective 10/1/2008 - 9/30/2009) (Continued)

State	Primary Destination	County	Begin	End	Lodging	M&IE	Total
Michigan	Benton Harbor / St. Joseph / Stevensville	Berrien			$74	$49	$123
Michigan	Charlevoix	Charlevoix			$74	$49	$123
Michigan	Detroit	Wayne			$107	$49	$156
Michigan	East Lansing / Lansing	Ingham and Eaton			$81	$39	$120
Michigan	Flint	Genessee			$80	$39	$119
Michigan	Grand Rapids	Kent			$84	$39	$123
Michigan	Holland	Ottawa			$82	$44	$126
Michigan	Kalamazoo / Battle Creek	Kalamazoo / Calhoun			$86	$44	$130
Michigan	Mackinac Island	Mackinac	10/01/08	06/30/09	$70	$49	$119
Michigan	Mackinac Island	Mackinac	07/01/09	08/31/09	$88	$49	$137
Michigan	Mackinac Island	Mackinac	09/01/09	09/30/09	$70	$49	$119
Michigan	Midland	Midland			$93	$39	$132
Michigan	Mount Pleasant	Isabella			$73	$44	$117
Michigan	Muskegon	Muskegon	10/01/08	05/31/09	$72	$39	$111
Michigan	Muskegon	Muskegon	06/01/09	08/31/09	$88	$39	$127
Michigan	Muskegon	Muskegon	09/01/09	09/30/09	$72	$39	$111
Michigan	Ontonagon / Baraga / Houghton	Ontonagon / Baraga / Houghton			$75	$39	$114
Michigan	Petoskey	Emmet	10/01/08	06/30/09	$71	$54	$125
Michigan	Petoskey	Emmet	07/01/09	08/31/09	$94	$54	$148
Michigan	Petoskey	Emmet	09/01/09	09/30/09	$71	$54	$125
Michigan	Pontiac / Auburn Hills	Oakland			$97	$44	$141
Michigan	South Haven	Van Buren	10/01/08	05/31/09	$70	$39	$109
Michigan	South Haven	Van Buren	06/01/09	08/31/09	$85	$39	$124
Michigan	South Haven	Van Buren	09/01/09	09/30/09	$70	$39	$109
Michigan	Traverse City and Leland	Grand Traverse and Leelanau	10/01/08	06/30/09	$70	$44	$114
Michigan	Traverse City and Leland	Grand Traverse and Leelanau	07/01/09	08/31/09	$118	$44	$162
Michigan	Traverse City and Leland	Grand Traverse and Leelanau	09/01/09	09/30/09	$70	$44	$114
Michigan	Warren	Macomb			$77	$39	$116
Minnesota	Duluth	St. Louis	10/01/08	05/31/09	$82	$49	$131
Minnesota	Duluth	St. Louis	06/01/09	08/31/09	$103	$49	$152
Minnesota	Duluth	St. Louis	09/01/09	09/30/09	$82	$49	$131
Minnesota	Eagan / Burnsville / Mendota Heights / Lakeville / Inver Grove Heights	Dakota			$90	$49	$139
Minnesota	Minneapolis / St. Paul	Hennepin and Ramsey			$130	$64	$194
Minnesota	Rochester	Olmsted			$95	$44	$139
Mississippi	Grenada	Grenada			$75	$44	$119
Mississippi	Gulfport / Biloxi	Harrison			$80	$44	$124
Mississippi	Hattiesburg	Forrest and Lamar			$76	$49	$125
Mississippi	Robinsonville	Tunica			$81	$44	$125
Mississippi	Southaven	Desoto			$91	$44	$135

Table 3. Maximum Federal Per Diem Rates (Effective 10/1/2008 - 9/30/2009) (Continued)

State	Primary Destination	County	Begin	End	Lodging	M&IE	Total
Mississippi	Starkville	Oktibbeha			$76	$44	$120
Missouri	Columbia	Boone			$79	$39	$118
Missouri	Kansas City	Jackson, Clay, Cass and Platte			$107	$49	$156
Missouri	Springfield	Greene			$76	$39	$115
Missouri	St. Louis	St. Louis, St. Louis City and St. Charles, Crawford, Franklin, Jefferson, Lincoln, Warren and Washington			$111	$59	$170
Montana	Big Sky / West Yellowstone	Gallatin	10/01/08	06/30/09	$82	$49	$131
Montana	Big Sky / West Yellowstone	Gallatin	07/01/09	08/31/09	$107	$49	$156
Montana	Big Sky / West Yellowstone	Gallatin	09/01/09	09/30/09	$82	$49	$131
Montana	Butte	Silver Bow			$80	$44	$124
Montana	Helena	Lewis and Clark			$77	$44	$121
Montana	Missoula / Polson / Kalispell	Missoula / Lake / Flathead	10/01/08	05/31/09	$84	$44	$128
Montana	Missoula / Polson / Kalispell	Missoula / Lake / Flathead	06/01/09	08/31/09	$106	$44	$150
Montana	Missoula / Polson / Kalispell	Missoula / Lake / Flathead	09/01/09	09/30/09	$84	$44	$128
Nebraska	Omaha	Douglas			$99	$49	$148
Nevada	Incline Village / Crystal Bay / Reno / Sparks	Washoe	10/01/08	06/30/09	$110	$49	$159
Nevada	Incline Village / Crystal Bay / Reno / Sparks	Washoe	07/01/09	08/31/09	$149	$49	$198
Nevada	Incline Village / Crystal Bay / Reno / Sparks	Washoe	09/01/09	09/30/09	$110	$49	$159
Nevada	Las Vegas	Clark	10/01/08	12/31/08	$105	$64	$169
Nevada	Las Vegas	Clark	01/01/09	05/31/09	$126	$64	$190
Nevada	Las Vegas	Clark	06/01/09	09/30/09	$105	$64	$169
Nevada	Stateline, Carson City	Douglas, Carson City			$103	$64	$167
New Hampshire	Concord	Merrimack	10/01/08	10/31/08	$94	$44	$138
New Hampshire	Concord	Merrimack	11/01/08	04/30/09	$85	$44	$129
New Hampshire	Concord	Merrimack	05/01/09	09/30/09	$94	$44	$138
New Hampshire	Conway	Caroll	10/01/08	05/31/09	$112	$49	$161
New Hampshire	Conway	Caroll	06/01/09	08/31/09	$145	$49	$194
New Hampshire	Conway	Caroll	09/01/09	09/30/09	$112	$49	$161
New Hampshire	Durham	Strafford			$94	$44	$138
New Hampshire	Laconia	Belknap	10/01/08	10/31/08	$99	$39	$138
New Hampshire	Laconia	Belknap	11/01/08	05/31/09	$86	$39	$125
New Hampshire	Laconia	Belknap	06/01/09	09/30/09	$99	$39	$138

Table 3. Maximum Federal Per Diem Rates (Effective 10/1/2008 - 9/30/2009) (Continued)

State	Primary Destination	County	Begin	End	Lodging	M&IE	Total
New Hampshire	Lebanon / Lincoln / West Lebanon / Franconia / Hanover / Holderness / Sunapee / Waterville Valley / North Woodstock / Plymouth	Grafton and Sullivan			$99	$49	$148
New Hampshire	Manchester	Hillsborough			$98	$44	$142
New Hampshire	Portsmouth	Rockingham	10/01/08	06/30/09	$102	$44	$146
New Hampshire	Portsmouth	Rockingham	07/01/09	09/30/09	$132	$44	$176
New Jersey	Atlantic City / Ocean City / Cape May	Atlantic and Cape May	10/01/08	10/31/08	$117	$54	$171
New Jersey	Atlantic City / Ocean City / Cape May	Atlantic and Cape May	11/01/08	04/30/09	$105	$54	$159
New Jersey	Atlantic City / Ocean City / Cape May	Atlantic and Cape May	05/01/09	09/30/09	$117	$54	$171
New Jersey	Belle Mead	Somerset			$127	$44	$171
New Jersey	Cherry Hill / Moorestown	Camden and Burlington			$94	$44	$138
New Jersey	Eatontown / Freehold	Monmouth			$125	$49	$174
New Jersey	Edison / Piscataway	Middlesex			$114	$44	$158
New Jersey	Flemington	Hunterdon			$113	$39	$152
New Jersey	Newark	Essex, Bergen, Hudson and Passaic			$133	$49	$182
New Jersey	Parsippany	Morris			$142	$49	$191
New Jersey	Princeton / Trenton	Mercer			$139	$44	$183
New Jersey	Springfield / Cranford / New Providence / Westfield / Clark / Summit / Linden	Union			$106	$49	$155
New Jersey	Tom's River	Ocean	10/01/08	05/31/09	$92	$39	$131
New Jersey	Tom's River	Ocean	06/01/09	08/31/09	$116	$39	$155
New Jersey	Tom's River	Ocean	09/01/09	09/30/09	$92	$39	$131
New Mexico	Albuquerque	Bernalillo			$80	$49	$129
New Mexico	Los Alamos	Los Alamos			$82	$49	$131
New Mexico	Santa Fe	Santa Fe			$86	$59	$145
New Mexico	Taos	Taos			$75	$59	$134
New York	Albany	Albany			$111	$49	$160
New York	Binghamton / Owego	Broome and Tioga			$87	$39	$126
New York	Buffalo	Erie			$92	$54	$146
New York	Floral Park / Garden City / Glen Cove / Great Neck / Roslyn	Nassau			$162	$64	$226
New York	Glens Falls	Warren	10/01/08	06/30/09	$98	$49	$147
New York	Glens Falls	Warren	07/01/09	08/31/09	$150	$49	$199
New York	Glens Falls	Warren	09/01/09	09/30/09	$98	$49	$147
New York	Ithaca / Waterloo / Romulus	Tompkins and Seneca			$102	$44	$146
New York	Kingston	Ulster			$96	$49	$145
New York	Lake Placid	Essex	10/01/08	05/31/09	$111	$54	$165
New York	Lake Placid	Essex	06/01/09	08/31/09	$150	$54	$204

Table 3. Maximum Federal Per Diem Rates (Effective 10/1/2008 - 9/30/2009) (Continued)

State	Primary Destination	County	Begin	End	Lodging	M&IE	Total
New York	Lake Placid	Essex	09/01/09	09/30/09	$111	$54	$165
New York	Manhattan (includes the boroughs of Manhattan, Brooklyn, the Bronx, Queens and Staten Island)	Bronx, Kings, New York, Queens, Richmond	10/01/08	12/31/08	$360	$64	$424
New York	Manhattan (includes the boroughs of Manhattan, Brooklyn, the Bronx, Queens and Staten Island)	Bronx, Kings, New York, Queens, Richmond	01/01/09	06/30/09	$285	$64	$349
New York	Manhattan (includes the boroughs of Manhattan, Brooklyn, the Bronx, Queens and Staten Island)	Bronx, Kings, New York, Queens, Richmond	07/01/09	08/31/09	$259	$64	$323
New York	Manhattan (includes the boroughs of Manhattan, Brooklyn, the Bronx, Queens and Staten Island)	Bronx, Kings, New York, Queens, Richmond	09/01/09	09/30/09	$360	$64	$424
New York	Niagara Falls	Niagara	10/01/08	04/30/09	$79	$44	$123
New York	Niagara Falls	Niagara	05/01/09	08/31/09	$97	$44	$141
New York	Niagara Falls	Niagara	09/01/09	09/30/09	$79	$44	$123
New York	Nyack / Palisades	Rockland			$117	$49	$166
New York	Poughkeepsie	Dutchess			$110	$54	$164
New York	Riverhead / Ronkonkoma / Melville / Smithtown / Huntington Station / Amagansett / East Hampton / Montauk / Southampton / Islandia / Commack / Medford / Stony Brook / Hauppauge / Centereach	Suffolk			$131	$64	$195
New York	Rochester	Monroe			$101	$44	$145
New York	Saratoga Springs / Schenectady	Saratoga and Schenectady	10/01/08	06/30/09	$106	$44	$150
New York	Saratoga Springs / Schenectady	Saratoga and Schenectady	07/01/09	08/31/09	$169	$44	$213
New York	Saratoga Springs / Schenectady	Saratoga and Schenectady	09/01/09	09/30/09	$106	$44	$150
New York	Syracuse	Onondaga			$94	$44	$138
New York	Tarrytown / White Plains / New Rochelle / Yonkers	Westchester			$164	$59	$223
New York	Troy	Rensselaer			$97	$39	$136
New York	West Point	Orange			$114	$44	$158
North Carolina	Asheville	Buncombe	10/01/08	10/31/08	$94	$49	$143
North Carolina	Asheville	Buncombe	11/01/08	06/30/09	$81	$49	$130
North Carolina	Asheville	Buncombe	07/01/09	09/30/09	$94	$49	$143
North Carolina	Atlantic Beach / Morehead City	Carteret	10/01/08	05/31/09	$76	$49	$125
North Carolina	Atlantic Beach / Morehead City	Carteret	06/01/09	08/31/09	$106	$49	$155
North Carolina	Atlantic Beach / Morehead City	Carteret	09/01/09	09/30/09	$76	$49	$125
North Carolina	Chapel Hill	Orange			$92	$49	$141
North Carolina	Charlotte	Mecklenburg			$97	$49	$146
North Carolina	Durham	Durham			$95	$49	$144
North Carolina	Fayetteville	Cumberland			$85	$49	$134
North Carolina	Greensboro	Guilford			$89	$44	$133

Table 3. Maximum Federal Per Diem Rates (Effective 10/1/2008 - 9/30/2009) (Continued)

State	Primary Destination	County	Begin	End	Lodging	M&IE	Total
North Carolina	Greenville	Pitt			$80	$39	$119
North Carolina	Kill Devil	Dare	10/01/08	04/30/09	$70	$54	$124
North Carolina	Kill Devil	Dare	05/01/09	09/30/09	$116	$54	$170
North Carolina	New Bern / Havelock	Craven			$89	$44	$133
North Carolina	Raleigh	Wake			$92	$54	$146
North Carolina	Wilmington	New Hanover	10/01/08	05/31/09	$93	$49	$142
North Carolina	Wilmington	New Hanover	06/01/09	07/31/09	$109	$49	$158
North Carolina	Wilmington	New Hanover	08/01/09	09/30/09	$93	$49	$142
North Carolina	Winston-Salem	Forsyth			$89	$44	$133
Ohio	Akron	Summit			$88	$49	$137
Ohio	Canton	Stark			$90	$44	$134
Ohio	Cincinnati	Hamilton and Clermont			$112	$54	$166
Ohio	Cleveland	Cuyahoga			$110	$54	$164
Ohio	Columbus	Franklin			$105	$49	$154
Ohio	Dayton / Fairborn	Greene, Darke and Montgomery			$84	$44	$128
Ohio	Hamilton	Butler and Warren			$91	$49	$140
Ohio	Mentor	Lake			$87	$44	$131
Ohio	Rittman	Wayne and Medina			$82	$39	$121
Ohio	Sandusky / Bellevue	Erie and Huron			$108	$39	$147
Ohio	Toledo	Lucas			$81	$44	$125
Ohio	Youngstown	Mahoning and Trumbull			$82	$39	$121
Oklahoma	Oklahoma City	Oklahoma			$83	$49	$132
Oklahoma	Tulsa	Tulsa, Creek, Osage, and Rogers			$79	$44	$123
Oregon	Ashland / Crater Lake	Jackson / Klamath			$87	$44	$131
Oregon	Beaverton	Washington			$98	$44	$142
Oregon	Bend	Deschutes	10/01/08	06/30/09	$90	$44	$134
Oregon	Bend	Deschutes	07/01/09	08/31/09	$124	$44	$168
Oregon	Bend	Deschutes	09/01/09	09/30/09	$90	$44	$134
Oregon	Clackamas	Clackamas			$85	$39	$124
Oregon	Eugene / Florence	Lane			$100	$44	$144
Oregon	Lincoln City	Lincoln	10/01/08	06/30/09	$86	$49	$135
Oregon	Lincoln City	Lincoln	07/01/09	08/31/09	$112	$49	$161
Oregon	Lincoln City	Lincoln	09/01/09	09/30/09	$86	$49	$135
Oregon	Portland	Multnomah			$116	$49	$165
Oregon	Seaside	Clatsop	10/01/08	06/30/09	$89	$54	$143
Oregon	Seaside	Clatsop	07/01/09	08/31/09	$132	$54	$186
Oregon	Seaside	Clatsop	09/01/09	09/30/09	$89	$54	$143
Pennsylvania	Allentown / Easton / Bethlehem	Lehigh and Northampton			$91	$44	$135
Pennsylvania	Bucks County	Bucks			$102	$59	$161
Pennsylvania	Chester / Radnor / Essington	Delaware			$107	$44	$151
Pennsylvania	Erie	Erie			$92	$39	$131
Pennsylvania	Gettysburg	Adams	10/01/08	10/31/08	$103	$54	$157
Pennsylvania	Gettysburg	Adams	11/01/08	03/31/09	$78	$54	$132

Table 3. Maximum Federal Per Diem Rates (Effective 10/1/2008 - 9/30/2009) (Continued)

State	Primary Destination	County	Begin	End	Lodging	M&IE	Total
Pennsylvania	Gettysburg	Adams	04/01/09	09/30/09	$103	$54	$157
Pennsylvania	Harrisburg	Daupin			$99	$44	$143
Pennsylvania	Hershey	City of Hershey	10/01/08	02/28/09	$91	$44	$135
Pennsylvania	Hershey	City of Hershey	03/01/09	05/31/09	$97	$44	$141
Pennsylvania	Hershey	City of Hershey	06/01/09	09/30/09	$159	$44	$203
Pennsylvania	Lancaster	Lancaster			$95	$49	$144
Pennsylvania	Malvern / Frazer / Berwyn / Phoenixville	Chester			$122	$49	$171
Pennsylvania	Mechanicsburg	Cumberland			$84	$54	$138
Pennsylvania	Montgomery County	Montgomery			$128	$59	$187
Pennsylvania	Philadelphia	Philadelphia	10/01/08	11/30/08	$166	$64	$230
Pennsylvania	Philadelphia	Philadelphia	12/01/08	08/31/09	$155	$64	$219
Pennsylvania	Philadelphia	Philadelphia	09/01/09	09/30/09	$166	$64	$230
Pennsylvania	Pittsburgh	Allegheny			$114	$54	$168
Pennsylvania	Reading	Berks			$98	$44	$142
Pennsylvania	Scranton	Lackawanna			$80	$39	$119
Pennsylvania	State College	Centre			$88	$44	$132
Rhode Island	East Greenwich / Warwick / North Kingstown	Kent and Washington			$103	$49	$152
Rhode Island	Jamestown / Middletown / Newport	Newport	10/01/08	05/31/09	$120	$64	$184
Rhode Island	Jamestown / Middletown / Newport	Newport	06/01/09	09/30/09	$178	$64	$242
Rhode Island	Providence	Providence			$145	$54	$199
South Carolina	Aiken	Aiken			$81	$39	$120
South Carolina	Charleston	Charleston, Berkeley and Dorchester			$141	$54	$195
South Carolina	Columbia	Richland	10/01/08	03/31/09	$92	$44	$136
South Carolina	Columbia	Richland / Lexington	04/01/08	09/30/09	$92	$44	$136
South Carolina	Greenville	Greenville			$92	$49	$141
South Carolina	Hilton Head	Beaufort	10/01/08	10/31/08	$114	$54	$168
South Carolina	Hilton Head	Beaufort	11/01/08	03/31/09	$98	$54	$152
South Carolina	Hilton Head	Beaufort	04/01/09	08/31/09	$144	$54	$198
South Carolina	Hilton Head	Beaufort	09/01/09	09/30/09	$114	$54	$168
South Carolina	Lexington County (See Columbia)	Lexington	10/01/08	03/31/09	$70	$39	$109
South Carolina	Myrtle Beach	Horry	10/01/08	10/31/08	$86	$54	$140
South Carolina	Myrtle Beach	Horry	11/01/08	02/28/09	$70	$54	$124
South Carolina	Myrtle Beach	Horry	03/01/09	08/31/09	$114	$54	$168
South Carolina	Myrtle Beach	Horry	09/01/09	09/30/09	$86	$54	$140
South Dakota	Hot Springs	Fall River and Custer	10/01/08	05/31/09	$70	$39	$109
South Dakota	Hot Springs	Fall River and Custer	06/01/09	08/31/09	$92	$39	$131
South Dakota	Hot Springs	Fall River and Custer	09/01/09	09/30/09	$70	$39	$109
South Dakota	Rapid City	Pennington	10/01/08	05/31/09	$70	$44	$114
South Dakota	Rapid City	Pennington	06/01/09	08/31/09	$109	$44	$153
South Dakota	Rapid City	Pennington	09/01/09	09/30/09	$70	$44	$114

Table 3. Maximum Federal Per Diem Rates (Effective 10/1/2008 - 9/30/2009) (Continued)

State	Primary Destination	County	Begin	End	Lodging	M&IE	Total
South Dakota	Sturgis / Spearfish	Meade, Butte and Lawrence	10/01/08	04/30/09	$70	$44	$114
South Dakota	Sturgis / Spearfish	Meade, Butte and Lawrence	05/01/09	08/31/09	$95	$44	$139
South Dakota	Sturgis / Spearfish	Meade, Butte and Lawrence	09/01/09	09/30/09	$70	$44	$114
Tennessee	Brentwood / Franklin	Williamson			$101	$49	$150
Tennessee	Chattanooga	Hamilton			$87	$44	$131
Tennessee	Knoxville	Knox			$83	$49	$132
Tennessee	Memphis	Shelby			$99	$49	$148
Tennessee	Nashville	Davidson			$117	$54	$171
Tennessee	Oak Ridge	Anderson			$86	$39	$125
Texas	Arlington / Fort Worth / Grapevine	Tarrant county and City limits of Grapevine			$149	$44	$193
Texas	Austin	Travis	10/01/08	03/31/09	$114	$54	$168
Texas	Austin	Travis	04/01/09	08/31/09	$107	$54	$161
Texas	Austin	Travis	09/01/09	09/30/09	$114	$54	$168
Texas	Beaumont	Jefferson			$82	$49	$131
Texas	College Station	Brazos			$86	$39	$125
Texas	Corpus Christi	Nueces			$89	$44	$133
Texas	Dallas	Dallas County and City of Dallas	10/01/08	12/31/08	$115	$59	$174
Texas	Dallas	Dallas County and City of Dallas	01/01/09	03/31/09	$129	$59	$188
Texas	Dallas	Dallas County and City of Dallas	04/01/09	09/30/09	$115	$59	$174
Texas	El Paso	El Paso			$92	$44	$136
Texas	Galveston	Galveston	10/01/08	05/31/09	$99	$49	$148
Texas	Galveston	Galveston	06/01/09	07/31/09	$121	$49	$170
Texas	Galveston	Galveston	08/01/09	09/30/09	$99	$49	$148
Texas	Houston (L.B. Johnson Space Center)	Montgomery, Fort Bend and Harris			$110	$59	$169
Texas	Hunt County	Hunt County			$81	$39	$120
Texas	Laredo	Webb			$88	$44	$132
Texas	McAllen	Hidalgo			$84	$44	$128
Texas	Plano	Collin			$108	$49	$157
Texas	Round Rock	Williamson			$95	$44	$139
Texas	San Antonio	Bexar			$117	$54	$171
Texas	South Padre Island	Cameron	10/01/08	05/31/09	$84	$44	$128
Texas	South Padre Island	Cameron	06/01/09	07/31/09	$110	$44	$154
Texas	South Padre Island	Cameron	08/01/09	09/30/09	$84	$44	$128
Texas	Waco	McLennan			$85	$39	$124
Utah	Park City	Summit	10/01/08	12/31/08	$91	$64	$155
Utah	Park City	Summit	01/01/09	03/31/09	$164	$64	$228
Utah	Park City	Summit	04/01/09	09/30/09	$91	$64	$155
Utah	Provo	Utah			$86	$49	$135
Utah	Salt Lake City	Salt Lake and Tooele	10/01/08	12/31/08	$102	$54	$156
Utah	Salt Lake City	Salt Lake and Tooele	01/01/09	03/31/09	$116	$54	$170

Table 3. Maximum Federal Per Diem Rates (Effective 10/1/2008 - 9/30/2009) (Continued)

State	Primary Destination	County	Begin	End	Lodging	M&IE	Total
Utah	Salt Lake City	Salt Lake and Tooele	04/01/09	09/30/09	$102	$54	$156
Vermont	Burlington / St. Albans	Chittenden and Franklin	10/01/08	10/31/08	$105	$49	$154
Vermont	Burlington / St. Albans	Chittenden and Franklin	11/01/08	04/30/09	$90	$49	$139
Vermont	Burlington / St. Albans	Chittenden and Franklin	05/01/09	09/30/09	$105	$49	$154
Vermont	Manchester	Bennington			$94	$59	$153
Vermont	Montpelier	Washington			$93	$54	$147
Vermont	Stowe	Lamoille	10/01/08	11/30/08	$121	$64	$185
Vermont	Stowe	Lamoille	12/01/08	03/31/09	$141	$64	$205
Vermont	Stowe	Lamoille	04/01/09	09/30/09	$121	$64	$185
Vermont	White River Junction	Windsor	10/01/08	02/28/09	$90	$54	$144
Vermont	White River Junction	Windsor	03/01/09	05/31/09	$82	$54	$136
Vermont	White River Junction	Windsor	06/01/09	09/30/09	$90	$54	$144
Virginia	Abingdon	Washington	10/01/08	03/31/09	$79	$49	$128
Virginia	Abingdon	Washington	04/01/09	05/31/09	$72	$49	$121
Virginia	Abingdon	Washington	06/01/09	09/30/09	$79	$49	$128
Virginia	Blacksburg	Montgomery			$80	$54	$134
Virginia	Charlottesville	City of Charlottesville, Albemarle, Greene			$100	$44	$144
Virginia	Chesapeake / Suffolk	Cities of Chesapeake and Suffolk	10/01/08	03/31/09	$89	$44	$133
Virginia	Chesapeake / Suffolk	Cities of Chesapeake and Suffolk	04/01/09	05/31/09	$97	$44	$141
Virginia	Chesapeake / Suffolk	Cities of Chesapeake and Suffolk	06/01/09	08/31/09	$107	$44	$151
Virginia	Chesapeake / Suffolk	Cities of Chesapeake and Suffolk	09/01/09	09/30/09	$89	$44	$133
Virginia	Chesterfield / Henrico Counties	Chesterfield / Henrico			$93	$49	$142
Virginia	Fredericksburg	City of Fredericksburg, Spotsylvania			$74	$54	$128
Virginia	Hampton City / Newport News	Cities of Hampton City and Newport News			$81	$44	$125
Virginia	James City and York Counties, Williamsburg	James City and York Counties, City of Williamsburg	10/01/08	03/31/09	$75	$54	$129
Virginia	James City and York Counties, Williamsburg	James City and York Counties, City of Williamsburg	04/01/09	08/31/09	$97	$54	$151
Virginia	James City and York Counties, Williamsburg	James City and York Counties, City of Williamsburg	09/01/09	09/30/09	$75	$54	$129
Virginia	Loudoun County	Loudoun			$140	$59	$199
Virginia	Lynchburg	Campbell, Lynchburg City			$78	$44	$122
Virginia	Manassas	City of Manassas			$101	$39	$140
Virginia	Norfolk / Portsmouth	Cities of Norfolk and Portsmouth			$96	$59	$155
Virginia	Richmond City	City of Richmond	10/01/08	10/31/08	$129	$54	$183
Virginia	Richmond City	City of Richmond	11/01/08	08/31/09	$123	$54	$177
Virginia	Richmond City	City of Richmond	09/01/09	09/30/09	$129	$54	$183

Table 3. Maximum Federal Per Diem Rates (Effective 10/1/2008 - 9/30/2009) (Continued)

State	Primary Destination	County	Begin	End	Lodging	M&IE	Total
Virginia	Roanoke	City limits of Roanoke			$96	$44	$140
Virginia	Stafford / Prince William Counties	Stafford / Prince William			$95	$44	$139
Virginia	Virginia Beach	City of Virginia Beach	10/01/08	05/31/09	$88	$54	$142
Virginia	Virginia Beach	City of Virginia Beach	06/01/09	08/31/09	$151	$54	$205
Virginia	Virginia Beach	City of Virginia Beach	09/01/09	09/30/09	$88	$54	$142
Virginia	Wallops Island	Accomack	10/01/08	06/30/09	$87	$49	$136
Virginia	Wallops Island	Accomack	07/01/09	08/31/09	$121	$49	$170
Virginia	Wallops Island	Accomack	09/01/09	09/30/09	$87	$49	$136
Virginia	Warrenton	Fauquier			$99	$44	$143
Virginia	Washington, DC Metro Area	Cities of Alexandria, Fairfax and Falls Church; Arlington and Fairfax	10/01/08	10/31/08	$233	$64	$297
Virginia	Washington, DC Metro Area	Cities of Alexandria, Fairfax and Falls Church; Arlington and Fairfax	11/01/08	06/30/09	$209	$64	$273
Virginia	Washington, DC Metro Area	Cities of Alexandria, Fairfax and Falls Church; Arlington and Fairfax	07/01/09	08/31/09	$165	$64	$229
Virginia	Washington, DC Metro Area	Cities of Alexandria, Fairfax and Falls Church; Arlington and Fairfax	09/01/09	09/30/09	$233	$64	$297
Washington	Anacortes / Camano Island / Coupeville / Mount Vernon / La Conner / Burlington / Friday Harbor / Oak Harbor	Skagit, Island, San Juan	10/01/08	05/31/09	$84	$59	$143
Washington	Anacortes / Camano Island / Coupeville / Mount Vernon / La Conner / Burlington / Friday Harbor / Oak Harbor	Skagit, Island, San Juan	06/01/09	08/31/09	$94	$59	$153
Washington	Anacortes / Camano Island / Coupeville / Mount Vernon / La Conner / Burlington / Friday Harbor / Oak Harbor	Skagit, Island, San Juan	09/01/09	09/30/09	$84	$59	$143
Washington	Bremerton	Kitsap			$83	$59	$142
Washington	Everett / Lynnwood	Snohomish			$99	$54	$153
Washington	Ocean Shores	Grays Harbor	10/01/08	06/30/09	$86	$44	$130
Washington	Ocean Shores	Grays Harbor	07/01/09	08/31/09	$109	$44	$153
Washington	Ocean Shores	Grays Harbor	09/01/09	09/30/09	$86	$44	$130
Washington	Olympia / Tumwater	Thurston			$86	$49	$135
Washington	Port Angeles / Port Townsend	Clallam and Jefferson	10/01/08	06/30/09	$92	$59	$151
Washington	Port Angeles / Port Townsend	Clallam and Jefferson	07/01/09	08/31/09	$129	$59	$188
Washington	Port Angeles / Port Townsend	Clallam and Jefferson	09/01/09	09/30/09	$92	$59	$151
Washington	Seattle	King			$158	$64	$222
Washington	Spokane	Spokane			$83	$49	$132
Washington	Tacoma	Pierce			$118	$59	$177
Washington	Vancouver	Clark, Cowlitz and Skamania			$120	$49	$169
West Virginia	Charleston	Kanawha			$95	$44	$139

Table 3. Maximum Federal Per Diem Rates (Effective 10/1/2008 - 9/30/2009) (Continued)

State	Primary Destination	County	Begin	End	Lodging	M&IE	Total
West Virginia	Morgantown	Monongalia			$83	$44	$127
West Virginia	Shepherdstown	Jefferson			$80	$44	$124
West Virginia	Wheeling	Ohio			$93	$44	$137
Wisconsin	Appleton	Outagamie			$81	$44	$125
Wisconsin	Brookfield / Racine	Waukesha / Racine			$92	$44	$136
Wisconsin	Green Bay	Brown			$75	$44	$119
Wisconsin	Lake Geneva	Walworth	10/01/08	04/30/09	$98	$54	$152
Wisconsin	Lake Geneva	Walworth	05/01/09	09/30/09	$146	$54	$200
Wisconsin	Madison	Dane			$90	$54	$144
Wisconsin	Milwaukee	Milwaukee			$99	$44	$143
Wisconsin	Sheboygan	Sheboygan			$79	$44	$123
Wisconsin	Sturgeon Bay	Door	10/01/08	06/30/09	$70	$49	$119
Wisconsin	Sturgeon Bay	Door	07/01/09	09/30/09	$88	$49	$137
Wisconsin	Wisconsin Dells	Columbia	10/01/08	06/30/09	$70	$64	$134
Wisconsin	Wisconsin Dells	Columbia	07/01/09	08/31/09	$86	$64	$150
Wisconsin	Wisconsin Dells	Columbia	09/01/09	09/30/09	$70	$64	$134
Wyoming	Cody	Park	10/01/08	04/30/09	$75	$44	$119
Wyoming	Cody	Park	05/01/09	09/30/09	$110	$44	$154
Wyoming	Evanston / Rock Springs	Sweetwater / Uinta			$91	$44	$135
Wyoming	Gillette	Campbell	10/01/08	06/30/09	$85	$49	$134
Wyoming	Gillette	Campbell	07/01/09	08/31/09	$104	$49	$153
Wyoming	Gillette	Campbell	09/01/09	09/30/09	$85	$49	$134
Wyoming	Jackson / Pinedale	Teton and Sublette	10/01/08	11/30/08	$104	$54	$158
Wyoming	Jackson / Pinedale	Teton and Sublette	12/01/08	06/30/09	$113	$54	$167
Wyoming	Jackson / Pinedale	Teton and Sublette	07/01/09	08/31/09	$164	$54	$218
Wyoming	Jackson / Pinedale	Teton and Sublette	09/01/09	09/30/09	$104	$54	$158
Wyoming	Sheridan	Sheridan	10/01/08	05/31/09	$70	$49	$119
Wyoming	Sheridan	Sheridan	06/01/09	08/31/09	$90	$49	$139
Wyoming	Sheridan	Sheridan	09/01/09	09/30/09	$70	$49	$119

NOTES:

(1) **Standard rate.** The standard rate of $109 ($70 for lodging and $39 for M&IE) applies to all locations within the continental United States (CONUS) not specifically listed below or encompassed by the boundary definition of a listed point. However, the standard CONUS rate applies to all locations within CONUS, including those defined below, for certain relocation allowances. (See parts 302-2, 302-4, and 302-5 of 41 CFR.)

(2) **Transition rule.** In lieu of the updated GSA rates that will be effective October 1, 2009 (Table 4), taxpayers may continue to use the CONUS rates in effect for the first 9 months of 2009 (Table 3) for expenses of all CONUS travel away from home that are paid or incurred during calendar year 2009. A taxpayer must consistently use either these rates or the updated rates for the period of October 1, 2009, through December 31, 2009.

(3) **Per diem locality.** Unless otherwise specified, the per diem locality is defined as "all locations within, or entirely surrounded by, the corporate limits of the key city, including independent entities located within those boundaries."

Per diem localities with county definitions shall include "all locations within, or entirely surrounded by, the corporate limits of the key city as well as the boundaries of the listed counties, including independent entities located within the boundaries of the key city and the listed counties (unless otherwise listed separately)."

When a military installation or Government-related facility (whether or not specifically named) is located partially within more than one city or county boundary, the applicable per diem rate for the entire installation or facility is the higher of the two rates which apply to the cities and/or counties, even though part(s) of such activities may be located outside the defined per diem locality.

Recognizing that all locations are not incorporated cities, the term "city limits" has been used as a general phrase to denote the commonly recognized local boundaries of the location cited.

(Sources: IRS Publication 1542, Per Diem Rates; U.S. General Services Administration, Domestic Per Diem Rates (available at http://www.gsa.gov))

Table 4. Maximum Federal Per Diem Rates (Effective 10/1/2009 - 9/30/2010)

State	Primary Destination	County	Begin	End	Lodging	M&IE	Total
	Standard CONUS Rate applies to all destinations or counties not specifically listed				$70	$46	$116
Alabama	Birmingham	Jefferson and Shelby			$92	$56	$148
Alabama	Gulf Shores	Baldwin	10/01/09	05/31/10	$111	$51	$162
Alabama	Gulf Shores	Baldwin	06/01/10	07/31/10	$137	$51	$188
Alabama	Gulf Shores	Baldwin	08/01/10	09/30/10	$111	$51	$162
Alabama	Huntsville	Madison and Limestone			$86	$51	$137
Alabama	Mobile	Mobile			$100	$51	$151
Alabama	Montgomery	Montgomery			$78	$51	$129
Arizona	Grand Canyon / Flagstaff	Coconino (except the city limits of Sedona), Yavapai	10/01/09	10/31/09	$95	$66	$161
Arizona	Grand Canyon / Flagstaff	Coconino (except the city limits of Sedona), Yavapai	11/01/09	02/28/10	$75	$66	$141
Arizona	Grand Canyon / Flagstaff	Coconino (except the city limits of Sedona), Yavapai	03/01/10	09/30/10	$95	$66	$161
Arizona	Kayenta	Navajo	10/01/09	04/30/10	$78	$46	$124
Arizona	Kayenta	Navajo	05/01/10	09/30/10	$96	$46	$142
Arizona	Phoenix / Scottsdale	Maricopa	10/01/09	12/31/09	$120	$71	$191
Arizona	Phoenix / Scottsdale	Maricopa	01/01/10	05/31/10	$140	$71	$211
Arizona	Phoenix / Scottsdale	Maricopa	06/01/10	08/31/10	$89	$71	$160
Arizona	Phoenix / Scottsdale	Maricopa	09/01/10	09/30/10	$120	$71	$191
Arizona	Sedona	City Limits of Sedona	10/01/09	02/28/10	$136	$66	$202
Arizona	Sedona	City Limits of Sedona	03/01/10	04/30/10	$149	$66	$215
Arizona	Sedona	City Limits of Sedona	05/01/10	09/30/10	$136	$66	$202
Arizona	Sierra Vista	Cochise			$83	$46	$129
Arizona	Tucson	Pima	10/01/09	01/31/10	$105	$56	$161
Arizona	Tucson	Pima	02/01/10	05/31/10	$127	$56	$183
Arizona	Tucson	Pima	06/01/10	08/31/10	$82	$56	$138
Arizona	Tucson	Pima	09/01/10	09/30/10	$105	$56	$161
Arizona	Yuma	Yuma			$84	$46	$130
Arkansas	Hot Springs	Garland			$102	$46	$148
Arkansas	Little Rock	Pulaski			$88	$61	$149
California	Antioch / Brentwood / Concord	Contra Costa			$110	$66	$176
California	Bakersfield / Delano (Naval Weapons Center and Ordnance Test Station, China Lake)	Kern			$79	$56	$135
California	Barstow / Ontario / Victorville	San Bernardino			$93	$56	$149
California	Benicia / Dixon / Fairfield	Solano			$93	$56	$149
California	Brawley / Calexico / El Centro	Imperial			$82	$51	$133
California	Death Valley	Inyo			$84	$46	$130
California	Eureka / Arcata / McKinleyville	Humboldt	10/01/09	05/31/10	$85	$61	$146
California	Eureka / Arcata / McKinleyville	Humboldt	06/01/10	08/31/10	$102	$61	$163
California	Eureka / Arcata / McKinleyville	Humboldt	09/01/10	09/30/10	$85	$61	$146
California	Fresno	Fresno			$94	$61	$155
California	Los Angeles	Los Angeles, Orange, Ventura, and Edwards AFB			$135	$71	$206
California	Mammoth Lakes	Mono	10/01/09	11/30/09	$114	$61	$175
California	Mammoth Lakes	Mono	12/01/09	01/31/10	$143	$61	$204

Table 4. Maximum Federal Per Diem Rates (Effective 10/1/2009 - 9/30/2010) (Continued)

State	Primary Destination	County	Begin	End	Lodging	M&IE	Total
California	Mammoth Lakes	Mono	02/01/10	09/30/10	$114	$61	$175
California	Mill Valley / San Rafael / Novato	Marin			$120	$56	$176
California	Modesto	Stanislaus			$88	$51	$139
California	Monterey	Monterey			$140	$71	$211
California	Napa	Napa	10/01/09	11/30/09	$163	$66	$229
California	Napa	Napa	12/01/09	03/31/10	$115	$66	$181
California	Napa	Napa	04/01/10	09/30/10	$163	$66	$229
California	Oakhurst	Madera	10/01/09	04/30/10	$74	$56	$130
California	Oakhurst	Madera	05/01/10	08/31/10	$93	$56	$149
California	Oakhurst	Madera	09/01/10	09/30/10	$74	$56	$130
California	Oakland	Alameda			$100	$61	$161
California	Palm Springs	Riverside	10/01/09	12/31/09	$111	$71	$182
California	Palm Springs	Riverside	01/01/10	05/31/10	$129	$71	$200
California	Palm Springs	Riverside	06/01/10	08/31/10	$90	$71	$161
California	Palm Springs	Riverside	09/01/10	09/30/10	$111	$71	$182
California	Point Arena / Gualala	Mendocino			$84	$66	$150
California	Redding	Shasta			$89	$61	$150
California	Sacramento	Sacramento			$109	$61	$170
California	San Diego	San Diego			$147	$71	$218
California	San Francisco	San Francisco	10/01/09	10/31/09	$192	$71	$263
California	San Francisco	San Francisco	11/01/09	08/31/10	$166	$71	$237
California	San Francisco	San Francisco	09/01/10	09/30/10	$192	$71	$263
California	San Luis Obispo	San Luis Obispo	10/01/09	06/30/10	$106	$66	$172
California	San Luis Obispo	San Luis Obispo	07/01/10	08/31/10	$126	$66	$192
California	San Luis Obispo	San Luis Obispo	09/01/10	09/30/10	$106	$66	$172
California	San Mateo / Foster City / Belmont	San Mateo			$125	$61	$186
California	Santa Barbara	Santa Barbara	10/01/09	06/30/10	$149	$66	$215
California	Santa Barbara	Santa Barbara	07/01/10	08/31/10	$199	$66	$265
California	Santa Barbara	Santa Barbara	09/01/10	09/30/10	$149	$66	$215
California	Santa Cruz	Santa Cruz	10/01/09	05/31/10	$99	$66	$165
California	Santa Cruz	Santa Cruz	06/01/10	08/31/10	$132	$66	$198
California	Santa Cruz	Santa Cruz	09/01/10	09/30/10	$99	$66	$165
California	Santa Monica	City limits of Santa Monica			$209	$71	$280
California	Santa Rosa	Sonoma			$119	$61	$180
California	South Lake Tahoe	El Dorado	10/01/09	11/30/09	$126	$71	$197
California	South Lake Tahoe	El Dorado	12/01/09	03/31/10	$140	$71	$211
California	South Lake Tahoe	El Dorado	04/01/10	06/30/10	$119	$71	$190
California	South Lake Tahoe	El Dorado	07/01/10	09/30/10	$126	$71	$197
California	Stockton	San Joaquin			$87	$56	$143
California	Sunnyvale / Palo Alto / San Jose	Santa Clara			$132	$56	$188
California	Tahoe City	Placer			$98	$61	$159
California	Truckee	Nevada	10/01/09	11/30/09	$97	$71	$168
California	Truckee	Nevada	12/01/09	02/28/10	$116	$71	$187
California	Truckee	Nevada	03/01/10	09/30/10	$97	$71	$168
California	Visalia / Lemoore	Tulare and Kings			$85	$61	$146
California	West Sacramento	Yolo			$99	$51	$150

Table 4. Maximum Federal Per Diem Rates (Effective 10/1/2009 - 9/30/2010) (Continued)

State	Primary Destination	County	Begin	End	Lodging	M&IE	Total
California	Yosemite National Park	Mariposa			$131	$71	$202
Colorado	Aspen	Pitkin	10/01/09	11/30/09	$92	$71	$163
Colorado	Aspen	Pitkin	12/01/09	04/30/10	$217	$71	$288
Colorado	Aspen	Pitkin	05/01/10	06/30/10	$105	$71	$176
Colorado	Aspen	Pitkin	07/01/10	08/31/10	$129	$71	$200
Colorado	Aspen	Pitkin	09/01/10	09/30/10	$92	$71	$163
Colorado	Boulder / Broomfield	Boulder and Broomfield	10/01/09	10/31/09	$124	$61	$185
Colorado	Boulder / Broomfield	Boulder and Broomfield	11/01/09	04/30/10	$103	$61	$164
Colorado	Boulder / Broomfield	Boulder and Broomfield	05/01/10	09/30/10	$124	$61	$185
Colorado	Colorado Springs	El Paso			$88	$66	$154
Colorado	Cortez	Montezuma	10/01/09	05/31/10	$85	$51	$136
Colorado	Cortez	Montezuma	06/01/10	08/31/10	$108	$51	$159
Colorado	Cortez	Montezuma	09/01/10	09/30/10	$85	$51	$136
Colorado	Crested Butte / Gunnison	Gunnison	10/01/09	03/31/10	$81	$51	$132
Colorado	Crested Butte / Gunnison	Gunnison	04/01/10	05/31/10	$74	$51	$125
Colorado	Crested Butte / Gunnison	Gunnison	06/01/10	08/31/10	$97	$51	$148
Colorado	Crested Butte / Gunnison	Gunnison	09/01/10	09/30/10	$81	$51	$132
Colorado	Denver / Aurora	Denver, Adams, Arapahoe, and Jefferson			$158	$66	$224
Colorado	Douglas County	Douglas			$108	$61	$169
Colorado	Durango	La Plata	10/01/09	05/31/10	$98	$61	$159
Colorado	Durango	La Plata	06/01/10	09/30/10	$133	$61	$194
Colorado	Fort Collins / Loveland	Larimer			$90	$56	$146
Colorado	Glenwood Springs / Grand Junction	Garfield / Mesa			$98	$51	$149
Colorado	Montrose	Montrose			$86	$56	$142
Colorado	Silverthorne / Breckenridge	Summit	10/01/09	11/30/09	$100	$56	$156
Colorado	Silverthorne / Breckenridge	Summit	12/01/09	03/31/10	$152	$56	$208
Colorado	Silverthorne / Breckenridge	Summit	04/01/10	09/30/10	$100	$56	$156
Colorado	Steamboat Springs	Routt	10/01/09	11/30/09	$108	$56	$164
Colorado	Steamboat Springs	Routt	12/01/09	03/31/10	$196	$56	$252
Colorado	Steamboat Springs	Routt	04/01/10	09/30/10	$108	$56	$164
Colorado	Telluride	San Miguel	10/01/09	11/30/09	$97	$71	$168
Colorado	Telluride	San Miguel	12/01/09	03/31/10	$187	$71	$258
Colorado	Telluride	San Miguel	04/01/10	05/31/10	$101	$71	$172
Colorado	Telluride	San Miguel	06/01/10	09/30/10	$141	$71	$212
Colorado	Vail	Eagle	10/01/09	11/30/09	$113	$71	$184
Colorado	Vail	Eagle	12/01/09	03/31/10	$271	$71	$342
Colorado	Vail	Eagle	04/01/10	08/31/10	$136	$71	$207
Colorado	Vail	Eagle	09/01/10	09/30/10	$113	$71	$184
Connecticut	Bridgeport / Danbury	Fairfield			$126	$71	$197
Connecticut	Cromwell / Old Saybrook	Middlesex			$87	$61	$148
Connecticut	Hartford	Hartford			$112	$56	$168
Connecticut	Lakeville / Salisbury	Litchfield			$97	$66	$163
Connecticut	New Haven	New Haven			$102	$61	$163
Connecticut	New London / Groton	New London			$101	$61	$162
Connecticut	Putnam / Danielson / Storrs	Windham / Tolland			$77	$56	$133
Delaware	Dover	Kent	10/01/09	04/30/10	$77	$46	$123

Table 4. Maximum Federal Per Diem Rates (Effective 10/1/2009 - 9/30/2010) (Continued)

State	Primary Destination	County	Begin	End	Lodging	M&IE	Total
Delaware	Dover	Kent	05/01/10	09/30/10	$96	$46	$142
Delaware	Lewes	Sussex	10/01/09	06/30/10	$84	$46	$130
Delaware	Lewes	Sussex	07/01/10	08/31/10	$123	$46	$169
Delaware	Lewes	Sussex	09/01/10	09/30/10	$84	$46	$130
Delaware	Wilmington	New Castle			$126	$56	$182
District of Columbia	District of Columbia	Washington DC (also the cities of Alexandria, Falls Church and Fairfax, and the counties of Arlington and Fairfax, in Virginia; and the counties of Montgomery and Prince George's in Maryland) (See also Maryland and Virginia)	10/01/09	10/31/09	$229	$71	$300
District of Columbia	District of Columbia	Washington DC (also the cities of Alexandria, Falls Church and Fairfax, and the counties of Arlington and Fairfax, in Virginia; and the counties of Montgomery and Prince George's in Maryland) (See also Maryland and Virginia)	11/01/09	02/28/10	$207	$71	$278
District of Columbia	District of Columbia	Washington DC (also the cities of Alexandria, Falls Church and Fairfax, and the counties of Arlington and Fairfax, in Virginia; and the counties of Montgomery and Prince George's in Maryland) (See also Maryland and Virginia)	03/01/10	06/30/10	$226	$71	$297
District of Columbia	District of Columbia	Washington DC (also the cities of Alexandria, Falls Church and Fairfax, and the counties of Arlington and Fairfax, in Virginia; and the counties of Montgomery and Prince George's in Maryland) (See also Maryland and Virginia)	07/01/10	08/31/10	$170	$71	$241
District of Columbia	District of Columbia	Washington DC (also the cities of Alexandria, Falls Church and Fairfax, and the counties of Arlington and Fairfax, in Virginia; and the counties of Montgomery and Prince George's in Maryland) (See also Maryland and Virginia)	09/01/10	09/30/10	$229	$71	$300
Florida	Altamonte Springs	Seminole			$93	$61	$154
Florida	Boca Raton / Delray Beach / Jupiter	Palm Beach	10/01/09	12/31/09	$93	$71	$164
Florida	Boca Raton / Delray Beach / Jupiter	Palm Beach	01/01/10	04/30/10	$123	$71	$194
Florida	Boca Raton / Delray Beach / Jupiter	Palm Beach	05/01/10	09/30/10	$93	$71	$164
Florida	Bradenton	Manatee	10/01/09	12/31/09	$87	$56	$143
Florida	Bradenton	Manatee	01/01/10	04/30/10	$105	$56	$161
Florida	Bradenton	Manatee	05/01/10	09/30/10	$87	$56	$143
Florida	Cocoa Beach	Brevard			$97	$51	$148
Florida	Daytona Beach	Volusia	10/01/09	01/31/10	$87	$51	$138
Florida	Daytona Beach	Volusia	02/01/10	07/31/10	$111	$51	$162
Florida	Daytona Beach	Volusia	08/01/10	09/30/10	$87	$51	$138
Florida	Fort Lauderdale	Broward	10/01/09	04/30/10	$168	$71	$239
Florida	Fort Lauderdale	Broward	05/01/10	09/30/10	$117	$71	$188

Table 4. Maximum Federal Per Diem Rates (Effective 10/1/2009 - 9/30/2010) (Continued)

State	Primary Destination	County	Begin	End	Lodging	M&IE	Total
Florida	Fort Myers	Lee	10/01/09	12/31/09	$85	$56	$141
Florida	Fort Myers	Lee	01/01/10	04/30/10	$114	$56	$170
Florida	Fort Myers	Lee	05/01/10	09/30/10	$85	$56	$141
Florida	Fort Pierce	Saint Lucie	10/01/09	01/31/10	$91	$51	$142
Florida	Fort Pierce	Saint Lucie	02/01/10	04/30/10	$108	$51	$159
Florida	Fort Pierce	Saint Lucie	05/01/10	09/30/10	$91	$51	$142
Florida	Fort Walton Beach / De Funiak Springs	Okaloosa and Walton	10/01/09	10/31/09	$120	$51	$171
Florida	Fort Walton Beach / De Funiak Springs	Okaloosa and Walton	11/01/09	02/28/10	$81	$51	$132
Florida	Fort Walton Beach / De Funiak Springs	Okaloosa and Walton	03/01/10	05/31/10	$133	$51	$184
Florida	Fort Walton Beach / De Funiak Springs	Okaloosa and Walton	06/01/10	07/31/10	$178	$51	$229
Florida	Fort Walton Beach / De Funiak Springs	Okaloosa and Walton	08/01/10	09/30/10	$120	$51	$171
Florida	Gainesville	Alachua			$92	$51	$143
Florida	Gulf Breeze	Santa Rosa	10/01/09	02/28/10	$96	$51	$147
Florida	Gulf Breeze	Santa Rosa	03/01/10	08/31/10	$130	$51	$181
Florida	Gulf Breeze	Santa Rosa	09/01/10	09/30/10	$96	$51	$147
Florida	Jacksonville / Jacksonville Beach / Mayport Naval Station	Duval, City of Jacksonville and Nassau			$88	$51	$139
Florida	Key West	Monroe	10/01/09	11/30/09	$155	$71	$226
Florida	Key West	Monroe	12/01/09	01/31/10	$188	$71	$259
Florida	Key West	Monroe	02/01/10	04/30/10	$199	$71	$270
Florida	Key West	Monroe	05/01/10	09/30/10	$155	$71	$226
Florida	Kissimmee	Osceola			$83	$46	$129
Florida	Lakeland	Polk			$87	$46	$133
Florida	Leesburg	Lake			$81	$46	$127
Florida	Miami	Miami-Dade	10/01/09	12/31/09	$128	$66	$194
Florida	Miami	Miami-Dade	01/01/10	03/31/10	$152	$66	$218
Florida	Miami	Miami-Dade	04/01/10	09/30/10	$117	$66	$183
Florida	Naples	Collier	10/01/09	12/31/09	$115	$61	$176
Florida	Naples	Collier	01/01/10	04/30/10	$164	$61	$225
Florida	Naples	Collier	05/01/10	09/30/10	$108	$61	$169
Florida	Ocala	Marion			$83	$46	$129
Florida	Orlando	Orange	10/01/09	12/31/09	$108	$56	$164
Florida	Orlando	Orange	01/01/10	03/31/10	$117	$56	$173
Florida	Orlando	Orange	04/01/10	09/30/10	$108	$56	$164
Florida	Panama City	Bay	10/01/09	02/28/10	$81	$51	$132
Florida	Panama City	Bay	03/01/10	05/31/10	$113	$51	$164
Florida	Panama City	Bay	06/01/10	07/31/10	$127	$51	$178
Florida	Panama City	Bay	08/01/10	09/30/10	$81	$51	$132
Florida	Pensacola / Pensacola Beach	Escambia			$109	$46	$155
Florida	Punta Gorda	Charlotte	10/01/09	01/31/10	$85	$51	$136
Florida	Punta Gorda	Charlotte	02/01/10	03/31/10	$99	$51	$150
Florida	Punta Gorda	Charlotte	04/01/10	09/30/10	$85	$51	$136
Florida	Sarasota	Sarasota	10/01/09	12/31/09	$93	$56	$149

Table 4. Maximum Federal Per Diem Rates (Effective 10/1/2009 - 9/30/2010) (Continued)

State	Primary Destination	County	Begin	End	Lodging	M&IE	Total
Florida	Sarasota	Sarasota	01/01/10	04/30/10	$117	$56	$173
Florida	Sarasota	Sarasota	05/01/10	09/30/10	$93	$56	$149
Florida	Sebring	Highlands	10/01/09	12/31/09	$85	$46	$131
Florida	Sebring	Highlands	01/01/10	03/31/10	$131	$46	$177
Florida	Sebring	Highlands	04/01/10	09/30/10	$85	$46	$131
Florida	St. Augustine	St. Johns			$105	$56	$161
Florida	Stuart	Martin	10/01/09	12/31/09	$85	$51	$136
Florida	Stuart	Martin	01/01/10	04/30/10	$108	$51	$159
Florida	Stuart	Martin	05/01/10	09/30/10	$85	$51	$136
Florida	Tallahassee	Leon			$90	$46	$136
Florida	Tampa / St. Petersburg	Pinellas and Hillsborough	10/01/09	12/31/09	$101	$51	$152
Florida	Tampa / St. Petersburg	Pinellas and Hillsborough	01/01/10	03/31/10	$120	$51	$171
Florida	Tampa / St. Petersburg	Pinellas and Hillsborough	04/01/10	09/30/10	$101	$51	$152
Florida	Vero Beach	Indian River	10/01/09	01/31/10	$89	$51	$140
Florida	Vero Beach	Indian River	02/01/10	03/31/10	$106	$51	$157
Florida	Vero Beach	Indian River	04/01/10	09/30/10	$89	$51	$140
Georgia	Athens	Clarke			$94	$46	$140
Georgia	Atlanta	Fulton, Dekalb and Cobb			$140	$56	$196
Georgia	Augusta	Richmond			$82	$51	$133
Georgia	Columbus	Muscogee			$91	$46	$137
Georgia	Conyers	Rockdale			$77	$46	$123
Georgia	Duluth / Norcross / Lawrenceville	Gwinnett			$81	$51	$132
Georgia	Jekyll Island / Brunswick	Glynn	10/01/09	11/30/09	$149	$56	$205
Georgia	Jekyll Island / Brunswick	Glynn	12/01/09	02/28/10	$108	$56	$164
Georgia	Jekyll Island / Brunswick	Glynn	03/01/10	09/30/10	$149	$56	$205
Georgia	Peachtree City / Jonesboro / Morrow	Fayette / Coweta / Clayton			$73	$51	$124
Georgia	Savannah	Chatham			$106	$56	$162
Idaho	Boise	Ada			$85	$51	$136
Idaho	Bonner's Ferry / Sandpoint	Bonner / Boundary / Shoshone	10/01/09	06/30/10	$77	$61	$138
Idaho	Bonner's Ferry / Sandpoint	Bonner / Boundary / Shoshone	07/01/10	08/31/10	$104	$61	$165
Idaho	Bonner's Ferry / Sandpoint	Bonner / Boundary / Shoshone	09/01/10	09/30/10	$77	$61	$138
Idaho	Coeur d'Alene	Kootenai	10/01/09	05/31/10	$72	$61	$133
Idaho	Coeur d'Alene	Kootenai	06/01/10	08/31/10	$107	$61	$168
Idaho	Coeur d'Alene	Kootenai	09/01/10	09/30/10	$72	$61	$133
Idaho	Driggs / Idaho Falls	Bonneville / Fremont / Teton			$76	$46	$122
Idaho	Sun Valley / Ketchum	Blaine	10/01/09	05/31/10	$84	$71	$155
Idaho	Sun Valley / Ketchum	Blaine	06/01/10	08/31/10	$99	$71	$170
Idaho	Sun Valley / Ketchum	Blaine	09/01/10	09/30/10	$84	$71	$155
Idaho	Twin Falls	Twin Falls			$87	$46	$133
Illinois	Bolingbrook / Romeoville / Lemont	Will			$92	$51	$143
Illinois	Chicago	Cook and Lake	10/01/09	11/30/09	$205	$71	$276
Illinois	Chicago	Cook and Lake	12/01/09	04/30/10	$158	$71	$229
Illinois	Chicago	Cook and Lake	05/01/10	06/30/10	$211	$71	$282
Illinois	Chicago	Cook and Lake	07/01/10	08/31/10	$176	$71	$247
Illinois	Chicago	Cook and Lake	09/01/10	09/30/10	$205	$71	$276
Illinois	Elgin / Aurora	City of Elgin, Kane			$90	$56	$146

Table 4. Maximum Federal Per Diem Rates (Effective 10/1/2009 - 9/30/2010) (Continued)

State	Primary Destination	County	Begin	End	Lodging	M&IE	Total
Illinois	Oak Brook Terrace	Dupage			$100	$61	$161
Illinois	O'Fallon / Fairview Heights / Collinsville	Bond, Calhoun, Clinton, Jersey, Macoupin, Madison, Monroe and St. Clair			$110	$56	$166
Illinois	Springfield	Sangamon			$83	$56	$139
Indiana	Bloomington	Monroe			$97	$56	$153
Indiana	Brownsburg / Plainfield	Hendricks			$83	$61	$144
Indiana	Ft. Wayne	Allen			$86	$56	$142
Indiana	Hammond / Munster / Merrillville	Lake			$94	$46	$140
Indiana	Indianapolis / Carmel	Marion, Hamilton, Fort Benjamin Harrison military base			$94	$61	$155
Indiana	Lafayette	Tippecanoe			$89	$51	$140
Indiana	Michigan City	La Porte			$79	$56	$135
Indiana	South Bend	St. Joseph			$96	$56	$152
Indiana	Valparaiso / Burlington Beach	Porter			$83	$51	$134
Iowa	Cedar Rapids	Linn			$87	$51	$138
Iowa	Des Moines	Polk			$86	$51	$137
Kansas	Kansas City / Overland Park	Wyandotte and Johnson			$107	$61	$168
Kansas	Wichita	Sedgwick			$91	$56	$147
Kentucky	Boone County	Boone			$98	$51	$149
Kentucky	Kenton County	Kenton			$123	$56	$179
Kentucky	Lexington	Fayette			$94	$61	$155
Kentucky	Louisville	Jefferson	10/01/09	05/31/10	$105	$61	$166
Kentucky	Louisville	Jefferson	06/01/10	08/31/10	$97	$61	$158
Kentucky	Louisville	Jefferson	09/01/10	09/30/10	$105	$61	$166
Louisiana	Baton Rouge	East Baton Rouge Parish			$103	$56	$159
Louisiana	Covington / Slidell	St. Tammany Parish			$99	$56	$155
Louisiana	Lafayette	Lafayette Consolidated Government			$89	$56	$145
Louisiana	Lake Charles	Calcasieu Parish			$82	$61	$143
Louisiana	New Orleans	Orleans, St. Bernard, Jefferson and Plaquemine Parishes	10/01/09	06/30/10	$133	$71	$204
Louisiana	New Orleans	Orleans, St. Bernard, Jefferson and Plaquemine Parishes	07/01/10	09/30/10	$104	$71	$175
Maine	Bar Harbor	Hancock	10/01/09	10/31/09	$109	$61	$170
Maine	Bar Harbor	Hancock	11/01/09	06/30/10	$84	$61	$145
Maine	Bar Harbor	Hancock	07/01/10	08/31/10	$156	$61	$217
Maine	Bar Harbor	Hancock	09/01/10	09/30/10	$109	$61	$170
Maine	Kennebunk / Kittery / Sanford	York	10/01/09	10/31/09	$96	$56	$152
Maine	Kennebunk / Kittery / Sanford	York	11/01/09	03/31/10	$70	$56	$126
Maine	Kennebunk / Kittery / Sanford	York	04/01/10	06/30/10	$87	$56	$143
Maine	Kennebunk / Kittery / Sanford	York	07/01/10	08/31/10	$132	$56	$188
Maine	Kennebunk / Kittery / Sanford	York	09/01/10	09/30/10	$96	$56	$152
Maine	Portland	Cumberland / Sagadahoc	10/01/09	06/30/10	$91	$56	$147
Maine	Portland	Cumberland / Sagadahoc	07/01/10	09/30/10	$115	$56	$171
Maine	Rockport	Knox	10/01/09	06/30/10	$70	$56	$126
Maine	Rockport	Knox	07/01/10	08/31/10	$83	$56	$139
Maine	Rockport	Knox	09/01/10	09/30/10	$70	$56	$126

Table 4. Maximum Federal Per Diem Rates (Effective 10/1/2009 - 9/30/2010) (Continued)

State	Primary Destination	County	Begin	End	Lodging	M&IE	Total
Maryland	Aberdeen / Bel Air / Belcamp	Harford			$83	$56	$139
Maryland	Annapolis	Anne Arundel			$120	$61	$181
Maryland	Baltimore City	Baltimore City	10/01/09	11/30/09	$161	$71	$232
Maryland	Baltimore City	Baltimore City	12/01/09	02/28/10	$135	$71	$206
Maryland	Baltimore City	Baltimore City	03/01/10	09/30/10	$161	$71	$232
Maryland	Baltimore County	Baltimore			$103	$61	$164
Maryland	Cambridge / St. Michaels	Dorchester and Talbot	10/01/09	10/31/09	$144	$61	$205
Maryland	Cambridge / St. Michaels	Dorchester and Talbot	11/01/09	03/31/10	$102	$61	$163
Maryland	Cambridge / St. Michaels	Dorchester and Talbot	04/01/10	05/31/10	$133	$61	$194
Maryland	Cambridge / St. Michaels	Dorchester and Talbot	06/01/10	08/31/10	$176	$61	$237
Maryland	Cambridge / St. Michaels	Dorchester and Talbot	09/01/10	09/30/10	$144	$61	$205
Maryland	Columbia	Howard			$123	$61	$184
Maryland	Frederick	Frederick			$92	$56	$148
Maryland	Hagerstown	Washington			$82	$56	$138
Maryland	La Plata / Indian Head	Charles			$93	$51	$144
Maryland	Lexington Park / Leonardtown / Lusby	St. Mary's and Calvert			$102	$61	$163
Maryland	Ocean City	Worcester	10/01/09	10/31/09	$104	$71	$175
Maryland	Ocean City	Worcester	11/01/09	03/31/10	$73	$71	$144
Maryland	Ocean City	Worcester	04/01/10	05/31/10	$91	$71	$162
Maryland	Ocean City	Worcester	06/01/10	08/31/10	$199	$71	$270
Maryland	Ocean City	Worcester	09/01/10	09/30/10	$104	$71	$175
Maryland	Washington, DC Metro Area	Montgomery and Prince George's	10/01/09	10/31/09	$229	$71	$300
Maryland	Washington, DC Metro Area	Montgomery and Prince George's	11/01/09	02/28/10	$207	$71	$278
Maryland	Washington, DC Metro Area	Montgomery and Prince George's	03/01/10	06/30/10	$226	$71	$297
Maryland	Washington, DC Metro Area	Montgomery and Prince George's	07/01/10	08/31/10	$170	$71	$241
Maryland	Washington, DC Metro Area	Montgomery and Prince George's	09/01/10	09/30/10	$229	$71	$300
Massachusetts	Andover	Essex			$88	$56	$144
Massachusetts	Boston / Cambridge	Suffolk, city of Cambridge	10/01/09	10/31/09	$240	$71	$311
Massachusetts	Boston / Cambridge	Suffolk, city of Cambridge	11/01/09	03/31/10	$168	$71	$239
Massachusetts	Boston / Cambridge	Suffolk, city of Cambridge	04/01/10	06/30/10	$231	$71	$302
Massachusetts	Boston / Cambridge	Suffolk, city of Cambridge	07/01/10	08/31/10	$205	$71	$276
Massachusetts	Boston / Cambridge	Suffolk, city of Cambridge	09/01/10	09/30/10	$240	$71	$311
Massachusetts	Burlington / Woburn	Middlesex			$121	$71	$192
Massachusetts	Falmouth	City limits of Falmouth	10/01/09	04/30/10	$98	$51	$149
Massachusetts	Falmouth	City limits of Falmouth	05/01/10	06/30/10	$108	$51	$159
Massachusetts	Falmouth	City limits of Falmouth	07/01/10	08/31/10	$152	$51	$203
Massachusetts	Falmouth	City limits of Falmouth	09/01/10	09/30/10	$98	$51	$149
Massachusetts	Hyannis	Barnstable	10/01/09	06/30/10	$86	$56	$142
Massachusetts	Hyannis	Barnstable	07/01/10	08/31/10	$125	$56	$181
Massachusetts	Hyannis	Barnstable	09/01/10	09/30/10	$86	$56	$142
Massachusetts	Martha's Vineyard	Dukes	10/01/09	10/31/09	$119	$71	$190
Massachusetts	Martha's Vineyard	Dukes	11/01/09	05/31/10	$105	$71	$176
Massachusetts	Martha's Vineyard	Dukes	06/01/10	08/31/10	$199	$71	$270
Massachusetts	Martha's Vineyard	Dukes	09/01/10	09/30/10	$119	$71	$190
Massachusetts	Nantucket	Nantucket	10/01/09	03/31/10	$115	$61	$176
Massachusetts	Nantucket	Nantucket	04/01/10	05/31/10	$130	$61	$191

Table 4. Maximum Federal Per Diem Rates (Effective 10/1/2009 - 9/30/2010) (Continued)

State	Primary Destination	County	Begin	End	Lodging	M&IE	Total
Massachusetts	Nantucket	Nantucket	06/01/10	09/30/10	$222	$61	$283
Massachusetts	Northampton	Hampshire			$92	$56	$148
Massachusetts	Pittsfield	Berkshire	10/01/09	06/30/10	$105	$61	$166
Massachusetts	Pittsfield	Berkshire	07/01/10	08/31/10	$132	$61	$193
Massachusetts	Pittsfield	Berkshire	09/01/10	09/30/10	$105	$61	$166
Massachusetts	Plymouth / Taunton / New Bedford	Plymouth / Bristol			$94	$56	$150
Massachusetts	Quincy	Norfolk			$124	$51	$175
Massachusetts	Springfield	Hampden			$97	$51	$148
Massachusetts	Worcester	Worcester			$96	$61	$157
Michigan	Ann Arbor	Washtenaw			$92	$56	$148
Michigan	Benton Harbor / St. Joseph / Stevensville	Berrien			$75	$51	$126
Michigan	Charlevoix	Charlevoix			$71	$61	$132
Michigan	Detroit	Wayne			$104	$56	$160
Michigan	East Lansing / Lansing	Ingham and Eaton			$84	$51	$135
Michigan	Flint	Genessee			$82	$51	$133
Michigan	Grand Rapids	Kent			$82	$51	$133
Michigan	Holland	Ottawa			$83	$56	$139
Michigan	Kalamazoo / Battle Creek	Kalamazoo / Calhoun			$89	$51	$140
Michigan	Mackinac Island	Mackinac	10/01/09	06/30/10	$70	$66	$136
Michigan	Mackinac Island	Mackinac	07/01/10	08/31/10	$87	$66	$153
Michigan	Mackinac Island	Mackinac	09/01/10	09/30/10	$70	$66	$136
Michigan	Midland	Midland			$97	$46	$143
Michigan	Mount Pleasant	Isabella			$74	$51	$125
Michigan	Muskegon	Muskegon	10/01/09	05/31/10	$74	$46	$120
Michigan	Muskegon	Muskegon	06/01/10	08/31/10	$99	$46	$145
Michigan	Muskegon	Muskegon	09/01/10	09/30/10	$74	$46	$120
Michigan	Ontonagon / Baraga / Houghton	Ontonagon / Baraga / Houghton			$75	$46	$121
Michigan	Petoskey	Emmet	10/01/09	06/30/10	$74	$51	$125
Michigan	Petoskey	Emmet	07/01/10	08/31/10	$98	$51	$149
Michigan	Petoskey	Emmet	09/01/10	09/30/10	$74	$51	$125
Michigan	Pontiac / Auburn Hills	Oakland			$97	$56	$153
Michigan	South Haven	Van Buren	10/01/09	05/31/10	$70	$56	$126
Michigan	South Haven	Van Buren	06/01/10	08/31/10	$86	$56	$142
Michigan	South Haven	Van Buren	09/01/10	09/30/10	$70	$56	$126
Michigan	Traverse City and Leland	Grand Traverse and Leelanau	10/01/09	06/30/10	$71	$51	$122
Michigan	Traverse City and Leland	Grand Traverse and Leelanau	07/01/10	08/31/10	$114	$51	$165
Michigan	Traverse City and Leland	Grand Traverse and Leelanau	09/01/10	09/30/10	$71	$51	$122
Michigan	Warren	Macomb			$77	$51	$128
Minnesota	Duluth	St. Louis	10/01/09	05/31/10	$84	$56	$140
Minnesota	Duluth	St. Louis	06/01/10	08/31/10	$104	$56	$160
Minnesota	Duluth	St. Louis	09/01/10	09/30/10	$84	$56	$140
Minnesota	Eagan / Burnsville / Mendota Heights	Dakota			$89	$56	$145
Minnesota	Minneapolis / St. Paul	Hennepin and Ramsey			$137	$71	$208
Minnesota	Rochester	Olmsted			$99	$51	$150
Mississippi	Grenada	Grenada			$79	$46	$125

Table 4. Maximum Federal Per Diem Rates (Effective 10/1/2009 - 9/30/2010) (Continued)

State	Primary Destination	County	Begin	End	Lodging	M&IE	Total
Mississippi	Gulfport / Biloxi	Harrison			$79	$56	$135
Mississippi	Hattiesburg	Forrest and Lamar			$80	$51	$131
Mississippi	Robinsonville	Tunica			$85	$51	$136
Mississippi	Southaven	Desoto			$91	$46	$137
Mississippi	Starkville	Oktibbeha			$86	$46	$132
Missouri	Columbia	Boone			$82	$51	$133
Missouri	Jefferson City	Cole			$78	$51	$129
Missouri	Kansas City	Jackson, Clay, Cass and Platte			$107	$56	$163
Missouri	Springfield	Greene			$78	$56	$134
Missouri	St. Louis	St. Louis, St. Louis City and St. Charles, Crawford, Franklin, Jefferson, Lincoln, Warren and Washington			$110	$66	$176
Missouri	St. Robert	Pulaski			$74	$46	$120
Montana	Big Sky / West Yellowstone	Gallatin	10/01/09	04/30/10	$77	$61	$138
Montana	Big Sky / West Yellowstone	Gallatin	05/01/10	09/30/10	$102	$61	$163
Montana	Butte	Silver Bow			$84	$51	$135
Montana	Helena	Lewis and Clark			$81	$56	$137
Montana	Missoula / Polson / Kalispell	Missoula / Lake / Flathead	10/01/09	06/30/10	$91	$51	$142
Montana	Missoula / Polson / Kalispell	Missoula / Lake / Flathead	07/01/10	08/31/10	$121	$51	$172
Montana	Missoula / Polson / Kalispell	Missoula / Lake / Flathead	09/01/10	09/30/10	$91	$51	$142
Nebraska	Omaha	Douglas			$101	$61	$162
Nevada	Incline Village / Reno / Sparks	Washoe	10/01/09	06/30/10	$104	$51	$155
Nevada	Incline Village / Reno / Sparks	Washoe	07/01/10	08/31/10	$130	$51	$181
Nevada	Incline Village / Reno / Sparks	Washoe	09/01/10	09/30/10	$104	$51	$155
Nevada	Las Vegas	Clark	10/01/09	12/31/09	$109	$71	$180
Nevada	Las Vegas	Clark	01/01/10	05/31/10	$118	$71	$189
Nevada	Las Vegas	Clark	06/01/10	09/30/10	$109	$71	$180
Nevada	Stateline, Carson City	Douglas, Carson City			$100	$61	$161
New Hampshire	Concord	Merrimack	10/01/09	10/31/09	$99	$51	$150
New Hampshire	Concord	Merrimack	11/01/09	05/31/10	$84	$51	$135
New Hampshire	Concord	Merrimack	06/01/10	09/30/10	$99	$51	$150
New Hampshire	Conway	Caroll	10/01/09	02/28/10	$124	$61	$185
New Hampshire	Conway	Caroll	03/01/10	06/30/10	$115	$61	$176
New Hampshire	Conway	Caroll	07/01/10	08/31/10	$161	$61	$222
New Hampshire	Conway	Caroll	09/01/10	09/30/10	$124	$61	$185
New Hampshire	Durham	Strafford			$96	$46	$142
New Hampshire	Laconia	Belknap	10/01/09	10/31/09	$102	$51	$153
New Hampshire	Laconia	Belknap	11/01/09	05/31/10	$87	$51	$138
New Hampshire	Laconia	Belknap	06/01/10	09/30/10	$102	$51	$153
New Hampshire	Lebanon / Lincoln / West Lebanon	Grafton / Sullivan			$101	$56	$157
New Hampshire	Manchester	Hillsborough			$93	$56	$149
New Hampshire	Portsmouth	Rockingham	10/01/09	06/30/10	$103	$61	$164
New Hampshire	Portsmouth	Rockingham	07/01/10	09/30/10	$134	$61	$195
New Jersey	Atlantic City / Ocean City / Cape May	Atlantic and Cape May	10/01/09	10/31/09	$114	$66	$180
New Jersey	Atlantic City / Ocean City / Cape May	Atlantic and Cape May	11/01/09	04/30/10	$104	$66	$170

Table 4. Maximum Federal Per Diem Rates (Effective 10/1/2009 - 9/30/2010) (Continued)

State	Primary Destination	County	Begin	End	Lodging	M&IE	Total
New Jersey	Atlantic City / Ocean City / Cape May	Atlantic and Cape May	05/01/10	09/30/10	$114	$66	$180
New Jersey	Belle Mead	Somerset			$127	$56	$183
New Jersey	Cherry Hill / Moorestown	Camden and Burlington			$96	$61	$157
New Jersey	Eatontown / Freehold	Monmouth			$121	$56	$177
New Jersey	Edison / Piscataway	Middlesex			$115	$51	$166
New Jersey	Flemington	Hunterdon			$114	$61	$175
New Jersey	Newark	Essex, Bergen, Hudson and Passaic			$130	$61	$191
New Jersey	Parsippany	Morris			$139	$56	$195
New Jersey	Princeton / Trenton	Mercer			$140	$61	$201
New Jersey	Springfield / Cranford / New Providence	Union			$107	$56	$163
New Jersey	Tom's River	Ocean	10/01/09	06/30/10	$90	$51	$141
New Jersey	Tom's River	Ocean	07/01/10	08/31/10	$122	$51	$173
New Jersey	Tom's River	Ocean	09/01/10	09/30/10	$90	$51	$141
New Mexico	Albuquerque	Bernalillo			$81	$56	$137
New Mexico	Los Alamos	Los Alamos			$85	$51	$136
New Mexico	Santa Fe	Santa Fe	10/01/09	05/31/10	$88	$71	$159
New Mexico	Santa Fe	Santa Fe	06/01/10	08/31/10	$109	$71	$180
New Mexico	Santa Fe	Santa Fe	09/01/10	09/30/10	$88	$71	$159
New Mexico	Taos	Taos			$77	$66	$143
New York	Albany	Albany			$110	$61	$171
New York	Binghamton / Owego	Broome and Tioga			$91	$46	$137
New York	Buffalo	Erie			$99	$56	$155
New York	Floral Park / Garden City / Great Neck	Nassau			$161	$66	$227
New York	Glens Falls	Warren	10/01/09	06/30/10	$98	$66	$164
New York	Glens Falls	Warren	07/01/10	08/31/10	$150	$66	$216
New York	Glens Falls	Warren	09/01/10	09/30/10	$98	$66	$164
New York	Ithaca / Waterloo / Romulus	Tompkins and Seneca			$117	$46	$163
New York	Kingston	Ulster			$103	$66	$169
New York	Lake Placid	Essex	10/01/09	11/30/09	$112	$61	$173
New York	Lake Placid	Essex	12/01/09	02/28/10	$131	$61	$192
New York	Lake Placid	Essex	03/01/10	06/30/10	$102	$61	$163
New York	Lake Placid	Essex	07/01/10	08/31/10	$160	$61	$221
New York	Lake Placid	Essex	09/01/10	09/30/10	$112	$61	$173
New York	Manhattan (includes the boroughs of Manhattan, Brooklyn, the Bronx, Queens and Staten Island)	Bronx, Kings, New York, Queens, Richmond	10/01/09	12/31/09	$340	$71	$411
New York	Manhattan (includes the boroughs of Manhattan, Brooklyn, the Bronx, Queens and Staten Island)	Bronx, Kings, New York, Queens, Richmond	01/01/10	03/31/10	$209	$71	$280
New York	Manhattan (includes the boroughs of Manhattan, Brooklyn, the Bronx, Queens and Staten Island)	Bronx, Kings, New York, Queens, Richmond	04/01/10	06/30/10	$318	$71	$389
New York	Manhattan (includes the boroughs of Manhattan, Brooklyn, the Bronx, Queens and Staten Island)	Bronx, Kings, New York, Queens, Richmond	07/01/10	08/31/10	$279	$71	$350

Table 4. Maximum Federal Per Diem Rates (Effective 10/1/2009 - 9/30/2010) (Continued)

State	Primary Destination	County	Begin	End	Lodging	M&IE	Total
New York	Manhattan (includes the boroughs of Manhattan, Brooklyn, the Bronx, Queens and Staten Island)	Bronx, Kings, New York, Queens, Richmond	09/01/10	09/30/10	$340	$71	$411
New York	Niagara Falls	Niagara	10/01/09	05/31/10	$78	$51	$129
New York	Niagara Falls	Niagara	06/01/10	08/31/10	$106	$51	$157
New York	Niagara Falls	Niagara	09/01/10	09/30/10	$78	$51	$129
New York	Nyack / Palisades	Rockland			$113	$61	$174
New York	Poughkeepsie	Dutchess			$110	$66	$176
New York	Riverhead / Ronkonkoma / Melville	Suffolk			$130	$71	$201
New York	Rochester	Monroe			$102	$51	$153
New York	Saratoga Springs / Schenectady	Saratoga and Schenectady	10/01/09	06/30/10	$106	$56	$162
New York	Saratoga Springs / Schenectady	Saratoga and Schenectady	07/01/10	08/31/10	$168	$56	$224
New York	Saratoga Springs / Schenectady	Saratoga and Schenectady	09/01/10	09/30/10	$106	$56	$162
New York	Syracuse	Onondaga			$97	$56	$153
New York	Tarrytown / White Plains / New Rochelle	Westchester			$164	$71	$235
New York	Troy	Rensselaer			$98	$51	$149
New York	West Point	Orange			$113	$51	$164
North Carolina	Asheville	Buncombe	10/01/09	10/31/09	$95	$51	$146
North Carolina	Asheville	Buncombe	11/01/09	06/30/10	$85	$51	$136
North Carolina	Asheville	Buncombe	07/01/10	09/30/10	$95	$51	$146
North Carolina	Atlantic Beach / Morehead City	Carteret	10/01/09	05/31/10	$84	$56	$140
North Carolina	Atlantic Beach / Morehead City	Carteret	06/01/10	08/31/10	$117	$56	$173
North Carolina	Atlantic Beach / Morehead City	Carteret	09/01/10	09/30/10	$84	$56	$140
North Carolina	Chapel Hill	Orange			$91	$56	$147
North Carolina	Charlotte	Mecklenburg			$100	$51	$151
North Carolina	Durham	Durham			$97	$51	$148
North Carolina	Fayetteville	Cumberland			$92	$51	$143
North Carolina	Greensboro	Guilford	10/01/09	10/31/09	$97	$56	$153
North Carolina	Greensboro	Guilford	11/01/09	03/31/10	$86	$56	$142
North Carolina	Greensboro	Guilford	04/01/10	09/30/10	$97	$56	$153
North Carolina	Greenville	Pitt			$86	$51	$137
North Carolina	Kill Devil	Dare	10/01/09	04/30/10	$70	$61	$131
North Carolina	Kill Devil	Dare	05/01/10	09/30/10	$114	$61	$175
North Carolina	New Bern / Havelock	Craven			$97	$46	$143
North Carolina	Raleigh	Wake			$92	$66	$158
North Carolina	Wilmington	New Hanover			$98	$56	$154
North Carolina	Winston-Salem	Forsyth			$92	$56	$148
Ohio	Akron	Summit			$91	$51	$142
Ohio	Canton	Stark			$93	$51	$144
Ohio	Cincinnati	Hamilton and Clermont			$115	$56	$171
Ohio	Cleveland	Cuyahoga			$109	$56	$165
Ohio	Columbus	Franklin			$101	$56	$157
Ohio	Dayton / Fairborn	Greene, Darke and Montgomery			$82	$56	$138
Ohio	Hamilton	Butler and Warren			$91	$51	$142
Ohio	Mentor	Lake			$92	$46	$138
Ohio	Rittman	Wayne and Medina			$86	$51	$137

Table 4. Maximum Federal Per Diem Rates (Effective 10/1/2009 - 9/30/2010) (Continued)

State	Primary Destination	County	Begin	End	Lodging	M&IE	Total
Ohio	Sandusky / Bellevue	Erie and Huron			$100	$46	$146
Ohio	Toledo	Lucas			$81	$51	$132
Ohio	Youngstown	Mahoning and Trumbull			$85	$51	$136
Oklahoma	Oklahoma City	Oklahoma			$84	$66	$150
Oklahoma	Tulsa	Tulsa, Creek, Osage, and Rogers			$81	$61	$142
Oregon	Ashland / Crater Lake	Jackson / Klamath			$88	$56	$144
Oregon	Beaverton	Washington			$96	$51	$147
Oregon	Bend	Deschutes	10/01/09	06/30/10	$93	$61	$154
Oregon	Bend	Deschutes	07/01/10	08/31/10	$120	$61	$181
Oregon	Bend	Deschutes	09/01/10	09/30/10	$93	$61	$154
Oregon	Clackamas	Clackamas			$91	$61	$152
Oregon	Eugene / Florence	Lane			$103	$51	$154
Oregon	Lincoln City	Lincoln	10/01/09	06/30/10	$87	$56	$143
Oregon	Lincoln City	Lincoln	07/01/10	08/31/10	$110	$56	$166
Oregon	Lincoln City	Lincoln	09/01/10	09/30/10	$87	$56	$143
Oregon	Portland	Multnomah			$120	$66	$186
Oregon	Seaside	Clatsop	10/01/09	06/30/10	$92	$51	$143
Oregon	Seaside	Clatsop	07/01/10	08/31/10	$132	$51	$183
Oregon	Seaside	Clatsop	09/01/10	09/30/10	$92	$51	$143
Pennsylvania	Allentown / Easton / Bethlehem	Lehigh and Northampton			$92	$51	$143
Pennsylvania	Bucks County	Bucks			$102	$71	$173
Pennsylvania	Chester / Radnor / Essington	Delaware			$109	$51	$160
Pennsylvania	Erie	Erie	10/01/09	05/31/10	$85	$46	$131
Pennsylvania	Erie	Erie	06/01/10	08/31/10	$97	$46	$143
Pennsylvania	Erie	Erie	09/01/10	09/30/10	$85	$46	$131
Pennsylvania	Gettysburg	Adams	10/01/09	10/31/09	$103	$51	$154
Pennsylvania	Gettysburg	Adams	11/01/09	03/31/10	$82	$51	$133
Pennsylvania	Gettysburg	Adams	04/01/10	09/30/10	$103	$51	$154
Pennsylvania	Harrisburg	Dauphin			$103	$51	$154
Pennsylvania	Hershey	City of Hershey	10/01/09	05/31/10	$99	$56	$155
Pennsylvania	Hershey	City of Hershey	06/01/10	08/31/10	$180	$56	$236
Pennsylvania	Hershey	City of Hershey	09/01/10	09/30/10	$99	$56	$155
Pennsylvania	Lancaster	Lancaster			$99	$56	$155
Pennsylvania	Malvern / Frazer / Berwyn	Chester			$126	$51	$177
Pennsylvania	Mechanicsburg	Cumberland			$88	$56	$144
Pennsylvania	Montgomery County	Montgomery			$128	$66	$194
Pennsylvania	Philadelphia	Philadelphia	10/01/09	11/30/09	$170	$66	$236
Pennsylvania	Philadelphia	Philadelphia	12/01/09	08/31/10	$153	$66	$219
Pennsylvania	Philadelphia	Philadelphia	09/01/10	09/30/10	$170	$66	$236
Pennsylvania	Pittsburgh	Allegheny			$119	$71	$190
Pennsylvania	Reading	Berks			$96	$56	$152
Pennsylvania	Scranton	Lackawanna			$83	$56	$139
Pennsylvania	State College	Centre			$92	$56	$148
Rhode Island	East Greenwich / Warwick / North Kingstown	Kent and Washington			$96	$56	$152
Rhode Island	Jamestown / Middletown / Newport	Newport	10/01/09	10/31/09	$166	$71	$237
Rhode Island	Jamestown / Middletown / Newport	Newport	11/01/09	04/30/10	$104	$71	$175

Table 4. Maximum Federal Per Diem Rates (Effective 10/1/2009 - 9/30/2010) (Continued)

State	Primary Destination	County	Begin	End	Lodging	M&IE	Total
Rhode Island	Jamestown / Middletown / Newport	Newport	05/01/10	09/30/10	$166	$71	$237
Rhode Island	Providence	Providence			$139	$71	$210
South Carolina	Aiken	Aiken			$86	$46	$132
South Carolina	Charleston	Charleston, Berkeley and Dorchester			$142	$56	$198
South Carolina	Columbia	Richland / Lexington			$93	$51	$144
South Carolina	Greenville	Greenville			$92	$56	$148
South Carolina	Hilton Head	Beaufort	10/01/09	10/31/09	$115	$61	$176
South Carolina	Hilton Head	Beaufort	11/01/09	03/31/10	$93	$61	$154
South Carolina	Hilton Head	Beaufort	04/01/10	08/31/10	$142	$61	$203
South Carolina	Hilton Head	Beaufort	09/01/10	09/30/10	$115	$61	$176
South Carolina	Myrtle Beach	Horry	10/01/09	10/31/09	$84	$51	$135
South Carolina	Myrtle Beach	Horry	11/01/09	02/28/10	$70	$51	$121
South Carolina	Myrtle Beach	Horry	03/01/10	05/31/10	$94	$51	$145
South Carolina	Myrtle Beach	Horry	06/01/10	08/31/10	$132	$51	$183
South Carolina	Myrtle Beach	Horry	09/01/10	09/30/10	$84	$51	$135
South Dakota	Hot Springs	Fall River and Custer	10/01/09	05/31/10	$70	$46	$116
South Dakota	Hot Springs	Fall River and Custer	06/01/10	08/31/10	$94	$46	$140
South Dakota	Hot Springs	Fall River and Custer	09/01/10	09/30/10	$70	$46	$116
South Dakota	Rapid City	Pennington	10/01/09	05/31/10	$70	$51	$121
South Dakota	Rapid City	Pennington	06/01/10	08/31/10	$118	$51	$169
South Dakota	Rapid City	Pennington	09/01/10	09/30/10	$70	$51	$121
South Dakota	Sturgis / Spearfish	Meade, Butte and Lawrence	10/01/09	04/30/10	$70	$51	$121
South Dakota	Sturgis / Spearfish	Meade, Butte and Lawrence	05/01/10	08/31/10	$99	$51	$150
South Dakota	Sturgis / Spearfish	Meade, Butte and Lawrence	09/01/10	09/30/10	$70	$51	$121
Tennessee	Brentwood / Franklin	Williamson			$102	$56	$158
Tennessee	Chattanooga	Hamilton			$87	$56	$143
Tennessee	Knoxville	Knox			$84	$56	$140
Tennessee	Memphis	Shelby			$100	$61	$161
Tennessee	Nashville	Davidson			$119	$66	$185
Tennessee	Oak Ridge	Anderson			$90	$46	$136
Texas	Arlington / Fort Worth / Grapevine	Tarrant county and City limits of Grapevine			$151	$56	$207
Texas	Austin	Travis	10/01/09	10/31/09	$121	$71	$192
Texas	Austin	Travis	11/01/09	08/31/10	$115	$71	$186
Texas	Austin	Travis	09/01/10	09/30/10	$121	$71	$192
Texas	Beaumont	Jefferson			$93	$51	$144
Texas	College Station	Brazos			$93	$56	$149
Texas	Corpus Christi	Nueces			$90	$51	$141
Texas	Dallas	Dallas County and City of Dallas	10/01/09	12/31/09	$117	$71	$188
Texas	Dallas	Dallas County and City of Dallas	01/01/10	03/31/10	$122	$71	$193
Texas	Dallas	Dallas County and City of Dallas	04/01/10	09/30/10	$117	$71	$188
Texas	El Paso	El Paso			$91	$51	$142
Texas	Galveston	Galveston	10/01/09	05/31/10	$108	$56	$164
Texas	Galveston	Galveston	06/01/10	07/31/10	$128	$56	$184
Texas	Galveston	Galveston	08/01/10	09/30/10	$108	$56	$164

Table 4. Maximum Federal Per Diem Rates (Effective 10/1/2009 - 9/30/2010) (Continued)

State	Primary Destination	County	Begin	End	Lodging	M&IE	Total
Texas	Houston (L.B. Johnson Space Center)	Montgomery, Fort Bend and Harris			$118	$71	$189
Texas	Hunt County	Hunt County			$87	$51	$138
Texas	Laredo	Webb			$85	$56	$141
Texas	McAllen	Hidalgo			$89	$56	$145
Texas	Plano	Collin			$116	$61	$177
Texas	Round Rock	Williamson			$97	$51	$148
Texas	San Antonio	Bexar			$117	$66	$183
Texas	South Padre Island	Cameron	10/01/09	05/31/10	$83	$56	$139
Texas	South Padre Island	Cameron	06/01/10	07/31/10	$107	$56	$163
Texas	South Padre Island	Cameron	08/01/10	09/30/10	$83	$56	$139
Texas	Waco	McLennan			$88	$51	$139
Utah	Park City	Summit	10/01/09	12/31/09	$96	$71	$167
Utah	Park City	Summit	01/01/10	03/31/10	$157	$71	$228
Utah	Park City	Summit	04/01/10	09/30/10	$96	$71	$167
Utah	Provo	Utah			$88	$51	$139
Utah	Salt Lake City	Salt Lake and Tooele			$106	$61	$167
Vermont	Burlington / St. Albans	Chittenden and Franklin	10/01/09	10/31/09	$112	$66	$178
Vermont	Burlington / St. Albans	Chittenden and Franklin	11/01/09	04/30/10	$93	$66	$159
Vermont	Burlington / St. Albans	Chittenden and Franklin	05/01/10	09/30/10	$112	$66	$178
Vermont	Manchester	Bennington			$93	$71	$164
Vermont	Middlebury	Addison			$116	$61	$177
Vermont	Montpelier	Washington			$101	$61	$162
Vermont	Stowe	Lamoille	10/01/09	03/31/10	$132	$71	$203
Vermont	Stowe	Lamoille	04/01/10	05/31/10	$105	$71	$176
Vermont	Stowe	Lamoille	06/01/10	09/30/10	$132	$71	$203
Vermont	White River Junction	Windsor	10/01/09	02/28/10	$102	$56	$158
Vermont	White River Junction	Windsor	03/01/10	05/31/10	$89	$56	$145
Vermont	White River Junction	Windsor	06/01/10	09/30/10	$102	$56	$158
Virginia	Abingdon	Washington			$82	$46	$128
Virginia	Blacksburg	Montgomery			$98	$46	$144
Virginia	Charlottesville	City of Charlottesville, Albemarle, Greene			$112	$56	$168
Virginia	Chesapeake / Suffolk	Cities of Chesapeake and Suffolk	10/01/09	05/31/10	$87	$56	$143
Virginia	Chesapeake / Suffolk	Cities of Chesapeake and Suffolk	06/01/10	08/31/10	$103	$56	$159
Virginia	Chesapeake / Suffolk	Cities of Chesapeake and Suffolk	09/01/10	09/30/10	$87	$56	$143
Virginia	Chesterfield / Henrico Counties	Chesterfield / Henrico			$92	$51	$143
Virginia	Fredericksburg	City of Fredericksburg, Spotsylvania			$78	$56	$134
Virginia	Hampton City / Newport News	Cities of Hampton City and Newport News			$80	$56	$136
Virginia	James City and York Counties, Williamsburg	James City and York Counties, City of Williamsburg	10/01/09	03/31/10	$72	$51	$123
Virginia	James City and York Counties, Williamsburg	James City and York Counties, City of Williamsburg	04/01/10	08/31/10	$94	$51	$145
Virginia	James City and York Counties, Williamsburg	James City and York Counties, City of Williamsburg	09/01/10	09/30/10	$72	$51	$123
Virginia	Loudoun County	Loudoun			$135	$61	$196
Virginia	Lynchburg	Campbell, Lynchburg City			$83	$51	$134

Table 4. Maximum Federal Per Diem Rates (Effective 10/1/2009 - 9/30/2010) (Continued)

State	Primary Destination	County	Begin	End	Lodging	M&IE	Total
Virginia	Manassas	City of Manassas			$93	$46	$139
Virginia	Norfolk / Portsmouth	Cities of Norfolk and Portsmouth			$95	$61	$156
Virginia	Richmond City	City of Richmond			$125	$66	$191
Virginia	Roanoke	City limits of Roanoke			$103	$51	$154
Virginia	Stafford / Prince William Counties	Stafford / Prince William			$95	$46	$141
Virginia	Virginia Beach	City of Virginia Beach	10/01/09	05/31/10	$89	$56	$145
Virginia	Virginia Beach	City of Virginia Beach	06/01/10	08/31/10	$148	$56	$204
Virginia	Virginia Beach	City of Virginia Beach	09/01/10	09/30/10	$89	$56	$145
Virginia	Wallops Island	Accomack	10/01/09	06/30/10	$87	$56	$143
Virginia	Wallops Island	Accomack	07/01/10	08/31/10	$128	$56	$184
Virginia	Wallops Island	Accomack	09/01/10	09/30/10	$87	$56	$143
Virginia	Warrenton	Fauquier			$101	$46	$147
Virginia	Washington, DC Metro Area	Cities of Alexandria, Fairfax and Falls Church; Arlington and Fairfax	10/01/09	10/31/09	$229	$71	$300
Virginia	Washington, DC Metro Area	Cities of Alexandria, Fairfax and Falls Church; Arlington and Fairfax	11/01/09	02/28/10	$207	$71	$278
Virginia	Washington, DC Metro Area	Cities of Alexandria, Fairfax and Falls Church; Arlington and Fairfax	03/01/10	06/30/10	$226	$71	$297
Virginia	Washington, DC Metro Area	Cities of Alexandria, Fairfax and Falls Church; Arlington and Fairfax	07/01/10	08/31/10	$170	$71	$241
Virginia	Washington, DC Metro Area	Cities of Alexandria, Fairfax and Falls Church; Arlington and Fairfax	09/01/10	09/30/10	$229	$71	$300
Washington	Anacortes / Coupeville / Oak Harbor	Skagit, Island, San Juan			$90	$61	$151
Washington	Bremerton	Kitsap			$83	$66	$149
Washington	Everett / Lynnwood	Snohomish			$100	$61	$161
Washington	Ocean Shores	Grays Harbor	10/01/09	06/30/10	$90	$51	$141
Washington	Ocean Shores	Grays Harbor	07/01/10	08/31/10	$111	$51	$162
Washington	Ocean Shores	Grays Harbor	09/01/10	09/30/10	$90	$51	$141
Washington	Olympia / Tumwater	Thurston			$89	$61	$150
Washington	Port Angeles / Port Townsend	Clallam and Jefferson	10/01/09	06/30/10	$98	$61	$159
Washington	Port Angeles / Port Townsend	Clallam and Jefferson	07/01/10	08/31/10	$142	$61	$203
Washington	Port Angeles / Port Townsend	Clallam and Jefferson	09/01/10	09/30/10	$98	$61	$159
Washington	Seattle	King			$159	$71	$230
Washington	Spokane	Spokane			$85	$61	$146
Washington	Tacoma	Pierce			$113	$61	$174
Washington	Vancouver	Clark, Cowlitz and Skamania			$125	$56	$181
West Virginia	Charleston	Kanawha			$101	$51	$152
West Virginia	Morgantown	Monongalia			$85	$46	$131
West Virginia	Shepherdstown	Jefferson			$81	$51	$132
West Virginia	Wheeling	Ohio			$99	$46	$145
Wisconsin	Appleton	Outagamie			$84	$46	$130
Wisconsin	Brookfield / Racine	Waukesha / Racine			$95	$56	$151
Wisconsin	Green Bay	Brown			$78	$51	$129
Wisconsin	Lake Geneva	Walworth	10/01/09	04/30/10	$89	$51	$140

Table 4. Maximum Federal Per Diem Rates (Effective 10/1/2009 - 9/30/2010) (Continued)

State	Primary Destination	County	Begin	End	Lodging	M&IE	Total
Wisconsin	Lake Geneva	Walworth	05/01/10	09/30/10	$132	$51	$183
Wisconsin	Madison	Dane			$93	$56	$149
Wisconsin	Milwaukee	Milwaukee			$104	$61	$165
Wisconsin	Sheboygan	Sheboygan			$84	$51	$135
Wisconsin	Sturgeon Bay	Door	10/01/09	06/30/10	$70	$56	$126
Wisconsin	Sturgeon Bay	Door	07/01/10	09/30/10	$89	$56	$145
Wisconsin	Wisconsin Dells	Columbia	10/01/09	06/30/10	$70	$61	$131
Wisconsin	Wisconsin Dells	Columbia	07/01/10	08/31/10	$89	$61	$150
Wisconsin	Wisconsin Dells	Columbia	09/01/10	09/30/10	$70	$61	$131
Wyoming	Cody	Park	10/01/09	05/31/10	$82	$51	$133
Wyoming	Cody	Park	06/01/10	09/30/10	$125	$51	$176
Wyoming	Evanston / Rock Springs	Sweetwater / Uinta			$85	$51	$136
Wyoming	Gillette	Campbell	10/01/09	05/31/10	$98	$51	$149
Wyoming	Gillette	Campbell	06/01/10	08/31/10	$123	$51	$174
Wyoming	Gillette	Campbell	09/01/10	09/30/10	$98	$51	$149
Wyoming	Jackson / Pinedale	Teton and Sublette	10/01/09	11/30/09	$109	$56	$165
Wyoming	Jackson / Pinedale	Teton and Sublette	12/01/09	06/30/10	$131	$56	$187
Wyoming	Jackson / Pinedale	Teton and Sublette	07/01/10	08/31/10	$174	$56	$230
Wyoming	Jackson / Pinedale	Teton and Sublette	09/01/10	09/30/10	$109	$56	$165
Wyoming	Sheridan	Sheridan	10/01/09	05/31/10	$74	$56	$130
Wyoming	Sheridan	Sheridan	06/01/10	08/31/10	$93	$56	$149
Wyoming	Sheridan	Sheridan	09/01/10	09/30/10	$74	$56	$130

NOTES:

(1) **Standard rate.** The standard rate of $116 ($70 for lodging and $46 for M&IE) applies to all locations within the continental United States (CONUS) not specifically listed below or encompassed by the boundary definition of a listed point. However, the standard CONUS rate applies to all locations within CONUS, including those defined below, for certain relocation allowances. (See parts 302-2, 302-4, and 302-5 of 41 CFR.)

(2) **Transition rule.** In lieu of the updated GSA rates that will be effective October 1, 2010, taxpayers may continue to use the CONUS rates in effect for the first 9 months of 2010 (Table 4) for expenses of all CONUS travel away from home that are paid or incurred during calendar year 2010. A taxpayer must consistently use either these rates or the updated rates for the period of October 1, 2010, through December 31, 2010.

(3) **Per diem locality.** Unless otherwise specified, the per diem locality is defined as "all locations within, or entirely surrounded by, the corporate limits of the key city, including independent entities located within those boundaries."

Per diem localities with county definitions shall include "all locations within, or entirely surrounded by, the corporate limits of the key city as well as the boundaries of the listed counties, including independent entities located within the boundaries of the key city and the listed counties (unless otherwise listed separately)."

When a military installation or Government-related facility (whether or not specifically named) is located partially within more than one city or county boundary, the applicable per diem rate for the entire installation or facility is the higher of the two rates which apply to the cities and/or counties, even though part(s) of such activities may be located outside the defined per diem locality.

Recognizing that all locations are not incorporated cities, the term "city limits" has been used as a general phrase to denote the commonly recognized local boundaries of the location cited.

(Sources: IRS Publication 1542, Per Diem Rates; U.S. General Services Administration, Domestic Per Diem Rates (available at http://www.gsa.gov))

Sample Weekly Traveling Expense and Entertainment Record

From: ____________________ To: ____________________ Name: ____________________

Expenses	SUN	MON	TUE	WED	THU	FRI	SAT	Total
Travel Expenses: Airlines								
Excess baggage								
Bus – Train								
Cab and Limousine								
Tips								
Porter								
Meals and Lodging: Breakfast								
Lunch								
Dinner								
Hotel and Motel (Detail in Section B)								
Entertainment (Detail in Section C)								
Other Expenses: Postage								
Telephone, Internet Access								
Stationery, Printing								
Stenographer								
Sample Room								
Advertising								
Assistant(s), Model(s)								
Trade Shows								
Car Expenses: (List all car expenses – the division between business and personal expenses may be made at the end of the year.) (Detail mileage in Section A)								
Gas, oil, lube, wash								
Repairs, parts								
Tires, supplies								
Parking fees, tolls								
Other (identify)								
Total								

Note: Attach receipted bills for (1) ALL lodging and (2) any other expenses of $75.00 or more.

Section A – Car								
Mileage: End								
Start								
Total								
Business Mileage								

Section B – Lodging									
Hotel or Motel	Name:								
	City:								

Section C – Entertainment

Date	Item	Place	Amount	Business Purpose	Business Relationship

WEEKLY REIMBURSEMENTS:

Travel and transportation expenses ____________

Other reimbursements ____________

TOTAL ____________

Form **2106** | Department of the Treasury Internal Revenue Service (99)

Employee Business Expenses

▶ See separate instructions.

▶ Attach to Form 1040 or Form 1040NR.

OMB No. 1545-0074

2009

Attachment Sequence No. 129

Your name	Occupation in which you incurred expenses	Social security number

Part I **Employee Business Expenses and Reimbursements**

Step 1 Enter Your Expenses		**Column A** Other Than Meals and Entertainment	**Column B** Meals and Entertainment
1 Vehicle expense from line 22 or line 29. (Rural mail carriers: See instructions.)	1		
2 Parking fees, tolls, and transportation, including train, bus, etc., that **did not** involve overnight travel or commuting to and from work	2		
3 Travel expense while away from home overnight, including lodging, airplane, car rental, etc. **Do not** include meals and entertainment	3		
4 Business expenses not included on lines 1 through 3. **Do not** include meals and entertainment	4		
5 Meals and entertainment expenses (see instructions)	5		
6 **Total expenses.** In Column A, add lines 1 through 4 and enter the result. In Column B, enter the amount from line 5	6		

Note: *If you were not reimbursed for any expenses in Step 1, skip line 7 and enter the amount from line 6 on line 8.*

Step 2 Enter Reimbursements Received From Your Employer for Expenses Listed in Step 1

7 Enter reimbursements received from your employer that were **not** reported to you in box 1 of Form W-2. Include any reimbursements reported under code "L" in box 12 of your Form W-2 (see instructions)	7		

Step 3 Figure Expenses To Deduct on Schedule A (Form 1040 or Form 1040NR)

8 Subtract line 7 from line 6. If zero or less, enter -0-. However, if line 7 is greater than line 6 in Column A, report the excess as income on Form 1040, line 7 (or on Form 1040NR, line 8)	8		
Note: If ***both columns*** *of line 8 are zero, you cannot deduct employee business expenses. Stop here and attach Form 2106 to your return.*			
9 In Column A, enter the amount from line 8. In Column B, multiply line 8 by 50% (.50). (Employees subject to Department of Transportation (DOT) hours of service limits: Multiply meal expenses incurred while away from home on business by 80% (.80) instead of 50%. For details, see instructions.)	9		

10 Add the amounts on line 9 of both columns and enter the total here. **Also, enter the total on Schedule A (Form 1040), line 21** (or on **Schedule A (Form 1040NR), line 9**). (Armed Forces reservists, qualified performing artists, fee-basis state or local government officials, and individuals with disabilities: See the instructions for special rules on where to enter the total.) ▶	10	

For Paperwork Reduction Act Notice, see instructions. Cat. No. 11700N Form **2106** (2009)

Part II Vehicle Expenses

Section A—General Information (You must complete this section if you are claiming vehicle expenses.)

			(a) Vehicle 1	(b) Vehicle 2
11	Enter the date the vehicle was placed in service	11	/ /	/ /
12	Total miles the vehicle was driven during 2009	12	miles	miles
13	Business miles included on line 12	13	miles	miles
14	Percent of business use. Divide line 13 by line 12	14	%	%
15	Average daily roundtrip commuting distance	15	miles	miles
16	Commuting miles included on line 12	16	miles	miles
17	Other miles. Add lines 13 and 16 and subtract the total from line 12	17	miles	miles

18	Was your vehicle available for personal use during off-duty hours?	☐ Yes	☐ No
19	Do you (or your spouse) have another vehicle available for personal use?	☐ Yes	☐ No
20	Do you have evidence to support your deduction?	☐ Yes	☐ No
21	If "Yes," is the evidence written?	☐ Yes	☐ No

Section B—Standard Mileage Rate (See the instructions for Part II to find out whether to complete this section or Section C.)

22	Multiply line 13 by 55¢ (.55). Enter the result here and on line 1	22	

Section C—Actual Expenses

			(a) Vehicle 1	(b) Vehicle 2
23	Gasoline, oil, repairs, vehicle insurance, etc.	23		
24a	Vehicle rentals	24a		
b	Inclusion amount (see instructions)	24b		
c	Subtract line 24b from line 24a	24c		
25	Value of employer-provided vehicle (applies only if 100% of annual lease value was included on Form W-2—see instructions)	25		
26	Add lines 23, 24c, and 25.	26		
27	Multiply line 26 by the percentage on line 14	27		
28	Depreciation (see instructions)	28		
29	Add lines 27 and 28. Enter total here and on line 1	29		

Section D—Depreciation of Vehicles (Use this section only if you owned the vehicle and are completing Section C for the vehicle.)

			(a) Vehicle 1	(b) Vehicle 2
30	Enter cost or other basis (see instructions)	30		
31	Enter section 179 deduction and special allowance (see instructions)	31		
32	Multiply line 30 by line 14 (see instructions if you claimed the section 179 deduction or special allowance)	32		
33	Enter depreciation method and percentage (see instructions)	33		
34	Multiply line 32 by the percentage on line 33 (see instructions)	34		
35	Add lines 31 and 34	35		
36	Enter the applicable limit explained in the line 36 instructions	36		
37	Multiply line 36 by the percentage on line 14	37		
38	Enter the **smaller** of line 35 or line 37. If you skipped lines 36 and 37, enter the amount from line 35. Also enter this amount on line 28 above	38		

Form **2106** (2009)

Form **2106-EZ**

Department of the Treasury
Internal Revenue Service (99)

Unreimbursed Employee Business Expenses

▶ **Attach to Form 1040 or Form 1040NR.**

OMB No. 1545-0074

2009

Attachment
Sequence No. **129A**

Your name	Occupation in which you incurred expenses	**Social security number**
		: :

You Can Use This Form Only if All of the Following Apply.

- You are an employee deducting ordinary and necessary expenses attributable to your job. An ordinary expense is one that is common and accepted in your field of trade, business, or profession. A necessary expense is one that is helpful and appropriate for your business. An expense does not have to be required to be considered necessary.
- You **do not** get reimbursed by your employer for any expenses (amounts your employer included in box 1 of your Form W-2 are not considered reimbursements for this purpose).
- If you are claiming vehicle expense, you are using the standard mileage rate for 2009.

Caution: *You can use the standard mileage rate for 2009* ***only if: (a)*** *you owned the vehicle and used the standard mileage rate for the first year you placed the vehicle in service,* ***or (b)*** *you leased the vehicle and used the standard mileage rate for the portion of the lease period after 1997.*

Part I Figure Your Expenses

1	Vehicle expense using the standard mileage rate. Complete Part II and multiply line 8a by 55¢ (.55) . . .	1		
2	Parking fees, tolls, and transportation, including train, bus, etc., that **did not** involve overnight travel or commuting to and from work . . .	2		
3	Travel expense while away from home overnight, including lodging, airplane, car rental, etc. **Do not** include meals and entertainment . . .	3		
4	Business expenses not included on lines 1 through 3. **Do not** include meals and entertainment . . .	4		
5	Meals and entertainment expenses: $ ________ × 50% (.50). (Employees subject to Department of Transportation (DOT) hours of service limits: Multiply meal expenses incurred while away from home on business by 80% (.80) instead of 50%. For details, see instructions.)	5		
6	**Total expenses.** Add lines 1 through 5. Enter here and on **Schedule A (Form 1040), line 21** (or on **Schedule A (Form 1040NR), line 9**). (Armed Forces reservists, fee-basis state or local government officials, qualified performing artists, and individuals with disabilities: See the instructions for special rules on where to enter this amount.) . . .	6		

Part II Information on Your Vehicle. Complete this part **only** if you are claiming vehicle expense on line 1.

7 When did you place your vehicle in service for business use? (month, day, year) ▶ .... / .... / ....

8 Of the total number of miles you drove your vehicle during 2009, enter the number of miles you used your vehicle for:

a Business .... **b** Commuting (see instructions) .... **c** Other ....

9 Was your vehicle available for personal use during off-duty hours? . . . ☐ **Yes** ☐ **No**

10 Do you (or your spouse) have another vehicle available for personal use? . . . ☐ **Yes** ☐ **No**

11a Do you have evidence to support your deduction?. . . ☐ **Yes** ☐ **No**

b If "Yes," is the evidence written?. . . ☐ **Yes** ☐ **No**

For Paperwork Reduction Act Notice, see page 4. Cat. No. 20604Q Form **2106-EZ** (2009)

What's New in 2009

Temporary Increase in IRC §179 Limits. The increased maximum IRC §179 deduction of $250,000 ($285,000 for qualified enterprise zone or renewal zone property) has been extended for 2009 by the American Recovery and Reinvestment Act of 2009 (P.L. 111-5). The threshold investment for a reduction in these limits is $800,000.

Qualified Section 179 Disaster Assistance Property. The IRC §179 expensing dollar limitation is increased by $100,000 (to $350,000 in 2009) for section 179 property that is "qualified section 179 disaster assistance property" for tax years after December 31, 2007. Qualified disaster assistance property is section 179 property which replaces property that is damaged or destroyed in a Presidentially declared disaster area.

Special Depreciation Allowance. Taxpayers can claim 50% bonus depreciation on qualifying property placed in service during the 2009 calendar year. The placed-in-service date is extended one year, through December 31, 2010, for property with a recovery period of 10 years or longer, for transportation property (tangible personal property used to transport people or property), and for certain aircraft.

Qualified Disaster Assistance Property. An additional 50-percent depreciation allowance can be claimed for qualified disaster assistance property that is purchased to rehabilitate or replace similar property that is destroyed or condemned as a result of a Presidentially declared disaster. The provision applies to property placed in service after December 31, 2007, with respect to disasters declared after that date and occurring before January 1, 2010.

Section at a Glance

Relevant IRS Publications

- ☐ IRS Publication 463, *Travel, Entertainment, Gift, and Car Expenses*
- ☐ IRS Publication 534, *Depreciating Property Placed in Service Before 1987*
- ☐ IRS Publication 535, *Business Expenses*
- ☐ IRS Publication 544, *Sales and Other Dispositions of Assets*
- ☐ IRS Publication 551, *Basis of Assets*
- ☐ IRS Publication 946, *How to Depreciate Property*

MACRS Property Classes for use on 2009 Returns

MACRS Class	Examples
3 years	Special manufacturing tools, race horses, tractors, and property with a class life of 4 years or less
5 years	Automobiles, trucks, computers and peripheral equipment (such as printers, external disk drives, and modems), typewriters, copiers, R&E equipment, and property with a class life of more than 4 years and less than 10 years
7 years	Office furniture, fixtures, office equipment, most machinery, motorsports facilities, property with a class life of 10 years or more but less than 16 years, and property with no assigned class life
10 years	Single-purpose agricultural and horticultural structures, assets used in petroleum refining and manufacturing of tobacco and certain food products, and property with a class life of 16 years or more but less than 20 years
15 years	Land improvements (such as sidewalks, roads, irrigation systems, sewers, fences, and landscaping), service stations, billboards, telephone distribution plants, qualified leasehold improvements, qualified restaurant property, and property with a class life of 20 years or more but less than 25 years
20 years	Municipal sewers and property with a class life of 25 years or more, farm buildings
27.5 years	Residential rental real estate, including apartment buildings, duplexes, etc.
39 years	Nonresidential real estate, including office buildings, warehouses, and factories

Filing Requirements

Form 4562, Depreciation and Amortization, is required for reporting:

- depreciation for property placed in service during the tax year;
- any IRC §179 expense deduction, including any carryover from a previous year;
- depreciation on a vehicle or other listed property including bonus or additional depreciation, regardless of when it was placed in service;
- a deduction for any vehicle reported on a form other than Schedule C or C-EZ of Form 1040; and
- amortization of costs beginning during 2009.

A separate Form 4562 should be filed for each business activity on the taxpayer's return. If the taxpayer is an employee deducting job-related vehicle expenses, use Form 2106, Employee Business Expenses (See Tab 6).

IRC §179 Deduction (Part I, Lines 1-13)

General Rule

The IRC §179 expense deduction is an election to deduct part or all of the cost of qualifying depreciable property (i.e., section 179 property) in the year that it is placed in service. All taxpayers other than estates and trusts are entitled to elect the IRC §179 expensing deduction. If a partnership or S corporation elects to use IRC §179, limitations on the deduction apply at both the entity and owner levels.

Planning Tip. In determining whether to use the IRC §179 expense deduction in any particular year, it is important to coordinate the deduction with net profit planning, the future income potential, and subsequent liquidation of the asset. Generally, a taxpayer will make the IRC §179 election on Form 4562 filed with their original return for the tax year the section 179 property is placed in service. However, a taxpayer can also make an election on an amended return that is filed within the three-year limitation period for filing an amended return. For tax years 2003 through 2010, a taxpayer may also revoke a IRC §179 election on an amended return without consent of the IRS. See MTG ¶1208.

Line 1, Maximum Amount

Generally, the maximum deduction allowed for section 179 property placed in service in 2009 is $250,000, as provided on Line 1 of Form 4562. This maximum amount is increased by an additional $35,000 to $285,000 for section 179 property placed in service in 2009 by a trade or business in qualified empowerment zones, renewal communities and the D.C. enterprise zone.

The IRC §179 expensing dollar limitation limitation is increased by $100,000 (to $350,000 in 2009) for section 179 property that is "qualified section 179 disaster assistance property" placed in service after December 31, 2007, with respect to disasters declared after December 31, 2007. In general, qualified disaster assistance property is section 179 property which replaces property that is damaged or destroyed in a Presidentially declared disaster area. Taxpayers may take either the increased deduction for qualified section 179 disaster assistance property or the increased deduction for qualified enterprise zone and renewal property, but not both.

Caution. Formerly, taxpayers could claim an increased IRC §179 expensing deduction for qualifying property placed in service in the GO Zone or Kansas disaster area. However, the increased expensing allowances for these areas have expired.

A discussion of qualifying empowerment zones and renewal communities can be found in the instructions to Form 8844, Empowerment Zone and Renewal Community Employment Credit, and also IRS Publication 954, Tax Incentives for Distressed Communities. To find out whether a business or employee residence is located in an empowerment zone, use the interactive address locator at www.hud.gov/crlocator or call 800-998-9999.

Caution. If any section 179 property placed in service during the tax year ceases to be used in a trade or business in a empowerment or renewal zone, then the increased IRC §179 deduction claimed for such property must be reported as "Other income" on Line 21 of Form 1040. Recapture is also required in any tax year during the recovery period that qualified section 179 disaster assistance property ceases to be qualified section 179 disaster assistance property.

Line 2, Total Cost of Section 179 Property

Line 2 of Form 4562 is used to enter the total cost of section 179 property placed in service during 2009. Include in this amount, the cost of any *listed property* (described on page 7-13) and 50% of the cost of section 179 property placed in service in a qualified enterprise or renewal zone. In the case of a married individual, also include the cost of section 179 property placed in service by his or her spouse, even if filing separately.

Eligible property. Property generally qualifies as section 179 property eligible for expensing if it is:

- tangible personal property (i.e., section 1245 property);
- depreciable under the Modified Accelerated Cost Recovery System or MACRS (see below); and
- acquired by purchase from a nonrelated party and used primarily (i.e., greater than 50%) in the active conduct of a trade or business (as opposed to property held for the production of income).

Off-the-shelf computer software that is placed in service in a tax year beginning after 2002 and before 2011 may be considered section 179 property. Section 179 property does not include air conditioners and heating units, nor property that is used:

- predominantly outside the United States;
- predominantly in connection with furnishing lodging;
- by a tax-exempt organization, unless it is used mainly in a unrelated taxable activity; or
- by a governmental unit, or a foreign person or entity.

For more information about qualifying and nonqualifying property, see MTG ¶1208.

Lines 3-4, Investment Limitation

The maximum allowable IRC §179 deduction for the tax year is reduced dollar for dollar for any section 179 property placed in service during the tax year that exceeds an investment threshold amount. For 2009, the threshold amount is $800,000. This threshold amount is increased by the lesser of $600,000 or the qualified section 179 disaster assistance property placed in service during the tax year, as provided on Line 3 of Form 4562. The amount of any reduction due to the investment limitation is recorded on Line 4.

Example. HMO Inc., a calendar-year taxpayer, purchases a piece of equipment to be used in its business. The cost of the machine is $810,000. Because this cost exceeds the investment threshold for 2009 by $10,000, HMO's dollar limitation for the section 179 property for 2009 must be reduced by $10,000 and HMO records $240,000 on Line 4, assuming it places no other section 179 property in service in 2009.

The reduction for the investment limitation is altered for section 179 property placed in service in a qualified enterprise or renewal zone, or for qualified section 179 disaster assistance property placed in service during the tax year. In these circumstances, the reduction in the maximum allowable deduction is computed by only taking into account one-half of the cost of property that is placed in service in the qualified zone.

Line 5, Dollar Limitation for the Tax Year

On Line 5, record the taxpayer's dollar limitation for the tax year (i.e., the maximum annual limit from Line 1, reduced by the investment limitation from Line 4, but not below zero). If the amount is zero, then the taxpayer cannot elect to deduct the cost of any section 179 property during the tax year. However, any disallowed deduction may be carried over to the next tax year (Line 13).

The dollar amount recorded on Line 5 must be shared by spouses filing separately. The couple may choose to allocate the limitation in any manner they wish (e.g., 50% to each, or 60% to wife and 40% to husband). In addition, the dollar limit on Line 5 must be allocated by a partnership or S corporation to its partners or shareholders according to their respective holdings in the entity.

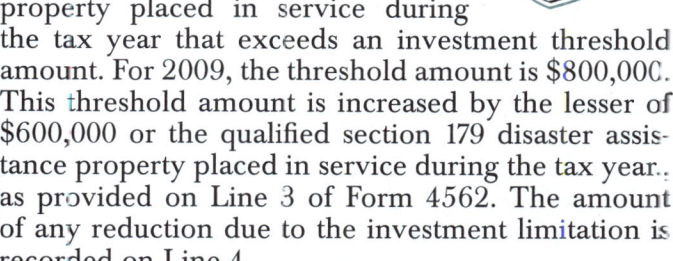

Planning Tip. If a partnership or S corporation elects to use IRC §179, then the annual dollar and investment limits are applied separately at the entity level and at the partner or shareholder level. For example, Mary and Linda form a business partnership that purchases equipment for $260,000 in 2009. Assuming that the equipment is section 179 property, the partnership may deduct $250,000 of the cost. Mary and Linda each may deduct $125,000, assuming they are both active in the conduct of the partnership's business. In addition, each may deduct an additional $125,000 (subject to the investment limitation) on any other section 179 property placed in service in 2009 individually or through another partnership.

Line 6, Description of Property, Cost and Elected Cost

Each item of section 179 property the taxpayer is electing to deduct the cost of during 2009 should be briefly described in Line 6. In column 6(a) provide the description of the property (e.g., type of equipment, office furniture).

Caution. Listed property should not be reported on Line 6. Instead it is included on Line 26. See page 7-13 for a discussion of listed property.

The total cost of section 179 property is reported in column 6(b). For this purpose, if the property was acquired in a like-kind exchange (e.g., a trade-in), only the excess of the cost of the property over the value of the property traded in is reported (i.e., the amount attributable to any boot given in the exchange). The portion of the new asset's basis attributable to the old asset cannot be expensed under IRC §179.

In column 6(c), the portion of the section 179 property's cost that the taxpayer elects to expense is reported. The taxpayer may allocate the IRC §179 allowance in any manner. Normally, the section 179 property that has the longest useful life and that would take the longest to depreciate is expensed. Note that any portion of the asset may be expensed. Any portion that is not expensed under IRC §179 may be depreciated in the normal manner.

Example. Tanya purchased five-year property for $255,000 and seven-year property for $195,000 during 2009. Both assets may be expensed subject to the limitations of IRC §179. The maximum amount that can be expensed in 2009 is $250,000. To maximize current tax savings from limited expensing and depreciation deductions, she should expense the full $195,000 of the seven-year property rather than the five-year property because the cost of the five-year property can then be recovered more quickly, resulting in higher depreciation. The remaining IRC §179 allowance of $55,000 should be used to expense the five-year property. In such case the total deduction for the five-year property in 2009 would be $95,000, computed as follows:

Original cost	$255,000
Expensed portion	– 55,000
Remaining depreciable basis	200,000
Depreciation percentage	× 20.00%
Depreciation deduction	40,000
IRC §179 deduction	+ 55,000
Total deduction	$ 95,000

Taxpayers who are entitled to a share of a IRC §179 expense deduction from a partnership or an S corporation should write "from Schedule K-1 (Form 1065)" or "from Schedule K-1 (Form 1120S)" across columns (a) and (b).

Line 7, Listed Property

The amount of any IRC §179 deduction that may be claimed for "listed property" is limited. To determine the amount of the deduction for "listed property," including motor vehicles, see the discussion beginning on page 7-13.

Line 8, Total Elected Cost of Section 179 Property

The sum of the amounts in column 6(c) and the cost of any listed property (see below) recorded on Line 7 is the total IRC §179 election reported on Line 8.

Line 9, Tentative Deduction

If this amount is less than the dollar limitation for the tax year on Line 5, then this is the taxpayer's tentative deduction for 2009 and should be reported on Line 9. However, if the sum is more than the taxpayer's dollar limitation for the tax year, then report the dollar limitation on Line 9.

Line 10, Carryover of Disallowed Prior-Year Deduction

If, in a prior year, the amount of the IRC §179 deduction was limited due to the taxable income limitation (see Line 11), the amount not used may be carried over to future years until there is sufficient taxable income to utilize it. The amount of carryover from the previous year to report on Line 10 is the amount from Line 13 of the taxpayer's 2008 Form 4562.

Line 11, Business Income Limitation

The IRC §179 deduction is limited to the aggregate taxable income derived from all of the taxpayer's trades or businesses during the year. Thus, the smaller of business income (but not less than zero) or Line 5 is entered on Line 11.

For this purpose, taxable income includes: section 1231 gains or losses (see Tab 4); interest from the working capital of a taxpayer's trade or business; and wages, salaries, tips, and other compensation earned as an employee. It is computed prior to consideration of the IRC §179 deduction, the deduction for self-employment tax, any net operating loss carryover and any unreimbursed employee business expense. Married individuals filing a joint return combine their incomes for this purpose.

Planning Tip. Any amount that cannot be deducted due to the taxable income limitation can be carried over indefinitely to following years to be used against future income. The maximum amount that can be expensed in subsequent years is not increased by the carryover amount, however. Rather than carry over the amount that could not be expensed because of the taxable income limitation, the taxpayer may want to consider reducing the election amount so that there is no carryover. This will allow an increased depreciation deduction in the current tax year.

Partnerships. In determining the taxable business income from a partnership or LLC, the taxpayer aggregates the partnership's items of income and expense from any trade or business that the partnership actively conducted. Items of tax-exempt income and the IRC §179 deduction are not taken into account in determining the partner's share of partnership income. Guaranteed payments from the partnership to the partner are generally treated as taxable business income to the partner only if such payments are for services or are otherwise treated as derived by the partner from the conduct of a trade or business.

S Corporations. In determining the taxable business income from an S corporation, the taxpayer aggregates the income and expense of the S corporation from any trade or business the corporation actively conducted. Items of tax-exempt income and the IRC §179 deduction are not considered in calculating the amount of taxable business income allocated to the shareholder by the S corporation. Wages received by a shareholder-employee of an S corporation are included in taxable business income.

Line 12, Total IRC §179 Expense Deduction

The sum of the current-year tentative deduction (Line 9) and carryover from prior years (Line 10) is entered on Line 12, if it does not exceed the amount on Line 11. Otherwise, the amount on Line 11 is also entered on Line 12 and the difference is reported on Line 13.

The reduction in the IRC §179 allowance for purchases exceeding $800,000 and the taxable income limitation apply to the taxpayer, and not to each separate business or activity. If the taxpayer has more than one business or activity, the allowable IRC §179 expense deduction may be allocated among them. To do so, the taxpayer should write "Summary" at the top of Part I of the separate Form 4562 filed for each business. The remainder of the form should not be completed. On Line 12 of the Form 4562 prepared for each separate business or activity, the amount allocated to the business or activity from the "Summary" should be reported. No other entry is required in Part I of the separate Form 4562.

Recapture. If section 179 property is no longer used more than 50% in a trade or business in a tax year during the property's recovery period, then the taxpayer may have to recapture all or part of the amount deducted under IRC §179 as ordinary income. The amount recaptured is equal to the excess of the amount deducted under IRC §179 over the amount of MACRS depreciation that would have been allowable on the property from the year it was placed in service, including the tax year of recapture. This calculation is made in Part IV of Form 4797. The taxpayer's basis in the property must also be increased by the recaptured amount.

In addition, the IRC §179 expense deduction will be treated as depreciation for recapture purposes. Thus, gain realized on the sale, exchange or other disposition of the property will be characterized as ordinary income to the extent of the IRC §179 deduction claimed, plus any depreciation claimed. If the property is disposed of through an installment sale, then the IRC §179 deduction is immediately recaptured as ordinary income to the extent gain is recognized on the disposition.

Line 13, Carryover of Disallowed Deduction to 2010

Any portion of the IRC §179 allowance that is disallowed due to the taxable income limitation is reported on Line 13 and may be carried over to the next year and deducted as if it were incurred in that year. There is no limit on the carryover period.

Special Depreciation Allowance and Other Depreciation (Part II, Lines 14-16)

Line 14, Special Depreciation Allowance

For certain qualified property, an additional special (bonus) depreciation allowance applies for the first year the property is placed in service. For 2009, taxpayers are allowed to claim bonus depreciation in the amount of 50% of the property's depreciable basis. In order to claim bonus depreciation on property, it must be one of the following: (1) property eligible for the modified accelerated cost recovery system (MACRS) with a depreciation period of 20 years or less; (2) water utility property; (3) computer software (off-the-shelf); or (4) qualified leasehold property. It generally must be purchased (i.e., original use) and place in service after December 31, 2007, and before January 1, 2010.

Planning Tip. The placed-in-service date is extended one year, through December 31, 2010, for property with a recovery period of 10 years or longer, for transportation property (tangible personal property used to transport people or property), and for certain aircraft.

Special Depreciation Allowance for Qualified Disaster Assistance Property. An additional 50-percent depreciation allowance can be claimed for qualified disaster assistance property that is purchased to rehabilitate or replace similar property that is destroyed or condemned as a result of a presidentially declared disaster. The provision applies to property placed in service after December 31, 2007, with respect to disasters declared after that date and occurring before January 1, 2010.

In order to be qualified disaster assistance property, an item must be MACRS recovery property with an recovery period of 20 years or less, computer software that is depreciable over three years, water utility property, or qualified leasehold improvement property, nonresidential real property or residential rental property. The property must rehabilitate property damaged, or replace property destroyed or condemned, as a result of the disaster.

Property is treated as replacing property destroyed or condemned if, as part of an integrated plan, it replaces property that is included in a continuous area that includes real property destroyed or condemned. The property must also be similar in nature to, and located in the same county as, the property being rehabilitated or replaced.

- The property must be acquired by the eligible taxpayer by purchase (as defined in IRC §179(d)), and original use must begin, on or after the applicable disaster date, but only if no written binding contract for the acquisition was in effect before that date. The property must be placed in service by the eligible taxpayer on or before the date that is the last day of the third calendar year following the applicable disaster date (or the fourth calendar year in the case of nonresidential real property and residential rental property).

Kansas Disaster Area. Taxpayers may claim an additional first-year depreciation allowance equal to 50 percent of the adjusted basis of nonresidential real property and residential rental property acquired on or after May 5, 2007, and placed in service on or before December 31, 2009 in the Kansas disaster area.

Additional GO Zone Depreciation. Taxpayers may claim an additional first-year depreciation allowance equal to 50 percent of the adjusted basis of qualified Gulf Opportunity Zone property that is nonresidential real property and residential rental property acquired on or after August 28, 2005, and placed in service on or before December 31, 2010, in a county or parish in which one or more hurricanes that occurred during 2005 damaged more than 60 percent of occupied housing units. The areas included are Hancock, Harrison, Jackson, Pearl River and Stone counties in Mississippi; and Calcasieu, Cameron, Orleans, Plaquemines, St. Bernard, St. Tammany and Washington parishes in Louisiana.

New York Liberty Zone Property. A taxpayer may expense 30% of the cost of qualified New York Liberty Zone nonresidential real and residential rental property if it was acquired by purchase after September 10, 2001, and placed in service before January 1, 2010. Qualified New York Liberty Zone nonresidential real and residential rental property includes certain real property to the extent it constitutes a rehabilitation or replacement of property destroyed or condemned as a result of the September 11, 2001, terrorist attack. Previously, the deduction was available for other types of Liberty Zone property (such as personal property), as well. However, this wider availability does not apply to property placed into service after December 31, 2006.

Caution. Qualified Liberty Zone leasehold improvement property does not qualify for additional special/bonus depreciation.

Planning Tip. Additional or bonus depreciation must be claimed unless a taxpayer makes an election out. An election applies to all property in the class or classes of property for which the election is made. Once made, the election out cannot be revoked without IRS consent.

Additional or bonus depreciation is computed by multiplying the depreciable basis of the property by 50%. It may be claimed *in addition* to any amount expensed under IRC §179. However, the IRC §179 deduction must be taken prior to the additional or bonus depreciation. Thus, the adjusted basis of qualified property is first reduced by any amount expensed under IRC §179.

The amount of the special depreciation allowance is entered on Line 14.

Line 15, Property Subject to Section 168(f)(1) Election

Depreciation for property the taxpayer elects to depreciate under the unit-of-production method or another method not based on a term of years is reported on Line 15. The election is made by reporting the taxpayer's depreciation for the property on Line 15 and attaching a statement to Form 4562 providing a description of the property and the depreciation method, as well as the taxpayer's adjusted basis in the property.

Line 16, Other Depreciation (Including ACRS)

If property may not be depreciated under the Modified Accelerated Cost Recovery System (MACRS) (see below), then total depreciation is reported on Line 16. This generally includes depreciation on the following types of property.

ACRS Property (pre-1987). Tangible personal property placed in service during 1981 through 1986 is normally depreciated using the Accelerated Cost Recovery System (ACRS). Certain antichurning rules exist to prevent taxpayers from taking advantage of MACRS for property owned or used prior to 1987. However, these rules do not apply to:

- residential rental property or nonresidential real property; and
- property for which in the tax year when it was placed in service, the deduction under ACRS was more than the deduction under MACRS using the half-year convention.

> **Planning Tip.** Improvements made after 1986 to property placed in service before 1987 must be depreciated using MACRS and not ACRS.

Personal property. Subject to the preceding exceptions, MACRS cannot be used for personal property (i.e., section 1245 property) if:

(1) the taxpayer or someone related to the taxpayer owned or used the property in 1986;

(2) the taxpayer acquired the property from a person who owned it in 1986 and the user of the property did not change as a result of the transaction;

(3) the taxpayer leased the property to a person (or someone related to the person) who owned or used the property in 1986; or

(4) the taxpayer acquired the property in a transaction in which the user of the property did not change, and the property was not MACRS property in the hands of the person from whom the taxpayer acquired it by virtue of restriction 2 or 3.

Real property. Subject to the exceptions to the antichurning rules, a taxpayer generally cannot use MACRS for real property (i.e., IRC §1250 property) if restrictions (1) and (3) applicable to personal property above apply. Also MACRS may not be used if the taxpayer acquired the real property in a like-kind exchange, involuntary conversion, or repossession of property that the taxpayer (or someone related to the taxpayer) owned in 1986. MACRS applies only to that part of the basis in the acquired real property that represents cash paid or unlike property given up. It does not apply to the carried-over part of the basis.

Property Placed in Service Before 1981. Property placed in service before 1981 generally is depreciated using a facts-and-circumstances method subject to certain limitations (e.g., property acquired from related persons).

Certain Nonrecognition Transactions. MACRS does not apply to property used before 1987 and transferred after 1986 to a corporation or partnership (except property the transferor placed in service after July 31, 1986, if MACRS was elected), to the extent its basis is carried over from the property's adjusted basis in the transferor's hands. The taxpayer must continue to use the same depreciation method as the transferor and figure depreciation as if the transfer had not occurred. However, if MACRS would otherwise apply, the taxpayer can use it to depreciate the part of the property's basis that exceeds the carried-over basis. The nontaxable transfers covered by this rule include:

- a distribution in complete liquidation of a subsidiary;
- a transfer to a corporation controlled by the transferor;
- an exchange of property solely for corporate stock or securities in a reorganization;
- a contribution of property to a partnership in exchange for a partnership interest; and
- a partnership distribution of property to a partner.

Intangibles. Intangibles are normally depreciated using the straight-line method. However, the income forecast method (discussed below) can be elected for certain property. See also the discussion of Amortization beginning on page 7-16.

Motor Vehicles. If a taxpayer elects to depreciate the cost of a motor vehicle for which the standard mileage rate had been used in a previous tax year, then the straight-line method must be used over the vehicle's estimated remaining useful life.

Certain Sound Recordings, Motion Pictures and Videotapes. MACRS cannot be used to depreciate sound recordings, motion picture films and video tapes. For this purpose, sound recordings are discs, tapes, or other phonorecordings resulting from the fixation of a series of sounds. Depreciation for this type of property is computed using the straight-line method or the income forecast method. Taxpayers in the business of renting videos can depreciate only those videos bought for rental. If the video has a useful life of one year or less, the cost may be deducted as a business expense.

Income Forecast Method. A taxpayer may choose to use the income forecast method or straight-line method to depreciate certain intangible property including sound recordings, motion pictures, videotapes, copyrights, books, and patents. Under the income forecast method, each year's depreciation deduction is equal to the cost of the property, less its salvage value, multiplied by a fraction. The numerator of the fraction is the current year's net income from the property, and the denominator is the total income anticipated from the property through the end of the 10th tax year following the tax year the property is placed in service.

MACRS Depreciation (Part III, Lines 17-20)

General Information

A taxpayer who buys or acquires a capital asset, such as a building, a machine or equipment, is generally not permitted to deduct the total cost of the item in the tax year of acquisition. Instead, the cost of such an item must be written off and deducted over a period of tax years that begins generally with the year of acquisition. This write-off is permitted by means of a depreciation deduction.

For this purpose, property is depreciable if:

- it is used in a trade or business or for the production of income;
- it has a useful life exceeding one year;
- if it is *tangible*, it is subject to wear and tear; and
- if it is *intangible*, it must generally be known to have a limited life that can be estimated with reasonable accuracy. See MTG ¶1201.

Trade or Business Requirement. No deduction is allowed for depreciation unless the property is used in a trade or business or other income-producing activity. In other words, no deduction is allowed for depreciation while property is being used for personal purposes.

If the taxpayer held property for personal use and subsequently converted it to business or income-producing use, the property can be depreciated. In such circumstances, the depreciable basis is the lesser of:

- the fair market value of the property on the date of the change in use; *or*
- the original cost increased by the cost of any permanent improvements or additions and other costs that must be added to basis, and decreased by any deductions the taxpayer claimed for casualty and theft losses and other items reducing the taxpayer's basis.

If an asset is used for *both* personal and business or income production purposes, the taxpayer is permitted to deduct depreciation on the portion of the asset used for business or production of income purposes. An allocation of the property's basis must be made to determine the portion of the asset that is subject to depreciation.

Determinable Life Requirement. The deduction for depreciation is permitted only for property that wears out or becomes obsolete. This requirement generally means that depreciation is allowed only for property that has a *determinable life*. Property, such as land, that does not wear out and that has no determinable life cannot be depreciated. The IRS takes the position that works of art cannot be amortized or depreciated since they normally have an indefinite life.

Modified Accelerated Cost Recovery System (MACRS)

For most tangible property placed in service after 1986, taxpayers must compute depreciation using the Modified Accelerated Cost Recovery System (MACRS). See MTG ¶1238. MACRS is not used to depreciate *intangible* assets, such as patents or copyrights, which are amortized using a straight-line depreciation method (see discussion on page 7-16).

Under MACRS, there are two depreciation systems, the general depreciation system (GDS) and the alternative depreciation system (ADS). Under both systems, the cost of tangible depreciable property (not including salvage value) must be recovered using the applicable depreciation method, recovery period, and accounting convention. The GDS normally will be used unless the taxpayer is specifically required by the Code or elects to use the ADS to compute their depreciation under MACRS.

General Depreciation System. Under the GDS, each piece of property is assigned to a prescribed asset class based on its useful life. For each asset class, an applicable depreciation method, recovery period and accounting convention are provided. A table of asset classes and applicable recovery periods under the GDS is provided beginning at page 7-19.

> **Caution.** Classification is critical because the recovery periods, methods, and accounting conventions to be used in calculating depreciation can vary among the different classes of property. Carefully review the class descriptions and the characteristics of the specific property.

The depreciation method and accounting convention that may be used in computing depreciation depends on the asset class the property is assigned and the recovery period for that class. The recovery period for a particular class is the number or years over which the taxpayer's cost or basis in the property may be recovered. There are generally eight recovery periods under the GDS including 3, 5, 7, 10, 15, 20, 27.5 and 39 years.

> **Caution.** Nonresidential real property placed in service before May 13, 1993, is depreciated under MACRS over 31.5 years.

Depreciation Methods. MACRS provides three depreciation methods under the GDS. The cost of property with a 3-, 5-, 7- or 10-year recovery period must be recovered using the 200% declining-balance depreciation method. The cost of property with a 15 or 20-year recovery period must be recovered using the 150%-declining-balance depreciation method. The cost of property recovered over 27.5 or 39 years is recovered using the straight-line method.

Declining-balance methods. Under the declining-balance methods, an applicable depreciation rate is determined by dividing the specified declining-balance percentage (i.e., 200 or 150 percent) by the applicable recovery period. This rate will then apply for each tax year in which the declining-balance method is used and applied to the unrecovered basis of the property. For example, the 200% declining-balance method applied to property with a 5-year recovery period results in an applicable depreciation rate of 40% in each of the five years.

Straight-line method. Under the straight-line method, a new applicable depreciation rate is determined for each tax year in the applicable recovery period. For any tax year, the applicable depreciation rate is determined by dividing one by the length of the recovery period remaining as of the beginning of the tax year. The rate is applied to the unrecovered basis of the property.

For example, the straight-line method applied to property with a 5-year recovery period results in applicable depreciation rates of 20, 25, 33.33, 50, and 100%, computed for five full years. If, as of the beginning of any tax year, the remaining recovery period is less than one year, the applicable depreciation rate for that year is 100%.

Special Elections. In lieu of using the applicable depreciation method, a taxpayer may irrevocably elect to use the straight-line method over any recovery period. A taxpayer may also elect to use the 150%-declining-balance depreciation method over the 3-, 5-, 7- or 10-year recovery period. If made, either election will apply to all property in the particular MACRS class that is placed in service during the tax year.

> **Caution.** If a taxpayer places personal property in service in a farming business during the tax year, then the 150%-declining-balance or straight-line depreciation methods must be used, unless the property must be depreciated under the ADS.

Accounting Conventions. Certain accounting conventions are used to determine the amount of depreciation in the year of acquisition and the year of disposition. Like the depreciation methods, what convention applies under the GDS is dependent on the applicable recovery period of the property.

Property with a 3-, 5-, 7-, 10-, 15- or 20-year recovery period must use the half-year convention (unless the mid-quarter convention applies). Property with 27.5 or 39 year recovery period must use a mid-month convention.

Half-Year Convention. Under the half-year convention, only one-half year of depreciation is allowed in the first tax year, regardless of when the asset is placed in service or sold during the year (i.e., ½ × the annual depreciation as normally computed). As a consequence, the recovery period is effectively extended one year so that the remaining one-half may be claimed. If the half-year convention applies, the depreciation tables automatically take this into account.

Mid-Month Convention. The mid-month convention is used for residential and nonresidential real property. Under the mid-month convention, one-half month of depreciation is allowed for the month the asset is placed in service or sold, and a full month of depreciation is allowed for each additional month of the year that the asset is in service.

For example, if a calendar-year taxpayer places a building in service on March 4, the annual depreciation allowed is 9.5/12 (a half-month's depreciation for March and nine months' depreciation for April through December). The MACRS depreciation tables automatically take this into account.

Mid-Month (MM) Convention

Month	Placed in Service	Disposed Of
1	0.9583	0.0417
2	0.8750	0.1250
3	0.7917	0.2083
4	0.7083	0.2917
5	0.6250	0.3750
6	0.5417	0.4583
7	0.4583	0.5417
8	0.3750	0.6250
9	0.2917	0.7083
10	0.2083	0.7917
11	0.1250	0.8750
12	0.0417	0.9583

Mid-Quarter Convention. The mid-quarter convention applies to tangible personal property only if more than 40% of the aggregate bases of all personal property placed in service during the tax year is placed in service during the last three months of the year. For this purpose, property placed in service and disposed of during the same tax year is not taken into account. Similarly, property that is not depreciated using MACRS is omitted.

Also not taken into account is any amount expensed under IRC §179 or property used for personal purposes. If the 40% test is satisfied, the mid-quarter convention applies to *all* personal property placed in service during the year (regardless of the quarter in which it was actually placed in service).

The mid-quarter convention treats all personal property as being placed in service in the middle of the quarter of the taxable year in which it was actually placed in service. Therefore, one-half of a quarter's depreciation–one-eighth (½ × ¼) or 12.5% of the annual depreciation–is allowed for the quarter in which the asset is placed in service or sold. In addition, a full quarter's depreciation is allowed for each additional quarter that the asset is in service.

For example, if the mid-quarter convention applies, personal property placed in service on March 3 would be treated as having been placed in service in the middle of the first quarter, and the taxpayer would be able to claim 3½ quarters–3.5/4 or 87.5%–of the annual amount of depreciation.

Mid-Quarter (MQ) Convention

Quarter	Placed in Service	Disposed Of
1	0.875	0.125
2	0.625	0.375
3	0.375	0.625
4	0.125	0.875

Alternative Depreciation System. Instead of depreciating property under the MACRS general depreciation system (GDS), a taxpayer may make an irrevocable election to use the alternative depreciation system (ADS) with respect to any classification of property for the tax year. The election will cover all property in the same property class placed in service in the tax year. However, for real property (i.e., nonresidential and residential rental property), the election may be made on a property-by-property basis.

ADS mandatory. The taxpayer must use ADS for depreciating the following property:

- "listed property" (see page 7-13) that is not used more than 50% for business purposes;
- tangible property used outside the United States during the tax year;
- property used by a tax-exempt entity;
- property financed by the issuance of tax-exempt bonds;
- property used predominantly in a farming business and placed in service during any tax year in which

Comparison of MACRS GDS and ADS

MACRS Property Class	MACRS GDS	ADS (Use ADS Life)	Accounting Convention
3-year, 5-year, 7-year, 10-year	200% DB 150% DB SL	SL	Half-year or mid-quarter
15-year, 20-year	150% DB SL	Choices: SL	Half-year or mid-quarter
Residential rental real estate	27.5 years SL	40 years SL	Mid-month
Nonresidential real estate	39 years SL	40 years SL	Mid-month

an election was made not to apply the uniform capitalization rules; and

- property imported into the United States for which an executive order of the president of the United States is in effect.

> **Planning Tip.** ADS must also be used for computing depreciation for purposes of the alternative minimum tax (AMT) and a corporation's earnings and profits.

> **Caution.** If a taxpayer is required to use ADS to depreciate property, then bonus depreciation may not be claimed for the property.

ADS is similar to GDS in that the same accounting conventions must be followed. The major difference between GDS and ADS is that ADS has longer recovery periods for most assets and the straight-line depreciation method is required for all classes of property.

Line 17, MACRS Deductions for Assets Placed in Service before 2009

For assets placed in service in tax years beginning before 2009, the amount of depreciation that may be claimed in 2009 under MACRS is reported on Line 17. Note that the taxpayer should maintain separate records of depreciation for each tax year. However, only the total amount of depreciation for all such assets is entered on Line 17. The taxpayer does not have to separately state the amount of depreciation for each asset placed in service before 2009.

Line 18, Election to Group Assets

To simplify the computation of MACRS depreciation, a taxpayer may establish *general asset accounts* (GAAs) for groups of assets and then depreciate each account as a single item. Each GAA must include only assets that are placed in service in the same tax year and have the same asset class, depreciation method, recovery period and convention.

Assets without an asset class, but which have the rest of the preceding characteristics in common, may be grouped in a single general asset account. In addition, the following rules apply in grouping property into GAAs:

- Property subject to the mid-quarter convention can be grouped only in a GAA with property placed in service in the same quarter.
- Property subject to the mid-month convention can be grouped only in a GAA with property placed in service in the same month.
- Passenger automobiles subject to the limits on passenger automobile depreciation must be grouped in a separate GAA (see Tab 8).
- A taxpayer cannot include property in a GAA if it is used for both personal and business purposes.
- Property that generates foreign-source income is subject to special rules.

Disposition of GAA Property. When a taxpayer disposes of property included in a GAA, the entire amount of the proceeds *realized* (i.e., the property is treated as having an adjusted basis of zero) is generally recognized as ordinary income. However, the unadjusted basis of the disposed property is left in the GAA to be fully recovered through depreciation in future years.

If all the assets, or the last asset, in a GAA are disposed of, then the taxpayer may treat the GAA as terminated. Under such circumstances, gain or loss for the GAA is the amount realized on the disposition over the adjusted basis of the GAA. A transfer of all of the assets in a GAA in a like-kind exchange or involuntary conversion, will be treated as a termination for this purpose.

> **Planning Tip.** Work with clients to discuss acquisitions and liquidations as they occur, rather than well after the fact or after the year end. Some projects run beyond the filing-year deadline and involved parties may or may not be available to assist you in return preparation.

Line 19, Assets Placed in Service During the 2009 Tax Year Using the General Depreciation System (Section B)

For property placed in service in 2009, a taxpayer uses Line 19 of Form 4562 to depreciate assets under the MACRS general depreciation system (GDS). The taxpayer must sort property into one of the nine classifications listed on Lines 19a-19i in column (a). A table of asset classes and applicable recovery periods under GDS is provided beginning at page 7-19 to help in this process.

Month and Year Placed in Service. In column (b), the month and year residential rental property and nonresidential real property was placed in service must be provided.

Basis for Depreciation. A taxpayer's adjusted basis in property placed in service during the tax year, is entered in column (c). If the asset is used for both business and personal purposes, only the portion of the basis attributable to business (or income-producing use) is depreciated.

Normally, a taxpayer's basis in property is the cost to purchase the asset. However, basis must be adjusted for several factors. For example, a taxpayer's basis in property must be reduced for any IRC §179 deduction claimed on the property on Line 12. In addition, basis must be reduced for any "additional special/bonus" depreciation claimed on the property on Line 14. Basis for depreciation purposes must also be reduced for: the deduction for removal of barriers to the disabled and elderly; disabled access credit; and the credit for employer-provided child-care facilities and services.

Recovery Period. The recovery period of the depreciable property must be entered in column (d). The recovery period generally follows the asset class of the property (e.g., 3-year property has a 3-year recovery period).

Convention. The accounting convention that must be used in computing depreciation is entered in column (e). If the half-year convention applies, then "HY" is entered. If the mid-month convention applies, then "MM" is entered. If the mid-quarter convention applies, then "MQ" is entered.

Method. The depreciation method that may be used in computing depreciation is entered in column (f). As noted before, the depreciation method used normally depends on the classification of the property. However, different options may be available for a particular class. If the taxpayer is using either the 200%- or 150%-declining-balance method, then enter "200 DB" or "150 DB" in the column. If the taxpayer is using the straight-line method, then enter "S/L" instead.

Depreciation Deduction. Computation of depreciation for each classification of property is made using the basis and the applicable statutory percentage provided in IRS tables. The tables incorporate the appropriate convention. The result is entered for each classification of property in column (g) of Line 19. Some of the most common used MACRS depreciation tables are reproduced beginning on page 7-29.

Example. On May 1, 2009, Daniel Muzrahi purchased a copier to be used solely for business for $10,000. It was his only acquisition during the year. The copier had an estimated useful life of four years. Under MACRS, the recovery period is specified based on the classification of the property. Copiers are considered five-year property, so the recovery period is five years.

Daniel has several options regarding the depreciation method: 200% or 150% declining balance, MACRS straight line using a five-year life, or ADS straight line using a six-year life. The accounting convention prescribed for five-year property is the half-year convention.

Daniel elects to compute his depreciation using the 200% declining-balance method (switching to straight line where appropriate), a five-year recovery period, and the half-year convention. Depreciation would be computed as follows:

Year	Unadjusted Recovery Basis	Accelerated Annual Percentage	Depreciation
2009	$10,000	20.00%	$2,000
2010	10,000	32.00	3,200
2011	10,000	19.20	1,920
2012	10,000	11.52	1,152
2013	10,000	11.52	1,152
2014	10,000	5.76	576
		100.00%	$10,000

Caution. Information needed to compute the depreciation deduction (basis, method, etc.) must be part of the permanent records even if it is not sent with the return. *The date placed in service is key to when a taxpayer may start taking the deduction.*

Line 20, Assets Placed in Service During 2009 Tax Year Using the Alternative Depreciation System (Section C)

A taxpayer uses Line 20 of Form 4562 if they elect to use the Alternative Depreciation System (ADS) under MACRS to depreciate property placed in service in 2009. Like the GDS, the taxpayer must sort property into the one of the classifications listed on Lines 20a-20c in column (a).

The depreciation for most property is based on the property's class life and is entered on Line 20a. A table of asset classes and applicable recovery periods under ADS is provided below to help in this process. Property that does not have a class life is entered as 12-year property on Line

20b. Nonresidential real property and residential rental property is entered as 40-year property on Line 20c.

The rest of Line 20 is completed similarly to Line 19 under the GDS. Column (b) is used to record the month and year nonresidential real property and residential rental property is placed in service. Column (c) is where basis is reported. The ADS recovery period is entered in column (d). Only straight-line depreciation is allowed to be used for ADS property.

The total ADS depreciation for each classification of property is entered on column (g) of Line 20. Computation of depreciation for each classification is made using the basis and the applicable statutory percentage provided in IRS tables. The tables are available in IRS Publication 946, How to Depreciate Property.

Depreciation Summary (Part IV, Lines 21-23)

The total amount of depreciation being claimed in 2009 is reported on Line 22. The total includes the sum of the amount of any:

- IRC §179 deduction (Line 12);
- bonus/additional depreciation (Line 14);
- depreciation under the unit-of-production method or another method not based on term of year (Line 15);
- depreciation not computed under MACRS (Line 16);
- depreciation under the MACRS general depreciation system (GDS) (Line 19(g));
- depreciation under the MACRS alternative depreciation system (ADS) (Line 20(g)); and
- depreciation on any listed property (Line 21).

A taxpayer that is a partnership or an S corporation, should not include any IRC §179 deduction in the total on Line 22. Instead, the deduction is passed through to each partner or shareholder (and reported on Schedule K-1) based on their respective interest in the entity. If any assets being depreciated in 2009 are subject to the uniform capitalization rules under IRC §263A, then the increase in basis from costs that the taxpayer must capitalize is entered on Line 23.

Recapture. If a taxpayer sells or otherwise disposes of property that was depreciated under MACRS, any gain on the sale may be recaptured as ordinary income up to the amount of the depreciation previously allowed. Generally, the gain treated as ordinary income is the *lesser* of: (1) the depreciation allowed or allowable on the property; or (2) the gain *realized* on the sale or disposition. Part III Form 4797 is used to figure this amount.

For this purpose, depreciation includes any additional special/bonus depreciation allowed, as well as any IRC §179 deduction claimed on the property. Since nonresidential real property and residential rental property are depreciated under MACRS using the straight-line method, there is no depreciation recapture upon the disposition of such property unless bonus depreciation was claimed.

Caution. All depreciation recapture is reported as ordinary income in the year the personal property is sold, even if the gain from the sale is reported using the installment method over the term of the contract. It may be advisable to make sure that the installment sale agreement includes an initial payment large enough to pay for any tax owed on the recapture income.

Listed Property (Part V, Lines 24-41)

Depreciation and Other Information (Section A)

The amount of depreciation as well as the IRC §179 deduction that may be claimed for "listed property" is limited if such property is not used predominantly (more than 50%) for business. If the property is not used more than 50% for business in the year it is placed in service, then:

- expensing under IRC §179 is not allowed; and
- the MACRS general depreciation system (GDS) may not be used, but instead the property must be depreciated using the MACRS alternative depreciation system (ADS).

In certain cases, depreciation may be denied.

For this purpose, "listed property" includes:

- passenger automobiles weighing 6,000 pounds or less (see Tab 8 for a discussion of depreciation limits for passenger automobiles);
- any property used for transportation if the nature of the property lends itself to personal use (e.g., motorcycles, pick-up trucks);
- any property used for entertainment or recreational purposes (e.g., photographic, phonographic, communication, and video recording equipment);
- cellular telephones or other similar telecommunications equipment; and
- computers or peripheral equipment.

Exceptions. Listed property does not include property used for entertainment or recreational purposes if it is used exclusively in a taxpayer's trade or business or at the taxpayer's regular business establishment. Computers and peripheral equipment are not listed property if used exclusively at a regular business establishment and owned or leased by the person who operates the business establishment. For this purpose, a portion of the taxpayer's home can be treated as a regular business establishment only if it meets the requirements for the home office deduction.

Line 24, Evidence for Use

A taxpayer cannot take any depreciation or IRC §179 deduction unless the business/investment use of the listed property is substantiated with adequate records or with sufficient evidence to support the taxpayer's own statements. The following information should be included in the records:

- the amount of each separate expenditure, such as the cost of acquiring the item, maintenance and repair costs, capital improvement costs, lease payments, and any other expenses;
- the amount of each business and investment use (based on an appropriate measure, such as mileage for vehicles and time for other listed property), and the total use of the property for the tax year;
- the date of the expenditure or use; and
- the business or investment purpose of the expenditure.

The information above should be recorded on a timely basis. The IRS takes the position that the expense must be recorded when the taxpayer has full knowledge of the elements of an expenditure. An expense account statement made from an account book, diary, or similar record prepared or maintained at or near the time of the expenditure or use generally is considered a timely record if, in the regular course of business:

- the statement is given by an employee to the employer; or
- the statement is given by an independent contractor to the client or customer.

For example, a log maintained on a weekly basis, that accounts for use during the week, will be considered a record made at or near the time of use.

Line 25, Special Depreciation Allowance

If the taxpayer placed listed property in service in the tax year and it is used more than 50% in a *qualified business use* (see below), any additional or bonus depreciation claimed on the property should be entered on Line 25. However, the amount of the deduction for passenger automobiles that may be claimed for the tax year is limited (see Tab 8). For a discussion of the special depreciation allowance, see page 7-5.

Lines 26–29, Depreciation for Listed Property

A taxpayer uses Line 26 to compute depreciation for listed property used more than 50% in a qualified business use. Line 27 is used to computed depreciation for listed property used 50% or less in a qualified business use.

In determining whether the property is used more than 50% for business, only *qualified business use* is considered. Generally, *qualified business use* means any use in a trade or business of the taxpayer, rather than use in an investment or other activity conducted for the production of income. Qualified business use does not include:

- leasing listed property to a five-percent owner or related person;
- use of listed property as compensation for services performed by a five-percent owner or related person (unless the property in question is an airplane, in which case use will be qualified business use if at least 25% of the total use during the tax year is for a qualifying business use); or
- use of listed property as compensation for services performed by any person (who is not a five-percent owner or related person), unless an amount is included in that person's income for the use of the property and, if required, income tax is withheld on that amount.

Employee's Use of Own Listed Property. An employee's use of his or her own listed property in connection with employment is not considered business use unless it is for the *convenience of the employer* and is *required as a condition of employment.* Thus, a statement by the employer expressly requiring the employee to use the property is insufficient for this purpose. Ordinarily, the property is considered required only if it enables the employee to properly perform the duties of his or her employment.

Computing Depreciation. The taxpayer must describe the type of listed property being depreciated in column (a) of Lines 26 and 27. Automobiles and other vehicles must be listed first, followed by any other listed property the taxpayer placed in service in the tax year.

The date on which depreciation begins is entered in column (b) of Lines 26 and 27. Depreciation begins when the asset is placed in service. This is not always the same as the time the asset is purchased. An asset is considered placed in service when it is in a state of readiness and availability for the assigned function of the activity.

In column (c) of Lines 26 and 27, the taxpayer enters the percentage of business/investment use (as opposed to personal use). For automobiles and other vehicles, this percentage is determined by dividing the number of miles driven during the tax year for trade or business purposes (or for the production of income) by the total number of miles driven for the tax year (see Tab 8). Commuting expenses are not included in business/investment use.

Basis for Depreciation. Column (d) of Lines 26 and 27 is used to record the taxpayer's basis (i.e., cost) of the listed property (unadjusted for prior years' depreciation). If the listed property was converted from personal use to business use, then the taxpayer's basis is the smaller of the property's adjusted basis or its fair market value on the date of conversion.

Filing Tip. For an automobile or other vehicle, the basis of the property is reduced for any qualified electric vehicle credit or deduction for clean-fuel vehicles claimed in previous years.

If the asset is used for both business and personal purposes, only the portion of the basis attributable to business (or income-producing) use is depreciated. This amount is entered in column (e) of Lines 26 and Line 27. It is calculated by multiplying the taxpayer's cost or other basis in column (d) by the percentage of business/investment use in column (c). This amount should then be reduced by any IRC §179 deduction, as well as the credit for employer-provided childcare facilities or service, and the investment tax credit.

Depreciation Methods. In columns (f) and (g) of Lines 26 and 27, the taxpayer should enter the appropriate recovery period, depreciation method and accounting convention. For listed property used more than 50% in qualified business use (Line 26), these are determined under the same rules for nonlisted property under MACRS (see page 7-8). For listed property used 50% or less in a qualified business use (Line 27), the taxpayer must use recovery periods under the MACRS alternative depreciation system (ADS) and the straight-line depreciation method.

Using the recovery period, depreciation method and accounting convention, compute the depreciation deduction for each listed property in column (h) of Lines 26 and 27 using the IRS tables (see page 7-29). However, the amount of the deduction for passenger automobiles that may be claimed for the tax year is limited (see Tab 8). Add the amount in column (h) for Lines 25, 26 and 27 (subject to the limits for automobiles), and enter the total on Line 28 and on Line 21.

IRC §179 Deduction. A taxpayer may elect the IRC §179 expense deduction for "listed property" that meets the 50-percent qualified business test (see above). The amount expensed is reported in column (i) of Line 26. The total expensed amount is entered on Line 29 and on Line 7. "Listed property" that fails to meet the 50-percent qualified business use requirement (Line 27) does not qualify for the IRC §179 deduction.

Expensing Limit for SUVs. A taxpayer may not expense more than $25,000 of the cost of certain motor vehicles, including a sport utility vehicle (SUV), under IRC §179. This rule applies to any vehicle:

- primarily designed or used to carry passengers over public streets, roads, or highways;
- not subject to the depreciation limits on motor vehicles (e.g., gross vehicle weight exceeds 6,000 pounds) (see discussion under Tab 8); and
- that has a gross vehicle weight not exceeding 14,000 pounds.

Recapture. If listed property is predominantly used (more than 50%) for business in the year in which it is placed in service but fails to be predominantly used for business in a later tax year, then the taxpayer will have to recapture depreciation deductions. The recaptured amount is equal to the excess of any MACRS deprecation allowable for tax years before business use fell to 50% or less, over the depreciation that would have been allowable in those years under the alternative depreciation system (ADS). Depreciation for this purpose includes any IRC §179 deduction claimed.

Form 4797 is used to figure the recapture amount and it is reported as other income on the same form or schedule on which the taxpayer claimed the depreciation deduction (Schedule C or Form 2106).

Information on Use of Vehicles (Section B)

If a motor vehicle is identified as "listed property" on Lines 26 and 27, then the taxpayer may have to provide certain information on the vehicle on Lines 30 through 36, including (see Tab 8 for a definition of some of these terms):

Line 30: Total business/investment miles

Line 31: Total commuting miles

Line 32: Total other personal miles

Line 33: Total miles

Line 34: Available for personal use

Line 35: Used by greater than five-percent owner

Line 36: Availability of another vehicle for personal use.

This information only has to be provided for vehicles used by a sole proprietor, a partner, any "more than 5% owner," or a related person. However, a taxpayer will be not required to complete Lines 30 through 36 if they provide the vehicle for use by their employees who are *not* a "more than 5% owner" or a related person and answer **Yes** to all of the requirements of Section C below.

Questions for Employers Who Provide Vehicles for Use by Their Employees (Section C)

Employers who provide vehicles to their employees must meet substantiation requirements by maintaining a written policy statement that either:

- prohibits personal use of a vehicle *including* commuting; or
- prohibits personal use of a vehicle *except* for commuting.

For either written policy statement, there must be evidence that would enable the IRS to determine whether use of the vehicle meets these conditions. An employee does not need to keep separate records for vehicles satisfying these written policy statement rules.

Line 37, Written Policy Prohibiting Personal Use (Including Commuting)

A written policy statement that prohibits personal use (including commuting) must meet *all* of the following conditions:

- The employer owns or leases the vehicle and provides it to one or more employees for use in the employer's trade or business.
- When the vehicle is not used in the employer's trade or business, it is kept on the employer's business premises, unless temporarily located elsewhere (e.g., for maintenance or because of a mechanical failure).
- No employee using the vehicle lives at the employer's business premises.
- No employee may use the vehicle for personal purposes, other than *de minimis* personal use (e.g., a stop for lunch between two business deliveries).
- Except for *de minimis* use, the employer reasonably believes that no employee uses the vehicle for any personal purpose.

Line 38, Written Policy Prohibiting Personal Use (Excluding Commuting)

A written policy statement that prohibits personal use (except for commuting) is *not* available if the commuting employee is an officer, director, or 1% or more owner. This policy must meet *all* of the following conditions:

- The employer owns or leases the vehicle and provides it to one or more employees for use in the employer's trade or business, and it is used in the employer's trade or business.
- For bona fide noncompensatory business reasons, the employer requires the employee to commute to and/or from work in the vehicle.
- The employer establishes a written policy under which the employee may not use the vehicle for personal purposes, other than commuting or de minimis personal use (e.g., a stop for a personal errand between a business delivery and the employee's home).
- Except for *de minimis* use, the employer reasonably believes that the employee does not use the vehicle for any personal purpose other than commuting.
- The value of commuting use is included in the employee's gross income.

Line 39, All Vehicle Use as Personal

If all use of vehicles by employees is treated as personal use (and is therefore included as taxable wages), check "Yes."

Line 40, More than Five Vehicles to Employees

An employer that provides more than five vehicles to its employees who are not 5% owners or related persons need not complete Section B for such vehicles. Instead, the employer must obtain the information from its employees and retain the information received.

Line 41, Qualified Automobile Demonstration

If an automobile is a demonstrator, the value of the automobile is a nontaxable fringe benefit to the employee and all of the related costs are deductible by the employer. An automobile meets the requirements for qualified demonstration use if the employer maintains a written policy statement that:

- prohibits use of the vehicle by individuals other than full-time automobile salespersons;
- prohibits use for personal vacation trips;
- prohibits storage of personal possessions in the automobile; and
- limits the total mileage outside the salesperson's normal working hours.

Amortization (Part VI, Lines 42-44)

Amortization is the recovery of certain capital expenditures that are not ordinarily deductible, over a fixed period of time. Amortization is therefore similar to straight-line depreciation. A taxpayer may elect to amortize certain property, while other property *must be* amortized.

Caution. The portion of the basis of property that is amortized, will not qualify for depreciation under MACRS or the IRC §179 deduction.

Line 42, Amortization of Costs for 2009 Tax Year

Line 42 is used to report the amortization of costs beginning during the tax year. Column (a) is used to provide a description of the costs. Columns (b), (c) and (e) are used to enter respectively, the date the amortization period begins, the total amount being amortized, and the amortization period or percentage (whichever applies). These are provided by various Code sections which permit the amortization of certain costs. The particular Code section must be entered in column (d).

The amortization deduction for 2009 is computed in column (f) in one of two ways:

- by dividing the total amortizable amount in column (c) by the number of months over which the costs are to be amortized in column (e) and multiplied by the number of the amortization months that occur in 2009; or
- by multiplying the total amortizable amount in column (c) by the amortizable percentage in column (e).

Section 197 Intangibles. One of the most common costs that are *required* to be amortized are section 197 intangibles. Such costs must be amortized over 15 years (180 months) starting with the month they were acquired or the month the trade or business activity engaged in begins, whichever is later. A longer amortization period may apply to section 197 intangibles leased to a tax-exempt organization, government, or foreign person.

A section 197 intangible includes:

- goodwill;
- going concern value;
- workforce in place;
- business books and records, operating systems, or any other information base;
- a patent, copyright, formula, process, design, pattern, know-how, format, or similar item;
- a customer-based intangible (e.g., composition of market or market share);
- a supplier-based intangible;
- any license, permit, or other right granted by a governmental unit;
- any covenant not to compete entered into in connection with the acquisition of a business; and
- any franchise (other than a sports franchise), trademark, or trade name.

Assets which are not section 197 intangibles and not eligible to be amortized include:

- any interest in a corporation, partnership, trust or estate;
- any interest in land;
- computer software; and
- any interest under an existing lease of tangible property, or a debt that was in existence when the interest was acquired.

Caution. A section 197 intangible will be treated as depreciable property used in the taxpayer's trade or business. Thus, a taxpayer who sells or otherwise disposes of a section 197 intangible held for more than one year may have to recapture any gain as ordinary income. Generally, the gain treated as ordinary income is the *lesser* of the amortization allowed or allowable on the property, or the gain realized on the sale or disposition.

If the taxpayer sells more than one section 197 intangible during the tax year, recapture must be calculated as if all of the taxpayer's section 197 intangibles sold or disposed of were a single asset. Thus, any gain realized on the sale or other disposition of the intangibles is recaptured as ordinary income to the extent of amortization claimed on any of the intangibles. For this purpose, the gain is calculated in Part III of Form 4797.

Start-Up Costs. A taxpayer may elect to deduct up to $5,000 of start-up expenses in the tax year in which they begin a trade or business. The deduction must be reduced on a dollar-by-dollar basis as the amount of expenses exceeds $50,000. Start-up expenses that are not currently deductible must be amortized over a 180-month period beginning with the month the taxpayer begins business operations.

For start-up expenses paid or incurred after September 8, 2008, a taxpayer is not required to attach a statement to its return or specifically identify the deducted amounts as start-up expenses. Rather, it will be deemed to have made such an election. A taxpayer can forego the deemed election by clearly electing to capitalize start-up expenses on a timely filed federal income tax return for the tax year in which the business begins operations. The election either to deduct start-up expenses or to capitalize such amounts is irrevocable and applies to all start-up expenses.

Start-up expenses are expenses paid or incurred in connection with: (1) investigating the creation or acquisition of an active trade or business; (2) creating an active trade or business; or (3) any activity engaged in for profit or for the production of income before the day on which the active trade or business begins.

In addition, start-up expenses must be allowable as a deduction if they were paid or incurred in connection with an existing active business in the same field as that entered into by the taxpayer. Start-up expenses do not include deductible interest, taxes or research and experimental expenses.

Caution. The deduction and amortization of start-up expenses is allowed to the taxpayer who incurs the start-up expenditures and subsequently enters the business. In the case of a sole proprietor, this means the deduction is allowed for the business with respect to which the start-up costs were incurred. If the business is organized into a corporation or partnership, then only the corporation or partnership may elect to deduct and amortize the start-up expenses it incurs. However, an individual taxpayer may elect to deduct and amortize expenses incurred to investigate an interest in an existing partnership, when the individual acquires the interest.

If the taxpayer does not subsequently enter the trade or business to which the start-up expenses relate, then the taxpayer may not deduct and amortize the expenses but instead must capitalize them. Similarly, if the trade or business is disposed of completely by the taxpayer before the end of the amortization period, then any remaining start-up expenses which were deferred through amortization are deductible only to the extent they qualify as a loss from a business.

Planning Tip. In addition to the deduction for start-up expenses, a corporation or partnership may deduct $5,000 of any organizational expenses in the tax year the business begins. This deduction is subject to the same $50,000 limitation as applies to start-up costs, and any remaining organizational expenses must be amortized over a 180-month period.

Other Amortizable Costs. Other costs which may be amortized include the following:

- Premiums paid on taxable bonds acquired after 1987 may be amortized over the life of the bond (IRC §171).
- Research and experimental expenditures may either be deducted as business expenses in the tax year incurred or amortized over a 60-month period or more (up to 120 months) (IRC §174).

Planning Tip. Any deduction for research expenditures must be reduced by the amount of the research tax credit under IRC §41 for the same expenses. Capitalized research expenses must also be reduced by the amount of the research credit that exceeds the amount otherwise allowable as a deduction for such expenses. As an alternative to reducing the otherwise allowable deduction or capitalized amount, the taxpayer may elect to claim a reduced credit on Form 6765. A taxpayer will want to calculate which alternative will allow them to achieve the lowest tax liability.

Caution. As of the date this publication went to press, the research credit was not available for amounts paid or incurred after December 31, 2009. However, Congress has extended the credit several times in the past. Determine the current state of the law if your client has research and experimental expenditures.

- The cost of acquiring a lease must be amortized over the term of the lease (IRC §178).
- Up to $10,000 of qualified reforestation costs may be deducted in the year incurred. Any remaining costs may be amortized over an 84-month period (IRC §194).
- One-half of qualified revitalization expenditures (i.e., incurred in a renewal community) may be deducted in the tax year the building is placed in service, or all such expenditures may be amortized over a 120-month period. This provision does not apply to any building placed in service after December 31, 2009 (IRC §1400I).
- Pollution control facilities may be amortized over a 60-month period (IRC §169).

Line 43, Amortization of Costs That Began In Prior Years

The amortization of costs that began before the tax year is reported on Line 43. However, if the taxpayer is not required to file Form 4562 for any other reason, then Form 4562 does not have to be filed merely to report these costs. Instead, the amortization of costs that began before the tax year are reported as "Other expenses" on Schedule C or F of Form 1040.

Line 44, Total Amortization Costs

The total amortization claimed for the tax year is reported on Line 44 (the sum of column (f) Lines 42 and 43). The total is reported as "Other expenses" on Schedule C or F of Form 1040.

Table B-1. **Table of Class Lives and Recovery Periods**

Asset class	Description of assets included	Recovery Periods (in years)		
		Class Life (in years)	**GDS (MACRS)**	**ADS**
	SPECIFIC DEPRECIABLE ASSETS USED IN ALL BUSINESS ACTIVITIES, EXCEPT AS NOTED:			
00.11	**Office Furniture, Fixtures, and Equipment:** Includes furniture and fixtures that are not a structural component of a building. Includes such assets as desks, files, safes, and communications equipment. Does not include communications equipment that is included in other classes.	10	7	10
00.12	**Information Systems:** Includes computers and their peripheral equipment used in administering normal business transactions and the maintenance of business records, their retrieval and analysis. Information systems are defined as: 1) Computers: A computer is a programmable electronically activated device capable of accepting information, applying prescribed processes to the information, and supplying the results of these processes with or without human intervention. It usually consists of a central processing unit containing extensive storage, logic, arithmetic, and control capabilities. Excluded from this category are adding machines, electronic desk calculators, etc., and other equipment described in class 00.13. 2) Peripheral equipment consists of the auxiliary machines which are designed to be placed under control of the central processing unit. Nonlimiting examples are: Card readers, card punches, magnetic tape feeds, high speed printers, optical character readers, tape cassettes, mass storage units, paper tape equipment, keypunches data entry devices, teleprinters, terminals, tape drives, disc drives, disc files, disc packs visual image projector tubes, card sorters, plotters, and collators. Peripheral equipment may be used on-line or off-line. Does not incude equipment that is an integral part of other capital equipment that is included in other classes of economic activity, i.e., computers used primarily for process or production control, switching, channeling, and automating distributive trades and services such as point of sale (POS) computer systems. Also, does not include equipment of a kind used primarily for amusement or entertainment of the user.	6	5	5
00.13	**Data Handling Equipment; except Computers:** Includes only typewriters, calculators, adding and accounting machines, copiers, and duplicating equipment.	6	5	6
00.21	**Airplanes (airframes and engines), except those used in commercial or contract carrying of passengers or freight, and all helicopters (airframes and engines)**	6	5	6
00.22	**Automobiles, Taxis**	3	5	5
00.23	**Buses**	9	5	9
00.241	**Light General Purpose Trucks:** Includes trucks for use over the road (actual weight less than 13,000 pounds)	4	5	5
00.242	**Heavy General Purpose Trucks:** Includes heavy general purpose trucks, concrete ready mix-trucks, and ore trucks, for use over the road (actual unloaded weight 13,000 pounds or more)	6	5	6
00.25	**Railroad Cars and Locomotives, except those owned by railroad transportation companies**	15	7	15
00.26	**Tractor Units for Use Over-The-Road**	4	3	4
00.27	**Trailers and Trailer-Mounted Containers**	6	5	6
00.28	**Vessels, Barges, Tugs, and Similar Water Transportation Equipment, except those used in marine construction**	18	10	18
00.3	**Land Improvements:** Includes improvements directly to or added to land, whether such improvements are section 1245 property or section 1250 property, provided such improvements are depreciable. Examples of such assets might include sidewalks, roads, canals, waterways, drainage facilities, sewers (not including municipal sewers in Class 51), wharves and docks, bridges, fences, landscaping shrubbery, or radio and television transmitting towers. Does not include land improvements that are explicitly included in any other class, and buildings and structural components as defined in section 1.48-1(e) of the regulations. Excludes public utility initial clearing and grading land improvements as specified in Rev. Rul. 72-403, 1972-2 C.B. 102.	20	15	20
00.4	**Industrial Steam and Electric Generation and/or Distribution Systems:** Includes assets, whether such assets are section 1245 property or 1250 property, providing such assets are depreciable, used in the production and/or distribution of electricity with rated total capacity in excess of 500 Kilowatts and/or assets used in the production and/or distribution of steam with rated total capacity in excess of 12,500 pounds per hour for use by the taxpayer in its industrial manufacturing process or plant activity and not ordinarily available for sale to others. Does not include buildings and structural components as defined in section 1.48-1(e) of the regulations. Assets used to generate and/or distribute electricity or steam of the type described above, but of lesser rated capacity, are not included, but are included in the appropriate manufacturing equipment classes elsewhere specified. Also includes electric generating and steam distribution assets, which may utilize steam produced by a waste reduction and resource recovery plant, used by the taxpayer in its industrial manufacturing process or plant activity. Steam and chemical recovery boiler systems used for the recovery and regeneration of chemicals used in manufacturing, with rated capacity in excess of that described above, with specifically related distribution and return systems are not included but are included in appropriate manufacturing equipment classes elsewhere specified. An example of an excluded steam and chemical recovery boiler system is that used in the pulp and paper manufacturing equipment classes elsewhere specified. An example of an excluded steam and chemical recovery boiler system is that used in the pulp and paper manufacturing industry.	22	15	22

Table B-2. **Table of Class Lives and Recovery Periods**

Asset class	Description of assets included	Recovery Periods (in years)		
		Class Life (in years)	GDS (MACRS)	ADS
	DEPRECIABLE ASSETS USED IN THE FOLLOWING ACTIVITIES:			
01.1	**Agriculture:** Includes machinery and equipment, grain bins, and fences but no other land improvements, that are used in the production of crops or plants, vines, and trees; livestock; the operation of farm dairies, nurseries, greenhouses, sod farms, mushroom cellars, cranberry bogs, apiaries, and fur farms; the performance of agriculture, animal husbandry, and horticultural services.	10	7	10
01.11	**Cotton Ginning Assets**	12	7	12
01.21	**Cattle, Breeding or Dairy**	7	5	7
01.221	**Any breeding or work horse that is 12 years old or less at the time it is placed in service****	10	7	10
01.222	**Any breeding or work horse that is more than 12 years old at the time it is placed in service****	10	3	10
01.223	**Any race horse that is more than 2 years old at the time it is placed in service****	*	3	12
01.224	**Any horse that is more than 12 years old at the time it is placed in service and that is neither a race horse nor a horse described in class 01.222****	*	3	12
01.225	**Any horse not described in classes 01.221, 01.222, 01.223, or 01.224**	*	7	12
01.23	**Hogs, Breeding**	3	3	3
01.24	**Sheep and Goats, Breeding**	5	5	5
01.3	**Farm buildings except structures included in Class 01.4**	25	20	25
01.4	**Single purpose agricultural or horticultural structures (within the meaning of section 168(i)(13) of the Code)**	15	10***	15
10.0	**Mining:** Includes assets used in the mining and quarrying of metallic and nonmetallic minerals (including sand, gravel, stone, and clay) and the milling, beneficiation and other primary preparation of such materials.	10	7	10
13.0	**Offshore Drilling:** Includes assets used in offshore drilling for oil and gas such as floating, self-propelled and other drilling vessels, barges, platforms, and drilling equipment and support vessels such as tenders, barges, towboats and crewboats. Excludes oil and gas production assets.	7.5	5	7.5
13.1	**Drilling of Oil and Gas Wells:** Includes assets used in the drilling of onshore oil and gas wells and the provision of geophysical and other exploration services; and the provision of such oil and gas field services as chemical treatment, plugging and abandoning of wells and cementing or perforating well casings. Does not include assets used in the performance of any of these activities and services by integrated petroleum and natural gas producers for their own account.	6	5	6
13.2	**Exploration for and Production of Petroleum and Natural Gas Deposits:** Includes assets used by petroleum and natural gas producers for drilling of wells and production of petroleum and natural gas, including gathering pipelines and related storage facilities. Also includes petroleum and natural gas offshore transportation facilities used by producers and others consisting of platforms (other than drilling platforms classified in Class 13.0), compression or pumping equipment, and gathering and transmission lines to the first onshore transshipment facility. The assets used in the first onshore transshipment facility are also included and consist of separation equipment (used for separation of natural gas, liquids, and in Class 49.23), and liquid holding or storage facilities (other than those classified in Class 49.25). Does not include support vessels.	14	7	14
13.3	**Petroleum Refining:** Includes assets used for the distillation, fractionation, and catalytic cracking of crude petroleum into gasoline and its other components.	16	10	16
15.0	**Construction:** Includes assets used in construction by general building, special trade, heavy and marine construction contractors, operative and investment builders, real estate subdividers and developers, and others except railroads.	6	5	6
20.1	**Manufacture of Grain and Grain Mill Products:** Includes assets used in the production of flours, cereals, livestock feeds, and other grain and grain mill products.	17	10	17
20.2	**Manufacture of Sugar and Sugar Products:** Includes assets used in the production of raw sugar, syrup, or finished sugar from sugar cane or sugar beets.	18	10	18
20.3	**Manufacture of Vegetable Oils and Vegetable Oil Products:** Includes assets used in the production of oil from vegetable materials and the manufacture of related vegetable oil products.	18	10	18
20.4	**Manufacture of Other Food and Kindred Products:** Includes assets used in the production of foods and beverages not included in classes 20.1, 20.2 and 20.3.	12	7	12
20.5	**Manufacture of Food and Beverages—Special Handling Devices:** Includes assets defined as specialized materials handling devices such as returnable pallets, palletized containers, and fish processing equipment including boxes, baskets, carts, and flaking trays used in activities as defined in classes 20.1, 20.2, 20.3 and 20.4. Does not include general purpose small tools such as wrenches and drills, both hand and power-driven, and other general purpose equipment such as conveyors, transfer equipment, and materials handling devices.	4	3	4

* Property described in asset classes 01.223, 01.224, and 01.225 are assigned recovery periods but have no class lives.

** A horse is more than 2 (or 12) years old after the day that is 24 (or 144) months after its actual birthdate.

*** 7 if property was placed in service before 1989.

Table B-2. **Table of Class Lives and Recovery Periods (Continued)**

Asset class	Description of assets included	Recovery Periods (in years)		
		Class Life (in years)	GDS (MACRS)	ADS
21.0	**Manufacture of Tobacco and Tobacco Products:** Includes assets used in the production of cigarettes, cigars, smoking and chewing tobacco, snuff, and other tobacco products.	15	7	15
22.1	**Manufacture of Knitted Goods:** Includes assets used in the production of knitted and netted fabrics and lace. Assets used in yarn preparation, bleaching, dyeing, printing, and other similar finishing processes, texturing, and packaging, are elsewhere classified.	7.5	5	7.5
22.2	**Manufacture of Yarn, Thread, and Woven Fabric:** Includes assets used in the production of spun yarns including the preparing, blending, spinning and twisting of fibers into yarns and threads, the preparation of yarns such as twisting, warping, and winding, the production of covered elastic yarn and thread, cordage, woven fabric, tire fabric, braided fabric, twisted jute for packaging, mattresses, pads, sheets, and industrial belts, and the processing of textile mill waste to recover fibers, flocks, and shoddies. Assets used to manufacture carpets, man-made fibers, and nonwovens, and assets used in texturing, bleaching, dyeing, printing, and other similar finishing processes, are elsewhere classified.	11	7	11
22.3	**Manufacture of Carpets and Dyeing, Finishing, and Packaging of Textile Products and Manufacture of Medical and Dental Supplies:** Includes assets used in the production of carpets, rugs, mats woven carpet backing, chenille, and other tufted products, and assets used in the joining together of backing with carpet yarn or fabric. Includes assets used in washing, scouring, bleaching, dyeing, printing, drying, and similar finishing processes applied to textile fabrics, yarns, threads, and other textile goods. Includes assets used in the production and packaging of textile products, other than apparel, by creasing, forming, trimming, cutting, and sewing, such as the preparation of carpet and fabric samples, or similar joining together processes (other than the production of scrim reinforced paper products and laminated paper products) such as the sewing and folding of hosiery and panty hose, and the creasing, folding, trimming, and cutting of fabrics to produce nonwoven products, such as disposable diapers and sanitary products. Also includes assets used in the production of medical and dental supplies other than drugs and medicines. Assets used in the manufacture of nonwoven carpet backing, and hard surface floor covering such as tile, rubber, and cork, are elsewhere classified.	9	5	9
22.4	**Manufacture of Textile Yarns:** Includes assets used in the processing of yarns to impart bulk and/or stretch properties to the yarn. The principal machines involved are falsetwist, draw, beam-to-beam, and stuffer box texturing equipment and related highspeed twisters and winders. Assets, as described above, which are used to further process man-made fibers are elsewhere classified when located in the same plant in an integrated operation with man-made fiber producing assets. Assets used to manufacture man-made fibers and assets used in bleaching, dyeing, printing, and other similar finishing processes, are elsewhere classified.	8	5	8
22.5	**Manufacture of Nonwoven Fabrics:** Includes assets used in the production of nonwoven fabrics, felt goods including felt hats, padding, batting, wadding, oakum, and fillings, from new materials and from textile mill waste. Nonwoven fabrics are defined as fabrics (other than reinforced and laminated composites consisting of nonwovens and other products) manufactured by bonding natural and/or synthetic fibers and/or filaments by means of induced mechanical interlocking, fluid entanglement, chemical adhesion, thermal or solvent reaction, or by combination thereof other than natural hydration bonding as occurs with natural cellulose fibers. Such means include resin bonding, web bonding, and melt bonding. Specifically includes assets used to make flocked and needle punched products other than carpets and rugs. Assets, as described above, which are used to manufacture nonwovens are elsewhere classified when located in the same plant in an integrated operation with man-made fiber producing assets. Assets used to manufacture man-made fibers and assets used in bleaching, dyeing, printing, and other similar finishing processes, are elsewhere classified.	10	7	10
23.0	**Manufacture of Apparel and Other Finished Products:** Includes assets used in the production of clothing and fabricated textile products by the cutting and sewing of woven fabrics, other textile products, and furs; but does not include assets used in the manufacture of apparel from rubber and leather.	9	5	9
24.1	**Cutting of Timber:** Includes logging machinery and equipment and roadbuilding equipment used by logging and sawmill operators and pulp manufacturers for their own account.	6	5	6
24.2	**Sawing of Dimensional Stock from Logs:** Includes machinery and equipment installed in permanent or well established sawmills.	10	7	10
24.3	**Sawing of Dimensional Stock from Logs:** Includes machinery and equipment in sawmills characterized by temporary foundations and a lack, or minimum amount, of lumberhandling, drying, and residue disposal equipment and facilities.	6	5	6
24.4	**Manufacture of Wood Products, and Furniture:** Includes assets used in the production of plywood, hardboard, flooring, veneers, furniture, and other wood products, including the treatment of poles and timber.	10	7	10
26.1	**Manufacture of Pulp and Paper:** Includes assets for pulp materials handling and storage, pulp mill processing, bleach processing, paper and paperboard manufacturing, and on-line finishing. Includes pollution control assets and all land improvements associated with the factory site or production process such as effluent ponds and canals, provided such improvements are depreciable but does not include buildings and structural components as defined in section 1.48-1(e)(1) of the regulations. Includes steam and chemical recovery boiler systems, with any rated capacity, used for the recovery and regeneration of chemicals used in manufacturing. Does not include assets used either in pulpwood logging, or in the manufacture of hardboard.	13	7	13

Table B-2. **Table of Class Lives and Recovery Periods (Continued)**

Asset class	Description of assets included	Recovery Periods (in years)		
		Class Life (in years)	GDS (MACRS)	ADS
26.2	**Manufacture of Converted Paper, Paperboard, and Pulp Products:** Includes assets used for modification, or remanufacture of paper and pulp into converted products, such as paper coated off the paper machine, paper bags, paper boxes, cartons and envelopes. Does not include assets used for manufacture of nonwovens that are elsewhere classified.	10	7	10
27.0	**Printing, Publishing, and Allied Industries:** Includes assets used in printing by one or more processes, such as letter-press, lithography, gravure, or screen; the performance of services for the printing trade, such as bookbinding, typesetting, engraving, photo-engraving, and electrotyping; and the publication of newspapers, books, and periodicals.	11	7	11
28.0	**Manufacture of Chemicals and Allied Products:** Includes assets used to manufacture basic organic and inorganic chemicals; chemical products to be used in further manufacture, such as synthetic fibers and plastics materials; and finished chemical products. Includes assets used to further process man-made fibers, to manufacture plastic film, and to manufacture nonwoven fabrics, when such assets are located in the same plant in an integrated operation with chemical products producing assets. Also includes assets used to manufacture photographic supplies, such as film, photographic paper, sensitized photographic paper, and developing chemicals. Includes all land improvements associated with plant site or production processes, such as effluent ponds and canals, provided such land improvements are depreciable but does not include buildings and structural components as defined in section 1.48-1(e) of the regulations. Does not include assets used in the manufacture of finished rubber and plastic products or in the production of natural gas products, butane, propane, and by-products of natural gas production plants.	9.5	5	9.5
30.1	**Manufacture of Rubber Products:** Includes assets used for the production of products from natural, synthetic, or reclaimed rubber, gutta percha, balata, or gutta siak, such as tires, tubes, rubber footwear, mechanical rubber goods, heels and soles, flooring, and rubber sundries; and in the recapping, retreading, and rebuilding of tires.	14	7	14
30.11	**Manufacture of Rubber Products—Special Tools and Devices:** Includes assets defined as special tools, such as jigs, dies, mandrels, molds, lasts, patterns, specialty containers, pallets, shells; and tire molds, and accessory parts such as rings and insert plates used in activities as defined in class 30.1. Does not include tire building drums and accessory parts and general purpose small tools such as wrenches and drills, both power and hand-driven, and other general purpose equipment such as conveyors and transfer equipment.	4	3	4
30.2	**Manufacture of Finished Plastic Products:** Includes assets used in the manufacture of plastics products and the molding of primary plastics for the trade. Does not include assets used in the manufacture of basic plastics materials nor the manufacture of phonograph records.	11	7	11
30.21	**Manufacture of Finished Plastic Products—Special Tools:** Includes assets defined as special tools, such as jigs, dies, fixtures, molds, patterns, gauges, and specialty transfer and shipping devices, used in activities as defined in class 30.2. Special tools are specifically designed for the production or processing of particular parts and have no significant utilitarian value and cannot be adapted to further or different use after changes or improvements are made in the model design of the particular part produced by the special tools. Does not include general purpose small tools such as wrenches and drills, both hand and power-driven, and other general purpose equipment such as conveyors, transfer equipment, and materials handling devices.	3.5	3	3.5
31.0	**Manufacture of Leather and Leather Products:** Includes assets used in the tanning, currying, and finishing of hides and skins; the processing of fur pelts; and the manufacture of finished leather products, such as footwear, belting, apparel, and luggage.	11	7	11
32.1	**Manufacture of Glass Products:** Includes assets used in the production of flat, blown, or pressed products of glass, such as float and window glass, glass containers, glassware and fiberglass. Does not include assets used in the manufacture of lenses.	14	7	14
32.11	**Manufacture of Glass Products—Special Tools:** Includes assets defined as special tools such as molds, patterns, pallets, and specialty transfer and shipping devices such as steel racks to transport automotive glass, used in activities as defined in class 32.1. Special tools are specifically designed for the production or processing of particular parts and have no significant utilitarian value and cannot be adapted to further or different use after changes or improvements are made in the model design of the particular part produced by the special tools. Does not include general purpose small tools such as wrenches and drills, both hand and power-driven, and other general purpose equipment such as conveyors, transfer equipment, and materials handling devices.	2.5	3	2.5
32.2	**Manufacture of Cement:** Includes assets used in the production of cement, but does not include assets used in the manufacture of concrete and concrete products nor in any mining or extraction process.	20	15	20
32.3	**Manufacture of Other Stone and Clay Products:** Includes assets used in the manufacture of products from materials in the form of clay and stone, such as brick, tile, and pipe; pottery and related products, such as vitreous-china, plumbing fixtures, earthenware and ceramic insulating materials; and also includes assets used in manufacture of concrete and concrete products. Does not include assets used in any mining or extraction processes.	15	7	15

Table B-2. **Table of Class Lives and Recovery Periods (Continued)**

Asset class	Description of assets included	Recovery Periods (in years)		
		Class Life (in years)	GDS (MACRS)	ADS
33.2	**Manufacture of Primary Nonferrous Metals:** Includes assets used in the smelting, refining, and electrolysis of nonferrous metals from ore, pig, or scrap, the rolling, drawing, and alloying of nonferrous metals; the manufacture of castings, forgings, and other basic products of nonferrous metals; and the manufacture of nails, spikes, structural shapes, tubing, wire, and cable.	14	7	14
33.21	**Manufacture of Primary Nonferrous Metals—Special Tools:** Includes assets defined as special tools such as dies, jigs, molds, patterns, fixtures, gauges, and drawings concerning such special tools used in the activities as defined in class 33.2, Manufacture of Primary Nonferrous Metals. Special tools are specifically designed for the production or processing of particular products or parts and have no significant utilitarian value and cannot be adapted to further or different use after changes or improvements are made in the model design of the particular part produced by the special tools. Does not include general purpose small tools such as wrenches and drills, both hand and power-driven, and other general purpose equipment such as conveyors, transfer equipment, and materials handling devices. Rolls, mandrels and refractories are not included in class 33.21 but are included in class 33.2.	6.5	5	6.5
33.3	**Manufacture of Foundry Products:** Includes assets used in the casting of iron and steel, including related operations such as molding and coremaking. Also includes assets used in the finishing of castings and patternmaking when performed at the foundry, all special tools and related land improvements.	14	7	14
33.4	**Manufacture of Primary Steel Mill Products:** Includes assets used in the smelting, reduction, and refining of iron and steel from ore, pig, or scrap; the rolling, drawing and alloying of steel; the manufacture of nails, spikes, structural shapes, tubing, wire, and cable. Includes assets used by steel service centers, ferrous metal forges, and assets used in coke production, regardless of ownership. Also includes related land improvements and all special tools used in the above activities.	15	7	15
34.0	**Manufacture of Fabricated Metal Products:** Includes assets used in the production of metal cans, tinware, fabricated structural metal products, metal stampings, and other ferrous and nonferrous metal and wire products not elsewhere classified. Does not include assets used to manufacture non-electric heating apparatus.	12	7	12
34.01	**Manufacture of Fabricated Metal Products—Special Tools:** Includes assets defined as special tools such as dies, jigs, molds, patterns, fixtures, gauges, and returnable containers and drawings concerning such special tools used in the activities as defined in class 34.0. Special tools are specifically designed for the production or processing of particular machine components, products, or parts, and have no significant utilitarian value and cannot be adapted to further or different use after changes or improvements are made in the model design of the particular part produced by the special tools. Does not include general small tools such as wrenches and drills, both hand and power-driven, and other general purpose equipment such as conveyors, transfer equipment, and materials handling devices.	3	3	3
35.0	**Manufacture of Electrical and Non-Electrical Machinery and Other Mechanical Products:** Includes assets used to manufacture or rebuild finished machinery and equipment and replacement parts thereof such as machine tools, general industrial and special industry machinery, electrical power generation, transmission, and distribution systems, space heating, cooling, and refrigeration systems, commercial and home appliances, farm and garden machinery, construction machinery, mining and oil field machinery, internal combustion engines (except those elsewhere classified), turbines (except those that power airborne vehicles), batteries, lamps and lighting fixtures, carbon and graphite products, and electromechanical and mechanical products including business machines, instruments, watches and clocks, vending and amusement machines, photographic equipment, medical and dental equipment and appliances, and ophthalmic goods. Includes assets used by manufacturers or rebuilders of such finished machinery and equipment in activities elsewhere classified such as the manufacture of castings, forgings, rubber and plastic products, electronic subassemblies or other manufacturing activities if the interim products are used by the same manufacturer primarily in the manufacture, assembly, or rebuilding of such finished machinery and equipment. Does not include assets used in mining, assets used in the manufacture of primary ferrous and nonferrous metals, assets included in class 00.11 through 00.4 and assets elsewhere classified.	10	7	10
36.0	**Manufacture of Electronic Components, Products, and Systems:** Includes assets used in the manufacture of electronic communication, computation, instrumentation and control system, including airborne applications; also includes assets used in the manufacture of electronic products such as frequency and amplitude modulated transmitters and receivers, electronic switching stations, television cameras, video recorders, record players and tape recorders, computers and computer peripheral machines, and electronic instruments, watches, and clocks; also includes assets used in the manufacture of components, provided their primary use is products and systems defined above such as electron tubes, capacitors, coils, resistors, printed circuit substrates, switches, harness cables, lasers, fiber optic devices, and magnetic media devices. Specifically excludes assets used to manufacture electronic products and components, photocopiers, typewriters, postage meters and other electromechanical and mechanical business machines and instruments that are elsewhere classified. Does not include semiconductor manufacturing equipment included in class 36.1.	6	5	6
36.1	**Any Semiconductor Manufacturing Equipment:** Includes equipment used in the manufacturing of semiconductors if the primary use of the semiconductors so produced is in products and systems of the type defined in class 36.0.	5	5	5

Table B-2. **Table of Class Lives and Recovery Periods (Continued)**

Asset class	Description of assets included	Recovery Periods (in years) Class Life (in years)	GDS (MACRS)	ADS
37.11	**Manufacture of Motor Vehicles:** Includes assets used in the manufacture and assembly of finished automobiles, trucks, trailers, motor homes, and buses. Does not include assets used in mining, printing and publishing, production of primary metals, electricity, or steam, or the manufacture of glass, industrial chemicals, batteries, or rubber products, which are classified elsewhere. Includes assets used in manufacturing activities elsewhere classified other than those excluded above, where such activities are incidental to and an integral part of the manufacture and assembly of finished motor vehicles such as the manufacture of parts and subassemblies of fabricated metal products, electrical equipment, textiles, plastics, leather, and foundry and forging operations. Does not include any assets not classified in manufacturing activity classes, e.g., does not include any assets classified in asset guideline classes 00.11 through 00.4. Activities will be considered incidental to the manufacture and assembly of finished motor vehicles only if 75 percent or more of the value of the products produced under one roof are used for the manufacture and assembly of finished motor vehicles. Parts that are produced as a normal replacement stock complement in connection with the manufacture and assembly of finished motor vehicles are considered used for the manufacture assembly of finished motor vehicles. Does not include assets used in the manufacture of component parts if these assets are used by taxpayers not engaged in the assembly of finished motor vehicles.	12	7	12
37.12	**Manufacture of Motor Vehicles—Special Tools:** Includes assets defined as special tools, such as jigs, dies, fixtures, molds, patterns, gauges, and specialty transfer and shipping devices, owned by manufacturers of finished motor vehicles and used in qualified activities as defined in class 37.11. Special tools are specifically designed for the production or processing of particular motor vehicle components and have no significant utilitarian value, and cannot be adapted to further or different use, after changes or improvements are made in the model design of the particular part produced by the special tools. Does not include general purpose small tools such as wrenches and drills, both hand and powerdriven, and other general purpose equipment such as conveyors, transfer equipment, and materials handling devices.	3	3	3
37.2	**Manufacture of Aerospace Products:** Includes assets used in the manufacture and assembly of airborne vehicles and their component parts including hydraulic, pneumatic, electrical, and mechanical systems. Does not include assets used in the production of electronic airborne detection, guidance, control, radiation, computation, test, navigation, and communication equipment or the components thereof.	10	7	10
37.31	**Ship and Boat Building Machinery and Equipment:** Includes assets used in the manufacture and repair of ships, boats, caissons, marine drilling rigs, and special fabrications not included in asset classes 37.32 and 37.33. Specifically includes all manufacturing and repairing machinery and equipment, including machinery and equipment used in the operation of assets included in asset class 37.32. Excludes buildings and their structural components.	12	7	12
37.32	**Ship and Boat Building Dry Docks and Land Improvements:** Includes assets used in the manufacture and repair of ships, boats, caissons, marine drilling rigs, and special fabrications not included in asset classes 37.31 and 37.33. Specifically includes floating and fixed dry docks, ship basins, graving docks, shipways, piers, and all other land improvements such as water, sewer, and electric systems. Excludes buildings and their structural components.	16	10	16
37.33	**Ship and Boat Building—Special Tools:** Includes assets defined as special tools such as dies, jigs, molds, patterns, fixtures, gauges, and drawings concerning such special tools used in the activities defined in classes 37.31 and 37.32. Special tools are specifically designed for the production or processing of particular machine components, products, or parts, and have no significant utilitarian value and cannot be adapted to further or different use after changes or improvements are made in the model design of the particular part produced by the special tools. Does not include general purpose small tools such as wrenches and drills, both hand and power-driven, and other general purpose equipment such as conveyors, transfer equipment, and materials handling devices.	6.5	5	6.5
37.41	**Manufacture of Locomotives:** Includes assets used in building or rebuilding railroad locomotives (including mining and industrial locomotives). Does not include assets of railroad transportation companies or assets of companies which manufacture components of locomotives but do not manufacture finished locomotives.	11.5	7	11.5
37.42	**Manufacture of Railroad Cars:** Includes assets used in building or rebuilding railroad freight or passenger cars (including rail transit cars). Does not include assets of railroad transportation companies or assets of companies which manufacture components of railroad cars but do not manufacture finished railroad cars.	12	7	12
39.0	**Manufacture of Athletic, Jewelry, and Other Goods:** Includes assets used in the production of jewelry; musical instruments; toys and sporting goods; motion picture and television films and tapes; and pens, pencils, office and art supplies, brooms, brushes, caskets, etc. **Railroad Transportation:** Classes with the prefix 40 include the assets identified below that are used in the commercial and contract carrying of passengers and freight by rail. Assets of electrified railroads will be classified in a manner corresponding to that set forth below for railroads not independently operated as electric lines. Excludes the assets included in classes with the prefix beginning 00.1 and 00.2 above, and also excludes any non-depreciable assets included in Interstate Commerce Commission accounts enumerated for this class.	12	7	12

Table B-2. **Table of Class Lives and Recovery Periods (Continued)**

Asset class	Description of assets included	Recovery Periods (in years) Class Life (in years)	GDS (MACRS)	ADS
40.1	**Railroad Machinery and Equipment:** Includes assets classified in the following Interstate Commerce Commission accounts: **Roadway accounts:** (16) Station and office buildings (freight handling machinery and equipment only) (25) TOFC/COFC terminals (freight handling machinery and equipment only) (26) Communication systems (27) Signals and interlockers (37) Roadway machines (44) Shop machinery **Equipment accounts:** (52) Locomotives (53) Freight train cars (54) Passenger train cars (57) Work equipment	14	7	14
40.2	**Railroad Structures and Similar Improvements:** Includes assets classified in the following Interstate Commerce Commission road accounts: (6) Bridges, trestles, and culverts (7) Elevated structures (13) Fences, snowsheds, and signs (16) Station and office buildings (stations and other operating structures only) (17) Roadway buildings (18) Water stations (19) Fuel stations (20) Shops and enginehouses (25) TOFC/COFC terminals (operating structures only) (31) Power transmission systems (35) Miscellaneous structures (39) Public improvements construction	30	20	30
40.3	**Railroad Wharves and Docks:** Includes assets classified in the following Interstate Commerce accounts: (23) Wharves and docks (24) Coal and ore wharves	20	15	20
40.4	**Railroad Track**	10	7	10
40.51	**Railroad Hydraulic Electric Generating Equipment**	50	20	50
40.52	**Railroad Nuclear Electric Generating Equipment**	20	15	20
40.53	**Railroad Steam Electric Generating Equipment**	28	20	28
40.54	**Railroad Steam, Compressed Air, and Other Power Plan Equipment**	28	20	28
41.0	**Motor Transport—Passengers:** Includes assets used in the urban and interurban commercial and contract carrying of passengers by road, except the transportation assets included in classes with the prefix 00.2.	8	5	8
42.0	**Motor Transport—Freight:** Includes assets used in the commercial and contract carrying of freight by road, except the transportation assets included in classes with the prefix 00.2.	8	5	8
44.0	**Water Transportation:** Includes assets used in the commercial and contract carrying of freight and passengers by water except the transportation assets included in classes with the prefix 00.2. Includes all related land improvements.	20	15	20
45.0	**Air Transport:** Includes assets (except helicopters) used in commercial and contract carrying of passengers and freight by air. For purposes of section 1.167(a)-11(d)(2)(iv)(a) of the regulations, expenditures for "repair, maintenance, rehabilitation, or improvement," shall consist of direct maintenance expenses (irrespective of airworthiness provisions or charges) as defined by Civil Aeronautics Board uniform accounts 5200, maintenance burden (exclusive of expenses pertaining to maintenance buildings and improvements) as defined by Civil Aeronautics Board accounts 5300, and expenditures which are not "excluded additions" as defined in section 1.167(a)-11(d)(2)(vi) of the regulations and which would be charged to property and equipment accounts in the Civil Aeronautics Board uniform system of accounts.	12	7	12
45.1	**Air Transport (restricted):** Includes each asset described in the description of class 45.0 which was held by the taxpayer on April 15, 1976, or is acquired by the taxpayer pursuant to a contract which was, on April 15, 1976, and at all times thereafter, binding on the taxpayer. This criterion of classification based on binding contract concept is to be applied in the same manner as under the general rules expressed in section 49(b)(1), (4), (5) and (8) of the Code (as in effect prior to its repeal by the Revenue Act of 1978, section 312(c)(1), (d), 1978-3 C.B. 1, 60).	6	5	6
46.0	**Pipeline Transportation:** Includes assets used in the private, commercial, and contract carrying of petroleum, gas and other products by means of pipes and conveyors. The trunk lines and related storage facilities of integrated petroleum and natural gas producers are included in this class. Excludes initial clearing and grading land improvements as specified in Rev. Rul. 72-403, 1972-2; C.B. 102, but includes all other related land improvements.	22	15	22

Table B-2. **Table of Class Lives and Recovery Periods (Continued)**

Asset class	Description of assets included	Recovery Periods (in years)		
		Class Life (in years)	GDS (MACRS)	ADS
48.11	**Telephone Communications:** Includes the assets classified below and that are used in the provision of commercial and contract telephonic services such as: **Telephone Central Office Buildings:** Includes assets intended to house central office equipment, as defined in Federal Communications Commission Part 31 Account No. 212 whether section 1245 or section 1250 property.	45	20	45
48.12	**Telephone Central Office Equipment:** Includes central office switching and related equipment as defined in Federal Communications Commission Part 31 Account No. 221. Does not include computer-based telephone central office switching equipment included in class 48.121. Does not include private branch exchange (PBX) equipment.	18	10	18
48.121	**Computer-based Telephone Central Office Switching Equipment:** Includes equipment whose functions are those of a computer or peripheral equipment (as defined in section 168(i)(2)(B) of the Code) used in its capacity as telephone central office equipment. Does not include private exchange (PBX) equipment.	9.5	5	9.5
48.13	**Telephone Station Equipment:** Includes such station apparatus and connections as teletypewriters, telephones, booths, private exchanges, and comparable equipment as defined in Federal Communications Commission Part 31 Account Nos. 231, 232, and 234.	10	7*	10*
48.14	**Telephone Distribution Plant:** Includes such assets as pole lines, cable, aerial wire, underground conduits, and comparable equipment, and related land improvements as defined in Federal Communications Commission Part 31 Account Nos. 241, 242.1, 242.2, 242.3, 242.4, 243, and 244.	24	15	24
48.2	**Radio and Television Broadcastings:** Includes assets used in radio and television broadcasting, except transmitting towers. **Telegraph, Ocean Cable, and Satellite Communications (TOCSC)** includes communications-related assets used to provide domestic and international radio-telegraph, wire-telegraph, ocean-cable, and satellite communications services; also includes related land improvements. If property described in Classes 48.31–48.45 is comparable to telephone distribution plant described in Class 48.14 and used for 2-way exchange of voice and data communication which is the equivalent of telephone communication, such property is assigned a class life of 24 years under this revenue procedure. Comparable equipment does not include cable television equipment used primarily for 1-way communication.	6	5	6
48.31	**TOCSC—Electric Power Generating and Distribution Systems:** Includes assets used in the provision of electric power by generation, modulation, rectification, channelization, control, and distribution. Does not include these assets when they are installed on customers premises.	19	10	19
48.32	**TOCSC—High Frequency Radio and Microwave Systems:** Includes assets such as transmitters and receivers, antenna supporting structures, antennas, transmission lines from equipment to antenna, transmitter cooling systems, and control and amplification equipment. Does not include cable and long-line systems.	13	7	13
48.33	**TOCSC—Cable and Long-line Systems:** Includes assets such as transmission lines, pole lines, ocean cables, buried cable and conduit, repeaters, repeater stations, and other related assets. Does not include high frequency radio or microwave systems.	26.5	20	26.5
48.34	**TOCSC—Central Office Control Equipment:** Includes assets for general control, switching, and monitoring of communications signals including electromechanical switching and channeling apparatus, multiplexing equipment patching and monitoring facilities, in-house cabling, teleprinter equipment, and associated site improvements.	16.5	10	16.5
48.35	**TOCSC—Computerized Switching, Channeling, and Associated Control Equipment:** Includes central office switching computers, interfacing computers, other associated specialized control equipment, and site improvements.	10.5	7	10.5
48.36	**TOCSC—Satellite Ground Segment Property:** Includes assets such as fixed earth station equipment, antennas, satellite communications equipment, and interface equipment used in satellite communications. Does not include general purpose equipment or equipment used in satellite space segment property.	10	7	10
48.37	**TOCSC—Satellite Space Segment Property:** Includes satellites and equipment used for telemetry, tracking, control, and monitoring when used in satellite communications.	8	5	8
48.38	**TOCSC—Equipment Installed on Customer's Premises:** Includes assets installed on customer's premises, such as computers, terminal equipment, power generation and distribution systems, private switching center, teleprinters, facsimile equipment and other associated and related equipment.	10	7	10
48.39	**TOCSC—Support and Service Equipment:** Includes assets used to support but not engage in communications. Includes store, warehouse and shop tools, and test and laboratory assets. **Cable Television (CATV):** Includes communications-related assets used to provide cable television community antenna television services. Does not include assets used to provide subscribers with two-way communications services.	13.5	7	13.5

* Property described in asset guideline class 48.13 which is qualified technological equipment as defined in section 168(i)(2) is assigned a 5-year recovery period.

Table B-2. **Table of Class Lives and Recovery Periods (Continued)**

Asset class	Description of assets included	Recovery Periods (in years)		
		Class Life (in years)	GDS (MACRS)	ADS
48.41	**CATV—Headend:** Includes assets such as towers, antennas, preamplifiers, converters, modulation equipment, and program non-duplication systems. Does not include headend buildings and program origination assets.	11	7	11
48.42	**CATV—Subscriber Connection and Distribution Systems:** Includes assets such as trunk and feeder cable, connecting hardware, amplifiers, power equipment, passive devices, directional taps, pedestals, pressure taps, drop cables, matching transformers, multiple set connector equipment, and convertors.	10	7	10
48.43	**CATV—Program Origination:** Includes assets such as cameras, film chains, video tape recorders, lighting, and remote location equipment excluding vehicles. Does not include buildings and their structural components.	9	5	9
48.44	**CATV—Service and Test:** Includes assets such as oscilloscopes, field strength meters, spectrum analyzers, and cable testing equipment, but does not include vehicles.	8.5	5	8.5
48.45	**CATV—Microwave Systems:** Inlcudes assets such as towers, antennas, transmitting and receiving equipment, and broad band microwave assets is used in the provision of cable television services. Does not include assets used in the provision of common carrier services.	9.5	5	9.5
49.11	**Electric, Gas, Water and Steam, Utility Services:** Includes assets used in the production, transmission and distribution of electricity, gas, steam, or water for sale including related land improvements. **Electric Utility Hydraulic Production Plant:** Includes assets used in the hydraulic power production of electricity for sale, including related land improvements, such as dams, flumes, canals, and waterways.	50	20	50
49.12	**Electric Utility Nuclear Production Plant:** Includes assets used in the nuclear power production and electricity for sale and related land improvements. Does not include nuclear fuel assemblies.	20	15	20
49.121	**Electric Utility Nuclear Fuel Assemblies:** Includes initial core and replacement core nuclear fuel assemblies (i.e., the composite of fabricated nuclear fuel and container) when used in a boiling water, pressurized water, or high temperature gas reactor used in the production of electricity. Does not include nuclear fuel assemblies used in breader reactors.	5	5	5
49.13	**Electric Utility Steam Production Plant:** Includes assets used in the steam power production of electricity for sale, combustion turbines operated in a combined cycle with a conventional steam unit and related land improvements. Also includes package boilers, electric generators and related assets such as electricity and steam distribution systems as used by a waste reduction and resource recovery plant if the steam or electricity is normally for sale to others.	28	20	28
49.14	**Electric Utility Transmission and Distribution Plant:** Includes assets used in the transmission and distribution of electricity for sale and related land improvements. Excludes initial clearing and grading land improvements as specified in Rev. Rul. 72-403, 1972-2 C.B. 102.	30	20	30
49.15	**Electric Utility Combustion Turbine Production Plant:** Includes assets used in the production of electricity for sale by the use of such prime movers as jet engines, combustion turbines, diesel engines, gasoline engines, and other internal combustion engines, their associated power turbines and/or generators, and related land improvements. Does not include combustion turbines operated in a combined cycle with a conventional steam unit.	20	15	20
49.21	**Gas Utility Distribution Facilities:** Includes gas water heaters and gas conversion equipment installed by utility on customers' premises on a rental basis.	35	20	35
49.221	**Gas Utility Manufactured Gas Production Plants:** Includes assets used in the manufacture of gas having chemical and/or physical properties which do not permit complete interchangeability with domestic natural gas. Does not include gas-producing systems and related systems used in waste reduction and resource recovery plants which are elsewhere classified.	30	20	30
49.222	**Gas Utility Substitute Natural Gas (SNG) Production Plant (naphtha or lighter hydrocarbon feedstocks):** Includes assets used in the catalytic conversion of feedstocks or naphtha or lighter hydrocarbons to a gaseous fuel which is completely interchangeable with domestic natural gas.	14	7	14
49.223	**Substitute Natural Gas—Coal Gasification:** Includes assets used in the manufacture and production of pipeline quality gas from coal using the basic Lurgi process with advanced methanation. Includes all process plant equipment and structures used in this coal gasification process and all utility assets such as cooling systems, water supply and treatment facilities, and assets used in the production and distribution of electricity and steam for use by the taxpayer in a gasification plant and attendant coal mining site processes but not for assets used in the production and distribution of electricity and steam for sale to others. Also includes all other related land improvements. Does not include assets used in the direct mining and treatment of coal prior to the gasification process itself.	18	10	18
49.23	**Natural Gas Production Plant**	14	7	14
49.24	**Gas Utility Trunk Pipelines and Related Storage Facilities:** Excluding initial clearing and grading land improvements as specified in Rev. Rul. 72-40.	22	15	22
49.25	**Liquefied Natural Gas Plant:** Includes assets used in the liquefaction, storage, and regasification of natural gas including loading and unloading connections, instrumentation equipment and controls, pumps, vaporizers and odorizers, tanks, and related land improvements. Also includes pipeline interconnections with gas transmission lines and distribution systems and marine terminal facilities.	22	15	22

Table B-2. **Table of Class Lives and Recovery Periods (Continued)**

Asset class	Description of assets included	Recovery Periods (in years)		
		Class Life (in years)	GDS (MACRS)	ADS
49.3	**Water Utilities:** Includes assets used in the gathering, treatment, and commercial distribution of water.	50	20***	50
49.4	**Central Steam Utility Production and Distribution:** Includes assets used in the production and distribution of steam for sale. Does not include assets used in waste reduction and resource recovery plants which are elsewhere classified.	28	20	28
49.5	**Waste Reduction and Resource Recovery Plants:** Includes assets used in the conversion of refuse or other solid waste or biomass to heat or to a solid, liquid, or gaseous fuel. Also includes all process plant equipment and structures at the site used to receive, handle, collect, and process refuse or other solid waste or biomass in a waterwall, combustion system, oil or gas pyrolysis system, or refuse derived fuel system to create hot water, gas, steam and electricity. Includes material recovery and support assets used in refuse or solid refuse or solid waste receiving, collecting, handling, sorting, shredding, classifying, and separation systems. Does not include any package boilers, or electric generators and related assets such as electricity, hot water, steam and manufactured gas production plants classified in classes 00.4, 49.13, 49.221, and 49.4. Does include, however, all other utilities such as water supply and treatment facilities, ash handling and other related land improvements of a waste reduction and resource recovery plant.	10	7	10
50.	**Municipal Wastewater Treatment Plant**	24	15	24
51.	**Municipal Sewer**	50	20***	50
57.0	**Distributive Trades and Services:** Includes assets used in wholesale and retail trade, and personal and professional services. Includes section 1245 assets used in marketing petroleum and petroleum products.	9	5	9*
57.1	**Distributive Trades and Services—Billboard, Service Station Buildings and Petroleum Marketing Land Improvements:** Includes section 1250 assets, including service station buildings and depreciable land improvements, whether section 1245 property or section 1250 property, used in the marketing of petroleum and petroleum products, but not including any of these facilities related to petroleum and natural gas trunk pipelines. Includes car wash buildings and related land improvements. Includes billboards, whether such assets are section 1245 property or section 1250 property. Excludes all other land improvements, buildings and structural components as defined in section 1.48-1(e) of the regulations. See *Gas station convenience stores* in chapter 3.	20	15	20
79.0	**Recreation:** Includes assets used in the provision of entertainment services on payment of a fee or admission charge, as in the operation of bowling alleys, billiard and pool establishments, theaters, concert halls, and miniature golf courses. Does not include amusement and theme parks and assets which consist primarily of specialized land improvements or structures, such as golf courses, sports stadia, race tracks, ski slopes, and buildings which house the assets used in entertainment services.	10	7	10
80.0	**Theme and Amusement Parks:** Includes assets used in the provision of rides, attractions, and amusements in activities defined as theme and amusement parks, and includes appurtenances associated with a ride, attraction, amusement or theme setting within the park such as ticket booths, facades, shop interiors, and props, special purpose structures, and buildings other than warehouses, administration buildings, hotels, and motels. Includes all land improvements for or in support of park activities (e.g., parking lots, sidewalks, waterways, bridges, fences, landscaping, etc.), and support functions (e.g., food and beverage retailing, souvenir vending and other nonlodging accommodations) if owned by the park and provided exclusively for the benefit of park patrons. Theme and amusement parks are defined as combinations of amusements, rides, and attractions which are permanently situated on park land and open to the public for the price of admission. This guideline class is a composite of all assets used in this industry except transportation equipment (general purpose trucks, cars, airplanes, etc., which are included in asset guideline classes with the prefix 00.2), assets used in the provision of administrative services (asset classes with the prefix 00.1) and warehouses, administration buildings, hotels and motels.	12.5	7	12.5
	Certain Property for Which Recovery Periods Assigned:			
	A. Personal Property With No Class Life		7	12
	Section 1245 Real Property With No Class Life		7	40
	B. Qualified Technological Equipment, as defined in section 168(i)(2).	**	5	5
	C. Property Used in Connection with Research and Experimentation referred to in section 168(e)(3)(B).	**	5	class life if no class life—12
	D. Alternative Energy Property described in sections 48(1)(3)(viii) or (iv), or section 48(1)(4) of the Code.	**	5	class life if no class life—12
	E. Biomass property described in section 48(1)(15) and is a qualifying small production facility within the meaning of section 3(17)(c) of the Federal Power Act (16 U.S.C. 796(17)(C)), as in effect on September 1, 1986.	**	5	class life if no class life—12

* Any high technology medical equipment as defined in section 168(i)(2)(C) which is described in asset guideline class 57.0 is assigned a 5-year recovery period for the alternate MACRS method.

** The class life (if any) of property described in classes B, C, D, or E is determined by reference to the asset guideline classes. If an item of property described in paragraphs B, C, D, or E is not described in any asset guideline class, such item of property has no class life.

*** Use straight line over 25 years if placed in service after June 12, 1996, unless placed in service under a binding contract in effect before June 10, 1996, and at all times until placed in service.

3-, 5-, 7-, 10-, 15-, and 20-Year Property
Half-Year Convention

Year	Depreciation rate for recovery period					
	3-year	5-year	7-year	10-year	15-year	20-year
1	33.33%	20.00%	14.29%	10.00%	5.00%	3.750%
2	44.45	32.00	24.49	18.00	9.50	7.219
3	14.81	19.20	17.49	14.40	8.55	6.677
4	7.41	11.52	12.49	11.52	7.70	6.177
5		11.52	8.93	9.22	6.93	5.713
6		5.76	8.92	7.37	6.23	5.285
7			8.93	6.55	5.90	4.888
8			4.46	6.55	5.90	4.522
9				6.56	5.91	4.462
10				6.55	5.90	4.461
11				3.28	5.91	4.462
12					5.90	4.461
13					5.91	4.462
14					5.90	4.461
15					5.91	4.462
16					2.95	4.461
17						4.462
18						4.461
19						4.462
20						4.461
21						2.231

Residential Rental Property
Mid-Month Convention
Straight Line—27.5 Years

Year	Month property placed in service											
	1	2	3	4	5	6	7	8	9	10	11	12
1	3.485%	3.182%	2.879%	2.576%	2.273%	1.970%	1.667%	1.364%	1.061%	0.758%	0.455%	0.152%
2–9	3.636	3.636	3.636	3.636	3.636	3.636	3.636	3.636	3.636	3.636	3.636	3.636
10	3.637	3.637	3.637	3.637	3.637	3.637	3.636	3.636	3.636	3.636	3.636	3.636
11	3.636	3.636	3.636	3.636	3.636	3.636	3.637	3.637	3.637	3.637	3.637	3.637
12	3.637	3.637	3.637	3.637	3.637	3.637	3.636	3.636	3.636	3.636	3.636	3.636
13	3.636	3.636	3.636	3.636	3.636	3.636	3.637	3.637	3.637	3.637	3.637	3.637
14	3.637	3.637	3.637	3.637	3.637	3.637	3.636	3.636	3.636	3.636	3.636	3.636
15	3.636	3.636	3.636	3.636	3.636	3.636	3.637	3.637	3.637	3.637	3.637	3.637
16	3.637	3.637	3.637	3.637	3.637	3.637	3.636	3.636	3.636	3.636	3.636	3.636
17	3.636	3.636	3.636	3.636	3.636	3.636	3.637	3.637	3.637	3.637	3.637	3.637
18	3.637	3.637	3.637	3.637	3.637	3.637	3.636	3.636	3.636	3.636	3.636	3.636
19	3.636	3.636	3.636	3.636	3.636	3.636	3.637	3.637	3.637	3.637	3.637	3.637
20	3.637	3.637	3.637	3.637	3.637	3.637	3.636	3.636	3.636	3.636	3.636	3.636
21	3.636	3.636	3.636	3.636	3.636	3.636	3.637	3.637	3.637	3.637	3.637	3.637
22	3.637	3.637	3.637	3.637	3.637	3.637	3.636	3.636	3.636	3.636	3.636	3.636
23	3.636	3.636	3.636	3.636	3.636	3.636	3.637	3.637	3.637	3.637	3.637	3.637
24	3.637	3.637	3.637	3.637	3.637	3.637	3.636	3.636	3.636	3.636	3.636	3.636
25	3.636	3.636	3.636	3.636	3.636	3.636	3.637	3.637	3.637	3.637	3.637	3.637
26	3.637	3.637	3.637	3.637	3.637	3.637	3.636	3.636	3.636	3.636	3.636	3.636
27	3.636	3.636	3.636	3.636	3.636	3.636	3.637	3.637	3.637	3.637	3.637	3.637
28	1.97	2.273	2.576	2.879	3.182	3.485	3.636	3.636	3.636	3.636	3.636	3.636
29							0.152	0.455	0.758	1.061	1.364	1.667

Nonresidential Real Property
Mid-Month Convention
Straight Line—31.5 Years

Year	Month property placed in service											
	1	2	3	4	5	6	7	8	9	10	11	12
1	3.042%	2.778%	2.513%	2.249%	1.984%	1.720%	1.455%	1.190%	0.926%	0.661%	0.397%	0.132%
2–7	3.175	3.175	3.175	3.175	3.175	3.175	3.175	3.175	3.175	3.175	3.175	3.175
8	3.175	3.174	3.175	3.174	3.175	3.174	3.175	3.175	3.175	3.175	3.175	3.175
9	3.174	3.175	3.174	3.175	3.174	3.175	3.174	3.175	3.174	3.175	3.174	3.175
10	3.175	3.174	3.175	3.174	3.175	3.174	3.175	3.174	3.175	3.174	3.175	3.174
11	3.174	3.175	3.174	3.175	3.174	3.175	3.174	3.175	3.174	3.175	3.174	3.175
12	3.175	3.174	3.175	3.174	3.175	3.174	3.175	3.174	3.175	3.174	3.175	3.174
13	3.174	3.175	3.174	3.175	3.174	3.175	3.174	3.175	3.174	3.175	3.174	3.175
14	3.175	3.174	3.175	3.174	3.175	3.174	3.175	3.174	3.175	3.174	3.175	3.174
15	3.174	3.175	3.174	3.175	3.174	3.175	3.174	3.175	3.174	3.175	3.174	3.175
16	3.175	3.174	3.175	3.174	3.175	3.174	3.175	3.174	3.175	3.174	3.175	3.174
17	3.174	3.175	3.174	3.175	3.174	3.175	3.174	3.175	3.174	3.175	3.174	3.175
18	3.175	3.174	3.175	3.174	3.175	3.174	3.175	3.174	3.175	3.174	3.175	3.174
19	3.174	3.175	3.174	3.175	3.174	3.175	3.174	3.175	3.174	3.175	3.174	3.175
20	3.175	3.174	3.175	3.174	3.175	3.174	3.175	3.174	3.175	3.174	3.175	3.174
21	3.174	3.175	3.174	3.175	3.174	3.175	3.174	3.175	3.174	3.175	3.174	3.175
22	3.175	3.174	3.175	3.174	3.175	3.174	3.175	3.174	3.175	3.174	3.175	3.174
23	3.174	3.175	3.174	3.175	3.174	3.175	3.174	3.175	3.174	3.175	3.174	3.175
24	3.175	3.174	3.175	3.174	3.175	3.174	3.175	3.174	3.175	3.174	3.175	3.174
25	3.174	3.175	3.174	3.175	3.174	3.175	3.174	3.175	3.174	3.175	3.174	3.175
26	3.175	3.174	3.175	3.174	3.175	3.174	3.175	3.174	3.175	3.174	3.175	3.174
27	3.174	3.175	3.174	3.175	3.174	3.175	3.174	3.175	3.174	3.175	3.174	3.175
28	3.175	3.174	3.175	3.174	3.175	3.174	3.175	3.174	3.175	3.174	3.175	3.174
29	3.174	3.175	3.174	3.175	3.174	3.175	3.174	3.175	3.174	3.175	3.174	3.175
30	3.175	3.174	3.175	3.174	3.175	3.174	3.175	3.174	3.175	3.174	3.175	3.174
31	3.174	3.175	3.174	3.175	3.174	3.175	3.174	3.175	3.174	3.175	3.174	3.175
32	1.720	1.984	2.249	2.513	2.778	3.042	3.175	3.174	3.175	3.174	3.175	3.174
33							0.132	0.397	0.661	0.926	1.190	1.455

Nonresidential Real Property
Mid-Month Convention
Straight Line—39 Years

Year	Month property placed in service											
	1	2	3	4	5	6	7	8	9	10	11	12
1	2.461%	2.247%	2.033%	1.819%	1.605%	1.391%	1.177%	0.963%	0.749%	0.535%	0.321%	0.107%
2–39	2.564	2.564	2.564	2.564	2.564	2.564	2.564	2.564	2.564	2.564	2.564	2.564
40	0.107	0.321	0.535	0.749	0.963	1.177	1.391	1.605	1.819	2.033	2.247	2.461

150% Declining Balance Method
Half-Year Convention

Year	Recovery periods in years												
	2.5	3	3.5	4	5	6	6.5	7	7.5	8	8.5	9	9.5
1	30.0%	25.0%	21.43%	18.75%	15.00%	12.50%	11.54%	10.71%	10.00%	9.38%	8.82%	8.33%	7.89%
2	42.0	37.5	33.67	30.47	25.50	21.83	20.41	19.13	18.00	16.99	16.09	15.28	14.54
3	28.0	25.0	22.45	20.31	17.85	16.41	15.70	15.03	14.40	13.81	13.25	12.73	12.25
4		12.5	22.45	20.31	16.66	14.06	13.09	12.25	11.52	11.22	10.91	10.61	10.31
5				10.16	16.66	14.06	13.09	12.25	11.52	10.80	10.19	9.65	9.17
6					8.33	14.06	13.09	12.25	11.52	10.80	10.19	9.64	9.17
7						7.03	13.08	12.25	11.52	10.80	10.18	9.65	9.17
8								6.13	11.52	10.80	10.19	9.64	9.17
9										5.40	10.18	9.65	9.17
10												4.82	9.16

(Continued)

Year	Recovery periods in years												
	10	10.5	11	11.5	12	12.5	13	13.5	14	15	16	16.5	17
1	7.50%	7.14%	6.82%	6.52%	6.25%	6.00%	5.77%	5.56%	5.36%	5.00%	4.69%	4.55%	4.41%
2	13.88	13.27	12.71	12.19	11.72	11.28	10.87	10.49	10.14	9.50	8.94	8.68	8.43
3	11.79	11.37	10.97	10.60	10.25	9.93	9.62	9.33	9.05	8.55	8.10	7.89	7.69
4	10.02	9.75	9.48	9.22	8.97	8.73	8.51	8.29	8.08	7.70	7.34	7.17	7.01
5	8.74	8.35	8.18	8.02	7.85	7.69	7.53	7.37	7.22	6.93	6.65	6.52	6.39
6	8.74	8.35	7.98	7.64	7.33	7.05	6.79	6.55	6.44	6.23	6.03	5.93	5.83
7	8.74	8.35	7.97	7.64	7.33	7.05	6.79	6.55	6.32	5.90	5.55	5.39	5.32
8	8.74	8.35	7.98	7.63	7.33	7.05	6.79	6.55	6.32	5.90	5.55	5.39	5.23
9	8.74	8.36	7.97	7.64	7.33	7.04	6.79	6.55	6.32	5.91	5.55	5.39	5.23
10	8.74	8.35	7.98	7.63	7.33	7.05	6.79	6.55	6.32	5.90	5.55	5.39	5.23
11	4.37	8.36	7.97	7.64	7.32	7.04	6.79	6.55	6.32	5.91	5.55	5.39	5.23
12			3.99	7.63	7.33	7.05	6.78	6.55	6.32	5.90	5.55	5.39	5.23
13					3.66	7.04	6.79	6.56	6.32	5.91	5.54	5.38	5.23
14							3.39	6.55	6.31	5.90	5.55	5.39	5.23
15									3.16	5.91	5.54	5.38	5.23
16										2.95	5.55	5.39	5.23
17											2.77	5.38	5.23
18													2.62

(Continued)

Year	Recovery periods in years												
	18	19	20	22	24	25	26.5	28	30	35	40	45	50
1	4.17%	3.95%	3.750%	3.409%	3.125%	3.000%	2.830%	2.679%	2.500%	2.143%	1.875%	1.667%	1.500%
2	7.99	7.58	7.219	6.586	6.055	5.820	5.500	5.214	4.875	4.194	3.680	3.278	2.955
3	7.32	6.98	6.677	6.137	5.676	5.471	5.189	4.934	4.631	4.014	3.542	3.169	2.866
4	6.71	6.43	6.177	5.718	5.322	5.143	4.895	4.670	4.400	3.842	3.409	3.063	2.780
5	6.15	5.93	5.713	5.328	4.989	4.834	4.618	4.420	4.180	3.677	3.281	2.961	2.697
6	5.64	5.46	5.285	4.965	4.677	4.544	4.357	4.183	3.971	3.520	3.158	2.862	2.616
7	5.17	5.03	4.888	4.627	4.385	4.271	4.110	3.959	3.772	3.369	3.040	2.767	2.538
8	4.94	4.69	4.522	4.311	4.111	4.015	3.877	3.747	3.584	3.225	2.926	2.674	2.461
9	4.94	4.69	4.462	4.063	3.854	3.774	3.658	3.546	3.404	3.086	2.816	2.585	2.388
10	4.94	4.69	4.461	4.063	3.729	3.584	3.451	3.356	3.234	2.954	2.710	2.499	2.316
11	4.94	4.69	4.462	4.063	3.729	3.583	3.383	3.205	3.072	2.828	2.609	2.416	2.246
12	4.95	4.69	4.461	4.063	3.729	3.584	3.383	3.205	2.994	2.706	2.511	2.335	2.179
13	4.94	4.69	4.462	4.064	3.730	3.583	3.383	3.205	2.994	2.590	2.417	2.257	2.114
14	4.95	4.69	4.461	4.063	3.729	3.584	3.383	3.205	2.994	2.571	2.326	2.182	2.050
15	4.94	4.69	4.462	4.064	3.730	3.583	3.383	3.205	2.994	2.571	2.253	2.110	1.989
16	4.95	4.69	4.461	4.063	3.729	3.584	3.383	3.205	2.994	2.571	2.253	2.039	1.929
17	4.94	4.69	4.462	4.064	3.730	3.583	3.383	3.205	2.994	2.571	2.253	2.005	1.871
18	4.95	4.70	4.461	4.063	3.729	3.584	3.383	3.205	2.994	2.571	2.253	2.005	1.815
19	2.47	4.69	4.462	4.064	3.730	3.583	3.383	3.205	2.994	2.571	2.253	2.005	1.806
20		2.35	4.461	4.063	3.729	3.584	3.384	3.205	2.993	2.571	2.253	2.005	1.806
21			2.231	4.064	3.730	3.583	3.383	3.205	2.994	2.571	2.253	2.005	1.806
22				4.063	3.729	3.584	3.384	3.205	2.993	2.571	2.253	2.005	1.806
23				2.032	3.730	3.583	3.383	3.205	2.994	2.571	2.253	2.005	1.806
24					3.729	3.584	3.384	3.205	2.993	2.571	2.253	2.004	1.806
25					1.865	3.583	3.383	3.205	2.994	2.571	2.253	2.005	1.806
26						1.792	3.384	3.205	2.993	2.571	2.253	2.004	1.806
27							3.383	3.205	2.994	2.571	2.253	2.005	1.806
28								3.205	2.993	2.572	2.253	2.004	1.806
29								1.602	2.994	2.571	2.253	2.005	1.806
30									2.993	2.572	2.253	2.004	1.806
31									1.497	2.571	2.253	2.005	1.806
32										2.572	2.253	2.004	1.806
33										2.571	2.252	2.005	1.806
34										2.572	2.253	2.004	1.806
35										2.571	2.252	2.005	1.806
36										1.286	2.253	2.004	1.806
37											2.252	2.005	1.806
38											2.253	2.004	1.806
39											2.252	2.005	1.806
40											2.253	2.004	1.806
41											1.126	2.005	1.806
42												2.004	1.805
43												2.005	1.806
44												2.004	1.805
45												2.005	1.806
46												1.002	1.805
47													1.806
48													1.805
49													1.806
50													1.805
51													0.903

Table A-8. **Straight Line Method Half-Year Convention**

Year	Recovery periods in years												
	2.5	3	3.5	4	5	6	6.5	7	7.5	8	8.5	9	9.5
1	20.0%	16.67%	14.29%	12.5%	10.0%	8.33%	7.69%	7.14%	6.67%	6.25%	5.88%	5.56%	5.26%
2	40.0	33.33	28.57	25.0	20.0	16.67	15.39	14.29	13.33	12.50	11.77	11.11	10.53
3	40.0	33.33	28.57	25.0	20.0	16.67	15.38	14.29	13.33	12.50	11.76	11.11	10.53
4		16.67	28.57	25.0	20.0	16.67	15.39	14.28	13.33	12.50	11.77	11.11	10.53
5				12.5	20.0	16.66	15.38	14.29	13.34	12.50	11.76	11.11	10.52
6					10.0	16.67	15.39	14.28	13.33	12.50	11.77	11.11	10.53
7						8.33	15.38	14.29	13.34	12.50	11.76	11.11	10.52
8								7.14	13.33	12.50	11.77	11.11	10.53
9										6.25	11.76	11.11	10.52
10												5.56	10.53

Table A-8. *(Continued)*

Year	Recovery periods in years												
	10	10.5	11	11.5	12	12.5	13	13.5	14	15	16	16.5	17
1	5.0%	4.76%	4.55%	4.35%	4.17%	4.0%	3.85%	3.70%	3.57%	3.33%	3.13%	3.03%	2.94%
2	10.0	9.52	9.09	8.70	8.33	8.0	7.69	7.41	7.14	6.67	6.25	6.06	5.88
3	10.0	9.52	9.09	8.70	8.33	8.0	7.69	7.41	7.14	6.67	6.25	6.06	5.88
4	10.0	9.53	9.09	8.69	8.33	8.0	7.69	7.41	7.14	6.67	6.25	6.06	5.88
5	10.0	9.52	9.09	8.70	8.33	8.0	7.69	7.41	7.14	6.67	6.25	6.06	5.88
6	10.0	9.53	9.09	8.69	8.33	8.0	7.69	7.41	7.14	6.67	6.25	6.06	5.88
7	10.0	9.52	9.09	8.70	8.34	8.0	7.69	7.41	7.14	6.67	6.25	6.06	5.88
8	10.0	9.53	9.09	8.69	8.33	8.0	7.69	7.41	7.15	6.66	6.25	6.06	5.88
9	10.0	9.52	9.09	8.70	8.34	8.0	7.69	7.41	7.14	6.67	6.25	6.06	5.88
10	10.0	9.53	9.09	8.69	8.33	8.0	7.70	7.40	7.15	6.66	6.25	6.06	5.88
11	5.0	9.52	9.09	8.70	8.34	8.0	7.69	7.41	7.14	6.67	6.25	6.06	5.89
12			4.55	8.69	8.33	8.0	7.70	7.40	7.15	6.66	6.25	6.06	5.88
13					4.17	8.0	7.69	7.41	7.14	6.67	6.25	6.06	5.89
14							3.85	7.40	7.15	6.66	6.25	6.06	5.88
15									3.57	6.67	6.25	6.06	5.89
16										3.33	6.25	6.06	5.88
17											3.12	6.07	5.89
18													2.94

Table A-8. *(Continued)*

Year	Recovery periods in years												
	18	**19**	**20**	**22**	**24**	**25**	**26.5**	**28**	**30**	**35**	**40**	**45**	**50**
1	2.78%	2.63%	2.5%	2.273%	2.083%	2.0%	1.887%	1.786%	1.667%	1.429%	1.25%	1.111%	1.0%
2	5.56	5.26	5.0	4.545	4.167	4.0	3.774	3.571	3.333	2.857	2.50	2.222	2.0
3	5.56	5.26	5.0	4.545	4.167	4.0	3.774	3.571	3.333	2.857	2.50	2.222	2.0
4	5.55	5.26	5.0	4.545	4.167	4.0	3.774	3.571	3.333	2.857	2.50	2.222	2.0
5	5.56	5.26	5.0	4.546	4.167	4.0	3.774	3.571	3.333	2.857	2.50	2.222	2.0
6	5.55	5.26	5.0	4.545	4.167	4.0	3.774	3.571	3.333	2.857	2.50	2.222	2.0
7	5.56	5.26	5.0	4.546	4.167	4.0	3.773	3.572	3.333	2.857	2.50	2.222	2.0
8	5.55	5.26	5.0	4.545	4.167	4.0	3.774	3.571	3.333	2.857	2.50	2.222	2.0
9	5.56	5.27	5.0	4.546	4.167	4.0	3.773	3.572	3.333	2.857	2.50	2.222	2.0
10	5.55	5.26	5.0	4.545	4.167	4.0	3.774	3.571	3.333	2.857	2.50	2.222	2.0
11	5.56	5.27	5.0	4.546	4.166	4.0	3.773	3.572	3.333	2.857	2.50	2.222	2.0
12	5.55	5.26	5.0	4.545	4.167	4.0	3.774	3.571	3.333	2.857	2.50	2.222	2.0
13	5.56	5.27	5.0	4.546	4.166	4.0	3.773	3.572	3.334	2.857	2.50	2.222	2.0
14	5.55	5.26	5.0	4.545	4.167	4.0	3.773	3.571	3.333	2.857	2.50	2.222	2.0
15	5.56	5.27	5.0	4.546	4.166	4.0	3.774	3.572	3.334	2.857	2.50	2.222	2.0
16	5.55	5.26	5.0	4.545	4.167	4.0	3.773	3.571	3.333	2.857	2.50	2.222	2.0
17	5.56	5.27	5.0	4.546	4.166	4.0	3.774	3.572	3.334	2.857	2.50	2.222	2.0
18	5.55	5.26	5.0	4.545	4.167	4.0	3.773	3.571	3.333	2.857	2.50	2.222	2.0
19	2.78	5.27	5.0	4.546	4.166	4.0	3.774	3.572	3.334	2.857	2.50	2.222	2.0
20		2.63	5.0	4.545	4.167	4.0	3.773	3.571	3.333	2.857	2.50	2.222	2.0
21			2.5	4.546	4.166	4.0	3.774	3.572	3.334	2.857	2.50	2.222	2.0
22				4.545	4.167	4.0	3.773	3.571	3.333	2.857	2.50	2.222	2.0
23				2.273	4.166	4.0	3.774	3.572	3.334	2.857	2.50	2.222	2.0
24					4.167	4.0	3.773	3.571	3.333	2.857	2.50	2.222	2.0
25					2.083	4.0	3.774	3.572	3.334	2.857	2.50	2.222	2.0
26						2.0	3.773	3.571	3.333	2.857	2.50	2.222	2.0
27							3.774	3.572	3.334	2.857	2.50	2.223	2.0
28								3.571	3.333	2.858	2.50	2.222	2.0
29								1.786	3.334	2.857	2.50	2.223	2.0
30									3.333	2.858	2.50	2.222	2.0
31									1.667	2.857	2.50	2.223	2.0
32										2.858	2.50	2.222	2.0
33										2.857	2.50	2.223	2.0
34										2.858	2.50	2.222	2.0
35										2.857	2.50	2.223	2.0
36										1.429	2.50	2.222	2.0
37											2.50	2.223	2.0
38											2.50	2.222	2.0
39											2.50	2.223	2.0
40											2.50	2.222	2.0
41											1.25	2.223	2.0
42												2.222	2.0
43												2.223	2.0
44												2.222	2.0
45												2.223	2.0
46												1.111	2.0
47–50													2.0
51													1.0

What's New in 2009

Mileage Deduction Increased. The 2009 standard mileage rate for business is 55¢ per mile for 2009. The rate for charitable miles driven is 14¢ per mile. For medical and moving miles, the rate is 24¢ per mile. For depreciation, the rate is 21¢ per mile.

Total Depreciation Limitation for Cars Remains Unchanged. The limitation on first-year depreciation of a car purchased in 2009 remains set at $2,960.

Total Depreciation Limitation for Trucks and Vans Decreased. The limitation on first-year depreciation of a truck or van purchased in 2009 decreases to $3,060.

Bonus Depreciation. In 2009, the special depreciation allowance ("bonus depreciation") increases by $8,000 the maximum depreciation deduction for business vehicles acquired and placed in service in 2009. Thus, the limit for first year depreciation, including bonus depreciation, is $10,960 for cars and $11,060 for trucks and vans.

Relevant IRS Publications

- ☐ IRS Publication 463, *Travel, Entertainment, Gift, and Car Expenses*
- ☐ IRS Publication 535, *Business Expenses*
- ☐ IRS Publication 544, *Sales and Other Dispositions of Assets*
- ☐ IRS Publication 551, *Basis of Assets*
- ☐ IRS Publication 946, *How to Depreciate Property*
- ☐ Form 2106, *Employee Business Expenses*

Section at a Glance

Tax Preparer's Checklist

- ☐ The following items are required: Logs of usage for all vehicles, cell phones, computers, etc., used in a small enterprise or home office; copy of lease, if applicable
- ☐ Vehicle type, date placed in service, and odometer readings on January 1, 2009, and December 31, 2009, in addition to all actual business travel in logs
- ☐ All receipts for vehicle expenses if actual expense method is elected or required. Invoice or other evidence of purchase or acquisition amount for each item of property

Vehicle Depreciation Percentages and 2009 Depreciation Limits*

	MACRS %	150% DB	Straight Line	Total Depreciation Limitation	
Year of Ownership	Assuming Half-Year Convention** (More than 50% Business Use)	Optional Method (More than 50% Business Use)	Optional Method or for 50% Business Use or Less	Car	Truck or Van
First year (bonus deprec.)	20.00%	15.00%	10.00%	10,960	11,060
First year (no bonus)	20.00%	15.00%	10.00%	2,960	3,060
Second year	32.00%	25.50%	20.00%	4,800	4,900
Third year	19.20%	17.85%	20.00%	2,850	2,950
Fourth year	11.52%	16.66%	20.00%	1,775	1,775
Fifth year	11.52%	16.66%	20.00%	1,775	1,775
Sixth year	5.76%	8.33%	10.00%	1,775	1,775
Seventh year and later	If vehicle is not fully depreciated after the sixth year, a maximum amount may be claimed based on business use percentage.			1,775	1,775

*Limits are for vehicles first placed in service in 2009.

**If using the mid-quarter convention, these amounts do not apply; see IRS Publication 463 for rates.

Business Vehicles

If a taxpayer purchases a vehicle for use in a business, or uses a personal vehicle for business purposes, all or a portion of the cost of owning and using that vehicle may be claimed as a business expense. Purchase cost and costs of having a vehicle overhauled or reconditioned are usually claimed through depreciation. Expenses and repairs related to business vehicles may also qualify to be deducted as a business expense.

Vehicle Recordkeeping

As for all deductions, substantiation requirements must be met when claiming vehicle expenses.

For every vehicle, records must indicate both general vehicle information and specific details of use:

- Vehicle make and model.
- Whether unloaded gross vehicle weight is more than or less than 6,000 pounds.
- Date of purchase and invoice, receipt, or other evidence of amount paid.
- Date vehicle was placed in service for business.
- Odometer readings on January 1 and December 31.
- All actual business travel, with mileage and date and purpose of trip (and which vehicle was used if more than one vehicle is in service).

If the vehicle was purchased or converted from solely personal use during the year, the odometer reading on the date placed in service may take the place of the January 1 reading.

Records must be kept at least as long as the statute of limitations on IRS examinations of returns runs or the item remains in use thereafter. Records of vehicle purchase and business use should be kept as long as the vehicle is owned, or at least three years after the last return is filed on which any deductions relating to that vehicle are taken, whichever is longer.

> **Caution.** Lines 20 and 21 of Part II of Form 2106 ask whether the taxpayer has evidence to support the deduction and whether that evidence is written. Lack of written records may lead to inability to take the deduction.

Choice of Deduction Method

Taxpayers can choose to deduct actual expenses, including depreciation, gas, registration fees, repairs, maintenance, and insurance. Or they can choose to use the standard mileage method. Either way, individuals can also deduct business-related tolls, parking fees, and personal property tax. Self-employed individuals can also deduct loan interest on business vehicles.

Business-Use Percentage

If a vehicle is used for both personal and business purposes, the costs related to the vehicle must be divided based on the mileage driven for each purpose.

> **Example.** Leo is the sole proprietor of a small business. He has only one vehicle, which he uses for both personal and business purposes. The odometer reading on January 1, 2009, was 31,522. The odometer reading on December 31, 2009, was 74,373. He keeps a log of each business trip, including miles driven, which indicates that he drove 18,130 miles on business during 2009. The business-use percentage for his vehicle is 18,130/(74,373 – 31,522) = 42.3%.

Some benefits are only available if a vehicle is used more than 50% for business. If business use varies from year to year, special rules may apply; see the discussion of depreciation recapture on page 8-12.

> **Planning Tip.** To maximize deductible business miles, to the extent that the taxpayer can plan out his or her day with multiple business trips, the first and last destinations should be closest to home. Also, taxpayers who use a vehicle for both business and personal use may consider the benefits of renting a vehicle for personal vacations, particularly if this prevents the business-use percentage from falling below 50%.

> **Caution.** The IRS assumes that individuals require a vehicle for personal use, so 100% business use of a vehicle in a situation where there is no other vehicle available is closely scrutinized. Line 19 of Part II of Form 2106 asks the question, "Do you (or your spouse) have another vehicle available for personal use?" Answering "No" may be incompatible with claiming 100% business use of the vehicle.

Qualified Business Use

Qualified business use is any use in a trade or business. Records must indicate the business purpose of each trip. Note that use of a vehicle for investment activities (use for production of income) is not a qualified business use, but mileage for investment activities

When Are Local Transportation Expenses Deductible?

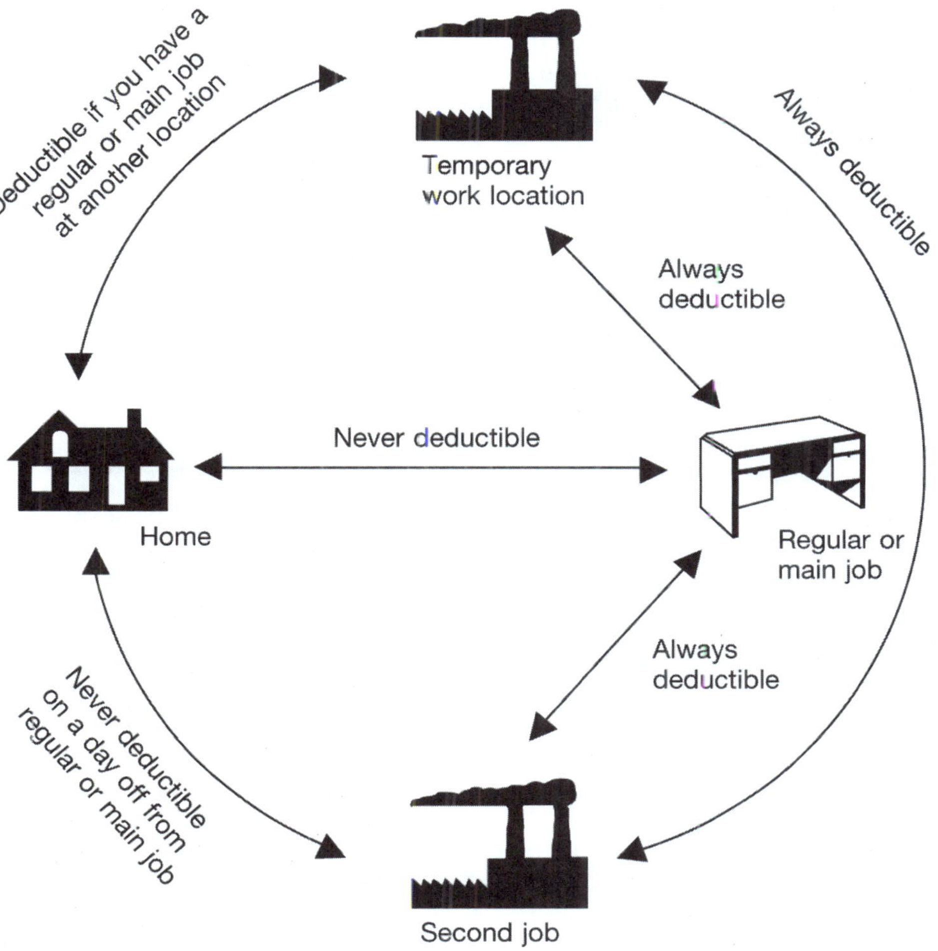

is combined with qualified business use in calculating the depreciation deduction.

Deductible Commuting

Transportation expenses for travel between jobs or to clients' locations are generally deductible. Travel between a regular job and a temporary jobsite, or between a regular job and a second job, is also deductible. Additionally, travel between a second job location and a temporary job or client's office is deductible. The general rule is that the travel must be for work, but not for the taxpayer's regular commute. The cost of travelling between the taxpayer's home and regular place of business is never deductible, even if the vehicle used displays advertising or if business telephone calls or business discussions are conducted while travelling.

Office in Home as Main Place of Work. If a taxpayer's main place of business is an office in the home, then the cost of travelling from there to clients' offices or other places of business is deductible. However, the cost of traveling to another main job location is not deductible.

See MTG ¶961 for further information.

Example. Donna has a regular place of business. The cost of traveling from her home to that business and back are not deductible. She is assigned to a different location for a week. The cost of travelling from her home to this temporary assignment is deductible.

Example. Frances does not have a regular place of business, nor does she have an office in her home. She leaves her home and visits several clients and then returns. The cost of travelling from her home to the first client and the cost of traveling from the last client back to her home is not deductible. The amount in between clients is deductible. If she had an office in her home, the entire trip would be deductible.

Mileage Deduction Methods

Either the standard mileage deduction may be taken or actual expenses may be used. Depreciation is included in the standard mileage method, so an election to use MACRS or another method of depreciation, or to claim any IRC §179 expense, requires that the actual expense method be used.

See MTG ¶947 for details.

Standard Mileage Method

The standard mileage method may be elected whether or not the taxpayer is reimbursed by an employer. It may be used for leased vehicles and for owned vehicles. If the taxpayer chooses to use the standard mileage method, he or she must generally do so in the first year the car is placed in service. In subsequent years, the standard mileage method or the actual expense method may be chosen.

If the taxpayer owns the vehicle, the decision to use the standard mileage method is usually made in the first year the car is placed in service. If the taxpayer leases the vehicle, and wishes to use the standard mileage method, it must be used for the duration of the lease.

The standard mileage method cannot be used if any of the following apply:

- The vehicle is used for hire.
- More than four vehicles are operated simultaneously in the business.
- Any depreciation other than straight line has been previously claimed for the vehicle.
- An IRC §179 deduction has been taken for the vehicle.
- Actual expenses on this vehicle have been claimed in a previous year and the vehicle is leased.
- The taxpayer is a rural mail carrier and received a qualified reimbursement.

Caution. Using the standard mileage method in the first year precludes using any accelerated depreciation methods in subsequent years (including IRC §179 deductions). Taking accelerated depreciation deductions on a vehicle (including IRC §179) precludes using the standard mileage method in future years.

Expenses Included in the Standard Mileage Allowance. The standard business allowance in 2009 is 55 cents per mile. This allowance is intended to cover all costs of operating the vehicle, and includes the following expenses:

- Depreciation.
- Maintenance and repairs.
- Gasoline and gasoline taxes.
- Oil.
- Insurance.
- Vehicle registration fees and license fees that are not personal property taxes.

Actual payments for these expenses may not be deducted in addition to the standard rate.

The standard mileage rate covers depreciation at 21 cents per mile for 2009. This portion of the deduction reduces the taxpayer's basis in the vehicle, but not below zero. Once the vehicle is fully depreciated, if the standard mileage method is continued, the full rate may still be taken, but none of it is considered depreciation.

Planning Tip. For maximum benefit, a taxpayer should consider the length of time vehicles are expected to be used when deciding whether to use the standard mileage method. If a vehicle will be used for many years, long after its full value is depreciated, the standard mileage method may be preferable to the immediate value of special depreciation and IRC §179 expense deduction, especially if the vehicle is relatively inexpensive.

Also, if the business-use percentage is expected to fall below 50% within the five-year cost-recovery period, the taxpayer may want to use the standard mileage method for all reimbursements. The recapture of IRC §179 expense as regular income in a later tax year may result in paying more tax if the taxpayer is in a higher tax bracket in the later year or if tax laws change.

Expenses Not Included in the Standard Mileage Allowance. Some expenses are not included in the standard rate. These include the following:

- Parking fees.
- Tolls.
- The personal property tax portion (if any) of license fees.
- Interest on auto loan.

These expenses may be deducted in addition to the standard mileage amount. Employees and statutory employees may not deduct interest on auto loans. They also may not include fees paid to park at their place of employment or tolls paid during their regular commute, as these are considered nondeductible commuting expenses. Other parking fees and tolls paid in the course of their work may be deductible job expenses.

Parking and tolls are deductible if paid in the course of business use. The portion of other expenses that is deductible is based on the percentage of use of the vehicle in business.

The personal property tax on the vehicle may be split on a pro rata basis. The business portion is deductible against self-employment income and the amount not related to business may be taken as an itemized deduction on Schedule A.

Actual Expense Method

The taxpayer must use the actual expense method if any accelerated depreciation (ACRS, MACRS, or any method other than straight line) or IRC §179 expense has been claimed on the vehicle, the vehicle is used for hire, more than four vehicles are operated simultaneously in the business, or actual expenses on this vehicle have been claimed in a previous year and the vehicle is leased (after 1997). Rural mail carriers who received a qualified reimbursement must also use the actual expense method.

If the taxpayer chooses to deduct actual expenses, this will include all costs of operating and maintaining the vehicle: gas, oil, maintenance, repairs, tires, licenses, registration, insurance, parking, tolls, garage fees, etc. Additionally, the taxpayer can take straight line or another form of depreciation on the vehicle. If the taxpayer uses the vehicle for both personal and business use, then the expenses must be either allocated between the two (as in the case of insurance) or traced directly to the type of use (as in the case of parking fees). Most expenses can be allocated on the basis of the number of miles driven for business and personal use.

Example. Oliver uses his car for both personal and business use. During the year he drove 12,000 personal miles and 18,000 business miles. He paid $800 for insurance for the year. The business portion of that insurance expense would be ($800 x 18/30) = $480. He also has several receipts for tolls paid. One was for $20 he paid while taking his family on vacation. Another is for $10 paid while making a sales call. The first one is a personal expense and not deductible. The $10 is deductible as a business expense.

Charitable Use of Automobile

If the taxpayer uses his or her car to drive to a qualified charity to perform volunteer work, a portion of the costs of the car's charitable use is deductible as a charitable expense. If the actual expense method is chosen, the costs must be directly related to the miles driven for a charitable purpose, such as gasoline. If the car is used exclusively for charitable purposes, maintenance and repairs on the car are deductible. If the car is used for both charitable and noncharitable purposes, no general maintenance or repairs can be deducted. Rather, only those costs directly attributable to the car's use for charitable purposes can be deducted.

If the taxpayer does not wish to track actual expenses, then a standard rate of 14 cents per mile may be used instead. Additionally, any parking fees or tolls incurred while using the vehicle for a charitable purpose may be deducted. Records must be kept to substantiate any deductions.

If the charitable travel is combined with personal pleasure time, it is generally not deductible.

Example. Quentin travels to San Francisco on a weekend pleasure outing. While he is there he volunteers at a qualified soup kitchen for half a day. He did not schedule the charity work before traveling to San Francisco. His mileage is not deductible.

Example. Ruth travels to Chicago to work at a qualified charity all day. On the way home she stops and watches a movie she has been wanting to see. The travel is deductible, but the cost of the movie is not.

Employer-Provided Vehicle

If an employee drives a vehicle provided by an employer, that is a fringe benefit and the value of the benefit is usually taxable. The employee can deduct actual expenses paid for use of the vehicle, such as for gasoline, that are in excess of what is reimbursed. The standard mileage method may not be used.

Planning Tip. Employer-provided vehicles may present unique difficulties if no other vehicle is available. If strictly a business vehicle and no personal vehicle exists, include the personal use as income on the person's W-2. If strictly business and another personal vehicle exists, then keep it that way—avoid any commuting.

Depreciating and Expensing Vehicles

A vehicle is a capital asset and thus can be depreciated if used for business. An IRC §179 deduction is also available. There are restrictions on depreciation and IRC §179 deductions based on the value of the vehicle, the type of usage, the percentage of business use, and who owns the vehicle.

A car (referred to in the statute as a "passenger automobile") is defined as a four-wheeled vehicle with an *unloaded* gross vehicle weight of 6,000 pounds or less and which is made primarily for use on public roads. A truck or van is considered to be a car if it has a *loaded* gross vehicle weight of 6,000 pounds or less. Vehicles with a weight in excess of this amount are not considered to be cars, and are subject to higher depreciation caps (discussed below). Also not considered to be cars are ambulances and hearses.

Trucks and vans (including SUVs and minivans that are built on a truck chassis) weighing less than 6,000 pounds while loaded are subject to a separate set of depreciation caps, which are slightly higher than those for cars.

A truck or van that is a "qualified nonpersonal use vehicle" is not considered to be a car, and is not subject to the annual depreciation cap. A qualified nonpersonal use vehicle is a vehicle which has been specially modified in such a way that more than a small amount of personal use is unlikely. One example of such vehicles would be taxis, while another would be delivery vans with built-in shelves and no passenger seating.

A taxpayer may elect to expense, rather than depreciate, a portion of the cost of business property for the first year that the property is placed in service. Expensing under IRC §179 (discussed further below) is usually subject to a limitation of $250,000 (for 2009).

For purposes of the IRC §179 expensing limitations, heavy SUVs (i.e., weighing more than 6,000 pounds) are ordinarily limited to $25,000. Trucks and vans in excess of 6,000 pounds are included in the statutory definition of SUV (and thus subject to the $25,000 expensing limitation) unless the truck or van has (a) seating for more than nine people behind the driver, (b) a bed (cargo area) of six feet or more in interior length, or (c) no seating behind the driver and no part of the vehicle body extending more than 30 inches past the windshield (i.e., cargo vans).

Caution. Simply placing advertising on a vehicle does not qualify it as a nonpersonal use vehicle, though it can result in advertising expenses qualified for deduction.

Limits

There are limits on depreciation as follows:

Purchased in 2009	Car	Truck or Van
General limit	$10,960	$11,060
If special depreciation allowance is not allowed or not taken	2,960	3,060
If the vehicle is used less than 100% for business, then the limit must be multiplied by the percentage of business use (for example, a vehicle with 60% business use that qualified and took the special depreciation allowance)	6,576 (for 60% business use)	6,636 (for 60% business use)

Limitations on depreciation for previous years are different. See MTG ¶1211 for depreciation limitations and further information.

If the taxpayer's vehicle weighs over 6,000 pounds, it is not subject to the same depreciation limitations. However, such vehicles are still listed property, and if the business use is below 50% they are therefore not eligible for accelerated depreciation or for IRC §179 expensing.

Basis

Basis is the amount paid for the vehicle, which includes cash, loan money, and property (or services) traded in. The total of sticker price, taxes, title and document fees, and a dealer's transportation charge is the basis in the purchased vehicle. Generally, to calculate depreciation, the basis must be used. However, sometimes the taxpayer's adjusted basis is used. If the vehicle was converted from personal use to business use, the basis is the lesser of the adjusted basis and fair market value.

Unadjusted Basis. Unadjusted basis, or "basis for depreciation," is the basis including sales tax, destination charge, and dealer preparation fees plus the cost of any significant improvements made that extend the value or life expectancy of the car (e.g., new engine or overhaul), less IRC §179 deductions, diesel fuel tax credit, clean-fuel vehicle deduction, and qualified electric vehicle credit.

Generally, when a vehicle is traded in on a new vehicle, and both cars are 100% business use, the basis is the adjusted basis in the old car plus the price paid for the new car.

Example. Gary has a car with an adjusted basis of $1,000 that he trades in along with $14,000 for a new car. Both cars are used exclusively for business. No IRC §179 deduction was taken for the old car; all proper elections made. The new car has a basis of $15,000.

Example. Hannah purchased a car exclusively for business in 2007 for $20,000. For 2007 through 2009, she deducted $10,810 for depreciation. On February 1, 2010, she traded in the car, along with $10,000 cash, for another car to be used exclusively in business. Under the half-year convention, she took $1,152 in depreciation for 2010. Her adjusted basis in the old car is ($20,000 – $10,810 – $1,152) = $8,038. Her basis in the new car is ($8,038 + $10,000) = $18,038. Note that the taxpayer could depreciate the $8,038 using the old schedule and for the old remaining life, while the $10,000 starts out as new MACRS property. Alternatively, the taxpayer could elect out of that method and could depreciate the entire $18,038 as new property.

Vehicle Depreciation Percentages and 2009 Depreciation Limits*					
Year of Ownership	MACRS %	150% DB	Straight Line	Total Depreciation Limitation	
	Assuming Half-Year Convention** (More than 50% Business Use)	Optional Method (More than 50% Business Use)	Optional Method or for 50% Business Use or Less	Car	Truck or Van
First year (bonus depr.)	20.00%	15.00%	10.00%	$10,960	$11,060
First year (no bonus)	20.00%	15.00%	10.00%	2,960	3,060
Second year	32.00%	25.50%	20.00%	4,800	4,900
Third year	19.20%	17.85%	20.00%	2,850	2,950
Fourth year	11.52%	16.66%	20.00%	1,775	1,775
Fifth year	11.52%	16.66%	20.00%	1,775	1,775
Sixth year	5.76%	8.33%	10.00%	1,775	1,775
Seventh year and later	If vehicle is not fully depreciated after the sixth year, a maximum amount may be claimed based on business use percentage.			1,775	1,775

*Limits are for vehicles first placed in service in 2009.

**If using the mid-quarter convention, these amounts do not apply; see IRS Publication 463 for rates.

Example. Isaac purchased a car that he uses 60% for business in 2007 and 2008 for $20,000. He did not claim any IRC §179 expense. In 2007 and 2008 he took a total of $4,776 in depreciation deductions. On February 1, 2009, he traded that car in for another car, paying an additional $10,000 cash. Under MACRS, he took a half-year's depreciation deduction for 2009 of $1,152 (the lesser of ($20,000 x 19.20% x 50% (for half-year convention) x 60% = $1,152) or ($2,850 x 60% = $1,710)). Actual depreciation taken for 2007, 2008, and 2009 was ($4,776 + $1,152) = $5,928. Isaac's adjusted basis in the old car was ($20,000 – $5,928) = $14,072, which is added to the amount paid for the new car for a preliminary basis of ($14,072 + $10,000) = $24,072. However, since the car was not 100% business use, he must calculate what the allowable depreciation on the old car would have been if it had been 100% business use:

2009	$20,000 x 19.20% x 50% (limit of $2,850)	$1,920
2008	$20,000 × 32% (limit of $4,900)	4,900
2007	$20,000 × 20% (limit of $3,060)	3,060
Total		$9,880

The excess of the allowable depreciation over actual depreciation taken is ($9,880 – $5,928) = $3,952. The adjusted basis on his old car was $14,072, but his adjusted basis in the new vehicle is ($24,072 – $3,952) = $20,120.

If the old car is not a 100% business-use vehicle, then an adjustment must be made to the basis of the trade-in vehicle. Add the adjusted basis of the old car to the amount paid for the new car then subtract the amount that would have been allowed as depreciation on the old car if it had been 100% business use to the extent that it exceeds the actual depreciation taken.

Date Placed in Service

A car is placed in service when it first becomes available to the taxpayer for use in his or her business or other income-producing activity. The date an order was placed is irrelevant. For a car that was personal use that is converted to business use, the date placed in service is the date of conversion (the earliest date used for business purposes).

IRC §179 Expensing

An IRC §179 deduction can only be claimed on a vehicle in the first year for which that vehicle was placed in service for business use (whether or not such use was made of it). The vehicle must be used for business more than 50% of the time. If the vehicle is used for personal use and then in a later year converted to business use, an IRC §179 deduction may not be taken for that vehicle.

Generally, up to $250,000 (for 2009) in IRC §179 deductions can be taken. However, there are limits on how much total IRC §179 and depreciation can be taken on individual vehicles:

- If the car was acquired in 2005 or 2006, the limit is $2,960.
- If the car was acquired in 2007, the limit is $3,060.
- If the car was acquired in 2008 or 2009, the limit is $2,960 (or $10,960 if special depreciation is taken).

The above limits are for passenger cars. Trucks and vans have somewhat higher limits. These limits are reduced ratably if the car is used less than 100% for business purposes.

See MTG ¶1208 and Tab 7 for more information about IRC §179 deductions.

The basis in the new car is limited to the cash paid for it plus the adjusted basis (not value) of the traded-in vehicle.

Caution. An IRC §179 deduction can only be taken in the year the vehicle was purchased AND placed in service. A personal use vehicle placed in service in subsequent years does not qualify.

Filing Tip. Employees elect to expense property under IRC §179 on Form 2106, Employee Business Expenses. Everyone else uses Form 4562, Depreciation and Amortization (Including Information on Listed Property).

Special Depreciation Allowance

For 2008 and 2009 the taxpayer is allowed to claim first-year bonus depreciation equal to 50 percent of the adjusted basis of qualifying property eligible for depreciation using the modified accelerated cost recovery system (MACRS) with a depreciation period of 20 years or less. The law also increases the vehicle depreciation limits to accommodate a modified version of the 50-percent bonus depreciation available to other MACRS property. The first-year limit on depreciation for vehicles placed in service in 2009 ($2,960 for passenger vehicles and $3,060 for vans and trucks) is increased by $8,000, for a total limit on vehicle depreciation of $10,960 for passenger vehicles and $11,060 for vans and trucks.

The special depreciation allowance is a deduction equal to 50% of the car's depreciable basis. The original use of the vehicle must begin with the taxpayer and must occur during 2009. Those who choose to claim this allowance must reduce the adjusted basis of the car by the amount of the allowance. The special depreciation allowance is calculated after the IRC §179 deduction, but before calculating the MACRS depreciation deduction. If the vehicle is not used predominately for business in a subsequent year, then the bonus depreciation taken must be recaptured.

Bonus depreciation must be claimed for both regular tax and alternative minimum tax liability, unless the taxpayer makes an election out. Once made, an election out cannot be revoked without IRS consent.

MACRS Calculation

Generally, cars are depreciated using the MACRS method. However, if the standard mileage method was used the

Example. Joanne buys a new car for 100% business use in 2009. She elects not to take an IRC §179 expensing deduction, and she elects out of special depreciation. Her basis in the car is $20,000. She elects to use the regular MACRS method. Her depreciation deductions are:

Year	Calculation	Amount of Depreciation	Limit	Depreciation Allowed	Basis after Depreciation
2009	$20,000 × 20%	$4,000	$2,960	$2,960	$17,040
2010	$20,000 × 32%	6,400	4,800	4,800	12,240
2011	$20,000 × 19.2%	3,840	2,850	2,850	9,390
2012	$20,000 × 11.52%	2,304	1,775	1,775	7,615
2013	$20,000 × 11.52%	2,304	1,775	1,775	5,840
2014	$20,000 × 5.76%	1,152	1,775	1,152	4,688
2015	$4,688 (unrecovered basis) × 100%	4,688	1,775	1,775	2,913
2016	$2,913 × 100%	2,913	1,775	1,775	1,138
2017	$1,138 × 100%	1,138	1,775	1,138	0

Example. The limitations on allowed deductions may make it advisable not to claim the IRC §179 expensing deduction. Lisa buys a new car for 100% business use in 2009. She elects not to expense any of its cost, and the car qualifies for the 50% first-year special depreciation allowance. Her basis in the car is $30,000. She elects to use the regular MACRS method. Her depreciation deductions are:

Year	Calculation	Amount of Depreciation	Limit	Depreciation Allowed	Basis after Depreciation
2009	Bonus depreciation	15,000			
	$15,000 x 20%	3,000	$10,960	$10,960	$19,040
2010	$15,000 x 32%	4,800	4,800	4,800	14,240
2011	$15,000 x 19.2%	2,880	2,850	2,850	11,390
2012	$15,000 x 11.52%	1,728	1,775	1,728	9,662
2013	$15,000 x 11.52%	1,728	1,775	1,728	7,934
2014	$15,000 x 5.76%	864	1,775	864	7,070
2015	$7,070 x 100%	7,070	1,775	1,775	5,295
2016	$5,295 x 100%	5,295	1,775	1,775	3,520
2017	$3,520 x 100%	3,520	1,775	1,775	1,745
2018	$1,745 x 100%	1,745	1,775	1,745	0

Even though Lisa is eligible to claim an IRC §179 deduction in addition to the special depreciation allowance, her first-year depreciation deductions have already reached the limit and it would do her no good.

Assume the same facts, except that the car's initial basis was $12,000. Without the IRC §179 deduction, her depreciation deductions are as follows:

Year	Calculation	Amount of Depreciation	Limit	Depreciation Allowed	Basis after Depreciation
2009	Bonus depreciation	$6.000			
	$6,000 x 20%	1.200	$10,960	$7,200	$4,800
2010	$6,000 x 32%	1.920	4,800	1,920	2,880
2011	$6,000 x 19.2%	1,152	2,850	1,152	1,728
2012	$6,000 x 11.52%	691	1,775	691	1,037
2013	$6,000 x 11.52%	691	1,775	691	346
2014	$6,000 x 5.76%	346	1,775	346	0

Here are the calculations for the same situation, but with the IRC §179 deduction taken into account:

Year	Calculation	Amount of Depreciation	Limit	Depreciation Allowed	Basis after Depreciation
2009	IRC §179 Expensing	$9,400			
	Bonus depreciation	1,300			
	$1,300 x 20%	260	$10,960	$10,960	$1,040
2010	$1,300 x 32%	416	4,800	416	624
2011	$1,300 x 19.2%	250	2,850	250	374
2012	$1,300 x 11.52%	150	1,775	150	224
2013	$1,300 x 11.52%	150	1,775	150	74
2014	$74 x 100%	74	1,775	74	0

In this case, Lisa is able to recover her basis in the car much faster with the IRC §179 deduction than without. The amount of IRC §179 deduction taken was that amount which, when added to the allowable special and regular depreciation deductions, reached the cap amount.

Example. Mark buys a used car in 2009 for $20,000. Because he plans to use it only 40% for business purposes, he is not eligible for bonus depreciation or IRC §179 expensing, and must use straight-line depreciation. His depreciation deductions are as follows:

Year	Calculation	Amount of Depreciation	Limit*	Depreciation Allowed	Basis after Depreciation
2009	$20,000 × 10% × 40%	$ 800	$1,184	$ 800	$18,000
2010	$20,000 × 20% × 40%	1,600	1,920	1,600	14,000
2011	$20,000 × 20% × 40%	1,600	1,140	1,140	11,150
2012	$20,000 × 20% × 40%	1,600	710	710	9,375
2013	$20,000 × 20% × 40%	1,600	710	710	7,600
2014	$20,000 × 10% × 40%	800	710	710	5,825
2015	$5,825 (unrecovered basis) × 40%	2,330	710	710	4,050
2016 and later would continue with the same calculation until the car has a basis of zero.					

*Limit is found by taking statutory limit and multiplying by the percentage of business use.

Example. Kevin buys a used car for 80% business use in 2009. He elects not to take IRC §179 expensing, and a used vehicle is ineligible for bonus depreciation. His basis in the car is $20,000. He elects to use the regular MACRS method. His depreciation deductions are:

Year	Calculation	Amount of Depreciation	Limit*	Depreciation Allowed	Basis after Depreciation
2009	$20,000 × 20% × 80%	$3,200	$2,368	$2,368	$17,040
2010	$20,000 × 32% × 80%	5,120	3,840	3,840	12,240
2011	$20,000 × 19.2% × 80%	3,072	2,280	2,280	9,390
2012	$20,000 × 11.52% × 80%	1,843	1,420	1,420	7,615
2013	$20,000 × 11.52%× 80%	1,843	1,420	1,420	5,840
2014	$20,000 × 5.76% × 80%	922	1,420	922	4,688
2015	$4,688 (unrecovered basis) × 80%	3,750	1,420	1,420	2,913
2016	$2,913 × 80%	2,330	1,420	1,420	1,138
2017 and later would continue with the same calculation until the car has a basis of zero.					

*Limit is calculated by taking statutory limit × 80% business use.

If business use varies from year to year, change the percentages and calculate the limits accordingly. Assume the same facts as in the previous example except that Kevin's business use changes from year to year. His depreciation deductions are:

Year	Percent Business Use	Calculation	Amount of Depreciation	Limit*	Depreciation Allowed	Basis after Depreciation
2009	80%	$20,000 × 20% × 80%	$3,200	$2,368	$2,368	$17,040
2010	60%	$20,000 × 32% × 60%	3,840	2,880	2,880	12,240
2011	70%	$20,000 × 19.2% × 70%	2,688	1,995	1,995	9,390
2012	80%	$20,000 × 11.52% × 80%	1,843	1,420	1,420	7,615
2013	60%	$20,000 × 11.52% × 60%	1,382	1,065	1,065	5,840
2014	70%	$20,000 × 5.76% × 70%	806	1,243	806	4,688
2015	80%	$4,688 (unrecovered basis) × 80%	3,750	1,420	1,420	2,913
2016 and later would continue with the same calculation until the car has a basis of zero.						

*Limit is calculated by taking statutory limit × the percentage of business use.

Example. Joanne buys a used car for 100% business use in 2009. She does not elect to take IRC §179 expensing. Her basis in the car is $20,000. She is not eligible for bonus depreciation, and elects to use the regular MACRS method. She planned to use the car solely for business, but in the fourth year the business use dropped to 40%. First, she must calculate how much depreciation would have been allowed in the first three years using the straight-line method:

Year	Calculation*	Amount of Depreciation	Limit	Depreciation Allowed	Basis after Depreciation
2009	$20,000 × 10%	$2,000	$2,960	$2,000	$18,000
2010	$20,000 × 20%	4,000	4,800	4,000	14,000
2011	$20,000 × 20%	4,000	2,850	2,850	11,150

*Because her first three years were at 100%, we don't have to worry about multiplying by business-use percentage here.

Her first three years looked like this before the business-use percentage dropped below 50%:

Year	Calculation	Amount of Depreciation	Limit	Depreciation Allowed	Basis after Depreciation
2009	$20,000 × 20%	$4,000	$2,960	$2,960	$17,040
2010	$20,000 × 32%	6,400	4,800	4,800	12,240
2011	$20,000 × 19.2%	3,840	2,850	2,850	9,390

She actually took ($2,960 + $4,800 + $2,850) = $10,610 depreciation. Under the straight-line method, she would only have been allowed ($2,000 + $4,000 + $2,850) = $8,850. Therefore she has to claim a recapture of ($10,610 – $8,850) = $1,760 on Form 4797. She adds the $1,760 basis back to her calculated basis to arrive at her new basis of ($1,760 + $9,390) = $11,150, which matches what her basis would have been if she'd used the straight-line method all along. For future years she continues with straight-line depreciation:

Year	Calculation	Amount of Depreciation	Limit	Depreciation Allowed	Basis after Depreciation
2012	$20,000 × 20% × 40%	$1,600	$710	$710	$9,375
2013	$20,000 × 20% × 40%	1,600	710	710	7,600
2014	$20,000 × 10% × 40%	800	710	710	5,825
2015	$5,825 (unrecovered basis) × 40%	2,330	710	710	4,050
2016 and later would continue with the same calculation until the car has a basis of zero					

*Limit is found by taking statutory limit and multiplying by business-use percentage.

The following example pertains to the trade-in of a business vehicle, which is discussed on page 8-12.

Example. Nina used the standard mileage method on her old car and is now trading it in along with an additional $15,000 cash payment on a new car. Her basis, before depreciation, in the old car was $12,000. Mileage and depreciation calculations are:

Year	Mileage	Rate	Depreciation
2009	11,200	0.21	$2,352
2008	10,600	0.21	2,226
2007	11,500	0.19	2,185
2006	10,750	0.17	1,828
2005	10,900	0.17	1,853
		Total	$10,444

Her new car's basis is $15,000 + ($12,000 – $10,444) = $16,556.

first year the car was placed in service, MACRS cannot be used. Additionally, the car must be used more than 50% for business in each of the recovery years. If the business use is less than 50%, MACRS cannot be used. If the business use falls below 50% in subsequent years, the taxpayer must switch to straight-line depreciation (and may have to recapture excess depreciation). Once the taxpayer has calculated the IRC §179 deduction, if any, he or she may then determine the amount of the MACRS deduction.

Filing Tip. If a car is placed in service and disposed of in the same year, no depreciation deduction may be taken on it.

Less than 50% Business Use. If the taxpayer's car is used less than 50% for business purposes, no IRC §179 deduction is allowed. Additionally, the straight-line method must be used. The other limits remain the same.

If the business percentage varies from year to year, just use the applicable rate in the calculations for the depreciation amount and for the limit.

Depreciation Recapture

If the taxpayer's car drops to below 50% business use in a year after MACRS or other accelerated depreciation has been taken, it must convert to straight line. Additionally, excess depreciation over straight line that has been taken in previous years must be recovered and added to income.

Disposition of Cars

Sale of Business Vehicle. The basis for computing gain or loss is generally the original cost reduced by the depreciation allowed. For vehicles that were used for both personal and business purposes, the gain or loss is computed by treating the vehicle as two separate pieces of property. The basis and selling price are allocated to two portions of the vehicle based on business-use percentage. Depreciation is allocated entirely to the business portion of the basis. The business-use percentage to be used in this calculation is determined for the entire life of the vehicle:

$$\text{Business use percentage} = \frac{\text{Sum of business miles driven in all years}}{\text{Total miles driven in all years}}$$

Trade-In of Business Vehicle. At the time of a trade in of one business vehicle for another, the basis of the old vehicle plus any amount paid for the new vehicle becomes the new vehicle's basis. The basis of the old vehicle must be reduced by any depreciation. If the standard mileage method was used, then a portion of that was for depreciation. The amount-per-mile considered allowed as depreciation is as follows:

Year	Amount
2008-2009	$0.21
2007	0.19
2005-2006	0.17
2003-2004	0.16
2001-2002	0.15

See MTG ¶1654.

Charitable Donation of Vehicle. If the taxpayer donates his or her vehicle to charity, it is deductible at fair market value. One source of information for the fair market value of a vehicle is the Blue Book Value, available at dealers and online. However, the condition of the vehicle and mileage must be taken into consideration. In the case of a donated vehicle with a value of greater than $500, the contribution must be substantiated by a contemporaneous written acknowledgment containing the name and taxpayer identification number of the donor, the vehicle identification number, and certain certifications. The acknowledgment must be obtained within 30 days of the contribution or the disposition of the vehicle by donee organization, as applicable. If the vehicle is valued at between $250 and $500, the general rules for substantiation of a charitable contribution of property valued at $250 or more must be met. If the vehicle is resold, the deduction is limited to the amount realized by the charity on resale.

Alternative Motor Vehicles

The alternative motor vehicle credit may be applied to property placed in service after December 31, 2005. This credit replaced the clean-fuel vehicle deduction, which was eliminated after 2005.

See MTG ¶1315 for additional information.

The alternative motor vehicle credit is the sum of five credits:

- Qualified fuel cell motor vehicle credit – for a vehicle using a hydrogen-oxygen-based fuel cell.
- Advanced lean burn technology motor vehicle credit – for a vehicle with an internal combustion engine with direct injection, using more air than is necessary for complete fuel combustion.
- Qualified hybrid motor vehicle credit – for a vehicle using both internal combustion and a rechargeable energy storage system.
- Qualified alternative fuel motor vehicle credit – for a vehicle fueled by an alternative fuel, such as liquefied natural gas, hydrogen, methanol, or a mixture of one of these with petroleum-based fuel that meets certain requirements.

- Plug-in conversion credit – for a vehicle which is converted to a plug-in electric drive motor vehicle.

Although these component credits have their own unique characteristics, they share in common the requirements that (1) the vehicle's original use begins with the taxpayer claiming the credit, (2) the vehicle is acquired for use or lease by the taxpayer, and not for resale, (3) the vehicle is made by a "manufacturer" (as defined at 42 USC 7550(1)), and (4) the vehicle is used primarily in the United States.

If the vehicle is used in a trade or business, the taxpayer will claim the credit as part of, and as subject to the rules governing, the general business credit. Any unused part of the credit can therefore be carried back three years or forward 20 years (although it cannot be carried back to years before the credit first became available).

The credit may also be claimed by an individual as a personal credit, subject to various limitations. Specifically, the credit is reduced by the amount of certain other credits, and is limited to the excess of the regular tax over the tentative minimum tax. If the personal portion of the credit cannot be used because of these limitations, it is lost, and may not be carried to other tax years.

Filing Tip. The claiming of the credit is at the election of the taxpayer. The credit is claimed by filing Form 8910, Alternative Motor Vehicle Credit, with one's tax return. This form includes separate sections for the "business/investment" and "personal use" parts of the vehicle.

Ordinarily, the credit is claimed by the buyer of the vehicle. However, if a qualified vehicle is sold (but not leased) to a tax-exempt entity, a governmental unit, or a foreign entity, the seller can claim the credit. To do so, the seller must give written notice to the buyer of the seller's intent to claim the credit, as well as the amount claimed.

The basis of a vehicle is reduced by the amount of alternative motor vehicle credit allowed. Also, the credit reduces the amount of any other deduction or credit applicable to the vehicle for the tax year.

Planning Tip. A qualified vehicle must comply with safety and air emissions standards. This includes more stringent emissions standards applicable in some states. The taxpayer should verify that the vehicle complies with the specific standards applicable in his or her state.

If the vehicle no longer qualifies for the credit, the taxpayer must recapture part or all of the credit.

Caution. In the case of the credit for a hybrid vehicle, the amount of the credit is limited based on sales of the vehicles. The credit amount will be phased out when a particular manufacturer has sold 60,000 vehicles. The full credit will be available for all certified hybrids sold during the calendar quarter in which 60,000 sales are reached. For the next two calendar quarters, the credit will be limited to 50 percent of the allowable credit. For the following two quarters, the credit will be limited to 25 percent. After that time, no credit will be allowed. For a chart showing the 2009 certified cars and the applicable credit amounts, see Tab 10.

Listed Property

Listed property is subject to deduction limitations if used partly for business and partly for personal use. Listed property includes the following types of assets:

- Any passenger vehicle as defined under "Business Vehicles"
- Any other property used for transportation, such as a trailer
- Any property generally used for entertainment, recreation, or amusement, such as video cameras, photography equipment, etc.
- Computer equipment and peripherals (unless used exclusively for business at a permanent business establishment)
- Cellular telephones

Although other listed property is not subject to the same dollar caps on depreciation as automobiles, all of the other requirements applicable to the automobiles also apply to these properties. Thus, the taxpayer must keep written documentation to support the deductions, and the 50% business-use tests apply. Thus if the taxpayer's initial use does not exceed 50% for business, he or she is limited to straight-line depreciation. If the initial use is greater than 50%, and then drops to that amount or less, the taxpayer may need to recapture prior deductions.

Business-use percentage is determined for listed property by hours of use.

See IRS Publication 946 and MTG ¶1211 for further information. See also Tab 7.

Lease or Buy Decision

Whether a client should buy or lease a vehicle may come up for discussion with the person who prepares their taxes. Following is a chart that briefly highlights the advantages both forms of acquisition pose. The answer, as always, depends on the client's preferences and awareness of the benefits of either mode.

Who Should Buy and Who Should Lease in 2009	
Buying is likely to be more favorable if . . .	**Leasing is likely to be more favorable if . . .**
The vehicle is driven more than 15,000 miles per year	The vehicle is driven less than 15,000 miles per year
The vehicle is primarily for personal use Interest not deductible Depreciation deductible Standard mileage rate is available	The vehicle is primarily for business use Interest deductible Greatly simplified calculation If standard mileage rate used, it must be for life of lease
The vehicle is less valuable (or used)	The vehicle is more valuable
Making a large down payment is possible	Down payment can be avoided
The vehicle will be kept longer than 3-4 years	The vehicle will be traded in 2-4 years
Changes in lifestyle and vehicle requirements are likely and flexibility is needed	Flexibility in terms of contract not needed
Poor credit rating is an issue	Credit rating is excellent
Higher monthly payments are acceptable to build equity	Lower monthly payments are a priority (30-60% lower)

Negotiating the Lease Agreement

The following list highlights some key points affecting the cost involved in leasing a vehicle.

Checklist for Lease Agreement
Early return: Terms may be negotiable; determine any penalty fees before signing.
Insurance: Be sure to get additional coverage to take care of the immediate, driving-off-the-lot depreciation. Otherwise, should the vehicle be stolen or severely damaged in the first few months, the insurance payoff would not be enough to make up for the difference between the vehicle's value and what you owe.
Lease Rate: This "money factor" is used to calculate the interest portion of the monthly payment. Just like interest rates for purchase, these are negotiable.
Residual Value: The anticipated market value of the vehicle at the end of the lease should be clearly spelled out in the lease contract.
Warranty: Verify that the warranty for the vehicle encompasses the whole time of the lease.

Leased Vehicle Tables

Limitations on deductions for leased vehicles are similar to those for vehicles that are owned by the taxpayer.

Vehicles (passenger cars, trucks and vans) with FMV greater than $18,500 that are leased in 2009 for a term of 30 days or more trigger an annual income inclusion amount.

The inclusion amount is determined by prorating the amount listed in the appropriate table for the number of days of the lease term that are included in the applicable year, prorated by the percentage of business and investment use for the year.

See IRS Publication 463 and MTG ¶1215 for further details.

Where to Report the Inclusion Amount

Self-employed taxpayers reduce their lease expense by the business-use portion of the lease inclusion amount and enter the result on line 20a of Schedule C.

Employees report the inclusion amount on lines 24a and 24b of Part II of Form 2106. See Tab 6 for instructions.

Inclusion Amounts for Passenger Automobiles (That Are Not Trucks or Vans) with a Lease Term Beginning in Calendar Year 2009

Fair Market Value		Tax Year during Lease[1]				
Over	Not Over	1st	2nd	3rd	4th	5th & later
$18,500	$19,000	9	19	28	34	38
19,000	19,500	10	21	32	38	43
19,500	20,000	11	24	36	42	48
20,000	20,500	12	27	39	46	54
20,500	21,000	13	29	43	51	58
21,000	21,500	15	31	47	55	64
21,500	22,000	16	34	50	60	68
22,000	23,000	17	38	56	66	76
23,000	24,000	20	42	64	75	86
24,000	25,000	22	47	71	84	96
25,000	26,000	24	52	78	93	107
26,000	27,000	26	58	85	101	117
27,000	28,000	29	62	93	110	127
28,000	29,000	31	67	100	119	138
29,000	30,000	33	72	108	128	147
30,000	31,000	35	77	115	137	157
31,000	32,000	38	82	122	146	167
32,000	33,000	40	87	129	155	178
33,000	34,000	42	92	137	163	188
34,000	35,000	44	97	144	172	199
35,000	36,000	47	102	151	181	208
36,000	37,000	49	107	159	189	219
37,000	38,000	51	112	166	199	228
38,000	39,000	53	117	173	208	239
39,000	40,000	56	122	180	216	250
40,000	41,000	58	127	188	225	259
41,000	42,000	60	132	195	234	269
42,000	43,000	62	137	203	242	280
43,000	44,000	65	141	210	252	290
44,000	45,000	67	146	218	260	300
45,000	46,000	69	151	225	269	311
46,000	47,000	71	157	232	278	320
47,000	48,000	74	161	240	286	331
48,000	49,000	76	166	247	296	340
49,000	50,000	78	171	255	304	351
50,000	51,000	80	176	262	313	361
51,000	52,000	83	181	269	322	371
52,000	53,000	85	186	276	331	381
53,000	54,000	87	191	284	339	392
54,000	55,000[2]	89	196	291	349	401

[1] For the last year of the lease, use the dollar amount for the preceding year.
[2] See IRS Publication 463 for inclusion amounts for vehicles with fair market value over $55,000.

Inclusion Amounts for Passenger Automobiles (That Are Not Trucks or Vans) with a Lease Term Beginning in Calendar Year 2008

Fair Market Value		Tax Year during Lease[1]				
Over	Not Over	1st	2nd	3rd	4th	5th & later
$18,500	$19,000	20	42	62	73	84
19,000	19,500	22	47	71	83	94
19,500	20,000	25	53	78	93	106
20,000	20,500	27	58	87	102	117
20,500	21,000	30	63	95	112	128
21,000	21,500	32	69	103	122	139
21,500	22,000	34	75	111	131	151
22,000	23,000	38	83	123	146	167
23,000	24,000	43	94	139	165	190
24,000	25,000	48	105	155	185	212
25,000	26,000	53	115	172	204	235
26,000	27,000	58	126	188	223	257
27,000	28,000	63	137	204	243	279
28,000	29,000	68	148	220	262	302
29,000	30,000	73	159	236	282	324
30,000	31,000	78	170	252	301	347
31,000	32,000	83	181	268	321	368
32,000	33,000	88	192	284	340	391
33,000	34,000	93	202	301	359	414
34,000	35,000	98	213	317	379	436
35,000	36,000	103	224	333	398	459
36,000	37,000	108	235	349	418	481
37,000	38,000	113	246	365	437	503
38,000	39,000	118	257	381	457	525
39,000	40,000	123	268	397	476	548
40,000	41,000	128	279	413	495	571
41,000	42,000	133	289	430	515	593
42,000	43,000	137	301	446	534	615
43,000	44,000	142	312	462	553	638
44,000	45,000	147	323	478	573	659
45,000	46,000	152	333	495	592	682
46,000	47,000	157	344	511	611	705
47,000	48,000	162	355	527	631	727
48,000	49,000	167	366	543	650	750
49,000	50,000	172	377	559	670	772
50,000	51,000	177	388	575	689	794
51,000	52,000	182	399	591	709	816
52,000	53,000	187	410	607	728	839
53,000	54,000	192	420	624	747	862
54,000	55,000[2]	197	431	640	767	884

[1] For the last year of the lease, use the dollar amount for the preceding year.

[2] See IRS Publication 463 for inclusion amounts for vehicles with fair market value over $55,000.

Inclusion Amounts for Passenger Automobiles (That Are Not Trucks or Vans) with a Lease Term Beginning in Calendar Year 2007

Fair Market Value		Tax Year during Lease[1]				
Over	Not Over	1st	2nd	3rd	4th	5th & later
$15,500	$15,800	2	5	11	11	13
15,800	16,100	4	10	17	19	22
16,100	16,400	6	14	24	28	31
16,400	16,700	9	18	31	35	41
16,700	17,000	11	23	37	43	50
17,000	17,500	13	29	46	54	62
17,500	18,000	17	37	56	68	77
18,000	18,500	20	44	68	81	93
18,500	19,000	24	51	80	94	108
19,000	19,500	27	59	90	108	124
19,500	20,000	30	67	101	121	139
20,000	20,500	34	74	113	134	154
20,500	21,000	37	82	123	148	170
21,000	21,500	41	89	135	161	185
21,500	22,000	44	97	146	174	201
22,000	23,000	49	108	163	194	224
23,000	24,000	56	123	185	221	255
24,000	25,000	63	138	207	248	285
25,000	26,000	70	153	229	275	316
26,000	27,000	77	168	251	302	347
27,000	28,000	83	183	274	328	378
28,000	29,000	90	198	296	355	409
29,000	30,000	97	213	318	382	439
30,000	31,000	104	228	341	408	470
31,000	32,000	111	243	363	435	501
32,000	33,000	118	258	385	461	532
33,000	34,000	125	273	407	488	563
34,000	35,000	131	288	430	515	593
35,000	36,000	138	303	452	542	624
36,000	37,000	145	318	474	568	656
37,000	38,000	152	333	496	595	686
38,000	39,000	159	348	519	621	717
39,000	40,000	166	363	541	648	748
40,000	41,000	172	378	564	674	779
41,000	42,000	179	393	586	701	810
42,000	43,000	186	408	608	728	840
43,000	44,000	193	423	630	755	871
44,000	45,000	200	438	652	782	902
45,000	46,000	207	453	674	809	933
46,000	47,000	213	468	697	835	964
47,000	48,000	220	483	719	862	995
48,000	49,000	227	498	742	888	1,025
49,000	50,000[2]	234	513	764	915	1,056

[1] For the last year of the lease, use the dollar amount for the preceding year.

[2] See IRS Publication 463 for inclusion amounts for vehicles with fair market value over $50,000.

Inclusion Amounts for Passenger Automobiles (That Are Not Trucks, Vans, or Electric Automobiles) with a Lease Term Beginning in Calendar Year 2006

Fair Market Value		Tax Year during Lease[1]				
Over	Not Over	1st	2nd	3rd	4th	5th & later
$15,200	$15,500	4	6	10	10	10
15,500	15,800	6	10	16	18	18
15,800	16,100	8	15	22	25	28
16,100	16,400	9	19	29	33	36
16,400	16,700	11	24	35	40	45
16,700	17,000	13	28	42	48	53
17,000	17,500	16	34	50	58	66
17,500	18,000	19	41	61	71	80
18,000	18,500	23	48	71	84	95
18,500	19,000	26	55	82	96	110
19,000	19,500	29	62	93	109	125
19,500	20,000	32	70	103	122	139
20,000	20,500	36	76	114	135	154
20,500	21,000	39	84	124	148	168
21,000	21,500	42	91	135	160	184
21,500	22,000	45	98	146	173	198
22,000	23,000	50	109	162	192	220
23,000	24,000	57	123	183	218	250
24,000	25,000	63	138	204	243	279
25,000	26,000	70	152	225	269	309
26,000	27,000	76	166	247	294	339
27,000	28,000	83	181	268	319	368
28,000	29,000	90	195	289	345	397
29,000	30,000	96	209	311	371	426
30,000	31,000	103	223	332	397	455
31,000	32,000	109	238	353	422	485
32,000	33,000	116	252	374	448	515
33,000	34,000	122	267	395	473	545
34,000	35,000	129	281	417	498	574
35,000	36,000	135	295	439	523	604
36,000	37,000	142	309	460	549	633
37,000	38,000	148	324	481	575	662
38,000	39,000	155	338	502	601	691
39,000	40,000	161	353	523	626	721
40,000	41,000	168	367	545	651	750
41,000	42,000	175	381	566	677	780
42,000	43,000	181	396	587	702	810
43,000	44,000	188	410	608	728	839
44,000	45,000	194	424	630	753	869
45,000	46,000	201	438	651	779	898
46,000	47,000	207	453	672	805	927
47,000	48,000	214	467	694	830	956
48,000	49,000	220	482	715	855	986
49,000	50,000[2]	227	496	736	881	1,016

[1] For the last tax year of the lease, use the dollar amount for the preceding year.

[2] See IRS Publication 463 for inclusion amounts for vehicles with fair market value over $50,000.

Inclusion Amounts for Passenger Automobiles (That Are Not Trucks, Vans, or Electric Automobiles) with a Lease Term Beginning in Calendar Year 2005

Fair Market Value		Tax Year during Lease[1]				
Over	Not Over	1st	2nd	3rd	4th	5th & Later
$15,200	$15,500	3	6	9	11	13
15,500	15,800	4	9	13	17	19
15,800	16,100	5	12	18	22	26
16,100	16,400	7	15	22	27	32
16,400	16,700	8	18	27	32	39
16,700	17,000	9	21	32	38	44
17,000	17,500	11	25	38	45	52
17,500	18,000	14	30	45	54	63
18,000	18,500	16	35	52	63	73
18,500	19,000	18	40	60	72	83
19,000	19,500	20	46	67	80	94
19,500	20,000	23	50	75	90	104
20,000	20,500	25	55	82	99	115
20,500	21,000	27	61	89	108	125
21,000	21,500	30	65	97	117	135
21,500	22,000	32	70	105	125	146
22,000	23,000	35	78	116	139	161
23,000	24,000	40	88	131	156	182
24,000	25,000	44	98	146	175	202
25,000	26,000	49	108	161	192	223
26,000	27,000	54	118	175	211	244
27,000	28,000	58	128	191	228	265
28,000	29,000	63	138	205	247	285
29,000	30,000	67	149	220	264	306
30,000	31,000	72	159	234	283	326
31,000	32,000	77	168	250	300	348
32,000	33,000	81	179	265	318	367
33,000	34,000	86	189	279	336	389
34,000	35,000	90	199	295	354	409
35,000	36,000	95	209	309	372	430
36,000	37,000	99	219	325	389	451
37,000	38,000	104	229	339	408	471
38,000	39,000	109	239	354	426	491
39,000	40,000	113	249	370	443	512
40,000	41,000	118	259	384	462	533
41,000	42,000	122	269	400	479	554
42,000	43,000	127	279	414	497	575
43,000	44,000	132	289	429	515	595
44,000	45,000	136	299	444	533	616
45,000	46,000	141	309	459	551	636
46,000	47,000	145	320	473	569	657
47,000	48,000	150	329	489	587	678
48,000	49,000	154	340	504	604	699
49,000	50,000[2]	159	350	518	623	719

[1] For the last tax year of the lease, use the dollar amount for the preceding year.
[2] See IRS Publication 463 for inclusion amounts for vehicles with fair market value over $50,000.

Inclusion Amounts for Trucks and Vans with a Lease Term Beginning in Calendar Year 2009

Fair Market Value		Tax Year during Lease[1]				
Over	Not Over	1st	2nd	3rd	4th	5th & later
$18,500	$18,000	8	17	25	30	35
19,000	19,500	9	19	29	35	40
19,500	20,000	10	22	33	38	45
20,000	20,500	11	25	36	43	50
20,500	21,000	12	27	40	48	55
21,000	21,500	13	30	43	52	60
21,500	22,000	15	32	47	56	66
22,000	23,000	16	36	52	64	72
23,000	24,000	18	41	60	72	83
24,000	25,000	21	45	68	81	93
25,000	26,000	23	50	75	90	103
26,000	27,000	25	56	82	98	114
27,000	28,000	27	61	89	107	124
28,000	29,000	30	65	97	116	134
29,000	30,000	32	70	104	125	144
30,000	31,000	34	75	112	134	154
31,000	32,000	36	80	119	143	164
32,000	33,000	39	85	126	151	175
33,000	34,000	41	90	134	160	184
34,000	35,000	43	95	141	169	195
35,000	36,000	45	100	148	178	205
36,000	37,000	48	105	155	187	215
37,000	38,000	50	110	163	195	226
38,000	39,000	52	115	170	204	236
39,000	40,000	55	120	177	213	246
40,000	41,000	57	125	185	221	256
41,000	42,000	59	130	192	231	266
42,000	43,000	61	135	199	240	276
43,000	44,000	64	139	207	249	286
44,000	45,000	66	144	215	257	296
45,000	46,000	68	149	222	266	307
46,000	47,000	70	155	229	274	317
47,000	48,000	73	159	237	283	327
48,000	49,000	75	164	244	292	338
49,000	50,000	77	169	251	301	348
50,000	51,000	79	174	259	310	357
51,000	52,000	82	179	266	318	368
52,000	53,000	84	184	273	328	378
53,000	54,000	86	189	281	336	388
54,000	55,000	88	194	288	345	399
55,000	56,000	91	199	295	354	408
56,000	57,000	93	204	302	363	419
57,000	58,000	95	209	310	371	429
58,000	59,000	97	214	317	381	439
59,000	60,000[2]	100	219	324	389	450

[1] For the last year of the lease, use the dollar amount for the preceding year.
[2] See IRS Publication 463 for inclusion amounts for vehicles with fair market value over $60,000.

Inclusion Amounts for Trucks and Vans with a Lease Term Beginning in Calendar Year 2008

Fair Market Value		Tax Year during Lease[1]				
Over	**Not Over**	**1st**	**2nd**	**3rd**	**4th**	**5th & later**
$19,000	$19,500	17	37	54	65	73
19,500	20,000	20	42	63	73	85
20,000	20,500	22	48	70	84	96
20,500	21,000	25	53	79	93	107
21,000	21,500	27	59	86	103	118
21,500	22,000	30	64	95	112	130
22,000	23,000	33	72	107	128	146
23,000	24,000	38	83	123	147	168
24,000	25,000	43	94	139	166	191
25,000	26,000	48	105	155	186	213
26,000	27,000	53	116	171	205	235
27,000	28,000	58	127	187	225	258
28,000	29,000	63	138	204	243	280
29,000	30,000	68	148	221	263	302
30,000	31,000	73	159	237	282	325
31,000	32,000	78	170	253	301	348
32,000	33,000	83	181	269	321	370
33,000	34,000	88	192	285	340	393
34,000	35,000	93	203	301	360	414
35,000	36,000	98	214	317	379	437
36,000	37,000	103	225	333	399	459
37,000	38,000	108	235	350	418	482
38,000	39,000	113	246	366	437	505
39,000	40,000	118	257	382	457	526
40,000	41,000	123	268	398	476	549
41,000	42,000	128	279	414	496	571
42,000	43,000	133	290	430	515	594
43,000	44,000	137	301	447	534	616
44,000	45,000	142	312	463	553	639
45,000	46,000	147	323	479	573	661
46,000	47,000	152	334	495	592	684
47,000	48,000	157	345	511	612	705
48,000	49,000	162	356	527	631	728
49,000	50,000	167	366	544	651	750
50,000	51,000	172	377	560	670	773
51,000	52,000	177	388	576	689	796
52,000	53,000	182	399	592	709	817
53,000	54,000	187	410	608	728	840
54,000	55,000	192	421	624	748	862
55,000	56,000	197	432	640	767	885
56,000	57,000	202	443	656	787	907
57,000	58,000	207	453	673	806	929
58,000	59,000	212	464	689	825	952
59,000	60,000[2]	217	475	705	845	974

[1] For the last year of the lease, use the dollar amount for the preceding year.

[2] See IRS Publication 463 for inclusion amounts for vehicles with fair market value over $60,000.

Inclusion Amounts for Trucks and Vans with a Lease Term Beginning in Calendar Year 2007

Fair Market Value		Tax Year during Lease[1]				
Over	Not Over	1st	2nd	3rd	4th	5th & later
$16,400	$16,700	2	4	8	10	11
16,700	17,000	4	9	15	17	21
17,000	17,500	6	15	24	28	33
17,500	18,000	10	22	35	42	48
18,000	18,500	13	30	46	55	64
18,500	19,000	17	37	57	69	79
19,000	19,500	20	45	68	82	94
19,500	20,000	24	52	80	95	109
20,000	20,500	27	60	90	109	125
20,500	21,000	30	67	102	122	141
21,000	21,500	34	75	113	135	156
21,500	22,000	37	82	124	149	171
22,000	23,000	42	94	140	169	194
23,000	24,000	49	109	163	195	225
24,000	25,000	56	123	186	222	256
25,000	26,000	63	138	208	249	286
26,000	27,000	70	153	230	276	317
27,000	28,000	77	168	252	302	349
28,000	29,000	83	184	274	329	379
29,000	30,000	90	199	296	356	410
30,000	31,000	97	214	318	383	440
31,000	32,000	104	228	342	408	472
32,000	33,000	111	243	364	435	503
33,000	34,000	118	258	386	462	534
34,000	35,000	125	273	408	489	564
35,000	36,000	131	289	430	515	595
36,000	37,000	138	304	452	542	626
37,000	38,000	145	318	475	569	657
38,000	39,000	152	333	497	596	688
39,000	40,000	159	348	520	622	718
40,000	41,000	166	363	542	649	749
41,000	42,000	172	379	563	676	780
42,000	43,000	179	394	586	702	811
43,000	44,000	186	409	608	729	842
44,000	45,000	193	423	631	756	872
45,000	46,000	200	438	653	783	903
46,000	47,000	207	453	675	810	934
47,000	48,000	213	469	697	836	965
48,000	49,000	220	484	719	863	996
49,000	50,000[2]	227	499	741	890	1,026

[1] For the last year of the lease, use the dollar amount for the preceding year.

[2] See IRS Publication 463 for inclusion amounts for vehicles with fair market value over $50,000.

Inclusion Amounts For Trucks and Vans with a Lease Term Beginning in Calendar Year 2006

Fair Market Value		Tax Year During Lease[1]				
Over	Not Over	1st	2nd	3rd	4th	5th & later
$16,700	$17,000	4	8	12	14	16
17,000	17,500	6	14	20	24	29
17,500	18,000	9	21	31	37	43
18,000	18,500	13	28	42	49	58
18,500	19,000	16	36	52	62	72
19,000	19,500	19	43	63	75	87
19,500	20,000	23	50	73	88	102
20,000	20,500	26	57	84	101	116
20,500	21,000	29	64	95	113	131
21,000	21,500	32	72	105	126	146
21,500	22,000	36	78	116	139	161
22,000	23,000	41	89	132	158	183
23,000	24,000	47	104	153	183	213
24,000	25,000	54	118	174	209	242
25,000	26,000	60	132	196	235	271
26,000	27,000	67	146	217	261	300
27,000	28,000	73	161	238	286	330
28,000	29,000	80	175	260	311	359
29,000	30,000	86	190	281	336	389
30,000	31,000	93	204	302	362	418
31,000	32,000	99	219	323	388	447
32,000	33,000	106	233	344	413	478
33,000	34,000	112	247	366	439	506
34,000	35,000	119	261	387	465	536
35,000	36,000	125	276	408	490	566
36,000	37,000	132	290	430	515	595
37,000	38,000	139	304	451	541	624
38,000	39,000	145	319	472	566	654
39,000	40,000	152	333	493	592	684
40,000	41,000	158	347	515	618	712
41,000	42,000	165	362	536	642	743
42,000	43,000	171	376	557	669	772
43,000	44,000	178	390	579	694	801
44,000	45,000	184	405	600	719	831
45,000	46,000	191	419	621	745	860
46,000	47,000	197	434	642	770	890
47,000	48,000	204	448	663	796	919
48,000	49,000	210	462	685	822	948
49,000	50,000[2]	217	476	707	847	977

1 For the last tax year of the lease, use the dollar amount for the preceding year

2 See IRS Publication 463 for inclusion amounts for vehicles with fair market value over $50,000.

Inclusion Amounts for Trucks and Vans with a Lease Term Beginning in Calendar Year 2005

Fair Market Value of Truck or Van		Tax Year during Lease[1]				
Over	Not Over	1st	2nd	3rd	4th	5th and Later
$16,700	$17,000	3	6	8	10	11
17,000	17,500	4	10	14	17	20
17,500	18,000	7	15	21	26	30
18,000	18,500	9	20	29	35	40
18,500	19,000	11	25	37	43	51
19,000	19,500	14	30	44	52	61
19,500	20,000	16	35	51	62	71
20,000	20,500	18	40	59	71	81
20,500	21,000	20	45	67	79	92
21,000	21,500	23	50	74	88	103
21,500	22,000	25	55	81	98	113
22,000	23,000	28	63	92	111	129
23,000	24,000	33	73	107	129	149
24,000	25,000	38	83	122	147	169
25,000	26,000	42	93	137	165	190
26,000	27,000	47	103	152	183	210
27,000	28,000	51	113	167	201	231
28,000	29,000	56	123	182	218	253
29,000	30,000	60	133	197	237	272
30,000	31,000	65	143	212	254	294
31,000	32,000	70	153	227	272	314
32,000	33,000	74	163	242	290	335
33,000	34,000	79	173	257	308	355
34,000	35,000	83	184	271	326	376
35,000	36,000	88	193	287	344	397
36,000	37,000	93	203	302	361	418
37,000	38,000	97	214	316	380	438
38,000	39,000	102	223	332	397	459
39,000	40,000	106	234	346	415	480
40,000	41,000	111	244	361	433	500
41,000	42,000	115	254	376	451	521
42,000	43,000	120	264	391	469	542
43,000	44,000	125	274	406	487	562
44,000	45,000	129	284	421	505	583
45,000	46,000	134	294	436	523	603
46,000	47,000	138	304	451	541	624
47,000	48,000	143	314	466	558	645
48,000	49,000	148	324	481	576	666
49,000	50,000[2]	152	334	496	594	687

[1] For the last tax year of the lease, use the dollar amount for the preceding year.
[2] See IRS Publication 463 for inclusion amounts for vehicles with fair market value over $50,000.

Inclusion Amounts For Electric Automobiles with a Lease Term Beginning in Calendar Year 2006						
Fair Market Value		Tax Year During Lease[1]				
Over	Not Over	1st	2nd	3rd	4th	5th and Later
$45,000	$46,000	4	8	11	12	12
46,000	47,000	10	22	33	37	42
47,000	48,000	17	36	54	63	72
48,000	49,000	24	51	74	89	101
49,000	50,000	30	65	96	114	131
50,000	51,000	37	79	118	139	160
51,000	52,000	43	94	139	165	189
52,000	53,000	50	108	160	190	219
53,000	54,000	56	123	181	216	248
54,000	55,000	63	137	202	242	277
55,000	56,000	69	151	224	267	307
56,000	57,000	76	165	245	293	337
57,000	58,000	82	180	266	318	367
58,000	59,000	89	194	288	343	396
59,000	60,000	95	209	309	369	425
60,000	62,000	105	230	341	407	470
62,000	64,000	118	259	383	459	528
64,000	66,000	131	288	425	510	587
66,000	68,000	144	316	469	560	646
68,000	70,000	158	345	510	612	705
70,000	72,000	171	373	554	662	764
72,000	74,000	184	402	596	713	823
74,000	76,000	197	431	638	765	881
76,000	78,000	210	459	682	815	940
78,000	80,000	223	488	724	866	1,000
80,000	85,000	246	538	798	956	1,103
85,000	90,000	278	610	905	1,083	1,250
90,000	95,000	311	682	1,011	1,211	1,397
95,000	100,000	344	753	1,118	1,338	1,544
100,000	110,000[2]	393	861	1,277	1,529	1,766

[1] For the last tax year of the lease, use the dollar amount for the preceding year.
[2] If the fair market value of the car is more than $110,000, see Revenue Procedure 2006-18 (2006-12 IRB 645).

KEY FACTS: Automobiles and Taxes

Automobiles for Personal Use: Expenses are generally not deductible.

- Interest on a home equity loan may be deductible, even if the amount is used to purchase personal-use items such as an automobile.
- Use of personal vehicles to obtain medical treatment and to do volunteer work is deductible, either as the actual portion of automobile expenses related, or at the standard medical/volunteer rate of 24¢ per mile.

Automobiles for Business Use: Business portion of expenses is generally deductible.

Documentation Required

Standard mileage method

- Total miles driven during year
- Business miles driven during year
- Date vehicle was placed in service
- Basis in vehicle

Actual expense method

All of the documentation required for standard mileage method, *plus* records of actual expenses paid during year

Choice of Method

Standard mileage method required if

- The vehicle is leased and the standard mileage method has previously been used for the same vehicle during the lease period
- Mileage records are available but actual expense records are not available

Actual expense method required if

- The vehicle is used for hire (such as a taxi)
- ACRS, MACRS, or any method other than straight-line depreciation has been claimed on the vehicle
- Section 179 expense has been claimed
- More than four vehicles are used in the business (before 2004, the rule was two or more)
- Actual expenses have been previously used

Standard Mileage Rate [The 2009 rates, per mile, are: 55¢ (business), 24¢ (medical/moving), and 14¢ (charitable)]

Includes: *(These expenses cannot be deducted in addition to the standard rate.)*

- Depreciation
- Maintenance and repairs
- Gasoline and gasoline taxes
- Oil
- Insurance
- Vehicle registration fees

Excludes: *(These expenses may be deducted in addition to the standard rate, if deductible.)*

- Parking fees
- Tolls
- Personal property taxes
- Interest on auto loan

Converting a Vehicle to or from Business Use:

To Business Use:

- If records are available for the entire year, business use percentage for the first year is calculated using mileage for the entire year.
- If records are not available for the portion of the year before the vehicle was placed in service, business use percentage must be annualized based on the portion of the year that the vehicle was used for business.

To Less Than 50% Business Use or Personal Use:

- Earlier MACRS deductions must be recaptured if the recovery period is not complete.
- When the vehicle is sold, a taxable gain over depreciated basis may be realized.

Social Security, Retirement and Financial Planning

What's New in 2009

IRA Contributions Limits. For 2009, the maximum contribution that can be made by an individual to all of his or her traditional and Roth IRAs is $5,000. The maximum amount of catch-up contributions that an individual can make is $1,000. The phaseout range to make contributions to a Roth IRA is $105,000 to $120,000 for single individuals and heads of household, and $166,000 to $176,000 for married individuals filing jointly. The phaseout range remains $0 to $10,000 for married individuals filing separately.

Traditional IRA Deduction Limits. For 2009, the phaseout range for the deduction of contributions to a traditional IRA by an individual who is an active participant in an employer provided retirement plan is $55,000 to $65,000 for single individuals and heads of household, and $89,000 and $109,000 for married individuals filing jointly. The phaseout range remains $0 to $10,000 for married individuals filing separately.

Elective Deferral Limit. For 2009, the maximum amount of elective deferrals that an employee can make to all of his or her 401(k) plans, 403(b) tax-sheltered annuities, or SARSEP IRAs is $16,500. The maximum amount of catch-up contributions that can be contributed is $5,500.

Waiver of RMDs. The required minimum distribution (RMD) rules are waived for calendar year 2009 for IRAs and defined contributions plans (including 401(k)s, 403(a) annuities, 403(b) tax-sheltered annuities, and 457 government plans).

Relevant IRS Publications

- ☐ IRS Publication 517, *Social Security and Other Information for Members of the Clergy and Religious Workers*
- ☐ IRS Publication 554, *Tax Guide for Seniors*
- ☐ IRS Publication 560, *Retirement Plans for Small Business (SEP, SIMPLE, and Qualified Plans)*
- ☐ IRS Publication 571, *Tax-Sheltered Annuity Plans (403(b) Plans)*
- ☐ IRS Publication 575, *Pension and Annuity Income*
- ☐ IRS Publication 590, *Individual Retirement Arrangements (IRAs)*
- ☐ IRS Notice 703, *Read This to See if Your Social Security Benefits May Be Taxable*
- ☐ IRS Publication 721, *Tax Guide to U.S. Civil Service Retirement Benefits*
- ☐ IRS Publication 915, *Social Security and Equivalent Railroad Retirement Benefits*
- ☐ IRS Publication 939, *General Rule for Pensions and Annuities*

Section at a Glance

Tax Preparer's Checklist

- ☐ The following items may be required:
- ☐ Forms RRB-1099 and SSA-1099
- ☐ Forms 1099-R, *Distributions from Pensions, Annuities, Retirement or Profit-Sharing Plans, IRAs, Insurance Contracts, etc.*
- ☐ Forms 1099-INT, *Interest Income*
- ☐ Form 5329, *Additional Taxes on Qualified Plans (Including IRAs) and Other Tax-Favored Accounts*
- ☐ Form 5498, *IRA Contribution Information*
- ☐ Form 8606, *Nondeductible IRAs*
- ☐ Estimation tools
- ☐ Documents showing the accumulated deposits and year-end balances in investment accounts, IRAs and employer plans

Retirement Contribution Limits for 2009 and 2010

Limit	2009	2010
IRA contributions	$5,000	$5,000
Catch-up IRA contributions	1,000	1,000
Total standard and designated Roth deferrals to 401(k), 403(b), and 501(c)(18) plans, SEPs and SIMPLEs	16,500 (no more than 11,500 in a SIMPLE)	16,500 (no more than 11,500 in a SIMPLE)
Catch-up deferrals	5,500	5,500

Social Security Disability and SSI Key Figures for 2009 and 2010		
Key Figure	**2009**	**2010**
Social Security disability thresholds for substantial gainful activity (SGA)		
Nonblind	$980/month	$1,000/month
Blind	$1,640/month	$1,640/month
Trial work period (TWP)	$700/month	$720/month
SSI federal payment standard		
Individual	$674/month	$674/month
Couple	$1,011/month	$1,011/month
SSI resources limits		
Individual	$2,000	$2,000
Couple	$3,000	$3,000
SSI student exclusion limits		
Monthly limit	$1,640	$1,640
Annual limit	$6,600	$6,600

Social Security

The Social Security system is a federal government program set up to provide retirement, survivor and disability benefits for workers and their families.

Basic Elements of the System

Individuals become eligible for Social Security benefits by accumulating credits. Credits are based on an individual's total wages and self-employment income during the year, no matter when the actual work is performed. The amount of earnings it takes to qualify for a credit changes each year. For 2009, one credit is given for each $1,090 of earnings, so that any individual who earns at least $4,360 during the year will get the maximum of four credits. For 2010, one credit will be given for each $1,120 of earnings, so any individual who earns at least $4,480 during the year will get the maximum of four credits.

Everyone born in 1929 or later needs 40 Social Security credits to be eligible for retirement benefits. Fewer credits are required for eligibility for survivor or disability benefits.

Estimated Average Monthly Social Security Benefits Payable in January 2010	
Recipient(s)	**Amount**
All retired workers	$1,153
Aged couple, both receiving benefits	1,876
Widowed mother and two children	2,399
Aged widow(er) alone	1,112
Disabled worker, spouse, and one or more children	1,793
All disabled workers	1,064

Paying into the System

Workers and employers pay into the Social Security system. Self-employed individuals, employers, and employees are taxed on earned income up to the Social Security wage base ($106,800 for 2009 and 2010). The Social Security tax rate is 12.4 percent. Employees and employers each contribute 6.2 percent, and self-

Comparison of Social Security Key Figures for 2009 and 2010		
Key Figure	**2009**	**2010**
Maximum earnings taxable		
Social Security	$106,800	$106,800
Medicare	No limit	No limit
Earnings required for one quarter of coverage	$1,090	$1,120
Maximum Social Security benefit		
Worker retiring at *full retirement age*	$2,323/month	$2,323/month
Retirement earnings test exempt amounts		
Under full retirement age[1]	$14,160/year ($1,180/month)	$14,160/year ($1,180/month)
Year individual reaches *full retirement age*[2]	$37,680/year ($3,140/month)	$37,680/year ($3,140/month)

[1] One dollar in benefits will be withheld for every $2 in earnings above the limit.
[2] Applies only to earnings for months prior to attaining full retirement age. One dollar in benefits will be withheld for every $3 in earnings above the limit. There is no limit on earnings beginning the month an individual attains full retirement age.

employed individuals pay the entire tax of 12.4 percent (both the employee's and employer's portions). See MTG ¶2648 for discussion of Social Security tax rates.

Similarly, workers and employers pay a Medicare tax to help fund Medicare benefits. There is no limit on wages subject to the Medicare tax. The Medicare tax rate is 2.9 percent. Again, employers and employees split the rate, each contributing 1.45 percent; self-employed individuals pay the entire 2.9 percent.

Employees pay Social Security and Medicare taxes through payroll withholding. Self-employed individuals pay self-employment tax (Social Security and Medicare taxes) by completing Schedule SE. See Tab 3 for more information.

Types of Benefits

Social Security provides more than just retirement benefits. Payments are also made to family members of retirees or deceased workers, and to disabled workers. The supplemental security income (SSI) program provides additional benefits to disabled, blind or elderly individuals who have low income and resources.

Retirement. Retirement benefits are paid on a monthly basis. The full amount of benefits available to an individual are paid if he or she waits until reaching full retirement age to begin receiving benefits. Full retirement age varies depending on the individual's year of birth. Individuals born between March 1, 1943 and December 31, 1943 reached full retirement age in 2009. The amount of the full benefit is determined by a complex formula that takes into account the individual's earnings during the 35 years in which the individual had the highest earnings (indexed for inflation).

Age to Receive Full Social Security Benefits (as of 2009)

Year of Birth	Full Retirement Age
1937 or earlier	65
1938	65 and 2 months
1939	65 and 4 months
1940	65 and 6 months
1941	65 and 8 months
1942	65 and 10 months
1943-1954	66
1955	66 and 2 months
1956	66 and 4 months
1957	66 and 6 months
1958	66 and 8 months
1959	66 and 10 months
1960 and later	67

An individual can choose to begin receiving Social Security benefits as early as age 62, instead of waiting until full retirement age. However, the monthly benefit received is permanently reduced if the individual chooses to begin receiving benefits before reaching full retirement age. This permanent reduction is intended to result, on average, in lifetime payments of the same total amount as full benefits beginning at full retirement age. The formula to determine the reduced benefits is complicated. An online calculator for computing benefits for specific combinations of retirement age and annual earnings can be found at www.ssa.gov/retire2/AnypiaApplet.html.

An additional temporary reduction may apply if an individual who chooses to begin receiving benefits early

Planning Tip. Consider the impact of beginning Social Security retirement benefits at different ages. Individuals age 62 and over (born in 1948 and earlier) can begin to receive benefits in 2010 if they so choose. Individuals born in 1944 will reach their full retirement age of 66 in 2010.

Individuals can choose to begin receiving their Social Security retirement benefits as early as age 62. Receiving retirement benefits before reaching full retirement age has a benefit and a drawback. On the positive side, a person will receive payments. However, the monthly benefit paid is permanently lower if payments begin before the recipient has reached full retirement age. Individuals born in 1948 and choosing to begin receiving retirement benefits at age 62 in 2010 will receive monthly benefits equal to about 75% of what they would have received if they had waited until full retirement age. By factoring in life expectancy and the time value of money, a person may compare these trade-offs.

For individuals who begin receiving benefits before they reach full retirement age, benefits are reduced further if their earned income exceeds an annual earned income limit. For 2010, the earned income limit is $14,160. For every $1 above that limit that a person receives as wages, salary, or self-employment income, his or her Social Security benefit is reduced by $0.50. A special version of the limit applies in the year in which the person reaches full retirement age. This reduction of benefits stops once the recipient reaches full retirement age.

Individuals who delay the start of their Social Security benefits past full retirement age receive larger monthly payments. Individuals reaching full retirement age in 2009 will increase their monthly benefits by as much as 32% if they delay the start of benefits until they reach age 70.

The Social Security Web site, at www.ssa.gov, is extremely helpful in planning for retirement. For a chart showing the effect of starting benefits at various ages, see: www.ssa.gov/OACT/ProgData/ar_drc.html

Example. Assuming that any Social Security money received can earn an 8% investment rate of return and is subject to a 3% inflation rate, a person who retires at 65 will have to collect benefits for 12 years before being better off than someone who retires at 62. A person who retires at 67 will go over their breakeven point after 14 years. So, if you know that you have a short time to live at age 62, it is probably a good idea to start claiming Social Security benefits right away.

is still working. The temporary reduction ceases once the individual reaches full retirement age. For an individual who is working and receiving benefits in 2010 but has not reached full retirement age by the end of the year, benefits are reduced by $1 for every $2 the individual earns over $14,160 ($1,180 per month). For an individual who reaches full retirement age during 2010, benefits are reduced by $1 for every $3 the individual earns over $37,680 ($3,140 per month) until the month the individual reaches retirement age.

If an individual delays the start of payments beyond full retirement age, then his or her monthly retirement benefit will be increased. Delaying the start of payments beyond age 70, however, has no additional effect. Individuals should sign up for Medicare when they reach age 65, even if they do not plan to begin receiving Social Security retirement benefits then.

Benefit Increases for Delaying Retirement to Age 70 (as of 2009)

Year of Birth	Yearly Rate of Increase
1917-1924	3.0%
1925-1926	3.5
1927-1928	4.0
1929-1930	4.5
1931-1932	5.0
1933-1934	5.5
1935-1936	6.0
1937-1938	6.5
1939-1940	7.0
1941-1942	7.5
1943 or later	8.0

Survivor. Social Security pays survivor benefits to certain family members of a deceased worker. Eligible survivors receive a percentage of the deceased worker's benefit. A family will receive about 150 to 180 percent of the deceased worker's benefit. Survivor benefits may be available to the following individuals:

- a surviving spouse who is age 60 or older;
- a disabled surviving spouse who is age 50 or older;
- a surviving spouse of any age who is caring for the deceased worker's child, if that child is younger than age 16 or disabled and receiving Social Security benefits;
- an unmarried child of the deceased who is under age 18, who is age 18 or 19 and not out of high school, or who becomes disabled before age 22;
- parents of the deceased, age 62 or older, who were dependent on the deceased for at least half of their support;
- a former spouse who reaches full retirement age (age 60 for reduced benefits or age 50 if disabled), if the marriage lasted at least 10 years.;
- a former spouse of any age who is caring for the deceased worker's child, if that child is eligible for benefits based on the deceased worker's record.

A former spouse can get these benefits only if she is not eligible for an equal or higher benefit based on her own work and she is not currently married (unless the remarriage occurred after age 60).

Disability and Supplemental Security Income. Social Security pays disability benefits to certain individuals who cannot work because they have a medical condition that is expected to last at least one year or result in death. The Social Security Administration (SSA) maintains an extensive list of conditions that qualify an individual for disability benefits. This list is provided in SSA Publication No. 64-039, entitled *Disability Evaluation under Social Security*, available online at www.ssa.gov/disability/professionals/bluebook.

A disabled adult qualifies for Social Security disability benefits if she satisfies two tests: a "duration of work" test to show that she worked long enough under Social Security; and a "recent work" test to show that she was working for significant portions of the period just prior to the time she became disabled. For example, an individual who becomes disabled at age 50 must have worked for at least seven years total and for five of the last 10 years. Certain blind workers only have to meet the "duration of work" test.

Disabled children can qualify for disability payments through the Supplemental Security Income (SSI) program. SSI is funded by general tax revenues and administered by the SSA. SSI benefits for children are payable to disabled children under age 18 who have limited income and resources, or who come from homes with limited income and resources.

A person who is disabled or blind may also receive SSI benefits if he or she has limited income and resources. The benefit available under this program is the same for all eligible individuals ($674 per month for 2009 and 2010). This amount may be supplemented by certain states. For more information, see SSA Publication No. 05-11011, *What You Need to Know When You Get Supplemental Security Income (SSI)* from www.ssa.gov/pubs/11011.html.

Social Security Statements

Each year, the SSA sends individually prepared Social Security statements to workers aged 25 and older. Each statement contains a brief explanation of Social Security and Medicare, the individual's estimated benefits (including his or her earnings record), and instructions on how to correct any misreported earnings. The estimated benefits portion of the statement specifies the estimated amount of benefits the taxpayer is eligible to receive per month for retirement (including early retirement) or disability, and his or her survivor benefits. The earnings record included in the statement provides a chart of the taxpayer's Social Security earnings and Medicare earnings for every year the taxpayer has worked.

If the earnings statement or any other information on the taxpayer's personalized statement is incorrect, the form provides a toll-free number to call (800-772-1213) to correct the information. A taxpayer who has not kept his or her statement handy can request a new one by following instructions at www.socialsecurity.gov/mystatement on the Internet, contacting any local Social Security office.

Social Security Benefit Planning

Maximizing Social Security Benefits. Workers do not lose accumulated Social Security benefits. However, a worker who has not earned the minimum number of credits may not be entitled to Social Security benefits. In addition, maximum benefits may not be earned if an individual ceases working prior to reaching full retirement age. An individual should determine whether continuing to work will result in increased earnings that would boost his or her average salary for the most lucrative 35 years of his or her working life, as this is the basis used to determine the individual's Social Security benefit. Review of the individual's annual Social Security Statement may be useful in making these decisions.

Diminishing Benefit from Increased Earnings. Social Security taxes are not imposed on income above the taxable wage base ($106,800 for 2009 and 2010). Workers who have 35 years of earnings at or above the taxable wage base should consider these maximums when deciding whether to continue working beyond the earliest age in which they could begin receiving Social Security benefits.

Taxation of Benefits

Social Security benefits are nontaxable for most recipients. However, a portion of the Social Security benefits received are taxable to individuals whose modified adjusted gross income (MAGI) exceeds certain thresholds.

Modified adjusted gross income is computed as follows:

	Adjusted gross income
+	1/2 of Social Security benefits
+	Tax-exempt income
+	Foreign earned income exclusion
	Modified adjusted gross income

Calculation of Taxable Portion of Social Security Benefits

	MAGI		
Filing Status	Over	But Not Over	Amount Taxed
Single, HOH, QW, or MFS (living apart from spouse for entire tax year)	$25,000	$34,000	*Step 1:* Lesser of (1) 50% of benefits or (2) 50% × (MAGI - $25,000)
	$34,000	Unlimited	*Step 2:* Lesser of (1) Step 1 amount not to exceed $4,500 + 85% × (MAGI - $34,000) or (2) 85% of benefits
MFJ	$32,000	$44,000	*Step 1:* Lesser of (1) 50% of benefits or (2) 50% × (MAGI - $32,000)
	$44,000	Unlimited	Step 2: Lesser of (1) Step 1 amount not to exceed $6,000 + 85% × (MAGI - $44,000) or (2) 85% of benefits
MFS (and lived with spouse for part of tax year)	Any		Lesser of (1) 85% MAGI or (2) 85% of benefits

> **Caution.** Note that certain tax-exempt interest is now reported to the IRS and the recipient. Review all Forms 1099-INT or substitute statements for tax-exempt interest to be included in the taxpayer's modified adjusted gross income.

Depending on the taxpayer's MAGI and filing status, the percentage of Social Security benefits to be taxed can be up to 85 percent. Taxpayers whose MAGI is less than the first threshold ($25,000 for unmarried taxpayers, $32,000 for joint filers) are not taxed on their Social Security benefits. If MAGI is between $25,000 and $34,000 for single filers, or $32,000 and $44,000 for joint filers, the amount of benefits taxed is the lesser of 50 percent of the Social Security benefits received or 50 percent of the excess of MAGI over the specified threshold. If the MAGI is higher than the second threshold ($34,000 for unmarried taxpayers, $44,000 for joint filers), up to 85 percent of the Social Security benefits could be taxable. The instructions to Forms 1040, 1040A, and 1040EZ include worksheets to be used to determine the amount of taxable Social Security benefits (see Tab 1). If any Social Security benefits are taxable, the taxpayer cannot use Form 1040EZ. See MTG ¶716 for discussion of the taxability of Social Security benefits.

Tax Planning Ideas

Managing the Retirement Portfolio. Taxpayers whose benefits are subject to tax may be able to reduce or avoid the tax by properly structuring their portfolios. Taxation of Social Security benefits is dependent on the taxpayer's MAGI. Taxation cannot be avoided merely by investing in securities that produce tax-exempt income, such as state and local bonds, since such income is included in the MAGI calculation. However, the unrealized appreciation of investments is not treated as income in calculating MAGI. Consequently, investment in growth stocks should be considered. Similarly, the growth element in series E or EE savings bonds is not included in income.

Managing Taxable Income. If Social Security benefits are included in gross income, the impact may be reduced or eliminated if the taxpayer is able to reduce overall taxable income (including Social Security benefits). For example, if a taxpayer has itemized deductions that offset their income, then the amount of tax due can be reduced. The taxpayer may be able to manage deductions (e.g., charitable contributions) in such a way that the standard deduction is used in one year and in the alternate year the taxpayer itemizes deductions.

Managing Distributions from Other Retirement Plans. Careful consideration should also be given to the effects on MAGI when the taxpayer makes withdrawals from retirement plans. Such income is generally included in the MAGI calculation. By reducing or eliminating such withdrawals, the amount of Social Security income that is taxed may be reduced. Alternatively, withdrawals prior to the receipt of Social Security benefits may help to minimize the impact such payments have on taxation.

Medicare

Medicare is a federal health insurance program, enacted by Congress in 1965, to benefit people 65 years of age and older and some disabled people under age 65. The program currently covers over 40 million people. An individual is eligible for Medicare if he or she worked for at least 10 years in Medicare-covered employment (or his or her spouse did so), is at least 65 years old, and is a citizen or permanent resident of the United States. Younger people may also qualify for coverage if they have a disability or end-stage renal disease. Medicare benefits include hospital insurance (Part A), medical insurance (Part B), Medicare Advantage plans (Part C), and prescription drug benefits (Part D).

The basic Medicare coverage is referred to as Part A compulsory hospitalization insurance. Financed through payroll taxes, it is provided free to anyone who qualifies for Medicare benefits. Individuals who do not qualify for free coverage can purchase Part A coverage. The premium for seniors with fewer than 30 quarters of covered employment is $443 per month (for 2009). Individuals should apply for Medicare benefits three months before their 65th birthday.

The deductible for hospitalization coverage under Part A is $1,068 per benefit period for 2009, and the required coinsurance for hospitalization is $267 a day for the 61st through 90th day of each benefit period, and $534 a day for each lifetime reserve day (the total of 60 lifetime reserve days is nonrenewable). All costs of hospitalization beyond 150 days are paid by the individual.

Part A also covers the full cost of the individual's first 20 days in a skilled nursing facility during a benefit period. For 2009, the individual pays $133.50 a day in coinsurance for days 21 through 100 in each benefit period. All costs of care in a skilled nursing facility beyond 100 days are paid by the individual.

A benefit period begins the day an individual goes to a hospital or skilled nursing facility. The benefit period ends when the individual has not received any hospital care or skilled care for 60 days in a row. If an individual goes into the hospital or a skilled nursing facility after one benefit period has ended, a new benefit period begins.

Medicare Part B, supplementary medical insurance, covers physician, outpatient and preventive services and is paid for by the insured individual via an enrollment program. For 2009 the monthly premium is $96.40. Individual beneficiaries with income over $85,000 (and married couples with income in excess of $170,000) pay higher premiums. Part B premiums are deductible as medical expenses. See MTG ¶1019. The coverage has a $135 annual deductible and a 20 percent-per-service coinsurance.

Medicare Part C, Medicare Advantage, is a collection of private plans, including HMOs and PPOs, that provide Part A, Part B and Part D benefits to enrollees. The costs for individuals electing to join a Medicare Advantage plan vary based on the terms of the plan.

Medicare Part D is a prescription drug benefit. Medicare recipients can join a prescription drug plan (and get other Medicare benefits from the traditional program) or join a Medicare Advantage plan, which will cover all Medicare benefits. Prescription drug plans are offered by private insurers and subsidized by Medicare. Each plan must offer at least the Medicare standard minimum level of coverage. At the minimum level of coverage, enrollees will pay a monthly premium expected to average around $30 for 2009.

Planning Tip. In choosing a Medicare drug plan, enrollees should keep in mind their current prescriptions, their location, and their preferred pharmacy. The Medicare website (www.medicare.gov) provides useful tools for comparing plans. Nevertheless, enrollees should double check with the plans they are considering to confirm that the information on the web is still correct. In particular, plans have great flexibility to change the list of drugs that they cover. An enrollee may change drug plans on a yearly basis.

The SSA determines entitlement to Medicare, and Medicare benefits are administered by the Centers for Medicare & Medicaid Services (CMS). For more information regarding Medicare benefits, call 800-MEDICARE or log on to www.cms.hhs.gov or www.medicare.gov.

Medigap Insurance

The private insurance industry has created special policies designed to supplement Medicare coverage, known as Medigap policies. There are 12 standard Medigap policies designated by the letters A through L. Medigap policies can be sold only in these 12 standardized plans. Medicare SELECT versions of the Medigap policies are available in some states. A Medicare SELECT policy pays full benefits only for care provided at specific hospitals and, in some cases, by specific doctors. Some basic benefits are included in all 12 Medigap plans; other benefits vary. The basic benefits include:

- Inpatient hospital care: Covers the Part A coinsurance and the cost of 365 extra days of hospital care during the insured's lifetime after coverage ends.
- Medical costs: Covers the Part B coinsurance (generally 20 percent of the Medicare-approved payment amount) after the insured has paid the annual deductible.
- Blood: Covers the first 3 pints of blood each year.
- Plans K and L also provide some hospice benefits as basic benefits. Plan K covers only 50 percent of the Part B coinsurance, blood and hospice costs. Plan L covers 75 percent of those costs.

Pensions and Retirement Plans

Individual Retirement Accounts (IRAs)

An IRA is a trust created or organized in the United States for the exclusive benefit of an individual or his or her beneficiaries. See MTG ¶2168 for discussion of IRAs. IRAs must meet the following requirements to receive tax-favored status:

- Annual contributions to the trust must not exceed the lesser of $5,000 for 2009 and 2010 (plus allowable catch-up contributions for individual's 50 years or older of $1,000 for 2009 and 2010) or the individual's compensation.
- The trustee must be a bank or other entity/person that demonstrates that the manner in which the trust is administered will be consistent with the statutory requirements, if such entity/person is approved by the IRS.
- The trust's investment funds cannot be invested in life insurance contracts.
- The account holder's interest in the trust must be nonforfeitable.
- The assets of the trust must be maintained separately from other funds.
- The trust must impose the minimum distribution rules required by the Code and regulations.

IRA Contributions. Contributions to a traditional IRA may be fully or partially deductible, depending on whether the individual is covered by an employer's plan and on the individual's gross income for the year. The maximum deduction may not exceed the *smaller* of the compensation includible in the taxpayer's gross income or the applicable statutory limit. If a married couple files jointly, the lower-paid spouse can take the higher paid spouse's compensation into account when calculating the compensation limit. See MTG ¶2170 for discussion of IRA deduction and contribution limits. Contributions to a Roth IRA are not deductible.

Caution. Although the deduction is generally limited to the amount of compensation included in the taxpayer's gross income, a special rule allows members of the armed forces to make deductible IRA contributions based on their excludable combat pay. For purposes of the deduction, excludable combat zone pay will be considered to be included in gross income.

Medigap Plans A through L												
Medigap Benefits	**A**	**B**	**C**	**D**	**E**	**F***	**G**	**H**	**I**	**J***	**K**	**L**
Medicare Part A Coinsurance and Medigap Coverage for Hospital Benefits	✓	✓	✓	✓	✓	✓	✓	✓	✓	✓	✓	✓
Medicare Part B Coinsurance or Copayment	✓	✓	✓	✓	✓	✓	✓	✓	✓	✓	✓ (50%)	✓ (75%)
Blood (First 3 Pints)	✓	✓	✓	✓	✓	✓	✓	✓	✓	✓	✓ (50%)	✓ (75%)
Hospice Care Coinsurance or Copayment											✓ (50%)	✓ (75%)
Skilled Nursing Facility Care Coinsurance			✓	✓	✓	✓	✓	✓	✓	✓	✓ (50%)	✓ (75%)
Medicare Part A Deductible		✓	✓	✓	✓	✓	✓	✓	✓	✓	✓ (50%)	✓ (75%)
Medicare Part B Deductible			✓			✓				✓		
Medicare Part B Excess Charges						✓	✓ (80%)		✓	✓		
Foreign Travel Emergency (Up to Plan Limits)**			✓	✓	✓	✓	✓	✓	✓	✓		
At-Home Recovery (Up to Plan Limits)				✓			✓		✓	✓		
Preventive Care Coinsurance (Included in the Part B Coinsurance)	✓	✓	✓	✓	✓	✓	✓	✓	✓	✓	✓	✓
Preventive Care not Covered by Medicare (Up to $120)					✓					✓		
	2009 out-of-pocket limit										$4,620***	$2,310***

* Medigap Plans F and J also offer a high-deductible option. You must pay the first $2,000 (high deductible in 2009) in Medigap-covered costs before the Medigap policy pays anything.

** You must also pay a separate deductible for foreign travel emergency ($250 per year).

***After you meet your out-of-pocket yearly limit and your yearly Part B deductible ($135 in 2009), the plan pays 100% of covered services for the rest of the calendar year.

Note: This chart does not apply if you live in Massachusetts, Minnesota, or Wisconsin. Call your state Insurance Department for more information on the policies that are offered in these states. Specific Medigap plan options available in each local area are listed at www.medicare.gov/mgcompare/home.asp.

Example. Irina who has no compensation, files a joint return with Oscar, who earns $42,000 (taxable compensation) in 2009 and plans to contribute the maximum $5,000 to his traditional IRA (Irina and Oscar are both under 50). Irina can contribute an additional $5,000 to her own IRA because this amount is smaller than Oscar's compensation ($42,000) plus her own ($0), minus Oscar's $5,000 contribution ($42,000 – $5,000 = $37,000).

IRA contributions for a tax year can be made until the due date (without extension) of the return for that year. Contributions for 2009 must be made by April 15, 2010. If total contributions to the IRA are less than the maximum allowed by law, the taxpayer *cannot* make up the difference after the due date of the return. If contributions exceed the legal limit, the excess portion may be withdrawn or applied to a later year in which total contributions would otherwise fall below the limit. However, if the excess contribution is not withdrawn before the date the return is due, a six percent tax applies.

Contributions may be made for any year before the taxpayer turns 70½ in which either the taxpayer or his or her spouse has compensation (i.e., wages, salary, commissions, self-employment income, etc.). A spouse's compensation can be taken into account only if the couple files a joint return.

Planning Note. A nonrefundable tax credit is available to assist low- and middle-income taxpayers in saving for retirement. The credit is in addition to the usual tax advantages of making contributions to a qualified retirement plan or an IRA. See Tab 10 for more information on the retirement savings contributions credit.

Withdrawals. IRA assets can be withdrawn at any time, though penalties are imposed to discourage early withdrawals. Distributions from a traditional IRA are generally taxable as ordinary income in the year received unless they are rolled over to another retirement arrangement. An additional 10 percent tax generally applies to any withdrawals made before the owner reaches the age of 59½. For 2009, distributions of up to $100,000 made directly to a charitable organization at the direction of the account owner can be excluded from the account owner's income. See Tab 1 for more information

An individual can elect to exclude from income an IRA distribution that is directly rolled over into his or her health savings account (HSA) in a trustee-to-trustee transfer. Generally, an individual is allowed to exclude only one such transfer during his or her lifetime. The dollar amount excluded from income cannot exceed the annual limit on the individual's HSA contribution for the year. If the individual ceases to be eligible to make HSA contributions within the 12 months following the HSA funding distribution, the exclusion is lost and an additional 10 percent tax also applies. The amount transferred is not deductible as an HSA contribution. See Tab 1 for more information.

Distributions from IRAs to which only deductible contributions were made are fully taxable, but distributions from IRAs that include some nondeductible contributions are only partly taxable. The portion of the distribution representing nondeductible contributions (the cost basis) is tax free and is calculated on Form 8606, Nondeductible IRAs.

Distributions representing income earned in a traditional IRA are taxed. Losses from an IRA investment can be recognized only if all the IRA assets have been distributed and their total is less than the unrecovered basis. The loss can be claimed as an itemized deduction on Schedule A, subject to the two-percent of adjusted gross income limit. See MTG ¶2178 for discussion of the taxation of IRA distributions.

Exceptions to the tax on early distributions. The 10 percent additional tax on distributions made before the owner reaches age 59½ does not apply to any withdrawal of contributions that occurs before the original due date of the return for the year in which the contributions were made. The additional tax also does not apply to early distributions if:

- the distributions are not more than the amount of the taxpayer's deductible medical expenses (even if the taxpayer does not itemize deductions);
- the distributions are not more than the cost of medical insurance (in certain unemployment situations);
- the taxpayer is disabled;
- the taxpayer is the beneficiary of a deceased IRA owner;
- the taxpayer is receiving distributions in the form of an annuity;
- the distributions are not more than certain higher education expenses for the taxpayer or the taxpayer's spouse, child or grandchild;
- the distributions (not exceeding $10,000 during the individual's lifetime) are used to buy, build, or rebuild a first home;
- the distribution is due to an IRS levy on the IRA; or
- the distribution was taken, while on active duty, by a reservist called to active duty for more than 179 days after September 11, 2001.

See MTG ¶2179 for discussion of the tax on early distributions from IRAs.

Required minimum distributions. IRA owners who are generally required to take minimum distributions from their accounts beginning April 1 of the calendar year following the year he or she turns 70½ and every year thereafter. The required minimum distribution (RMD) for a given year is determined by dividing the account balance as of the end of the preceding year by the applicable distribution period or life expectancy generally determined in tables in IRS Publication 590, *Individual Retirement Arrangements (IRAs).* See MTG ¶2177 for more information.

A 50 percent excise tax is assessed on amounts not distributed as required. Any distributions exceeding the RMD for a given year may not be credited against the minimum for a later year. RMDs also cannot be rolled over into another qualified plan or IRA. When an individual who is receiving RMDs passes away, the entire RMD for the year of death must still be made.

Planning Note. The minimum distribution rules are waived for calendar year 2009 for IRAs and certain other employer-provided retirement plans. The waiver even applies if an IRA owner turns 70 1/2 in 2009 and delays the 2009 RMD until April 1, 2010. However, it does not apply RMDs for 2008, even if the IRA owner turned 70 1/2 in 2008 and delay the 2008 RMD until April 1, 2009. A beneficiary receiving distributions from an IRA over a required five-year period may waive the distribution for 2009, in essence taking distributions over a six-year period. If an IRA owner or beneficiary received a distribution from an IRA in 2009 that otherwise would have been a RMD, then he or she has 60 days from the date of distribution to roll it over into another IRA or eligible retirement plan.

IRA Facts for 2009		
Attribute	**Traditional IRA**	**Roth IRA**
Age limit on contributions	Taxpayer must not have reached age 70½ by the end of the year.	Any age.
Limit on contributions (if the taxpayer earned more than the dollar limit)	For 2009, a taxpayer can contribute $5,000 ($6,000 if 50 or older by the end of 2009) to his or her traditional and Roth IRAs.	For 2009, a taxpayer may be able to contribute $5,000 ($6,000 if 50 or older by the end of 2009) to a Roth IRA but the amount may be less than that depending on income, filing status, and whether contributions are made to a traditional IRA.
Contributions deductible?	Yes. Contributions to a traditional IRA are deductible, depending on income, filing status, and whether the taxpayer (or his or her spouse) is covered by a retirement plan at work.	No. Contributions to a Roth IRA are never deductible.
Form to file when contributions are made	None, unless nondeductible contributions are made to a traditional IRA. In that case, Form 8606, *Nondeductible IRAs*, must be filed.	None. Although no form must be filed when the taxpayer contributes to a Roth IRA, records of the amount and date of contributions must be kept.
Required distributions	The taxpayer must begin receiving required minimum distributions by April 1 of the year following the year he or she reaches age 70½.	The owner of a Roth IRA is not required to take any distributions regardless of age.
Tax treatment of distributions	Distributions from a traditional IRA are taxed as ordinary income, but if nondeductible contributions were made, not all of the distribution is taxable.	Distributions from a Roth IRA are not taxed as long as certain criteria are met.
Form to file when distributions are received	None, unless nondeductible contributions have been made. In that case file Form 8606.	File Form 8606 when distributions are received from a Roth IRA (other than a rollover, recharacterization, certain qualified distributions, or a return of certain contributions).

Rollovers and Trustee-to-Trustee Transfers. IRA assets are held by a trustee, usually a bank or mutual fund company. The account owner can choose to move IRA assets from one trustee to another. If the transfer of assets is accomplished by a trustee-to-trustee transfer (without a distribution to the account owner), there is no distribution, and no taxable event. If the account owner actually receives a distribution, it will be subject to tax, and possibly to the additional tax on early distributions, unless it is rolled over to another IRA or eligible plan within 60 days. Required distributions cannot be rolled over. Rollover contributions to an IRA or other plan cannot be deducted but must be reported on the return for the tax year in which they occur. See MTG ¶2186 for discussion of rollovers.

IRA-to-IRA rollovers may be made from or moved into a particular IRA only once per year. The time period begins on the date a distribution is received by the account owner. Trustee-to-trustee transfers are not subject to this limitation.

Distributions from any of the following types of arrangements may be rolled over into a traditional or Roth IRA:

- a traditional IRA;
- an employer-provided qualified retirement plan;
- a Section 457 plan (discussed later); or
- a tax-sheltered annuity (Section 403) plan (discussed later).

Distributions from a traditional IRA may be rolled over to any of those types of plans, if the plan allows it. Distributions from a traditional IRA or employer plan may also be contributed to a new or existing Roth IRA account, or all or a portion of a traditional IRA may be converted to a Roth IRA. Such contributions or conversions are not allowed if the taxpayer has adjusted gross income (apart from the amount being moved to a Roth IRA) exceeding $100,000. The taxable portion of the amount converted must be included in income.

Penalties and Additional Taxes. Penalties or additional taxes may be imposed if IRA funds are used for prohibited transactions or if one of the following occurs:

- investment in collectibles;
- excess contributions;
- early withdrawals;
- failure to take required minimum distributions.

Additional taxes on these events are reported on Form 5329.

Prohibited transactions involving a traditional IRA include the following:

- borrowing money from the account;
- selling property to the account;

- receiving unreasonable compensation for managing the account;
- using it as security for a loan; or
- buying property for personal use with IRA funds.

If the account owner or a beneficiary engages in a prohibited transaction with an IRA, the account ceases to be an IRA, and it is treated as if its assets were distributed to the holder of the account.

Types of IRAs (Employee Funded)

Traditional. A traditional IRA is any IRA that is not a Roth IRA or a SIMPLE IRA. See MTG ¶2168 for discussion of traditional IRAs.

Eligibility to Make Contributions–An individual who has compensation (or whose spouse has compensation, if filing a joint return), and has not reached age 70½ by the end of the year is eligible to make contributions to a traditional IRA.

Contribution Limits–For 2009, an eligible individual may contribute the *lesser* of $5,000 ($6,000 if the individual was born before January 1, 1960) *or* an amount equal to the individual's compensation for the tax year to their traditional and/or Roth IRAs. A married couple filing jointly can make IRA contributions on behalf of both spouses, even if one has no compensation for the year. For the lower compensated spouse, the limit is the *smaller* of the dollar limit *or* the total compensation of both spouses, reduced by the traditional and Roth IRA contributions made on behalf of the higher paid spouse.

Phaseout Ranges for Deductible Contributions–Contributions to traditional IRAs are generally deductible. However, the deduction is reduced or eliminated completely for high-income individuals who are covered by an employer's retirement plan or who file jointly with a spouse who is covered by such a plan. The deduction is phased out over a range of modified adjusted gross incomes (MAGI), with different ranges depending on the individual's filing status. For individuals who are not covered by an employer plan, but file jointly with a spouse who is covered, the phaseout range is from MAGI of $166,000 to $176,000 for 2009 and 2010.

Distributions–Distributions from a traditional IRA are taxable as ordinary income, except for the return of nondeductible contributions. Minimum distributions are required once the account owner has died or reached age 70½.

Pre-Retirement Liquidity–The account owner may withdraw amounts from a traditional IRA, but a 10 percent additional tax may be imposed (in addition to the regular income tax). The additional tax is not imposed after age 59½ or if another exception applies.

Roth. A Roth IRA is an IRA that the owner has designated to be a Roth IRA. See MTG ¶2180 for discussion of Roth IRAs.

Eligibility to Make Contributions–An individual who has compensation (or whose spouse has compensation, if filing a joint return) is eligible to make contributions to a Roth IRA. Contributions can be made after age 70½. Eligibility to make Roth IRA contributions is eliminated by a phaseout based on the taxpayer's modified adjusted gross income (MAGI).

Roth IRA Contribution Phaseout Ranges

Filing Status	2009 MAGI	2010 MAGI
MFJ or QW	$166,000-$176,000	$167,000-$177,000
Single, HOH	105,000-120,000	105,000-120,000
MFS	0-10,000	0-10,000

Traditional IRA Deduction Phaseout Ranges

Filing Status	2009 MAGI	2010 MAGI
MFJ or QW	$89,000-$109,000	$89,000-$109,000
Single, HOH	55,000-65,000	56,000-66,000
MFS	0-10,000	0-10,000

Annual Retirement Contribution Limits for Individuals

	2009	2010
IRA contributions	$5,000	$5,000*
Catch-up IRA contributions	1,000	1,000*
Total standard deferrals to 401(k), 403(b), and 501(c)(18) plans, SIMPLEs and SEPs	15,500/10,500	16,500*/11,500*
Standard deferrals to SIMPLEs	10,500	11,500*
Catch-up deferrals to SIMPLE accounts	2,500	2,500*
Catch-up deferrals to 401(k), 403(b) and 457 plans	5,000	5,500*

* Subject to inflation adjustments for later years.

Contribution Limits–For 2009, an eligible individual may contribute the lesser of $5,000 ($6,000 if the individual was born before January 1, 1960) *or* an amount equal to the individual's compensation for the tax year to their traditional and/or Roth IRAs. As with traditional IRAs, joint filers can "share" their compensation.

> **Planning Note.** When a member of the military is killed in action or during training, his survivor may receive a military death gratuity or payment under the Servicemembers' Group Life Insurance Program. The survivor can make a Roth IRA contribution up to the amount of such payments received without regard to the annual limit on contributions or the income-based phaseout of that limit. The contribution must be made within one year of the survivor's receipt of the underlying payment.

Deductibility–Contributions to Roth IRAs are not deductible.

Distributions–Qualified distributions are not taxable. A distribution is qualified if it is made after the five year period beginning with the first tax year for which a contribution was made to a Roth IRA by or on behalf of the taxpayer, and is made:

- on or after the taxpayer attains age 59½;
- because the taxpayer is disabled;
- to the estate or beneficiary of the account owner after his or her death; or
- in compliance with the requirements for the first-time homebuyer exception to the 10 percent additional tax on early distributions.

The minimum distribution requirements do not apply to Roth IRAs while the account owner is alive. Minimum distribution requirements do apply after the account owner's death.

Pre-Retirement Liquidity–Amounts may be withdrawn from a Roth IRA at any time. Qualified distributions are completely excluded from income. Withdrawals that are not qualified are tax free up to the amount of the regular after-tax contributions to the account. Nonqualified withdrawals of earnings may be taxable, and may be subject to the additional 10 percent tax on early withdrawals, which is computed and reported on Form 5329.

Qualified Defined Contribution Plans

General Principles. Qualified defined contribution plans are employer (or union) sponsored retirement plans that provide benefits based on participants' individual account balances. See MTG ¶2103 for discussion of defined contribution plans. The accounts are increased by contributions made by the employer and/or employee. The account balance will also fluctuate depending on investment earnings and fees assessed to the account. If investments perform poorly, the participant's account decreases, and the reverse is true if investments perform well. Therefore, investment risk is borne by the employee.

For 2009 and 2010, the maximum annual addition to a participant's account is the lesser of $49,000 or 100% of the participant's compensation. Annual additions include employer and employee contributions and any forfeitures. Employer contributions and an employee's elective deferrals to a defined contribution plan (such as a 401(k) plan) are generally excluded from the employee's income. For 2009 and 2010 the maximum elective deferral that an employee can make is $16,500 ($22,000 for individuals age 50 or older). The employer's contributions are deductible. However, the employer's deduction is limited to 25 percent of the compensation paid or accrued during the tax year to plan participants.

Penalty for Excess Contributions. Excess contributions to a defined contribution plan may be taxed and penalized. An employer that contributes more to a plan than it can deduct may be permitted to carry over the excess contribution to the next year. However, depending on the circumstances, an excise penalty may also apply.

Excess elective deferrals are not excluded from the employee's income, and are subject to tax again upon distribution. Excess deferrals by an employee should be returned to the employee by April 15 of the tax year immediately following the year in which the deferral is made. If excess deferrals are not properly returned to participants, the plan's tax-favored status may be jeopardized. Excess contributions on behalf of highly compensated employees will subject the employer to a 10 percent excise tax.

Setup and Administration. A defined contribution plan is generally sponsored by an employer. The employer must comply with the Employee Retirement Income Security Act of 1974 (ERISA) and the Internal Revenue Code in order to maintain a retirement plan. Plan design requirements are very complicated (e.g., eligibility requirements, employer contributions, vesting requirements, funding obligations). See MTG ¶2117 and following paragraphs. The employer must ensure the plan is administered in a manner consistent with regulations issued by the Internal Revenue Service and the Department of Labor.

A tax credit may be available for certain start-up costs associated with creation of a new plan. The small employer pension start-up cost credit is an amount equal to 50 percent of the qualified start-up costs paid or incurred by the taxpayer during the taxable year. The credit may not exceed $500 for the first credit year and each of the two tax years immediately following the first credit year, and is not available for any other tax year. A small employer is defined as one that had no more than 100 employees who received at least $5,000 of compensation from the employer for the preceding year. A qualified start-up cost is an ordinary and necessary expense of an employer that is paid or incurred in connection with the establishment or administration of an employer plan or the retirement-related education of employees with respect to such a plan. See MTG ¶1365U for discussion of the credit.

Types of Defined Contribution Plans

SEP IRA. A simplified employee pension (SEP) plan allows a small employer to contribute to employees' IRAs without setting up a profit-sharing or other type of qualified plan. Contributions must be made on behalf of every eligible employee. This includes any individual who is 21 years old, has been employed by the employer during at least three of the last five years, and receives at least $550 in compensation from the employer during the year (for 2009 and 2010). Employers are permitted to contribute to the SEP the lesser of 25 percent of an employee's compensation or $49,000 (for 2009 and 2010). See MTG ¶2184 for discussion of SEPs.

Pre-Retirement Liquidity. Withdrawals are permitted prior to retirement to the extent allowed under the IRA rules. In addition, the 10 percent additional tax is imposed on certain early withdrawals.

Caution. Since contribution limits apply to all retirement plan contributions, employers should require employees to certify that they will disclose their participation in any other qualified retirement plans.

SIMPLE IRA. A savings incentive match plan for employees (SIMPLE) IRA may be sponsored by an employer that employs fewer than 100 employees (regardless of their eligibility to participate in the plan) who received $5,000 or more in compensation for the preceding plan year, and that does not sponsor any other qualified plans (except for collective bargaining plans) from the start-up year of the SIMPLE plan. Any employee who received at least $5,000 in compensation during any two earlier years and is reasonably expected to receive $5,000 in the current calendar year is eligible to participate. An employer sponsoring a SIMPLE IRA plan can choose to impose less restrictive eligibility requirements. See MTG ¶2185 for discussion of SIMPLEs.

Contribution Limits. Under a SIMPLE IRA plan, employees are allowed to make elective deferrals, and the employer must make either matching contributions on behalf of employees who make deferrals or nonelective contributions on behalf of all employees. Elective deferrals under a SIMPLE IRA are limited to $11,500 for 2009 and 2010 ($14,000 for employees age 50 orolder). Employers generally must make either matching contributions of up to three percent of an employee's compensation, or fixed nonelective contributions equal to two percent of each eligible employee's compensation.

Pre-Retirement Liquidity. Withdrawals are permitted prior to retirement to the extent allowed under the IRA rules. However, the 10 percent additional tax is imposed on certain early withdrawals and the 10 percent rate is increased to 25 percent for withdrawals made within the first two years of plan participation.

401(k) Plan. Employers, including self-employed individuals, can set up 401(k) plans. Employees will be permitted to participate in the plan according to the plan's written document. The plan will also be required to provide for protection of plan assets (e.g., via a trust document, annuity, etc.). A 401(k) plan allows eligible employees to make elective deferrals of salary. The amounts deferred are excluded from the employees' incomes. A 401(k) plan may also allow participants to treat all or a portion of their contributions as designated Roth contributions. Designated Roth contributions are included in the employee's current income, but qualified distributions of such contributions and the income on them are excluded from income. See MTG ¶2108 for discussion of 401(k) plans.

Contribution Limits. For 2009 and 2010, participants are limited to contributing $16,500 ($22,000 for employees age 50 or older) to their 401(k) accounts. Contributions in excess of the annual limit are included in the employee's income, but may be withdrawn before April 15 of the year following the year they were included as income. A 10-percent additional tax is imposed on the employer for excess contributions, unless the excess is recharacterized or distributed within two months following the applicable plan year. In addition, the employer is free to make matching contributions that are not subject to the annual limit on elective deferrals. Matching contributions and elective deferrals are subject to special discrimination tests.

Pre-Retirement Liquidity. In-service withdrawals are permitted, but are included in gross income and subject to the additional 10 percent tax if the withdrawal occurs prior to the participant's reaching age 59½. The 10-percent additional tax does not apply if the participant has separated from service after reaching age 55. Loans may also be permitted, depending on provisions of the plan document.

Section 457 Plan. An employer that is a state or local government or nongovernmental tax-exempt entity may sponsor a Section 457 plan under which participants may defer part of their compensation. See MTG ¶2197B for discussion of Section 457 plans.

Contribution Limits. For 2009 and 2010, participants are allowed to contribute the lesser of 100 percent of includible compensation or $16,500 ($22,000 for participants age 50 or older). Additional catch-up contributions calculated under a special formula are permitted for each of the last three years ending before the participant reaches normal retirement age under the plan.

Distributions. Amounts deferred under a Section 457 plan must not be distributed before the calendar year in which the participant turns 70½, is severed from employment, or is faced with an unforeseen emergency. Distributions before age 59½ are normally subject to the same 10-percent additional tax as early distributions from 401(k) plans. However, the exclusion for distributions after severance from employment after age 55 is expanded to cover distributions from governmental plans to former public safety officers (police officers, firefighters, and emergency medical services technicians) who separate from service after attaining age 50. Also, a retired public safety officer may elect to have up to $3,000 deducted from distributions from a government plan and paid directly to an insurance company or self-insured plan for health insurance without such amounts excluded from income.

403(b) Plan. Certain nonprofit entities [e.g., public schools, colleges, universities, churches, public hospitals, or IRC §501(c)(3) entities] are permitted to sponsor 403(b) tax-sheltered annuity plans. See MTG ¶2167 for discussion of Section 403(b) plans.

Contribution Limits. The annual additions that may be made to an employee's 403(b) account are limited. Annual additions include elective contributions by the employee, nonelective contributions by the employer, and after-tax contributions by the employee. For 2009 and 2010, the annual addition cannot exceed the lesser of $49,000 or 100 percent of the employee's compensation.

For 2009 and 2010, an employee's elective deferrals are limited to $16,500 ($22,000 for employees age 50 or older). All of an individual's elective deferrals under any 401(k) plan, SIMPLE, SEP or 403(b) plan are combined and compared against this limit. See IRS Publication 571, *Tax-Sheltered Annuity Plans (403(b) Plans).*

Pre-Retirement Liquidity. Generally, distributions are not permitted until the employee attains age 59½, severs from employment, dies or becomes disabled. Elective deferral amounts may be distributable upon financial hardship.

Money Purchase Plans. Money purchase plans involve mandatory employer contributions that are set by the plan document. Employers, including self-employed individuals, can set up a money purchase plan. Employees will be permitted to participate in the plan according to the plan's written document. The plan will also be required to provide protection of plan assets (e.g., through a trust document, annuity, etc.). See MTG ¶2106 for discussion of money purchase plans.

Contribution Limits. For 2009 and 2010, employer contributions to a money purchase plan are limited to the lesser of $49,000 or 100 percent of a participant's compensation.

Pre-Retirement Liquidity. In-service withdrawals are permitted, but are included in gross income and subject to the 10-percent additional tax if the withdrawal occurs prior to the participant's reaching age 59½. The 10-percent additional tax does not apply if the participant has separated from service after reaching age 55. Loans may also be permitted, depending on the plan document.

Caution. Due to the mandatory nature of the employer contributions, certain funding requirements must be satisfied for money purchase plans.

Profit-Sharing Plans. Profit-sharing plans are defined contribution plans funded by discretionary employer contributions. Employees will be permitted to participate in the plan according to the plan's written document. The plan will also be required to provide protection of plan assets (e.g., by means of a trust document, annuity, etc.). See MTG ¶2105 for discussion of profit-sharing plans.

Contribution Limits. For 2009 and 2010, the maximum annual additions to a profit sharing plan on account of a particular employee are limited to the lesser of $49,000 or 100 percent of the participant's compensation. Annual additions include both employer and employee contributions and any forfeitures. Employer contributions must be allocated to employees according to a specific written formula. The employer's contributions are deductible. However, the deduction is limited to 25 percent of the compensation paid or accrued during the tax year to plan participants.

Pre-Retirement Liquidity. In-service withdrawals are permitted, but are included in gross income and subject to the 10-percent additional tax if the withdrawal occurs prior to the participant's reaching age 59½. The 10-percent additional tax does not apply if the participant has separated from service after reaching age 55. Loans may also be permitted, depending on the plan document.

Qualified Defined Benefit Plans

Defined benefit plans are retirement plans that do not maintain individual accounts for each participant. Instead, benefits are calculated based on the plan's for-

KEY FACTS: Retirement Plans Side by Side

Comparison of Features	SEP IRA	SIMPLE IRA	Profit-Sharing Plan	401(k) (pre-tax and Roth)	Defined Benefit Plan
Eligibility	Anyone with SE income, or employee 21 or over with income >$550 for 2009 and 2010	Employer must have <100 employees and no other retirement programs; must be offered to all employees who earn >$5,000	Plan can restrict participation to employees at least 21 with one year of service	Plan can restrict participation to employees at least 21 with one year of service	Plan can restrict participation to employees at least 21 with one year of service
Maximum employee contribution (for 2009 and 2010	N/A; note that SEP IRAs do not count against individual IRA limits	Lesser of $11,500 or earned income; catch-up (over 50), $2,500	N/A	$16,500; catch-up (over 50), $5,500	N/A
Maximum employer contribution	25% of wages up to $49,000, or 20% of SE net income	(a) 2% of compensation (for all employees) or (b) matching contribution up to 3% for employees making a deferral contribution	Lesser of $49,000 or 100% of compensation; deduction limit, 25% of total compensation of participants	Employer/employee total: Lesser of 25% of compensation or $49,000	Actuarially determined (annual benefit promised cannot exceed $195,000)
Penalties for early withdrawal	10%	10% (25% if in first 2 years of program)	10%	10%	10%
Penalties for excess contributions	6% SE and employees; 10% employers	10%	10%	10% if not distributed within 2.5 months after end of year	10%
When withdrawals must begin	70½ (but contributions can still be made if there is earned income)	70½ (but contributions can still be made if there is earned income)	70½ or year of retirement, whichever is later	70½ or year of retirement, whichever is later	70½ or year of retirement, whichever is later

Qualified distributions from each of these plans generally can be rolled over into IRAs or qualified employer plans. In addition, a 401(k) can be rolled into another employer's 401(k).

Key Facts: Principal Characteristics of IRAs and 401(k)s

<table>
<tr><th rowspan="2">Characteristic</th><th rowspan="2">Traditional IRA</th><th rowspan="2">Roth IRA</th><th colspan="2">401(k)</th></tr>
<tr><th>Traditional</th><th>Roth</th></tr>
<tr><td>Age Limitations on Contributions or Participation</td><td>No contributions allowed if participant will be 70½ by year-end</td><td>No age requirement for ending contributions</td><td colspan="2">Plan may impose minimum age and service requirements (up to age 21 and 1 year of service) for participation. Contributions may continue as long as participant is employed.</td></tr>
<tr><td>Due Date of Contributions</td><td>April 15th of following year</td><td>April 15th of following year</td><td>Employer must deposit deferred amounts as soon as is reasonably possible, and not later than the 15th day of the following month.</td><td></td></tr>
<tr><td>Deductibility of Contributions</td><td>Full deduction available in current year unless individual participates in employer-sponsored retirement plan
If participating in employer plan, deduction for 2008 contributions phases out for modified AGI:
S, HOH $55,000-65,000
MFJ, QW $89,000-109,000
MFS $0 -10,000</td><td>Contributions are not deductible</td><td>Elective deferrals are excluded from income</td><td>Designated Roth contributions are included in income</td></tr>
<tr><td>Taxability of Distributions</td><td>Distributions taxable</td><td>Qualified distributions nontaxable</td><td colspan="2">Distributions taxable
Qualified distributions nontaxable</td></tr>
<tr><td>Contribution Limits for 2009</td><td>Lesser of taxable compensation and $5,000 for those under age 50 or $6,000 for those age 50 or over</td><td>Contribution limits same as for traditional IRA
AGI phaseouts for contributions
S, HOH $105,000 120,000
MFJ, QW $166,000 176,000
MFS $0 10,000</td><td colspan="2">Total elective contributions capped at $16,500, or $22,000 for those age 50 or over. Employer deduction cannot exceed 25% of all compensation. Total contributions cannot exceed 100% of wages up to $49,000.</td></tr>
<tr><td>Distributions Permitted</td><td>Distributions permitted without penalty:
• After participant turns 59½
• At death or disability
• For qualified college costs
• For qualified medical costs exceeding 7.5% of AGI
• For qualified first-time home buyers
• Distributions in the form of an annuity</td><td>Return of basis always tax free.
Distributions made after five years of participation are qualified (tax-free) if made:
• After participant turns 59½
• At death or disability
• For qualified first-time home buyers</td><td colspan="2">Distributions permitted without penalty:
• After participant turns 59½
• At death or disability
• After severance from employment after age 55
Hardship distributions from a traditional 401(k) are subject to income tax and the penalty for early withdrawals unless an exception applies. Hardship distributions from a designated Roth account are qualified (and excluded from income) if made after five years of participation and after participant turns 59½ or becomes disabled.</td></tr>
<tr><td>Distributions Required</td><td>Distributions must begin by April 1 following the year participant turns 70½</td><td>Distributions required only at death of participant</td><td colspan="2">Withdrawals required to begin at later of age 70½ or retirement</td></tr>
<tr><td>Penalty for Early Withdrawal</td><td>10% penalty on nonqualified distributions</td><td>10% penalty for withdrawal before age 59½</td><td>10% penalty for withdrawal before age 59½ or for failure to distribute excess within 2½ months after close of plan year</td><td></td></tr>
<tr><td>Rollovers</td><td>Rollover into another IRA or an employer plan permitted. Rollover into Roth IRA requires income recognition</td><td>Rollover to another Roth IRA permitted</td><td>Rollover to IRA or another employer plan permitted. Rollover into Roth IRA requires income recognition</td><td>Rollover to a Roth IRA or other employer Roth 401(k) permitted in some circumstances</td></tr>
</table>

What Retirement Plan Rollovers Are Allowed in 2009

ROLL FROM:	ROLL TO: IRA	SEP-IRA	SIMPLE IRA	Roth IRA	457(b)	403(b)	Qualified plan	Designated Roth Account (Roth 401(k))
IRA	Yes	Yes	No	Yes, but must be included in income.	Yes, if destination 457(b) has separate accounts.	Yes	Yes	No
SEP-IRA	Yes	Yes	No	Yes, but must be included in income.	Yes, if destination 457(b) has separate accounts.	Yes	Yes	No
SIMPLE IRA	Yes, after two years of participation.	Yes, after two years of participation.	Yes	Yes, after two years of participation. Must be included in income.	Yes, after two years of participation. Destination 457(b) must have separate accounts.	Yes, after two years of participation.	Yes, after two years of participation.	No
Roth IRA	No	No	No	Yes	No	No	No	No
457(b)	Yes	Yes	No	Yes. Must be included in income.	Yes	Yes	Yes	No
403(b)	Yes	Yes	No	Yes. Must be included in income.	Yes, if destination 457(b) has separate accounts.	Yes	Yes	No
Qualified plan	Yes	Yes	No	Yes. Must be included in income.	Yes, if destination 457(b) has separate accounts.	Yes	Yes	No
Designated Roth Account (Roth 401(k))	No	No	No	Yes	No	No	No	Yes, via direct trustee-to-trustee transfer only.

mula, and usually take the form of a monthly pension based on the employee's wages and years of service. Employers are required to contribute to the plan based on actuarial calculations of the amount necessary to fund the promised benefits. If investment returns are poor, the employer must contribute an increased amount to the trust to maintain the proper level of funding. However, if market returns are better than expected, the employer reaps the reward and may contribute less to maintain the proper level of funding. Therefore, unlike the defined contribution plans, the employer bears the investment risk associated with defined benefit plans. See MTG ¶2103 for discussion of defined benefit plans.

Defined benefit plans vary in plan design. Participants should carefully review the plan's summary description and ask for clarification by the plan administrator where needed.

Social Security and Railroad Retirement. See discussion above and IRS Publication 915, *Social Security and Equivalent Railroad Retirement Benefits*, for information regarding taxation of these benefits.

Civil Service. See IRS Publication 721, *Tax Guide to U.S. Civil Service Retirement Benefits*, for information regarding taxation of these benefits.

412(i) Plans. Defined benefit plans that are fully insured and funded are Section 412(i) plans. These plans must be fully guaranteed by insurance products and are eligible for greater tax deductions than other defined benefit plans.

Caution. How retirement plans interact when you are participating in more than one plan must be examined. Be aware of overall contribution limits.

Planning Tip. Retirement planning for one's spouse as a Schedule C employee may be advantageous.

Pension and Retirement Plan Income

Taxable Distributions

Distributions received from traditional IRAs, qualified retirement plans, or nonqualified plans (including annuities) are taxable to the extent they have not been previously taxed. For example, if nondeductible contributions have been made to an IRA, the taxpayer will need to calculate the taxable portion of distributions from the account. The taxpayer will be responsible for paying taxes only on the amount of the distribution that has not been previously taxed. Specifically, the taxable portion of the distribution will include any before-tax contributions and earnings on before- or after-tax contributions.

Taxation of Annuity Benefits. If the taxpayer has no basis in a periodic distribution from a retirement plan (an annuity), the entire amount of each payment is taxable. If the taxpayer has a basis in a periodic distribution, a portion of that basis is recovered in each payment, determined under either the "simplified method" or the "general rule." The appropriate method is set at the time payments begin and cannot be changed.

The simplified method must be used if the payments are from a qualified plan or tax-sheltered annuity if the annuity starting date is after November 18, 1996, and on that date the recipient was under age 75 or was entitled to less than five years of guaranteed payments. Under this method, the nontaxable portion of a distribution is calculated by dividing the cost by the expected number of payments. The expectation is based on either the lifetime of the recipient (in which case life expectancy tables are used) or the set number of payments for the annuity. The instructions to Form 1040 include a worksheet for using the simplified method. The worksheet is reproduced at page 9-42.

Individuals with annuity starting dates before November 19, 1996, but after July 1, 1986, had the option to choose either the simplified method or the general rule if they met the requirements for the simplified method described above and the annuity was payable for life (or for the lives of the annuitant and one survivor). The taxable portion of other types of distributions, most notably distributions from nonqualified plans, is determined under the general rule.

The general rule calculates the nontaxable portion of each payment by dividing the cost by the total expected return, and multiplying that by the amount of each payment. Examples of this calculation are provided in IRS Publication 939, *General Rule for Pensions and Annuities.*

Taxation of Nonperiodic Payments. A nonperiodic distribution (any distribution other than an annuity payment) must be taxed when distributed unless some portion of the distribution has already been taxed. A nonperiodic distribution received after annuity payments have started will be treated as fully taxable unless it results in a reduction of the annuity payments received. A nonperiodic distribution received before annuity payments have begun is treated as a pro rata return of capital.

Generally, taxable lump-sum distributions are treated as ordinary income and taxed at ordinary income tax rates. However, certain older taxpayers may be eligible to tax a portion of their distributions at capital gains tax rates and may employ a 10-year tax option on the portion of the distribution not taxed at capital gains rates. This optional method is available only to taxpayers born before January 2, 1936. See MTG ¶2155 for discussion of the 10-year tax option. In addition, certain distributions will not qualify for the optional method treatment, regardless of the taxpayer's date of birth. For a list of such distributions, see IRS Publication 575, *Pension and Annuity Income.* If the optional method is elected, the taxpayer must use Form 4972, *Tax on Lump-Sum Distributions,* to report the distributions. Form 4972 should be completed and attached to the taxpayer's Form 1040 or 1040A.

If a taxpayer's entire cost is not recovered before his or her benefit is fully distributed, the taxpayer may claim the loss on his or her tax return. However, the loss may be recouped only if the taxpayer itemizes deductions. The loss should be reported on the taxpayer's Schedule A as a miscellaneous deduction.

Required Minimum Distributions. Taxpayers must generally begin receiving minimum distributions from traditional IRAs and other retirement plans by April 1 of the year that follows the later of year of the taxpayer's retirement from the employer maintaining the plan or the year the taxpayer reaches age 70½. Required minimum distributions (RMDs) are subject to the general rules for taxation of distributions.

> **Planning Note.** The minimum distribution rules are waived for calendar year 2009 for IRAs and certain other employer-provided retirement plans. The waiver even applies if an IRA owner turns 70 1/2 in 2009 and delays the 2009 RMD until April 1, 2010. However, it does not apply RMDs for 2008, even if the employee turned 70 1/2 in 2008 and delay the 2008 RMD until April 1, 2009. A beneficiary receiving distributions from a retirement plan over a required five-year period may waive the distribution for 2009, in essence taking distributions over a six-year period. If the employee or beneficiary received a distribution from an reitrement plan in 2009 that otherwise would have been a RMD, then he or she has 60 days from the date of distribution to roll it over into another IRA or eligible retirement plan.

Divorce Issues and QDROs. Qualified domestic relations orders (QDROs) are court orders instructing a retirement plan to assign a plan participant's retirement benefits to an alternate payee. Generally, ERISA preempts state law interference with qualified retirement plans; however, if a court order qualifies as a QDRO, the plan must comply with the order. ERISA and the Internal Revenue Code have specific requirements regarding the qualifications for a QDRO. The specificity is intended to ensure that the plan has clear directions regarding whom to pay benefits to and how much of the participant's benefit should be directed to that alternate payee. Distributions to a spouse or former spouse under a QDRO are taxable to the alternate payee who receives them, and not to the employee. A distribution to a child or other dependent under a QDRO is taxable to the employee. For further discussion of QDROs, see Tab 13 and MTG ¶2166.

Financial Planning

The Financial Planning Process

Careful financial planning allows people to anticipate opportunities, prepare for contingencies, and navigate competently through the life stages of education, employment, marriage and divorce, home ownership, parenting, eldercare, retirement, and ultimately death. Wherever a person is in life, the financial planning process includes several basic steps:

- taking an inventory of current assets, income, expenditures, debt, and existing planning documents;
- identifing and quantify goals;
- determining a path that will meet these goals;
- implementing the plan, and
- review and revising the plan as necessary and as circumstances change.

A simple financial planning system will take anyone through these basic steps.

Starting Point

Financial planning primarily focuses on the future, but knowledge of one's financial past and the present circumstances it has produced is critical for effective planning.

Inventory of Assets and Liabilities. The first step in determining a financial planning starting point is to create an organized list of current assets and liabilities. The list of assets need not be the type of detailed, whole-house inventory that might be done in connection with a homeowner's or renter's insurance policy (though it is a good idea to have that as well). It is simply a list of all major assets, indicating the date acquired, purchase price, current value, and what income (if any) they generate. The emphasis of this list is on investments, that is, assets that are held with a view to their likely appreciation in value (such as real estate or collectible coins or stamps) and/or generation of income (such as stocks or bonds). Married couples should also note whether each asset is owned by one spouse or jointly.

Similarly, the list of liabilities should include a brief description of each liability, including to whom the debt is owed, when it was incurred, the interest rate, the amount of the unpaid balance, the amount of each payment and the frequency of payments (such as monthly), the date when the debt is expected to be completely repaid, and, if the debt is secured, the security or collateral (such as a house or car).

Net worth is the sum of assets less the sum of liabilities. If liabilities are more than assets, net worth is negative. Individuals may use the personal financial statement on page 9-38 to account for their current financial situation.

Assemble Current Documents

Existing legal documents and arrangements will have an effect on future financial plans. Documents such as wills, trusts, business contracts, and alimony agreements are an important part of the snapshot of any current financial situation. Some of these arrangements may be readily changeable, such as wills, trusts, and powers of attorney. Others, such as contracts and marriage dissolution agreements, may be difficult or impossible to amend. Still others can be changed for a fee, such as variable annuities, or mortgages that can be refinanced.

Existing legal arrangements have an impact on the current cash flow situation and also affect the types of choices available. The following are some of the legal documents that must be taken into consideration wherever they would be relevant to life planning, investments, and estate planning:

- marriage dissolution agreements, including alimony, property settlements, prenuptial agreements, and child support agreements;
- business organization documents and materials for the self-employed;
- business transfer/continuation agreements and plans, including insurance policies;
- contracts;
- wills and trusts;
- property tax records, including information about jointly owned property;
- evidence of gifts of money or property worth more than $10,000 to individuals or charitable organizations;
- insurance policies;
- living wills;
- powers of attorney; and
- tax returns.

Setting Goals

To create a workable personal financial plan and follow through long enough to reap the benefits, it is important to identify personal financial goals. Goal setting is important because it identifies the correct financial direction and provides a way to measure progress. Goals must meet certain criteria to be useful for financial planning:

- list several goals and clearly prioritize them;
- have some goals that are short term and some that are long term;
- goals must be realistic; if they are too easy to achieve, little benefit is gained; if they are so difficult that they are practically impossible to reach, sticking with the plan will be difficult;
- concrete images motivate people emotionally; envisioning a goal is important for creating the drive to make financial sacrifices;
- goals must be measurable; in order to make progress measurable, reduce the goal to a monetary amount and set a deadline to reach the goal.

Build a Budget

A personal budget is a tool to help individuals reach their personal financial goals. It is intended to be an organized way to compare income and expenditures over a relatively short time frame (often one month or one year), and to forecast income and expenses, monitor progress, and make changes as needed to achieve stated goals.

A personal budget provides a detailed picture of how money comes in and how it is spent. Be sure to include income fluctuations, especially if any income is from self-employment.

Keeping track of all expenditures–no matter how small–is the key to effective budgeting. The best way to do this is to track payments shown in checkbooks and on credit card statements for the last six months or so, to determine how much is spent each month in various categories of expenses. To account for out-of-pocket cash expenses, it may make sense to record actual expenses for a week or more and compare these amounts to cash withdrawals. The following general categories should be considered:

- **Housing.** For most people, housing expenses are the major drain on their finances. This category includes all housing-related expenses: rent, mortgage payments, utilities (gas, water, electricity), telephone, garbage disposal, property taxes, home maintenance and repairs, and furnishings.
- **Taxes.** This includes federal, state, and local taxes on income and property, including employment taxes.
- **Food.** This includes grocery purchases, beverage purchases (alcoholic and nonalcoholic), and restaurant costs.

- **Clothing.** Annualize costs.
- **Support of children and other relatives.** These expenses can be included in other categories, if paid in conjunction with those personal expenses.

- **Entertainment.** These costs are often individually small, but can add up over a month's or year's time.
- **Transportation.** Given the increasing cost of gas, these expenses are a big chunk of most people's budget. Other costs to factor in are car payments; vehicle modifications due to physical handicap; car repairs; licenses, registration, and fees; tolls; parking; and public transportation.

- **Personal care.** This category includes the costs of personal grooming items, cosmetics, haircuts, manicures, facials, pedicures, mud baths, and body wraps.
- **Health care.** These costs cover everything from routine medical and dental check-ups, glasses, and prescription and nonprescription medicines to major surgery.

- **Insurance.** Include the various forms of personal insurance. Usually, this includes health, auto, home, life, and disability insurance.
- **Debt.** Payment toward credit cards and other debt not included in other categories must be included in the overall budget.
- **Gifts.** Charitable donations and gifts to family members should be included in budget planning.

- **Retirement savings.** Include individual accounts and amounts withheld by an employer.
- **Savings (other than for retirement).** This category should not be considered "leftover;" pay yourself first.
- **Miscellaneous.** The specific categories probably cover most major expenses. However, there may be other expenses to consider.

A personal budget can be used to match income with expenses to clearly show what needs cutting back, or where increases must be made. An interactive electronic budget is easier to use and provides more useful information than a budget done on paper. It is also easier to update and saves time.

Fundamentals of Financial Planning

Time Value of Money

The time value of money is the foundation of all financial planning. A dollar received today is worth more than a dollar to be received at some point in the future, because today's dollar can earn interest starting now (and inflation has not eroded the value of today's dollar). A variety of financial calculators are available that help with the understanding and use of this important concept.

Compounding Interest. The two most common methods of calculating interest are the simple interest and compound interest formulas. Simple interest is based on the amount borrowed (the principal), the interest rate, and the amount of time for which the principal is borrowed. The formula used to find simple interest is

$$\text{Interest} = \text{Principal} \times \begin{array}{c}\text{Rate of}\\ \text{Interest}\end{array} \times \begin{array}{c}\text{Amount of time}\\ \text{the loan}\\ \text{is outstanding}\end{array}$$

or $I = P \times R \times t$. The future repayment amount is the principal plus interest, so $F = P \times (1 + Rt)$.

Unlike simple interest, compound interest calculates interest not only on the principal, but also on all interest already accrued. The formula for calculating compound interest is

$$\begin{array}{c}\text{Future Repayment}\\ \text{value}\end{array} = \text{Principal} \times \left(1 + \begin{array}{c}\text{Rate of}\\ \text{interest}\end{array}\right)^{\text{amount of time}}$$

or

$$F = P \times (1 + R)^{t}$$

Most consumer loans use monthly or even daily compounding. The interest rate used in the calculation must be the rate for the period of compounding, and the time must be in the same units.

Example. Adam borrows $1,000 at 10 percent simple annual interest and repays it in one lump sum at the end of three years. He will pay interest of $1,000 × 0.10 × 3 = $300 in addition to the principal, for a total payment due of $1,300.

Suppose instead Adam borrows $1,000 at 10% interest, compounded monthly, and repays it in one lump sum at the end of three years. To find the amount that must be repaid, he first converts the 10 percent annual interest rate into a monthly interest rate: 0.10/12 = 0.00833

Plugging this number into the formula yields

$$\begin{aligned} F &= \$1{,}000 \times (1 + .00833)^{36} \\ &= \$1{,}000 \times (1.00833)^{36} \\ &= \$1{,}000 \times (1.34802) \\ &= \$1{,}348.02 \end{aligned}$$

The monthly compounding added $48.02 to the cost of the loan.

Discounting. The time value of money is a two-way street. Discounting is based on the premise that a future dollar is worth less in today's terms. Discounting is a way of expressing the loss of interest income and/or erosion by inflation that occurs before money is received at some future time. Discount rates can be determined by using a financial calculator or from standard tables.

The following table gives the present value of $1 at various interest rates if it is to be received after a given number of years.

Net Present Value of a Dollar

Number of Years	9.0%	9.5%	10.0%	10.5%
1	$0.917431	$0.913242	$0.909091	$0.904977
2	0.841680	0.834011	0.826446	0.818984
3	0.772183	0.761654	0.751315	0.741162
4	0.708425	0.695574	0.683013	0.670735
5	0.649931	0.635228	0.620921	0.607000
6	0.596267	0.580117	0.564474	0.549321
7	0.547034	0.529787	0.513158	0.497123
8	0.501866	0.483824	0.466507	0.449885
9	0.460428	0.441848	0.424098	0.407136
10	0.422411	0.403514	0.385543	0.368449
11	0.387533	0.368506	0.350494	0.333438
12	0.355535	0.336535	0.318631	0.301754

Example. Erica is designing a building for a big client who wants her to agree to wait for payment of her fees until the building is built and rented out. The client needs five years for this. If Erica expects to earn 10 percent interest on her money, she would use the 10 percent column of the Present Value table and find the value of $1 in the 5-year row. Since the payment in five years is worth only 62 cents, she chooses to charge a higher fee for this delayed-payment scenario.

Opportunity Costs. Opportunity cost is the cost of choosing one use of money over another. Spending money on a party rather than investing it in a CD yielding four percent has an opportunity cost of four percent. There are also other, less obvious and more difficult-to-calculate opportunity costs.

Other opportunity costs include failure to use available sources of money, such as life insurance cash value and low-interest loans. However, opportunity cost is not the only factor to consider in saving money. The security of the investment and the risk of unguaranteed returns are also relevant considerations.

Example. Alice has decided that she will need to replace her current automobile in about two years. Moreover, anticipated changes in her lifestyle are going to dictate the need for a roomier vehicle capable of carrying more people and their things. Alice has chosen a vehicle that will probably cost $25,000 two years from now. Alice wants to pay for her new auto outright, instead of over time through a loan.

Alice has $60,000 in a secure low-interest savings account paying 3.5 percent annually, but feels uncomfortable liquidating any more than one-third of her account for the new vehicle. So she decides to move some money into a higher-interest investment to make up the shortfall in savings. She puts $20,000 into a mutual fund that ends up yielding 11.5 percent each of those two years, yielding a final value of $24,864.50. Had she left her $20,000 car purchase allowance in the savings account, she would have only $21,424.50 to spend on her new vehicle. If Alice had left the money where it was, her opportunity cost in terms of the annual interest rate would have been eight percent (11.5 – 3.5). In terms of dollars, her opportunity cost for doing nothing would have been $3,440.

Inflation

It is easy to overlook inflation when planning one's financial future. An inflation rate of four percent might not seem like much, but its effect on the purchasing power of money over the long term is substantial. Over 20 years, four percent inflation annually would drive the value of a dollar down to $0.44.

Factors for inflation rate calculations are provided in the table below. Multiply the amount of money at issue by an inflation factor from the table corresponding to the expected inflation rate and the number of years. For example, to have the same buying power as $1,000 today, $1,280 will be needed five years from now, assuming a five percent inflation rate ($1,000 × 1.28).

Inflation Factors for Selected Annual Inflation Rates over a Number of Years			
Years	3% Inflation Rate	4% Inflation Rate	5% Inflation Rate
5	1.16	1.22	1.28
10	1.34	1.48	1.63
15	1.56	1.80	2.08
20	1.81	2.19	2.65
25	2.09	2.67	3.39
30	2.43	3.24	4.32
35	2.81	3.95	5.52
40	3.26	4.80	7.04

Procrastination Is Expensive

Compounding of interest makes early action the key to sound financial planning. Consider two 30-year-old individuals with different attitudes toward saving for retirement. One begins to save $100 per month, earning eight percent interest, compounded monthly. The other postpones saving until age 40. Even if the early saver stops contributing to his retirement nest egg after 10 years, he will have one and one-half times as much at age 65 as the procrastinator. It is never too early to start saving, and the bigger the goal, the more time is likely needed to achieve it.

Comparison of Early and Late Start—Savings of $100 per Month (8% Interest)				
	Saves $100 per Month Starting at Age 30		Saves $100 per Month Starts Saving at Age 40	
Age	Contributions	Balance	Contributions	Balance
31	$ 1,200	$ 1,253	$ 0	$ 0
35	4,800	7,397	0	0
40	6,000	18,417	0	0
41	0	19,946	1,200	1,253
45	0	27,438	4,800	7,397
50	0	40,879	6,000	18,417
55	0	60,904	6,000	34,835
60	0	90,737	6,000	59,295
65	0	135,184	6,000	95,737
Total invested	$12,000		$24,000	

Monthly Savings to Accumulate $100,000	
Number of Years of Savings	Monthly Savings Required to Accumulate $100,000 (8% interest)
10	$550
20	170
30	70
40	30

Risk Tolerance

In implementing an investment plan, the first factor to consider is the risk level. Generally speaking, the riskier an investment is, the higher its expected return will have to be in order to entice investors. Factors affecting risk tolerance include the individual's family situation, age, business or employment situation, debt and liquidity, insurance, and emotional factors. Changes in any of these areas should be considered whenever the plan is updated.

Investments

Investing always involves forecasting the future. It is never possible to guarantee that predicted events will occur or that unexpected setbacks will not, but with more information, risk can be evaluated and kept within limits.

Requirements

Certain basic financial needs should be met before other investment strategies can be implemented:

- stable income (from employment, self-employment, or other sources);
- an emergency savings fund sufficient to cover three to six months of living expenses;
- a budget and financial plan; and
- adequate insurance coverage.

Diversification

A general rule is that a diversified group of investment holdings is the best protection against investment disaster. A diversified investment portfolio is another way of managing risk–having several kinds of investments, such as stocks, bonds (government and corporate), real estate, and precious metals greatly reduces the chance that a particular economic or legal change will devastate one's entire investment fund.

A diversified portfolio requires knowledge of the various investment vehicles. The different types of investments available include bank accounts, stocks, bonds, mutual funds, investments for education, real estate, and insurance. It is important to understand the basics about the types of investments available and to carefully investigate the options to achieve the best result.

Dollar-Cost Averaging. Dollar-cost averaging, that is, investing a specific amount of money in a specific mutual fund or stock on a regular schedule (usually monthly), is a method of diversifying by time. A good example of dollar-cost averaging is contributing to a 401(k) retirement plan through salary withholding.

The benefits are twofold. First, an investor using dollar-cost averaging buys more shares of his selected investment when its price is low, and fewer when the price is high. Second, a dollar-cost averaging program provides a schedule of regular investing, which provides necessary discipline for many investors. The disadvantage of dollar-cost averaging is that it eliminates the opportunity for the investor to take advantage of situations where the investor has determined that a particular security is underpriced at a particular time. Given the difficulty of making such determinations consistently, perhaps this is not a disadvantage for most investors.

Types of Investments

The general rule is that the safer the investment (the less likely the investor is to lose the principal invested), the lower the return. Investments offering greater potential returns will generally have a greater risk of loss.

Savings and Checking Accounts. An interest-bearing savings or checking account at a local bank or credit union is an investment. Bank accounts are a simple and important part of successful financial planning. Traditional savings accounts earn compound interest at a low rate. The federal government, through the Federal Deposit Insurance Corporation (FDIC), guarantees bank and credit union accounts for amounts up to $250,000 per depositor per insured bank. Most of these types of accounts allow withdrawals and deposits of funds without penalty.

A vital part of anyone's financial planning is an emergency savings fund, and a traditional savings account is the perfect place for it. A great way to have an emergency fund earn interest is to find a bank or credit union that offers checking accounts that earn interest. Usually a higher minimum balance is required for interest-bearing checking. Interest earned on savings and checking accounts is considered income for tax purposes.

Certificates of Deposit. Certificates of deposit (CDs) are accounts that require an investment of money for a specific time period. CDs from insured banks are also insured by the FDIC. CDs usually have terms that range from three months to four years, but they can be shorter or longer. Some CDs are set up to automatically roll over, or reinvest the principal and interest in a new CD of the same term at the current interest rate. If this is the case, investors must keep track of the end-of-term dates if they want to withdraw funds to use or to invest elsewhere.

The disadvantage of CDs is their early withdrawal penalty, which can be substantial. CDs also tend to have a low interest rate. It is best to lock in the rate at a time when interest rates are relatively high. CD rates are generally higher than rates for saving accounts. Interest earned on CDs is considered income for tax purposes.

Money Market Accounts. Money market accounts are bank accounts that invest in vehicles such as government securities. There are two sources of money market accounts: mutual funds and savings institutions. This discussion concerns money markets through institutions such as banks and credit unions.

Money market accounts are very similar to traditional savings accounts offered by financial institutions. They may be guaranteed by the federal government up to $250,000 per account, and there is no penalty for early withdrawals. Like CDs, money market accounts typically earn higher interest than traditional savings accounts.

Money market accounts require a minimum deposit. The minimum starting deposit and minimum balance is typically $500, and often $1,000. Many financial institutions offer interest rates based on the amount in the money market account, so that a money market account with a $100,000 balance will earn a higher interest rate than a money market account with a $5,000 balance.

Some money market accounts function as checking accounts as well. Some financial institutions charge a maintenance fee for their money market accounts. Money market accounts are a safe, stable investment and a good alternative to traditional savings accounts for sizable deposit amounts. Money market accounts are not subject to the restrictions that come with investing in a CD, but their interest rates are comparable and usually higher than those of traditional savings accounts. Interest earned on money market accounts is considered income for tax purposes.

Stocks and Equities. A company's stock represents a piece, or a share, of that company. The stockholders of a company are its owners. This is the reason stocks are considered equity investments. Most individual investors buy and sell securities through brokerage firms that are registered with the NASD. Registered stockbrokers buy and sell stocks through traders on the appropriate stock exchange. There are basic two types of stock: common stock and preferred stock.

Common stock is categorized by its expected rate of growth and income. For example, common stock can be in the low-income category, but be characterized as aggressive growth. Conversely, high-income stock can be in the low-growth category.

Preferred stock is so labeled because it has priority over common stock. If dividends are paid or the company is liquidated, owners of preferred stock are paid before owners of common stock. Preferred stock in a company usually carries a higher price tag than common stock in the same company.

Stock options are the right to purchase or sell a specific amount of shares in a company for a specific price and for a defined time period. The price is generally the stock's market price at the time the option is granted. Stock options fall in an investment vehicle category known as derivatives. For most investors, unless their mutual funds participate in stock options, involvement with stock options is limited to employee benefit plans.

Derivatives include options contracts or futures contracts that enable or obligate the holder to buy or sell stock at a certain price. Options and futures contracts are called derivatives because the price is derived from the value and characteristics of some underlying asset.

The two primary stock investment goals are income and growth. Although growth and income may coexist in a particular stock investment, most stocks have one primary strength.

Growth stock is stock in a company that does not pay cash dividends, but instead reinvests its profits into the company in hopes of "growing" the value of the business and the stock price. Income stock is stock in well-established companies that do not need to reinvest their profits internally and therefore use them to pay dividends to stockholders. Income stock is often more expensive than most growth stock because the income stream and security of the investment is greater.

Stock investing is sometimes seen as a get-rich-quick scheme. However, the only strategy that has proven successful for investing in stocks is to pick wisely, and then hold on for the long term. Bull markets (when the stock market is on an upswing) and bear markets (when stock prices are going down) are part of the inevitable cycle that is the stock market. No one–not even the experts–can reliably predict which way the market is headed until it is too late to turn a quick profit.

Bonds. Bonds are a way to invest by loaning money to an entity such as a corporation or the government, whether federal, state, or local. Bonds usually pay interest at a fixed rate for a fixed period of time, from a few months to over 20 years. When the bond matures, the borrower pays the face amount of the bond to the holder.

In general, when interest rates go up, bonds decrease in value. Conversely, when interest rates go down, bonds are more valuable because their interest rate is higher than the interest rate available from other investments. Investing in bonds carries varying degrees of risk depending on the type of bond.

Municipal bonds are bonds that are issued by state and local governments. The interest earned on municipal bonds is not subject to federal income tax. In addition, residents of the state or locality that issues the bonds generally do not have to pay state and local income tax. Because of this attractive tax feature, municipal bonds typically pay interest at rates lower than other types of bonds. However, for those in higher tax brackets, the tax savings may offset the lower interest rate.

Zero coupon bonds are bonds that are sold at a discount, and when they mature, the owner receives the full face value of the bond. Zero coupon bonds do not make periodic interest payments. However, the interest is taxed as it is earned. Investing in zero coupon bonds has the primary advantage of locking in a good interest rate. But the locking-in feature of zero coupon bonds can also be its downfall if interest rates are rising.

Treasury bonds are sold by the U.S. government at auction and have a set interest rate for 30 years. The minimum amount they are issued for is $100. Interest is paid every six months.

Treasury notes are sold by the U.S. government at auction and have a set interest rate for a specific term that ranges from two to 10 years. The minimum amount they are issued for is $100. Interest is paid every six months.

Treasury bills (T-bills) are sold by the U.S. government at auction and do not have a set interest rate. Investors purchase these bills for less than face value, and when the term is over, the investor receives the full face value of the T-bill. T-bills are available in $100 increments, with a minimum purchase amount of $100. Treasury bills are issued with terms of four, 13 and 26 weeks. Cash management bills may be issued for shorter or irregular terms.

Treasury inflation-protected securities (TIPS) are sold by the U.S. government at auction, with terms of five, 10, or 20 years, and with the interest rate determined at the auction. TIPS are sold in $100 increments. Interest is paid every six months. The interest rate is fixed, but the principal amount is adjusted for inflation (and deflation) throughout the term of the note, so that the amount of interest fluctuates as well. The principal paid at maturity is the greater of the adjusted principal or the original principal.

Collectively, Treasury bonds, bills, TIPS, and notes are referred to as "Treasuries" and are considered one of the lowest-risk investments because they are backed by the U.S. government. Treasuries can be purchased directly from the federal government or through a bank or brokerage. Treasuries can be held until they mature or be sold on the secondary market.

The interest on Treasuries is not taxed at the state or local level. This may help to offset the major disadvantage of Treasuries, namely that the interest rates that they pay are on the lower end of the scale. However, a low interest rate is to be expected with such a low-risk security.

U.S. savings bonds are also issued by the federal government. Series EE and series I U.S. savings bonds are currently available for purchase directly from the U.S. Treasury online or at banks, credit unions, and other financial institutions. Online purchases can be made in any amount from $25 up to the maximums. Some employers offer payroll programs where deductions are made to purchase savings bonds.

Series EE savings bonds are sold as paper bonds or as electronic bonds. Interest on the bonds is not actually paid until the bonds are cashed in. Federal income tax is not due until the bonds are cashed in. See Tab 2 for reporting of savings bond interest. In addition, the interest earned is exempt from state and local taxes. Series EE paper bonds are currently issued at a price of half their face value, in denominations ranging from $50 to $10,000. Electronic bonds, purchased through www.treasurydirect.gov are currently issued priced at face value. The buyer can choose any dollar amount between $25 and $5,000. Buyers can purchase up to $5,000 in electronic bonds and $5,000 worth of paper bonds each year. Series EE savings bonds earn interest for 30 years. They can be redeemed at any time after one year has passed for the purchase price and any accrued interest, except that if they are redeemed before five years have passed, the last three months of interest is forfeited.

Series EE savings bonds issued after April 1997 and before May 2005 earn interest based on 90 percent of the average yields on five-year Treasury securities for the preceding six months. These bonds increase in value every month and interest is compounded semiannually. Their interest rate is adjusted every six months, on May 1 and November 1. Series EE bonds issued after April 2005 earn a fixed rate of interest. This rate has ranged from 1.4 to 3.7 percent.

Series I bonds are designed to protect the bondholder against inflation. Paper I bonds can be purchased at face value in denominations ranging from $50 to $5,000, up to a maximum of $5,000 per calendar year; electronic I bonds can be purchased at face value in any amount from $25 to $5,000, up to a maximum of $5,000 per calendar year. Upon redemption the holder of an I bond receives the face value of the bond plus accrued interest.

Caution. Effective September 1, 2004, series HH savings bonds are no longer available to the public. Series HH savings bonds issued through August 2004 will continue to earn interest until they reach maturity 20 years after issue.

Corporate bonds are issued by a company at a specific interest rate for a specific period of time. Corporate bonds have maturity dates ranging anywhere from 10 to 30 years. The interest rate on corporate bonds depends on several factors, including the length of the maturity. Generally, longer-term bonds pay higher interest rates as an incentive for investors to lock in their funds for such a long period of time.

The interest rate on corporate bonds depends even more heavily on the strength of a corporation's finances. The stronger a corporation's credit record is, the lower the interest rate on bonds it issues. The safest bonds, those issued by financially strong corporations, will attract investors for the safety of their investment. Credit ratings issued by firms such as Standard & Poor's and Moody's Investors Service, which assign letter grades to the credit history of corporations, range from a high of AAA all the way down to C.

In general, corporate bonds pay higher interest rates than Treasuries that mature in the same time period. As safe an investment as the best-rated corporate bond may be, a comparable Treasury will be safer still with the U.S. government as its backer. Therefore, investors have to sacrifice a higher interest rate for less risk if they choose Treasuries over corporate bonds.

Junk bonds are simply corporate bonds that are considered to be particularly high risk. This means that bond-rating services such as Standard & Poor's and Moody's Investors Service have assigned them a low rating in terms of the company's ability to meet its obligations. To offset the risk involved, these bonds offer higher interest rates than other corporate bonds.

Mutual Funds. Most people invest in securities through mutual funds, which pool investors' money to invest in stocks, bonds, and other assets. Many people are introduced to mutual fund investing by the opportunity to choose investments for their account under an employer's 401(k) plan. The most important advantages of investing in mutual funds are diversification, simplicity, and professional management. Index mutual funds are often excellent choices because they generally have lower administrative costs than actively managed funds.

The choice of a particular fund should be based on several factors, including:

- performance, measured by annual average return over an appropriate period;
- performance record of individuals managing the fund;
- investment objective (growth vs. income);
- risk tolerance;
- reliability and customer service of fund family
- fees.

Load fees are actually a sales charge paid to the financial advisor or broker who sells Class A shares in a mutual fund. There are no-load funds, in which shares are purchased directly from the mutual fund company. These are Class B or Class C shares, which may have back-end load fees or redemption charges if shares are sold within a specific time period, usually four to six years.

Management fees are fees that mutual fund investors pay for management services (for example, salaries and expenses). Management fees range from less than 0.5 to three percent of the value of an investor's fund. Generally, they are automatically deducted annually.

Many funds charge an annual marketing fee (also known as a 12b-1 fee) of generally 0.25 to one percent of assets managed. No-load funds are particularly likely to charge a marketing fee (although it must be below a certain percentage in order for the fund to be labeled no-load) to make up for not charging load fees.

The length of time a manager has been with a fund and whether there is high turnover in a fund's management are also important factors. If a fund's management changes, the methodology it uses to achieve its objective can change, and it may not be as successful or as good a fit for a particular investor.

Mutual funds can be categorized by their general investment strategies. Some mutual funds invest in companies of a particular size, as measured by the companies' total market values, or market capitalization. Other funds are categorized by the weight their investment strategy places on seeking growth or income. The two goals are not mutually exclusive, but many actively managed funds focus heavily on one or the other.

Growth funds have the primary objective of a high return on investment in the form of appreciation. This type of fund is generally not aimed at obtaining an income stream, such as dividends.

Growth and income funds or equity return funds are a more conservative version of a basic growth fund, usually investing in companies that consistently pay dividends and are also expected to grow.

Income funds have the primary objective of a high return on investment in the form of dividends and interest, rather than capital appreciation.

Funds are also categorized by other dimensions of their strategies.

Index funds are mutual funds that invest in all the stocks in a particular stock index. For example, a mutual fund that uses the Standard & Poor's 500 stock index would buy stock in all the companies that make up the index. Investment management fees for index funds are much lower than for actively managed funds. An index fund will generally not beat the market, but it will usually outperform most of the actively managed funds owning a similar mix of securities.

Balanced funds are mutual funds that invest in both stocks and bonds. In order to be considered a balanced fund, federal securities law requires that a fund have at least 25 percent of its holdings in bonds and 25 percent of its holdings in stocks. The remaining holdings can vary but are usually based on how the stock market is doing at that particular time. Balanced funds are more stable than growth funds and produce higher returns than bond funds.

Foreign equity funds or international equity funds invest in stocks of companies outside the United States. Funds that invest in the stock of companies in one country outside the United States are known as single-country or country funds.

Global equity funds invest in the stock of both domestic and international companies.

Sector funds invest in one particular industry or sector of the economy. Examples of these sectors include technology, financial services, and precious metals. The greatest risk inherent in sector funds is lack of diversification. A sector fund may invest in several different companies, but all the companies will be in the same line of business. The performance of the fund tends to go up and down based on how the industry is doing as a whole.

Socially responsible funds or conscious funds are mutual funds that are defined more by what they do not invest in than by what they do invest in. Socially responsible funds choose not to invest in companies that engage in activities that go against a particular social cause, political ideology, or value system. Examples of the types of companies that these funds may not buy stock in are drug companies that conduct tests on animals, tobacco companies, and gun manufacturers.

Option funds invest in stock options as opposed to actually purchasing stocks. A variation on basic option funds are funds that actually purchase stocks and then issue options on the stocks they purchased. This type of option fund can produce dividends for investors because of the options being sold, but does not rate highly in terms of growth, because the options are exercised if the price of the stock purchased goes up.

Money market funds invest in items such as certificates of deposit and Treasuries. The most common type of money market fund invests in various items, including Treasuries, certificates of deposit, and commercial paper. Some money market funds invest in securities guaranteed by the federal government. Money market funds are the one of the safest types (and can be the safest depending on what items make up the fund) of mutual fund. Also, money market funds usually have conveniences attached, such as the ability to write checks on the account. They provide little opportunity for growth of the investor's capital.

Investment Real Estate

For most people, the single largest investment they have is their home. Investing in other real estate also has its advantages.

Fixer-uppers. Buying houses, condominiums, or other buildings that need some work at a bargain price and fixing them up is a common method of investing in real estate. Different tax rules apply to the purchase and sale of a home if it is not used as the owner's principal residence.

Rental Property. Rental real estate can produce income. In addition, if the property appreciates in value, the investor may be able to sell it at a profit. Some investors hire a property manager or management company to manage their investment real estate.

Planning Tip. A popular method of investing in real estate for many investors is to not sell their present home when they buy a new one, but rent it out instead. This is especially common for those who move from a condominium or starter home to a bigger home in the same general area. If the proceeds from the sale of the present home are not needed to purchase a new home, this may be an investment alternative. However, keeping the home as a rental for more than three years will eliminate the opportunity to exclude any gain realized on the sale of the property under Code Sec. 121. (See Tab 4.)

Seller financing, or holding a mortgage for a new homeowner and receiving an income stream from his or her mortgage payments, is another alternative for those who own a home outright with no mortgage liens.

Second Homes. Second homes or vacation homes should be purchased primarily for vacation purposes, not investment purposes. Most people end up with a loss on their vacation home properties because the costs of owning the home often exceed the rental income it produces, and resale values in resort areas may be more vulnerable to the effects of a general economic downturn.

Timeshares. Timeshares are best defined as the purchase of a set period of time (usually one or two weeks) during a certain time of the year at a certain location (for example, a condominium in Florida or a villa in France). This provides a fixed vacation cost each year, and often weeks and locations can be traded with other timeshare owners in the same company. Approach such "investments" as vacation rentals, not as investments. It may be telling that in bankruptcy cases, timeshares are often assigned zero value as an asset.

Real Estate Investment Trusts (REITs). These trusts invest in real estate through actual property or mortgage portfolios. Pooling investor funds for REITs also allows investors to invest in larger-scale properties such as hotels and office buildings, which would be financially impossible for most of us to do on our own dime. Another important selling point for using a REIT to invest in real estate is liquidity. It is much easier to sell or transfer a share of a REIT than to sell or transfer actual real estate. Like real estate, REITs may provide an income stream from rents and offer a very good possibility of long-term appreciation if the real estate market goes up.

Investments for Education

Investments for education, including Coverdell education savings accounts (CESAs), state-sponsored educational investment accounts and prepaid tuition plans, and education savings bonds, college certificates of deposit, and financial aid are covered in Tab 13 and IRS Publication 970, *Tax Benefits for Higher Education.*

Planning for Retirement

Most people have done little or no planning for retirement. With people living longer and retiring earlier, many may spend as much as a third of their lives in retirement.

Most individuals who consider themselves financially successful rely on the "three-legged stool" of personal savings and holdings, company retirement benefits, and Social Security to fund retirement. It is important to actually estimate what retirement income and expenses will be rather than to simply take a comfortable retirement on faith.

Being Late Is Never Better. People often start planning for retirement later in life. Although it is never too late to begin retirement planning, the number of options available decreases with time.

Company Retirement Benefits Alone Are Not Always Enough. People commonly misunderstand how company retirement benefits work and what they offer.

Social Security Is Not a Safety Net. The Social Security system has never been and never will be a safety net for those who retire with no assets or income. At most, it provides a cushion to soften the blow when employees retire.

Planning Tip. Social Security benefits will not be decreased by the amount of employer-provided pensions an individual receives if Social Security taxes were paid on the earnings from that employer. On the other hand, pensions based on work that is not covered by Social Security (such as the federal civil service and some state, local, or foreign government systems) will probably reduce the amount of Social Security benefits.

Medicare Is Not Enough to Cover Health Care Costs. For most older individuals, Medicare will be the main source of health insurance coverage. Unfortunately, Medicare costs increase regularly, and any shortfall in coverage will have to come from individual retirees.

It Does Not Cost Less to Live During Retirement. In addition to increased health care costs, leisure and entertainment costs tend to increase sharply after retirement. Families who started having children late in life may find their resources strained under the burden of funding college tuition. Finally, inflation becomes a major factor.

Retirement Needs as a Percentage of Income

The simplest method for estimating future retirement needs is to use a percentage of current income. The general rule of thumb is that retirement expenses will be 60 to 80 percent of after-tax preretirement income.

Using a factor of 80 percent or more provides a more conservative approach to estimating potential retirement expenses. Conversely, the lower the percentage used in the calculations, the lower the safety cushion. Using any percentage below 60 percent would be likely to lead to a major shortfall in retirement funds.

Another method of figuring how much is needed for retirement involves the use of budget calculations, by comparing a current budget with a projected retirement budget. Although more time consuming and complicated, this method can provide a more realistic idea of what will be needed during retirement.

Pension Benefits. These benefits include income from employer-provided retirement plans, self-employed plans, and savings from the various forms of IRAs.

Meeting Your Savings Goal

Your Age	Annual Savings Necessary to Reach $100,000 by Age 65 (8% Interest Rate)	Your Age	Annual Savings Necessary to Reach $100,000 by Age 65 (8% Interest Rate)
18	$ 204	37	$ 962
19	221	38	1,049
20	239	39	1,145
21	259	40	1,251
22	280	41	1,368
23	303	42	1,498
24	329	43	1,642
25	356	44	1,803
26	386	45	1,983
27	419	46	2,185
28	454	47	2,413
29	492	48	2,570
30	534	49	3,298
31	580	50	3,683
32	630	51	4,130
33	685	52	4,652
34	745	53	5,270
35	811	54	6,008
36	883		

Unlike Social Security benefits, an individual has some control over this potential source of income. The amount of control, however, is limited to participating (as opposed to not participating) in a plan, selecting investment options, and switching to employers that offer better retirement benefits.

Personal Savings. If either of the other legs in the model comes up short, it is personal savings that will have to support the three-legged stool.

401(k) Plans. As an employee, there really is no downside to contributing to a 401(k) plan as long as the plan offers investment choices appropriate for the individual. As an initial benefit, contributions to a 401(k) are made on a pretax basis, so the employee sees an immediate tax savings. In addition, the money in a 401(k) will grow on a tax-deferred basis, making it even easier to save for retirement. Yet another benefit of most 401(k) plans is that the employer will match employee contributions or otherwise make additional contributions to the plan.

Credit and Debt

Personal credit, if used wisely, has its advantages. Consumer credit falls into two broad categories: closed-end and open-end. Closed-end credit is used for a specific purpose, for a specific amount, and for a specific period of time. Payments are usually of equal amounts. Mortgage loans and automobile loans are common examples of closed-end credit. With open-end, or revolving, credit, loans are made on a continuous basis, and the lender bills the borrower periodically to make at least partial payment. Credit cards issued by a store, bank cards such as VISA or MasterCard, and overdraft protection are examples of open-end credit.

Debit cards deduct payments directly from a bank account and are not considered credit cards because funds are not borrowed.

Cost of Credit

Credit costs money. Because a dollar invested today can earn interest over time, a dollar today is worth more than a dollar at some point in the future. Many people think that the cheapest loan is the one with the lowest interest rate and the lowest payments. However, the length of the loan and its fees are essential in figuring the loan's real cost.

The Consumer Credit Protection Act requires creditors to state the cost of borrowing in a common language so that the consumer understands exactly what the charges will be. With that information, consumers can compare costs and shop around for the best credit deal.

Annual Percentage Rate. The Annual Percentage Rate (APR) combines the fees with a year of interest charges to give the true annual interest rate. All lenders are required to disclose the effective annual percentage rate as well as the total finance charge in dollars. In this way, credit alternatives can be compared on equal terms.

The APR is the ratio of the total finance charge, not just the interest charge, to the average amount of credit in use during the life of the loan and is expressed as a percentage rate per year. The calculation of the APR depends on whether the loan is repaid in a single payment or in installments.

Debt and Income Tax Laws. The cost of credit is increased because individuals cannot generally deduct interest paid on auto, credit cards, education, and other consumer loans.

In addition, only a limited amount of qualified residence (mortgage) interest is deductible. Qualified residence interest is the interest paid or accrued on acquisition or home equity loans with respect to an individual's principal residence and one other residence, usually a "vacation home." The total amount of acquisition loans is limited to $1 million and the total amount of home equity loans is limited to $100,000. Interest on any debt over these limits is considered to be personal, consumer interest that is not deductible. See Tab 2 for details about the home mortgage interest deduction.

Tips to Lower Credit Card Costs

There are effective strategies for minimizing the cost of credit in any financial situation:

- pay off the entire amount within the grace period if at all possible;
- pay off card balances as quickly as possible; paying only the minimum payment required each month may prolong the debt for a decade or more;
- charge new purchases on lower-interest-rate cards;
- carry only one or two cards for emergencies (such as gas and telephone cards) and only a few selected store or bank cards, arranged in a way to remind you which cards offer the lowest rates;
- cancel any unneeded cards, especially those that charge annual fees;
- pay off high-interest, high-fee card balances first;
- avoid late-payment and overlimit penalties;
- use overnight delivery or on-line payments to save charges and fees if necessary. Because many credit card companies now assess hefty late payment fees ($15, $20, or more), consider whether you could avoid these fees by sending a payment by overnight delivery; and
- negotiate with creditors for better credit terms.

Credit Reports and Credit Bureaus

Every consumer should review his or her credit report periodically to ensure that no errors have slipped in, and also to uncover fraud or identity theft. Credit reports contain the name, address, Social Security number, birth date, information about past and current employers and incomes, home ownership information, and detailed credit information of an individual.

Creditors inform the credit bureaus of account numbers and the amount and type of credit and payments, the outstanding balance, the number and the amounts of payments past due, and the frequency of 30-, 60, or 90-day lateness. Commonly, credit files indicate the largest amount of credit an individual has had and each inquiry and credit refusal. Any lawsuits, judgments, or tax liens may appear as well.

Creditors who deny credit to an applicant must send a written rejection notice within 30 days of the decision, stating the specific reasons for the rejection and providing the name and address of any credit bureau that issued a report. Consumers have the right to view their credit files.

Caution. Small business owners often have more trouble than employees in obtaining personal credit. One of the reasons for this is that creditors may feel that the income stream from a small business is less secure than income received as an employee. Also, the creditors may worry about verifying the amount of income actually generated by the small business. Faced with these difficulties in obtaining credit, some small business owners may be tempted to "fudge" their income numbers, that is, inflate the amount received from their businesses. Such "creative accounting" is ill advised: Not only can a loan be denied if untrue information is supplied, but the applicant can be criminally prosecuted.

At the center of the credit reporting system are three national credit bureaus: Equifax, Experian, and TransUnion. The credit bureaus are private, for-profit businesses. Under federal law consumers may obtain a free copy of their credit report from each of these companies once each year. The free reports are available through a single website sponsored by the credit bureaus, at www.annualcreditreport.com, by calling 1-877-322-8228, or by filling out and mailing in a request form (available at the website). Consumers may obtain additional credit reports from any of the credit bureaus by visiting their websites–www.equifax.com, www.transunion.com, and www.experian.com.

The credit bureaus simply collect and collate credit information and make it available to businesses that subscribe to their service. They do not deny credit; they merely report the information they have gathered.

Time Limits on Adverse Data. Most of the information in an individual's credit file may be reported for only seven years. Personal bankruptcy, however, may be reported for 10 years. After that time, the past information in a credit file cannot be disclosed by a credit-reporting agency except with regard to an application for credit of $150,000 or more, to purchase life insurance for $150,000 or more, or for employment at an annual salary of $75,000 or more. In those situations, the time limits on releasing the information in a credit file do not apply. Nor do those time limits apply if the creditor chooses to use prior adverse information to deny a credit application.

Incorrect Credit File Information. Credit bureaus are required to follow reasonable procedures to ensure that subscribing creditors report information accurately. However, mistakes do occur. When a consumer notifies a credit bureau that he or she disputes the accuracy of information, the credit bureau must investigate and modify or remove inaccurate data. If investigation does not resolve the dispute, a consumer may place a statement of 100 words or less in his or her file explaining why the record is inaccurate. The credit bureau must then include the statement about disputed data or a coded version of that statement with the credit report.

Mortgage Credit

Mortgage lenders traditionally use a 28/36 ratio test to figure out the mortgage an applicant qualifies for. That is, the sum of the monthly mortgage payment, homeowner's insurance, and property taxes should equal no more than 28 percent of household monthly gross income. The second part of the ratio is that monthly debts, including the mortgage payment, should equal no more than 36 percent of monthly income.

$$\text{Gross monthly income} \times 0.28 = \text{Maximum monthly mortgage payment}$$

$$\text{Gross monthly income} \times 0.36 = \text{Maximum total monthly debt}$$

For information on the tax advantages of owning a home, see Tab 2.

Managing Substantial Debt

Overwhelming debt has become a common problem in America. There are a number of solutions, with bankruptcy as a last resort.

Information Is Key. The book NCLC Guide to Surviving Debt, from the National Consumer Law Center, is available through most local libraries or from NCLC at (617) 542-9595.

Consumer credit counseling services (CCCSs) are not-for-profit organizations that provide debt counseling services for families and individuals with serious financial problems, for a modest fee. A credit counselor meets with debtors and analyzes their total financial situation. The counselor may develop a repayment plan and contact creditors to arrange new repayment terms. These services also offer education and help design a budget.

The IRS has been reviewing the not-for-profit status of many of these organizations and has revoked that status in many cases, on the grounds that the organization was operating for a profit rather than engaged in educational activities for the benefit of the public. Consumers are encouraged to check that the organization offers advice and counseling, rather than promises of easy escape from debt for a fee.

Loan Consolidation. Loan consolidation companies specialize in loaning people money to pay off all their other debts. The advantages include having to deal with only one creditor and one payment each month, the fact that loans are usually long term, and the monthly payments often being lower than before consolidation. However, the interest charged by loan consolidators may be very high, and there may be a fee for paying off the loan ahead of schedule. Another danger is that a consolidation loan does nothing to resolve the habits and tendencies that may have caused the credit problems in the first place.

Home Equity Loans. The most common loan consolidation technique is to roll as much debt as possible into a home equity loan, which may have tax advantages (see Tab 2).

Most credit counselors advocate the general rule that individuals should not convert unsecured debt to secured debt. Following this rule would mean not using home equity to collateralize credit card debt. Although this is certainly a logical and prudent rule, there are exceptions. For instance, a home equity loan may be appropriate if most or all of the following factors are true:

- you have been able to make only the minimum monthly payment required on your credit cards;
- your credit card debt carries very high interest rates compared with what you could obtain for a home equity loan;
- you meet the qualifications that would make interest paid on the home equity loan deductible on your federal income tax return;
- you will pay back the home equity loan on a relatively short payment schedule–preferably five years, but no more than 10 years;
- you have an adequate and dependable source of income available to repay the home equity loan; and
- you have made the adjustments to your lifestyle and personal finances necessary to ensure that you will not slide back into the credit card debt morass once (or worse, before) your existing credit balances are extinguished.

Bankruptcy: The Last Resort

The United States Constitution provides a method whereby individuals burdened by excessive debt can obtain a fresh financial start and pursue newly productive lives unimpaired by past financial problems. It is an important alternative for persons mired deep in financial difficulty.

The federal bankruptcy laws were enacted to provide debtors with a fresh start and to establish a ranking and equity among all the creditors who are clamoring for the debtor's limited resources. Bankruptcy helps people avoid the kind of permanent discouragement that can prevent them from ever reestablishing themselves as hard-working members of society. Also, creditors are ranked so that the debtor's nonexempt property can be fairly distributed according to established rules guaranteeing identical treatment to all creditors of the same rank.

This discussion is intended only as a brief overview of the types of bankruptcy filings and of what a bankruptcy filing can and cannot do. Anyone considering this course of action is encouraged to seek the advice and assistance of an attorney specializing in bankruptcy law.

Types of Bankruptcy. The Bankruptcy Code is divided into chapters. The chapters that usually apply to consumer debtors are Chapter 7, known as a liquidation, and Chapter 13, known as an adjustment of the debts of an individual with regular income.

An important feature applicable to all types of bankruptcy filings is the automatic stay. The automatic stay means that the mere request for bankruptcy protection automatically "stays," or forces an abrupt halt to, repossessions, foreclosures, evictions, garnishments, attachments, utility shut-offs, and debt collection harassment. Creditors cannot take any further action against the debtor or the property without permission from the bankruptcy court.

Chapter 7. In a Chapter 7, or liquidation, case, the bankruptcy court appoints a trustee to examine the debtor's assets and divide them into exempt and nonexempt property. Exempt property is limited to a certain amount of equity in the debtor's residence, motor vehicle, household goods, life insurance, health aids, specified future earnings such as Social Security benefits and alimony, and certain other personal property. The trustee may then sell the nonexempt property and distribute the proceeds among the unsecured creditors. Although a liquidation case can rarely help with secured debt (the secured creditor still has the right to repossess the collateral), the debtor will be discharged from the legal obligation to pay unsecured debts such as credit card debts, medical bills, and utility arrearages. Certain types of unsecured debt are allowed special treatment and cannot be discharged. These include some student loans, alimony, child support, criminal fines, and some taxes.

Chapter 13. In a Chapter 13 case, the debtor puts forward a plan, following the rules set forth in the bankruptcy laws, to repay all creditors over a period of time, usually from future income. A Chapter 13 case may be advantageous in that the debtor is allowed to get caught up on mortgages or car loans without the threat of foreclosure or repossession and is allowed to keep both exempt and nonexempt property. The debtor's plan is a simple document outlining to the bankruptcy court how the debtor proposes to pay current expenses while paying off all the old debt balances. The debtor's property is protected from seizure from creditors, including mortgage and other lien holders, as long as the proposed payments are made. The plan generally requires monthly payments to the bankruptcy trustee over a period of three to five years. Arrangements can be made to have these payments made automatically through payroll deductions.

For information about bankruptcy and taxes, see Tab 12.

Insurance

In most cases, risks that are large or unpredictable are best transferred to a reliable insurance carrier. Lines of insurance such as homeowner's or renter's, auto, life, disability, health, and business coverage protect individuals from varying degrees of risk depending on the likelihood of an adverse occurrence.

Health Insurance

Private health insurance costs have risen much more than inflation in recent years. Many employees receive insurance under group policies provided or subsidized by their employers; others must seek individual policies or do without. Medicare is a federal health insurance program for people 65 years of age and older and some disabled people under age 65. For discussion of Medicare costs and coverages, see the discussion earlier in this Tab.

Disability Insurance

There are two types of disability insurance: short-term and long-term.

Short-term disability insurance is designed to provide income to employees who become disabled due to sickness or an accident, and are unable to work after an initial waiting period (generally, one to seven days). Short-term benefits are usually expressed in terms of the maximum number of weeks that the plan will pay (the industry standard is 26 weeks). These benefits typically replace 50 percent to 67 percent of an employee's income.

Long-term disability policies take up where short-term coverage leaves off for those who become disabled and unable to work for longer periods of time (generally six months or longer), and typically provide 50 percent to 60 percent of pay. In most plans, benefits are paid for the duration of the disability up to the age of 65.

Life Insurance and Annuities

Life insurance offers important benefits, including income replacement for survivors, forced savings, possible collateral, and a ready source of emergency cash.

Term versus Cash Value? Life insurance policies can be divided into two main categories, term insurance and cash-value insurance.

Term Insurance. Term insurance provides a death benefit only. If the insured dies within the specified term, the insurance company pays the benefit amount. Such a policy is pure protection only; it has no investment (cash value) component to it. Although it is called "term" insurance because the coverage runs for a specified term (such as a year), many modern term policies may be renewed at the option of the insured for as long as he or she is willing to pay the premiums. Term insurance is generally less expensive than cash-value insurance.

The simplest form of term insurance must be renewed annually. Many term policies are now written for much longer terms (five, 10, or 15 years). Although the cost of term insurance usually rises as the insured gets older, level-term policies are also available. These policies keep the premium at the same dollar amount throughout the term (although the premium would jump more sharply for the next term than would be the case for the year-to-year rise for an annual term policy).

Cash-Value Insurance. There sometimes appear to be a nearly unlimited number of types of cash-value (or whole-life) policies. Although they have important differences, they all boil down to this: They provide a death benefit (equivalent to term protection) and they also provide a savings feature in their cash value. Cash-value insurance is much more expensive than term (particularly at younger ages) but typically provides insurance throughout the insured's lifetime at a level premium. The extra expense of cash-value insurance (over term insurance) funds the cash value feature.

A policyholder normally can receive the benefit of the cash value during lifetime in one of two ways: (1) by taking a loan against them or (2) by cashing in the policy (the policy will no longer be in force, but the policyholder will receive the cash surrender value). If the cash value remains in the policy, it increases without any tax consequence to the policyholder. Thus, an individual who lacks the discipline to follow through on an independent investment plan may benefit from the "forced savings" under a cash-value insurance policy.

Annuities. An annuity is sometimes referred to as an "upside-down life insurance policy." With a life insurance policy, the insured's relatively small periodic payments (premiums) are invested to fund a large sum to be paid in the future. With an annuity the purchaser makes one or more payments to fund a series of periodic payments (starting immediately or at some point in the future) over an extended period of time. A life insurance policy primarily protects the insured's dependents against the economic harm of premature death. An annuity is meant to protect individuals (and their dependents) from the economic harm of outliving their life savings and other resources.

Annuities are available in various forms. A fixed annuity is one designed to assure the buyer of a lifetime (or other fixed period) of payments of a guaranteed set amount. The amount of these payments is based on the age of the annuitant (the person whose life the annuity is computed on) at the time the payments are to commence, the sex of the annuitant, and the rate of interest that the insurer assumes will be made from the purchase funds paid by the annuitant.

A variable annuity (also known as a "market value account") is one in which the insurer invests the premiums (less investment charges) in a portfolio of securities. The value of the annuity provided varies with the performance of the portfolio. A variable annuity is purchased with the hope that the performance of the underlying securities will outstrip the return that would have been obtained from a fixed annuity.

Both the amounts that build up within the annuity (during the accumulation phase) and the amounts that are received as annuity payments (during the distribution phase) can qualify for favorable federal income tax treatment. Thus, purchasing an annuity can become a tax-deferred method of saving for retirement.

Homeowner's Insurance

There are several different types of homeowner's policies in terms of the risks that are covered. The most common type of homeowner's policy in use today (known as "comprehensive coverage," or HO-3 in the insurance industry) covers a variety of risks. Here are some of the major kinds of risks that are covered by a comprehensive-coverage homeowner's policy:

- damage to home and personal property caused by fire, lightning, wind, or storm;
- medical payments for occupants for injuries caused by fire, lightning, wind, or storm;
- medical and legal liabilities to persons injured by accident while in the home;
- loss or theft of personal property, even if not in the home, with some restrictions on things like jewelry or laptop computers;
- liability to others for accidental damage to their property, even if not in the home;
- liability for unintentional personal injury to others caused by the homeowner or his or her family;
- liability for intentional personal injury to others caused by the homeowner's children who are below a specified age;
- liability to others hurt because of the homeowner's participation in a sporting event (for example, while playing golf, the homeowner accidentally strikes someone with a golf ball);
- liability for damage or injury caused by pets (but damage caused by exotic pets is not covered);
- damage caused by vandalism, riot, or civil unrest; and
- damage caused by falling objects (such as tree limbs).

What's Not Covered by a Homeowner's Policy? It is important to know the types of risks a homeowner's policy does not cover. The main risks that a comprehensive policy normally does not cover are the following:

- flood damage (including the water damage caused by a hurricane);
- damage caused by ground movement (such as earthquakes and soil erosion); and
- claims arising from a business use of the premises.

Claims arising from a business use of the premises are, by far, the most important exclusion for home business operators.

The phrase "normally does not cover" is used because some states require insurance companies to cover some of these risks (for example, California requires coverage of earthquakes) and because coverage can often be obtained by purchasing a policy rider, at an additional premium cost, or other specific insurance, such as through the National Flood Insurance Program.

Caution. Home-based business owners should consult with their insurance advisors to be sure that their home and business needs are all covered.

Auto Insurance

Auto insurance has two main components: liability insurance and insurance for property damage. Liability insurance is the most important. It provides compensation to persons who would be able to sue for personal injuries, medical payments, loss of earnings, or damage to their property arising out of an auto accident.

Property damage insurance includes collision and comprehensive coverage, which compensates the policyholder for assorted damage to the car caused by collisions and such things as fire, theft, and vandalism.

Business Insurance

General liability insurance will protect you from payments required to be made for bodily injury or property damage to a third party, for medical expenses arising from the underlying incident, for the cost of defending lawsuits including investigations and settlements, and for any bonds or judgments required during an appeal procedure.

This type of coverage comes with exclusions and limitations. The exclusions typically include war and sometimes property of others entrusted to you (such as clothing if you own a dry-cleaning business). Liability for the property of others can be removed as an exclusion, usually for an additional premium or via separate coverage. Limitations will be akin to those on your personal auto policy–for example, $100,000 per person and $300,000 per accident. In addition to general liability coverage, depending on what kind of business you are in, you may need one or more of the other kinds of liability coverage.

Product liability insurance can cover products you may manufacture or sell or your services if you are, say, a mechanic or house painter. Under the name of malpractice insurance, this is the classification of coverage that will cover physicians, dentists, accountants, and lawyers. In today's world, a minimum of $1 million is the recommended coverage for businesses dealing with the general public. It is also a good idea to have the name of your business added to your supplier's insurance riders as an "additional named" insured. This adds another explicit layer of protection should a product liability suit arise, generally costs nothing, and has become common practice for companies in food retailing, wholesaling, marketing, and manufacturing.

Auto liability insurance for a business, just as for your personal vehicles, should be of the comprehensive type. This is especially important if you have employees who drive for your business.

Workers' compensation insurance is required by law in all states and protects an employer from liability for an accident involving an employee. This type of insurance will pay for medical expenses and lost wages for an injured employee and, in cases of death or disability, provide lump sums or annuities. Maintaining a safe working environment will go a long way toward controlling the cost of this type of coverage, but a careless or accident-prone employee can raise your insurance rates out of the realm of affordability very quickly. Proper selection and training must be practiced to minimize this risk. In some states this coverage is not required for family members who may be working in the business. Your agent will know if any exceptions apply to your situation.

Umbrella liability insurance is an all-inclusive option that can cover enormous liabilities exceeding the normal limits of your basic policy at a fairly low cost. This coverage is almost always worth considering since it provides a valuable safety net for you and your business.

Malpractice, errors and omissions (E&O), or professional liability coverage is needed if you provide advice or services to the public where significant liability could result if something went wrong. You may want to consider obtaining professional insurance for a couple of reasons. First, depending on your profession, you may be required to carry such insurance by law. Second, certain policies will provide you with low-cost legal representation in the event you are sued.Even if your work is flawless, a customer could still claim that you did something wrong. A good professional insurance policy would help you defray the costs of any lawsuit, regardless of whether the underlying claim has merit.

Planning Investments for Tax Advantages

Tax planning is a process of looking at various tax options in order to determine when, whether, and how to conduct business and personal transactions so that taxes are eliminated or reduced. There are countless tax planning strategies available, particularly for small-business owners. Regardless of how simple or how complex a tax strategy is, it will be based on structuring the transaction to accomplish one or more of these goals:

- reducing the amount of taxable income;
- reducing the tax rate;
- controlling the time when the tax must be paid;
- claiming any available tax credits; and
- controlling the effects of the alternative minimum tax.

Tax-Favored Investments

In addition to deductions and exclusions from income, certain items (generally, capital gains (other than gains on collectibles) and qualified dividends) are taxed at lower rates.

Tax Avoidance

Tax evasion is illegal. Tax avoidance is the legal planning of transactions to take full advantage of the tax laws. Frequently, what sets tax evasion apart from tax avoidance is the IRS's finding that there was some fraudulent intent on the part of the taxpayer. The following are four areas commonly identified by IRS examiners as pointing to possible fraud:

- a failure to report substantial amounts of income, such as a shareholder's failure to report dividends, or a store owner's skimming from the cash register without including it in the daily business receipts;
- a claim for fictitious or improper deductions on a return, such as a sales representative's substantial overstatement of travel expenses, or a taxpayer's claim of a large deduction for charitable contributions when no verification exists;
- accounting irregularities, such as a business's failure to keep adequate records, or a discrepancy between amounts reported on a corporation's return and amounts reported on its financial statements; and
- improper allocation of income to a related taxpayer who is in a lower tax bracket, such as where a corporation makes distributions to the controlling shareholder's children.

A "How Much Life Insurance Do You Need?" Worksheet

1. Estimated annual living expenses of survivors (spouse, children, etc.) Estimate 75% of current family living expenses	$________(1)
2. Less expected annual benefits	
A. Social Security benefits	$________
B. Survivor's pension benefits	$________
C. Survivor's earned income	$________
D. Other income	$________
Total expected annual benefits	$________(2)
3. Net living expense shortage (or surplus) (1) MINUS (2) =	$________(3)
4. Amount of capital required to cover living expense shortage: Inflation-adjusted rate of return (example: 8% interest less 3% inflation = 5%)	________%
$________ (3) DIVIDED BY ________% =	$________(4)
5. Plus other lump-sum expenses	
A. Final expenses/estate costs	$________
B. Mortgage cancellation	$________
C. Education fund or other	$________
D. Emergency fund	$________
Total lump-sum expenses	$________(5)
6. Total capital required (4) PLUS (5) =	$________(6)
7. Less present capital	
A. Income-producing assets	$________
B. Present life insurance	$________
Total present capital	$________(7)
8. Additional life insurance needed (6) MINUS (7) =	$________

In contrast, the following techniques may result in a lower tax bill without breaking the law:

- shifting income from a high-bracket taxpayer to a lower-bracket taxpayer (such as a child); one fairly simple way to do this is to shift investment assets to minor children; owners of small businesses can hire their children; another possibility is to make one or more children part owners of a small business, so that net profits of the business are shared among a larger group; the tax laws limit the usefulness of this strategy for shifting *unearned* income to children under age 18, but some tax saving opportunities still exist (see Tab 13);
- structuring an investment or transaction so that payments are classified as capital gains. Long-term capital gains earned by noncorporate taxpayers are subject to lower tax rates than other income; and
- choosing the optimal form of organization for a business (such as sole proprietorship, partnership, or corporation); if business income is under $75,000 and the business is not a personal-service business such as medicine, law, architecture, engineering, accounting, the arts, or consulting, incorporating may result in tax savings; otherwise, the sole proprietorship or pass-through entities (partnerships, LLCs, S corporations) usually offer more tax benefits; of course, nontax factors must be taken into account as well.

Timing of Income and Deductions

In broad terms, taxes can be minimized in the current year by postponing the receipt of income so that more of it will be taxed next year, and by accelerating deductions into the current year.

Postponing Income, Accelerating Deductions. If the current year's tax bracket is expected to be as high or higher than next year's, strategies for postponing taxable income until the next tax year will reduce current tax liability. Even if the tax bracket is expected to stay the same, because of the time value of money, it is often best to postpone tax liability. There are several methods to do this:

- **Delay collections**–Year-end billings can be delayed until late enough in the year that payments come in the following year.

- **Delay dividends**–Corporations may arrange for any dividends to be paid after the end of the year.
- **Delay capital gains**–Sell assets that have appreciated in value after the first of the year.
- **Accelerate payments**–Where possible, prepay deductible business expenses, including rent, interest, taxes, insurance, etc.
- **Accelerate large purchases**–Close the purchase of depreciable personal property or real estate within the current year.
- **Accelerate operating expenses**–Accelerate the purchase of equipment, supplies, or the making of repairs.
- **Accelerate depreciation**–Elect to expense the cost of new equipment if eligible to do so, rather than to depreciate the equipment.

Many of these strategies are much easier to accomplish under the cash method of accounting. Although strategies aimed at changing the year in which income and deductions will be accounted for are usually more difficult to accomplish using the accrual method, this does not mean that they cannot be done.

To delay an accrual basis taxpayer's recognition of an item of income, make sure that all events fixing the liability for payment of that income are not met by year's end. For instance, when selling goods, delay shipment until next year.

To accelerate a deductible expense into the current year, make sure that all events fixing the liability and amount of payment as well as the economic performance have been completed by year's end. If purchasing goods, services, or the use of property, make sure that a valid contract covering all necessary terms is in effect and that the goods, services, or properties are delivered, performed, or used by year's end.

Accelerating Income, Postponing Deductions. If the current year's tax bracket is expected to be lower than next year's, maximize the amount of income that will be taxed in the present tax year. This can be accomplished by accelerating income and postponing expenses into the following year. In most cases, the opposite of the suggestions listed in the previous section apply. For example, instead of delaying billings, send out year-end bills early and try to collect payments before year's end.

Planning Tip. Watch for changes in the tax laws that affect tax brackets. The tax rates are scheduled to increase in 2011, but shifting political winds make even the near future of the rates difficult to predict at this time. Be sure also to keep in mind the applicability of the alternative minimum tax, discussed in Tab 10.

FINANCIAL PLANNING CHECKUP STATEMENT

CONFIDENTIAL

Personal Financial Statement as of ____________

Name(s): ________________________________ E-Mail–Home: ________________________________

____

Home Address: ________________________________ E-Mail–Office: ________________________________

________________________________ Social Security #: ________________________________

Home Phone: ________________________________ Spouse's Social Security #: ________________________________

Assets	Amount	Liabilities and Net Worth	Amount
Cash on hand and in banks–See Schedule A	$	Notes payable–See Schedule A	$
U.S. government securities–See Schedule B		Notes payable–Relatives	
Listed securities–See Schedule B		Notes payable–Other	
Unlisted securities–See Schedule B		Accounts and bills due	
Other equity interests–See Schedule B		Unpaid taxes	
Accounts and notes receivable		Real estate mortgages payable–See Schedule C or D	
Real estate owned–See Schedule C		Land contracts payable–See Schedule C or D	
Mortgages and land contracts receivable–See Schedule D		Life insurance loans–See Schedule E	
Cash value life insurance–See Schedule E		Other liabilities: Itemize	
Retirement accounts–See Schedule F			
Other assets: Itemize			
TOTAL ASSETS	$	TOTAL LIABILITIES	$
		NET WORTH	$
		TOTAL LIABILITIES AND NET WORTH	$

Sources of Income	Amount	General Information	
Salary	$	Employer	
Bonus and Commissions		Position or Profession	No. Years
Dividends		Employer's Address	
Real Estate Income			
*Other Income: Itemize		Phone No.	
TOTAL INCOME	$	Partner, officer, or owner in any other venture? No ___ Yes ____ If so, explain:	
		Are any assets pledged? No ___ Yes ___ (Detail in Schedule A)	
		Income taxes settled through (Date)	

*Alimony, child support, or separate maintenance payments need not be disclosed unless relied upon as a basis for extension of credit. If disclosed, payments received under: (circle) court order written agreement oral understanding.

Contingent Liabilities	Amount	General Information (Continued)
As endorser, comaker, or guarantor	$	Are you a defendant in any suits or legal action? No ___ Yes ___
On leases		If so, explain:
Legal claims		Have you ever filed for bankruptcy? No ___ Yes ___
Provision for federal income taxes		If so, explain:
Other special debt, e.g., recourse or repurchase liability		Do you have a will? No ___ Yes ___ With whom?
		Do you have a trust? No ___ Yes ___ With whom?
TOTAL	$	Number of dependents ______ Age(s) _______________

Schedule A: Banks, Brokers, Savings & Loan Associations, Finance Companies, or Credit Unions

List the names of all the institutions at which you maintain a deposit account and/or where you have obtained loans.

Name of Institution	Name on Account	Balance on Deposit	High Credit	Amount Owing	Monthly Payment	Secured by What Assets
	TOTAL					

Schedule B: Stocks (Listed & Unlisted), Bonds (Gov't & Comm.), and Partnership Interests (General & Ltd.)

Number of Shares, Face Value (Bonds), or % of Ownership	Indicate: 1. Agency or name of company issuing security or name of partnership 2. Type of investment or equity classification 3. Number of shares, bonds or % of ownership held 4. Basis of valuation*	In Name Of	*Market Value	Pledged	
				Yes	No
		TOTAL			

*If unlisted security or partnership interest, provide current financial statements to support basis for valuation.

Schedule C: Real Estate Owned (and related debt, if applicable)

Description of Property or Address	Name on Title	Date Acquired	Cost Improvements	Present Mkt. Value	Mortgage or Land Contract Payable		
					Bal. Owing	Mo. Payt.	Holder
		TOTAL					

Schedule D: Real Estate: Mortgages & Land Contracts Receivable (and related debt, if applicable)							
Description of Property or Address	Name on Title	Date Acquired	Balance Receivable	Monthly Payment	Mortgage or Land Contract Payable		
					Bal. Owing	Mo. Payt.	Holder
		TOTAL					

Schedule E: Life Insurance Carried				
Name of Company	Beneficiary	Cash Surrender Value	Loans	Face Amount
			TOTAL	

Schedule F: Retirement Accounts				
Description of Account	Institution	Beneficiary	Balance	Nondeductible Contributions
			TOTAL	

Social Security Benefits Worksheet—Lines 20a and 20b

Keep for Your Records

Before you begin:

√ Complete Form 1040, lines 21 and 23 through 32, if they apply to you.
√ Figure any write-in adjustments to be entered on the dotted line next to line 36 (see the instructions for line 36 on page 35).
√ If you are married filing separately and you lived apart from your spouse for all of 2009, enter "D" to the right of the word "benefits" on line 20a. If you do not, you may get a math error notice from the IRS.
√ Be sure you have read the **Exception** on page 27 to see if you can use this worksheet instead of a publication to find out if any of your benefits are taxable.

1. Enter the total amount from **box 5** of **all** your **Forms SSA-1099** and **Forms RRB-1099.** Also, enter this amount on Form 1040, line 20a . . . . . . **1.** ______
2. Enter one-half of line 1 . . . . **2.** ______
3. Enter the total of the amounts from Form 1040, lines 7, 8a, 9a, 10 through 14, 15b, 16b, 17 through 19, and 21 . . . . **3.** ______
4. Enter the amount, if any, from Form 1040, line 8b . . . . **4.** ______
5. Add lines 2, 3, and 4 . . . . **5.** ______
6. Enter the total of the amounts from Form 1040, lines 23 through 32, plus any write-in adjustments you entered on the dotted line next to line 36 . . . . **6.** ______
7. Is the amount on line 6 less than the amount on line 5?
   ☐ **No.** STOP None of your social security benefits are taxable. Enter -0- on Form 1040, line 20b.
   ☐ **Yes.** Subtract line 6 from line 5 . . . . **7.** ______
8. If you are:
   - Married filing jointly, enter $32,000
   - Single, head of household, qualifying widow(er), or married filing separately and you **lived apart** from your spouse for all of 2009, enter $25,000
   - Married filing separately and you lived with your spouse at any time in 2009, skip lines 8 through 15; multiply line 7 by 85% (.85) and enter the result on line 16. Then go to line 17

   . . . . **8.** ______
9. Is the amount on line 8 less than the amount on line 7?
   ☐ **No.** STOP None of your social security benefits are taxable. Enter -0- on Form 1040, line 20b. If you are married filing separately and you **lived apart** from your spouse for all of 2009, be sure you entered "D" to the right of the word "benefits" on line 20a.
   ☐ **Yes.** Subtract line 8 from line 7 . . . . **9.** ______
10. Enter: $12,000 if married filing jointly; $9,000 if single, head of household, qualifying widow(er), or married filing separately and you **lived apart** from your spouse for all of 2009 . . **10.** ______
11. Subtract line 10 from line 9. If zero or less, enter -0- . . . . **11.** ______
12. Enter the **smaller** of line 9 or line 10 . . . . **12.** ______
13. Enter one-half of line 12 . . . . **13.** ______
14. Enter the **smaller** of line 2 or line 13 . . . . **14.** ______
15. Multiply line 11 by 85% (.85). If line 11 is zero, enter -0- . . . . **15.** ______
16. Add lines 14 and 15 . . . . **16.** ______
17. Multiply line 1 by 85% (.85) . . . . **17.** ______
18. **Taxable social security benefits.** Enter the **smaller** of line 16 or line 17. Also enter this amount on Form 1040, line 20b . . . . **18.** ______

TIP *If any of your benefits are taxable for 2009* ***and*** *they include a lump-sum benefit payment that was for an earlier year, you may be able to reduce the taxable amount. See Pub. 915 for details.*

Simplified Method Worksheet—Lines 16a and 16b

Keep for Your Records

Before you begin: √ If you are the beneficiary of a deceased employee or former employee who died **before** August 21, 1996, include any death benefit exclusion that you are entitled to (up to $5,000) in the amount entered on line 2 below.

Note. If you had more than one partially taxable pension or annuity, figure the taxable part of each separately. Enter the total of the taxable parts on Form 1040, line 16b. Enter the total pension or annuity payments received in 2009 on Form 1040, line 16a.

1. Enter the total pension or annuity payments received in 2009. Also, enter this amount on Form 1040, line 16a . . . . . . **1.** ______

2. Enter your cost in the plan at the annuity starting date . . . . . . **2.** ______

Note. If you completed this worksheet last year, skip line 3 and enter the amount from line 4 of last year's worksheet on line 4 below (even if the amount of your pension or annuity has changed). Otherwise, go to line 3.

3. Enter the appropriate number from **Table 1** below. **But** if your annuity starting date was **after** 1997 **and** the payments are for your life and that of your beneficiary, enter the appropriate number from **Table 2** below . . . . . . **3.** ______

4. Divide line 2 by the number on line 3 . . . . . . **4.** ______

5. Multiply line 4 by the number of months for which this year's payments were made. If your annuity starting date was **before** 1987, skip lines 6 and 7 and enter this amount on line 8. Otherwise, go to line 6 . . . . . . **5.** ______

6. Enter the amount, if any, recovered tax free in years after 1986. If you completed this worksheet last year, enter the amount from line 10 of last year's worksheet . . . . . . **6.** ______

7. Subtract line 6 from line 2 . . . . . . **7.** ______

8. Enter the **smaller** of line 5 or line 7 . . . . . . **8.** ______

9. **Taxable amount.** Subtract line 8 from line 1. Enter the result, but not less than zero. Also, enter this amount on Form 1040, line 16b. If your Form 1099-R shows a larger amount, use the amount on this line instead of the amount from Form 1099-R. If you are a retired public safety officer, see *Insurance Premiums for Retired Public Safety Officers* on page 25 before entering an amount on line 16b. . . . . . . **9.** ______

10. Was your annuity starting date before 1987?

☐ **Yes.** STOP Leave line 10 blank.

☐ **No.** Add lines 6 and 8. This is the **amount you have recovered tax free** through 2009. You will need this number when you fill out this worksheet next year . . . . . . **10.** ______

Table 1 for Line 3 Above

IF the age at annuity starting date (see page 25) was . . .	**AND your annuity starting date was—** **before** November 19, 1996, enter on line 3 . . .	**after** November 18, 1996, enter on line 3 . . .
55 or under	300	360
56–60	260	310
61–65	240	260
66–70	170	210
71 or older	120	160

Table 2 for Line 3 Above

IF the combined ages at annuity starting date (see page 25) were . . .	**THEN enter on line 3 . . .**
110 or under	410
111–120	360
121–130	310
131–140	260
141 or older	210

What's New in 2009

AMT Exemption Amounts Increased. The alternative minimum tax (AMT) exemption amount has been increased for 2009 to $70,950 for joint filers; $46,700 for unmarried individuals; and $35,475 for married filing separate. However, the phase out amounts continue to remain the same.

First-Time Homebuyer Credit. A refundable credit equal to the lesser of 10 percent of the purchase price or $8,000 is available to qualified first-time homebuyers who purchase a principal residence in 2009. Unlike the credit in 2008, the credit in 2009 does not have to be recaptured unless the home ceases to be the taxpayer's principal residence within three years of the date of purchase.

Credits Against AMT Liability. Use of nonrefundable personal tax credits against an individual's regular tax and AMT liability has been extended to 2009.

Additional Child Tax Credit. For 2009 and 2010, the earned income amount for purposes of claiming the additional refundable child tax credit is lowered to $3,000.

American Opportunity Credit. The American Opportunity Credit, which is available for 2009 and 2010, is a modified version of the Hope scholarship tax credit, The maximum credit amount is $2,500 With an increased threshold phase out amount of $80,000 for single filers ($160,000 for joint filers).

Making Work Pay Credit. A $400 ($800 for joint filers) credit is available to all taxpayers in 2009 and 2010 with earned income. The credit is received through out the year from reduced withholding for income taxes.

Tax Preparer's Checklist

- ☐ Interview client to see whether anything affecting the tax credits claimed last year has changed or created the potential for claiming additional tax credit.
- ☐ Verify that clients receiving Social Security and/or railroad retirement benefits, veteran's compensation or certain pension annuity payments received their economic recovery payment.
- ☐ Review AGI phaseout limitation of credits.
- ☐ Review the alternative minimum tax rules and exemption amounts for potential AMT liability.
- ☐ Review prior year return for any long-term unused alternative minimum tax credit, part or all of which may be refundable.
- ☐ Review tax planning to maximize the use of tax credits and flexible spending arrangements.

Section at a Glance

Relevant IRS Publications

- ☐ IRS Publication 378, *Fuel Tax Credits and Refunds*
- ☐ IRS Publication 502, *Medical and Dental Expenses (Including the Coverage Tax Credit)*, and Form 8885, *Health Coverage Tax Credit*
- ☐ IRS Publication 503, *Child and Dependent Care Expenses,* and Form 2441, *Child and Dependent Care Expenses*
- ☐ IRS Publication 514, *Foreign Tax Credit for Individuals,* Publication 901, *U.S. Tax Treaties,* and Form 1116, *Foreign Tax Credit (Individual, Estate, or Trust)*
- ☐ IRS Publication 524, *Credit for the Elderly or the Disabled,* and Schedule R of Form 1040, *Credit for the Elderly or the Disabled*
- ☐ IRS Publication 530, *Tax Information for First-Time Homeowners,* Form 5405, *First-Time Homebuyer Credit,* and Form 8396, *Mortgage Interest Credit*
- ☐ IRS Publication 590, *Individual Retirement Arrangements (IRAs),* and Form 8880, *Credit for Qualified Retirement Savings Contributions*
- ☐ IRS Publication 596, *Earned Income Credit,* and Schedule EIC of Form 1040, *Earned Income Credit Qualifying Child Information*
- ☐ IRS Publication 968, *Tax Benefits for Adoption,* and Form 8839, *Qualified Adoption Expenses*
- ☐ IRS Publication 970, *Tax Benefits for Education,* and Form 8863, *Education Credits (Hope and Lifetime Learning Credits)*
- ☐ IRS Publication 972, *Child Tax Credit,* and Form 8812, *Additional Child Tax Credit*

Tax Credits

Tax credits are subtracted directly from a taxpayer's tax liability and they reduce the tax, dollar for dollar, by the amount of the allowable credit. The advantage of a tax credit over a tax deduction is that the credit amount is subtracted from the tax liability rather than from taxable income. Thus, a tax credit results in a greater benefit than a tax deduction of the same dollar amount. Tax credits also allow all taxpayers who qualify to obtain a tax benefit, regardless of whether they itemize or take the standard deduction, since credits are available even to those who do not itemize on Schedule A of Form 1040.

A refundable credit will generate a refund in the amount that it exceeds the current year's tax liability. A nonrefundable credit that exceeds the tax liability of the current year will not generate a refund. However, some nonrefundable credits may be carried back or forward to offset income taxes in other years.

See MTG Chapter 13, Tax Credits.

Nonrefundable Credits

Filing Tip. The ability to use the nonrefundable personal credits against the sum of the regular tax liability (reduced by the foreign tax credit, if any) and the minimum tax liability (AMT) is extended for 2009.

The order in which the nonrefundable credits are claimed, which is specified in the Internal Revenue Code, is important both because credit amounts are limited by the taxpayer's tax liability and because not *all* credits allow carryback or carryforward treatment. The nonrefundable credits are:

- the foreign tax credit,
- the child and dependent care credit,
- the elderly and disabled credit,
- the educational credits,
- the retirement savings contributions credit,
- the child tax credit,
- the adoption credit,
- the home mortgage interest credit,
- the residential energy credit,
- the District of Columbia first-time homebuyer credit,
- the alternative motor vehicle credit (personal use portion),
- the alternative fuel vehicle refueling property credit (residential installation), and
- the credit for prior year alternative minimum tax credit.

Child and Dependent Care Credit

A nonrefundable credit is allowed for a portion of qualifying child or dependent care expenses paid for the purpose of allowing the taxpayer to be gainfully employed (IRC §21). The credit is claimed by filing Form 2441, *Child and Dependent Care Expense,* and reporting the credit on Form 1040, line 48.

Eligibility. To be eligible for the child and dependent care credit, the taxpayer must maintain a household for him- or herself and one of the following individuals:

1. A dependent as defined in IRC §152(a)(1), i.e., a qualifying child, that has not yet attained the age of 13. See Tab 1 for the definition of a qualifying child.
2. A dependent of the taxpayer who is physically or mentally incapable of caring for himself or herself and has the same principal place of abode as the taxpayer for more than one-half of the year.
3. The taxpayer's spouse who is physically or mentally incapable of caring for himself or herself and has the same principal place of abode of more than one-half of the year.

Taxpayers must provide each dependent's taxpayer identification number, usually their Social Security number, and the identifying number of the service provider (either their Social Security number or their employer identification number (EIN)) in order to claim the credit.

The maximum amount of qualifying expenses eligible for the child and dependent care credit is $3,000 for taxpayers with one qualifying individual and $6,000 for taxpayers with two or more qualifying individuals. Eligible expenses are further limited to smaller of the earned income of either the taxpayer or their spouse. Generally, if one spouse is not working, no credit is allowed. However, if the nonworking spouse is a full-time student at an educational institution for at least five months during the calendar year or is mentally or physically incapable of self-care, the law assumes for each month of disability or school attendance an earned income of $250 if there is one qualifying child or dependent and $500 if there are two or more qualifying children or dependents.

Planning Tip. Depending on the tax bracket of the taxpayer, the number of dependents, and amount of qualifying expenses, comparing the use of the dependent care credit to an employer's dependent care benefit plan is in order to help the taxpayer maximize their tax benefits.

Expenses paid for child and dependent care may qualify for tax benefits under the following methods:

- Taxpayer claims a credit on Form 1040, line 48 (and attaches Form 2441, *Child and Dependent Care Expenses*).
- Taxpayer's employer provides a dependent care benefit (DCB) plan that may be either;
  - an employer paying incurred expenses for the care of a qualifying dependent directly to the taxpayer or his/her care provider,
  - receiving the fair market value for use of an employer-provided daycare center, or
  - pre-tax contributions made by the taxpayer to a daycare flexible spending arrangement (FSA).

The maximum amount of dollars that may be set aside under an employer's DCB plan to cover qualifying dependent care is $5,000 ($2,500 if MFS).

Caution. The credit may *not* be claimed for expenses that were paid with pre-tax employer-provided benefits or with funds from a pre-tax dependent care flexible spending account. Even though you may be unable to use these expenses to claim a credit, the pre-tax benefits must be reconciled on Form 2441.

Example. Gina paid $8,000 in qualifying child care expenses for two children during 2009. Her employer reimbursed her for $2,500 of those expenses. The $6,000 maximum is reduced by the $2,500 reimbursement, leaving $3,500 of expenses eligible for the credit.

Married Taxpayers Who File Separate Returns Are Generally Ineligible. Generally, a married taxpayer must file a joint return to claim the credit. However, a married person living apart from his or her spouse may be considered unmarried for this purpose, unless the spouse was a member of the household during the last six months of the tax year. The requirements for being considered unmarried for this purpose are the same as those for Head of Household filing status described in Tab 1.

Divorced Taxpayers. A divorced or legally separated taxpayer with custody of a child who is disabled or under the age of 13 is entitled to the credit even though the taxpayer has released the right to a dependency exemption for the child.

Amount of the Credit. The amount of the child and dependent care credit is from 20% to 35% of eligible expenses, depending on the taxpayer's AGI. To calculate the credit, multiply the amount of qualifying expenses by the percentage (%) for the appropriate AGI range. Qualifying expenses are limited to $3,000 for one qualifying individual or $6,000 for two or more qualifying individuals.

Child and Dependent Care Credit Rates

Adjusted Gross Income (AGI)	%	Adjusted Gross Income (AGI)	%
$ 0 - 15,000	0.35	$29,001 - 31,000	0.27
15,001 - 17,000	0.34	31,001 - 33,000	0.26
17,001 - 19,000	0.33	33,001 - 35,000	0.25
19,001 - 21,000	0.32	35,001 - 37,000	0.24
21,001 - 23,000	0.31	37,001 - 39,000	0.23
23,001 - 25,000	0.30	39,001 - 41,000	0.22
25,001 - 27,000	0.29	41,001 - 43,000	0.21
27,001 - 29,000	0.28	43,001 - No limit	0.20

Caution. If an employee's W-2 form includes an amount for DCB, Part III of Form 2441 must be completed to report qualified expenses incurred, even if the child and dependent care credit is not claimed. DCBs may result in taxable income if not enough qualified expenses are paid for child or dependent care.

Example. Tony had $4,000 in pretax earnings withheld through a DCB plan. He was reimbursed for the entire $4,000, but incurred only $3,500 of qualified child care expenses for the year. Result: $500 of benefits must be included on line 7 of Form 1040 as taxable income.

See MTG ¶1301.

Credit for the Elderly or the Disabled

A 15% nonrefundable credit is available to low-income taxpayers who are age 65 or older, or permanently and totally disabled and retired (IRC §22). The credit is claimed by filing Schedule R, *Credit for the Elderly and Disabled.* The credit amount is reported on Form 1040, line 53 by checking box c and writing "Sch R" in space next to the box. The maximum amount of this credit is $1,125.

To qualify, the AGI must be equal to or less than;

- the cutoff for the taxpayer's filing status, or
- the total of nontaxable income from Social Security and other nontaxable pensions must be equal to or less than the cutoff for the taxpayer's filing status.

See the following chart for the cutoff amounts for each filing status.

AGI Limitations for the Elderly or the Disabled Credit

Filing Status	AGI Cutoff	Cutoff for Total of Nontaxable Social Security and Other Nontaxable Pensions
Single, Head of Household, or Qualifying Widow(er)	$17,500	$5,000
Married Filing Jointly **and** both spouses qualify	$25,000	$7,500
Married Filing Jointly **and** only one spouse qualifies	$20,000	$5,000
Married Filing Separately **and** spouses did not live together at any time during the year	$12,500	$3,750

Individuals are considered retired on disability if they have stopped working because of a permanent and total disability, even if they did not formally retire. A physician must complete a statement certifying that the permanent and total disability existed on the date of retirement and is expect to last at least 12 months or more. This statement should be retained with their income tax records. For more information, see IRS Publication 554, *Credit for the Elderly or the Disabled,* and MTG ¶1302.

Unless they lived apart at all times during the tax year, married taxpayers must file a joint tax return to claim the credit.

Amount of the Credit. For individuals age 65 or older, the initial amount of allowable credit varies with filing status (see the chart below). This initial amount is then reduced by amounts received as pension, annuity or disability benefits that are excludable from gross income and are payable under the Social Security Act (Title II), the Railroad Retirement Act of 1974, or a Veterans Administration program, or that are excludable under a non-Code provision. No reduction is made for pension, annuity or disability benefits for personal injuries or sickness resulting from active service in the armed forces of any country, the National Oceanic and Atmospheric Administration, the Public Health Service, or as a disability annuity payable under the provisions of §808 of the Foreign Service Act of 1980.

Amounts Required to Calculate the Credit for the Elderly or the Disabled

Filing Status	Age and Disability Status	Initial (Maximum) Amount	Reduced by One-Half of AGI Over
Single, Head of Household, or Qualifying Widow(er)	Age 65 or older or under age 65 and retired on permanent and total disability[1]	$5,000	$7,500
Married Filing Jointly	Both age 65 or older or one age 65 or older and the other retired on permanent and total disability or both retired on permanent and total disability[1]	$7,500	$10,000
Married Filing Jointly	Both under age 65 and one retired on permanent and total disability[1] or one 65 or older and the other under age 65 and not retired on permanent and total disability[1]	$5,000	$10,000
Married Filing Separately and spouses did not live together at any time during the year	Age 65 or older or under age 65 and retired on permanent and total disability[1]	$3,750	$5,000

[1]For permanently and totally disabled individuals under age 65, the applicable initial amount may not exceed the amount of taxable disability income.

Education Credits—Hope, American Opportunity (modified Hope), and Lifetime Learning Credits

Two nonrefundable tax credits are available to persons who incur expenses for higher education (IRC §25A). Taxpayers claim an education credit on Form 8863, *Education Credits (American Opportunity, Hope and Lifetime Learning Credits),* and enter the amounts on Line 49 of Form 1040.

Requirements and Rules for Education Credits. The credits are available for qualified tuition and related expenses of the taxpayer, the taxpayer's spouse, or a dependent of the taxpayer claimed on the taxpayer's return. The credits are not available to married taxpayers filing separate returns, unless one of the taxpayers can qualify under the filing status rules as unmarried for filing purposes.

The Hope credit phases out in 2009 for modified AGI between $80,000 and $90,000 if Single, Head of Household or Qualifying Widow(er), or between $160,000 and $180,000 if Married Filing Jointly. The lifetime learning credit phases out in 2009 for modified AGI between $50,000 and $60,000 if Single, Head of Household or Qualifying Widow(er), or between $100,000 and $120,000 if Married Filing Jointly. AGI must be increased by any exclusion or deduction for foreign earned income, foreign housing cost, income for residents of American Samoa and income from Puerto Rico.

A taxpayer may not claim both a Hope and lifetime learning credit for the same student in the same year.

A taxpayer may claim either the tuition and fees deduction under IRC §222 or an educational credit, but not both, for the same student in the same year. See Tab 13 for information on the tuition and fees deduction.

Dependent Claimed on Another Person's Return. If a parent claims a child as a dependent, only that parent, or, in some cases, the other parent (see IRS Publication 970, *Tax Benefits for Education*), may claim the education credit for the child. If the parent does not claim an eligible child, who is a student, as a dependent, only the student can claim the education credit. Qualifying expenses paid by a student are considered to have been paid by the parent if the student is claimed as a dependent on the parent's tax return.

Planning Tip. It may be advantageous for an upper income parents, whose adjusted gross income either partially or completely phases out the educational credit and most or all of the dependency exemption, to forego claiming the eligible child, who is a student, as a dependent. This would allow the child to claim the full amount of the education credit, assuming the child has a tax liability. This would result in a lower family tax liability than if the parents claimed the student as a dependent.

Caution. If upper income parents forego claiming an eligible child, who is a student, as a dependent, to maximize the use of an education credit, this does not mean the child may claim the personal exemption for themselves.

Third-Party Tuition Payments. If a third party (such as a grandparent) makes a payment directly to an eligible educational institution for a student's qualified expenses, the student is treated as receiving the payment from a third party and, in turn, paying the qualified expenses. If the student is not claimed as a dependent on another person's return, the student claims the education credit (if otherwise eligible). If the student is claimed as a dependent on another person's return, the expenses treated as paid by the student are treated as paid by the person claiming the dependency deduction and that person claims the education credit.

Qualified Expenses. The taxpayer may include tuition and fees required for the enrollment or attendance of a student at an eligible educational institution. Fees are included only if the fees must be paid to the institution as a condition of enrollment or attendance. For 2009 and 2010, qualifying expenses will also include course materials (IRC §25A(i)(3)).

Expenses qualify in the tax year paid. Payments must be for an academic period (such as a quarter, semester, or trimester) that begins either in the same tax year or in the first three months of the following tax year. For institutions that use credit hours or clock hours and not academic periods, each payment period may be treated as an academic period.

An eligible educational institution is any accredited college, university, vocational school or other accredited post-secondary education institution.

See Tab 13 and MTG ¶1303.

Payment with Borrowed Funds. The Hope and lifetime learning credits can be claimed for qualified tuition and related expenses paid with the proceeds of a loan. The expenses are used to figure the credit for the year in which the expenses are paid, not the year in which the loan is repaid.

American Opportunity Credit. For 2009 and 2010, a modified version of the Hope scholarship credit, called the American Opportunity tax credit, is available. The amount of the credit is 100 percent of the tuition and related expenses paid by the taxpayer during the tax year for education furnished to the eligible student during any academic period beginning in the tax year up to $2,000, and 25 percent of the next $2,000 of the same expenses, for a maximum credit of $2,500. Qualified expenses are the same as for purposes of the Hope scholarship credit, except that they include course materials, whether or not they are required as a condition of enrollment. The American Opportunity credit is allowed for first four years of post-secondary education per student at an eligible educational institution (IRC §25A(i)).

Unlike the Hope credit, the American Opportunity credit is allowed against the alternative minimum tax (AMT). In addition, 40 percent of the credit is refundable. However, no portion of the credit is refundable for any taxpayer that is subject to the kiddie tax.

Filing Tip. Taxpayers with students attending a college or university located in the Midwestern disaster area may elect out of claiming the American Opportunity credit. The Hope and the lifetime learning credits have been double for students attending educational institutions located in the Midwestern disaster area for 2008 and 2009. See Tab 16 for a definition of the Midwestern disaster area.

Caution. Parents with two or more dependents in college must take care in electing out of the American Opportunity credit. If the parents elects out to claim double the regular Hope credit for a student at a qualified Midwestern educational institution, the election effects all their dependent students regardless of where they are attending college.

Hope Scholarship Credit. The Hope scholarship credit is a nonrefundable tax credit of 100% of the first $1,200 and 50% of the next $1,200 for each of the first two years of post-secondary tuition and fees. The amount of tuition and fees to be used each year in calculating the credit amount is adjusted for inflation. The maximum annual credit for 2009 is $1,800 per eligible student (Rev. Proc. 2008-66, 2008-45 I.R.B. 1107).

The following restrictions apply to the Hope credit:

- Students must be enrolled in a program that leads to a degree, certificate, or other recognized educational credential.
- Student must take at least one-half of the normal full-time workload for the student's course of study for at least one academic period beginning during the year.
- The student must be free of any felony conviction for possessing or distributing a controlled substance.
- The first two years of post-secondary education may include two one-year certificate programs. A student who completes a one-year post-secondary certificate program and in a later year completes another one-year post-secondary certificate program may claim the Hope credit for both years if all other requirements are met.

Planning Tip. The Hope credit is claimed per student per year. A family may have more than one eligible student in a year.

Lifetime Learning Credit. The lifetime learning credit is a nonrefundable tax credit of 20% of up to $10,000 of qualified tuition and fees paid during the tax year. The maximum credit allowed is $2,000. There is no limit on the number of years for which the credit can be claimed. The credit is "per taxpayer," and does not vary based on the number of students in a family. The credit is not workload-based; it is allowed for students taking one or more courses. Both degree and nondegree courses are counted. The credit is available for undergraduate, graduate, and professional degree students and for students acquiring or improving job skills.

Planning Tip. Compare taking an education credit with taking a tuition and fees deduction on line 34, Form 1040. Also, see Tab 13 for more information on education tax breaks and planning opportunities.

Residential Energy Credits

Nonbusiness (Residential) Energy Property Credit

Caution. The American Recovery and Reinvestment Act of 2009 (P.L. 111-5) has extended the nonbusiness energy credit through 2010.

This credit is to assist taxpayers in defraying the expenses of either improving their principal residence's energy efficiency or replacing heating and cooling systems with more efficient units (IRC §25C). The credit amount is equal to 30 percent of the sum of (a) taxpayer's residential energy property expenditures, plus (b) the cost of qualified energy efficiency improvements for the tax year. The amount of credit a taxpayer may claim is limited to a maximum of $1500 for both 2009 and 2010. In addition, the credit is to be treated as a nonrefundable personal credit allowing the credit to be claimed against both a taxpayer's regular and alternative minimum tax liabilities.

The taxpayer must be the original owner and place the property into use before December 31, 2007, and between January 1 and December 31, 2010. Any increase in the basis of the residential property must be reduced by the credit amount claimed. The credit will be claimed on Form 5695, *Residential Energy Credits.*

Qualified energy efficiency improvements include the following building envelope components that are installed on or in the taxpayer's main home located in the United States:

- any insulation material or system that is specifically and primarily designed to reduce the heat loss or gain of a home when installed in or on that home;
- exterior doors, including certain storm doors; and
- any metal roof installed on a home, but only if this roof has appropriate pigmented coatings or cooling granules that are specifically and primarily designed to reduce the heat gain of the home.

These components must be new, and they must be expected to remain in use for at least five years.

> **Caution.** The costs for onsite preparation, assembly or original installation of the qualified energy efficiency improvements *cannot* be included in the amounts used to determine the amount of credit.

Qualified residential energy property is any of the following:

- certain electric heat pump water heaters, electric heat pumps, central air conditioners, and natural gas, propane, oil water, or biomass fueled heaters;
- qualified natural gas, propane, or oil furnaces or hot water boilers; and
- certain advanced main air circulating fans used in natural gas, propane, or oil furnaces.

The costs of onsite preparation, assembly, or original installation of residential energy property (unlike such costs related to qualified energy efficiency improvements) are included in the amount of costs to be used for determining the credit amount.

> **Planning Tip.** For married taxpayers who maintain separate main residences but still file jointly, they each can claim the nonbusiness energy property credit. Each figures their credit amount on their own Form 5695, which are attached to the Form 1040. The total amount is written in on line 50 with the phrase "more than one main home" written on the dotted line to the left of the box.

> **Caution.** Qualified nonbusiness energy property must meet certain energy performance and quality standards to be able to claim the credit. The manufacturer's written certification may be relied upon but should be retained with tax records.

For further information on the nonbusiness (residential) energy property credit, see MTG at ¶1341.

Residential Energy Efficient Property Credit

This energy credit, available through 2016, allows taxpayers to claim a credit in an amount equal to 30 percent of the expenditures, including installation costs, for qualified solar water heating, solar electric equipment, including but not limited to photovoltaic equipment, fuel cell energy property, geothermal heat pump property, and small wind energy property (IRC §25D). For tax years beginning after 2008, the credit limitation has been eliminated except for fuel cell property, which remains at $500 per half kilowatt of capacity. Any unused credit due to the tax liability limitation rules may be carried forwarded to succeeding tax years. The property must be installed and used in a home in the United States. The credit will also be claimed on Form 5695, *Residential Energy Credits.*

> **Planning Tip.** Qualified residential solar energy property installed and used in a home in the United States does *not* have to be on the taxpayer's principal or main home.

Qualified solar water heating property expenditures are for property used to heat water for use in a home, with at least one-half of the energy used being derived from the sun. The property must be certified by the nonprofit Solar Rating Certification Corporation or a comparable entity endorsed by the government of the state in which the property is installed.

> **Caution.** Costs allocated to solar water heating property of a swimming pool, hot tub, or any other energy storage medium which has a function other than storage do not qualify for purposes of claiming the residential energy efficient property credit.

Qualified solar electric property expenditures are for property that uses solar energy to generate electricity for use in a home and includes costs related to solar panels or other property installed as a roof or a portion of a roof.

> **Planning Tip.** There is no lifetime maximum, as for the nonbusiness energy credit, for the residential energy efficient property credit. A taxpayer could install a solar heating system and a solar electrical system in the same year and potentially be eligible to claim the full amount of both credits.

Qualified fuel cell property expenditures are for an integrated system comprising a fuel cell stack assembly and associated balance of plant components that converts a fuel into electricity using electrochemical means. The fuel cell property must have a nameplate capacity of at least one-half kilowatt of electricity using an electrochemical process and the electricity-only generation efficiency of greater than 30 percent to qualify for the credit.

> **Caution.** If installing qualified fuel cell property, the installation must be in a home located in the United States and the taxpayer's principal residence. This is different than from the installation of solar water heating or electrical generation property, which only requires installation in a home used by the taxpayer in the United States.

Qualifying small wind energy property expenditures are for property that uses a wind turbine to generate electricity for use in connection with the taxpayer's residence located in the United States. If the residence is occupied by two or more taxpayers, the total credit amount for the year *cannot* exceed the annual maximum limit.

Qualifying geothermal heat pump property expenditures are for property that uses the ground water as a thermal energy source to heat a U.S. residential dwelling unit, or as a thermal heat energy sink to cool the unit that meets the Energy Star program requirements.

For further information on the residential energy efficient property credit, see MTG at ¶1341

> **Planning Tip.** The residential energy efficient property credit may be used to offset the sum of the regular tax liability and the minimum tax liability.

Foreign Tax Credit

A taxpayer may choose between claiming a foreign tax credit (IRC §27) or a tax deduction on Schedule A of Form 1040 for taxes paid to a foreign government or a U.S. possession on income that is also subject to U.S. federal income tax. A taxpayer cannot take both the credit and claim the deduction on the same foreign tax. However, the deduction on Schedule A is allowed for certain taxes that do not qualify for the foreign tax credit due to boycott provisions or limitations imposed by IRC §901(j)(2).

Election Not to File Form 1116, Foreign Tax Credit. Taxpayers are allowed to claim the foreign tax credit on line 47 of Form 1040 without regard to the foreign tax credit limitation and without filing Form 1116 if all of the following apply:

1. The foreign taxes paid or accrued during the year do not exceed $300 ($600 for joint filers).
2. All foreign income is "passive income" (such as dividends, interest, annuities, and rents and royalties not from an active trade or business).
3. All foreign income is reported on Form 1099-DIV, 1099-INT, or a similar statement.

No excess foreign taxes may be carried over to or from a tax year to which the election applies, but carryovers to and from other years are unaffected.

Form 1116, Foreign Tax Credit. A separate Form 1116 must be filed for each category of income listed above Part I of the form.

In *Part I, Taxable Income or Loss From Sources Outside the United States,* the taxpayer begins by entering the gross income from sources within the country named for the category of income designated on the form. This does not include any income that has been excluded on Form 2555, *Foreign Earned Income.*

> **Caution.** The taxpayer must include income even if it is not taxable by the foreign country.

Deductions and losses definitely related to earning this income, plus a pro-rata share of other expenses and losses, are then subtracted from the gross income figure.

In *Part II, Foreign Taxes Paid or Accrued,* the taxpayer must enter the foreign tax paid in both the foreign currency denominations and converted to U.S. dollars. Foreign tax on passive income does not have to be entered in foreign currency amounts.

In *Part III, Figuring the Credit,* the foreign taxes paid, from Part II, are adjusted to arrive at total foreign taxes available for credit. Adjustments include carrybacks and carryovers of foreign taxes and taxes on income excluded on Form 2555. If only part of the taxpayer's income is excluded on Form 2555, pro-rate the adjustment for this item. Adjustments are also made for dividends and lump sum distributions. The maximum foreign tax credit is generally limited to the allocated amount of U.S. tax imposed on the foreign income or the actual foreign tax paid, whichever is less.

Part IV, Summary of Credits from Separate Parts III, is filled out if more than one Form 1116 is being filed. Combine the credits from each form and enter the total in Part IV.

Child Tax Credit

The child tax credit allows an individual to claim a credit for each qualifying child as defined under IRC §152(c) who is under age 17 on the last day of the tax year (IRC §24). See Tab 1 for the definition of a qualifying child. The child tax credit amount is $1,000 per qualifying child through 2010.

> **Caution.** A child is a qualifying child of the taxpayer only if the taxpayer *can and does* claim an exemption for the child.

> **Caution.** Beginning in 2009, the child must be younger than the taxpayer.

Phaseout Based on Modified AGI. The child tax credit is phased out for individuals with modified AGI over $75,000 for single taxpayers, $110,000 for married individuals filing jointly, and $55,000 for married individuals filing separately. Specifically, the credit is reduced by $50 for each $1,000 (or fraction thereof) of modified AGI (MAGI) over the threshold. Therefore, a $1,000 credit will be completely phased out at $20,000 of income over the threshold, but because excess income must be increased to the next $1,000 rather than being rounded down, the full benefit actually is lost at $19,001 of income over the threshold amount. Thus, the actual phaseout range for a single individual with one qualifying child is between $75,000 and $94,001 of MAGI. The actual phaseout range for a single individual with two qualifying children is between $75,000 and $114,001. MAGI (modified adjusted gross income) is adjusted gross income determined without regard to the exclusion for foreign earned income, the exclusion for foreign housing costs, and exclusion of income from certain U.S. possessions and Puerto Rico.

Additional Child Tax Credit May Be Available. The additional child tax credit allows a portion of the child tax credit to be refundable for certain taxpayers who get less than the full amount of the child tax credit. Only taxpayers with at least one qualifying child are eligible. For details, see *Additional Child Tax Credit* under **Refundable Credits**.

See the IRS worksheets reproduced at pages 10-23 through 10-25.

Tax Liability Limitation. The child tax credit may be claimed in an amount equal to the regular tax liability reduced by any foreign tax credit allowed plus the alternative minimum tax liability. It should be noted that for tax years after 2009 the amount of child tax credit will be limited to the excess of the sum of the regular tax liability plus the alternative minimum tax liability over all the other nonrefundable credits except this credit, the adoption credit, the retirement savings contributions credit and the foreign tax credit.

Retirement Savings Contributions Credit

This nonrefundable credit is targeted toward low- and middle-income taxpayers who make contributions to a retirement plan (IRC §25B). The credit amount is determined by multiplying the applicable percentage for the taxpayer's filing status and AGI (see the table on page 10-9) by their contribution amount to a qualified retirement plan, except that the total amount of credit claimed cannot exceed $2,000. Taxpayers are allowed both a deduction for contributions to a qualified retirement plan and an exclusion for the retirement savings contributions credit (also referred to as the "saver's credit"). The credit amount that may be claimed cannot exceed the total of the regular tax liability and the alternative minimum tax liability less all other nonrefundable personal credits except this credit, the adoption credit and the foreign tax credit when IRC §26(a)(2) does not apply. Form 8880, *Credit for Qualified Retirement Savings Contributions,* is used to claim the credit.

Mortgage Interest Credit

This nonrefundable credit is targeted toward low-income homeowners who obtain qualified mortgage credit certificates (MCCs) from state or local governments (IRC §25). The credit amount is equal to the percentage as listed on the MCC of the interest paid on the mortgage amount. Only the taxpayer's main home/principal residence is eligible. The credit rate is provided on the MCC and cannot be less than 10% or more than 50%. If the certificate credit rate is more than 20%, a $2,000 limit applies to the credit. Any unused credit amount due to the tax liability limitation rule imposed by IRC §26 may be carried forward for

Retirement Savings Credit Limitations

Adjusted Gross Income			% of AGI Allowed as Credit
MFJ	HOH	Single, MFS, QW	
$0 - $33,000	$0 - $24,750	$0 - $16,500	50%
$33,001 - $36,000	$24,751 - $27,000	$16,501 - $18,000	20%
$36,001 - $55,000	$27,001 - $41,625	$18,001 - $27,750	10%
$55,001 or more	$41,626 or more	$27,751 or more	0%

three years. Mortgage interest deducted on Schedule A, Form 1040 must be reduced by any credit allowed under this provision. Form 8396, *Mortgage Interest Credit,* is used to claim the credit.

See MTG ¶ 1308.

Planning Tip. Taxpayers need to be aware that if the main home/principal residence upon which the mortgage interest certificate is issued is disposed of before the tenth year, a portion of the credit amount must be recaptured under the formula in IRC §143(m).

District of Columbia First-Time Homebuyer Credit

First-time homebuyers who had purchased a principal residence in the District of Columbia are eligible to claim a credit of up to $5,000 ($2,500 in the case of a married person filing separately) (IRC §1400C). The credit is phased out ratably between AGI of $70,000 and $90,000 ($110,000 to $130,000, for joint filers). The residence must have been purchased before January 1, 2010, but any unused credit is carried forward indefinitely. The taxpayer's basis in the home must be reduced by the amount of credit claimed. The credit is claimed on Form 8859, *District of Columbia First-Time Homebuyer Credit.*

See MTG ¶ 1310.

Caution. The District of Columbia first-time homebuyer credit is coordinated with the refundable first-time homebuyer credit under IRC §36.

Adoption Credit

Adoptive parents may be able to take either a credit (IRC §23) or an adoption assistance income exclusion (IRC §137) for qualifying adoption expenses incurred in the legal adoption of a child under age 18 or an incapacitated or special needs person. Both a credit and an exclusion may be claimed for the same adoption; however, the same expenses cannot be used to claim both the credit and the exclusion. For 2009, there is a $12,150 per child maximum on qualifying expenses. The credit is phased out for modified AGI between $182,180 and $222,180. The credit amount for year 2009 is limited to the excess of the sum of the taxpayer's regular tax liability reduced by the foreign tax credit over the alternative minimum tax. The credit amount in years after 2009 will be limited to the excess of the sum of the regular tax liability plus the alternative minimum tax under IRC §55 over the sum of all other nonrefundable personal credits other than this credit plus the foreign tax credit. Any unused credit may be carried forward for up to five years. File Form 8839, *Qualified Adoption Expenses,* to claim the credit or exclusion. Also, see IRS Publication 968, *Tax Benefits for Adoption,* for expense limitations, eligibility requirements, and other rules.

Alternative Motor Vehicle Credit

To encourage taxpayers to use cars powered by alternative fuel sources, the alternative motor vehicle credit was enacted. The credit is actually the sum of four separate credits each based on the alternative propulsion system used to power the car (IRC §30B). The credit amounts are determined by the IRS using numerous factors including, but not limited to, the car's weight, the annual fuel consumption and the percentage increase in miles per gallon over the base year, 2002. The amount of the credit that may be claimed is further limited by the tax liability limitation under IRC §30B(g)(2). For individual taxpayers, the credit amount cannot exceed the excess of the regular tax liability reduced by all the nonrefundable personal credits and the foreign tax credit over the alternative minimum tax liability. The credit for all the components of the alternative motor vehicle credit will be claimed on Form 8910, *Alternative Motor Vehicle Credit.* Currently, their are several vehicles certified under the hybrid motor vehicle credit component, the alternative fuel motor vehicle credit component, and the lean-burn technology credit component. See MTG ¶ 1345-¶ 1349.

Hybrid Motor Vehicle Credit

A credit of potentially up to $3,400 is available for new hybrid motor vehicles which are either a passenger automobile or light truck with a gross vehicle weight of not more than 8,500 pounds if purchased prior to January 1, 2011 (IRC §30B(d) and (j)). A new hybrid vehicle is a vehicle that receives its propulsion from both an internal combustion or heat engine using a consumable fuel and a rechargeable energy storage source. In addition, the vehicle must meet certain standards of the Clean Air Act or exceed the equivalent qualifying California low emission vehicle standards.

The hybrid motor vehicle credit is subject to a phaseout calculation based on the number of hybrid vehicles sold during the year. The credit amount that may be claimed is reduced once a manufacturer sells 60,000 vehicles. The phaseout schedule is as follows:

- in the quarter that the 60,000th vehicle is sold and the following quarter - 100 percent of the credit amount;
- in the next two quarters (the second and third quarters following the quarter in which the 60,000th vehicle is sold) - 50 percent of the credit amount;
- in the next two quarters (the fourth and fifth quarters following the quarter in which the 60,000th vehicle is sold) - 25 percent of the credit amount; and
- for all quarters thereafter, no credit is available.

Filing Tip. The original use of the hybrid vehicle must commence with the taxpayer and the vehicle has to be assembled by a manufacturer; no retrofitting.

Caution. The credit cannot be claimed by taxpayers who lease a hybrid vehicle, but rather only by the leasing company that purchased the vehicle for lease.

The following table contains the vehicles that have been certified and the credit amount assigned at the time of publication.

Model Year	Make and Model	Credit Amount
2010	Cadillac Escalade Hybrid (2 & 4 WD)	$2,200
	Chevrolet Malibu Hybrid	$1,550
	Chevrolet Silverado Hybrid C15 (2WD)	$2,200
	Chevrolet Silverado Hybrid K15 (4WD)	$2,200
	Chevrolet Tahoe Hybrid C15 (2WD)	$2,200
	Chevrolet Tahoe Hybrid K15 (4WD)	$2,200
	Ford Escape Hybrid 4x2	$3,000*
	Ford Escape Hybrid 4x4	$2,600**
	Ford Fusion Hybrid	$3,400***
	GMC Sierra Hybrid C15 (2WD)	$2,200
	GMC Sierra Hybrid K15 (4WD)	$2,200
	GMC Yukon Hybrid C1500 (2WD)	$2,200
	GMC Yukon Hybrid K1500 (4WD)	$2,200
	GMC Denali Hybrid C1500 (2WD)	$2,200
	GMC Denali Hybrid K1500 (4WD)	$2,200
	Mercury Mariner Hybrid 4x2	$3,000*
	Mercury Mariner Hybrid 4x4	$2,600**
	Mercury Milan Hybrid	$3,400***
	Nissan Altima Hybrid	$2,350
2009	Cadillac Escalade Hybrid (2WD)	$2,200
	Cadillac Escalade Hybrid All-Wheel Drive	$1,800
	Chevrolet Tahoe Hybrid C1500 (2WD)	$2,200
	Chevrolet Tahoe Hybrid K1500 (4WD)	$2,200
	Chevrolet Tahoe Hybrid C15 (4WD)	$2,200
	Chevrolet Tahoe Hybrid K15 (4WD)	$2,200
	Chevrolet Malibu Hybrid	$1,500
	Chrysler Aspen Hybrid	$2,200
	Dodge Durango Hybrid	$2,200
	Ford Escape Hybrid (2WD)	$3,000
	Ford Escape Hybrid (4WD)	$1,950
	GMC Sierra Hybrid C15 (2WD)	$2,200
	GMC Sierra Hybrid K15 (4WD)	$2,200
	GMC Yukon Hybrid C1500 (2WD)	$2,200
	GMC Yukon Hybrid K1500 (4WD)	$2,200
	Mazda Tribute Hybrid (2WD)	$3,000
	Mazda Tribute Hybrid (4WD)	$1,950
	Mercury Mariner Hybrid (2WD)	$3,000
	Mercury Mariner Hybrid (4WD)	$1,950
	Nissan Altima Hybrid	$2,350
	Saturn Aura Hybrid	$1,550
	Saturn Vue Hybrid	$1,550
2008	Chevrolet Malibu Hybrid	$1,300
	Chevrolet Tahoe Hybrid (2 & 4 WD)	$2,200
	Ford Escape Hybrid (2WD)	$3,000
	Ford Escape Hybrid (4WD)	$2,200
	GMC Yukon Hybrid	$2,200
	Mazda Tribute 2WD	$3,000
	Mazda Tribute 4WD	$2,200
	Mercury Mariner Hybrid 2WD	$3,000
	Mercury Mariner Hybrid 4WD	$2,200
	Nissan Altima Hybrid	$2,350
	Saturn Aura Hybrid	$1,300
	Saturn Vue Green Hybrid	$1,550

* If purchased before April 1, 2009; $1,500 if purchased after April 1, 2009 but before October 1, 2009; $750 if purchased after October 1, 2009, but before April 1, 2010; no credit is available if purchased on or after April 1, 2010.

** If purchased before April 1, 2009; $1,300 if purchased after April 1, 2009 but before October 1, 2009; $650 if purchased after October 1, 2009, but before April 1, 2010; no credit is available if purchased on or after April 1, 2010.

*** If purchased before April 1, 2009; $1,700 if purchased after April 1, 2009 but before October 1, 2009; $850 if purchased after October 1, 2009, but before April 1, 2010; no credit is available if purchased on or after April 1, 2010.

Caution. Toyota, which wholly owns Lexus, and American Honda Motor Company, Inc. have exceeded the phase out threshold and the hybrid vehilce credit is no longer available for any model of their vehicles.

Caution. Ford Motor Company sold its 60,000 hybrid vehicle in the fourth quarter of 2008. Thus, the alternative hybrid motor vehicle credit began to phase out on April 1, 2009. The phase out will be complete on March 31, 2010.

Alternative Fuel Motor Vehicle Credit

The alternative fuel motor vehicle credit is available to automobiles that are operated using an alternative fuel, such as compressed natural gas. As with the hybrid vehicle credit (IRC §30B(d)), the IRS will determine the credit amount upon certifying the vehicles. At the time of publication, there is only one make and model vehicle that has been certified;

- the 2009 Honda Civic GX with a credit amount of $4,000, and
- the 2009 Honda FCX Clarity Fuel Cell with a credit amount of $12,000.

As with the hybrid vehicle credit, the original use of the alternative fuel vehicle must be by the taxpayer and the vehicle has to be assembled by the manufacturer, not retrofitted.

Planning Tip. There is no phaseout for the alternative fuel motor vehicle credit. The full credit amount will be available through 2010.

Advanced Lean Burn Technology

Lean burn technology vehicles are either passenger automobiles or light trucks that have an internal combustion engine that: (1) is designed to incorporate more air than is necessary for complete combustion, (2) is fuel injected, and (3) achieves at least 125 percent of the 2002 model year fuel economy (IRC §30B(b)). As well as meeting the standard three requirements of all components of the alternative motor vehicle credit, e.g., first use by the taxpayer, not purchased for resale, and assembled by a manufacturer, certain Clean Air Act standards or their state equivalents must be satisfied for 2004 and later vehicles. The credit amount is potentially up to $3,400, but the amount is phased out in conjunction with the hybrid vehicle credit component. The credit will be available for certified vehicles purchased before January 1, 2011. At the time of publication, these models and their credit amounts are:

Model Year	Make and Model	Credit Amount
2010	Audi A3 2.0L TDI Automatic	$1,300
	Audi Q7 3.0L TDI	$1,150
	Volkswagon Golf 2.0L TDI (2 & 4 Door) Automatic	$1,700
	Volkswagon Golf 2.0L TDI (2 & 4 Door) Manual	$1,300
	Volkswagon Golf 2.0L TDI (Manual & Automatic)	$1,300
	Volkswagon Golf 2.0L TDI SportWagon (Manual & Automatic)	$1,300
	Volkswagon Touareg 3.0L TDI	$1,150
2009	Audi Q7 3.0L TDI	$1,150
	BMW 335d Sedan	$ 900
	BMW x5xDrive35dSports Activity Vehicle	$1,800
	Mercedes GL 320 BLUE TEC	$1,550
	Mercedes R 320 Blue TEC	$1,550
	Mercedes ML 320 Blue TEC	$ 900
	Volkswagon Jetta 2.0L TDI Sedan (Manual & Automatic)	$1,300
	Volkswagon Jetta 2.0L TDI SportsWagon (Manual & Automatic)	$1,300
	Volkswagon Touareg 3.0L TDI	$1,150

Qualified Alternative Fuel Motor Vehicles (QAFMV) and Heavy Hybrid Vehicles

Vehicles with a gross vehicle weight rating of 8,500 pounds or more qualify for additional credit amounts of the hybrid vehicle credit or the alternative fuel vehicle credit. The vehicles must still meet all the requirements for each credit and be certified by the IRS. A complete list of qualifying vehicles can be found on the IRS website at http://www.irs.gov/businesses/article/0,,id=175456,00.html.

Plug-In Conversion Credit

The American Recovery and Reinvestment Act of 2009 (P.L. 111-5) added a new credit to the alternative motor vehicle credit to encourage taxpayers to convert their vehicles to electric drive motors. The credit amount is equal to 10 percent of the first $40,000 of conversion expenses to meet the requirements of a qualified plug-in electric drive motor vehicle as defined in IRC §30D (IRC §30B(i)). The credit is allowed with respect to motor vehicles whose cost may have been used in earlier years to claim any other alternative motor vehicle credit.

Alternative Fuel Vehicle Refueling Property Credit

The alternative fuel vehicle refueling credit is also available to taxpayers who install in their residence the necessary equipment to refuel their alternative fuel motor vehicles (IRC §30C). For 2009 and 2010, the credit amount is equal to 30 percent of the cost of the hydrogen-related refueling property placed into service during the year. The credit amount for non-hydrogen-related property during 2009 and 2010 is 50 percent. This credit replaced the clean-fuel refueling property credit under IRC §179A but adopts many of the same rules. The credit amount for hydrogen-related property is limited to $1,000 ($2,000 for non-hydrogen related property) for residential installation. This amount could be further reduced by the tax liability limitation, which limits the credit amount that may be claimed to the excess of the regular tax liability less the sum of all nonrefundable personal credits, the foreign tax credit, and the alternative motor vehicle credit over the alternative minimum tax (IRC §30C(d)(2)). The credit will be claimed on Form 8911, *Alternative Fuel Vehicle Refueling Property Credit.*

Electric Drive Motor Vehicle Credits

Plug-in Electric Drive Motor Vehicle Credit

A new credit is available for qualified plug-in electric drive motor vehicles placed in service after December 31, 2008 and before January 1, 2010. The amount of the credit is $2,500, plus $417 for each kilowatt hour of traction battery capacity in excess of four kilowatt hours. A new qualified plug-in electric drive motor vehicle must meet requirements similar to those of under the alternative motor vehicle credit. For the purposes of the credit, a vehicle;

- is first used by taxpayer,
- is acquired for use or lease and not resale,
- is made by a manufacturer,
- draws propulsion using a traction battery with at least a four hour kilowatt capacity,
- uses an offboard source of energy to recharge such battery, and
- with a gross vehicle weight rating (GVWR) of not more than 8,500 pounds meets or exceeds the qualifying California low emission vehicle standard under the Clean Air Act and, if the GVWR is 6,000 or less, it meets the Bin 5 Tier II emission standards proscribed by the Environmental Protection Agency, or, if the GVWR is greater than 6,000 pounds, it meets the Bin 8, Tier II emission standards proscribed by the Environmental Protection Agency.

The plug-in electric drive motor vehicle credit is limited based on the weight of the vehicle and the number of vehicles sold. The maximum credit amount that may be claimed for new qualified plug-in electric drive motor vehicle is:

- $7,500 for a vehicle with a gross vehicle weight rating (GVWR) of not more than 10,000 pounds;
- $10,000 if the GVWR is more than 10,000 pounds and not more than 14,000 pounds;
- $12,500 if the GVWR is more than 14,000 pounds and not more than 26,000 pounds; and
- $15,000 if the GVWR is more than 26,000 pounds.

The credit begins to phase-out after 250,000 vehicles have been sold in the United States.

For further information, see MTG ¶1350.

Planning Tip. The American Recovery and Reinvestment Act of 2009 (P.L. 111-5) rewrote this credit effective for new qualified electric drive motor vehicles purchased after December 31, 2009. The maximum credit amount will be limited to $7,500 regardless of the GVWR of the vehicle and the phase out threshold is lowered to 200,000 qualified vehicles sold in the United States. The phase out regime is the same as used in the hybrid and advance lean burn alternative motor vehicle credit.

Certain Plug-In Electric Vehicles

The electric motor vehicle credit has been replaced by the certain plug-in electric drive vehicles credit (IRC §30). Vehicles covered by this credit are two and three wheel electric vehicles and low power electric golf carts. The credit amount is equal to 10 percent of the cost with a maximum credit amount of no more than $2,500. A qualified plug-in vehicle is defined in a similar matter to a new qualified electric drive motor vehicle with the lower power requirements. The credit is available for automobiles purchased after February 17, 2009, and before January 1, 2012.

For more information, see MTG ¶1354.

Credit for Prior Year Minimum Tax

This credit, which now includes a refundable aspect for unused long-term credit amount (see *Refundable AMT Credit*, page 10-22), can be carried forward indefinitely and is for the amount of the AMT that was attributable to deferral items (timing preferences and adjustments). Any amount of the AMT generated by "exclusion items," including but not limited to state and local taxes, employee business and investment expenses, personal exemptions, and private activity bond interest does *not* generate a prior year minimum tax credit amount. Form 8801, *Credit for Prior Year Minimum Tax–Individuals, Estates, and Trusts,* is used to claim the credit.

General Business Credit

The general business credit is a limited nonrefundable credit against income tax that is claimed after all other nonrefundable credits. Part I of Form 3800, *General Business Credit,* lists the various credits that are summarized and reported to the IRS. Part II calculates the allowable credit for the current year. Form 3800 is required if the taxpayer has more than one of the credits listed on the lines in Part I.

Generally, if the taxpayer cannot use part or all of the credit because of the tax liability limit, he or she may carry the unused credit back one tax year. To carry back an unused credit, file an amended Form 1040 for the prior tax year or apply for a tentative refund on Form 1045, *Application for Tentative Refund.*

If the taxpayer has unused credit after carrying it back, he or she may carry it forward to each of the 20 tax years after the year of the credit.

Filing Tip. Several of the general business credits are no longer subject to the general business credit limitation rule (IRC §38(c)(4)). The limitation on the amount of these credits is calculated separately and the tentative tax is to be treated as zero. This will allow for the maximum use of these credits against both the regular and the alternative minimum tax liabilities. These credits are:

- the alcohol used as fuels credit;
- the low income housing credit to the extent attributable to buildings placed in service after December 31, 2007.
- the electricity produced from certain renewable sources credit, including refined coal, produced at facilities originally placed into service after October 22, 2004, and during the four-year period beginning on the date the facility was originally placed in service;
- the credit for portion of employer Social Security taxes paid with respect to employee cash tips determined in tax years beginning after December 31, 2006 and to any carrybacks of such credits;
- the railroad tax maintenance credit;
- the investment credit, to the extent attributable to the energy credit or to the rehabilitation (for periods after December 31, 2007); and
- the work opportunity tax credit determined in tax years beginning after December 31, 2006, and to any carrybacks of such credits.

For further information, see MTG ¶1365-¶1365KK.

Caution. The effective date language would indicate that for any carryforwards of these credits from prior years would still be subject to the tax liability limitation rule of the general business credit in effect in the year the credit amount was generated.

Planning Tip. Certain of the general business credits are allowed to taken as a deduction in the year after the taxpayer ceases to exist or the 20-year carryforward period ends (IRC §196).

Tax Liability Limitation

Limitation on the Use of Nonrefundable Personal Credits

For 2009, the aggregate amount of nonrefundable personal credits shall not exceed the sum of the regular tax liability reduced by the foreign tax credit, if any, plus the alternative minimum tax (IRC §26(a)(2)). In years that IRC §26(a)(2) does not apply, the aggregate amount of nonrefundable personal credits other than the adoption credit, the child tax credit, the American Opportunity credit, the retirement savings credit. the residential energy efficient credit, the certain plug-in electric vehicle credit, the alternative motor vehicle credit and the new qualified electric drive motor vehicle credit, cannot exceed the excess of the regular tax liability over the tentative minimum tax liability determined without regard to the alternative minimum foreign tax credit (IRC §26(a)(1)).

Filing Tip. The personal alternative motor vehicle credit is to be treated like a nonrefundable personal credit in tax years beginning in 2009.

Refundable Credits

Recovery Rebate Credit.

The Recovery Rebate Credit is no longer available. The advanced payment of the credit was on taxpayers' 2007 income tax returns. The advance payment was reconciled on the 2008 income tax return.

Making Work Pay and Government Retiree Credits

Working taxpayers for 2009 and 2010 are eligible to claim the making work pay credit (IRC §36A). The credit amount is equal to the lesser of:

(1) 6.2 percent of the taxpayer's earned income, or
(2) $400 ($800 for joint filers).

The credit will be phased out for single taxpayers with a modified adjusted gross income (MAGI) that exceeds $75,000 ($150,000 for joint filers) at the rate of two percent of the excess MAGI over the threshold amount. MAGI is adjusted gross income increased by excluded foreign or U.S. possessions earned income and foreign housing expenses. The credit cannot be claimed by taxpayers who can be claimed as a dependent on another taxpayer's return, or who fail to include their social security number on their return.

The making work pay credit amount is coordinated with the economic recovery payment and the government retiree credit to avoid certain taxpayers from receiving excess tax benefits.

Caution. The making work pay credit initial wording indicated that taxpayers would have an election to either decrease their withholding through out the year or claim the entire credit at once on their 2009 income tax return. For administrative reason, the IRS modified the withholding tables effective April 1, 2009 to account for the making work pay credit. For individuals working two or more jobs, working married couples that file jointly, individuals that claim Social Security or railroad retirement benefits, receive veteran's compensation or certain pension benefits, unless they adjusted their withholding, have the potential to have their 2009 tax liability under withheld.

Government Retiree Credit

For 2009 only, certain government retirees can claim a refundable $250 tax credit ($500 on a joint return if both spouses are eligible). To take the credit, the taxpayer must:

(1) during his/her first tax year beginning in 2009, have received an amount from a pension or annuity for service performed in the employ of the United States, any state, or any instrumentality thereof, which is not considered employment for purposes of the Federal Insurance Contributions Act (FICA),
(2) have not received an economic recovery payment during the tax year, and
(3) include his/her social security number on the return (a joint return must include the social security number of at least one of the spouses).

Economic Recovery Payment

Eligible adults were qualified to receive a one-time payment of $250 in 2009. Although not a credit, the payment is to be coordinated with the claiming of the making work pay credit to avoid an individual from receiving excess tax benefits. An eligible individual is one who;

(1) during any of the months of November and December 2008 or January 2009 were eligible to receive benefits from a qualifying program and
(2) has a current address of record in one of the 50 states, the District of Columbia, Puerto Rico, Guam, the U.S. Virgin Islands, American Samoa, and the Northern Mariana Islands.

Qualifying programs are the Social Security program, the Railroad Retirement Act program, veteran's compensation or pension payments and certain supplemental Social Security programs.

Filing Tip. The making work pay and the government retiree credits are reconciled with the economic recovery payment on new Schedule M of Form 1040.

First-Time Homebuyer Credit.

The American Recovery and Reinvestment Act (P.L. 111-5) modified and extended the first-time homebuyer refundable credit for homes purchased in 2009. The credit amount remains at 10 percent of the purchase price but the maximum amount was increased to $8,000 (IRC §36). The credit is claimed on Form 5405, *First-Time Homebuyer Credit* (the draft version is reproduced on page 10-50). The 2009 credit amount will be limited to no more than $4,000 for those couples using married filing separate status. The same applies for two unrelated taxpayers purchasing a home together, the total credit amount claimed cannot exceed $8,000 per house. Purchases completed in 2009 may be treated as having been completed in 2008, allowing these taxpayers to file an amended return to receive any additional refund earlier.

Planning Tip. The IRS issued Notice 2009-12 explaining how the first-time homebuyer credit may be allocated among unmarried individuals purchasing a principal residence together. As stated earlier, the total credit cannot exceed the 2009 credit limitation amount of $8,000. The IRS will accept any reasonable method of allocation as long as no portion of the credit is allocated to a party who does not qualify to claim the credit.

Unlike first-time homebuyers who purchased a home in 2008, first-time homeowners who purchased a home in 2009 are not required to recapture the credit amount unless the home ceases to be the principal residence with in three years of closing.

A first-time homebuyer for purposes of this credit is an individual who had no present interest in a principal residence in the last three years measured from the date of closing. The home purchased must be used as a principal residence. Certain rules limit or disallow the credit if the purchase is from a related individual. In addition, no credit amount may be claimed if:

- the taxpayer is a nonresident alien, or
- before the end of the tax year of purchase, the taxpayer sells the residence or the home ceases to be the principal residence of the taxpayer.

The credit begins to phase out when the taxpayer's modified adjusted gross income is at the threshold amount of

$75,000 ($150,000 for joint filers). The credit is reduced by the ratio that the excess of the taxpayer's modified AGI over $75,000 ($150,000 for joint filers) bears to $20,000. Modified AGI is a taxpayer's AGI increased by the foreign income and housing exclusions and the exclusions for income from Puerto Rico and certain U.S. possessions. The credit amount is reduced to zero when the modified AGI is at $95,000 ($170,000 for joint filers).

Example. Jane is single and first-time homebuyer who purchases a condo as her principal residence in March 2009 for $150,000. Her modified AGI is $70,000. She qualifies and elects to claim a $8,000 first-time homebuyer credit on her 2009 tax return. As long as Jane does not dispose of the condo within 36 months from the date of the purchase (or cease to maintain the condo as her principal residence), she is not required to recapture the credit. Jane can elect to claim the credit on an amended 2008 tax return.

Caution. The modifications to the first-time homebuyer credit regarding recapture were not made retroactive. For purchases made between April 8, 2008, and December 31, 2008, the original recapture rules still apply.

Recapture of First-Time Homebuyer Credit. Taxpayers who purchased and claimed a the first-time homebuyer credit in 2008 will begin to recapture the credit amount claimed in the second year after claiming the credit. The recapture period is 15 years. The recapture amount is equal to one fifteenth (or six and two-thirds percent) of the credit amount claimed. The recapture of the credit amount is accelerated if the home is disposed of or ceases to be the taxpayer's principal residence. Thus, in the year of the sale or cessation of use as the taxpayer's principal residence, the tax liability for the year is increased by the balance of the credit amount. A safe harbor for taxpayers is that the recapture amount cannot exceed the amount of gain from the sale of the home. For purposed of determining the amount of gain, which might limit the accelerated recapture amount, the taxpayer's basis in the home before the sale is reduced by the amount of unrecaptured credit amount.

There are three exceptions to the accelerated recapture of the first-time homebuyer credit:

- in the event of the death of the taxpayer,
- upon an involuntary or compulsory conversion of the home, as long as a new principal residence is acquired within two years, and
- upon transfer of the property to a spouse or former spouse incident to a divorce.

Planning Tip. For taxpayers who purchased and claimed the maximum first-time homebuyer credit in 2008, will begin to recapture the credit amount on their 2010 income tax return. The recapture amount is $500 and will be an addition to tax. Advising these clients to adjust their withholding now will prevent unpleasant surprises at tax time next year.

Earned Income Credit

A refundable credit is available to certain low-income individuals who have earned income, meet adjusted gross income thresholds, and do not have disqualifying income (IRC §32). The IRS has developed an online assistant, the Earned Income Tax Credit Assistant, to assist taxpayers, as well as professional tax preparers, in determining eligibility for the earned income credit. The online assistant is available at www.irs.gov/individuals/article/0,,id=130102,00.html.

Qualifying Taxpayer

To qualify for the EIC, a taxpayer must meet the following requirements:

1. The taxpayer has earned income.
2. The taxpayer's investment income is not more than $3,100 in 2009.
3. The taxpayer's filing status is not Married Filing Separately (MFS).
4. The taxpayer, his or her spouse (if married), and any qualifying children have Social Security numbers. Other identifying numbers, such as ITINs, do not qualify.
5. Neither the taxpayer nor his or her spouse (if married) is the qualifying child of another person.
6. The taxpayer did not exclude any 2009 income by filing Form 2555 or Form 2555-EZ.
7. The taxpayer was not a nonresident alien for any part of the year. (See IRS Publication 596, *Earned Income Credit (EIC)*, for exceptions to this rule.)

Filing Tip. Special rules apply for military personnel stationed outside the U.S. See IRS Publication 596, *Earned Income Credit*, for more information.

See the reproduced worksheets for Lines 64a and 64b of Form 1040 beginning on page 10-26.

Taxpayers without Qualifying Children

The following additional rules apply to taxpayers without qualifying children:

1. The taxpayer's earned income and AGI for 2009 must each be less than $13,440 ($18,440 for joint filers).
2. The taxpayer must be at least 25 years old but less than 65 years old at the end of the tax year. If married, either spouse can meet the age requirement.
3. The taxpayer (and spouse, if married) cannot qualify as a dependent on any other return.
4. The taxpayer cannot be a qualifying child for another person.
5. The taxpayer's main home must be in the U.S. for more than half the year.

Taxpayers with Qualifying Children

The following additional rules apply to taxpayers with qualifying children:

1. The taxpayer's earned income and AGI must each be less than $35,463 ($40,463 for joint filers) with one qualifying child, or $40,295 ($45,295 for joint filers) with two qualifying children or $43,279 ($48,279 for joint filers) with three or more qualifying children.
2. Schedule EIC must be completed and attached to the taxpayer's return to provide information about qualifying child(ren).

The qualifying child must meet the requirements under the uniform definition of a qualifying child, which are:

1. Relationship–the child must be the taxpayer's:
   - Son, daughter, adopted child, stepchild, or a descendant (for example, grandchild) of any of them, or eligible foster child; or
   - Brother, sister, stepbrother, stepsister, or a descendant (for example, niece or nephew) of any of them.
2. Age–the qualifying child must be:
   - Under age 19 at the end of 2009 or under 24 and a student or permanently and totally disabled at any time during the year, regardless of age.

> **Example.** Jack's son turned 19 on December 10. Unless he was disabled or a full-time student, he is not a qualifying child because, at the end of the year, he was not under age 19.

3. Residency–has the same principal place of abode with the taxpayer for more than one-half of the year.
4. Income–child has not provided more than one-half of his or her own support during the year.
5. Dependency–claimed by the taxpayer as a dependent on line 6c of Form 1040 or 1040A.

Foster/Adopted Child

A foster child is eligible only if the child is placed with the taxpayer by any authorized placement agency or by judgment or decree of a court of competent jurisdiction. An adopted child is eligible only if the child is either legally adopted by the taxpayer or placed by an authorized agency with the taxpayer for adoption.

Kidnapped Child

A kidnapped child is treated as having lived with the taxpayer for more than one-half of the year if the child resided with the taxpayer for more than one-half of the year prior to the date of the kidnapping. Additionally, authorities must determine that the child was not kidnapped by a person related to the child. A taxpayer may continue to claim a kidnapped child until the child either has been determined to be deceased or has reached his or her 18th birthday.

> **Caution.** The tie-breaker rules beginning in 2009 apply when two or more taxpayers can claim the same qualifying child. It will no longer be a requirement that two or more taxpayers actually do claim the same child.

Tie-Breaker Rules

Sometimes a child is a qualifying child of more than one person for purposes of the EIC. However, only one person can treat that child as a qualifying child in order to claim the earned income credit. If two or more persons have the same qualifying child, they must decide who will claim the credit using that qualifying child. But if they cannot agree and two or more persons wish to claim the credit using the same child, the tie-breaker rule applies. If the other person is a spouse and they file a joint return, this rule does not apply.

Under the tie-breaker rule, only the following taxpayers may treat the child as a qualifying child:

1. The parents, if they file a joint return.
2. The parent, if only one of the persons is the child's parent.
3. The parent with whom the child lived the longest during the tax year, if two of the persons are the child's parents and they do not file a joint return together.
4. The parent with the highest AGI if the child lived with each parent for the same amount of time during the tax year and they do not file a joint return together.
5. The person with the highest AGI, if none of the persons is the child's parent.
6. For 2009 and later years, if the parents of an individual may claim the individual as a qualifying child but neither actually do so, the individual may be claimed as the qualifying child of another taxpayer if the adjusted gross income of the taxpayer is higher than the highest adjusted gross income of either parent.

Caution. The IRS issued Notice 2006-86 clarifying the tie-breaker rules. It is important to note that if two taxpayers may claim a qualifying child only the taxpayer actually claiming the child may claim any of the tax benefits that adopted the uniform definition of a child. The only exception that will allow the tax benefits to be divided between two taxpayers is for the child's parents that meet the requirements under IRC §152(e):

- the child is in the custody of one or both parents for more than one-half of the year;
- the child receives over one-half of the child's support during the calendar year from the child's parents; and
- the parents are separated or divorced under a written decree or separation agreement, or have lived separate and apart at all times during the last six months of the calendar year.

Investment Income

Disqualified income, $3,100 for 2009, includes an individual's capital gain net income and net passive income in addition to interest, dividends, tax-exempt interest, and nonbusiness rents or royalties.

Earned Income Defined

This credit is based on earned income, which includes all wages, salaries, tips, and other employee compensation (including strike benefits), plus the amount of the taxpayer's net earnings from self-employment, determined with regard to the deduction for one-half of self-employment taxes. Earned income is determined without regard to community property laws.

Caution. Remember the rental value of housing or the housing allowance for ministers that is provided as part of their compensation is excludable for income tax purposes, but is includible in net earnings for self-employment purposes. Thus, for earned income credit purposes, the rental value or housing allowance is includible in earned income.

Earned income does **not** include:

- Interest and dividends
- Welfare benefits (including AFDC payments)
- Veteran's benefits
- Pensions or annuities
- Alimony and child support
- Social Security and railroad retirement benefits
- Worker's compensation
- Unemployment compensation
- Taxable scholarships or fellowships that are not reported on Form W-2
- Income of nonresident alien individuals not connected with U.S. business
- Amounts received for services performed by prison inmates while in prison
- Salary deferrals, such as contributions to 401(k) plans
- Nontaxable military pay (including combat pay (but see exception following), the Basic Allowance for Housing (BAH), and the Basic Allowance for Subsistence (BAS))

Exception for Nontaxable Combat Pay

Members of the military are allowed to elect to include nontaxable combat pay in their earned income for purposes of the earned income tax credit. The purpose of this election is to increase the amounts of earned income tax credit available to families where the majority of their income is excludable combat pay.

Filing Tip. To ensure that the maximum amount of the earned income tax credit for military taxpayers is claimed, the credit should be calculated twice: once electing to include nontaxable combat pay as earned income and once excluding nontaxable combat pay in earned income.

Caution. The IRS will treat a claimed earned income credit as a mathematical error if the Federal Case Registry of Child Support Orders shows that the taxpayer is the noncustodial parent of a child claimed as a qualifying child for EIC or the qualifying child's social security number and last name fails to match the information on file with the Social Security Administration.

Additional Child Tax Credit

Though the child tax credit is generally nonrefundable, a portion of the credit is refundable regardless of the amount of the taxpayer's regular tax or alternative minimum tax liability (IRC §24(d)).

The child tax credit is refundable to the extent of 15 percent of the taxpayer's earned income in excess of $8,050 up to the per-child amount. The amount of the nonrefundable credit is reduced by the amount of the refundable credit.

For taxpayers with one or more qualifying children, the additional child tax credit is the smaller of:

1. The amount of the child tax credit remaining after reducing regular tax and AMT to zero, or
2. Fifteen percent of the taxpayer's earned income in excess of $3,000.

Filing Tip. The earned income amount for the purpose of claiming the additional refundable child tax credit was lowered to $3,000 for 2009 and 2010 by the American Recovery and Reinvestment Act of 2009 (P.L. 111-15).

For taxpayers with three or more qualifying children, the additional child tax credit is the greater of:

1. The result of the above calculation for all taxpayers with one or more qualifying children, or
2. The taxpayer's employee share of FICA taxes (plus one-half SE tax liability, if any) in excess of the Earned Income Credit (EIC), limited to the amount of the child tax credit remaining after reducing regular tax and AMT to zero.

For purposes of the additional child tax credit, earned income is defined as it is for the EIC, but only to the extent included in taxable income.

Taxpayers who have more than $3,000 of earned income must complete Form 8812, *Additional Child Tax Credit,* to compute the refundable portion of the credit

Credit for Federal Tax Paid on Fuels

Use Form 4136, *Credit for Federal Tax Paid on Fuels,* to claim a credit for fuel used on a farm, for off-highway business use, and for other qualifying uses (IRC §34). For claims for credit or payment made on or after May 15, 2008, no credit is allowed if the fuel or mixture is produced outside the United States for use outside the United States (IRC §6426(i) and 6427(e)(5)).

Health Coverage Tax Credit

A credit of up to 65% (80% between May 2009 and December 2010) of health insurance premiums paid is available to members of the following groups:

- Eligible Trade Adjustment Assistance (TAA) recipients under Act Sec. 231 of the Trade Act of 1974
- Eligible alternative TAA recipients as defined under Act Sec. 246 of the Trade Act of 1974
- Eligible Pension Benefit Guaranty Corporation (PBGC) recipients (IRC §35).

Qualified individuals will claim the health coverage tax credit using Form 8885, *Health Coverage Tax Credit.*

See MTG ¶1328.

Alternative Minimum Tax (AMT)

Congress enacted the alternative minimum tax (AMT) in 1969 in an effort to ensure that wealthy taxpayers are unable to avoid significant federal tax liability through the use of tax shelters and other means. This was the response of Congress after learning that, in the 1966 tax year, 155 taxpayers with adjusted gross income of $200,000 or more paid no federal income tax at all.

An unintended result in more recent years has been that more and more middle-income taxpayers must complete Form 6251, *Alternative Minimum Tax–Individuals,*

Example. In 2009, a married New York resident with three children earned $20,000, received $50,000 as a lump-sum settlement from a job-related discrimination lawsuit, and incurred legal fees of $26,400 for the settlement. He reports 100% of the settlement income and deducts the $26,400 legal fees as miscellaneous itemized deductions on Schedule A. (Assume for simplicity that he has no other itemized deductions.) If he is married and files a joint return (and his spouse has no income), he owes no AMT and his total tax is $3,181. If he is married and files a separate liability return (claiming his children as dependents), he would be required to file using MFS status and would have an AMT of $4,831 and a total tax liability of $8,977. If the man is not married and has custody of his three children, he would file as HOH and be liable for $2,092 in AMT and a total tax liability of $6,058.

Example: AMT and Filing Status

Filing Status	MFJ	MFS	HOH
Adjusted Gross Income	$70,000	$70,000	$70,000
Schedule A Miscellaneous Deductions subject to 2%-of-AGI floor	$26,400	$26,400	$26,400
Tentative Minimum Tax	$0	$8,977	$6,058
Regular Tax (2009 tax rates)	$3,181	$4,146	$3,956
AMT	$0	$4,831	$2,092
Total Tax	$3,181	$8,977	$6,058

and pay AMT. Congress has repeatedly provided short-term relief to some taxpayers, extended the increased AMT exemption amounts and provided waivers that ensure that the AMT did not render personal tax credits useless. Despite these past modifications, many more taxpayers still found themselves paying AMT. Although Congress enacted many technical changes over past decades, the basic AMT rules have remained intact.

Gray Area. The difficulty of projecting AMT tax liability in advance makes it challenging for taxpayers to compute it for the purpose of making required estimated tax payments; this can result in penalties. The "no estimate" safe harbor is the safest bet; see Tab 11.

Specific Provisions

The AMT is a separate system from the regular income tax, with its own rules governing taxable and nontaxable income and the timing of deductions and credits (IRC §55).

Complex Computation. For most taxpayers, the first step for determining whether they must complete Form 6251, *Alternative Minimum Tax – Individuals*, is to either fill out a 18-line worksheet in the instructions to Form 1040, following instructions more complicated than the basic Form 1040 requirements, or to use the web-based AMT assistant provided by the IRS, which is found at http://www.irs.gov/businesses/small/article/0,,id=150703,00.html. Then, taxpayers may have to complete a 55-line form, possibly to find out they owe little or no AMT. Other taxpayers, those claiming one or more of the general business credits, must complete the 55-line form even though they are not subject to the AMT, simply to substantiate their entitlement to the tax credits.

Taxpayers subject to the AMT must calculate their tax twice, once under the regular income tax rules and again under AMT rules. The mechanics and computation of AMT tax liability are so complex that many taxpayers may not even realize they are subject to the tax.

The determination of AMT liability involves the following steps:

1. Calculate the taxpayer's regular tax. The regular income tax rules provide preferred treatment for certain types of income and allow taxpayers to claim certain exemptions, deductions, exclusions, and credits.
2. Determine whether the taxpayer is subject to additional tax under the AMT system. The 18-line worksheet provided in the Instruction to Form 1040 may be used for this purpose or the web-based assistant at http://www.irs.gov/businesses/small/article/0,,id=150703,00.html.
3. Compute the alternative minimum taxable income (AMTI) on Form 6251, using the first 28 lines of the form. This computation generally requires taxpayers to give up the benefit of tax preference items to which they are entitled under the regular income tax system. These items commonly include dependency exemptions; the standard deduction; and itemized deductions for medical and dental expenses, state and local taxes, and miscellaneous deductions on line 27, Schedule A (Form 1040).
4. Determine the "exemption amount" to which the taxpayer is entitled based on filing status. The "exemption amount" replaces both the standard deduction and the personal exemption for purposes of computing the AMT. For 2009 only, the exemption amounts are as follows: joint filer, $70,950; unmarried individuals, $46,700; and married filing separately, $35,475.

Filing Tip. The exemption amounts will revert to their pre-2001 levels after December 31, 2009. Thus, for 2010 and later years, absent Congressional action, the AMT exemption amount is $45,000 for taxpayers whose filing status is married filing jointly or surviving spouse, $22,500 for married filing separately, and $33,750 for single or head-of-household.

5. Compute the "taxable excess" by subtracting the exemption amount from the AMTI.
6. Taxpayers with a positive "taxable excess" must compute the "tentative minimum tax" on line 34, Form 6251. A "taxable excess" of $175,000 or less is taxed at a 26% rate and any additional "taxable excess" is taxed at a 28% rate. The total amount is the tentative minimum tax.
7. Compute the "alternative minimum tax." The AMT is equal to the excess of the taxpayer's tentative minimum tax, if any, over the regular tax liability (reduced by any tax from Form 4972, *Tax on Lump-Sum Distributions* and the foreign tax credit, if any) from Form 1040. If the net result is a negative number or zero, the taxpayer does not owe AMT.
8. If the taxpayer owes AMT, compute the final tax liability by adding the regular income tax and the AMT liability.

Who Must File Form 6251

Most taxpayers are exempt from AMT. Higher-income taxpayers and those who itemize deductions are the primary targets of this tax. Form 6251 is also used to figure the tax liability limit on any of the general business credits, the empowerment zone and renewal community employment credit, the qualified electric vehicle credit, the alternative motor vehicle credit, the alternative fuel vehicle refueling property credit, or the credit for prior-year minimum tax, which now includes the refundable AMT credit (see *Refundable AMT Credit* discussion following).

Form 6251 must be attached to any return if deductions taken are greater than AGI, or alternative minimum taxable income (AMTI) is above the exemption amount for the taxpayer's filing status, or if any general business credits, the empowerment zone and renewal community employment credit, the qualified electric vehicle credit, the alternative motor vehicle credit, the alternative fuel vehicle refueling property credit, or the credit for prior-year minimum tax is claimed.

AMT Exemption Amounts

Filing Status	2009
Single	$46,700
Head of Household	$46,700
Joint Return	$70,950
Surviving Spouse	$70,950
Married Filing Separately	$35,475

Caution. Even though the exemption amounts have been increased, the exemption phaseout threshold amounts have not. The exemption phase out threshold amount remains at $150,000 for joint filers and surviving spouses, $112,500 for singles or heads-of-household, and $75,000 for married filing separately.

Caution. There has been no recent rate reduction for AMT rates (26% on the first $175,000 of AMT income and 28% on AMT income over $175,000) as there has for regular income tax rates.

See the Example on page 10-19 for the different AMT results from different filing statuses.

Nonresident Aliens. If you are a nonresident alien and you disposed of U.S. real property interests at a gain, you must make a special computation. Fill in Form 6251 through line 31. If your net gain from the disposition of U.S. real property interests and the amount on line 29 are both greater than the tentative amount you figured for line 31, replace the amount on line 31 with the smaller of that net gain or the amount on line 29. Also, write "RPI" on the dotted line next to line 31. Otherwise, do not change line 31.

Filing Tip. If you are filing Form 1040NR, treat any reference in these instructions or on Form 6251 to a line on Form 1040 as a reference to the corresponding line on Form 1040NR.

Planning Tip. For effective tax planning, it is essential to identify clients who may be subject to the AMT. The AMT and Regular Income Tax Compared chart on page 10-21 shows the most common differences between the AMT and regular income tax bases. For a complete list of adjustments, see IRC §56 and §57.

AMT and Regular Income Tax Compared

AMT Computation		Regular Income Tax Computation	
Adjusted Gross Income		Adjusted Gross Income	
Plus	AMT adjustments and preferences	Less	Regular income tax personal and dependency exemptions
Less	AMT itemized deductions	Less	The greater of total itemized deductions or the standard deduction
Equals	AMT income	Equals	Taxable income
Less	AMT exemption	Times	Regular tax rate
Equals	AMT base	Equals	Regular income tax before credits
Times	AMT tax rate	Plus	Actual AMT
Equals	Tentative AMT liability	Less	Nonrefundable credits followed by refundable credits
Less	Regular income tax before credits	Plus	Other taxes
Equals	Actual AMT	Equals	Total tax

Caution. The AMT basis in stock acquired through an incentive stock option is likely to differ from the regular tax basis. Therefore, adequate records are required for both the AMT and regular tax so that adjusted gain or loss can be determined.

Example. Jennifer, a single individual, has regular taxable income of $80,000 in 2009 and tax preference items (TPIs) totaling $125,000. Her regular tax on the regular taxable income using tax rate schedules is $16,188. To compute her AMT, she must first establish her AMTI by adding her TPIs to her regular taxable income ($205,000). Next, her tentative minimum tax must be computed by first subtracting her pro rata exemption amount of $23,575 from AMTI of $205,000 to arrive at the amount of $181,425. Since $181,425 exceeds $175,000, multiply 28% times $181,425 to arrive at a tentative minimum tax of $50,799. Assuming there is no alternative minimum tax foreign tax credit, the $34,611 excess of the $50,799 tentative minimum tax over the $16,188 regular tax is Jennifer's AMT and must be paid in addition to her regular tax.

A taxpayer who is subject to the AMT accrues AMT credits. However, these credits are generated only by timing items, not to exclusion items. Timing items are those accounted for in different tax years in the regular tax and AMT systems. For example, the AMT in some instances requires taxpayers to depreciate property over a longer period of time. Exclusion items are adjustments and tax preference items that result in the permanent disallowance of certain tax benefits such as the standard deduction, personal exemption, and certain itemized deductions. AMT credits can only be used when the regular tax liability, reduced by other nonrefundable credits, exceeds the tentative minimum tax for the year. However for tax years 2007 through 2012, unused long-term AMT credits are refundable; see the following discussion.

Refundable AMT Credit

The refundable AMT credit was enacted to give relief to individuals who exercised incentive stock options that lost all or a significant portion of their value in later years. Since the difference between the fair market value and the option price is a preference item for AMT purposes, these taxpayers paid an increased amount of tax and generated a credit for use in later years when, hopefully, the stock was sold for a profit. The loss in value of the stocks resulted in these individuals being unable to use a portion, if any, of the sizable amounts of AMT credit to offset their tax liability, and they would simply carry the amount forward to the next year with similar result.

For tax years beginning after December 31, 2007, the Emergency Economic Stabilization Act of 2008 (P.L. 110-343) increased the amount of long-term unused minimum tax credit that can be claimed. The minimum credit allowed will be not less than the greater of the amount of the AMT refundable credit amount determined for the preceding year or 50 percent of the unused credit.

The minimum tax credit is the amount of AMT attributable to these deferral-type adjustments to reduce the taxpayer's regular tax liability in a tax year by some or all for the AMT paid in previous years. Unused long-term minimum credit amount is defined as that portion of the minimum tax credit attributable to the adjusted minimum tax for tax years before the third tax year immediately preceding such tax year. Thus, for 2009, taxpayers may be able to claim a refundable amount for credits generated from paying the alternative minimum tax in 2005.

To claim the AMT credit, including the refundable portion, taxpayers must complete Form 8801, *Credit For Prior Year Minimum Tax – Individuals, Estates, and Trusts.*

Additional Amount of Refundable AMT Credit

The Emergency Economic Stabilization Act of 2008 (P.L. 110-343) also instructed the IRS to abate collection of any underpayment of tax still outstanding as of January 1, 2008, which is attributable to application of IRC §56(b)(3), the treatment of stock options. The abatement of collection also extends to penalties and interest arising from this underpayment of tax. As additional relief to those taxpayers who paid the penalties and interest, they may increase each of their AMT refundable credit amount and their minimum tax credit for 2008 and 2009 by 50 percent of the aggregate of the penalties and interest paid before 2008 which would have been so abated.

Planning Tip. The purpose of this additional amount of refundable AMT credit is to insure all taxpayers are treated equally, since many who have been fighting the IRS will not have to pay anything. This additional amount will allow those who have paid the additional tax due with penalties and interest to recoup their penalties and interest payments over a two-year period.

Planning Options

Schedule A itemized deductions continue to be a source of inconsistent treatment for middle-income taxpayers. Because the AMT does not treat itemized deductions uniformly, the type of Schedule A itemized deduction is a key factor in determining whether an AMT obligation is triggered. A married couple with three children living in a high-tax area or incurring high employee business expenses is more likely to owe AMT than a similar family that had other itemized deductions, such as mortgage interest or charitable contributions, which are not taken into account for AMT purposes.

Taxpayers who are subject to the AMT may consider accelerating income so that it is subject to the AMT rates, which are still lower than the regular tax rates. Taxpayers who are not subject to the AMT may consider accelerating deductions, such as itemized deductions and state income tax payments, that would otherwise trigger the AMT. These taxpayers will still be able to enjoy the full benefit of these deductions.

Because certain expenses are treated as deferral items that give rise to a minimum tax credit, taxpayers who are subject to the AMT may wish to adopt a strategy of incurring expenses that are not deductible for AMT purposes. This can provide a benefit in future years. Examples of deferral items include depletion, certain depreciation, and the spread between the exercise and market value prices of incentive stock options.

Caution. Taxpayers with incentive stock options (ISOs) need to work carefully with tax professionals to time the exercise of their options, since the spread between the value of the option and the exercise price is an adjustment to income for AMT purposes and could trigger or increase AMT liability.

Line 51—Child Tax Credit

Three Steps To Take the Child Tax Credit!

Step 1. Make sure you have a qualifying child for the child tax credit. Follow Steps 1 through 3 in the instructions for line 6c on page 17.

Step 2. Make sure you checked the box on Form 1040, line 6c, column (4), for each qualifying child.

Step 3. Answer the questions on this page to see if you can use the worksheet on pages 43 and 44 to figure your credit or if you must use Pub. 972.

Question **Who Must Use Pub. 972**

1. Are you claiming any of the following credits?
   - Mortgage interest credit, Form 8396.
   - Adoption credit, Form 8839.
   - District of Columbia first-time homebuyer credit, Form 8859.
   - Residential energy efficient property credit, Form 5695, Part II.

   ☐ **Yes.** STOP You must use Pub. 972 to figure your child tax credit. You will also need the form(s) listed above for any credit(s) you are claiming.

   ☐ **No.** Continue

2. Are you excluding income from Puerto Rico or are you filing any of the following forms?
   - Form 2555 or 2555-EZ (relating to foreign earned income).
   - Form 4563 (exclusion of income for residents of American Samoa).

   ☐ **Yes.** STOP You must use Pub. 972 to figure your credit.

   ☐ **No.** Use the worksheet on pages 43 and 44 to figure your credit.

Child Tax Credit Worksheet—Line 51

Keep for Your Records

CAUTION

- To be a qualifying child for the child tax credit, the child must be your dependent, **under age 17** at the end of 2009, and meet all the conditions in Steps 1 through 3 on page 17.
- **Do not** use this worksheet if you answered "Yes" to question 1 or 2 on page 42. Instead, use Pub. 972.

Part 1

1. Number of qualifying children: ________ × $1,000. Enter the result. **1** ______

2. Enter the amount from Form 1040, line 38. **2** ______

3. Enter the amount shown below for your filing status.

- Married filing jointly — $110,000
- Single, head of household, or qualifying widow(er) — $75,000
- Married filing separately — $55,000

3 ______

4. Is the amount on line 2 more than the amount on line 3?

☐ **No.** Leave line 4 blank. Enter -0- on line 5, and go to line 6. **4** ______

☐ **Yes.** Subtract line 3 from line 2.
If the result is not a multiple of $1,000, increase it to the next multiple of $1,000. For example, increase $425 to $1,000, increase $1,025 to $2,000, etc.

5. Multiply the amount on line 4 by 5% (.05). Enter the result. **5** ______

6. Is the amount on line 1 more than the amount on line 5?

☐ **No.** STOP
You cannot take the child tax credit on Form 1040, line 51. You also cannot take the additional child tax credit on Form 1040, line 65. Complete the rest of your Form 1040.

☐ **Yes.** Subtract line 5 from line 1. Enter the result. **6** ______
Go to Part 2 on the next page.

Before you begin Part 2: √ Figure the amount of any credits you are claiming on Form 5695, Part I; Form 8834, Part I; Form 8910; Form 8936; or Schedule R.

Part 2

7. Enter the amount from Form 1040, line 46. **7** ______

8. Add the following amounts from

Form 1040, line 47 ______

Form 1040, line 48 + ______

Form 1040, line 49 + ______

Form 1040, line 50 + ______

Form 5695, line 11 + ______

Form 8834, line 22 + ______

Form 8910, line 21 + ______

Form 8936, line 14 + ______

Schedule R, line 24 + ______ Enter the total. **8** ______

9. Are the amounts on lines 7 and 8 the same?

☐ **Yes.** STOP
You cannot take this credit because there is no tax to reduce. However, you may be able to take the **additional child tax credit.** See the **TIP** below.

☐ **No.** Subtract line 8 from line 7. **9** ______

10. Is the amount on line 6 more than the amount on line 9?

☐ **Yes.** Enter the amount from line 9. Also, you may be able to take the **additional child tax credit.** See the **TIP** below.

☐ **No.** Enter the amount from line 6.

This is your child tax credit. **10** ______

Enter this amount on Form 1040, line 51.

TIP You may be able to take the **additional child tax credit** on Form 1040, line 65, if you answered "Yes" on line 9 **or** line 10 above.

- First, complete your Form 1040 through lines 64a and 64b.
- Then, use Form 8812 to figure any additional child tax credit.

Lines 64a and 64b—Earned Income Credit (EIC)

What Is the EIC?

The EIC is a credit for certain people who work. The credit may give you a refund even if you do not owe any tax.

TIP *Special rules may apply for people who had to relocate because of the storms, tornadoes, or flooding in a Midwestern disaster area. For details, see Pub. 4492-B.*

To Take the EIC:

- Follow the steps below.
- Complete the worksheet that applies to you or let the IRS figure the credit for you.
- If you have a qualifying child, complete and attach Schedule EIC.

For help in determining if you are eligible for the EIC, go to *www.irs.gov/eitc* and click on "EITC Assistant." This service is available in English and Spanish.

CAUTION *If you take the EIC even though you are not eligible and it is determined that your error is due to reckless or intentional disregard of the EIC rules, you will not be allowed to take the credit for 2 years even if you are otherwise eligible to do so. If you fraudulently take the EIC, you will not be allowed to take the credit for 10 years. See* Form 8862, who must file, *that begins on page 50. You may also have to pay penalties.*

Step 1 All Filers

1. If, in 2009:
   - 3 or more children lived with you, is the amount on Form 1040, line 38, less than $43,279 ($48,279 if married filing jointly)?
   - 2 children lived with you, is the amount on Form 1040, line 38, less than $40,295 ($45,295 if married filing jointly)?
   - 1 child lived with you, is the amount on Form 1040, line 38, less than $35,463 ($40,463 if married filing jointly)?
   - No children lived with you, is the amount on Form 1040, line 38, less than $13,440 ($18,440 if married filing jointly)?

   ☐ **Yes.** Continue ☐ **No.** STOP You cannot take the credit.

2. Do you, and your spouse if filing a joint return, have a social security number that allows you to work or is valid for EIC purposes (see page 51)?

   ☐ **Yes.** Continue ☐ **No.** STOP You cannot take the credit. Enter "No" on the dotted line next to line 64a.

3. Is your filing status married filing separately?

   ☐ **Yes.** STOP You cannot take the credit. ☐ **No.** Continue

4. Are you filing Form 2555 or 2555-EZ (relating to foreign earned income)?

   ☐ **Yes.** STOP You cannot take the credit. ☐ **No.** Continue

5. Were you or your spouse a nonresident alien for any part of 2009?

   ☐ **Yes.** See *Nonresident aliens* on page 51. ☐ **No.** Go to Step 2.

Step 2 Investment Income

1. Add the amounts from Form 1040:

Line 8a		______
Line 8b	+	______
Line 9a	+	______
Line 13*	+	______
Investment Income	=	☐

*If line 13 is a loss, enter -0-.

2. Is your investment income more than $3,100?

   ☐ **Yes.** Continue ☐ **No.** Skip question 3; go to question 4.

3. Are you filing Form 4797 (relating to sales of business property)?

   ☐ **Yes.** See *Form 4797 filers* on page 50. ☐ **No.** STOP You cannot take the credit.

4. Do any of the following apply for 2009?
   - You are filing Schedule E.
   - You are a member of a qualified joint venture that is a passive activity reporting rental real estate income not subject to self-employment tax on Schedule C or C-EZ.
   - You are reporting income from the rental of personal property not used in a trade or business.
   - You are reporting income on Form 1040, line 21, from Form 8814 (relating to election to report child's interest and dividends).

   ☐ **Yes.** You must use Worksheet 1 in Pub. 596 to see if you can take the credit. ☐ **No.** Go to Step 3.

Step 3 Qualifying Child

A qualifying child for the EIC is a child who is your...

Son, daughter, stepchild, foster child, brother, sister, stepbrother, stepsister, or a descendant of any of them (for example, your grandchild, niece, or nephew)

AND

was ...

Under age 19 at the end of 2009 and younger than you (or your spouse, if filing jointly)

or

Under age 24 at the end of 2009, a student (see page 51), and younger than you (or your spouse, if filing jointly)

or

Any age and permanently and totally disabled (see page 51)

AND

Who is not filing a joint return for 2009 (or is filing a joint return for 2009 only as a claim for refund)

AND

Who lived with you in the United States for more than half of 2009.
If the child did not live with you for the required time, see *Exception to time lived with you* on page 50.

CAUTION *If the child meets the conditions to be a qualifying child of any other person (other than your spouse if filing a joint return) for 2009, or the child was married, see page 51.*

1. Do you have at least one child who meets the conditions to be your qualifying child?

   ☐ **Yes.** The child must have a valid social security number (SSN) as defined on page 51 unless the child was born and died in 2009. If at least one qualifying child has a valid SSN (or was born or died in 2009), go to question 2. Otherwise, you cannot take the credit.

   ☐ **No.** Skip question 2; go to Step 4.

2. Could you, or your spouse if filing a joint return, be a qualifying child of another person in 2009?

   ☐ **Yes.** STOP You cannot take the credit. Enter "No" on the dotted line next to line 64a.

   ☐ **No.** Skip Step 4; go to Step 5 on page 50.

Step 4 Filers Without a Qualifying Child

1. Is the amount on Form 1040, line 38, less than $13,440 ($18,440 if married filing jointly)?

   ☐ **Yes.** Continue ↓

   ☐ **No.** STOP You cannot take the credit.

2. Could you, or your spouse if filing a joint return, be a qualifying child of another person in 2009?

   ☐ **Yes.** STOP You cannot take the credit. Enter "No" on the dotted line next to line 64a.

   ☐ **No.** Continue ↓

3. Can you, or your spouse if filing a joint return, be claimed as a dependent on someone else's 2009 tax return?

   ☐ **Yes.** STOP You cannot take the credit.

   ☐ **No.** Continue ↓

4. Were you, or your spouse if filing a joint return, at least age 25 but under age 65 at the end of 2009? If your spouse died in 2009, see Pub. 596 before you answer.

   ☐ **Yes.** Continue ↓

   ☐ **No.** STOP You cannot take the credit.

5. Was your home, and your spouse's if filing a joint return, in the United States for more than half of 2009? Members of the military stationed outside the United States, see page 51 before you answer.

   ☐ **Yes.** Go to Step 5 on page 50.

   ☐ **No.** STOP You cannot take the credit. Enter "No" on the dotted line next to line 64a.

Continued

Step 5 Earned Income

1. Are you filing Schedule SE because you were a member of the clergy or you had church employee income of $108.28 or more?

   ☐ **Yes.** See *Clergy* or *Church employees,* whichever applies, on this page. ☐ **No.** Continue ↓

2. Figure earned income:

Form 1040, line 7	________
Subtract, if included on line 7, any: • Taxable scholarship or fellowship grant not reported on a Form W-2. • Amount received for work performed while an inmate in a penal institution (enter "PRI" and the amount subtracted on the dotted line next to Form 1040, line 7). • Amount received as a pension or annuity from a nonqualified deferred compensation plan or a nongovernmental section 457 plan (enter "DFC" and the amount subtracted on the dotted line next to Form 1040, line 7). This amount may be shown in box 11 of Form W-2. If you received such an amount but box 11 is blank, contact your employer for the amount received as a pension or annuity.	− ________
Add all of your nontaxable combat pay if you elect to include it in earned income. Also enter this amount on Form 1040, line 64b. See *Combat pay, nontaxable* on this page.	+ ________

CAUTION *Electing to include nontaxable combat pay may increase or decrease your EIC. Figure the credit with and without your nontaxable combat pay before making the election.*

Earned Income = ☐

3. Were you self-employed at any time in 2009, or are you filing Schedule SE because you were a member of the clergy or you had church employee income, or are you filing Schedule C or C-EZ as a statutory employee?

   ☐ **Yes.** Skip question 4 and Step 6; go to Worksheet B on page 53. ☐ **No.** Continue ↓

4. If you have:
   - 3 or more qualifying children, is your earned income less than $43,279 ($48,279 if married filing jointly)?
   - 2 qualifying children, is your earned income less than $40,295 ($45,295 if married filing jointly)?
   - 1 qualifying child, is your earned income less than $35,463 ($40,463 if married filing jointly)?
   - No qualifying children, is your earned income less than $13,440 ($18,440 if married filing jointly)?

   ☐ **Yes.** Go to Step 6. ☐ **No.** STOP You cannot take the credit.

Step 6 How To Figure the Credit

1. Do you want the IRS to figure the credit for you?

   ☐ **Yes.** See *Credit figured by the IRS* on this page. ☐ **No.** Go to Worksheet A on page 52.

Worksheet A—Earned Income Credit (EIC)—Lines 64a and 64b *Keep for Your Records*

Before you begin: √ Be sure you are using the correct worksheet. Use this worksheet only if you answered "No" to Step 5, question 3, on page 50. Otherwise, use Worksheet B that begins on page 53.

Part 1

All Filers Using Worksheet A

1. Enter your earned income from Step 5 on page 50. **1** ______

2. Look up the amount on line 1 above in the EIC Table on pages 55–71 to find the credit. Be sure you use the correct column for your filing status and the number of children you have. Enter the credit here. **2** ______

If line 2 is zero, STOP You cannot take the credit. Enter "No" on the dotted line next to line 64a.

3. Enter the amount from Form 1040, line 38. **3** ______

4. Are the amounts on lines 3 and 1 the same?

☐ **Yes.** Skip line 5; enter the amount from line 2 on line 6.

☐ **No.** Go to line 5.

Part 2

Filers Who Answered "No" on Line 4

5. If you have:

- No qualifying children, is the amount on line 3 less than $7,500 ($12,500 if married filing jointly)?
- 1 or more qualifying children, is the amount on line 3 less than $16,450 ($21,450 if married filing jointly)?

☐ **Yes.** Leave line 5 blank; enter the amount from line 2 on line 6.

☐ **No.** Look up the amount on line 3 in the EIC Table on pages 55–71 to find the credit. Be sure you use the correct column for your filing status and the number of children you have. Enter the credit here. **5** ______

Look at the amounts on lines 5 and 2. Then, enter the **smaller** amount on line 6.

Part 3

Your Earned Income Credit

6. **This is your earned income credit.** **6** ______

Enter this amount on Form 1040, line 64a.

Reminder—

√ If you have a qualifying child, complete and attach Schedule EIC.

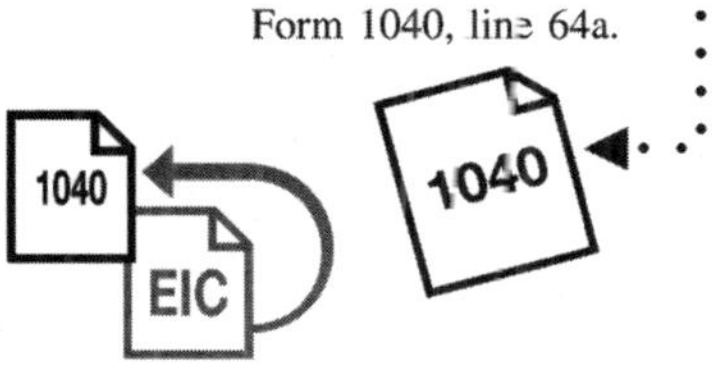

CAUTION *If your EIC for a year after 1996 was reduced or disallowed, see page 50 to find out if you must file Form 8862 to take the credit for 2009.*

Worksheet B—Earned Income Credit (EIC)—Lines 64a and 64b

Keep for Your Records

Use this worksheet if you answered "Yes" to Step 5, question 3, on page 50.

√ Complete the parts below (Parts 1 through 3) that apply to you. Then, continue to Part 4.

√ If you are married filing a joint return, include your spouse's amounts, if any, with yours to figure the amounts to enter in Parts 1 through 3.

Part 1

Self-Employed, Members of the Clergy, and People With Church Employee Income Filing Schedule SE

1a. Enter the amount from Schedule SE, Section A, line 3, or Section B, line 3, whichever applies.		1a	
b. Enter any amount from Schedule SE, Section B, line 4b, and line 5a.	+	1b	
c. Combine lines 1a and 1b.	=	1c	
d. Enter the amount from Schedule SE, Section A, line 6, or Section B, line 13, whichever applies.	–	1d	
e. Subtract line 1d from 1c.	=	1e	

Part 2

Self-Employed NOT Required To File Schedule SE

For example, your net earnings from self-employment were less than $400.

2. Do not include on these lines any statutory employee income, any net profit from services performed as a notary public, any amount exempt from self-employment tax as the result of the filing and approval of Form 4029 or Form 4361, or any income or loss from a qualified joint venture reporting only rental real estate income not subject to self-employment tax.

a. Enter any net farm profit or (loss) from Schedule F, line 36, and from farm partnerships, Schedule K-1 (Form 1065), box 14, code A*.		2a	
b. Enter any net profit or (loss) from Schedule C, line 31; Schedule C-EZ, line 3; Schedule K-1 (Form 1065), box 14, code A (other than farming); and Schedule K-1 (Form 1065-B), box 9, code J1*.	+	2b	
c. Combine lines 2a and 2b.	=	2c	

*Reduce any Schedule K-1 amounts by any partnership section 179 expense deduction claimed, unreimbursed partnership expenses claimed, and depletion claimed on oil and gas properties. If you have any Schedule K-1 amounts, complete the appropriate line(s) of Schedule SE, Section A. Enter your name and social security number on Schedule SE and attach it to your return.

Part 3

Statutory Employees Filing Schedule C or C-EZ

3. Enter the amount from Schedule C, line 1, or Schedule C-EZ, line 1, that you are filing as a statutory employee.	3	

Part 4

All Filers Using Worksheet B

Note. If line 4b includes income on which you should have paid self-employment tax but did not, we may reduce your credit by the amount of self-employment tax not paid.

4a. Enter your earned income from Step 5 on page 50.	4a	
b. Combine lines 1e, 2c, 3, and 4a. **This is your total earned income.**	4b	

If line 4b is zero or less, STOP You cannot take the credit. Enter "No" on the dotted line next to line 64a.

5. If you have:

- 3 or more qualifying children, is line 4b less than $43,279 ($48,279 if married filing jointly)?
- 2 qualifying children, is line 4b less than $40,295 ($45,295 if married filing jointly)?
- 1 qualifying child, is line 4b less than $35,463 ($40,463 if married filing jointly)?
- No qualifying children, is line 4b less than $13,440 ($18,440 if married filing jointly)?

☐ **Yes.** If you want the IRS to figure your credit, see page 50. If you want to figure the credit yourself, enter the amount from line 4b on line 6 (page 54).

☐ **No.** STOP You cannot take the credit. Enter "No" on the dotted line next to line 64a.

Part 5

All Filers Using Worksheet B

6. Enter your total earned income from Part 4, line 4b, on page 53. **6** ______

7. Look up the amount on line 6 above in the EIC Table on pages 55–71 to find the credit. Be sure you use the correct column for your filing status and the number of children you have. Enter the credit here. **7** ______

If line 7 is zero, STOP You cannot take the credit. Enter "No" on the dotted line next to line 64a.

8. Enter the amount from Form 1040, line 38. **8** ______

9. Are the amounts on lines 8 and 6 the same?

☐ **Yes.** Skip line 10; enter the amount from line 7 on line 11.

☐ **No.** Go to line 10.

Part 6

Filers Who Answered "No" on Line 9

10. If you have:

- No qualifying children, is the amount on line 8 less than $7,500 ($12,500 if married filing jointly)?
- 1 or more qualifying children, is the amount on line 8 less than $16,450 ($21,450 if married filing jointly)?

☐ **Yes.** Leave line 10 blank; enter the amount from line 7 on line 11.

☐ **No.** Look up the amount on line 8 in the EIC Table on pages 55–71 to find the credit. Be sure you use the correct column for your filing status and the number of children you have. Enter the credit here. **10** ______
Look at the amounts on lines 10 and 7.
Then, enter the **smaller** amount on line 11.

Part 7

Your Earned Income Credit

11. This is your earned income credit. **11** ______

Enter this amount on Form 1040, line 64a.

Reminder—

√ If you have a qualifying child, complete and attach Schedule EIC.

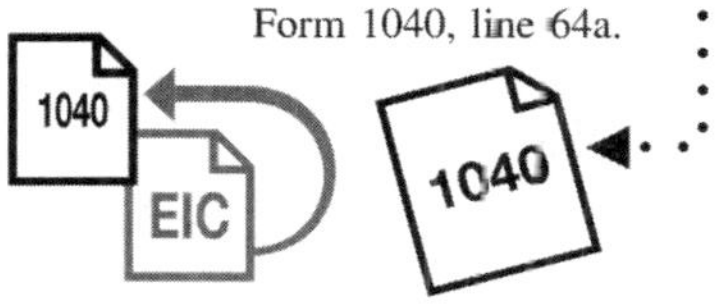

CAUTION

If your EIC for a year after 1996 was reduced or disallowed, see page 50 to find out if you must file Form 8862 to take the credit for 2009.

2009 Earned Income Credit (EIC) Table

Caution. This is **not** a tax table.

1. To find your credit, read down the "At least - But less than" columns and find the line that includes the amount you were told to look up from your EIC Worksheet.

2. Then, go to the column that includes your filing status and the number of qualifying children you have. Enter the credit from that column on your EIC Worksheet.

Example. If your filing status is single, you have one qualifying child, and the amount you are looking up from your EIC Worksheet is $2,455, you would enter $842.

If the amount you are looking up from the worksheet is—		And your filing status is— Single, head of household, or qualifying widow(er) and you have—			
		No children	One child	Two children	Three children
At least	But less than	Your credit is—			
2,400	2,450	186	825	970	1,091
2,450	2,500	189	842	990	1,114

If the amount you are looking up from the worksheet is–		And your filing status is– Single, head of household, or qualifying widow(er) and you have–				Married filing jointly and you have–			
		No Children	One Child	Two Children	Three Children	No Children	One Child	Two Children	Three Children
At least	But less than	Your credit is–				Your credit is–			
$1	$50	$2	$9	$10	$11	$2	$9	$10	$11
50	100	6	26	30	34	6	26	30	34
100	150	10	43	50	56	10	43	50	56
150	200	13	60	70	79	13	60	70	79
200	250	17	77	90	101	17	77	90	101
250	300	21	94	110	124	21	94	110	124
300	350	25	111	130	146	25	111	130	146
350	400	29	128	150	169	29	128	150	169
400	450	33	145	170	191	33	145	170	191
450	500	36	162	190	214	36	162	190	214
500	550	40	179	210	236	40	179	210	236
550	600	44	196	230	259	44	196	230	259
600	650	48	213	250	281	48	213	250	281
650	700	52	230	270	304	52	230	270	304
700	750	55	247	290	326	55	247	290	326
750	800	59	264	310	349	59	264	310	349
800	850	63	281	330	371	63	281	330	371
850	900	67	298	350	394	67	298	350	394
900	950	71	315	370	416	71	315	370	416
950	1,000	75	332	390	439	75	332	390	439
1,000	1,050	78	349	410	461	78	349	410	461
1,050	1,100	82	366	430	484	82	366	430	484
1,100	1,150	86	383	450	506	86	383	450	506
1,150	1,200	90	400	470	529	90	400	470	529
1,200	1,250	94	417	490	551	94	417	490	551
1,250	1,300	98	434	510	574	98	434	510	574
1,300	1,350	101	451	530	596	101	451	530	596
1,350	1,400	105	468	550	619	105	468	550	619
1,400	1,450	109	485	570	641	109	485	570	641
1,450	1,500	113	502	590	664	113	502	590	664
1,500	1,550	117	519	610	686	117	519	610	686
1,550	1,600	120	536	630	709	120	536	630	709
1,600	1,650	124	553	650	731	124	553	650	731
1,650	1,700	128	570	670	754	128	570	670	754
1,700	1,750	132	587	690	776	132	587	690	776
1,750	1,800	136	604	710	799	136	604	710	799
1,800	1,850	140	621	730	821	140	621	730	821
1,850	1,900	143	638	750	844	143	638	750	844
1,900	1,950	147	655	770	866	147	655	770	866
1,950	2,000	151	672	790	889	151	672	790	889
2,000	2,050	155	689	810	911	155	689	810	911
2,050	2,100	159	706	830	934	159	706	830	934
2,100	2,150	163	723	850	956	163	723	850	956
2,150	2,200	166	740	870	979	166	740	870	979
2,200	2,250	170	757	890	1,001	170	757	890	1,001
2,250	2,300	174	774	910	1,024	174	774	910	1,024
2,300	2,350	178	791	930	1,046	178	791	930	1,046
2,350	2,400	182	808	950	1,069	182	808	950	1,069
2,400	2,450	186	825	970	1,091	186	825	970	1,091
2,450	2,500	189	842	990	1,114	189	842	990	1,114

2009 Earned Income Credit (EIC) Table–*Continued* (**Caution.** This is **not** a tax table.)

If the amount you are looking up from the worksheet is–		And your filing status is–							
		Single, head of household, or qualifying widow(er) and you have–				Married filing jointly and you have–			
		No Children	One Child	Two Children	Three Children	No Children	One Child	Two Children	Three Children
At least	But less than	Your credit is–				Your credit is–			
2,500	2,550	193	859	1,010	1,136	193	859	1,010	1,136
2,550	2,600	197	876	1,030	1,159	197	876	1,030	1,159
2,600	2,650	201	893	1,050	1,181	201	893	1,050	1,181
2,650	2,700	205	910	1,070	1,204	205	910	1,070	1,204
2,700	2,750	208	927	1,090	1,226	208	927	1,090	1,226
2,750	2,800	212	944	1,110	1,249	212	944	1,110	1,249
2,800	2,850	216	961	1,130	1,271	216	961	1,130	1,271
2,850	2,900	220	978	1,150	1,294	220	978	1,150	1,294
2,900	2,950	224	995	1,170	1,316	224	995	1,170	1,316
2,950	3,000	228	1,012	1,190	1,339	228	1,012	1,190	1,339
3,000	3,050	231	1,029	1,210	1,361	231	1,029	1,210	1,361
3,050	3,100	235	1,046	1,230	1,384	235	1,046	1,230	1,384
3,100	3,150	239	1,063	1,250	1,406	239	1,063	1,250	1,406
3,150	3,200	243	1,080	1,270	1,429	243	1,080	1,270	1,429
3,200	3,250	247	1,097	1,290	1,451	247	1,097	1,290	1,451
3,250	3,300	251	1,114	1,310	1,474	251	1,114	1,310	1,474
3,300	3,350	254	1,131	1,330	1,496	254	1,131	1,330	1,496
3,350	3,400	258	1,148	1,350	1,519	258	1,148	1,350	1,519
3,400	3,450	262	1,165	1,370	1,541	262	1,165	1,370	1,541
3,450	3,500	266	1,182	1,390	1,564	266	1,182	1,390	1,564
3,500	3,550	270	1,199	1,410	1,586	270	1,199	1,410	1,586
3,550	3,600	273	1,216	1,430	1,609	273	1,216	1,430	1,609
3,600	3,650	277	1,233	1,450	1,631	277	1,233	1,450	1,631
3,650	3,700	281	1,250	1,470	1,654	281	1,250	1,470	1,654
3,700	3,750	285	1,267	1,490	1,676	285	1,267	1,490	1,676
3,750	3,800	289	1,284	1,510	1,699	289	1,284	1,510	1,699
3,800	3,850	293	1,301	1,530	1,721	293	1,301	1,530	1,721
3,850	3,900	296	1,318	1,550	1,744	296	1,318	1,550	1,744
3,900	3,950	300	1,335	1,570	1,766	300	1,335	1,570	1,766
3,950	4,000	304	1,352	1,590	1,789	304	1,352	1,590	1,789
4,000	4,050	308	1,369	1,610	1,811	308	1,369	1,610	1,811
4,050	4,100	312	1,386	1,630	1,834	312	1,386	1,630	1,834
4,100	4,150	316	1,403	1,650	1,856	316	1,403	1,650	1,856
4,150	4,200	319	1,420	1,670	1,879	319	1,420	1,670	1,879
4,200	4,250	323	1,437	1,690	1,901	323	1,437	1,690	1,901
4,250	4,300	327	1,454	1,710	1,924	327	1,454	1,710	1,924
4,300	4,350	331	1,471	1,730	1,946	331	1,471	1,730	1,946
4,350	4,400	335	1,488	1,750	1,969	335	1,488	1,750	1,969
4,400	4,450	339	1,505	1,770	1,991	339	1,505	1,770	1,991
4,450	4,500	342	1,522	1,790	2,014	342	1,522	1,790	2,014
4,500	4,550	346	1,539	1,810	2,036	346	1,539	1,810	2,036
4,550	4,600	350	1,556	1,830	2,059	350	1,556	1,830	2,059
4,600	4,650	354	1,573	1,850	2,081	354	1,573	1,850	2,081
4,650	4,700	358	1,590	1,870	2,104	358	1,590	1,870	2,104
4,700	4,750	361	1,607	1,890	2,126	361	1,607	1,890	2,126
4,750	4,800	365	1,624	1,910	2,149	365	1,624	1,910	2,149
4,800	4,850	369	1,641	1,930	2,171	369	1,641	1,930	2,171
4,850	4,900	373	1,658	1,950	2,194	373	1,658	1,950	2,194
4,900	4,950	377	1,675	1,970	2,216	377	1,675	1,970	2,216
4,950	5,000	381	1,692	1,990	2,239	381	1,692	1,990	2,239
5,000	5,050	384	1,709	2,010	2,261	384	1,709	2,010	2,261
5,050	5,100	388	1,726	2,030	2,284	388	1,726	2,030	2,284
5,100	5,150	392	1,743	2,050	2,306	392	1,743	2,050	2,306
5,150	5,200	396	1,760	2,070	2,329	396	1,760	2,070	2,329
5,200	5,250	400	1,777	2,090	2,351	400	1,777	2,090	2,351
5,250	5,300	404	1,794	2,110	2,374	404	1,794	2,110	2,374
5,300	5,350	407	1,811	2,130	2,396	407	1,811	2,130	2,396
5,350	5,400	411	1,828	2,150	2,419	411	1,828	2,150	2,419
5,400	5,450	415	1,845	2,170	2,441	415	1,845	2,170	2,441
5,450	5,500	419	1,862	2,190	2,464	419	1,862	2,190	2,464

2009 Earned Income Credit (EIC) Table–*Continued* (**Caution.** This is **not** a tax table.)

If the amount you are looking up from the worksheet is–		And your filing status is– Single, head of household, or qualifying widow(er) and you have–				Married filing jointly and you have–			
		No Children	One Child	Two Children	Three Children	No Children	One Child	Two Children	Three Children
At least	But less than	Your credit is–				Your credit is–			
5,500	**5,550**	423	1,879	2,210	2,486	423	1,879	2,210	2,486
5,550	**5,600**	426	1,896	2,230	2,509	426	1,896	2,230	2,509
5,600	**5,650**	430	1,913	2,250	2,531	430	1,913	2,250	2,531
5,650	**5,700**	434	1,930	2,270	2,554	434	1,930	2,270	2,554
5,700	**5,750**	438	1,947	2,290	2,576	438	1,947	2,290	2,576
5,750	**5,800**	442	1,964	2,310	2,599	442	1,964	2,310	2,599
5,800	**5,850**	446	1,981	2,330	2,621	446	1,981	2,330	2,621
5,850	**5,900**	449	1,998	2,350	2,644	449	1,998	2,350	2,644
5,900	**5,950**	453	2,015	2,370	2,666	453	2,015	2,370	2,666
5,950	**6,000**	457	2,032	2,390	2,689	457	2,032	2,390	2,689
6,000	**6,050**	457	2,049	2,410	2,711	457	2,049	2,410	2,711
6,050	**6,100**	457	2,066	2,430	2,734	457	2,066	2,430	2,734
6,100	**6,150**	457	2,083	2,450	2,756	457	2,083	2,450	2,756
6,150	**6,200**	457	2,100	2,470	2,779	457	2,100	2,470	2,779
6,200	**6,250**	457	2,117	2,490	2,801	457	2,117	2,490	2,801
6,250	**6,300**	457	2,134	2,510	2,824	457	2,134	2,510	2,824
6,300	**6,350**	457	2,151	2,530	2,846	457	2,151	2,530	2,846
6,350	**6,400**	457	2,168	2,550	2,869	457	2,168	2,550	2,869
6,400	**6,450**	457	2,185	2,570	2,891	457	2,185	2,570	2,891
6,450	**6,500**	457	2,202	2,590	2,914	457	2,202	2,590	2,914
6,500	**6,550**	457	2,219	2,610	2,936	457	2,219	2,610	2,936
6,550	**6,600**	457	2,236	2,630	2,959	457	2,236	2,630	2,959
6,600	**6,650**	457	2,253	2,650	2,981	457	2,253	2,650	2,981
6,650	**6,700**	457	2,270	2,670	3,004	457	2,270	2,670	3,004
6,700	**6,750**	457	2,287	2,690	3,026	457	2,287	2,690	3,026
6,750	**6,800**	457	2,304	2,710	3,049	457	2,304	2,710	3,049
6,800	**6,850**	457	2,321	2,730	3,071	457	2,321	2,730	3,071
6,850	**6,900**	457	2,338	2,750	3,094	457	2,338	2,750	3,094
6,900	**6,950**	457	2,355	2,770	3,116	457	2,355	2,770	3,116
6,950	**7,000**	457	2,372	2,790	3,139	457	2,372	2,790	3,139
7,000	**7,050**	457	2,389	2,810	3,161	457	2,389	2,810	3,161
7,050	**7,100**	457	2,406	2,830	3,184	457	2,406	2,830	3,184
7,100	**7,150**	457	2,423	2,850	3,206	457	2,423	2,850	3,206
7,150	**7,200**	457	2,440	2,870	3,229	457	2,440	2,870	3,229
7,200	**7,250**	457	2,457	2,890	3,251	457	2,457	2,890	3,251
7,250	**7,300**	457	2,474	2,910	3,274	457	2,474	2,910	3,274
7,300	**7,350**	457	2,491	2,930	3,296	457	2,491	2,930	3,296
7,350	**7,400**	457	2,508	2,950	3,319	457	2,508	2,950	3,319
7,400	**7,450**	457	2,525	2,970	3,341	457	2,525	2,970	3,341
7,450	**7,500**	457	2,542	2,990	3,364	457	2,542	2,990	3,364
7,500	**7,550**	452	2,559	3,010	3,386	457	2,559	3,010	3,386
7,550	**7,600**	449	2,576	3,030	3,409	457	2,576	3,030	3,409
7,600	**7,650**	445	2,593	3,050	3,431	457	2,593	3,050	3,431
7,650	**7,700**	441	2,610	3,070	3,454	457	2,610	3,070	3,454
7,700	**7,750**	437	2,627	3,090	3,476	457	2,627	3,090	3,476
7,750	**7,800**	433	2,644	3,110	3,499	457	2,644	3,110	3,499
7,800	**7,850**	430	2,661	3,130	3,521	457	2,661	3,130	3,521
7,850	**7,900**	426	2,678	3,150	3,544	457	2,678	3,150	3,544
7,900	**7,950**	422	2,695	3,170	3,566	457	2,695	3,170	3,566
7,950	**8,000**	418	2,712	3,190	3,589	457	2,712	3,190	3,589
8,000	**8,050**	414	2,729	3,210	3,611	457	2,729	3,210	3,611
8,050	**8,100**	410	2,746	3,230	3,634	457	2,746	3,230	3,634
8,100	**8,150**	407	2,763	3,250	3,656	457	2,763	3,250	3,656
8,150	**8,200**	403	2,780	3,270	3,679	457	2,780	3,270	3,679
8,200	**8,250**	399	2,797	3,290	3,701	457	2,797	3,290	3,701
8,250	**8,300**	395	2,814	3,310	3,724	457	2,814	3,310	3,724
8,300	**8,350**	391	2,831	3,330	3,746	457	2,831	3,330	3,746
8,350	**8,400**	387	2,848	3,350	3,769	457	2,848	3,350	3,769
8,400	**8,450**	384	2,865	3,370	3,791	457	2,865	3,370	3,791
8,450	**8,500**	380	2,882	3,390	3,814	457	2,882	3,390	3,814

2009 Earned Income Credit (EIC) Table–*Continued* (**Caution.** This is **not** a tax table.)

If the amount you are looking up from the worksheet is–		And your filing status is– Single, head of household, or qualifying widow(er) and you have–				Married filing jointly and you have–			
At least	But less than	No Children	One Child	Two Children	Three Children	No Children	One Child	Two Children	Three Children
		Your credit is–				Your credit is–			
8,500	8,550	376	2,899	3,410	3,836	457	2,899	3,410	3,836
8,550	8,600	372	2,916	3,430	3,859	457	2,916	3,430	3,859
8,600	8,650	368	2,933	3,450	3,881	457	2,933	3,450	3,881
8,650	8,700	365	2,950	3,470	3,904	457	2,950	3,470	3,904
8,700	8,750	361	2,967	3,490	3,926	457	2,967	3,490	3,926
8,750	8,800	357	2,984	3,510	3,949	457	2,984	3,510	3,949
8,800	8,850	353	3,001	3,530	3,971	457	3,001	3,530	3,971
8,850	8,900	349	3,018	3,550	3,994	457	3,018	3,550	3,994
8,900	8,950	345	3,035	3,570	4,016	457	3,035	3,570	4,016
8,950	9,000	342	3,043	3,590	4,039	457	3,043	3,590	4,039
9,000	9,050	338	3,043	3,610	4,061	457	3,043	3,610	4,061
9,050	9,100	334	3,043	3,630	4,084	457	3,043	3,630	4,084
9,100	9,150	330	3,043	3,650	4,106	457	3,043	3,650	4,106
9,150	9,200	326	3,043	3,670	4,129	457	3,043	3,670	4,129
9,200	9,250	322	3,043	3,690	4,151	457	3,043	3,690	4,151
9,250	9,300	319	3,043	3,710	4,174	457	3,043	3,710	4,174
9,300	9,350	315	3,043	3,730	4,196	457	3,043	3,730	4,196
9,350	9,400	311	3,043	3,750	4,219	457	3,043	3,750	4,219
9,400	9,450	307	3,043	3,770	4,241	457	3,043	3,770	4,241
9,450	9,500	303	3,043	3,790	4,264	457	3,043	3,790	4,264
9,500	9,550	299	3,043	3,810	4,286	457	3,043	3,810	4,286
9,550	9,600	296	3,043	3,830	4,309	457	3,043	3,830	4,309
9,600	9,650	292	3,043	3,850	4,331	457	3,043	3,850	4,331
9,650	9,700	288	3,043	3,870	4,354	457	3,043	3,870	4,354
9,700	9,750	284	3,043	3,890	4,376	457	3,043	3,890	4,376
9,750	9,800	280	3,043	3,910	4,399	457	3,043	3,910	4,399
9,800	9,850	277	3,043	3,930	4,421	457	3,043	3,930	4,421
9,850	9,900	273	3,043	3,950	4,444	457	3,043	3,950	4,444
9,900	9,950	269	3,043	3,970	4,466	457	3,043	3,970	4,466
9,950	10,000	265	3,043	3,990	4,489	457	3,043	3,990	4,489
10,000	10,050	261	3,043	4,010	4,511	457	3,043	4,010	4,511
10,050	10,100	257	3,043	4,030	4,534	457	3,043	4,030	4,534
10,100	10,150	254	3,043	4,050	4,556	457	3,043	4,050	4,556
10,150	10,200	250	3,043	4,070	4,579	457	3,043	4,070	4,579
10,200	10,250	246	3,043	4,090	4,601	457	3,043	4,090	4,601
10,250	10,300	242	3,043	4,110	4,624	457	3,043	4,110	4,624
10,300	10,350	238	3,043	4,130	4,646	457	3,043	4,130	4,646
10,350	10,400	234	3,043	4,150	4,669	457	3,043	4,150	4,669
10,400	10,450	231	3,043	4,170	4,691	457	3,043	4,170	4,691
10,450	10,500	227	3,043	4,190	4,714	457	3,043	4,190	4,714
10,500	10,550	223	3,043	4,210	4,736	457	3,043	4,210	4,736
10,550	10,600	219	3,043	4,230	4,759	457	3,043	4,230	4,759
10,600	10,650	215	3,043	4,250	4,781	457	3,043	4,250	4,781
10,650	10,700	212	3,043	4,270	4,804	457	3,043	4,270	4,804
10,700	10,750	208	3,043	4,290	4,826	457	3,043	4,290	4,826
10,750	10,800	204	3,043	4,310	4,849	457	3,043	4,310	4,849
10,800	10,850	200	3,043	4,330	4,871	457	3,043	4,330	4,871
10,850	10,900	196	3,043	4,350	4,894	457	3,043	4,350	4,894
10,900	10,950	192	3,043	4,370	4,916	457	3,043	4,370	4,916
10,950	11,000	189	3,043	4,390	4,939	457	3,043	4,390	4,939
11,000	11,050	185	3,043	4,410	4,961	457	3,043	4,410	4,961
11,050	11,100	181	3,043	4,430	4,984	457	3,043	4,430	4,984
11,100	11,150	177	3,043	4,450	5,006	457	3,043	4,450	5,006
11,150	11,200	173	3,043	4,470	5,029	457	3,043	4,470	5,029
11,200	11,250	169	3,043	4,490	5,051	457	3,043	4,490	5,051
11,250	11,300	166	3,043	4,510	5,074	457	3,043	4,510	5,074
11,300	11,350	162	3,043	4,530	5,096	457	3,043	4,530	5,096
11,350	11,400	158	3,043	4,550	5,119	457	3,043	4,550	5,119
11,400	11,450	154	3,043	4,570	5,141	457	3,043	4,570	5,141
11,450	11,500	150	3,043	4,590	5,164	457	3,043	4,590	5,164

2009 Earned Income Credit (EIC) Table–*Continued* (**Caution.** This is **not** a tax table.)

If the amount you are looking up from the worksheet is–		And your filing status is– Single, head of household, or qualifying widow(er) and you have–				Married filing jointly and you have–			
		No Children	One Child	Two Children	Three Children	No Children	One Child	Two Children	Three Children
At least	But less than	Your credit is–				Your credit is–			
11,500	**11,550**	146	3,043	4,610	5,186	457	3,043	4,610	5,186
11,550	**11,600**	143	3,043	4,630	5,209	457	3,043	4,630	5,209
11,600	**11,650**	139	3,043	4,650	5,231	457	3,043	4,650	5,231
11,650	**11,700**	135	3,043	4,670	5,254	457	3,043	4,670	5,254
11,700	**11,750**	131	3,043	4,690	5,276	457	3,043	4,690	5,276
11,750	**11,800**	127	3,043	4,710	5,299	457	3,043	4,710	5,299
11,800	**11,850**	124	3,043	4,730	5,321	457	3,043	4,730	5,321
11,850	**11,900**	120	3,043	4,750	5,344	457	3,043	4,750	5,344
11,900	**11,950**	116	3,043	4,770	5,366	457	3,043	4,770	5,366
11,950	**12,000**	112	3,043	4,790	5,389	457	3,043	4,790	5,389
12,000	**12,050**	108	3,043	4,810	5,411	457	3,043	4,810	5,411
12,050	**12,100**	104	3,043	4,830	5,434	457	3,043	4,830	5,434
12,100	**12,150**	101	3,043	4,850	5,456	457	3,043	4,850	5,456
12,150	**12,200**	97	3,043	4,870	5,479	457	3,043	4,870	5,479
12,200	**12,250**	93	3,043	4,890	5,501	457	3,043	4,890	5,501
12,250	**12,300**	89	3,043	4,910	5,524	457	3,043	4,910	5,524
12,300	**12,350**	85	3,043	4,930	5,546	457	3,043	4,930	5,546
12,350	**12,400**	81	3,043	4,950	5,569	457	3,043	4,950	5,569
12,400	**12,450**	78	3,043	4,970	5,591	457	3,043	4,970	5,591
12,450	**12,500**	74	3,043	4,990	5,614	457	3,043	4,990	5,614
12,500	**12,550**	70	3,043	5,010	5,636	452	3,043	5,010	5,636
12,550	**12,600**	66	3,043	5,028	5,657	449	3,043	5,028	5,657
12,600	**12,650**	62	3,043	5,028	5,657	445	3,043	5,028	5,657
12,650	**12,700**	59	3,043	5,028	5,657	441	3,043	5,028	5,657
12,700	**12,750**	55	3,043	5,028	5,657	437	3,043	5,028	5,657
12,750	**12,800**	51	3,043	5,028	5,657	433	3,043	5,028	5,657
12,800	**12,850**	47	3,043	5,028	5,657	430	3,043	5,028	5,657
12,850	**12,900**	43	3,043	5,028	5,657	426	3,043	5,028	5,657
12,900	**12,950**	39	3,043	5,028	5,657	422	3,043	5,028	5,657
12,950	**13,000**	36	3,043	5,028	5,657	418	3,043	5,028	5,657
13,000	**13,050**	32	3,043	5,028	5,657	414	3,043	5,028	5,657
13,050	**13,100**	28	3,043	5,028	5,657	410	3,043	5,028	5,657
13,100	**13,150**	24	3,043	5,028	5,657	407	3,043	5,028	5,657
13,150	**13,200**	20	3,043	5,028	5,657	403	3,043	5,028	5,657
13,200	**13,250**	16	3,043	5,028	5,657	399	3,043	5,028	5,657
13,250	**13,300**	13	3,043	5,028	5,657	395	3,043	5,028	5,657
13,300	**13,350**	9	3,043	5,028	5,657	391	3,043	5,028	5,657
13,350	**13,400**	5	3,043	5,028	5,657	387	3,043	5,028	5,657
13,400	**13,450**	*	3,043	5,028	5,657	384	3,043	5,028	5,657
13,450	**13,500**	0	3,043	5,028	5,657	380	3,043	5,028	5,657
13,500	**13,550**	0	3,043	5,028	5,657	376	3,043	5,028	5,657
13,550	**13,600**	0	3,043	5,028	5,657	372	3,043	5,028	5,657
13,600	**13,650**	0	3,043	5,028	5,657	368	3,043	5,028	5,657
13,650	**13,700**	0	3,043	5,028	5,657	365	3,043	5,028	5,657
13,700	**13,750**	0	3,043	5,028	5,657	361	3,043	5,028	5,657
13,750	**13,800**	0	3,043	5,028	5,657	357	3,043	5,028	5,657
13,800	**13,850**	0	3,043	5,028	5,657	353	3,043	5,028	5,657
13,850	**13,900**	0	3,043	5,028	5,657	349	3,043	5,028	5,657
13,900	**13,950**	0	3,043	5,028	5,657	345	3,043	5,028	5,657
13,950	**14,000**	0	3,043	5,028	5,657	342	3,043	5,028	5,657
14,000	**14,050**	0	3,043	5,028	5,657	338	3,043	5,028	5,657
14,050	**14,100**	0	3,043	5,028	5,657	334	3,043	5,028	5,657
14,100	**14,150**	0	3,043	5,028	5,657	330	3,043	5,028	5,657
14,150	**14,200**	0	3,043	5,028	5,657	326	3,043	5,028	5,657
14,200	**14,250**	0	3,043	5,028	5,657	322	3,043	5,028	5,657

*If the amount you are looking up from the worksheet is at least $13,400 but less than $13,440, your credit is $2. Otherwise, you cannot take the credit.

2009 Earned Income Credit (EIC) Table–*Continued* (**Caution.** This is **not** a tax table.)

If the amount you are looking up from the worksheet is–		And your filing status is– Single, head of household, or qualifying widow(er) and you have–				Married filing jointly and you have–			
At least	But less than	No Children	One Child	Two Children	Three Children	No Children	One Child	Two Children	Three Children
		Your credit is–				Your credit is–			
14,250	**14,300**	0	3,043	5,028	5,657	319	3,043	5,028	5,657
14,300	**14,350**	0	3,043	5,028	5,657	315	3,043	5,028	5,657
14,350	**14,400**	0	3,043	5,028	5,657	311	3,043	5,028	5,657
14,400	**14,450**	0	3,043	5,028	5,657	307	3,043	5,028	5,657
14,450	**14,500**	0	3,043	5,028	5,657	303	3,043	5,028	5,657
14,500	**14,550**	0	3,043	5,028	5,657	299	3,043	5,028	5,657
14,550	**14,600**	0	3,043	5,028	5,657	296	3,043	5,028	5,657
14,600	**14,650**	0	3,043	5,028	5,657	292	3,043	5,028	5,657
14,650	**14,700**	0	3,043	5,028	5,657	288	3,043	5,028	5,657
14,700	**14,750**	0	3,043	5,028	5,657	284	3,043	5,028	5,657
14,750	**14,800**	0	3,043	5,028	5,657	280	3,043	5,028	5,657
14,800	**14,850**	0	3,043	5,028	5,657	277	3,043	5,028	5,657
14,850	**14,900**	0	3,043	5,028	5,657	273	3,043	5,028	5,657
14,900	**14,950**	0	3,043	5,028	5,657	269	3,043	5,028	5,657
14,950	**15,000**	0	3,043	5,028	5,657	265	3,043	5,028	5,657
15,000	**15,050**	0	3,043	5,028	5,657	261	3,043	5,028	5,657
15,050	**15,100**	0	3,043	5,028	5,657	257	3,043	5,028	5,657
15,100	**15,150**	0	3,043	5,028	5,657	254	3,043	5,028	5,657
15,150	**15,200**	0	3,043	5,028	5,657	250	3,043	5,028	5,657
15,200	**15,250**	0	3,043	5,028	5,657	246	3,043	5,028	5,657
15,250	**15,300**	0	3,043	5,028	5,657	242	3,043	5,028	5,657
15,300	**15,350**	0	3,043	5,028	5,657	238	3,043	5,028	5,657
15,350	**15,400**	0	3,043	5,028	5,657	234	3,043	5,028	5,657
15,400	**15,450**	0	3,043	5,028	5,657	231	3,043	5,028	5,657
15,450	**15,500**	0	3,043	5,028	5,657	227	3,043	5,028	5,657
15,500	**15,550**	0	3,043	5,028	5,657	223	3,043	5,028	5,657
15,550	**15,600**	0	3,043	5,028	5,657	219	3,043	5,028	5,657
15,600	**15,650**	0	3,043	5,028	5,657	215	3,043	5,028	5,657
15,650	**15,700**	0	3,043	5,028	5,657	212	3,043	5,028	5,657
15,700	**15,750**	0	3,043	5,028	5,657	208	3,043	5,028	5,657
15,750	**15,800**	0	3,043	5,028	5,657	204	3,043	5,028	5,657
15,800	**15,850**	0	3,043	5,028	5,657	200	3,043	5,028	5,657
15,850	**15,900**	0	3,043	5,028	5,657	196	3,043	5,028	5,657
15,900	**15,950**	0	3,043	5,028	5,657	192	3,043	5,028	5,657
15,950	**16,000**	0	3,043	5,028	5,657	189	3,043	5,028	5,657
16,000	**16,050**	0	3,043	5,028	5,657	185	3,043	5,028	5,657
16,050	**16,100**	0	3,043	5,028	5,657	181	3,043	5,028	5,657
16,100	**16,150**	0	3,043	5,028	5,657	177	3,043	5,028	5,657
16,150	**16,200**	0	3,043	5,028	5,657	173	3,043	5,028	5,657
16,200	**16,250**	0	3,043	5,028	5,657	169	3,043	5,028	5,657
16,250	**16,300**	0	3,043	5,028	5,657	166	3,043	5,028	5,657
16,300	**16,350**	0	3,043	5,028	5,657	162	3,043	5,028	5,657
16,350	**16,400**	0	3,043	5,028	5,657	158	3,043	5,028	5,657
16,400	**16,450**	0	3,043	5,028	5,657	154	3,043	5,028	5,657
16,450	**16,500**	0	3,034	5,016	5,645	150	3,043	5,028	5,657
16,500	**16,550**	0	3,026	5,006	5,634	146	3,043	5,028	5,657
16,550	**16,600**	0	3,018	4,995	5,624	143	3,043	5,028	5,657
16,600	**16,650**	0	3,010	4,985	5,613	139	3,043	5,028	5,657
16,650	**16,700**	0	3,002	4,974	5,603	135	3,043	5,028	5,657
16,700	**16,750**	0	2,994	4,964	5,592	131	3,043	5,028	5,657
16,750	**16,800**	0	2,986	4,953	5,582	127	3,043	5,028	5,657
16,800	**16,850**	0	2,978	4,943	5,571	124	3,043	5,028	5,657
16,850	**16,900**	0	2,970	4,932	5,561	120	3,043	5,028	5,657
16,900	**16,950**	0	2,962	4,922	5,550	116	3,043	5,028	5,657
16,950	**17,000**	0	2,954	4,911	5,540	112	3,043	5,028	5,657
17,000	**17,050**	0	2,946	4,901	5,529	108	3,043	5,028	5,657
17,050	**17,100**	0	2,938	4,890	5,519	104	3,043	5,028	5,657
17,100	**17,150**	0	2,930	4,880	5,508	101	3,043	5,028	5,657
17,150	**17,200**	0	2,922	4,869	5,497	97	3,043	5,028	5,657
17,200	**17,250**	0	2,914	4,858	5,487	93	3,043	5,028	5,657

2009 Earned Income Credit (EIC) Table–*Continued* (**Caution.** This is **not** a tax table.)

If the amount you are looking up from the worksheet is–		And your filing status is– Single, head of household, or qualifying widow(er) and you have–				Married filing jointly and you have–			
At least	But less than	No Children	One Child	Two Children	Three Children	No Children	One Child	Two Children	Three Children
		Your credit is–				Your credit is–			
17,250	**17,300**	0	2,906	4,848	5,476	89	3,043	5,028	5,657
17,300	**17,350**	0	2,898	4,837	5,466	85	3,043	5,028	5,657
17,350	**17,400**	0	2,890	4,827	5,455	81	3,043	5,028	5,657
17,400	**17,450**	0	2,882	4,816	5,445	78	3,043	5,028	5,657
17,450	**17,500**	0	2,874	4,806	5,434	74	3,043	5,028	5,657
17,500	**17,550**	0	2,866	4,795	5,424	70	3,043	5,028	5,657
17,550	**17,600**	0	2,858	4,785	5,413	66	3,043	5,028	5,657
17,600	**17,650**	0	2,850	4,774	5,403	62	3,043	5,028	5,657
17,650	**17,700**	0	2,842	4,764	5,392	59	3,043	5,028	5,657
17,700	**17,750**	0	2,834	4,753	5,382	55	3,043	5,028	5,657
17,750	**17,800**	0	2,826	4,743	5,371	51	3,043	5,028	5,657
17,800	**17,850**	0	2,818	4,732	5,361	47	3,043	5,028	5,657
17,850	**17,900**	0	2,810	4,722	5,350	43	3,043	5,028	5,657
17,900	**17,950**	0	2,803	4,711	5,340	39	3,043	5,028	5,657
17,950	**18,000**	0	2,795	4,701	5,329	36	3,043	5,028	5,657
18,000	**18,050**	0	2,787	4,690	5,318	32	3,043	5,028	5,657
18,050	**18,100**	0	2,779	4,679	5,308	28	3,043	5,028	5,657
18,100	**18,150**	0	2,771	4,669	5,297	24	3,043	5,028	5,657
18,150	**18,200**	0	2,763	4,658	5,287	20	3,043	5,028	5,657
18,200	**18,250**	0	2,755	4,648	5,276	16	3,043	5,028	5,657
18,250	**18,300**	0	2,747	4,637	5,266	13	3,043	5,028	5,657
18,300	**18,350**	0	2,739	4,627	5,255	9	3,043	5,028	5,657
18,350	**18,400**	0	2,731	4,616	5,245	5	3,043	5,028	5,657
18,400	**18,450**	0	2,723	4,606	5,234	*	3,043	5,028	5,657
18,450	**18,500**	0	2,715	4,595	5,224	0	3,043	5,028	5,657
18,500	**18,550**	0	2,707	4,585	5,213	0	3,043	5,028	5,657
18,550	**18,600**	0	2,699	4,574	5,203	0	3,043	5,028	5,657
18,600	**18,650**	0	2,691	4,564	5,192	0	3,043	5,028	5,657
18,650	**18,700**	0	2,683	4,553	5,182	0	3,043	5,028	5,657
18,700	**18,750**	0	2,675	4,543	5,171	0	3,043	5,028	5,657
18,750	**18,800**	0	2,667	4,532	5,161	0	3,043	5,028	5,657
18,800	**18,850**	0	2,659	4,522	5,150	0	3,043	5,028	5,657
18,850	**18,900**	0	2,651	4,511	5,139	0	3,043	5,028	5,657
18,900	**18,950**	0	2,643	4,500	5,129	0	3,043	5,028	5,657
18,950	**19,000**	0	2,635	4,490	5,118	0	3,043	5,028	5,657
19,000	**19,050**	0	2,627	4,479	5,108	0	3,043	5,028	5,657
19,050	**19,100**	0	2,619	4,469	5,097	0	3,043	5,028	5,657
19,100	**19,150**	0	2,611	4,458	5,087	0	3,043	5,028	5,657
19,150	**19,200**	0	2,603	4,448	5,076	0	3,043	5,028	5,657
19,200	**19,250**	0	2,595	4,437	5,066	0	3,043	5,028	5,657
19,250	**19,300**	0	2,587	4,427	5,055	0	3,043	5,028	5,657
19,300	**19,350**	0	2,579	4,416	5,045	0	3,043	5,028	5,657
19,350	**19,400**	0	2,571	4,406	5,034	0	3,043	5,028	5,657
19,400	**19,450**	0	2,563	4,395	5,024	0	3,043	5,028	5,657
19,450	**19,500**	0	2,555	4,385	5,013	0	3,043	5,028	5,657
19,500	**19,550**	0	2,547	4,374	5,003	0	3,043	5,028	5,657
19,550	**19,600**	0	2,539	4,364	4,992	0	3,043	5,028	5,657
19,600	**19,650**	0	2,531	4,353	4,982	0	3,043	5,028	5,657
19,650	**19,700**	0	2,523	4,342	4,971	0	3,043	5,028	5,657
19,700	**19,750**	0	2,515	4,332	4,960	0	3,043	5,028	5,657
19,750	**19,800**	0	2,507	4,321	4,950	0	3,043	5,028	5,657
19,800	**19,850**	0	2,499	4,311	4,939	0	3,043	5,028	5,657
19,850	**19,900**	0	2,491	4,300	4,929	0	3,043	5,028	5,657
19,900	**19,950**	0	2,483	4,290	4,918	0	3,043	5,028	5,657
19,950	**20,000**	0	2,475	4,279	4,908	0	3,043	5,028	5,657

*If the amount you are looking up from the worksheet is at least $18,400 but less than $18,440, your credit is $2. Otherwise, you cannot take the credit.

2009 Earned Income Credit (EIC) Table–*Continued* (**Caution.** This is **not** a tax table.)

If the amount you are looking up from the worksheet is–		And your filing status is–							
		Single, head of household, or qualifying widow(er) and you have–				Married filing jointly and you have–			
At least	But less than	No Children	One Child	Two Children	Three Children	No Children	One Child	Two Children	Three Children
		Your credit is–				Your credit is–			
20,000	**20,050**	0	2,467	4,269	4,897	0	3,043	5,028	5,657
20,050	**20,100**	0	2,459	4,258	4,887	0	3,043	5,028	5,657
20,100	**20,150**	0	2,451	4,248	4,876	0	3,043	5,028	5,657
20,150	**20,200**	0	2,443	4,237	4,866	0	3,043	5,028	5,657
20,200	**20,250**	0	2,435	4,227	4,855	0	3,043	5,028	5,657
20,250	**20,300**	0	2,427	4,216	4,845	0	3,043	5,028	5,657
20,300	**20,350**	0	2,419	4,206	4,834	0	3,043	5,028	5,657
20,350	**20,400**	0	2,411	4,195	4,824	0	3,043	5,028	5,657
20,400	**20,450**	0	2,403	4,185	4,813	0	3,043	5,028	5,657
20,450	**20,500**	0	2,395	4,174	4,803	0	3,043	5,028	5,657
20,500	**20,550**	0	2,387	4,163	4,792	0	3,043	5,028	5,657
20,550	**20,600**	0	2,379	4,153	4,781	0	3,043	5,028	5,657
20,600	**20,650**	0	2,371	4,142	4,771	0	3,043	5,028	5,657
20,650	**20,700**	0	2,363	4,132	4,760	0	3,043	5,028	5,657
20,700	**20,750**	0	2,355	4,121	4,750	0	3,043	5,028	5,657
20,750	**20,800**	0	2,347	4,111	4,739	0	3,043	5,028	5,657
20,800	**20,850**	0	2,339	4,100	4,729	0	3,043	5,028	5,657
20,850	**20,900**	0	2,331	4,090	4,718	0	3,043	5,028	5,657
20,900	**20,950**	0	2,323	4,079	4,708	0	3,043	5,028	5,657
20,950	**21,000**	0	2,315	4,069	4,697	0	3,043	5,028	5,657
21,000	**21,050**	0	2,307	4,058	4,687	0	3,043	5,028	5,657
21,050	**21,100**	0	2,299	4,048	4,676	0	3,043	5,028	5,657
21,100	**21,150**	0	2,291	4,037	4,666	0	3,043	5,028	5,657
21,150	**21,200**	0	2,283	4,027	4,655	0	3,043	5,028	5,657
21,200	**21,250**	0	2,275	4,016	4,645	0	3,043	5,028	5,657
21,250	**21,300**	0	2,267	4,006	4,634	0	3,043	5,028	5,657
21,300	**21,350**	0	2,259	3,995	4,624	0	3,043	5,028	5,657
21,350	**21,400**	0	2,251	3,984	4,613	0	3,043	5,028	5,657
21,400	**21,450**	0	2,243	3,974	4,602	0	3,043	5,028	5,657
21,450	**21,500**	0	2,235	3,963	4,592	0	3,034	5,016	5,645
21,500	**21,550**	0	2,227	3,953	4,581	0	3,026	5,006	5,634
21,550	**21,600**	0	2,219	3,942	4,571	0	3,018	4,995	5,624
21,600	**21,650**	0	2,211	3,932	4,560	0	3,010	4,985	5,613
21,650	**21,700**	0	2,203	3,921	4,550	0	3,002	4,974	5,603
21,700	**21,750**	0	2,195	3,911	4,539	0	2,994	4,964	5,592
21,750	**21,800**	0	2,187	3,900	4,529	0	2,986	4,953	5,582
21,800	**21,850**	0	2,179	3,890	4,518	0	2,978	4,943	5,571
21,850	**21,900**	0	2,171	3,879	4,508	0	2,970	4,932	5,561
21,900	**21,950**	0	2,163	3,869	4,497	0	2,962	4,922	5,550
21,950	**22,000**	0	2,155	3,858	4,487	0	2,954	4,911	5,540
22,000	**22,050**	0	2,147	3,848	4,476	0	2,946	4,901	5,529
22,050	**22,100**	0	2,139	3,837	4,466	0	2,938	4,890	5,519
22,100	**22,150**	0	2,131	3,827	4,455	0	2,930	4,880	5,508
22,150	**22,200**	0	2,123	3,816	4,444	0	2,922	4,869	5,497
22,200	**22,250**	0	2,115	3,805	4,434	0	2,914	4,858	5,487
22,250	**22,300**	0	2,107	3,795	4,423	0	2,906	4,848	5,476
22,300	**22,350**	0	2,099	3,784	4,413	0	2,898	4,837	5,466
22,350	**22,400**	0	2,091	3,774	4,402	0	2,890	4,827	5,455
22,400	**22,450**	0	2,083	3,763	4,392	0	2,882	4,816	5,445
22,450	**22,500**	0	2,075	3,753	4,381	0	2,874	4,806	5,434
22,500	**22,550**	0	2,067	3,742	4,371	0	2,866	4,795	5,424
22,550	**22,600**	0	2,059	3,732	4,360	0	2,858	4,785	5,413
22,600	**22,650**	0	2,051	3,721	4,350	0	2,850	4,774	5,403
22,650	**22,700**	0	2,043	3,711	4,339	0	2,842	4,764	5,392
22,700	**22,750**	0	2,035	3,700	4,329	0	2,834	4,753	5,382
22,750	**22,800**	0	2,027	3,690	4,318	0	2,826	4,743	5,371
22,800	**22,850**	0	2,019	3,679	4,308	0	2,818	4,732	5,361
22,850	**22,900**	0	2,011	3,669	4,297	0	2,810	4,722	5,350
22,900	**22,950**	0	2,004	3,658	4,287	0	2,803	4,711	5,340
22,950	**23,000**	0	1,996	3,648	4,276	0	2,795	4,701	5,329

2009 Earned Income Credit (EIC) Table–*Continued* (**Caution.** This is **not** a tax table.)

If the amount you are looking up from the worksheet is–		And your filing status is– Single, head of household, or qualifying widow(er) and you have–				Married filing jointly and you have–			
At least	But less than	No Children	One Child	Two Children	Three Children	No Children	One Child	Two Children	Three Children
		Your credit is–				Your credit is–			
23,000	23,050	0	1,988	3,637	4,265	0	2,787	4,690	5,318
23,050	23,100	0	1,980	3,626	4,255	0	2,779	4,679	5,308
23,100	23,150	0	1,972	3,616	4,244	0	2,771	4,669	5,297
23,150	23,200	0	1,964	3,605	4,234	0	2,763	4,658	5,287
23,200	23,250	0	1,956	3,595	4,223	0	2,755	4,648	5,276
23,250	23,300	0	1,948	3,584	4,213	0	2,747	4,637	5,266
23,300	23,350	0	1,940	3,574	4,202	0	2,739	4,627	5,255
23,350	23,400	0	1,932	3,563	4,192	0	2,731	4,616	5,245
23,400	23,450	0	1,924	3,553	4,181	0	2,723	4,606	5,234
23,450	23,500	0	1,916	3,542	4,171	0	2,715	4,595	5,224
23,500	23,550	0	1,908	3,532	4,160	0	2,707	4,585	5,213
23,550	23,600	0	1,900	3,521	4,150	0	2,699	4,574	5,203
23,600	23,650	0	1,892	3,511	4,139	0	2,691	4,564	5,192
23,650	23,700	0	1,884	3,500	4,129	0	2,683	4,553	5,182
23,700	23,750	0	1,876	3,490	4,118	0	2,675	4,543	5,171
23,750	23,800	0	1,868	3,479	4,108	0	2,667	4,532	5,161
23,800	23,850	0	1,860	3,469	4,097	0	2,659	4,522	5,150
23,850	23,900	0	1,852	3,458	4,086	0	2,651	4,511	5,139
23,900	23,950	0	1,844	3,447	4,076	0	2,643	4,500	5,129
23,950	24,000	0	1,836	3,437	4,065	0	2,635	4,490	5,118
24,000	24,050	0	1,828	3,426	4,055	0	2,627	4,479	5,108
24,050	24,100	0	1,820	3,416	4,044	0	2,619	4,469	5,097
24,100	24,150	0	1,812	3,405	4,034	0	2,611	4,458	5,087
24,150	24,200	0	1,804	3,395	4,023	0	2,603	4,448	5,076
24,200	24,250	0	1,796	3,384	4,013	0	2,595	4,437	5,066
24,250	24,300	0	1,788	3,374	4,002	0	2,587	4,427	5,055
24,300	24,350	0	1,780	3,363	3,992	0	2,579	4,416	5,045
24,350	24,400	0	1,772	3,353	3,981	0	2,571	4,406	5,034
24,400	24,450	0	1,764	3,342	3,971	0	2,563	4,395	5,024
24,450	24,500	0	1,756	3,332	3,960	0	2,555	4,385	5,013
24,500	24,550	0	1,748	3,321	3,950	0	2,547	4,374	5,003
24,550	24,600	0	1,740	3,311	3,939	0	2,539	4,364	4,992
24,600	24,650	0	1,732	3,300	3,929	0	2,531	4,353	4,982
24,650	24,700	0	1,724	3,289	3,918	0	2,523	4,342	4,971
24,700	24,750	0	1,716	3,279	3,907	0	2,515	4,332	4,960
24,750	24,800	0	1,708	3,268	3,897	0	2,507	4,321	4,950
24,800	24,850	0	1,700	3,258	3,886	0	2,499	4,311	4,939
24,850	24,900	0	1,692	3,247	3,876	0	2,491	4,300	4,929
24,900	24,950	0	1,684	3,237	3,865	0	2,483	4,290	4,918
24,950	25,000	0	1,676	3,226	3,855	0	2,475	4,279	4,908
25,000	25,050	0	1,668	3,216	3,844	0	2,467	4,269	4,897
25,050	25,100	0	1,660	3,205	3,834	0	2,459	4,258	4,887
25,100	25,150	0	1,652	3,195	3,823	0	2,451	4,248	4,876
25,150	25,200	0	1,644	3,184	3,813	0	2,443	4,237	4,866
25,200	25,250	0	1,636	3,174	3,802	0	2,435	4,227	4,855
25,250	25,300	0	1,628	3,163	3,792	0	2,427	4,216	4,845
25,300	25,350	0	1,620	3,153	3,781	0	2,419	4,206	4,834
25,350	25,400	0	1,612	3,142	3,771	0	2,411	4,195	4,824
25,400	25,450	0	1,604	3,132	3,760	0	2,403	4,185	4,813
25,450	25,500	0	1,596	3,121	3,750	0	2,395	4,174	4,803
25,500	25,550	0	1,588	3,110	3,739	0	2,387	4,163	4,792
25,550	25,600	0	1,580	3,100	3,728	0	2,379	4,153	4,781
25,600	25,650	0	1,572	3,089	3,718	0	2,371	4,142	4,771
25,650	25,700	0	1,564	3,079	3,707	0	2,363	4,132	4,760
25,700	25,750	0	1,556	3,068	3,697	0	2,355	4,121	4,750
25,750	25,800	0	1,548	3,058	3,686	0	2,347	4,111	4,739
25,800	25,850	0	1,540	3,047	3,676	0	2,339	4,100	4,729
25,850	25,900	0	1,532	3,037	3,665	0	2,331	4,090	4,718
25,900	25,950	0	1,524	3,026	3,655	0	2,323	4,079	4,708
25,950	26,000	0	1,516	3,016	3,644	0	2,315	4,069	4,697

If the amount you are looking up from the worksheet is—		And your filing status is—							
		Single, head of household, or qualifying widow(er) and you have—				Married filing jointly and you have—			
		No Children	One Child	Two Children	Three Children	No Children	One Child	Two Children	Three Children
At least	But less than	Your credit is—				Your credit is—			
26,000	26,050	0	1,508	3,005	3,634	0	2,307	4,058	4,687
26,050	26,100	0	1,500	2,995	3,623	0	2,299	4,048	4,676
26,100	26,150	0	1,492	2,984	3,613	0	2,291	4,037	4,666
26,150	26,200	0	1,484	2,974	3,602	0	2,283	4,027	4,655
26,200	26,250	0	1,476	2,963	3,592	0	2,275	4,016	4,645
26,250	26,300	0	1,468	2,953	3,581	0	2,267	4,006	4,634
26,300	26,350	0	1,460	2,942	3,571	0	2,259	3,995	4,624
26,350	26,400	0	1,452	2,931	3,560	0	2,251	3,984	4,613
26,400	26,450	0	1,444	2,921	3,549	0	2,243	3,974	4,602
26,450	26,500	0	1,436	2,910	3,539	0	2,235	3,963	4,592
26,500	26,550	0	1,428	2,900	3,528	0	2,227	3,953	4,581
26,550	26,600	0	1,420	2,889	3,518	0	2,219	3,942	4,571
26,600	26,650	0	1,412	2,879	3,507	0	2,211	3,932	4,560
26,650	26,700	0	1,404	2,868	3,497	0	2,203	3,921	4,550
26,700	26,750	0	1,396	2,858	3,486	0	2,195	3,911	4,539
26,750	26,800	0	1,388	2,847	3,476	0	2,187	3,900	4,529
26,800	26,850	0	1,380	2,837	3,465	0	2,179	3,890	4,518
26,850	26,900	0	1,372	2,826	3,455	0	2,171	3,879	4,508
26,900	26,950	0	1,364	2,816	3,444	0	2,163	3,869	4,497
26,950	27,000	0	1,356	2,805	3,434	0	2,155	3,858	4,487
27,000	27,050	0	1,348	2,795	3,423	0	2,147	3,848	4,476
27,050	27,100	0	1,340	2,784	3,413	0	2,139	3,837	4,466
27,100	27,150	0	1,332	2,774	3,402	0	2,131	3,827	4,455
27,150	27,200	0	1,324	2,763	3,391	0	2,123	3,816	4,444
27,200	27,250	0	1,316	2,752	3,381	0	2,115	3,805	4,434
27,250	27,300	0	1,308	2,742	3,370	0	2,107	3,795	4,423
27,300	27,350	0	1,300	2,731	3,360	0	2,099	3,784	4,413
27,350	27,400	0	1,292	2,721	3,349	0	2,091	3,774	4,402
27,400	27,450	0	1,284	2,710	3,339	0	2,083	3,763	4,392
27,450	27,500	0	1,276	2,700	3,328	0	2,075	3,753	4,381
27,500	27,550	0	1,268	2,689	3,318	0	2,067	3,742	4,371
27,550	27,600	0	1,260	2,679	3,307	0	2,059	3,732	4,360
27,600	27,650	0	1,252	2,668	3,297	0	2,051	3,721	4,350
27,650	27,700	0	1,244	2,658	3,286	0	2,043	3,711	4,339
27,700	27,750	0	1,236	2,647	3,276	0	2,035	3,700	4,329
27,750	27,800	0	1,228	2,637	3,265	0	2,027	3,690	4,318
27,800	27,850	0	1,220	2,626	3,255	0	2,019	3,679	4,308
27,850	27,900	0	1,212	2,616	3,244	0	2,011	3,669	4,297
27,900	27,950	0	1,205	2,605	3,234	0	2,004	3,658	4,287
27,950	28,000	0	1,197	2,595	3,223	0	1,996	3,648	4,276
28,000	28,050	0	1,189	2,584	3,212	0	1,988	3,637	4,265
28,050	28,100	0	1,181	2,573	3,202	0	1,980	3,626	4,255
28,100	28,150	0	1,173	2,563	3,191	0	1,972	3,616	4,244
28,150	28,200	0	1,165	2,552	3,181	0	1,964	3,605	4,234
28,200	28,250	0	1,157	2,542	3,170	0	1,956	3,595	4,223
28,250	28,300	0	1,149	2,531	3,160	0	1,948	3,584	4,213
28,300	28,350	0	1,141	2,521	3,149	0	1,940	3,574	4,202
28,350	28,400	0	1,133	2,510	3,139	0	1,932	3,563	4,192
28,400	28,450	0	1,125	2,500	3,128	0	1,924	3,553	4,181
28,450	28,500	0	1,117	2,489	3,118	0	1,916	3,542	4,171
28,500	28,550	0	1,109	2,479	3,107	0	1,908	3,532	4,160
28,550	28,600	0	1,101	2,468	3,097	0	1,900	3,521	4,150
28,600	28,650	0	1,093	2,458	3,086	0	1,892	3,511	4,139
28,650	28,700	0	1,085	2,447	3,076	0	1,884	3,500	4,129
28,700	28,750	0	1,077	2,437	3,065	0	1,876	3,490	4,118
28,750	28,800	0	1,069	2,426	3,055	0	1,868	3,479	4,108
28,800	28,850	0	1,061	2,416	3,044	0	1,860	3,469	4,097
28,850	28,900	0	1,053	2,405	3,033	0	1,852	3,458	4,086
28,900	28,950	0	1,045	2,394	3,023	0	1,844	3,447	4,076
28,950	29,000	0	1,037	2,384	3,012	0	1,836	3,437	4,065

2009 Earned Income Credit (EIC) Table–*Continued* (**Caution.** This is **not** a tax table.)

If the amount you are looking up from the worksheet is–		And your filing status is–							
		Single, head of household, or qualifying widow(er) and you have–				Married filing jointly and you have–			
		No Children	One Child	Two Children	Three Children	No Children	One Child	Two Children	Three Children
At least	But less than	Your credit is–				Your credit is–			
29,000	**29,050**	0	1,029	2,373	3,002	0	1,828	3,426	4,055
29,050	**29,100**	0	1,021	2,363	2,991	0	1,820	3,416	4,044
29,100	**29,150**	0	1,013	2,352	2,981	0	1,812	3,405	4,034
29,150	**29,200**	0	1,005	2,342	2,970	0	1,804	3,395	4,023
29,200	**29,250**	0	997	2,331	2,960	0	1,796	3,384	4,013
29,250	**29,300**	0	989	2,321	2,949	0	1,788	3,374	4,002
29,300	**29,350**	0	981	2,310	2,939	0	1,780	3,363	3,992
29,350	**29,400**	0	973	2,300	2,928	0	1,772	3,353	3,981
29,400	**29,450**	0	965	2,289	2,918	0	1,764	3,342	3,971
29,450	**29,500**	0	957	2,279	2,907	0	1,756	3,332	3,960
29,500	**29,550**	0	949	2,268	2,897	0	1,748	3,321	3,950
29,550	**29,600**	0	941	2,258	2,886	0	1,740	3,311	3,939
29,600	**29,650**	0	933	2,247	2,876	0	1,732	3,300	3,929
29,650	**29,700**	0	925	2,236	2,865	0	1,724	3,289	3,918
29,700	**29,750**	0	917	2,226	2,854	0	1,716	3,279	3,907
29,750	**29,800**	0	909	2,215	2,844	0	1,708	3,268	3,897
29,800	**29,850**	0	901	2,205	2,833	0	1,700	3,258	3,886
29,850	**29,900**	0	893	2,194	2,823	0	1,692	3,247	3,876
29,900	**29,950**	0	885	2,184	2,812	0	1,684	3,237	3,865
29,950	**30,000**	0	877	2,173	2,802	0	1,676	3,226	3,855
30,000	**30,050**	0	869	2,163	2,791	0	1,668	3,216	3,844
30,050	**30,100**	0	861	2,152	2,781	0	1,660	3,205	3,834
30,100	**30,150**	0	853	2,142	2,770	0	1,652	3,195	3,823
30,150	**30,200**	0	845	2,131	2,760	0	1,644	3,184	3,813
30,200	**30,250**	0	837	2,121	2,749	0	1,636	3,174	3,802
30,250	**30,300**	0	829	2,110	2,739	0	1,628	3,163	3,792
30,300	**30,350**	0	821	2,100	2,728	0	1,620	3,153	3,781
30,350	**30,400**	0	813	2,089	2,718	0	1,612	3,142	3,771
30,400	**30,450**	0	805	2,079	2,707	0	1,604	3,132	3,760
30,450	**30,500**	0	797	2,068	2,697	0	1,596	3,121	3,750
30,500	**30,550**	0	789	2,057	2,686	0	1,588	3,110	3,739
30,550	**30,600**	0	781	2,047	2,675	0	1,580	3,100	3,728
30,600	**30,650**	0	773	2,036	2,665	0	1,572	3,089	3,718
30,650	**30,700**	0	765	2,026	2,654	0	1,564	3,079	3,707
30,700	**30,750**	0	757	2,015	2,644	0	1,556	3,068	3,697
30,750	**30,800**	0	749	2,005	2,633	0	1,548	3,058	3,686
30,800	**30,850**	0	741	1,994	2,623	0	1,540	3,047	3,676
30,850	**30,900**	0	733	1,984	2,612	0	1,532	3,037	3,665
30,900	**30,950**	0	725	1,973	2,602	0	1,524	3,026	3,655
30,950	**31,000**	0	717	1,963	2,591	0	1,516	3,016	3,644
31,000	**31,050**	0	709	1,952	2,581	0	1,508	3,005	3,634
31,050	**31,100**	0	701	1,942	2,570	0	1,500	2,995	3,623
31,100	**31,150**	0	693	1,931	2,560	0	1,492	2,984	3,613
31,150	**31,200**	0	685	1,921	2,549	0	1,484	2,974	3,602
31,200	**31,250**	0	677	1,910	2,539	0	1,476	2,963	3,592
31,250	**31,300**	0	669	1,900	2,528	0	1,468	2,953	3,581
31,300	**31,350**	0	661	1,889	2,518	0	1,460	2,942	3,571
31,350	**31,400**	0	653	1,878	2,507	0	1,452	2,931	3,560
31,400	**31,450**	0	645	1,868	2,496	0	1,444	2,921	3,549
31,450	**31,500**	0	637	1,857	2,486	0	1,436	2,910	3,539
31,500	**31,550**	0	629	1,847	2,475	0	1,428	2,900	3,528
31,550	**31,600**	0	621	1,836	2,465	0	1,420	2,889	3,518
31,600	**31,650**	0	613	1,826	2,454	0	1,412	2,879	3,507
31,650	**31,700**	0	605	1,815	2,444	0	1,404	2,868	3,497
31,700	**31,750**	0	597	1,805	2,433	0	1,396	2,858	3,486
31,750	**31,800**	0	589	1,794	2,423	0	1,388	2,847	3,476
31,800	**31,850**	0	581	1,784	2,412	0	1,380	2,837	3,465
31,850	**31,900**	0	573	1,773	2,402	0	1,372	2,826	3,455
31,900	**31,950**	0	565	1,763	2,391	0	1,364	2,816	3,444
31,950	**32,000**	0	557	1,752	2,381	0	1,356	2,805	3,434

2009 Earned Income Credit (EIC) Table—*Continued* (**Caution.** This is **not** a tax table.)

If the amount you are looking up from the worksheet is–		And your filing status is–							
		Single, head of household, or qualifying widow(er) and you have–				Married filing jointly and you have–			
		No Children	One Child	Two Children	Three Children	No Children	One Child	Two Children	Three Children
At least	But less than	Your credit is–				Your credit is–			
32,000	**32,050**	0	549	1,742	2,370	0	1,348	2,795	3,423
32,050	**32,100**	0	541	1,731	2,360	0	1,340	2,784	3,413
32,100	**32,150**	0	533	1,721	2,349	0	1,332	2,774	3,402
32,150	**32,200**	0	525	1,710	2,338	0	1,324	2,763	3,391
32,200	**32,250**	0	517	1,699	2,328	0	1,316	2,752	3,381
32,250	**32,300**	0	509	1,689	2,317	0	1,308	2,742	3,370
32,300	**32,350**	0	501	1,678	2,307	0	1,300	2,731	3,360
32,350	**32,400**	0	493	1,668	2,296	0	1,292	2,721	3,349
32,400	**32,450**	0	485	1,657	2,286	0	1,284	2,710	3,339
32,450	**32,500**	0	477	1,647	2,275	0	1,276	2,700	3,328
32,500	**32,550**	0	469	1,636	2,265	0	1,268	2,689	3,318
32,550	**32,600**	0	461	1,626	2,254	0	1,260	2,679	3,307
32,600	**32,650**	0	453	1,615	2,244	0	1,252	2,668	3,297
32,650	**32,700**	0	445	1,605	2,233	0	1,244	2,658	3,286
32,700	**32,750**	0	437	1,594	2,223	0	1,236	2,647	3,276
32,750	**32,800**	0	429	1,584	2,212	0	1,228	2,637	3,265
32,800	**32,850**	0	421	1,573	2,202	0	1,220	2,626	3,255
32,850	**32,900**	0	413	1,563	2,191	0	1,212	2,616	3,244
32,900	**32,950**	0	406	1,552	2,181	0	1,205	2,605	3,234
32,950	**33,000**	0	398	1,542	2,170	0	1,197	2,595	3,223
33,000	**33,050**	0	390	1,531	2,159	0	1,189	2,584	3,212
33,050	**33,100**	0	382	1,520	2,149	0	1,181	2,573	3,202
33,100	**33,150**	0	374	1,510	2,138	0	1,173	2,563	3,191
33,150	**33,200**	0	366	1,499	2,128	0	1,165	2,552	3,181
33,200	**33,250**	0	358	1,489	2,117	0	1,157	2,542	3,170
33,250	**33,300**	0	350	1,478	2,107	0	1,149	2,531	3,160
33,300	**33,350**	0	342	1,468	2,096	0	1,141	2,521	3,149
33,350	**33,400**	0	334	1,457	2,086	0	1,133	2,510	3,139
33,400	**33,450**	0	326	1,447	2,075	0	1,125	2,500	3,128
33,450	**33,500**	0	318	1,436	2,065	0	1,117	2,489	3,118
33,500	**33,550**	0	310	1,426	2,054	0	1,109	2,479	3,107
33,550	**33,600**	0	302	1,415	2,044	0	1,101	2,468	3,097
33,600	**33,650**	0	294	1,405	2,033	0	1,093	2,458	3,086
33,650	**33,700**	0	286	1,394	2,023	0	1,085	2,447	3,076
33,700	**33,750**	0	278	1,384	2,012	0	1,077	2,437	3,065
33,750	**33,800**	0	270	1,373	2,002	0	1,069	2,426	3,055
33,800	**33,850**	0	262	1,363	1,991	0	1,061	2,416	3,044
33,850	**33,900**	0	254	1,352	1,980	0	1,053	2,405	3,033
33,900	**33,950**	0	246	1,341	1,970	0	1,045	2,394	3,023
33,950	**34,000**	0	238	1,331	1,959	0	1,037	2,384	3,012
34,000	**34,050**	0	230	1,320	1,949	0	1,029	2,373	3,002
34,050	**34,100**	0	222	1,310	1,938	0	1,021	2,363	2,991
34,100	**34,150**	0	214	1,299	1,928	0	1,013	2,352	2,981
34,150	**34,200**	0	206	1,289	1,917	0	1,005	2,342	2,970
34,200	**34,250**	0	198	1,278	1,907	0	997	2,331	2,960
34,250	**34,300**	0	190	1,268	1,896	0	989	2,321	2,949
34,300	**34,350**	0	182	1,257	1,886	0	981	2,310	2,939
34,350	**34,400**	0	174	1,247	1,875	0	973	2,300	2,928
34,400	**34,450**	0	166	1,236	1,865	0	965	2,289	2,918
34,450	**34,500**	0	158	1,226	1,854	0	957	2,279	2,907
34,500	**34,550**	0	150	1,215	1,844	0	949	2,268	2,897
34,550	**34,600**	0	142	1,205	1,833	0	941	2,258	2,886
34,600	**34,650**	0	134	1,194	1,823	0	933	2,247	2,876
34,650	**34,700**	0	126	1,183	1,812	0	925	2,236	2,865
34,700	**34,750**	0	118	1,173	1,801	0	917	2,226	2,854
34,750	**34,800**	0	110	1,162	1,791	0	909	2,215	2,844
34,800	**34,850**	0	102	1,152	1,780	0	901	2,205	2,833
34,850	**34,900**	0	94	1,141	1,770	0	893	2,194	2,823
34,900	**34,950**	0	86	1,131	1,759	0	885	2,184	2,812
34,950	**35,000**	0	78	1,120	1,749	0	877	2,173	2,802

2009 Earned Income Credit (EIC) Table–*Continued* (**Caution.** This is **not** a tax table.)

If the amount you are looking up from the worksheet is–		And your filing status is–							
		Single, head of household, or qualifying widow(er) and you have–				**Married filing jointly and you have–**			
		No Children	One Child	Two Children	Three Children	No Children	One Child	Two Children	Three Children
At least	But less than	**Your credit is–**				**Your credit is–**			
35,000	**35,050**	0	70	1,110	1,738	0	869	2,163	2,791
35,050	**35,100**	0	62	1,099	1,728	0	861	2,152	2,781
35,100	**35,150**	0	54	1,089	1,717	0	853	2,142	2,770
35,150	**35,200**	0	46	1,078	1,707	0	845	2,131	2,760
35,200	**35,250**	0	38	1,068	1,696	0	837	2,121	2,749
35,250	**35,300**	0	30	1,057	1,686	0	829	2,110	2,739
35,300	**35,350**	0	22	1,047	1,675	0	821	2,100	2,728
35,350	**35,400**	0	14	1,036	1,665	0	813	2,089	2,718
35,400	**35,450**	0	6	1,026	1,654	0	805	2,079	2,707
35,450	**35,500**	0	*	1,015	1,644	0	797	2,068	2,697
35,500	**35,550**	0	0	1,004	1,633	0	789	2,057	2,686
35,550	**35,600**	0	0	994	1,622	0	781	2,047	2,675
35,600	**35,650**	0	0	983	1,612	0	773	2,036	2,665
35,650	**35,700**	0	0	973	1,601	0	765	2,026	2,654
35,700	**35,750**	0	0	962	1,591	0	757	2,015	2,644
35,750	**35,800**	0	0	952	1,580	0	749	2,005	2,633
35,800	**35,850**	0	0	941	1,570	0	741	1,994	2,623
35,850	**35,900**	0	0	931	1,559	0	733	1,984	2,612
35,900	**35,950**	0	0	920	1,549	0	725	1,973	2,602
35,950	**36,000**	0	0	910	1,538	0	717	1,963	2,591
36,000	**36,050**	0	0	899	1,528	0	709	1,952	2,581
36,050	**36,100**	0	0	889	1,517	0	701	1,942	2,570
36,100	**36,150**	0	0	878	1,507	0	693	1,931	2,560
36,150	**36,200**	0	0	868	1,496	0	685	1,921	2,549
36,200	**36,250**	0	0	857	1,486	0	677	1,910	2,539
36,250	**36,300**	0	0	847	1,475	0	669	1,900	2,528
36,300	**36,350**	0	0	836	1,465	0	661	1,889	2,518
36,350	**36,400**	0	0	825	1,454	0	653	1,878	2,507
36,400	**36,450**	0	0	815	1,443	0	645	1,868	2,496
36,450	**36,500**	0	0	804	1,433	0	637	1,857	2,486
36,500	**36,550**	0	0	794	1,422	0	629	1,847	2,475
36,550	**36,600**	0	0	783	1,412	0	621	1,836	2,465
36,600	**36,650**	0	0	773	1,401	0	613	1,826	2,454
36,650	**36,700**	0	0	762	1,391	0	605	1,815	2,444
36,700	**36,750**	0	0	752	1,380	0	597	1,805	2,433
36,750	**36,800**	0	0	741	1,370	0	589	1,794	2,423
36,800	**36,850**	0	0	731	1,359	0	581	1,784	2,412
36,850	**36,900**	0	0	720	1,349	0	573	1,773	2,402
36,900	**36,950**	0	0	710	1,338	0	565	1,763	2,391
36,950	**37,000**	0	0	699	1,328	0	557	1,752	2,381
37,000	**37,050**	0	0	689	1,317	0	549	1,742	2,370
37,050	**37,100**	0	0	678	1,307	0	541	1,731	2,360
37,100	**37,150**	0	0	668	1,296	0	533	1,721	2,349
37,150	**37,200**	0	0	657	1,285	0	525	1,710	2,338
37,200	**37,250**	0	0	646	1,275	0	517	1,699	2,328
37,250	**37,300**	0	0	636	1,264	0	509	1,689	2,317
37,300	**37,350**	0	0	625	1,254	0	501	1,678	2,307
37,350	**37,400**	0	0	615	1,243	0	493	1,668	2,296
37,400	**37,450**	0	0	604	1,233	0	485	1,657	2,286
37,450	**37,500**	0	0	594	1,222	0	477	1,647	2,275
37,500	**37,550**	0	0	583	1,212	0	469	1,636	2,265
37,550	**37,600**	0	0	573	1,201	0	461	1,626	2,254
37,600	**37,650**	0	0	562	1,191	0	453	1,615	2,244
37,650	**37,700**	0	0	552	1,180	0	445	1,605	2,233
37,700	**37,750**	0	0	541	1,170	0	437	1,594	2,223

*If the amount you are looking up from the worksheet is at least $35,450 but less than $35,463, your credit is $1. Otherwise, you cannot take the credit.

2009 Earned Income Credit (EIC) Table–*Continued* (**Caution.** This is **not** a tax table.)

If the amount you are looking up from the worksheet is–		And your filing status is–							
		Single, head of household, or qualifying widow(er) and you have–				Married filing jointly and you have–			
		No Children	One Child	Two Children	Three Children	No Children	One Child	Two Children	Three Children
At least	But less than	Your credit is–				Your credit is–			
37,750	**37,800**	0	0	531	1,159	0	429	1,584	2,212
37,800	**37,850**	0	0	520	1,149	0	421	1,573	2,202
37,850	**37,900**	0	0	510	1,138	0	413	1,563	2,191
37,900	**37,950**	0	0	499	1,128	0	406	1,552	2,181
37,950	**38,000**	0	0	489	1,117	0	398	1,542	2,170
38,000	**38,050**	0	0	478	1,106	0	390	1,531	2,159
38,050	**38,100**	0	0	467	1,096	0	382	1,520	2,149
38,100	**38,150**	0	0	457	1,085	0	374	1,510	2,138
38,150	**38,200**	0	0	446	1,075	0	366	1,499	2,128
38,200	**38,250**	0	0	436	1,064	0	358	1,489	2,117
38,250	**38,300**	0	0	425	1,054	0	350	1,478	2,107
38,300	**38,350**	0	0	415	1,043	0	342	1,468	2,096
38,350	**38,400**	0	0	404	1,033	0	334	1,457	2,086
38,400	**38,450**	0	0	394	1,022	0	326	1,447	2,075
38,450	**38,500**	0	0	383	1,012	0	318	1,436	2,065
38,500	**38,550**	0	0	373	1,001	0	310	1,426	2,054
38,550	**38,600**	0	0	362	991	0	302	1,415	2,044
38,600	**38,650**	0	0	352	980	0	294	1,405	2,033
38,650	**38,700**	0	0	341	970	0	286	1,394	2,023
38,700	**38,750**	0	0	331	959	0	278	1,384	2,012
38,750	**38,800**	0	0	320	949	0	270	1,373	2,002
38,800	**38,850**	0	0	310	938	0	262	1,363	1,991
38,850	**38,900**	0	0	299	927	0	254	1,352	1,980
38,900	**38,950**	0	0	288	917	0	246	1,341	1,970
38,950	**39,000**	0	0	278	906	0	238	1,331	1,959
39,000	**39,050**	0	0	267	896	0	230	1,320	1,949
39,050	**39,100**	0	0	257	885	0	222	1,310	1,938
39,100	**39,150**	0	0	246	875	0	214	1,299	1,928
39,150	**39,200**	0	0	236	864	0	206	1,289	1,917
39,200	**39,250**	0	0	225	854	0	198	1,278	1,907
39,250	**39,300**	0	0	215	843	0	190	1,268	1,896
39,300	**39,350**	0	0	204	833	0	182	1,257	1,886
39,350	**39,400**	0	0	194	822	0	174	1,247	1,875
39,400	**39,450**	0	0	183	812	0	166	1,236	1,865
39,450	**39,500**	0	0	173	801	0	158	1,226	1,854
39,500	**39,550**	0	0	162	791	0	150	1,215	1,844
39,550	**39,600**	0	0	152	780	0	142	1,205	1,833
39,600	**39,650**	0	0	141	770	0	134	1,194	1,823
39,650	**39,700**	0	0	130	759	0	126	1,183	1,812
39,700	**39,750**	0	0	120	748	0	118	1,173	1,801
39,750	**39,800**	0	0	109	738	0	110	1,162	1,791
39,800	**39,850**	0	0	99	727	0	102	1,152	1,780
39,850	**39,900**	0	0	88	717	0	94	1,141	1,770
39,900	**39,950**	0	0	78	706	0	86	1,131	1,759
39,950	**40,000**	0	0	67	696	0	78	1,120	1,749
40,000	**40,050**	0	0	57	685	0	70	1,110	1,738
40,050	**40,100**	0	0	46	675	0	62	1,099	1,728
40,100	**40,150**	0	0	36	664	0	54	1,089	1,717
40,150	**40,200**	0	0	25	654	0	46	1,078	1,707
40,200	**40,250**	0	0	15	643	0	38	1,068	1,696
40,250	**40,300**	0	0	*	633	0	30	1,057	1,686
40,300	**40,350**	0	0	0	622	0	22	1,047	1,675
40,350	**40,400**	0	0	0	612	0	14	1,036	1,665
40,400	**40,450**	0	0	0	601	0	6	1,026	1,654
40,450	**40,500**	0	0	0	591	0	**	1,015	1,644

*If the amount you are looking up from the worksheet is at least $40,250 but less than $40,295, your credit is $5. Otherwise, you cannot take the credit.

**If the amount you are looking up from the worksheet is at least $40,450 but less than $40,463, your credit is $1. Otherwise, you cannot take the credit.

2009 Earned Income Credit (EIC) Table–*Continued* (**Caution.** This is **not** a tax table.)

If the amount you are looking up from the worksheet is–		And your filing status is–							
		Single, head of household, or qualifying widow(er) and you have–				Married filing jointly and you have–			
At least	But less than	No Children	One Child	Two Children	Three Children	No Children	One Child	Two Children	Three Children
		Your credit is–				Your credit is–			
40,500	40,550	0	0	0	580	0	0	1,004	1,633
40,550	40,600	0	0	0	569	0	0	994	1,622
40,600	40,650	0	0	0	559	0	0	983	1,612
40,650	40,700	0	0	0	548	0	0	973	1,601
40,700	40,750	0	0	0	538	0	0	962	1,591
40,750	40,800	0	0	0	527	0	0	952	1,580
40,800	40,850	0	0	0	517	0	0	941	1,570
40,850	40,900	0	0	0	506	0	0	931	1,559
40,900	40,950	0	0	0	496	0	0	920	1,549
40,950	41,000	0	0	0	485	0	0	910	1,538
41,000	41,050	0	0	0	475	0	0	899	1,528
41,050	41,100	0	0	0	464	0	0	889	1,517
41,100	41,150	0	0	0	454	0	0	878	1,507
41,150	41,200	0	0	0	443	0	0	868	1,496
41,200	41,250	0	0	0	433	0	0	857	1,486
41,250	41,300	0	0	0	422	0	0	847	1,475
41,300	41,350	0	0	0	412	0	0	836	1,465
41,350	41,400	0	0	0	401	0	0	825	1,454
41,400	41,450	0	0	0	390	0	0	815	1,443
41,450	41,500	0	0	0	380	0	0	804	1,433
41,500	41,550	0	0	0	369	0	0	794	1,422
41,550	41,600	0	0	0	359	0	0	783	1,412
41,600	41,650	0	0	0	348	0	0	773	1,401
41,650	41,700	0	0	0	338	0	0	762	1,391
41,700	41,750	0	0	0	327	0	0	752	1,380
41,750	41,800	0	0	0	317	0	0	741	1,370
41,800	41,850	0	0	0	306	0	0	731	1,359
41,850	41,900	0	0	0	296	0	0	720	1,349
41,900	41,950	0	0	0	285	0	0	710	1,338
41,950	42,000	0	0	0	275	0	0	699	1,328
42,000	42,050	0	0	0	264	0	0	689	1,317
42,050	42,100	0	0	0	254	0	0	678	1,307
42,100	42,150	0	0	0	243	0	0	668	1,296
42,150	42,200	0	0	0	232	0	0	657	1,285
42,200	42,250	0	0	0	222	0	0	646	1,275
42,250	42,300	0	0	0	211	0	0	636	1,264
42,300	42,350	0	0	0	201	0	0	625	1,254
42,350	42,400	0	0	0	190	0	0	615	1,243
42,400	42,450	0	0	0	180	0	0	604	1,233
42,450	42,500	0	0	0	169	0	0	594	1,222
42,500	42,550	0	0	0	159	0	0	583	1,212
42,550	42,600	0	0	0	148	0	0	573	1,201
42,600	42,650	0	0	0	138	0	0	562	1,191
42,650	42,700	0	0	0	127	0	0	552	1,180
42,700	42,750	0	0	0	117	0	0	541	1,170
42,750	42,800	0	0	0	106	0	0	531	1,159
42,800	42,850	0	0	0	96	0	0	520	1,149
42,850	42,900	0	0	0	85	0	0	510	1,138
42,900	42,950	0	0	0	75	0	0	499	1,128
42,950	43,000	0	0	0	64	0	0	489	1,117
43,000	43,050	0	0	0	53	0	0	478	1,106
43,050	43,100	0	0	0	43	0	0	467	1,096
43,100	43,150	0	0	0	32	0	0	457	1,085
43,150	43,200	0	0	0	22	0	0	446	1,075
43,200	43,250	0	0	0	11	0	0	436	1,064

2009 Earned Income Credit (EIC) Table–*Continued* (**Caution.** This is **not** a tax table.)

If the amount you are looking up from the worksheet is–		**And your filing status is–**							
		Single, head of household, or qualifying widow(er) and you have–				**Married filing jointly and you have–**			
		No Children	One Child	Two Children	Three Children	No Children	One Child	Two Children	Three Children
At least	But less than	**Your credit is–**				**Your credit is–**			
43,250	**43,300**	0	0	0	*	0	0	425	1,054
43,300	**43,350**	0	0	0	0	0	0	415	1,043
43,350	**43,400**	0	0	0	0	0	0	404	1,033
43,400	**43,450**	0	0	0	0	0	0	394	1,022
43,450	**43,500**	0	0	0	0	0	0	383	1,012
43,500	**43,550**	0	0	0	0	0	0	373	1,001
43,550	**43,600**	0	0	0	0	0	0	362	991
43,600	**43,650**	0	0	0	0	0	0	352	980
43,650	**43,700**	0	0	0	0	0	0	341	970
43,700	**43,750**	0	0	0	0	0	0	331	959
43,750	**43,800**	0	0	0	0	0	0	320	949
43,800	**43,850**	0	0	0	0	0	0	310	938
43,850	**43,900**	0	0	0	0	0	0	299	927
43,900	**43,950**	0	0	0	0	0	0	288	917
43,950	**44,000**	0	0	0	0	0	0	278	906
44,000	**44,050**	0	0	0	0	0	0	267	896
44,050	**44,100**	0	0	0	0	0	0	257	885
44,100	**44,150**	0	0	0	0	0	0	246	875
44,150	**44,200**	0	0	0	0	0	0	236	864
44,200	**44,250**	0	0	0	0	0	0	225	854
44,250	**44,300**	0	0	0	0	0	0	215	843
44,300	**44,350**	0	0	0	0	0	0	204	833
44,350	**44,400**	0	0	0	0	0	0	194	822
44,400	**44,450**	0	0	0	0	0	0	183	812
44,450	**44,500**	0	0	0	0	0	0	173	801
44,500	**44,550**	0	0	0	0	0	0	162	791
44,550	**44,600**	0	0	0	0	0	0	152	780
44,600	**44,650**	0	0	0	0	0	0	141	770
44,650	**44,700**	0	0	0	0	0	0	130	759
44,700	**44,750**	0	0	0	0	0	0	120	748
44,750	**44,800**	0	0	0	0	0	0	109	738
44,800	**44,850**	0	0	0	0	0	0	99	727
44,850	**44,900**	0	0	0	0	0	0	88	717
44,900	**44,950**	0	0	0	0	0	0	78	706
44,950	**45,000**	0	0	0	0	0	0	67	696
45,000	**45,050**	0	0	0	0	0	0	57	685
45,050	**45,100**	0	0	0	0	0	0	46	675
45,100	**45,150**	0	0	0	0	0	0	36	664
45,150	**45,200**	0	0	0	0	0	0	25	654
45,200	**45,250**	0	0	0	0	0	0	15	643
45,250	**45,300**	0	0	0	0	0	0	**	633
45,300	**45,350**	0	0	0	0	0	0	0	622
45,350	**45,400**	0	0	0	0	0	0	0	612
45,400	**45,450**	0	0	0	0	0	0	0	601
45,450	**45,500**	0	0	0	0	0	0	0	591
45,500	**45,550**	0	0	0	0	0	0	0	580
45,550	**45,600**	0	0	0	0	0	0	0	569
45,600	**45,650**	0	0	0	0	0	0	0	559
45,650	**45,700**	0	0	0	0	0	0	0	548
45,700	**45,750**	0	0	0	0	0	0	0	538
45,750	**45,800**	0	0	0	0	0	0	0	527
45,800	**45,850**	0	0	0	0	0	0	0	517
45,850	**45,900**	0	0	0	0	0	0	0	506
45,900	**45,950**	0	0	0	0	0	0	0	496
45,950	**46,000**	0	0	0	0	0	0	0	485

*If the amount you are looking up from the worksheet is at least $43,250 but less than $43,279, your credit is $3. Otherwise, you cannot take the credit.

**If the amount you are looking up from the worksheet is at least $45,250 but less than $45,295, your credit is $5. Otherwise, you cannot take the credit.

2009 Earned Income Credit (EIC) Table–*Continued* (**Caution.** This is **not** a tax table.)

If the amount you are looking up from the worksheet is–		And your filing status is– Single, head of household, or qualifying widow(er) and you have–				Married filing jointly and you have–			
At least	But less than	No Children	One Child	Two Children	Three Children	No Children	One Child	Two Children	Three Children
		Your credit is–				Your credit is–			
46,000	46,050	0	0	0	0	0	0	0	475
46,050	46,100	0	0	0	0	0	0	0	464
46,100	46,150	0	0	0	0	0	0	0	454
46,150	46,200	0	0	0	0	0	0	0	443
46,200	46,250	0	0	0	0	0	0	0	433
46,250	46,300	0	0	0	0	0	0	0	422
46,300	46,350	0	0	0	0	0	0	0	412
46,350	46,400	0	0	0	0	0	0	0	401
46,400	46,450	0	0	0	0	0	0	0	390
46,450	46,500	0	0	0	0	0	0	0	380
46,500	46,550	0	0	0	0	0	0	0	369
46,550	46,600	0	0	0	0	0	0	0	359
46,600	46,650	0	0	0	0	0	0	0	348
46,650	46,700	0	0	0	0	0	0	0	338
46,700	46,750	0	0	0	0	0	0	0	327
46,750	46,800	0	0	0	0	0	0	0	317
46,800	46,850	0	0	0	0	0	0	0	306
46,850	46,900	0	0	0	0	0	0	0	296
46,900	46,950	0	0	0	0	0	0	0	285
46,950	47,000	0	0	0	0	0	0	0	275
47,000	47,050	0	0	0	0	0	0	0	264
47,050	47,100	0	0	0	0	0	0	0	254
47,100	47,150	0	0	0	0	0	0	0	243
47,150	47,200	0	0	0	0	0	0	0	232
47,200	47,250	0	0	0	0	0	0	0	222
47,250	47,300	0	0	0	0	0	0	0	211
47,300	47,350	0	0	0	0	0	0	0	201
47,350	47,400	0	0	0	0	0	0	0	190
47,400	47,450	0	0	0	0	0	0	0	180
47,450	47,500	0	0	0	0	0	0	0	169
47,500	47,550	0	0	0	0	0	0	0	159
47,550	47,600	0	0	0	0	0	0	0	148
47,600	47,650	0	0	0	0	0	0	0	138
47,650	47,700	0	0	0	0	0	0	0	127
47,700	47,750	0	0	0	0	0	0	0	117
47,750	47,800	0	0	0	0	0	0	0	106
47,800	47,850	0	0	0	0	0	0	0	96
47,850	47,900	0	0	0	0	0	0	0	85
47,900	47,950	0	0	0	0	0	0	0	75
47,950	48,000	0	0	0	0	0	0	0	64
48,000	48,050	0	0	0	0	0	0	0	53
48,050	48,100	0	0	0	0	0	0	0	43
48,100	48,150	0	0	0	0	0	0	0	32
48,150	48,200	0	0	0	0	0	0	0	22
48,200	48,250	0	0	0	0	0	0	0	11
48,250	48,279	0	0	0	0	0	0	0	3

Worksheet To See if You Should Fill in Form 6251—Line 45

Keep for Your Records

Before you begin:

✓ Be sure you have read the **Exception** on page 40 to see if you must fill in Form 6251 instead of using this worksheet.

✓ If you are claiming the foreign tax credit (see the instructions for Form 1040, line 47, on page 40), enter that credit on line 47.

1. Are you filing **Schedule A?**
   - ☐ **No.** Enter the amount from Form 1040, line 38.
   - ☐ **Yes.** Enter the amount from Form 1040, line 41.

   .... **1.** ______
2. Enter any amount from Form 8914, line 6 .... **2.** ______
3. If filing **Schedule L**, enter the total of lines 6 and 20 from Schedule L. Otherwise, enter -0- .. **3.** ______
4. Add lines 2 and 3 .... **4.** ______
5. Subtract line 4 from line 1 .... **5.** ______
6. If filing Schedule A, enter the **smaller** of the amount on Schedule A, line 4, or 2.5% (.025) of the amount on Form 1040, line 38 (but not less than zero). Otherwise, enter -0- .... **6.** ______
7. If filing Schedule A, enter the total of the amounts from Schedule A, lines 5, 6, 8, and 27. Otherwise, enter -0- .. **7.** ______
8. Add lines 5 through 7 .... **8.** ______
9. Enter any tax refund from Form 1040, lines 10 and 21 .... **9.** ______
10. Subtract line 9 from line 8 .... **10.** ______
11. Enter the amount shown below for your filing status.
    - Single or head of household—$46,700
    - Married filing jointly or Qualifying widow(er)—$70,950
    - Married filing separately—$35,475

    .... **11.** ______
12. Is the amount on line 10 more than the amount on line 11?
    - ☐ **No.** STOP You do not need to fill in Form 6251.
    - ☐ **Yes.** Subtract line 11 from line 10 .... **12.** ______
13. Enter the amount shown below for your filing status.
    - Single or head of household—$112,500
    - Married filing jointly or qualifying widow(er)—$150,000
    - Married filing separately—$75,000

    .... **13.** ______
14. Is the amount on line 10 more than the amount on line 13?
    - ☐ **No.** Skip lines 14 and 15; enter on line 16 the amount from line 12, and go to line 17.
    - ☐ **Yes.** Subtract line 13 from line 10 .... **14.** ______
15. Multiply line 14 by 25% (.25) and enter the **smaller** of the result or line 11 above .... **15.** ______
16. Add lines 12 and 15 .... **16.** ______
17. Is the amount on line 16 more than $175,000 ($87,500 if married filing separately)?
    - ☐ **Yes.** STOP Fill in Form 6251 to see if you owe the alternative minimum tax.
    - ☐ **No.** Multiply line 16 by 26% (.26) .... **17.** ______
18. Enter the amount from Form 1040, line 44, minus the total of any tax from Form 4972 and any amount on Form 1040, line 47. If you used Schedule J to figure your tax, the amount for Form 1040, line 44, must be refigured without using Schedule J .... **18.** ______

Next. Is the amount on line 17 more than the amount on line 18?
- ☐ **Yes.** Fill in Form 6251 to see if you owe the alternative minimum tax.
- ☐ **No.** You do not owe alternative minimum tax and do not need to fill in Form 6251. Leave line 45 blank.

Form **5405**

Department of the Treasury
Internal Revenue Service

First-Time Homebuyer Credit and Repayment of the Credit

▶ Attach to Form 1040

OMB No. 1545-0074

2009

Attachment Sequence No. **58**

Name(s) shown on return | **Your social security number**

CAUTION: Skip Parts I and II and go to Part III if you are filing this form to report a disposition or change of your main home for which you claimed the credit for 2008.

Part I General Information

A Address of home qualifying for the credit (if different from the address shown on page 1 of Form 1040)

B Date acquired (MM/DD/YYYY) (must be after December 31, 2008, and before December 1, 2009) (see instructions)

Part II Credit

1 Enter the **smaller** of:
- $8,000 ($4,000 if married filing separately), or
- 10% of the purchase price of the home.

If someone other than a spouse also held an interest in the home, enter only your share of this amount (see instructions) . . . **1**

2 Enter your modified adjusted gross income (see instructions) . . **2**

3 Is line 2 more than $75,000 ($150,000 if married filing jointly)?
No. Skip lines 3 through 5 and enter the amount from line 1 on line 6.
Yes. Subtract $75,000 ($150,000 if married filing jointly) from the amount on line 2 and enter the result . . . **3**

4 Divide line 3 by $20,000 and enter the result as a decimal (rounded to at least three places). **Do not** enter more than 1.000 . . . **4** X .

5 Multiply line 1 by line 4 . . . **5**

6 Subtract line 5 from line 1. This is your **credit.** Enter here and on Form 1040, line 67 . . . **6**

Part III Disposition or Change of Main Home

7 Enter the date the home for which you claimed the credit ceased to be your main home (MM/DD/YYYY) ▶ ___/___/___

8 Check the box below that applies to you. See the instructions for the definition of "related person."

a ☐ I sold the home to an unrelated person and had a gain on the sale (as figured after reducing the basis of my home by the credit I claimed). Go to Part IV below.

b ☐ I sold the home to an unrelated person and did not have a gain on the sale (as figured after reducing the basis of my home by the credit I claimed). No repayment of the credit is required. Stop here.

c ☐ I sold the home to a related person. Go to Part IV below.

d ☐ I converted the home to a rental or business use OR I still own the home but no longer use it as my main home. Go to Part IV below.

e ☐ I transferred the home to my ex-spouse as part of my divorce settlement. The full name of my ex-spouse is ▶ ______

The responsibility for repayment of the credit is transferred to your ex-spouse. Stop here.

f ☐ My home was destroyed, condemned, or disposed of under threat of condemnation and I acquired or plan to acquire a new home within 2 years of the event. Repayment of the credit over a 15-year period will begin next year if you purchased your home in 2008. If you purchased your home in 2009, you do not have to repay the credit. Stop here.

g ☐ My home was destroyed, condemned, or disposed of under threat of condemnation and I do not plan to acquire a new home within 2 years of the event. Go to Part IV below.

h ☐ The taxpayer who claimed the credit died in 2009. No repayment of the credit is required of the deceased taxpayer. If the decedent is filing a joint return, see instructions. Otherwise, stop here.

Part IV Repayment of Credit

9 Enter the amount of the credit you claimed on line 6 of your 2008 Form 5405. See instructions if you filed a joint return for 2008. If you checked box 8a above, go to line 10. Otherwise, skip line 10 and enter the amount from line 9 on line 11 . . . **9**

10 Enter the gain on the sale of your main home (as figured after reducing your basis by the amount on line 9 above) . . . **10**

11 Enter the smaller of line 9 or line 10 here and include it on Form 1040, line 60. On the dotted line to the left of line 60, enter "FTHCR" . . . **11**

For Paperwork Reduction Act Notice, see page 3. Cat. No. 11880I Form **5405** (2009)

Estimated Payments, Penalties, and Amended Returns

What's New in 2009

Last Estimated Tax Payment. An individual is not required to make the fourth and final installment payment of 2009 estimated tax if his or her return for 2009 is filed no later than February 1, 2010, and any balance of tax is paid at that time. Fiscal-year filers may file their returns by the last day of the first month after the end of their fiscal year instead of paying the last installment. Farmers and fishermen need not make the January 15, 2010 payment if they file and pay the entire tax due by March 1, 2010.

Tax Preparer's Checklist

- Prior year's returns provide much of the information necessary for determining estimated tax requirements and safe harbor calculations.
- All Form 1040-ES vouchers, canceled checks, etc., should be available.
- Ensure that clients understand the civil and criminal penalties for tax code violations.

Section at a Glance

Estimated Payments ... 11-2
Taxpayer Penalties ... 11-8
Tax Return Preparer Penalties 11-10
Amended Returns ... 11-13

Relevant IRS Publications

- IRS Publication 505, *Tax Withholding and Estimated Tax*
- Instructions for Form 1040-ES, *Estimated Tax for Individuals*
- Instructions for Form 2210, *Underpayment of Estimated Tax by Individuals, Estates, and Trusts*

Rates for Individual (Noncorporate) Overpayments and Underpayment 2006-2009

Calendar Quarter	Interest Rate
1-1-06 to 3-31-06	7
4-1-06 to 6-30-06	7
7-1-06 to 9-30-06	8
10-1-06 to 12-31-06	8
1-1-07 to 3-31-07	8
4-1-07 to 6-30-07	8
7-1-07 to 9-30-07	8
10-1-07 to 12-31-07	8
1-1-08 to 3-31-08	7
4-1-08 to 6-30-08	6
7-1-08 to 9-30-08	5
10-1-08 to 12-31-08	6
1-1-09 to 3-31-09	5
4-1-09 to 6-30-09	4
7-1-09 to 9-30-09	4
10-1-09 to 12-31-09	4

Rates for Large Corporate Overpayments and Underpayment 2007-2009

Quarter	Overpayment Interest Rate	Underpayment Interest Rate
1-1-07 to 3-31-07	5.5	10
4-1-07 to 6-30-07	5.5	10
7-1-07 to 9-30-07	5.5	10
10-1-07 to 12-31-07	5.5	10
1-1-08 to 3-31-08	4.5	9
4-1-08 to 6-30-08	3.5	8
7-1-08 to 9-30-08	2.5	7
10-1-08 to 12-31-08	3.5	8
1-1-09 to 3-31-09	2.5	7
4-1-09 to 6-30-09	1.5	6
7-1-09 to 9-30-09	1.5	6
10-1-09 to 12-31-09	1.5	6

Estimated Payment Due Dates for 2009 and 2010

Installment	2009	2010	Fiscal - Year Filers
1	April 15, 2009	April 15, 2010	15th day of fourth month after tax year ends
2	June 15, 2009	June 15, 2010	15th day of sixth month after tax year ends
3	September 15, 2009	September 15, 2010	15th day of ninth month after tax year ends
4	January 15, 2010	January 18, 2011	15th day of the first month after tax year ends

Estimated Payments

Federal income tax is a pay-as-you-go tax. Unless the total tax shown on the taxpayer's return (line 60 of 2009 Form 1040) minus the amount paid through withholding will be less than $1,000, the taxpayer generally must make quarterly estimated tax payments. Taxpayers whose entire income is subject to withholding and who do not owe special taxes, such as household employment taxes, generally do not need to make separate estimated payments. IRS Publication 505, *Tax Withholding and Estimated Tax*, provides more information.

Who Must Make Estimated Payments

Taxpayers who have income that is not subject to withholding (earnings from self-employment, interest, dividends, rents, alimony, etc.) must determine whether they are required to make estimated payments. In addition, estimated tax payments may be required on unemployment compensation and the taxable portion of Social Security benefits if the taxpayer did not elect voluntary withholding.

Increased Withholding Preferable. There are advantages to increasing withholding rather than making estimated payments. The IRS assesses penalties for late payment, or underpayment, of estimated tax, even when the total amount paid for the year meets or exceeds the tax liability for that year. Withholding is credited ratably against each respective quarter's required estimated tax payment even if the tax was not withheld evenly throughout the year. Therefore, increased withholding later in the year may make up a shortfall that would otherwise result in an underpayment penalty for an earlier quarter. Taxpayers may elect to treat withheld taxes as paid on the date withheld. If they choose this option, they must file Form 2210.

Filing Tip. Taxpayers who have some income subject to withholding may choose to increase the amount of income tax withheld from wages in order to reduce the anticipated tax due with their tax return to below the amount at which quarterly payments are required (generally $1,000).

How to Increase Withholding. To increase the amount of tax withheld from wages, the taxpayer files Form W-4, *Employee's Withholding Allowance Certificate*, with his or her employer. Taxpayers may also choose to have tax withheld from pension or annuity payments (Form W-4P, *Withholding Certificate for Pension or Annuity Payments*), from sick pay that is received from a party other than the taxpayer's employer (Form W-4S, *Request for Federal Income Tax Withholding from Sick Pay*), and from certain government payments, including Social Security payments (Form W-4V, *Voluntary Withholding Request*). Most farm income is not subject to withholding, although voluntary withholding may be elected on certain government payments. IRS Publication 225, *Farmer's Tax Guide*, explains the tax treatment of commodity credit loans and crop disaster payments.

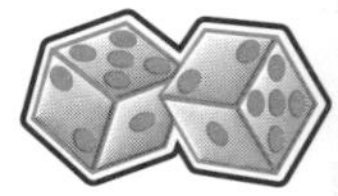

Gambling Winnings. Gambling winnings of more than $5,000 from sweepstakes, wagering pools, or lotteries are subject to income tax withholding at a flat rate. Poker tournament sponsors are required to report, but not withhold, winnings of more than $5,000. Any other wager is subject to withholding if the proceeds are at least 300 times the amount of the bet. Gambling winnings from bingo, keno, and slot machines are generally not subject to withholding. Taxpayers who receive gambling winnings not subject to withholding may need to pay estimated tax.

General Rule

The general rule is that at least 90% of an individual's final income tax is to be paid through either withholding or estimated tax payments. The estimated tax is the amount of income and self-employment tax (as well as other taxes reported on Form 1040–including household employment taxes computed on Form 1040, Schedule H) that an individual estimates will have to be paid for the tax year after subtracting any estimated credits against tax.

Planning Tip. Windfalls, unanticipated revenues, multiple W-2s from different employers, and variable cash flow from self-employment all affect the estimated tax process in various ways. Practitioners must obtain current information from clients. Taxpayers should contact their tax preparers if their situation changes and estimates may need to be revised.

No underpayment penalty is assessed if the tax shown on the tax return for the year (or, if no return is filed, the tax due), reduced by income tax withheld from wages (including excess Social Security and railroad retirement tax withholding), is less than $1,000.

Also, an individual who was a U.S. citizen or resident for the entire previous tax year need not pay estimated tax if he or she had no tax liability for that tax year, provided it was a 12-month period.

Caution. Rules for individuals are different from rules for corporations, estates, trusts, and taxable income of tax-exempt organizations—don't assume the same treatment! See MTG ¶225 for corporations, MTG ¶518 for estates and trusts, and MTG ¶658 for tax-exempt organizations.

Under circumstances of hardship or following an individual's retirement or disability, the penalty for underpayment of estimated tax may be waived. Form 2210, *Underpayment of Estimated Tax by Individuals*, must be filed when a waiver of the penalty is requested.

Safe Harbor Estimates

Individuals may avoid the penalty for failure to pay estimated tax by meeting one of the three "safe harbor" provisions:

1. Estimated payments and withholding are at least 90% of the tax shown on the current year's return.
2. Estimated payments and withholding are at least 100% of the tax shown on the prior year's return (the no-estimate safe harbor), provided the prior year's return covered a 12-month period. An individual with adjusted gross income in excess of $150,000 ($75,000 for a married individual filing separately) in 2009 can avoid the estimated tax penalty by paying 110% of the amount of tax shown on the prior year's tax return, provided the prior year was a full year. No estimation of current year's income is required if this option is available.
3. Installments are made on a current basis under an annualized income installment method.

Individual Small Business Taxpayers. The no-estimate safe harbor (2, above) is modified for tax years beginning in 2009 for certain individuals with income from a small business. Instead of paying 100 percent (or 110 percent) of the tax shown on the individual's prior year return, the individual can pay 90 percent of the tax shown if (1) his or her adjusted gross income on the prior year return was less than $500,000 ($250,000 in the case of married individuals filing separate returns), and (2) the individual certifies that more than 50 percent of the gross income shown on the return was income from a small business. A small business, for this purpose, is a trade or business with fewer than 500 employees. To certify that he or she qualifies for this tax relief, an individual must check box F in Part II on Form 2210 or, for a farmer or fisherman, box C on Form 2210-F.

Married Couples

Married couples may make joint estimated tax payments, even if they are not living together and even if they file separate returns. Married couples cannot make joint estimated tax payments if any of the following three criteria applies:

1. They are legally separated under a decree of divorce or separate maintenance.
2. Either spouse is a nonresident alien (unless an election is made under Code Sec. 6013 to treat the spouse as a resident alien or the spouse becomes a resident alien during the tax year).
3. The spouses have different tax years.

Whether joint or separate estimated tax payments are made will not affect the choice of filing a joint tax return or separate returns. Form 2210 must be filed if 2009 tax is used to figure 2010 estimated payments and a joint return is filed for only one of the years.

2009 Separate Returns and 2010 Joint Return. Taxpayers who plan to file a joint return for 2010, but filed separate returns for 2009, must use the total of the tax shown on the separate 2009 returns in calculating 2009 tax for the no-estimate safe harbor. Returns filed as single, head of household, or married filing separately are considered separate returns.

2009 Joint Return and 2010 Separate Returns. If the taxpayer plans to file a separate return for 2010, but filed a joint return for 2009, the 2009 tax is his or her share of the tax on the joint return.

To figure each spouse's share of the tax on a joint return, first figure the tax both spouses would have paid had they filed separate returns for 2009 using the same filing status as they intend to use for 2010. Then multiply the tax on the joint return by the following fraction:

$$\frac{\text{The tax one spouse would have paid had separate returns been filed}}{\text{The total tax both spouses would have paid had separate returns been filed}}$$

Farmers and Fishermen

Farmers and fishermen may ignore the first three installment due dates and either: 1) pay all their estimated tax by January 15, 2010, and file their tax return by the regular due date; or 2) file their tax return by March 1, 2010, and pay all tax that is due. Estimated payments and withholding need only be two-thirds of the tax liability in 2009. The rule that 110% of the prior year's tax must be used for taxpayers with higher gross income for 2009 does not apply to farmers and fishermen.

An individual is a farmer or fisherman if at least two-thirds of their gross income for 2009 or 2010 is from farming or fishing. Installments may be based on 66 2/3 percent of the tax shown on the return (or the tax due if no return is filed) for the current tax year.

Gross Income from Farming. Income from cultivating the soil or raising agricultural commodities is considered income from farming. It includes the following amounts:

1. Income from operating a stock, dairy, poultry, bee, fruit, or truck farm
2. Income from a plantation, ranch, nursery, range, orchard, or oyster bed
3. Crop shares for the use of the taxpayer's land

4. Gains from sales of draft, breeding, dairy, or sporting livestock

These amounts may be shown on Schedule F of Form 1040, *Profit or Loss From Farming;* on Form 4835, *Farm Rental Income and Expenses;* as the taxpayer's share of a partnership's or S corporation's gross income from farming; or as the taxpayer's share of distributable net income from farming of an estate or trust. Gains from sales of draft, breeding, dairy, or sporting livestock are normally shown on Form 4797, *Sales of Business Property.*

Caution. Wages received as a farm employee and wages received from a farm corporation are not gross income from farming.

Gross Income from Fishing. Income from catching, taking, harvesting, cultivating, or farming any kind of fish, shellfish (for example, clams or mussels), crustaceans (for example, lobsters, crabs, or shrimp), sponges, seaweeds, or other aquatic forms of animal and vegetable life is considered income from fishing.

Gross income from fishing includes the following amounts:

1. Income for services as an officer or crew member of a vessel while the vessel is engaged in fishing;
2. The taxpayer's share of a partnership's or S corporation's gross income from fishing;
3. Income for services normally performed in connection with fishing, such as shore service as an officer or crew member of a vessel engaged in fishing, and services that are necessary for the immediate preservation of the catch, such as cleaning, icing, and packing the catch.

See MTG ¶2691 for estimated tax information for farmers and fishermen.

Nonresident Aliens

Generally, a foreign person is subject to U.S. tax withholding on all U.S.-source income. Most types of U.S.-source income received by a foreign person are subject to U.S. tax of 30%. A reduced rate, including exemption, may apply if there is a tax treaty between the foreign person's country of residence and the United States. The tax is generally withheld (NRA withholding) from the payment made to the foreign person.

If too little tax is withheld, three estimated tax payments are required of most nonresident aliens: first installment, 50%, due June 15; second installment, 25%, due September 15; and third installment, 25%, due the following January 15. However, if any wages are subject to the same withholding rules that apply to U.S. citizens, the due dates for U.S. citizens apply. Nonresident aliens must pay estimated payments or withholding of at least (1) 90% of the tax to be shown on the current year's income tax return, or (2) 100% (110% if adjusted gross income for 2009 was more than $150,000, or $75,000 for married filing separately) of the tax shown on the prior year's income tax return, if that return covered 12 months and U.S. tax was owed.

Nonresident aliens use Form 1040-ES (NR) to figure and pay estimated tax, unless they expect to be a resident of Puerto Rico during the entire year, in which case they must use Form 1040-ES or Forma 1040-ES (in Spanish).

Estimated Payment Calculation

Form 1040-ES includes worksheets to figure the amount to pay. A simplified worksheet is included on page 11-6. All taxable income, including the taxable portion of Social Security and railroad retirement benefits, must be included in gross income used to figure estimated payments. See Tab 9 for a table to figure the taxable portion of these benefits. Itemized deductions and adjustments to income may be taken into consideration when calculating estimated payments.

Taxpayers whose income varies during the year may choose to use the annualized income method to estimate tax (see next section).

Unexpected Income

If a taxpayer has unexpected income after March 31 or was not liable for estimated tax on March 31, but, after that date, his or her tax situation changes, the amount of tax must be recalculated and estimated taxes paid ratably over the remaining installment due dates.

Caution. Tax rate schedules or tax tables, deductions, and credits for the year in which income is earned must be used to figure estimated payment amounts. Do not use rates or amounts from the prior year.

Annualized Income Method of Estimating Tax

The annualization method is suitable for taxpayers whose income is received or accrued more heavily in one part of the year.

When Unexpected Changes in Income During 2010 Affect Estimated Payments		
Estimated Tax Refigured	**First Installment Due Date**	**Affect Estimated Payments**
After March 31 but before June 1	June 15	50
After May 31 but before September 1	September 15	75
After August 31 but before December 31	January 18, 2011	100

Gray Area. Annualization may or may not result in lower estimated tax payments. The option is always available, but its use should be weighed carefully.

Estimated tax penalties are computed from the quarter in which a shortfall in the required payment occurs. Normally, this means that the year's income tax is allocated equally across all four quarters. If a taxpayer uses the annualized income installment alternative to calculate the amount of a quarterly installment, he or she can avoid the estimated tax penalty even if an installment of estimated tax is lower than the otherwise required installment. Under this alternative, any difference between an earlier installment paid and the amount required must be made up by increasing the next installment so that the applicable percentage of tax is paid as of that time.

Installment	Applicable Percentage
1	22.5
2	45
3	67.5
4	90

If the annualized income installment method is used to figure estimated tax payments, Form 2210 ***must be*** filed with the taxpayer's return.

When Estimated Payments Are Due

Any underpayment of tax must be made up by a payment with the final return, and any overpayment is either refunded or credited against the estimated tax for the next year, whichever the taxpayer elects.

See MTG ¶2685 and table on page 11-1.

Where to File Taxes for Form 1040-ES During 2010	
Taxpayer's State of Residence	**Send to: Internal Revenue Service**
Florida, Georgia, North Carolina, South Carolina	P.O. Box 105225 Atlanta, GA 30348-5225
Alabama, Kentucky, Louisiana, Mississippi, Tennessee, Texas	P. O Box 1300 Charlotte, NC 28201-1300
Alaska, Arizona, California, Colorado, Hawaii, Nevada, New Mexico, Oregon, Utah, Washington	P.O. Box 510000 San Francisco, CA 94151-5100
Idaho, Illinois, Indiana, Iowa, Kansas, Michigan, Minnesota, Montana, Nebraska, North Dakota, Oklahoma, South Dakota, Wisconsin, Wyoming	P.O. Box 802502 Cincinnati, OH 45280-2502
Arkansas, Connecticut, Delaware, District of Columbia, Maryland, Missouri, Ohio, Rhode Island, Virginia, West Virginia	P.O. Box 970006 St. Louis, MO 63197-0006
Maine, Massachusetts, New Hampshire, New Jersey, New York, Pennsylvania, Vermont	P.O. Box 37007 Hartford, CT 06176-0007
American Samoa, the Commonwealth of the Northern Mariana Islands, nonpermanent residents of Guam or the Virgin Islands, Puerto Rico (or if excluding foreign income under Internal Revenue Code Section 933), dual status taxpayers, non-resident aliens, U.S. citizens or tax residents in a foreign country, all APO or FPO addresses and anyone filing Form 2555, 2555EZ, or 4563	P. O. Box 1300 Charlotte, NC 28201-1300 USA
Guam: Permanent residents (should not use Form 1040-V)	Department of Revenue and Taxation Government of Guam P.O. Box 23607 GMF, GU 96921
Virgin Islands: Permanent residents (should not use Form 1040-V)	V.I. Bureau of Internal Revenue 9601 Estate Thomas, Charlotte Amalie St. Thomas, VI 00802

Example. Garrett, a single taxpayer who itemizes deductions, has adjusted gross income from January 1, 2010, to March 31, 2010, of $6,500 and applicable itemized deductions for the period of $1,000. His annualized income minus annualized deductions for the year is $22,000 [($6,500 –$1,000) × 12/3]. He is entitled to a $3,650 personal exemption; therefore, his taxable income is $18,350. The tax on $18,350 is projected to be $2,334 for a single taxpayer. The first annualized installment equals $525 ($2,334 × 22.5%). To compute the second installment, Garrett must use his adjusted gross income from January 1 through May 31, which is $17,000, and his itemized deductions for the same period, which total $5,700. The annualized amount is $27,120 ($11,300 × 12/5), and his annualized taxable income is $23,450. The tax on $23,450 is projected to be $3,099. His second annualized installment is $870 [($3,099 × 45%) – $525].

2010 Estimated Tax Worksheet

If filing a joint return, enter combined amounts.

1	Adjusted gross income expected in 2010. It may be easiest to estimate this by starting with 2009 AGI and adding and subtracting changes expected to take effect in 2010.	1
2	Estimated standard deduction for 2010 filing status ($5,700 for Single or MFS, $8,400 for HOH, or $11,400 for MFJ or QW) or total of estimated itemized deductions for 2009.	2
3	Subtract line 2 from line 1.	3
4	Exemptions. Multiply $3,650 by the number of personal exemptions.	4
5	Subtract line 4 from line 3.	5
6	Tax for the amount on line 5 from the 2010 Tax Rate Schedules (see back cover for schedules). Also include tax on qualified dividends and net capital gains.	6
7	Alternative minimum tax from Form 6251.	7
8	Add lines 6 and 7. Also include any tax from Forms 4972 and 8814 and any recapture of education credits.	8
9	Credits. Do not include any income tax withholding on this line. Do not include credits listed on line 13b below.	9
10	Subtract line 9 from line 8. If zero or less, enter -0-.	10
11	Self-employment tax. If estimate of 2010 net earnings (92.35% of total net profit) from self-employment is $106,800 or less, multiply the amount by 15.3%; if more than $106,800, multiply the amount by 2.9%, add $13,243.20 to the result, and enter the total. For a joint return, figure the self-employment tax separately for each spouse and add the amounts. Caution: If any wages are also subject to social security tax, the amount of self-employment tax may be reduced if the total income subject to social security tax is $106,800 or more.	11
12	Other taxes. Enter all other taxes expected to be owed in 2010, including taxes on IRA distributions. Include household employment taxes owed in 2010 only if Federal income tax will be withheld on some income or estimated tax payments would be required, even if these taxes were not included. Do not include: • Social Security and Medicare tax on unreported tip income • Tax on recapture of a Federal mortgage subsidy • Uncollected employee Social Security and Medicare tax on RRTA tax on tips or group-term life insurance	12
13a	Add lines 10 through 12.	13a
b	Earned income credit, additional child tax credit, and credits from Form 4136, Form 5405, Form 8801 (current year nonrefundable credit), and Form 8885.	b
c	Total 2010 estimated tax. Subtract line 13b from line 13a. If zero or less, enter -0-.	c
14a	Multiply line 13c by 90% (66.67% for farmers and fishermen).	14a
b	Enter the tax shown on the taxpayer's 2009 return (110% of that amount if not a farmer or fisherman and the AGI shown on that return is more than $150,000 or, if married filing separately for 2010, more than $75,000.	b
c	Required annual payment to avoid a penalty. Enter the smaller of line 14a or 14b. Income tax withheld and estimated to be withheld during 2009 (including income tax withholding on pensions, annuities, certain deferred income, etc.).	c
15	Income tax estimated to be withheld during 2010 (including income tax withholding on pensions, annuities, certain deferred income, etc.). If line 13c minus line 15 is less than $1,000, no estimated payments are required.	15
16	Subtract line 15 from line 14c. If the amount on line 16 is zero or less, no estimated payments are required.	16
17	If the first payment is due April 15, 2010, enter 25% of line 16 (minus any 2009 overpayment that was applied to this installment) here, and on the payment voucher(s). Household employers, subtract any amount paid to household employees as advance EIC payments during the period.	17

Last Estimated Tax Payment. A taxpayer is not required to make the fourth installment payment if his or her return for the year is filed on or before February 1, 2010, and any balance of tax is paid at that time. Fiscal-year filers may file their returns by the last day of the first month after the end of their fiscal year instead of paying the last installment. Farmers and fishermen need not make the January 15 payment if they file and pay the entire tax due by March 1, 2010.

See Tab 12 for information about collections, extensions of time to pay, and payment options for taxpayers unable to pay the full amount due.

How to File Estimated Payments

There are five ways to pay estimated tax.

1. **Credit an overpayment** on the previous year's return to the current year's estimated tax. If the taxpayer asks that an overpayment be credited to his or her estimated tax for the next year, the payment is considered to have been made on the due date of the first estimated tax installment (April 15 for calendar-year taxpayers). The taxpayer cannot have any of that amount refunded to him or her, or use that overpayment in any other way, after that due date until the close of that tax year.
2. **Mail each payment** with a payment voucher from Form 1040-ES to the appropriate address shown in the table. Make checks payable to "United States Treasury."
3. **Pay electronically** using the Electronic Federal Tax Payment System (EFTPS). For EFTPS information, call 800-316-6541 (individuals) or 800-555-4477 (businesses).
4. **Use electronic funds withdrawal** if Form 1040 or Form 1040A is filed electronically. Taxpayers may make a 2010 estimated tax payment when they electronically file their 2009 Form 1040 or Form 1040A by authorizing an electronic funds withdrawal from a checking or savings account. Whether or not a balance is due on the 2009 electronically filed tax return, the taxpayer may schedule **one** estimated tax payment with an effective date of April 15, 2010, June 15, 2010, or September 15, 2010. *Do not* send in a Form 1040-ES payment voucher when an estimated tax payment by electronic funds withdrawal is scheduled.
5. **Pay by credit card** using a pay-by-phone system or the Internet. American Express®, Discover®, MasterCard®, or Visa® credit cards may be used to make estimated tax payments. Call or access by Internet one of the service providers listed in Tab 1 and follow the instructions of the provider. Each provider will charge a convenience fee based on the amount of the payment.

> **Example.** When Kathleen filed her 2008 tax return, it showed that she had overpaid her taxes by $750. Kathleen knew that she would owe additional tax in 2009, so she credited $600 of the overpayment to her 2009 estimated tax and had the remaining $150 refunded to her. In September, she amended her 2008 return by filing Form 1040X, *Amended U.S. Individual Income Tax Return.* It turned out that she owed $250 more in tax than she had thought. This reduced her 2008 overpayment from $750 to $500. Because the $750 had already been applied to her 2009 estimated tax or refunded to her, the IRS billed her for the additional $250 she owed, plus penalties and interest. Kathleen could not use any of the $600 she had credited to her 2009 estimated tax to pay this bill.

Interest

The interest rate that taxpayers must pay for underpayment of taxes is equal to the federal short-term rate plus three percentage points (short-term rate plus five percentage points for large corporate underpayments). In case of overpayment of taxes, the amount of interest owed by the Treasury is also equal to the federal short-term rate plus three percentage points (short-term rate plus 0.5 percentage points for large corporate overpayments). These interest rates are adjusted quarterly, with the new rates becoming effective two months after the date of each adjustment.

Abatement of Interest

The IRS may abate interest if it is excessive, if it is assessed after the statute of limitations on collections expires, or if it is illegally or erroneously assessed. Interest may also be abated if collection of a small balance would not be cost-effective. In addition, unreasonable delays or errors caused by IRS personnel performing ministerial or managerial acts may be cause for abatement of interest.

Interest is not charged during the period of extension designated for presidentially declared disaster areas. For erroneous refunds less than $50,000 made due to IRS error, interest is abated until the date the IRS demands payment.

A taxpayer may request an abatement of interest attributable to IRS delays by filing Form 843, *Claim for Refund and Request for Abatement* (see page 11-18).

If the IRS denies a request for abatement of interest, eligible taxpayers may bring action in Tax Court within 180 days after the date the IRS mails its final determination not to abate interest. Generally, individuals with net worth up to $2 million and businesses with net worth up to $7 million are eligible.

Gray Area. As the instructions for the form state, there are several ways to calculate penalties on Form 2210. Annualized or other calculations may be applied if they conform to IRS regulations and their use can be supported. It is to the taxpayer's advantage to calculate the penalty using each allowable method to determine which results in the lowest penalty.

Taxpayer Penalties

The law allows for penalties for improperly reporting information on tax returns, for failure to file a return, for failure to pay tax or to make timely estimated tax payments, and for other infractions. These penalties are in addition to interest charged on unpaid balances.

Calculation of Penalties

Taxpayers may calculate the late-filing and late-payment penalty owed on Form 2210, *Underpayment of Estimated Tax by Individuals, Estates, and Trusts*, or may let the IRS calculate the penalty and bill them. Interest is not charged if the taxpayer's return is timely filed and any penalty is paid by the due date on the bill.

Date Return Considered Filed and Tax Considered Paid

To calculate penalties and interest owed, the date returns are filed and tax payments are considered paid is determined according to the following rules:

- Returns and payments received by the IRS on or before the due date are considered filed and paid on the due date.
- Returns and payments postmarked on or before due date are considered paid on the due date (either the original due date or that of an extension). This "mailbox rule" also applies to original returns claiming a refund postmarked before the three-year deadline. An amended return is considered filed on the postmark date.
- Returns and payments postmarked after the due date are considered filed or paid when received by the IRS.

For the purposes of the mailbox rule, a return or payment is "postmarked" on the date of a U.S. mail postmark, on the date of another official foreign country's postmark, on the date of the electronic postmark if the return is e-filed, or the date received by a private delivery service designated by the IRS. There are 16 designated private delivery services provided by three carriers:

Civil and Criminal Taxpayer Penalties Applicable in 2009

Code Section	Violation	Amount of Penalty
6651(a)(1)	Failure to file return	• 5% for each month or fraction thereof that the return is late, up to a maximum of 25% of the tax owed, less any penalty for failure to pay tax for the same month • A minimum of $135 or the tax due, whichever is less, if the return is more than 60 days late
6651(a)(2), 6651(a)(3), 6651(d), and 6651(h)	Failure to pay tax	• 0.5% for each month or fraction thereof that there is an unpaid balance, up to a maximum of 25% of tax owed, less any failure to file penalty for the same return for the same month • 1% per month after notice and demand for immediate payment is given, or 10 days after the IRS issues a notice of intent to levy, whichever date is earlier • 0.25% per month if an installment agreement is in effect, the return was filed on time, and payments are current For amounts not shown on a return, the penalty begins 21 calendar days from the date the IRS demands payment (10 business days if amount is $100,000 or more)
6651(f)	Fraudulent failure to file return	• 15% for each month or fraction thereof that the return is late, up to a maximum of 75% of the tax owed, less any penalty for failure to pay tax for the same month • A minimum of $100 or the tax due, whichever is less, if the return is more than 60 days late
6652(b)	Failure to report tips	50% of the employee's portion of the FICA tax or railroad retirement tax for the tip amount not reported

Civil and Criminal Taxpayer Penalties Applicable in 2009 (Continued)

Code Section	Violation	Amount of Penalty
6654 and 6655	Underpayment of estimated tax	Interest at federal rate (see tables on page 11-1)
6662	Accuracy-related penalty, including negligence, substantial understatement (10% of tax required to be shown on return or $5,000, whichever is greater) of tax, substantial overstatement of pension liabilities	20% of the portion of the underpayment
6663	Fraud	75% of the portion of the underpayment attributable to fraud
6673	Frivolous or delaying Tax Court actions	Up to $10,000 for frivolous actions, up to $25,000 for actions brought primarily for delay
6682	False information on Form W-4 (including claims of withholding allowances that reduce the amount of tax withheld)	$500 for each false statement (W-4)
6702	Filing a frivolous return, including alteration or deletion of "penalty of perjury" statement	$5,000 per return deemed to be frivolous
7201	Willful attempt to evade or defeat tax	Felony punishable by a fine of up to $100,000 ($500,000 for corporations), imprisonment up to five years, or both, and costs of prosecution
7203	Willful failure to pay tax or file a return	Misdemeanor punishable by a fine of up to $25,000 ($100,000 for corporations), imprisonment up to one year, or both, and costs of prosecution
7205	Fraudulent withholding exemption certificate or statement that backup withholding does not apply	Misdemeanor punishable by a fine of up to $1,000, imprisonment of up to one year, or both
7206	Fraud	Felony punishable by a fine up to $100,000 ($500,000 for corporations), up to three years in prison, or both

- DHL Express (DHL): DHL Same Day Service; DHL Next Day 10:30 am; DHL Next Day 12:00 pm; DHL Next Day 3:00 pm; and DHL 2nd Day Service
- Federal Express (FedEx): FedEx Priority Overnight, FedEx Standard Overnight, FedEx 2Day, FedEx International Priority, and FedEx International First
- United Parcel Service (UPS): UPS Next Day Air, UPS Next Day Air Saver, UPS 2nd Day Air, UPS 2nd Day Air A.M., UPS Worldwide Express Plus, and UPS Worldwide Express

Reasonable Cause for Late Filing and Late Payments

The IRS will waive the penalties for late filing and late payment if the taxpayer can show that delay was due to reasonable cause and not willful neglect. Although there is no clear definition of reasonable cause that applies to all penalty provisions, there is a recognized list of circumstances that the IRS considers to be "administratively acceptable" as justification for abatement of a penalty. Reasonable cause for filing a late return includes death or illness of the taxpayer or a close relative, unavoidable absence of the taxpayer, and destruction of the taxpayer's residence, business, or records due to fire, hurricane, etc. Reasonable cause for late payment of tax may be related to unexpected financial circumstances, but the taxpayer must show that he or she exercised ordinary business care and prudence. Standards used by the IRS for determining "reasonable cause" are set out in Internal Revenue Manual §20.1.1.3.1 (2-22-08).

What Is and What Is Not Reasonable Cause. Forgetfulness, reliance on another person to perform required acts, and ignorance of the law are generally not accepted as reasonable cause for delay absent special circumstances. However, reliance on the advice of a competent tax advisor or on written advice of the IRS generally constitutes reasonable cause. In evaluating reasonable cause, IRS agents evaluate each case on its own merits.

Taxpayers request abatement of late-filing and late-payment penalties by submitting a written statement to the director of the service center where the return was filed stating the cause and a signed declaration similar to the "penalties of perjury" statement on Form 1040, or, after paying the penalty, by filing Form 843, *Claim for Refund or Abatement.*

> **Planning Tip.** Whenever there is sufficient doubt as to a taxpayer's liability or circumstances regarding tax penalties, practitioners may apply for abatement for the taxpayer.

Abatement of Accuracy-Related and Fraud Penalties

Accuracy-related penalties and penalties for fraudulent failure to file a return and fraud may be abated if they were illegally or erroneously assessed [IRC §6404(a)] or if the taxpayer can prove that the penalty does not apply under the statute. IRS agents consider payment patterns, penalty history, and whether the taxpayer acted with ordinary business care and prudence when considering an abatement request. A repetition of a penalty situation could indicate lack of ordinary business care and prudence. The Internal Revenue Manual sets out the standards for determining "ordinary business care and prudence" under the circumstances in §20.1.1.3.1.2 (2-22-08).

Appeals. Penalties can be appealed through a claim for refund if the penalty has been paid, or after assessment through the post-assessment penalty appeal program.

The taxpayer may appeal a denial of a request for abatement or nonassertion. This is done by filing a protest to the Office of Appeals in the standard manner of income tax protests. It is important to note that the time for filing such appeals is usually very short, sometimes within 15 days of issuance of denial.

The case is then submitted to an appeals officer, and a conference is held, following which Appeals will either sustain the penalty, reject it, or compromise. After that, the only route left to contest a penalty is by paying the penalty and filing a claim for refund.

Tax Return Preparer Penalties

Signing Prepared Returns

If the client retains the right to make all final decisions on the return, the preparer may not have to sign the return. For example, a certified public accountant who was asked to review a client's income tax return and to furnish a recommendation affecting an entry on the return was not a tax return preparer required to sign the client's return. In this case the client's tax director had retained the right to make all final decisions on the return.

Final Review. A final comprehensive review will likely result in bestowing a reviewer with primary responsibility if it includes (1) evaluating the information provided by other preparers; (2) applying to this information the final reviewer's knowledge of the taxpayer's affairs, if any; (3) observing that the preparer-employer's policies and practices have been followed; and (4) making the final determinations with respect to the proper application of the tax laws to the taxpayer's tax liability.

The fact that a return preparer is the last person to look at the return does not mean that he or she is the preparer with primary responsibility for its accuracy.

If a taxpayer sends a person his or her books and records and the person sends back a composite statement of all the necessary information so that it is merely a mechanical process for the taxpayer to fill out the return, the individual is an income tax return preparer with a duty to sign the return.

When Preparers Sign. The preparer must sign the completed return before its presentation to the taxpayer for signature, thereby ensuring that the taxpayer has had an opportunity to review the final return before signing it.

> **Example.** Andrey and Andrey, an accounting partnership, entered into an agreement with Mark Young Inc. to prepare income tax returns for its clients. Under the agreement, where the law was unclear, the partnership was to resolve questions of law in favor of Young's clients if a reasonable justification for that position existed. Although the partnership prepared the returns, the partners were not responsible for the overall substantive accuracy of the returns because, prior to completion, questionable entries on the returns were discussed with Young and, after completion, the returns were submitted to Young for final review. Therefore, the partners were not required to sign the returns.

Specific Penalties. Behavior that would have been subject to the former return preparer's penalty for negligent or intentional disregard of rules and regulations continues to be subject to the penalty for unreasonable return positions.

The Fifth Amendment protection against self-incrimination may not be claimed by tax return preparers in actions where the penalties imposed against them are civil and not criminal in nature. See the table on page 11-11 for a list of current penalties.

Regarding penalties for failure to perform a required act or for negotiating a client's refund check, an income tax return preparer can appeal the imposition of these penalties only after payment. Form

6118, *Claim for Refund of Income Tax Return Preparer Penalties*, may be used for this purpose.

See MTG ¶2518, ¶2521, and ¶2894 for further information.

Unreasonable Positions and Willful Understatement

If a tax return preparer is assessed a penalty based upon understatements due to unreasonable positions (Code Sec. 6694(a)) or to willful or reckless conduct (Code Sec. 6694(b)), the IRS generally will issue a 30-day letter notifying the preparer of the proposed penalty and giving the preparer an opportunity to pursue administrative remedies prior to the assessment of the penalty. If the penalty is assessed, the preparer must, within 30 days, either pay the assessment in full or pay at least 15% of the penalty and file a claim for refund of the amount paid. The IRS may counterclaim for the balance of the penalty. Form 6118 is also used for this purpose. If the IRS denies the claim for refund, or if six months have passed since the day the claim was filed and the IRS has not made a determination, the return preparer must file suit in U.S. District Court within 30 days after the date the claim was denied or the six-month period expired, whichever is sooner, if he or she wants to pursue the claim further.

If a final administrative or judicial action determines that there was no understatement of the liability for which the penalty was assessed, any penalty assessed against a preparer for the understatement will be abated or, if paid, refunded.

Fraud

In its hunt for return preparer fraud, the IRS is looking for (1) inflated or bogus personal or business expenses, (2) false deductions, (3) unallowable or bogus credits, and (4) excessive exemptions.

The agency's Criminal Investigation Division has a special program that focuses on enforcing compliance among return preparers. In FY 2008, the IRS initiated 214 investigations into preparer fraud. 134 cases were recommended to the Justice Department for prosecution, resulting in 142 indictments/informations. Sentences were handed down in 124 cases.

Assessment of Penalties-Limitations Periods

A penalty may be assessed against a return preparer at any time during a three-year period following the filing of the return. The three-year period begins to run on the statutory due date of the return, in the case of an early or timely filed return, and on the actual date the return was filed, for a late-filed return. Extensions of the three-year period may be arranged by agreement between the IRS and the return preparer. The IRS may assess return preparer penalties prior to the statutory due date of a return where the return has been filed before such date. Although premature assessments are not usually made, the power to make them is necessary to permit the processing of returns before the due date.

The filing of a second, correct return prior to the statutory due date of the first return will cure preparer deficiencies on the first return. A letter or a list filed by the return preparer may also be accepted by the IRS as curing an incorrect first return, although the IRS is not required to accept anything less than a complete return.

Advertising Restrictions

The IRS has issued rules regarding advertising and solicitation of employment in tax-related matters by attorneys, certified public accountants, and enrolled agents, allowing tax practitioners a freedom to advertise that is roughly equivalent to that currently enjoyed by lawyers and CPAs in general.

Permissible Advertising. Among the permissible forms of solicitation under these rules are the announcement of fixed fees for specific, routine tax services and the use of professional listings, telephone directory listings, and the print media, radio, and television. If fees are advertised, the practitioner has to state clearly that they apply only to matters of average complexity and that they may vary for more involved matters (if applicable). Radio and television commercials must be prerecorded, and the practitioner must maintain a recording of the advertisements. A preparer is not prohibited from indicating a past or present connection with the IRS.

Civil and Criminal Tax Return Preparer Penalties Applicable in 2009

Code Section	Violation	Applies to Employer (including Partnerships) and Self-Employed Preparer	Applies to Employee Preparer (including Partners)	Amount of Penalty
6694(a)	Understatement of taxpayer's liability due to unreasonable positions (including negligence)	Yes	Yes	Greater of $1,000 or 50% of the income derived (or to be derived) by the preparer with respect to the return

Civil and Criminal Tax Return Preparer Penalties Applicable in 2009 (Continued)

Code Section	Violation	Applies to Employer (including Partnerships) and Self-Employed Preparer	Applies to Employee Preparer (including Partners)	Amount of Penalty
6694(b)	Willful attempt to understate liability or reckless or intentional disregard of rules or regulations	Yes	Yes	Greater of $5,000 or 50% of the income derived (or to be derived) by the preparer with respect to the return, reduced by penalty paid under Code Sec. 6694(a)
6695(a)	Failure to furnish copy of return to taxpayer	Yes	No	$50 per failure, up to $25,000 per preparer
6695(b)	Failure of preparer to sign return	Yes	Yes	$50 per failure, up to $25,000 per preparer
6695(c)	Failure to furnish identifying numbers	Yes	No	$50 per failure, up to $25,000 per preparer
6695(d)	Failure to maintain copies of returns prepared or to maintain a listing	Yes	No	$50 per failure, up to $25,000 per preparer
6695(e)	Failure to (1) retain and make available a record of the preparers employed (or engaged) during a return period and (2) set forth an item, as required by Code Sec. 6060	Yes	No	$50 per failure, up to $25,000 per preparer
6695(f)	Endorsing or negotiating a tax refund check	Yes	Yes	$500 per check
6695(g)	Failure to be dilligent in determining eligibility for the earned income tax credit	Yes	No	$100 per failure
6701	Aiding and abetting understatements	Yes	Yes	$1,000 per return ($10,000 per corporate return) per preparer
7206	Fraud and false statements	Yes	Yes	Maximum $100,000 fine ($500,000 for corporations), or three years imprisonment, or both, and prosecution costs
7207	Willful delivery or disclosure of fraudulent documents or information to IRS	Yes	Yes	Maximum $10,000 fine ($50,000 for corporations), or one year imprisonment, or both
7216	Unauthorized disclosure of taxpayer information	Yes	Yes	Maximum $1,000 fine, or one year imprisonment, or both, and prosecution costs

The IRS supports individual electronic return originators' (EROs) advertising and promotional efforts by annually creating and distributing an IRS e-file Marketing Tool Kit. New EROs receive a kit when they are accepted into the IRS e-file program. The kit contains professionally developed material that EROs can customize for use in advertising campaigns and promotional efforts.

Caution. Advertising language requires careful scrutiny. Testimonials are allowed, but promising more than can be delivered or exaggerating possible results is not.

False Advertising. An individual tax return preparer is prohibited from using any advertising containing a false, fraudulent, misleading, deceptive, unduly influencing, coercive, or unfair statement or claim.

The IRS is concerned about false statements used to induce taxpayers to use a particular service, rather than general statements suggesting the need for help because of the complexity of the tax law. For instance, false claims as to the qualifications of the tax return preparer or statements implying that the tax return preparer has a special relationship with the IRS would be objectionable. Also unacceptable would be the use of misleading figures regarding the number of self-prepared returns that err in the government's favor and of exaggerated refund statistics to make it appear that the tax preparation firm has a special ability to obtain refunds.

A tax return preparer who engages in false or deceptive advertising may be subject to an injunction or suspension or disbarment from practice before the IRS.

Electronic Filers

Electronic filing must be done through the IRS or through an electronic filing participant. Upon acceptance into the electronic filing program, a participant is referred to as an authorized IRS e-file provider. There are five categories of electronic filers, and, depending on the functions performed, an electronic filer may fall into more than one category at a time.

1. Electronic return originators (EROs) originate the electronic submission of income tax returns.
2. Software developers develop software for the purposes of formatting the electronic portion of returns according to Publication 1346 and/or transmitting the electronic portion of returns directly to the IRS. The IRS and participating states require that all software pass a series of tests each year. Software developers must also register and test with participating state electronic filing programs.
3. Transmitters transmit the electronic portion of a return directly to the IRS.
4. Intermediate service providers receive tax return information from EROs or from taxpayers who file electronically from home via an Internet site or commercial tax preparation software. The intermediate service provider processes the return and either forwards the information to a transmitter or sends the information back to the ERO or taxpayer.
5. Reporting agents are accounting services, banks, or others that comply with IRS procedures and are authorized to electronically prepare a Form 940/941 for a taxpayer.

Filing Tip. Free File, developed through an agreement between the Treasury Department and the Office of Management and Budget, is in its seventh year. This program generally provides individual taxpayers, with an adjusted gross income of less than a designated amount ($56,000 for 2008 returns), a free interview-based software option for online filing. An alternative Free File Fillable Tax Forms option is open to virtually all individual taxpayers, regardless of income. This option offers "self-service" online versions of paper forms that can be e-filed for free. Information is available at www.irs.gov.

Electronic filing provides the following advantages to taxpayers: (1) electronic returns are filed simultaneously and are easier to process than paper returns; (2) the taxpayer receives confirmation from the IRS within one or two days that the return was accurately received; and (3) the time period for receipt of a refund is shortened from 12 weeks to about 3 weeks. The IRS also finds electronic filing advantageous because electronic returns have a lower error rate, are easier to store and retrieve, and are processed at a lower cost compared with paper returns. More information is available for tax return preparers and e-filers in IRS Publication 1345, *Handbook for Electronic Filers of Individual Income Tax Returns.*

Planning Tip. Technology such as Check 21 (effective October 28, 2004) and new compliance rules drive the industry toward electronic filing and EFTPS depository practices. Educating taxpayers is essential.

Amended Returns

Taxpayers should file an amended return if filing status, total income, deductions, or credits were reported incorrectly. Taxpayers may also want to file an amended return to take advantage of changes in the tax law that are retroactive. However, an amended return cannot be filed to make retroactive changes in accounting method or as a means of obtaining a notice of deficiency required to bring an action in Tax Court.

Also, taxpayers who suffered losses in a presidentially declared disaster area can claim disaster-related casualty losses on either their current year's tax return or the return for last year. If using last year's return, taxpayers should put the disaster designation in red ink at the top of the Form 1040X.

Taxpayers may use Form 1045, *Application for Tentative Refund*, instead of Form 1040X to apply for a refund based on a net operating loss, a general business credit carryback, a net Section 1256 contracts loss, or a claim of right adjustment under Section 1341(b)(1). Form 1045 must be filed within one year after the end of the year in which the loss, credit, or claim of right adjustment arose. For more details, see the instructions for Form 1045.

How to Fill Out Form 1040X

Enter the year of the return being amended at the top of Form 1040X. If amended returns are being submitted for more than one tax return, use a separate 1040X for each one and mail each in a separate envelope.

Form 1040X (see pages 11-16 and 11-17) has three columns. Column A is used to show original or adjusted figures from the original return. Column C is used to show the corrected figures. The difference between the figures in columns A and C is shown in column B. There is an area on the back of the form for explaining the specific changes being made on the return and the reason for each change; the reason for filing the amended return should be clearly stated. If the changes involve another schedule or form, attach it to the 1040X.

Filing Tip. The IRS sends a notice that 1040X changes have been accepted (or not). Taxpayers may choose to wait until they receive this notice before filing a state amended return. Most states require notification of changes made to Federal returns that affect state liabilities.

Filing Tip. When preparing amended returns, try to provide the person reviewing the return all the documentation they might need to evaluate the taxpayer's claim and quickly make a decision to accept it. Failure to do so may result in delays, lack of acceptance, or worse yet, the desire by the IRS to delve more completely into the taxpayer's return.

Deceased Taxpayer. If filing an amended return for a deceased taxpayer, enter "Deceased," the deceased taxpayer's name, and the date of death across the top of Form 1040X. A surviving spouse should enter "Filing as surviving spouse" in the signature area of the return. If someone else is the personal representative, he or she must also sign. If a refund is claimed by anyone other than a surviving spouse, Form 1310, *Statement of Person Claiming Refund Due a Deceased Taxpayer*, is required.

When to File an Amended Return

Taxpayers who wish to file a claim for an additional refund should wait until they have received the original refund before filing Form 1040X. If additional tax is owed, Form 1040X should be filed and the tax paid by the due date of the original return to avoid any penalty and interest.

Generally, to claim a refund, Form 1040X must be filed within three years from the date the original return was filed or within two years from the date the tax was paid, whichever is later. A Form 1040X based on a bad debt or worthless security generally must be filed within seven years after the due date of the return for the tax year in which the debt or security became worthless.

Gray Area. Filing old returns (more than three years from date original return filed) with credits rolled forward may effectively extend the statute of limitations for obtaining a credit, but generally not a refund.

Only the original return operates to start or extend the limitations period for assessment and collection. A second return is merely an amendment or supplement to a return already in the files and does not toll a limitation period that has begun to run.

The open-ended assessment period applicable to fraudulent returns cannot be cut off by the later filing of a nonfraudulent amended return.

See MTG ¶2759 and ¶2760 for information about amended returns.

Where to File Form 1040X During 2010

State of Taxpayer's Residence	Filing Address
Florida, Georgia, North Carolina, South Carolina	Internal Revenue Service Atlanta, GA 39901
Alabama, Kentucky, Louisiana, Mississippi, Tennessee, Texas	Internal Revenue Service Austin, TX 73301
Alaska, Arizona, California, Colorado, Hawaii, Idaho, Illinois, Indiana, Iowa, Kansas, Michigan, Minnesota, Montana, Nebraska, Nevada, New Mexico, North Dakota, Oklahoma, Oregon, South Dakota, Utah, Washington, Wisconsin, Wyoming	Internal Revenue Service Fresno, CA 93888-0422
Arkansas, Connecticut, Delaware, District of Columbia, Maine, Maryland, Massachusetts, Missouri, New Hampshire, New Jersey, New York, Ohio, Pennsylvania, Rhode Island, Vermont, Virginia, West Virginia	Internal Revenue Service Kansas City, MO 64999
American Samoa, the Commonwealth of the Northern Mariana Islands, non-permanent residents of Guam or the Virgin Islands, Puerto Rico (or if excluding foreign income under Internal Revenue Code Section 933), dual status taxpayers, non-resident aliens, U.S. citizens or tax residents in a foreign country, all APO or FPO addresses and anyone filing Form 2555, 2555EZ, or 4563	Internal Revenue Service Austin, TX 73301-0215
Guam: Permanent residents	Department of Revenue and Taxation Government of Guam PO Box 23607 GMF, GU 96921
Virgin Islands: Permanent residents	V.I. Bureau of Internal Revenue 9601 Estate Thomas, Charlotte Amalie St. Thomas, VI 00802

Form **1040X** (Rev. December 2009)

Department of the Treasury—Internal Revenue Service

Amended U.S. Individual Income Tax Return

▶ See separate instructions.

OMB No. 1545-0074

Your first name and middle initial	Your last name	Your social security number
If a joint return, your spouse's first name and middle initial	Your spouse's last name	Your spouse's social security number
Your current home address (number and street) or P.O. box if mail is not delivered to you	Apt. no.	Your phone number
Your city, town or post office, state, and ZIP code. If you have a foreign address, see page 3 of instructions.		

All filers must complete lines A, B, and C.

A **Amended return filing status.** You must check one box even if you are not changing your filing status. ***Caution.*** *You cannot change your filing status from joint to separate returns after the due date.*

☐ Single ☐ Married filing jointly ☐ Married filing separately
☐ Qualifying widow(er) ☐ Head of household (If the qualifying person is a child but not your dependent, see page 3 of instructions.)

B **This return is for calendar year** ☐ 2009 ☐ 2008 ☐ 2007 ☐ 2006
Other year. Enter one: calendar year ______ **or** fiscal year (month and year ended): ______

C **Explanation of changes.** In the space provided below, tell us why are you filing Form 1040X.

Income and Deductions		**Correct Amount**
1 Adjusted gross income (see page 3 of instructions). If net operating loss (NOL) carryback is included, check here ☐	1	
2 Itemized deductions or standard deduction (see page 4 of instructions)	2	
3 Subtract line 2 from line 1	3	
4 Exemptions. **If changing, complete the Exemptions section on the back and enter the amount from line 30** (see page 4 of instructions)	4	
5 Taxable income. Subtract line 4 from line 3	5	
Tax Liability		
6 Tax (see page 5 of instructions). Enter method used to figure tax:	6	
7 Credits (see page 5 of instructions). If general business credit carryback is included, check here ☐	7	
8 Subtract line 7 from line 6. If the result is zero or less, enter -0-	8	
9 Other taxes (see page 5 of instructions)	9	
10 Total tax. Add lines 8 and 9	10	
Payments		
11 Federal income tax withheld and excess social security and tier 1 RRTA tax withheld (**if changing**, see page 5 of instructions)	11	
12 Estimated tax payments, including amount applied from prior year's return (See page 7 of instructions)	12	
13 Earned income credit (EIC) (See page 7 of instructions)	13	
14 Refundable credits from ☐ Schedule M or Forms ☐ 2439 ☐ 4136 ☐ 5405 ☐ 8801 ☐ 8812 ☐ 8863 ☐ 8885 or ☐ other (specify):	14	
15 Total amount paid with request for extension of time to file, tax paid with original return, and additional tax paid after return was filed (see page 5 of instructions)	15	
16 Total payments. Add lines 11 through 15	16	
Refund or Amount You Owe (Note. Allow 8–12 weeks to process Form 1040X.)		
17 Overpayment, if any, as shown on original return or as previously adjusted by the IRS (see page 8 of instructions)	17	
18 Subtract line 17 from line 16 (see page 6 of instructions)	18	
19 **Amount you owe.** If line 10 is more than line 18, enter the difference (see page 6 of instructions)	19	
20 If line 10 is less than line 18, enter the difference. This is the amount **overpaid** on this return	20	
21 Amount of line 20 you want **refunded to you**	21	
22 Amount of line 20 you want **applied to your (enter year):** ______ **estimated tax** 22		

Complete and sign this form on Page 2.

For Paperwork Reduction Act Notice, see page 9 of instructions. Cat. No. 11360L Form **1040X** (Rev. 12-2009)

Exemptions

Complete this part **only** if you are:

- Increasing or decreasing the number of exemptions (personal and dependents) claimed on line 6d of the return you are amending, or
- Increasing or decreasing the exemption amount for housing individuals displaced by Hurricane Katrina or a Midwestern disaster.

See *Form 1040 or Form 1040A instructions* and page 8 of Form 1040X instructions.

			Correct Number or Amount
23	Yourself and spouse. **Caution.** If someone can claim you as a dependent, you cannot claim an exemption for yourself	23	
24	Your dependent children who lived with you	24	
25	Your dependent children who did not live with you due to divorce or separation	25	
26	Other dependents	26	
27	Total number of exemptions. Add lines 23 through 26	27	
28	Multiply the number of exemptions claimed on line 27 by the exemption amount shown in the instructions for line 28	28	
29	If you are claiming an exemption amount for housing individuals displaced by Hurricane Katrina, enter the amount from Form 8914, line 6 for 2006. If you are claiming an exemption amount for housing individuals displaced by a Midwestern disaster, enter the amount from Form 8914, line 2 for 2008, or line 6 for 2009.	29	
30	Add lines 28 and 29. Enter the result here and on line 4 on page 1 of this form	30	

31 List ALL dependents (children and others) claimed on this amended return. If more than 4 dependents, see instructions.

(a) First name	Last name	**(b)** Dependent's social security number	**(c)** Dependent's relationship to you	**(d)** Check box if qualifying child for child tax credit (see page 6 of instructions)
				☐
				☐
				☐
				☐

Presidential Election Campaign Fund

Checking below will not increase your tax or reduce your refund.

☐ Check here if you did not previously want $3 to go to the fund but now want to.

☐ Check here if this is a joint return and your spouse did not previously want $3 to go to the fund but now wants to.

Checklist

Before mailing this form, remember to

☐ Complete name, address, and social security number

☐ Complete lines A, B, and C on page 1

☐ Complete lines 1 through 22 on page 1

☐ Complete lines 23 through 31 on page 2, if required

☐ Attach any supporting documents and new or changed forms and schedules

☐ Sign and date this form

Sign Here

Remember to keep a copy of this form for your records.

Under penalties of perjury, I declare that I have filed an original return and that I have examined this amended return, including accompanying schedules and statements, and to the best of my knowledge and belief, this amended return is true, correct, and complete. Declaration of preparer (other than taxpayer) is based on all information about which the preparer has any knowledge.

Your signature | Date | Spouse's signature. If a joint return, **both** must sign. | Date

Paid Preparer's Use Only

Preparer's signature | Date

Firm's name (or yours if self-employed), address, and ZIP code

Preparer's SSN or PTIN | ☐ Check if self-employed | Phone number | EIN

Form **843** (Rev. February 2009) Department of the Treasury Internal Revenue Service

Claim for Refund and Request for Abatement

▶ See separate instructions.

OMB No. 1545-0024

Use Form 843 if your claim or request involves:

(a) a refund of one of the taxes (other than income taxes and an employer's claim for FICA tax, RRTA tax, or income tax withholding), shown on line 3,

(b) an abatement of FUTA tax or certain excise taxes, or

(c) a refund or abatement of interest, penalties, or additions to tax for one of the reasons shown on line 5a.

Do not use Form 843 if your claim or request involves:

(a) an overpayment of income taxes or an employer's claim for FICA tax, RRTA tax, or income tax withholding (use the appropriate amended tax return),

(b) a refund of excise taxes based on the nontaxable use or sale of fuels, or

(c) an overpayment of excise taxes reported on Form(s) 11-C, 720, 730, or 2290.

Name(s)	Your social security number
Address (number, street, and room or suite no.)	Spouse's social security number
City or town, state, and ZIP code	Employer identification number (EIN)
Name and address shown on return if different from above	Daytime telephone number ( )
1 Period. Prepare a separate Form 843 for each tax period From / / to / /	**2 Amount** to be refunded or abated $

3 Type of tax. Indicate the type of tax to be refunded or abated or to which the interest, penalty, or addition to tax is related.

☐ Employment ☐ Estate ☐ Gift ☐ Excise ☐ Income

4 Type of penalty. If the claim or request involves a penalty, enter the Internal Revenue Code section on which the penalty is based (see instructions). IRC section: ________

5a Interest, penalties, and additions to tax. Check the box that indicates your reason for the request for refund or abatement. (If none apply, go to line 6.)

☐ Interest was assessed as a result of IRS errors or delays.

☐ A penalty or addition to tax was the result of erroneous written advice from the IRS.

☐ Reasonable cause or other reason allowed under the law (other than erroneous written advice) can be shown for not assessing a penalty or addition to tax.

b Date(s) of payment(s) ▶ ________

6 Original return. Indicate the type of return filed to which the tax, interest, penalty, or addition to tax relates.

☐ 706 ☐ 709 ☐ 940 ☐ 941 ☐ 943 ☐ 945

☐ 990-PF ☐ 1040 ☐ 1120 ☐ 4720 ☐ Other (specify) ▶

7 Explanation. Explain why you believe this claim or request should be allowed and show the computation of the amount shown on line 2. If you need more space, attach additional sheets.

Signature. If you are filing Form 843 to request a refund or abatement relating to a joint return, both you and your spouse must sign the claim. Claims filed by corporations must be signed by a corporate officer authorized to sign, and the officer's title must be shown.

Under penalties of perjury, I declare that I have examined this claim, including accompanying schedules and statements, and, to the best of my knowledge and belief, it is true, correct, and complete. Declaration of preparer (other than taxpayer) is based on all information of which preparer has any knowledge.

Signature (Title, if applicable. Claims by corporations must be signed by an officer.) Date

Signature (spouse, if joint return) Date

Paid Preparer's Use Only			
Preparer's signature ▶	Date	Check if self-employed ☐	Preparer's SSN or PTIN
Firm's name (or yours if self-employed), address, and ZIP code ▶		EIN	
		Phone no. ( )	

For Privacy Act and Paperwork Reduction Act Notice, see separate instructions. Cat. No. 10180R Form **843** (Rev. 02-2009)

Tax Representation Issues and Filings

What's New in 2009

Filing Deadlines Extended. The deadline for furnishing recipients with copies of Form 1099-S and Form 1099-MISC (proceeds paid to attorney or substitute dividends) has been extended to February 15, 2010.

IRS Extends Suspension of Code Sec. 6707A Penalty Collection. Legislation in 2004 imposed penalties for failure to disclose information on a "reportable transaction" that is also a "listed transaction." The IRS suspended collection enforcement actions where the tax benefit was below a given amount, and this suspension has been extended through the end of 2009.

IRS Mediation Procedures Updated. The IRS has updated its mediation procedures for cases in the Appeals administrative process.

Section at a Glance

Tax Preparer's Checklist

- ☐ The Internal Revenue Manual, Audit Technique Guides, and other instructions the IRS provides to examiners are freely available. In addition, the IRS website offers numerous calculators and other practice aids to help preparers.
- ☐ Authorization to file Form 2848, *Power of Attorney and Declaration of Representative*, and Form 8821, *Tax Information Authorization*, are available electronically to those who file five or more returns.
- ☐ The IRS offers "Free File," which allows taxpayers with adjusted gross income of less than a given amount (for 2008 the maximum was $56,000) to choose a preparer's website on which they can prepare their tax return.
- ☐ The IRS now offers the Oral Disclosure Consent (ODC) and the Oral Tax Information Authorization (OTIA), which allow disclosure of tax information to a designee of the taxpayer.

Relevant IRS Publications

- ☐ Treasury Department Circular No. 230, *Regulations Governing the Practice of Attorneys, Certified Public Accountants, Enrolled Agents, Enrolled Actuaries, and Appraisers before the Internal Revenue Service*
- ☐ IRS Publication 1, *Your Rights as a Taxpayer*
- ☐ IRS Publication 5, *Your Appeal Rights and How to Prepare a Protest If You Don't Agree*
- ☐ IRS Publication 556, *Examination of Returns, Appeal Rights, and Claims for Refund*
- ☐ IRS Publication 594, *The IRS Collection Process*
- ☐ IRS Publication 947, *Practice Before the IRS and Power of Attorney*
- ☐ IRS Publication 3498, *The Examination Process*
- ☐ IRS Publication 4245, *Power of Attorney*
- ☐ Form 656-B, *Offer in Compromise Booklet*
- ☐ Instructions for Form 2848, *Power of Attorney and Declaration of Representative*
- ☐ Form 8821, *Tax Information Authorization*

Statute of Limitations Effective in 2009

Action	Period of Limitation
IRS examination of return and assessment of additional tax	Later of 3 years from due date of timely filed return or 3 years from receipt of late filed returns
Claim for credit or refund	Later of 3 years from date return filed or 2 years from date tax was paid, extended by any period during which the taxpayer was unable to manage his or her affairs due to terminal or prolonged illness that began during that time
Income not reported that is more than 25% of the gross income shown on return	6 years
Fraudulent return	Unlimited
Return not filed	Unlimited
Claim for a loss from worthless securities or a bad debt deduction	7 years
IRS collection action	10 years from assessment

Taxpayer Representation

Taxpayers have the right to representation during IRS examinations of tax returns and when dealing with other tax matters before the IRS. The taxpayer's representative may be an attorney, a certified public accountant, an enrolled agent, or any other person permitted to practice before the IRS who has written power of attorney to act on the taxpayer's behalf.

Practice before the IRS

Matters relating to presentations to the IRS or any of its officers or employees relating to a taxpayer's rights, privileges, or liabilities under laws or regulations administered by the IRS are "practice before the IRS." Preparing and filing documents, corresponding and communicating with the IRS, and representing a taxpayer at conferences, hearings, and meetings are all considered practice before the IRS. "Practice before the IRS" also includes the rendering of written advice on any entity, transaction, plan, or arrangement which has a potential for tax avoidance or evasion. However, attorneys and CPAs are not required to file a power of attorney (Form 2848) in order to issue that advice.

Treasury Department Circular 230, *Regulations Governing the Practice of Attorneys, Certified Public Accountants, Enrolled Agents, Enrolled Actuaries, and Appraisers Before the Internal Revenue Service* (Title 31 CFR Subtitle A, Part 10, revised as of April 2008), provides regulations governing tax practice.

Who Can Practice Before the IRS. There are six categories of individuals who may practice before the IRS (see Circular 230 for details).

- **Attorneys** who are not currently under suspension or disbarment from practice before the IRS may file a written declaration stating that they are currently qualified as an attorney and authorized to represent the party or parties on whose behalf they act.
- **Certified Public Accountants** who are not currently under suspension or disbarment from practice before the IRS and who are qualified to practice public accountancy in any state may file a written declaration that they are currently qualified as a certified public accountant and are authorized to represent the party or parties on whose behalf they act.
- **Enrolled Agents** who are not currently under suspension or disbarment from practice before the IRS may file a written declaration stating that they are authorized to represent the party or parties on whose behalf they act.
- **Enrolled Actuaries** who are enrolled by the Joint Board for the Enrollment of Actuaries pursuant to 29 U.S.C. 1242 and are not currently under suspension or disbarment from practice before the IRS may practice before the IRS by filing a written declaration stating that they are currently qualified as an enrolled actuary and are authorized to represent the party or parties on whose behalf they act. Practice as an enrolled actuary is limited to representation with respect to issues involving certain specified statutory provisions requiring actuarial expertise, generally those relating to employee retirement plans.
- **Enrolled Retirement Plan Agents** are individuals who provide technical services to plan sponsors to maintain a plan's tax qualified status. Practice is limited to representation with respect to issues involving forms filed by plans and certain IRS employee plans programs, including the Determination Letter program, the Compliance Resolution System, and the Prototype and Volume Submitter program.
- **Unenrolled Return Preparers and Individual Taxpayers** practicing in limited capacity. Those in this category may practice before the IRS in very limited situations. Individuals may appear on their own behalf. In addition, unenrolled individuals may practice before the IRS with limited authority in the following circumstances:
  - An individual may represent a member of his or her immediate family.
  - An employer may be represented by a regular full-time employee.
  - A partnership may be represented by a general partner or a regular full-time employee of the partnership.
  - An association, corporation (including a parent, subsidiary, or affiliated corporation), or other organized group may be represented by an officer or full-time employee of the group.
  - A trust, receivership, guardianship, or estate may be represented by a trustee, receiver, guardian, personal representative, administrator, executor, or regular full-time employee.
  - An officer or a regular employee of a governmental unit, authority, or agency may, in the course of his or her official duties, represent that governmental unit.
  - An individual may represent anyone before personnel of the IRS if those personnel are located outside of the United States.
  - A tax preparer who prepares and, if required, signs the return of a taxpayer may represent the taxpayer before IRS customer service representatives, revenue agents, and examination officers with regard to the taxpayer's liability for the period covered by the return. An unenrolled tax preparer may not represent the taxpayer in appeals or collections procedures or any other area.

The Director, Office of Professional Responsibility, may authorize any person, even if not otherwise eligible to practice before the IRS, to represent another without enrollment with respect to a particular matter.

The IRS's Office of Professional Responsibility (OPR) reviews applications from individuals and administers the rules for practice before the IRS as set forth in Treasury Department Circular 230. OPR, formed in January 2003, is the successor office to the former Director of Practice organization. Unenrolled preparers are regulated by the Small Business/Self-Employed (SB/SE) Compliance Division of the IRS.

The IRS maintains a computerized system of records, called CAF, that contains information on authorized representatives of taxpayers. A CAF number is assigned to a tax practitioner when a Form 2848 or Form 8821 is filed.

Who Cannot Practice before the IRS. Some individuals are not allowed to practice before the IRS.

- Any individual who has been disbarred from professional practice is prohibited from practicing before the IRS.
- An officer or employee of the executive, legislative, or judicial branch of the U.S. government; an officer or employee of the District of Columbia; a Member of Congress; or a Resident Commissioner may not practice before the IRS if such practice violates 18 U.S.C. 203 or 205.
- An officer or employee of any state, or subdivision of any state, whose duties require him or her to pass upon, investigate, or deal with tax matters for such state or subdivision, may not practice before the IRS, if such employment may disclose facts or information applicable to federal tax matters.

Power of Attorney

Form 2848, *Power of Attorney and Declaration of Representative,* is used to confer necessary powers on the taxpayer's representative. A Form 2848 must be signed and dated by the taxpayer, and also signed by the representative. A non-IRS form containing the same information may be used in place of the Form 2848. Power of attorney allows the taxpayer's representative to act in all matters relating to IRS issues. If the appointed representative is not qualified to sign the form, however, the form will not be honored. The IRS no longer treats such invalid forms as authority for the person named to receive tax information.

Third Party Designee

A taxpayer may designate another person to discuss his or her tax return with the IRS by checking the "Yes" box in the *Third Party Designee* area of the return. This checkbox authority may be used to allow an employee of the taxpayer's business, a return preparer, a friend, a family member, or another third party to discuss the tax return with the IRS. The taxpayer must enter the designee's name, phone number, and any five numbers as a personal identification number (PIN).

Preparer as Designee. To allow the paid preparer who signed the return to discuss it with the IRS, "*Preparer*" is entered in the space for the designee's name, and no other information is required.

Scope of Authorization. Designation of a third party authorizes the IRS to call the designee to answer any questions relating to the information reported on the tax return. It also authorizes the designee to:

- Exchange information concerning the return with the IRS,
- Call the IRS for information about the processing of the return or the status of any refund or payments,
- Request and receive written tax return information relating to the tax return, including copies of notices, correspondence, and account transcripts, and
- Respond to certain IRS notices about math errors, offsets, and return preparation.

A designee is not authorized to receive any refund check, bind the taxpayer to anything (including additional tax liability), or otherwise represent the taxpayer before the IRS. Power of attorney is required to expand the designee's authority.

Automatic Expiration. The designee authorization automatically expires on the due date for the next year's tax return (for the 2009 return, that would be April 15, 2010, for most people). The authorization may be revoked by the taxpayer (or the representative may withdraw) during this time by sending a written statement of revocation to the Internal Revenue Service Center at the address where the return was filed. The statement of revocation must indicate that the authority of the designee is revoked, list the tax return, and be signed and dated by the taxpayer or designee.

Disclosure of Returns

The IRS is generally prohibited from disclosing tax returns and tax return information in its files, but it may disclose tax returns to persons having a material interest under specified circumstances. The right to inspect an income tax return in the possession of the IRS is statutorily conferred on a limited number of persons, all of whom must have a material interest in the contents of that return.

Information subject to the disclosure rules is of two types: returns and return information. The former includes any tax or information return, declaration of estimated tax, or claim for refund, together with any amendments, supplements, supporting schedules, attachments, or lists that were part of such returns. "Return information" includes the taxpayer's identity and the nature, source, or amount of the taxpayer's income, payments, receipts, deductions, exemptions, credits, assets, liabilities, net worth, tax liability, tax withheld, deficiencies, overassessments, or tax payments.

The IRS may also disclose returns and return information to any person for purposes of tax administration, in connection with the processing, storage, transmission, or reproduction of returns. The regulation allowing this has been held to allow the IRS to contract out the processing of tax returns to third parties. Recent amendments to this regulation clarify the circumstances in which disclosure is allowed, and also set forth appropriate safeguards and notification requirements which must be met by those to whom the information is disclosed. Finally, these requirements apply regardless of the form of the contract under which the third party will process the returns.

Taxpayer. An individual taxpayer is entitled to inspect his or her own return. If a joint return was filed, either spouse may examine it. A spouse who files a joint return has waived the right to confidentiality of return information with respect to the other spouse.

A copy of a return and all attachments to a return may be obtained by submitting Form 4506, along with the $57 fee, to the IRS RAIVS Team address given in the instructions for Form 4506 for the state in which the taxpayer lived when the return was filed.

Form 4506-T may be used to request a transcript of information for a tax year. A return transcript includes most of the line items on the return as filed. An account transcript contains information on the financial status of the account. Transcripts of W-2s, 1099s and other information returns filed for a year are also available. There is no charge for a transcript.

An individual may file Form 8821, *Tax Information Authorization*, to allow another person (an appointee) to view his or her tax information. A Form 8821 appointee is not empowered to represent the taxpayer unless Form 2848 is also filed.

Spouses and Children. A spouse who filed a joint return is entitled to examine the return, but spouses who file separate returns are not entitled to examine each other's returns. A separation agreement that requires a taxpayer to furnish his or her tax returns to the ex-spouse for the purpose of ensuring compliance with alimony and child support obligations would most likely not be sufficient to authorize disclosure. Regulations require that a taxpayer's authorization for disclosure be in the form of a separate written document pertaining solely to the authorized disclosure. The document must also, at the time it is signed, state the taxable years it covers.

If a deficiency with respect to a joint return is assessed, and the individuals filing the return are no longer married or sharing the same household, the IRS must disclose its collection activities, including whether the other party was contacted and how much of the debt has been paid, upon the written request of one of the individuals. The IRS may omit the current home address and business location of a former spouse.

A child or a child's legal representative is considered a person having a material interest in the disclosure of returns or return information and may examine the parents' returns. This rule is to facilitate the administration of the rules under which unearned income of certain minor children is subject to tax at a parent's tax rate.

Others Who May Examine Returns. Returns of partnerships, corporations, estates (including bankruptcy estates), and trusts may be examined by individuals who have a material interest in the returns.

- In the case of a partnership, one who was a partner during any part of the time covered by a partnership return is permitted to examine such return. However, a partner of a partnership, or a shareholder of an S corporation, is not entitled to the disclosure of information regarding tax deficiency challenges filed by other partners or shareholders since the disclosure of such information constitutes the disclosure of the individuals' and not the entity's confidential return information.

Caution. Some practitioners routinely distribute copies of 1120/1120S/1065 returns to all shareholders or partners at the time of preparation. This is generally acceptable. However, it is important to be aware of other information related to partnerships and S corporations that may require permission for disclosure.

- In bankruptcy proceedings, the trustee of the bankruptcy estate of an individual may examine any returns of the debtor for the tax year in which the bankruptcy proceedings are commenced or for any prior years by making a written request. If the bankruptcy is involuntary, the court's permission is required for such examination. With regard to prior years' returns, a finding by the IRS that the returns contain relevant information is required.
- Estate returns may be examined by the administrator, executor, or trustee of the estate. Estate returns may also be examined by any heir at law, next of kin, or beneficiary under the will of the

decedent if the IRS determines that such person has a material interest that will be affected by the information contained in the return. This rule applies even if the decedent died intestate. However, the Tax Court has the power to issue a protective order preventing the IRS from giving information sought from a decedent's estate when such disclosure will contribute to harassment of the estate with spurious and protracted litigation and when the requestor can obtain such information through subsequent discovery proceedings in any civil action he may bring.

- Returns of a decedent may be examined by the same people who are entitled to examine his estate return.
- Trust returns may be inspected by the trustee or trustees, and by any individual who was a beneficiary of the trust during any part of the time covered by the return, if the IRS finds that the trust beneficiary has a material interest that will be affected by return information.
- A corporate return may be examined by (1) any person designated by action of its board of directors, (2) any officer or employee upon written request signed by any principal officer and attested to by the secretary or other officer, (3) the attorney in fact, (4) in the case of a dissolved corporation, any person who might have inspected at the date of dissolution, (5) the receiver or trustee in bankruptcy holding the property, or his attorney in fact, and (6) a bona fide shareholder of record owning 1 percent or more of the outstanding stock (the 1 percent requirement does not apply in the case of an S corporation). No power of attorney can be accepted, however, because the privilege to the shareholder is personal. The executor of an estate holding 2 percent of a corporation's outstanding stock is regarded as the shareholder and is entitled to inspect the corporate return.
- If an individual is legally incompetent, the committee, trustee, or guardian of his estate is entitled to inspect his or her return.

Privilege

Communications between a taxpayer and his or her federally authorized representative are protected by privilege similar to the privilege that exists between clients and attorneys. The representative may not be compelled to disclose the information in court unless the taxpayer waives the privilege. This confidentiality applies to all facts communicated by the taxpayer in the process of seeking tax advice from the representative, in an area within the scope of the representative's authority to practice before the IRS. Confidentiality does not apply to communications relating to the preparation of tax returns, general accounting services, or business advice, or to any information that can be obtained from other sources.

Caution. Taxpayers have for some time been able to treat communications with federally authorized tax practitioners as confidential and privileged (with some exceptions, in the case of criminal matters). The privilege, however, does not apply to any written communication regarding tax shelters. This exception to the privilege formerly applied only to communications regarding corporate tax shelters, but has now been expanded to include any tax shelter.

The Kovel Doctrine. Communications by a client with a nonattorney tax professional engaged by counsel to perform services to assist the attorney in rendering legal services (i.e., providing legal advice regarding tax matters) may be protected from disclosure by the attorney-client privilege. The landmark case in this area is *U.S. v. Kovel*, 62-1 USTC ¶9111, 296 F2d 918 (2nd Cir. 1961).

Information Return Filing Requirements

Taxpayers engaged in a trade or business are required to file various information returns if they make or receive certain payments. It is important for taxpayers to be aware of information returns that may be filed by financial institutions, government agencies, and businesses with which they conduct transactions because the IRS compares information on these returns with individual tax returns.

Taxpayer Responsibilities

Recordkeeping. Taxpayers are required to keep adequate records relating to items reported on tax returns for at least the period covered by the statute of limitations for assessment of tax relating to the return, usually three years. Some records must be kept longer. The absence of adequate books and records may be treated as evidence of intent to engage in civil fraud or commit tax crimes. Records do not have to be kept in any specific form; any records that reflect income adequately and clearly on the basis of an annual accounting period are sufficient.

Example. A farmer sells depreciable farming equipment at auction for $75,000. He had not maintained any books or records as to the assets' original costs, useful lives, or dates of acquisition. Because he is unable to furnish any written proof that the farm equipment had a remaining basis at the time of the sale, he is subject to 100 percent recapture, and the auction proceeds are taxable as ordinary income.

After a sale or exchange, a lack of records can result in a zero basis and a large taxable gain.

Individual taxpayers who derive their incomes from the business of farming, or from salaries, wages, and similar compensation for personal services, need not maintain formal, permanent books, but they must maintain records sufficient to determine the correct amount of their taxable incomes and to prove any deductions or credits claimed on any return.

An approximation of business expenses based on credible evidence other than actual documentation was allowed in *Cohan* [39 F.2d 540 (2nd Cir. 1930)]. The Cohan rule may be applied in cases where records are incomplete or inadequate unless stricter substantiation requirements are specified by statute. Also, if a taxpayer has established that records have been lost due to circumstances beyond the taxpayer's control, such as destruction by fire or flood, then the taxpayer has the right to substantiate claimed deductions by a reasonable reconstruction of the financial information.

Information Return Filing Requirements as of 2009

Form	Who Must File	Information Reportable	Where Filed	Due Date
W-2	Employer required to withhold	Employee names, wages, tips, other compensation, certain fringe benefits, advance earned income credit (EIC) payments, withheld income, Medicare, and FICA taxes	Social Security Administration (PA) Data Operations Center	March 1 (paper) March 31 (electronic) (to recipient February 1)
W-2G	Payers of gambling winnings from bingo, lotteries, horse racing, dog racing, jai alai, poker tournaments, etc.	Generally, payments of $600 or more if winnings are at least 300 times the amount of the wager; $1,200 or more in bingo or slot machine winnings; $1,500 or more in keno winnings; $5,000 or more in poker winnings	See instructions for form 1099, etc.	March 1 (paper) March 31 (electronic) (to recipient February 1)
W-3	Employer required to withhold	Total of amounts reported on wage and tax statements	Social Security Administration (PA) Data Operations Center	March 1 (paper) March 31 (electronic)
W-8	Noncitizens and nonresidents having gain not effectively connected with a U.S. trade or business, who meet certain residency requirements	Qualifications for exemption or notice of change in status	With payer of the qualifying income who is the withholding agent	Before a payment is made
W-9	Taxpayers desiring to avoid backup withholding on interest and dividends and other forms of nonwage income	Taxpayer Identification Number (TIN)	With payer, middleman, broker, or barter exchange	When TIN is requested
56	Fiduciary	Identification, authority, tax notices, revocation or termination of notice, and court or administrative proceedings	Service Center for principal's tax return	When a fiduciary relationship is first created or when it is terminated
90-22.1	U.S. person having authority over, or interest in, a foreign financial account valued at over $10,000	Name, institution, location, valuation of account	U.S. Treasury Dept., Detroit, MI, or hand carry to local IRS office	June 30 of the year following the calendar year reported
90-22.47	Financial institutions	Suspicious activities	Detroit Computing Center	No later than 30 days after initial detection
926	Transferor of property to foreign corporation	Foreign transferee information, indication if transfer was exempt from excise tax, and calculation of excise tax	Service Center for tax return	Due date of transferor's return

Information Return Filing Requirements as of 2009 (Continued)				
Form	**Who Must File**	**Information Reportable**	**Where Filed**	**Due Date**
945	Persons who withhold tax from nonpayroll payments (employers)	Income tax withheld from nonpayroll payments, including pensions, annuities, IRAs, military retirement, gambling winnings, voluntary withholding on certain government payments, and backup withholding	See instructions for form	February 1 February 10 if timely deposits made in full payment of taxes
972	Shareholder evidencing consent to receive dividend (with corporation claiming deduction)	Amount of dividend, name and address of corporations, shares, class of stock	Office for income tax return as attachment to Form 973	Due date of corporation's return
973	Corporation claiming a deduction for consent dividends	Class of stock, amount of shares, amount of dividends distributed	Office for income tax return as an attachment to return	Due date of corporation's return
990	Organizations exempt under Code Sec. 501(c)	Income, expenses, balance sheet, contributions, substantial contributors, and other information	Service Center, Ogden, UT	Fifteenth day of fifth month after accounting period of organization ends
1040-C, 2063	Departing alien	Income (for certificate of compliance)	Local IRS office	No later than two weeks before departure
1041-A	Trusts claiming charitable deductions and split-interest trusts, including charitable remainder trusts and pooled income funds	Income, deductions, accumulations, distributions, and balance sheet	Service Center, Ogden, UT	April 15
1042-S	Withholding agent for nonresident aliens	Name and address of payee and agent, gross amount and nature of income paid, withholding, per-country analysis	Philadelphia Service Center	March 15
1065	Limited liability company	Income, shareholders, shares	See instructions for form	April 15
1065	Partnership	Income, partners, shares	See instructions for form	April 15
1065	Religious or apostolic association/corporation	Members, shares of main office	See instructions for form	April 15
1096	Payers, brokers, trustees of IRAs, mortgage interest recipients, barterers, creditors, persons reporting real estate transactions, and lenders who acquire an interest in secured property	Transmittals of Forms W-2G, 1098, 1099, 3921, 3922, 5498, 5498-ESA and 5498-SA	See instructions for form	March 1 (W-2G, 1098, 1099, 3921, 3922) June 1 (5498, 5498-ESA, 5498-SA)
1098	Mortgage lender	Mortgage interest payments of $600 or more received in course of trade or business, including certain points	See instructions for form	March 1 (paper) March 31 (electronic) (to payer/borrower February 1)
1098-C	Donees of contributed motor vehicles, boats, or airplanes valued at over $500	Information about a donated motor vehicle, boat, or airplane; gross proceeds over $500	See instructions for form	March 1 (paper) March 31 (electronic) To donor within 30 days of donation

Information Return Filing Requirements as of 2009 (Continued)				
Form	**Who Must File**	**Information Reportable**	**Where Filed**	**Due Date**
1098-E	Payees of student loan payments	Qualified educational student loan interest payments of $600 or more during a covered period	See instructions for form	March 1 (paper) March 31 (electronic) (to payer/borrower February 1)
1098-T	Qualified educational institutions	Amount of qualified tuition and related expenses received on behalf of individual, amounts of refunds and reimbursements, and amounts of grants received by student that were processed through the institution	See instructions for form	March 1 (paper) March 31 (electronic) (to student February 1)
1099-A	Secured lender	Information about the acquisition or abandonment of property that is security for a debt	See instructions for form	March 1 (paper) March 31 (electronic) (to borrower February 1)
1099-B	Brokers and barter exchanges	Sales or redemptions of securities, futures transactions, commodities, and bartering exchange transactions	See instructions for form	March 1 (paper) March 31 (electronic) (to recipient February 1)
1099-C	Lender	Amount of canceled debt of $600 or more owed to a financial institution, credit union, RTC, FDIC, NCUA, or federal governmental agency	See instructions for form	March 1 (paper) March 31 (electronic) (to borrower February 1)
1099-CAP	Domestic corporations after acquisition of control or substantial change in capital structure, unless exempt	Information about cash, stock, or other property from acquisition of control or change in capital structure of corporation	See instructions for form	March 1 (paper) March 31 (electronic) (to recipient February 1; if clearinghouse, January 10)
1099-DIV	Corporations (or associations taxable as such) or stockholders	Distributions, such as dividends (including ESOP dividends), capital gains or nontaxable distributions, that were paid on stock and that totaled $10 or more, distributions in liquidation of $600 or more, foreign tax paid on certain distributions and federal income tax withheld under the backup withholding rules	See instructions for form	March 1 (paper) March 31 (electronic) (to recipient February 1)
1099-G	Payer	Unemployment compensation and state and local income tax refunds aggregating $10 or more, or agricultural payments and taxable grants for $600 or more	See instructions for form	March 1 (paper) March 31 (electronic) (to recipient February 1)
1099-H	Payers	Health insurance premiums paid on behalf of certain individuals	See instructions for form	March 1 (paper) March 31 (electronic) (to recipient February 1)

Information Return Filing Requirements as of 2009 (Continued)				
Form	**Who Must File**	**Information Reportable**	**Where Filed**	**Due Date**
1099-INT	Corporations, banks, and savings and loan institutions	Interest, not including interest on an IRA, generally aggregating $10 or more ($600 or more for certain interest paid in the course of a trade or business)	See instructions for form	March 1 (paper) March 31 (electronic) (to recipient February 1)
1099-INT	Real estate mortgage investment conduits, issuers of CDOs and broker-nominees holding interests in REMICs or CDOs	Interest, other than original issue discount, accrued to a REMIC regular interest holder	See instructions for form	March 1 (paper) March 31 (electronic) (to recipient March 15)
1099-LTC	Payers	Payments from long-term care insurance plans or accelerated death benefits	See instructions for form	March 1 (paper) March 31 (electronic) (to insured and policyholder February 1)
1099-MISC	Payers	Attorney fees over $600 and gross proceeds paid to an attorney in any amount	See instructions for form	March 1 (paper) March 31 (electronic) (to recipient February 16)
1099-MISC	Businesses, including nonprofit organizations	Amounts aggregating $600 or more such as rent, prizes, and awards, and $10 in royalty or broker payments	See instructions for form	March 1 (paper) March 31 (electronic) (to recipient February 1)
1099-MISC	Fishing boat owners and operators	Amounts paid to crew members as proceeds from sale of fish	See instructions for form	March 1 (paper) March 31 (electronic) (to recipient February 1)
1099-MISC	Persons in a trade or business	Payments aggregating $600 or more for services performed for a trade or business by people not treated as its employees, such as subcontractors or directors, including golden parachute payments	See instructions for form	March 1 (paper) March 31 (electronic) (to recipient February 1)
1099-MISC	Businesses making payments for services received	Payments aggregating $600 or more, with name, address, and identification number of service recipient	See instructions for form	March 1 (paper) March 31 (electronic) (to recipient February 1)
1099-MISC	Payers under health plan	Payments aggregating $600 or more to physicians, physicians' corporations, or others providing health and medical services	See instructions for form	March 1 (paper) March 31 (electronic) (to recipient February 1)
1099-MISC	Brokers	Substitute dividend and tax-exempt interest payments of $10 or more	See instructions for form	March 1 (paper) March 31 (electronic) (to recipient February 16)
1099-MISC	Direct sellers	Direct sales of $5,000 or more of consumer goods for resale	See instructions for form	March 1 (paper) March 31 (electronic) (to recipient February 1)

Information Return Filing Requirements as of 2009 (Continued)				
Form	**Who Must File**	**Information Reportable**	**Where Filed**	**Due Date**
1099-MISC	Crop insurers	Crop insurance proceeds of $600 or more paid by an insurance company	See instructions for form	March 1 (paper) March 31 (electronic) (to recipient February 1)
1099-OID	Bond, CD issuers, other institutions accepting deposits, brokers, nominees	Original issue discount aggregating $10 or more	See instructions for form	March 1 (paper) March 31 (electronic) (to recipient February 1)
1099-OID	REMICs and issuers of collateralized debt obligations	Accrued original issue discount of $10 or more	See instructions for form	March 1 (paper) March 31 (electronic) (to recipient February 1)
1099-PATR	Cooperatives	Patronage dividends aggregating $10 or more	See instructions for form	March 1 (paper) March 31 (electronic) (to recipient February 1)
1099-Q	Qualified tuition programs and account trustees	Distributions from qualified tuition programs or Coverdell education savings accounts	See instructions for form	March 1 (paper) March 31 (electronic) (to recipient February 1)
1099-R	Employers, plan administrators, and issuers of insurance or annuity contracts	All distributions aggregating more than $10 from retirement or profit-sharing plans, IRAs, SEPs, or insurance contracts	See instructions for form	March 1 (paper) March 31 (electronic) (to recipient February 1)
1099-S	Person responsible for closing certain real estate transactions	Gross proceeds from sale or exchange of certain real estate	See instructions for form	March 1 (paper) March 31 (electronic) (to transferor February 16)
1099-SA	Payers	Distributions, including earnings, from medical savings accounts	See instructions for form	March 1 (paper) March 31 (electronic) (to recipient February 1)
1120S	S corporation	Income, deductions, cost of goods sold, and each shareholder's pro rata share of each subchapter S item	See instructions for form	March 15
2438	Regulated investment companies (RICs) and real estate investment trusts (REITs) for each mutual fund	Undistributed capital gains	Service Center, Covington, KY	30 days after close of the fund's tax year
3520	Grantor or fiduciary of foreign trusts	Preparer, name of trust or estate, country of creation, dates of creation and termination, foreign trustee, list of property transferred to trust, beneficiaries	Service Center, Ogden, UT	April 15
3520-A	Foreign trust with at least one U.S. owner	Preparer, name of trust, U.S. agent and foreign trustee, income and expenses, balance sheet, owner and beneficiary statement	Service Center, Ogden, UT	March 15 (file Form 3520-A, send copy of owner statement to grantor, send copy of beneficial statement to each beneficiary)

Information Return Filing Requirements as of 2009 (Continued)				
Form	**Who Must File**	**Information Reportable**	**Where Filed**	**Due Date**
5227	Split-interest trusts treated the same as private foundations, e.g., pooled income funds, charitable remainder trusts, or charitable lead trusts	Income, deductions and capital gains or losses (for charitable remainder trusts), balance sheet, information on charitable activities and distribution	Service Center, Ogden, UT	April 15
5471	A U.S. citizen or resident who is an officer or director of a foreign corporation in which a U.S. person (citizen or resident or domestic partnership, corporation, estate or trust) initially acquires 10% or more stock ownership or subsequently acquires an additional 10% or more (by value or voting power) of the outstanding stock	Identifying information, Schedules G and O (Part I)	File with income tax return	March 15 for corporations; April 15 for individuals
5471	A U.S. person (a U.S. citizen, resident, partnership, corporation, estate, or trust) who, with respect to a foreign corporation; (1) acquires 10% ownership; (2) acquires additional stock that increases ownership to 10%; or (3) disposes of stock reducing ownership below 10%; also, a person who (1) is treated as a U.S shareholder under Code Sec. 953(c); or (2) becomes a U.S. person while meeting the 10% ownership requirement	Identifying information, Schedules A, B, C, E, F, G, and O (Pt II); statement on related person indebtedness and shareholder information	File with income tax return	March 15 for corporations; April 15 for individuals
5471	Controlling (50% or more) shareholders (a U.S. citizen, resident, partnership, corporation, estate, or trust) of a foreign corporation that exercised control for an uninterrupted period of at least 30 days during its annual accounting period	Identifying information, Schedules A, B, C, E, F, G, H, I, J, and M	File with income tax return	March 15 for corporations; April 15 for individuals

Information Return Filing Requirements as of 2009 (Continued)				
Form	**Who Must File**	**Information Reportable**	**Where Filed**	**Due Date**
5471	A U.S. person (a U.S. citizen, resident, partnership, corporation, estate, or trust) who owns 10% of a controlled foreign corporation (CFC), or any stock of a CFC that is a captive insurance company, for 30 days during the CFC's tax year, as well as on the last day of that year.	Identifying information, Schedules G, H, I, and J	File with income tax return	March 15 for corporations; April 15 for individuals
5472	All foreign corporations engaged in a U.S. trade or business and all domestic corporations that are at least 25% foreign owned that engage in a reportable transaction	Sales and purchases of stock or other tangible property in trade, rents and royalties paid or received, consideration paid for specified services, commissions paid and received, amounts loaned or borrowed, interest, premiums for insurance and reinsurance	Same as corporation's income tax return, duplicate at Ogden Service Center	Same as corporation's income tax return
5498	Trustees or issuers of individual retirement arrangements (IRAs) or simplified employee pensions (SEPs)	Participant's name, address, SSN, amount of IRA or SEP contributions, cost of life insurance and value of IRA or SEP account	See instructions for form	June 1 (to participant February 1 for value of account and June 1 for contributions)
5498-ESA	Trustees or custodians of Coverdell ESAs	Participant's name, address, SSN, amount of Coverdell ESA contributions (including rollovers), and value of accounts	See instructions for form	June 1 (to beneficiary April 30)
5498-SA	Trustees or custodians of MSAs, HSAs, Medicare Advantage MSAs	Participant's name, address, SSN, amount of MSA or HSA contributions, year for which contribution is made, rollovers, fair market value of account	See instructions for form	June 1 (to participant June 1)
5500	Pension plan administrators and sponsors who maintain an employee benefit plan subject to ERISA	Specified information on the plan	Lawrence, KS (see Form 5500 instructions)	The last day of the seventh month after the plan year ends
8027/ 8027-T	Existing large food or beverage establishments where tipping is customary and more than 10 persons are normally employed and new large food or beverage establishments where the average number of hours worked each business day by all employees during any two consecutive months exceeded 80 hours	Gross food and beverage sales receipts, total charge receipts, charged tips, number of tipped employees, wages paid and tips reported by each employee, allocation of employee tip income	Cincinnati Service Center	March 1 (paper) March 31 (electronic) (allocable tips shown on W-2, furnished to recipients February 1)

Information Return Filing Requirements as of 2009 (Continued)				
Form	**Who Must File**	**Information Reportable**	**Where Filed**	**Due Date**
8038	Issuers of certain tax-exempt private activity bonds	Date and type of issue, description of obligations including maturity date, total face amount of obligations and stated annual interest rate, description of financed property and its principal users unless a student, and approval of issue if industrial development bonds	Ogden Service Center	Fifteenth day of second month after the calendar quarter during which the bond was issued
8300	Persons engaged in a trade or business	Payment of over $10,000 in cash or foreign currency received in one transaction or two or more related transactions in the course of a trade or business; cash payments received with respect to the same transaction or a related transaction exceeding $10,000 in a 12-month period in the course of a trade or business	Detroit Computing Center or hand-carry to local office	Within 15 days after date of transaction (to payer February 1)
8300	Clerks of federal or state courts	Cash payment for bail of over $10,000 in aggregate for certain criminal offenses	Detroit Computing Center or hand-carry to local office	Within 15 days after date of transaction, or if multiple payments, 15 days after date of transaction that causes aggregate to exceed $10,000 (to payer February 1)
8300	Casinos	Payment of over $10,000 in cash or foreign currency received in one transaction or two or more related transactions for nongaming activities (restaurants, shops, etc.)	Detroit Computing Center or hand-carry to local office	Within 15 days after date of transaction (to payer February 1)
8308	Partnership	Sale or exchange of partnership interest involving unrealized receivables or substantially appreciated inventory items	Service Center of main office	Attach and file by due date of Form 1065 (to transferor and transferee February 1)

Note: Form 8809 is used to request a 30-day extension of time to file Forms 1042-S, 1098, 1099, 3921, 3922, 5498 and 8027 with the IRS or Form W-2 with the Social Security Administration. An extension of time to furnish required statements to recipients may be requested by sending a letter to the Enterprise Computing Center (see General Instructions, Forms 1099, 1098, 3921, 3922, 5498, and W-2G).

Audits

Audits, also called examinations, are the main tool of the IRS for ensuring taxpayer compliance with tax laws.

The IRS reviews all returns it receives. Mathematical or clerical errors are corrected, and a notice of the correction is sent to the taxpayer along with a refund of any overpayment or a demand for payment of any additional tax resulting from the correction. A notice of correction does not give the taxpayer the right to appeal to the Tax Court.

Problems with returns that are treated as mathematical or clerical errors include:

- Failure to include a correct TIN for the taxpayer, spouse, or any dependent when claiming an exemption or when claiming the child care credit, child tax credit, any higher education credit, the earned income credit (EIC), etc.
- Failure to pay the proper amount of self-employment tax on returns on which the EIC is claimed on net earnings from self-employment.
- EIC claim by noncustodial parent.

- S corporation shareholder's return inconsistent with the corporation's return.
- In most cases, estate or trust beneficiary's return inconsistent with estate's or trust's return.

The IRS Restructuring and Reform Act of 1998 has driven many recent changes in the conduct of IRS audits, including a dramatic decline in individual and corporate audit rates. The Act provided that the IRS Mission Statement was to emphasize serving and educating the public and satisfying the needs of taxpayers rather than enforcement.

Selection of Returns for Audit

The IRS assigns an activity code that categorizes each return by the type of form used and by the level of the taxpayer's income, gross receipts, or assets (the "size" of the return). Under an annual examination plan IRS employees select a predetermined percentage of the highest-risk returns within each activity code.

The discriminant index function (sometimes called the discriminant inventory function) (DIF), the unreported income discriminant index function (UI DIF), and the National Research Program (NRP) are important features of the current return selection process.

DIF Score. The IRS determines which are the highest-risk returns using the DIF, a complex, computer-based technique that evaluates multiple items on returns to determine the potential for changes, based on the IRS's past experience with similar returns. After all the relevant items on a return are scored, a total DIF score is calculated as a sum of the individual item scores. The higher the DIF score, the greater the audit potential for that return. The UI DIF uses similar methods to measure the potential for unreported income.

IRS Research Programs. The IRS uses data collected in the NRP to determine the DIF and UI DIF scores. The NRP employs annual individual studies using a multi-year rolling methodology. Audits under the NRP are similar to regular IRS examinations, and are less intrusive and time-consuming than those conducted under prior research programs.

Audit Technique Guides. The IRS offers Audit Technique Guides (ATGs) in order to train its examiners for a particular market segment. The ATGs include examination techniques, unique or common industry issues, business practices, terminology specific to particular industries, and other information that may assist examiners in performing examinations.

Planning Tip. No rules limit the information or documentation that can be attached to a return. If there is concern that a particular return item may increase audit potential, consider attaching a detailed explanation and some verification for that item. It may be possible to avoid an audit by taking advantage of the IRS's pre-audit screening process.

Examinations of Related or Associated Taxpayers. Sometimes the examining agent commences the audit with a substantial amount of information, documentary and sometimes testimonial, developed during the course of examining a third party's return.

A prime example would be the audit of a local check-cashing agency that routinely cashes the checks of its customers. While conducting a compliance audit of the check-cashing agency, the IRS would collect substantial information about the agency's customers, mindful that they may not have appropriately reported proceeds from the cashed checks as gross receipts. Similarly, audits of related taxpayers or the taxpayer's vendors or customers often lead to an audit of the taxpayer if the taxpayer has significant interactions with them.

Public Records and Government Agencies. Audits and examinations sometimes arise from a government agent's review of newspaper articles; local, state, or national publicity sources; or court records. There are also many information-sharing arrangements between the IRS and other federal agencies as well as various state agencies (including state taxing authorities).

Other Outside Sources. Many audits are prompted by information from people somehow connected to the taxpayer. Informants typically include disgruntled employees, ex-business partners, business competitors, ex-spouses, and others. The IRS may reward the informant a percentage of the tax and penalty ultimately recovered and is precluded from disclosing the informant's identity.

Information-Reporting Project (IRP). The IRS typically tries to match all information on a taxpayer's Form 1099, W-2, and Schedule K-1 with information in the taxpayer's return. If these do not match, and the taxpayer's response to an initial inquiry is insufficient, an audit may ensue.

Compliance Projects. Increased requirements for transaction and information reporting have provided the IRS with a great deal of information about currency-related transactions. The IRS performs compliance checks, or audits of businesses to determine whether information reporting requirements are being met. Audit potential is often determined during the compliance check. Currency and banking transaction information reports collected from all federal agencies are consolidated in the Currency and Banking Transaction Reporting System of the IRS. Many former IRS and Treasury forms are now used by (and renamed for) the Financial Crimes Enforcement Network (FinCEN). These information reports include the following:

- **FinCEN Form 104,** *Currency Transaction Report* (formerly Form 4789) is filed by financial institutions reporting currency transactions (deposits and withdrawals) in excess of $10,000.
- **FinCEN Form 105** (formerly U.S. Customs Form 4790) details the international transportation of currency or monetary instruments, either by persons traveling to or from the United States, or by mail or other shipping method.
- **IRS/FinCEN Form 8300** is an information return filed by any business that receives cash in excess of $10,000 in one transaction or in two or more related transactions within 15 days of receiving the cash. The form identifies the customer by name, taxpayer identification number, address, the transaction involved, method of payment, and other related information. The definition of cash for purposes of filing this report includes multiple cashier's checks, traveler's checks, money orders, and bank checks in amounts of less than $10,000. The Patriot Act requires that Form 8300 be filed with both the IRS and the Financial Crimes Enforcement Network (FinCEN). Because this form is no longer filed solely with the IRS, some of the stringent disclosure restrictions are relaxed, and the information contained in Form 8300 may be available to any local, state, or federal employee investigating someone on a civil, criminal, or regulatory matter. In addition, there is a place on Form 8300 to indicate that the person filing the form believes he or she has witnessed a suspicious transaction, which includes any transaction in which there is an indication of possible illegal activity.
- **FinCEN Form 103** (formerly Form 8362) is completed by casinos engaged in currency transactions with individuals.
- **Treasury Form TD F 90-22.1** is required of all entities and individuals having a financial interest in or signature authority over a foreign bank account or financial account with an aggregate value of more than $10,000.
- **FinCEN Form 107** (formerly Treasury Form TD F 90-22.55) is required of all businesses issuing or redeeming money orders or traveler's checks involving more than $1,000.
- **FinCEN Form 109** (formerly Treasury Form TD F 90-22.56) *Suspicious Activity Report by Money Services Business.* Federally insured institutions are required to report to the appropriate federal authorities any suspicious transactions of their customers. The report requires the institution to identify the customer and provide a detailed description of the suspicious conduct.

The Patriot Act and recent Treasury rules have greatly increased the amount of information that businesses must collect and maintain about their customers' financial lives; more businesses are required to report suspicious activities; and new rules step up information sharing between financial institutions and the government.

Financial Status Audits. Information not specifically related to an individual's tax return, such as a taxpayer's standard of living and credit reports, are considered by the IRS if it already has a reasonable indication that there is a likelihood of unreported income.

IRS Audit Priorities

In September 2002, the IRS announced that it was realigning its audit resources to focus on key, high-risk areas of noncompliance. These new priority areas include the following:

- Offshore credit card users
- High-risk, high-income taxpayers
- Abusive schemes and promoter investigations
- High-income nonfilers
- Filers with likely unreported income
- National Research Program

When the IRS Will Perform Examinations

The general statutory limitation on the IRS's power to assess additional taxes is three years from the due date of a timely filed return, or three years from the receipt of a return filed late.

A taxpayer will generally be notified that a return is going to be examined during the 26 months (27 months in the case of a corporation) after the date the return was due or filed. The statute of limitations begins running on the date the return was due if the return is filed on time or early, or on the date the return was received if the return was filed late.

If the IRS cannot complete an examination within the period of limitation, it may seek to extend the statute of limitations, subject to the consent of the taxpayer.

> **Planning Tip.** Extending the statute of limitations is not necessarily detrimental to a taxpayer. If the taxpayer does not agree to the extension, it is likely that the IRS will issue a notice of deficiency.

How Audits Are Conducted

Audits may take place through correspondence, at an IRS office, or at the taxpayer's home or place of business or the place of business of the taxpayer's representative (a field examination). The IRS is required to conduct its examination of taxpayers and their books and records in a reasonable fashion that does not unduly inconvenience the taxpayers.

Taxpayer Rights

During an IRS examination of a taxpayer's return, the taxpayer has specific rights.

- The IRS must provide a written statement detailing the taxpayer's rights and the IRS's obligations during the audit, appeals, refund, and collection process. The IRS must also explain the audit and collection process.
- A taxpayer is guaranteed the right to be represented by any individual currently permitted to practice before the IRS, unless the IRS notifies the taxpayer that the representative is responsible for unreasonable delay or hindrance. Further, unless it issues an administrative summons, the IRS cannot require the taxpayer to accompany the representative to the interview.
- If a taxpayer goes to an audit without a representative, any interview must be suspended when the taxpayer clearly requests the right to consult with a representative.
- The taxpayer has the right to make an audio recording of any in-person interview conducted by the IRS, upon 10 days' advance notice.
- The IRS is entitled to inspect the taxpayer's books only once, unless the taxpayer requests reexamination or the IRS provides written notification.
- The taxpayer has the right to claim additional deductions not claimed on the return during the audit if entitled to the deductions.
- The taxpayer may invoke his or her constitutional rights if questioned about possible criminal violations.
- After an audit, the taxpayer has the right to get a copy of the IRS's file. Case workpapers compiled by the examiner do not become a permanent part of the file, but may be obtained by the taxpayer after the examination is completed and before an appeal is filed. The taxpayer's right to his or her file is covered by the Freedom of Information Act, and the taxpayer may file a FOIA request with the responsible IRS official, as indicated in the regulation.

Planning Tip. Fifth Amendment protection is not available in regard to civil matters or as a method for taxpayers to avoid providing required information to the IRS. Its use must be carefully weighed.

Taxpayer Representation During an Audit

During the course of an audit, the representative must remain aware of the many issues that might arise and any privileges that may apply. The representative must attempt to respond to each request for information in a timely manner. Effective representation requires adequate preparation, an understanding of the taxpayer's business, a fair presentation of the relevant facts and legal authorities, and a realistic evaluation of the relative hazards in the event of litigation.

Among a representative's key audit objectives should be to limit the scope of the agent's inquiry; maintain the appearance of reasonable cooperation; avoid presenting false or misleading information or statements; make certain no privileges are waived; and maintain a detailed schedule of all information and documents provided to the agent.

The IRS has the power to issue a summons to any person who has information that may be relevant to an IRS inquiry. This power may be invoked to require a person to produce books and records or to give testimony.

Unagreed Issues

If, as a result of an audit, adjustments are proposed with which the taxpayer does not agree, the taxpayer is given an opportunity to appeal the examiner's conclusions. If the examination takes place at an IRS office, the taxpayer may request a meeting with the examiner's supervisor. If that meeting fails to resolve the disagreement, or if the audit did not take place at an IRS office, the taxpayer may request an appeal. If the taxpayer requests such consideration, the case will be referred to the Appeals Office, which will afford the taxpayer the opportunity for a conference. The determination of tax liability by the Appeals Office is final insofar as the taxpayer's appeal rights within the IRS are concerned.

Caution. Signing the examiner's report constitutes agreement with the findings of the examination. If the taxpayer does not agree that the tax is owed, he or she should not sign the report. The taxpayer cannot appeal a signed report within the IRS or in Tax Court.

Fast-Track Mediation

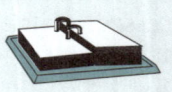

If a taxpayer disagrees with the findings of an examination, or in certain other circumstances, it may be possible to resolve the issue with a mediator, outside of the federal court system. Most cases that are not docketed in any court qualify for fast-track mediation. IRS Publication 3605, *Fast Track Mediation*, describes the exceptions and procedure. In addition, the IRS offers specific fast-track mediation programs targeted toward business taxpayers. Small business/self-employed (SB/SE) fast-track mediation is an expedited process to resolve disputes within 40 days, compared to several months or longer for the regular appeals process. Large/mid-size business (LMSB) fast-track mediation aims to resolve issues within 120 days.

Filing Tip. If fast-track mediation fails to resolve a dispute, the taxpayer retains the option of continuing with the traditional appeals process.

Collections

The IRS charges a late-payment penalty of 0.5% per month as well as interest at the federal rate on past-due tax payments. In addition, if a return is not filed by the due date, a late-filing penalty of 5% per month, up to 25% of the tax due, is charged. Extensions of time to file are obtained using Form 4868; see Tab 1. An extension of time to pay tax may be obtained using Form 1127, *Application for Extension of Time for Payment of Tax*. The taxpayer must show that timely payment would result in undue hardship.

Liens

A lien is a claim against property for the satisfaction of a debt. The IRS has an automatic lien on a taxpayer's property if the taxpayer owes tax that is not currently being disputed. The IRS may file a Notice of Federal Tax Lien to protect its right to the taxpayer's property if the tax is not paid.

The IRS must notify any person subject to a lien of the existence of the lien within five days of the lien being filed, with a notice given in person, left at the taxpayer's home or place of business, or sent by certified or registered mail to the person's last known address. The notice must explain (1) the amount of the unpaid tax, (2) the person's right to request a hearing during the 30-day period beginning on the fifth day after the lien is filed, (3) the available administrative appeals and their procedures, and (4) the procedures relating to the release of liens.

Any tax lien against an individual's property will be released within 30 days after the tax (along with applicable penalties and interest) is paid. In some circumstances, the IRS will release a tax lien while the tax is still owed. See IRS Publication 783, *Instructions on How to Apply for a Certificate of Discharge of Property from Federal Tax Lien*, and IRS Publication 1660, *Collection Appeal Rights*, for more information.

Levies

A levy is a seizure of property to satisfy a debt. The IRS must give 30 days' notice of its intent to seize a taxpayer's property. The IRS may generally levy any property the taxpayer owns at the time of the levy. Certain property is exempt from levy:

- Clothing and school books needed by the taxpayer and family members
- Furniture and personal effects in the taxpayer's household up to $8,230 in value (for 2009)
- Books and tools of the taxpayer's trade, business, or profession up to $4,120 in value (for 2009)
- Unemployment benefits, including any portion payable with respect to dependents
- Undelivered mail
- Annuity or pension payments under the Railroad Retirement Act; benefits under the Railroad Unemployment Insurance Act; special pension payments received by a person whose name has been entered on the Army, Navy, Air Force, and Coast Guard Medal of Honor roll; and annuities based on retired or retainer pay under chapter 73 of title 10 USC

- Worker's compensation, including any portion payable with respect to dependents
- Salary, wages, or other income necessary to comply with any child support judgment
- Wages or salary received by an individual for personal services, or income from other sources, up to the "exempt amount" stated in the statute This amount consists of the sum of the individual's standard deduction and personal exemption for the tax year, divided by the number of payments during the year (for example, 52 in the case of weekly wage or salary payments).
- Certain amounts payable to an individual as a service-connected disability benefit
- Any amount payable to an individual as a recipient of public assistance under supplemental security income for the aged, blind, and disabled of the Social Security Act, or state or local government public assistance or public welfare programs for which eligibility is determined by a needs or income test
- Any amount payable to a participant under the Job Training Partnership Act (29 U.S.C. 1501 et seq.) from funds appropriated pursuant to that Act
- If the amount of the levy does not exceed $5,000, the residence of the taxpayer; or any real property of the taxpayer (other than that which is rented) used by any other individual as a residence
- The principal residence of the taxpayer (unless the levy is approved by a judge or magistrate of a federal district court), as well as tangible personal or real property (other than that which is rented) used in the trade or business of an individual taxpayer (unless the levy is approved by an appropriate IRS official, or it is determined that the collection of the tax is in jeopardy)

Personal property that is exempt from levy is not exempt from attachment by a federal tax lien.

Relief from Collection Activity

Delays of Collection Activities

If a taxpayer's income is below an amount based on the HHS poverty guidelines, the IRS may delay collection activities. Low-income taxpayers may file Form 433-A, *Collection Information Statement for Wage Earners and Self-Employed Individuals*, or Form 433-B, *Collection Information Statement for Businesses*, to prove that their income is insufficient to pay the tax owed and also meet basic living expenses, and that the taxpayer has no assets the IRS might levy to secure payment of the tax.

Taxpayer Advocate Service

Collection activity may be suspended if the taxpayer faces significant hardship. The Taxpayer Advocate Service assists taxpayers who have an issue that has not been resolved through normal channels. The taxpayer advocate independently represents taxpayer interests and concerns within the IRS. Taxpayer advocates are independent of other divisions of the IRS and report directly to the National Taxpayer Advocate. This service is provided for the following situations:

- The taxpayer is suffering, or is about to suffer, a significant hardship as a result of administration of the tax laws.
- The taxpayer is facing an immediate threat of adverse action.
- The taxpayer will incur significant costs in resolving the tax problem through normal channels (including fees for professional representation).
- The taxpayer will suffer irreparable injury or long-term adverse impact as a result of IRS action.
- There has been a delay of more than 30 days beyond normal processing times to resolve a tax account problem.
- A response has not been received by the date promised.

Situations are reviewed on a case-by-case basis. An issue is submitted for consideration by the taxpayer advocate service in one of three ways:

- By phone at 877-777-4778 (for TTY/TTD, call 800-829-4059).
- By filing Form 911, *Request for Taxpayer Advocate Service Assistance (and Application for Taxpayer Assistance Order)*, with the Taxpayer Advocate Service.
- By a written request for assistance or in person at the local Taxpayer Advocate office.

Injured Spouse Claim

The IRS may offset overpayments of taxes for past-due federal debts, child support payments, and some other debts. If the debt is attributable to one spouse, and a joint return was filed, the other spouse may be entitled to receive a refund of his or her share of the overpayment by filing Form 8379, *Injured Spouse Claim and Allocation.*

Innocent Spouse Relief

If a joint return is filed, each spouse is responsible for the accuracy of the return and for the payment of the tax. Under certain circumstances, one spouse may claim relief by filing Form 8857, *Request for Innocent Spouse Relief*, no later than two years after the date on which the IRS first attempted to collect the tax. Married taxpayers who live in community property states may qualify for relief even if a joint return is not filed.

The following conditions must be met to qualify for innocent spouse relief:

1. The joint return had an understatement of tax due to erroneous items of the spouse or former spouse.
2. At the time the spouse requesting relief signed the joint return, he or she did not know or have reason to know that there was an understatement of tax.
3. Taking into account all the facts and circumstances, it would be unfair to hold the spouse requesting relief liable for the understatement of tax.

Relief by Separation of Liability. Under separation of liability, income, deductions, credits, and other items are allocated to each spouse in a method similar to that which would have been used if the spouses had filed separate returns, and each spouse is liable only for his or her portion of the tax. Only unpaid liabilities may be treated in this way. If the tax has been paid, relief by separation of liability is not available.

This type of relief applies only if the spouses are divorced or legally separated (or the other spouse has died), or if the spouses were not members of the same household at any time during the last 12 months. Also, the spouse applying for relief must not have had actual knowledge of the disputed items.

Equitable Relief. Spouses who do not qualify for innocent spouse relief or relief by separation of liability may qualify for equitable relief. The IRS automatically considers whether equitable relief is appropriate if an application for another form of relief is received and declined. This type of relief may apply to both understatement of tax and to underpayment of tax. For example, if the taxpayer believed that his or her spouse paid the tax but the tax has in fact not been paid.

See IRS Publication 971, *Innocent Spouse Relief (and Separation of Liability and Equitable Relief)*, for more details.

Appeals of Collections

There are various collection appeal procedures available to taxpayers who have received a bill or notice of deficiency from the IRS. The two main procedures are the Collection Due Process (CDP) hearing and the Collection Appeals Program (CAP).

Installment Agreements

Installment agreements are used when a taxpayer cannot fully and immediately pay the amount due. The IRS will generally grant an installment agreement in cases where the liability can be paid within three years and in "small dollar" cases, defined now as "streamlined agreements." A $105 fee is charged by the IRS for setting up an installment agreement ($52 for those with a direct debit agreement; $43 for those below a certain income level). If a taxpayer has an installment agreement restructured or reinstated, the user fee is $45. An installment agreement reduces the late-payment penalty to 0.25% per month.

The IRS is authorized to enter into installment agreements with taxpayers that provide for partial payment of the tax liability (in contrast to prior law, which required an installment agreement to provide for payment in full of the tax liability). The IRS is required to review partial payment agreements every two years. If payment in full can be made within three years, however, and the taxpayer's liability is less than $10,000 (and if certain other conditions are met), the IRS can only accept an agreement providing for full payment, and the partial payment option is not available.

Offers in Compromise

Sometimes the IRS settles tax collection matters for less than the full amount of tax due. There are three potential grounds for an offer in compromise: doubt as to collectibility, doubt as to liability, and effective tax administration or special circumstances.

A taxpayer makes an offer using Form 656, *Offer in Compromise*, or, if the offer is based on doubt as to liability, Form 656-L *Offer in Compromise (Doubt as to Liability)*. A $150 application fee is required, but the fee may be waived for low-income taxpayers who file Form 656-A, *Income Certification for Offer in Compromise Application Fee*. If Form 656-L is filed, the fee may be waived. See Form 656-B, *Offer in Compromise Booklet*.

If an offer is accepted based on doubt as to collectibility, the IRS will determine the reasonable collection potential of a case (an amount less than the total debt owed), taking into account the taxpayer's basic living expenses. In addition, the agency may accept less than that amount if there are special circumstances. However, if a taxpayer's tax liability can be paid in full in a lump sum or through an installment agreement, the taxpayer will not be considered for an offer in compromise. The only exception is if the taxpayer can demonstrate special circumstances that would show the full payment of the liability would result in economic hardship or be detrimental to voluntary compliance.

In a case where the IRS accepts an offer based on the promotion of effective tax administration (that is, the IRS has decided that collecting the full amount owed would be possible, but would create economic hardship for the taxpayer or would be unfair or inequitable), the decision will be based on the taxpayer's individual circumstances. The structure of these agreements is based on the IRS's goal of collecting as much of the tax as possible in situations in which the taxpayer lacks the resources to meet the tax liability.

A taxpayer is required to make partial payments while an offer in compromise is being considered. If the offer is of a lump sum payment, then the taxpayer must make a nonrefundable downpayment of 20 percent of the amount of the offer. The relevant fee must also be submitted with the appropriate partial payment; that amount will be applied to the taxpayer's tax liability.

Bankruptcy and Taxes

A separate estate, for tax purposes, is created for an individual who files a petition under Chapter 7 or 11 of the Bankruptcy Code. A separate estate is not created under Chapter 12 or 13 of the Bankruptcy Code.

The individual taxpayer should continue to file the same federal income tax return, reporting all income received and deducting all allowable expenses. Debt canceled because of bankruptcy is not included in income, but may reduce certain losses and credits (to the extent that the taxpayer has them).

The estate is represented by a trustee appointed by the bankruptcy court to administer the estate and liquidate nonexempt assets. In Chapter 11, the debtor usually remains in control of the assets as a "debtor-in-possession."

A bankruptcy estate may produce its own income as well as incur its own expenses, and the trustee must file a tax return on Form 1041, *U.S. Income Tax Return for Estates and Trusts*, for the estate if its income is greater than the sum of the personal exemption amount and the basic standard deduction for a married individual filing separately. If a return is required, the trustee (or debtor-in-possession) completes the identification area at the top of the Form 1041 and lines 23-29 (the total tax amount on line 23 is taken from Form 1040), and signs and dates it. For bankruptcy estates, Form 1041 is used as a transmittal for Form 1040, *U.S. Individual Income Tax Return.* Complete Form 1040 and figure the tax using the tax rate schedule for a married person filing separately. In the top margin of Form 1040, write "Attachment to Form 1041. DO NOT DETACH." Attach Form 1040 to the Form 1041.

Payment Options Comparison Chart

	Total of All Liabilities	Time Frame for Full Payment	Other Basic Requirements	Financial Information	Verification of Financial Information
Guaranteed Installment Agreement (IA)*	Below $10,000	Within 36 months	Must stay current with all future taxes	Limited	No
Streamlined IA*	Below $25,000	Within 60 months	Must stay current with all future taxes	Limited	No
Full Pay IA < 60 months**	No limit	Up to 60 months	Leverage equity in assets Must stay current with all future taxes Conditional expenses may be allowed	Complete	Yes
Full Pay IA > 60 months**	No limit	61 months and up, prior to expiration of collection statute	Leverage equity in assets Must stay current with all future taxes Transition period for conditional expenses may be allowed for up to 12 months	Complete	Yes
Partial Pay IA	No limit	Payments made until collection statute expires	Leverage equity in assets Must stay current with all future taxes No conditional expenses allowed No transition period	Complete	Yes
Deferred Payment Offer in Compromise	No limit	Payments made until statute date or until accepted offer amount received	Net realizable equity must be accounted for in amount offered No conditional expenses allowed Must stay current with all future taxes	Complete	Yes

* 98 percent of all IA taxpayers fall into these first two categories** Length of installment agreement determined by the financial analysis

Advantages and Disadvantages of Tax Code and Bankruptcy Code Remedies as of 2009

Remedy	Advantages	Disadvantages
Statute of Limitation on Collection	• Discharge of the tax liability without payment and release of underlying liens.	• Difficulty of withstanding 10 years of collection activity. • Heightened collection activity prior to the statute's expiration. • The IRS may renew the taxpayer's liability with a court proceeding.
Installment Agreement	• Creation of breathing space free from examination by the IRS. • Possibility of full payment. • Possibility of hardship status when payment is not possible. • Partial payment in satisfaction of liability may be accepted by IRS.	• Impossibly strict budget. • Likelihood that a notice of tax lien will be filed.

Advantages and Disadvantages of Tax Code and Bankruptcy Code Remedies as of 2009 (Continued)		
Remedy	**Advantages**	**Disadvantages**
Offer in Compromise	• Discharge by the taxpayer of unsecured liabilities that are nondischargeable in bankruptcy. • Discharge of liabilities without payment in full. • Removal of the tax lien, which might otherwise remain attached to property after a Chapter 7 filing.	• Formulating an acceptable offer is incredibly difficult. • A taxpayer must find an outside source to fund/offer with cash equal to the proceeds that could be generated from a liquidation of the taxpayer's assets plus the net present value of a five-year installment agreement. • Taxpayer's tax refunds for all tax years up through and including the year in which the offer is accepted are taken by the IRS. • Filing of an offer stays the statute of limitation on collection, and the IRS receives an additional year (beyond the 10 it is already granted) to collect the tax if the offer is rejected, or if the offer is accepted and the taxpayer does not fulfill the obligation • Interest continues to accrue. • Installment payments are required while offer is being considered by the IRS.
Chapter 7 Bankruptcy	• Discharge of unsecured income tax liabilities, regardless of size, for which the statute of limitation on assessment for the underlying tax year has run and the liability was neither assessed within the last 240 days nor the subject of an offer in compromise. • Payments above asset liquidation value are not required. • Bankruptcy Code exemptions are larger than the Tax Code exemptions used by the IRS for computing an offer. The taxpayer's tax refund may be protected.	• Provides no relief for relatively fresh tax liabilities. • It provides no relief for the Code Sec. 6672 responsible person penalty, regardless of assessment date. • It provides no relief from secured tax debt. • Relief against unsecured debt is limited in scope. • No relief if taxpayer did not file his or her tax returns for the tax years in question. Also, the returns must have been filed more than two years before the filing of the bankruptcy.
Chapter 11 Bankruptcy	• Chapter 11 can be used when a taxpayer does not qualify for Chapter 13, cannot age Type 1 obligations into Type 3 obligations, and cannot pay priority taxes under terms and conditions available in an installment agreement.	• Chapter 11 is relatively uncommon for individuals. The Chapter 11 plan of reorganization is often more complicated, more expensive, and more time-consuming than Chapters 7 and 13. • All priority taxes must be paid.
Chapter 13 Bankruptcy	• Because of its $336,900 noncontingent, liquidated unsecured debt and $1,010,650 secure debt limitations, Chapter 13 works best to discharge moderate amounts of debt. Type 2 and Type 3 claims need only be paid out of disposable income for a three-year period. As compared with Chapter 7, this is an especially favorable treatment for the Type 2 claims. • Under current law old income tax liabilities (liabilities for tax periods over three years old) are dischargeable in Chapter 13 even if the taxpayer failed to file tax returns for one or more of the tax periods in question.	• Because a separate taxable entity is not created, the debtor retains tax attributes until the plan is completed and debt is discharged. Type 1 claims must be paid in full but without interest, at least during the life of the plan. Type 2 tax claims must be paid in full.
"Chapter 20" Bankruptcy	• "Chapter 20" is a Chapter 7 bankruptcy followed by a Chapter 13 (or vice versa); no Chapter 20 exists in the Bankruptcy Code. Chapter 20 works when the taxpayer has both large Type 3 claims that prevent the use of Chapter 13 and Type 1 claims that can be paid over the applicable three-year Chapter 13 period. The Type 3 claims are discharged in Chapter 7, the Type 2 claims are discharged in Chapter 13, and the Type 1 claims are paid in Chapter 13.	• In using Chapter 20, practitioners must be aware of case law increasing Bankruptcy Code time periods for determining priority and dischargeability by the time spent in the first bankruptcy. In addition, a court will scrutinize the second filing to ensure that the statutory good faith filing requirement is met. • Recent legislation requires a minimum of four years between Chapter 7 and Chapter 13 filings. This will reduce the likelihood that a Chapter 20 will be of any use to a taxpayer.

Employer Identification Number. The trustee (or debtor-in-possession) must obtain an employer identification number (EIN) for the bankruptcy estate if the estate must file any form, statement, or document with the IRS. The trustee uses this EIN on any tax return filed for the bankruptcy estate, including estimated tax returns. The trustee can obtain an EIN for a bankruptcy estate by filing Form SS-4, *Application for Employer Identification Number.*

Election to End Tax Year. Individuals who file a petition in bankruptcy court have the option of ending their tax year on the day before the bankruptcy petition is filed. This allows the tax due on that short-period return to be a claim against the bankruptcy estate. The election to end the tax year is made by filing Form 1040 for the short tax year on or before the fifteenth day of the fourth full month after the end of the short tax year. To avoid delays in processing the return, "Section 1398 Election" should be written at the top of the return. The taxpayer may also make the election by attaching a statement to an application for extension of time to file a tax return (Form 4868 or other) by the due date of the return for the short tax year ending on the day before the filing date of the bankruptcy. A debtor's spouse may also choose to elect the same short tax year, but only if the spouses file a joint return.

Tax Assessment during Bankruptcy

Generally, the automatic stay rules prevent a creditor (including the IRS) from taking actions to collect prepetition debts. However, the automatic stay does not apply to:

- An audit to determine tax liability.
- A demand for tax returns.
- The issuance of a notice of deficiency to the debtor.
- The making of an assessment for any tax and the sending of a notice and demand for payment of the tax assessed.

Under the Bankruptcy Abuse Prevention and Consumer Protection Act of 2005, postpetition actions are never barred by the automatic stay in a bankruptcy proceeding. The bankruptcy court may now determine not only postpetition tax liabilities, but also which taxable periods will be subject to the automatic stay.

In bankruptcy, debts are assigned priorities for payment. Most unsecured tax debts existing before the bankruptcy case was filed are classified as eighth-priority claims, including:

- Income taxes for tax years ending on or before the date of filing the bankruptcy petition, for which a return is due (including extensions) within three years of the filing date.
- Income taxes assessed within 240 days before the date of filing the petition. This 240-day period is increased by any time during which an offer in compromise that was made within 240 days after the assessment was pending, plus 30 days.
- Income taxes that were assessable but not assessed before the petition date, unless these taxes were still assessable solely because no return, a late return (within two years of the filing of the bankruptcy petition), or a fraudulent return was filed.
- Withholding taxes for which the debtor is liable in any capacity.
- Employer's share of employment taxes on wages, salaries, or commissions (including vacation, severance, and sick leave pay) paid as priority claims or for which a return is due within three years of the filing of the bankruptcy petition, including a return for which an extension of the filing date was obtained.
- Excise taxes on transactions occurring before the date of filing the bankruptcy petition, for which a return, if required, is due (including extensions) within three years of the filing of the bankruptcy petition. If a return is not required, these excise taxes include only those on transactions occurring during the three years immediately before the date of filing the petition.

Different rules apply to payment of eighth-priority prepetition taxes under Chapters 11, 12, and 13:

- Under Chapter 11, the debtor can pay these taxes over a period of six years from the date of assessment, including interest.
- Under Chapter 12, the debtor can pay such tax claims in deferred cash payments over time.
- Under Chapter 13, the debtor can pay such taxes over three years (or over five years with court approval).

Dismissal of Bankruptcy Case. If an individual's bankruptcy case began but was later dismissed by the bankruptcy court, the estate is not treated as a separate entity, and the taxpayer is treated as if the bankruptcy petition had never been filed in the first place. The taxpayer must file amended returns on Form 1040X to replace any returns previously filed. Include on any amended returns items of income, deductions, or credits that were or would have been reported by the bankruptcy estate on its returns. Administrative expenses the former estate could have claimed may be deductible. Also, the bankruptcy exclusion cannot be used to exclude debt that was canceled while the individual was under the bankruptcy court's protection. The other exclusions (such as insolvency) may apply.

Return Preparer Requirements

E-Filing Requirements

More and more preparers are choosing to, or are being required to, file their returns electronically. Preparers seeking to become authorized e-filers should review IRS Publication 3112, IRS e-file Application and Participation, and can file the e-file application electronically from the IRS website. Authorized e-filers can electronically transmit tax returns according to the procedures outlined in IRS Publication 1345, Handbook for Authorized IRS e-File Providers of Individual Income Tax Returns. Also useful is IRS Publication 1345A, Filing Season Supplement for Authorized IRS e-file Providers.

Enrolled Agents

The Director, Office of Professional Responsibility, issues an enrollment card to each individual whose application for enrollment to practice before the Internal Revenue Service is approved after July 26, 2002. To maintain active enrollment to practice before the Internal Revenue Service, each individual enrolled is required to renew his or her enrollment every three years.

Special Enrollment Examination. An individual may become an enrolled agent by getting a passing score on each part of the Special Enrollment Examination. The individual must then apply for enrollment and undergo a background check by the IRS. A new computer-based version of the Special Enrollment Examination (SEE) is now available. The new examination will be developed and administered by a nationwide private testing firm, Thomson Prometric. The examination will comprise three parts, Individuals, Businesses, and Representation, Practice, and Procedures. Each part will contain approximately 100 questions. The first testing window began in October, 2006.

Renewal of Enrollment. Forms required for renewal may be obtained from the Director, Office of Professional Responsibility, Internal Revenue Service, 1111 Constitution Avenue, NW, Washington, DC 20224. The three-year enrollment cycle applies to enrolled agents according to the last digit of his or her SSN or TIN:

- All enrolled individuals whose SSN or TIN ends with the number 0, 1, 2, or 3 must apply for renewal between November 1, 2009, and January 31, 2010. The renewal will be effective April 1, 2010.
- All enrolled individuals whose SSN or TIN ends with the number 4, 5, or 6 must apply for renewal between November 1, 2010, and January 31, 2011. The renewal will be effective April 1, 2011.
- All enrolled individuals whose SSN or TIN ends with the number 7, 8, or 9 must apply for renewal between November 1, 2011, and January 31, 2012. The renewal will be effective April 1, 2012.

Applications for renewal will be required between November 1 and January 31 of every subsequent third year according to the last number of the individual's SSN or TIN. Those individuals who receive initial enrollment after November 1 and before April 2 of the applicable renewal period will not be required to renew their enrollment before the first full renewal period following the receipt of their initial enrollment. The fee for renewal of enrollment is $125 (for actuaries, $250).

Computerized Return Preparation Services

A person who furnishes services consisting of typing, reproducing, or other mechanical assistance is not considered to be an income tax return preparer. However, persons or firms that furnish computerized tax return preparation services to tax practitioners are deemed to be return preparers, if the programs go beyond mere mechanical assistance.

Example: A program that calculates the amount of applicable depreciation deductions goes beyond mechanical assistance, and the person or firm offering this service is a return preparer.

Continuing Professional Education

To qualify for renewal of enrollment, an individual enrolled to practice before the IRS must certify on the application for renewal form that he or she has satisfied the continuing professional education (CPE) requirements. For renewed enrollment effective after April 1, 2007, the following CPE requirements must be met:

- A minimum of 72 hours of continuing education credit during each three-year renewal period (enrollment cycle).
- A minimum of 16 hours of continuing education credit, including 2 hours of ethics or professional conduct, in each year of an enrollment cycle.
- An individual who receives initial enrollment during an enrollment cycle must complete two (2) hours of qualifying continuing education credit for each month enrolled during the enrollment cycle. Enrollment for any part of a month is considered enrollment for the entire month.

Qualifying Programs. To qualify for CPE credit, a course of learning must be a qualifying program designed to enhance professional knowledge in federal taxation or federal tax-related matters and be conducted by a qualifying sponsor. A list of qualifying sponsors is published by the Director, Office of Professional Responsibility, on a regular basis.

Qualifying programs are formal, correspondence, or individual study programs that meet the criteria outlined in Circular 230. Generally, the programs must qualify in three areas:

- Registration or attendance must be required. Formal program sponsors must provide each attendee with a certificate of attendance. Other programs must provide a means of measuring completion by participants.
- Formal programs must be conducted by a qualified instructor, discussion leader, or speaker.
- Programs must provide or require a written outline, textbook, or suitable electronic educational materials.

Continuing education coursework is measured in contact hours. One contact hour is 50 minutes of continuous participation in a program. Credit is granted only for a full contact hour, i.e., 50 minutes or multiples thereof. For example, a program lasting more than 50 minutes but less than 100 minutes counts as one contact hour. No programs lasting less than 50 minutes earn CPE credit. Individual segments at continuous conferences, conventions, etc. will be considered one total program.

For university or college courses, each semester hour credit equals 15 contact hours and a quarter-hour credit equals 10 contact hours.

CPE Credit for Instructors. An instructor, discussion leader, or speaker will be awarded up to three hours of CPE credit (up to two for subject preparation and one for the course itself) for every contact hour completed as an instructor, discussion leader, or speaker at qualifying programs. It is the responsibility of the individual claiming such credit to maintain records to verify preparation time. The maximum credit for instruction and preparation may not exceed 50% of the continuing education requirement for an enrollment cycle. In addition, an instructor, discussion leader, or speaker who makes more than one presentation on the same subject matter during an enrollment cycle, will receive continuing education credit for only one such presentation for the enrollment cycle.

CPE Credit for Publication. Continuing education credit will be awarded for published books, articles, etc. on federal taxation or tax-related matters, provided the content of such publications is current and designed for the enhancement of the professional knowledge of an individual enrolled to practice before the IRS. One hour of credit will be allowed for each hour of preparation time for the material. It is the responsibility of the person claiming the credit to maintain records to verify preparation time. The maximum credit for publications may not exceed 25% of the continuing education requirement of any enrollment cycle.

Recordkeeping Requirements. Each individual applying for renewal must retain records supporting qualifying CPE credits for a period of three years following the date of renewal of enrollment.

CPE Waivers. Waiver of the CPE requirements for a given period may be granted by the Director, Office of Professional Responsibility, for health reasons; for extended active military duty; for extended absence from the United States due to employment or other reasons, provided the individual does not practice before the IRS during such absence; and for other compelling reasons, considered on a case-by-case basis.

Individuals placed in inactive enrollment status and individuals ineligible to practice before the Internal Revenue Service may not state or imply that they are enrolled to practice before the Internal Revenue Service, or use the term "enrolled agent," the designation "E. A.," or other form of reference to eligibility to practice before the Internal Revenue Service. An individual placed in an inactive status may be reinstated to an active enrollment status by filing an application for renewal of enrollment and providing evidence of the completion of all required continuing professional education hours for the enrollment cycle.

Contingent Fees

A contingent fee is any fee that is based, in whole or in part, on whether or not a position taken on a tax return or other filing avoids challenge by the IRS or is sustained either by the IRS or in litigation. A contingent fee includes any fee arrangement in which the practitioner will reimburse the client for all or a portion of the client's fee in the event that a position taken on a tax return or other filing is challenged by the IRS or is not sustained, whether pursuant to an indemnity agreement, a guarantee, rescission rights, or any other arrangement with a similar effect.

In general, a practitioner may not charge a contingent fee for services rendered in connection with any matter before the IRS. This prohibition encompasses the preparation or filing of an original return, or an amended return, as well as a claim for credit or refund. However, a practitioner is permitted to charge a contingent fee for services rendered in connection with any of the following:

- An IRS challenge to, or audit of, an original return;
- An IRS challenge to, or audit of, an amended return, or a claim for refund or credit, if the amended return or claim is filed within 120 days of the examination notice (or if filed before the notice is given; written notice from the IRS is not a prerequisite to charging a contingent fee);
- A credit or refund claim filed solely to determine statutory interest or penalties assessed by the IRS;

- A whistleblower claim; or
- Any judicial proceeding arising under the Code.

Caution. Practitioners who prepare tax returns to generate fees rather than informing the taxpayer that no return is required, such as by emphasizing the fact that a return may be filed even if not required, are subject to particular scrutiny.

Reasonable Belief Standard and Reliance on Information from Clients

A practitioner may not sign a tax return as a preparer if the return contains an understatement of liability due to a position, the preparer lacks a reasonable belief that the position would more likely than not be sustained on its merits, and the position was either not disclosed or had no reasonable basis. However, the practitioner will not be penalized if there was reasonable cause for the understatement and the practitioner acted in good faith.

A practitioner advising a client to take a position on a tax return, or preparing or signing a tax return as a preparer, must inform the client of the penalties reasonably likely to apply to the client with respect to the position advised, prepared, or reported. The practitioner must inform the client of any opportunity to avoid any such penalty by disclosure, if relevant, and of the requirements for adequate disclosure.

A practitioner generally may rely in good faith, without verification, on information furnished by the client. The practitioner may not, however, ignore the implications of information furnished to, or actually known by, the practitioner, and must make reasonable inquiries if the information appears to be incorrect, inconsistent with an important fact or another factual assumption, or incomplete.

Conflicts of Interest

A practitioner must be aware of possible conflicts of interest with respect to a particular taxpayer. A conflict exists if representation of one client of the practitioner's would be adverse to another client of the practitioner's. A conflict may exist if there is a significant risk that the representation of a client will be materially limited by the practitioner's responsibilities to another client, a former client, or a third party, or by a personal interest of the practitioner. However, the practitioner may represent a client despite a conflict if the practitioner believes he or she will be able to provide competent representation to each affected client, the representation is not otherwise prohibited, and if each affected client gives informed, written consent. Examples of such situations include spouses on a joint return; former spouses, parent, and child on 1040s; trustee and beneficiaries on 1041s; limited and general partners on 1065s; and parent and child on gift tax returns.

Appeals Within the IRS

If a client disagrees with a proposed adjustment by an IRS tax examiner, a tax practitioner has several options. The most commonly used is to make a verbal or written appeal to the appropriate IRS Appeals Office. Alternatively, the taxpayer may skip over the IRS appeals process and proceed directly to Tax Court or, after payment in full of the deficiency, District or Claims Court. Similarly, if the IRS Appeals Office and the taxpayer cannot come to an agreement, the taxpayer may then proceed to court.

After an examination, if the return is accepted as filed, the taxpayer receives a "no change" letter. If the examiner proposes an adjustment, the taxpayer is informed by being sent a copy of the examination report, a transmittal letter (the "30-day letter"), information on appeal rights and procedures, and the appropriate waiver form for the taxpayer to sign if he or she agrees with the proposed adjustment. The most common form is Form 870, *Waiver of Restrictions on Assessment and Collection of Deficiency in Tax and Acceptance of Overassessment,* and its variations (870-E, 870-AD, etc.).

Written Request for Appeal and Protest. If the taxpayer disagrees with the examiner's findings, the taxpayer can respond with a request that the Appeals Office review the findings of the examiner. This requires a written request and a written protest, except in the cases of an office or correspondence examination, or a field examination where the amount of additional tax is $2,500 or less for a taxable period. The protest must contain:

- The name, address, and telephone number of the taxpayer;
- A statement that the taxpayer wants to appeal the conclusions of the IRS examiner to the Appeals Office;
- A copy of the letter showing the proposed changes and findings with which the taxpayer disagrees;
- The years or tax periods involved;
- A list of the changes with which the taxpayer disagrees, and the reasons for disagreement;
- The facts supporting the taxpayer's position on any issue with which the taxpayer disagrees;
- The law or authority on which the taxpayer intends to rely; and
- The taxpayer's signature, which must be under penalty of perjury.

The taxpayer must swear to the statement of facts under penalties of perjury. If the protest is prepared or filed by an attorney or agent, a substitute declaration may be used. The attorney or agent must state under penalty of perjury that he or she prepared the protest and knows of his or her own knowledge that the information contained in the protest is true.

Appeals Conference. The conference with the Appeals Office is held in an informal manner, by correspondence or telephone, or at a personal conference. The taxpayer is not required to have representation, but may choose to do so. He or she may be represented by an attorney, a CPA, an enrolled agent, or an enrolled actuary. The representative must be qualified to practice before the IRS. In general, the same confidentiality protection an individual has with an attorney is also applicable to communications between a taxpayer and a federally authorized practitioner.

Planning Tip. A taxpayer can be represented by an attorney or agent at the Appeals conference. It may, in fact, be appropriate for the taxpayer not to attend with the representative, depending on the circumstances of the case and the temperment of the taxpayer. In some cases, the taxpayer's memory of relevant events will make his or her presence necessary. On the other hand, if the taxpayer is nervous, excessively timid or emotional, or too self-conscious, the attorney or agent might prefer to attend the conference alone. Similarly, a belligerent attitude on the part of the taxpayer might antagonize the IRS representative. This choice should be left to the judgment of the attorney or agent.

If the taxpayer is not going to attend the conference with the representative, the taxpayer must execute a power of attorney and provide it to the IRS before the representative can receive or inspect confidential information. The taxpayer may bring documents or witnesses supporting the taxpayer's position to the conference with the Appeals Office.

At the conference, the taxpayer and/or representative should be prepared to discuss all disputed issues. The Appeals officer will be prepared to be flexible, and both the taxpayer (or representative) and the officer will likely concede some issues to advance their position as to other issues. Most differences are settled at this stage. The reasons for disagreement must come within the scope of the tax law (that is, the so-called "tax protester" arguments, based on previously rejected constitutional, religious, moral, political, or philosophical claims, will not be considered by the IRS at any point, including at an Appeals conference).

Appeals Mediation. Some issues being considered by the IRS Appeals Office may be resolved through mediation. This option is generally available only after settlement discussions have failed and, in most cases, when all issues other than that for which mediation is requested have been resolved. Mediation is available for legal issues, factual issues, Compliance or Appeals Coordinated Issues, early referral issues where an agreement has not been reached, issues for which a request for competent authority assistance has not yet been filed, unsuccessful attempts to enter into a closing agreement under Code Sec. 7121, and certain offer-in-compromise and trust fund recovery penalty cases. Mediation is not available for cases where mediation is inappropriate, issues designated for litigation, issues docketed in a court, most collection cases (the offer-in-compromise and trust fund recovery cases are exceptions), issues governed by closing agreements or judicial decisions, frivolous issues, "whipsaw" issues, cases where the taxpayer has not acted in good faith during settlement negotiations, or issues expressly excluded from mediation by the IRS.

Mediation is optional, and may be requested by the Appeals Office or the taxpayer. If the request to mediate is approved, the parties must enter into a written agreement to mediate. The taxpayer must also consent to disclosure of tax return information to the mediator. The mediator is an employee of the Appeals Office trained as a mediator. The IRS will pay all costs associated with the mediation process, although the taxpayer may, at his or her own expense, choose to use a co-mediator who is not an IRS employee.

What's New in 2009

Qualifying Child Definition Modified. The definition of a qualifying child is modified as follows; the child must be younger than the taxpayer claiming the child, the tiebreaker rules must be applied if two or more taxpayers can claim a qualifying child, and a qualifying child for child tax credit purposes must be the taxpayer's dependent.

Refundable Portion of Child Tax Credit Increased. Taxpayers with qualifying children are eligible for a refundable child tax credit equal to 15 percent of their earned income in excess of $3,000, up to the per child amount, if their allowable child tax credit exceeds their total tax liability (regular and alternative minimum tax).

Hope Scholarship Credit Modified. The modified Hope educational tax credit, referred to as the American Opportunity Tax Credit, is increased to a maximum of $2,500 per eligible student; qualifying expenses include text books and course materials; the credit is available for up to four years per eligible student; the income phaseout range is expanded; and up to 40 percent of the credit amount may be refundable.

Earned Income Tax Credit Amounts Increased. The maximum earned income tax credit amounts for 2009 are for taxpayers: with three or more children, $5,657; with two qualifying children, $5,028; with one qualifying child, $3,043; and with no children, $457.

Phaseout Thresholds for Earned Income Tax Credit Increased. The earned income tax credit phaseout threshold amount for single, head of household and surviving spouse filers begins at $16,420 for taxpayers with one or more children and $7,470 for taxpayer with no children. The phaseout is complete at $43,281 for taxpayers with three or more children, $40,295 with two children, $35,463 with one child and $13,440 with no children. For joint filers, the phaseout begins at $21,420 with one or more children and $12,470 with no children, The earned income credit completely phases out at $48,279 with three or more children,$43,415 with two children, $38,583 with only one qualifying child, and with no qualifying children at $18,440.

Section at a Glance

Relevant IRS Publications

- ☐ IRS Publication 501, *Exemptions, Standard Deduction, and Filing Information*
- ☐ IRS Publication 503, *Child and Dependent Care Expenses*
- ☐ IRS Publication 504, *Divorced or Separated Individuals*
- ☐ IRS Publication 929, *Tax Rules for Children and Dependents*
- ☐ IRS Publication 970, *Tax Benefits for Education*
- ☐ IRS Publication 972, *Child Tax Credit*

Tax Preparer's Checklist

- ☐ Date of birth, Social Security number, and accurate spelling of last name as it appears in Social Security records of all dependents.
- ☐ All Forms W-2, 1098, and 1099 applicable to dependents.
- ☐ Form 1098-T, Tuition Statement, from school for students.
- ☐ Tuition, books, fees, and scholarship and fellowship documentation.
- ☐ Verify whether the dependent has already filed and, if so, whether they claimed a personal exemption.

Limits and Phaseout Ranges for Certain Education Tax Benefits

Benefit	Tuition and Fees Deduction	Student Loan Interest Deduction	American Opportunity (Modified Hope Credit)**	Lifetime Learning Credit
Limit	$4,000*	$2,500	$2,500 per student	$2,000 per family
Phaseout	$65,000 ($130,000 for MFJ)	$60,000-$75,000 ($120,000-$150,000 for MFJ)	$80,000 ($160,00 for MFJ)	$50,000 ($100,000 for MFJ)

* The deduction is limited to $2,000 for taxpayers with adjusted gross income exceeding $65,000 ($130,000 if filing jointly) but less than $80,000 ($160,000 if filing jointly).
** Available only during tax years beginning in 2009 and 2010.

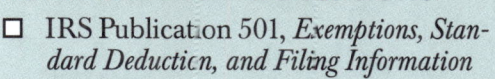

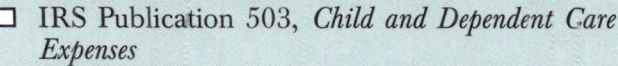

Children and Taxes

Taxpayers with children may enjoy tax advantages in many areas:

- **Filing status.** Taxpayers considered unmarried may be able to file as Head of Household if they have a qualifying child. See Tab 1.
- **Exemption for dependents.** If the child qualifies as a dependent, the taxpayer may be able to claim the dependency exemption. See Tab 1.
- **Other deductions.** Medical expenses, tuition and fee expenses, student loan interest, and child care expenses may all be deductible. See Tabs 1 and 2 for more information about deductions. Education deductions are discussed beginning on page 13-15.
- **Credits.** The child tax credit and additional child tax credit, child and dependent care expense credit, earned income credit, adoption credit and educational credits may be available. These tax credits are discussed later in this Tab, and are also covered in Tab 10.
- **Exceptions to additional tax for IRA early distribution.** The 10% additional tax for early withdrawals from an individual retirement account (IRA) does not apply if the funds are used to pay the higher education expenses of a child and/or the health insurance premiums for an unemployed taxpayer's dependents.

Caution. The exception to the early distribution penalty only applies to IRAs, not to other types of qualified deferred plans or retirement accounts. Although the Tax Court sympathized with the taxpayer who received incorrect advice from the IRS, they noted that the law clearly states only withdrawals from IRAs may be exempted from the penalty.

Who Qualifies as a Dependent?

A child is the taxpayer's dependent if he or she meets either the requirements for a qualifying child or for a qualifying relative (see Tab 1). The major difference is that a qualifying child must have a closer relationship to the taxpayer than a qualifying relative.

Planning Tip. The IRS in Notice 2008-5 clarified their position on the claiming of a dependent child that is a qualifying child for one taxpayer and a qualifying relative of another. Essentially, the IRS adopted the position they had taken prior to the passage of the Working Families Tax Relief Act of 2004 (P.L. 108-311). Thus, an unrelated child may be claimed as a qualifying relative dependent by a taxpayer provided that the taxpayer for whom the child would be a qualifying child dependent does not file a return or only files a return to obtain a refund.

A child born at any time during a tax year is considered a dependent for the entire tax year. If a child dies shortly after birth, the full exemption amount is taken. The question of what constitutes a child's being born alive depends on state or local law. To claim a dependency exemption for a child who was born and died during the same tax year, the taxpayer should have a birth certificate or other official documentation to show that the child was born alive (see Tab 1).

If a dependent dies during the tax year, a full dependency exemption is allowed. The exemption amount is not prorated.

Persons who could be claimed as dependents by other taxpayers cannot also claim personal exemptions for themselves if they file their own returns.

Taxpayers generally cannot claim an exemption for a dependent who files a joint return with a spouse, unless the joint return is filed merely as a claim for a refund and neither spouse would have had a tax liability if they were to file separately.

Caution. Once an individual has been classified as a dependent, other tax consequences follow. Filing requirements differ, and some credits and deductions are not available to dependent individuals who file their own returns.

Each claimed dependent, including those born during the current tax year, must have a taxpayer identification number (TIN) or Social Security number. Resident and nonresident alien dependents who do not qualify for a Social Security number must have an individual taxpayer identification number (ITIN).

Filing Tip. To obtain a Social Security number, file Form SS-5. For an ITIN, file Form W-7.

Filing Tip. Be sure to always enter the name on the return exactly as it appears on the Social Security card. A mismatch will prevent electronic filing and delay any refund.

Caution. Failure to provide the taxpayer identification number will be treated as a mathematical error. The IRS will recalculate the tax liability as if no exemption had been claimed, and may change the filing status or eliminate any deductions or credits related to the claimed exemption. This may reduce any refund amount or create a larger tax liability.

Adopted Children. An adopted child is always treated as the taxpayer's own child, even if the adoption is not final, provided the child has been placed for adoption with the taxpayer by a qualified adoption agency.

Filing Tip. To claim a child during the adoption process before the Social Security number is issued, the taxpayer will need to obtain an adoption taxpayer identification number (ATIN) by filing Form W-7A.

Students. A dependency exemption is allowed for a taxpayer's child who is a full-time student if they are under the age of 24, do not file a joint return with their spouse and, regardless of the child's gross income, their earned income does not exceed more than half of their own support. A full-time student is a student enrolled for at least the minimum number of hours or credits determined by the school to be considered in full-time attendance for some part of at least five months during the calendar year. The school must have:

- a regular teaching staff,
- an established curriculum, and
- a regularly enrolled body of students.

A school may be:

- an elementary school,
- a junior or senior high school,
- a college or university, or
- a technical, trade, or mechanical school.

On-the-job training courses, correspondence schools, online institutions and night schools do not qualify. However, individuals taking full-time on-farm training through an educational institution qualify as students. Vocational high school students who work on jobs in private industry as part of their education are considered to be full-time students.

Planning Tip. Parents and college students should discuss in advance how to properly coordinate the filing of their income tax returns to avoid errors or confusion and minimize the family total tax liability. Many college students often file their income tax returns before their parents do and mistakenly believe they are entitled to claim a personal exemption which entitles them to a refund. When the parents, who are legally entitled to claim the child as a dependent, later file and claim the student as a dependent, they learn that the student's/child's SSN has already been claimed resulting in an unexpected increase in their tax liability.

Gray Area. Medical students, interns, and residents at hospitals are not considered students. However, an individual enrolled at a nursing school was considered to be a student even though part of the training included doing nursing work in a hospital.

Kidnapped Children. A kidnapped child under age 18 can be a qualifying child if the dependency tests and the qualifying child tests are met for the portion of the calendar year preceding the date of the kidnapping and the child is presumed by law enforcement officials to have been kidnapped by someone who is not a family member of the child or the taxpayer. The child is no longer a qualifying person in the calendar year in which the child is determined to be deceased or after the child would have turned 18.

Children of Divorced or Separated Parents. Generally, as long as at least half of a child's support is provided by one or both parents, the parent who has custody of a child is entitled to the exemption. The exemption, however, may be relinquished by the custodial parent to the noncustodial parent. A child may be treated as the qualifying child of the noncustodial parent only if:

- the couple is divorced, legally separated, separated under a written separation agreement, or lived apart at all times during the last six months of the calendar year;
- one spouse (or both combined) provides more than half of the child's total support for the calendar year (determined without regard to any multiple support agreement);
- one spouse (or both combined) has custody of the child for more than half of the calendar year; and

- the custodial parent makes a written declaration that he or she will not claim the exemption and the noncustodial parent attaches the declaration to his or her tax return for each year the exemption is claimed.

Filing Tip. A signed Form 8332, *Release of Claim to Exemption for Child of Divorced or Separated Parents*, must be used by for this purpose. A divorce or separate maintenance agreement has no effect on allocating a dependency exemption.

Can a Child's Income Be Included on a Parent's Return?

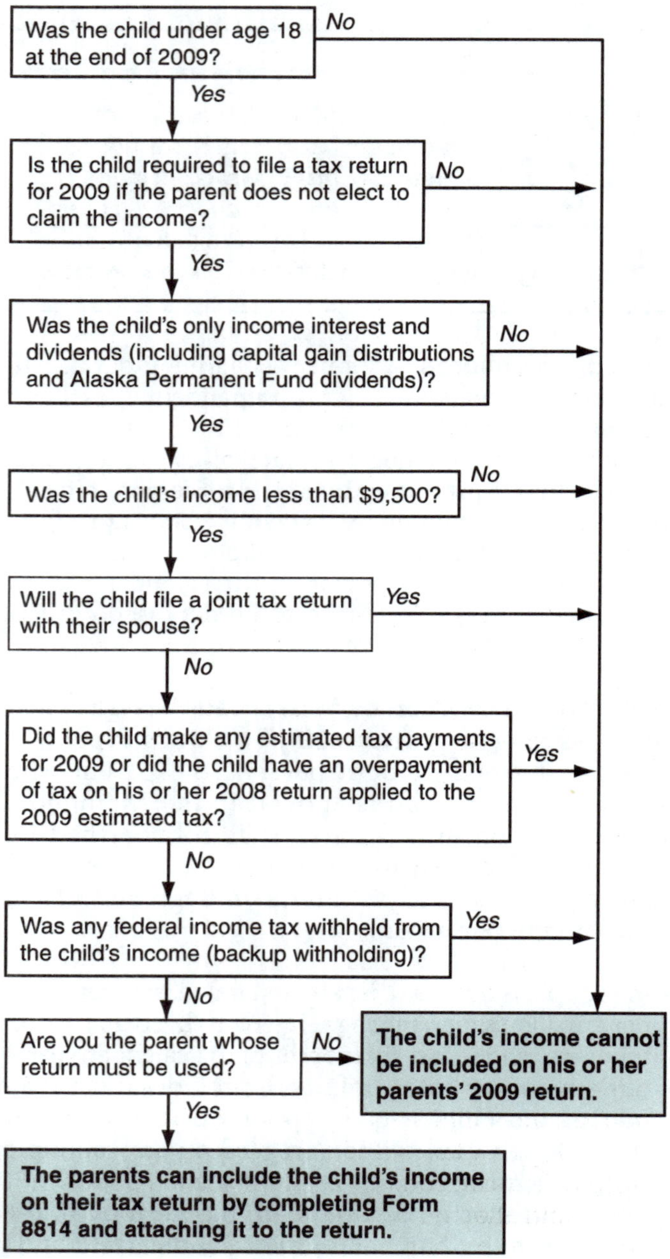

Was the child under age 18 at the end of 2009?
No
Yes
Is the child required to file a tax return for 2009 if the parent does not elect to claim the income?
No
Yes
Was the child's only income interest and dividends (including capital gain distributions and Alaska Permanent Fund dividends)?
No
Yes
Was the child's income less than $9,500?
No
Yes
Will the child file a joint tax return with their spouse?
Yes
No
Did the child make any estimated tax payments for 2009 or did the child have an overpayment of tax on his or her 2008 return applied to the 2009 estimated tax?
Yes
No
Was any federal income tax withheld from the child's income (backup withholding)?
Yes
No
Are you the parent whose return must be used?
No
The child's income cannot be included on his or her parents' 2009 return.
Yes
The parents can include the child's income on their tax return by completing Form 8814 and attaching it to the return.

Taxation of a Child's Income

Most children are considered qualifying children for purposes of being claimed as dependents. See Tab 1 for filing requirements for dependents. If any federal income tax was withheld from a child's wages, the child should file a return to claim a refund of the withheld taxes even if they are not required to file a return.

If a child cannot sign his or her return, a parent or guardian can sign it in the space provided, followed by "By (signature), parent (or guardian) of minor child."

Caution. A child with income, who qualifies as a dependent on the parents' tax return, cannot claim a personal exemption on his or her own tax return. The exemption can only be claimed by the parents, even if they choose not to claim it.

Special rules govern taxation on income of children under age 19 or students under age 24 who have more than $1,900 in unearned income. See "**Special Rules for Children Under 19 or Students Under 24**" following.

Earned and Unearned Income. To determine whether a dependent must file a return, the amount of earned and unearned income must be known.

Earned income is money received as pay for work that was done, as well as certain scholarships, fellowships, and grants. It includes:

- Salaries and wages, including wages received as a household employee,
- Tips,
- Professional fees, and
- Taxable scholarships and fellowship grants (see **"Education Tax Benefits,"** following).

For federal tax purposes, the income a child receives for his or her labor is considered his or her own, even if state law says it belongs to the parent. If a minor child does not pay tax on the income, the parent is liable.

Unearned income is income from investments, trusts and other payments that are not compensation for services. It includes:

- Interest,
- Dividends,
- Capital gains,
- Distributions from a trust, and
- Taxable Social Security payments.

Example. Robert and Ellen O'Connor maintain several investments for their eight-year-old son Joseph. Joseph did not have any earned income in 2009 but he did have taxable interest income of $2,000, tax-exempt interest of $35, and taxable dividend income of $2,500. Instead of filing a separate return for Joseph, Robert and Ellen, after determining the effect on their adjusted gross income dependent calculations, elect to report his income on their own joint return by attaching a completed Form 8814.

The first $950 of a child's unearned income is not taxable (this is equal to the standard deduction for dependents). The next $950 is taxed at the child's tax rate, and the amount greater than $1,900 is taxed at the parents' marginal tax rate. This is commonly known as the "kiddie tax." Kiddie tax is computed by adding the child's investment income to the income of the parents, so it is possible that the child's income will be taxed at a higher rate than the parents' income.

For purposes of imposing the "kiddie tax" on a child's unearned income of less than $9,500, the child must be:

- under the age of 18;
- under the age of 19 and whose earned income does not exceed one half of their own support; or
- under the age of 24, a full-time student, and whose earned income does not exceed one half of their own support.

See MTG ¶114 and ¶706.

Filing Tip. A child who is the beneficiary of a disability trust can treat the distributions as earned income. This income will not be subject to the "kiddie tax" rules.

Filing Tip. An account in a child's name and SSN, such as one set up under the Uniform Gifts to Minors Act, may be held by someone other than the child's parents, frequently a grandparent. Parents and tax preparers must ensure that all Forms 1099-DIV are received and included when calculating the child's tax liability.

Special Rules for Children Under 19 or Full-Time Students Under 24.
If a child is required to file a return, parents may elect to report the child's income on their return if all of the following apply to their child:

1. The child is under age 19 at the end of 2009, or a full-time student under age 24.
2. The child has income only from interest and dividends (including Alaska Permanent Fund dividends and capital gain distributions).
3. The child's gross income is less than $9,500.
4. The child has no federal income tax withheld and did not make estimated tax payments for 2009.
5. The child does not file a joint tax return for the year.

Who Declares Income (Child or Parents)? Generally, a child under age 18, or a child under 19 or a full-time student under age 24 whose earned income does not exceed one half of their support must declare investment income of more than $1,900 by filing Form 8615, *Tax for Certain Children Who Have Investment Income of More Than $1,900.*

Filing Tip. The minor child will need to file their own return if the unearned income amount is $9,500 or greater.

However, taxpayers may elect to be taxed on their children's unearned income, if the child's income only comes from interest and dividends and is less than $9,500. These taxpayers will use Form 8814, *Parents' Election to Report Child's Interest and Dividends,* to determine the additional amount of tax to be added to the taxpayer's Form 1040 tax liability. If this election is made, then the child will not have to file a return or Form 8615. The amount on Form 8814 must be entered in the space provided on line 44 of Form 1040.

If a married couple decides to file separate returns and wishes to include the unearned income of a child, only the parent with the higher taxable income can make the election. Thus, the child's tax liability will be determined using the parent with the higher taxable income.

Example. Aaron and Julia are married and will file separate tax returns for 2009. Their only child, Roxanne, is five years old. Roxanne received a Form 1099-INT showing $4,700 taxable interest income. Her parents decide to include that income on one of their returns so they will not have to file a return for Roxanne.

First, Aaron and Julia each figure their taxable income without regard to Roxanne's income. Aaron's taxable income is $141,200 and Julia's is $259,300. Because Julia's taxable income is greater, Roxanne's income is included on her return. She fills out Form 8814 and attaches it to her return.

Who Is a Qualifying Person for the Child and Dependent Care Credit?

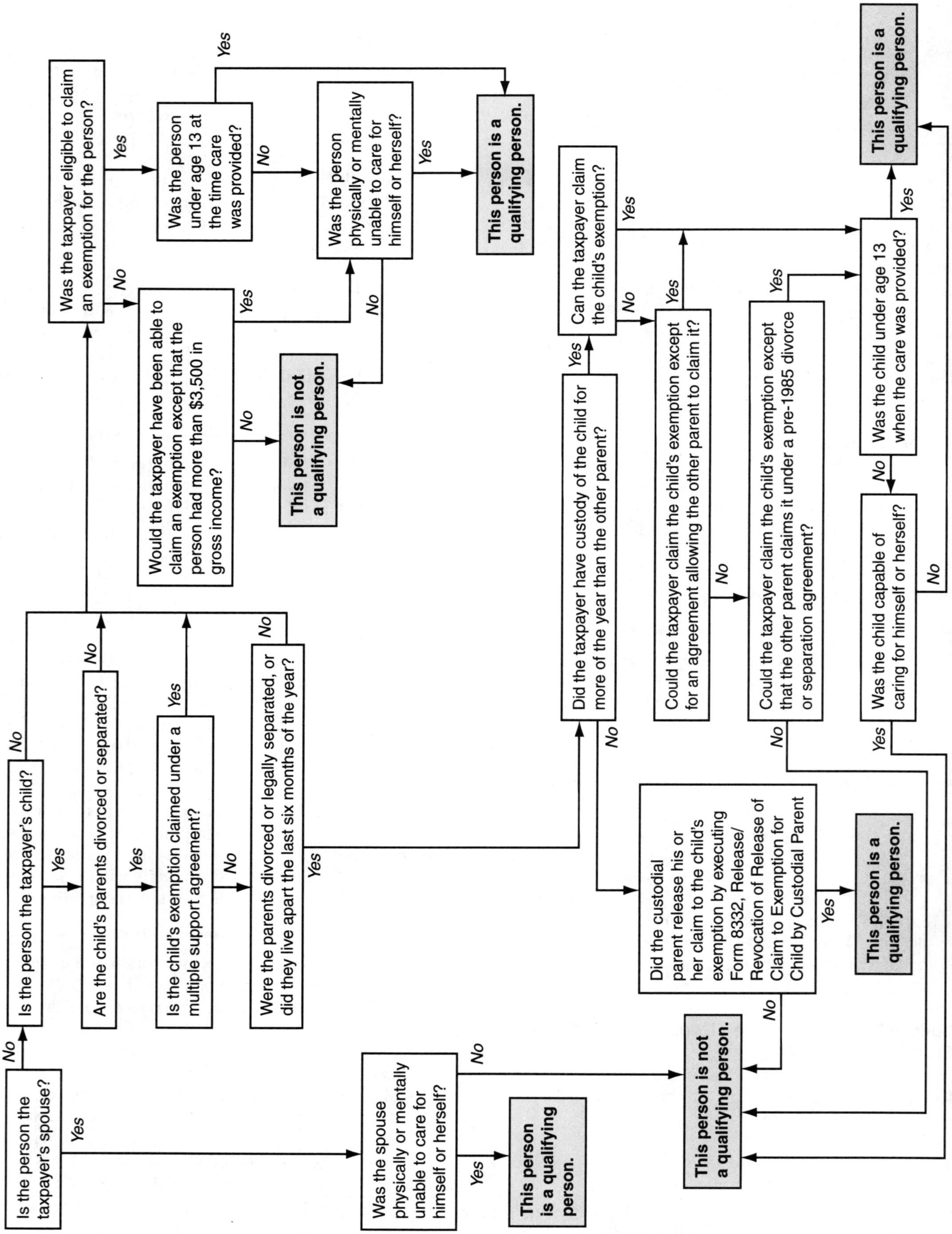

Can a Taxpayer Claim the Child and Dependent Care Credit?

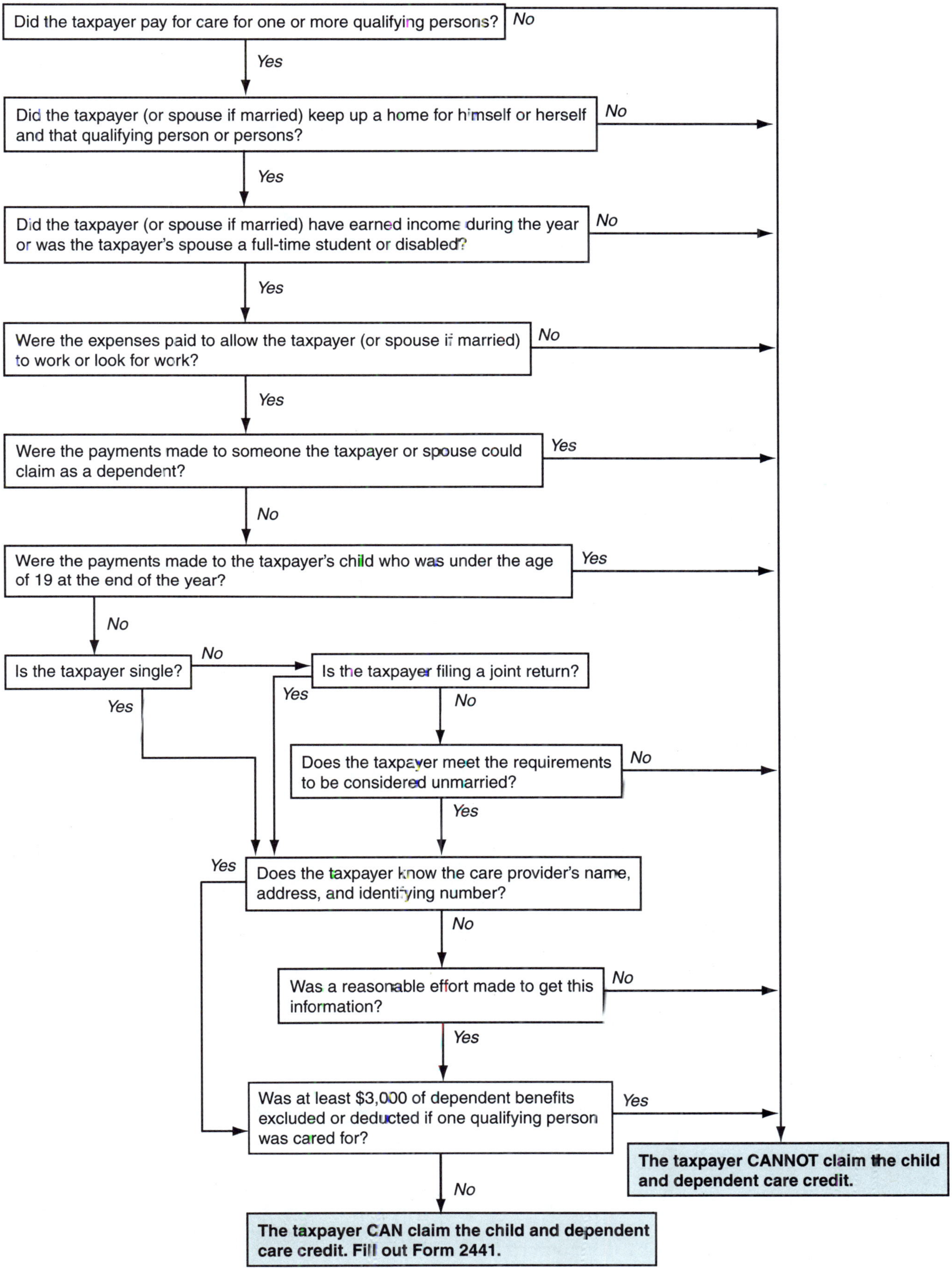

Caution. Including the child's income on the parent's return affects AGI-sensitive calculations (e.g., the medical expense and miscellaneous itemized deductions), adjustments to gross income (e.g., the phaseout of the tuition and fees deduction), and credits (e.g., the phaseout of the educational credits). The additional preparation time it takes to do the child's return is often rewarded with lower overall family tax liability.

These rules do *not* apply if either of the following is true:

- The child is *not* required to file a tax return.
- Neither of the child's parents were living at the end of the tax year.

For more information, see IRS Publication 17, *Your Federal Income Tax*, IRS Publication 929, *Tax Rules for Children and Dependents*, and MTG ¶706.

Planning Tip. When investing for children, proper tax planning is essential to minimize the potential effects of the "kiddie tax." Two possible investment strategies are:

Growth Investments. Invest in something that appreciates in value but does not pay dividends. The gain of investments of this nature is not realized until the asset is sold.

Savings Bonds. Put money in investments that accrue tax-deferred or tax-free interest. See Tab 4 and Tab 9 and MTG ¶730 for a discussion of the tax advantages of U.S. savings bonds.

Credits for Families with Children

Child Tax Credit. The maximum child tax credit is $1,000 for each qualifying child of the taxpayer for which the taxpayer claims a dependency exemption.

A qualifying child for purposes of the child tax credit must:

1. be the taxpayer's child, stepchild, adopted or foster child, sibling, stepbrother, stepsister, or descendant of any of them;
2. not have attained the age of 17 by the end of the calendar year;
3. share a home with the taxpayer for more than half of the year;
4. have not provided over one-half of their support for the calendar year;
5. be claimed as a dependent on the taxpayer's 2009 return; and
6. not have filed a joint return with their spouse other than to claim a refund.

The $1,000 credit amount is reduced by $50 for each $1,000, or fraction thereof, by which the taxpayer's modified adjusted gross income exceeds a threshold amount of $75,000 ($55,000 if MFS, $110,000 if MFJ). The child tax credit may be used against both the regular and alternative minimum tax liability. However, the credit may not reduce the tax owed below zero, but the additional child tax credit is refundable (see Tab 10 for a detailed discussion of the refundable additional child tax credit).

For more information, see details in IRS Publication 972, *Child Tax Credit*, Form 8812, *Additional Child Tax Credit*, MTG ¶1302, and Tab 10.

Child and Dependent Care Credit. If a taxpayer resides in a household that includes a dependent child under the age of 13, or a dependent or spouse who is mentally or physically incapable of self-care, the taxpayer may claim this credit for expenses paid to provide such care to enable the taxpayer to be employed or look for work. Generally:

- The credit ranges from 20% to 35% of qualifying expenses.
- Qualifying expenses must be paid to provide for the care and well-being of a dependent under the age of 13, or a dependent or spouse unable to care for themselves, to allow the taxpayer to work or look for work.
- The maximum 35% is available to taxpayers whose adjusted gross income (AGI) is less than $15,000. The credit is reduced by one percent for each $2,000 increase in AGI. Thus, taxpayers with AGI greater than $43,000 are limited to the minimum 20% credit for such expenses.
- The limit on the amount of eligible expenses is $3,000 for one qualifying individual and $6,000 for two or more qualifying individuals.

The amount on which the credit is computed is limited to the lower of eligible expenses, or, for married couples, the earned income of the lower-paid spouse. If the spouse is either a full-time student or not able to care for himself or herself, the amount of income he or she is treated as having earned is $250 a month if there is one qualifying person and $500 a month if there are two or more qualifying persons.

Planning Tip. A dependent care flexible spending account (FSA) may offer significant tax savings. For two or more qualifying individuals $5,000 could be withheld from a paycheck on a pre-tax basis. Should day care expenses exceed $5,000, up to $1,000 of the excess could be used to claim the dependent care credit.

Flow charts are provide on pages 13-6 and 13-7 to help determine whether an individual is a qualifying person for purposes of the dependent care credit and whether the taxpayer can claim the credit.

The child and dependent care credit is calculated on Form 2441, *Child and Dependent Care Expenses*, and reported on line 48 of Form 1040, *U.S. Individual Income Tax Return*. For more information, see Publication 503, *Child and Dependent Care Expenses*, MTG ¶1301 and Tab 10.

Caution. Failure to reconcile dependent care benefits on page 2 of Form 2441 could result in the IRS recalculating the dependent care credit, adding the dependent care benefits back into income and sending a bill for tax due to the client.

Adoption Credit. Taxpayers may claim a nonrefundable credit on Form 8839, *Qualified Adoption Expenses*, of up to $12,150 for qualified adoption expenses for each eligible child, though the credit is phased out ratably for taxpayers with modified gross incomes between $182,180 and $222,180. The credit amount is then reported on line 52 of Form 1040.

Taxpayers who adopt a child with special needs can claim an adoption credit of $12,150 regardless of actual expenses paid or incurred in the year the adoption becomes final.

The following expenses are *not* eligible for the adoption credit:

- Expenses incurred in connection with the adoption of a spouse's child.
- Costs associated with a surrogate parenting arrangement.

The adoption credit is coordinated with employer-provided adoption assistance programs. Expenses can only be used once either for claiming the exclusion under an assistance program or for claiming the credit.

See MTG ¶1306.

Foster Care

Tax-Free Payments. Payments received from a state, political subdivision, or qualified foster care placement agency for providing foster care in the home are excluded from gross income as long as care is for:

- No more than five individuals over age 18; or
- In the case of any difficulty-of-care payments, no more than 10 individuals under age 19 and five individuals age 19 or older.

Taxable Payments. All foster care payments are taxable if the taxpayer:

- Maintains space in his or her home for emergency foster care;
- Provides care for more than five individuals age 19 or older; or
- In the case of difficulty-of-care payments, provides care for more than 10 qualified foster care individuals under the age of 19 and five individuals over the age of 19.

See MTG ¶883.

Filing Tip. Taxpayers receiving payments for more than 10 foster children must report the amounts on Schedule C, *Sole Proprietorship*, and pay self-employment tax since they will be considered to be in the trade or business of providing foster care.

Foster Children as Dependents. A foster child may qualify as a dependent of the taxpayer if the dependency qualifications are met.

Family Income Tax Planning

Most families want to take steps to maximize their benefits–and minimize their tax liability–under the income tax laws. Careful planning and awareness of the requirements for specific tax credits and deductions will result in the most advantageous tax situation.

Shifting Income

Families can reduce their aggregate tax liability by shifting income from a higher-bracket family member to a lower-bracket family member, often from parents to children. There was a time when shifting income involved merely transferring assets from a family member in a higher tax bracket to a family member in a lower tax bracket. However, the kiddie tax limits this planning opportunity by taxing a child's net unearned income at the parents' marginal tax rate.

Employing Family Members. Taxpayers who operate their own business can shift income by employing other family members. A taxpayer who employs his or her child can deduct the wages paid as a business expense, and the child's earned income is not subject to the kiddie tax. In addition, if the taxpayer's business is a sole proprietorship or partnership, and the employed child is under age 18, the child's earned income is not subject to Social Security or Medicare.

Caution. Income and asset shifting must be legitimate. Transfers carried out solely for the purpose of income tax avoidance that do not meet the requirements for the type of transfer, such as payment of wages to a child when no work is performed, are not legitimate and the IRS may disallow tax advantages resulting from such payments.

Wages paid to a parent employed by his or her child are not subject to federal unemployment tax (FUTA) (IRS Publication 15, Circular E).

Filing Tip. Taxpayers should consider hiring children in the family business for wages that are at least enough to contribute to their own traditional IRA plus the standard deduction for a single filer. The result is tax-free income to the children and an early start for their retirement, which will maximize under the power of compounding.

Gifting Issues

The first $13,000 of gifts made by a donor during the 2009 calendar year to any donee is not included in the total amount of the donor's taxable gifts during the year and therefore is neither taxed nor uses up any of the donor's lifetime gift tax credit.

The annual exclusion is not allowed for gifts of future interests in property. Future interests include any interest, whether vested or contingent, that is not available for the donee's use, possession, or enjoyment until some future date or time.

Gifts to Minors

The annual exclusion is allowed for an outright gift to a minor whether made to the minor's legal guardian or to a custodian under a state statute such as the Uniform Gifts to Minors Act.

Uniform Gifts to Minors Act (UGMA) Accounts. The Uniform Gifts to Minors Act and Uniform Transfers to Minors Act allow taxpayers to set up custodial accounts for minors. Under state UGMA accounts, the custodian, often a parent, is responsible for managing the account, which is then transferred to the child when he or she is no longer a minor (age 18 or 21, depending on the state).

A transfer of property for the benefit of a minor pursuant to the Uniform Transfers to Minors Act, the Uniform Gifts to Minors Act, or the Model Gifts of Securities to Minors Act is considered to be a completed gift of the full fair market value of the property. No taxable gift occurs by reason of a subsequent resignation of the custodian or termination of the custodianship for federal gift tax purposes. Such a gift also qualifies for the annual gift tax exclusion ($13,000 in 2009).

Generation-Skipping Gifts

If a donor makes a generation-skipping transfer to a grandchild or lower generation, the transfer is a gift subject to the regular gift tax, and it may also be subject to the generation-skipping transfer tax. In computing the regular gift tax on such a transfer, the annual exclusion and gift-splitting provisions are available. Further, the regular gift tax is computed by using the unified tax rates based on cumulative gifts. If the generation-skipping transfer tax is applicable, it is payable as an additional tax in the year the transfer occurs. The annual exclusion and gift-splitting provisions are available in computing the amount subject to the generation-skipping transfer tax.

Income-Producing Assets

Families can also shift income by giving income-producing property to a lower-bracket family member. When the donor retains no interest in the transferred property, the recipient generally is taxed on all the income generated by the property. In the case of minor children where the income discharges the parents' legal obligation of support, the income is taxed to the parents.

Caution. Shifting assets to save income taxes could hurt college financial aid eligibility and could impact future support tests.

General Gifting Issues for Families

Gifts of property to members of a family, often motivated by a desire to spread the income and thereby reduce the tax on the donor and on the family as a whole, are not prohibited but may be carefully scrutinized by the IRS. The essential elements of a valid intra-family gift are:

1. A donor competent to make the gift.
2. A donee capable of receiving the gift.
3. A clear and unmistakable intention on the part of the donor to divest title, dominion, and control of the subject matter of the gift, immediately, absolutely, and irrevocably.
4. The irrevocable transfer of the present legal title and of the dominion and control of the entire gift to the donee, so the donor can exercise no further act of dominion or control over it.
5. A delivery by the donor to the donee of the subject of the gift or of the most effectual means of commanding dominion over it.
6. Acceptance of the gift by the donee.

An assignment of income alone will be disregarded for tax purposes unless the taxpayer also assigns the income-producing property. For example, a taxpayer may not escape tax on wages by assigning part of a salary under a legally enforceable contract.

The gift itself results in no income to the recipient and is not deductible by the donor unless the gift qualifies as a deductible charitable contribution (see MTG ¶1058), but it may result in liability of the donor for a gift tax (see MTG ¶2903). Additionally, although the value of a gift is excluded from the recipient's income, any income from the gift, such as profit resulting from a sale of the gift, is taxable to the recipient (see MTG ¶849).

Family Loans

One effective means of shifting income from a high-bracket taxpayer to a low-bracket taxpayer is through use of an interest-free or below-market-interest loan. Upon receipt of the funds, the borrower can invest them in income-producing assets. Although the borrower must pay taxes on the income produced by the assets, the loan results in an overall lower tax liability within the family unit because the income is shifted away from the high-bracket taxpayer and taxed at lower rates.

Gift Loans

In the case of a below-market term loan that is a gift loan because the forgone interest is in the nature of a gift, the excess of the amount loaned over the present value of all the payments is treated for gift tax purposes as being transferred to the borrower on the date the loan is made. Similar to the rule for demand loans, the amount deemed to be retransferred to the lender is the forgone interest and the interest forgone during a calendar year is deemed to be retransferred to the lender on the last day of such calendar year. The lender must pay tax on the forgone interest.

See MTG ¶795 for the exceptions to gift loans.

Separation and Divorce

Divorce has many tax consequences. Issues of alimony, child support, and transfer of property all affect income tax. IRS Publication 504, *Divorced or Separated Individuals,* covers divorce-related tax issues in detail.

Filing Status

If the taxpayer is considered unmarried, his or her filing status is Single (or Head of Household if he or she qualifies according to the rules outlined in Tab 1). If the taxpayer is considered married, the status is either Married Filing Jointly or Married Filing Separately.

Situations in which taxpayers are considered unmarried:

- They have obtained a full decree of divorce, as determined by the law of their state of residence, by the last day of the tax year.
- They have obtained an annulment.

> **Filing Tip.** If a marriage has been annulled by a court, the marriage is ruled to never have legally existed. Any tax returns filed as married must be amended to reflect the taxpayers' single status if the tax year is still open under statute of limitations laws (generally three years).

Situations in which taxpayers are considered married:

- They are separated but have not obtained a final divorce decree by the end of the tax year.
- Their common-law marriage is recognized by their state of residence.

There are exceptions to these general rules:

- If the husband and wife plan to remarry within one year, they may be considered married.
- In certain circumstances, if a couple lives apart they may be considered unmarried for tax purposes.

Alimony

Alimony is payment to or for a spouse or former spouse under a divorce or separation instrument. It is deductible by the payer and must be included in the recipient's income. Alimony payments made are deducted on line 31a of Form 1040 along with the former spouse's Social Security number. Alimony payments received are reported as income on line 11 of Form 1040.

> **Caution.** If a taxpayer deducting alimony does not include the spouse's Social Security number, a $50 penalty may be incurred, and the deduction may be disallowed.

Only cash payments, including checks and money orders, qualify as alimony. The following do *not* qualify:

- Transfers of services or property (including a debt instrument of a third party or an annuity contract)
- Execution of a debt instrument by the payor
- The use of property

Not all payments under a divorce or separation instrument are considered alimony. Alimony does *not* include the following:

- Child support.
- Noncash property settlements.
- Payments that are the spouse or former spouse's part of community income.
- Payments to keep up the payor's property.
- Use of property.

See MTG ¶771.

Example. Under a written separation agreement, Donna lives rent-free in a home Josh owns. Josh must pay the mortgage, real estate taxes, insurance, repairs, and utilities for the home. Because Josh owns the home and the debts belong to him, these payments are not alimony. Neither is the value of Donna's use of the home. If the home were jointly owned, different rules would apply.

Underpayment of Alimony. If both child support and alimony are owed, and the taxpayer pays less than is required, the payments apply first to child support and then to alimony.

Recapture of Alimony. In the event that alimony payments are reduced during the first three calendar years, the taxpayer may be subject to the alimony recapture rule. The rule is invoked if the alimony payments:

- decrease by more than $15,000 from the second to the third year; or
- decrease by more than $15,000 over the entire first three calendar years; or
- terminate.

Filing Tip. The recapture of alimony rules are not triggered by either the death of either spouse or the remarriage of the recipient spouse.

Taxpayers subject to this rule must include in income in the third year part of the alimony payments that were previously deducted. The spouse can deduct in the third year part of the alimony payments he or she previously included in income. See MTG ¶774 for further details.

The three-year period starts with the first calendar year during which the taxpayer makes a payment qualifying as alimony. No recapture is required if payments stop because of the death of either spouse or the remarriage of the payee, or if the amount of payments fluctuates because it is based on a fixed portion of a variable income.

Reasons for reduction or termination of alimony payments that can require a recapture include:

- Change in the divorce or separation instrument.
- Failure to make timely payments.
- Reduction in taxpayer's ability to provide support.
- Reduction in the spouse's support needs.

Expenses for a Jointly-Owned Home in A Divorce: Who May Deduct on 2009 Form 1040?

Ownership of Home	Expenses Considered Alimony if Paid by One Spouse for the Benefit of the Other	Expenses that Qualify as Itemized Deductions of Payor	Expenses That Qualify as Itemized Deductions of Other Spouse
Joint Tenancy	Half of the total mortgage payments (principal and interest) paid by spouse	Half of the interest as interest expense (if the home is a qualified home)	Half of the interest as interest expense (if the home is a qualified home)
Tenancy in Common	Half of the total real estate taxes and home insurance payments paid by spouse	Half of the real estate taxes	Half of the real estate taxes
Tenancy by the Entirety	None of the payments	All of the real estate taxes if required to pay by the divorce decree	Depends on the provisions of the divorce decree

Recapture of Alimony Worksheet	
Note: Do not enter less than zero on any line.	
1. Alimony paid in **2nd year**	1.
2. Alimony paid in **3rd year**	2.
3. Floor	3. $ 15,000
4. Add lines 2 and 3	4.
5. Subtract line 4 from line 1	5.
6. Alimony paid in **1st year**	6.
7. Subtract line 1 from line 5	7.
8. Alimony paid in **3rd year**	8.
9. Add lines 7 and 8	9.
10. Divide line 9 by 2	10.
11. Floor	11. $15,000
12. Add lines 10 and 11	12.
13. Subtract line 12 from line 6	13.
14. **Recaptured alimony.** Add lines 5 and 13	14. *

* If you deducted alimony paid, report this amount as income on line 11, Form 1040. If you reported alimony received, deduct this amount on line 31a on 2009 Form 1040.

Child Support

Child support paid by the noncustodial parent is considered used for the child's support, even if it actually pays for other things. Child support is neither deductible by the payer nor taxable to the recipient. See MTG ¶776.

Individual Retirement Arrangements and Medical Savings Accounts

- **Spousal IRA:** If a couple is divorced by the end of the tax year, the taxpayer cannot deduct contributions to the former spouse's traditional individual retirement account (IRA). All taxable alimony received is treated as compensation for the contribution and deduction limits of traditional IRAs, so a former spouse who receives alimony can make and, if the general requirements are satisfied, deduct IRA contributions. See Tab 9.
- **Transfer of interest in an IRA to a spouse or former spouse:** The transfer of an interest in an IRA to a spouse or former spouse under a divorce or separation agreement is not considered a taxable transfer. Starting from the date of the transfer, the interest is treated as the former spouse's IRA.
- **Transfer of interest in an Archer medical savings account:** Similarly, the transfer of an interest in an Archer medical savings account (MSA) is not considered a taxable transfer. After the transfer, the interest is considered part of the spouse or former spouse's MSA.

Caution. Be sure to advise the client that any transfers from individual retirement accounts or medical savings accounts need to be a trustee-to-trustee transfer to avoid serious tax consequences. Moneys withdrawn from such accounts to be directly paid to the other spouse will be taxed to the account holder with penalties and interest.

Property Settlements

There is no recognized gain or loss in the transfer of property between spouses or former spouses in the case of divorce. Retirement benefits held in a qualified plan are frequently a major asset of a divorcing

Property Transferred Pursuant to Divorce—Where to Report on the Return

Nature of Property	Payor	Recipient	For More Information
Income-producing property (such as an interest in a business, rental property, stocks, or bonds)	Include on tax return any profit or loss, rental income or loss, dividends, or interest generated or derived from the property during the year until the property is transferred	Report any income or loss generated or derived after the property is transferred	Instructions for appropriate schedule (Schedule C, D, E, or F)
Interest in a passive activity with unused passive activity losses	Cannot deduct accumulated unused passive activity losses allocable to the transferred interest	Increase the adjusted basis of the transferred interest by the amount of the unused losses	IRS Publication 925, Passive Activity and At-Risk Rules
Investment credit property with recapture potential	Does not have to recapture any part of the credit	May have to recapture part of the credit if he or she disposes of the property or changes its use before the end of the recapture period	Form 4255, Recapture of Investment Credit
Nonstatutory stock options and nonqualified deferred compensation	Does not include any amount in gross income upon the transfer	Include an amount in gross income when the stock options are exercised or when the deferred compensation is paid or made available	IRS Publication 525, Taxable and Nontaxable Income, Rev. Rul. 2002-22, and Rev. Rul. 2004-60

couple. The plan will generally require that any division of retirement benefits earned by a participant be made in accordance with a qualified domestic relations order.

Qualified Domestic Relations Orders. A qualified domestic relations order (QDRO) is a judgment, decree, or court order under a domestic relations law that:

- allows someone other than the participant to receive benefits under a retirement plan, such as a tax-sheltered annuity, and most pension or profit-sharing plans;
- relates to payment of child support, alimony, or marital property rights to spouse, former spouse, child, or other dependent; and
- specifies the amount or portion of the participant's benefits to be transferred to the alternate payee.

Benefits paid to the participant's dependent or child are treated as though they are paid to the participant. Benefits paid to a spouse or former spouse must be included in the their income. If the participant contributed to the retirement plan, the participant's cost is allocated to the payments to determine the taxable amount. See Tab 9.

See MTG ¶2166 for more information about QDROs.

Transfer of S Corporation Losses to Spouse or Incident to Divorce

Generally, suspended losses and deductions are disallowed and are not available to anyone once an S corporation shareholder transfers all of his or her shares to another person. However, if a shareholder's stock is transferred to his or her spouse, or to a former spouse incident to divorce, any suspended loss or deduction with respect to that stock will be treated as incurred by the S corporation in the succeeding tax year with respect to the transferee. Reg. §1.1366-2(a)(5)(ii) provides guidance on the handling of losses prior to and in the year of the transfer of stock incident to a divorce under IRC §1041(a).

Costs of Divorce

Taxpayers cannot deduct legal fees and court costs related to the divorce. However, taxpayers may be able to deduct legal fees paid for tax advice in connection with a divorce, and legal fees to get alimony. Deductions may also be taken for payments to appraisers, actuaries, and accountants for tax purposes or for help in obtaining alimony.

Planning Tip. Because some fees may be tax-deductible and others not, based on the service for which the fee is paid, taxpayers should always request a breakdown of fees for each service performed by attorneys, accountants, and other professionals.

Education Tax Benefits

A variety of tax incentives are available for educational expenses, including exclusion of scholarships, grants, and certain other income used for qualified education expenses from taxable income; two major above-the-line deductions (adjustments to gross income); and two major education tax credits.

For a summary of educational tax benefits, see the chart on page 13-18.

General Information

Qualified Education Expenses. For tax purposes, qualified education expenses generally include the following:

- Tuition and certain related expenses required to enroll in an eligible institution.
- Student activity fees and expenses for course-related books, supplies and equipment are included in qualified expenses only if the fees and expenses must be paid to the institution as a condition of enrollment.
- Expenses that do not qualify include room and board, travel, and clerical help.

Example. Charlie received a scholarship of $16,000 and has wages of $7,500 in 2009. He is not a dependent of any other taxpayer. His tuition, fees, and other expenses required for enrollment in his degree program totaled $13,500. He used the remaining $2,500 of his scholarship money toward his $5,000 expense for room and board (this use was allowed under the terms of the scholarship). He must include the $2,500 amount (and his wages) as taxable income on line 7 of Form 1040.

If he reports $10,000 taxable income, he may not claim any deduction or credit for education expenses because all qualifying expenses were paid with nontaxable income. After his $3,650 personal exemption and $5,700 standard deduction as a Single filer, he has taxable income of $650 and pays $66 of tax.

Assume Charlie reports $12,000 taxable income on line 7 of Form 1040 (electing not to exclude an additional $2,000 of his scholarship, applying it to room and board rather than tuition). He then has $2,000 in qualifying education expenses for the the American Opportunity (modified Hope) tax credit, and can claim a $2,000 credit on line 49 of Form 1040. His tax on the taxable income of $2,650 is $266, but after he subtracts the American Opportunity credit, he owes no tax for 2009 (and can claim a full refund of any tax withheld from his wages by his employer).

Eligible Educational Institution. An eligible educational institution is one that maintains a regular facility and curriculum and normally has a regularly enrolled body of students.

Modified Adjusted Gross Income (MAGI). For most taxpayers, MAGI is adjusted gross income as figured on the federal income tax return. When using Form 1040A, it is on line 21. On Form 1040, it is on line 37, modified by adding back any:

- Foreign earned income exclusion.
- Foreign housing exclusion.
- Exclusion of income for residents of Guam, the Northern Mariana Islands, and American Samoa.
- Exclusion of income from Puerto Rico.

> **Planning Tip.** Students who have taxable income from any education benefits may need to make estimated tax payments if the payer does not withhold enough income tax. See Tab 11 for information about estimated tax.

No Double Benefits. When taking education-related deductions, taxpayers may not deduct the same expenses twice or claim both a credit and a deduction for the same expenses. The following double benefits are specifically disallowed:

- Claim of an American Opportunity (modified Hope) or lifetime learning credit and deduction of tuition and fees expenses for the same student in the same year.
- Claim of an American Opportunity (modified Hope) or lifetime learning credit based on the same expenses used to figure the tax-free portion of a distribution from a Coverdell education savings account (ESA) or a qualified tuition program (QTP).
- Claim of a credit based on qualified education expenses paid with a tax-free scholarship, grant, or employer-provided educational assistance.
- Claim of an exclusion of interest from U.S. Savings bonds for qualified educational expenses either used to claim another tax benefit or paid with a tax-free scholarship, grant, or employer-provided educational assistance.

Tax-Free Benefits

The taxability of various kinds of education assistance available while studying, teaching, or researching in the United States is covered in detail in IRS Publication 970, *Tax Benefits for Education.* Most scholarships, fellowships, need-based grants, and qualified tuition reductions are tax-free if they are used to pay qualified education expenses.

Scholarships and Fellowships. Generally, scholarships and fellowships received by a degree candidate and used for qualified education expenses are nontaxable. Taxpayers do not have to file a tax return if their only income is tax-free scholarships or fellowships. If all or part of the scholarships or fellowships is taxable, the taxpayer must file a return.

Other forms of educational assistance that may be tax-free include the following:

- Pell grants and other Title IV need-based education grants are treated like scholarships and are tax-free when used for qualified education expenses.
- Fulbright scholarships are generally treated as a scholarship or fellowship in figuring out how much of the grant is tax-free.
- Veterans' benefits received for education, training, or subsistence under any law administered by the Department of Veterans Affairs are tax-free.
- Payments to Service Academy cadets may be deductible if used for education expenses related to study at a U.S. military academy. Appointment to a U.S. military academy is now treated as a scholarship or fellowship. Payments for services as a cadet or midshipman are included as taxable income.

Taxpayers may elect not to exclude scholarship or fellowship grants that can be used for room and board and other expenses. If these payments are reported as taxable income, they do not reduce the amount of qualifying expenses for the purpose of the American Opportunity (modified Hope) and lifetime learning credits.

Employer-Provided Assistance Excluded. Taxpayers who receive educational assistance benefits from their employer under an educational assistance program can exclude as much as $5,250 of those benefits each year. See MTG ¶871.

> **Caution.** The election to treat nontaxable scholarships as taxable does not extend to restricted scholarships, which must be used only for tuition and fees. Qualifying expenses must be reduced by the amount of these scholarships.

Education Tax Deductions

Above-the-line deductions (or adjustments to gross income) that are related to education are the student loan interest and the tuition and fees deductions. In addition, work-related education may be deductible as a business expense.

Student Loan Interest Deduction. This deduction is taken as a reduction in income on line 33 of Form 1040, so it can also be claimed even if taxpayers do not itemize. The maximum deduction is $2,500. The deduction is phased out for taxpayers with adjusted gross income between $60,000 and $75,000 ($120,000 and $150,000 for MFJ). See MTG ¶1082.

Work-Related Education Deduction. Some education expenses are deductible as employee business expenses. See Tab 6 and MTG ¶1082.

Tuition and Fees Deduction. The deduction for tuition and fees can reduce the taxpayer's adjusted gross income by as much as $4,000 for tax years ending on or before December 31, 2009. Since it is taken as a reduction in income, it is available to taxpayers who do not itemize deductions.

To qualify, the taxpayer must pay qualified education expenses for an eligible student who is the taxpayer, the taxpayer's spouse, or a dependent for whom the taxpayer can claim an exemption. The taxpayer may *not* claim the tuition and fees deduction if any of the following apply:

- The taxpayer's filing status is Married, Filing Separately (MFS).
- Another person claims the taxpayer as an exemption on his or her tax return.
- The taxpayer's modified adjusted gross income (MAGI) is more than $80,000 ($160,000, if Married, Filing Jointly (MFJ)).
- The taxpayer claims a Hope or lifetime learning credit for the same expenses.
- The taxpayer is a nonresident alien and did *not* elect to be treated as a resident alien for tax purposes.

The amount of qualified education expenses that can be deducted is $4,000 if MAGI is not more than $65,000 ($130,000, if MFJ). For taxpayers with a MAGI of $65,000 ($130,000, if MFJ) but less than $80,000 ($160,000, if MFJ), the maximum tuition and fees deduction is $2,000. No tuition and fees deduction is allowed for taxpayers is allowed for taxpayers whose MAGI is larger than $80,000 (160,000, if (MFJ).

Tax-Free Transactions

Canceled Student Loans. Although the cancellation of a debt is usually treated as income to the debtor, certain cancellations of student loans are excluded from this rule. To qualify for tax-free treatment on a canceled loan, the loan must contain a provision that all or part will be forgiven if the taxpayer works for a certain period of time, in certain professions, and for any of a broad class of employers. Also, the loan generally must have been made by a government, a public corporation operating a hospital, or an educational institution. See MTG ¶791.

Student Loan Repayment Assistance. Student loan repayment assistance provided through the National Health Service Corps Loan Repayment Program or similar state programs is excluded from gross income. These programs provide subsidies to individuals providing primary health services in underserved areas. The IRS recently expanded the exclusion to include recent law school graduates who accept loan repayment assistance from their law schools to enter public service, the non-profit sector, and underserved areas.

Qualified Tuition Programs (QTP) or 529 Plans. Qualified tuition programs, also known as 529 plans, are programs established by states or educational institutions that allow taxpayers to either prepay or contribute to an account for paying a student's qualified higher education expenses. Earnings in a qualified tuition program also accumulate tax-free. No tax is due on a distribution from a QTP unless the amount distributed is greater than the beneficiary's qualified higher education expenses. Excess distributions are included in the recipient's income and also subject to an additional tax of 10%.

Contributions to a QTP cannot be more than the amount necessary to provide for the qualified education expenses of the beneficiary. See MTG ¶899.

Planning Tip. This change in the age for imposition of the "kiddie tax" makes the use of 529 plans more desirable for saving for a child's college education.

For ratings of various plans, see http://www.finaid.org/savings/.

Savings Bonds Used for Education. Taxpayers who cash series EE or I savings bonds issued after 1989 can exclude the interest from their income if they pay qualified education expenses for themselves, their spouse, or a dependent during the year. Qualified education expenses include college tuition and fees, contributions to a qualified tuition program, and contributions to a Coverdell education savings account. The exclusion phases out for taxpayers with 2009 modified adjusted gross income in excess of $104,900 (if married filing jointly) or $69,950 (for other filers). The phase-out is complete at $134,900 for joint filers and $84,950 for other filers. Form 8815, *Exclusion of Interest from Series EE or I U.S. Savings Bonds Issued after 1989*, is used to calculate the exclusion.

To qualify for the exclusion, the bonds must be issued in the name of the taxpayer or the names of the taxpayer and the taxpayer's spouse, as co-owners, and the taxpayer must have been 24 or older when the bonds were issued. A bond purchased by a parent and issued in the name of his or her child under age 24 does *not* qualify for the exclusion by the parent or the child. See MTG ¶730A.

Coverdell Education Savings Accounts (ESAs). Taxpayers can create a Coverdell ESA on behalf of a particular beneficiary and contribute to it as much as $2,000 per year. Contributions to the ESA are not deductible, but accumulations are tax-deferred until distributed. Beneficiaries must be under 18 or have special needs. Any individual, including the beneficiary, can contribute as long as their modified AGI is less than $110,000 (or $220,000 if filing a joint return). The $2,000 amount is phased out for MAGI between $95,000 and $110,000 ($190,000 to $220,000 for MFJ).

The $2,000 annual limit also applies to all Coverdell ESAs set up for any one beneficiary. Contributions in excess of the $2,000 limit per contributor or per beneficiary are subject to a 6% excise tax if not withdrawn by June 1 of the following year.

Coverdell ESA distributions can be used to pay elementary and secondary education expenses, as well as higher learning expenses.

If distributions exceed qualified educational expenses not paid with tax-free assistance, the remainder is allocated to taxable earnings and return of contributions. Earnings are taxable, but the amount attributable to the contributed basis in the account is not. IRS Publication 970 contains a worksheet to calculate the taxable amount of the distribution. Withdrawals in excess of qualified educational expenses are also subject to a 10% penalty, which is calculated on Form 5329, *Additional Taxes on Qualified Plans (Including IRAs) and Other Tax Favored Accounts.*

Any balance remaining in a Coverdell ESA must be withdrawn within 30 days after the beneficiary's thirtieth birthday, unless the beneficiary has special needs that extend the length of time required for his or her education, or within 30 days after the beneficiary's death if he or she dies before reaching age 30. Rollovers to the following family members (who are under age 30 at the time of the rollover) of the beneficiary are allowed:

- Son, daughter, or descendant of son or daughter
- Stepson or stepdaughter
- Brother, sister, or son or daughter of a brother or sister
- Stepbrother or stepsister
- Father, mother, or ancestor of either
- Stepfather or stepmother
- Brother or sister of father or mother
- First cousin
- Son-in-law, daughter-in-law, brother-in-law, sister-in-law, mother-in-law, or father-in-law
- Spouse of original beneficiary or any relative listed except first cousin

Rollovers must be deposited within 60 days of withdrawal to avoid the 10% penalty. See MTG ¶898.

Education Tax Credits

American Opportunity (Modified Hope) Tax Credit and Lifetime Learning Credit. These two tax credits offset the cost of higher education by reducing the amount of income tax a student or his/her parents pays.

The American Opportunity (modified Hope) tax credit is available for the first four-years of higher education, with a maximum credit amount of $2,500, includes the expenses of course materials as qualified expenses, and the phaseout threshold amount is increased to $80,000 for single filers ($160,000 for joint filers). However, the Hope credit is modified for tax years beginning in 2009 and 2010. For taxpayers with low or no tax liability, 40 percent of the credit amount may be claimed as a refundable credit. A student must be pursuing an undergraduate degree and must be enrolled at least half-time for an academic period beginning during the year to have his/her expenses qualify to be claim the American Opportunity (modified Hope) credit.

Planning Tip. Students attending colleges in a Midwestern disaster area may elect to claim the credit under the previous rules for the Hope credit. The Emergency Economic Stabilization Act of 2008 (P.L. 110-343) extended the educational credit relief under IRC §1400O for 2009. This relied doubled the normal Hope credit amounts. Those students are eligible for a total credit of up to $3,600 for 2009.

Caution. All students claiming a Hope credit must used the previous rules if anyone student elects to claim the higher credit amount due to attendance at a college in the Midwestern disaster area. The lifetime learning credit has a maximum credit amount of up to $2,000 per return and is available for all years of postsecondary education including courses to acquire or improve job skills.

The credits are calculated on Form 8863, *Education Credits,* and reported on line 49 of Form 1040. Students may not claim both in the same year. Generally, the lifetime learning credit and the American Opportunity (modified Hope) credit are allowed for payments made in 2009 for an academic period beginning in 2009 or the first three months of 2010.

See Tab 10 and MTG ¶1303 for details.

Highlights of Tax Benefits for Education

	Scholarships, Fellowships, Grants, and Tuition Reductions	American Opportunity (Modified Hope Credit)**	Lifetime Learning Credit	Student Loan Interest Deduction	Tuition and Fees Deduction	Coverdell Educational Savings Accounts (ESAs)*	Qualified Tuition Programs (QTPs)*	Education Savings Bond Program*	Employer-Provided Educational Assistance*	Educational Exception on Early IRA Distributions*
Benefit	Amounts received may not be taxable	Credit can reduce amount of tax owed	Credit can reduce amount of tax owed	Deduction can reduce taxable income	Deduction can reduce taxable income	Earning accumulate tax free	Earning accumulate tax free	Interest not taxed	Employer benefits not taxed	No 10% penalty on early distribution
Annual Contribution Limit	None	$2,500 per student***	$2,000 per family	Up to $2,500	Up to $4,000	Up to $2000 per beneficiary	None	Amount of qualified education expenses	$5,250 exclusion	Amount of qualified education expenses
Adjusted Gross Income Phase Out Range	No phase out	Single — $80,000–$90,000; MFJ — $160,000–$180,000 (for 2009 & 2010 only)	Single — $50,000–$60,000; MFJ — $100,000–$120,000	Single — $60,000–$75,000; MFJ — $120,000–$150,000	Single — $65,000–$80,000; MFJ — $130,000–$160,000	Single — $95,000–$110,000; MFJ — $190,000–$220,000	No phase out	Single — $69,950–$84,950; MFJ — $104,900–$134,950	No phase out	No phase out
Qualifying Education	K – 12, undergraduate and graduate	1st 4 years of undergraduate (2009 & 2010 only)	Undergraduate and graduate courses to acquire or improve job skills	Undergraduate and graduate	Undergraduate and graduate	K – 12, undergraduate and graduate	Undergraduate and graduate	Undergraduate and graduate	Under-graduate and graduate	Under-graduate and graduate
Qualifying Expenses (In addition to tuition and required enrollment fees)	Required books, supplies, and equipment	Course Materials (2009 & 2010 only)	None	Required books, supplies, & equipment; room & board, transportation, & other necessary expenses	None	Required books, supplies, & equipment; expenses for special needs services; payments to QTPs; Higher Education: Room and board, if at least a half-time student; K–12: Tutoring, room & board, uniforms, transportation, computer access, and supplementary expenses	Required books, supplies and equipment; room and board, if at least a half-time student, & expenses for special needs services	Payments to Coverdell ESAs and QTPs	Required books, supplies, and equipment	
Additional Requirements	• Must be a degree or vocational program • Payment of tuition and fees allowed under grant	• No felony drug conviction(s) • At least half-time in degree program	None	Must have been at least a half-time student in a degree program	Cannot claim deduction and an educational credit for same student in year	Assets must be distributed at age 30 unless special needs beneficiary	None	Applies only to qualified series EE bonds issued after 1989 and series I bonds	None	None

*Any nontaxable distribution is limited to the amount that does not exceed qualified educational expenses.

**Available only during the tax years beginning in 2009 and 2010.

***Student attending colleges in the Midwestern disaster area are still eligible for relief authorized under the Emergency Economic Stabilization Act of 2008. They may claim a total credit amount of up to $3,600.

What's New in 2009

Maximum Tax Rate remains the same. The maximum estate and gift tax rate for decedents dying in 2009 is 45%.

GST Exemption Equal to Increased Exclusion Amount. For estates of decedents dying and generation-skipping transfers (GSTs) occurring after December 31, 2003, the GST exemption is equal to the applicable exclusion amount. For 2009, the applicable exclusion amount is $3,500,000. The applicable exclusion amount for gifts remains at $1,000,000 for 2009.

Various dollar amounts relevant to Form 706 are indexed for inflation. For decedents dying in 2009, the following amounts have increased: the ceiling on special-use valuation is $1,000,000; and the amount used in computing the 2% portion of estate tax payable in installments is $1,330,000.

Tax Preparer's Checklist

Information Needed by Personal Representative or Executor

- ☐ Will
- ☐ Trust agreements
- ☐ Listing of assets and debts
- ☐ Decedent's checkbooks and bank statements for period including death
- ☐ Life insurance policies
- ☐ Recent credit card statements
- ☐ Titles to assets
- ☐ Inventory of safe deposit boxes
- ☐ Prior gift tax returns
- ☐ Death certificate
- ☐ Income tax returns for prior three years
- ☐ Buy-sell agreements (closely held corporations or partnerships)
- ☐ Prenuptial agreements and divorce decrees, if applicable
- ☐ For sole proprietorship:
  - Balance sheet for valuation date and five preceding years
  - Income statement for five preceding years
- ☐ Names, addresses, Social Security numbers, citizenship information, and dates of birth of heirs
- ☐ Basis of decedent in retirement accounts and annuities
- ☐ Amount of consideration provided by decedent for property owned jointly with individuals other than spouse
- ☐ Casualty insurance policies

Section at a Glance

Relevant IRS Publications

- ☐ IRS Publication 559, *Survivors, Executors, and Administrators*
- ☐ IRS Publication 950, *Introduction to Estate and Gift Taxes*

Due Dates of Required Forms for 2009

Form	Date
Form 1040, *U.S. Individual Income Tax Return*	Date the return would have been due if decedent were still alive
Form 1041, *U.S. Income Tax Return for Estates and Trusts*	15th day of 4th month after close of the tax year
Form 706, *United States Estate (and Generation-Skipping Transfer) Tax Return*	9 months after date of death
Form 709, *United States Gift (and Generation-Skipping Transfer) Tax Return*	Earlier of Form 1040 due date or Form 706 due date

Estate and Trust Income Tax Rates for 2009

If taxable income is:			
Over	**But not over**	**The tax is**	**of the amount: Over**
$0	$2,300	$0 + 15%	$0
$2,300	$5,350	$345 + 25%	$2,300
$5,350	$8,200	$1,107.50 + 28%	$5,350
$8,200	$11,150	$1,905.50 + 33%	$8,200
$11,150		$2,879 + 35%	$11,150

What Tax Returns Must be Filed for a Deceased Taxpayer?

Form 1040, *U.S. Individual Income Tax Return*

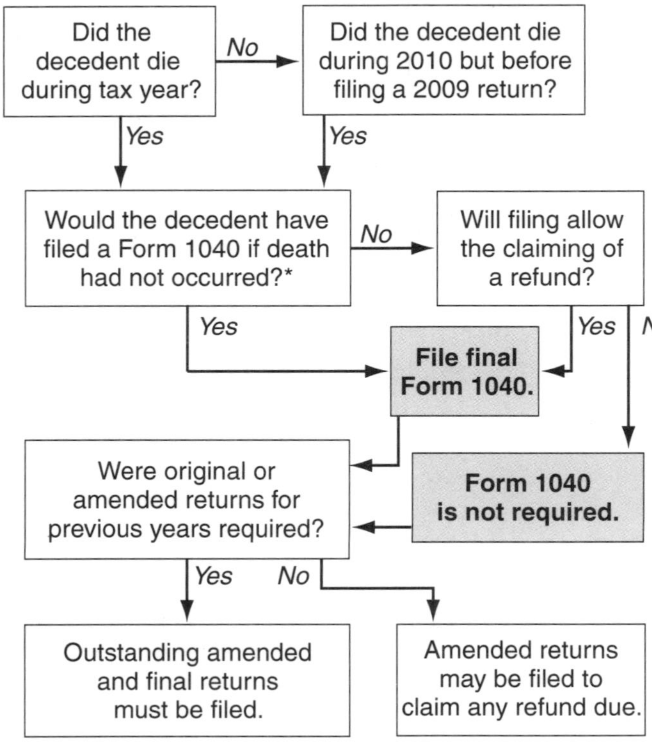

*If taxpayer was married and would have filed jointly with his or her spouse, see p.14–5.

Form 706, *United States Estate (and Generation-Skipping Transfer) Tax Return*

Form 1041, *U.S. Income Tax Return for Estates and Trusts*

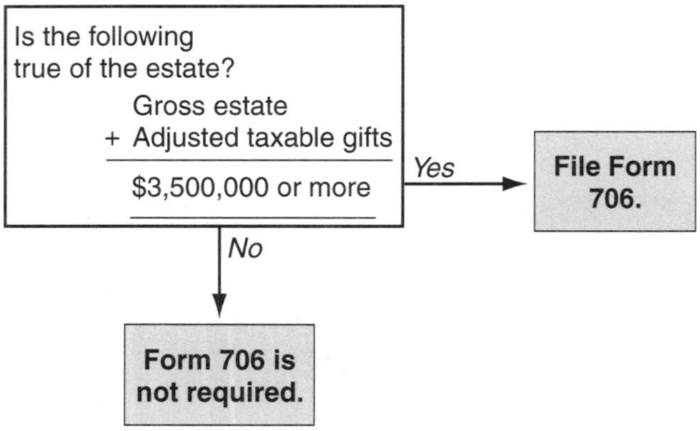

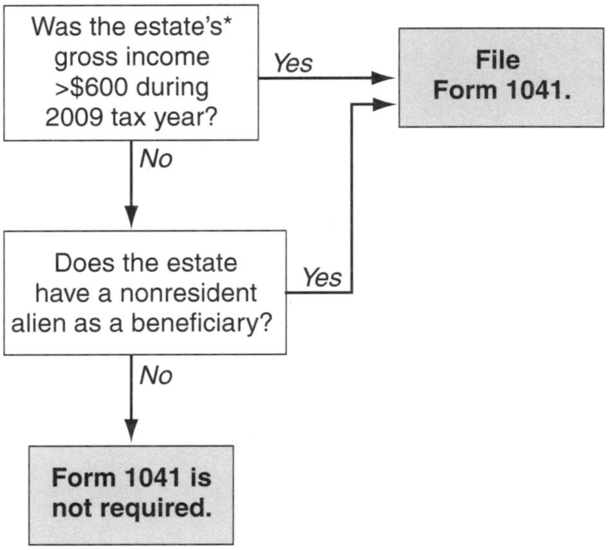

*Qualified revocable trusts may make an election to be treated as an estate; see Form 8855 and IRC §645.

Form 709, *United States Gift (and Generation-Skipping Transfer) Tax Return*

Death of a Taxpayer

This section discusses tax and other financial considerations concerning a taxpayer's death and related planning. One must understand what happens to a decedent's property at, and subsequent to, death.

This section provides planning and other considerations to achieve one's goals for one's property. It also provides a checklist of actions that can be taken by a personal representative to minimize estate and income taxes when a person dies.

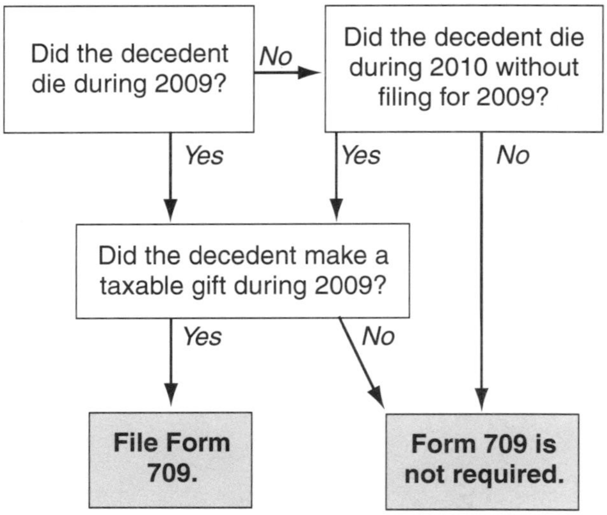

Understanding Probate and Asset Administration

Person Responsible. Upon the death of an individual, a determination must be made as to who will be named the decedent's personal representative – the person responsible for handling the financial affairs of the decedent. This person is then charged with the following tasks:

- Accounting for all assets of the decedent
- Collecting all income due during the period of administration
- Paying all liabilities of the decedent
- Paying expenses incurred during administration
- Ensuring that the remaining assets of the decedent are transferred according to the decedent's will

If the decedent had no will, the distribution of assets is governed by state law. The applicable law for real and tangible personal property is that of the state in which it is located. The laws of the state of residence of the decedent at the time of death are applicable for all other property.

If the decedent had a will, the will specifies who is to be executor (i.e., the person responsible for carrying out the directions in the will). If the decedent had no will, then local law provides rules as to who is to be the personal representative. In either event, application is made to the court with jurisdiction to validate the will and/or appoint the personal representative. This is documented by the court issuing *letters testamentary* or *letters of administration*.

The Probate Process. The formality of accounting for assets and liabilities of the decedent and the amount of court supervision depend on the total value of assets subject to probate and may also depend on any anticipated controversy among heirs or creditors or questions of title to assets.

Assets Subject to Probate. Assets subject to probate, generally, are any assets owned by the decedent at death to which title does not automatically pass to another person. Such assets must be reported to the probate court, which must authorize or approve the transfer or sale of such assets.

Examples of Probate Assets. Assets only in name of decedent:
- Checking account(s)
- Savings account(s)
- Brokerage account(s)
- Residence
- Other real estate
- Partnership interests
- Coin collection(s)

Assets owned as tenants-in-common:
- Life insurance
- Annuities
- Retirement accounts with no designated beneficiaries or for which the estate is named as beneficiary

When Probate Is Required. Probate is generally required only when the total *probate* assets exceed a threshold amount, depending on the state of jurisdiction (for example, $100,000). For probate estates under the threshold, a small estate affidavit or other similar procedure may be followed, obviating a formal probate procedure.

Examples of Non-Probate Assets. Assets with beneficiary designations (other than the estate):
- Life insurance
- Retirement accounts [IRA, 401(k), 403(b), 457, SEP, SIMPLE]
- Annuities
- Annuities and other income interests that terminate on death
- Accounts that are "payable on death"
- Beneficial interests in trusts created by others
- Land trusts
- Living trusts
- Social Security benefits
- Veterans Administration benefits
- Assets owned as joint tenants or as tenants-by-the-entirety

Duties of Personal Representative. The personal representative is responsible for ensuring that the following actions are completed:

- Publish notice of probate and acceptance of claims.
- Notify creditors of death and provide information for making claims.
- List, value, and collect all assets subject to probate.

Filing Tip. Review decedent's prior income tax returns to make sure all sources of income have been identified and the related assets accounted for.

Caution. Once it is determined that the creation of an estate or trust is needed, obtain a tax identification number for the entity. This is required to open a separate checking account for the trust. After establishing a separate checking account for the estate or trust, deposit all income and proceeds from the liquidation of assets and pay all expenses from this account.

- File tax returns and pay taxes and other debts of decedent.
- Provide to the court and all heirs an accounting of assets and income collected and claims and expenses paid.

Caution. It may, depending on the terms of the will, be important to keep track of income separately from other receipts. Also, net income for probate purposes may not be the same as for income tax purposes.

- Make a distribution of remaining assets according to the will or, if there is no will, according to the succession laws of the state of jurisdiction.
- Obtain a discharge of responsibility from the court.

Determining States Requiring Probate. The decedent's domicile within a state establishes jurisdiction. If the decedent owned real property or tangible personal property out of state, then what is known as an "ancillary" administration in the state in which such property is located may be required.

Caution. Depending on the property, an income tax return and/or an inheritance or estate tax return may also be required by the state.

Forms Required upon Death. The personal representative will need the following:

- Employer identification number (Form SS-4)–Required for any income-producing assets of the decedent's estate. This can be obtained online by going to www.irs.gov/businesses and clicking on more topics under *Business Topics* and selecting *Employer ID Numbers*. Or call the IRS at 1-800-829-4933.

Filing Tip. Advise all payers of income as soon as you receive a tax identification number for the estate. This will reduce problems later when filing income tax returns.

- Notice of fiduciary relationship (Form 56)–File with the IRS Service Center where the person for whom you are acting is required to file tax returns. For the final 1040 and the 1041, note that more that one Form 56 may need to be filed. A separate Form 56 must be filed for each person for whom you are acting in a fiduciary capacity.

Income Tax Filing Requirements for Year of Death

The personal representative must file a final income tax return (Form 1040) for the year of death and for any prior years that have not been filed as of the date of death.

IRS Publication 559, *Survivors, Executors, and Administrators*, contains further details.

Example. Joe Black died July 15, 2009. He was married to Mabel at the time of his death. He received salary prior to death of $50,000. A payroll check for the month of his death and for unused sick and vacation pay was issued after his death for $15,237.75 ($16,500, less Social Security (6.2%) and Medicare (1.45%) taxes of $1,262.25). The check was made payable to his estate. Mabel had wages of $55,000 for the year; $27,500 was earned prior to Joe's death. Joe and Mabel earned $1,200 on a joint savings account; $650 of this was earned prior to Joe's death. Joe owned stock on which he received $600 in dividends prior to death. A Form 1099 was received in Joe's name for $1,300, which included $700 of dividends paid to Joe's estate after death.

The first installment of property taxes on Joe and Mabel's residence, of $1,800, was paid prior to death. The residence was owned jointly. Mabel paid the second installment of $1,800 after Joe's death. In addition, Joe owned a vacation home in Florida. Mabel paid property taxes of $3,000 on this in November. Joe and Mabel can file a joint return for 2009. The joint return would include the following income:

- Joe's salary prior to death, $50,000
- Mabel's salary for the entire 12 months, $55,000
- Interest income on joint savings, $1,200
- Dividend income of $600 [$1,300 should be reported but then reduced by $700 as income not taxable in the final Form 1040 (reportable by Joe's estate)]

Income not includible in the final joint Form 1040:

- Final salary check of $15,237.75 (reportable in Joe's estate's Form 1041 as IRD)
- Dividend income of $700 (reportable in Joe's estate's Form 1041 as IRD)

The final joint return would include a deduction for property taxes of $3,600 but would not include the property taxes on the Florida property. The Florida property taxes would be deductible by Joe's estate on Form 1041 (and also on Form 706, if required).

Example. John Smith, an unmarried taxpayer, died March 31, 2010, without having filed his 2009 income tax return. His personal representative must file a return for 2009 and a separate return for the period January 1, 2010, through John's date of death, March 31, 2010. The 2009 return is due April 15, 2010, and the 2010 return is due April 15, 2011.

If the decedent was married at the time of death and a joint return is to be filed, then the surviving spouse can sign the return as "Surviving Spouse." Note that the determination regarding the filing status of the decedent's final return is made by the personal representative of the estate, not the surviving spouse, unless he or she is also the personal representative. The return for the year of death will include income and deductions of the decedent up to the date of death and the income and deductions of the surviving spouse for the entire year. See MTG ¶168, ¶178 and ¶182.

A widow or widower may qualify to use the lower Married Filing Jointly tax rates for the two years following the year of death if:

- He or she was entitled to file a joint return with the deceased spouse in the spouse's year of death.
- He or she must not remarry before the end of the tax year.
- He or she has a child, stepchild, or foster child who qualifies as a dependent for the tax year.
- He or she provides more than half of the cost of maintaining the home, which is the principal residence of the child for the entire year except for temporary absences.

See MTG ¶175.

Planning Tip. A tax practitioner should consider working with an attorney whenever dealing with the financial affairs of a decedent, executor, or surviving spouse or other family members. State laws dictate requirements.

Decedent's Final Income Tax Return (2009 Form 1040) Checklist

The purpose of this checklist is to ensure that all matters incident to death are considered in preparing the decedent's final income tax return.

1. Determine if a final tax return is required and the marital status at date of death. Check Form 1040 general instructions.
2. Separate all taxable income items actually or constructively received (per Treas. Reg. §1.451-2) to the date of death from items considered income in respect of decedent that are reportable on estate income tax return. See IRS Publication 559, Table B, Worksheet to Reconcile Amounts Reported in Name of Decedent on Information Returns.
3. If decedent had series E, EE, H, HH, or I savings bond interest, IRC §454(a) permits election of reporting all accrued interest on the final return.
4. Carryovers
   - A. Capital loss–lost if not used on final return.
   - B. Passive loss–additional passive losses may be allowed if suspended losses exceed the step-up in basis.
   - C. Net operating loss–lost if not used on final return.
   - D. Investment interest expense–lost if not used on final return.
   - E. Charitable contribution–lost if not used on final return.
5. Complete preparation of return
   - A. Input the same occupation as prior year in the "occupation" space of return.
   - B. Enter date of death.
   - C. Determine whether medical expenses of decedent paid by estate within one year after death will be deducted on Form 1040 or Form 706.
   - D. Spouse can elect to treat deceased spouse's IRA as his or her own.
   - E. Deduct any unamortized loan costs.
   - F. Deduct any unrecovered basis in annuities.
6. Tax credit carryovers
   - A. May deduct any unused "qualified business credits."
   - B. Foreign tax credit carryovers may be used by decedent's estate or heirs.

Decedent's Final Income Tax Return (2009 Form 1040) Checklist (Continued)
7. If joint return is to be filed: A. Determine if payment of executor commissions to surviving spouse should be accelerated to the final joint return. B. Enter "Filing as surviving spouse" in the area where the surviving spouse will sign on behalf of the deceased tax payer. Also write "Deceased" and the name and date of death above the "taxpayer's name" area. C. Determine the decedent's separate share of the joint tax liability (debt of decedent) as provided by Treas. Reg. §20.2053-6(f). The estate is liable for the decedent's allocable share of tax liability. D. Determine the surviving spouse's estimated tax obligation based on his or her separate share of income and expense items and estimated distributions from decedent's estate or trust. E. Consider the deduction for estate tax attributable to income in respect of a decedent.
8. If a refund is due, determine if Form 1310, Statement of Person Claiming Refund Due a Deceased Taxpayer (and corresponding state form) is necessary (see Form 1310 instructions).
9. Are Social Security numbers on Forms 1099 correct?
10. Are amounts on Forms 1099 correctly reported between individual and estate? If not, disclose in return amount per 1099 in return and then subtract amount not includible in return.
11. Are estimated tax vouchers for the succeeding year in the surviving spouse's name and Social Security number?
12. For taxation of and reporting of income subsequent to death, see "Income Taxation after Death" on page 14-15.

Gift Tax Return Requirements for Year of Death

If the decedent made any reportable gifts in the year of death or any prior year, the personal representative is responsible for filing a gift tax return using Form 709, *United States Gift (and Generation-Skipping Transfer) Tax Return.* The personal representative can consent to "splitting" gifts with the decedent's spouse. See the discussion of gift tax beginning on page 14-14.

A gift tax is generally due by April 15 in the year following the date of the gift. An exception exists where the gift and the decedent's death occur in the same year. In such cases, the gift tax return is due the earlier of the following two dates:

- April 15 following the year of gift or
- The due date of the estate tax return, Form 706

Example. Ben Newman makes a reportable gift on February 15, 2009. He dies March 1, 2009. The gift tax return is due December 1, 2009. However, if the gift consists of interests in property that would otherwise be included in Ben's gross estate because he retained a power to amend or revoke the gift, see page 14–8 and MTG ¶2913.

Estate Taxation and Reporting, Form 706

The federal estate tax is a tax on the transfer of the decedent's property. It is in addition to and separate from the income tax. The federal gift tax is also a tax on the transfer of property during one's lifetime. The gift tax is "integrated" with the estate tax; that is, transfers made by a person during life are included in the computation of that person's estate tax liability at death.

Prior to 2004, the applicable exclusion amount was the same for both gift and estate tax purposes, making the transfer tax system truly unified. Hence, the Internal Revenue Code (IRC) refers to a "unified credit." Beginning in 2004, however, the gift and estate tax applicable exclusion amounts are no longer the same. In 2009, the gift tax applicable exclusion amount is $1 million and the estate tax applicable exclusion amount is $3.5 million. Thus, it is no longer technically accurate to speak of the transfer tax system as being completely "unified." However, many people continue to use the "unified" terminology and the IRC itself still refers to a "unified credit" against the estate tax.

The personal representative of the decedent is responsible for determining what transfers of assets are taxable at death and, depending on the value of total cumulative transfers, filing a federal estate tax return (Form 706) and paying any estate tax that may be due. In addition to the federal estate tax, it is necessary to determine whether the decedent will owe any state estate or inheritance tax requiring a separate tax return.

The federal estate tax (but not the gift tax) is scheduled to be repealed for decedents dying after 2009. However, the estate tax is scheduled to be reinstated for decedents dying in 2011 and thereafter.

See IRS Publication 950, *Introduction to Estate and Gift Taxes,* for more information.

> **Example.** Margot Jones is the personal representative for John Smith, who died in 2009. To file Form 706 for John's estate, she calculates the estate tax as follows:
>
> | | |
> |---|---|
> | Gross estate | $4,500,000 |
> | Less: Allowable deductions | (60,000) |
> | Taxable estate | 4,440,000 |
> | Plus: Taxable gifts | 100,000 |
> | Total | $4,540,000 |
> | Tentative tax on total | 1,923,800 |
> | Less: Gift tax paid by decedent | 0 |
> | Gross estate tax | 1,923,800 |
> | Maximum unified credit | (1,455,800) |
> | Total | $ 468,000 |
> | Net federal estate tax | $ 468,000 |
>
> *State death tax deduction not taken into account. Example illustrates federal estate tax only.

Federal Estate Tax

The following individuals are subject to federal estate tax:

- U.S. citizens, regardless of whether they are domiciled in the United States;
- Resident aliens; and
- Nonresident aliens, to the extent they own assets located in the United States.

Filing Requirements. Form 706 is required if the gross estate, plus adjusted taxable gifts and specific exemptions, exceeds the applicable exclusion amount ($3,500,000 in 2009). A return is required, even though there may be no tax liability.

Due Date. Form 706 is due nine months after the date of death. An automatic extension of six months is available with the filing of Form 4768.

> **Example.** Hemberto Ruiz died in 2009. Prior to his death he had made $100,000 of taxable gifts. His gross estate is $3,450,000. His estate has deductions of $60,000. His personal representative is required to file Form 706, even though there is no federal estate tax liability, because his gross estate plus his amount of taxable gifts exceeds the applicable exclusion of $3.5 million.

> **Caution.** Extending the time for filing does not extend the due date for payment of tax. See page 14–13 regarding provisions for extending the time for payment of tax.

> **Filing Tip.** If it is determined, subsequent to filing, that an election was not made that should have been made (e.g., special use valuation under IRC §2032A), see Treas. Reg. §§301.9100-1–3.

Tax Preparer's Checklist.
Assets includible in gross estate:

- ❖ Accrued interest
- ❖ Amounts due on sales contracts
- ❖ Annuities, IRAs, other retirement accounts
- ❖ Archer Medical Savings Accounts (MSA) or Health Savings Accounts (HSA)
- ❖ Autos, boats, etc.
- ❖ Bonds, certificates of deposit, savings accounts, etc.
- ❖ Cash
- ❖ Coin collections, other collectibles
- ❖ Dividends payable
- ❖ Gift tax paid on gifts within three years of death
- ❖ Includible portions of jointly owned property
- ❖ Jewelry, other significant personal property (review insurance policy)
- ❖ Life insurance on another
- ❖ Life insurance on decedent (need Form 712 from insurance company)
- ❖ Loans due decedent
- ❖ Partnership interests
- ❖ Property over which decedent had a general power of appointment
- ❖ Real estate
- ❖ Revocable transfers
- ❖ Section 529 gifts exceeding annual exclusion amounts
- ❖ Share of final income tax refund
- ❖ Stocks
- ❖ Transfers made for less than full and adequate consideration
- ❖ Transfers made within three years of death (see IRC §2035(a))
- ❖ Transfers taking effect after death (see IRC §2037)
- ❖ Unpaid salary
- ❖ Value of interest in qualified terminable interest property (QTIP) trust established upon prior death of spouse

Gross Estate

The gross estate includes all assets owned by the decedent as well as certain legal rights or interests discussed in this section.

Caution. The gross estate is not the same as the probate estate; it includes property, such as life insurance and retirement benefits, that is not part of probate but is includible in the decedent's gross estate.

Filing Tip. Review the decedent's income tax returns for the last few years prior to death to make sure all property and sources of income have been identified and accounted for on the estate tax return. Also use these returns to identify all liabilities that may exist at the date of death.

Inventory the Contents of Safe Deposit Boxes. The IRS assumes the contents are owned by the decedent unless it is established to the contrary.

Property Owned Jointly with a Non-Spouse. The percentage of the cost of such property contributed by the decedent determines the amount includible in the decedent's estate.

Transfers during Life. Review any trusts created during the decedent's lifetime to determine if these are includible in the gross estate.

Powers of Appointment. Review trust agreements for any trusts in which the decedent had an interest. Determine if these are includible in the gross estate as the result of a general power of appointment.

Gifts Made within Three Years of Death. The decedent's gross estate includes the amount of gift tax paid on any gift made within three years of death (IRC §2035(b)).

In addition, if the decedent transfers an interest in property (or relinquishes a power with respect to property) within three years of death, and the property would have been included in the decedent's gross estate under certain IRC sections if the transferred property had been retained by the decedent, then the property is included in the gross estate. See IRC §2035(a). For example, if the decedent transfers a life insurance policy in which he has "incidents of ownership" within three years of death, the policy proceeds are includible in the decedent's gross estate. See IRC §2042. See the discussion at MTG ¶2914.

Valuation

When Valued. Generally, assets includible in the gross estate must be valued as of the date of death. An "alternate" valuation election can be made to value property as of six months after the date of death (or for property disposed of prior to that date, the value at the date of disposition). This election should be considered if it results in reduced estate tax liability. The election is made by checking a box on Form 706. See MTG ¶1642 and ¶2922.

2009 Valuation Guide

Asset	Guide
Real estate	Attach copy of appraisal from qualified real estate appraiser to Form 706. • Be sure that the appraiser breaks out buildings and other land improvements from the land. On farms, break out the value of drainage tiling (depreciable). • If an undivided or fractional interest is owned, consider if a discount for lack of marketability and/or cost to partition is appropriate. See, e.g., *E. Pillsbury Est.*, 64 TCM 284, CCH Dec. 48,378(M), TC Memo. 1992-425. • Consider whether the estate qualifies for special use valuation. See example on page 14–9. See Schedule A-1 and related instructions for Form 706. • Consider whether an exclusion for a qualified conservation easement applies. See Schedule U of Form 706.
Art, collectibles	Appraisal needed for any article valued in excess of $3,000 or for any collection of similar articles valued in excess of $10,000. Review the insurance policy for any riders.

2009 Valuation Guide (Continued)

Asset	Guide
Closely held business	• Valuation needed of underlying business and assets, plus appraisal of decedent's ownership interest (i.e., stock or partnership interest). See Treas. Reg. §20.2031-2 when valuing stock and Reg. §20.2031-3 when valuing other business interests. • Determine if any buy-sell agreement exists. See *G. Blount Est.*, CA-11, 2005-2 USTC ¶60,509, aff'd in part and rev'd and rem'd in part, 87 TCM 1303, CCH Dec. 56,636(M), TC Memo. 2004-116, for a recent case on factors for determining when the price set in a buy-sell agreement controls.
Stocks, bonds	Determine the mean between lowest and highest selling prices for publicly traded securities quoted on the valuation date.
Life insurance on another	Obtain Form 712 from insurance company for each policy.

Filing Tip. The alternate valuation election is not available unless Form 706 is required and the election would decrease both the value of the gross estate and the amount of the net estate tax due. "Default" valuation is fair market value as of the date of death.

Valuation Rules. Fair market value is the standard used to value the decedent's property. See MTG ¶1695, ¶1697 and ¶2922.

Filing Tip. To establish basis, an appraisal is recommended even if no estate tax return is required. This applies to valuation for estate tax purposes and for stepped-up basis realization.

A "stepped-up" basis rule applies to inherited property.

The stepped-up basis at death rule is currently scheduled to be repealed for individuals who die after December 31, 2009. Records indicating basis and appraisal value are important.

No step-up in basis is allowed for appreciated property acquired by the decedent through gift within one year of death if the property passes, directly or indirectly, from the donee-decedent to the original donor or the donor's spouse. See IRC §1014(e).

Planning Tip. Family limited partnerships (FLPs) have been the subject of much attention and litigation between taxpayers and the IRS. The primary estate and gift tax benefit of an FLP is the ability to claim substantial discounts on the value of the partnership interest in some cases. FLPs, if properly set up and operated, are still an effective estate planning tool. See, *e.g., D. Kimbell, Sr., Exr.*, CA-5, 2004-1 USTC ¶60,486, 371 F.3d 257. Rev'g and rem'g DC Tex, 2003-1 USTC ¶60,455, 244 F Supp2d 700.

Example. Dick Brown, a widower, owns farmland worth $3,000,000, which he leases on a crop-share basis to a tenant. He has owned this land for 40 years. He is active in the management of the farm and shares crop expenses with the tenant. He reports the farm income as self-employment income. He has other assets of $2,000,000. His will provides that the farm land go to his two children equally. His son Darrell is interested in the farm and plans to take over the management of the farm upon his father's death. His other son, Dave, is not interested in the farm management. A farm management fee will be paid to Darrell based on a percentage of farm income.

Upon Dick's death, his estate will be able to make an election to have the farm land valued pursuant to IRC § 2032A. The property's value under the special use valuation provision is $1.5 million. The gross estate will be reduced by only $1,000,000. Although the difference in value is $1.5 million ($3 million less $1.5 million), the reduction in the value of the land will be limited to $1,000,000 if Dick dies in 2009. Thus, Dick's taxable estate would be $4,000,000. The federal estate tax savings of electing §2032A will be $450,000.

*State death tax deduction not taken into account. Example illustrates federal estate tax only.

Note that the basis of the land to Dick's sons is reduced by the special-use reduction (i.e., the basis in the land would be $1,500,000).

To avoid losing this benefit, the farm must continue to be owned and managed by members of Dick's family for 10 years.

Example. John Farmer transfers $2,000,000 of farmland to a family limited partnership. He then makes gifts of 10% interests in the partnership. Although the value of the farmland allocable to the 10% interests is $200,000, the value of a minority partnership interest is $120,000 if a 40% discount is applied.

Planning Tip. A sole proprietor operating an ongoing business whose heirs may or may not be interested in continuing the business should discuss the handling of the business with legal counsel. Options available may include rolling the enterprise into the estate for disposition or creating a new entity to enable business continuation.

Deductions

Specified expenses (see the table above) are deductible in determining the taxable estate.

Planning Tip. If expenses are of no benefit on Form 706 (e.g., not a taxable estate), consider claiming them as income tax deductions for the estate. See Treas. Reg. §1.642(g)-1 for the statement required to be attached to the income tax return.

Also deductible are any casualty losses incurred by the estate.

Planning Tip. State death taxes are deductible for individuals dying after 2004.

2009 Expense Guide

Expense	Guide
Funeral	Reduce by any amounts that were reimbursed, such as VA or Social Security death benefits.
Attorney, accountant	OK to estimate reasonable amount if exact amount not determined at time of filing.
Executor commissions	If one is the sole beneficiary of the estate, it may be advantageous to claim these since the estate tax benefit will be more than the income tax cost. Generally, such fees are subject to income tax but not self-employment tax (if no business is being managed for the estate).
Maintaining or storing estate property	Deductible if it is not possible to immediately distribute property to beneficiaries. See Treas. Reg. §20.2053-3(d)(1). Also see *M. Millikin Est.*, 76 TCM 1076, CCH Dec. 53,009(M), TC Memo. 1998-456.
Selling expenses	Deductible if necessary to pay estate tax liabilities and expenses. Must not be for the benefit of beneficiaries. See Treas. Reg. §20.2053-3(d)(2) and *M. Millikin Est., supra.*

2009 Liability Guide

Liability	Guide
Mortgage and accrued interest expenses	Reference to the real property to which it relates on appropriate schedule.
Property taxes	Limited to the taxes accrued before death of decedent. See Treas. Reg. §20.2053-6(b).
State income taxes	Include for year of death and any prior year unpaid as of death. For Married Filing Jointly, determine decedent's share of joint liability. See Treas. Reg. §20.2053-6(f).
State intangible, personal property, other taxes	Determine if liability existed as of death.
Unpaid child support or alimony	Review divorce decree and property settlement.
Outstanding checks	If they are in discharge of bona fide legal obligations or for charitable purposes and honored by the bank after death, then they reduce the bank balance. Gifts to noncharitable donees in the form of a check that are not paid until after the death of the decedent are includible in the gross estate. See, e.g., *J. Gagliardi Est.*, 89 TC 1207, CCH Dec. 44,393.

Specified debts are deductible in determining the taxable estate.

Filing Tip. Some liabilities (e.g., property taxes, state income tax liability) are deductible on both Form 706 and for income tax purposes.

Filing Tip. Review amounts paid for at least six months after death to determine if the liability existed at the date of death. If it did not, then consider whether payment qualifies as an administrative expense.

State Death Taxes. For decedents dying after 2004, a deduction is available for state death taxes paid. This replaces the credit for state death taxes that was phased out as a result of EGTRRA.

Marital Deduction. A married person's estate is allowed a deduction for property (both probate and non-probate) passing to the surviving spouse. Such amounts are reported on Schedule M of Form 706.

Assets that pass tax-free to a spouse in this way include the following:

- Jointly owned property;
- Life insurance;
- Retirement benefits; and
- Bequests in the will or property passing in trust.

Caution. If the spouse is not a citizen of the United States, then the marital deduction may not be available. But see IRC §2056A.

If a surviving spouse is provided an income interest (only) in property, either outright or via a trust, then the personal representative needs to consider making a "QTIP" election in order to qualify the interest for the marital deduction. See IRC §2056(b)(7).

Example. Mark Thompson's will provides that all of his property, net of taxes and expenses, is to go to a trust. His wife is entitled to all the income of the trust, to be paid quarterly. Upon her death, the trust terminates and passes to Mark's children by his first marriage. Mark dies in 2009. Mark's gross estate less expenses is $4,500,000. If the QTIP election is not made with Mark's estate tax return, his estate will owe federal tax of $450,000. By making the QTIP election as to one-third of the trust ($1,500,000/$4,500,000), no estate taxes will be payable on Mark's death. One-third of the value of the trust at the time of his wife's death will be taxable in her estate. The estate taxes attributable to the inclusion of a portion of the trust in her estate are reimbursable out of the trust.

*State death tax deduction not taken into account. Example illustrates federal estate tax only.

Caution. The marital deduction is reduced to the extent it is chargeable for estate taxes or expenses.

Charitable Deductions. Amounts passing outright to qualified charitable organizations are fully deductible. If a partial interest is provided for (e.g., an income interest or a remainder interest to a charity), then specific requirements must be met to qualify for the estate tax charitable deduction.

The charitable deduction is reduced by any administrative expenses and death taxes allocable to the property being transferred to the charity. However, if the expenses are payable out of income generated during administration by assets allocable to a charitable trust, then the deduction is not reduced. See *O. Hubert Est.*, S.Ct., 97-1 USTC ¶60,261, 117 S.Ct. 1124.

Caution. Property passing to a charity by will cannot be deducted on the income tax return of the estate. Conversely, property transferred to a charity, but not pursuant to the will, does not qualify as an estate tax deduction but may be deductible for income tax purposes.

Be sure that charitable beneficiaries qualify for the deduction. Resources can be found on the Web at www.irs.gov under "Charities & Non-Profits." Also, IRS Publication 78, *Cumulative List of Organizations Described in Section 170(c) of the Internal Revenue Code of 1986*, is available on the IRS Web site and at public libraries.

Tax

The estate tax is based on the taxable estate. The taxable estate equals the gross estate less all allowable deductions and losses. To the taxable estate, add any taxable gifts made after December 31, 1976. The resulting sum is the amount on which the tentative estate tax is calculated.

Credits against Tax

The following credits are available to reduce the estate tax:

- Applicable credit;
- Credit for gift taxes on pre-1977 gifts;
- Credit for foreign death taxes; and
- Credit for tax on prior transfers.

Applicable Credit. The applicable credit and exclusion are based on the year of death.

Applicable Credit and Exclusion 2003-2010

Year	Exclusion	Credit
2003	$1,000,000	$ 345,800
2004-2005	1,500,000	555,800
2006-2008	2,000,000	780,800
2009	3,500,000	1,455,800
2010	No tax	No tax

Transfer Tax Rate Schedule for 2009

Taxable Amount			
Over	Not Over	Tax	Rate of Tax on Excess over Lower Number of Taxable Amount Range (%)
$ 0 –	10,000	$ 0	18
10,000 –	20,000	1,800	20
20,000 –	40,000	3,800	22
40,000 –	60,000	8,200	24
60,000 –	80,000	13,000	26
80,000 –	100,000	18,200	28
100,000 –	150,000	23,800	30
150,000 –	250,000	38,800	32
250,000 –	500,000	70,800	34
500,000 –	750,000	155,800	37
750,000 –	1,000,000	248,300	39
1,000,000 –	1,250,000	345,800	41
1,250,000 –	1,500,000	448,300	43
1,500,000 –	2,000,000	555,800	45
2,000,000 –	3,500,000	780,800	45
>3,500,000		1,455,800	45

Credit for Taxes on Pre-1977 Gifts. A credit is allowed for gift taxes paid on pre-1977 gifts includible in the donor's gross estate under any one of the estate tax provisions that make prior gifts includible in the donor's estate. The credit is generally the same as the estate tax attributable to including the gift in the estate, but cannot be more than the gift tax paid.

Estate and Gift Tax Maximum Rates 2003-2010

2003	49%
2004	48%
2005	47%
2006	46%
2007-2009	45%
2010	Estate tax repealed Gift tax top rate = 35% on cumulative gifts >$500,000; however, $1 million gift tax exclusion applies

Credit for Foreign Death Taxes. A credit is available for foreign death taxes paid on property located in a foreign country but included in the gross estate of a U.S. citizen or resident. Because the United States has entered into estate tax conventions with many countries, determine whether a treaty applies. The estate must file Form 706-CE to claim the credit.

Credit for Prior Transfers. If the decedent owned property acquired from a person who died within 10 years before his or her death or 2 years after, then a credit, limited to the additional estate tax resulting from inclusion in the decedent's estate, is available for estate tax paid on the property in the transferor's estate.

State Estate Tax

Prior to 2002. Every state imposed an estate tax equal to the maximum credit allowed by the federal estate tax prior to the enactment of EGTRRA. Generally, a separate return was required by the state with payment at the same time as the federal tax.

Changes Enacted by EGTRRA. The EGTRRA phased out the benefit of the credit for state estate taxes as follows:

- For 2002, the reduction in the state death credit was 25%.
- For 2003, the reduction in the state death tax credit was 50%.
- For 2004, it was 75%.
- For 2005, the credit was fully phased out and replaced with a deduction.

As a result of the phaseout many states have "de-coupled" from the federal tax law and reestablished the state estate tax as an amount equal to the federal credit before the phaseout. Specific state statutes should be examined.

Caution. As a result of states de-coupling from the federal estate tax, the marginal rate of the combined federal and state death tax has increased. Although the federal marginal rate has decreased, this decrease has generally been more than offset by the increase in the state tax in those states that have de-coupled.

Planning Tip. Most states do not impose a gift tax. Thus, making gifts is an effective way to avoid state estate or inheritance tax. In some cases, "deathbed" gifts should be considered.

States Currently De-coupled from EGTRRA

The following jurisdictions are currently taxing according to exclusion levels that existed prior to EGTRRA:

District of Columbia	Minnesota	Rhode Island
Illinois	New Jersey	Vermont
Maine	New York	
Maryland	North Carolina	
Massachusetts	Oregon	

The exclusion levels prior to EGTRRA are as follows:

Year	Exclusion	Credit
2002-2003	$700,000	$229,800
2004	$850,000	$287,300
2005	$950,000	$326,300
2006 and later	$1,000,000	$345,800

Differences among De-coupled States. Not all of the de-coupled states follow the above format. For deaths occuring in 2009, the following differences apply: In the District of Columbia and in Maryland, the exclusion (credit) is $1,000,000 ($345,800). In North Carolina and Vermont, the current exclusion (credit) under the Internal Revenue Code is used, $3,500,000 ($1,455,800). New Jersey and Rhode Island both use their own tax table for the additional estate tax, and the filing threshold is $675,000, after a $60,000 exemption. It should also be noted that in Connecticut, applicable to estates of decedents dying on or after January 1, 2005, there is a uniform estate and gift tax, with a lifetime combined exemption of $2,000,000 and, in Washington, effective January 1, 2009, the filing threshold for completing an estate tax return is $2,000,000 or more.

Payment of Estate Tax

Generally, the federal estate tax liability is due with the filing of the return, 9 months after the date of death. The IRS may extend the time for payment up to 12 months or, if reasonable cause exists, up to 10 years.

Election to Pay Estate Tax in Installments. If the value of a farm or other closely held business exceeds 35% of the "adjusted gross estate," then an election can be made to defer the tax attributable to such property. The tax subject to the election can be deferred up to 5 years (paying interest only) with installments payable after that up to 10 years. The adjusted gross estate for this purpose is:

Gross estate
− Expenses, debts, and taxes
− Losses
Adjusted gross estate

Conditions

- Must be an active business (i.e., must not consist of passive assets) except for persons holding real estate investments who have an active role in the property's management. (See Rev. Rul. 2006-34).
- If an interest in a partnership or corporation, then such interest must represent 20% or more of the capital of a partnership or 20% or more of the value of the voting interests in the corporation.
- An aggregate disposition of 50% or more of the closely held business will result in an acceleration of the tax due.

Interest is payable on the unpaid tax as follows:

- 2% on the amount of estate tax if the taxable estate was $1,330,000 (for decedents dying in 2009) plus the exemption equivalent amount ($3,500,000 for 2009) minus the applicable credit amount ($1,455,800 for 2009). The maximum amount eligible for the two-percent rate for 2009 is $598,000 (a $2,054,300 tentative tax on $4,830,000 less the applicable credit of $1,455,800). See Code Sec. 6601(j).
- The interest rate on any tax deferred in excess of the above amount is 45% of the IRS rate being charged on underpayments, determined quarterly per IRC §6621. For fourth quarter 2009, the rate is 4%; therefore the §6166 rate is 1.80% (45% × 4%).

Caution. The interest expense is not deductible for income or estate tax purposes.

Example. Richard Freeman died June 30, 2009, owning 100% of the stock of Freeman, Inc., which is an active business. The value of the stock at his date of death is $3,500,000. Richard's other assets, net of expenses, total $1,500,000. Thus, his adjusted gross and taxable estate is $5,000,000. His federal estate tax is $675,000. The portion of this tax eligible for deferral under IRC §6166 is $472,500 ($675,000 × $3,500,000/$5,000,000). The balance of $202,500 is due March 31, 2009. The portion of the deferred tax eligible for the 2% interest rate is the entire amount of the deferral, $472,500, since this is less than the maximum amount eligible for the 2% rate, $598,500.

* State death tax deduction not taken into account. Example illustrates federal estate tax only.

Redemption of Stock to Pay Estate Tax. If stock in a closely held corporation is 35% or more of the gross estate, then the corporation may redeem part or all of the stock to pay estate taxes and administrative expenses. A portion of the distribution in redemption qualifies for sale or exchange treatment (usually resulting in capital gain).

Federal Gift Tax

General Rule. The primary purpose of the gift tax is to prevent persons from avoiding the estate tax by gifting away their property during their lifetime. To that end, the gift tax is imposed, using the same rate structure as the federal estate tax.

A three-year look-back rule applies to some gifts given in the three years prior to a death, if it was a gift of life insurance or a gift of an interest in property over which the decedent retained powers. See MTG ¶2914.

Valuation. Generally the same considerations apply to determining the amount of a gift as are used in determining one's gross estate (see page 14-8). The amount of a gift is the excess of the value of property transferred over any consideration received.

Deductions

Annual Exclusion. Each person is allowed an annual exclusion of up to $13,000 per donee. The amount of the annual exclusion is subject to adjustment based on changes in the consumer price index. If a spouse consents to "splitting" a gift, then a person can give up to $26,000 per donee. A separate gift tax return must be filed for each spouse to effect the splitting.

A person can pay another's educational or medical expenses and not have this count against the annual exclusion.

Caution. Educational or medical expenses of another person must be paid directly to the provider of services to be excludable from the annual tax-free gift limit.

To qualify for the annual exclusion, the gift must be of a present interest and not a future interest. For example, if one transfers property to a trust and keeps the income for 10 years and then provides that the property go to his son, the remainder interest passing to the son would not qualify as a present interest. An exception to this is a gift to a trust for the benefit of a minor if the minor will be entitled to the assets of the trust at age 21.

Gray Area. The U.S. Court of Appeals for the 7th Circuit held in *A. Hackl*, CA-7, 2003-2 USTC ¶60,465, 335 F.3d 664, that gifts of membership interests in a limited liability company that owned tree farms did not qualify for the annual exclusion because they were gifts of future interests. In light of this case, consider giving donees of such interests a right to withdrawal assets (*Crummey* power) or gift cash and then sell the interests to the donees.

Marital Gifts. A person can make unlimited gifts to his or her spouse provided the spouse is a citizen. No return is required for gifts to a citizen spouse.

Charitable Gifts. Outright transfers to qualifying organizations are not subject to gift tax or reporting requirements. See the discussion on page 14-11 regarding charitable transfers for estate tax purposes.

Planning Tip. Charitable gifts of appreciated assets are deductible for income tax purposes at their fair market value. No tax is payable on the appreciation.

Gift Tax Exemption. Each person has a lifetime exemption from tax on taxable gifts up to $1,000,000. This exemption is not indexed for inflation. Unlike the federal estate tax, the gift tax is not scheduled for repeal.

Return Filing Requirements. An annual gift tax return is required for reporting any taxable gift and/or effecting gift splitting between spouses. Form 709 is due April 15 following the year of the gift. Any tax is payable at that time also.

Filing the 2009 Return and Paying the GST Tax			
Type of Transfer	**Where Reported**	**When Due**	**Person Responsible**
Direct skips at death	Form 706, Schedules R and R-1	With estate tax, generally nine months after death (IRC §6166 deferral may be available)	Executor or personal representative
Direct skips during life	Form 709	April 15 following year of transfer	Transferor
Taxable distributions	Form 706-GS(D)	April 15 following year of transfer	Transferee
Taxable terminations	Form 706-GS(T)	April 15 following year of transfer	Trustee

Basis to Recipients of Gifts. The donor's cost basis and holding period generally carry over to the recipient.

Filing Tip. Be sure to notify, in writing, the persons to whom you made gifts of your basis in the asset, the fair market value at the date of the gift, and the date you acquired the property.

Exception. If the fair market value of the property is less than the donor's basis at the date of gift, then upon a subsequent disposition of the property by the donee: (1) the basis, for purposes of determining loss, is the fair market value and (2) for purposes of computing gain, the basis is equal to the donor's basis in the transferred property.

Federal Generation-Skipping Transfer Tax

The purpose of the generation-skipping transfer tax is to prevent families from avoiding estate tax in younger generations by skipping a generation and transferring property to the next generation. For example, suppose Jack Green dies with a $10,000,000 estate and leaves all his property in trust with income payable to his children, and upon their death the trust assets go to his grandchildren. Jack's estate will be subject to the estate tax. However, on the subsequent death of his children, none of the trust property will be taxable in the children's estate; the family would have "skipped" a generation of estate taxes. The generation-skipping transfer tax is designed to minimize this result by imposing a tax comparable to the estate tax on the "skip."

Transfers Subject. There are three types of transfers subject to the generation-skipping transfer tax:

- Direct skip (e.g., a transfer from grandparent to grandchild)
- Taxable distribution (e.g., in the above Jack Green example, if the trust made a distribution of principal to the grandchildren)
- Taxable termination (e.g., in the above Jack Green example, upon the termination of the trust)

Exclusions. As is the case with the gift tax, an annual exclusion from the GST tax of $13,000 is generally available as well as the exclusion for payment of medical and educational expenses. However, for gifts to trusts, the annual exclusion may not be available unless the trust provides the beneficiaries the right to withdraw an amount that does not exceed the gift tax annual exclusion amount.

Exemption. Each individual has a lifetime exemption from the GST tax. For 2004 through 2009, the exemption is the same as the estate tax exemption ($3,500,000 in 2009).

Rate of Tax. After 2010, the generation-skipping tax is scheduled to return as in effect for 2001.

Generation-Skipping Tax Rate 2003-2010	
Year	**Rate**
2003	49%
2004	48%
2005	47%
2006	46%
2007	45%
2008	45%
2009	45%
2010	Repealed

Income Taxation After Death

Who Is Liable for Tax?

Income and expenses up to the date of death are reportable in the final Form 1040 of the decedent (and spouse, if filing jointly). (See page 14-4 for discussion.) Income and expenses subsequent to death depend on the asset and the reason for the expense.

Probate Assets. Generally, probate assets do not pass directly to heirs but are subject to administration as part of the decedent's estate. Income on any assets that are subject to probate must be accounted for separately and reported on a fiduciary income tax return (Form 1041) for the estate. A separate estate checking account should be opened shortly after death by the personal representative and all income and expenses paid out of that account. Also, all payers of income on probate assets should be notified as soon as possible of the change in ownership of the estate and provided with the estate's employer identification number. (See page 14-3 for examples of probate assets. See page 14-4 for how to obtain a number. See below for general income tax considerations of the estate.)

Correspondingly, when probate assets are transferred to the heirs of the estate, the payers of income should be notified of the transfer. Income and expenses related to such assets after transfer to the heir are reportable by the recipient.

Non-Probate Assets. The recipient of any assets passing outside of probate is responsible for reporting any income and related expenses subsequent to death.

Example. Jack Green owned 100 shares of XYZ company as a joint tenant with his son, Jim. Jack died on April 9, 2009. A dividend of $50 was paid to John and Tom on April 30, 2009. This dividend should be reported by Tom in his 2009 individual income tax return.

Basis of Assets Acquired from Decedent

The basis of assets acquired from a decedent, whether by probate or otherwise, is necessary in determining the following:

- Gain or loss on the subsequent disposition of the property.
- Depreciation on depreciable assets.

Current Law

In General. Under current law, the basis of assets acquired from a decedent is generally the fair market value at the date of death. If an estate tax return (Form 706) was filed and the alternate valuation election was made (see above), then the basis is the value used for that purpose.

Example. Shirley makes a gift of XYZ stock on February 28, 2009, to her daughter. She originally purchased the stock on January 14, 2002, for $12,000. At the time of her gift, the value of the stock was $10,000. Her daughter sells the stock on March 15, 2009, for $9,000. Her daughter recognizes a long-term capital loss of $1,000. If she had sold it for $13,500, she would have recognized a long-term capital gain of $500. If she had sold it for $11,000, she would not have recognized a gain or a loss.

Example. Bob and Mary Carver owned, as joint tenants with the right of survivorship, a residential rental property that they had acquired for $150,000. They had allocated $15,000 to the cost of land and depreciated the balance of $135,000 using 27.5-year MACRS. Bob died on June 29, 2009. The property was appraised at $200,000, with $20,000 of that allocable to land. For the period prior to his death, Bob and Mary would be entitled to depreciation, using the mid-month convention, of $135,000/ 27.5 years × 5.5 months/12 months = $2,250. For the period subsequent to death, two calculations are necessary.

Calculation 1: Depreciation on Bob's interest would be based on one-half of the value at the date of his death (i.e., $90,000/27.5 years × 6.5 months/12 months, or $1,772.73).

Calculation 2: Depreciation on Mary's interest would be calculated using the MACRS depreciation formula used before Bob's death (i.e., $67,500/27.5 years × 6.5 months/12 months, or $1,329.55). Mary's interest in half of the property would continue to be reduced by one-half of the accumulated depreciation that had been claimed on the property prior to Bob's death.

Thus total depreciation to be claimed on the 2009 joint return would be $2,250.00 + $1,772.73 + $1,329.55 = $5,352.28.

Planning Tip. As a matter of "deathbed" planning, consider selling "loss" assets prior to death.

Filing Tip. Be sure to report to heirs the basis of assets distributed to or received by them.

Caution. Although the adjustment of basis to fair market value at the date of death is referred to as "stepped-up basis," it can also result in a "step down" in basis if the fair market value is less than the decedent's basis.

Special Rules. The basis of property that is "income in respect of a decedent" (IRD) is not adjusted. See below for a discussion of IRD and how it is taxed.

One-half of the basis of property jointly owned with a spouse is adjusted to fair market value. The survivor's half is determined by reference to the basis prior to death.

Caution. If the jointly owned property was acquired prior to 1977, then up to 100% of the property may be eligible for adjustment to fair market value at the date of death. See *T. Hahn*, 110 TC 140, CCH Dec. 52,606 (Acq.).

For property that was purchased and jointly owned with a nonspouse, the percentage of the cost of the property that the decedent contributed determines the amount includible in the decedent's estate. Basis is adjusted to this extent.

The surviving spouse's share of community property takes the same basis as the decedent's if at least one-half of the entire community interest is included in the gross estate. Thus, 100% of the basis is adjusted.

The basis of property subject to the special-use election is reduced by the amount of reduction in value. See the example on page 14-9.

Scheduled Law Change. In conjunction with the scheduled repeal of the estate tax in 2010, the step-up in basis rules will generally be replaced by carryover basis. See IRC §1022.

Holding Period

Property acquired from a decedent is deemed to have been owned for more than one year, thus qualifying for more favorable long-term capital gain treatment.

Example. John Smith owned 100 shares of XYZ company as a joint tenant with his son, Tom. John died on April 9, 2009. John had paid $2,000 for 100% of the stock. The value at the date of John's death was $5,000. Tom sells the stock on September 14, 2009, for $6,000. Tom has a long-term capital gain of $1,000.

Income and Deductions in Respect of a Decedent

Definition. Income in respect of a decedent (IRD) is any right to receive income as of the date of a decedent's death that, if the decedent had received it prior to death, would have been includible in the decedent's gross income.

Examples of Income in Respect of Decedent

- Salary received after death
- Retirement income from IRAs (other than Roth), 401(k) plans, 403(b) plans, qualified profit sharing plans, etc.
- Interest income accrued but not paid as of death
- Dividends that are payable after death even though declared prior to death
- Increase in redemption value (interest) of U.S. savings bonds (series E, EE, H, HH, or I) if IRC §454(a) election to recognize income is not made
- Crops on hand held by landlord
- Installment obligations
- Life insurance commissions

Life insurance proceeds do not represent income in respect of a decedent and are not subject to income tax when received.

Deductions in respect of a decedent are obligations of the decedent that, had they been paid prior to death, would have been deductible by the decedent.

Examples of Deductions in Respect of a Decedent

- State income taxes due on final state income tax form
- Property taxes
- Business expenses

Income Taxation. Any IRD is taxable to the person who receives it. Thus, if the item is an asset subject to probate and the estate receives it, it is reportable by the estate. If it is received by a trust, then it is reportable by the trust. If received by an individual, then it is taxable to the individual when received.

The character of the income is the same as it would have been in the hands of the decedent (e.g., ordinary or capital gain).

For distributions from retirement plans, it is the actual distribution from the plan that is taxable, not the transfer of the interest in the plan.

Any item of IRD is taxable only to the extent it would have been taxable to the decedent (i.e., the decedent's basis in the item carries over).

Example. Jay Norris contributed $2,000 to a nondeductible IRA. At the date of his death, the IRA had a value of $8,000. John's estate receives a $1,000 distribution from the IRA, at which time it is still worth $8,000. Of the $1,000, 25% ($2,000/$8,000), or $250, is a nontaxable recovery of basis. The balance of $750 is taxable as income in respect of a decedent.

Gray Area. The receipt of a covenant not-to-compete payment after death was held to be taxable as ordinary income in respect of a decedent in *J. C. Coleman,* 87 TCM 1367, CCH Dec. 55,647(M), TC Memo. 2004-126. Both payments made to estates and those to other individuals in respect of decedents must be clearly documented.

Deductions in respect of a decedent are deductible when paid by the estate or the person who is liable for the obligation.

Deduction for Estate Tax Attributable to IRD. The person receiving and reporting an item of IRD is entitled to a deduction for the estate tax attributable to the income. See IRC §691(c). This is determined as follows:

1. Subtract all deductions in respect of a decedent from all items of income in respect of a decedent.
2. Determine estate tax on taxable estate excluding the net amount in step 1.
3. Subtract amount in step 2 from total estate tax.
4. Divide the amount of IRD being reported in the current return by the total IRD of the estate and multiply the result times the amount in step 3.

For individuals, the amount is deductible as an itemized deduction (not subject to the 2% limitation on miscellaneous itemized deductions). It is also deductible for alternative minimum tax purposes.

For estates, the amount is fully deductible.

Example. Jack Sage used the cash method of accounting. At the time of his death, he was entitled to receive $12,000 from clients for his services and he had accrued bond interest of $8,000, for a total income in respect of the decedent of $20,000. He also owed $5,000 for business expenses for which his estate is liable. The income and expenses are reported on Jack's estate tax return. The tax on Jack's estate is $11,250 after credits. The net value of the items included as income in respect of the decedent is $15,000 ($20,000 – $5,000). The estate tax determined without including the $15,000 in the taxable estate is $4,500, after credits. The estate tax that qualifies for the deduction is $6,750 ($11,250 – $4,500).

Recipient's deductible part. Wilma Krause is the recipient. Figure her part of the deductible estate tax by dividing the estate tax value of the items of income in respect of the decedent included in her income (the numerator) by the total value of all items included in the estate that represents income in respect of the decedent (the denominator). If the amount included in the recipient's income is less than the estate tax value of the item, use the lesser amount in the numerator.

As the beneficiary of Jack's estate, Wilma collects the $12,000 accounts receivable from his clients. She will include the $12,000 in her income in the tax year she receives it. If she itemizes her deductions in that tax year, she can claim an estate tax deduction of $4,050, figured as follows:

$$\frac{\text{Value included in income}}{\text{Total value of IRD}} \times \text{The overall amount of estate tax that qualified for the deduction} = \text{Deduction}$$

$$\frac{\$12{,}000}{\$20{,}000} \times \$6{,}750 = \$4{,}050$$

If the amount Wilma collects for the accounts receivable turns out to be more than $12,000, she would still claim $4,050 as an estate tax deduction because only the $12,000 actually reported on the estate tax return can be used in the above computation. However, if she collected less than the $12,000 reported on the estate tax return, she would use the smaller amount to figure the estate tax deduction.

Income Tax Considerations of an Estate

An estate is a separate taxable entity that must file a separate income tax return, Form 1041, if it has gross income of $600 or more. As discussed previously, income on any assets that are subject to probate must be accounted for separately and reported by the estate.

The estate is generally entitled to the same deductions as an individual, with a few exceptions which are described in this section.

Administrative Expenses. Amounts paid in the administration of the estate are deductible for income tax purposes unless they have been claimed on Form 706 as deductions in arriving at the taxable estate.

Planning Tip. If the estate is subject to estate tax, then it will generally be preferable to claim administrative expenses on Form 706 since the effective estate tax bracket will generally be higher than the estate or beneficiary income tax brackets.

Filing Tip. In order to claim administrative expenses on the income tax return, it is required that a statement be filed in duplicate stating that the expenses have not been allowed as deductions for estate tax purposes and waiving the right to claim them on Form 706. The statement can be filed with the income tax return or at any time prior to the expiration of the statute of limitations applicable to the tax year for which the deduction is sought.

If administrative expenses are incurred in excess of what was claimed on Form 706, consideration should be given to filing an amended estate tax return.

Exemption. An estate is entitled to an exemption of $600 even if the return is for a period of less than 12 months.

Investment Expenses. Investment expenses of an individual are subject to the 2%-of-adjusted-gross-income floor on miscellaneous itemized deductions. However, expenses that would not have been incurred if the property were not held by the estate are fully deductible.

Gray Area. The U.S. Court of Appeals for the 6th Circuit held that investment fees are fully deductible (*William J. O'Neill, Jr. Irrevocable Trust*, CA-6, 93-1 USTC ¶50,332, 994 F.2d 302). However, the IRS has continued to litigate this issue with success. See AOD CC-1994-006, September 12, 1994; *Mellon Bank N.A., et al.*, FedCl, 2000-2 USTC ¶50,642; *Scott, J.H., et al.*, CA-4 2003-1 USTC ¶50,428, 328 F.3d 132, aff'g DC Va, 186 F. Supp. 2d 664, 2002-1 USTC ¶50,364; *William L. Rudkin Testamentary Trust*, CA-2, 2006-2 USTC ¶50,369, 467 F.3d 149, aff'd 124 TC 304, CCH Dec. 56,073.

Charitable Deductions. An estate is entitled to an unlimited charitable deduction for amounts that are paid or permanently set aside, pursuant to the will, out of gross income during the tax year. Amounts that are bequeathed per the will and are paid out of principal under state law are not deductible for income tax purposes.

Distributions to Beneficiaries. Income distributions made by an estate that are not payments of specific bequests are deductible by the estate and taxable to the beneficiaries. The amount of the income distributions deduction is limited to distributable net income as determined on Schedule B of Form 1041. The character of income to the beneficiaries is determined by reference to the character of the income to the estate.

Generally, capital gains are not includible in distributable net income and, therefore, are taxable to the estate. However, any capital gains in the year of termination are considered distributed to the beneficiaries and taxable to them. Details are outlined in the individual trust agreement and must be handled on a case-by-case basis based on a careful reading of the documents.

Treatment of Payments after End of Tax Year. An estate can elect to treat distributions made up to 65 days after year end as made on the last day of the estate's taxable year.

Planning Tip. Because the estate income tax brackets are very compressed (in 2009 the 35% bracket applies to taxable income over $11,150), the taxable income of the estate should be determined (or at least estimated) before expiration of the 65-day period and consideration given to making deductible distributions of income to the beneficiaries if they are expected to be in lower income tax brackets.

Be particularly alert if the estate has received any items of IRD, including withdrawals from qualified retirement plans.

Asset Distribution. An estate can distribute assets in lieu of cash to beneficiaries, in which case the distribution amount is the fair market value of the property at the time of distribution. No gain or loss is recognized on the distribution of property unless either of the following applies:

1. The distribution is in satisfaction of a specific bequest or designated amount.
2. The estate elects to recognize the gain or loss.

Caution. Losses recognized on the distribution of property are not deductible because of the related-party rules of IRC §267(b).

If the estate has deductions in excess of income or net capital losses in its final year, they are passed on to the residuary beneficiaries in the year of termination.

Depreciation and Depletion. Depreciation and depletion of estate property is apportioned between the estate and its beneficiaries based on the income that is allocable to each. See IRC §167(h).

Example. An estate has income on a rental property before depreciation of $50,000. Of this income, $20,000 is distributed to the beneficiaries of the estate. Depreciation for the year is $10,000. Depreciation of $4,000 is allocable to the beneficiaries (on Schedule K-1) ($10,000 × $20,000/ $50,000); the balance of the depreciation, $6,000, is deductible by the estate.

Tax Year of an Estate. An estate's tax year starts with the date of the decedent's death. It can adopt any fiscal year end (not more than 12 months later).

Example. Josh Burns dies February 21, 2009. The estate can adopt any month end as a fiscal year end up to January 31, 2010.

Distributions of income are deemed to be made on the last day of the tax year of the estate.

Planning Tip. With the adoption of a fiscal year ending, January 31 in the above example, distributions of income made in 2009 would not be taxable to the beneficiaries until 2010.

Filing of Estate Income Tax Return and Payment of Tax. An estate income tax return is due the 15th day of the fourth month after year end. Any estate income tax due is payable at such time. An estate is not required to pay estimated income tax for its first two tax years.

Caution. For the year of termination of the estate, the final income tax return is due the 15th day of the fourth month after the month of termination.

Income Tax Considerations of Trusts

General Definition and Types of Trusts. A trust is a separate taxable entity for federal income tax purposes. A trust can be created pursuant to a trust agreement executed during one's lifetime or upon death pursuant to one's will (testamentary). The trustee takes title to the property in order to protect or conserve it for the beneficiaries pursuant to the directions of the grantor or decedent as expressed in the trust agreement or will.

Income Taxation. As a separate taxable entity, a trust reports all income received on assets owned by it and deducts all expenses paid by it that are otherwise deductible. It does so on Form 1041. However, if the grantor has sufficient control of trust income or principal as set forth in IRC §§673–677, the income is taxed directly to the grantor. A so-called grantor trust does become a separate entity upon the death of the grantor. See below for election to be treated as an estate.

Like an estate, a trust is entitled to a deduction for distributions made to its beneficiaries. Also like an estate, a trust must apportion depreciation between the trust and beneficiaries based on the income apportioned to each. However, if the trust agreement or applicable state law requires that the trust reserve from income an amount for depreciation, then depreciation, to that extent, is allocated to the trust.

A trust is entitled to an annual exemption of $300 if it is required under its terms to distribute all income currently (i.e., a simple trust); otherwise the exemption is $100.

Example. A trust has income on a rental property, before depreciation, of $50,000. Of this income $20,000 is distributed to the beneficiaries of the trust. Depreciation for the year is $10,000. State law requires that the trustee reserve from income an amount for depreciation. Depreciation of $10,000 is so reserved. The $10,000 of depreciation is deductible only by the trust. The $20,000 distribution is fully taxable to the beneficiaries. The trust taxable income before exemption is $20,000 ($50,000 income less $10,000 depreciation and a deduction for distribution to beneficiaries of $20,000).

Calendar Year. Unlike an estate, a trust (other than certain charitable trusts) must be on a calendar-year basis.

Election to Be Treated as an Estate. A revocable trust, upon the death of the grantor, can elect, along with the estate, to be treated as part of the estate for income tax purposes. Making this election qualifies the trust for favorable tax treatment which includes:

- The ability to report on a fiscal-year basis
- No estimated income tax requirements for two tax years
- Charitable deduction for amounts permanently set aside for charitable purposes
- Deductibility of passive losses for first two tax years
- Qualification for amortization of reforestation expenses

The election is made by filing Form 8855 and, once made, cannot be revoked. A taxpayer identification number is necessary. This election allows the electing trust to be treated and taxed as part of its related estate during the election period. That period begins at the decedent's death and lasts for a minimum of two years. If an executor is appointed to the related estate after the election is made, the executor must agree to the election or it will terminate.

See Treas. Reg. §1.645-1 for more information on how and when to make the election.

Helping Clients Prepare Financially for Their Own Death

This discussion is intended to provide a basic understanding of what happens financially upon one's death:

- The probate process.
- The administration of one's financial affairs, including accounting for all assets, paying all claims, collecting income, and paying expenses during the period of administration.
- The income and transfer tax laws as they apply in the year of death and to the subsequent period of administration.

Based on this information, one must then plan for one's death. Failure to do so can have disastrous consequences both financially and in terms of the survivors' well-being.

Will

The first and most important step in planning for death is to make a will. A will is a legal document that allows an individual to determine the administration and distribution of his or her estate. It also allows the individual to designate who will be responsible for his or her minor children.

Other Documents

Other documents to consider at the time of preparing or updating one's will are:

- **Living trust**–A living trust is a trust created to hold title to an individual's assets. The benefits include:
  - Continuity of management of assets should the individual become incapacitated and unable to take care of his or her financial affairs.
  - Avoidance of probate.
  - Privacy as to one's assets upon his or her death. Without a living trust, an inventory of the decedent's assets subject to probate may be a matter of public record.
  - Possible reduced cost, time, and aggravation in settling one's estate.
- **Durable power of attorney**–This is a legal document in which an individual appoints a person to act as his or her agent as to certain personal and financial matters in the event of specified events or at a specified time.
- **Living will**–A living will usually expresses an individual's desire not to receive extraordinary medical treatment and specifies the kind of medical care he or she would prefer under given circumstances.
- **Durable power of attorney for health care**–In this legal document, an individual designates someone to make health care decisions in the event he or she is unable to do so.

Ownership of Assets

Without careful preparation, an individual's assets at death may not go where he or she intended. Because of this, it is important to do a careful review of how one's assets are currently held. A will or living trust controls assets solely in an individual's name or in the trust's name as well as his or her portion of certain assets owned jointly with others. Assets in joint tenancy or tenancy by the entirety pass to the surviving joint owner pursuant to state law and not according to an individual's will. Assets owned as tenants in common are subject to an individual's will to the extent of his or her interest in the property.

A careful review should include beneficiary designations on the following:

- Life insurance
- Group term life insurance
- Annuities
- IRAs and other retirement accounts
- Deferred compensation contracts

Individuals who are divorced should be especially alert to this. Although divorce generally terminates an ex-spouse's interest in probate assets, it does not terminate beneficiary designations.

It is important to consider providing for contingent or secondary beneficiaries in case the primary beneficiary predeceases the individual or does not wish to take ownership of the asset.

Business Succession Planning

If an individual owns an interest in a closely held business, it is critically important to provide for disposition of the interest in the business and to provide for an orderly transition after an individual's death. If the business is unincorporated, such as rental real estate or farming, the individual may wish to consider transferring it to a family partnership or corporation. This may prevent the assets of the business from having to be divided up among the individual's heirs and may facilitate management by those heirs that are active in the business.

Buy-Sell Agreement. A buy-sell agreement provides a set of rules as to what is to happen to each owner's interest in the event of any of the following:

- Death
- Disability
- Termination of employment
- The desire of an owner to dispose of his or her interest during his or her lifetime

This document should be reviewed at least once a year to make sure all parties are in agreement with it and understand it.

The price provided for in the agreement may be controlling as to the value to be reported in a deceased owner's estate.

> **Caution.** See *G. Blount Est.*, 87 TCM 1303, CCH Dec. 55,626(M), TC Memo 2004-116, aff'd in part and rev'd and rem'd in part, CA-11, 2005-2 USTC ¶60,509, for how not to prepare a buy-sell agreement and a discussion of factors that apply in determining whether a price in a buy-sell agreement is controlling for estate tax valuation purposes.

Estate Tax Planning

One of the purposes of estate tax planning is to ensure that an individual's assets go to whom he or she chooses with the least federal and state estate tax cost. It is also important to consider the income tax consequences of the planned disposition of assets.

Inventory All Assets and Liabilities. The first step in estate tax planning is to prepare an inventory of all of the individual's assets and their approximate values. Note ownership (i.e., whether jointly owned and if so with whom). Also list all mortgages and other liabilities.

> **Caution.** Don't assume anything. Verify ownership and beneficiary designation by reference to written documents.

Who Is to Receive Income and/or Assets? Effective estate tax planning involves consideration of who is to receive interests in property and under what conditions:

- Spouse
- Children
- Other
- Charitable causes

Project Estate Tax. Based on the preceding information, project the potential estate and income taxes upon death. For a married couple, this needs to be done under two scenarios: the husband predeceasing the wife, and the wife predeceasing the husband.

Project Liquidity. Will there be enough cash to pay estate taxes and final expenses? Tax planning hopefully will reduce the need for cash, but, even after planning, the availability of sufficient cash should be evaluated.

Checklist of Estate Planning Strategies under Current Law

Gifting

- Gifts up to the annual exclusion amount ($13,000 in 2009) completely avoid federal gift and estate tax (MTG ¶2905). Also, future appreciation on, and income from, the property gifted avoid estate tax.
- Gifts for educational and medical purposes paid directly to the institution can be made in addition to the annual exclusion amount. There is no limit on the amount of such gifts. See MTG ¶2907 for details.
- With a spouse's consent, one-half of gifts made by one spouse are deemed made by the other spouse. This increases the annual amount that can be given with no transfer tax consequences from $13,000 to $26,000.
- Gifts to 529 plans, used to fund college education, avoid gift tax (MTG ¶899). Up to five times the annual exclusion amount (i.e., $65,000) can be funded up front with no gift tax over a five year period. If the donor lives five years, then the transfer is estate tax free also. Joining with a spouse can increase this limit to $130,000.
- Gifts in excess of the annual exclusion amounts should be considered. Although such gifts use some of the donor's lifetime exemption ($1,000,000 in 2009), subsequent appreciation on such gifts avoids gift and estate taxes.

> **Example.** Assume Jason Hamilton gifted $600,000 over and above his annual exclusion in 2000, using up $192,800 of his lifetime exemption. Assume the property appreciates to $1,000,000 by the time of his death in 2009. Also assume his remaining taxable estate is $4,500,000. His federal estate tax is $720,000. If he had not made the gift, his federal estate tax would have been $900,000—a savings of $180,000.
>
> *State death tax deduction not taken into account. Example illustrates federal estate tax only.

- It is important to make sure that each spouse has enough assets in his or her own name to ensure that the benefit of each spouse's applicable credit is maximized. Furthermore, estate planners want to "equalize" estates between spouses. Both goals can be accomplished by gifts from the spouse with more assets to the other spouse.
- For a discussion of gifts in contemplation of death, see page 14-14.

Provide for and Optimize Marital Deduction

- The will or revocable trust can provide a formula for minimizing the amount of property passing to the surviving spouse while avoiding estate tax on the estate of the first spouse to die (i.e., maximizing the benefit of the decedent's applicable credit).
- Alternatively, a QTIP trust can be created by requiring, among other factors, that all income be payable at least annually to the surviving spouse (MTG ¶2926). Then, in connection with the filing of the estate tax return (Form 706) for the first spouse to die, a QTIP election can be made as to part or all of the trust property. This qualifies the property subject to the election for the marital deduction. On the death of the surviving spouse, the portion of the trust subject to the election is taxable to the surviving spouse's estate. (Provision should be made in the surviving spouse's will that taxes attributable to the QTIP are to be payable out of the QTIP trust.)
- Upon the death of the first spouse, a qualified disclaimer (MTG ¶2903) can be made as to property otherwise passing to the surviving spouse to keep it out of his or her taxable estate and to get full benefit of the decedent's applicable credit.

> **Example.** John Smith has assets of $7,000,000. His wife has assets of $200,000. Assuming a testamentary plan that optimizes the marital deduction, then upon John's death (in 2008) $3,500,000 goes to his wife outright and the balance of his estate goes to a "bypass" trust. Upon her subsequent death (assuming no change in the value of the assets and that she dies in 2009), her federal estate tax (assuming a non-decoupled state) would be $90,000 (on a taxable estate of $3,700,000). However, if Mrs. Smith predeceases her husband and he inherits the $200,000 outright, then, although no estate tax would be payable on her death, the estate tax on Mr. Smith's subsequent death would be $1,665,000, a cost of $1,575,000.
>
> * State death tax deduction not taken into account. Example illustrates federal estate tax only.

Sever and Avoid Joint Tenancy. Joint tenancy "preempts" any planning done through a will or living trust.

Charitable Planning. If a person has charitable interests, there are several planning considerations.

- Outright charitable bequests are fully deductible for estate tax and gift tax purposes.
- If a person wants to retain some amount of cash flow either for himself or for an heir or heirs, a charitable trust may be appropriate (MTG ¶2932). For example, one could provide that upon his death his daughter would get an annuity equal to 5% of the amount going to a charitable trust. His estate would be entitled to a charitable deduction based on the value of the remainder interest going to the charity.
- By transfering a remainder interest in a residence or farm to a qualifying charity, one is entitled to an income tax charitable deduction and an estate tax charitable deduction.
- Consider naming a charity as beneficiary of qualified retirement plans. Upon death, qualified retirement plan assets are estate taxable as well as income taxable. By designating a charity as beneficiary of part or all of such assets, those assets go to the charity without any income or estate tax.

Life Insurance. If life insurance is a significant amount, then planning is obviously important.

- *Life insurance trust.* A life insurance trust is very effective in removing the death benefit from estate tax. An irrevocable trust is used that acquires ownership of the life insurance. Premiums are paid by the trust, usually from gifts received from the insured. Beneficiaries are usually given a right (*Crummey* power) to withdraw any gifts to the trust for a limited period of time in order to qualify the gifts as a present interest eligible for the annual exclusion amount ($13,000 in 2009). Upon the insured's death, the proceeds are paid to the trust. The trust can purchase nonliquid assets from the estate to provide cash to pay estate taxes. Such a trust usually provides for income to the surviving spouse as well as the ability to spend principal for education, medical expenses, or support and maintenance of the surviving spouse. Upon the surviving spouse's subsequent death, the trust may terminate and go to children and/or charity.

Example. Ted Blue has a taxable estate of $4,000,000. He also owns $2,500,000 of life insurance with his wife as beneficiary. His will provides for a maximum marital deduction and a bypass trust. Upon Ted's death in 2008, there is no estate tax payable since the life insurance qualifies for the marital deduction and his will provides for a maximum marital deduction of his other property. Assume Mrs. Blue dies in 2009. Her taxable estate will include $2,000,000 from Ted's estate plus the life insurance of $2,500,000, a total of $4,500,000; federal estate taxes of $450,000 are due.

If Ted had used a life insurance trust to acquire and own the life insurance, there would have been no estate taxes payable on either his death or his wife's.

* State death tax deduction not taken into account. Example illustrates federal estate tax only.

- *Second-to-die life insurance.* This insurance contract covers both spouses and does not pay a benefit until the second spouse dies. It is less expensive than normal life insurance. It provides funds to pay estate taxes when needed, which is usually on the second death.

Valuation. There are significant strategies to be considered that take advantage of either statutory reductions in value or valuation discounting principles.

- By qualifying for IRC §2032A, a significant discount (limited to $1,000,000 in 2009) can be achieved for qualifying farm land (MTG ¶2922).
- One should monitor the threshold requirement of 50% (i.e., qualifying farmland must meet or exceed 50% of the adjusted gross estate as defined). If one is close to this, then gifting of non-farm assets or purchasing additional farm land should be considered.
- Be sure to meet the material participation requirements either as to the owner or by providing for material participation by a "qualified heir."
- If properly structured and used, interests in family partnerships may be subject to significant discounts from the proportionate share of underlying assets.
- A properly structured buy-sell agreement can be effective to fix the value of a closely held business interest. See *H.A. True Jr., Est.,* 82 TCM 27, CCH Dec. 54 398(M), TC Memo. 2001-167. Aff'd CA-10, 2004-2 USTC ¶60,495, 30 F3d 1210.

Payment of Taxes. Provisions exist that may assist the estate and heirs in financing the payment of estate taxes.

- IRC §6166. If a closely held business interest is more than 35% of the adjusted gross estate, then taxes allocable to such interest are eligible for up to a 14-year maximum payment period with a favorable interest rate. See page 14-13.
- IRC §303 provides that qualifying interests in closely held corporations may be redeemed by the corporation to provide cash to pay estate taxes and administrative expenses. Absent qualification under IRC §303, redemptions of stock may be treated as taxable dividend income to the estate.
- Consider acquiring life insurance if there will not be sufficient liquidity of an estate to pay taxes and expenses.

Generation Skipping. If the children of an individual already have sizable estates, then passing part of the individual's estate to a generation-skipping trust will avoid additional estate tax on the children's death. Each individual has a generation-skipping transfer exemption ($3,500,000 in 2009). This is the maximum amount that can be transferred to the grandchildren without incurring generation-skipping transfer tax.

Example. George Street, a widower, has a $4,500,000 estate. His son Tom has an estate of $10,000,000. Tom has three children. If George dies in 2009 and leaves his estate to Tom, then Tom's estate is increased by $4,050,000 ($4,500,000 less $450,000 in federal estate taxes). Assuming a marginal estate tax bracket (federal) of 45%, this would result in $1,822,500 in additional taxes for Tom's estate. By providing that $3,500,000 of George's estate is to go to a generation-skipping trust, $1,575,000 of taxes could be avoided on Tom's death. The trust could provide for income to be payable to Tom or to Tom's children.

*State death tax deduction not taken into account. Example illustrates federal estate tax only.

Deathbed Planning. See below for techniques for saving on income and estate taxes if a person is in failing health.

Loans. Loans to family members can effectively transfer wealth to heirs reducing estate taxes.

- A person can loan up to $10,000 at no interest. If the loan recipient has less than $1,000 of investment income, up to $100,000 can be loaned interest free.

- Individuals can assist children and other heirs by loaning money (e.g., to purchase a house) at an interest rate based on the IRS adjusted federal rate (AFR), which is lower than the commercial rate that the child would otherwise borrow at. The AFR for short-term loans (three years or less) with monthly payments is published monthly.

Effect of Sunset Legislation—Importance of Flexibility. The EGTRRA schedules the estate tax for repeal in 2010, but, because of the sunset nature of EGTRRA, the estate tax, as in effect prior to the legislation, would be reinstated in 2011. EGTRRA provided for the phaseout of the estate tax by providing for scheduled increases in the exemption equivalent as follows:

Year of Death	Exemption Equivalent
2004 or 2005	$1,500,000
2006-2008	$2,000,000
2009	$3,500,000

The gift tax was not repealed. The current exemption is $1,000,000.

Congress has considered making the repeal of the estate tax permanent, but, as of this time, has not done so. The status of the law leads to much uncertainty in estate planning and puts an emphasis on flexibility. Techniques that lend themselves to flexibility are:

- **Disclaimer**–By planning for the ability of survivors to disclaim part or all of their interest in the decedent's estate, one can take into account the estate and income tax law as of the time of death and use disclaimers to minimize estate tax.
- **QTIP interest**–The ability to vary the amount of property subject to the QTIP election provides the flexibility to take into account the estate and income tax law and financial factors at the time of death.

Deathbed Planning

The following strategies should be considered when a person is in failing health and/or does not expect to live much longer. If the person is not able to act because of incapacity, then an agent may be able to take action if he or she has authority pursuant to a power of attorney or as trustee of the individual's living trust.

Accelerate Distributions from Annuities and Retirement Plans. Generally, the amount in an annuity or retirement plan will be subject to income tax when received by the individual or by his or her heirs after the individual's death. Although the amount of the retirement account is taxable in one's estate, the income tax on the income (IRD) that is later payable by the heirs is not deductible for estate tax purposes. However, if the individual incurs the income tax liability prior to death, this reduces his or her taxable estate.

Charitable Gifts. Bequests provided for in one's will to a qualified charity will result in a deduction for estate tax purposes but not for income tax purposes. By making such gifts prior to death, the individual gets an income tax deduction (subject to the limitations based on adjusted gross income) and removes the gift from his or her estate.

Annual Exclusion Gifts. If the individual makes gifts that do not exceed the annual exclusion of $13,000 (in 2009) per donee, the amount gifted is not includible in his or her estate.

> **Caution.** Checks written as gifts prior to death must be cashed by the donees prior to death to be effective.

Additional Gifts. With the "de-coupling" of state estate taxes from the federal tax system, and given that most states do not impose a gift tax, additional gifts shortly prior to death can result in significant savings in estate taxes.

Recognize Losses. If the individual has unrealized losses, consider selling the assets with the losses prior to death. Upon death the loss evaporates, with the adjustment of the basis to the (lower) fair market value at death. Taking the loss prior to death may offset other income in the individual's income tax return. Capital losses (e.g., on the sale of securities) are available only to offset capital gains and up to $3,000 of ordinary income. Potential ordinary (or IRC §1231) losses, such as on rental real estate used in a trade or business, are not limited. Also consider that the disposition of property with suspended passive losses prior to death will trigger full deductibility of the suspended loss (MTG ¶2076). Otherwise, the suspended loss is deductible in the year of death only to the extent it exceeds any increase in basis as a result of death.

> **Example.** Ted Flynn dies in 2009. At the time of his death he owns a rental property (passive activity) with a basis of $26,000 and suspended passive activity losses of $40,000. The property is appraised at $60,000 as of the date of John's death. Of the suspended loss, only $6,000 [$40,000 – increase in basis of $34,000 ($60,000 – $26,000)] is deductible on John's final individual income tax return.

Post-Mortem Tax Planning

Planning prior to death can be very effective. However, often either planning is not done or the plan created is not kept current with changes in one's financial situation and tax laws. After death, however, there are still many opportunities to minimize taxes.

Preparing the Final Form 1040

The decedent's final tax return is discussed on pages 14-4 to 14-6. Post-mortem information must be included on the decedent's final Form 1040:

- Medical expenses incurred prior to death, but paid within 12 months after death can be claimed on the final Form 1040.
- The election to report accrued series E and EE savings bond interest annually, rather than when received, may be made. In the year the election is made, previously unreported E and EE bond interest is recognized. This can be beneficial if the marginal income tax bracket of the decedent in his or her final return is lower than that of the estate or the ultimate beneficiaries.

Preparing the Estate Tax Return

The estate tax return, Form 706, is discussed on page 14-6.

- The election for alternate valuation can be made on a timely filed return, including extensions.
- An estate containing qualified farm or closely held business property passing to a qualified heir may use special valuation methods that value the property at its present use rather than its highest and best use (MTG ¶2922). The total reduction in value is limited to $1,000,000 for individuals dying in 2009.
- Personal representative's commissions, attorney's and accountant's fees, appraisal fees, court expenses, and other administrative costs can be claimed on either Form 706 or Form 1041.
- Consider maximizing executor fees if the marginal estate tax bracket is greater than the anticipated income tax bracket of the executor and the executor is the sole residuary beneficiary.
- The personal representative may elect to include in the marital deduction the value of qualified terminable interest property (QTIP), that is, property passing to the spouse, who is entitled to all the income from the property for life.
- A qualified disclaimer can be made, thus keeping the disclaimed property out of the estate of the person disclaiming and resulting in a tax-free transfer to those succeeding to the disclaimer's interest or in a charitable deduction to the estate. The disclaimer must be made within nine months of death.
- An extension of time to pay the estate tax due may be elected in the following circumstances:
  - For reasonable cause or undue hardship (extension up to 10 years, with interest at the statutory rate) (see IRC §6161.).
  - When a closely held business is a significant part of the estate (extension up to 14 years, with interest on part of the tax at 2% and on the remainder at 45% of the federal underpayment rate) (MTG ¶2939).
  - When a remainder or reversionary interest is included in the estate (extension up to six months after the precedent interest terminates, with interest at the statutory rate) (See IRC §6163).

Consider redeeming stock in a closely held corporation to provide funds to pay estate taxes and administrative expenses.

Preparing the Fiduciary Income Tax Return

A fiduciary (trustee or executor) files Form 1041 if required (see flowchart on page 14-2).

- Proper selection of a fiscal year may avoid bunching income into one taxable year and allow deferral of income to the beneficiaries.
- All or part of the administration expenses may be deducted on Form 1041 as an income tax deduction rather than on Form 706 as an estate tax deduction (MTG ¶529).
- The partnership basis-adjustment election may be made in a timely filed partnership return. This results in an adjustment to fair market value to the extent of the deceased partner's interest in partnership assets (MTG ¶456).
- A distribution during administration, even a distribution of principal, is treated as a distribution of income (which is taxable to the beneficiaries in the year in which the estate's year ends) to the extent of the estate's distributable net income. But, this does not apply to a payment of a specific bequest of money that is distributed in not more than three installments (MTG ¶564).
- Consider distributions to spread income among the estate and beneficiaries.
- Consider the election of a revocable trust to be treated as an estate (see discussion above). See MTG ¶516.

Retirement Plan Accounts

IRAs require special attention at death. See Tab 9.

- Determine who the beneficiaries are and advise them of minimum distribution requirements; see Treas. Reg. §§1.401(a)(9)-1 to 5 and 1.408-8.
- Advise beneficiaries of basis, if any, in the accounts and any related deduction for estate tax attributable to income in respect of a decedent (IRD).
- Consider a spousal rollover or the election to have a decedent's account treated as that of the spouse.
- Consider dividing IRA accounts so that each account has one beneficiary.

ALABAMA

2009 tax rate schedule:

Single, HOF, MFS:

$ 0 –	500	×	2%	minus	$	0.00
501 –	3,000	×	4	minus		10.00
3,001 +		×	5	minus		40.00

MFJ:

$ 0 –	1,000	×	2%	minus	$	0.00
1,001 –	6,000	×	4	minus		20.00
6,001 +		×	5	minus		80.00

Tax assistance: 334.242.2677

Other information: E-mail requests by using the form at www.ador.state.al.us/mailform.cfm. Other assistance is available at Taxpayer Service Centers located in Auburn/Opelika, Birmingham, Dothan, Gadsden, Huntsville, Mobile, Montgomery, Muscle Schoals, and Tuscaloosa; addresses and phone numbers of these centers are available at www.revenue.alabama.gov/servcenters.html.

Forms request: 334.242.2677
Fax requests 334.242.0064

Alabama Department of Revenue
Income Tax Forms
P.O. Box 327470
Montgomery, AL 36132-7470

Web site: www.ador.state.al.us

Download: www.ador.state.al.us/incometax/Itformsindex.htm

e~file www.ador.state.al.us/incometax/efilemain.htm

Who can e-file? All filers using an approved software provider or a certified electronic return originator (ERO)

Who must e-file? Tax preparers who prepared 50 or more Alabama resident or part-year resident individual income tax returns for the calendar using tax preparation software are required to e-file all of their current-year individual returns.

Filing requirements:

Filing status options: Single, Married Filing Jointly, Married Filing Separately, and Head of Family (same meaning as Head of Household for federal purposes).

Residents: Residents must file if gross income for the year is at least $4,000 for Single, $5,250 for Married Filing Separately, or $7,700 for Head of Family. Those whose filing status is Married Filing Jointly and whose gross income for the year is at least $10,500 must file an Alabama income tax return.

Part-year residents: Part-year residents must file if annual gross income meets the thresholds listed for Residents above while an Alabama resident. Those whose filing status is Married Filing Jointly must file if annual gross income is at least $10,500 while an Alabama resident.

Nonresidents: Nonresidents must file a return if Alabama income exceeds the allowable prorated personal exemption. Multiply the appropriate amount by the percentage of adjusted total income earned in Alabama.

Forms to file:

Residents and part-year residents: Form 40, *Alabama Individual Income Tax Return.* Part-year residents who receive Alabama income while not living in state must also file Form 40NR.

Nonresidents: Form 40NR, *Alabama Individual Income Tax Return (Nonresidents Only)*

Where to send returns:

Form 40, balance due:
Alabama Department of Revenue
P.O. Box 2401
Montgomery, AL 36140-0001

Form 40, refund due:
Alabama Department of Revenue
P.O. Box 154
Montgomery, AL 36135-0001

Form 40NR:
Alabama Department of Revenue
P.O. Box 327469
Montgomery, AL 36132-7469

IRC conformity: IRC incorporated by reference as currently amended to extent of provisions directly referenced by state code.

Starting point for calculation of income: Gross income.

Attach other state returns? Yes, if claiming credit for tax paid to other state(s).

Federal attachments: If filed with federal return, Schedules C and F, Forms 2106, 3903, 4684, 4797, 6252, and 8283. If taxpayer is claiming a federal tax liability deduction, attach page 2 of Form 1040. Complete copy of federal return must be attached to nonresident return if federal tax deduction is claimed.

Estimated tax payments: Required if nonwage income over $1,875 ($3,750 if married filing jointly) or estimated tax $100 or over.

Extensions: Automatic six-month extension allowed.

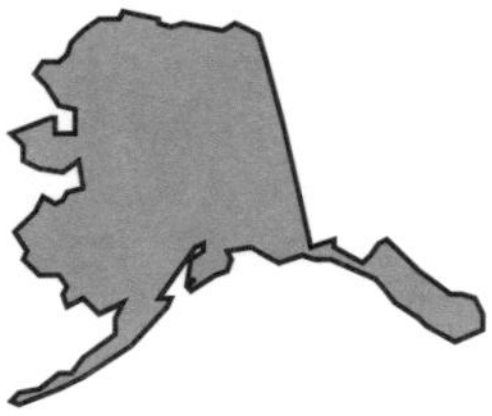

ALASKA

2009 tax rate schedule: The state of Alaska does not have an individual income tax.

Tax assistance:	Juneau: 907.465.2320 Anchorage: 907.269.6620
Forms request:	Juneau: 907.465.2320 Anchorage: 907.269.6620 *Juneau office:* 333 W. Willoughby Ave. 11 Fl. Side B P.O. Box 110420 Juneau, AK 99811-0420 *Anchorage office:* 550 W. 7th Ave. Ste. 500 Anchorage, AK 99501-3555
Web site:	www.revenue.state.ak.us
Download:	www.revenue.state.ak.us/FORMS/index.htm

Filing requirements: Although there is no individual state income tax, Alaska does have a corporate state income tax, and also all partnerships with at least one corporate partner must file an information return.

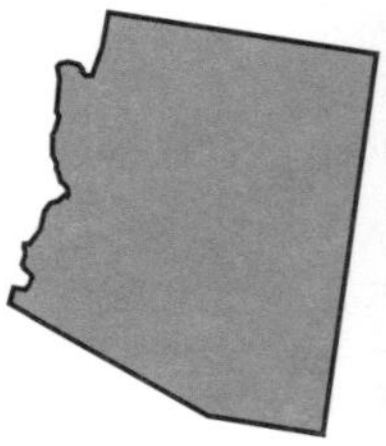

ARIZONA

2009 tax rate schedule:

Single, MFS:

$ 0	–	10,000	×	2.59%	minus	$	0.00
10,001	–	25,000	×	2.88	minus		29.00
25,001	–	50,000	×	3.36	minus		149.00
50,001	–	150,000	×	4.24	minus		589.00
150,001 +			×	4.54	minus		1,039.00

MFJ, HOH:

$ 0	–	20,000	×	2.59%	minus	$	0.00
20,001	–	50,000	×	2.88	minus		58.00
50,001	–	100,000	×	3.36	minus		298.00
100,001	–	300,000	×	4.24	minus		1,178.00
300,001 +			×	4.54	minus		2,078.00

Tax assistance:	602.255.3381 or 800.352.4090
Forms request:	602.542.4260 FORMS Arizona Department of Revenue 1600 W. Monroe Phoenix, AZ 85007-2650
Web site:	www.revenue.state.az.us
Tax Practitioner Web site:	www.revenue.state.az.us/Taxpro/Taxpro%20menu.asp
Download:	www.azdor.gov/Forms/individualforms.asp
e~file	see www.azdor.gov/Eservice/individual.asp

Who can e-file? Individual tax returns may be electronically filed.

Who must e-file? No conditions.

Filing requirements:
Filing status options: Single, Married Filing Jointly, Married Filing Separately, and Unmarried Head of Household, including Surviving Spouse.

Residents: If your Arizona gross income (this is the federal adjusted gross income minus income not taxed in Arizona) is at least $15,000, you must file an Arizona income tax return. Also, you must file an Arizona income tax return if your Arizona adjusted gross income is at least $11,000 for married filing jointly or $5,500 for those filing as single, head of household, or married filing separately.

Part-year residents: Report all income received during AZ residency plus AZ-source income received during nonresidency. Same gross income limits apply as for residents.

Nonresidents: Report income received from AZ sources. Same gross income limits apply as for residents.

Forms to file: Form 140, *Resident Personal Income Tax Return*

Part-year residents: Form 140PY, *Part-Year Resident Personal Income Tax Return*

Nonresidents: Form 140NR, *Nonresident Personal Income Tax Return*

Where to send returns:

Refund or no tax due:
Arizona Department of Revenue
P.O. Box 52138
Phoenix, AZ 85072-2138

Payment due:
Arizona Department of Revenue
P.O. Box 52016
Phoenix, AZ 85072-2016

IRC conformity: IRC incorporated by reference as of January 1, 2009.

Starting point for calculation of income: Federal adjusted gross income.

Attach other state returns?

Yes, if claiming credit for tax paid to other state(s).

Federal attachments: Schedule A, if taxpayer itemized deductions on federal return.

Estimated tax payments: Required if expected gross income exceeds $75,000 in current or preceding year ($150,000, if married filing jointly).

Extensions: A federal extension for filing income taxes will also extend taxpayer's time to file Arizona income taxes. However, in the absence of a federal extension or if making a tax payment with the extension request, taxpayer must use the Arizona extension form (Form 204).

Length of extension: Automatic six months. Taxpayer must pay 100% of tax liability by original due date of return to avoid late payment penalty. 90% of tax liability must be paid by original due date of return to avoid extension underpayment penalty.

Mailing address:

No payment enclosed:
Arizona Department of Revenue
P.O. Box 52138
Phoenix, AZ 85072-2138

Payment enclosed:
Arizona Department of Revenue
P.O. Box 52016
Phoenix, AZ 85072-2016

ARKANSAS

Caution: The 2008 tax rate schedule appears below. At the time of publication, the 2009 tax rate schedule has not been released by the state. However, it will be reproduced at *tax.cchgroup.com/Express Answers* as soon as it is available.

2008 Individual Tax Rate Schedule

$ 0	–	3,799	×	1.0 %	minus	$	0.00
3,800	–	7,599	×	2.5	minus		56.99
7,600	–	11,399	×	3.5	minus		132.98
11,400	–	18,999	×	4.5	minus		246.97
19,000	–	31,699	×	6.0	minus		531.95
31,700	+		×	7.0	minus		848.94

MFS combined-status couples calculate taxes separately and add the results.

Tax assistance: 501.682.1100 or 501.682.7225 or 800.882.9275 (AR)

Forms request: 501.682.1100

State of Arkansas Income Tax
Forms Supply
P.O. Box 3628
Little Rock, AR 72203-3628

Web site: www.state.ar.us/dfa/your_taxes.html

Download: www.state.ar.us/dfa/income_tax/tax_individual.html

e~file http://www.state.ar.us/dfa/income_tax/tax_efile_providers.html

Who can e-file? Tax preparers accepted in the IRS e-file program who submit federal and state return together using approved software. Arkansas also participates in State only filing provided through the IRS.

Who must e-file? No conditions.

Filing requirements:
Filing status options: Single, Married Filing Jointly, Married Filing Separately on Same Return, Married Filing Separately on Different Returns, Qualifying Widow or Widower with Dependent Child, and Head of Household.

Residents: Taxpayers filing as Single must file if gross income is at least $7,800 ($9,300 for age 65 or older). Taxpayers with Head of Household status must file if gross income is at least $12,100 ($13,000 for age 65 or older). Married Filing Jointly taxpayers must file if gross income is at least $15,500 (both spouses under age 65), $15,600 (one spouse age 65 or older), or $16,200 (both spouses age 65 or older). Taxpayers with Married Filing Separately status must file if gross income is at least $3,999. Those with qualified widow(er) status must file if gross income is at least $15,500 ($16,000 for age 65 or older).

Part-year residents: Must file for gross income of at least $1 while resident (any age or filing status).

Nonresidents: Must file for gross income of at least $1 from AR source (any age or filing status).

Forms to file: Form AR 1000, *Arkansas Individual Income Tax Return*

Part-year residents and nonresidents: Form AR 1000NR, *Arkansas Individual Income Tax Return, Nonresident and Part-Year Resident*

Where to send returns:

Refund:
Arkansas State Income Tax
P.O. Box 1000
Little Rock, AR 72203-1000

Balance due:
Arkansas State Income Tax
P.O. Box 2144
Little Rock, AR 72203-2144

No tax due:
Arkansas State Income Tax
P.O. Box 8026
Little Rock, AR 72203-8026

IRC conformity: Only certain IRC provisions are incorporated as amended through specified dates.

Starting point for calculation of income: Gross income.

Attach other state returns? Yes, if claiming credit for tax paid to other state(s).

Federal attachments:
Residents: Schedules C-F and Forms 2106, 2441, 3903, 4684, 4797, 4952, 5329, 8283, 8606, 8839.

Part-year residents and nonresidents: Copy of federal income tax return.

Estimated tax payments: Required if expected liability over $1,000.

Extensions: Automatic extension if federal extension filed by original due date or file Form AR1055, *Request for Extension of Time for Filing Income Tax Returns.*

Length of extension: Six months if filed federal extension; 180-day extension if filed Form AR1055.

Mailing address:
Individual Income Tax Section
P.O. Box 3628
Little Rock, AR 72203-3628

CALIFORNIA

2009 Individual Tax Rate Schedule

Single, MFS, RDPFS:

$ 0	–	7,060	×	1.25 %	minus	$ 0.00
7,061	–	16,739	×	2.25	minus	70.60
16,740	–	26,419	×	4.25	minus	405.38
26,420	–	36,675	×	6.25	minus	933.76
36,676	–	46,349	×	8.25	minus	1,667.25
46,350 +			×	9.55	minus	2,269.79

MFJ, RDPFJ, QW:

$ 0	–	14,120	×	1.25 %	minus	$ 0.00
14,121	–	33,478	×	2.25	minus	141.20
33,479	–	52,838	×	4.25	minus	810.76
52,839	–	73,350	×	6.25	minus	1,867.52
73,351	–	92,698	×	8.25	minus	3,334.52
92,699 +			×	9.55	minus	4,539.59

HOH:

$ 0	–	14,130	×	1.25 %	minus	$ 0.00
14,131	–	33,479	×	2.25	minus	141.30
33,480	–	43,157	×	4.25	minus	810.87
43,158	–	53,412	×	6.25	minus	1,674.01
53,413	–	63,089	×	8.25	minus	2,742.25
63,090 +			×	9.55	minus	3,562.41

An additional 1% tax is imposed on taxable income over $1 million for all filing statuses.

Tax assistance: 800.852.5711

Forms request: 800.338.0505

Franchise Tax Board
Tax Forms Request Unit
P.O. Box 307
Rancho Cordova, CA 95741-0307

Web site: www.ftb.ca.gov

Tax Practitioner Web site: www.ftb.ca.gov

Tax Practitioner Hotline: 916.845.7057

Download: http://www.ftb.ca.gov/forms/index.html

e~file www.ftb.ca.gov/individuals/index.shtml

Who can e-file? No restrictions.

Who must e-file? Tax preparers who prepared more than 100 California individual income tax returns in any year after 2002 and who prepared one or more current-year returns using tax preparation software. Subject to $50 penalty per return if no e-file due to willful neglect and not reasonable cause.

Filing requirements:

Filing status options: Single, Married/Resident Domestic Partner Filing Jointly, Married/Resident Domestic Partner Filing Separately, Head of Household, and Qualifying Widow(er) with Dependent Child.
Residents, part-year residents, and nonresidents: Residents must file if they meet the filing thresholds. Part-year residents and nonresidents must file if they have any California-source income and their income from all sources exceeds the filing thresholds. If CA gross income or CA AGI is more than the standard deduction, filing is required. Filing is also mandatory if taxpayer owes:

- Alternative minimum tax
- Tax on lump-sum distribution
- Tax on qualified retirement plan, medical savings account, or IRA
- Tax for child under 14 with more than $1,800 of investment income
- Tax on selected installment obligations
- Recapture taxes
- Tax on nonqualified education savings plan distributions
- Tax on an accumulation distribution from a trust

CA gross income more than:	Number of dependents: 0	1	2 or more
Single, HOH, QW under age 65	$14,622	$17,889	$20,339
Single, HOH, QW age 65+	19,522	21,972	23,932
MFJ, RDP filing jointly or separately, MFS: both under age 65	29,245	32,512	34,962
MFJ, RDP filing jointly or separately, MFS: one age 65+	34,145	36,595	38,555
MFJ, RDP filing jointly or separately, MFS: both age 65+	39,045	41,495	43,455
or CA AGI more than:			
Single, HOH, QW under age 65	$11,698	$14,965	$17,415
Single, HOH, QW age 65+	16,598	19,048	21,008
MFJ, RDP filing jointly or separately, MFS: both under age 65	23,396	26,663	29,113
MFJ, RDP filing jointly or separately, MFS: one age 65+	28,296	30,746	32,706
MFJ, RDP filing jointly or separately, MFS: both age 65+	33,196	35,646	37,606

Forms to file: Form 540, *California Resident Income Tax Return*

Part-year residents and nonresidents: Form 540NR, *California Nonresident or Part-Year Resident Income Tax Return*

Where to send returns:

Refund, no tax due:
Franchise Tax Board
P.O. Box 942840
Sacramento, CA 94240-0002

Balance due:
Franchise Tax Board
P.O. Box 942867
Sacramento, CA 94267-0001

IRC conformity: IRC incorporated as of January 1, 2005, with modifications.

Starting point for calculation of income: Adjusted gross income.

Attach other state returns? Yes, if claiming credit for tax paid to other state(s).

Federal attachments: Copy of federal return required for part-year residents and nonresidents. Resident taxpayers who attach federal forms or schedules other than Schedule A or B to federal Form 1040 must attach federal Form 1040 and all supporting schedules and forms. Taxpayers who itemize for state purposes, but not for federal purposes, must attach a pro forma copy of federal Schedule A to their state return. If applicable, attach federal Form 8886 (Reportable Transaction Disclosure Statement).

Estimated tax payments: Required if expected liability over $500 ($250 for married filing separately) or less than 90% of preceding year's tax or current year's estimated tax paid through withholding.

Extensions: Six months automatic (file Form FTB 3519 if tax due).

COLORADO

2009 tax rate schedule: Income tax rate is 4.63% of federal taxable income for all filers.

Tax assistance:	303.238.7378
Forms request:	303.238.3278 Colorado Dept. of Revenue 1375 Sherman St. Denver, CO 80261-0008
Web site:	www.colorado.gov/revenue
Tax Practitioner Web site:	www.colorado.gov/cs/Satellite/Revenue/REVX/1176842266474
Download:	www.colorado.gov/cs/Satellite/Revenue/REVX/1177017542056
e~file	http://www.colorado.gov/revenue/tax

Who can e-file? All filers who use approved software or vendors.

Who must e-file? No conditions.

Filing requirements:
Filing status options: Single, Married Filing Jointly, Married Filing Separately, Head of Household, and Qualifying Widow(er) with Dependent Child.

Residents: All full-year residents must file who filed a federal return or had a CO income tax liability for the tax year.

Part-year residents: Must file if taxable income was earned during CO residency and if required to file federal return or there is a CO tax liability for current year.

Nonresidents: Must file if received CO-source income and if required to file federal return or there is a CO tax liability for current year.

Forms to file: Form 104, *Colorado Individual Income Tax Return*

Part-year residents and nonresidents: Form 104PN, *Part-Year Resident/Nonresident Tax Calculation Schedule* (attachment)

Where to send returns:
Colorado Department of Revenue
Denver, CO 80261-0005

IRC conformity: IRC incorporated by reference as currently amended.

Starting point for calculation of income: Federal taxable income.

Attach other state returns? Yes, if claiming credit for taxes paid to other state(s).

Federal attachments: None required.

Estimated tax payments: Required if expected liability over $1000.

Extensions: Six months automatic (file Form 158-I if tax due).

CONNECTICUT

2009 Individual Tax Rate Schedule

Single, MFS:							
$ 0	–	10,000	×	3.0 %	minus	$	0.00
10,001	–	500,000	×	5.0	minus		200.00
500,001	+		×	6.5	minus		7,700.00
HOH:							
$ 0	–	16,000	×	3.0 %	minus	$	0.00
16,001	–	800,000	×	5.0	minus		320.00
800,001	+		×	6.5	minus		12,320.00
MFJ, QW:							
$ 0	–	20,000	×	3.0 %	minus	$	0.00
20,001	–	1,000,000	×	5.0	minus		400.00
1,000,001	+		×	6.5	minus		400.00

Tax assistance:	Connecticut Department of Revenue Services Taxpayer Services Division 25 Sigourney St. Hartford, CT 06106-5032 860.297.5962 or 800.382.9463 (CT)

Forms request: 860.297.5962 or 800.382.9463 (CT)
Fax: 860.297.5698

Connecticut Department
of Revenue Services
Forms Division
25 Sigourney St.
Hartford, CT 06106

Web site: www.ct.gov/drs

Download: www.ct.gov/drs

e~file http://www.ct.gov/drs/site/default.asp

Who can e-file? Anyone who uses approved software or vendors. Online filing also available.

Who must e-file? Tax preparers who prepared 50 or more Connecticut individual income tax returns during the previous tax year.

Filing requirements:
Filing status options: Single, Filing Jointly for Federal and Connecticut, Filing Jointly for Connecticut Only, Filing Separately for Federal and Connecticut, Filing Separately for Connecticut Only, Head of Household, and Qualifying Widow(er) with Dependent Child.

Residents: Taxpayers must file who had gross income exceeding:

- $13,000 (Single)
- $12,000 (Married Filing Separately)
- $19,000 (Head of Household)
- $24,000 (Married Filing Jointly)

Part-year residents: Taxpayers must file who:

- Had CT income tax withheld or
- Made estimated tax payments to CT or
- Meet the gross income test for CT resident or had a federal alternative minimum tax liability

Nonresidents: Taxpayers must file who:

- Had CT income tax withheld or
- Made estimated tax payments to CT or
- Had CT-source income and meet the gross income test for CT resident or had a federal alternative minimum tax liability

Forms to file: Form CT-1040, *Connecticut Resident Income Tax Return*

Part-year residents and nonresidents: Form CT-1040NR/PY, *Connecticut Nonresident or Part-Year Resident Income Tax Return*

Where to send returns:
Refunds, no tax due:
Full-year residents:
Connecticut Department of Revenue Services
P.O. Box 2976
Hartford, CT 06104-2976

Nonresident or part-year resident:
Connecticut Department of Revenue Services
P.O. Box 2968
Hartford, CT 06104-2968

Balance due:
Full-year residents:
Connecticut Department of Revenue Services
P.O. Box 2977
Hartford, CT 06104-2977

Nonresident or part-year resident:
Connecticut Department of Revenue Services
P.O. Box 2969
Hartford, CT 06104-2969

Federal attachments: None required.

IRC conformity: IRC incorporated by reference as currently amended.

Starting point for calculation of income: Federal adjusted gross income.

Attach other state returns? Yes, if claiming credit for taxes paid to other state(s).

Estimated tax payments: Required if CT taxable income, other than wages on which tax withheld, expected to exceed $500.

Extensions: Form CT-1040-EXT if making payment. Federal extension extends time to file Connecticut return if no payment due.

Length of extension: Six months.

Mailing address:
Connecticut Department of Revenue Services
P.O. Box 2977
Hartford, CT 06104-2977

DELAWARE

2009 tax rate schedule:

$	0 –	2,000	×	0 %	minus	$	0.00
	2,001 –	5,000	×	2.20	minus		44.00
	5,001 –	10,000	×	3.90	minus		129.00
	10,001 –	20,000	×	4.80	minus		219.00
	20,001 –	25,000	×	5.20	minus		299.00
	25,001 –	60,000	×	5.55	minus		386.50
	60,001 +		×	5.95	minus		626.50

Tax assistance:	Delaware Division of Revenue Carvel State Office Building 820 N. French Street Wilmington, DE 19801 302. 577.8200
Forms request:	302.577.8201 Delaware Division of Revenue Carvel State Office Building 820 N. French Street, M/S 29 Wilmington, DE 19801
Web site:	http://revenue.delaware.gov
Download:	http://revenue.delaware.gov
e~file	http://revenue.delaware.gov

Who can e-file? Electronic filing allowed for residents, nonresidents, and part-year residents.

Who must e-file? No conditions.

Filing requirements:
Filing status options: Single, including Divorced and Widow(er); Married Filing Jointly; Married Filing Separately; Married and Filing Combined Separately on Form; and Head of Household.

Residents:

Filing status	Age	AGI at least:
Single, MFS, HOH	Under 60	$ 9,400
	60–64	12,200
	65+ or blind	14,700
	65+ and blind	17,200
MFJ Under	60	15,450
	60–64	17,950
	65+ or blind	20,450
	65+ and blind	22,950
Dependent on another's return	Under 60	5,250
	60–64	5,250
	65+ or blind	7,750
	65+ and blind	10,250

Part-year residents: Must file if any income was received from DE source while resident or nonresident, or if income received from any source while a DE resident.

Nonresidents: Must file if any income was received from DE source.

Forms to file: Form 200-01, *Delaware Individual Resident Income Tax Return*

Part-year residents: Form 200-01 or Form 200-02

Nonresidents: Form 200-02, *Delaware Individual Non-Resident Income Tax Return*

Where to send returns:
Balance due:
Residents:
Delaware Division of Revenue
P.O. Box 508
Wilmington, DE 19899-0508

Nonresidents:
Delaware Division of Revenue
P.O. Box 8752
Wilmington, DE 19899-8752

Zero balance:
Residents: and Nonresidents:
Delaware Division of Revenue
P.O. Box 8711
Wilmington, DE 19899-8711

Refund due:
Residents:
Delaware Division of Revenue
P.O. Box 8765
Wilmington, DE 19899-8765

Nonresidents:
Delaware Division of Revenue
P.O. Box 8772
Wilmington, DE 19899-8772

IRC conformity: IRC incorporated by reference as currently amended.

Starting point for calculation of income: Federal adjusted gross income.

Attach other state returns? Copy of signed income tax return(s) if credit for taxes paid to other state(s) is claimed.

Federal attachments: Copy of federal return not required. Copies of all schedules required to be filed with federal return must be attached. Taxpayers must attach the following federal schedules and forms, if applicable: Form 2106 or 2106EZ (unreimbursed employee expense credit); Form 2441 or 1040A Schedule 2 (child and dependent care expense credit); Schedule A; 1100S Schedule A-1 (credit for taxes paid by S corporations); and Schedule EIC and pages 1 and 2 of federal 1040 if claiming earned income credit.

Due Date: April 30

Estimated tax payments: Required if expected liability over $400.

Extensions: Form 1027 or six-month automatic if federal extension is filed by original due date.

Length of extension: Five and one-half months, and can extend to federal extension date if copy of approved federal extension is filed by expiration of Form 1027 extension. Six months if federal extension is filed.

Mailing address:

Payment:
Delaware Division of Revenue
P.O. Box 508
Wilmington, DE 19899-0508

No payment:
Delaware Division of Revenue
P.O. Box 8711
Wilmington, DE 19899-8711

Refund:
Delaware Division of Revenue
P.O. Box 8765
Wilmington, DE 19899-8765

DISTRICT OF COLUMBIA

2009 Individual Tax Rate Schedule

$ 0	–	10,000	×	4.0 %	minus	$	0.00
10,001	–	40,000	×	6.0	minus		200.00
40,001	+		×	8.5	minus		1,200.00

Excludes SS income and the first $3,000 of military retirement pay and DC and federal pension income.

Tax assistance:	Office of Tax and Revenue Customer Service Center 941 North Capitol Street, NE, 1st Floor Washington, DC 20002 202.727.4829
Tax Practitioner Hotline:	202.727.1435
Forms request:	202.442.6546 Office of Tax and Revenue Customer Service Center 941 North Capitol Street, NE, 1st Floor Washington, DC 20002
Web site:	www.cfo.dc.gov/otr/site/default.asp
e~file	http://otr.cfo.dc.gov/otr/site/default.asp

Who can e-file? Any taxpayer or authorized practitioner.

Who must e-file? Electronic payments required from third-party bulk filers taxpayers with monthly employer personal income tax withholding and quarterly corporation franchise estimated tax payments if outstanding tax liability for the filing period exceeds $25,000.

Filing requirements:
Filing status options: Single, Married Filing Jointly, Married Filing Separately, Dependent Claimed by Someone Else, Married Filing Separately on Same Return, Head of Household, Registered Domestic Partners Filing Jointly, and Registered Domestic Partners Filing Separately on Same Form.

Residents: Taxpayers must file who:

- Are DC residents required to file a federal income tax return
- Maintained a permanent residence in DC for part or all of the tax year
- Resided in DC for 183 days or more in the tax year
- Are members of armed forces for whom DC was home of record for part or all of the tax year
- Are spouses of exempt members of armed forces or other exempt individuals and one of the above conditions applies

Part-year residents: Must file if resident of DC for part of the year.

Nonresidents: Not required to file DC return.

Forms to file: Form D-40, *Individual Income Tax Return*

Where to send returns: (Balance Due)
Office of Tax and Revenue
P.O. Box 7182
Washington, DC 20044-7182
(Refund, no payment)
Office of Tax and Revenue
P.O. Box 209
Washington, DC 20044-0209

IRC conformity: IRC incorporated by reference as currently amended.

Starting point for calculation of income: Federal gross income.

Attach other state returns? Yes.

Federal attachments: None required.

Estimated tax payments: Required if expected liability over $100.

Extensions: Form FR-127.

Length of extension: Six months; additional six months if living or traveling outside the U.S.

Mailing address:
Office of Tax and Revenue
P.O. Box 59
Washington, DC 20044-0059

FLORIDA

2009 tax rate schedule: Florida does not impose a personal income tax. Florida does impose corporate income taxes and intangible personal property taxes.

Tax assistance:	850.488.6800 or 800.352.3671
Forms request:	850.488.8422 or 800.352.3671 Fax: 850.922.2208 Taxpayer Services FL Department of Revenue 1379 Blountstown Hwy. Tallahassee, FL 32304-2716
Web site:	http://dor.myflorida.com/dor/
Download:	www.myflorida.com/dor/forms
e~file	www.state.fl.us/dor/eservices

Florida does not impose a personal income tax.

GEORGIA

2009 tax rate schedule:

Single:

$ 0 –	750	× 1.0%	minus	$	0.00
751 –	2,250	× 2.0	minus		7.50
2,251 –	3,750	× 3.0	minus		30.00
3,751 –	5,250	× 4.0	minus		67.50
5,251 –	7,000	× 5.0	minus		120.00
7,001 +		× 6.0	minus		190.00

MFJ, HOH:

$ 0 –	1,000	× 1.0%	minus	$	0.00
1,001 –	3,000	× 2.0	minus		10.00
3,001 –	5,000	× 3.0	minus		40.00
5,001 –	7,000	× 4.0	minus		90.00
7,001 –	10,000	× 5.0	minus		160.00
10,001 +		× 6.0	minus		260.00

MFS:

$ 0 –	500	× 1.0%	minus	$	0.00
501 –	1,500	× 2.0	minus		5.00
1,501 –	2,500	× 3.0	minus		20.00
2,501 –	3,500	× 4.0	minus		45.00
3,501 –	5,000	× 5.0	minus		80.00
5,001 +		× 6.0	minus		130.00

Tax assistance:	404.417.4477 or 877.602.8477
Forms request:	404.417.2409 Georgia Income Tax Forms P.O. Box 29369 Atlanta, GA 30359
Web site:	www.etax.dor.ga.gov
Download:	www.etax.dor.ga.gov/inctax/individual_income_tax_forms.aspx
e~file	www.etax.dor.ga.gov/inctax/efile/electronicfile.aspx

Who can e-file? All taxpayers, regardless of filing or residency status

Who must e-file? No conditions.

Filing requirements:
Filing status options: Single, Married Filing Jointly, Married Filing Separately, Head of Household, and Qualifying Widow(er) with Dependent Child.

Residents: Taxpayers must file if:
- Filing of federal income tax return required
- Income subject to GA income tax but not federal income tax
- Income exceeds the standard deduction and personal exemptions

Part-year residents: Must file if filing of federal income tax return required and legal GA resident for part of the year.

Nonresidents: Must file if employed in GA or received GA-source income and required to file federal return unless only profitable activity involves services for GA employer where wages do not exceed the lesser of 5% of total income for year or $5,000.

Filing status	Age	Income more than:
Single, HOH, QW	Under 65, not blind	$ 5,000
	Under 65 and blind	6,300
	65+, not blind	6,300
	65+ and blind	7,600
MFJ	Both under 65, not blind	8,400
	One 65+, not blind	9,700
	Under 65, both blind	11,000
	Both 65+, not blind	11,000
	One 65+ and blind	11,000
	One 65+, both blind	12,300
	Both 65+ and blind	13,600
MFS	Under 65, not blind	4,200
	Under 65 and blind	5,500
	65+, not blind	5,500
	65+ and blind	6,800

Forms to file: Form 500, *Individual Income Tax Return*

Where to send returns:

Refunds:
Georgia Department of Revenue
Processing Center
P.O. Box 740380
Atlanta, GA 30374-0380

Balance, no tax due:
Georgia Department of Revenue
Processing Center
P.O. Box 740399
Atlanta, GA 30374-0399

Where to send 2D barcode returns:

Refunds:
Georgia Department of Revenue
Processing Center
P.O. Box 105597
Atlanta, GA 30348-5597

Payments:
Georgia Department of Revenue
Processing Center
P.O. Box 105613
Atlanta, GA 30348-5613

IRC conformity: IRC incorporated by reference as of January 1, 2009, except: most bonus depreciation provisions; extended net operating loss carryback periods; shortened depreciation recovery periods for retail improvements, qualified restaurant property, and new farm equipment; shortened depreciation recovery periods for retail improvements, qualified restaurant property, and new farm equipment; the domestic production activities deduction; depreciation, losses, and other benefits relating to certain disaster areas and zones; and special rules that allow financial institutions to treat losses from the sale of certain preferred stock as ordinary rather than capital losses.

Starting point for calculation of income: Federal adjusted gross income.

Attach other state returns? Yes, if credit claimed for taxes paid to another state.

Federal attachments: Copy of federal return generally not required. However, taxpayers must attach the following federal schedules and forms, if applicable: pages 1 and 2 of federal Form 1040, if federal adjusted gross income is $40,000 or more, or less than the total income on W-2(s); Form 2441 or 1040A Schedule 2 (child and dependent care expense credit); Schedule A (itemized deductions); and copy of federal return when claiming combat zone pay exclusion.

Estimated tax payments: Required if expected gross income exceeding personal exemption, plus credit for dependents, plus estimated deductions, plus $1,000 income not subject to withholding.

Extensions: Form IT-303 or attach federal extension.

Length of extension: Six months.

Mailing address:
Georgia Department of Revenue, Processing Center
P.O. Box 740320
Atlanta, GA 30374-0320

HAWAII

2009 Individual Tax Rate Schedule

Single, MFS:

$ 0	–	2,400	×	1.40 %	minus	$ 0.00
2,401	–	4,800	×	3.20	minus	43.20
4,801	–	9,600	×	5.50	minus	153.60
9,601	–	14,400	×	6.40	minus	240.00
14,401	–	19,200	×	6.80	minus	297.60
19,201	–	24,000	×	7.20	minus	374.40
24,001	–	36,000	×	7.60	minus	470.40
36,001	–	48,000	×	7.90	minus	578.40
48,001	–	150,000	×	8.25	minus	746.40
150,001	–	175,000	×	9.00	minus	1,871.40
175,001	–	200,000	×	10.00	minus	3,621.40
200,001	+		×	11.00	minus	5,621.40

MFJ, Surviving Spouse:

$ 0	–	4,800	×	1.40 %	minus	$ 0.00
4,801	–	9,600	×	3.20	minus	86.40
9,601	–	19,200	×	5.50	minus	307.20
19,201	–	28,800	×	6.40	minus	480.00
28,801	–	38,400	×	6.80	minus	595.20
38,401	–	48,000	×	7.20	minus	748.80
48,001	–	72,000	×	7.60	minus	940.80
72,001	–	96,000	×	7.90	minus	1,156.80
96,001	–	300,000	×	8.25	minus	1,492.80
300,001	–	350,000	×	9.00	minus	3,742.80
350,001	–	400,000	×	10.00	minus	7,242.80
400,001	+		×	11.00	minus	11,242.80

HOH:

$ 0	–	3,600	×	1.40 %	minus	$ 0.00
3,601	–	7,200	×	3.20	minus	64.80
7,201	–	14,400	×	5.50	minus	230.40
14,401	–	21,600	×	6.40	minus	360.00
21,601	–	28,800	×	6.80	minus	446.40
28,801	–	36,000	×	7.20	minus	561.60
36,001	–	54,000	×	7.50	minus	705.60
54,001	–	72,000	×	7.90	minus	867.60
72,001	–	225,000	×	8.25	minus	1,119.60
225,001	–	262,500	×	9.00	minus	2,807.10
262,501	–	300,000	×	10.00	minus	5,432.10
300,001	+		×	11.00	minus	8,432.10

Tax assistance:	808.587.4242 or 800.222.3229
Forms request:	808.587.7572 or 800.222.7572 Department of Taxation P.O. Box 259 Honolulu, HI 96809-0259
Web site:	www.state.hi.us/tax
Download:	www.state.hi.us/tax/a1_forms.htm
e~file	www.eHawaii.gov/efile

Who can e-file? Resident, nonresident, and part-year resident returns accepted

Who must e-file? No conditions.

Filing requirements:
Filing status options: Single, Married Filing Jointly, Married Filing Separately, Head of Household, and Qualifying Widow(er) with Dependent Child. Reciprocal beneficiaries may elect Married Filing Jointly status.

Residents:

- All individuals doing business in Hawaii
- All individuals earning more than the following gross income amounts:

Filing status	Age	Income more than:
Single	Under 65	$2,540
	65+	3,580
MFS	Under 65	1,990
	65+	3,030
HOH	Under 65	2,690
	65+	3,730
QW with dependent child	Under 65	2,940
	65+	3,980
MFJ	Under 65	3,980
	One 65 +	5,020
	65+	6,060

Nonresidents: Threshold amounts above must be multiplied by ratio of HI AGI to AGI from all sources to determine filing requirement.

Forms to file: Form N-11, *Individual Income Tax Return - Resident*

Part-year residents and nonresidents: Form N-15, *Individual Income Tax Return - Nonresident and Part-Year Resident*

Where to send returns:

Balance due:
Hawaii Department of Taxation
Attn: Payment Section
P.O. Box 1530
Honolulu, HI 96806-1530

Refund, no tax due:
Hawaii Department of Taxation
P.O. Box 3559
Honolulu, HI 96811-3559

IRC conformity: IRC incorporated by reference as amended through December 31, 2008.

Starting point for calculation of income: Federal adjusted gross income.

Attach other state returns? Yes, if claiming credit for tax paid to other state(s).

Federal attachments: Any forms used as a substitute for state forms.

Due Date: April 20

Estimated tax payments: Required if tax liability is $500 or more.

Extensions: Automatic extension; file Form N101A with payment.

Length of extension: Six months automatic.

Mailing address:
Hawaii Department of Taxation
P.O. Box 1530
Honolulu, HI 96806-1530

IDAHO

2009 Individual Tax Rate Schedule

Single, MFS:

$ 0	–	1,320	×	1.6 %	minus	$ 0.00
1,321	–	2,641	×	3.6	minus	26.40
2,642	–	3,962	×	4.1	minus	39.60
3,963	–	5,283	×	5.1	minus	79.22
5,284	–	6,603	×	6.1	minus	132.05
6,604	–	9,906	×	7.1	minus	198.09
9,907	–	26,417	×	7.4	minus	227.81
26,418	+		×	7.8	minus	333.48

MFJ, HOH, QW:

$ 0	–	2,641	× 1.6 %	minus	$	0.00
2,642	–	5,283	× 3.6	minus		52.82
5,284	–	7,925	× 4.1	minus		79.24
7,926	–	10,567	× 5.1	minus		158.49
10,568	–	13,207	× 6.1	minus		264.16
13,208	–	19,813	× 7.1	minus		396.22
19,814	–	52,835	× 7.4	minus		455.66
52,836	+		× 7.8	minus		667.00

Tax brackets are adjusted annually based on the consumer price index.

Tax assistance: Idaho State Tax Commission
P.O. Box 36
Boise, ID 83722-0410
208.334.7660 or 800.972.7660

Forms request: 208.334.7660 or 800.972.7660

Idaho State Tax Commission
P.O. Box 36
Boise, ID 83722-0410

Web site: www.tax.idaho.gov

Tax Practitioner Web site: www.tax.idaho.gov/tax_pros.htm

Download: www.tax.idaho.gov/forms.htm

e~file www.tax.idaho.gov/filing_individual.htm

Who can e-file? Electronic filing is allowed for residents, nonresidents, and part-year residents.

Who must e-file? No conditions.

Filing requirements:
Filing status options: Single, Married Filing Jointly, Married Filing Separately, Head of Household, and Qualifying Widow(er) with Dependent Child.

Residents: Taxpayers must file who are Idaho residents required to file federal income tax return.

Part-year residents: Must file if gross income from all sources during residency and from ID-sources during nonresidency exceeds $2,500.

Nonresidents: Must file if ID source income exceeds $2,500.

Forms to file: Form 40, *Idaho Individual Income Tax Return*

Part-year residents and nonresidents: Form 43, *Idaho Part-Year Resident & Nonresident Income Tax Return*

Where to send returns:
Idaho State Tax Commission
P.O. Box 56
Boise, ID 83756-0056

IRC conformity: IRC incorporated by reference as amended on February 17, 2009.

Starting point for calculation of income: Federal adjusted gross income.

Attach other state returns? Yes, if claiming credit for taxes paid to other state(s).

Federal attachments: Copy of federal income tax return.

Estimated tax payments: Voluntary.

Extensions: Six months automatic (file Form 51 if tax due).

ILLINOIS

2009 tax rate schedule: Illinois income tax rate is 3% for all individuals.

Tax assistance: Illinois Department of Revenue
Williard Ice Building
101 West Jefferson Street
Springfield, IL 62702
800.732.8866 or 217.782.3336

Illinois Department of Revenue
James R. Thompson Center
100 West Randolph Street
Chicago, Il 60601-3274
312.814.5232

Forms request: 800.356.6302

Illinois Department of Revenue
P.O. Box 19010
Springfield, IL 62794-9010

Web site: www.revenue.state.il.us

Tax Practitioner Web site: www.revenue.state.il.us/TaxProfessionals/index.htm

Electronic Services: www.revenue.state.il.us/ElectronicServices/Individuals/index.htm

Download: www.revenue.state.il.us/taxforms/index.htm

e~file www.revenue.state.il.us/ElectronicServices/Individuals/index.htm

Who can e-file? Resident, nonresident, and part-year resident returns allowed.

Who must e-file? No conditions.

Filing requirements:
Filing status options: Single, Married Filing Jointly, Married Filing Separately, Head of Household, and Qualifying Widow(er) with Dependent Child.

Residents: Filing is required of any Illinois resident who:

- Filed a federal income tax return or had Illinois base income exceeding the Illinois exemption allowance
- Worked in Kentucky, Iowa, Michigan, or Wisconsin or
- Was claimed as a dependent on another's return and has base income greater than $2,000 or wants a refund of IL income tax withheld from pay

Part-year residents: All individuals must file who:
- Earned income from any source while a resident
- Earned income from IL source while not a resident or
- Want a refund of IL tax withheld

Nonresidents: All individuals must file who:
- Resided in Kentucky, Iowa, Michigan, or Wisconsin and earned income in IL other than wages, salaries, tips, or commissions or want a refund of IL tax withheld
- Earned enough income from IL sources to have a tax liability or
- Want a refund of IL tax withheld in error

Forms to file: IL-1040, Individual Income Tax Return

Part-year residents and nonresidents: Schedule NR, *Nonresident and Part-Year Resident Computation of Illinois Tax* (attachment)

Where to send returns:

Payment:
Illinois Department of Revenue
Springfield, IL 62726-0001

No payment:
Illinois Department of Revenue
P.O. Box 1040
Galesburg, IL 61402-1040

IRC conformity: IRC incorporated by reference as currently amended.

Starting point for calculation of income: Federal adjusted gross income.

Attach other state returns? Yes, if claiming credit for taxes paid to other state(s).

Federal attachments: Copy of federal return not required. Taxpayers must attach the following federal schedules and forms, if applicable: page 1 of Form 1040 or 1040A (Social Security, government disability benefits, and retirement income); and Schedule D, pages 1 and 2 (capital gains and losses). Taxpayers must file a copy of any federal disclosure statement with respect to reportable transactions.

Estimated tax payments: Required if expected liability at least $500 after subtracting IL withholding, the earned income credit, credits from Schedule 1299-C, and credits for income tax paid to other states, IL property tax paid, and education expenses.

Extensions: Six months automatic (file Form IL-505-I if tax due).

INDIANA

2009 tax rate schedule: All taxpayers are subject to an income tax rate of 3.4%.

Tax assistance:	317.232.2240
Forms request:	317.615.2581 Fax: 317.233.2329 Indiana Department of Revenue 100 N. Senate Ave. Indianapolis, IN 46204
Web site:	www.in.gov/dor
Download:	www.in.gov/dor/3489.htm
e~file	http://www.in.gov/dor/3336.htm

Who can e-file? Individuals can electronically file their state returns using I-File, or individuals may electronically file their federal and state returns together by working through an approved tax professional.

Who must e-file? Tax preparers who filed more than 100 resident/nonresident returns in the previous calendar year.

Filing requirements:
Filing status options: Single, Married Filing Jointly, and Married Filing Separately. If a joint return is filed by a surviving spouse, the surviving spouse should sign and write "Filing as Surviving Spouse."

Residents: Residents must file if gross income exceeds exemptions.

Part-year residents: Must file if income earned during IN residency.

Nonresidents: Must file if income received from IN source, except certain interest, dividends, or retirement income.

Forms to file: Form IT-40, *Indiana Full-Year Resident Individual Income Tax Return*

Part-year residents and nonresidents: Form IT-40PNR, *Indiana Part-Year or Full-Year Nonresident Individual Income Tax Return*

Where to send returns:
Indiana Department of Revenue
P.O. Box 40
Indianapolis, IN 46206-0040

Payment:
Indiana Department of Revenue
P.O. Box 7224
Indianapolis, IN 46207-7224

IRC conformity: IRC incorporated by reference as amended on January 1, 2008.

Starting point for calculation of income: Federal adjusted gross income.

Attach other state returns? Yes, if claiming credit for tax paid to other state(s).

Federal attachments: Form 4868; Form 4972; Schedule A from federal Form 1045; Schedule R.

Estimated tax payments: Required if expected liability of $400 or more.

Extensions: Form IT-9 (or Federal Form 4868)

Length of extension: 60 days if Form IT-9, 7 months if federal extension is filed (30 days after the federal extension date).

Mailing address: (if payment due)
Indiana Department of Revenue
P.O. Box 6117
Indianapolis, IN 46206-6117

IOWA

2009 Individual Tax Rate Schedule

$ 0	–	1,407	×	0.36 %	minus	$ 0.00
1,408	–	2,814	×	0.72	minus	5.06
2,815	–	5,628	×	2.43	minus	53.18
5,629	–	12,663	×	4.50	minus	169.68
12,664	–	21,105	×	6.12	minus	374.82
21,106	–	28,140	×	6.48	minus	450.79
28,141	–	42,210	×	6.80	minus	540.84
42,211	–	63,315	×	7.92	minus	1,013.59
63,316	+		×	8.98	minus	1,684.73

Tax assistance:
Taxpayer Services
Iowa Department of Revenue
P.O. Box 10457
Des Moines, IA 50306-0457
515.281.3114 or 800.367.3388 (IA)

idr@iowa.gov

Forms request: 515.281.7239 or 800.532.1531 (IA)
Fax: 800.572.3943

Web site: www.iowa.gov/tax

Download: www.iowa.gov/tax/forms/indinc.html

e~file www.state.ia.us/tax/elf/elfchoic.html

Who can e-file? Anyone can file from a PC using approved software or through an authorized tax preparer.

Who must e-file? No conditions.

Filing requirements:
Filing status options: Single, Married Filing Jointly, Married Filing Separately, Married and Filing Separately on Same Form, Head of Household, and Qualifying Widow(er) with Dependent Child. Same sex married couples may file jointly, married filing separately on a combined return, or married filing separately.

Residents:

- Filing status of single and net income over $9,000 ($18,001 if 65 or older)
- Filing status other than single and net income over $13,500 ($24,001 if 65 or older)
- Claimed as dependent on another's IA return and net income at least $5,000
- Subject to IA lump-sum tax or IA alternative minimum tax or
- In military service with IA given as legal residence

Part-year residents: Same conditions as for residents but net income from IA sources of at least $1,000

Nonresidents: Net income from IA sources of at least $1,000 or subject to IA lump-sum tax or IA alternative minimum tax

Forms to file: IA 1040, *Iowa Individual Income Tax Long Form*

Part-year residents and nonresidents: Form IA 126, *Iowa Nonresident and Part-Year Resident Credit* (in addition to IA 1040)

Where to send returns:
Refund:
Iowa Income Tax–Refund Processing
Hoover State Office Building
Des Moines, IA 50319-0120

Payment:
Iowa Income Tax–Document Processing
P.O. Box 9187
Des Moines, IA 50306-9187

IRC conformity: IRC incorporated by reference as of January 1, 2008.

Starting point for calculation of income: Federal adjusted gross income.

Attach other state returns? Yes, if claiming credit for tax paid to other states (available only to residents and to part-year residents whose income during IA residency was taxed by another state).

Federal attachments: Taxpayers must attach federal return if claiming nonresident or part-year resident credit, or if Illinois resident requesting refund from Iowa income tax withheld in error.

Due Date: April 30

Estimated tax payments: Required if expected liability over $200.

Extensions: Six months automatic.

KANSAS

2009 tax rate schedule:

MFJ:

$ 0 – 30,000	×	3.50%	minus	$ 0.00
30,001 – 60,000	×	6.25	minus	825.00
60,001 +	×	6.45	minus	945.00

Single, HOH, MFS:

$ 0 – 15,000	×	3.50%	minus	$ 0.00
15,001 – 30,000	×	6.25	minus	412.50
30,001 +	×	6.45	minus	472.50

Tax assistance: Tax Assistance
Docking State Office Building
915 SW Harrison St., Room 150
Topeka, KS 66612
785.368.8222
Fax: 785.291.3614

Forms request: 785.296.4937
forms@kdor.state.ks.us

Forms/Correspondence Unit
Kansas Department of Revenue
915 SW Harrison St.
Topeka, KS 66612

Web site: www.ksrevenue.org

Tax Practitioner Web site: www.ksrevenue.org/taxprac.htm

Download: www.ksrevenue.org/formsii.htm

e~file www.ksrevenue.org/eservices.htm

Who can e-file? All individuals using approved software or the services of an IRS-authorized tax preparer

Who must e-file? Any paid tax preparer that prepares 50 or more Kansas individual income tax returns during any calendar year must e-file 90% of the returns prepared

Filing requirements:

Filing status options: Single, Married Filing Jointly, Married Filing Separately, Head of Household, and Qualifying Widow(er) with Dependent Child. If federal filing status is Qualifying Widow(er) with Dependent Child, check "Head of Household" box.

Residents: Kansas residents must file:

- If a federal income tax return was filed
- If income exceeds the combined total of the Kansas standard deduction and the personal exemption amount
- If claimed as a dependent on another's return and unearned income is more than $500 or if base income exceeds $3,000
- If requesting a refund of taxes withheld
- If military home of record is Kansas or
- If any of the following minimum income requirements are met:

Filing status	Age	AGI more than:
Single, MFS	Under 65	$ 5,250
	65+ or blind	6,100
	65+ and blind	6,950
MFJ	Both spouses under 65	10,500
	One spouse 65+ or blind	11,200
	Both spouses 65+ or blind	11,900
	One spouse 65+ and blind	11,900
	One spouse 65+ or blind and one spouse 65+ and blind	12,600
	Both spouses 65+ and blind	13,300
HOH	Under 65	9,000
	65+ or blind	9,850
	65+ and blind	10,700

Part-year residents: May be treated as residents or nonresidents.

Nonresidents: Must file a Kansas income tax return if there is any income from Kansas sources, or to request refund of Kansas taxes withheld by employer in error.

Forms to file: Form K-40, *Kansas Individual Income Tax and/or Food Sales Tax Refund*

Nonresidents: Schedule S, Part B, *Nonresident Allocation* (Form K-40 attachment)

Where to send returns:

Individual Income Tax/Food Sales Tax
Kansas Department of Revenue
915 SW Harrison Street
Topeka, KS 66699-1000

IRC conformity: IRC incorporated by reference as currently amended.

Starting point for calculation of income: Federal adjusted gross income.

Attach other state returns? Yes, in order to claim a credit on the KS return.

Federal attachments: Taxpayers must attach federal return if claiming child and dependent care expense credit or earned income credit; or if taxpayer's Form K-40 address is not in Kansas, along with applicable Schedules A-F. Taxpayers must attach federal Form 1116 (foreign tax credit), if applicable.

Estimated tax payments: Required if expected liability over $500, and withholding plus credits less than the smaller of 90% of the year's tax or 100% of last year's tax.

Extensions: Attach copy of federal extension.

Length of extension: Six months.

Mailing address:

Kansas Department of Revenue
915 SW Harrison Street
Topeka, KS 66699-1000

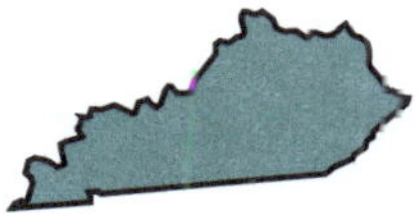

KENTUCKY

2009 tax rate schedule:

$ 0	–	3,000	×	2.0%	minus	$ 0.00
3,001	–	4,000	×	3.0	minus	30.00
4,001	–	5,000	×	4.0	minus	70.00
5,001	–	8,000	×	5.0	minus	120.00
8,001	–	75,000	×	5.8	minus	184.00
75,001	+		×	6.0	minus	334.00

After computing tax, deduct $20 for each tax credit claimed.

Tax assistance:	502.564.4581
Forms request:	502.564.3658
Web site:	www.revenue.ky.gov
Download:	www.revenue.ky.gov/forms
e~file	www.revenue.ky.gov

Who can e-file? Electronic filing is allowed for resident individual income tax returns.

Who must e-file? No conditions.

Filing Requirements:

Filing status options: Single, Married Filing Jointly, Married Filing Separately, and Married Filing Separately on Combined Return.

Residents: A Kentucky resident must file an individual tax return if modified gross income exceeds the amount in Chart A and Kentucky adjusted gross income exceeds the amount in Chart B.

Chart A

Family Size	Modified Gross income more than:
One	$10,400
Two	14,000
Three	17,600
Four +	21,200

Chart B

Filing status	Age	Kentucky AGI more than:
Single	Under 65	$3,140
	65+ or blind	5,140
	65+ and blind	6,410
Husband and Wife	Both under 65	4,140
	One 65+	5,810
	Both 65+	6,910

Taxpayers with self-employment income must file an individual income tax return regardless of the amount of Kentucky adjusted gross income if gross receipts from self-employment exceed the amount of modified gross income for the taxpayer's family size listed in Chart A.

Part-year residents and Nonresidents: Part-year residents and nonresidents must file if (1) they had any income from Kentucky sources in excess of modified gross income for their family size listed in Chart A, or (2) Kentucky gross receipts from self-employment in excess of modified gross income for their family size.

Forms to file: Form 740, *Kentucky Individual Income Tax Return*

Part-year residents and nonresidents: Form 740-NP, *Kentucky Income Tax Return: Nonresident or Part-Year Resident*

Where to send returns:

Refund:

Kentucky Department of Revenue
Frankfort, KY 40618-0006

Payment:

Kentucky Department of Revenue
Frankfort, KY 40619-0008

IRC conformity: IRC incorporated by reference as amended on December 31, 2006.

Starting point for calculation of income: Federal adjusted gross income.

Attach other state returns? Yes, if claiming credit for tax paid to other state(s).

Federal attachments: Copy of federal return generally not required. However, resident taxpayers must attach complete copy of federal return if taxpayer received farm, business, or rental income or loss. Nonresident and part-year resident taxpayers must attach copy of federal return and all supporting schedules. Taxpayers must attach the following federal schedules and forms, if applicable: Form 2106 or Form 2106-EZ (unreimbursed employee expense deduction); Form 2120 (individuals supported by more than one taxpayer); Form 2441(child and dependent care expense credit); Form 4562 (depreciation deduction); Form 4684 (casualty or theft losses); Form 4952 (investment interest); Form 8283 (charitable contributions over $500); and Form 8332 (noncustodial parent dependent deduction). In addition, nonresident and part-year resident taxpayers must attach the following federal schedules and forms, if applicable: Schedules C (business income and losses), D (capital gains and losses), E (rent, royalty, partnership income), and F (farm income or losses); Form 4797 (for any gains and losses reported on sales of business property); and Form 8889 (for any health savings account deduction).

Estimated tax payments: Required if expected liability over $500.

Extensions: Taxpayers with federal extensions attach copy of federal Form 4868. Taxpayers without federal extensions must attach Kentucky Form 40A102.

Length of extension: Six-month automatic extension if federal extension is filed by original due date of return. Six-month state extension may be granted for reasonable cause if Form 40A102 is filed by original due date of return. Inability to pay is not a valid reason.

Mailing address:

Kentucky Department of Revenue
P.O. Box 1190
Frankfort, KY 40620-1190

LOUISIANA

2009 Individual Tax Rate Schedule

Single, MFS, HOH:

$ 0	–	12,500	×	2.0 %	minus	$	0.00
12,501	–	50,000	×	4.0	minus		250.00
50,001	+		×	6.0	minus		1,250.00

MFJ or qualified surviving spouse:

$ 0	–	25,000	×	2.0 %	minus	$	0.00
25,001	–	100,000	×	4.0	minus		500.00
100,001	+		×	6.0	minus		2,500.00

Tax assistance:	225.219.0102
Forms request:	225.219.2690 Louisiana Department of Revenue 617 N. Third St. Baton Rouge, LA 70802
Web site:	www.rev.state.la.us
Tax Practitioner Web site:	www.revenue.louisiana.gov/sections/preparer/default.aspx
Download:	www.rev.state.la.us
e~file	www.rev.state.la.us/sections/eservices/default.asp#fsef

Who can e-file? Resident, nonresident, part-year resident returns accepted

Who must e-file? Mandate for tax preparers that prepare more than 100 tax returns in any calendar year as follows:

- 30% of authorized individual returns due on or after January 1, 2008;
- 60% of returns due on or after January 1, 2010; and
- 90% of returns due on or after January 1, 2012

Filing requirements:

Filing status options: Single, Married Filing Jointly, Married Filing Separately, Head of Household, and Qualifying Widow(er) with Dependent Child.

Residents: A tax return must be filed by:

- Any resident who is required to file a federal income tax return
- Any resident who had state income tax withheld
- A taxpayer who has overpaid tax through withholding, declaration of estimated tax, or composite partnership payments and who wishes to obtain a refund or credit

Part-year residents and nonresidents:

- Anyone with income from LA sources who is required to file a federal income tax return
- Anyone who has overpaid tax through withholding, declaration of estimated tax, or composite partnership payments and who wishes to obtain a refund or credit
- Military personnel whose home of record is LA and who meet one of the requirements above

Forms to file: Form IT-540, *Louisiana Resident Income Tax Return*

Nonresidents and part-year residents: Form IT-540B, *Louisiana Nonresident and Part-Year Resident Income Tax Return*

Where to send returns:

Refund:
Louisiana Department of Revenue
P.O. Box 3440
Baton Rouge, LA 70821-3440

Payment:
Louisiana Department of Revenue
P.O. Box 3550
Baton Rouge, LA 70821-3550

IRC conformity: IRC incorporated by reference as currently amended.

Starting point for calculation of income: Federal adjusted gross income.

Attach other state returns? Yes, if claiming credit for taxes paid to other state(s).

Federal attachments: Copy of federal return generally not required. However, taxpayers must attach federal return if Louisiana income tax withheld exceeds 10% of federal adjusted gross income. Taxpayers must attach copies of federal return, federal Form 3800, and appropriate IRS form substantiating credit amount if claimed federal disaster relief credits on federal return as a result of Hurricane Katrina or Hurricane Rita, which may have been carried forward.

Due Date: May 15

Estimated tax payments: Required if expected liability over $500.

Extensions: For extension granted by IRS, attach copy of federal extension. For additional one-month extension, use Form R-2868.

Length of extension: Six months if federal extension; one month beyond the federal extended due date if file Form R-2868.

Mailing address:
Louisiana Department of Revenue
P.O. Box 3440
Baton Rouge, LA 70821-3440

MAINE

2009 Individual Tax Rate Schedule

Single, MFS:

$ 0	–	5,049	×	2.0 %	minus	$	0.00
5,050	–	10,049	×	4.5	minus		126.23
10,050	–	20,149	×	7.0	minus		377.45
20,150	+		×	8.5	minus		679.68

HOH:

$ 0	–	7,599	×	2.0 %	minus	$	0.00
7,600	–	15,099	×	4.5	minus		189.98
15,100	–	30,249	×	7.0	minus		567.45
30,250	+		×	8.5	minus		1,021.18

MFJ:

$ 0	–	10,149	×	2.0 %	minus	$	0.00
10,150	–	20,149	×	4.5	minus		253.73
20,150	–	40,349	×	7.0	minus		757.45
40,350	+		×	8.5	minus		1,362.68

Tax assistance: 207.626.8475

Tax Practitioner Hotline: 207.626.8458

Forms request: 207.624.7894

Maine Revenue Services
P.O. Box 9100
Augusta, ME 04332-9100

Web site: www.maine.gov/revenue

Download: www.maine.gov/revenue/forms/homepage.html

e~file http://www.maine.gov/revenue/netfile/gateway2.htm

Who can e-file? Any individual or participating preparer using approved software.

Who must e-file? Electronic filing is mandated for tax preparers who submitted more than 50 returns for tax year 2008.

Filing requirements:
Filing status options: Single, Married Filing Jointly, Married Filing Separately, Head of Household, and Qualifying Widow(er) with Dependent Child.

Residents: Residents who are required to file a federal income tax return or are subject to Maine income tax resulting in a Maine income tax liability must file a return, unless (1) Maine taxable income is $2,000 or less, (2) taxpayer is claimed as an exemption on his or her own return, and (3) taxpayer is not subject to the Maine minimum tax. Residents who do not have state income tax liability and who file a federal income tax return for the sole purpose of claiming a federal earned income credit are not required to file.

Part-year residents: Must file if income from ME source is reported on federal return.

Nonresidents: Must file return if performed personal services in Maine for more than 10 days regardless of amount of income.

Forms to file: Form 1040ME, *Maine Individual Income Tax*

Nonresidents and part-year residents: Attach Schedule NR, *Schedule for Calculating the Nonresident Credit,* or Schedule NRH, *Schedule for Calculating the Nonresident Credit for Married Person Electing to File Single*

Where to send returns:

Refund:
Maine Revenue Services
P.O. Box 9111
Augusta, ME 04332-9111

Balance, no tax due:
Maine Revenue Services
P.O. Box 1067
Augusta, ME 04332-1067

IRC conformity: IRC incorporated by reference as amended on February 17, 2009.

Starting point for calculation of income: Federal adjusted gross income.

Attach other state returns? Yes, if claiming credit for taxes paid to other state(s).

Federal attachments: Copy of federal return generally not required. However, taxpayers must attach federal Schedule K-1 (fiduciary adjustment), if applicable. In addition, taxpayers claiming nonresident credit must attach complete copy of federal return, including all schedules and worksheets.

Estimated tax payments: Required if expected liability $1,000 or more after withholding and allowable credits and if prior year liability also exceeded $1,000.

Extensions: Six months automatic (file Form 1040EXT-ME if tax due). Additional time to file, up to 8 months, may be requested in writing prior to expiration of automatic extension period.

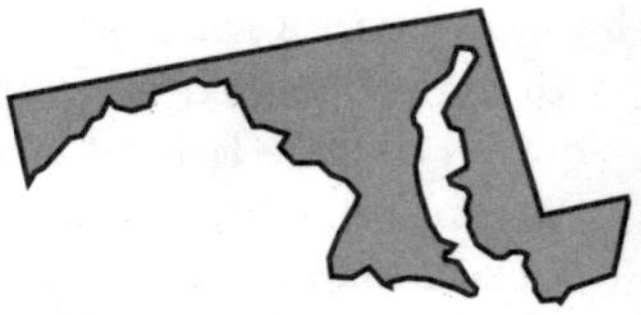

MARYLAND

2009 Individual Tax Rate Schedule

Single, MFS:

$ 0 –	1,000	× 2.00 %	minus	$	0.00
1,001 –	2,000	× 3.00	minus		10.00
2,001 –	3,000	× 4.00	minus		30.00
3,001 –	150,000	× 4.75	minus		52.50
150,001 –	300,000	× 5.00	minus		427.50
300,001 –	500,000	× 5.25	minus		1,177.50
500,001 –	1,000,000	× 5.50	minus		2,427.50
1,000,001 +		× 6.25	minus		9,927.50

MFJ, HOH, QW:

$ 0 –	1,000	× 2.00 %	minus	$	0.00
1,001 –	2,000	× 3.00	minus		10.00
2,001 –	3,000	× 4.00	minus		30.00
3,001 –	200,000	× 4.75	minus		52.50
200,001 –	350,000	× 5.00	minus		552.50
350,001 –	500,000	× 5.25	minus		1,427.50
500,001 –	1,000,000	× 5.50	minus		2,677.50
1,000,001 +		× 6.25	minus		10,177.50

Maryland counties and Baltimore City may levy a local income tax ranging from 1.25% to 3.15% of taxable income.

Tax assistance: 800.638.2937

Forms request: 410.260.7980

Comptroller of Maryland
Revenue Administration Division
80 Calvert St.
Annapolis, MD 21401

Web site: http://individuals.marylandtaxes.com/

Tax Practitioner Web site: http://taxpros.marylandtaxes.com

Download: http://individuals.marylandtaxes.com/taxforms/default.asp

e~file http://individuals.marylandtaxes.com/filinginfo/efile.asp

Who can e-file? Any individual with the approved software, except amended returns.

Electronic filing may also be accomplished using a designated software vendor or certified tax preparer.

Who must e-file? Electronic filing mandated for tax preparer who for compensation prepares more than 300 personal income tax returns in prior year. Threshold decreases to more than 200 for tax year 2010, and more than 100 in any tax year after 2010.

Filing requirements:
Filing status options: Single, Married Filing Jointly, Married Filing Separately, Head of Household, and Qualifying Widow(er) with Dependent Child. Includes limited domestic partnership relationships. Single individuals who may be claimed as a dependent on another's tax return must use the filing status "Dependent Taxpayer."

Residents:

Filing status	Age	Gross income at least:
Single	Under 65	$ 8,950
	65+	10,300
MFJ	Under 65	17,900
	One spouse 65+	18,950
	Both spouses 65+	20,000
MFS	Under 65	3,500
	65+	3,500
HOH	Under 65	11,500
	65+	12,850
QW	Under 65	14,400
	65+	15,450
Dependent Taxpayer	Single person claimed as dependent on federal return of other	8,950

Also, taxpayers wanting a refund of MD taxes must file, or if required to file federal form.

Part-year residents: Same as for residents.

Nonresidents: Individuals with income from MD source who meet the gross income criteria above.

Forms to file: Form 502, *Maryland Resident Tax Return*

Nonresidents: Form 505, *Maryland Nonresident Tax Return*

Where to send returns:
Comptroller of Maryland
Revenue Administration Division
Annapolis, MD 21411-0001

IRC conformity: IRC incorporated by reference as currently amended, unless the Comptroller determines that impact of federal amendment on state income tax revenue for the fiscal year that begins during the calendar year in which amendment is enacted will be greater than $5 million.

Starting point for calculation of income: Federal adjusted gross income.

Attach other state returns? Yes, if claiming a credit for taxes paid to other state(s).

Federal attachments: None required.

Estimated tax payments: Required if expected liability over $500.

Extensions: No form required if federal extension has been approved and no taxes are due. Form 502E must be filed if tax is due.

Length of extension: Six months automatic.

Mailing address:
Comptroller of Maryland
Revenue Administration Division
Annapolis, MD 21411-0001

MASSACHUSETTS

2009 Individual Tax Rate Schedule

Income tax:
State taxes income at 5.3%, barring an election to be taxed at 5.85%. This election does not apply to 12% taxes.

Capital Gains:
Short-term capital gains and losses, long-term gains on collectibles and pre-1996 installment sales classified as capital gain income for Massachusetts purposes, and gains on the sale of property used in a trade or business (4797 property) held for one year or less are taxed at 12%.

Long-term capital gains excluding collectibles are taxed at 5.3%.

Tax assistance:	617.887.6367 or 800.392.6089 (MA)
Forms request:	617.887.6367 or 800.392.6089 (MA)
Web site:	www.dor.state.ma.us
Download:	www.dor.state.ma.us
e~file	www.dor.state.ma.us

Who can e-file? Electronic filing is allowed for resident, part-year resident, and nonresident returns.

Who must e-file? Preparers who completed 100 or more returns during the previous calendar year, unless the taxpayer specifically directs that the filing be on paper and signs Form EFO.

Filing requirements:
Filing status options: Single, Married Filing Jointly, Married Filing Separately, and Head of Household. Same sex couples should choose Married Filing Jointly and combine figures from separate federal returns.

Residents: Residents with gross income over $8,000 must file.

Part-year residents: Same as for residents.

Nonresidents: If MA-source income exceeds your personal exemption amount multiplied by ratio of MA income to total income, or gross income was more than $8,000, you must file.

Forms to file: Form 1, *Massachusetts Resident Income Tax Return*

Part-year residents and nonresidents: Form 1-NR/PY, *Massachusetts Nonresident/Part-Year Resident Income Tax Return*

Where to send returns:

Refund, no tax due:
Massachusetts Department of Revenue
P.O. Box 7000
Boston, MA 02204-7000

Balance due:
Massachusetts Department of Revenue
P.O. Box 7003
Boston, MA 02204-7003

IRC conformity: IRC incorporated as amended on January 1, 2005, with exceptions.

Starting point for calculation of income: Federal gross income.

Attach other state returns? No.

Federal attachments: Copy of federal return not required. Taxpayers may attach federal Schedule C-EZ (business/profession income or loss) in place of MA Schedule C, and must attach federal Schedule F (farm income or loss), if applicable.

Estimated tax payments: Required if expected liability over $200.

Extensions: Automatic unless tax due, then Form M-4868. Any extension request must be submitted electronically if includes a payment of $5,000 or more, or electronic filing is optional if no payment with request.

Length of extension: Six months.

Mailing address:
Massachusetts Department of Revenue
P.O. Box 7070
Boston, MA 02204-7070

MICHIGAN

2009 tax rate schedule: Income tax rate is 4.35% for all filers.

Tax assistance:	800.827.4000
Forms request:	800.827.4000 Michigan Department of Treasury Lansing, MI 48922
Web site:	http://www.michigan.gov/taxes
Tax Practitioner Web site:	www.michigan.gov/taxes/0,1607,7-238-43549---,00.html
Download:	http://www.michigan.gov/taxes
e~file	http://www.michigan.gov/taxes/0,1607,7-238-43689-118045--,00.html

Who can e-file? Generally, all Michigan taxpayers are eligible, but see website for exceptions.

Who must e-file? Tax preparers that file 200 or more returns.

Filing requirements:
Filing status options: Single, Married Filing Jointly, and Married Filing Separately. File as Single if federal return was filed as Head of Household or Qualifying Widow(er).

Residents: All MI residents who owe tax or are due a refund, or whose AGI exceeds the personal exemption amount, must file. Also, all those who file a federal return should file. Also, for all residents claimed as dependents by other filers, a state return must be filed if status is Single or MFS and AGI exceeds $1,500, or if status is MFJ and AGI exceeds $3,000. In addition, if taxable income is less than the personal exemption allowance, you must file to claim a refund of any MI tax withheld.

Part-year residents: Must file if income was earned, received, or accrued during MI residency.

Nonresidents: Must file if received income from MI sources regardless of income level.

Forms to file: Form MI-1040, *Individual Income Tax Return*

Part-year residents and nonresidents: Schedule NR, *Nonresident and Part-Year Resident Schedule* (attachment to Form MI-1040)

Where to send returns:

Refund, credit, no tax due:
Michigan Department of Treasury
Lansing, MI 48956

Balance due:
Michigan Department of Treasury
Lansing, MI 48929

IRC conformity: IRC incorporated as amended on January 1, 1996 or, at the option of the taxpayer, IRC in effect for current taxable year.

Starting point for calculation of income: Federal adjusted gross income.

Attach other state returns? Yes, if credit claimed for taxes paid to other state(s).

Federal attachments: Copy of federal return not required. However, taxpayers must attach the following schedules and forms, if applicable: Schedule B or 1040A Schedule 1 (interest and dividend income if over $5,000); Schedule C or C-EZ (business income and losses); Schedule D (gains and losses); Schedule E (rent, royalty, partnership income); Schedule F (farm income or losses); Schedule R or 1040A Schedule 3 (credit for elderly or disabled); Form 1040NR (Nonresident Alien Income Tax Return); Form 2555 (foreign earned income); Form 3903 or 3903-F (moving expenses); Form 4797 (gains and losses); Form 6198 (deductible loss from activity); Form 8829 (expenses for business use of home); and Form 8839 (adoption expenses). In addition, taxpayers claiming credit for repayment of amounts previously reported as income must attach pages 1 and 2 of federal Form 1040 and Schedule A, if applicable.

Estimated tax payments: Required if expected liability over $500. Estimated tax payments not required if taxpayer expects withholding for current year to be at least 90% of taxpayer's total liability for the current year (or 66 2/3% if the taxpayer is a qualified farmer, fisherman, or seafarer), 100% of tax liability for previous tax year, or 110% of previous year liability if taxpayer's AGI for previous year was more than $150,000 ($75,000 for married filing separately).

Extensions: Copy of approved federal extension or state Form 4.

Length of extension: Six months.

Mailing address:
Michigan Department of Treasury
P.O. Box 30774
Lansing, MI 48909

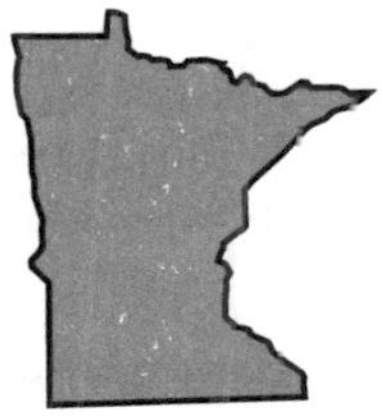

MINNESOTA

2009 Individual Tax Rate Schedule

Single:					
$ 0 –	22,730	× 5.35 %	minus	$	0.00
22,731 –	74,650	× 7.05	minus		386.41
74,651 +		× 7.85	minus		985.61
MFJ:					
$ 0 –	33,220	× 5.35 %	minus	$	0.00
33,221 –	131,970	× 7.05	minus		564.74
131,971 +		× 7.85	minus		1,620.50
MFS:					
$ 0 –	16,610	× 5.35 %	minus	$	0.00
16,611 –	65,990	× 7.05	minus		282.37
65,991 +		× 7.85	minus		810.29
HOH:					
$ 0 –	27,980	× 5.35 %	minus	$	0.00
27,981 –	112,420	× 7.05	minus		475.66
112,421 +		× 7.85	minus		1,375.02

Tax assistance:	651.296.3781
Forms request:	651.296.4444 Minnesota Tax Forms Mail Station 1421 St. Paul, MN 55146-1421
Web site:	www.taxes.state.mn.us
Download:	www.taxes.state.mn.us
e~file	http://www.taxes.state.mn.us/taxes/e-file/index.shtml

Who can e-file? Electronic filing is allowed for resident, part-year resident, and nonresident returns.

Who must e-file? Tax preparers who filed more than 100 returns during the previous year.

Filing requirements:
Filing status options: Single, Married Filing Jointly, Married Filing Separately, Head of Household, and Qualifying Widow(er) with Dependent Child.

Residents: Residents who filed a federal tax return or wish to claim credits, or whose employer withheld MN income tax.

Part-year residents: (1) Determine total income from all sources while a MN resident; (2) Determine income from following sources while a MN nonresident:

- Wages, salaries, commissions, fees, tips, or bonuses for work done in MN
- Rents and royalties received from MN property
- Gains from sale of land or other tangible property in MN
- Gains from sale of partnership interest, to the extent partnership had property or sales in MN
- Gain on sale of goodwill or income from agreement not to compete in connection with business operating in MN
- MN gross income from business or profession conducted partly or entirely in MN
- Gross winnings from gambling in MN

Add items above. If total is $8,950 or more, you must file Form M1 and Schedule M1NR. If total is less than $8,950 and you had taxes withheld or paid estimated tax, you must file Form M1 and Schedule M1NR to receive a refund.

Nonresidents: Same as for part-year residents.

Forms to file: Form M1, *Minnesota Individual Income Tax Return*

Part-year residents and nonresidents: Schedule M1NR (attachment to Form M1)

Where to send returns:
Minnesota Individual Income Tax
Mail Station 0010
St. Paul, MN 55145-0010

IRC conformity: IRC incorporated by reference as of March 31, 2009.

Starting point for calculation of income: Federal taxable income.

Attach other state returns? Yes, if resident of state with reciprocity agreement with Minnesota (i.e., Michigan, North Dakota, and Wisconsin).

Federal attachments: Copies of federal return and all schedules must be attached.

Estimated tax payments: Required if expected liability of $500 or more, and withholding and credits less than the smaller of 90% of current year liability (farmers, 66.7%) or 100% of previous year liability (110% if federal AGI was more than $150,000).

Extensions: Form M13 if payment due.

Length of extension: Six months automatic.

Mailing address:
Minnesota Revenue
P.O. Box 64058
St. Paul, MN 55164-0058

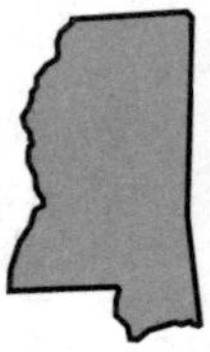

MISSISSIPPI

2009 tax rate schedule:

$ 0	–	5,000	×	3.0%	minus	$ 0.00
5,001	–	10,000	×	4.0	minus	50.00
10,001	+		×	5.0	minus	150.00

Tax assistance:	601.923.7089
Forms request:	601.923.7815 State Tax Commission Office of Revenue P.O. Box 1033 Jackson, MS 39215-1033
Web site:	www.mstc.state.ms.us
Tax Practitioner Web site:	www.mstc.state.ms.us/txpreprs/main.htm
Tax Practitioner Hotline:	601.923.7089
Download:	www.mstc.state.ms.us
e~file	http://www.mstc.state.ms.us/taxareas/individ/efiling/main.htm

Who can e-file? Anyone who uses an approved MS e-file tax preparer or an approved online service provider.

Who must e-file? No conditions.

Filing requirements:
Filing status options: Single, Married Filing Joint or Combined Return, Married Spouse Died, Married Filing Separate Returns, and Head of Family Individual.

Residents:

- You have MS income tax withheld from your wages or gambling winnings
- *Single or MFS:* Gross income of more than $8,300 plus $1,500 for each dependent
- *HOH:* Gross income of more than $12,900 plus $1,500 for each dependent
- *Married:* Combined gross income of more than $16,600 plus $1,500 for each dependent
- *Minor:* Gross income exceeds the personal exemption plus the standard deduction according to filing status
- *Working out of state or outside United States:* Must report total gross income

Part-year residents: You have income taxed by MS excluding gambling income.

Nonresidents: You have income taxed by MS excluding gambling income.

Forms to file: Form 80-105, *Mississippi Resident Individual Income Tax Return*

Part-year residents and nonresidents: Form 80-205, *Mississippi Non-Resident or Part-Year Resident Individual Income Tax Return*

Where to send returns:

Balance, no tax due:

Office of Revenue
P.O. Box 23050
Jackson, MS 39225-3050

Refund:

Office of Revenue
P.O. Box 23058
Jackson, MS 39225-3058

IRC conformity: IRC not incorporated.

Starting point for calculation of income: Gross income.

Attach other state returns? Yes, if claiming a credit for taxes paid to other state(s).

Federal attachments: Copy of federal return not required. However, taxpayers must attach the following federal schedules and forms, if applicable: Schedule C or C-EZ (business income and losses); Schedule D (gains and losses); Schedule E (rent, royalty, partnership income); Schedule F (farm income or losses); Form 2106 (unreimbursed employee expense deduction); Form 3903 or 3903-F (moving expenses); and Form 4684 (casualty and theft losses). In addition, if amount of state taxable income entered on Form 80-105 differs from amount of federal taxable income entered on a federal return, separate reconciling schedules must be attached.

Estimated tax payments: Required if expected liability over $200 and less than 80% of tax covered by withholding.

Extensions: Form 80-180 if tax due or automatic if federal extension.

Length of extension: Six months automatic.

Mailing address:

Office of Revenue
P.O. Box 23075
Jackson, MS 39225-3075

MISSOURI

2009 tax rate schedule:

$ 0	– 1,000	×	1.5%	minus	$0.00
1,001	– 2,000	×	2.0	minus	5.00
2,001	– 3,000	×	2.5	minus	15.00
3,001	– 4,000	×	3.0	minus	30.00
4,001	– 5,000	×	3.5	minus	50.00
5,001	– 6,000	×	4.0	minus	75.00
6,001	– 7,000	×	4.5	minus	105.00
7,001	– 8,000	×	5.0	minus	140.00
8,001	– 9,000	×	5.5	minus	180.00
9,001 +		×	6.0	minus	225.00

Tax assistance: 573.751.7191

Forms request: 800.877.6881

Missouri Department of Revenue
Taxation Division
P.O. Box 3022
Jefferson City, MO 65105-3022

Web site: www.dor.mo.gov/tax

Download: www.dor.mo.gov/tax/forms

e~file www.dor.mo.gov/tax/personal/electronic.htm

Who can e-file? Resident, nonresident, and part-year resident returns accepted.

Individuals may also file using a preparer who is a certified Electronic Return Originator.

Who must e-file? No conditions.

Filing requirements:
Filing status options: Single, Married Filing Jointly, Married Filing Separately, Head of Household, Qualifying Widow(er) with Dependent Child, taxpayer claimed as dependent on another person's federal tax return, and Married Taxpayers Filing Separately whose spouse had no income and was claimed as an exemption on taxpayer's federal return and was not a dependent of someone else.

Residents: All residents who are required to file a federal tax return and have at least $1,200 in MO AGI or have MO AGI more than the standard deduction plus exemption for the individual's filing status or desire a refund of MO income tax withheld.

Part-year residents: Treated as nonresidents but may determine tax as residents for entire year.

Nonresidents: Must have at least $600 of MO income.

Forms to file: Form MO-1040, *Individual Income Tax Return*

Part-year residents and nonresidents: Form MO-NRI, *Missouri Income Percentage* (attachment to Form MO-1040)

Where to send returns:

Refund or no balance due:
Department of Revenue
P.O. Box 500
Jefferson City, MO 65106-0500

Balance due:
Department of Revenue
P.O. Box 329
Jefferson City, MO 65107-0329

IRC conformity: IRC incorporated by reference as currently amended.

Starting point for calculation of income: Federal adjusted gross income.

Attach other state returns? Yes, if claiming credit for taxes paid to other state(s).

Federal attachments: Copy of pages 1 and 2 of federal return must be attached, if applicable (capital gain exclusion on sale of low income housing, itemized deductions, dependents, long-term care insurance deduction, pension exemption, alternative minimum and other federal taxes, state income tax refund). Copy of federal return required for part-year residents and nonresidents calculating their state income percentage on Form MO-NRI. Taxpayers must also attach the following federal schedules and forms, if applicable: Schedule A (itemized deductions); Form 1045 (net operating loss); Form 4255 (recapture taxes); Form 4797 (capital gain exclusion on sale of low income housing); Form 4972 (lump sum distribution); Form 8611 (recapture taxes); Form 8826 (disabled access credit); Form 8828 (recapture taxes); and K-1. In addition, while not listed as a requirement in Form MO-1040 Instructions, MO Department of Revenue recommends attaching federal Form 8886, if applicable.

Estimated tax payments: Required if expected liability at least $100.

Extensions: Form MO-60 or automatic with federal extension.

Length of extension: Six months automatic.

Mailing address:
Missouri Department of Revenue
P.O. Box 3400
Jefferson City, MO 65105-3400

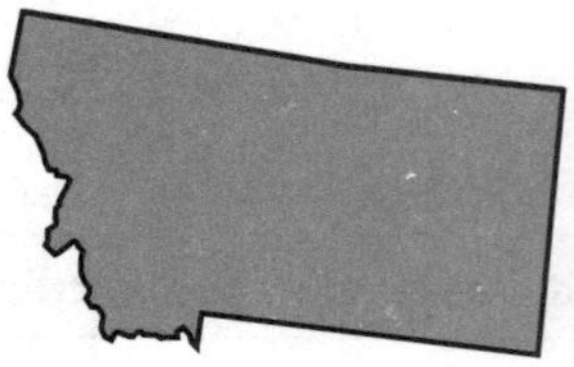

MONTANA

2009 Individual Tax Rate Schedule

$ 0	–	2,600	×	1.0 %	minus	$ 0.00
2,601	–	4,500	×	2.0	minus	26.00
4,501	–	6,900	×	3.0	minus	71.00
6,901	–	9,300	×	4.0	minus	140.00
9,301	–	12,000	×	5.0	minus	233.00
12,001	–	15,400	×	6.0	minus	353.00
15,401	+		×	6.9	minus	492.00

Capital Gains:
Capital gains tax credit: 1%

Tax assistance: 406.444.6900

Forms request: 406.444.6900

Montana Department of Revenue
Attn: Income Taxes
P.O. Box 5805
Helena, MT 59604-5805

Web site: www.mt.gov/revenue

Download: www.mt.gov/formsandresources/forms.asp

e~file http://mt.gov/revenue/forindividuals/electronicfiling/electronicfiling.asp

Who can e-file? Taxpayers can file individual income tax returns using approved software, an approved online service provider, or an authorized tax professional.

Who must e-file? No conditions.

Filing requirements:

Filing status options: Single, Married Filing Jointly, Married Filing Separately on Same Form, Married Filing Separately on Separate Forms, Married Filing Separately and Spouse Not Filing, and Head of Household.

Residents:

Filing status	Age	Gross income at least:
Single, MFS	Under 65	$ 3,920
	65+	6,060
MFJ	Both under 65	7,840
	One spouse 65+	9,880
	Both spouses 65+	12,120
HOH	Under 65	5,700
	65+	7,840

Increase federal gross income required to file by $1,980 if eligible for the blind exemption.

Part-year residents: Taxed on all income derived from or connected to Montana sources. Additionally, part-year residents are taxed on all non-Montana-source income generated during or attributable to the period of the tax year in which they resided in Montana.

Nonresidents: Taxed on all income derived from or connected to Montana sources.

Forms to file: Form 2, *Montana Individual Income Tax Return*

Part-year residents and nonresidents: Schedule IV, *Nonresident/Part-Year Resident Tax*

Where to send returns:

Returns with payments:

Dept. of Revenue
P.O. Box 6308
Helena, MT 59604-6308

All other returns:

Dept. of Revenue
P.O. Box 6577
Helena, MT 59604-6577

IRC conformity: IRC incorporated by reference as currently amended.

Starting point for calculation of income: Federal adjusted gross income.

Attach other state returns? No.

Federal attachments: Complete copy of federal return must be attached for taxpayers required to disclose tax shelters, reportable transactions, and similar activities for federal purposes. Taxpayers using head-of-household filing status must attach pages 1 and 2 of federal return. Nonresident and part-year resident taxpayers must attach copy of federal return including all forms and schedules. Taxpayers must also attach the following federal schedules and forms, if applicable: Schedule B (interest and dividend income); Schedule C or C-EZ (business income and losses); Schedule D (gains and losses); Schedule E (rent, royalty, partnership income); Schedule F (farm income or losses); Schedule SE (self-employment tax); Form 1040 (federal estimated tax payment paid); Form 2106 or 2106-EZ (unreimbursed employee business expenses); Form 3468 (historic property preservation credit); Form 3903 or 3903-F (moving expenses); Form 4684 (casualty and theft losses); Form 4797 (gains and losses); Form 4952 (investment interest); Form 4972 (lump sum distribution); Form 8839 (adoption expenses); Form 8889 (health savings account deduction); and Form 8903 (domestic production activities).

Estimated tax payments: Required if expected liability of $500 or more after subtracting credits and withholding.

Extensions: Automatic with federal extension. Complete Form EXT if tax owed. Attach copies of federal extension forms when filing state return, unless return is filed electronically.

Length of extension: Six months automatic.

Mailing address:

Dept. of Revenue
P.O. Box 6308
Helena, MT 59604-6308

NEBRASKA

2009 Individual Tax Rate Schedule

Single:

$ 0	–	2,400	× 2.56 %	minus	$ 0.00
2,401	–	17,500	× 3.57	minus	24.24
17,501	–	27,000	× 5.12	minus	295.49
27,001	+		× 6.84	minus	759.89

MFJ and surviving spouses:

$ 0	–	4,800	× 2.56 %	minus	$ 0.00
4,801	–	31,000	× 3.57	minus	48.80
35,001	–	54,000	× 5.12	minus	590.98
54,001	+		× 6.84	minus	1,519.78

MFS:

$ 0	–	2,400	× 2.56 %	minus	$ 0.00
2,401	–	17,500	× 3.57	minus	24.40
17,501	–	27,000	× 5.12	minus	295.49
27,001	+		× 6.84	minus	759.89

HOH:

$ 0	–	4,500	× 2.56 %	minus	$ 0.00
4,501	–	28,000	× 3.57	minus	45.45
28,001	–	40,000	× 5.12	minus	479.45
40,001	+		× 6.84	minus	1,167.45

There is an additional tax on taxpayers with federal AGI of more than $166,800 ($83,400 for MFS).

Tax assistance: 800.742.7474 (NE and IA) or 402.471.5729

Forms request: 800.742.7474

Nebraska Department of Revenue
P.O. Box 94818
Lincoln, NE 68509-4818

Web site: www.revenue.state.ne.us

Download: www.revenue.state.ne.us/tax/forms.htm

e~file www.revenue.state.ne.us/electron/e-file.htm

Who can e-file? Any taxpayer who uses an approved tax preparer, approved software, or the state-offered Nebfile program.

Who must e-file? Electronic filing is mandated for tax returns due on or after January 1, 2010, for tax preparers that file 25 or more returns in the prior calendar year.

Filing requirements:
Filing status options: Single, Married Filing Jointly, Married Filing Separately, Head of Household, and Qualifying Widow(er) with Dependent Child.

Residents, part-year residents, and nonresidents: The following taxpayers are required to file:

- Those required to file a federal return or report a federal liability, or
- Those who have $5,000 or more of Nebraska adjustments to federal AGI

Forms to file: Form 1040N, *Nebraska Individual Income Tax Return*

Part-year residents and nonresidents: Schedule III (attachment to Form 1040N), *Computation of Nebraska Tax for Nonresidents and Partial-Year Residents Only*

Where to send returns:

Refund:
Nebraska Department of Revenue
P.O. Box 98912
Lincoln, NE 68509-8912

Payment:
Nebraska Department of Revenue
P.O. Box 98934
Lincoln, NE 68509-8934

IRC conformity: IRC incorporated by reference as currently amended.

Starting point for calculation of income: Federal adjusted gross income.

Attach other state returns? Yes, if claiming credit for taxes paid to other state(s)

Federal attachments: Copy of federal return generally not required. However, copy of pages 1 and 2 of federal return must be attached if claiming earned income credit. Taxpayers must also attach the following federal schedules and forms, if applicable: Schedule D (special capital gain deduction); Schedule R or 1040A Schedule 3 (credit for elderly or disabled); Form 2441 or 1040A Schedule 2 (child/dependent care credit); Form 4972 (lump sum distributions); Form 5329 or copy of federal return if Form 5329 not required (early retirement plan distributions); and Form 6251 (alternative minimum tax recalculated under Revenue Ruling 22-03-1).

Estimated tax payments: Required if expected liability of $300 or more.

Extensions: Copy of approved federal extension or state Form 4868N.

Length of extension: Six months with federal extension; seven months with Form 4868N.

Mailing address:
Nebraska Department of Revenue
P.O. Box 94818
Lincoln, NE 68509-4818

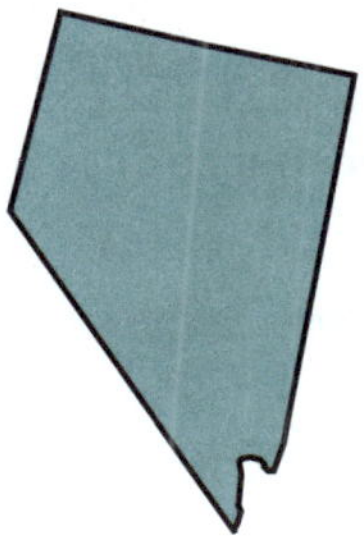

NEVADA

Tax assistance: 775.684.2000

Forms request: 775.684.2000

Nevada Department of Taxation
1550 College Parkway, Suite 115
Carson City, NV 89706

Web site: www.tax.state.nv.us

Download: www.tax.state.nv.us

Filing requirements: Nevada does not impose an income tax.

NEW HAMPSHIRE

2009 tax rate schedule: 5% on interest and dividend income

Tax assistance: 603.271.2191

Forms request: 603.271.2192

New Hampshire Department of Revenue Administration
P.O. Box 637
Concord, NH 03302-0637

Web site: www.nh.gov/revenue

Download: www.nh.gov/revenue/forms/index.htm

e~file www.revenue.nh.gov/index.htm

Who can e-file? Electronic filing is allowed for residents and part-year residents.

Who must e-file? No conditions.

Filing requirements:
Filing status options: Individual, Joint, Partnership, and Fiduciary. Applies to Interest and Dividend Tax.

Residents and part-year residents: Filing is required for residents and part-year residents with interest and dividend taxable income of more than $2,400 annually ($4,800 for joint filers).

Forms to file: Form DP-10, *Interest and Dividends Tax Return*

Where to send returns:
New Hampshire Department of Revenue Administration
Document Processing Division
P.O. Box 2072
Concord, NH 03302-2072

IRC conformity: IRC incorporated.

Starting point for calculation of income: Gross income (tax on interest and dividends only).

Attach other state returns? No

Federal attachments: None required

Estimated tax payments: Required if expected liability of $500 or more.

Extensions: Form DP-59-A

Length of extension: An automatic seven-month extension is granted if 100% of the taxes are paid by the due date for the tax.

Mailing address:
New Hampshire Department of Revenue Administration
P.O. Box 2072
Concord, NH 03302-2072

NEW JERSEY

2009 Individual Tax Rate Schedule

Single, MFS:

$ 0	–	20,000	×	1.400 %	minus	$	0.00
20,001	–	35,000	×	1.750	minus		70.00
35,001	–	40,000	×	3.500	minus		682.50
40,001	–	75,000	×	5.525	minus		1,492.50
75,001	–	400,000	×	6.370	minus		2,126.25
400,001	–	500,000	×	8.000	minus		8,646.25
500,001	–	1,000,000	×	10.250	minus		19,896.25
1,000,001	+		×	10.750	minus		24,896.25

MFJ, HOH, QW:

$ 0	–	20,000	×	1.400 %	minus	$	0.00
20,001	–	50,000	×	1.750	minus		70.00
50,001	–	70,000	×	2.450	minus		420.00
70,001	–	80,000	×	3.500	minus		1,155.00
80,001	–	150,000	×	5.525	minus		2,775.00
150,001	–	400,000	×	6.370	minus		4,042.50
400,001	–	500,000	×	8.000	minus		10,562.50
500,001	–	1,000,000	×	10.250	minus		21,812.50
1,000,001	+		×	10.750	minus		26,812.50

Tax assistance: 609.292.6400

Forms request: 800.323.4400
Fax: 609.826.4500

NJ Division of Taxation
Taxpayer Forms Services
P.O. Box 269
Trenton, NJ 08695-0269

Web site: www.state.nj.us/treasury/taxation

Download: www.state.nj.us/treasury/taxation/taxprnt.shtml

e~file http://www.state.nj.us/treasury/taxation/online.shtml

Who can e-file? Resident, nonresident, and part-year resident returns accepted.

Who must e-file? Tax preparers that filed 25 or more resident returns for prior taxable year.

Filing requirements:
Filing status options: Single, Married/Civil Union Filing Jointly, Married/Civil Union Partner Filing Separately, Head of Household, and Qualifying Widow(er)/Surviving Civil Union Partner.

Residents, part-year residents, and nonresidents: Residents, part-year residents, and nonresidents must file if:

- Filing status of Single or MFS and gross income over $10,000
- Filing status of MFJ, HOH, or QW and gross income over $20,000

Forms to file: *Residents and part-year residents:* Form NJ-1040, *State of New Jersey Income Tax--Resident Return*

Part-year residents and nonresidents (if NJ-source income received during nonresidency): Form NJ-1040NR, *State of New Jersey Income Tax--Nonresident Return*

Where to send returns:
Resident, part-year resident:

Payment:
State of New Jersey
Division of Taxation
Revenue Processing Center
P.O. Box 111
Trenton, NJ 08645-0111

Refund:
State of New Jersey
Division of Taxation
Revenue Processing Center
P.O. Box 555
Trenton, NJ 08647-0555

Nonresident:
State of New Jersey-TGI
Division of Taxation
Revenue Processing Center
P.O. Box 244
Trenton, NJ 08646-0244

IRC conformity: IRC not incorporated.

Starting point for calculation of income: Gross income.

Attach other state returns? No

Federal attachments: Copy of federal return generally not required. However, part-year residents with income below annual filing threshold must attach copy of federal return. Taxpayers must also attach the following federal schedules and forms, if applicable: Schedule B (interest and dividend income); Schedule C or C-EZ (business income and losses); Schedule F (farm income or losses); Form 2106 or 2106-EZ (unreimbursed employee business expenses); Form 3903 or 3903-F (moving expenses); Form 8283 (qualified conservation contributions); Form 8853 (Archer MSA contributions); and Schedule K-1.

Estimated tax payments: Required if expected liability of more than $400.

Extensions: Form NJ-630

Length of extension: A taxpayer can receive an extension of up to six months if at least 80% of the tax due is paid by the original due date. The taxpayer must attach the federal application for automatic extension to the return or file Form NJ-630, *Application for Extension of Time to File New Jersey Gross Income Tax Return.*

Mailing address:

State of New Jersey
Division of Taxation
Revenue Processing Center
P.O. Box 282
Trenton, NJ 08646-0282

NEW MEXICO

2009 tax rate schedule:

Single:

$	0 –	5,500	×	1.7%	minus	$	0.00
	5,501 –	11,000	×	3.2	minus		82.50
	11,001 –	16,000	×	4.7	minus		247.50
	16,001 +		×	4.9	minus		279.50

MFJ, QW:

$	0 –	8,000	×	1.7%	minus	$	0.00
	8,001 –	16,000	×	3.2	minus		120.00
	16,001 –	24,000	×	4.7	minus		360.00
	24,001 +		×	4.9	minus		408.00

MFS:

$	0 –	4,000	×	1.7%	minus	$	0.00
	4,001 –	8,000	×	3.2	minus		60.00
	8,001 –	12,000	×	4.7	minus		180.00
	12,001 +		×	4.9	minus		204.00

HOH:

$	0 –	8,000	×	1.7%	minus	$	0.00
	8,001 –	16,000	×	3.2	minus		120.00
	16,001 –	24,000	×	4.7	minus		360.00
	24,001 +		×	4.9	minus		408.00

Tax assistance: 505.827.0827

Forms request: 505.827.2206

New Mexico Taxation and Revenue Department
P.O. Box 630
Santa Fe, NM 87504-0630

Web site: www.tax.state.nm.us/trd_home.htm

Tax Practitioner Web site: www.tax.state.nm.us/taxprac.htm

Download: www.tax.state.nm.us/trd_form.htm

e~file www.tax.state.nm.us/eser.htm

Who can e-file? Most taxpayers, although certain restrictions apply.

Who must e-file? Tax preparers filing more than 25 returns per year.

Filing requirements:
Filing status options: Single, Married Filing Jointly, Married Filing Separately, Head of Household, and Qualifying Widow(er) with Dependent Child.

Residents: Must file if they:

- Are required to file a federal income tax return
- Want to claim a refund of any New Mexico state income tax withheld from pay
- Want to claim any New Mexico rebates or credits

Nonresidents and part-year residents: Must file if they:

- Are required to file a federal income tax return
- Received income or incurred loss from New Mexico sources

Forms to file: Form PIT-1, *New Mexico Personal Income Tax Return*

Part-year residents and nonresidents: PIT-B, *New Mexico Allocation and Apportionment of Income Schedule* (attachment)

Where to send returns:

Refund, no payment:
New Mexico Taxation and Revenue Department
P.O. Box 25122
Santa Fe, NM 87504-5122

Payment:
New Mexico Taxation and Revenue Department
P.O. Box 8390
Santa Fe, NM 87504-8390

IRC conformity: IRC incorporated by reference as currently amended.

Starting point for calculation of income: Federal adjusted gross income.

Attach other state returns? Yes, if claiming credit for taxes paid to other state(s).

Federal attachments: Copy of federal return generally not required. However, Taxation and Revenue Department may require taxpayer to furnish copy of federal return and attachments. If filing joint nonresident federal return, and taxpayer's spouse not required to have SSN or ITIN, taxpayer must submit copy of federal nonresident return. Copy of federal Form(s) 8886 (Reportable Transaction Disclosure Statement) must be attached to return and checkbox on return must be marked, if Form 8886 required to be attached with federal return.

Due Date: April 15 (April 30 if taxes are filed and paid electronically).

Estimated tax payments: Required if expected liability of less than $500 and 90% of tax shown for current year, or 100% of tax shown on the prior year's return.

Extensions: No form required for six-month extension if federal extension has been approved; otherwise, file New Mexico Form RPD-41096.

Length of extension: Six-month automatic extension if federal extension is filed by original due date of return. Additional extension for good cause may be requested on Form RPD-41096.

Sixty-day automatic extension if Form RPD-41096 is postmarked by original due date of return. Additional extension up to 12 months may be granted upon showing of good cause.

Mailing address:

Revenue Processing Division
New Mexico Taxation and Revenue Department
P.O. Box 630
Santa Fe, NM 87504-0630

NEW YORK

2009 Individual Tax Rate Schedule

Single, MFS:

$ 0	– 8,000	× 4.00 %	minus	$ 0.00
8,001	– 11,000	× 4.50	minus	40.00
11,001	– 13,000	× 5.25	minus	122.50
13,001	– 20,000	× 5.90	minus	207.00
20,001	– 200,000	× 6.85	minus	397.00
200,001	– 500,000	× 7.85	minus	2,397.00
500,001	+	× 8.97	minus	7,997.00

MFJ, QW:

$ 0	– 16,000	× 4.00 %	minus	$ 0.00
16,001	– 22,000	× 4.50	minus	80.00
22,001	– 26,000	× 5.25	minus	245.00
26,001	– 40,000	× 5.90	minus	414.00
40,001	– 300,000	× 6.85	minus	794.00
300,001	– 500,000	× 7.85	minus	3,794.00
500,001	+	× 8.97	minus	9,394.00

HOH:

$ 0	– 11,000	× 4.00 %	minus	$ 0.00
11,001	– 15,000	× 4.50	minus	55.00
15,001	– 17,000	× 5.25	minus	167.50
17,001	– 30,000	× 5.90	minus	278.00
30,001	– 250,000	× 6.85	minus	563.00
250,001	– 500,000	× 7.85	minus	3,063
500,001	+	× 8.97	minus	8,663.00

Note that a supplemental tax (the tax table benefit recapture) is computed for taxpayers with certain levels of income. Also, a separate New York City tax rate schedule applies to New York City residents.

Tax assistance:	800.225.5829
Forms request:	800.462.8100 Fax: 800.748.3676 NYS Tax Department OSB-Forms Control Section 8 W.A. Harriman Campus Albany, NY 12227
Web site:	www.tax.state.ny.us
Tax Practitioner Web site:	www.tax.state.ny.us/tp
Download:	www.tax.state.ny.us/forms/default.htm
e~file	www.tax.state.ny.us/elf

Who can e-file? Most taxpayers using approved software or online service provider. For exceptions, see website.

Who must e-file? Tax preparers that filed more than 100 combined individual or partnership returns in the prior tax year and that prepare one or more individual and/or partnership returns for tax year 2008 in calendar year 2009 using tax software.

Filing requirements:
Filing status options: Single; Married Filing Jointly if one spouse is state resident but other is nonresident or part-year resident, taxpayer is unable to file jointly for state purposes because address or whereabouts of one spouse is unknown, or one spouse refuses to sign joint state return; Married Filing Separately; Head of Household; and Qualifying Widow(er) with Dependent Child.

Residents: All residents who:

- Must file a federal return
- Did not have to file a federal return, but:

Federal filing status would have been:	Federal adjusted gross income (plus New York additions) was more than:
Single, and can be claimed as a dependent on another's federal return	$3,000
Single and cannot be claimed as a dependent on another's federal return, *or* married filing joint return, *or* married filing separate return, *or* head of household, *or* qualifying widow(er)	4,000

Filing is also required of residents who:

- Are subject to the minimum income tax
- Are subject to the separate tax on lump-sum distributions
- Want to claim a refund of any New York State, city of New York, or city of Yonkers income taxes withheld or
- Want to claim a refund of certain New York State, city of New York, or city of Yonkers credits

Part-year residents and nonresidents: Must file if:

Federal filing status is:	Taxpayer had New York source income, and New York adjusted gross income is more than:
Single, and can be claimed as a dependent on another's federal return	$ 3,000
Single, and cannot be claimed as a dependent on another's federal return	7,500
Married filing joint return	15,000
Married filing separate return	7,500
Head of household	10,500
Qualifying widow(er)	15,000

Filing is also required of nonresidents and part-year residents who:

- Are subject to the minimum income tax
- Are subject to the separate tax on lump-sum distributions
- Want to claim a refund of any New York State, city of New York, or city of Yonkers income taxes withheld
- Want to claim a refund of certain New York State, city of New York, or city of Yonkers credits or
- Incurred a net operating loss for New York State personal income tax purposes for the tax year, without incurring a similar net operating loss for federal income tax purposes

Forms to file: IT-201, *Resident Income Tax Return*

Part-year residents and nonresidents: IT-203, *Nonresident and Part-Year Resident Income Tax Return*

Where to send returns:
State Processing Center
P.O. Box 61000
Albany, NY 12261-0001

IRC conformity: IRC not incorporated by reference but federal adjusted gross income is starting point for calculating state tax.

Starting point for calculation of income: Federal adjusted gross income.

Attach other state returns? No

Federal attachments: Schedules C, D, E, and F; Forms 4797, 8886.

Estimated tax payments: Required if expected liability less than the smaller of (a) 90% of the tax shown for the current tax year, or (b) 100% of the tax shown on the prior year's return (110% of that amount if not a farmer or fisherman and NY current year AGI is more than $150,000, or $75,000 if married filing separately).

Extensions: Form IT-370 or federal Form 4868

Length of extension: Six months automatic.

Mailing address:

Payment:
Extension Request
P.O. Box 4125
Binghamton, NY 13902-4125

No payment:
Extension Request--NR
P.O. Box 4126
Binghamton, NY 13902-4126

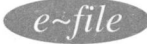

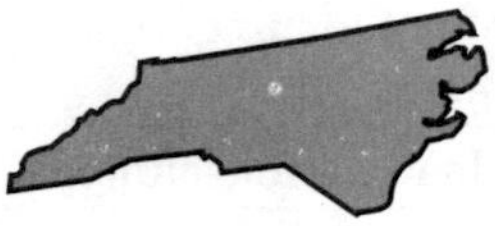

NORTH CAROLINA

2009 Individual Tax Rate Schedule

Single:

$ 0	–	12,750	×	6.00 %	minus	$	0.00
12,751	–	60,000	×	7.00	minus		127.50
60,001	+		×	7.75	minus		577.50

MFJ, QW:

$ 0	–	21,250	×	6.00 %	minus	$	0.00
21,251	–	100,000	×	7.00	minus		212.50
100,001	+		×	7.75	minus		962.50

HOH:

$ 0	–	17,000	×	6.00 %	minus	$	0.00
17,001	–	80,000	×	7.00	minus		170.00
80,001	+		×	7.75	minus		770.00

MFS:

$ 0	–	10,625	×	6.00 %	minus	$	0.00
10,626	–	50,000	×	7.00	minus		106.25
50,001	+		×	7.75	minus		481.25

2% surcharge imposed during 2009 and 2010 tax years for the following taxpayers: joint filers or surviving spouses with taxable incomes greater than $100,000 and up to $250,000; heads of households with taxable incomes greater than $80,000 and up to $200,000; single filers with taxable incomes greater than $60,000 and up to $150,000; married filing separately with taxable incomes greater than $50,000 and up to $125,000. 3% surcharge imposed during 2009 and 2010 tax years for the following taxpayers: joint filers and surviving spouses with taxable incomes greater than $250,000; heads of households with taxable incomes greater than $200,000; single filers with taxable incomes greater than $150,000; married filing separately filers with taxable incomes greater than $125,000.

Tax assistance: 877.252.3052

Forms request: 877.252.3052

North Carolina Department
of Revenue
P.O. Box 25000
Raleigh, NC 27640-0640

Web site: www.dor.state.nc.us

Tax Practitioner Hotline: 919.754.2500

Download: www.dor.state.nc.us/downloads/individual.html

e~file www.dor.state.nc.us/electronic

Who can e-file? Most taxpayers can file from a PC using approved software or through an authorized tax preparer.

Who must e-file? No conditions.

Filing requirements:
Filing status options: Single, Married Filing Jointly, Married Filing Separately, Head of Household, and Qualifying Widow(er) with Dependent Child.

Residents: Residents are required to file if:

Filing status	Age	Gross income at least:
Single	Under 65	$ 5,500
	65+	6,250
MFJ	Both under 65	11,000
	One 65+	11,600
	Both 65+	12,200
MFS	Any age	2,500
HOH	Under 65	6,900
	65+	7,650
QW	With dependent child	8,500
	65+	9,100

Part-year residents and nonresidents: Part-year residents must file if they received income while a NC resident or had NC source income while a nonresident and income from all sources exceeds filing threshold. Nonresidents must file if they have NC source income and their income from all sources exceeds the filing threshold.

Forms to file: Form D-400, *Individual Income Tax Return*

Where to send returns:

Refund:
North Carolina Department of Revenue
P.O. Box R
Raleigh, NC 27634-0001

Balance, no tax due:
North Carolina Department of Revenue
P.O. Box 25000
Raleigh, NC 27640-0640

IRC conformity: IRC incorporated by reference as of May 1, 2009.

Starting point for calculation of income: Federal taxable income.

Attach other state returns? Yes, if claiming credit for tax paid to other state(s).

Federal attachments: If filed joint return federally and separate return for NC and using a non-NC address. Federal return must be attached unless federal return reflects a NC address or the taxpayer files electronically.

Estimated tax payments: Required if expected liability of $1,000 or more.

Extensions: Form D-410

Length of extension: Six months if form is filed by the due date of the return.

Mailing address:
North Carolina Department of Revenue
P.O. Box 25000
Raleigh, NC 27640-0635

NORTH DAKOTA

2009 Individual Tax Rate Schedule

Single:

$ 0 –	33,950	× 1.84 %	minus	$ 0.00
33,951 –	82,850	× 3.44	minus	543.20
82,851 –	171,550	× 3.81	minus	849.75
171,551 –	372,950	× 4.42	minus	1,896.20
372,951 +		× 4.86	minus	3,537.18

MFJ, QW:

$ 0 –	56,750	× 1.84 %	minus	$ 0.00
56,751 –	137,050	× 3.44	minus	908.00
137,051 –	208,850	× 3.81	minus	1,415.09
208,851 –	372,950	× 4.42	minus	2,689.07
372,950 +		× 4.86	minus	4,330.05

MFS:

$ 0 –	28,375	× 1.84 %	minus	$ 0.00
28,376 –	68,525	× 3.44	minus	454.00
68,526 –	104,425	× 3.81	minus	707.54
104,426 –	186,475	× 4.42	minus	1,344.54
186,476 +		× 4.86	minus	2,165.03

HOH:

$ 0 –	45,500	× 1.84 %	minus	$ 0.00
45,501 –	117,450	× 3.44	minus	728.00
117,451 –	190,200	× 3.81	minus	1,162.56
190,201 –	372,950	× 4.42	minus	2,322.78
372,951 +		× 4.86	minus	3,963.76

Tax assistance: 701.328.1247

Forms request: 701.328.1243
Office of State Tax Commissioner
600 E. Boulevard Ave., Dept. 127
Bismarck, ND 58505-0599

Web site: www.nd.gov/tax

Tax Practitioner Web site: www.nd.gov/tax/vendor

Download: www.nd.gov/tax/indincome/forms

e~file www.nd.gov/tax/indincome/elecfiling

Who can e-file? Resident, nonresident, part-year resident returns accepted.

Who must e-file? No conditions.

Filing requirements:
Filing status options: Single, Married Filing Jointly, Married Filing Separately, Head of Household, and Qualifying Widow(er) with Dependent Child.

Residents: Anyone who is required to file a federal tax return.

Part-year residents: Those who have federal income tax filing requirement and derive gross income from North Dakota or derive gross income from any source while a North Dakota resident.

Nonresidents: Those who have federal income tax filing requirement and derive gross income from North Dakota (exceptions: certain Minnesota and Montana residents and certain nonresidents employed by interstate commerce carriers).

Forms to file: Form ND-1, *Individual Income Tax Return*

Part-year residents and nonresidents: Schedule ND-1NR, *Tax Calculation for Nonresidents and Part-Year Residents* (attachment)

Where to send returns:
State Tax Commissioner
P.O. Box 5621
Bismarck, ND 58506-5621

IRC conformity: IRC incorporated by reference as currently amended.

Starting point for calculation of income: Federal taxable income.

Attach other state returns? No.

Federal attachments: Attach a complete copy of federal income tax return.

Estimated tax payments: Required if expected liability over $500 or more and current year withholding equals the smaller of 90% of current year net tax liability or 100% of preceding year net tax liability.

Extensions: Federal Form 4868; or state Form 101 (extension granted only if there is good cause)

Length of extension: Six months automatic with federal extension; state extension at taxpayer's request, pending approval.

Mailing address:
Office of State Tax Commissioner
600 E. Boulevard Ave., Dept. 127
Bismarck, ND 58505-0599

OHIO

2009 Individual Tax Rate Schedule

$ 0 –	5,000	× 0.587 %	minus	$	0.00
5,001 –	10,000	× 1.174	minus		29.35
10,001 –	15,000	× 2.348	minus		146.75
15,001 –	20,000	× 2.935	minus		234.80
20,001 –	40,000	× 3.521	minus		352.00
40,001 –	80,000	× 4.109	minus		587.20
80,001 –	100,000	× 4.695	minus		1,056.00
100,001 –	200,000	× 5.451	minus		1,812.00
200,001 +		× 5.925	minus		2,760.00

Ohio individual income tax rates will drop 4.2% each year through 2009.

Tax assistance: 800.282.1780

Forms request: 800.282.1782
Forms Printing Division
P.O. Box 2476
Columbus, OH 43216-2476

Web site: www.tax.ohio.gov

Tax Practitioner Web site: www.tax.ohio.gov/channels/other/tax_professional.stm

Tax Practitioner Hotline: 614.728.1055

Download: www.tax.ohio.gov/forms/index.stm

e~file http://tax.ohio.gov/divisions/communications/electronic_filing_options.stm

Who can e-file? Available to most taxpayers. See www.tax.ohio.gov/online_services/index.stm for exceptions.

Who must e-file? Electronic filing is mandated for tax preparers who file 25 or more returns.

Filing requirements:
Filing status options: Single, Married Filing Jointly, Married Filing Separately, Head of Household, and Qualifying Widow(er) with Dependent Child.

Residents, part-year residents, and nonresidents:

Filing status	Age	AGI at least:
Single	65+	$11,500
MFJ	65+	13,000

Residents, part-year residents, and nonresidents are also required to file if they:

- Have completed Schedule A (on the back of the Ohio Form IT-1040)
- Had Ohio tax withheld
- Are due an Ohio income tax refund

Exceptions: Individuals are not required to file if:

- Their only source of income is retirement income eligible for the retirement income credit *and* the credit is the same or larger than tax before credits, or
- Their exemption amount is the same as or more than their Ohio adjusted gross income.

Forms to file: Form IT-1040, *Individual Income Tax Return*

Part-year residents and nonresidents: Schedule D, *Nonresident/Part-Year Resident Credit*

Where to send returns:

Payment:
Ohio Department of Taxation
P.O. Box 2057
Columbus, OH 43270-2057

No payment:
Ohio Department of Taxation
P.O. Box 2679
Columbus, OH 43270-2679

IRC conformity: IRC incorporated by reference as amended on October 16, 2009.

Starting point for calculation of income: Federal adjusted gross income.

Attach other state returns? No.

Federal attachments: Copy of federal return generally not required. However, taxpayers with zero or negative federal adjusted gross income must attach copy of page 1 of federal return to state return. Investors in pass-through entities claiming credit for tax paid on Ohio Form IT-4708 or IT-1140 must attach federal Form K-1s that reflect amount of Ohio tax paid.

Estimated tax payments: Required if expected liability over $500 after withholding, current year withholding is less than 90% of current year estimated tax liability and less than 100% of preceding year tax as reported on preceding year return.

Extensions: Automatic if federal extension. Copy of federal extension form, extension confirmation number, or extension acknowledgement must be attached to return when filed. Use Ohio Form IT-40P to make tax payments by due date.

Length of extension: Six months automatic.

Mailing address:

Payment enclosed:
Ohio Department of Taxation
P.O. Box 182131
Columbus, OH 43218-2131

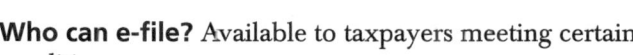

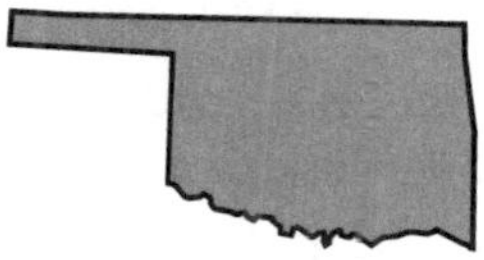

OKLAHOMA

2009 Individual Tax Rate Schedule

Single, MFS:

$ 0	–	1,000	×	0.5 %	minus	$ 0.00
1,001	–	2,500	×	1.0	minus	5.00
2,501	–	3,750	×	2.0	minus	30.00
3,751	–	4,900	×	3.0	minus	67.50
4,901	–	7,200	×	4.0	minus	116.50
7,201	–	8,700	×	5.0	minus	188.50
8,701	+		×	5.5	minus	232.00

MFJ, QW, HOH:

$ 0	–	2,000	×	0.5 %	minus	$ 0.00
2,001	–	5,000	×	1.0	minus	10.00
5,001	–	7,500	×	2.0	minus	60.00
7,501	–	9,800	×	3.0	minus	135.00
9,801	–	12,200	×	4.0	minus	233.00
12,201	–	15,000	×	5.0	minus	355.00
15,001	+		×	5.5	minus	430.00

Tax assistance: 405.521.3160 or 800.522.8165

Forms request: 405.521.3108 or 800.522.8165

Oklahoma Tax Commission
Income Tax Forms
511 Northeast 31st Street
Oklahoma City, Oklahoma
73105-4007

Web site: www.oktax.state.ok.us

Download: www.oktax.state.ok.us/itforms.html

e~file http://www.tax.ok.gov/itfile.html

Who can e-file? Available to taxpayers meeting certain conditions.

Who must e-file? Tax preparers that filed more than 50 resident returns for prior tax year.

Filing requirements:
Filing status options: Single; Married Filing Jointly, but if one taxpayer is a resident and the other is a nonresident (nonmilitary) state filing status must be: Married Filing Separately or Married Filing Jointly as if both taxpayers were residents; Married Filing Separately; Head of Household; and Qualifying Widow(er) with Dependent Child.

Residents: Residents who must file a federal tax return are required to file.

Part-year residents and nonresidents: Must file if they have gross income of $1,000 or more from Oklahoma sources.

Forms to file: Form 511, *State of Oklahoma Income Tax Return*

Part-year residents and nonresidents: Form 511NR, *State of Oklahoma Income Tax Return: Nonresident or Part-Year Resident*

Where to send returns:
Oklahoma Tax Commission
Income Tax
P.O. Box 26800
Oklahoma City, OK 73126-0800

IRC conformity: IRC incorporated by reference as currently amended.

Starting point for calculation of income: Federal adjusted gross income.

Attach other state returns? Yes, if claiming credit for tax paid to other state(s).

Federal attachments: Copy of federal return must be attached if: state AGI differs from federal; claiming earned income credit; claiming child care credit; medical or health savings account deduction; Police Corps Program deduction; claiming Indian Employment Credit; claiming exemption for housing displaced person from Midwestern disaster area; social security benefits subtracted; lump sum distributions added; out-of-state income; or claiming exception to estimated payment requirements due to at least 66-2/3% of gross income this year or last year from farming. In addition, nonresidents and part-year residents must attach copy of federal return. Taxpayers must also attach the following federal schedules and forms, if applicable: Schedule A (itemized deductions); Schedule D (gains from exempt federal obligations, capital gains); Schedule E (rent, royalty, partnership income); Schedule F (farm income); Form 2441 or 1040A Schedule 2 (child care expense credit); Form 4562 (depreciation); Form 8606 (nondeductible IRAs); Form 8845 and Form 3800 (Indian Employment Credit); and copy of federal NOL computation.

Due Date: April 15 (April 20 for calendar year electronic filers).

Estimated tax payments: Required if expected liability of $500 and current year withholding is less than the smaller of 70% of current year estimated tax liability or 100% of preceding taxable year of 12 months.

Extensions: Attach copy of federal extension or file state Form 504 if tax owed.

Length of extension: Six months.

Mailing address:
Oklahoma Tax Commission
Income Tax
P.O. Box 26800
Oklahoma City, Oklahoma 73126-0800

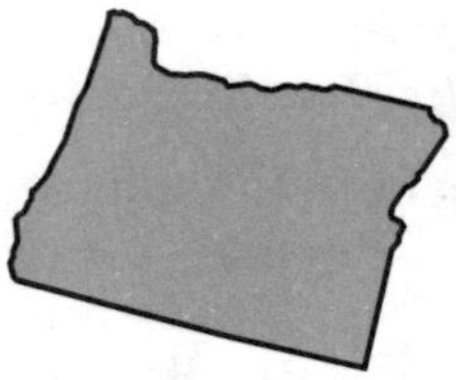

OREGON

2009 Individual Tax Rate Schedule

Single, MFS:

$ 0	–	2,000	× 5.0 %	minus	$ 0.00
2,001	–	5,000	× 7.0	minus	40.00
5,001	–	125,000	× 9.0	minus	140.00
125,001	–	250,000	× 10.8	minus	2,390.00
250,001	+		× 11.0	minus	2,890.00

MFJ, HOH, QW:

$ 0	–	4,000	× 5.0 %	minus	$ 0.00
4,001	–	10,000	× 7.0	minus	80.00
10,001	–	250,000	× 9.0	minus	280.00
250,001	–	500,000	× 10.8	minus	4,780.00
500,001	+		× 11.0	minus	5,780.00

Tax assistance:	503.378.4988 or 800.356.4222
Forms request:	503.378.4988 or 800.356.4222 Oregon Department of Revenue P.O. Box 14999 Salem, OR 97309-0990
Web site:	www.oregon.gov/DOR
Tax Practitioner Web site:	www.oregon.gov/DOR/TAXPRO/index.shtml
Tax Practitioner Hotline:	503.945.8655 prac.revenue@state.or.us
Download:	www.oregon.gov/DOR/PERTAX/formspit.shtml
e~file	www.oregon.gov/DOR/ESERV/elf-individuals.shtml

Who can e-file? Resident, nonresident, and part-year resident returns accepted.

Who must e-file? No conditions.

Filing requirements:
Filing status options: Single, Married Filing Jointly, Registered Domestic Partners Filing Jointly, Married Filing Separately, Registered Domestic Partner Filing Separately, Head of Household, and Qualifying Widow(er) with Dependent Child.

Residents: Must file if they are:
- Required to file a federal return
- Had $1 or more of Oregon income tax withheld from wages

Residents, part-year residents, and nonresidents must file if:

Filing status	Age	Residents: Gross income exceeds:	Part-year residents and nonresidents: Oregon income exceeds:
Single and can be claimed on another's return	Any	$ 900[1]	$ 900[1]
Single	Under 65	5,110	1,865
	65+	6,310	3,065
HOH	Under 65	6,385	3,005
	65+	7,585	4,205
MJF	Both under 65	10,220	3,735
	One 65+	11,220	4,735
	Both 65+	12,220	5,735
MFS	Under 65	5,110	1,865[2]
	65+	6,110	2,865[2]
QW	Under 65	7,115	3,735
	65+	8,115	4,735

[1]The greater of $900 or earned income plus $300, up to the standard deduction amount.

[2]$0 if spouse itemizes deductions.

Forms to file: Form 40, *Oregon Individual Income Tax Return: Full-Year Residents Only*

Part-year residents: Form 40P, *Oregon Individual Income Tax Return: Part-Year Resident*

Nonresidents: Form 40N, *Oregon Individual Income Tax Return: Nonresident*

Where to send returns:
Refund, no tax due:
REFUND
P.O. Box 14700
Salem, OR 97309-0930

Balance due:
Oregon Department of Revenue
P.O. Box 14555
Salem, OR 97309-0940

IRC conformity: May 1, 2009 for transactions or activities occurring after May 1, 2009, in tax years beginning on or after January 1, 2009. May 1, 2009 for tax years after 2010, or if related to definition of taxable income, as applicable to tax year of taxpayer.

Starting point for calculation of income: Federal taxable income.

Attach other state returns? Yes, if claiming a credit for taxes paid to other state(s).

Federal attachments: Copy of Form 1040.

Estimated tax payments: Required if expected liability of $1,000 or more after withholding and current year withholding is less than the smaller of 90% of current year tax liability, 100% of preceding year tax as reported on preceding year return, or 90% of tax on annualized income.

Extensions: Automatic with federal extension if no tax due, or use state Form 40-EXT to make payment.

Length of extension: Six months automatic.

Mailing address:
Extension Clerk
Oregon Department of Revenue
P.O. Box 14950
Salem, OR 97309-0950

PENNSYLVANIA

2009 tax rate schedule: The income tax rate is 3.07% for all filers.

Tax assistance:	717.787.8201 or 888.728.2937
Forms request:	800.362.2050 or 888.728.2937 Pennsylvania Department of Revenue Tax Forms Service Unit 711 Gibson Blvd. Harrisburg, PA 17104-3200
Web site:	www.revenue.state.pa.us
Download:	www.revenue.state.pa.us

e~file www.doreservices.state.pa.us

Who can e-file? Available to most taxpayers. See www.doreservices.state.pa.us for details.

Who must e-file? No conditions.

Filing requirements:
Filing status options: Single, Married Filing Jointly, Married Filing Separately, Final Return, and Deceased.

Residents, part-year residents, and nonresidents: Residents, part-year residents, and nonresidents must file if they:
- Received more than $33 total PA gross taxable income, even if no tax is due; and/or
- Incurred a loss from any transaction as an individual, sole proprietor, partner in a partnership, or PA S corporation shareholder, or association member

Forms to file: Form PA-40, *Pennsylvania Income Tax Return*

Where to send returns:

Payment:
Pennsylvania Department of Revenue
Payment Enclosed
1 Revenue Place
Harrisburg, PA 17129-0001

Refund:
Pennsylvania Department of Revenue
Refund/Credit Requested
3 Revenue Place
Harrisburg, PA 17129-0003

No payment/no refund:
Pennsylvania Department of Revenue
No Payment/No Refund
2 Revenue Place
Harrisburg, PA 17129-0002

IRC conformity: IRC incorporated by reference as amended to January 1, 1997.

Starting point for calculation of income: Gross income.

Attach other state returns? Yes, if claiming credit for taxes paid to other state(s).

Federal attachments: Copy of federal return not required. However, taxpayer must attach all applicable federal schedules, where allowed, if state schedules are not used. Federal Schedule K-1 must be attached if taxpayer did not receive the corresponding PA K-1, if applicable. Page 1 of federal Form 1040 must be attached if claiming deduction for medical savings account or health savings account contributions. Nonresident and part-year resident taxpayers who file paper copies of the PA-40 must also include a copy of page 1 of federal return.

Estimated tax payments: Required if current year withholding is less than the smaller of 90% (farmers, 66 2/3%) of expected current year tax liability (after employer incentive payments credit, job creation tax credit, research and development credit, special tax forgiveness credit, and credit for income tax paid to other states), or 100% of preceding year taxable income.

Extensions: Automatic with federal extension, or use state Form REV-276.

Length of extension: Automatic six-month with federal extension. Six-month extension if Form Rev-276 is filed before original due date of return and adequate explanation of reason for delay is provided.

Mailing address:
Pennsylvania Department of Revenue
Bureau of Individual Taxes
Dept. 280504
Harrisburg, PA 17128-0504

RHODE ISLAND

2009 Individual Tax Rate Schedule

Single:

$ 0 –	33,950	× 3.75 %	minus	$ 0.00
33,951 –	82,250	× 7.00	minus	1,103.38
82,251 –	171,550	× 7.75	minus	1,720.25
171,551 –	372,950	× 9.00	minus	3,864.63
372,951 +		× 9.90	minus	7,221.18

MFJ, QW:

$ 0 –	56,700	× 3.75 %	minus	$ 0.00
56,701 –	137,050	× 7.00	minus	1,842.75
137,051 –	208,850	× 7.75	minus	2,870.63
208,851 –	372,950	× 9.00	minus	5,481.25
372,951 +		× 9.90	minus	8,837.80

MFS:

$ 0 –	28,350	× 3.75 %	minus	$ 0.00
28,351 –	68,525	× 7.00	minus	921.38
68,526 –	104,425	× 7.75	minus	1,435.31
104,426 –	186,475	× 9.00	minus	2,740.63
186,476 +		× 9.90	minus	4,418.90

HOH:

$ 0 –	45,500	× 3.75 %	minus	$ 0.00
45,501 –	117,450	× 7.00	minus	1,478.75
117,451 –	190,200	× 7.75	minus	2,359.63
190,201 –	372,950	× 9.00	minus	4,737.13
372,951 +		× 9.90	minus	8,093.68

Taxpayers may elect to compute income tax liability based on a flat rate equal to 6.5% or a graduated rate schedule based on 25% of the federal income tax rates, including capital gains rates and any other special rates for other types of income, that were in effect prior to enactment of the Economic Growth and Tax Relief Reconciliation Act of 2001.

Tax assistance:	401.574.8829
Forms request:	401.574.8970 Rhode Island Division of Taxation One Capitol Hill Providence, RI 02908-5801
Web site:	www.tax.state.ri.us
Download:	www.tax.state.ri.us/taxforms/personal.php
e~file	http://www.tax.state.ri.us/misc/efile.php

Who can e-file? Resident, nonresident, and part-year resident returns accepted.

Who must e-file? Beginning January 1, 2009, electronic filing is mandated for tax preparers who prepare more than 100 returns in the previous year.

Filing requirements:
Filing status options: Single, Married Filing Jointly, Married Filing Separately, Head of Household, and Qualifying Widow(er) with Dependent Child.

Residents: Must file if:
- Required to file federal income tax return, or
- Not required to file federal income tax return but income for taxable year is greater than federal personal exemption

Part-year residents: Must file if:
- Required to file federal income tax return, or
- Not required to file federal income tax return but have Rhode Island income increasing their federal adjusted gross income

Nonresidents: Must file if:
- Required to file federal income tax return and received Rhode Island income, or
- Not required to file federal income tax return but have Rhode Island income increasing their federal adjusted gross income

Forms to file: Form RI-1040, *Rhode Island Resident Individual Income Tax Return*

Part-year residents and nonresidents: Form RI-1040 NR, *Rhode Island Nonresident Individual Income Tax Return*

Where to send returns:
Residents:
State of Rhode Island
Division of Taxation
One Capitol Hill
Providence, RI 02908-5806

Part-year residents and nonresidents:
State of Rhode Island
Division of Taxation
One Capitol Hill
Providence, RI 02908-5814

IRC conformity: IRC incorporated by reference as currently amended.

Starting point for calculation of income: Federal adjusted gross income.

Attach other state returns? Yes, if claiming credit for taxes paid to other state(s).

Federal attachments: None.

Estimated tax payments: Required if expected liability of $250 or more.

Extensions: Automatic with federal extension; for state extension, use Form RI-4868. Copy of extension must be attached to front of return when filed. If federal extension was filed electronically, acknowledgement must be attached to front of return when filed.

Length of extension: Six months automatic.

Mailing address:
State of Rhode Island
Division of Taxation
One Capitol Hill
Providence, RI 02908-5806

SOUTH CAROLINA

2009 Individual Tax Rate Schedule

$ 0	–	2,740	×	0.0 %	minus	$	0.00
2,741	–	5,480	×	3.0	minus		82.00
5,481	–	8,220	×	4.0	minus		137.00
8,221	–	10,960	×	5.0	minus		220.00
10,961	–	13,700	×	6.0	minus		329.00
13,701	+		×	7.0	minus		466.00

Tax assistance:	803.898.5709
Forms request:	800.768.3676 (SC) or 803.898.5320
Web site:	www.sctax.org
Download:	www.sctax.org/Forms+and+Instructions

e~file http://www.sctax.org/Electronic+Services/default.htm

Who can e-file? Available to most taxpayers.

Who must e-file? Tax preparers that filed 100 or more returns for a tax period for the same tax year.

Filing requirements:
Filing status options: Single, Married Filing Jointly, Married Filing Separately, Head of Household, and Qualifying Widow(er) with Dependent Child.

Residents: Residents under age 65 who:
- Earn income in South Carolina and are required to file a federal return
- Have South Carolina income taxes withheld from wages

Residents over age 65 are not required to file if:
- Gross income is less than the federal filing requirement plus $15,000 ($30,000 if MFJ and both spouses are over 65)
- No South Carolina income taxes withheld from wages

Part-year residents and nonresidents: Must file if they:
- Earn income that is taxable by South Carolina
- Have South Carolina income taxes withheld from wages

Forms to file: Form SC1040, *South Carolina Individual Income Tax Return*

Part-year residents and nonresidents: Schedule NR, *Nonresident Schedule* (attachment to Form SC1040)

Where to send returns:

Refund, no tax due:
Long Form Processing Center
P.O. Box 101100
Columbia, SC 29211-0100

or:
Short Form Processing Center
P.O. Box 101104
Columbia, SC 29211-0104

Balance due:
Taxable Processing Center
P.O. Box 101105
Columbia, SC 29211-0105

IRC conformity: IRC incorporated by reference through December 31, 2008.

Starting point for calculation of income: Federal taxable income.

Attach other state returns? Yes, if claiming credit for tax paid to other state(s).

Federal attachments: Complete copy of federal return and schedules must be attached if taxpayer has income or loss on federal Schedules C, D, E, or F or if filing Schedule NR (part year/nonresident), Form SC1040TC (non-refundable credits), Form I-319 (tuition tax credit), or Form I-335 (active trade or business income). Taxpayers must attach federal Form 8332 (release of claim to exemption), if applicable.

Estimated tax payments: Required if expected liability of $1,000 or more.

Extensions: Automatic with federal extension; for state extension or to make payment, use Form SC-4868.

Length of extension: Six months automatic.

Mailing address:
South Carolina Department of Revenue
Income Tax
Columbia, SC 29214-0013

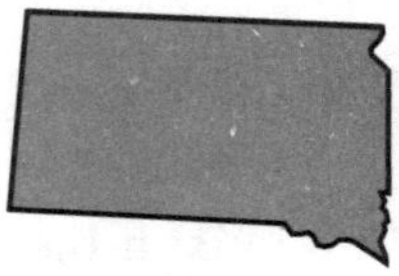

SOUTH DAKOTA

Tax assistance:	800.829.9188
Forms request:	800.829.9188 South Dakota Department of Revenue and Regulation 445 E. Capitol Avenue Pierre, SD 57501
Web site:	www.state.sd.us/drr2/revenue.html
Download:	www.state.sd.us/drr2/drrforms.htm

Filing requirements: South Dakota does not have an individual income tax.

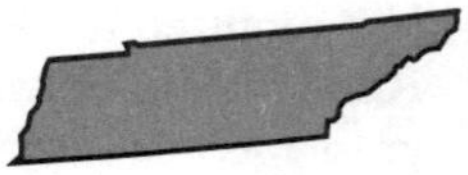

TENNESSEE

2009 Individual Tax Rate Schedule
There is a 6% tax on interest and dividend income.

Tax assistance:	615.253.0600 or 800.342.1003 (TN)
Tax Practitioner Hotline:	615.253.0700 or 800.397.8395 (TN)
Forms request:	615.253.0600 or 800.342.1003 (TN) Tennessee Department of Revenue Attention: Taxpayer Services 500 Deaderick Street Nashville, TN 37242
Web site:	www.state.tn.us/revenue/

Download:	www.state.tn.us/revenue/forms/index.htm
e~file	www.tennesseeanytime.org/etax

Who can e-file? Electronic filing is allowed for residents, nonresidents, and part-year residents.

Who must e-file? No conditions.

Filing requirements:
Filing status options: Single, Married Filing Jointly, and Married Filing Separately.

Residents and part-year residents: Residents and part-year residents are required to file if taxable interest and dividend income exceeds $1,250 ($2,500 if Married Filing Jointly).

Nonresidents: Nonresidents are required to file if they:

- Maintained a residence in Tennessee for more than six months, *and*
- Have taxable interest and dividend income exceeding $1,250 ($2,500 if Married Filing Jointly)

Forms to file: Form INC 250, *Individual Income Tax Return*

Where to send returns:
Tennessee Department of Revenue
Andrew Jackson State Office Building
500 Deaderick Street
Nashville, TN 37242

IRC conformity: IRC not incorporated.

Starting point for calculation of income: Certain dividends and interest income.

Attach other state returns? No

Federal attachments: None

Estimated tax payments: Voluntary.

Extensions: Automatic with federal extension, or state Form INC-251. Copy of extension must be attached to return when filed.

Length of extension: Six months automatic.

Mailing address:
Tennessee Department of Revenue
Andrew Jackson State Office Building
500 Deaderick Street
Nashville, TN 37242

TEXAS

Tax assistance:	800.252.1381
Forms request:	800.531.1441 Texas Comptroller of Public Accounts P.O. Box 13528, Capitol Station Austin, TX 78711-3528
Web site:	www.cpa.state.tx.us
Download:	www.cpa.state.tx.us/taxinfo/taxforms/00-forms.html

Filing requirements: Texas does not have an income tax.

UTAH

2009 tax rate schedule: All taxpayers are subject to an income tax rate of 5%.

Tax assistance:	801.297.2200 or 800.662.4335 (UT)
Forms request:	801.297.6700 or 800.662.4335, ext. 6700 (UT) Utah State Tax Commission 210 North 1950 West Salt Lake City, UT 84134
Web site:	www.tax.utah.gov
Download:	http://tax.utah.gov/forms
e~file	http://incometax.utah.gov/ifiling.php

Who can e-file? Anyone can file from a PC using approved software or through an authorized tax preparer. Taxpayers meeting certain conditions can use the free TaxExpress service.

Who must e-file? Tax preparers that filed 101 or more returns in any calendar year after 2004.

Filing requirements:
Filing status options: Single, Married Filing Jointly, Married Filing Separately, Head of Household, and Qualifying Widow(er) with Dependent Child.

Residents: Required to file if they:
- Must file a federal income tax return
- Request a refund

Part-year residents and nonresidents: Required to file if they:
- Have income from Utah sources and are required to file a federal return,
- Request a refund

Forms to file: Form TC-40, *Utah Individual Income Tax Return*

Part-year residents and nonresidents: Form TC-40B, *Non or Part-year Resident Utah Income Schedule* (attachment to Form TC-40)

Where to send returns:

Refund:
Utah State Tax Commission
210 N 1950 W
Salt Lake City, UT 84134-0260

Payments and/or all other returns:
Utah State Tax Commission
210 N 1950 W
Salt Lake City, UT 84134-0266

IRC conformity: IRC incorporated by reference as currently amended.

Starting point for calculation of income: Federal adjusted gross income.

Attach other state returns? No.

Federal attachments: Copy of federal return not required. However, taxpayers must attach a copy of federal Form 8379 to the front of return if claiming provisions of an injured spouse. Checkbox on return must be marked if taxpayer filed federal Form 8886 (Reportable Transaction Disclosure Statement) with the IRS.

Estimated tax payments: Voluntary.

Extensions: No form needed for extension. If payment is required, use Form TC-546.

Length of extension: Automatic six-month extension.

Mail completed form to:
Income Tax Prepayment
Utah State Tax Commission
210 N 1950 W
Salt Lake City, UT 84134-0266

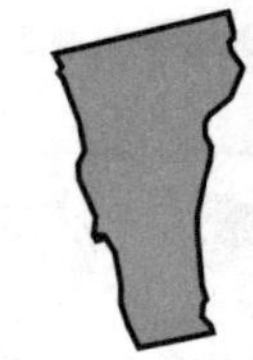

VERMONT

2009 Individual Tax Rate Schedule

Single:

$ 0 –	33,950	×	3.55 %	minus	$	0.00
33,951 –	82,250	×	7.0	minus		1,171.27
82,251 –	171,550	×	8.25	minus		2,199.40
171,551 –	372,950	×	8.9	minus		3,314.47
372,951 +		×	9.4	minus		5,179.22

MFJ, QW, Civil Union Filing Jointly:

$ 0 –	56,700	×	3.55 %	minus	$	0.00
56,701 –	137,050	×	7.0	minus		1,956.15
137,051 –	208,850	×	8.25	minus		3,669.28
208,851 –	372,950	×	8.9	minus		5,026.80
372,951 +		×	9.4	minus		6,891.55

MFS, Civil Union Filing Separately:

$ 0 –	28,350	×	3.55 %	minus	$	0.00
28,351 –	68,525	×	7.0	minus		978.07
68,526 –	104,425	×	8.25	minus		1,834.63
104,426 –	186,475	×	8.9	minus		2,513.40
186,476 +		×	9.4	minus		3,445.77

HOH:

$ 0 –	45,500	×	3.55 %	minus	$	0.00
45,501 –	117,450	×	7.0	minus		1,569.75
117,451 –	190,200	×	8.25	minus		3,037.87
190,201 –	372,950	×	8.9	minus		4,274.17
372,951 +		×	9.4	minus		6,138.72

Tax assistance: 866.828.2865 or 802.828.2865

Forms request: 802.828.2551 or 866.828.2865 (toll-free in VT)
Fax: 802.828.5787

VT Department of Taxes
133 State St.
Montpelier, VT 05633-1401

Web site: www.state.vt.us/tax/index.shtml

Download: www.state.vt.us/tax/forms.shtml

e~file www.state.vt.us/tax/efile.shtml

Who can e-file? Electronic filing is allowed for residents, nonresidents, and part-year residents.

Who must e-file? No conditions.

Filing requirements:
Filing status options: Single, Married Filing Jointly, Civil Union Partner Filing Jointly, Married Filing Separately, Civil Union Filing Separately, Head of Household, and Qualifying Widow(er) with Dependent Children.

Residents: VT residents must file who are required to file a federal tax return *and* who received at least $100 of VT income *or* who received at least $1,000 in gross income.

Part-year residents: Must file if they are required to file a federal tax return and received at least $100 of VT income or received at least $1,000 in gross income from VT sources.

Nonresidents: Must file if they are required to file a federal tax return and received at least $100 of VT income or received at least $1,000 in gross income from VT sources.

Forms to file: Form IN-111, *Vermont Income Tax Return*

Part-year residents and nonresidents: Form IN-113, *Income Adjustment Schedules* (attachment to Form IN-111)

Where to send returns:

Balance due:
Vermont Department of Taxes
P.O. Box 1779
Montpelier, VT 05601-1779

Refund, no tax due:
Vermont Department of Taxes
P.O. Box 1881
Montpelier, VT 05601-1881

IRC conformity: IRC incorporated by reference as in effect for 2008 taxable year.

Starting point for calculation of income: Federal taxable income.

Attach other state returns? Yes, if claiming credit for taxes paid to other state(s).

Federal attachments: Copy of pages 1 and 2 of federal Form 1040 and federal schedules reporting state income or loss must be attached, if applicable. If taxpayer sold real estate in state and tax was withheld, taxpayer must attach copy of pages 1 and 2 of federal return and any federal schedule documenting income or loss from sale. Taxpayers must also attach the following federal schedules and forms, if applicable: Schedule SE (self-employment); Form 1116 (foreign tax credit); Form 1310 (person claiming refund due a deceased taxpayer); Form 2210 (underpayment of estimated tax); Form 2441 (child and dependent care expenses); and Form 6252 (gain from installment sale of real estate).

Estimated tax payments: Required if liability exceeds credits plus tax withheld.

Extensions: Form IN-151.

Length of extension: Six months automatic.

Mailing address:
Vermont Department of Taxes
P.O. Box 1779
Montpelier, VT 05601-1779

VIRGINIA

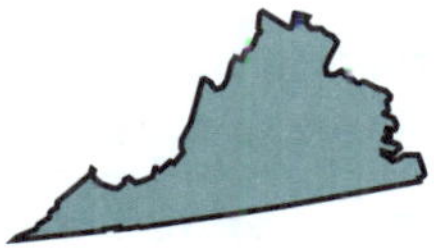

2009 tax rate schedule:

$ 0 –	3,000	×	2.00%	minus	$	0.00
3,001 –	5,000	×	3.00	minus		30.00
5,001 –	17,000	×	5.00	minus		130.00
17,001 +		×	5.75	minus		257.50

Tax assistance: 804.367.8031

Forms request: 804.440.2541

Virginia Department of Taxation
Forms Request Unit
P.O. Box 1317
Richmond, VA 23218-1317

Web site: www.tax.virginia.gov

Download: www.tax.virginia.gov/site.cfm?alias=indforms

e~file www.tax.virginia.gov/site.cfm?alias=ElectronicFilingOptions

Who can e-file? Any filer using approved software or software vendor.

Who must e-file? Electronic filing is mandated for tax preparers that file 100 or more returns in a tax year.

Filing requirements:

Filing status options: Single, Married Filing Jointly, and Married Filing Separately.

Residents, part-year residents, and nonresidents:

Filing status	VA adjusted gross income at least:
Single	$11,250
MFJ	22,500
MFS	11,250

Forms to file: Form 760, *Virginia Resident Individual Income Tax Return*

Part-year residents: Form 760PY, *Virginia Part-Year Resident Income Tax Return*

Nonresidents: Form 763, *Virginia Nonresident Income Tax Return*

Where to send returns: Mail to city or county of filer's residence. See Form 760 instructions for a list of addresses.

IRC conformity: IRC incorporated by reference as of December 31, 2008.

Starting point for calculation of income: Federal adjusted gross income.

Attach other state returns? Yes, if claiming credit for tax paid to other state(s).

Federal attachments: Copy of federal return generally not required. However, nonresident and part-year resident taxpayers must attach complete copy of federal return. Taxpayers must also attach federal Schedules C, C-EZ, E and F, and Form 1310 (person claiming refund due a deceased taxpayer), if applicable.

Due Date: May 1 (15th day of 4th month for fiscal year filers).

Estimated tax payments: Required if expected liability over $150 and expected VA AGI is $5,000 or more, if single ($8,000 or more if married filing jointly, or $4,000 or more if married filing separately).

Extensions: No application required, but must pay at least 90% of tax liability by original due date to avoid penalties with Form 760IP.

Length of extension: Six months automatic.

Mailing address:
Department of Taxation
P.O. Box 760
Richmond, VA 23218-0760

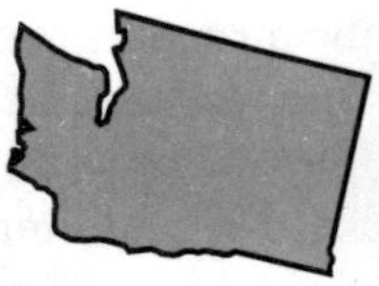

WASHINGTON

Tax assistance: 800.647.7706

Forms request: 800.647.7706

Department of Revenue
P.O. Box 47478
Olympia, WA 98504-7478

Web site: www.dor.wa.gov/Content/Home/Default.aspx

Download: www.dor.wa.gov/content/GetAFormOrPublication

Filing requirements: Washington does not impose a personal income tax.

WEST VIRGINIA

2009 tax rate schedule:

Single, HOH, MFJ, QW:

$ 0 –	10,000	×	3.0%	minus	$	0.00
10,001 –	25,000	×	4.0	minus		100.00
25,001 –	40,000	×	4.5	minus		225.00
40,001 –	60,000	×	6.0	minus		825.00
60,001 +		×	6.5	minus		1,125.00

MFS:

$ 0 –	5,000	×	3.0%	minus	$	0.00
5,001 –	12,500	×	4.0	minus		50.00
12,501 –	20,000	×	4.5	minus		112.50
20,001 –	30,000	×	6.0	minus		412.50
30,001 +		×	6.5	minus		562.50

Tax assistance: 304.558.3333 or 800.982.8297

West Virginia State Tax Department
Taxpayer Services Division
P.O. Box 3784
Charleston, WV 25337-3784

Forms request: 304.344.2068 or 800.422.2075 (WV)

West Virginia State Tax Department
Taxpayer Services Division
Attn: Form Orders
P.O. Box 3784
Charleston, WV 25337-3784

Web site: www.wvtax.gov/index.html

Download: www.wvtax.gov/personalIncomeTaxes.html

e~file http://www.wvtax.gov/electronicServices.html

Who can e-file? All filers using approved software.

Who must e-file? Tax preparers filing more than 100 returns in previous year and who use tax preparation software must e-file.

Filing requirements:
Filing status options: Single, Married Filing Jointly, Married Filing Separately, Head of Household, and Qualifying Widow(er) with Dependent Child.

Residents: Residents must file who are required to file a federal income tax return, have WV AGI exceeding the exemption allowance or $500 if zero exemptions, or are claiming a refund. Not required if taxpayer and/or spouse are 65 or older and total income is less than $2,000 exemption allowance plus senior citizen subtraction modification of up to $8,000 of income received by each taxpayer who is 65 or older.

Part-year residents and nonresidents: Must file if any WV income was received during nonresidency, if income from any source was received during residency and WV AGI exceeds exemption allowance or $500 if zero exemptions, or if a refund is due. Not required if taxpayer and/or spouse are 65 or older and total income is less than $2,000 exemption allowance plus senior citizen subtraction modification of up to $8,000 of income received by each taxpayer who is 65 or older.

Forms to file: Form IT-140, *West Virginia Resident Income Tax Return*

Part-year residents and nonresidents: Form IT-140NR/PY, *West Virginia Nonresident/Part-Year Resident Income Tax Return*

Where to send returns:

Refund:
West Virginia State Tax Dept.
P.O. Box 1071
Charleston, WV 25324-1071

Balance Due:
West Virginia State Tax Dept.
P.O.Box 3694
Charleston, WV 25336-3694

IRC conformity: IRC and federal laws relating to determination of federal taxable income in effect after December 31, 2007 and prior to February 18, 2009, adopted for purposes of computing taxable income.

Starting point for calculation of income: Federal adjusted gross income.

Attach other state returns? Yes, if claiming credit for tax paid to other state(s).

Federal attachments: Copy of federal return not required. Copy of federal Schedule R (Part II) may be substituted for WV Schedule H (disabled taxpayer). If applicable, attach federal Form 8886 (Reportable Transaction Disclosure Statement).

Estimated tax payments: Required if current year withholding is less than 90% of expected current year tax liability (after exemption allowance and allowable credits).

Extensions: Automatic if federal extension or file Schedule L if no federal extension or if payment due. Copy of federal extension must be enclosed with return when filed.

Length of extension: Six months automatic.

Mailing address:
West Virginia State Tax Department
Internal Auditing Division
P.O. Box 2585
Charleston, WV 25329-2585

WISCONSIN

2009 Individual Tax Rate Schedule

Single, HOH:

$ 0 –	10,220	× 4.60 %	minus	$ 0.00
10,221 –	20,440	× 6.15	minus	158.41
20,441 –	153,280	× 6.50	minus	229.95
153,280 –	225,000	× 6.75	minus	613.15
225,001 +		× 7.75	minus	2,863.15

MFJ:

$ 0 –	13,620	× 4.60 %	minus	$ 0.00
13,621 –	27,250	× 6.15	minus	211.11
27,251 –	204,370	× 6.50	minus	306.48
204,371 –	300,000	× 6.75	minus	817.40
300,001 +		× 7.75	minus	3,817.40

MFS:

$ 0 –	6,810	× 4.60 %	minus	$ 0.00
6,811 –	13,620	× 6.15	minus	105.55
13,621 –	102,190	× 6.50	minus	153.22
102,191 –	150,000	× 6.75	minus	408.69
150,001 +		× 7.75	minus	1,908.69

Tax assistance: 608.266.2772

Wisconsin Department of Revenue
Individual Income Tax Assistance
P.O. Box 8906
Madison, WI 53708-8906

Forms request:	608.266.1961 Forms Request Office Wisconsin Department of Revenue P.O. Box 8949 Madison, WI 53708-8949
Web site:	www.dor.state.wi.us/
Tax Practitioner Web site:	www.dor.state.wi.us/taxpro/
Download:	www.dor.state.wi.us/html/formpub.html
e~file	www.dor.state.wi.us/eserv/

Who can e-file? Electronic filing allowed for self-filers.

Who must e-file? Tax preparers that filed 100 or more returns for the prior tax year.

Filing requirements:

Filing status options: Single, Married Filing Jointly, Married Filing Separately, and Head of Household.

Caution: The 2008 filing information appears below. At the time of publication, the 2009 filing information has not been released by the state. However, it will be reproduced at *tax.cchgroup.com/Express Answers* as soon as it is available.

Residents: Residents must file if:

Filing status	Age	Gross income at least
Single	Under 65	$ 9,660
	65+	9,910
MFJ	Both or one under 65	18,000
	Both 65+	18,040
MFS	All	9,000 (each spouse)
HOH	Under 65	12,050
	65+	12,300

Also, any resident who could be claimed as a dependent on another's return must file if he or she had income of more than $900 with at least $301 of unearned income or had gross income of more than:

- $8,960 (Single)
- $11,570 (HOH)
- $16,140 (MFJ)
- $7,660 (MFS)

Also, any resident must file who owes a penalty on an IRA, retirement plan, medical savings account, or Coverdell education savings account.

Part-year residents and nonresidents: Gross income (or combined gross income if married) of at least $2,000.

Forms to file: Form 1, *Wisconsin Income Tax*

Part-year residents and nonresidents: Form 1NPR, *Wisconsin Income Tax: Nonresident and Part-Year Resident*

Where to send returns:

Balance due:
Wisconsin Department of Revenue
P.O. Box 268
Madison, WI 53790-0001

Refund, no tax due:
Wisconsin Department of Revenue
P.O. Box 59
Madison, WI 53785-0001

Homestead credit claimed:
Wisconsin Department of Revenue
P.O. Box 34
Madison, WI 53786-0001

IRC conformity: IRC incorporated as amended to December 31, 2008, with exclusions.

Starting point for calculation of income: Federal adjusted gross income.

Attach other state returns? Yes, if claiming a credit for tax paid to other state(s).

Federal attachments: Complete copy of federal return with supporting schedules and forms must be attached. However, taxpayers itemizing deductions on federal, but not state, return are not required to attach federal Schedule A.

Estimated tax payments: Required if expected liability of $200 or more after withholding and credits, and current year withholding is less than the smaller of 90% of current year tax as shown on current year form (including alternative minimum tax and recycling surcharge), 100% of preceding year tax as reported on preceding year return form (including alternative minimum tax and recycling surcharge), or 90% of tax shown on current year return, computed by annualizing taxable income alternative minimum taxable income.

Extensions: No extension application form necessary. Include with return a copy of federal extension application or a statement indicating which federal extension provision you wish to apply for state purposes.

Length of extension: Six month automatic or may vary with federal extension provision.

WYOMING

Tax assistance: 307.777.5287

Forms request: 307.777.5287

Department of Revenue
122 W. 25th St.
Cheyenne, WY 82002-0110

Web site: http://revenue.state.wy.us

Download: http://revenue.state.wy.us

Filing requirements: Wyoming does not impose an individual or corporate income tax.

Sales and Use Tax Table of Rates

State tax rates generally applicable to the retail sale of tangible personal property are listed below. Special rates may apply to specific categories of tangible personal property, and are not noted in this chart. Most states also authorize local jurisdictions to adopt sales and use taxes in addition to the state tax set forth below.

The following states do not impose a general sales and use tax: Alaska, Delaware, Montana, New Hampshire, and Oregon. Delaware imposes a merchants' and manufacturers' license tax and a use tax on leases.

	Sales	Use
Alabama	4%	4%
Arizona	5.6%	5.6%
Arkansas	6%	6%
California[11]	7.25%	7.25%
Colorado	2.9%	2.9%
Connecticut[1]	6%	6%
District of Columbia[1,13]	6%	6%
Florida	6%	6%
Georgia	4%	4%
Hawaii	4%[2]	4%[2]
Idaho	6%	6%
Illinois	6.25%	6.25%
Indiana[1]	7%[3]	7%[3]
Iowa	6%[9]	6%[9]
Kansas	5.3%	5.3%
Kentucky	6%	6%
Louisiana	4%	4%
Maine[1]	5%	5%
Maryland[1]	6%[4]	6%[4]
Massachusetts[1,12]	6.25%	6.25%
Michigan[1]	6%	6%
Minnesota	6.875%[10]	6.875%[10]
Mississippi[1]	7%	7%
Missouri	4.225%[5]	4.225%[5]
Nebraska	5.5%	5.5%
Nevada	6.85%[6]	6.85%[6]
New Jersey	7%	7%
New Mexico	5%	5%
New York	4%	4%
North Carolina	5.75%[7]	5.75%[7]
North Dakota	5%	5%
Ohio	5.5%	5.5%
Oklahoma	4.5%	4.5%
Pennsylvania	6%	6%
Rhode Island[1]	7%	7%
South Carolina	6%	6%
South Dakota	4%	4%
Tennessee	7%	7%
Texas	6.25%	6.25%
Utah	4.7%[8]	4.7%[8]
Vermont	6%	6%
Virginia	4%	4%
Washington	6.5%	6.5%
West Virginia[1]	6%	6%
Wisconsin	5%	5%
Wyoming	4%	4%

1 Local general sales/use taxes not authorized or imposed. (Local governments may be authorized, however, to levy miscellaneous local taxes on specific types of transactions.)
2 Hawaii: Rate for wholesalers/manufacturers is 0.5%.
3 Indiana: 6% prior to April 1, 2008.
4 Maryland: 5% prior to January 3, 2008.
5 Missouri: Total rate of 4.225% consists of general sales/use tax of 4%, additional sales tax of 0.10% for soil/water conservation and state parks, and additional sales tax of 0.125% for wildlife conservation.
6 Nevada: 6.5% prior to July 1, 2009 and after June 30, 2011. Tax rate consists of a 2% state rate under the general Sales and Use Tax Act, a 2.6% state rate under the Local School Support Tax Law, and a 2.25% state-mandated local rate under the City-County Relief Tax Law.
7 North Carolina: 5.5% in September 2009; 4.5% prior to September 1, 2009.
8 Utah: 4.65% prior to January 1, 2009.
9 Iowa: 5% prior to July 1, 2008.
10 Minnesota: 6.5% prior to July 1, 2009.
11 California: 6.25% prior to April 1, 2009.
12 Massachusetts: 5% prior to August 1, 2009.
13 District of Columbia: 5.75% prior to October 1, 2009 and after September 30, 2012.

What's New in 2009

New Tax Laws. Non-itemizers who purchase a new motor vehicle between February 17 and December 31, 2009, can claim an additional standard deduction for sales and excise taxes attributed to the first $49,500 of the purchase price.

For the earned income tax credit in 2009 (and 2010), the applicable credit percentage for taxpayers with three or more qualifying children is 45 percent (up from 40 percent). Also, the phaseout amount is increased by $5,000 for joint filers.

The definition of "qualified child" has been revised.

The first-time homebuyer credit is extended to purchases before December 1, 2009, is increased to a maximum of $8,000, and is not recaptured unless the taxpayer sells the home or stops using it as a principal residence within 36 months of the purchase.

The Making Work Pay credit must be reported on new Schedule M.

Section at a Glance

Tax Preparer's Checklist

- ☐ Use the Taxpayer Interview Form on page 16–15 to gather current tax information in one place.

Key Tax Law Changes for Individual Tax Returns

Area	Effective Date	Provisions of New Law
10% tax bracket, expansion of	2009	For 2009, the 10% tax bracket applies to the first $8,350 of taxable income for taxpayers filing as unmarried individuals or as married filing separately (MFS), and to the first $16,700 of taxable income of taxpayers filing as married individuals filing joint returns (MFJ). The 10% bracket applies to the first $11,950 for taxpayers filing as head-of-household (HOH).
Adoption credit	2009	In 2009, the maximum refundable credit for qualified adoption expenses is $12,150 per each eligible child. The credit is phased-out ratably in 2009 for taxpayers with modified AGI between $182,180 and $222,180. For tax year 2009, the limitation on the allowable amount of the adoption credit based on the amount of tax does not apply (see Tabs 1, 10 and 13).
Alternative fuel vehicle refueling property credit	2009	For 2009 and 2010, the alternative fuel vehicle refueling property credit is increased for certain property. For qualified hydrogen-related property subject to depreciation, the maximum credit amount increases to $200,000 per location; if not subject to depreciation (e.g., refueling property installed at a residence), the maximum credit remains at $1,000. For qualified non-hydrogen-related property, the credit percentage increases to 50%. If property is subject to depreciation, the maximum credit is $50,000 per location; if the property is installed at a residence, the maximum credit increases to $2,000. The credit is claimed on Form 8911 (see Tab 10).
AMT, long-term unused minimum tax credit	2009	A tax liability (including related penalties and interest) arising from AMT adjustments for incentive stock options (ISOs) and outstanding on October 3, 2008, is abated. If the liability was paid as of October 3, 2008, then for the taxpayer's first two tax years beginning after 2007, the AMT refundable credit amount and minimum tax credit are each increased by 50% of the aggregate amount of the interest and penalties (but not tax) that would have been abated but for the payment.

Key Tax Law Changes for Individual Tax Returns (Continued)

Area	Effective Date	Provisions of New Law
AMT, relief from	2009	For 2009, the AMT exemption amounts for individuals are: (1) $70,950 for married individuals filing a joint return and surviving spouses; (2) $46,700 for unmarried individuals; and (3) $35,475 for married individuals filing separate returns. However, the threshold levels for calculating the 2009 exemption phase-out remain unchanged. The minimum exemption in 2009 for a child subject to the "kiddie tax" is $6,700. Also for 2009, nonrefundable personal tax credits (including the alternative motor vehicle credit and the qualified plug-in electric vehicle credit) are allowed to the full extent of the taxpayer's regular tax (reduced by any applicable foreign tax credit) and AMT liability. The personal use portion of the nonrefundable tax credit for alternative fuel vehicle refueling property may only be used against the excess of the taxpayer's regular tax liability, reduced by all other nonrefundable credits plus the foreign or U.S. possession tax credit, over the tentative minimum tax. Bonds issued in 2009 and 2010 are not treated as "private activity bonds" for AMT purposes, and tax-exempt interest on such bonds is not a tax preference item. While a refunding bond (whether current or advance refunding) will be treated as issued on the date of issuance of the refunded bond (or, in the case of a series of refundings, on the date of issuance of the original bond), this treatment will not apply to any refunding bond issued to refund any bond that was issued after 2003 and before 2009. If a taxpayer claims the standard deduction for certain disaster losses and/or qualified motor vehicle taxes, these deductions may also be claimed in calculating the taxpayer's AMT liability (see Tab 10).
Build America Bonds	February 17, 2009	Build America Bonds are bonds issued after February 17, 2009, and before January 1, 2011, which qualify as tax-exempt bonds that are not private activity bonds, and for which an election is made by the bond issuer. The bondholder can claim a tax credit of 35% of the interest payable on a Build America Bonds, but not if the issuer elects to receive a direct payment in lieu of the credit to the bondholder. The credit amount is taxable interest income to the bondholder. Any unused credit can be carried forward to later tax years. Taxpayers use Form 8912 to claim the credit.
Cancellation of debt Revenue Procedure Section 108(i)	2009	At the election of the taxpayer, income from the discharge of indebtedness in connection with the reacquisition of an applicable debt instrument in 2009 or 2010 can be deferred, and included in gross income *ratably* over a five-tax-year period beginning with (1) the fifth tax year following the reacquisition year for a reacquisition occurring in 2009; and (2) the fourth tax year following the reacquisition year for a reacquisition occurring in 2010. This treatment applies to debt discharged in connection with the reacquisition in 2009 or 2010 of a corporate or business debt instrument. If the election is made, then for the tax year of the election or any later tax year, the taxpayer cannot exclude the income from cancellation of debt based on a bankruptcy case, insolvency, qualified farm indebtedness or qualified real property business indebtedness.

Key Tax Law Changes for Individual Tax Returns (Continued)		
Area	**Effective Date**	**Provisions of New Law**
"Cash for clunkers" program	2009	Under the "Cash for Clunkers" program, eligible individuals can receive a tax-free voucher to offset the purchase price or lease amount of a new car or truck when they trade in their current vehicle for a more fuel-efficient one. A voucher or any payments made for a voucher are *not included* in an eligible purchaser's gross income for federal tax purposes, but might be included in gross income for state tax purposes. The voucher amount is either $3,500 or $4,500, based on the new vehicle's fuel economy compared to that of the traded-in vehicle. The program applies to eligible new vehicle purchases completed from July 1, 2009, through 8:00 p.m. EDT on August 24, 2009; the program ended before the original November 1, 2009 termination date because government funds were exhausted. The voucher is provided through registered dealers, and is only available if the trade-in vehicle is in drivable condition, has been continuously insured under state law, is not more than 25 years old on the trade-in date, and has a combined fuel economy of 18 miles per gallon or less. The number of vouchers is limited to one per customer, including joint, registered owners of a single eligible trade-in vehicle. The manufacturer's suggested retail price for the new fuel-efficient vehicle cannot exceed $45,000. Domestic and foreign vehicles are eligible for the program.
Casualty or theft losses (generally)	2009	For any casualty or theft occurring in 2009, the personal casualty or theft loss deduction is limited to the amount of the loss that exceeds $500, instead of the usual $100 floor (see Tab 2). The floor goes back to $100 after 2009.
Casualty or theft losses (investment fraud)	2009	IRS guidance provides that investors with losses from criminally fraudulent investment arrangements in the form of "Ponzi" schemes can claim a theft loss rather than a capital loss, because the scheme perpetrators actually deprive investors of money by criminal acts. The loss is on a transaction entered into for profit, is not subject to the personal loss or itemized deduction limits, and is deductible in the year discovered (Rev. Rul. 2009-9). The IRS also issued a safe harbor procedure that allows taxpayers to deduct up to 95% of qualified losses from a fraudulent investment scheme as theft losses, calculated according to detailed definitions and formulas, if certain requirements and circumstances are satisfied. The safe harbor is for loss discovery years beginning after 2007 (Rev. Proc. 2009-20).
Child tax credit	2009	For 2009 (and 2010), the child tax credit is refundable to the extent of 15% of the taxpayer's earned income in excess of $3,000, up to the per child credit amount, if the taxpayer has a total tax liability (regular and alternative minimum) of less than his or her allowable child tax credit minus nonrefundable credits previously taken. The threshold requirements for the 15% of earned income refundable component of the child tax credit are: (1) a total tax liability (regular plus alternative minimum), minus nonrefundable credits previously taken, of less than the taxpayer's allowable child tax credit ($1,000 per qualifying child); and (2) earned income in excess of $3,000 (see Tabs 1 and 10). For 2009 and later years, a taxpayer cannot claim the child tax credit for a child unless the taxpayer is allowed to and does claim the child as a dependent. For 2009, the nonrefundable portion of the child tax credit cannot exceed the taxpayer's regular income tax liability (reduced by the foreign tax credit), plus alternative minimum tax (AMT) liability. (Barring Congressional action, this will change beginning in 2010.)

Key Tax Law Changes for Individual Tax Returns (Continued)

Area	Effective Date	Provisions of New Law
COBRA premium assistance	February 17, 2009	Effective for periods of coverage beginning after February 16, 2009, assistance eligible individuals who are involuntarily terminated from their employment are treated as having paid the required COBRA coverage premium if the individual pays 35% of the premium. In effect, the individual is provided with a 65% reduction in premiums. An "assistance eligible individual" is defined as any qualified beneficiary if: • at any time during the period beginning on September 1, 2008, and ending on December 31, 2009, the qualified beneficiary is eligible for COBRA continuation coverage; • the beneficiary elects such coverage; and • the qualifying event for which the beneficiary would otherwise lose health plan coverage is the involuntary termination of the covered employee's employment during such period. The 65% premium reduction is excluded from the individual's gross income. Neither the health coverage tax credit (HCTC) nor the advance payment program for the HCTC is available for any month that an individual receives a premium reduction for COBRA continuing coverage. If the covered taxpayer's modified AGI for the tax year exceeds $125,000 ($250,000 for joint returns), then the income tax imposed on the taxpayer is increased by the amount of the assistance. This recapture is phased-in ratably, and becomes complete when modified AGI reaches $145,000 ($290,000 for joint returns). High-income individuals can elect to waive assistance and avoid recapture. Any tax increase as a result of recapture is not treated as a part of regular tax liability and, therefore, may not be offset by tax credits. Employers are provided a credit against payroll taxes for amounts of COBRA continuation coverage premiums not paid by involuntarily terminated employees who qualify for premium reductions.
Dependency exemption ("qualifying child")	2009	Starting in 2009, the definition of "qualifying child" has been revised. An age test requires a qualifying child to be younger than the taxpayer claiming the child as a dependent. A joint return test requires that a qualifying child cannot file a joint return (except to claim a refund) in the same calendar year as the taxpayer claiming the child. If the parents can claim the qualifying child but neither does so, another taxpayer may claim the qualifying child but only if the other taxpayer's adjusted gross income (AGI) is higher than the highest AGI of either of the qualifying child's parents. The tie-breaker rules will apply whenever two or more taxpayers *can* claim the qualifying child, regardless of whether they actually *do* so (see Tab 1).
Dependency exemption (release of exemption claim)	2009	For tax years beginning after July 2, 2008, if a custodial parent revokes a release of claim to exemption that was previously released to the noncustodial parent on Form 8332, Release/Revocation of Release of Claim to Exemption for Child by Custodial Parent (or similar form), the revocation is effective no earlier than the tax year beginning in the calendar year following the calendar year in which the custodial parent provides, or makes reasonable efforts to provide, the noncustodial parent with written notice of the revocation. In other words, if the custodial parent provides notice of revocation in 2009, the revocation is not effective until 2010. Noncustodial parents may no longer attach a court decree or separation agreement executed after July 2, 2008, to a tax return to claim a dependency exemption (see Tabs 1 and 13).

Key Tax Law Changes for Individual Tax Returns (Continued)

Area	Effective Date	Provisions of New Law
District of Columbia first-time homebuyer's credit	2009	An eligible taxpayer who purchases a principal residence in the District of Columbia after December 31, 2008, and before December 1, 2009, cannot claim the Code Sec. 1400C credit for first-time homebuyers in the District of Columbia if the Code Sec. 36 first-time homebuyer credit is allowable to the taxpayer or the taxpayer's spouse (see "First-time homebuyer's credit," infra).
Economic recovery payment	2009	In 2009, an adult may receive a one-time economic recovery payment of $250 if: • during the months of November 2008, December 2008 or January 2009, the individual person was eligible to receive Social Security benefits, supplemental Social Security benefits, Railroad Retirement Act benefits, or veterans compensation or pension benefits; and • the individual is a resident of the United States or certain U.S. territories. (Certain restrictions on eligibility apply.) If the adult is married and his or her spouse also meets these requirements, they each may receive a $250 payment. The payment is *not* considered gross income for income tax purposes, is generally protected from assignment and garnishment, and is not taken into account in computing the individual's eligibility for aid under any federal program, or any state program funded with federal funds. If the individual is also eligible for the Making Work Pay credit (see infra), that credit is reduced by the individual's economic recovery payment amount.
Electric drive motor vehicle credit, plug-in	2009	Starting in 2009, a credit is available for new qualified plug-in electric drive motor vehicles placed in service after 2008 and before 2015. The credit amount is $2,500, plus $417 for each kilowatt hour of traction battery capacity in excess of four kilowatt hours. The credit amount for 2009 is limited based on the weight of the vehicle, with the maximum credit that may be claimed being $15,000 for a vehicle with a gross vehicle weight rating of more than 26,000 pounds. Sale of 250,000 new qualified plug-in electric drive motor vehicles for use in the U.S. triggers the phase-out of the credit. The vehicle's basis is reduced by the amount of credit claimed. Taxpayers can elect not to claim the credit for a vehicle that otherwise qualifies. To qualify as a new plug-in electric drive motor vehicle, the vehicle must (1) have at least four wheels; (2) be made by a manufacturer for use on public streets, roads, and highways, (3) be acquired for use or lease, but not resale; (4) have its original use begin with the taxpayer; (5) have a traction battery propulsion source with at least 4 kilowatt hours capacity; (6) have an offboard energy source to recharge the battery; and (7) have a certificate of conformity under the Clean Air Act, and meet or exceed certain California emission standards. A vehicle is not eligible unless it complies with the Federal and State environmental and safety laws for the applicable make and model year. (Some of these requirements will change after 2009.) No credit is allowed if the vehicle is used predominately outside the U.S., or for any portion of the vehicle cost which is deducted under Code Sec. 179. If the vehicle is used in a trade or business (and is, therefore, subject to depreciation), the credit allowed for the business use portion is treated as part of the general business credit and subject to the tax liability limitation and carry over rules. If the vehicle is considered personal property, the credit is treated as part of the nonrefundable personal credits. The credit is claimed on Form 8936 (see Tab 10).

Key Tax Law Changes for Individual Tax Returns (Continued)

Area	Effective Date	Provisions of New Law
Electric drive motor vehicle credit, plug-in, conversion	February 17, 2009	A new 10% plug-in conversion credit may be claimed on the cost of converting any motor vehicle (new or used) to a qualified plug-in electric drive motor vehicle (see supra), for property placed in service after February 17, 2009. The maximum credit is $4,000 per vehicle. The credit is treated as part of the alternative motor vehicle credit (AMVC), and may be claimed even if another AMVC was claimed for the same vehicle in any preceding tax year. The credit will not apply to conversions made after 2011. The credit is claimed on Form 8910 (see Tab 10).
Electric vehicle credit, plug-in	February 17, 2009	A new 10% credit can be claimed for the cost of a new plug-in electric vehicle acquired after February 17, 2009. The credit is generally modeled on the plug-in electric drive motor vehicle credit (see supra), but applies to certain electrically powered two-wheeled, three-wheeled and low-speed vehicles. The credit is available for the tax year in which the qualifying vehicle is put into service, and terminates after 2011. The vehicle's basis is reduced by the amount of credit claimed. Taxpayers can elect not to claim the credit for a vehicle that otherwise qualifies. The credit is capped at $2,500, and can offset regular tax and AMT liabilities in 2009. To qualify, a vehicle must (1) be made by a manufacturer for use on public streets, roads, and highways, (2) be acquired for use or lease, but not resale; (3) have its original use begin with the taxpayer; (4) be propelled to a significant extent by an electric motor powered by a battery with capacity of at least 2-1/2 kilowatt hours for a 2- or 3-wheel vehicle, and at least 4 kilowatt hours capacity for other vehicles; (5) have a gross vehicle weight rating of less than 14,000 pounds; and (6) be capable of being recharged by an external electricity source. No credit is allowed if the vehicle is used predominately outside the U.S. If the vehicle is used in a trade or business (and is therefore subject to depreciation), the credit allowed for the business use portion is treated as part of the general business credit and subject to the tax liability limitation and carry over rules. If the vehicle is considered personal property, the credit is treated as part of the nonrefundable personal credits. The credit is claimed on Form 8834 (see Tab 10).
Estimated tax	2009	Starting in 2009, estimated tax payments of a qualified individual with a small businesses may be based on 90% of the individual's prior year's tax liability. An individual is a "qualified individual" if: (1) the AGI shown on the individual's return for the preceding tax year is less than $500,000 ($250,000 for MFS in the tax year for which the installment is being determined), and (2) the person certifies that more than 50% of the gross income shown on his or her return for the preceding tax year is from a business which employed less than 500 employees on average during the calendar year that ends with or within the individual's preceding tax year. To certify that he or she qualifies, the taxpayer must check box F in Part II on Form 2210 or box C on Form 2210-F (see Tab 11).

Key Tax Law Changes for Individual Tax Returns (Continued)

Area	Effective Date	Provisions of New Law
Exclusion of gain from sale of principal residence	2009	Starting in 2009, gain from the sale or exchange of a principal residence is not excludable if that gain is allocable to periods of nonqualified use. "Nonqualified use" is generally any use other than as a principal residence. Thus, this limitation restricts the availability of the exclusion for second homes and vacation homes significantly. However, a "period of nonqualified use" does not include: • any period before January 1, 2009; • any portion of the five-year period ending on the date of the sale or exchange that is after the last date that the taxpayer or his or her spouse uses the property as a principal residence (for example, a period starting the day after the taxpayer moves out and ending on the date he or she sells the home); • any period of 10 years or less when the taxpayer or his or her spouse is serving on "qualified official extended duty" as an armed forces member, a Foreign Service officer or an intelligence community employee; or • any period of two years or less for temporary absence due to a change of employment, health conditions or other unforeseen circumstances. The portion of the gain allocated to the period of nonqualified use equals the gain multiplied by the ratio of the total periods of nonqualified use during ownership after 2008 divided by the entire period the property was owned by the taxpayer (see Tab 4).
Exemptions	2009	For 2009, the exemption amount that may be claimed by a taxpayer for himself or herself and for each dependent is $3,650. The limitation on personal and dependency exemptions for high-income taxpayers is being phased out until it is fully repealed effective for tax years beginning after 2009. (Note that, barring Congressional action, the limit is currently set to return to its 2001 level for tax years beginning after 2010.) For 2009, the otherwise applicable exemption phaseout reduction amount is reduced by 2/3; thus, only 1/3 of the reduction will apply. In 2009, each exemption cannot be reduced to less than $2,433.33 (2/3 x $3,650) (see Tab 1).
First-time homebuyer's credit	2009	Effective for residential property purchased after December 31, 2008: • the maximum first-time homebuyer credit increases from $7,500 to $8,000 (from $3,750 to $4,000 for MFS); • the purchase date is extended through November 30, 2009; and • recapture is waived unless, within 36 months of the purchase date, the property is sold or the taxpayer (and his or her spouse, if married) does not use the property as a principal residence. The credit will be allowed to homebuyers that used tax-exempt financing options. Additionally, for purchases after 2008 and before December 1, 2009, qualified homebuyers in the District of Columbia must claim the credit under Code Sec. 36, *not* the first-time homebuyer credit for D.C. under Code Sec. 1400C. Taxpayers may still elect to treat a purchase made in 2009 as having been completed on December 31, 2008, but the restrictions for purchases completed prior to January 1, 2009, will apply except for the repayment provision. The taxpayer claims the credit on Form 5405 and attaches that form to his or her return (see Tab 10).

Key Tax Law Changes for Individual Tax Returns (Continued)

Area	Effective Date	Provisions of New Law
Government retiree credit	2009	For the 2009 tax year, a government retiree is eligible to claim a refundable $250 tax credit ($500 for MFJ if both spouses are eligible) if the retiree: • has received a pension or annuity amount in 2009 for service performed in the employ of the United States, or any state or instrumentality thereof, which is not considered employment for purposes of the Federal Insurance Contributions Act (FICA); • has *not* received the $250 economic recovery payment during the tax year (see supra); and • includes his or her social security number on the tax return (a joint return must include the social security number of at least one spouse). Form 1040 filers calculate and report the credit on Schedule M (see Tab 10).
Health coverage tax credit	2009	In order to make the health coverage tax credit (HCTC) more favorable for eligible individuals and their qualifying family members, several modifications have been made: • the credit amount is increased to 80% of the premium amounts in eligible coverage months after April 2009 but before January 2011; • newly-enrolled monthly participants are allowed retroactive payments for premiums paid before the advance payments of credit begin; • eligibility for the credit and types of coverage has been expanded; • there is a favorable pre-certification rule for determining a 63-day lapse in coverage; • notice requirements have been enhanced; and • surveys, studies and reports will be undertaken to assess the credit. The HCTC modifications are coordinated with COBRA premium assistance provision (see supra) to prevent double benefits. The modifications do not extend beyond 2010 (see Tab 10).
Health saving account (HSA), maximum contribution	2009	For 2009, the maximum aggregate annual contribution is $3,000 for an individual with self-only coverage under a HDHP, and $5,950 for an individual with family coverage under a HDHP. Individuals age 55 or older can increase their annual contribution by $1,000 (see Tabs 1 and 9).
Household employees	2009	A taxpayer employer must withhold and pay FICA taxes (social security and Medicare) for a household employee only if the employer has paid the employee $1,700 or more in cash wages during 2009 (see Tab 1).
IRA contributions	2009	For 2009, the maximum annual contribution to traditional IRAs is $5,000 ($6,000 for individuals who are age 50 or older by the end of 2009). For 2009, the deduction for IRA contributions begins to phase out when the taxpayer is an active member of his or her employer's retirement plan and modified adjusted gross income (MAGI) is over $55,000 for single or HOH (complete phase-out at $65,000 MAGI); $89,000 for MFJ with both spouses actively participating in an employer's retirement plan (complete phase-out at $109,000 MAGI); and $0 for MFS (complete phase-out at $10,000 MAGI). If the taxpayer either lives with his or her spouse or files a joint return, and the spouse is covered by a retirement plan at work but the taxpayer is not, then the 2009 deduction begins to phase out when MAGI is over $166,000, and completely phases out when MAGI reaches $176,000. Starting in 2009, compensation for IRA purposes includes differential wage payments by employers to individuals who are on active military service for periods of more than 30 days (see Tab 9).

Key Tax Law Changes for Individual Tax Returns (Continued)

Area	Effective Date	Provisions of New Law
Itemized deductions	2008	For 2009, itemized deductions begin to be reduced when a taxpayer's AGI reaches $166,800 ($83,400 for MFS). In 2009, the limit on itemized deductions for high-income taxpayers is being phased out until it is fully repealed effective for tax years beginning after 2009. (Note that, barring Congressional action, the limit is currently set to return to its 2001 level for tax years beginning after 2010.) For 2009, the regular reduction amount is reduced by 2/3; thus, the amount by which itemized deductions are reduced is only 1/3 of the reduction amount that would otherwise have applied (see Tab 2).
Kiddie tax	2009	For purposes of the "kiddie tax," under which a child's 2009 net investment income may be taxed at his or her parents' highest marginal tax rate, the child's net investment income is his or her total investment income for the year reduced by the larger of: • (1) $950 plus the itemized deductions connected with producing the investment income; or • (2) $1,900. The amount of net investment income subject to the parent's marginal tax rate cannot exceed the child's taxable income for the year (see Tab 13).
Making Work Pay credit	2009	For 2009 and 2010, many individuals with earned income can claim a refundable Making Work Pay credit, equal to the lesser of: • (1) 6.2% of the taxpayer's earned income; or • (2) $400 ($800 for joint filers). The credit begins to phase-out for single taxpayers with a modified adjusted gross income (MAGI) over $75,000 ($150,000 for MFJ), and is not available to taxpayers with MAGI of $95,000 or more ($190,000 or more for MFJ). MAGI is adjusted gross income increased by excluded foreign earned income, U.S. possessions income and housing allowance. The credit is also reduced if in 2009 the taxpayer receives a $250 economic recovery payment or claims the government retiree credit (see discussion of these benefits, supra). The credit is not available to nonresident aliens, taxpayers who can be claimed as a dependent on another taxpayer's return, or estates or trusts. To claim the credit, a taxpayer must include his or her social security number on the tax return (a joint return must include the social security number of at least one spouse). An identification number issued by the IRS does *not* qualify as a social security number. While most people who receive a paycheck will benefit from the credit through reduced withholding, the credit must be claimed on the taxpayer's return. Filers of Form 1040 must calculate and report the credit on Schedule M (see Tab 10).
Marriage penalty relief (15% tax bracket)	2005-2010	In tax years through 2010, the size of the 15% rate bracket for joint returns is twice that of the corresponding rate bracket for single returns. For 2009, the 15% bracket for MFJ begins at $16,701 and ends at $67,900.
Marriage penalty relief (standard deduction)	2005-2010	In tax years through 2010, the basic standard deduction for joint returns will be twice the basic standard deduction for single returns. For 2009, the standard deduction for MFJ is $11,400.

Key Tax Law Changes for Individual Tax Returns (Continued)

Area	Effective Date	Provisions of New Law
Motor vehicle taxes	February 17, 2009	Taxpayers can claim an itemized deduction for state or local sales or excise taxes paid on purchases of new (not used) automobiles, light trucks and motorcycles with a gross vehicle weight of no more than 8,500 pounds, as well as motor homes, but only for purchases made after February 16, 2009, and before 2010. The deduction is not available to taxpayers who elect to deduct state and local sales taxes in lieu of state and local income taxes. Taxpayers who do not itemize can claim the deduction as an increase to the standard deduction (see "Standard deduction," infra). New motor vehicle buyers in states that do not have a sales tax can claim the deduction for other fees and taxes imposed on the purchase. Qualifying fees or taxes must (1) be assessed on the purchase of the vehicle; and (2) be either a per-unit fee or based on the price of the vehicle. The deduction is allowed only for taxes on the first $49,500 of the vehicle's purchase price. The deduction begins to phase-out for a taxpayer with modified adjusted gross income (MAGI) over $125,000 ($250,000 for MFJ), and is reduced to zero when MAGI reaches $135,000 ($260,000 for MFJ). MAGI for this purpose is the taxpayer's AGI plus any excluded income of a United States citizen or resident living abroad, and any excluded income from sources within Guam, American Samoa, the Northern Mariana Islands or Puerto Rico (see Tabs 1 and 2).
Required minimum distributions (RMDs)	2009	For 2009, the required minimum distribution (RMD) requirements generally applicable to retirement plans are suspended for certain defined contribution arrangements. The suspension applies to most defined contribution retirement plans, and to traditional and Roth IRAs. As a result, individual participants or beneficiaries will not be required to take any required distributions for the 2009 year. The waiver also applies to those individuals who turn 70-1/2 in 2009 and delay their 2009 RMD until April 1, 2010. This waiver does *not* apply to RMDs for 2008, even for individuals who turned 70-1/2 in 2008 and choose to take the 2008 RMD by April 1, 2009. In applying the RMD rules in years after 2009, each individual's required beginning date will be determined without regard to the temporary waiver. Therefore, if an individual turned 70-1/2 on October 15, 2009, he is *not* required to take any distribution *for 2009* by April 1, 2010, but he *must* take a distribution *for 2010* by December 31, 2010. (see Tab 9).
Residential energy credits (nonbusiness energy property)	2009	The *nonbusiness energy property credit* has been reinstated and is available for certain qualified energy efficiency improvements or residential energy property expenditures made in 2009. (The credit will also be available in 2010.) The credit amount is 30% of the sum of expenditures for qualified energy efficiency improvements (building envelope components) and qualified energy property (furnaces and certain fans, central air conditioners, water heaters, certain heat pumps, biomass stoves) placed in service in 2009. The total nonbusiness energy property credit allowed for 2009 and 2010 cannot exceed $1,500 (see Tab 10).

Key Tax Law Changes for Individual Tax Returns (Continued)

Area	Effective Date	Provisions of New Law
Residential energy credits (residential energy efficient property)	2009	Beginning in 2009, the *residential energy efficient property credit* maximums are eliminated through 2016 for solar hot water heaters, for each half-kilowatt of electric capacity generated by a wind turbine, and for geothermal heat pumps. However, the maximum annual credit for each half-kilowatt of electricity from fuel cell plants remains at $500. The rule that any expenditures made with funds obtained from subsidized energy financing are ineligible for the credit has also been eliminated. Also, a taxpayer may temporarily elect to claim the energy credit portion of the investment tax credit in lieu of the residential energy efficient property credit (see Tab 10).
Retirement savings contributions credit ("savers' credit")	2009	For 2009, the retirement savings contribution credit (i.e., the "savers' credit") is completely phased-out when modified AGI is over $55,500 for MFJ, over $41,625 for HOH, and over $27,750 for singles and MFS. For 2009, the savers' credit cannot exceed the taxpayer's regular income tax liability (reduced by the foreign tax credit), plus AMT liability (see Tabs 1 and 10).
Roth IRAs	2009	For 2009, the maximum annual contribution to Roth IRAs is $5,000 ($6,000 for individuals who are age 50 or older by the end of 2009). In 2009, the maximum Roth IRA contribution begins to phase out for a single person with modified adjusted gross income (MAGI) of $105,000 (complete phase-out at $120,000), for MFJ with MAGI of $166,000 (complete phase-out at $176,000), and for MFS with MAGI of $0 (complete phase-out at $10,000) (see Tab 9).
Section 179 expensing, generally	2009	For depreciable property placed in service in 2009, the Section 179 dollar limitation remains at $250,000, and the investment limitation remains at $800,000 (see Tab 7). Note that in 2010, the dollar limitation will be $125,000 and the investment limitation will be $500,000; these amounts will be indexed for inflation. Starting in 2011, the maximum dollar limitation will be $25,000 per year, and the investment limitation will be $200,000 per year; barring Congressional action, these amounts will *not* be adjusted for inflation.
Small business stock	February 17, 2009	The exclusion of gain from the sale or exchange of qualified small business stock (IRC §1202) is increased to 75% regarding the sale or exchange of stock acquired after February 17, 2009 and before January 1, 2011 (see Tab 4).
Standard deduction	2009	Homeowners who do not itemize deductions may claim an additional standard deduction for state and local real property taxes for any tax year beginning in 2009. The deduction is the lesser of: (1) the allowable deduction amount for state and local real property taxes if the taxpayer had itemized deductions, or (2) $500 ($1,000 for MFJ). Taxes taken into account when computing AGI are not taken into account for these purposes (see Tab 1). Non-itemizers can also claim an additional standard deduction for their "net disaster loss" amount in 2009. A net disaster loss is the excess of (1) personal casualty losses due to a federally declared disaster occurring before 2010 in a disaster area, over (2) personal casualty gains (see Tabs 1 and 2). Non-itemizers who purchase a new motor vehicle between February 17 and December 31, 2009, can also claim an additional standard deduction in 2009 for their state or local sales and excise taxes attributed to the first $49,500 of the purchase price (see "Motor vehicle taxes," supra, and Tab 1). In 2009, taxpayers who increase their standard deductions by state or local real estate taxes, new motor vehicle taxes, or net disaster losses must file Schedule L (see Tab 1).

Key Tax Law Changes for Individual Tax Returns (Continued)		
Area	**Effective Date**	**Provisions of New Law**
State and local sales taxes	2009	Taxpayers who elect to deduct state and local general sales taxes in lieu of state and local income taxes may not also claim the itemized deduction allowed for state or local sales or excise taxes paid on certain new vehicles (see "Motor vehicle taxes," supra).
Teachers' expenses	2009	Elementary and secondary school teachers and other education workers can take an above-the-line deduction in 2009 of up to $250 for certain out-of-pocket classroom expenses. The deduction covers expenses for books, supplies (other than nonathletic supplies for health or physical education courses), computer equipment (including related software and services) and other equipment, and supplementary materials used in the classroom (see Tab 1). After 2009, barring Congressional action, these expenses will be deductible only as miscellaneous itemized deductions subject to the 2%-of-AGI floor.
Transportation fringe benefits	2009	In January and February 2009, employees may exclude a maximum of $120 per month for the value of employer-provided transit passes or vanpooling in an employer-provided commuter highway vehicle. Starting in March 2009, the maximum exclusion for transit passes and vanpooling is increased to $230 per month. In 2009, employees may exclude up to $230 per month from gross income for the value of employer-provided qualified parking. Starting in 2009, employees may exclude reimbursements for reasonable qualified bicycle commuting expenses. The exclusion is limited to a per employee annual limitation of $20 multiplied by the number of qualified bicycle commuting months during the calendar year. A qualified bicycle commuting month is any month the employee regularly uses the bicycle to commute between his or her residence and place of employment and does not receive a reimbursement or subsidy for the other transportation fringe benefits. The reasonable expenses must be for the purchase of a bicycle and bicycle improvements, repair and storage if the bicycle is regularly used for commuting. The exclusion is not available if the reimbursement is made under an elective salary reduction agreement.
Tuition and fees deduction	2009	An above-the-line deduction is available in 2009 for tuition and fees paid which are required for enrollment or attendance by the taxpayer or his or her spouse or dependent at an accredited post-secondary institution. A $4,000 deduction is available to single taxpayers with AGI of $65,000 or less ($130,000 for joint filers). A $2,000 deduction is available to single taxpayers with AGI up to $80,000 ($160,000 for joint filers). Taxpayers taking this deduction cannot also claim the Hope or Lifetime Learning credits for the same student. Taxpayers claiming this deduction must complete Form 8917 and attach it to their return (see Tabs 1 and 13). After 2009, barring Congressional action, these expenses will no longer be deductible.
Unemployment compensation	2009	For tax years beginning in 2009, an individual can exclude from gross income up to $2,400 of unemployment compensation received during the year (see Tab 1).

Key Tax Figures 2006-2010					
Year	**2010**	**2009**	**2008**	**2007**	**2006**
Income Threshold for Requirement to File Form 1040					
Single, under age 65	9,350	9,350	8,950	8,750	8,450
Single, age 65 or over	10,750	10,750	10,300	10,050	9,700
HOH, under age 65	12,050	12,000	11,500	11,250	10,850
HOH, age 65 or over	13,450	13,400	12,850	12,550	12,100
MFJ, under age 65, (both spouses)	18,700	18,700	17,900	17,500	16,900
MFJ, age 65 or over (one spouse)	19,800	19,800	18,950	18,550	17,900
MFJ, age 65 or over (both spouses)	20,900	20,900	20,000	19,600	18,900
MFS, any age	3,650	3,650	3,500	3,400	3,300
QW, under age 65	15,050	15,050	14,400	14,100	13,600
QW, age 65 or over	16,150	16,150	15,450	15,150	14,600
Standard Deduction					
MFJ or QW	11,400	11,400	10,900	10,700	10,300
Single	5,700	5,700	5,450	5,350	5,150
HOH	8,400	8,350	8,000	7,850	7,550
MFS	5,700	5,700	5,450	5,350	5,150
Additional for age 65 or over, or blind each (MFJ, QW, MFS)	1,100	1,100	1,050	1,050	1,000
Additional for age 65 or over, or blind each (Single, HOH)	1,400	1,400	1,350	1,300	1,250
Personal and Dependent Exemption					
Amount of deduction	3,650	3,650	3,500	3,400	3,300
Phaseout begins, MFJ or QW	No Phaseout	250,200	239,950	234,600	225,750
Phaseout begins, Single	No Phaseout	166,800	159,950	156,400	150,500
Phaseout begins, HOH	No Phaseout	208,500	199,950	195,500	188,150
Phaseout begins, MFS	No Phaseout	125,100	119,975	117,300	112,875
Maximum Earnings Subject To					
Social Security tax	106,800	106,800	102,000	97,500	94,200
Medicare tax	No Limit	No Limit	No Limit	No Limit	No Limit
Maximum Tax Paid For					
Employee Social Security	6,621.60	6,621.60	6,324	6,045	5,840.40
Employee Medicare	No Limit	No Limit	No Limit	No Limit	No Limit
SE Social Security	13,243.20	13,243.20	12,648	12,090	11,680.80
SE Medicare	No Limit	No Limit	No Limit	No Limit	No Limit
Maximum Earnings Allowed Without Reduction of Social Security Benefits					
Under full retirement age, benefits reduced by $1 for each $2 earned over:	14,160	14,160	13,560	12,960	12,480
Full retirement age and over	No Limit	No Limit	No Limit	No Limit	No Limit
Maximum Deductible 401(k) Contribution					
Under age 50	16,500	16,500	15,500	15,500	15,000
Age 50 or older	22,000	22,000	20,500	20,500	20,000
Auto Standard Mileage Allowances (cents per mile)					
Business	N/A	55	50.5/58.5[1]	48.5	44.5

Key Tax Figures 2006-2010 (Continued)					
Year	**2010**	**2009**	**2008**	**2007**	**2006**
Medical/moving	N/A	24	19/27[1]	20	18
Charity work	N/A	14	14/36/41[2]	14	14/32/44.5[3]

[1] Before 7-1-08: business rate is 50.5¢ per mile, medical/moving rate is 19¢ per mile. After 6-30-08: business rate is 58.5¢ per mile, medical/moving rate is 27¢ per mile.

[2] The 2008 mileage rate for charity work is generally 14¢ per mile. However, for charity work related to the Midwestern disaster area, the rate is 36¢ per mile from the date the relevant storms occurred through 6-30-08, and 41¢ per mile from 7-1-08 through 12-31-08. For determining the amount excluded from income by taxpayers who are reimbursed for use of an automobile in charity work related to the Midwestern disaster area, the business rate for the applicable period applies.

[3] The 2006 mileage rate for charity work is generally 14¢ per mile. However, the rate is 32¢ per mile for charity work related to Hurricane Katrina, and 44.5¢ per mile for determining the amount excluded from income by taxpayers who are reimbursed for use of an automobile in charity work related to Hurricane Katrina.

Year	2010	2009	2008	2007	2006
Itemized Deduction Phaseout Begins					
MFJ or QW	No Phaseout	166,800	159,950	156,400	150,500
Single or HOH	No Phaseout	166,800	159,950	156,400	150,500
MFS	No Phaseout	83,400	79,975	78,200	75,250
Earned Income Credit					
One qualifying child					
Earned income amount	8,970	8,950	8,580	8,390	8,080
Maximum credit	3,050	3,043	2,917	2,853	2,747
Threshold phaseout	16,450	16,420	15,740	15,390	14,810
Complete phaseout	35,535	35,463	33,995	33,241	32,001
Threshold (MFJ)	21,460	21,420	18,740	17,390	16,810
Complete (MFJ)	40,545	40,463	36,995	35,241	34,001
Two qualifying children					
Earned income amount	12,590	12,570	12,060	11,790	11,340
Maximum credit	5,036	5,028	4,824	4,716	4,536
Threshold phaseout	16,450	16,420	15,740	15,390	14,810
Complete phaseout	40,363	40,295	38,646	37,783	36,348
Threshold (MFJ)	21,460	21,420	18,740	17,390	16,810
Complete (MFJ)	45,373	45,295	41,646	39,783	38,348
Three or more qualifying children					
Earned income amount	12,590	12,570	12,060	11,790	11,340
Maximum credit	5,666	5,657	4,824	4,716	4,536
Threshold phaseout	16,450	16,420	15,740	15,390	14,810
Complete phaseout	43,352	43,279	38,646	37,783	36,348
Threshold (MFJ)	21,460	21,420	18,740	17,390	16,810
Complete (MFJ)	48,362	48,279	41,646	39,783	38,348
No qualifying children					
Earned income amount	5,980	5,970	5,720	5,590	5,380
Maximum credit	457	457	438	428	412
Threshold phaseout	7,480	7,470	7,160	7,000	6,740
Complete phaseout	13,460	13,440	12,880	12,590	12,120
Threshold (MFJ)	12,490	12,470	10,160	9,000	8,740
Complete (MFJ)	18,470	18,440	15,880	14,590	14,120
Kiddie Tax					
Unearned income thresholds	950/1,900	950/1,900	900/1,800	850/1,700	850/1,700
Child Tax Credit Refund Threshold					
Amount per child	3,000	3,000	8,500	11,750	11,300

Taxpayer Interview

Personal

Name: ______________	Occupation: _______	SSN: __________	
Single	Married, living w/spouse	Separated	Divorced
Spouse: ______________	Occupation: _______	SSN: __________	
Blind/disabled	Spouse blind/disabled		

Children: Name	Birthdate	SSN	Gross Income	Months in Home	% Support from Child

Filing status in 2008:	Single	MFJ	MFS	HOH	QW
List dependent children who filed an income tax return in 2008: ________________					
List dependent children who have unearned income > $950 in 2009: ________________					
Changes in exemptions from 2008: ____________________________________					
Educational expenses: _______________________	Documentation? ________________________________				

Income

[Self] How many Forms W-2? ___________	Have them all? _________	
[Spouse] How many Forms W-2? ________	Have them all? _________	
[Both] How many Forms 1099? _________	Have them all? _________	
Income from mutual funds? ___________	Complete records? ______________	
Income from sales of stock? __________	Basis information available? ______________	
Income from municipal bonds? ________	Amount from "private activity" bonds: _____________	
Income from sales of personal assets? _____	Basis information available? ______________	
Forgiveness of debt? _______________	Loans with interest below AFR? _________	Gifts? ______
Rental Income–How many properties?_________	Income/expense records available? ________	
Retirement–How many Forms 1099-R? ____	Forms SSA-1099 or RRB-1099? _____________	
Other Income: Forms 1099-G: _________	Gambling: _____________	Alimony: ________
Tax refunds: ______	Tips: ______________	Other not on W-2: _______

Business Income, Deductions, and Credits

Business activity: _______	Name: ______	Product: _______	Gain or loss: _______
Records clear and complete? __________________		Multiple businesses' records kept separately? ______________	
Business jointly owned with spouse? _________________		Is spouse an employee? ____________	
Gross income from sales: _______		Other income: ______	
Income from sales of assets? _____	Basis information: ______	Recapture applicable? ____	
Insurance expenses: ________________			
Casualty/theft losses? ________	Insurance proceeds paid: ____	Insurance proceeds expected? ______	
Bad debts written off in 2009? __________________			

Office in home (% of home)? ________________		Mortgage/rent on buildings: ____________	
Depreciable equipment? ____	Auto(s)/other vehicle(s)? _____	Records of use? _____	
Records of taxes paid: ________	Records of purchases: _______	Records of improvements since purchase? _________	
Records of travel/lodging expenses? ____________________________			
Other expenses: ____			
Was any of the income related to farming? ___		Specific farming activities: _________	
Credits. Rehabilitation: _________	Energy: _____________	Employment: _____	Research: _________
Disabled access: __________________		Other: ________________	

Personal Deductions

IRA contributions made? _____	Can they be made now? _____	HSA/MSA? ____
Student loan interest paid? ____	Tuition/fees paid? ________	
Alimony paid? ________		
Itemized deductions in past? ____	Big change in medical expenses/living quarters in 2009? ____	
Medical. Whose medical expenses did you pay? ____________	Special-needs dependents? ____	
Medical expenses (less insurance): Major work: _____ Glasses: ____ Dental _____ Routine medical: ______ Prescription drugs: ________ Insurance premiums (list all) _____ Medical transportation: _______ Other: ____________		
Taxes. State income taxes paid in 2009: ______ Local taxes: ______ Property taxes _____ Records of sales taxes paid? ______ Real property taxes on home: _______ Other real property taxes: ______ Personal property taxes: ______		
Casualty Losses. Was property used in a business (% used)? _______	Insurance proceeds paid: _____	Insurance proceeds expected ______
Charitable Contributions. Money directly donated: ______ To whom? ____________ ____		Records? ________
Incidental expenses while donating services? _______	Goods donated: ______________	Records? ______________
Other. Employee expenses–Did you incur expenses for the convenience of your employer? ___	Auto: ______ Travel/lodging: ______ Auto expenses: ________ Telephone: _____ Supplies/tools: ______ Equipment: ________ Uniforms: _______	
Job-seeking expenses: ____________	Investment expenses: ________	Records? ______
Gambling losses: _________		
Other: ____		

Payments and Credits

Estimated federal 2009 tax payments: Q1_______ Q2 _______ Q3 _________ Q4 ________	
Estimated state 2009 tax payments: Q1_______ Q2 _______ Q3 _________ Q4 ________	
Amount applied to estimated payments from 2008 return: ___________	
Contributions to retirement funds:	
Child care expenses: _________	Any provided tax-free by employer? _________
Advance child credit payments received? ________	Adoption in 2009? _____
Taxes paid to foreign government? _________	
Family members in first 4 years of higher education? _______ Any family members in higher education? _______	
Certificate for mortgage interest credit? _____	
Paid AMT in prior 5 years? ________	

Miscellaneous

Tax returns and records available how far back?	Worker employed in home?

Requirements at a Glance: Filing Returns for Recently Deceased Taxpayers

2009 Forms That May Be Required When Filing for Recently Deceased Taxpayers				
Form	**Form Title**	**Required If...**	**Date Due**	**Special Requirements**
1040	*U.S. Individual Income Tax Return*	If decedent dies after end of calendar year but before due date of tax return (usually after January 1 and before April 15), and would normally have filed for the previous year, that return would have to be filed. *Example.* George dies on March 10, 2010. His return for 2009 (assuming he would have had to file a 2009 return if he had lived) must still be filed by April 15, 2010. A return may be filed to claim a refund or a refundable credit even if the return isn't required. A return must be filed if either of the following is true: • Decedent's income from beginning of tax year through date of death was large enough to require filing of Form 1040. • Decedent was required to file for some other reason (such as SE income); see Tab 1 for details. • Decedent did not have to file, but had tax withheld. *Example.* Assume George in the previous example had $12,000 of income in 2010 before dying. The final return for George (i.e., his 2010 return) would have to be filed by April 15, 2011.	Same date that the decedent's return would have been due if still alive (usually April 15 in the year of death)	Write the words "Deceased," the decedent's name, and the date of death across the top margin of the tax return. If refund is requested, and not filing MFJ, attach Form 1310, *Statement of Person Claiming Refund Due a Deceased Taxpayer*, to the return. If filing MFJ, enter "filing as surviving spouse" in the area where you sign the return.
1041	*U.S. Income Tax Return for Estates and Trusts*	File if either of the following is true: • The estate had more than $600 of income in the tax year. • Any beneficiary of the estate is a nonresident alien.	For fiscal-year filers, 15th day of fourth month following the end of the estate's tax year (beginning on the date of death). For calendar-year filers, April 15, 2010.	Note that the gross income of an estate consists of all items of income received, i.e., dividends, interest, rents, royalties, gain from the sale of property (including personal residence if paid to the probate estate), and income from business, partnerships, trusts, and any other sources earned and received after the date of death.
706	*Estate Tax Return*	Gross estate over $3.5 million for those dying in 2009; barring Congressional action, estate tax repealed for those dying in 2010.	Nine months after decedent's date of death	Automatic six-month extension available by filing Form 4768
709	*U.S. Gift (and Generation-Skipping Transfer) Tax Return*	The decedent made a taxable gift in either the year of death, or in the year preceding death without yet filing a return. Also, returns required for preceding years must be filed if decedent had not filed them.	Form 706 deadline (if Form 706 required), or same date that decedent's return would have been due if still alive (April 15, 2010), whichever is earlier	Extension to file decedent's federal income tax return (Form 4868 or 2350) automatically extends time to file gift tax return. Otherwise, use Form 8892 to request automatic six-month filing extension.

KEY FACTS: Comparing Tax Benefits of Education Options

Tax Benefits for K–12

Tuition is NEVER deductible, except when required for special-needs children. Coverdell ESAs (formerly education IRAs) can be used for tuition along with all other qualified expenses.

Coverdell ESA:

- Trust established to cover qualified education expenses of beneficiary
- Limited to contributions of $2,000 per child under 18 (exception: special-needs child)
- Elementary, secondary, postsecondary, and graduate education
- Tuition, books, supplies, equipment, registration fees, room and board (for attendance at least half-time), and qualified tuition program payments, as long as distribution is not used for expenses for which credit is claimed
- Hope or lifetime learning credit can be claimed in the same year a Coverdell ESA distribution is excluded from income
- Contributions not deductible
- Earnings tax deferred
- Distributions tax-free
- 6% excise tax on excess contributions (including earnings) not withdrawn by June of next year
- Phaseouts: MFJ, $190,000–220,000; others (except MFS), $95,000–110,000

Tax Credits for Higher Education

Attribute	Hope Credit (American Opportunity Tax Credit)	Lifetime Learning Credit
Benefit	Covers 100% of the first $2,000 ($2,400*) and 25% (50%*) of the second $2,000 ($2,400*) of qualified expenses	Credit equals 20% (40%*) of the first $10,000 of qualified education expenses for all eligible students
Limit	Limited to $2,500 ($3,600*) per student	Limited to $2,000 ($4,000*) per student
Education covered	Available through completion of first four post-secondary years	Available through all postsecondary years, and for job improvement or skill attainment coursework
Years covered	Limited to 4 years of education	Unlimited number of years of education
Qualifying expenses	Tuition; related expenses (e.g., student-activity fees, course-related books, supplies, and equipment) only if they must be paid to the institution as a condition of enrollment or attendance. In 2009 and 2010, Hope Credit also covers "course materials" (e.g., books, supplies and equipment needed for a course of study whether or not they are purchased from the institution as a condition of enrollment or attendance).	
Qualifying education	Must be used in pursuit of undergraduate degree or other recognized credential; student must be enrolled at least half-time for academic period beginning in tax year	Cannot claim both Hope and Lifetime Learning credit for the same student in the same year.
Other requirements	No felony drug conviction on student's record	
Type of credit	Up to 40% refundable; 0% refundable if taxpayer claiming the credit is a child subject to the "kiddie tax"	Nonrefundable tax credit
Phaseout	MFJ: $160,000-$180,000; Others: $80,000-$90,000; MFS: $0	MFJ: $100,000-$120,000; Others: $50,000-$60,000; MFS: $0

* Increased amounts and percentages are for students attending eligible educational institutions located in the Midwestern Disaster Area during tax year 2009; qualified expenses also expanded. Eligible taxpayers can elect to waive American Opportunity Tax Credit provisions and claim the higher amounts allowed in 2009 for Midwestern Disaster Area institutions.

Other Education Benefits

Qualified Tuition Program (Shop Around!!)

- No AGI limitations
- Distributions not exceeding costs of higher education excluded from income
- Can be used in conjunction with Coverdell ESA
- States and even private universities may offer programs; shopping around advisable
- In 2009 and 2010, includes expenses for certain computer technology or equipment, and certain internet services

Scholarships and Fellowships

- Generally excluded from income unless payments for services are included
- No AGI limits

Series EE and I Savings Bonds

- All or part of interest excluded from income if used to cover college tuition or fees
- EE bond must have been issued since 12/31/89

What's New in 2009

Partial Exclusion of Unemployment Compensation Benefits. An individual may exclude up to $2,400 of unemployment compensation received from gross income for 2009.

Limitation on Qualified Transportation Fringe Benefits. The limitation on the amount employees may exclude for transportation in a commuter highway vehicle and transit passes provided by an employer is temporarily increased to equal the limitation on the exclusion for qualified parking ($230 for 2009).

Code Sec. 179 Expense Election for 2009. The increased Code Sec. 179 expensing allowance provided for tax years beginning in 2008 is extended one additional year. Thus, for 2009, the Code Sec. 179 dollar limitation is $250,000, and the investment limitation is $800,000.

Section at a Glance

Qualified Dividends and Capital Gain Tax Worksheet—Line 44

Keep for Your Records

Before you begin:

√ See the instructions for line 44 that begin on page 37 to see if you can use this worksheet to figure your tax.

√ If you do not have to file Schedule D and you received capital gain distributions, be sure you checked the box on line 13 of Form 1040.

1. Enter the amount from Form 1040, line 43. However, if you are filing Form 2555 or 2555-EZ (relating to foreign earned income), enter the amount from line 3 of the worksheet on page 38 .... 1. ______
2. Enter the amount from Form 1040, line 9b* .... 2. ______
3. Are you filing Schedule D?*
   - ☐ **Yes.** Enter the **smaller** of line 15 or 16 of Schedule D. If either line 15 or line 16 is a loss, enter -0-
   - ☐ **No.** Enter the amount from Form 1040, line 13 } 3. ______
4. Add lines 2 and 3 .... 4. ______
5. If you are claiming investment interest expense on Form 4952, enter the amount from line 4g of that form. Otherwise, enter -0- .... 5. ______
6. Subtract line 5 from line 4. If zero or less, enter -0- .... 6. ______
7. Subtract line 6 from line 1. If zero or less, enter -0- .... 7. ______
8. Enter the **smaller** of:
   - The amount on line 1, or
   - $33,950 if single or married filing separately, $67,900 if married filing jointly or qualifying widow(er), $45,500 if head of household. } .... 8. ______
9. Is the amount on line 7 equal to or more than the amount on line 8?
   - ☐ **Yes.** Skip lines 9 and 10; go to line 11 and check the "No" box.
   - ☐ **No.** Enter the amount from line 7 .... 9. ______
10. Subtract line 9 from line 8 .... 10. ______
11. Are the amounts on lines 6 and 10 the same?
    - ☐ **Yes.** Skip lines 11 through 14; go to line 15.
    - ☐ **No.** Enter the **smaller** of line 1 or line 6 .... 11. ______
12. Enter the amount from line 10 (if line 10 is blank, enter -0-) .... 12. ______
13. Subtract line 12 from line 11 .... 13. ______
14. Multiply line 13 by 15% (.15) .... 14. ______
15. Figure the tax on the amount on line 7. Use the Tax Table or Tax Computation Worksheet, whichever applies .... 15. ______
16. Add lines 14 and 15 .... 16. ______
17. Figure the tax on the amount on line 1. Use the Tax Table or Tax Computation Worksheet, whichever applies .... 17. ______
18. **Tax on all taxable income.** Enter the **smaller** of line 16 or line 17. Also include this amount on Form 1040, line 44. If you are filing Form 2555 or 2555-EZ, do not enter this amount on Form 1040, line 44. Instead, enter it on line 4 of the worksheet on page 38 .... 18. ______

**If you are filing Form 2555 or 2555-EZ, see the footnote in the worksheet on page 38 before completing this line.*

2009 Tax Table

CAUTION *See the instructions for line 44 that begin on page 37 to see if you must use the Tax Table below to figure your tax.*

Example. Mr. and Mrs. Brown are filing a joint return. Their taxable income on Form 1040, line 43, is $25,300. First, they find the $25,300–25,350 taxable income line. Next, they find the column for married filing jointly and read down the column. The amount shown where the taxable income line and filing status column meet is $2,964. This is the tax amount they should enter on Form 1040, line 44.

Sample Table

At least	But less than	Single	Married filing jointly *	Married filing separately	Head of a household
		Your tax is—			
25,200	25,250	3,366	2,949	3,366	3,186
25,250	25,300	3,374	2,956	3,374	3,194
25,300	25,350	3,381	(2,964)	3,381	3,201
25,350	25,400	3,389	2,971	3,389	3,209

If line 43 (taxable income) is— / And you are—

At least	But less than	Single	Married filing jointly *	Married filing separately	Head of a household
		Your tax is—			
0	5	0	0	0	0
5	15	1	1	1	1
15	25	2	2	2	2
25	50	4	4	4	4
50	75	6	6	6	6
75	100	9	9	9	9
100	125	11	11	11	11
125	150	14	14	14	14
150	175	16	16	16	16
175	200	19	19	19	19
200	225	21	21	21	21
225	250	24	24	24	24
250	275	26	26	26	26
275	300	29	29	29	29
300	325	31	31	31	31
325	350	34	34	34	34
350	375	36	36	36	36
375	400	39	39	39	39
400	425	41	41	41	41
425	450	44	44	44	44
450	475	46	46	46	46
475	500	49	49	49	49
500	525	51	51	51	51
525	550	54	54	54	54
550	575	56	56	56	56
575	600	59	59	59	59
600	625	61	61	61	61
625	650	64	64	64	64
650	675	66	66	66	66
675	700	69	69	69	69
700	725	71	71	71	71
725	750	74	74	74	74
750	775	76	76	76	76
775	800	79	79	79	79
800	825	81	81	81	81
825	850	84	84	84	84
850	875	86	86	86	86
875	900	89	89	89	89
900	925	91	91	91	91
925	950	94	94	94	94
950	975	96	96	96	96
975	1,000	99	99	99	99
1,000					
1,000	1,025	101	101	101	101
1,025	1,050	104	104	104	104
1,050	1,075	106	106	106	106
1,075	1,100	109	109	109	109
1,100	1,125	111	111	111	111
1,125	1,150	114	114	114	114
1,150	1,175	116	116	116	116
1,175	1,200	119	119	119	119
1,200	1,225	121	121	121	121
1,225	1,250	124	124	124	124
1,250	1,275	126	126	126	126
1,275	1,300	129	129	129	129
1,300	1,325	131	131	131	131
1,325	1,350	134	134	134	134
1,350	1,375	136	136	136	136
1,375	1,400	139	139	139	139
1,400	1,425	141	141	141	141
1,425	1,450	144	144	144	144
1,450	1,475	146	146	146	146
1,475	1,500	149	149	149	149
1,500	1,525	151	151	151	151
1,525	1,550	154	154	154	154
1,550	1,575	156	156	156	156
1,575	1,600	159	159	159	159
1,600	1,625	161	161	161	161
1,625	1,650	164	164	164	164
1,650	1,675	166	166	166	166
1,675	1,700	169	169	169	169
1,700	1,725	171	171	171	171
1,725	1,750	174	174	174	174
1,750	1,775	176	176	176	176
1,775	1,800	179	179	179	179
1,800	1,825	181	181	181	181
1,825	1,850	184	184	184	184
1,850	1,875	186	186	186	186
1,875	1,900	189	189	189	189
1,900	1,925	191	191	191	191
1,925	1,950	194	194	194	194
1,950	1,975	196	196	196	196
1,975	2,000	199	199	199	199
2,000					
2,000	2,025	201	201	201	201
2,025	2,050	204	204	204	204
2,050	2,075	206	206	206	206
2,075	2,100	209	209	209	209
2,100	2,125	211	211	211	211
2,125	2,150	214	214	214	214
2,150	2,175	216	216	216	216
2,175	2,200	219	219	219	219
2,200	2,225	221	221	221	221
2,225	2,250	224	224	224	224
2,250	2,275	226	226	226	226
2,275	2,300	229	229	229	229
2,300	2,325	231	231	231	231
2,325	2,350	234	234	234	234
2,350	2,375	236	236	236	236
2,375	2,400	239	239	239	239
2,400	2,425	241	241	241	241
2,425	2,450	244	244	244	244
2,450	2,475	246	246	246	246
2,475	2,500	249	249	249	249
2,500	2,525	251	251	251	251
2,525	2,550	254	254	254	254
2,550	2,575	256	256	256	256
2,575	2,600	259	259	259	259
2,600	2,625	261	261	261	261
2,625	2,650	264	264	264	264
2,650	2,675	266	266	266	266
2,675	2,700	269	269	269	269
2,700	2,725	271	271	271	271
2,725	2,750	274	274	274	274
2,750	2,775	276	276	276	276
2,775	2,800	279	279	279	279
2,800	2,825	281	281	281	281
2,825	2,850	284	284	284	284
2,850	2,875	286	286	286	286
2,875	2,900	289	289	289	289
2,900	2,925	291	291	291	291
2,925	2,950	294	294	294	294
2,950	2,975	296	296	296	296
2,975	3,000	299	299	299	299
3,000					
3,000	3,050	303	303	303	303
3,050	3,100	308	308	308	308
3,100	3,150	313	313	313	313
3,150	3,200	318	318	318	318
3,200	3,250	323	323	323	323
3,250	3,300	328	328	328	328
3,300	3,350	333	333	333	333
3,350	3,400	338	338	338	338
3,400	3,450	343	343	343	343
3,450	3,500	348	348	348	348
3,500	3,550	353	353	353	353
3,550	3,600	358	358	358	358
3,600	3,650	363	363	363	363
3,650	3,700	368	368	368	368
3,700	3,750	373	373	373	373
3,750	3,800	378	378	378	378
3,800	3,850	383	383	383	383
3,850	3,900	388	388	388	388
3,900	3,950	393	393	393	393
3,950	4,000	398	398	398	398
4,000					
4,000	4,050	403	403	403	403
4,050	4,100	408	408	408	408
4,100	4,150	413	413	413	413
4,150	4,200	418	418	418	418
4,200	4,250	423	423	423	423
4,250	4,300	428	428	428	428
4,300	4,350	433	433	433	433
4,350	4,400	438	438	438	438
4,400	4,450	443	443	443	443
4,450	4,500	448	448	448	448
4,500	4,550	453	453	453	453
4,550	4,600	458	458	458	458
4,600	4,650	463	463	463	463
4,650	4,700	468	468	468	468
4,700	4,750	473	473	473	473
4,750	4,800	478	478	478	478
4,800	4,850	483	483	483	483
4,850	4,900	488	488	488	488
4,900	4,950	493	493	493	493
4,950	5,000	498	498	498	498

* This column must also be used by a qualifying widow(er).

2009 Tax Table—*Continued*

If line 43 (taxable income) is— / And you are—

At least	But less than	Single	Married filing jointly *	Married filing separately	Head of a household
		Your tax is—			
5,000					
5,000	5,050	503	503	503	503
5,050	5,100	508	508	508	508
5,100	5,150	513	513	513	513
5,150	5,200	518	518	518	518
5,200	5,250	523	523	523	523
5,250	5,300	528	528	528	528
5,300	5,350	533	533	533	533
5,350	5,400	538	538	538	538
5,400	5,450	543	543	543	543
5,450	5,500	548	548	548	548
5,500	5,550	553	553	553	553
5,550	5,600	558	558	558	558
5,600	5,650	563	563	563	563
5,650	5,700	568	568	568	568
5,700	5,750	573	573	573	573
5,750	5,800	578	578	578	578
5,800	5,850	583	583	583	583
5,850	5,900	588	588	588	588
5,900	5,950	593	593	593	593
5,950	6,000	598	598	598	598
6,000					
6,000	6,050	603	603	603	603
6,050	6,100	608	608	608	608
6,100	6,150	613	613	613	613
6,150	6,200	618	618	618	618
6,200	6,250	623	623	623	623
6,250	6,300	628	628	628	628
6,300	6,350	633	633	633	633
6,350	6,400	638	638	638	638
6,400	6,450	643	643	643	643
6,450	6,500	648	648	648	648
6,500	6,550	653	653	653	653
6,550	6,600	658	658	658	658
6,600	6,650	663	663	663	663
6,650	6,700	668	668	668	668
6,700	6,750	673	673	673	673
6,750	6,800	678	678	678	678
6,800	6,850	683	683	683	683
6,850	6,900	688	688	688	688
6,900	6,950	693	693	693	693
6,950	7,000	698	698	698	698
7,000					
7,000	7,050	703	703	703	703
7,050	7,100	708	708	708	708
7,100	7,150	713	713	713	713
7,150	7,200	718	718	718	718
7,200	7,250	723	723	723	723
7,250	7,300	728	728	728	728
7,300	7,350	733	733	733	733
7,350	7,400	738	738	738	738
7,400	7,450	743	743	743	743
7,450	7,500	748	748	748	748
7,500	7,550	753	753	753	753
7,550	7,600	758	758	758	758
7,600	7,650	763	763	763	763
7,650	7,700	768	768	768	768
7,700	7,750	773	773	773	773
7,750	7,800	778	778	778	778
7,800	7,850	783	783	783	783
7,850	7,900	788	788	788	788
7,900	7,950	793	793	793	793
7,950	8,000	798	798	798	798
8,000					
8,000	8,050	803	803	803	803
8,050	8,100	808	808	808	808
8,100	8,150	813	813	813	813
8,150	8,200	818	818	818	818
8,200	8,250	823	823	823	823
8,250	8,300	828	828	828	828
8,300	8,350	833	833	833	833
8,350	8,400	839	838	839	838
8,400	8,450	846	843	846	843
8,450	8,500	854	848	854	848
8,500	8,550	861	853	861	853
8,550	8,600	869	858	869	858
8,600	8,650	876	863	876	863
8,650	8,700	884	868	884	868
8,700	8,750	891	873	891	873
8,750	8,800	899	878	899	878
8,800	8,850	906	883	906	883
8,850	8,900	914	888	914	888
8,900	8,950	921	893	921	893
8,950	9,000	929	898	929	898
9,000					
9,000	9,050	936	903	936	903
9,050	9,100	944	908	944	908
9,100	9,150	951	913	951	913
9,150	9,200	959	918	959	918
9,200	9,250	966	923	966	923
9,250	9,300	974	928	974	928
9,300	9,350	981	933	981	933
9,350	9,400	989	938	989	938
9,400	9,450	996	943	996	943
9,450	9,500	1,004	948	1,004	948
9,500	9,550	1,011	953	1,011	953
9,550	9,600	1,019	958	1,019	958
9,600	9,650	1,026	963	1,026	963
9,650	9,700	1,034	968	1,034	968
9,700	9,750	1,041	973	1,041	973
9,750	9,800	1,049	978	1,049	978
9,800	9,850	1,056	983	1,056	983
9,850	9,900	1,064	988	1,064	988
9,900	9,950	1,071	993	1,071	993
9,950	10,000	1,079	998	1,079	998
10,000					
10,000	10,050	1,086	1,003	1,086	1,003
10,050	10,100	1,094	1,008	1,094	1,008
10,100	10,150	1,101	1,013	1,101	1,013
10,150	10,200	1,109	1,018	1,109	1,018
10,200	10,250	1,116	1,023	1,116	1,023
10,250	10,300	1,124	1,028	1,124	1,028
10,300	10,350	1,131	1,033	1,131	1,033
10,350	10,400	1,139	1,038	1,139	1,038
10,400	10,450	1,146	1,043	1,146	1,043
10,450	10,500	1,154	1,048	1,154	1,048
10,500	10,550	1,161	1,053	1,161	1,053
10,550	10,600	1,169	1,058	1,169	1,058
10,600	10,650	1,176	1,063	1,176	1,063
10,650	10,700	1,184	1,068	1,184	1,068
10,700	10,750	1,191	1,073	1,191	1,073
10,750	10,800	1,199	1,078	1,199	1,078
10,800	10,850	1,206	1,083	1,206	1,083
10,850	10,900	1,214	1,088	1,214	1,088
10,900	10,950	1,221	1,093	1,221	1,093
10,950	11,000	1,229	1,098	1,229	1,098
11,000					
11,000	11,050	1,236	1,103	1,236	1,103
11,050	11,100	1,244	1,108	1,244	1,108
11,100	11,150	1,251	1,113	1,251	1,113
11,150	11,200	1,259	1,118	1,259	1,118
11,200	11,250	1,266	1,123	1,266	1,123
11,250	11,300	1,274	1,128	1,274	1,128
11,300	11,350	1,281	1,133	1,281	1,133
11,350	11,400	1,289	1,138	1,289	1,138
11,400	11,450	1,296	1,143	1,296	1,143
11,450	11,500	1,304	1,148	1,304	1,148
11,500	11,550	1,311	1,153	1,311	1,153
11,550	11,600	1,319	1,158	1,319	1,158
11,600	11,650	1,326	1,163	1,326	1,163
11,650	11,700	1,334	1,168	1,334	1,168
11,700	11,750	1,341	1,173	1,341	1,173
11,750	11,800	1,349	1,178	1,349	1,178
11,800	11,850	1,356	1,183	1,356	1,183
11,850	11,900	1,364	1,188	1,364	1,188
11,900	11,950	1,371	1,193	1,371	1,193
11,950	12,000	1,379	1,198	1,379	1,199
12,000					
12,000	12,050	1,386	1,203	1,386	1,206
12,050	12,100	1,394	1,208	1,394	1,214
12,100	12,150	1,401	1,213	1,401	1,221
12,150	12,200	1,409	1,218	1,409	1,229
12,200	12,250	1,416	1,223	1,416	1,236
12,250	12,300	1,424	1,228	1,424	1,244
12,300	12,350	1,431	1,233	1,431	1,251
12,350	12,400	1,439	1,238	1,439	1,259
12,400	12,450	1,446	1,243	1,446	1,266
12,450	12,500	1,454	1,248	1,454	1,274
12,500	12,550	1,461	1,253	1,461	1,281
12,550	12,600	1,469	1,258	1,469	1,289
12,600	12,650	1,476	1,263	1,476	1,296
12,650	12,700	1,484	1,268	1,484	1,304
12,700	12,750	1,491	1,273	1,491	1,311
12,750	12,800	1,499	1,278	1,499	1,319
12,800	12,850	1,506	1,283	1,506	1,326
12,850	12,900	1,514	1,288	1,514	1,334
12,900	12,950	1,521	1,293	1,521	1,341
12,950	13,000	1,529	1,298	1,529	1,349
13,000					
13,000	13,050	1,536	1,303	1,536	1,356
13,050	13,100	1,544	1,308	1,544	1,364
13,100	13,150	1,551	1,313	1,551	1,371
13,150	13,200	1,559	1,318	1,559	1,379
13,200	13,250	1,566	1,323	1,566	1,386
13,250	13,300	1,574	1,328	1,574	1,394
13,300	13,350	1,581	1,333	1,581	1,401
13,350	13,400	1,589	1,338	1,589	1,409
13,400	13,450	1,596	1,343	1,596	1,416
13,450	13,500	1,604	1,348	1,604	1,424
13,500	13,550	1,611	1,353	1,611	1,431
13,550	13,600	1,619	1,358	1,619	1,439
13,600	13,650	1,626	1,363	1,626	1,446
13,650	13,700	1,634	1,368	1,634	1,454
13,700	13,750	1,641	1,373	1,641	1,461
13,750	13,800	1,649	1,378	1,649	1,469
13,800	13,850	1,656	1,383	1,656	1,476
13,850	13,900	1,664	1,388	1,664	1,484
13,900	13,950	1,671	1,393	1,671	1,491
13,950	14,000	1,679	1,398	1,679	1,499

* This column must also be used by a qualifying widow(er).

If line 43 (taxable income) is— At least	But less than	And you are— Single	Married filing jointly *	Married filing separately	Head of a household
		Your tax is—			
14,000					
14,000	14,050	1,686	1,403	1,686	1,506
14,050	14,100	1,694	1,408	1,694	1,514
14,100	14,150	1,701	1,413	1,701	1,521
14,150	14,200	1,709	1,418	1,709	1,529
14,200	14,250	1,716	1,423	1,716	1,536
14,250	14,300	1,724	1,428	1,724	1,544
14,300	14,350	1,731	1,433	1,731	1,551
14,350	14,400	1,739	1,438	1,739	1,559
14,400	14,450	1,746	1,443	1,746	1,566
14,450	14,500	1,754	1,448	1,754	1,574
14,500	14,550	1,761	1,453	1,761	1,581
14,550	14,600	1,769	1,458	1,769	1,589
14,600	14,650	1,776	1,463	1,776	1,596
14,650	14,700	1,784	1,468	1,784	1,604
14,700	14,750	1,791	1,473	1,791	1,611
14,750	14,800	1,799	1,478	1,799	1,619
14,800	14,850	1,806	1,483	1,806	1,626
14,850	14,900	1,814	1,488	1,814	1,634
14,900	14,950	1,821	1,493	1,821	1,641
14,950	15,000	1,829	1,498	1,829	1,649
15,000					
15,000	15,050	1,836	1,503	1,836	1,656
15,050	15,100	1,844	1,508	1,844	1,664
15,100	15,150	1,851	1,513	1,851	1,671
15,150	15,200	1,859	1,518	1,859	1,679
15,200	15,250	1,866	1,523	1,866	1,686
15,250	15,300	1,874	1,528	1,874	1,694
15,300	15,350	1,881	1,533	1,881	1,701
15,350	15,400	1,889	1,538	1,889	1,709
15,400	15,450	1,896	1,543	1,896	1,716
15,450	15,500	1,904	1,548	1,904	1,724
15,500	15,550	1,911	1,553	1,911	1,731
15,550	15,600	1,919	1,558	1,919	1,739
15,600	15,650	1,926	1,563	1,926	1,746
15,650	15,700	1,934	1,568	1,934	1,754
15,700	15,750	1,941	1,573	1,941	1,761
15,750	15,800	1,949	1,578	1,949	1,769
15,800	15,850	1,956	1,583	1,956	1,776
15,850	15,900	1,964	1,588	1,964	1,784
15,900	15,950	1,971	1,593	1,971	1,791
15,950	16,000	1,979	1,598	1,979	1,799
16,000					
16,000	16,050	1,986	1,603	1,986	1,806
16,050	16,100	1,994	1,608	1,994	1,814
16,100	16,150	2,001	1,613	2,001	1,821
16,150	16,200	2,009	1,618	2,009	1,829
16,200	16,250	2,016	1,623	2,016	1,836
16,250	16,300	2,024	1,628	2,024	1,844
16,300	16,350	2,031	1,633	2,031	1,851
16,350	16,400	2,039	1,638	2,039	1,859
16,400	16,450	2,046	1,643	2,046	1,866
16,450	16,500	2,054	1,648	2,054	1,874
16,500	16,550	2,061	1,653	2,061	1,881
16,550	16,600	2,069	1,658	2,069	1,889
16,600	16,650	2,076	1,663	2,076	1,896
16,650	16,700	2,084	1,668	2,084	1,904
16,700	16,750	2,091	1,674	2,091	1,911
16,750	16,800	2,099	1,681	2,099	1,919
16,800	16,850	2,106	1,689	2,106	1,926
16,850	16,900	2,114	1,696	2,114	1,934
16,900	16,950	2,121	1,704	2,121	1,941
16,950	17,000	2,129	1,711	2,129	1,949
17,000					
17,000	17,050	2,136	1,719	2,136	1,956
17,050	17,100	2,144	1,726	2,144	1,964
17,100	17,150	2,151	1,734	2,151	1,971
17,150	17,200	2,159	1,741	2,159	1,979
17,200	17,250	2,166	1,749	2,166	1,986
17,250	17,300	2,174	1,756	2,174	1,994
17,300	17,350	2,181	1,764	2,181	2,001
17,350	17,400	2,189	1,771	2,189	2,009
17,400	17,450	2,196	1,779	2,196	2,016
17,450	17,500	2,204	1,786	2,204	2,024
17,500	17,550	2,211	1,794	2,211	2,031
17,550	17,600	2,219	1,801	2,219	2,039
17,600	17,650	2,226	1,809	2,226	2,046
17,650	17,700	2,234	1,816	2,234	2,054
17,700	17,750	2,241	1,824	2,241	2,061
17,750	17,800	2,249	1,831	2,249	2,069
17,800	17,850	2,256	1,839	2,256	2,076
17,850	17,900	2,264	1,846	2,264	2,084
17,900	17,950	2,271	1,854	2,271	2,091
17,950	18,000	2,279	1,861	2,279	2,099
18,000					
18,000	18,050	2,286	1,869	2,286	2,106
18,050	18,100	2,294	1,876	2,294	2,114
18,100	18,150	2,301	1,884	2,301	2,121
18,150	18,200	2,309	1,891	2,309	2,129
18,200	18,250	2,316	1,899	2,316	2,136
18,250	18,300	2,324	1,906	2,324	2,144
18,300	18,350	2,331	1,914	2,331	2,151
18,350	18,400	2,339	1,921	2,339	2,159
18,400	18,450	2,346	1,929	2,346	2,166
18,450	18,500	2,354	1,936	2,354	2,174
18,500	18,550	2,361	1,944	2,361	2,181
18,550	18,600	2,369	1,951	2,369	2,189
18,600	18,650	2,376	1,959	2,376	2,196
18,650	18,700	2,384	1,966	2,384	2,204
18,700	18,750	2,391	1,974	2,391	2,211
18,750	18,800	2,399	1,981	2,399	2,219
18,800	18,850	2,406	1,989	2,406	2,226
18,850	18,900	2,414	1,996	2,414	2,234
18,900	18,950	2,421	2,004	2,421	2,241
18,950	19,000	2,429	2,011	2,429	2,249
19,000					
19,000	19,050	2,436	2,019	2,436	2,256
19,050	19,100	2,444	2,026	2,444	2,264
19,100	19,150	2,451	2,034	2,451	2,271
19,150	19,200	2,459	2,041	2,459	2,279
19,200	19,250	2,466	2,049	2,466	2,286
19,250	19,300	2,474	2,056	2,474	2,294
19,300	19,350	2,481	2,064	2,481	2,301
19,350	19,400	2,489	2,071	2,489	2,309
19,400	19,450	2,496	2,079	2,496	2,316
19,450	19,500	2,504	2,086	2,504	2,324
19,500	19,550	2,511	2,094	2,511	2,331
19,550	19,600	2,519	2,101	2,519	2,339
19,600	19,650	2,526	2,109	2,526	2,346
19,650	19,700	2,534	2,116	2,534	2,354
19,700	19,750	2,541	2,124	2,541	2,361
19,750	19,800	2,549	2,131	2,549	2,369
19,800	19,850	2,556	2,139	2,556	2,376
19,850	19,900	2,564	2,146	2,564	2,384
19,900	19,950	2,571	2,154	2,571	2,391
19,950	20,000	2,579	2,161	2,579	2,399
20,000					
20,000	20,050	2,586	2,169	2,586	2,406
20,050	20,100	2,594	2,176	2,594	2,414
20,100	20,150	2,601	2,184	2,601	2,421
20,150	20,200	2,609	2,191	2,609	2,429
20,200	20,250	2,616	2,199	2,616	2,436
20,250	20,300	2,624	2,206	2,624	2,444
20,300	20,350	2,631	2,214	2,631	2,451
20,350	20,400	2,639	2,221	2,639	2,459
20,400	20,450	2,646	2,229	2,646	2,466
20,450	20,500	2,654	2,236	2,654	2,474
20,500	20,550	2,661	2,244	2,661	2,481
20,550	20,600	2,669	2,251	2,669	2,489
20,600	20,650	2,676	2,259	2,676	2,496
20,650	20,700	2,684	2,266	2,684	2,504
20,700	20,750	2,691	2,274	2,691	2,511
20,750	20,800	2,699	2,281	2,699	2,519
20,800	20,850	2,706	2,289	2,706	2,526
20,850	20,900	2,714	2,296	2,714	2,534
20,900	20,950	2,721	2,304	2,721	2,541
20,950	21,000	2,729	2,311	2,729	2,549
21,000					
21,000	21,050	2,736	2,319	2,736	2,556
21,050	21,100	2,744	2,326	2,744	2,564
21,100	21,150	2,751	2,334	2,751	2,571
21,150	21,200	2,759	2,341	2,759	2,579
21,200	21,250	2,766	2,349	2,766	2,586
21,250	21,300	2,774	2,356	2,774	2,594
21,300	21,350	2,781	2,364	2,781	2,601
21,350	21,400	2,789	2,371	2,789	2,609
21,400	21,450	2,796	2,379	2,796	2,616
21,450	21,500	2,804	2,386	2,804	2,624
21,500	21,550	2,811	2,394	2,811	2,631
21,550	21,600	2,819	2,401	2,819	2,639
21,600	21,650	2,826	2,409	2,826	2,646
21,650	21,700	2,834	2,416	2,834	2,654
21,700	21,750	2,841	2,424	2,841	2,661
21,750	21,800	2,849	2,431	2,849	2,669
21,800	21,850	2,856	2,439	2,856	2,676
21,850	21,900	2,864	2,446	2,864	2,684
21,900	21,950	2,871	2,454	2,871	2,691
21,950	22,000	2,879	2,461	2,879	2,699
22,000					
22,000	22,050	2,886	2,469	2,886	2,706
22,050	22,100	2,894	2,476	2,894	2,714
22,100	22,150	2,901	2,484	2,901	2,721
22,150	22,200	2,909	2,491	2,909	2,729
22,200	22,250	2,916	2,499	2,916	2,736
22,250	22,300	2,924	2,506	2,924	2,744
22,300	22,350	2,931	2,514	2,931	2,751
22,350	22,400	2,939	2,521	2,939	2,759
22,400	22,450	2,946	2,529	2,946	2,766
22,450	22,500	2,954	2,536	2,954	2,774
22,500	22,550	2,961	2,544	2,961	2,781
22,550	22,600	2,969	2,551	2,969	2,789
22,600	22,650	2,976	2,559	2,976	2,796
22,650	22,700	2,984	2,566	2,984	2,804
22,700	22,750	2,991	2,574	2,991	2,811
22,750	22,800	2,999	2,581	2,999	2,819
22,800	22,850	3,006	2,589	3,006	2,826
22,850	22,900	3,014	2,596	3,014	2,834
22,900	22,950	3,021	2,604	3,021	2,841
22,950	23,000	3,029	2,611	3,029	2,849
23,000					
23,000	23,050	3,036	2,619	3,036	2,856
23,050	23,100	3,044	2,626	3,044	2,864
23,100	23,150	3,051	2,634	3,051	2,871
23,150	23,200	3,059	2,641	3,059	2,879
23,200	23,250	3,066	2,649	3,066	2,886
23,250	23,300	3,074	2,656	3,074	2,894
23,300	23,350	3,081	2,664	3,081	2,901
23,350	23,400	3,089	2,671	3,089	2,909
23,400	23,450	3,096	2,679	3,096	2,916
23,450	23,500	3,104	2,686	3,104	2,924
23,500	23,550	3,111	2,694	3,111	2,931
23,550	23,600	3,119	2,701	3,119	2,939
23,600	23,650	3,126	2,709	3,126	2,946
23,650	23,700	3,134	2,716	3,134	2,954
23,700	23,750	3,141	2,724	3,141	2,961
23,750	23,800	3,149	2,731	3,149	2,969
23,800	23,850	3,156	2,739	3,156	2,976
23,850	23,900	3,164	2,746	3,164	2,984
23,900	23,950	3,171	2,754	3,171	2,991
23,950	24,000	3,179	2,761	3,179	2,999
24,000					
24,000	24,050	3,186	2,769	3,186	3,006
24,050	24,100	3,194	2,776	3,194	3,014
24,100	24,150	3,201	2,784	3,201	3,021
24,150	24,200	3,209	2,791	3,209	3,029
24,200	24,250	3,216	2,799	3,216	3,036
24,250	24,300	3,224	2,806	3,224	3,044
24,300	24,350	3,231	2,814	3,231	3,051
24,350	24,400	3,239	2,821	3,239	3,059
24,400	24,450	3,246	2,829	3,246	3,066
24,450	24,500	3,254	2,836	3,254	3,074
24,500	24,550	3,261	2,844	3,261	3,081
24,550	24,600	3,269	2,851	3,269	3,089
24,600	24,650	3,276	2,859	3,276	3,096
24,650	24,700	3,284	2,866	3,284	3,104
24,700	24,750	3,291	2,874	3,291	3,111
24,750	24,800	3,299	2,881	3,299	3,119
24,800	24,850	3,306	2,889	3,306	3,126
24,850	24,900	3,314	2,896	3,314	3,134
24,900	24,950	3,321	2,904	3,321	3,141
24,950	25,000	3,329	2,911	3,329	3,149
25,000					
25,000	25,050	3,336	2,919	3,336	3,156
25,050	25,100	3,344	2,926	3,344	3,164
25,100	25,150	3,351	2,934	3,351	3,171
25,150	25,200	3,359	2,941	3,359	3,179
25,200	25,250	3,366	2,949	3,366	3,186
25,250	25,300	3,374	2,956	3,374	3,194
25,300	25,350	3,381	2,964	3,381	3,201
25,350	25,400	3,389	2,971	3,389	3,209
25,400	25,450	3,396	2,979	3,396	3,216
25,450	25,500	3,404	2,986	3,404	3,224
25,500	25,550	3,411	2,994	3,411	3,231
25,550	25,600	3,419	3,001	3,419	3,239
25,600	25,650	3,426	3,009	3,426	3,246
25,650	25,700	3,434	3,016	3,434	3,254
25,700	25,750	3,441	3,024	3,441	3,261
25,750	25,800	3,449	3,031	3,449	3,269
25,800	25,850	3,456	3,039	3,456	3,276
25,850	25,900	3,464	3,046	3,464	3,284
25,900	25,950	3,471	3,054	3,471	3,291
25,950	26,000	3,479	3,061	3,479	3,299
26,000					
26,000	26,050	3,486	3,069	3,486	3,306
26,050	26,100	3,494	3,076	3,494	3,314
26,100	26,150	3,501	3,084	3,501	3,321
26,150	26,200	3,509	3,091	3,509	3,329
26,200	26,250	3,516	3,099	3,516	3,336
26,250	26,300	3,524	3,106	3,524	3,344
26,300	26,350	3,531	3,114	3,531	3,351
26,350	26,400	3,539	3,121	3,539	3,359
26,400	26,450	3,546	3,129	3,546	3,366
26,450	26,500	3,554	3,136	3,554	3,374
26,500	26,550	3,561	3,144	3,561	3,381
26,550	26,600	3,569	3,151	3,569	3,389
26,600	26,650	3,576	3,159	3,576	3,396
26,650	26,700	3,584	3,166	3,584	3,404
26,700	26,750	3,591	3,174	3,591	3,411
26,750	26,800	3,599	3,181	3,599	3,419
26,800	26,850	3,606	3,189	3,606	3,426
26,850	26,900	3,614	3,196	3,614	3,434
26,900	26,950	3,621	3,204	3,621	3,441
26,950	27,000	3,629	3,211	3,629	3,449
27,000					
27,000	27,050	3,636	3,219	3,636	3,456
27,050	27,100	3,644	3,226	3,644	3,464
27,100	27,150	3,651	3,234	3,651	3,471
27,150	27,200	3,659	3,241	3,659	3,479
27,200	27,250	3,666	3,249	3,666	3,486
27,250	27,300	3,674	3,256	3,674	3,494
27,300	27,350	3,681	3,264	3,681	3,501
27,350	27,400	3,689	3,271	3,689	3,509
27,400	27,450	3,696	3,279	3,696	3,516
27,450	27,500	3,704	3,286	3,704	3,524
27,500	27,550	3,711	3,294	3,711	3,531
27,550	27,600	3,719	3,301	3,719	3,539
27,600	27,650	3,726	3,309	3,726	3,546
27,650	27,700	3,734	3,316	3,734	3,554
27,700	27,750	3,741	3,324	3,741	3,561
27,750	27,800	3,749	3,331	3,749	3,569
27,800	27,850	3,756	3,339	3,756	3,576
27,850	27,900	3,764	3,346	3,764	3,584
27,900	27,950	3,771	3,354	3,771	3,591
27,950	28,000	3,779	3,361	3,779	3,599
28,000					
28,000	28,050	3,786	3,369	3,786	3,606
28,050	28,100	3,794	3,376	3,794	3,614
28,100	28,150	3,801	3,384	3,801	3,621
28,150	28,200	3,809	3,391	3,809	3,629
28,200	28,250	3,816	3,399	3,816	3,636
28,250	28,300	3,824	3,406	3,824	3,644
28,300	28,350	3,831	3,414	3,831	3,651
28,350	28,400	3,839	3,421	3,839	3,659
28,400	28,450	3,846	3,429	3,846	3,666
28,450	28,500	3,854	3,436	3,854	3,674
28,500	28,550	3,861	3,444	3,861	3,681
28,550	28,600	3,869	3,451	3,869	3,689
28,600	28,650	3,876	3,459	3,876	3,696
28,650	28,700	3,884	3,466	3,884	3,704
28,700	28,750	3,891	3,474	3,891	3,711
28,750	28,800	3,899	3,481	3,899	3,719
28,800	28,850	3,906	3,489	3,906	3,726
28,850	28,900	3,914	3,496	3,914	3,734
28,900	28,950	3,921	3,504	3,921	3,741
28,950	29,000	3,929	3,511	3,929	3,749
29,000					
29,000	29,050	3,936	3,519	3,936	3,756
29,050	29,100	3,944	3,526	3,944	3,764
29,100	29,150	3,951	3,534	3,951	3,771
29,150	29,200	3,959	3,541	3,959	3,779
29,200	29,250	3,966	3,549	3,966	3,786
29,250	29,300	3,974	3,556	3,974	3,794
29,300	29,350	3,981	3,564	3,981	3,801
29,350	29,400	3,989	3,571	3,989	3,809
29,400	29,450	3,996	3,579	3,996	3,816
29,450	29,500	4,004	3,586	4,004	3,824
29,500	29,550	4,011	3,594	4,011	3,831
29,550	29,600	4,019	3,601	4,019	3,839
29,600	29,650	4,026	3,609	4,026	3,846
29,650	29,700	4,034	3,616	4,034	3,854
29,700	29,750	4,041	3,624	4,041	3,861
29,750	29,800	4,049	3,631	4,049	3,869
29,800	29,850	4,056	3,639	4,056	3,876
29,850	29,900	4,064	3,646	4,064	3,884
29,900	29,950	4,071	3,654	4,071	3,891
29,950	30,000	4,079	3,661	4,079	3,899
30,000					
30,000	30,050	4,086	3,669	4,086	3,906
30,050	30,100	4,094	3,676	4,094	3,914
30,100	30,150	4,101	3,684	4,101	3,921
30,150	30,200	4,109	3,691	4,109	3,929
30,200	30,250	4,116	3,699	4,116	3,936
30,250	30,300	4,124	3,706	4,124	3,944
30,300	30,350	4,131	3,714	4,131	3,951
30,350	30,400	4,139	3,721	4,139	3,959
30,400	30,450	4,146	3,729	4,146	3,966
30,450	30,500	4,154	3,736	4,154	3,974
30,500	30,550	4,161	3,744	4,161	3,981
30,550	30,600	4,169	3,751	4,169	3,989
30,600	30,650	4,176	3,759	4,176	3,996
30,650	30,700	4,184	3,766	4,184	4,004
30,700	30,750	4,191	3,774	4,191	4,011
30,750	30,800	4,199	3,781	4,199	4,019
30,800	30,850	4,206	3,789	4,206	4,026
30,850	30,900	4,214	3,796	4,214	4,034
30,900	30,950	4,221	3,804	4,221	4,041
30,950	31,000	4,229	3,811	4,229	4,049
31,000					
31,000	31,050	4,236	3,819	4,236	4,056
31,050	31,100	4,244	3,826	4,244	4,064
31,100	31,150	4,251	3,834	4,251	4,071
31,150	31,200	4,259	3,841	4,259	4,079
31,200	31,250	4,266	3,849	4,266	4,086
31,250	31,300	4,274	3,856	4,274	4,094
31,300	31,350	4,281	3,864	4,281	4,101
31,350	31,400	4,289	3,871	4,289	4,109
31,400	31,450	4,296	3,879	4,296	4,116
31,450	31,500	4,304	3,886	4,304	4,124
31,500	31,550	4,311	3,894	4,311	4,131
31,550	31,600	4,319	3,901	4,319	4,139
31,600	31,650	4,326	3,909	4,326	4,146
31,650	31,700	4,334	3,916	4,334	4,154
31,700	31,750	4,341	3,924	4,341	4,161
31,750	31,800	4,349	3,931	4,349	4,169
31,800	31,850	4,356	3,939	4,356	4,176
31,850	31,900	4,364	3,946	4,364	4,184
31,900	31,950	4,371	3,954	4,371	4,191
31,950	32,000	4,379	3,961	4,379	4,199

* This column must also be used by a qualifying widow(er).

* This column must also be used by a qualifying widow(er).

2009 Tax Table—*Continued*

If line 43 (taxable income) is— At least	But less than	And you are— Single	Married filing jointly *	Married filing separately	Head of a household
		Your tax is—			
32,000					
32,000	32,050	4,386	3,969	4,386	4,206
32,050	32,100	4,394	3,976	4,394	4,214
32,100	32,150	4,401	3,984	4,401	4,221
32,150	32,200	4,409	3,991	4,409	4,229
32,200	32,250	4,416	3,999	4,416	4,236
32,250	32,300	4,424	4,006	4,424	4,244
32,300	32,350	4,431	4,014	4,431	4,251
32,350	32,400	4,439	4,021	4,439	4,259
32,400	32,450	4,446	4,029	4,446	4,266
32,450	32,500	4,454	4,036	4,454	4,274
32,500	32,550	4,461	4,044	4,461	4,281
32,550	32,600	4,469	4,051	4,469	4,289
32,600	32,650	4,476	4,059	4,476	4,296
32,650	32,700	4,484	4,066	4,484	4,304
32,700	32,750	4,491	4,074	4,491	4,311
32,750	32,800	4,499	4,081	4,499	4,319
32,800	32,850	4,506	4,089	4,506	4,326
32,850	32,900	4,514	4,096	4,514	4,334
32,900	32,950	4,521	4,104	4,521	4,341
32,950	33,000	4,529	4,111	4,529	4,349
33,000					
33,000	33,050	4,536	4,119	4,536	4,356
33,050	33,100	4,544	4,126	4,544	4,364
33,100	33,150	4,551	4,134	4,551	4,371
33,150	33,200	4,559	4,141	4,559	4,379
33,200	33,250	4,566	4,149	4,566	4,386
33,250	33,300	4,574	4,156	4,574	4,394
33,300	33,350	4,581	4,164	4,581	4,401
33,350	33,400	4,589	4,171	4,589	4,409
33,400	33,450	4,596	4,179	4,596	4,416
33,450	33,500	4,604	4,186	4,604	4,424
33,500	33,550	4,611	4,194	4,611	4,431
33,550	33,600	4,619	4,201	4,619	4,439
33,600	33,650	4,626	4,209	4,626	4,446
33,650	33,700	4,634	4,216	4,634	4,454
33,700	33,750	4,641	4,224	4,641	4,461
33,750	33,800	4,649	4,231	4,649	4,469
33,800	33,850	4,656	4,239	4,656	4,476
33,850	33,900	4,664	4,246	4,664	4,484
33,900	33,950	4,671	4,254	4,671	4,491
33,950	34,000	4,681	4,261	4,681	4,499
34,000					
34,000	34,050	4,694	4,269	4,694	4,506
34,050	34,100	4,706	4,276	4,706	4,514
34,100	34,150	4,719	4,284	4,719	4,521
34,150	34,200	4,731	4,291	4,731	4,529
34,200	34,250	4,744	4,299	4,744	4,536
34,250	34,300	4,756	4,306	4,756	4,544
34,300	34,350	4,769	4,314	4,769	4,551
34,350	34,400	4,781	4,321	4,781	4,559
34,400	34,450	4,794	4,329	4,794	4,566
34,450	34,500	4,806	4,336	4,806	4,574
34,500	34,550	4,819	4,344	4,819	4,581
34,550	34,600	4,831	4,351	4,831	4,589
34,600	34,650	4,844	4,359	4,844	4,596
34,650	34,700	4,856	4,366	4,856	4,604
34,700	34,750	4,869	4,374	4,869	4,611
34,750	34,800	4,881	4,381	4,881	4,619
34,800	34,850	4,894	4,389	4,894	4,626
34,850	34,900	4,906	4,396	4,906	4,634
34,900	34,950	4,919	4,404	4,919	4,641
34,950	35,000	4,931	4,411	4,931	4,649
35,000					
35,000	35,050	4,944	4,419	4,944	4,656
35,050	35,100	4,956	4,426	4,956	4,664
35,100	35,150	4,969	4,434	4,969	4,671
35,150	35,200	4,981	4,441	4,981	4,679
35,200	35,250	4,994	4,449	4,994	4,686
35,250	35,300	5,006	4,456	5,006	4,694
35,300	35,350	5,019	4,464	5,019	4,701
35,350	35,400	5,031	4,471	5,031	4,709
35,400	35,450	5,044	4,479	5,044	4,716
35,450	35,500	5,056	4,486	5,056	4,724
35,500	35,550	5,069	4,494	5,069	4,731
35,550	35,600	5,081	4,501	5,081	4,739
35,600	35,650	5,094	4,509	5,094	4,746
35,650	35,700	5,106	4,516	5,106	4,754
35,700	35,750	5,119	4,524	5,119	4,761
35,750	35,800	5,131	4,531	5,131	4,769
35,800	35,850	5,144	4,539	5,144	4,776
35,850	35,900	5,156	4,546	5,156	4,784
35,900	35,950	5,169	4,554	5,169	4,791
35,950	36,000	5,181	4,561	5,181	4,799
36,000					
36,000	36,050	5,194	4,569	5,194	4,806
36,050	36,100	5,206	4,576	5,206	4,814
36,100	36,150	5,219	4,584	5,219	4,821
36,150	36,200	5,231	4,591	5,231	4,829
36,200	36,250	5,244	4,599	5,244	4,836
36,250	36,300	5,256	4,606	5,256	4,844
36,300	36,350	5,269	4,614	5,269	4,851
36,350	36,400	5,281	4,621	5,281	4,859
36,400	36,450	5,294	4,629	5,294	4,866
36,450	36,500	5,306	4,636	5,306	4,874
36,500	36,550	5,319	4,644	5,319	4,881
36,550	36,600	5,331	4,651	5,331	4,889
36,600	36,650	5,344	4,659	5,344	4,896
36,650	36,700	5,356	4,666	5,356	4,904
36,700	36,750	5,369	4,674	5,369	4,911
36,750	36,800	5,381	4,681	5,381	4,919
36,800	36,850	5,394	4,689	5,394	4,926
36,850	36,900	5,406	4,696	5,406	4,934
36,900	36,950	5,419	4,704	5,419	4,941
36,950	37,000	5,431	4,711	5,431	4,949
37,000					
37,000	37,050	5,444	4,719	5,444	4,956
37,050	37,100	5,456	4,726	5,456	4,964
37,100	37,150	5,469	4,734	5,469	4,971
37,150	37,200	5,481	4,741	5,481	4,979
37,200	37,250	5,494	4,749	5,494	4,986
37,250	37,300	5,506	4,756	5,506	4,994
37,300	37,350	5,519	4,764	5,519	5,001
37,350	37,400	5,531	4,771	5,531	5,009
37,400	37,450	5,544	4,779	5,544	5,016
37,450	37,500	5,556	4,786	5,556	5,024
37,500	37,550	5,569	4,794	5,569	5,031
37,550	37,600	5,581	4,801	5,581	5,039
37,600	37,650	5,594	4,809	5,594	5,046
37,650	37,700	5,606	4,816	5,606	5,054
37,700	37,750	5,619	4,824	5,619	5,061
37,750	37,800	5,631	4,831	5,631	5,069
37,800	37,850	5,644	4,839	5,644	5,076
37,850	37,900	5,656	4,846	5,656	5,084
37,900	37,950	5,669	4,854	5,669	5,091
37,950	38,000	5,681	4,861	5,681	5,099
38,000					
38,000	38,050	5,694	4,869	5,694	5,106
38,050	38,100	5,706	4,876	5,706	5,114
38,100	38,150	5,719	4,884	5,719	5,121
38,150	38,200	5,731	4,891	5,731	5,129
38,200	38,250	5,744	4,899	5,744	5,136
38,250	38,300	5,756	4,906	5,756	5,144
38,300	38,350	5,769	4,914	5,769	5,151
38,350	38,400	5,781	4,921	5,781	5,159
38,400	38,450	5,794	4,929	5,794	5,166
38,450	38,500	5,806	4,936	5,806	5,174
38,500	38,550	5,819	4,944	5,819	5,181
38,550	38,600	5,831	4,951	5,831	5,189
38,600	38,650	5,844	4,959	5,844	5,196
38,650	38,700	5,856	4,966	5,856	5,204
38,700	38,750	5,869	4,974	5,869	5,211
38,750	38,800	5,881	4,981	5,881	5,219
38,800	38,850	5,894	4,989	5,894	5,226
38,850	38,900	5,906	4,996	5,906	5,234
38,900	38,950	5,919	5,004	5,919	5,241
38,950	39,000	5,931	5,011	5,931	5,249
39,000					
39,000	39,050	5,944	5,019	5,944	5,256
39,050	39,100	5,956	5,026	5,956	5,264
39,100	39,150	5,969	5,034	5,969	5,271
39,150	39,200	5,981	5,041	5,981	5,279
39,200	39,250	5,994	5,049	5,994	5,286
39,250	39,300	6,006	5,056	6,006	5,294
39,300	39,350	6,019	5,064	6,019	5,301
39,350	39,400	6,031	5,071	6,031	5,309
39,400	39,450	6,044	5,079	6,044	5,316
39,450	39,500	6,056	5,086	6,056	5,324
39,500	39,550	6,069	5,094	6,069	5,331
39,550	39,600	6,081	5,101	6,081	5,339
39,600	39,650	6,094	5,109	6,094	5,346
39,650	39,700	6,106	5,116	6,106	5,354
39,700	39,750	6,119	5,124	6,119	5,361
39,750	39,800	6,131	5,131	6,131	5,369
39,800	39,850	6,144	5,139	6,144	5,376
39,850	39,900	6,156	5,146	6,156	5,384
39,900	39,950	6,169	5,154	6,169	5,391
39,950	40,000	6,181	5,161	6,181	5,399
40,000					
40,000	40,050	6,194	5,169	6,194	5,406
40,050	40,100	6,206	5,176	6,206	5,414
40,100	40,150	6,219	5,184	6,219	5,421
40,150	40,200	6,231	5,191	6,231	5,429
40,200	40,250	6,244	5,199	6,244	5,436
40,250	40,300	6,256	5,206	6,256	5,444
40,300	40,350	6,269	5,214	6,269	5,451
40,350	40,400	6,281	5,221	6,281	5,459
40,400	40,450	6,294	5,229	6,294	5,466
40,450	40,500	6,306	5,236	6,306	5,474
40,500	40,550	6,319	5,244	6,319	5,481
40,550	40,600	6,331	5,251	6,331	5,489
40,600	40,650	6,344	5,259	6,344	5,496
40,650	40,700	6,356	5,266	6,356	5,504
40,700	40,750	6,369	5,274	6,369	5,511
40,750	40,800	6,381	5,281	6,381	5,519
40,800	40,850	6,394	5,289	6,394	5,526
40,850	40,900	6,406	5,296	6,406	5,534
40,900	40,950	6,419	5,304	6,419	5,541
40,950	41,000	6,431	5,311	6,431	5,549

* This column must also be used by a qualifying widow(er).

2009 Tax Table—*Continued*

If line 43 (taxable income) is— At least	But less than	And you are— Single	Married filing jointly *	Married filing separately	Head of a household
		Your tax is—			
41,000					
41,000	41,050	6,444	5,319	6,444	5,556
41,050	41,100	6,456	5,326	6,456	5,564
41,100	41,150	6,469	5,334	6,469	5,571
41,150	41,200	6,481	5,341	6,481	5,579
41,200	41,250	6,494	5,349	6,494	5,586
41,250	41,300	6,506	5,356	6,506	5,594
41,300	41,350	6,519	5,364	6,519	5,601
41,350	41,400	6,531	5,371	6,531	5,609
41,400	41,450	6,544	5,379	6,544	5,616
41,450	41,500	6,556	5,386	6,556	5,624
41,500	41,550	6,569	5,394	6,569	5,631
41,550	41,600	6,581	5,401	6,581	5,639
41,600	41,650	6,594	5,409	6,594	5,646
41,650	41,700	6,606	5,416	6,606	5,654
41,700	41,750	6,619	5,424	6,619	5,661
41,750	41,800	6,631	5,431	6,631	5,669
41,800	41,850	6,644	5,439	6,644	5,676
41,850	41,900	6,656	5,446	6,656	5,684
41,900	41,950	6,669	5,454	6,669	5,691
41,950	42,000	6,681	5,461	6,681	5,699
42,000					
42,000	42,050	6,694	5,469	6,694	5,706
42,050	42,100	6,706	5,476	6,706	5,714
42,100	42,150	6,719	5,484	6,719	5,721
42,150	42,200	6,731	5,491	6,731	5,729
42,200	42,250	6,744	5,499	6,744	5,736
42,250	42,300	6,756	5,506	6,756	5,744
42,300	42,350	6,769	5,514	6,769	5,751
42,350	42,400	6,781	5,521	6,781	5,759
42,400	42,450	6,794	5,529	6,794	5,766
42,450	42,500	6,806	5,536	6,806	5,774
42,500	42,550	6,819	5,544	6,819	5,781
42,550	42,600	6,831	5,551	6,831	5,789
42,600	42,650	6,844	5,559	6,844	5,796
42,650	42,700	6,856	5,566	6,856	5,804
42,700	42,750	6,869	5,574	6,869	5,811
42,750	42,800	6,881	5,581	6,881	5,819
42,800	42,850	6,894	5,589	6,894	5,826
42,850	42,900	6,906	5,596	6,906	5,834
42,900	42,950	6,919	5,604	6,919	5,841
42,950	43,000	6,931	5,611	6,931	5,849
43,000					
43,000	43,050	6,944	5,619	6,944	5,856
43,050	43,100	6,956	5,626	6,956	5,864
43,100	43,150	6,969	5,634	6,969	5,871
43,150	43,200	6,981	5,641	6,981	5,879
43,200	43,250	6,994	5,649	6,994	5,886
43,250	43,300	7,006	5,656	7,006	5,894
43,300	43,350	7,019	5,664	7,019	5,901
43,350	43,400	7,031	5,671	7,031	5,909
43,400	43,450	7,044	5,679	7,044	5,916
43,450	43,500	7,056	5,686	7,056	5,924
43,500	43,550	7,069	5,694	7,069	5,931
43,550	43,600	7,081	5,701	7,081	5,939
43,600	43,650	7,094	5,709	7,094	5,946
43,650	43,700	7,106	5,716	7,106	5,954
43,700	43,750	7,119	5,724	7,119	5,961
43,750	43,800	7,131	5,731	7,131	5,969
43,800	43,850	7,144	5,739	7,144	5,976
43,850	43,900	7,156	5,746	7,156	5,984
43,900	43,950	7,169	5,754	7,169	5,991
43,950	44,000	7,181	5,761	7,181	5,999
44,000					
44,000	44,050	7,194	5,769	7,194	6,006
44,050	44,100	7,206	5,776	7,206	6,014
44,100	44,150	7,219	5,784	7,219	6,021
44,150	44,200	7,231	5,791	7,231	6,029
44,200	44,250	7,244	5,799	7,244	6,036
44,250	44,300	7,256	5,806	7,256	6,044
44,300	44,350	7,269	5,814	7,269	6,051
44,350	44,400	7,281	5,821	7,281	6,059
44,400	44,450	7,294	5,829	7,294	6,066
44,450	44,500	7,306	5,836	7,306	6,074
44,500	44,550	7,319	5,844	7,319	6,081
44,550	44,600	7,331	5,851	7,331	6,089
44,600	44,650	7,344	5,859	7,344	6,096
44,650	44,700	7,356	5,866	7,356	6,104
44,700	44,750	7,369	5,874	7,369	6,111
44,750	44,800	7,381	5,881	7,381	6,119
44,800	44,850	7,394	5,889	7,394	6,126
44,850	44,900	7,406	5,896	7,406	6,134
44,900	44,950	7,419	5,904	7,419	6,141
44,950	45,000	7,431	5,911	7,431	6,149
45,000					
45,000	45,050	7,444	5,919	7,444	6,156
45,050	45,100	7,456	5,926	7,456	6,164
45,100	45,150	7,469	5,934	7,469	6,171
45,150	45,200	7,481	5,941	7,481	6,179
45,200	45,250	7,494	5,949	7,494	6,186
45,250	45,300	7,506	5,956	7,506	6,194
45,300	45,350	7,519	5,964	7,519	6,201
45,350	45,400	7,531	5,971	7,531	6,209
45,400	45,450	7,544	5,979	7,544	6,216
45,450	45,500	7,556	5,986	7,556	6,224
45,500	45,550	7,569	5,994	7,569	6,234
45,550	45,600	7,581	6,001	7,581	6,246
45,600	45,650	7,594	6,009	7,594	6,259
45,650	45,700	7,606	6,016	7,606	6,271
45,700	45,750	7,619	6,024	7,619	6,284
45,750	45,800	7,631	6,031	7,631	6,296
45,800	45,850	7,644	6,039	7,644	6,309
45,850	45,900	7,656	6,046	7,656	6,321
45,900	45,950	7,669	6,054	7,669	6,334
45,950	46,000	7,681	6,061	7,681	6,346
46,000					
46,000	46,050	7,694	6,069	7,694	6,359
46,050	46,100	7,706	6,076	7,706	6,371
46,100	46,150	7,719	6,084	7,719	6,384
46,150	46,200	7,731	6,091	7,731	6,396
46,200	46,250	7,744	6,099	7,744	6,409
46,250	46,300	7,756	6,106	7,756	6,421
46,300	46,350	7,769	6,114	7,769	6,434
46,350	46,400	7,781	6,121	7,781	6,446
46,400	46,450	7,794	6,129	7,794	6,459
46,450	46,500	7,806	6,136	7,806	6,471
46,500	46,550	7,819	6,144	7,819	6,484
46,550	46,600	7,831	6,151	7,831	6,496
46,600	46,650	7,844	6,159	7,844	6,509
46,650	46,700	7,856	6,166	7,856	6,521
46,700	46,750	7,869	6,174	7,869	6,534
46,750	46,800	7,881	6,181	7,881	6,546
46,800	46,850	7,894	6,189	7,894	6,559
46,850	46,900	7,906	6,196	7,906	6,571
46,900	46,950	7,919	6,204	7,919	6,584
46,950	47,000	7,931	6,211	7,931	6,596
47,000					
47,000	47,050	7,944	6,219	7,944	6,609
47,050	47,100	7,956	6,226	7,956	6,621
47,100	47,150	7,969	6,234	7,969	6,634
47,150	47,200	7,981	6,241	7,981	6,646
47,200	47,250	7,994	6,249	7,994	6,659
47,250	47,300	8,006	6,256	8,006	6,671
47,300	47,350	8,019	6,264	8,019	6,684
47,350	47,400	8,031	6,271	8,031	6,696
47,400	47,450	8,044	6,279	8,044	6,709
47,450	47,500	8,056	6,286	8,056	6,721
47,500	47,550	8,069	6,294	8,069	6,734
47,550	47,600	8,081	6,301	8,081	6,746
47,600	47,650	8,094	6,309	8,094	6,759
47,650	47,700	8,106	6,316	8,106	6,771
47,700	47,750	8,119	6,324	8,119	6,784
47,750	47,800	8,131	6,331	8,131	6,796
47,800	47,850	8,144	6,339	8,144	6,809
47,850	47,900	8,156	6,346	8,156	6,821
47,900	47,950	8,169	6,354	8,169	6,834
47,950	48,000	8,181	6,361	8,181	6,846
48,000					
48,000	48,050	8,194	6,369	8,194	6,859
48,050	48,100	8,206	6,376	8,206	6,871
48,100	48,150	8,219	6,384	8,219	6,884
48,150	48,200	8,231	6,391	8,231	6,896
48,200	48,250	8,244	6,399	8,244	6,909
48,250	48,300	8,256	6,406	8,256	6,921
48,300	48,350	8,269	6,414	8,269	6,934
48,350	48,400	8,281	6,421	8,281	6,946
48,400	48,450	8,294	6,429	8,294	6,959
48,450	48,500	8,306	6,436	8,306	6,971
48,500	48,550	8,319	6,444	8,319	6,984
48,550	48,600	8,331	6,451	8,331	6,996
48,600	48,650	8,344	6,459	8,344	7,009
48,650	48,700	8,356	6,466	8,356	7,021
48,700	48,750	8,369	6,474	8,369	7,034
48,750	48,800	8,381	6,481	8,381	7,046
48,800	48,850	8,394	6,489	8,394	7,059
48,850	48,900	8,406	6,496	8,406	7,071
48,900	48,950	8,419	6,504	8,419	7,084
48,950	49,000	8,431	6,511	8,431	7,096
49,000					
49,000	49,050	8,444	6,519	8,444	7,109
49,050	49,100	8,456	6,526	8,456	7,121
49,100	49,150	8,469	6,534	8,469	7,134
49,150	49,200	8,481	6,541	8,481	7,146
49,200	49,250	8,494	6,549	8,494	7,159
49,250	49,300	8,506	6,556	8,506	7,171
49,300	49,350	8,519	6,564	8,519	7,184
49,350	49,400	8,531	6,571	8,531	7,196
49,400	49,450	8,544	6,579	8,544	7,209
49,450	49,500	8,556	6,586	8,556	7,221
49,500	49,550	8,569	6,594	8,569	7,234
49,550	49,600	8,581	6,601	8,581	7,246
49,600	49,650	8,594	6,609	8,594	7,259
49,650	49,700	8,606	6,616	8,606	7,271
49,700	49,750	8,619	6,624	8,619	7,284
49,750	49,800	8,631	6,631	8,631	7,296
49,800	49,850	8,644	6,639	8,644	7,309
49,850	49,900	8,656	6,646	8,656	7,321
49,900	49,950	8,669	6,654	8,669	7,334
49,950	50,000	8,681	6,661	8,681	7,346

* This column must also be used by a qualifying widow(er).

If line 43 (taxable income) is— At least	But less than	And you are— Single	Married filing jointly *	Married filing separately	Head of a household
		Your tax is—			
50,000					
50,000	50,050	8,694	6,669	8,694	7,359
50,050	50,100	8,706	6,676	8,706	7,371
50,100	50,150	8,719	6,684	8,719	7,384
50,150	50,200	8,731	6,691	8,731	7,396
50,200	50,250	8,744	6,699	8,744	7,409
50,250	50,300	8,756	6,706	8,756	7,421
50,300	50,350	8,769	6,714	8,769	7,434
50,350	50,400	8,781	6,721	8,781	7,446
50,400	50,450	8,794	6,729	8,794	7,459
50,450	50,500	8,806	6,736	8,806	7,471
50,500	50,550	8,819	6,744	8,819	7,484
50,550	50,600	8,831	6,751	8,831	7,496
50,600	50,650	8,844	6,759	8,844	7,509
50,650	50,700	8,856	6,766	8,856	7,521
50,700	50,750	8,869	6,774	8,869	7,534
50,750	50,800	8,881	6,781	8,881	7,546
50,800	50,850	8,894	6,789	8,894	7,559
50,850	50,900	8,906	6,796	8,906	7,571
50,900	50,950	8,919	6,804	8,919	7,584
50,950	51,000	8,931	6,811	8,931	7,596
51,000					
51,000	51,050	8,944	6,819	8,944	7,609
51,050	51,100	8,956	6,826	8,956	7,621
51,100	51,150	8,969	6,834	8,969	7,634
51,150	51,200	8,981	6,841	8,981	7,646
51,200	51,250	8,994	6,849	8,994	7,659
51,250	51,300	9,006	6,856	9,006	7,671
51,300	51,350	9,019	6,864	9,019	7,684
51,350	51,400	9,031	6,871	9,031	7,696
51,400	51,450	9,044	6,879	9,044	7,709
51,450	51,500	9,056	6,886	9,056	7,721
51,500	51,550	9,069	6,894	9,069	7,734
51,550	51,600	9,081	6,901	9,081	7,746
51,600	51,650	9,094	6,909	9,094	7,759
51,650	51,700	9,106	6,916	9,106	7,771
51,700	51,750	9,119	6,924	9,119	7,784
51,750	51,800	9,131	6,931	9,131	7,796
51,800	51,850	9,144	6,939	9,144	7,809
51,850	51,900	9,156	6,946	9,156	7,821
51,900	51,950	9,169	6,954	9,169	7,834
51,950	52,000	9,181	6,961	9,181	7,846
52,000					
52,000	52,050	9,194	6,969	9,194	7,859
52,050	52,100	9,206	6,976	9,206	7,871
52,100	52,150	9,219	6,984	9,219	7,884
52,150	52,200	9,231	6,991	9,231	7,896
52,200	52,250	9,244	6,999	9,244	7,909
52,250	52,300	9,256	7,006	9,256	7,921
52,300	52,350	9,269	7,014	9,269	7,934
52,350	52,400	9,281	7,021	9,281	7,946
52,400	52,450	9,294	7,029	9,294	7,959
52,450	52,500	9,306	7,036	9,306	7,971
52,500	52,550	9,319	7,044	9,319	7,984
52,550	52,600	9,331	7,051	9,331	7,996
52,600	52,650	9,344	7,059	9,344	8,009
52,650	52,700	9,356	7,066	9,356	8,021
52,700	52,750	9,369	7,074	9,369	8,034
52,750	52,800	9,381	7,081	9,381	8,046
52,800	52,850	9,394	7,089	9,394	8,059
52,850	52,900	9,406	7,096	9,406	8,071
52,900	52,950	9,419	7,104	9,419	8,084
52,950	53,000	9,431	7,111	9,431	8,096

If line 43 (taxable income) is— At least	But less than	And you are— Single	Married filing jointly *	Married filing separately	Head of a household
		Your tax is—			
53,000					
53,000	53,050	9,444	7,119	9,444	8,109
53,050	53,100	9,456	7,126	9,456	8,121
53,100	53,150	9,469	7,134	9,469	8,134
53,150	53,200	9,481	7,141	9,481	8,146
53,200	53,250	9,494	7,149	9,494	8,159
53,250	53,300	9,506	7,156	9,506	8,171
53,300	53,350	9,519	7,164	9,519	8,184
53,350	53,400	9,531	7,171	9,531	8,196
53,400	53,450	9,544	7,179	9,544	8,209
53,450	53,500	9,556	7,186	9,556	8,221
53,500	53,550	9,569	7,194	9,569	8,234
53,550	53,600	9,581	7,201	9,581	8,246
53,600	53,650	9,594	7,209	9,594	8,259
53,650	53,700	9,606	7,216	9,606	8,271
53,700	53,750	9,619	7,224	9,619	8,284
53,750	53,800	9,631	7,231	9,631	8,296
53,800	53,850	9,644	7,239	9,644	8,309
53,850	53,900	9,656	7,246	9,656	8,321
53,900	53,950	9,669	7,254	9,669	8,334
53,950	54,000	9,681	7,261	9,681	8,346
54,000					
54,000	54,050	9,694	7,269	9,694	8,359
54,050	54,100	9,706	7,276	9,706	8,371
54,100	54,150	9,719	7,284	9,719	8,384
54,150	54,200	9,731	7,291	9,731	8,396
54,200	54,250	9,744	7,299	9,744	8,409
54,250	54,300	9,756	7,306	9,756	8,421
54,300	54,350	9,769	7,314	9,769	8,434
54,350	54,400	9,781	7,321	9,781	8,446
54,400	54,450	9,794	7,329	9,794	8,459
54,450	54,500	9,806	7,336	9,806	8,471
54,500	54,550	9,819	7,344	9,819	8,484
54,550	54,600	9,831	7,351	9,831	8,496
54,600	54,650	9,844	7,359	9,844	8,509
54,650	54,700	9,856	7,366	9,856	8,521
54,700	54,750	9,869	7,374	9,869	8,534
54,750	54,800	9,881	7,381	9,881	8,546
54,800	54,850	9,894	7,389	9,894	8,559
54,850	54,900	9,906	7,396	9,906	8,571
54,900	54,950	9,919	7,404	9,919	8,584
54,950	55,000	9,931	7,411	9,931	8,596
55,000					
55,000	55,050	9,944	7,419	9,944	8,609
55,050	55,100	9,956	7,426	9,956	8,621
55,100	55,150	9,969	7,434	9,969	8,634
55,150	55,200	9,981	7,441	9,981	8,646
55,200	55,250	9,994	7,449	9,994	8,659
55,250	55,300	10,006	7,456	10,006	8,671
55,300	55,350	10,019	7,464	10,019	8,684
55,350	55,400	10,031	7,471	10,031	8,696
55,400	55,450	10,044	7,479	10,044	8,709
55,450	55,500	10,056	7,486	10,056	8,721
55,500	55,550	10,069	7,494	10,069	8,734
55,550	55,600	10,081	7,501	10,081	8,746
55,600	55,650	10,094	7,509	10,094	8,759
55,650	55,700	10,106	7,516	10,106	8,771
55,700	55,750	10,119	7,524	10,119	8,784
55,750	55,800	10,131	7,531	10,131	8,796
55,800	55,850	10,144	7,539	10,144	8,809
55,850	55,900	10,156	7,546	10,156	8,821
55,900	55,950	10,169	7,554	10,169	8,834
55,950	56,000	10,181	7,561	10,181	8,846

If line 43 (taxable income) is— At least	But less than	And you are— Single	Married filing jointly *	Married filing separately	Head of a household
		Your tax is—			
56,000					
56,000	56,050	10,194	7,569	10,194	8,859
56,050	56,100	10,206	7,576	10,206	8,871
56,100	56,150	10,219	7,584	10,219	8,884
56,150	56,200	10,231	7,591	10,231	8,896
56,200	56,250	10,244	7,599	10,244	8,909
56,250	56,300	10,256	7,606	10,256	8,921
56,300	56,350	10,269	7,614	10,269	8,934
56,350	56,400	10,281	7,621	10,281	8,946
56,400	56,450	10,294	7,629	10,294	8,959
56,450	56,500	10,306	7,636	10,306	8,971
56,500	56,550	10,319	7,644	10,319	8,984
56,550	56,600	10,331	7,651	10,331	8,996
56,600	56,650	10,344	7,659	10,344	9,009
56,650	56,700	10,356	7,666	10,356	9,021
56,700	56,750	10,369	7,674	10,369	9,034
56,750	56,800	10,381	7,681	10,381	9,046
56,800	56,850	10,394	7,689	10,394	9,059
56,850	56,900	10,406	7,696	10,406	9,071
56,900	56,950	10,419	7,704	10,419	9,084
56,950	57,000	10,431	7,711	10,431	9,096
57,000					
57,000	57,050	10,444	7,719	10,444	9,109
57,050	57,100	10,456	7,726	10,456	9,121
57,100	57,150	10,469	7,734	10,469	9,134
57,150	57,200	10,481	7,741	10,481	9,146
57,200	57,250	10,494	7,749	10,494	9,159
57,250	57,300	10,506	7,756	10,506	9,171
57,300	57,350	10,519	7,764	10,519	9,184
57,350	57,400	10,531	7,771	10,531	9,196
57,400	57,450	10,544	7,779	10,544	9,209
57,450	57,500	10,556	7,786	10,556	9,221
57,500	57,550	10,569	7,794	10,569	9,234
57,550	57,600	10,581	7,801	10,581	9,246
57,600	57,650	10,594	7,809	10,594	9,259
57,650	57,700	10,606	7,816	10,606	9,271
57,700	57,750	10,619	7,824	10,619	9,284
57,750	57,800	10,631	7,831	10,631	9,296
57,800	57,850	10,644	7,839	10,644	9,309
57,850	57,900	10,656	7,846	10,656	9,321
57,900	57,950	10,669	7,854	10,669	9,334
57,950	58,000	10,681	7,861	10,681	9,346
58,000					
58,000	58,050	10,694	7,869	10,694	9,359
58,050	58,100	10,706	7,876	10,706	9,371
58,100	58,150	10,719	7,884	10,719	9,384
58,150	58,200	10,731	7,891	10,731	9,396
58,200	58,250	10,744	7,899	10,744	9,409
58,250	58,300	10,756	7,906	10,756	9,421
58,300	58,350	10,769	7,914	10,769	9,434
58,350	58,400	10,781	7,921	10,781	9,446
58,400	58,450	10,794	7,929	10,794	9,459
58,450	58,500	10,806	7,936	10,806	9,471
58,500	58,550	10,819	7,944	10,819	9,484
58,550	58,600	10,831	7,951	10,831	9,496
58,600	58,650	10,844	7,959	10,844	9,509
58,650	58,700	10,856	7,966	10,856	9,521
58,700	58,750	10,869	7,974	10,869	9,534
58,750	58,800	10,881	7,981	10,881	9,546
58,800	58,850	10,894	7,989	10,894	9,559
58,850	58,900	10,906	7,996	10,906	9,571
58,900	58,950	10,919	8,004	10,919	9,584
58,950	59,000	10,931	8,011	10,931	9,596

* This column must also be used by a qualifying widow(er).

If line 43 (taxable income) is— At least	But less than	And you are— Single	Married filing jointly *	Married filing separately	Head of a household
		Your tax is—			
59,000					
59,000	59,050	10,944	8,019	10,944	9,609
59,050	59,100	10,956	8,026	10,956	9,621
59,100	59,150	10,969	8,034	10,969	9,634
59,150	59,200	10,981	8,041	10,981	9,646
59,200	59,250	10,994	8,049	10,994	9,659
59,250	59,300	11,006	8,056	11,006	9,671
59,300	59,350	11,019	8,064	11,019	9,684
59,350	59,400	11,031	8,071	11,031	9,696
59,400	59,450	11,044	8,079	11,044	9,709
59,450	59,500	11,056	8,086	11,056	9,721
59,500	59,550	11,069	8,094	11,069	9,734
59,550	59,600	11,081	8,101	11,081	9,746
59,600	59,650	11,094	8,109	11,094	9,759
59,650	59,700	11,106	8,116	11,106	9,771
59,700	59,750	11,119	8,124	11,119	9,784
59,750	59,800	11,131	8,131	11,131	9,796
59,800	59,850	11,144	8,139	11,144	9,809
59,850	59,900	11,156	8,146	11,156	9,821
59,900	59,950	11,169	8,154	11,169	9,834
59,950	60,000	11,181	8,161	11,181	9,846
60,000					
60,000	60,050	11,194	8,169	11,194	9,859
60,050	60,100	11,206	8,176	11,206	9,871
60,100	60,150	11,219	8,184	11,219	9,884
60,150	60,200	11,231	8,191	11,231	9,896
60,200	60,250	11,244	8,199	11,244	9,909
60,250	60,300	11,256	8,206	11,256	9,921
60,300	60,350	11,269	8,214	11,269	9,934
60,350	60,400	11,281	8,221	11,281	9,946
60,400	60,450	11,294	8,229	11,294	9,959
60,450	60,500	11,306	8,236	11,306	9,971
60,500	60,550	11,319	8,244	11,319	9,984
60,550	60,600	11,331	8,251	11,331	9,996
60,600	60,650	11,344	8,259	11,344	10,009
60,650	60,700	11,356	8,266	11,356	10,021
60,700	60,750	11,369	8,274	11,369	10,034
60,750	60,800	11,381	8,281	11,381	10,046
60,800	60,850	11,394	8,289	11,394	10,059
60,850	60,900	11,406	8,296	11,406	10,071
60,900	60,950	11,419	8,304	11,419	10,084
60,950	61,000	11,431	8,311	11,431	10,096
61,000					
61,000	61,050	11,444	8,319	11,444	10,109
61,050	61,100	11,456	8,326	11,456	10,121
61,100	61,150	11,469	8,334	11,469	10,134
61,150	61,200	11,481	8,341	11,481	10,146
61,200	61,250	11,494	8,349	11,494	10,159
61,250	61,300	11,506	8,356	11,506	10,171
61,300	61,350	11,519	8,364	11,519	10,184
61,350	61,400	11,531	8,371	11,531	10,196
61,400	61,450	11,544	8,379	11,544	10,209
61,450	61,500	11,556	8,386	11,556	10,221
61,500	61,550	11,569	8,394	11,569	10,234
61,550	61,600	11,581	8,401	11,581	10,246
61,600	61,650	11,594	8,409	11,594	10,259
61,650	61,700	11,606	8,416	11,606	10,271
61,700	61,750	11,619	8,424	11,619	10,284
61,750	61,800	11,631	8,431	11,631	10,296
61,800	61,850	11,644	8,439	11,644	10,309
61,850	61,900	11,656	8,446	11,656	10,321
61,900	61,950	11,669	8,454	11,669	10,334
61,950	62,000	11,681	8,461	11,681	10,346

If line 43 (taxable income) is— At least	But less than	And you are— Single	Married filing jointly *	Married filing separately	Head of a household
		Your tax is—			
62,000					
62,000	62,050	11,694	8,469	11,694	10,359
62,050	62,100	11,706	8,476	11,706	10,371
62,100	62,150	11,719	8,484	11,719	10,384
62,150	62,200	11,731	8,491	11,731	10,396
62,200	62,250	11,744	8,499	11,744	10,409
62,250	62,300	11,756	8,506	11,756	10,421
62,300	62,350	11,769	8,514	11,769	10,434
62,350	62,400	11,781	8,521	11,781	10,446
62,400	62,450	11,794	8,529	11,794	10,459
62,450	62,500	11,806	8,536	11,806	10,471
62,500	62,550	11,819	8,544	11,819	10,484
62,550	62,600	11,831	8,551	11,831	10,496
62,600	62,650	11,844	8,559	11,844	10,509
62,650	62,700	11,856	8,566	11,856	10,521
62,700	62,750	11,869	8,574	11,869	10,534
62,750	62,800	11,881	8,581	11,881	10,546
62,800	62,850	11,894	8,589	11,894	10,559
62,850	62,900	11,906	8,596	11,906	10,571
62,900	62,950	11,919	8,604	11,919	10,584
62,950	63,000	11,931	8,611	11,931	10,596
63,000					
63,000	63,050	11,944	8,619	11,944	10,609
63,050	63,100	11,956	8,626	11,956	10,621
63,100	63,150	11,969	8,634	11,969	10,634
63,150	63,200	11,981	8,641	11,981	10,646
63,200	63,250	11,994	8,649	11,994	10,659
63,250	63,300	12,006	8,656	12,006	10,671
63,300	63,350	12,019	8,664	12,019	10,684
63,350	63,400	12,031	8,671	12,031	10,696
63,400	63,450	12,044	8,679	12,044	10,709
63,450	63,500	12,056	8,686	12,056	10,721
63,500	63,550	12,069	8,694	12,069	10,734
63,550	63,600	12,081	8,701	12,081	10,746
63,600	63,650	12,094	8,709	12,094	10,759
63,650	63,700	12,106	8,716	12,106	10,771
63,700	63,750	12,119	8,724	12,119	10,784
63,750	63,800	12,131	8,731	12,131	10,796
63,800	63,850	12,144	8,739	12,144	10,809
63,850	63,900	12,156	8,746	12,156	10,821
63,900	63,950	12,169	8,754	12,169	10,834
63,950	64,000	12,181	8,761	12,181	10,846
64,000					
64,000	64,050	12,194	8,769	12,194	10,859
64,050	64,100	12,206	8,776	12,206	10,871
64,100	64,150	12,219	8,784	12,219	10,884
64,150	64,200	12,231	8,791	12,231	10,896
64,200	64,250	12,244	8,799	12,244	10,909
64,250	64,300	12,256	8,806	12,256	10,921
64,300	64,350	12,269	8,814	12,269	10,934
64,350	64,400	12,281	8,821	12,281	10,946
64,400	64,450	12,294	8,829	12,294	10,959
64,450	64,500	12,306	8,836	12,306	10,971
64,500	64,550	12,319	8,844	12,319	10,984
64,550	64,600	12,331	8,851	12,331	10,996
64,600	64,650	12,344	8,859	12,344	11,009
64,650	64,700	12,356	8,866	12,356	11,021
64,700	64,750	12,369	8,874	12,369	11,034
64,750	64,800	12,381	8,881	12,381	11,046
64,800	64,850	12,394	8,889	12,394	11,059
64,850	64,900	12,406	8,896	12,406	11,071
64,900	64,950	12,419	8,904	12,419	11,084
64,950	65,000	12,431	8,911	12,431	11,096

If line 43 (taxable income) is— At least	But less than	And you are— Single	Married filing jointly *	Married filing separately	Head of a household
		Your tax is—			
65,000					
65,000	65,050	12,444	8,919	12,444	11,109
65,050	65,100	12,456	8,926	12,456	11,121
65,100	65,150	12,469	8,934	12,469	11,134
65,150	65,200	12,481	8,941	12,481	11,146
65,200	65,250	12,494	8,949	12,494	11,159
65,250	65,300	12,506	8,956	12,506	11,171
65,300	65,350	12,519	8,964	12,519	11,184
65,350	65,400	12,531	8,971	12,531	11,196
65,400	65,450	12,544	8,979	12,544	11,209
65,450	65,500	12,556	8,986	12,556	11,221
65,500	65,550	12,569	8,994	12,569	11,234
65,550	65,600	12,581	9,001	12,581	11,246
65,600	65,650	12,594	9,009	12,594	11,259
65,650	65,700	12,606	9,016	12,606	11,271
65,700	65,750	12,619	9,024	12,619	11,284
65,750	65,800	12,631	9,031	12,631	11,296
65,800	65,850	12,644	9,039	12,644	11,309
65,850	65,900	12,656	9,046	12,656	11,321
65,900	65,950	12,669	9,054	12,669	11,334
65,950	66,000	12,681	9,061	12,681	11,346
66,000					
66,000	66,050	12,694	9,069	12,694	11,359
66,050	66,100	12,706	9,076	12,706	11,371
66,100	66,150	12,719	9,084	12,719	11,384
66,150	66,200	12,731	9,091	12,731	11,396
66,200	66,250	12,744	9,099	12,744	11,409
66,250	66,300	12,756	9,106	12,756	11,421
66,300	66,350	12,769	9,114	12,769	11,434
66,350	66,400	12,781	9,121	12,781	11,446
66,400	66,450	12,794	9,129	12,794	11,459
66,450	66,500	12,806	9,136	12,806	11,471
66,500	66,550	12,819	9,144	12,819	11,484
66,550	66,600	12,831	9,151	12,831	11,496
66,600	66,650	12,844	9,159	12,844	11,509
66,650	66,700	12,856	9,166	12,856	11,521
66,700	66,750	12,869	9,174	12,869	11,534
66,750	66,800	12,881	9,181	12,881	11,546
66,800	66,850	12,894	9,189	12,894	11,559
66,850	66,900	12,906	9,196	12,906	11,571
66,900	66,950	12,919	9,204	12,919	11,584
66,950	67,000	12,931	9,211	12,931	11,596
67,000					
67,000	67,050	12,944	9,219	12,944	11,609
67,050	67,100	12,956	9,226	12,956	11,621
67,100	67,150	12,969	9,234	12,969	11,634
67,150	67,200	12,981	9,241	12,981	11,646
67,200	67,250	12,994	9,249	12,994	11,659
67,250	67,300	13,006	9,256	13,006	11,671
67,300	67,350	13,019	9,264	13,019	11,684
67,350	67,400	13,031	9,271	13,031	11,696
67,400	67,450	13,044	9,279	13,044	11,709
67,450	67,500	13,056	9,286	13,056	11,721
67,500	67,550	13,069	9,294	13,069	11,734
67,550	67,600	13,081	9,301	13,081	11,746
67,600	67,650	13,094	9,309	13,094	11,759
67,650	67,700	13,106	9,316	13,106	11,771
67,700	67,750	13,119	9,324	13,119	11,784
67,750	67,800	13,131	9,331	13,131	11,796
67,800	67,850	13,144	9,339	13,144	11,809
67,850	67,900	13,156	9,346	13,156	11,821
67,900	67,950	13,169	9,356	13,169	11,834
67,950	68,000	13,181	9,369	13,181	11,846

* This column must also be used by a qualifying widow(er).

2009 Tax Table—*Continued*

If line 43 (taxable income) is—		And you are—			
At least	But less than	Single	Married filing jointly *	Married filing separately	Head of a household
		Your tax is—			
68,000					
68,000	68,050	13,194	9,381	13,194	11,859
68,050	68,100	13,206	9,394	13,206	11,871
68,100	68,150	13,219	9,406	13,219	11,884
68,150	68,200	13,231	9,419	13,231	11,896
68,200	68,250	13,244	9,431	13,244	11,909
68,250	68,300	13,256	9,444	13,256	11,921
68,300	68,350	13,269	9,456	13,269	11,934
68,350	68,400	13,281	9,469	13,281	11,946
68,400	68,450	13,294	9,481	13,294	11,959
68,450	68,500	13,306	9,494	13,306	11,971
68,500	68,550	13,319	9,506	13,319	11,984
68,550	68,600	13,331	9,519	13,333	11,996
68,600	68,650	13,344	9,531	13,347	12,009
68,650	68,700	13,356	9,544	13,361	12,021
68,700	68,750	13,369	9,556	13,375	12,034
68,750	68,800	13,381	9,569	13,389	12,046
68,800	68,850	13,394	9,581	13,403	12,059
68,850	68,900	13,406	9,594	13,417	12,071
68,900	68,950	13,419	9,606	13,431	12,084
68,950	69,000	13,431	9,619	13,445	12,096
69,000					
69,000	69,050	13,444	9,631	13,459	12,109
69,050	69,100	13,456	9,644	13,473	12,121
69,100	69,150	13,469	9,656	13,487	12,134
69,150	69,200	13,481	9,669	13,501	12,146
69,200	69,250	13,494	9,681	13,515	12,159
69,250	69,300	13,506	9,694	13,529	12,171
69,300	69,350	13,519	9,706	13,543	12,184
69,350	69,400	13,531	9,719	13,557	12,196
69,400	69,450	13,544	9,731	13,571	12,209
69,450	69,500	13,556	9,744	13,585	12,221
69,500	69,550	13,569	9,756	13,599	12,234
69,550	69,600	13,581	9,769	13,613	12,246
69,600	69,650	13,594	9,781	13,627	12,259
69,650	69,700	13,606	9,794	13,641	12,271
69,700	69,750	13,619	9,806	13,655	12,284
69,750	69,800	13,631	9,819	13,669	12,296
69,800	69,850	13,644	9,831	13,683	12,309
69,850	69,900	13,656	9,844	13,697	12,321
69,900	69,950	13,669	9,856	13,711	12,334
69,950	70,000	13,681	9,869	13,725	12,346
70,000					
70,000	70,050	13,694	9,881	13,739	12,359
70,050	70,100	13,706	9,894	13,753	12,371
70,100	70,150	13,719	9,906	13,767	12,384
70,150	70,200	13,731	9,919	13,781	12,396
70,200	70,250	13,744	9,931	13,795	12,409
70,250	70,300	13,756	9,944	13,809	12,421
70,300	70,350	13,769	9,956	13,823	12,434
70,350	70,400	13,781	9,969	13,837	12,446
70,400	70,450	13,794	9,981	13,851	12,459
70,450	70,500	13,806	9,994	13,865	12,471
70,500	70,550	13,819	10,006	13,879	12,484
70,550	70,600	13,831	10,019	13,893	12,496
70,600	70,650	13,844	10,031	13,907	12,509
70,650	70,700	13,856	10,044	13,921	12,521
70,700	70,750	13,869	10,056	13,935	12,534
70,750	70,800	13,881	10,069	13,949	12,546
70,800	70,850	13,894	10,081	13,963	12,559
70,850	70,900	13,906	10,094	13,977	12,571
70,900	70,950	13,919	10,106	13,991	12,584
70,950	71,000	13,931	10,119	14,005	12,596

If line 43 (taxable income) is—		And you are—			
At least	But less than	Single	Married filing jointly *	Married filing separately	Head of a household
		Your tax is—			
71,000					
71,000	71,050	13,944	10,131	14,019	12,609
71,050	71,100	13,956	10,144	14,033	12,621
71,100	71,150	13,969	10,156	14,047	12,634
71,150	71,200	13,981	10,169	14,061	12,646
71,200	71,250	13,994	10,181	14,075	12,659
71,250	71,300	14,006	10,194	14,089	12,671
71,300	71,350	14,019	10,206	14,103	12,684
71,350	71,400	14,031	10,219	14,117	12,696
71,400	71,450	14,044	10,231	14,131	12,709
71,450	71,500	14,056	10,244	14,145	12,721
71,500	71,550	14,069	10,256	14,159	12,734
71,550	71,600	14,081	10,269	14,173	12,746
71,600	71,650	14,094	10,281	14,187	12,759
71,650	71,700	14,106	10,294	14,201	12,771
71,700	71,750	14,119	10,306	14,215	12,784
71,750	71,800	14,131	10,319	14,229	12,796
71,800	71,850	14,144	10,331	14,243	12,809
71,850	71,900	14,156	10,344	14,257	12,821
71,900	71,950	14,169	10,356	14,271	12,834
71,950	72,000	14,181	10,369	14,285	12,846
72,000					
72,000	72,050	14,194	10,381	14,299	12,859
72,050	72,100	14,206	10,394	14,313	12,871
72,100	72,150	14,219	10,406	14,327	12,884
72,150	72,200	14,231	10,419	14,341	12,896
72,200	72,250	14,244	10,431	14,355	12,909
72,250	72,300	14,256	10,444	14,369	12,921
72,300	72,350	14,269	10,456	14,383	12,934
72,350	72,400	14,281	10,469	14,397	12,946
72,400	72,450	14,294	10,481	14,411	12,959
72,450	72,500	14,306	10,494	14,425	12,971
72,500	72,550	14,319	10,506	14,439	12,984
72,550	72,600	14,331	10,519	14,453	12,996
72,600	72,650	14,344	10,531	14,467	13,009
72,650	72,700	14,356	10,544	14,481	13,021
72,700	72,750	14,369	10,556	14,495	13,034
72,750	72,800	14,381	10,569	14,509	13,046
72,800	72,850	14,394	10,581	14,523	13,059
72,850	72,900	14,406	10,594	14,537	13,071
72,900	72,950	14,419	10,606	14,551	13,084
72,950	73,000	14,431	10,619	14,565	13,096
73,000					
73,000	73,050	14,444	10,631	14,579	13,109
73,050	73,100	14,456	10,644	14,593	13,121
73,100	73,150	14,469	10,656	14,607	13,134
73,150	73,200	14,481	10,669	14,621	13,146
73,200	73,250	14,494	10,681	14,635	13,159
73,250	73,300	14,506	10,694	14,649	13,171
73,300	73,350	14,519	10,706	14,663	13,184
73,350	73,400	14,531	10,719	14,677	13,196
73,400	73,450	14,544	10,731	14,691	13,209
73,450	73,500	14,556	10,744	14,705	13,221
73,500	73,550	14,569	10,756	14,719	13,234
73,550	73,600	14,581	10,769	14,733	13,246
73,600	73,650	14,594	10,781	14,747	13,259
73,650	73,700	14,606	10,794	14,761	13,271
73,700	73,750	14,619	10,806	14,775	13,284
73,750	73,800	14,631	10,819	14,789	13,296
73,800	73,850	14,644	10,831	14,803	13,309
73,850	73,900	14,656	10,844	14,817	13,321
73,900	73,950	14,669	10,856	14,831	13,334
73,950	74,000	14,681	10,869	14,845	13,346

If line 43 (taxable income) is—		And you are—			
At least	But less than	Single	Married filing jointly *	Married filing separately	Head of a household
		Your tax is—			
74,000					
74,000	74,050	14,694	10,881	14,859	13,359
74,050	74,100	14,706	10,894	14,873	13,371
74,100	74,150	14,719	10,906	14,887	13,384
74,150	74,200	14,731	10,919	14,901	13,396
74,200	74,250	14,744	10,931	14,915	13,409
74,250	74,300	14,756	10,944	14,929	13,421
74,300	74,350	14,769	10,956	14,943	13,434
74,350	74,400	14,781	10,969	14,957	13,446
74,400	74,450	14,794	10,981	14,971	13,459
74,450	74,500	14,806	10,994	14,985	13,471
74,500	74,550	14,819	11,006	14,999	13,484
74,550	74,600	14,831	11,019	15,013	13,496
74,600	74,650	14,844	11,031	15,027	13,509
74,650	74,700	14,856	11,044	15,041	13,521
74,700	74,750	14,869	11,056	15,055	13,534
74,750	74,800	14,881	11,069	15,069	13,546
74,800	74,850	14,894	11,081	15,083	13,559
74,850	74,900	14,906	11,094	15,097	13,571
74,900	74,950	14,919	11,106	15,111	13,584
74,950	75,000	14,931	11,119	15,125	13,596
75,000					
75,000	75,050	14,944	11,131	15,139	13,609
75,050	75,100	14,956	11,144	15,153	13,621
75,100	75,150	14,969	11,156	15,167	13,634
75,150	75,200	14,981	11,169	15,181	13,646
75,200	75,250	14,994	11,181	15,195	13,659
75,250	75,300	15,006	11,194	15,209	13,671
75,300	75,350	15,019	11,206	15,223	13,684
75,350	75,400	15,031	11,219	15,237	13,696
75,400	75,450	15,044	11,231	15,251	13,709
75,450	75,500	15,056	11,244	15,265	13,721
75,500	75,550	15,069	11,256	15,279	13,734
75,550	75,600	15,081	11,269	15,293	13,746
75,600	75,650	15,094	11,281	15,307	13,759
75,650	75,700	15,106	11,294	15,321	13,771
75,700	75,750	15,119	11,306	15,335	13,784
75,750	75,800	15,131	11,319	15,349	13,796
75,800	75,850	15,144	11,331	15,363	13,809
75,850	75,900	15,156	11,344	15,377	13,821
75,900	75,950	15,169	11,356	15,391	13,834
75,950	76,000	15,181	11,369	15,405	13,846
76,000					
76,000	76,050	15,194	11,381	15,419	13,859
76,050	76,100	15,206	11,394	15,433	13,871
76,100	76,150	15,219	11,406	15,447	13,884
76,150	76,200	15,231	11,419	15,461	13,896
76,200	76,250	15,244	11,431	15,475	13,909
76,250	76,300	15,256	11,444	15,489	13,921
76,300	76,350	15,269	11,456	15,503	13,934
76,350	76,400	15,281	11,469	15,517	13,946
76,400	76,450	15,294	11,481	15,531	13,959
76,450	76,500	15,306	11,494	15,545	13,971
76,500	76,550	15,319	11,506	15,559	13,984
76,550	76,600	15,331	11,519	15,573	13,996
76,600	76,650	15,344	11,531	15,587	14,009
76,650	76,700	15,356	11,544	15,601	14,021
76,700	76,750	15,369	11,556	15,615	14,034
76,750	76,800	15,381	11,569	15,629	14,046
76,800	76,850	15,394	11,581	15,643	14,059
76,850	76,900	15,406	11,594	15,657	14,071
76,900	76,950	15,419	11,606	15,671	14,084
76,950	77,000	15,431	11,619	15,685	14,096

* This column must also be used by a qualifying widow(er).

2009 Tax Table—*Continued*

If line 43 (taxable income) is—		And you are—			
At least	But less than	Single	Married filing jointly *	Married filing separately	Head of a household
		Your tax is—			
77,000					
77,000	77,050	15,444	11,631	15,699	14,109
77,050	77,100	15,456	11,644	15,713	14,121
77,100	77,150	15,469	11,656	15,727	14,134
77,150	77,200	15,481	11,669	15,741	14,146
77,200	77,250	15,494	11,681	15,755	14,159
77,250	77,300	15,506	11,694	15,769	14,171
77,300	77,350	15,519	11,706	15,783	14,184
77,350	77,400	15,531	11,719	15,797	14,196
77,400	77,450	15,544	11,731	15,811	14,209
77,450	77,500	15,556	11,744	15,825	14,221
77,500	77,550	15,569	11,756	15,839	14,234
77,550	77,600	15,581	11,769	15,853	14,246
77,600	77,650	15,594	11,781	15,867	14,259
77,650	77,700	15,606	11,794	15,881	14,271
77,700	77,750	15,619	11,806	15,895	14,284
77,750	77,800	15,631	11,819	15,909	14,296
77,800	77,850	15,644	11,831	15,923	14,309
77,850	77,900	15,656	11,844	15,937	14,321
77,900	77,950	15,669	11,856	15,951	14,334
77,950	78,000	15,681	11,869	15,965	14,346
78,000					
78,000	78,050	15,694	11,881	15,979	14,359
78,050	78,100	15,706	11,894	15,993	14,371
78,100	78,150	15,719	11,906	16,007	14,384
78,150	78,200	15,731	11,919	16,021	14,396
78,200	78,250	15,744	11,931	16,035	14,409
78,250	78,300	15,756	11,944	16,049	14,421
78,300	78,350	15,769	11,956	16,063	14,434
78,350	78,400	15,781	11,969	16,077	14,446
78,400	78,450	15,794	11,981	16,091	14,459
78,450	78,500	15,806	11,994	16,105	14,471
78,500	78,550	15,819	12,006	16,119	14,484
78,550	78,600	15,831	12,019	16,133	14,496
78,600	78,650	15,844	12,031	16,147	14,509
78,650	78,700	15,856	12,044	16,161	14,521
78,700	78,750	15,869	12,056	16,175	14,534
78,750	78,800	15,881	12,069	16,189	14,546
78,800	78,850	15,894	12,081	16,203	14,559
78,850	78,900	15,906	12,094	16,217	14,571
78,900	78,950	15,919	12,106	16,231	14,584
78,950	79,000	15,931	12,119	16,245	14,596
79,000					
79,000	79,050	15,944	12,131	16,259	14,609
79,050	79,100	15,956	12,144	16,273	14,621
79,100	79,150	15,969	12,156	16,287	14,634
79,150	79,200	15,981	12,169	16,301	14,646
79,200	79,250	15,994	12,181	16,315	14,659
79,250	79,300	16,006	12,194	16,329	14,671
79,300	79,350	16,019	12,206	16,343	14,684
79,350	79,400	16,031	12,219	16,357	14,696
79,400	79,450	16,044	12,231	16,371	14,709
79,450	79,500	16,056	12,244	16,385	14,721
79,500	79,550	16,069	12,256	16,399	14,734
79,550	79,600	16,081	12,269	16,413	14,746
79,600	79,650	16,094	12,281	16,427	14,759
79,650	79,700	16,106	12,294	16,441	14,771
79,700	79,750	16,119	12,306	16,455	14,784
79,750	79,800	16,131	12,319	16,469	14,796
79,800	79,850	16,144	12,331	16,483	14,809
79,850	79,900	16,156	12,344	16,497	14,821
79,900	79,950	16,169	12,356	16,511	14,834
79,950	80,000	16,181	12,369	16,525	14,846

If line 43 (taxable income) is—		And you are—			
At least	But less than	Single	Married filing jointly *	Married filing separately	Head of a household
		Your tax is—			
80,000					
80,000	80,050	16,194	12,381	16,539	14,859
80,050	80,100	16,206	12,394	16,553	14,871
80,100	80,150	16,219	12,406	16,567	14,884
80,150	80,200	16,231	12,419	16,581	14,896
80,200	80,250	16,244	12,431	16,595	14,909
80,250	80,300	16,256	12,444	16,609	14,921
80,300	80,350	16,269	12,456	16,623	14,934
80,350	80,400	16,281	12,469	16,637	14,946
80,400	80,450	16,294	12,481	16,651	14,959
80,450	80,500	16,306	12,494	16,665	14,971
80,500	80,550	16,319	12,506	16,679	14,984
80,550	80,600	16,331	12,519	16,693	14,996
80,600	80,650	16,344	12,531	16,707	15,009
80,650	80,700	16,356	12,544	16,721	15,021
80,700	80,750	16,369	12,556	16,735	15,034
80,750	80,800	16,381	12,569	16,749	15,046
80,800	80,850	16,394	12,581	16,763	15,059
80,850	80,900	16,406	12,594	16,777	15,071
80,900	80,950	16,419	12,606	16,791	15,084
80,950	81,000	16,431	12,619	16,805	15,096
81,000					
81,000	81,050	16,444	12,631	16,819	15,109
81,050	81,100	16,456	12,644	16,833	15,121
81,100	81,150	16,469	12,656	16,847	15,134
81,150	81,200	16,481	12,669	16,861	15,146
81,200	81,250	16,494	12,681	16,875	15,159
81,250	81,300	16,506	12,694	16,889	15,171
81,300	81,350	16,519	12,706	16,903	15,184
81,350	81,400	16,531	12,719	16,917	15,196
81,400	81,450	16,544	12,731	16,931	15,209
81,450	81,500	16,556	12,744	16,945	15,221
81,500	81,550	16,569	12,756	16,959	15,234
81,550	81,600	16,581	12,769	16,973	15,246
81,600	81,650	16,594	12,781	16,987	15,259
81,650	81,700	16,606	12,794	17,001	15,271
81,700	81,750	16,619	12,806	17,015	15,284
81,750	81,800	16,631	12,819	17,029	15,296
81,800	81,850	16,644	12,831	17,043	15,309
81,850	81,900	16,656	12,844	17,057	15,321
81,900	81,950	16,669	12,856	17,071	15,334
81,950	82,000	16,681	12,869	17,085	15,346
82,000					
82,000	82,050	16,694	12,881	17,099	15,359
82,050	82,100	16,706	12,894	17,113	15,371
82,100	82,150	16,719	12,906	17,127	15,384
82,150	82,200	16,731	12,919	17,141	15,396
82,200	82,250	16,744	12,931	17,155	15,409
82,250	82,300	16,757	12,944	17,169	15,421
82,300	82,350	16,771	12,956	17,183	15,434
82,350	82,400	16,785	12,969	17,197	15,446
82,400	82,450	16,799	12,981	17,211	15,459
82,450	82,500	16,813	12,994	17,225	15,471
82,500	82,550	16,827	13,006	17,239	15,484
82,550	82,600	16,841	13,019	17,253	15,496
82,600	82,650	16,855	13,031	17,267	15,509
82,650	82,700	16,869	13,044	17,281	15,521
82,700	82,750	16,883	13,056	17,295	15,534
82,750	82,800	16,897	13,069	17,309	15,546
82,800	82,850	16,911	13,081	17,323	15,559
82,850	82,900	16,925	13,094	17,337	15,571
82,900	82,950	16,939	13,106	17,351	15,584
82,950	83,000	16,953	13,119	17,365	15,596

If line 43 (taxable income) is—		And you are—			
At least	But less than	Single	Married filing jointly *	Married filing separately	Head of a household
		Your tax is—			
83,000					
83,000	83,050	16,967	13,131	17,379	15,609
83,050	83,100	16,981	13,144	17,393	15,621
83,100	83,150	16,995	13,156	17,407	15,634
83,150	83,200	17,009	13,169	17,421	15,646
83,200	83,250	17,023	13,181	17,435	15,659
83,250	83,300	17,037	13,194	17,449	15,671
83,300	83,350	17,051	13,206	17,463	15,684
83,350	83,400	17,065	13,219	17,477	15,696
83,400	83,450	17,079	13,231	17,491	15,709
83,450	83,500	17,093	13,244	17,505	15,721
83,500	83,550	17,107	13,256	17,519	15,734
83,550	83,600	17,121	13,269	17,533	15,746
83,600	83,650	17,135	13,281	17,547	15,759
83,650	83,700	17,149	13,294	17,561	15,771
83,700	83,750	17,163	13,306	17,575	15,784
83,750	83,800	17,177	13,319	17,589	15,796
83,800	83,850	17,191	13,331	17,603	15,809
83,850	83,900	17,205	13,344	17,617	15,821
83,900	83,950	17,219	13,356	17,631	15,834
83,950	84,000	17,233	13,369	17,645	15,846
84,000					
84,000	84,050	17,247	13,381	17,659	15,859
84,050	84,100	17,261	13,394	17,673	15,871
84,100	84,150	17,275	13,406	17,687	15,884
84,150	84,200	17,289	13,419	17,701	15,896
84,200	84,250	17,303	13,431	17,715	15,909
84,250	84,300	17,317	13,444	17,729	15,921
84,300	84,350	17,331	13,456	17,743	15,934
84,350	84,400	17,345	13,469	17,757	15,946
84,400	84,450	17,359	13,481	17,771	15,959
84,450	84,500	17,373	13,494	17,785	15,971
84,500	84,550	17,387	13,506	17,799	15,984
84,550	84,600	17,401	13,519	17,813	15,996
84,600	84,650	17,415	13,531	17,827	16,009
84,650	84,700	17,429	13,544	17,841	16,021
84,700	84,750	17,443	13,556	17,855	16,034
84,750	84,800	17,457	13,569	17,869	16,046
84,800	84,850	17,471	13,581	17,883	16,059
84,850	84,900	17,485	13,594	17,897	16,071
84,900	84,950	17,499	13,606	17,911	16,084
84,950	85,000	17,513	13,619	17,925	16,096
85,000					
85,000	85,050	17,527	13,631	17,939	16,109
85,050	85,100	17,541	13,644	17,953	16,121
85,100	85,150	17,555	13,656	17,967	16,134
85,150	85,200	17,569	13,669	17,981	16,146
85,200	85,250	17,583	13,681	17,995	16,159
85,250	85,300	17,597	13,694	18,009	16,171
85,300	85,350	17,611	13,706	18,023	16,184
85,350	85,400	17,625	13,719	18,037	16,196
85,400	85,450	17,639	13,731	18,051	16,209
85,450	85,500	17,653	13,744	18,065	16,221
85,500	85,550	17,667	13,756	18,079	16,234
85,550	85,600	17,681	13,769	18,093	16,246
85,600	85,650	17,695	13,781	18,107	16,259
85,650	85,700	17,709	13,794	18,121	16,271
85,700	85,750	17,723	13,806	18,135	16,284
85,750	85,800	17,737	13,819	18,149	16,296
85,800	85,850	17,751	13,831	18,163	16,309
85,850	85,900	17,765	13,844	18,177	16,321
85,900	85,950	17,779	13,856	18,191	16,334
85,950	86,000	17,793	13,869	18,205	16,346

* This column must also be used by a qualifying widow(er).

2009 Tax Table—*Continued*

If line 43 (taxable income) is—		And you are—			
At least	But less than	Single	Married filing jointly *	Married filing sepa-rately	Head of a house-hold
		Your tax is—			
86,000					
86,000	86,050	17,807	13,881	18,219	16,359
86,050	86,100	17,821	13,894	18,233	16,371
86,100	86,150	17,835	13,906	18,247	16,384
86,150	86,200	17,849	13,919	18,261	16,396
86,200	86,250	17,863	13,931	18,275	16,409
86,250	86,300	17,877	13,944	18,289	16,421
86,300	86,350	17,891	13,956	18,303	16,434
86,350	86,400	17,905	13,969	18,317	16,446
86,400	86,450	17,919	13,981	18,331	16,459
86,450	86,500	17,933	13,994	18,345	16,471
86,500	86,550	17,947	14,006	18,359	16,484
86,550	86,600	17,961	14,019	18,373	16,496
86,600	86,650	17,975	14,031	18,387	16,509
86,650	86,700	17,989	14,044	18,401	16,521
86,700	86,750	18,003	14,056	18,415	16,534
86,750	86,800	18,017	14,069	18,429	16,546
86,800	86,850	18,031	14,081	18,443	16,559
86,850	86,900	18,045	14,094	18,457	16,571
86,900	86,950	18,059	14,106	18,471	16,584
86,950	87,000	18,073	14,119	18,485	16,596
87,000					
87,000	87,050	18,087	14,131	18,499	16,609
87,050	87,100	18,101	14,144	18,513	16,621
87,100	87,150	18,115	14,156	18,527	16,634
87,150	87,200	18,129	14,169	18,541	16,646
87,200	87,250	18,143	14,181	18,555	16,659
87,250	87,300	18,157	14,194	18,569	16,671
87,300	87,350	18,171	14,206	18,583	16,684
87,350	87,400	18,185	14,219	18,597	16,696
87,400	87,450	18,199	14,231	18,611	16,709
87,450	87,500	18,213	14,244	18,625	16,721
87,500	87,550	18,227	14,256	18,639	16,734
87,550	87,600	18,241	14,269	18,653	16,746
87,600	87,650	18,255	14,281	18,667	16,759
87,650	87,700	18,269	14,294	18,681	16,771
87,700	87,750	18,283	14,306	18,695	16,784
87,750	87,800	18,297	14,319	18,709	16,796
87,800	87,850	18,311	14,331	18,723	16,809
87,850	87,900	18,325	14,344	18,737	16,821
87,900	87,950	18,339	14,356	18,751	16,834
87,950	88,000	18,353	14,369	18,765	16,846
88,000					
88,000	88,050	18,367	14,381	18,779	16,859
88,050	88,100	18,381	14,394	18,793	16,871
88,100	88,150	18,395	14,406	18,807	16,884
88,150	88,200	18,409	14,419	18,821	16,896
88,200	88,250	18,423	14,431	18,835	16,909
88,250	88,300	18,437	14,444	18,849	16,921
88,300	88,350	18,451	14,456	18,863	16,934
88,350	88,400	18,465	14,469	18,877	16,946
88,400	88,450	18,479	14,481	18,891	16,959
88,450	88,500	18,493	14,494	18,905	16,971
88,500	88,550	18,507	14,506	18,919	16,984
88,550	88,600	18,521	14,519	18,933	16,996
88,600	88,650	18,535	14,531	18,947	17,009
88,650	88,700	18,549	14,544	18,961	17,021
88,700	88,750	18,563	14,556	18,975	17,034
88,750	88,800	18,577	14,569	18,989	17,046
88,800	88,850	18,591	14,581	19,003	17,059
88,850	88,900	18,605	14,594	19,017	17,071
88,900	88,950	18,619	14,606	19,031	17,084
88,950	89,000	18,633	14,619	19,045	17,096
89,000					
89,000	89,050	18,647	14,631	19,059	17,109
89,050	89,100	18,661	14,644	19,073	17,121
89,100	89,150	18,675	14,656	19,087	17,134
89,150	89,200	18,689	14,669	19,101	17,146
89,200	89,250	18,703	14,681	19,115	17,159
89,250	89,300	18,717	14,694	19,129	17,171
89,300	89,350	18,731	14,706	19,143	17,184
89,350	89,400	18,745	14,719	19,157	17,196
89,400	89,450	18,759	14,731	19,171	17,209
89,450	89,500	18,773	14,744	19,185	17,221
89,500	89,550	18,787	14,756	19,199	17,234
89,550	89,600	18,801	14,769	19,213	17,246
89,600	89,650	18,815	14,781	19,227	17,259
89,650	89,700	18,829	14,794	19,241	17,271
89,700	89,750	18,843	14,806	19,255	17,284
89,750	89,800	18,857	14,819	19,269	17,296
89,800	89,850	18,871	14,831	19,283	17,309
89,850	89,900	18,885	14,844	19,297	17,321
89,900	89,950	18,899	14,856	19,311	17,334
89,950	90,000	18,913	14,869	19,325	17,346
90,000					
90,000	90,050	18,927	14,881	19,339	17,359
90,050	90,100	18,941	14,894	19,353	17,371
90,100	90,150	18,955	14,906	19,367	17,384
90,150	90,200	18,969	14,919	19,381	17,396
90,200	90,250	18,983	14,931	19,395	17,409
90,250	90,300	18,997	14,944	19,409	17,421
90,300	90,350	19,011	14,956	19,423	17,434
90,350	90,400	19,025	14,969	19,437	17,446
90,400	90,450	19,039	14,981	19,451	17,459
90,450	90,500	19,053	14,994	19,465	17,471
90,500	90,550	19,067	15,006	19,479	17,484
90,550	90,600	19,081	15,019	19,493	17,496
90,600	90,650	19,095	15,031	19,507	17,509
90,650	90,700	19,109	15,044	19,521	17,521
90,700	90,750	19,123	15,056	19,535	17,534
90,750	90,800	19,137	15,069	19,549	17,546
90,800	90,850	19,151	15,081	19,563	17,559
90,850	90,900	19,165	15,094	19,577	17,571
90,900	90,950	19,179	15,106	19,591	17,584
90,950	91,000	19,193	15,119	19,605	17,596
91,000					
91,000	91,050	19,207	15,131	19,619	17,609
91,050	91,100	19,221	15,144	19,633	17,621
91,100	91,150	19,235	15,156	19,647	17,634
91,150	91,200	19,249	15,169	19,661	17,646
91,200	91,250	19,263	15,181	19,675	17,659
91,250	91,300	19,277	15,194	19,689	17,671
91,300	91,350	19,291	15,206	19,703	17,684
91,350	91,400	19,305	15,219	19,717	17,696
91,400	91,450	19,319	15,231	19,731	17,709
91,450	91,500	19,333	15,244	19,745	17,721
91,500	91,550	19,347	15,256	19,759	17,734
91,550	91,600	19,361	15,269	19,773	17,746
91,600	91,650	19,375	15,281	19,787	17,759
91,650	91,700	19,389	15,294	19,801	17,771
91,700	91,750	19,403	15,306	19,815	17,784
91,750	91,800	19,417	15,319	19,829	17,796
91,800	91,850	19,431	15,331	19,843	17,809
91,850	91,900	19,445	15,344	19,857	17,821
91,900	91,950	19,459	15,356	19,871	17,834
91,950	92,000	19,473	15,369	19,885	17,846
92,000					
92,000	92,050	19,487	15,381	19,899	17,859
92,050	92,100	19,501	15,394	19,913	17,871
92,100	92,150	19,515	15,406	19,927	17,884
92,150	92,200	19,529	15,419	19,941	17,896
92,200	92,250	19,543	15,431	19,955	17,909
92,250	92,300	19,557	15,444	19,969	17,921
92,300	92,350	19,571	15,456	19,983	17,934
92,350	92,400	19,585	15,469	19,997	17,946
92,400	92,450	19,599	15,481	20,011	17,959
92,450	92,500	19,613	15,494	20,025	17,971
92,500	92,550	19,627	15,506	20,039	17,984
92,550	92,600	19,641	15,519	20,053	17,996
92,600	92,650	19,655	15,531	20,067	18,009
92,650	92,700	19,669	15,544	20,081	18,021
92,700	92,750	19,683	15,556	20,095	18,034
92,750	92,800	19,697	15,569	20,109	18,046
92,800	92,850	19,711	15,581	20,123	18,059
92,850	92,900	19,725	15,594	20,137	18,071
92,900	92,950	19,739	15,606	20,151	18,084
92,950	93,000	19,753	15,619	20,165	18,096
93,000					
93,000	93,050	19,767	15,631	20,179	18,109
93,050	93,100	19,781	15,644	20,193	18,121
93,100	93,150	19,795	15,656	20,207	18,134
93,150	93,200	19,809	15,669	20,221	18,146
93,200	93,250	19,823	15,681	20,235	18,159
93,250	93,300	19,837	15,694	20,249	18,171
93,300	93,350	19,851	15,706	20,263	18,184
93,350	93,400	19,865	15,719	20,277	18,196
93,400	93,450	19,879	15,731	20,291	18,209
93,450	93,500	19,893	15,744	20,305	18,221
93,500	93,550	19,907	15,756	20,319	18,234
93,550	93,600	19,921	15,769	20,333	18,246
93,600	93,650	19,935	15,781	20,347	18,259
93,650	93,700	19,949	15,794	20,361	18,271
93,700	93,750	19,963	15,806	20,375	18,284
93,750	93,800	19,977	15,819	20,389	18,296
93,800	93,850	19,991	15,831	20,403	18,309
93,850	93,900	20,005	15,844	20,417	18,321
93,900	93,950	20,019	15,856	20,431	18,334
93,950	94,000	20,033	15,869	20,445	18,346
94,000					
94,000	94,050	20,047	15,881	20,459	18,359
94,050	94,100	20,061	15,894	20,473	18,371
94,100	94,150	20,075	15,906	20,487	18,384
94,150	94,200	20,089	15,919	20,501	18,396
94,200	94,250	20,103	15,931	20,515	18,409
94,250	94,300	20,117	15,944	20,529	18,421
94,300	94,350	20,131	15,956	20,543	18,434
94,350	94,400	20,145	15,969	20,557	18,446
94,400	94,450	20,159	15,981	20,571	18,459
94,450	94,500	20,173	15,994	20,585	18,471
94,500	94,550	20,187	16,006	20,599	18,484
94,550	94,600	20,201	16,019	20,613	18,496
94,600	94,650	20,215	16,031	20,627	18,509
94,650	94,700	20,229	16,044	20,641	18,521
94,700	94,750	20,243	16,056	20,655	18,534
94,750	94,800	20,257	16,069	20,669	18,546
94,800	94,850	20,271	16,081	20,683	18,559
94,850	94,900	20,285	16,094	20,697	18,571
94,900	94,950	20,299	16,106	20,711	18,584
94,950	95,000	20,313	16,119	20,725	18,596
95,000					
95,000	95,050	20,327	16,131	20,739	18,609
95,050	95,100	20,341	16,144	20,753	18,621
95,100	95,150	20,355	16,156	20,767	18,634
95,150	95,200	20,369	16,169	20,781	18,646
95,200	95,250	20,383	16,181	20,795	18,659
95,250	95,300	20,397	16,194	20,809	18,671
95,300	95,350	20,411	16,206	20,823	18,684
95,350	95,400	20,425	16,219	20,837	18,696
95,400	95,450	20,439	16,231	20,851	18,709
95,450	95,500	20,453	16,244	20,865	18,721
95,500	95,550	20,467	16,256	20,879	18,734
95,550	95,600	20,481	16,269	20,893	18,746
95,600	95,650	20,495	16,281	20,907	18,759
95,650	95,700	20,509	16,294	20,921	18,771
95,700	95,750	20,523	16,306	20,935	18,784
95,750	95,800	20,537	16,319	20,949	18,796
95,800	95,850	20,551	16,331	20,963	18,809
95,850	95,900	20,565	16,344	20,977	18,821
95,900	95,950	20,579	16,356	20,991	18,834
95,950	96,000	20,593	16,369	21,005	18,846
96,000					
96,000	96,050	20,607	16,381	21,019	18,859
96,050	96,100	20,621	16,394	21,033	18,871
96,100	96,150	20,635	16,406	21,047	18,884
96,150	96,200	20,649	16,419	21,061	18,896
96,200	96,250	20,663	16,431	21,075	18,909
96,250	96,300	20,677	16,444	21,089	18,921
96,300	96,350	20,691	16,456	21,103	18,934
96,350	96,400	20,705	16,469	21,117	18,946
96,400	96,450	20,719	16,481	21,131	18,959
96,450	96,500	20,733	16,494	21,145	18,971
96,500	96,550	20,747	16,506	21,159	18,984
96,550	96,600	20,761	16,519	21,173	18,996
96,600	96,650	20,775	16,531	21,187	19,009
96,650	96,700	20,789	16,544	21,201	19,021
96,700	96,750	20,803	16,556	21,215	19,034
96,750	96,800	20,817	16,569	21,229	19,046
96,800	96,850	20,831	16,581	21,243	19,059
96,850	96,900	20,845	16,594	21,257	19,071
96,900	96,950	20,859	16,606	21,271	19,084
96,950	97,000	20,873	16,619	21,285	19,096
97,000					
97,000	97,050	20,887	16,631	21,299	19,109
97,050	97,100	20,901	16,644	21,313	19,121
97,100	97,150	20,915	16,656	21,327	19,134
97,150	97,200	20,929	16,669	21,341	19,146
97,200	97,250	20,943	16,681	21,355	19,159
97,250	97,300	20,957	16,694	21,369	19,171
97,300	97,350	20,971	16,706	21,383	19,184
97,350	97,400	20,985	16,719	21,397	19,196
97,400	97,450	20,999	16,731	21,411	19,209
97,450	97,500	21,013	16,744	21,425	19,221
97,500	97,550	21,027	16,756	21,439	19,234
97,550	97,600	21,041	16,769	21,453	19,246
97,600	97,650	21,055	16,781	21,467	19,259
97,650	97,700	21,069	16,794	21,481	19,271
97,700	97,750	21,083	16,806	21,495	19,284
97,750	97,800	21,097	16,819	21,509	19,296
97,800	97,850	21,111	16,831	21,523	19,309
97,850	97,900	21,125	16,844	21,537	19,321
97,900	97,950	21,139	16,856	21,551	19,334
97,950	98,000	21,153	16,869	21,565	19,346
98,000					
98,000	98,050	21,167	16,881	21,579	19,359
98,050	98,100	21,181	16,894	21,593	19,371
98,100	98,150	21,195	16,906	21,607	19,384
98,150	98,200	21,209	16,919	21,621	19,396
98,200	98,250	21,223	16,931	21,635	19,409
98,250	98,300	21,237	16,944	21,649	19,421
98,300	98,350	21,251	16,956	21,663	19,434
98,350	98,400	21,265	16,969	21,677	19,446
98,400	98,450	21,279	16,981	21,691	19,459
98,450	98,500	21,293	16,994	21,705	19,471
98,500	98,550	21,307	17,006	21,719	19,484
98,550	98,600	21,321	17,019	21,733	19,496
98,600	98,650	21,335	17,031	21,747	19,509
98,650	98,700	21,349	17,044	21,761	19,521
98,700	98,750	21,363	17,056	21,775	19,534
98,750	98,800	21,377	17,069	21,789	19,546
98,800	98,850	21,391	17,081	21,803	19,559
98,850	98,900	21,405	17,094	21,817	19,571
98,900	98,950	21,419	17,106	21,831	19,584
98,950	99,000	21,433	17,119	21,845	19,596
99,000					
99,000	99,050	21,447	17,131	21,859	19,609
99,050	99,100	21,461	17,144	21,873	19,621
99,100	99,150	21,475	17,156	21,887	19,634
99,150	99,200	21,489	17,169	21,901	19,646
99,200	99,250	21,503	17,181	21,915	19,659
99,250	99,300	21,517	17,194	21,929	19,671
99,300	99,350	21,531	17,206	21,943	19,684
99,350	99,400	21,545	17,219	21,957	19,696
99,400	99,450	21,559	17,231	21,971	19,709
99,450	99,500	21,573	17,244	21,985	19,721
99,500	99,550	21,587	17,256	21,999	19,734
99,550	99,600	21,601	17,269	22,013	19,746
99,600	99,650	21,615	17,281	22,027	19,759
99,650	99,700	21,629	17,294	22,041	19,771
99,700	99,750	21,643	17,306	22,055	19,784
99,750	99,800	21,657	17,319	22,069	19,796
99,800	99,850	21,671	17,331	22,083	19,809
99,850	99,900	21,685	17,344	22,097	19,821
99,900	99,950	21,699	17,356	22,111	19,834
99,950	100,000	21,713	17,369	22,125	19,846

$100,000 or over — use the Tax Computation Worksheet on page 89

* This column must also be used by a qualifying widow(er).

* This column must also be used by a qualifying widow(er)

2009 Tax Rate Schedules

CAUTION

The Tax Rate Schedules are shown so you can see the tax rate that applies to all levels of taxable income. Do not use them to figure your tax. Instead, see the instructions for line 44 that begin on page 37.

Schedule X—If your filing status is **Single**

If your taxable income is: Over—	But not over—	The tax is:	of the amount over—
$0	$8,350	.... 10%	$0
8,350	33,950	$835.00 + 15%	8,350
33,950	82,250	4,675.00 + 25%	33,950
82,250	171,550	16,750.00 + 28%	82,250
171,550	372,950	41,754.00 + 33%	171,550
372,950	....	108,216.00 + 35%	372,950

Schedule Y-1—If your filing status is **Married filing jointly** or **Qualifying widow(er)**

If your taxable income is: Over—	But not over—	The tax is:	of the amount over—
$0	$16,700	.... 10%	$0
16,700	67,900	$1,670.00 + 15%	16,700
67,900	137,050	9,350.00 + 25%	67,900
137,050	208,850	26,637.50 + 28%	137,050
208,850	372,950	46,741.50 + 33%	208,850
372,950	....	100,894.50 + 35%	372,950

Schedule Y-2—If your filing status is **Married filing separately**

If your taxable income is: Over—	But not over—	The tax is:	of the amount over—
$0	$8,350	.... 10%	$0
8,350	33,950	$835.00 + 15%	8,350
33,950	68,525	4,675.00 + 25%	33,950
68,525	104,425	13,318.75 + 28%	68,525
104,425	186,475	23,370.75 + 33%	104,425
186,475	....	50,447.25 + 35%	186,475

Schedule Z—If your filing status is **Head of household**

If your taxable income is: Over—	But not over—	The tax is:	of the amount over—
$0	$11,950	.... 10%	$0
11,950	45,500	$1,195.00 + 15%	11,950
45,500	117,450	6,227.50 + 25%	45,500
117,450	190,200	24,215.00 + 28%	117,450
190,200	372,950	44,585.00 + 33%	190,200
372,950	....	104,892.50 + 35%	372,950

2009 Tax Computation Worksheet—Line 44

CAUTION *See the instructions for line 44 that begin on page 37 to see if you must use the worksheet below to figure your tax.*

Note. If you are required to use this worksheet to figure the tax on an amount from another form or worksheet, such as the Qualified Dividends and Capital Gain Tax Worksheet, the Schedule D Tax Worksheet, Schedule J, Form 8615, or the Foreign Earned Income Tax Worksheet, enter the amount from that form or worksheet in column (a) of the row that applies to the amount you are looking up. Enter the result on the appropriate line of the form or worksheet that you are completing.

Section A—Use if your filing status is **Single.** Complete the row below that applies to you.

Taxable income. If line 43 is—	(a) Enter the amount from line 43	(b) Multiplication amount	(c) Multiply (a) by (b)	(d) Subtraction amount	**Tax.** Subtract (d) from (c). Enter the result here and on Form 1040, line 44
At least $100,000 but not over $171,550	$	× 28% (.28)	$	$ 6,280.00	$
Over $171,550 but not over $372,950	$	× 33% (.33)	$	$ 14,857.50	$
Over $372,950	$	× 35% (.35)	$	$22,316.50	$

Section B—Use if your filing status is **Married filing jointly** or **Qualifying widow(er).** Complete the row below that applies to you.

Taxable income. If line 43 is—	(a) Enter the amount from line 43	(b) Multiplication amount	(c) Multiply (a) by (b)	(d) Subtraction amount	**Tax.** Subtract (d) from (c). Enter the result here and on Form 1040, line 44
At least $100,000 but not over $137,050	$	× 25% (.25)	$	$ 7,625.00	$
Over $137,050 but not over $208,850	$	× 28% (.28)	$	$ 11,736.50	$
Over $208,850 but not over $372,950	$	× 33% (.33)	$	$ 22,179.00	$
Over $372,950	$	× 35% (.35)	$	$ 29,638.00	$

Section C—Use if your filing status is **Married filing separately.** Complete the row below that applies to you.

Taxable income. If line 43 is—	(a) Enter the amount from line 43	(b) Multiplication amount	(c) Multiply (a) by (b)	(d) Subtraction amount	**Tax.** Subtract (d) from (c). Enter the result here and on Form 1040, line 44
At least $100,000 but not over $104,425	$	× 28% (.28)	$	$ 5,868.25	$
Over $104,425 but not over $186,475	$	× 33% (.33)	$	$ 11,089.50	$
Over $186,475	$	× 35% (.35)	$	$ 14,819.00	$

Section D—Use if your filing status is **Head of household.** Complete the row below that applies to you.

Taxable income. If line 43 is—	(a) Enter the amount from line 43	(b) Multiplication amount	(c) Multiply (a) by (b)	(d) Subtraction amount	**Tax.** Subtract (d) from (c). Enter the result here and on Form 1040, line 44
At least $100,000 but not over $117,450	$	× 25% (.25)	$	$ 5,147.50	$
Over $117,450 but not over $190,200	$	× 28% (.28)	$	$ 8,671.00	$
Over $190,200 but not over $372,950	$	× 33% (.33)	$	$ 18,181.00	$
Over $372,950	$	× 35% (.35)	$	$ 25,640.00	$

A

B

C

D

E

F

G

H

I

N

Q

R

T

U

V

W

Z